Technical Writing
A Practical Approach

THIRD EDITION

William S. Pfeiffer
Southern College of Technology

Prentice Hall
Upper Saddle River, New Jersey   Columbus, Ohio

Library of Congress Cataloging-in-Publication Data

Pfeiffer, William S.
　　Technical writing: a practical approach / William S. Pfeiffer. —
3rd ed.
　　　　p. cm.
　　Includes bibliographical references and index.
　　ISBN 0–13–455339–X (alk. paper)
　　1. English language—Technical English. 2. English language-
-Rhetoric. I. Title.
PE1475.P47 1997
808'.0666—dc20

95-52175
CIP

Cover art: Paul Klee/Superstock
Editor: Steven Helba
Production Editor: Mary M. Irvin
Design Coordinator: Jill Bonar
Text Designer: Rebecca Bobb
Cover Designer: Brian Deep
Production Manager: Pamela A. Bennett
Marketing Manager: Danny Hoyt

This book was set in Meridien by Carlisle Communications, Inc., and was printed and bound by R. R. Donnelley/Virginia. The cover was printed by Phoenix Color Corp.

Photo credits: pp. 3, 99, 129, 173, 207, 287, 333, 393, 465, 507, and 547, Todd Yarrington/Merrill/Prentice Hall; pp. 43, 73, 249, 435, Anthony Magnacca/Merrill/Prentice Hall. "McDuff" color insert: page 2: Photo courtesy of Ohio Department of Natural Resources; Page 3: Photo courtesy of Schlumberger/Sedco Forex; Page 4: Photo courtesy of Grant Medical Center, Columbus, Ohio; Page 5: Photo property of the Houston Oilers; Page 6: (c) 1993 Terence E. Seidel; Page 7: Photo courtesy of U.S. Council for Energy Awareness; Page 8: (c) 1993 Todd Yarrington.

Printed in the United States of America

10 9 8 7 6 5 4 3 2 1

ISBN: 0-13-455339-0
Prentice-Hall International (UK) Limited, *London*
Prentice-Hall of Australia Pty. Limited, *Sydney*
Prentice-Hall of Canada, Inc., *Toronto*
Prentice-Hall Hispanoamericana, S. A., *Mexico*
Prentice-Hall of India Private Limited, *New Delhi*
Prentice-Hall of Japan, Inc., *Tokyo*
Simon & Schuster Asia Pte. Ltd., *Singapore*
Editora Prentice-Hall do Brasil, Ltda., *Rio de Janeiro*

Preface

*E*very student who plans to work in business and industry must master the art of technical writing. Good writing will make your organization more effective and your society more productive. Just as important, skill in writing will lead to a good deal of personal satisfaction as well as considerable advancement throughout your career. Indeed, as we close in on the next century, writing will remain a major contributor to success in your profession.

MAIN FEATURES OF THIS BOOK

To help you become an excellent writer, this book stresses one simple principle: you learn to write best by *doing* as much writing as possible. Thus *Technical Writing: A Practical Approach* aims to provide the basic tools to get you started on various writing tasks.

Like the first two editions, the third edition continues to emphasize these five main features:

- A "textbook company"—McDuff, Inc.—that forms the basis for most assignments and examples
- Easy-to-use, numbered guidelines for every document covered
- Annotated models to give students clear direction
- Dozens of realistic writing assignments
- A clear prose style that puts into practice what the book preaches

The third edition adds some new features as well. Here are the main changes:

■ *Change 1: "Communication Challenge" Sidebars in All 15 Chapters*

This new feature adds a McDuff case study to the end of every chapter. Each "challenge" presents a realistic problem—either an ethical dilemma to address or a communication problem to solve. The cases are directly related to the material in the chapters in which they appear, providing a springboard for class discussion and writing assignments.

■ *Change 2: New Sections on Ethics and Global Communication*

The revised chapter 2 includes new overviews of two topics: ethics and international communication. Both are crucial issues in modern technical communication. Then the rest of the book offers assignments and cases involving ethics in the workplace and global communication. By using the McDuff structure—with its 15 worldwide offices and diverse group of employees—to illustrate these topics, the new edition makes concrete what could otherwise be abstract topics.

■ *Change 3: New Research Information on Automated Libraries*

The chapter on technical research has been brought into the electronic age. As before, the chapter includes a running case study on a McDuff employee completing an on-the-job research project. However, in this edition much of the text and many examples relate to technical advances such as CD-ROM databases, on-line catalogs, and Internet research. Automated libraries and on-line research are here to stay.

■ *Change 4: More Collaborative and Computer Assignments*

Practical assignments are the hallmark of this book. The new edition includes many more writing projects—some for individual writing but many for collaborative work. Most assignments make good use of McDuff, Inc. In fact, a special effort was made to connect assignments to seven projects described in the chapter 2 color insert. In some projects, students will use e-mail and other forms of electronic communication.

■ *Change 5: Updated Models in Several Chapters*

The new formal report in chapter 9 is easier to use than the report it replaced. It describes the results of an "adopt-a-stream" program, wherein a resident monitored the cleanup of a polluted waterway in his community. Another new example is the chapter 5 technical description. Other models were fine-tuned, and all continue to be grouped at the end of each chapter, for easy reference.

ACKNOWLEDGMENTS

Many generous clients and colleagues helped strengthen this book. Four companies allowed me to use written material gathered during my consulting work: Fugro-McClelland, Law Engineering and Environmental Services, McBride-Ratcliff and Associates, and Westinghouse Environmental and Geotechnical Services. Though this book's fictional firm, McDuff, Inc., does have features of the world I observed as a consultant, I want to emphasize that McDuff is truly an invention.

Many friends at Southern College of Technology and other organizations offered excellent suggestions used in this book. I want to thank Saul Carliner, George Ferguson, Dory Ingram, Chuck Keller, Jo Lundy, Randy Nipp, Ken Rainey, Hattie Schumaker, Herb Smith, James Stephens, John Ulrich, Steven Vincent, and Tom Wiseman. In particular, the following six colleagues greatly influenced the third edition: Bob Harbort (who introduced me to the Internet while we canoed down the Chattahoochee), Mark Stevens and Shawn Tonner (who helped me understand automated libraries), Minoru Moriguchi (who reviewed the ethics and international sections), Alan Gabrielli (who showed me the intricacies of Bunsen burners), and Becky Kelly (who provided advice that kept me on track in several chapters). In addition, these reviewers from other schools provided their assistance with the project: Susan Chin, DeVry Institute of Technology; Betty Cramton, Kansas State University at Salina.

I also appreciate the help of the following students for allowing me to adapt their written work for use in this book: Michael Alban, Becky Austin, Corey Baird, Natalie Birnbaum, Cedric Bowden, Gregory Braxton, Ishmael Chigumira, Bill Darden, Jeffrey Daxon, Rob Duggan, William English, Joseph Fritz, Jon Guffey, Sam Harkness, Gary Harvey, Lee Harvey, Hammond Hill, Sudhir Kapoor, Steven Knapp, Wes Matthews, Kim Meyer, James Moore, James Porter, James Roberts, Mort Rolleston, Chris Ruda, Barbara Serkedakis, Tom Skywark, Tom Smith, DaTonja Stanley, James Stephens, Chris Swift, and Jeff Woodward. Special thanks go to Chris Owen, whose real report I used as the basis for the new formal report example in chapter 9.

For all three editions, it has been my good fortune to have the same outstanding development editor, Monica Ohlinger. She always has winning ideas. I must add that Monica has mastered the art of friendly persuasion better than anyone I know. Also, I want to give special thanks to my Prentice Hall executive editor, Steve Helba, for his continuing faith in my book. Other Prentice Hall people who contributed to the project include Mary Irvin, production editor, and Jill Bonar, design coordinator.

Finally, deepest thanks go to my family—Evelyn, Zachary, and Katie—for their love and support throughout this and every writing project I take on. They made the personal sacrifices that gave me the opportunity to write *Technical Writing*. I only hope I have it in me to return the favor when they write their books.

A FINAL NOTE TO STUDENTS

I'll close this preface with the same comment made in the last edition: At the start of my classes, I sometimes ask students to describe their professional goals for the next 10 years. As you might expect, their comments suggest they hope to rise to important positions in the workplace and make genuine contributions to their professions. Such long-term thinking is crucial, keeping you on course in your life.

Yet, ultimately, the way you handle the small, daily details of life most influences the real contribution you make in the long run. If you do good technical work, believe in what you do, and communicate well with others—both interpersonally and in writing—success will come your way. The author Robert Pirsig put it this way in his 1971 work, *Zen and the Art of Motorcycle Maintenance:*

> The place to improve the world is first in one's own heart and head and hands, and then work outward from there.

I believe—and this book tries to show—that clear, concise, and honest writing is one of the most powerful tools of your heart, head, *and* hands.

Contents

Technical Writing
A Practical Approach

THIRD EDITION

PART 1

1

Process in Technical Writing

A McDuff engineer collects data for a technical report. This task is part of the planning stage of writing. The other two stages are drafting and revising.

G ood communication skills are essential in any career you choose. Jobs, promotions, raises, and professional prestige result from your ability to write and speak effectively. With so much at stake, you need a simple road map to direct you toward writing excellence. *Technical Writing: A Practical Approach* is such a map.

The four chapters in Part 1 give you an overview of technical writing and prepare you to complete the assignments in this book:

Chapter 1: Defines technical writing and describes the writing process. As shown in Figure 1–1, the technical writing process has three main parts: planning, drafting, and revising. Careful completion of this *process* is the best guarantee of a successful *product*—the final document.

Chapter 2: Introduces you to life in the corporate world and to the fictional company of McDuff, Inc. This organization will provide the framework for most examples and assignments in this book.

Chapter 3: Focuses on organizing information for diverse readers who are often very busy and unfamiliar with a project.

Chapter 4: Describes techniques for using the best elements of page design and computer technology in the writing process.

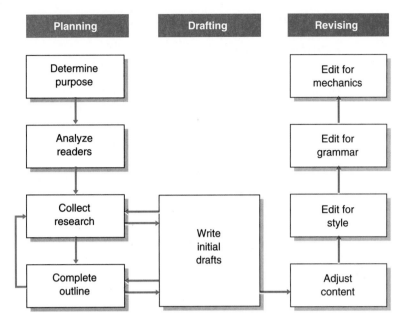

FIGURE 1-1
Flowchart for the technical writing process

So that you can begin writing early in the course, preliminaries are kept to a minimum. Now let's take a closer look at the nature of technical writing.

GETTING FROM HERE TO THERE

You probably learned how to write short essays in previous writing courses. This book helps you transfer that basic knowledge to the kind of writing done on the job. In the process, you will discover that learning technical writing is a bit like studying a foreign language, with a new set of rules. Yet career writing is so practical, so well grounded in common sense, that it will seem to proceed smoothly from your previous work. This section highlights features of both traditional academic writing and job-related technical writing.

Features of Academic Writing

Writing you have done in school probably has had these characteristics:

- **Purpose:** Demonstrating what you know about the topic, in a way that justifies a high grade
- **Your knowledge of topic:** Less than the teacher who evaluates the writing

- **Audience:** Teacher who requests the assignment and who will read it from beginning to end
- **Criteria for evaluation:** Depth, logic, clarity, unity, and grammar

Academic writing requires that you display your learning to someone who knows more about the subject than you do. Because this person's job is to evaluate your work, you have what might be called a "captive audience." Here are two common situations in which academic writing would be appropriate, along with brief examples:

▪ Example 1: Essays for English Class

In a typical high school or college writing class, you write short essays based on your experience or readings. Instructors expect you to (1) state the topic, purpose, and main points in the introduction, (2) develop the supporting points in the body, and (3) wrap up the paper in the conclusion. Your reader wants a coherent, unified, grammatically sound, and interesting piece of writing. What follows is the first paragraph from one such essay. The student was asked to attend and then comment on a local cultural event.

> The recent exhibit at Atlanta's High Museum of Art, "Masterpieces of the American West," gives the viewer a small glimpse of the beautiful land and fascinating peoples that confronted the explorer-artists who ventured west in the 1800s. This paper will describe my response to three works—Catlin's *Mandan Dance,* Bierstadt's *Rocky Mountain Waterfall,* and Remington's *Turn Him Loose, Bill.* The first portrays the Indian culture; the second, Western landscape; and the third, the encroaching civilization from the East.

▪ Example 2: Exams and Papers in General Studies Courses

Courses like history and science often require that you write analytical papers and exams. As in essays for a writing class, these papers should start with a topic statement that outlines main points and then proceed with supporting paragraphs. For example, you may be asked to describe both the immediate and long-term reasons for a particular event. Here is the first paragraph of a cause-effect essay in environmental science. The writer must define and give causes for the "greenhouse effect."

> The term *greenhouse effect* refers to the global warming trend of the earth. It occurs when the sun's reflected heat is unable to escape the earth's atmosphere into space, because of a buildup of carbon monoxide and other gases in the atmosphere. This essay will describe these main reasons for the dramatic increase in the greenhouse effect: the burning of rain forests in the Amazon, accelerated emission of auto pollutants around the world, and increases in the use of coal-fired plants.

In both examples, the *purpose* is to demonstrate knowledge, and the *audience* is someone already familiar with the subject or approach. In this sense, academic writing shows your command of information to someone more knowledgeable about the subject than you are. The next section examines a different kind of writing—the kind you will be doing in your career and in this course. The purpose and audience differ considerably from those of academic writing.

Features of Technical Writing

The ground rules for writing shift somewhat when you begin your career. Those unprepared for this change often flounder for years, never quite understanding the new rules. *Technical writing* is a generic term for all written communications done on the job—whether in business, industry, or other professions. It is particularly identified with jobs in technology, engineering, science, the health professions, and other fields with specialized vocabularies. The terms *technical writing, professional writing, business writing,* and *occupational writing* all mean essentially the same thing—writing done in your career. Here are the main characteristics of technical writing:

- **Purpose:** Getting something done within an organization (completing a project, persuading a customer, pleasing your boss, etc.)
- **Your knowledge of topic:** Usually greater than that of the reader
- **Audience:** Often several people, with differing technical backgrounds
- **Criteria for evaluation:** Clear and simple organization of ideas, in a format that meets the needs of busy readers

Contrast these features with those of academic writing, listed earlier. In particular, note the following main differences:

1. Technical writing has a practical role on the job, whereas academic writing aims only to display your knowledge.
2. Technical writing is done by an informed writer conveying needed information to an uninformed reader, whereas academic writing is done by a student as learner for a teacher as source of knowledge.
3. Technical writing often is read by many readers, whereas academic writing aims to satisfy only one person, the teacher.

Finally, technical writing places greater emphasis on techniques of organization and format that help readers find important information as quickly as possible.

Figure 1–2 lists some typical on-the-job writing assignments. While not exhaustive, the list does include many of the writing projects you will encounter. Also, see Figure 1–3 for an example of a short technical document.

Besides projects that involve writing, you will also have speaking responsibilities during your career—for example, formal speeches at conferences and informal presentations at meetings. The term *technical communication* is used to include both the writing and speaking tasks involved with any job.

Although technical communication plays a key role in the success of all technical professionals and managers, the amount of time you devote to it will depend on your job. A 1989 survey of technical managers gives some idea of the time involved. Conducted by the National Aeronautics and Space Administration (NASA), the survey canvassed managers in profit-making and

---

Correspondence: In-House or External
- Memos to your boss and to your subordinates
- Routine letters to customers, vendors, etc.
- "Good news" letters to customers
- "Bad news" letters to customers
- Sales letters to potential customers
- Electronic mail (e-mail) messages to coworkers or customers over a computer network

Short Reports: In-House or External
- Analysis of a problem
- Recommendation
- Equipment evaluation
- Progress report on project or routine periodic report
- Report on the results of laboratory or field work
- Description of the results of a company trip

Long Reports: In-House or External
- Complex problem analysis, recommendation, or equipment evaluation
- Project report on field or laboratory work
- Feasibility study

Other Documents
- Proposal to boss for new product line
- Proposal to boss for change in procedures
- Proposal to customer to sell a product, service, or idea
- Proposal to funding agency for support of research project
- Abstract or summary of technical article
- Technical article or presentation
- Operation manual or other manual

FIGURE 1–2
Examples of technical writing

nonprofit organizations in the field of aeronautics. As Figure 1–4 shows, 100% of the profit managers and 98% of the nonprofit managers in the study consider technical communication a "somewhat important" or "very important" part of their jobs.

Even more telling is the amount of time the NASA survey respondents spend communicating. Figure 1–4 indicates that they use (1) over one-third of their work time conveying information *to* others and (2) another one-third working with technical information sent to them *by* others. Based on a 40-hour week, therefore, both groups spend roughly *two-thirds* of their working week on job duties associated with technical communication.

Now that you know the nature and importance of technical writing, the next section examines the first part of the planning stage: determining a document's purpose.

Mc Duff, Inc.   MEMORANDUM

DATE: December 6, 1996
TO: Holly Newsome
FROM: Michael Allen *MA*
SUBJECT: Printer Recommendation

Introductory Summary

Recently you asked for my evaluation of the Hemphill LaserFast printer currently used in my department. Having analyzed the printer's features, print quality, and cost, I am quite satisfied with its performance.

Features

Among the LaserFast's features. I have found these five to be most useful:
1. Portrait and landscape print modes
2. Selectable character sizes (10/12/16.7 characters per inch)
3. 1.5 megabytes of print-buffer memory
4. Selectable paper sizes (letter, legal, half-letter)
5. Print speed of six pages per minute

In addition, the LaserFast printer is equipped with two built-in fonts and accepts several additional fonts from specially purchased cartridges. This combination of features makes the LaserFast a most versatile printer.

Print Quality

The Hemphill LaserFast printer produces laser-sharp clarity that rivals professional typeset quality. The print resolution is an amazing 300 x 300 dots per inch, among the highest attainable in current desktop printers. This memo was printed on LaserFast, and, as you can see, the quality speaks for itself.

Cost

Considering the features and quality, the LaserFast is an excellent printer for the money. At a retail price of $2500, it is one of the lowest-priced laser printers. In fact, the highest-quality daisy wheel and dot matrix printers cost just $500 less than the LaserFast, yet neither offers the superior features or quality of a laser printer.

Conclusion

On the basis of my observation, I strongly recommend that our firm continue to use and purchase the LaserFast printer. Please call me at ext. 204 if you want further information about this excellent machine.

FIGURE 1–3
Short report

FIGURE 1–4
Data from NASA aeronautics
survey
Source: Thomas E. Pinelli et al.,
*Technical Communications in
Aeronautics: Results of an Exploratory
Study—An Analysis of Profit Managers'
and Nonprofit Managers' Responses*
(Washington, D.C.: National
Aeronautics and Space
Administration, NASA TM-101626,
October 1989), 71. (Available from
NTIS Springfield, Va.)

TABLE 1. Importance of Technical Communications

How Important	Profit Managers		Nonprofit Managers	
	No.	%	No.	%
Very	86	92.5	43	84.3
Somewhat	7	7.5	7	13.7
Not at all	0	0.0	1	2.0
Total	93	100.0	51	100.0

TABLE 2. Time Spent Communicating Technical Information to Others

Time Spent Per Week, Hours	Profit Managers		Nonprofit Managers	
	No.	%	No.	%
5 or less	13	14.3	9	18.0
6 to 10	33	36.2	16	30.0
11 to 20	37	40.7	21	42.0
21 or more	8	8.8	5	10.0
Total	91	100.0	51	100.0
Mean	13.5		13.9	

TABLE 3. Time Spent Working with Technical Information Received from Others

Time Spent Per Week, Hours	Profit Managers		Nonprofit Managers	
	No.	%	No.	%
5 or less	8	8.7	6	12.0
6 to 10	42	46.2	23	46.0
11 to 20	36	39.6	18	36.0
21 or more	5	5.5	3	6.0
Total	91	100.0	50	100.0
Mean	13.0		13.0	

DISCOVERING YOUR PURPOSE

Kate Paulsen works as a training supervisor for the Boston office of McDuff, Inc., a firm described in more detail in chapter 2. The company is growing so quickly that hiring, training, and retraining employees have become major goals. Kate recently flew to Cleveland to attend a workshop sponsored by a major professional training organization. The workshop emphasized a new in-house procedure for surveying the training needs of a company's employees. After returning to Boston, Kate must write her manager a trip report that describes the survey technique. She ponders three different approaches to the report:

- **Giving an overview** of the survey procedure she studied during the three-day workshop—stressing a few key points so that her manager could decide whether to inquire further
- **Providing details** of exactly how the survey procedure could be applied to her firm—with enough specifics for her manager to see exactly how the survey could be used at McDuff
- **Proposing** that the procedure for conducting the needs survey be used at McDuff—in language that argues strongly for adoption

For Kate, the first step is to decide what she wants to accomplish. Likewise, every piece of *your* writing should have a specific reason for being. The purpose may be dictated by someone else or selected by you. In either case, it must be firmly understood *before* you start writing. Purpose statements guide every decision you make while you plan, draft, and revise.

Kate Paulsen's three choices indicate some of your options, but there are others. Your choice of purpose will fall somewhere within this continuum:

For example, when reporting to your boss on the feasibility of adding a new wing to your office building, you should be quite objective. You must provide facts that can lead to an informed decision by someone else. If you are an outside contractor proposing to construct such a wing, however, your purpose is more persuasive. You will be trying to convince readers that your firm should receive the construction contract.

When preparing to write, therefore, you need to ask yourself two related questions about your purpose.

■ *Question 1: Why Am I Writing This Document?*

This question should be answered in just one or two sentences, even in complicated projects. Often the resulting purpose statement can be moved "as is" to the beginning of your outline and later to the first draft.

For example, Kate Paulsen finally decides on the following purpose statement, which becomes the first passage in her trip report: "This memo will highlight main features of the training needs survey introduced at the workshop I attended in Cleveland. I will focus on several possible applications you might want to consider for our office training." Note that Kate's purpose would rest about halfway across the persuasive continuum shown earlier. Though she will not be strongly advocating McDuff's use of the survey, she will be giving information that suggests the company might benefit by using it.

■ *Question 2: What Response Do I Want from Readers?*

The first question about purpose leads inevitably to the second about results. Again, your response should be only one or two sentences long. Though brief, it should pinpoint exactly what you want to happen as a result of your document. Are you just giving data for the file? Will information you provide help others do their jobs? Will your document recommend a major change?

In Kate Paulsen's case, she decides on this results statement: "Though I'm not yet sure if this training survey is worth purchasing for McDuff, I want my boss to consider it." Unlike the purpose statement, the results statement may not go directly into your document. Kate's statement hints at a "hidden" agenda that may be implicit in her trip report but will not be explicitly stated. This statement, written for her own use, becomes an essential part of her planning. It is a concrete goal to keep in mind as she writes.

The answers to these two questions about purpose and results are included on the Planning Form your instructor may ask you to use for assignments. Figure 1–5 on pages 14 and 15 includes a copy of the form, along with instructions for using it. The last page of this book contains another copy you can duplicate for use with assignments.

Having established your purpose, you are now ready to consider the next part of the writing process: audience analysis.

ANALYZING YOUR READERS

One cardinal rule governs all on-the-job writing:

> ### WRITE FOR YOUR READER, NOT FOR YOURSELF.

This rule especially applies to science and technology because many readers may know little about your field. In fact, experts on writing agree that most technical writing assumes too much knowledge on the part of the reader. The key to avoiding this problem is to examine the main obstacles readers face and adopt a strategy for overcoming them.

This section (1) highlights problems that readers have understanding technical writing, (2) suggests techniques to prevent these problems, and (3) describes some main classifications of technical readers. At first, analyzing your audience might seem awkward and even unproductive. You are forced out of your own world to consider that of your reader, before you even put pen to paper. The payoff, however, will be a document that has clear direction and gives the audience what it wants.

Obstacles for Readers

As purchasing agent for McDuff, Inc., Charles Blair must recommend one automobile sedan for fleet purchase by the firm's sales force and executives. First, he will conduct some research—interviewing car firm representatives, reading car evaluations in consumer magazines, and inquiring about the needs of his firm's salespeople. Then he will submit a recommendation report to the selection committee consisting of the company president, the accounting manager, several salespeople, and the supervisor of company maintenance. As Charles will discover, readers of all backgrounds often have these four problems when reading any technical document:

1. Constant interruptions
2. Impatience finding information they need
3. A different technical background from the writer
4. Shared decision-making authority with others

If you think about these obstacles every time you write, you will be better able to understand and respond to your readers.

■ *Obstacle 1: Readers Are Always Interrupted*

As a professional, how often will you have the chance to read a report or other document without interruption? Such times are rare. Your reading time will be interrupted by meetings and phone calls, so a report often gets read in several sittings. Aggravating this problem is the fact that readers may have forgotten details of the project.

■ *Obstacle 2: Readers Are Impatient*

Many readers lose patience with vague or unorganized writing. They are thinking "What's the point?" or "So what?" as they plod through memos, letters, reports, and proposals. They want to know the significance of the document right away.

■ *Obstacle 3: Readers Lack Your Technical Knowledge*

In college courses, the readers of your writing are professors who usually have knowledge of the subject on which you are writing. In your career, however, you will write to readers who lack the information and background you have. They expect a technically sophisticated response, but in language they can understand. If you write over their heads, you will not accomplish your purpose. Think of yourself as an educator; if readers do not learn from your reports, you have failed in your objective.

■ *Obstacle 4: Most Documents Have More Than One Reader*

If you always wrote to only one person, technical writing would be much easier than it is. Each document could be tailored to the background, interests, and technical education of just that individual. However, this is not the case in the actual

PLANNING FORM

NAME: _____   ASSIGNMENT: _____

I. Purpose: Answer each question in one or two sentences.

   A. Why are you writing this document?_____

   _____

   B. What response do you want from readers? _____

   _____

II. Reader Matrix: Fill in names and positions of people who may read the document.

	Decision-Makers	Advisers	Receivers
Managers			
Experts			
Operators			
General Readers			

III. Information on Individual Readers: Answer these questions about selected members of your audience. Attach additional sheets as is necessary.

   1. What is this reader's technical or educational background?

   _____

   _____

   2. What main question does this person need answered?

   _____

   _____

   3. What main action do you want this person to take?

   _____

   _____

   4. What features of this person's personality might affect his or her reading?

   _____

   _____

   5. What features does this person prefer in

     Format?_____

     Style?_____

     Organization? _____

IV. Outline: Attach an outline (topic) to use in drafting the **BODY** of this document.

FIGURE 1–5

Planning Form for all technical documents

Instructions for Completing "Planning Form"

The Planning Form is for your use in preparing assignments in your technical writing course. It focuses only on the planning stage of writing. Complete it before you begin your first draft.

1. Use the Planning Form to help plan your strategy for all writing assignments. Your instructor may or may not require that it be submitted with assignments.

2. Photocopy the form on the back page of this book or write the answers to questions on separate sheets of paper, whatever option your instructor prefers. (Your instructor may hand out enlarged, letter-size copies of the form, which are included in the Instructor's Resource Manual.)

3. Answer the two purpose questions in one or two sentences each. Be as specific as possible about the purpose of the document and the response you want—especially from the decision-makers.

4. Note that the reader matrix classifies each reader by two criteria: (a) technical levels (shown on the vertical axis) and (b) relationship to the decision-making process (shown on the horizontal axis). Some of the boxes will be filled with one or more names, while others may be blank. How you fill out the form depends on the complexity of your audience and, of course, on the directions of your instructor.

5. Refer to Chapter 2 for any McDuff positions and titles you may want to use in the reader matrix, if your paper is based on a simulated case from McDuff, Inc.

6. Note that questions in the "Information on Individual Readers" section can be filled out for one or more readers, depending on what your instructor requires.

7. Complete the topic outline after you have collected whatever information or research your document requires. The outline should be specific and should include two or three levels (see Figure 1-8 and Figure 1-9).

FIGURE 1–5
continued

world of business and industry. Readers usually share decision-making authority with others, who may read all or just part of the text. Thus you must respond to the needs of many individuals—most of whom have a hectic schedule, are impatient, and have a technical background different from yours.

Ways to Understand Readers

Obstacles to communication can be frustrating. Yet there are techniques for overcoming them. First, you must try to find out exactly what information each reader needs. Think of the problem this way—would you give a speech without learning about the background of your audience? Writing depends just as much, if not more, on such analysis. Follow these four steps to determine your readers' needs:

■ *Audience Analysis Step 1: Write Down
What You Know About Your Reader*

To build a framework for analyzing your audience, you need to write down—not just casually think about—the answers to these questions for each reader:

1. What is this reader's technical or educational background?
2. What main question does this person need answered?
3. What main action do you want this person to take?
4. What features of this person's personality might affect his or her reading?
5. What features does this reader prefer in
   Format?
   Style?
   Organization?

The Planning Form in Figure 1–5 includes these five questions.

■ *Audience Analysis Step 2: Talk with Colleagues
Who Have Written to the Same Readers*

Often your best source of information about your readers is a colleague where you work. Ask around the office or check company files to discover who else may have written to the same audience. Useful information could be as close as the next office.

■ *Audience Analysis Step 3: Find Out
Who Makes Decisions*

Almost every document requires action of some kind. Identify decision-makers ahead of time so that you can design the document with them in mind. Know the needs of your *most important* reader.

■ *Audience Analysis Step 4: Remember That All Readers Prefer Simplicity*

Even if you uncover little specific information about your readers, you can always rely on one basic fact: Readers of all technical backgrounds prefer concise, simple writing. The popular KISS principle (Keep It Short and Simple) is a worthy goal.

Types of Readers

You have learned some typical problems readers face and some general solutions to these problems. To complete the audience-analysis stage, this section shows you how to classify readers by two main criteria: knowledge and influence. Specifically, you need to answer two questions about every potential reader:

1. How much does this reader already know about the subject?
2. What part will this reader play in making decisions?

Then use the answers to these questions to plan your document. Figure 1–6 (adapted from the Planning Form in Figure 1–5) provides a reader matrix by which you can quickly view the technical levels and decision-making roles of all your readers. For complex documents, your audience may include many of the 12 categories shown on the matrix. Also, you may have more than one person in each box—that is, there may be more than one reader with the same background and decision-making role.

Technical Levels. On-the-job writing requires that you translate technical ideas into language that nontechnical people can understand. This task can be very

Technical Level	Decision-Making Level		
	Decision-Makers	Advisors	Recievers
Managers			
Experts			
Operators			
General Readers			

FIGURE 1–6
Reader matrix

complicated because you often have several readers, each with different levels of knowledge about the topic. If you are to "write for your reader, not for yourself," you must identify the technical background of *each* reader. Four categories will help you classify each reader's knowledge of the topic.

■ *Reader Group 1: Managers*

Many technical professionals aspire to become managers. Once into management, they may be removed from hands-on technical details of their profession. Instead, they manage people, set budgets, and make decisions of all kinds. Thus you should assume that management readers will not be familiar with fine technical points, will have forgotten details of your project, or both. These managers often need:

- Background information
- Definitions of technical terms
- Lists and other format devices that highlight points
- Clear statements about what is supposed to happen next

In chapter 3, we will discuss an all-purpose "ABC format" for organization that responds to the needs of managers.

■ *Reader Group 2: Experts*

Experts include anyone with a good understanding of your topic. They may be well educated—as with engineers and scientists—but that is not necessarily the case. In the example mentioned earlier, the maintenance supervisor with no college training could be considered an "expert" about selecting a new automobile for fleet purchase. That supervisor will understand any technical information about car models and features. Whatever their educational levels, most experts in your audience need:

- Thorough explanations of technical details
- Data placed in tables and figures
- References to outside sources used in writing the report
- Clearly labeled appendices for supporting information

■ *Reader Group 3: Operators*

Because decision-makers are often managers or technical experts, they tend to get most of the attention. However, many documents also have readers who are operators. They may be technicians in a field crew, workers on an assembly line, salespeople in a department store, or drivers for a trucking firm—anyone who puts the ideas in your document into practice. These readers expect:

- A clear table of contents for locating sections that relate to them
- Easy-to-read listings for procedures or instructions
- Definitions of technical terms
- A clear statement of exactly how the document affects their jobs

■ *Reader Group 4: General Readers*

General readers, also called "laypersons," often have the least amount of information about your topic or field. For example, a report on the environmental impact of a toxic waste dump might be read by general readers who are home owners in the surrounding area. Most will have little technical understanding of toxic wastes and associated environmental hazards. These general readers often need:

- Definitions of technical terms
- Frequent use of graphics like charts and photographs
- A clear distinction between facts and opinions

Like managers, general readers need to be assured that (1) all implications of the document have been put down on paper and (2) important information has not been buried in overly technical language.

Decision-Making Levels. Figure 1–6 shows that your readers, whatever their technical level, also can be classified by the degree to which they make decisions based on your document. Pay special attention to those most likely to use your report to create change. Use three levels to classify your audience during the planning process:

■ *First-Level Audience: Decision-Makers*

The first-level audience must act on the information. If you are proposing a new fax machine for your office, first-level readers will decide whether to accept or reject the idea. If you are comparing two computer systems for storing records at a hospital, the first-level audience will decide which unit to purchase. If you are describing electrical work your firm completed in a new office building, it will decide whether the project has fulfilled agreed-upon guidelines.

In other words, decision-makers translate information into action. They are usually, but not always, managers within the organization. One exception occurs in highly technical companies, wherein decision-makers may be technical experts with advanced degrees in science or engineering. Another exception occurs when decision-making committees consist of a combined audience. For example, the deacons' committee of a church may be charged with the task of choosing a firm to build a new addition to the sanctuary.

■ *Second-Level Audience: Advisers*

This second group could be called "influencers." Although they don't make decisions themselves, they read the document and give advice to those who will decide. Often the second-level audience comprises experts such as engineers and accountants, who are asked to comment on technical matters. After reading the summary, a decision-making manager may refer the rest of the document to advisers for their comments.

■ *Third-Level Audience: Receivers*

Some readers do not take part in the decision-making process. They only receive information contained in the document. For example, a report recommending changes in the hiring of fast-food workers may go to the store managers after it has been approved, just so they can put the changes into effect. This third-level audience usually includes readers defined as "operators" in the previous section—that is, those who may be asked to follow guidelines or instructions contained in a report.

Using all this information about technical and decision-making levels, you can analyze each reader's (1) technical background with respect to your document and (2) potential for making decisions after reading what you present. Then you can move on to the research and outline stages of writing.

COLLECTING INFORMATION

Having established a clear sense of purpose and your readers' needs, you're ready to collect information for writing. Although you may want to use a scratch outline to guide the research process, a detailed outline normally gets written *after* you have collected research necessary to support the document.

This section lays out a general strategy for research. Details about research are included in chapter 13 ("Technical Research").

■ *Research Step 1: Decide What Kind of Information You Need*

There are two types of research—primary and secondary. Primary research is that which you collect on your own, whereas secondary information is generated by others and found in books, periodicals, or other sources. Figure 1–7 gives examples of both types. Use the kind of research that will be most helpful in supporting the goals of your project. Here are two examples:

- **Report context for using primary research:** A recommendation report to purchase new light tables for the drafting department is supported by your survey of the office drafters. All of them recommend the brand of table you have selected.

- **Report context for using secondary research:** Your report on light tables depends on data found in several written sources, such as an article in a mechanical engineering journal that contrasts features of three tables. On the basis of this article, you recommend a particular table.

■ *Research Step 2: Devise a Research Strategy*

Before you start searching through libraries or conducting interviews, you need a plan. In its simplest form, this plan may list the questions that you expect to

Primary	Secondary
1. **Interviews** 2. **Surveys** 3. **Laboratory Work** 4. **Field Work** 5. **Personal Observation**	1. **Bibliographies** (lists of possible sources— in print or on computer data bases) 2. **Periodical Indexes** (lists of journal and magazine articles, by subject) 3. **Newspaper Indexes** 4. **Books** 5. **Journals** 6. **Newspapers** 7. **Reference Books** (encyclopedias, dictionaries, directories, etc.) 8. **Government Reports** 9. **Company Reports**

FIGURE 1–7
Research sources

answer in your quest for information. For example, a research strategy for a report on office chairs for word-processing operators might pose these questions:

- What kind of chair design do experts in the field of workplace environment recommend for word processors?
- Are there any data that connect the design of chairs with the efficiency of operators?
- Have any specific chair brands been recommended by experts?
- Is there information that suggests a connection between poor chair design and specific health problems?

■ *Research Step 3: Record Notes Carefully*

See chapter 13 for the variety of resources available to you at a well-stocked library. Once you have located the information you need in these sources, you must be very careful incorporating it into your own document. As chapter 13 denotes, you must clearly distinguish direct quotations, paraphrasing, and summaries in your notes. Then, when you are ready to translate these notes into a first draft, you will know exactly how much borrowed information you have used and in what form.

■ *Research Step 4: Acknowledge Your Sources*

The care that you took in step 3 must be accompanied by thorough acknowledgment of the specific sources. Chapter 13 demonstrates one citation system.

■ *Research Step 5: Keep a Bibliography for Future Use*

Consider any research you do for a writing project as an investment in later efforts. Even after your research for a project is complete and you have submitted the report, keep active files on any subjects that relate to your work. Update these files every time you complete a research-related project, such as the two mentioned previously on chair design and light tables. If you or a colleague wants to examine the subject later, you will have developed your own database from which to start.

WRITING AN OUTLINE

After determining purpose and audience and completing your research, you are ready to write an outline. Outlines provide the best method for planning any piece of writing, especially long documents. They do not have to be pretty; they just have to guide your writing of the draft. If you conscientiously use outlines now, you will find it easier to organize and write documents of all kinds throughout your career. Refer to the following steps in preparing functional outlines. Figures 1–8 and 1–9 show the outline process in action.

■ *Outline Step 1: Record Your Random Ideas Quickly*

At first, ideas need *not* be placed in a pattern. Just jot down as many major and minor points as possible. For this exercise, try to use only one piece of paper, even if it is oversized. Putting points on one page helps prepare the way for the next step, in which you begin to make connections among points.

■ *Outline Step 2: Show Relationships*

Next you need to connect related ideas. Using your brainstorming sheet, follow these three steps:

1. Circle or otherwise mark the points that will become main sections.
2. Connect each main point with its supporting ideas, using lines or arrows.
3. Delete material that seems irrelevant to your purpose.

Figure 1–8 shows the results of applying steps 1 and 2 to a writing project at McDuff, Inc., the company used throughout this book. Diane Simmons, office services manager at the Baltimore branch, plans to recommend a change in food service. She uses the brainstorming technique to record her major and minor points. First, she circles the six main ideas. As it happens, these ideas include three main problems and three possible solutions, so she labels them P#1 through P#3 (problems) and S#1 through S#3 (solutions). Second, she draws arrows between each main point and its related minor points. In this case, there is no material to be deleted. Although the result is messy, it prepares her for the next step of writing the formal outline.

Like Diane Simmons, you will face one main question as you plan your outline: What pattern of organization best serves the material? Chapter 3 presents an "ABC format" that applies to overall structure. Each document should start with

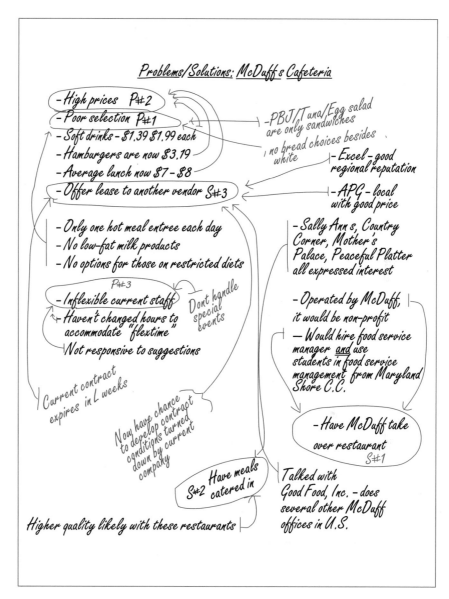

FIGURE 1–8
The outlining process: Early stage

an **A**bstract (summary), move to the **B**ody (discussion), and end with a **C**onclusion. However, outlines usually cover only the *body* of a document. Here are some common patterns to consider in outlining the middle part, or body, of a report or proposal. The examples all relate to a decision by McDuff, Inc., to revamp its photocopying system:

PROBLEMS AND SOLUTIONS: CURRENT CAFETERIA IN BUILDING

I. Problem #1: Poor selection
  A. Only one hot meal entree each day
  B. Only three sandwiches—PBJ, egg salad, and tuna
  C. Only one bread—white
  D. No low-fat milk products (milk, yogurt, LF cheeses, etc.)
  E. No options for those with restricted diets
II. Problem #2: High prices
  A. Soft drinks from $1.39 to $1.99 each
  B. Hamburgers now $3.19
  C. Average lunch now $7–$8
III. Problem #3: Inflexible staff
  A. Unwilling to change hours to meet McDuff's flexible work schedule
  B. Have not acted on suggestions
  C. Not willing to cater special events in building
IV. Solution #1: End lease and make food service a McDuff department
  A. Hire food service manager
  B. Use students enrolled in food service management program at
     Maryland Shore Community College
  C. Operate as nonprofit operation—just cover expenses
V. Solution #2: Hire outside restaurant to cater meals in to building
  A. Higher quality likely
  B. Initial interest by four nearby restaurants
    1. Sally Ann's
    2. Country Corner
    3. Mother's Palace
    4. Peaceful Platter
VI. Solution #3: Continue leasing space but change companies
  A. Initial interest by three vendors
    1. Excel—good regional reputation for quality
    2. APG—close by and local, with best price
    3. Good Food, Inc.—used by two other McDuff offices with good
       results
  B. Current contract over in two months
  C. Chance to develop contract not acceptable to current company

---

FIGURE 1–9
The outlining process: Later stage

- **Chronological:** The writer wants to describe the step-by-step procedure for completing a major photocopying project, from receiving copy at the copy center to sending it out the next day.
- **Parts of an object:** The writer wants to provide a part-by-part description of the current photocopying machine, along with a list of parts that have been replaced in three years of service calls.

- **Simple to complex or vice versa:** The writer wants to describe problems associated with the current photocopying procedure, working from minor to major problems or vice versa.
- **Specific to general (inductive):** The writer wants to begin by listing about 20 individual complaints about the present photocopying machine, later arriving at three general groupings into which all the individual complaints fall.
- **General to specific (deductive):** The writer wants to lead off with some generalizations about photocopying problems at McDuff, followed by a description of incidents related to poor copies, missed deadlines, and high service bills.

■ *Outline Step 3: Draft a Final Outline*

Once related points are clustered, it is time to transform what you have done into a somewhat ordered outline. (See Figure 1–9, which continues with the report context used in Figure 1–8.) This step allows you to (1) refine the wording of your points and (2) organize them in preparation for writing the draft. Although you need not produce the traditional outline with Roman numerals, etc., some structure is definitely needed. Abide by these basic rules:

- **Depth:** Make sure every main point has enough subpoints so that it can be developed thoroughly in your draft.
- **Balance:** When you decide to subdivide a point, have at least two breakdowns (because *any* object that is divided will have at least two parts). This same rule applies to headings and subheadings in the final document. (In fact, a good outline will provide you with the wording for headings and subheadings. The outline even becomes the basis for a table of contents in formal documents.)
- **Parallel Form:** For the sake of consistency, phrase your points in either topic or sentence form. Sentences give you a head start on the draft, but they may lock you into wording that needs revision later. Most writers prefer the topic approach; topics take up less space on the page and are easier to revise as you proceed through the draft.

WRITING INITIAL DRAFTS

With your research and outline completed, you are ready to begin the draft. This stage in the writing process should go quickly *if* you have planned well. Yet many writers have trouble getting started. The problem is so widespread that it has its own name—"writer's block." If you suffer from it, you are in good company; some of the best and most productive writers often face the "block."

In business and industry, the worst result of writer's block is a tendency to delay the start of writing projects, especially proposals. These delays can lead to rushed final drafts and editing errors. Outlining and other planning steps are wasted if you fail to complete drafting on time. The suggestions that follow can help you to start writing and then to keep the words flowing.

■ *Drafting Step 1: Schedule at Least a One-Hour Block of Drafting Time*

Most writers can keep the creative juices flowing for at least an hour *if* distractions are removed. Rather than writing for three or four hours with your door open and thus with constant interruptions, schedule an hour or two of uninterrupted writing time. Most other business can wait an hour, especially considering the importance of good writing to your success. Colleagues and staff members will adjust to your new strategy for drafting reports. They may even adopt it themselves.

■ *Drafting Step 2: Do Not Stop to Edit*

Later, you will have time to revise your writing; that time is not now. Instead, force yourself to get ideas from the outline to paper or computer screen as quickly as possible. Most writers have trouble getting back into their writing pace once they have switched gears from drafting to revising.

■ *Drafting Step 3: Begin with the Easiest Section*

In writing the body of the document, you need not move chronologically from beginning to end. Because the goal is to write the first draft quickly, you may want to start with the section that flows best for you. Later, you can piece together sections and adjust content.

■ *Drafting Step 4: Write Summaries Last*

As already noted, the outline used for drafting covers just body sections of the document. Only after you have drafted them should you write overview sections like summaries. You cannot summarize a report until you have actually completed it. Because most writers have trouble with the summary—a section that is geared mainly for decision-makers in the audience—they may get bogged down if they begin writing it prematurely.

REVISING DRAFTS

You may have heard the old saw, "There is no writing, only rewriting." In technical writing, as in other types of communication, careful revision breeds success. The term *revision* encompasses four tasks that transform early drafts into final copy:

1. Adjusting and reorganizing content
2. Editing for style
3. Editing for grammar
4. Editing for mechanics

Following are some broad-based suggestions for revising your technical prose. For more details, consult chapter 15, "Style in Technical Writing," or the Handbook at the end of the book. Also, chapter 4 examines the use of word processing during the revision process.

■ *Revision Step 1: Adjust and Reorganize Content*

In this step, go back through your draft to (1) expand sections that deserve more attention, (2) shorten sections that deserve less, and (3) change the location of sentences, paragraphs, or entire sections. The use of word processing has made this step considerably easier than it used to be.

■ *Revision Step 2: Edit for Style*

The term *style* refers to changes that make writing more engaging, more interesting, more readable. Such changes are usually matters of choice, not correctness. For example, you might want to:

- Shorten paragraphs
- Rearrange a paragraph to place the main point first
- Change passive-voice sentences to active
- Shorten sentences
- Define technical terms
- Add headings, lists, or graphics

One stylistic error deserves special mention because of its frequency: long, convoluted sentences. As a rule, you should simplify a sentence if its meaning cannot easily be understood in one reading. Also, be wary of sentences that are so long you must take a breath before you complete them.

■ *Revision Step 3: Edit for Grammar*

You probably know your main grammatical weaknesses. Perhaps comma placement or subject-verb agreement gives you problems. Or maybe you have trouble distinguishing couplets like imply/infer, effect/affect, or complementary/complimentary. In editing the document for grammar, focus on the particular errors that have given you problems in the past.

■ *Revision Step 4: Edit for Mechanics*

Your last revision pass should be for mechanical errors such as misspelled words, misplaced pages, incorrect page numbers, missing illustrations, and errors in numbers (especially cost figures). Word-processing software can help prevent some of these errors, such as most misspellings, but computer technology has not eliminated the need for at least one final proofing check.

This four-stage revision process will produce final drafts that reflect well on you, the writer. Here are two final suggestions that apply to all stages of the process:

1. Depend on another set of eyes besides your own. One strategy is to form a partnership with another colleague, whether in a technical writing class or on the job. In this arrangement, you both agree that you will carefully review each other's writing. This "buddy system" works better than simply asking favors of friends and colleagues. Choose a colleague in whom you have some confidence and from whom you can expect consistent editing quality. However, never make changes suggested by another person unless you fully understand the reason for doing so. After all, it is *your* writing.

2. Remember the importance of completing each step separately. Revising in stages yields the best results.

WRITING IN GROUPS

Writing can seem like a lonely act at times. Your own experience in school may reinforce the image of the solitary writer—with sweat on brow—toiling away on research, outlines, and drafts. In fact, this description does *not* typify much writing in the working world outside college. Writing in teams is the rule rather than the exception in many professions and organizations.

Group writing (also called collaborative writing) can be defined in this way:

> **Group writing:** the effort by two or more people to produce one document, with each member *sharing* in the writing process. The term assumes all members actually help with the drafting process, as opposed to (1) the writing of a document by one person, after all group members have met to discuss the project, or (2) group editing of something written by one person. The team must have clear goals and effective leadership to achieve results. Group work can be done in person, over the phone, or through electronic mail (e-mail) on the computer.

This section further defines group writing, highlighting benefits of the strategy and noting some pitfalls to avoid. Then you are given guidelines for using group writing in your classes and on the job.

Benefits and Drawbacks of Group Writing

Most organizations rely on people working together throughout the writing process to produce documents. The success of writing projects depends on information and skills contributed by varied employees. For example, a proposal writing team may include technical specialists, marketing experts, graphic designers, word processors, and technical editors. The company depends on all these individuals working together to produce the final product, a first-rate proposal.

In group writing, however, the whole is greater than the sum of the parts. In other words, benefits go beyond the collective specialties and experience of individual group members. Participants create *new* knowledge as they plan, draft, and edit their work together. They become better contributors and faster learners simply by being a part of the social process of a team. Discussion with fellow participants moves them toward new ways of thinking and inspires them to contribute their best. This collaborative effort yields ideas, writing strategies, and editorial decisions that result from the mixing of many perspectives.

Of course, group writing does have drawbacks. Most notably, the group must make decisions without falling into time traps that slow down the process. There must be procedures for getting everyone's ideas on the table *and* for reaching decisions on time. A leader with good interpersonal skills will help the group reach its potential, whereas an indecisive or autocratic leader will be an obstacle to progress. Good leadership rests at the core of every effective writing team.

In addition to good leadership, shared decision-making is at the heart of every successful writing team. Group writing is not one writer simply getting information from many people before he or she writes a draft. Nor is it one person writing a draft for the editorial red pen of individuals at higher levels. These two models may have their place in some types of company writing, but they do not constitute group writing. Instead, participants in a group must work together during the planning, drafting, and revising stages of writing. Although the degree of collaboration may vary, all forms of group writing differ considerably from the model of one person writing with only occasional help from others.

Guidelines for Group Writing

This section offers six pointers for group writing, to be used in this course and throughout your career. The suggestions concern the writing process as well as interpersonal communication.

■ Group Guideline 1: Get to Know Your Group

Most people are sensitive about strangers evaluating their writing. Before collaborating on a writing project, therefore, learn as much as you can about those with whom you will be working. Drop by their offices before your first meeting, or talk informally as a group before the writing process begins. In other words, first establish a personal relationship. This familiarity will help set the stage for the spirited dialogue, group criticism, and collaborative writing to follow.

■ Group Guideline 2: Set Clear Goals and Ground Rules

Every writing group needs a common understanding of its objectives and procedures for doing business. Either before or during the first meeting, these questions should be answered:

1. What is the group's main objective?
2. Who will serve as team leader?

3. What exactly will be the leader's role in the group?
4. How will the group's activities be recorded?
5. How will responsibilities be distributed?
6. How will conflicts be resolved?
7. What will the schedule be?
8. What procedures will be followed for planning, drafting, and revising?

The guidelines that follow offer suggestions for answering the preceding questions.

■ *Group Guideline 3: Use Brainstorming Techniques for Planning*

The term *brainstorming* means to pool ideas in a *nonjudgmental* fashion. In this early stage, participants should feel free to suggest ideas without criticism by colleagues in the group. This nonjudgmental approach does not come naturally to most people. Thus the leader may have to establish ground rules for brainstorming before the group proceeds.

Here is one sample approach to brainstorming:

Step 1: The group recorder takes down ideas as quickly as possible.
Step 2: Ideas are written on large pieces of paper affixed to walls around the meeting room so all participants can see how major ideas fit together.
Step 3: Members use ideas as springboards for suggesting others.
Step 4: The group takes some time to digest ideas generated during the first session, before meeting again.

Results of a brainstorming session might look much like a nonlinear outline produced during a solo writing project (see Figure 1–8). The goal of both is to generate as many ideas as possible; these ideas can be culled and organized later.

■ *Group Guideline 4: Use Storyboarding Techniques for Drafting*

Storyboarding helps propel participants from the brainstorming stage toward completion of a first draft. It also makes visuals an integral part of the document. Originating in the screenwriting trade in Hollywood, a storyboard is a sheet of paper that contains (1) one draft-quality illustration and (2) a series of sentences about one topic. (See Figure 1–10.) As applied to technical writing, the technique involves six main steps:

Step 1: The group or its leader assembles a topic outline from ideas brought forth during the brainstorming session.
Step 2: All group members are given one or more topics to develop on storyboard forms.

DOCUMENT TITLE: McDuff's Training Needs
STORYBOARD TOPIC: Results of employee survey
STORYBOARD WRITER: Susan Hernandez

1. In one sentence, summarize this section of the document.

The recent survey of employees showed a strong preference for nontechnical over technical training.

2. In sentence form, include the key points to be developed in this document section. Use same order that points will appear in document.

A. The greatest interest was in the area of sales and marketing training — engineers, in particular, feel deficient here.

B. Many employees also wanted further training in project management — with emphasis on scheduling, accounting practices, and basic management.

C. The third most called-for training area was communication skills — that is, report writing, grammar, and oral presentations.

D. Many employees want training in stress management, to reduce or manage on-the-job pressures and make work more enjoyable.

E. The fifth area of interest was technical training in the respondents' own area of expertise.

3. Include an illustration that supports the text in this document section.

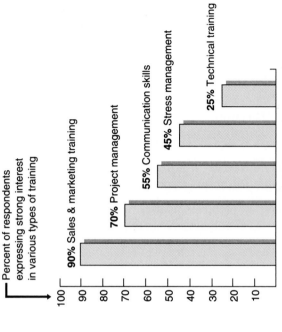

— Percent of respondents expressing strong interest in various types of training

90% Sales & marketing training
70% Project management
55% Communication skills
45% Stress management
25% Technical training

Caption: Training Interests of McDuff Employees

(The 5 most popular training topics, according to company-wide employee survey.)

FIGURE 1–10
Completed storyboard

Step 3: Each member works independently on the boards, creating an illustration and a series of subtopics for each main topic (see Figure 1–10).

Step 4: Members meet again to review all completed storyboards, modifying them where necessary and agreeing on key sentences.

Step 5: Individual members develop draft text and related graphics from their own storyboards.

Step 6: The group leader or the entire group assembles the draft from the various storyboards.

■ *Group Guideline 5: Agree on a Thorough Revision Process*

As with drafting, all members usually help with revision. Team editing can be difficult, however, as members strive to reach consensus on matters of style. Here are some suggestions for keeping the editing process on track:

- Avoid making changes simply for the sake of individual preference.
- Search for areas of agreement among group members, rather than areas of disagreement.
- Make only those changes that can be supported by accepted rules of style, grammar, and usage.
- Ask the group's best all-round stylist to do a final edit.

This review will help produce a uniform document, no matter how many people work on the draft.

■ *Group Guideline 6: Use Computers to Communicate*

When team members are at different locations, computer technology can be used to complete some or all of the project. Team members must have personal computers and the software to connect their machines to a network, allowing members to send and receive information on-line. This section describes three specific computer applications that can improve communication among members of a group-writing project: e-mail, computer conference, and groupware. Chapter 4 ("Page Design") will discuss how the individual writer can use computers to plan, draft, and revise copy. Chapter 7 ("Letters and Memos") will discuss stylistic features of electronic mail.

- **Electronic Mail (e-mail):** Individuals can send and receive messages from their office computers or from remote locations. Like written memos, e-mail messages usually include the date, sender, receiver, and subject. Unlike written memos, the style is often quite informal. Messages are sent at a time convenient for the sender and saved until a time that readers check their mail.
- **Computer Conference:** Members of a group can make their own comments and respond to comments of others on a specific topic or project. Computer

conferences may be open to all interested users or open only to a particular group. For the purposes of group writing, the conference probably would be open only to members of the writing team. A leader may be chosen to monitor the contributions and keep the discussion focused. Contributions may be made over a long period, as opposed to a conventional face-to-face meeting wherein all team members are present at the same time. Accumulated comments in the conference can be organized or indexed by topic. The conference may be used to brainstorm and thus to generate ideas for a project, or it may be used for comments at a later stage of the writing project.

- **Groupware:** Team members using this software can work at the same time, or different times, on any part of a specific document. Groupware that permits contributions at the same time is called "synchronous"; that which permits contributions at different times is called "asynchronous." Because team members are at different locations, they may also be speaking on the phone at the same time they are writing or editing with synchronous groupware. Such sophisticated software gives writers a much greater capability than simply sending a document over a network for editing or comment. They can collaborate with team members on a document at the same time, almost as if they were in the same room. With several windows on the screen, they can view the document itself on one screen and make comments and changes on another screen.

Computers can be used to overcome many obstacles for writers and editors in different locations. Indeed, electronic communication can help to accomplish all the guidelines just noted. Specifically, (1) e-mail can be used by group members to get to know each other, (2) e-mail or a computer conference can be used to establish goals and ground rules, (3) synchronous, or real-time, groupware can help a team brainstorm about approaches to the project (and may, in fact, encourage more openness than a face-to-face brainstorming session), (4) computer conferences combined with groupware can approximate the storyboard process, and (5) either synchronous or asynchronous groupware can be used to approximate the editing process.

Granted, such techniques lack the body language used in face-to-face meetings. Yet when personal meetings are not possible, computerized communication can provide a substitute that allows writers in different locations to work together to meet their deadline.

Of course, computers can create problems during a group writing project, if you are not careful. When different parts of a document have been written and stored by different writers, your group must be vigilant during the final editing and proofreading stages. Before submitting it, review the document for consistency and correctness.

Team writing may play an important part in your career. If you use the preceding techniques, you and your team members will build on each other's strengths to produce top-quality writing.

COMMUNICATION CHALLENGE

"A Group Project Gone Bad"

Professor Sam Crosby's technical writing class was assigned a group writing project. Each of the five groups was to (1) learn about the documents produced by a particular office on their campus, Irwin State, (2) produce a written report on their findings, and (3) give a short presentation to highlight their findings to the class. Professor Crosby announced that he would give the same grade to all members of the same group. As part of his introduction to the assignment, he covered the guidelines for group writing included in this chapter. The groups had about 10 days from the time they were assigned the project, on Wednesday, until the time they had to hand in the paper and give a speech, the following Friday.

As is sometimes the case in group projects, one of the teams in Crosby's class encountered problems with the assignment. What follows are details about (1) Group 4's make-up as well as its field activities during the project, (2) the group's preparation for the oral and written report, (3) response to the grade by members of the group, and (4) questions for discussion.

Group 4 Fieldwork

Group 4—composed of Hester Pinn, Bob Simpson, Hector Lopez, and Miranda Arons—was assigned to the Public Relations (PR) Department. To complete its project, the group planned to (1) conduct some library research on PR writing, (2) interview the director of the PR staff, (3) write a short report on its research and interviews, and (4) deliver a panel presentation in which all four members would speak. At its first meeting in class on Wednesday, Group 4 selected a team leader (Miranda), set up a tentative schedule of activities, and agreed to meet the next day at noon at the library to begin its research.

The next day all members except Bob showed up on time. After waiting 10 minutes, the other three members went to the library computer terminals and began locating research sources. By the time Bob arrived a half hour later, the group had jotted down eight periodical sources. They divided up the list of sources and split up to find, read, and photocopy two articles each. Later they reconvened to discuss what they found. They agreed to write one-paragraph summaries of their articles and meet again the next day in the library.

When they met the next day, everyone arrived on time. However, Hester brought only one of the two summaries, noting that the other article was too difficult to read and summarize in the time she had. She promised to finish the second summary that night. Then all four group members proceeded to read the seven summaries and agree on a list of questions to ask the PR director on the content, format, and production of PR documents at Irwin State. Bob, however, wanted to make the report more interesting for the class and suggested they expand their questions to include several about career possibilities in public relations for Irwin State graduates. Although the other team members worried that his questions would be off the assigned topic, they agreed to include them in the interview.

Group 4 arranged to meet the PR director, Rachelle Cochran, on Monday at noon in the cafeteria. Both Bob and Hester arrived late, so Miranda and Hector conducted the first half of the interview on their own. Then Bob and Hester arrived, the interview was completed, and the PR director returned to her office.

Work on the Oral Presentation and Written Report

After Ms. Cochran left the cafeteria, Group 4 stayed in the cafeteria a few more minutes to discuss remaining tasks and to write a scratch outline for the report. Failing to get volunteers, Miranda said she would write the first draft of the report and present it to the others for editing at a meeting at the campus word-processing center the next day, Tuesday. Both Hector and Hester said they had other obligations on Tuesday and Wednesday, so Miranda reluctantly agreed to delay the editing meeting until Thursday, the day before the project was due.

As for the panel presentation, the group decided that (1) Bob and Hester would give an overview of the library research conducted by the group, (2) Hector would discuss the results of the interview with Rachelle Cochran, and (3) Miranda would summarize the findings and conclusions of the project. Because the report was being edited the day before the deadline, they decided there would be no time to practice the presentation together. Instead, the other three members said they would call Miranda to summarize what they intended to cover. If she saw inconsistencies in the four parts, she could suggest changes. In short, they planned to "wing it" during their panel.

The members of Group 4 submitted their report and gave their presentation on time. Professor Crosby gave them a "C" on the written report, noting that there were some good ideas but that the editing needed work and the paper lacked a clear focus. He gave them a "C-" on the presentation, commenting that the panel seemed poorly coordinated.

Response to the Group Grade

Bob and Hester seemed satisfied with the grades and quickly left the classroom. Hector was disappointed. But because he had never participated in a successful group project, he had low expectations and shrugged his shoulders as he left the room. Miranda, however, was furious about the grade. She didn't know who to blame—the instructor, the other group members, or herself. Later that day she visited Professor Crosby and complained that having three weak members on her team doomed her to a mediocre project. Then she asked if she could complete an extra credit paper to replace her group project grade or at least to be added in with her other grades. Professor Crosby turned her down. He explained that as group leader, she should have exerted more leadership. Furthermore, he noted that if there were major problems, she should have told him before the project was submitted.

Questions for Discussion

Consider the following questions for class discussion. Base your responses on details from the case study and on information from this chapter's guidelines on group work.

1. From beginning to end, what are the various ways that this group project broke down?
2. What, if anything, could have been done to ensure, or at least to encourage, better participation by all group members?
3. One member of the group, Bob Simpson, clearly did not participate to the same degree as the others, and several other group members were lacking at times. What could have been done? Did the group leader, Miranda, have any special responsibilities in this regard?
4. Professor Crosby assigned Group 4 members with a final grade of "C" on the report and "C-" on the panel presentation. Which of the responses to the grade by the group members were appropriate? In particular, discuss Miranda's strategy in her meeting with Professor Crosby.
5. Did Professor Crosby provide adequate direction in the assignment and give an appropriate response to Miranda in their meeting?
6. What are some specific techniques that can be used within a group for keeping all members contributing adequately to the completion of the task?
7. What can a professor do to ensure or encourage the most effective operation of groups in a writing project?

CHAPTER SUMMARY

Technical writing refers to the many kinds of writing you will do in your career. In contrast to most academic writing, technical writing aims to get something done (not just to demonstrate knowledge), relays information from someone more knowledgeable about the topic (you) to someone less knowledgeable about it (the reader), and is read by people from mixed technical and decision-making levels.

For each writing project, you should complete a three-stage process of planning, drafting, and revising. Planning involves understanding your purpose, knowing the readers' needs, collecting information, and outlining major and minor points. In the drafting stage, you use the outline to write a first draft as quickly as possible—without stopping to make changes. Finally, the revision process requires that you adjust content and then edit for style, grammar, and mechanics.

Technical writing can be completed by you alone or by you as a member of a writing team. The latter approach is common in companies, for it exploits the strengths of the varied professionals within an organization. In group writing you work closely with your team during the planning, drafting, and revising processes.

ASSIGNMENTS

Your instructor will indicate whether assignments 1 through 6 should serve as the basis for class discussion, for a written exercise, or for both. Assignments 7, 8, 9, and 10 require a written response. Assignment 11 requires a brief oral presentation by groups.

1. Features of Academic Writing.

Option A. Select an example of writing that you wrote for a high school or college course other than this one. Then prepare a brief analysis in which you explain (1) the purpose of the writing sample, (2) the audience for which it was intended, and (3) the ways in which it differs from technical writing, as defined in this chapter.

Option B. As an alternative to using your own example, complete the assignment by using the following example. Assume that the passage was written as homework or as an in-class essay in an environmental science class in college.

There are many different responses that are possible in the event toxic waste contamination is suspected or discovered at a site. First, you can simply monitor the site by periodically taking soil and/or water samples to check for contamination. This approach doesn't solve the problem and may not prove politically acceptable when contamination is obvious to the community, but it does help determine the extent of the problem. A second approach—useful when contamination is likely or proved—is to contain the toxic waste by sealing off the site in some fashion, such as by building barriers between it and the surrounding area or by "capping" it in some manner (as in the case of a toxic waste pit). Basically, this alternative depends on the ability to isolate the toxic substances effectively. A third strategy, useful when the contamination is liquified (as with toxic groundwater), is to pump the water from under the ground or from surface ponds and then transport it to treatment systems.

A fourth method is appropriate when toxic substances need to be treated on-site, in which case they can be incinerated or they can be solidified at the site in some way. Then they can be placed in a landfill at the site. Fifth, waste can be hauled to another location where it can be incinerated or placed in some kind of secure landfill—when an off-site disposal approach is needed.

2. Features of Technical Writing.

Option A. Locate an example of technical writing (such as by borrowing it from a family member or an acquaintance who works in a technical profession). Then prepare a brief analysis in which you explain (1) the purpose for which the piece was written, (2) the apparent readers and their needs, (3) the way in which the example differs from typical academic writing, and (4) the relative success with which the piece satisfies this chapter's guidelines.

Option B. Using the following brief example of technical writing, prepare the analysis requested in Option A.

DATE: June 15, 1995
TO: Pat Jones, Office Coordinator
FROM: Sean Parker, Word-Processing Operator
SUBJECT: New Word-Processing Software

Introductory Summary

As you requested, I have examined the WordWonder word-processing software we are considering. On the basis of my observations, I recommend we secure one copy of WordWonder and test it in our office for two months. Then after comparing it to the other two packages we have tested, we can choose one of the three word-processing packages to use throughout the office.

Features of WordWonder

As we agreed, my quick survey of WordWonder involved reading the user's manual, completing the orientation disk, and meeting with a salesperson from the company. Here are the five features of the package that seemed most relevant to our needs:

1. Formatting Flexibility: WordWonder includes diverse "style sheets" to meet our needs in producing reports, proposals, letters, memos, articles, and even brochures. By engaging just one command on the keyboard, the user can change style sheets—whereby the program will automatically place text in a specified format.

2. Mailers: For large mailings, we can take advantage of WordWonder's "Mail Out" feature that automatically places names from mailing lists on form letters.

3. Documentation: To accommodate our staff's research needs, WordWonder has the capacity to renumber and rearrange footnotes as text is being edited.

4. Page Review: This package's "PagePeek" feature permits the user to view an entire written page on the screen. Without having to print the document, he or she can then see how every page of text will actually look on the page.

5. Tables of Contents: WordWonder can create and insert page numbers on tables of contents, created from the headings and subheadings in the text.

Conclusion

Though I gave WordWonder only a brief look, my survey suggests that it may be a strong contender for use in our office. If you wish to move to the next step of starting a two-month office test, just let me know. Then I will make arrangements with the manufacturer for us to receive a complimentary trial copy.

---

3. **Purpose and Audience.** The following examples deal with the same topic in four different ways. Using this chapter's guidelines on purpose and audience, determine the main reason for which each excerpt was written and the technical level of the intended readers.

   A. You can determine the magnitude of current flowing through a resistor by use of this process:
      - Connect the circuit (power supply, resistor, ammeter, voltmeter).
      - Set the resistor knob to a setting of "1."

- Turn the voltage adjusting knob to the left until it stops rotating.
- Switch the voltmeter to "on" and make sure it reads 0.00 volts.
- Switch the power supply to "on."
- Slowly increase the voltage on the voltmeter from 0 to 10 volts.
- Take the reading from the ammeter to determine the amount of current flowing through the resistor.

B. After careful evaluation of several testers, I strongly recommend that Langston Electronics Institute purchase 100 Mantra Multitesters for use in our laboratories in Buffalo, Albany, and Syracuse.

C. Selected specifications for the Ames Multitester are as follows:

- Rangers 43
- DC Voltage 0–125–250mV 1.25–2.5–10–5–125–500–1000V
- AC Voltage 0–5–25–125–250–500–1000V
- DC Current 0–25–50μA–2.5–5–25–50–250–500mA–10amperes
- Resistance . . . . .0–2K–20K–200K–20 Mega ohms
- Decibels . . . .−20 to +62 in db 8 ranges
- Accuracy . . . .±3% on DC measurements
  ±4% on AC measurements
  ±3% on scale length on resistance
- Batteries . . . . .one type AA penlight cell
- Fuse . . . . .0.75A at 250V

Note that the accuracy rate for the Ames is within our requirements of ±6%, and is considerably lower than the three other types of testers currently used by our staff.

D. Having used the Ames Multitester in my own home laboratory for the last few months, I found it extremely reliable during every experiment. In addition, it is quite simple to operate and includes clear instructions. As a demonstration of this operational ease, my 10-year-old son was able to follow the instructions that came with the device to set up a functioning circuit.

4. **Interview.** Interview a friend, relative, or recent college graduate who works as a technical professional or manager. Gather specific information on these topics:

   - The percentage of the workweek spent on writing
   - Types of documents that are written and their purpose
   - Specific types of readers of these documents

5. **Contrasting Styles.** Find two articles on the same topic in a professional field that interests you. One article should be taken from a newspaper or magazine of general interest, such as one you would find on a newsstand. The other should be from a magazine or journal written mainly for professionals in the field you have chosen. Now contrast the two articles according to purpose, intended audience, and level of technicality.

6. **Contrasting Audiences.** Photocopy three articles from the same Sunday issue of a local or national newspaper. Choose each article from a different section of the paper—for example, you could use the sections on automobiles, business, travel, personal computers, national political events, local events, arts, editorials, or employment. Describe the intended audience of each article. Then explain why you think the author has been successful, or unsuccessful, in reaching the particular audience for each article.

7. **Rewrite for Different Audience.** Locate an excerpt from a technical article or textbook, preferably on a topic that interests you because of your background or col-

lege major. Rewrite all or part of the selection so that it can be understood by readers who have no previous knowledge of the topic.

8. **Group Writing #1.** Your instructor will divide you into groups of three to five members for completing this assignment. Follow the guidelines for group writing in this chapter. (If your instructor decides that the storyboarding rule is impractical for this exercise, bypass that step.)

   Your objective is to write a brief evaluation of the teaching effectiveness of either the room in which your class is held or some other room or building of your instructor's choice. In following the tasks listed in this chapter, the group must establish criteria for evaluation, apply these criteria, and report on the results.

   Your brief report should have three parts: (1) a one-paragraph summary of the room's effectiveness, (2) a list of the criteria used for evaluation, and (3) details of how the room met or did not meet the criteria you established.

   Besides preparing the written report, be prepared to discuss the relative effectiveness with which the group followed this chapter's guidelines for group writing. What problems were encountered? How did you overcome them? How would you do things differently next time?

9. **Group Writing #2.** For this assignment, use either the draft below or the draft of a paper provided by your instructor. Your instructor will divide the class into working groups. Using this chapter's guidelines for revision and for group work, revise the draft. Focus your efforts on (a) eliminating excess words, (b) shortening sentences, and (c) dividing the passage into several paragraphs.

Most of us who fly in planes either take the safety of this particular mode of transportation for granted or resign ourselves to the fact that if a plane does manage to crash then we cannot do anything about it so we tend either to try hard to enjoy the flight while we're on it or to keep so busy during it such that our mind is preoccupied with other thoughts; however, when we do hear about a plane emergency that has occurred, we tend to wonder how we ourselves would respond in a similar situation or event. An example or instance for possible consideration might be the April 4, 1979, incident in which a flight traveling from New York to Minneapolis experienced a severe emergency situation that caused the plane to go into a nosedive, from its cruising altitude of almost 40,000 feet down to about a mile from the surface of the earth, while at the same time rolling completely over two times and diving at a speed so fast that passengers experienced G forces that forced them into the back of their seats without the ability to move their bodies. The captain, who was an experienced pilot, and his copilot and his flight engineer tried a number of different emergency techniques and responses during the over 40 seconds that they were careering toward the earth, but nothing seemed to work until at the last minute as a last resort they lowered the landing gear, which slowed the plane down to the point where the pilot was able to level off somewhat and prevent a fiery explosion into the earth, and after making a number of other emergency moves, the pilot was able to land at the Detroit airport without any serious injuries to the passengers or flight crew. It appeared after some investigating that the incident was caused by leaks in the plane's hydraulic system, which then caused various failures in the plane that affected its ability to fly correctly, and although these kinds of events do not happen very often or frequently, when they do occur, they make us wonder how we would ourselves respond if we were in the cockpit or if we were among the passengers or if we were among the flight attendants.

---

10. **Computerized Communication #1.** If your campus computer facilities permit, set up an e-mail system with members of a writing group to which you have been assigned by your instructor. Decide on a topic upon which you and your team members will comment. Each member should make four comments, or "postings." At least one posting should be an original comment, and at least one should be a response to another member's comment. Print the group's copy and submit it to your instructor. Depending on the instructions you have been given, this assignment may be independent or it may be related to a larger group-writing assignment.

11. **Computerized Communication #2.** Using the working groups your instructor has established, collect information on collaborative learning and then make a brief oral presentation on your findings to the entire class. Your sources may involve print media or computer sources such as Internet.

2 McDuff, Inc., and the Global Workplace

Most employees at McDuff's corporate office in Baltimore depend on good writing for success in their jobs.

*C*hapter 1 defines technical writing and outlines the writing process. This second chapter introduces you to the fictional company, McDuff, Inc., used in examples and assignments throughout this book. Then chapters 3 and 4 cover organization and page design, respectively. Together, this four-chapter package provides the foundation for your work in the rest of the book.

The use of McDuff is intended to yield two main benefits for you as a student:

- **Real-World Context:** McDuff provides you with an extended case study in modern technical communication. By placing you in actual working roles, the text prepares you for writing and speaking tasks ahead in your career.
- **Continuity:** The use of McDuff material will lend continuity to class assignments and discussions throughout the term. Your frequent use of this international organization in assignments and class will emphasize the connections among all on-the-job assignments.

Thus McDuff gives you a window into an international organization similar to one where you may work soon. The rest of this chapter addresses four main topics related to McDuff—(1) an overview of corporate culture in the 1990s, (2) background of McDuff and its types of projects, (3) activities and positions at the corporate and branch offices, (4) typical writing tasks at McDuff—plus ethical guidelines for work and writing.

CORPORATE CULTURE IN THE '90S

As a preface to information about McDuff, the first part of this section presents three features common to the culture of any organization that may employ you. Then the second and third parts concentrate on two corporate trends of special note: the drive for quality and the focus on the global workplace.

Elements of a Company's Culture

Unless you become self-employed, you will work for some sort of business enterprise or nonprofit organization after you leave college. For simplicity here, we'll use the term *company* or *firm* to refer to any organization where you may work. As noted in chapter 1, the writing you do in a company differs greatly from the writing you do in college. The stakes on the job are much higher than a grade on your college transcript. Writing will directly influence your performance evaluations, your professional reputation, and your company's productivity and success in the marketplace. Given these high stakes, let's look at typical features of the organizations wherein you may spend your career.

Starting a job is both exciting and , sometimes, a bit intimidating. Although you look forward to practicing skills learned in college, you also wonder just how you will fare in new surroundings. Soon you discover that any organization you join has its own personality. This personality, or "culture," can be defined as follows:

> **Company culture:** term for the main features of life at a particular company. A company's culture is influenced by the firm's history, type of business, management style, values, attitude toward customers, and attitude toward its own employees. Taken together, all features of a particular company's culture create a definable quality of life within the working world of that company.

Before examining the culture at McDuff, let's look more closely at three features mentioned in the preceding definition: a firm's history, its type of business, and its management style.

■ Feature 1: Company History

A firm's origin often is central to its culture. On the one hand, the culture of a 100-year-old steel firm will depend on accumulated traditions to which most employees are accustomed. On the other hand, the culture of a recently established home electronics firm may depend more on the entrepreneurial spirit of its founders. Thus the facts, and even the mythology, of a company's origin may be central to its culture, especially if the person starting the firm remained at the helm for a long time. WalMart, for instance, possesses a culture very much connected to the dreams, aspirations, and open management style of its founder, the late Sam Walton. And IBM, while facing many changes in the computer marketplace during its history, still reflects the strong research-and-development orientation of its early leaders.

■ *Feature 2: Type of Business*

Culture is greatly influenced by a company's type of business. Many computer software firms, for example, are known for their flexible, nontraditional, and sometimes chaotic culture. Such firms encourage constant change and innovation. The industry's well-known competitiveness probably inspires this cultural trait. Some of the large computer hardware firms, however, have a culture focused more on tradition, formality, and custom. Yet both hardware and software companies share the same cultural trait of a high level of customer service.

■ *Feature 3: Management Style*

A major component of a company's culture is its style of leadership. Some companies run according to a rigid hierarchy, with all decisions coming from the top. Other companies have fewer top-down pronouncements from upper management. Instead, they involve a wide range of employees in the decision-making process. As you might expect, most firms have a decision-making culture somewhere between these two extremes.

These three features give you some idea of what makes up the culture of any company. A company's culture influences who is hired and promoted at the firm, how decisions are made, and even how company documents are written and reviewed. Now let's examine one particular feature—the emphasis on quality—which is becoming a part of the life of many companies throughout the world, including McDuff.

The Search for Quality

"Total quality management (TQM)," "continuous improvement," and similar phrases have become buzzwords in today's workplace. They signal industry's effort to give customers better goods and services. The many spokespersons in this movement agree that the search for quality must permeate every part of an organization. It especially applies to employee productivity and customer service. This section highlights several features of this quality revolution, with special emphasis on relevance to written and oral communications.

■ *Quality Feature 1: Putting the Customer First*

Most quality experts agree that any successful company must keep its finger on the pulse of customers, never taking them for granted. Putting the customer first starts with the design of products and services. It also is reflected in the efficiency and sincerity with which complaints are handled.

In the area of communication, this responsiveness to the customer can be seen in the way a writer strives to understand the reader's needs before a report is written. The reader may be a manager within the writer's company, or a customer outside the firm. From the quality perspective, both internal and external readers alike are "customers" who deserve first-class treatment.

■ *Quality Feature 2: Stressing Teamwork Over Internal Competition*

Many quality experts believe we spend too much time pitting employees against each other, as in the way we distribute merit raises and give commissions on sales. These experts suggest that companies should focus attention on team goals, to promote the good of the entire company.

In communication, teamwork can translate into the need to increase the use of group writing (see chapter 1). Collaborative efforts help draw on specialties of writers, technical experts, editors, graphics specialists, and others to produce the best possible document. A culture that encourages group writing reduces the "lone ranger" mentality in communication. Employees work *together* for the good of the final written product.

■ *Quality Feature 3: Giving People the Freedom to Do Their Jobs*

Too often, management gets in the way of employee productivity by drawing a box around each person's responsibilities. Quality-centered firms, instead, give everyone more power to suggest changes that will improve the overall business. If employees believe their opinions are important to the overall plan of the company, they will be motivated to work harder and smarter.

In communication, this quality feature might mean that a good word processor should feel comfortable recommending improvements in writing style, rather than simply typing words without regard for the quality of the product. It might also mean that new hires, right out of school, would be encouraged to apply writing skills they learned in college to improve the company's report format, rather than simply following whatever format is handed to them by supervisors. Quality-based firms give all employees the authority to suggest improvements in the way the company does business.

■ *Quality Feature 4: Thinking Long Term, Not Short Term*

Most quality experts agree that focusing on short-term profits works against the long-term well-being of organizations. Instead, companies should cultivate permanent, trusting relationships with suppliers and with customers. Although such relationships may not produce immediate profits or savings, they will pay off in the end by reducing cyclical ups and downs in profits. Another long-term strategy is to support company training of all types for *all* levels of employees. In particular, people can be cross-trained in other jobs to avoid burnout, to help them understand more about the firm's business, and to prepare them for career advancement.

In communication, investing in the long term can mean training employees to write and speak well. One such investment is to produce an up-to-date writing manual. This manual should specify guidelines for format and style and provide excellent models of all company documents. Most important, it should be followed by employees at all levels.

The concern for quality may change the culture of companies throughout the world, including the ones where you may work. Now let's explore another corporate trend today—the move toward globalism.

The Global Workplace

Very possibly, you will work for an organization that does some business beyond the borders of its home country, one that may even have international offices, as does McDuff. Such organizations face opportunities and challenges of diversity among employees, customers, or both. They seek employees who can view issues from the perspective of people outside their culture. This section examines work in the global marketplace by posing 10 questions to ask when you communicate with someone from another country or culture. Asking and answering these questions may determine your personal success and that of your organization.

Let's start with the most important point, one that seems obvious and yet is often forgotten:

> People in different cultures have different ways of thinking, different ways of acting, and different expectations in communication.

To be sure, there are a few basic ethical guidelines evident in most cultures with which you will do business. But other than these core values, differences abound that should be studied by employees of multinational firms. Then these differences must be reflected in communication with colleagues, vendors, and customers. At the close of their excellent text, Iris Varner and Linda Beamer list five recommendations to help organizations with intercultural business communication:

1. "Train employees in intercultural business communication skills and distribute this training . . . to . . . employees at all levels. . . .

2. Send more people to foreign subsidiaries and don't restrict travel to top executives. Foreign travel should not be a perk but [instead] should meet specific business goals. . . .

3. Train employees in intercultural communication skills early in their careers. At this point employees are less costly and more flexible. . . .

4. Carefully evaluate employees as they are hired. . . . Interpersonal skills, language ability, a sense of adventure, and an open attitude may be much more important than specific technical skills. . . .

5. Above all, encourage a climate of excitement and adventure."[1]

Perhaps you will work for a firm that takes Varner and Beamer's enlightened view toward interculturalism. To prepare you for that possibility, this section includes some questions to ask about those with whom you communicate outside your own culture. Consider these questions to be a starting point for your journey toward understanding communication in the global workplace.

Question 1—*Work:* What are their views about work and work rules?

Question 2—*Time:* What is their approach to time, especially with regard to starting and ending times for meetings, being on time for appointments, expected response time for action requests, hours of the regular workday, etc.?

Question 3—*Beliefs:* What are the dominant religious and philosophical belief systems in the culture, and how do they affect the workplace?

Question 4—*Gender:* What are their views of equality of men and women in the workplace, and how do these views affect their actions?

Question 5—*Personal Relationships:* What degree of value is placed on close personal relationships among people doing business with each other?

Question 6—*Teams:* What part does teamwork have in their business, and, accordingly, how is individual initiative viewed?

Question 7—*Communication Preferences:* What types of business communication are valued most—formal writing, informal writing, formal presentations, casual meetings, e-mail, phone conversations?

Question 8—*Negotiating:* What are their expectations for the negotiation process, and, more specifically, how do they convey negative information?

Question 9—*Body Language:* What types of body language are most common in the culture, and how do they differ from your own?

Question 10—*Writing Options:* What writing conventions are most important to them, especially in prose style and the organization of information? How important is the design of the document in relationship to content and organization?

---

[1] Iris Varner and Linda Beamer, *Intercultural Communication in the Global Workplace* (Chicago: Irvin, 1995), 306-308. The ten questions in this section are gleaned from information in two excellent sources for the student of international communication: the Varner/Beamer text and *International Business Communication,* by David A. Victor (New York: HarperCollins, 1992).

To be sure, asking these questions does not mean we bow to attitudes that conflict with our own ethical values, as in the equal treatment of women in the workplace. It only means that we first seek to comprehend cultures with which we are dealing before we operate within them. Intercultural knowledge translates into power in the international workplace. If we are aware of diversity, then we will be best prepared to act.

It might help to see how some of these issues were addressed by Sarah Logan, a marketing specialist who transferred to McDuff's Tokyo office three years ago. In her effort to find new clients for McDuff's services, she discovered much about the Japanese culture that helped her and her colleagues do business in Japan. For example, she learned that Japanese workers at all levels depend more on their identification with a group than on their individual identity. Thus Sarah's marketing prospects in Japan felt most comfortable discussing their work in a corporate department or team, rather than their individual interests or accomplishments—at least until a personal relationship was established.

Sarah learned that an essential goal of Japanese employees is what they call "Wa"—harmony among members of a group and, for that matter, between the firm and those doing business with it. Accordingly, her negotiations with the Japanese often took an indirect path. Personal relationships usually were established and social customs usually observed before any sign of business occurred. A notable exception, she discovered, occurred among the smaller, more entrepreneurial Japanese firms, where employees often displayed a "Western" predisposition toward getting right down to business.

She also discovered that Japanese business is dominated by men more than in her own culture and that there tends to be more separation of men and women in social contexts. Although this cultural feature occasionally frustrated her, she tried to focus on understanding behavior rather than judging it from her own perspective. Moreover, she knew Japan is making changes in the role of women. Indeed, her own considerable success in getting business for McDuff suggested that Japanese value ability and hard work most of all.

Like Sarah Logan, you should enter every intercultural experience with a mind open to learning about those with whom you will work. Adjust your communication strategies so that you have the best chance of succeeding in the international marketplace. Intercultural awareness does *not* require that you jettison your own ethics, customs, or standards. Instead, it provides you with a wonderful opportunity to learn about, empathize with, and show respect for the views of others.

BACKGROUND AND TYPES OF PROJECTS

Today McDuff, Inc., is trying hard to develop a company culture based on a concern for quality and intercultural awareness. The firm's management believes such an effort is crucial to the success of the firm. This section takes a detailed look at

McDuff, first with a brief overview of its history and then with a description of its major project types.

History of McDuff, Inc.

Just out of Georgia Tech in 1950, Rob McDuff spent several years as a civil engineer in the U.S. Army Corps of Engineers during the Korean War. Then in 1954, he started a small engineering consulting firm in Baltimore, Maryland, where he had grown up. This firm's specialty was doing consulting work for construction firms and real estate developers. Specifically, McDuff, Inc., tested soils and then recommended foundation designs for structures that were being proposed.

In the early days, Rob McDuff did much of the fieldwork himself. He also analyzed the data, wrote reports, and did the marketing for new business. Work progressed well, and his new company earned a reputation for high-quality service. Now Rob McDuff nostalgically looks back upon those days as some of the most satisfying of his career. He had seized the opportunity to fulfill a dream that many people still have today: starting a business and then using skill, hard work, and imagination to make it grow.

From its founding in 1954 until about 1958, the company worked mostly for construction firms in the Baltimore area. Each job—whether a building, dam, or highway—involved tasks like those listed in Figure 2–1. The work was not glamorous. Yet it provided an important service. By the early 1960s, the firm enjoyed

---

McDuff Sequence of Tasks
Typical Construction Job:
1954-1958

1. **Reviewing** whatever information was already on file about the construction site

2. **Visiting** the site to observe and record surface features such as rock formations or waste dumps

3. **Drilling** one or more borings (deep, cylindrical holes) into the earth, using special equipment to collect the dirt and rock samples from various depths

4. **Testing** the samples back in the office laboratory

5. **Analyzing** the laboratory data to come up with recommendations for foundation design

6. **Writing** a report that records project activities and specific recommendations for the client

7. **Observing** construction activities, like the pouring of concrete slabs, to be sure correct procedures are followed

---

FIGURE 2–1
McDuff sequence of tasks, typical construction job

a first-rate reputation. It had offices in Baltimore and Boston and about 80 employees.

McDuff, Inc., kept growing steadily, with a large spurt in the mid-1960s and another in the 1980s. The first was tied to increased oil exploration in all parts of the world. Oil firms needed experts to test soils, especially in offshore areas. The results of these projects were used to position oil rigs at locations where they could withstand rough seas. The second growth period was tied to environmental work required by the federal government, state agencies, and private firms. McDuff became a major player in the waste-management business, consulting with clients about ways to store or clean up hazardous waste.

Today, as it nears its fiftieth birthday, McDuff, Inc., has about 2,500 employees. There are nine offices in the United States and six overseas, as well as a corporate headquarters in Baltimore that is separate from the Baltimore branch office. McDuff in the late 1990s performs a wide variety of work. What started as a consulting engineering firm has expanded into one that does both technical and nontechnical work for a variety of customers.

Projects

Every company must improve its products and services to stay in business. McDuff is no exception. If it had stayed just with soils testing work, the company would be stagnant today. Periodic slowdowns in the construction and oil industries would have taken their toll. Fortunately, the company diversified. These are its seven main project areas today:

1. Soils work on land: Still the company's bread-and-butter work, these projects involve (a) taking soil samples, (b) testing samples in the laboratory, and (c) making design recommendations for foundations and other parts of office buildings, dams, factories, subdivisions, reservoirs, and mass transit systems. When done well, this kind of work helps to prevent later problems, like cracks in building walls.

2. Soils work at sea: Now a smaller market than it was in the 1970s and early 1980s, this geological and engineering work used to be done exclusively for oil and gas companies. It helped them to place offshore platforms at safe locations or to select drilling locations with the best chance of hitting oil. Now, however, McDuff also is hired by countries and states who want to preserve the ecologically sensitive offshore environment. By collecting and analyzing data from its ship, *Dolphin,* McDuff helps clients decide whether an offshore area should be preserved or developed.

3. Construction monitoring: Besides designing parts of structures, McDuff also helps observe construction. Here are some services it offers during the construction process:

- Checking the quality of concrete being poured into structures like cooling towers for nuclear power plants

- Watching construction workers to make sure they follow proper procedures
- Testing the strength of concrete and other foundation materials, once they are put in place

4. Construction management: About 10 years ago, McDuff got into the business of actually supervising projects other than its own jobs. Large construction companies hire McDuff to orchestrate all parts of a project so that it is completed on time. The work involves these activities:

- Establishing a schedule
- Observing the work of subcontractors
- Regularly informing contractors about job progress

5. Environmental management: In the mid-1970s, Rob McDuff began to realize that garbage—all kinds of it—could mean big business for his firm. Suddenly the United States and other countries faced major problems caused by the volume of current wastes and by improper disposal of wastes since World War II. As McDuff's fastest growing market, environmental management work can involve one or more of these tasks:

- Testing surface soil and water for toxic wastes
- Drilling borings to see if surface pollution has filtered into the groundwater
- Designing a cleanup plan
- Supervising the cleanup
- Predicting the impact of proposed projects on the environment
- Analyzing the current environmental health of wetlands, beaches, national forests, lakes, and other areas

As Rob McDuff had hoped, managing wastes and determining the environmental impact of proposed projects proved to be excellent markets. Although there is growing competition, the company got into the business early enough to establish a good reputation for reliable, affordable work.

6. Equipment development: Here the firm departs from its traditional emphasis on services and instead produces products. The ED group, as it is known, designs and builds specialized equipment, both for McDuff's own project needs and for its clients. As the company's newest and most innovative group, it takes on a variety of projects. For example, it is building mechanisms as diverse as a prototype for a new device to test water pollution levels, on the one hand, and a new instrument gauge to install in tractors, on the other. Although the ED group is based in the Baltimore corporate office, it is mobile enough to go to other offices—even in other countries—to complete projects.

7. Training: McDuff entered the training business about five years ago, when it realized that there was a good market for technical training in skills represented by the firm. Recently the Training Department also started offering nontechnical training in areas such as report writing, since the company employs several writers who are excellent trainers.

These seven project areas reflect McDuff's diversity. Though starting as a traditional engineering firm, McDuff has sought out new markets and become a scrappy competitor in many areas. Still an active company president at age 68, Rob McDuff likes to think that the entrepreneurial spirit thrives in this company he started out of his basement almost 50 years ago.

CORPORATE AND BRANCH OFFICES

Headquarters

McDuff, Inc., has fifteen branch offices and a corporate headquarters. Though not a large company by international standards, it has become well known within its own fields. The company operates as a kind of loose confederation. Each office enjoys a good measure of independence. Yet some corporate structure is required for these purposes:

1. To coordinate projects that involve employees from several offices
2. To prevent duplication of the same work at different offices
3. To ensure fairness, consistency, and quality in the handling of human resources issues throughout the firm (salaries, benefits, workload, and so forth)

The corporate office gives special attention to problems related to international communications. Among its non-U.S. clients and employees, it must respond to differences in cultures and ways of doing business. This effort can mean the difference between success or failure in negotiating deals, completing projects, hiring employees, and so forth.

The corporate office in Baltimore is housed in a building across the street from the Baltimore branch office. In Rob McDuff's mind, this separation is important. He likes to keep the mostly "overhead" functions of the corporate office distinct from the mostly profit-generating functions of the branches. Also, he believes the physical separation is symbolic to offices outside of Baltimore, which already suspect that the large Baltimore branch office receives special treatment from corporate headquarters. Figure 2–2 shows an organization chart for this office. What follows is a brief description of the responsibilities of each service group in the corporate office.

■ Service 1: Human Resources

The Human Resources Department performs mostly personnel-related tasks. Its main work covers these four fields:

1. **Employment:** The office handles job advertisements, ensures that branch offices follow government guidelines that apply to hiring, gives legal advice on workers' compensation, and visits college campuses to recruit prospective graduates.

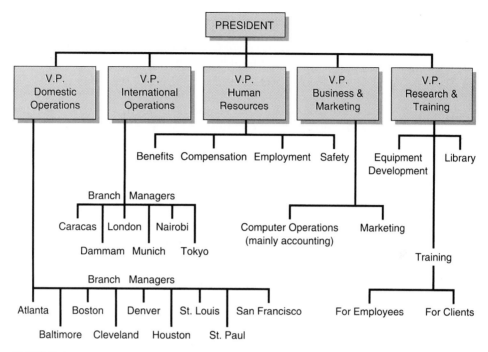

FIGURE 2–2
McDuff's corporate office

2. Benefits: Two staff members are responsible for handling company benefits. They send information to employees, check the accuracy of benefit deductions from paychecks, stay current about the newest benefits available for McDuff employees, and make recommendations to the corporate staff about benefit changes.

3. Safety: Given the company's interest in waste management, safety is crucial. The company hired a manager of safety in 1980 to complete these tasks:

- Educate employees about the importance of safe work practices
- Provide proper equipment and training
- Visit job sites to make safety checks
- Respond to questions by government agencies

4. Compensation: The compensation expert has three main duties:

- Monitoring salaries at all offices to ensure some degree of uniformity within the job classifications
- Researching salary guidelines in all professions represented in the firm, to make sure the company's salaries are competitive
- Monitoring branch offices to make sure performance evaluation interviews are done each year for each employee, before salary decisions are made

■ *Service 2: Project Coordination*

With fifteen offices spread over a wide geographical area, the company sometimes falls into the trap of the left hand not knowing what the right hand is doing. Specifically, individual offices may not know what project resources exist in another office. If a large project requires experts from several offices, the corporate office can assemble the team. To make this system work, the office keeps an accurate record of current projects at each office.

■ *Service 3: Marketing*

By working closely with clients, the engineers and scientists at every branch help to secure repeat work from current clients. Yet their technical responsibilities keep them from spending much time on marketing for *new* clients. The corporate office, however, has a marketing and proposal-writing staff that works extensively on seeking new business. Also, it helps branch offices write proposals requested by current clients.

■ *Service 4: Computer Operations*

The corporate office houses the company's two mainframe computers. These units are used mainly for the firm's accounting databases. Each branch office has terminals tied into the mainframes, giving them direct access to corporate databases in Baltimore. All employees can reach all other employees through e-mail. Of course, each branch also uses its own stand-alone computer systems for word processing and some other functions.

■ *Service 5: Research*

The term *research* at McDuff covers the services of the Equipment Development (ED) Group and the library. The ED lab is housed in the corporate office; it is the only group in the building that could be considered profit-generating. However, this young department is a start-up operation that does not make much money yet. It also retains the important "overhead" function of designing and building tools and other mechanisms that McDuff employees use on their projects. As for the McDuff library, two full-time librarians maintain a modest corporate collection that includes these items:

- Copies of all company reports and proposals since 1954
- Over 100 technical, business, and general periodicals
- Many reference works in technology and the sciences

McDuff employees around the world can receive information the same day they request it—by either phone or fax. In addition, each branch office usually keeps a small reference and periodical collection for its own use.

■ *Service 6: Training*

As noted earlier, McDuff now performs two types of training: in-house courses for its own employees, and external training for clients who need training in a number of technical and nontechnical subjects in which McDuff is proficient. The Training Department directs these efforts. Also, it helps McDuff employees find useful outside training or college courses.

Branches

Each McDuff branch is unique in its particular combination of technical and nontechnical positions. Yet all fifteen branches include a common management structure, as shown in Figure 2–3. A branch manager, who reports to one of two corporate vice presidents, supervises a group of four or more department managers. These managers, in turn, supervise the technical and nontechnical employees at the branch.

Branch positions below the manager can be grouped into four categories:

1. Technical professional
2. Nontechnical professional
3. Technical staff
4. Nontechnical staff

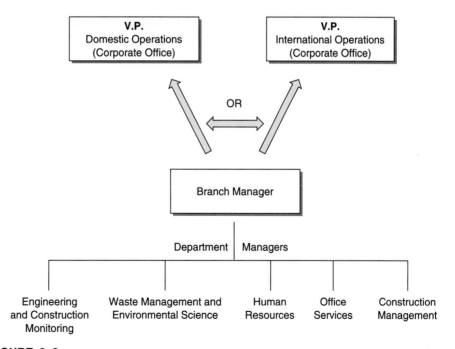

FIGURE 2–3
Branch office: Typical management structure

Figures 2–4 through 2–7 list some of the positions in these four groupings. Although all these employees are under the supervision of their respective branch managers, some interact closely with employees at the corporate level. For example, each human resources manager reports to his or her respective branch manager *and* works closely with the corporate vice president of human resources.

Most McDuff positions designated "professional" (Figures 2–4 and 2–5) require bachelor's degrees or higher in an appropriate field. Positions designated "staff" require at least a high-school education and sometimes more (such as a certificate program, vocational-technical training, or two-year college degree). Although these categories apply just to our fictional firm of McDuff, some may resemble jobs that exist in a real organization where you now work or will work.

Now that you have viewed McDuff's structure, you need to be made aware of a continuing management problem at the company—one common to many firms with widely spread offices and a corporate office. Branch employees often question whether the corporate people really understand and respond to their needs. Indeed, it is easy to feel misunderstood and even neglected when you work hundreds or thousands of miles from the company's hub. Effective written and

Position	Typical Education (Minimum)	Main Duties
1. Department Manager	• B.S. in engineering or science • M.S. in engineering or science **or** M.B.A.	• Oversees entire technical department in engineering or science
2. Project Manager	• B.S. in engineering or science or engineering technology	• Oversees entire projects in engineering, waste management, construction, etc.
3. Research Engineer (Equipment Development)	• B.S. in engineering or design • M.S. or Ph.D. in engineering or design	• Designs new tools, mechanisms, or other equipment at ED lab at corporate office
4. Field Engineer	• B.S. in engineering or engineering technology	• Completes site work for projects and then completes remaining work at office
5. Field Scientist	• B.S. in biology, chemistry, environmental science, etc.	• Completes site work for hazardous waste projects and then completes remaining work back at office

FIGURE 2–4
Sample positions: Technical professionals

Position	Typical Education (Minimum)	Main Duties
1. Office Services Manager	• B.S./B.A. in business	• Oversees accounting, word processing, purchasing, physical plant, etc.
2. Human Resources Manager	• B.S./B.A. in liberal arts or in human resources	• Oversees benefits, safety, employment, compensation
3. Technical Writer	• B.S./B.A. in technical communication **or** in liberal arts	• Helps write and edit reports, proposals, and other branch documents
4. Marketing Specialist	• B.S./B.A. in business **or** in liberal arts	• Writes to and visits potential clients • Helps with proposals
5. Training Specialist	• B.S./B.A. in education **or** in liberal arts	• Works with corporate office to plan in-house training **and** external training for clients

FIGURE 2–5
Sample positions: Nontechnical professionals

Position	Typical Education (Minimum)	Main Duties
1. Field/Lab Technician	• Vo-tech or associate's degree (in technical field)	• Recovers samples from site • Completes lab tests
2. Computer Operator	• Vo-tech or associate's degree (in technical field)	• Inputs data
3. Field Hand	• High school diploma	• Operates and maintains equipment • Orders and picks up supplies
4. Research Technician	• Vo-tech or associate's degree (in technical field)	• Assists research engineers in work at the Equipment Development Lab
5. Warehouse Supervisor	• Vo-tech or associate's degree (in technical field)	• Keeps track of, and maintains, equipment in a branch office

FIGURE 2–6
Sample positions: Technical staff

Position	Typical Education (Minimum)	Main Duties
1. Word-Processing Operator	• High school diploma **or** associate's degree	• Produces drafts of all company documents
2. Secretary	• High school diploma **or** associate's degree	• Handles paperwork for professional workers • Does some typing • Has some client contact
3. Receptionist	• High school diploma	• Oversees all of switchboard operation
4. Library Assistant	• High school diploma	• Helps librarian with cataloging, ordering books, etc.
5. Training Assistant	• High school diploma	• Helps orchestrate training activities of all kinds

FIGURE 2–7
Sample positions: Nontechnical staff

spoken communication can go a long way toward bridging the gaps between McDuff's local and central offices.

WRITING AT MCDUFF

Good writing is crucial to McDuff's existence. First, one of its main products is a written report. After the company completes a technical project, the project report stands as a permanent statement about, and reflection of, the quality of McDuff's work. Second, many company projects result from written proposals. Third, most routine activity within the firm is preceded or followed by memos, reports, in-house proposals, and manuals. As an employee at McDuff, you would be writing to readers in these groups:

- Superiors at your own McDuff branch
- Subordinates at your McDuff branch
- Employees at other branches or at the corporate office
- Clients
- Subcontractors and vendors

As pointed out in chapter 1, you often write to a mixed group of readers, all with different needs and backgrounds. Likewise, at McDuff, readers of the same document could come from more than one of the groups just listed. For example, assume McDuff's corporate training manager needs to send a memo to 20 employees officially confirming their attendance at an upcoming training seminar at the corporate office. Coming to Baltimore from all domestic offices, these employees need a seminar schedule as well as information about the course. Copies of the memo would have to be sent to (1) the participants' managers, who need to be reminded that they will be minus an employee for three days; (2) the vice president for research and training, who likes to be made aware of any company-wide training; and (3) a training assistant, who needs to make room arrangements for the seminar.

This memo is not unique. Most documents at McDuff and other companies are read by persons from different levels. Listed next are more examples of McDuff writing directed to diverse readers. Some of these projects resemble the examples and assignments in later chapters.

Examples of Internal Writing

1. Memo about changes in benefits—from a manager of human resources at a branch to all employees at that branch
2. Memo about changes in procedures for removing asbestos from buildings—from a project manager to field engineers and technicians
2. Orientation booklet on McDuff—from the manager of employment to all new employees at the firm
4. Internal proposal for funds to develop a new piece of equipment—from a technician to the Equipment Development lab manager
5. Draft of a project report—written by a project manager for review by a department manager (before being submitted to the client)
6. Long report on future markets for McDuff—from the vice president of business and marketing to all 2,500 McDuff employees
7. Memo on new procedure for compensating domestic employees who work on overseas projects—from the corporate manager of compensation to all branch managers
8. Manual on new accounting procedures—from the corporate manager of computer operations to all branch managers
9. Article on an interesting environmental project at a national park—from a project manager to all employees who read the company's monthly newsletter
10. Trip report on a professional conference—from a biologist in the environmental science area to the corporate manager of training

Examples of External Writing

1. Sales letter—to potential client
2. McDuff brochure describing technical services—to potential client
3. Proposal—to potential client

4. Progress report—to client
5. Final project report—to client
6. Refresher letter—to previous client
7. Complaint letter—to supplier
8. Article on technical subject—for technical periodical
9. Training manual—for client
10. Affirmative-action report—for government

Writing and speaking tasks, like many responsibilities at McDuff, present ethical dilemmas. The last section of this chapter describes an ethical framework within which technical work—and technical writing, in particular—can be completed at organizations where you may work.

ETHICS ON THE JOB

This section outlines the ethical context in which all workers, like those at McDuff, do their jobs. The goal is (1) to present one main ethical principle and four related guidelines for the workplace and (2) to show how ethical guidelines can be applied to a specific activity at McDuff—writing. Then at the end of the chapter, and throughout this book, you will find assignments in which your own ethical decisions play an important role.

Ethical Guidelines for Work

Like your personal life, your professional life will hold many opportunities for demonstrating your views of what is right or wrong. There is no way to escape these ethical challenges. Most of them occur daily, without much fanfare, but cumulatively they compose our personal approach to morality. Thus our belief systems, or lack thereof, will be revealed by the manner in which we respond to this continuous barrage of ethical dilemmas.

Obviously, not everyone in the same company—let alone the same industry or profession—has the same ethical beliefs. Nor should they. After all, each person's understanding of right and wrong flows from individual experiences, upbringing, religious beliefs, and cultural values. Some "ethical relativists" even argue that ethics only makes sense as a descriptive study of what people *do* believe, not a prescriptive study of what they *should* believe. Yet there are some basic ethical guidelines that, in this author's view, should be part of the decision-making process in every organization. These guidelines apply to small employers, just as they apply to large multinational organizations. Although they may be displayed in different ways in different cultures, they should transcend national identity, cultural background, and family beliefs. In other words, these guidelines represent what, ideally, should be the *core* values for employees at international companies like McDuff.

The guidelines in this section flow from one main tenet that Peter Singer calls the principle of Equal Consideration of Interests (ECI):

> **ECI:** You should make judgments and act in ways that treat the interests and well-being of others as no less important than your own.*

Note that the ECI principle resembles similar principles espoused by religions and philosophies worldwide. That fact makes ECI especially useful as a bedrock principle for multinational organizations. Now let's examine four guidelines that flow from this principle.

■ *Ethics Guideline 1: Be Honest*

First, you should relate information accurately and on time—to your colleagues, to customers, and to outside parties, such as government regulators. This guideline also means you should not mislead listeners or readers by leaving out important information that relates to a situation, product, or service. In other words, give those with whom you communicate the same information that you would want presented to you.

This guideline does *not* prescribe the manner or form in which information will be delivered. Indeed, issues such as format, organization, and presentation will change from culture to culture. The need for accurate and timely information, however, will not change.

■ *Ethics Guideline 2: Do No Harm*

The most healthy, productive, and enjoyable workplaces are those with a positive, constructive atmosphere. One way to achieve such a working environment is to avoid words or actions calculated to harm others. For example, avoid negative, rumor-laden conversations that hurt feelings, spread unsupported information, or waste time.

Of course, different cultures and countries differ in the degree to which personal, familiar chatting takes place at work. But this cultural difference does not change the fact that you should consider the impact words and deeds have on colleagues, clients, and competitors. Our ideal goal should be to make the working world a better place at the end of each day; however, a minimum goal should be to leave the world at least as good as we found it.

■ *Ethics Guideline 3: Keep Your Commitments*

People expect that you will keep your word. Be careful about the commitments you make to superiors, subordinates, customers, and others. When you do make

---

*This definition is a slightly condensed form of the one in Singer's *Practical Ethics* (Cambridge, England: Cambridge Univ. Press, 1979) 19, as included in Raymond S. Pfeiffer and Ralph P. Forsberg's *Ethics on the Job* (Belmont, CA: Wadsworth, 1993) 4. The four guidelines that follow are paraphrased from six rules included in *Ethics on the Job*, 12-17.

a legitimate commitment, follow through on it. "Legitimate" means a commitment wherein you do not violate other ethical guidelines, such as those of being honest and doing no harm.

Cultural guidelines differ on exactly what makes up a commitment, and you should be sensitive to such variations. In one country, a comment in a meeting may seal an agreement from the perspective of some participants. In another, multiple legal contracts are required. Make sure you know what constitutes a commitment with your audience, and then make sure you abide by it.

■ *Ethics Guideline 4: Be Independent*

Make no mistake, teamwork will be crucial to the success of organizations for which you work. Group efforts, however, do not relieve you from the personal responsibility for making decisions that come with your job and then accepting the resulting blame or credit. We cannot simply "go along with" group decisions if we have ethical reservations. This phenomenon of excessive conformity within teams has its own name—"groupthink"—and it can be dangerous. Effective teamwork is more important than ever, but it is only as valid as the strength of individual contributors.

If you do business in non-Western countries, such as Japan, you will learn that some cultures emphasize teamwork to the point where individuals seem to be absorbed into the fabric of the group. If you are part of such teams, you may need to alter your style to adapt to a pattern of decision-making that is highly consensual. Yet such cultural adjustments don't change the importance of being assertive, when appropriate, and taking individual responsibility. Although you should be cooperative in teamwork, you cannot sacrifice your own values on the altar of group consensus. Be clear and direct, while still listening and adjusting to others' views.

Now let's examine the manner in which ethical considerations play a part in the *writing* responsibilities at companies such as McDuff, Inc.

Ethics in Writing

In your career you should develop and apply your own code of ethics, making certain it follows the four guidelines already noted. Writing—whether on paper, audiotape, videotape, or computer screen—presents a special ethical challenge for demonstrating your personal code of ethics. Along with speaking, there may be no more important way you display your beliefs during your career. The following section will (1) list some ethical questions related to specific documents and (2) provide responses based on the ethical guidelines noted earlier.

Being honest, doing no harm, keeping commitments, showing independence of thought and action—all four of these ethical guidelines apply to written communication. Here are some typical examples from the working world of McDuff:

Lab Report: Should you mention a small, possibly insignificant percentage of the data that was collected but that doesn't support your conclusions?

Answer: Yes. Readers deserve to see all the data, even (and perhaps especially) any information that doesn't support your conclusion. They need a true picture of the lab study so that they can draw their own decisions.

Trip Report: Should you mention the fact that one client you visited expressed dissatisfaction with the service he received from your group?

Answer: Yes. Assuming that your report was supposed to present an accurate reflection of your activities, your reader deserves to hear about *all* your client contacts—good news and bad news. You can counter any critical comments by indicating how your group plans to remedy the problem.

Proposal: Should you include cost information, even though cost is not a strong point in your proposal?

Answer: Almost assuredly yes. Most clients expect complete and clear cost data in a proposal. It is best to be forthright about costs, even if they are not your selling point. Then you can highlight features that are exemplary about your firm so that the customer is encouraged to look beyond costs to matters of quality, qualifications, scheduling, experience, etc.

Feasibility Study: Should you list all the criteria you used in comparing three products, even though one criterion could not be applied adequately in your study?

Answer: Yes. It is unethical to adjust criteria after the fact to accommodate your inability to apply them consistently. Besides, information about a project dead end may be useful to the reader.

Technical Article: Should you acknowledge ideas you derived from another article, even though you quoted no information from the piece?

Answer: Yes. Your reliance on *all* borrowed ideas should be noted, whether the ideas are quoted, paraphrased, or summarized. The exception is "common knowledge," which is general information that is found in many sources. Such common knowledge need not be footnoted.

Statement of Qualifications (SOQ): Should you feel obligated to mention technical areas in which your firm does *not* have extensive experience?

Answer: Probably not, as long as you believe the customer is not expecting such information in the statement of qualifications. Ethical guidelines do not require you to tell everything about your firm, especially in a marketing document like an SOQ. They only require that you provide the information that the client requests or expects.

Of course, many other types of technical writing require careful ethical evaluation. You might even consider performing an "ethical review" during the final process of drafting a document. Other parts of this book cover topics that apply to specific stages of such an ethical review, as well as to ethics in spoken communication. For ethics in argumentation, see chapter 5; for ethics in instructions, see chapter 6; for ethics in the use of graphics, see chapter 11; for ethics in the research process, see chapter 13; and for ethics in negotiation, see chapter 14.

In the final analysis, acting ethically on the job means thinking constantly about the way in which people will be influenced by what you do, say, and write. Peter Singer's ECI principle embodies this approach perfectly: "Make judgments and act in ways that treat the interests and well-being of others as no less important than your own." These "others" can include your colleagues, your customers, your employers, or the general public. Show them your very best self.

COMMUNICATION CHALLENGE

"McDuff's Moscow Buyout: Global Dilemmas"

McDuff has steadily grown to the point where it now has 15 branches, along with its corporate office in Baltimore, Maryland. Though conservative in its approach to growth, the McDuff corporate staff is still looking for ways to add international offices so that it can expand its business. A recent international opportunity is being considered by Rob McDuff and his staff. What follows is (1) background on the possible buyout of a Moscow firm, (2) issues that the buyout study has raised, and (3) questions and comments for discussion.

Background on the Moscow Buyout

With the breakup of the former Soviet Union in December 1991, the 15 republics that made up one of the largest and most powerful countries in the world became a series of separate nations. Actually, economic changes had begun several years earlier with the start of "glasnost" (the new openness to other cultures and ideas) and "perestroika" (the economic restructuring of the country). Out of the economic change that followed came many new companies run by a new class of entrepreneurs called "biznesmeny." One member of this group, Vlad Gorky, joined with some former government engineers and scientists to establish an engineering firm called, in translation, Moscow Technical Services (MTS). Since 1991 the firm has grown to 75 employees.

Interested in the potential for work in Russia and other former Soviet republics, Rob McDuff has met with Vlad Gorky several times in the United States and in Moscow. The stage has been set for McDuff, Inc., to buy out MTS soon. All government and regulatory requirements have been met in both the United States and Russia. The only remaining obstacle is approval by (1) a McDuff committee consisting of high-level corporate staff and representative employees from various levels and offices and (2) an MTS committee made up of the six principals of that firm. Both groups are meeting this week to discuss important issues related to the purchase. The thorniest of these issues are summarized below.

Problems with the Buyout

In many ways, the buyout appears to be a "win-win" for both firms. McDuff wants an avenue into the growing markets of Russia—especially in construction and environmental work. MTS, for its part, needs additional capital to expand its operation and wants the stability associated with being part of an international firm. Yet the buyout committees in both firms are struggling with the following issues, among others:

Language. When it started acquiring international offices, McDuff adopted a policy that all internal documents would be written in English, to reduce communication barriers within the company. Most external documents, like reports and proposals, are also in English, unless of course clients request otherwise. The policy of English-only internal documents bothers the MTS committee. It sees no reason why MTS cannot continue to write internal memos, reports, procedures, and other documents in Russian. Although most MTS employees have a fair reading and writing knowledge of English and all employees have some, there is the issue of pride at work. Moreover, the MTS buyout committee sees no strong rationale for the English-only policy. To them it smacks of the kind of arbitrary centralized control that they remember all too well.

Work Rules. Like many new entrepreneurial firms around the world, MTS has remained unstructured in its approach to work rules—office hours, lunch breaks, vacation time, job duties, policies and procedures, etc. The firm was started by a creative, innovative scientist who has attracted many like-minded colleagues. Work rules were not on the top of their list. McDuff, however, has a Human Resources Manual that is quite specific about issues such as work hours (whether regular or flextime), vacation time, office dress, required training, and safety. Because the manual has been adopted by all 15 branch offices, McDuff would want it to be used in the Moscow branch.

Perceptions of Undue Influence. McDuff knows that many of the MTS principals, especially those in the environmental field, were formerly a part of the communist technical bureaucracy. They still have strong friendships with present-day officials and do a considerable amount of work for the government. Indeed, MTS continues to hire technical specialists who leave the government for higher-paying jobs at the firm. This "revolving door" practice is considered "business as usual" by the firm, providing MTS with well-educated workers who know where the work is. Although no one at McDuff is uncomfortable with being friends with clients, some members of the McDuff buyout committee are worried about the perception, if not the reality, of undue influence at MTS caused by close associations with, and the "revolving door" hiring of, government officials. At the very least, they worry that the buyout may appear to be an effort by McDuff to gain Russian projects through unfair means. That perception may be held by Russian officials or it may be held by international competitors of McDuff.

Questions and Comments for Discussion

Answer the following questions from your own point of view. Before doing so, however, make sure you have carefully considered the perspective of both McDuff and MTS.

1. Is McDuff's English-only policy justified? Is there any compromise that would satisfy both groups in this dispute?
2. Elaborate on some of the general language problems multinational firms can face.
3. The use of English does not by itself break down communication barriers with colleagues and customers at global firms. That is, English is spoken around the world by people from many different cultures. Its use does not mean that people necessarily think, write, or speak by the same conventions. Examine this view. Putting aside obvious dialect and vocabulary differences, how can one's culture and national background affect the use of English in writing and speaking?
4. How can the work rules controversy be solved? How might the way this issue is resolved affect the success of the entire buyout? Indeed, give your opinion on the degree to which common work rules and practices are important at McDuff's domestic offices.
5. Give your views of the dilemma posed by the close association of MTS and the government. What are the real and perceived problems here? Which problems most concern McDuff and why? Is there a solution that would satisfy both sides?

CHAPTER SUMMARY

This book uses the fictional firm of McDuff, Inc., to lend realism to your study of technical writing. The many McDuff examples and assignments give you a purpose, an audience, and an organizational context that simulate what you will face in your career.

Like other organizations where you might work, McDuff has developed its own personality, or "culture." A company's culture can be influenced by many features including its history, type of business, and management style. Two particular features that many organizations have in common today are (1) an interest in improving the quality of their services or products and (2) the need to operate in a global environment.

This chapter looks specifically at the culture of McDuff, Inc. Though started as an engineering consulting firm with a narrow focus, McDuff is now an international company with 2,500 employees, fifteen branches, and a corporate office. The firm works in seven main project areas: soils engineering on land, soils engineering at sea, construction monitoring, construction management, waste management (environmental science), equipment development, and training. The color insert gives summary information about specific McDuff projects in all seven areas.

McDuff's corporate office is in Baltimore, Maryland. It helps the branch offices in the areas of human resources, project coordination, marketing, computer operations, research, and training. Each of the fifteen offices is run by a branch manager. At each branch, employees are grouped into four categories: technical professionals, nontechnical professionals, technical staff, and nontechnical staff.

McDuff employees at all levels do a good deal of writing, both to superiors and subordinates within the organization and to clients and other outside readers. Documents often have multiple readers with different backgrounds, making writing even more challenging. McDuff employees who meet this challenge will have the best chance of doing valuable work for the company and succeeding in their careers.

Another major concern at McDuff—and at all organizations—is ethical behavior in the workplace. Companies and their employees should follow some basic ethical guidelines in all their work, including communication with colleagues and customers.

ASSIGNMENTS

1. **Intercultural Communication.** Refer to the 10 questions in "The Global Workplace" section of this chapter. Using them as the basis for your investigation, conduct your own research project on the cultural features of employees of a specific country. Consider using some or all of the following sources: campus library, travel agencies, consulate offices, international students office on your campus, or individuals who have worked in or visited the country. Your instructor will indicate whether your report should be presented orally or in writing.

2. **Company Profile.** Having read the information in this chapter about McDuff, conduct your own profile of a multinational company in your region. Collect information from some sources such as the following: corporate annual reports, newspaper or magazine articles, or personal contacts. Consider some or all of the following subtopics: company history, types of projects, corporate structure, common types of writing produced, and special features of the company (such as an international market or workforce). Your instructor will indicate whether your report should be presented orally or in writing.

3. **Group Project: Ethics.** For this assignment your instructor will place you into a group, with the goal of presenting an oral or written report.

   Option A: Your group is to investigate the ethical climate in one or more organizations that are in the same type of business. You may decide to (a) collect company codes of ethics, (b) do research on ethical guidelines issued by professional associations to which the organizations belong, (c) interview employees about ethical decisions they face on the job, and/or (d) read any available information on ethics related to the companies or profession.

Option B: For this option your group will select (or be assigned) one of the seven projects sheets in the color insert. Perform a "brainstorming" session in your group by which you arrive at numerous potential ethical dilemmas related to your project. For example, you may want to consider some of these concerns: (a) decisions to be made by and about employees on the job, (b) technical questions related to the project, (c) interaction with clients, and (d) communication with any parties or agencies that are not directly connected with the project but that may be influenced by it.

The following assignments can be completed either as individual exercises or as group projects, depending on the directions of your instructor. Prepare a response that can be delivered as an oral presentation for discussion in class.

Analyze the context of each case by considering what you learned in chapter 1 about the context of technical writing *and* what you learned in this chapter about McDuff. In particular, answer these five questions:

- What is the purpose of the document to be written?
- What result will you hope to achieve by writing it?
- Who will be your readers and what will they want from your document?
- What method of organization will be most useful?
- What tone and choice of language will be most effective?

4. **Analysis: Memo Changing Supplies Policy.** As the office services manager at the St. Louis office, you have a problem. In the last fiscal year, the office has used significantly more bond paper, computer paper, pens, mechanical pencils, eraser fluid, and file folders than in previous fiscal years. After going back through the year's projects, you can find no business-related reason why the office has bought $12,000 more of these items. Given that everyone has easy access to the supplies, you have concluded that some employees are taking them home. Putting the best face on it, you assume they may be "borrowing" supplies to complete company business they take home with them, then just keeping items at home. Putting the worst face on it, you wonder whether some employees are stealing from the company.

After consulting with the branch manager and some other managers, you decide to restrict access to office supplies. Starting next month, these supplies must be signed out through secretaries in the various departments. First, you plan to meet with the secretaries to explain how to make the system work. Then on the following day, you will send a memo explaining the change to *all employees*.

Would you change your approach in this memo if it were to be sent to a *specific* audience in the office? Why or why not? Answer this question with regard to the four employee groups shown in Figure 2–4 ("Technical Professionals"), Figure 2–5 ("Nontechnical Professionals"), Figure 2–6 ("Technical Staff"), and Figure 2–7 ("Nontechnical Staff").

5. **Analysis: Letter Requesting Testimonials.** As a writer in the corporate marketing department, you spend a good deal of your time preparing materials to be used in sales letters, brochures, and company proposals. Yesterday you were assigned the task of asking 20 customers if they will write "testimonial letters" about their satisfaction with McDuff's work. In all cases, these clients have used McDuff for many projects and have informally expressed satisfaction with the work. Now you are going to ask them

to express their satisfaction in the form of a letter, which McDuff could use as a testimonial to secure other business.

Your strategy is to write a "personalized" form letter to the 20 clients, and then follow it up with phone calls.

6. **Analysis: Memo on Inventory Control.** For five years, you have supervised the supply warehouse at the Houston office. Your main job is to maintain equipment and see that it is returned after jobs are completed. When checking out equipment, each project manager is supposed to fill out part of a project equipment form that lists all equipment used on the job and the date of checkout. Upon returning the equipment, the project manager should complete the form by listing the date of return and any damage, no matter how small, that needs to be repaired before the equipment is used again. This equipment ranges from front-end loaders and pickup trucks to simple tools like hammers, wrenches, and power drills.

Lately you have noticed that many forms you receive are incomplete. In particular, project managers are failing to record fully any equipment damage that occurred on the job. For example, if someone fails to report that a truck's alignment is out, the truck will not be in acceptable shape for the next project for which it could be used.

Your oral comments to project managers have not done much good. Apparently, the project managers do not take the warehouse problem seriously, so you believe it is time to put your concerns in writing. The goal is to inform all technical professionals who manage projects that from now on the form must be correctly filled out. You have no "authority," as such, over the managers; however, you know that their boss would be very concerned about this problem if you chose to bring it to his or her attention.

At this point, you have decided to ask nicely one more time—this time in writing. You want your memo to emphasize issues of safety and profitability, as well as the need to follow a procedure that has helped you to maintain a first-rate warehouse.

7. **Analysis: Memo Report on Flextime.** As branch manager of the Atlanta office, you have always tried to give employees as much flexibility as possible in their jobs—as long as the jobs got done. Recently you have had many requests to adopt flextime. In this arrangement, the office would end its standard 8:00 A.M. to 4:30 P.M. workday (with a half-hour lunch break). Instead, each employee would fit her or his eight-hour day within the following framework: 7:00 A.M. to 8:30 A.M. arrival, a half hour or full hour for lunch, and 3:30 P.M. to 5:30 P.M. departure.

Two conditions would prevail if flextime were adopted. First, each employee's supervisor would have to agree on the hours chosen, since the supervisor would need to make sure that departmental responsibilities were covered. Second, each employee would "lock in" a specific flextime schedule until another was negotiated with the supervisor. In other words, an employee's hours would not change from day to day.

Before you spend any more time considering this change, you want to get the views of employees. You decide to write a short memo report that (1) explains the changes being considered and the conditions (see previous paragraph); (2) solicits their views in writing, by a certain date; and (3) asks what particular work hours they would prefer, if given the choice. Also, you want your short report to indicate that later there may be department meetings and finally a general office meeting on the subject, depending on the degree of interest expressed by employees in their memos to you.

3 Organizing Information

This McDuff committee discusses ways to organize information in its upcoming long report.

*T*om Kent asks the department secretary to hold his calls. Closing his door, he reaches for the report draft written by one of his staff members and sits down to read it. As a McDuff manager for 10 years, he has reviewed and signed off on every major report written by members of his department. Of all the problems that plague the drafts he reads, poor organization bothers him the most.

This problem is especially annoying at the beginning of a document and the beginning of individual sections. Sometimes he has no idea where the writer is going. His people don't seem to understand that they are supposed to be "telling a story," even in a technical report. Grammar and style errors are annoying to him, but organization problems are much more troublesome. They require extensive rewriting and time-consuming meetings with the report writer. Reaching for his red pen, Tom hopes for the best as he begins to read yet another report.

You, too, will face internal reviewers like Tom Kent when you write on the job. To help you avoid organization problems, this chapter offers strategies for organizing information as you plan, draft, and revise your writing. It builds on the discussion of the three stages of writing covered in chapter 1. Then the next chapter will complete your introduction to technical writing by showing you how to use effective page design to keep readers' attention.

IMPORTANCE OF ORGANIZATION

In a survey of engineering professionals, respondents named "organizing information" the most important topic for any undergraduate technical writing course [Pinelli, T. E., M. Glassman, R. O. Barclay, and W. E. Oliu. 1989. *Technical communications in aeronautics: Results of an exploratory study—an analysis of profit managers' and nonprofit managers' responses. (NASA TM–101626, p. 28.)* Washington, DC:

Option A
Organize information
for technical readers

Option B
Organize information
for less technical readers

Option C
Organize information
for *all* readers

FIGURE 3–1
Options for organizing information

National Aeronautics and Space Administration]. This research is backed up by the experience of many communication consultants—including the author of this textbook, who for 18 years has helped companies improve their employees' writing. Overwhelmingly, these firms have cited poor organization as the main writing problem among both new and experienced employees. That concern underlies all the suggestions in this chapter.

As you learned in chapter 1, your documents will be read by varied readers with diverse technical backgrounds. Chapter 2 displays this technical range within McDuff and refers to an even broader technical spectrum among McDuff's clients. Given this reader diversity, this chapter aims to answer one essential question: How can you best organize information to satisfy so many different people?

Figure 3–1 shows you three possible options for organizing information for a mixed technical audience, but only one is recommended in this book. Some writers, usually those with technical backgrounds themselves, choose Option A. They direct their writing to the *most* technical people. Other writers choose Option B. They respond to the dilemma of a mixed technical audience by finding the lowest common denominator—that is, they write to the level of the *least* technical person. Option A and B each satisfies one segment of readers at the expense of the others.

Option C is preferred in technical writing for mixed readers. It encourages you to organize documents so that **all** readers—both technical and nontechnical—get what they need. The rest of this chapter provides strategies for developing this option. It describes general principles of organization and guidelines for organizing entire documents, individual document sections, and paragraphs.

THREE PRINCIPLES OF ORGANIZATION

Good organization starts with careful analysis of your audience. Most readers are impatient and skip around as they read. Think about how you examine a weekly newsmagazine or an airline magazine. You are likely to take a quick look at articles of special interest to you; then you might read them more thoroughly, if there is time. That approach also resembles how *your* audience treats technical reports and other work-related documents. If important points are buried in long paragraphs or sections, busy readers may miss them. Three principles respond realistically to the needs of your readers:

■ *Principle 1: Write Different Parts for Different Readers*

The longer the document, the less likely it is that any of your readers will read it from beginning to end. As shown in Figure 3–2, they use a "speed-read" approach that includes these steps:

Step 1: **Quick scan.** Readers scan easy-to-read sections like executive summaries, introductory summaries, introductions, tables of contents, conclusions, and recommendations. They pay special attention to beginning and ending sections, especially in documents longer than a page or two, and to illustrations.

Step 2: **Focused search.** Readers go directly to parts of the document body that will give them what they need at the moment. To find information quickly, they search for format devices like subheadings, listings, and white space in margins to guide their reading. (See chapter 4 for a discussion of page design.)

Step 3: **Short follow-ups.** Readers return to the document, when time permits, to read or re-read important sections.

Your job is to write in a way that responds to this nonlinear, episodic reading process of your audience. Most important, you should direct each section to those in the audience most likely to read that particular section. Shift the level of technicality as you move from section to section *within* the document, to meet the needs of each section's specific readers. On the one hand, managers and general readers favor less technical language and depend most heavily on overviews at the beginning of documents. On the other hand, experts and operators expect more

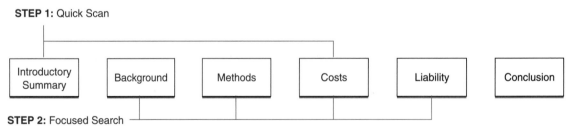

FIGURE 3–2
Sample speed-read approach to short proposal

technical jargon and pay more attention than others to the body sections of documents.

Of course, you walk a thin line in designing different parts of the document for different readers. Although technical language and other stylistic features may change from section to section, your document must hang together as one piece of work. Common threads of organization, theme, and tone must keep it from appearing fragmented or pieced together.

This approach breaks the rules of nontechnical writing, which strives for dogged consistency throughout the same document. However, technical writing marches to the beat of a different drummer.

■ *Principle 2: Emphasize Beginnings and Endings*

Suspense fiction relies on the interest and patience of readers to piece together important information. The writer usually drops hints throughout the narrative before finally revealing who did what to whom. Technical writing operates differently. Busy readers expect to find information in predictable locations without having to search for it. Their first-choice locations for important information are as follows:

- The beginning of the entire document
- The beginnings of report sections
- The beginnings of paragraphs

The reader interest curve in Figure 3–3 reflects this focus on beginnings. But the curve also shows that the readers' second choice for reading is the ends of documents, sections, and paragraphs. That is, most readers tend to remember best the first and last things they read. The ending is a slightly less desirable location than the beginning because it is less accessible, especially in long sections or documents.

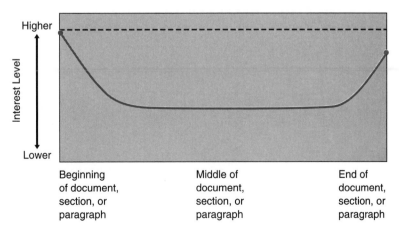

FIGURE 3–3
Reader interest curve

Of course, some readers inevitably will read the last part of a document first, for they may have the habit of fanning pages when first seeing a document. Their thumb first locks on the last section of the report. Thus, although there is no guarantee that the first document section will be read first, you can be fairly sure that *either* the beginning *or* the ending will get first attention.

Emphasizing beginnings and endings responds to the reading habits and psychological needs of readers. At the beginning, they want to know where you're heading. They need a simple "road map" for the rest of the passage. In fact, if you don't provide something important at the beginnings of paragraphs, sections, and documents, readers will start guessing the main point themselves. It is in your best interest to direct the reader to what *you* consider most important in what they are about to read, rather than to encourage them to guess at the importance of the passage. At the ending, readers expect some sort of wrap-up or transition; your writing shouldn't simply drop off. The following paragraph begins and ends with such information:

> *The proposed word-processing software has two other features that will help our writers: a dictionary and a thesaurus.* When the built-in dictionary is engaged, it compares each word in a document with the same word in the system's dictionary. Differences are then highlighted so that they can be corrected by the operator of the system. The thesaurus also can help our writers by offering alternative word selections. When just the right word is escaping the writer, he or she can trigger the system to provide a list of related words or synonyms. *Both the dictionary and thesaurus are very quick and thus far superior to their counterparts in book format.*

The first sentence gives readers an immediate impression of the two topics to be covered in the paragraph. The paragraph body explores details of both topics. Then the last sentence flows smoothly from the paragraph body by reinforcing the main point about features of the dictionary and thesaurus.

Why does this top-down pattern, which seems so logical from the reader's perspective, frequently get ignored in technical writing? The answer arises from the difference between the way you complete your research or fieldwork and the way busy readers expect results of your work to be conveyed in a report. Figure 3–4 illustrates this difference. Having moved logically from data to conclusions and recommendations in technical work, many writers assume they should take this same approach in their report. They reason that the reader wants and needs all the supporting details before being confronted with conclusions and recommendations that result from these data.

Such reasoning is wrong. Readers want the results placed first, followed by details that support your main points. Of course, you must be careful not to give *detailed* conclusions and recommendations at the beginning; most readers want and expect only a brief summary. This overview will provide a framework within which readers can place the details presented later. In other words, readers of technical documents want the "whodunit" answer at the beginning. Recall the motto in chapter 1: *Write for your reader, not for yourself.* Now you can see that this rule governs the manner in which you organize information in everything you write.

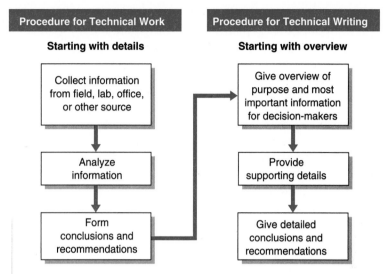

FIGURE 3–4
Technical *work* vs. technical *writing*

■ *Principle 3: Repeat Key Points*

You have learned that different people focus on different sections of a document. Sometimes no one carefully reads the *entire* report. For example, managers may have time to read only the summary, whereas technical experts may skip the lead-off sections and go directly to "meaty" technical sections with supporting information. These varied reading patterns require a *redundant* approach to organization—you must repeat important information in different sections for different readers.

For example, assume you are a McDuff employee in Denver and are writing a report to the University of Colorado on choosing sites for several athletic fields. Having examined five alternatives, your report recommends one site for final consideration. Your 25-page report compares and contrasts all five alternatives according to criteria of land cost, nearness to other athletic locations, and relative difficulty of grading the site and building the required facilities. Given this context, where will your recommendation appear in the report? Here are five likely spots:

1. Executive summary
2. Cost section in the body
3. Location section in the body
4. Grading/construction section of the body
5. Concluding section

Our assumption, you recall, is that few readers move straight through a report. Because they often skip to the section most interesting to them, you need to make main sections somewhat self-contained. In the University of Colorado report, that would mean placing the main recommendation at the beginning, at the end, and at one or more points within each main section. In this way, readers of all sections would encounter your main point.

What about the occasional readers who read all the way through your report, word for word? Will they be put off by the restatement of main points? No, they won't. Your strategic repetition of a major finding, conclusion, or recommendation gives helpful reinforcement to readers always searching for an answer to the "So what?" question as they read. Fiction and nonfiction may be alike in this respect—writers of both genres are "telling a story." The theme of this story must periodically reappear to keep readers on track.

Now we're ready to be more specific about how the three general principles of organization apply to documents, document sections, and paragraphs.

ABC FORMAT FOR DOCUMENTS

You have learned the three principles of organization: (1) write different parts of the document for different readers, (2) emphasize beginnings and endings, and (3) repeat key points. Now let's move from principles to practice. Here we will develop an all-purpose pattern of organization for writing entire documents. (The next major section covers document sections and paragraphs.)

Technical documents should assume a three-part structure that consists of a beginning, a middle, and an end. This book labels this structure the "ABC Format" (for **A**bstract, **B**ody, and **C**onclusion). Visually, think of this pattern as a three-part diamond structure, as shown in Figure 3–5:

- **Abstract:** A brief beginning component is represented by the narrow top of the diamond, which leads into the body.

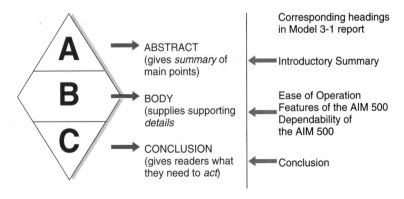

FIGURE 3–5
ABC format for all documents

- **Body:** The longer middle component is represented by the broad, expansive portion of the diamond figure.
- **Conclusion:** A brief ending component is represented by the narrow bottom of the diamond, which leads away from the body.

Model 3–1 (pp. 94–95) includes a memo report that conforms to this structure. The following sections discuss the three ABC components in detail.

Document Abstract: The "Big Picture" for Decision-Makers

Every document should begin with an overview. As used in this text, *abstract* is defined as follows:

> **Abstract:** brief summary of a document's main points. Although its makeup varies with the type and length of the document, an abstract always includes (1) a clear purpose statement for the document and (2) the most important points for decision-makers. It may also note the main document sections that follow. As a capsule version of the entire document, the abstract should answer readers' typical mental questions, such as the following: "How does this document concern me? What's the bottom line? So what?"

Abstract information is provided under different headings, depending on the document's length and degree of formality. Some common headings are "Summary," "Executive Summary," "Introductory Summary," and "Overview." The abstract may vary in length from a short paragraph to a page or so. Its purpose, however, is always the same: to provide decision-makers with highlights of the document.

For example, assume you are an engineer who has evaluated environmental hazards for the potential purchaser of a shopping mall site. The abstract information in your report should include (1) a brief project summary, (2) a statement of findings, and (3) an indication of sections to follow. In effect, this summary should answer three questions:

- What are the major risks at the site?
- Are these risks great enough to warrant not buying the land?
- What major sections does the rest of the report contain?

Here is how the summary might read:

> As you requested, we have examined the possibility of environmental contamination at the site being considered for the new Klinesburg Mall. Our field exploration revealed two locations with deposits of household trash, which can be easily cleaned up. Another spot has a more serious deposit problem of 10 barrels of industrial waste. However, our inspection of the containers and soil tests revealed no leaks.
>
> Given these limited observations and tests, we conclude that the site poses no major environmental risks and recommend development of the mall. The rest of this report details our field activities, test analyses, conclusions, and recommendations.

This general abstract, or overview, is mainly for decision-makers. Highlights must be brief, yet free of any possible misunderstanding. On some occasions, you may need to state that further clarification is included in the text, even though that point may seem obvious. For example, if your report concerns matters of safety, the overview may not be detailed enough to prevent or eliminate risks. In this case, state this point clearly so that the reader will not misunderstand or exaggerate the purpose of the abstract.

Later chapters in this book contain guidelines for writing the following specific types of abstracts:

- Introductory summaries for short reports (chapter 8)
- Executive summaries for formal reports (chapter 9)
- Introductory summaries for short proposals (chapter 10)
- Executive summaries for formal proposals (chapter 10)
- Abstracts of technical articles (chapter 13)

Document Body: Details for All Readers

The longest part of any document is the body. As used in this book, the body is defined as follows:

> **Body:** the middle section(s) of the document providing supporting information to readers, especially those with a technical background. Unlike the abstract and conclusion, the body component allows you to write expansively about items such as (1) the background of the project, (2) field, lab, office, or any other work upon which the document is based, and (3) details of any conclusions, recommendations, or proposals that might be highlighted at the beginning or end of the document. The body answers this main reader question: "What support is there for points put forth in the abstract at the beginning of the document?"

Managers may read much of the body, especially if they have a technical background and if the document is short. Yet the more likely readers are technical specialists who (1) verify technical information for the decision-makers or (2) use your document to do their jobs. In writing the body, use the following guidelines:

- **Separate fact from opinion.** Never leave the reader confused about where opinions begin and end. Body sections usually move from facts to opinions that are based on facts. To make the distinction clear, preface opinions with phrases such as "We believe that," "I feel that, "It is our opinion that," and the like. Such wording gives a clear signal to readers that you are presenting judgments, conclusions, and other nonfactual statements.
- **Adopt a format that reveals much structure.** Use frequent headings and subheadings to help busy readers locate important information immediately. (Chapter 4 covers these and other elements of page design.)

- **Use graphics whenever possible.** Use graphics to draw attention to important points. Today more than ever, readers expect visual reinforcement of your text, particularly in more persuasive documents like proposals. (Chapter 11 deals with graphical elements in technical documents.)

By following these guidelines, which apply to any document, you will make detailed body sections as readable as possible. They keep ideas from becoming buried in text and show readers what to do with the information they find.

Document Conclusion: Wrap-Up Leading to Next Step

Your conclusion deserves special attention, for readers often recall first what they have read last. We define the conclusion component as follows:

> **Conclusion:** the final section(s) of the document bringing readers—especially decision-makers—back to one or more central points already mentioned in the body. Occasionally, it may include one or more points not previously mentioned. In any case, the conclusion provides closure to the document and often leads to the next step in the writer's relationship with the reader.

The conclusion component may have any one of several headings, depending on the type and length of the document. Possibilities include "Conclusion," "Closing," "Closing Remarks," and "Conclusions and Recommendations." The chapters in Part 2 of this text describe the options for short and long documents of many kinds. In general, however, a conclusion component answers these sorts of questions:

- What major points have you made?
- What problem have you tried to solve?
- What should the reader do next?
- What will you do next?
- What single idea do you want to leave with the reader?

Because readers focus on beginnings and endings of documents, you want to exploit the opportunity to drive home your message—just as you did in the abstract. Format can greatly affect the impact you make on decision-makers. Although specific formats vary, most conclusions take one of these two forms:

- **Listings:** This format is especially useful when pulling together points mentioned throughout the document. Whereas the abstract often gives readers the big picture in narrative format, the conclusion may instead depend on listings of findings, conclusions, and/or recommendations. (Chapter 4 gives suggestions on using bulleted and numbered listings.)
- **Summary paragraph(s):** When a listing is not appropriate, you may want to write a concluding paragraph or two. Here you can leave readers with an important piece of information and make clear the next step to be taken.

Whichever alternative you choose, your goal is to return to the main concerns of the most important readers—decision-makers. Both the abstract and conclusion, in slightly different ways, should respond to the needs of this primary audience.

TIPS FOR ORGANIZING SECTIONS AND PARAGRAPHS

First and foremost, the ABC format pertains to the organization of entire documents. Yet the same "beginning-middle-end" strategy applies to the next smaller units of discourse—document sections and paragraphs. In fact, you can view the entire document as a series of interlocking units, with each responding to reader expectations as viewed on the reader interest curve in Figure 3–3.

Document Sections

As mentioned earlier, readers often move from the document abstract to the specific body sections they need to solve their problem or answer their immediate question. Just as they need abstracts and conclusions in the whole document, they need "mini-abstracts" and brief wrap-ups at the start and finish of each major section.

To see how a section abstract works, we must first understand the dilemma of readers. Refer to Model 3–2 on page 96, which contains one section from a long report. Some readers may read it from beginning to end, but others might not have the time or interest to do so in one sitting. Instead, they would look to a section beginning for an abstract, and then move around within that section at will. Thus the beginning must provide them with a map of what's ahead. Here are the two items that should be part of every section abstract:

1. **Interest grabber:** a sentence or more that captures the attention of the reader. Your grabber may be one sentence or an entire paragraph, depending on the overall length of the document.
2. **Lead-in:** a list, in sentence or bullet format, that indicates main topics to follow in the section. If the section contains subheadings, your lead-in may include the same wording as the subheadings and be in the same order.

The first part of the section gives readers everything they need to read on. First, you get their attention with a grabber. Then you give them an outline of the main points to follow so that they can move to the part of the section that interests them most. As in Model 3–2 on page 96, the section abstract immediately precedes the first subheading when subheads are used.

Sections also should end with some sort of closing thought, rather than just dropping off after the last supporting point has been stated. For example, you can (1) briefly restate the importance of the information in the section or (2) provide a transition to the section that follows. Model 3–2 (p. 96) takes the latter approach by suggesting the main topic for the next section. Whereas the section lead-in provides a map to help readers navigate through the section, the closing gives a sense of an ending so that readers are ready to move on.

Paragraphs

Paragraphs represent the basic building blocks of any document. Organizing them is not much different in technical writing than it is in nontechnical prose. Most paragraphs contain these elements:

1. **Topic sentence:** This sentence states the main idea to be developed in the paragraph. Usually it appears first. Do not delay or bury the main point, for busy readers may read only the beginnings of paragraphs. If you fail to put the main point there, they may miss it entirely.
2. **Development of main idea:** Sentences that follow the topic sentence develop the main idea with examples, narrative, explanation, or other details. Give the reader concrete supporting details, not generalizations.
3. **Transitional elements:** Structural transitions help the paragraph flow smoothly. Use transitions in the form of repeated nouns and pronouns, contrasting conjunctions, and introductory phrases.
4. **Closing sentence:** Most paragraphs, like sections and documents, need closure. Use the last sentence for a concluding point about the topic or a transitional point that links the paragraph with the one following it.

Model 3–3 on page 97 shows two paragraphs that follow this pattern of organization. The paragraphs are from a McDuff recommendation report. McDuff was hired to suggest ways for a hospital to modernize its physical plant. Each paragraph is a self-contained unit addressing a specific topic, while being linked to surrounding paragraphs (not shown) by theme and transitional elements.

This suggested format applies to many, but not to all, paragraphs included in technical documents. In one common exception, you may choose to delay statement of a topic sentence until you engage the reader's attention with the first few sentences. In other cases, the paragraph may be short and serve only as an attention grabber or a transitional device between several longer paragraphs. Yet for most paragraphs in technical writing, the beginning-middle-end model described here will serve you well. Remember these other points as well as you organize paragraphs in technical writing:

- *Length:* Keep the typical length of paragraphs at around 6 to 10 lines. Many readers won't read long blocks of text, no matter how well organized the information may be. If you see that your topic requires more than 10 lines for its development, split the topic, and develop it in two or more paragraphs.
- *Listings:* Use short listings of three or four items to break up long paragraphs. Readers lose patience when they realize information could have been more clearly presented in listings. The next chapter offers detailed suggestions on using lists.

- *Use of Numbers:* Paragraphs are the worst format for presenting technical data of any kind, especially numbers that describe costs. Readers may ignore or miss data packed into paragraphs. Usually tables or figures would be a more clear and appropriate format. Also, be aware that some readers may think that cost data couched in paragraph form represent an attempt to hide important information.

This chapter mostly concerns the ordering of ideas within paragraphs, sections, and whole documents. Good organization helps make your writing successful. Organization alone, however, will not win the day. Readers also expect a visually appealing document. The next chapter describes technical devices for creating the best possible design of your pages.

COMMUNICATION CHALLENGE

"Telecommuting: The Last Frontier?"

Calling themselves the "Commute Group," five managers at McDuff's Boston office have been meeting to discuss telecommuting (that is, permitting some or all employees to do part of their work at home). The branch manager, Janet Remington, has expressed interest in the group's work and suggested that group members write a report proposing a pilot project at the branch. The report would be read by Janet and by members of the McDuff corporate staff in Baltimore—especially Kerry Camp, vice president for domestic operations, Janet's boss. Any change in branch work schedules must be approved by corporate headquarters.

The Commute Group now must decide (1) what to include in its report to Janet Remington and (2) how to *organize* information for maximum impact. What follows are some details on the audience for the report, the group's reasons for favoring telecommuting, some problems discussed by the group, and questions that remain about the organization of the report. Although the group has made progress in discussing telecommuting, it has been unable to decide on a structure for its report.

Report Audience

The group has spent much time discussing what points would be most persuasive with the primary audience, Janet Remington and Kerry Camp. Janet has been open to new ideas since being chosen for the manager job a year ago. She meets often with all departments in the office and shows a genuine interest in creating a more comfortable workplace. For example, she recently accepted recommendations by department managers to purchase office chairs and desks that will allow employees to work with less physical strain.

Yet Janet knows that her boss, Kerry Camp, will evaluate her largely on the financial performance of the branch, not on the comfort level of her staff. Indeed, Kerry is a 60-year-old engineer, with a master's degree in finance, who keeps a close eye on the "bottom line" of each branch. He is interested in exploring new work practices only if they may improve employee productivity. More than likely, he will be the final decision-maker about the pilot project.

Rationale for Pilot Project

The Commute Group spent much time discussing two topics: branch jobs that would be best suited to telecommuting and specific arguments in support of a telecommute policy.

Group members agreed that employees who do much independent work, especially on the computer, would be the best candidates for a pilot project. In particular, members of the technical and scientific staff often spend half their days at personal computers, either performing technical calculations or drafting sections of reports and proposals.

Next the group discussed reasons for adopting a telecommute pilot project. The group first met to discuss the issue after a series of horrible rush hours over the holiday season in December. Bad weather forced most of the 125 branch employees either to miss some workdays during the period or to arrive up to two hours late several days. Most employees already have a one-way commute of at least one hour, since there is little affordable housing close to the office location in downtown Boston. Thus the heavy holiday traffic prompted the discussion about telecommuting.

In its deliberations, the Commute Group focused mostly on the kind of work that could be done by employees at home. What follows are some of the points discussed by the group, in random order.

- Telecommuting will save time either by eliminating commuting (on days the employee works exclusively at home) or by reducing commuting time (on days when the employee comes to the office for part of the day and thus avoids one or both rush-hour periods that day).
- Employees can write and edit reports and proposals at home for several hours at a time, without the usual office interruptions of meetings, phone calls, drop-in visitors, etc. Some experts claim that writers are most productive during the drafting stage if they have uninterrupted blocks of writing time.
- Morale will improve as long as there is a clear rationale for adopting the policy and selecting participants for the pilot project. Employees chosen should be those who work well independently, whose jobs can be handled through telecommuting, and who have already made significant contributions to their departments.
- If McDuff adopts a telecommuting policy after the pilot project, the firm may attract an additional pool of excellent employees.
- Telecommuting will improve some employees' productivity by allowing them to work when they are recovering from an illness at home or when family members are ill—in other words, times when the employee would normally be on sick leave.
- The company would benefit from the increase in computer literacy among both the telecommuters and those who work with them back at the office. The firm would begin to take advantage of the considerable investment it already has

made in computer technology—personal computers, networking, software for electronic mail, Internet connections, modems, etc. In particular, e-mail would become a way of life. Up until now, many employees have been reluctant to replace time-consuming meetings, phone calls, and memos with e-mail.

- If telecommuting were to become a regular way of doing business, it might reduce the amount of work space needed at the office and thus reduce overhead. For example, several employees could share the same office work space if much of their work time were spent at home.
- Even some noncomputer tasks, like phone calls to clients, could be done best in the quiet environment of the home, as opposed to the hectic environment of the office where noise and interruptions are a part of doing business.
- If a telecommuting policy were adopted, McDuff would gain public support by showing that it is part of the solution to the central problems of traffic congestion and air pollution. Even some potential clients might be attracted by the firm's progressive policies.

Possible Problems with Telecommuting

The Commute Group also addressed problems that might arise with the pilot project and with telecommuting in general. Group members were unsure how or if the problems should be woven into the fabric of the report. Here are some concerns that were discussed:

- The right employees must be selected for the pilot project. Whereas some employees might improve their productivity at home, others might find it difficult to stay on task, either because of their own work habits or because of their home environment. Some kind of appropriate screening device would be in order.
- The branch must determine how to evaluate the success of the pilot project, perhaps by some combination of (a) self-evaluation by the employee, (b) performance evaluations by the employees' supervisors, (c) productivity assessment by the corporate office, or (d) opinions gathered by surveying employees who are not part of the pilot project but who interact regularly with the employees who are telecommuting.
- Good communication is central to the project. Employees must be involved in selecting participants, planning the study, conducting the project on a day-to-day basis, and evaluating its success.

Organization of the Report

The Commute Group has agreed on the audience for the report, the likely qualifications for participation in the pilot study, advantages of telecommuting, and some possible problems with the study and with telecommuting in general. But the group has *not* resolved two main questions: (1) what part of the information assembled should be included in the report and (2) what order this information should assume. In other words, the group must wrestle with matters of *organization*. Indeed, disagreements about these two issues created a stumbling block in the group's work.

Assume that you have been called in by the Commute Group to help get it back on track. Answer the following questions, remembering that you are not to be concerned with specific report sections or headings described later in this book. Instead, this exercise concerns only the generic ABC (**A**bstract/**B**ody/**C**onclusion) structure explained in this chapter.

1. Briefly, how would you describe an overall ABC structure that would work in this report? Your answer should take into account the intended purpose and audience of the report.
2. More specifically, what points would you suggest be included in the abstract component? What issues need *not* be addressed? Why?
3. What points would you suggest be included in the body? Why? In what order? Explain the rationale for the order you suggest. If you have excluded some information discussed by the committee, explain why.
4. Given what you've read so far, what one main purpose should be served by the conclusion component of the group's report? To accomplish this purpose, what information should be included? Why?
5. What issues, if any, remain to be discussed by the Commute Group before it writes its recommendation report?

CHAPTER SUMMARY

Good technical writing calls on special skills, especially in organization. Writers should follow three guidelines for organizing information: (1) write different parts of the document for different readers, (2) place important information at the beginnings and endings, and (3) repeat key points throughout the document.

This chapter recommends the "ABC format" for organizing technical documents. This format includes an **A**bstract (summary), a **B**ody (supporting details), and a **C**onclusion (wrap-up and transition to next step). The abstract section is particularly important because most readers give special attention to the start of a document.

Individual sections and paragraphs also require attention to organization. Sections need overviews and closing passages so that busy readers can find information quickly. Most paragraphs should contain a topic sentence, supporting details, transitional words and phrases, and a closing sentence that leads into the next paragraph.

ASSIGNMENTS

1. **Overall Organization.** Find an example of technical writing directed to more than one reader. Prepare a written or an oral report (your instructor's choice) that explains how well the excerpt follows this chapter's guidelines for organization.

2. Evaluating an Abstract. Read the following abstract and evaluate the degree to which it follows the guidelines in this chapter.

As one of the buyers for of Randall Auto Parts, I constantly search for new products that I feel can increase our sales. I recently attended an electronics convention to see what new products were available. One product that caught my eye was the new Blaupunkt BMA5350B amplifier. I recommend that we adopt this amplifier into our line of car audio products.

This proposal supports my recommendation and includes the following sections:

1. Features of the Blaupunkt BMA5350B
2. Customer Benefits
3. Cost
4. Conclusions

---

3. Section Organization. As a graphics specialist at McDuff, you have written a recommendation report on ways to upgrade the graphics capabilities of the firm. One section of the report describes a new desktop publishing system, which you believe will make McDuff proposals and reports much more professional looking. Your report section describes technical features of the system, the free training that comes with purchase, and the cost.

Write a lead-in paragraph for this section of your report. If necessary, invent additional information for writing the paragraph.

4. Paragraph Organization: Analysis. Select a paragraph from each of four different articles taken from periodicals in your campus library. Choose one from a nationally known newspaper (like the *New York Times*), one from a popular magazine (like *Time* or *Sports Illustrated*), one from a business magazine (like *Forbes* or *Business Week*), and one from a technical journal (like *IEEE Transactions on Professional Communication*). Explain in writing how each of the paragraphs does or does not follow the top-down pattern of organization discussed in this chapter. If a paragraph does not follow the top-down pattern, indicate whether you believe the writer made the right or wrong decision in organizing the paragraph. In other words, was there a legitimate reason to depart from the ABC pattern? If so, what was the reason? If not, how would you revise the paragraph to make it fit the ABC model?

5. Paragraph Organization: Writing. With the following list of related information, write a paragraph that follows the organizational guidelines in this chapter. Use all the information, change any of the wording when necessary, and add appropriate transitions. Assume that this the paragraph is part of an internal McDuff document suggesting ways to improve work schedules.

- Four-day weeks may lower job stress—employees have long weekends with families and may avoid worst part of rush hour.
- A four-day, 10-hour-a-day workweek may not work for some service firms, where projects and clients need five days of attention.
- Standard five-day, eight-hour-a-day workweeks increase on-the-job stress, especially considering commuter time and family obligations.
- McDuff is considering a pilot program for one office, whereby the office would depart from the standard 40-hour workweek.
- There are also other strategies McDuff is considering to improve work schedules of employees.

- The 40-hour workweek came into being when many more families had one parent at home while the other worked.
- Some firms have gone completely to a four-day week (with 10-hour days).
- McDuff's pilot program would be for one year, after which it would be evaluated.

6. **Writing an Abstract: Individual Work.** The following short report lacks an abstract that states the purpose and provides the main conclusion or recommendation from the body of the report. Write a brief abstract for this report.

DATE: June 13, 1996
TO: Ed Simpson
FROM: Jeff Radner
SUBJECT: Creation of an Operator Preventive Maintenance Program

The Problem

The lack of operator involvement in the equipment maintenance program has caused the reliability of equipment to decline. Here are a few examples:

- A tractor was operated without adequate oil in the crankcase, resulting in a $15,000 repair bill after the engine locked.
- Operators have received fines from police officers because safety lights were not operating. The bulbs were burned out and had not been replaced. Brake lights and turn-signal malfunctions have been cited as having caused rear-end collisions.
- A small grass fire erupted at a construction site. When the operator of the vehicle nearest to the fire attempted to extinguish the blaze, he discovered that the fire extinguisher had already been discharged.

When the operator fails to report deficiencies to the mechanics, dangerous consequences may result.

The Solution

The goal of any maintenance program is to maintain the company equipment so that the daily tasks can be performed safely and on schedule. Since the operator is using the equipment on a regular basis, he or she is in the position to spot potential problems before they become serious. For a successful maintenance program, the following recommendations should be implemented:

- Hold a mandatory four-hour equipment maintenance training class conducted by mechanics in the motor pool. This training would consist of a hands-on approach to preventive maintenance checks and services at the operator level.
- Require operators to perform certain checks on a vehicle before checking it out of the motor pool. A vehicle checklist would be turned in to maintenance personnel.

The attached checklist would require 5 to 10 minutes to complete.

Conclusion

I believe the cost of maintaining the vehicle fleet at McDuff will be reduced when potential problems are detected and corrected before they become serious. Operator training and the vehicle pretrip inspection checklist will ensure that preventable accidents are avoided. I will call you this week to answer any questions you may have about this proposal.

McDuff, Inc.
Fleet Maintenance Division
Vehicle Checklist
Pretrip Inspection

Inspected by: _____   Date: _____

Vehicle #: _____   Odometer: _____

Fluid Levels, Full/Low   Comments

_____ Engine Oil   _____

_____ Transmission Fluid   _____

_____ Brake Fluid   _____

_____ Power Steering   _____

_____ Radiator Level   _____

Before Cranking Vehicle

_____ Tire Condition   _____

_____ Battery Terminals   _____

_____ Fan Belts   _____

_____ Bumper and Hitch   _____

_____ Trailer Plug-in   _____

_____ Safety Chains   _____

After Cranking Vehicle

_____ Parking Brakes   _____

_____ Lights   _____

_____ All Gauges   _____

_____ Seat Belts   _____

_____ Mirrors/Windows/Wipers   _____

_____ Clutch   _____

_____ Fire Ext. Mounted and Charged   _____

_____ Two-Way Radio Working   _____

Additional Comments: _____

_____

_____

7. **Writing an Abstract: Conventional Group Work.** For this assignment your instructor will divide the class into groups. Using one of the seven project sheets included in the color insert, your group will write a generic abstract for a report of the completed project. Follow the guidelines in this chapter.

8. **Writing an Abstract: Group Work Using Computer Communication.** As in assignment 7, for this assignment you will (a) work in groups established by your instructor, (b) write a generic abstract for a report on one of the seven project sheets included in the color insert, and (c) follow the abstract guidelines included in this chapter. In addition, you are to conduct at least part of your team business by e-mail.

The degree to which your team uses e-mail will depend on the technical resources of team members and the campus. At a minimum, you should plan for each member to send a message to every other member concerning, for example, the drafting or editing process. At a maximum, and if computer resources permit, you may develop on-screen "windows" whereby you conduct a conversation with each fellow member in one window and make changes in text in another window. The point of this assignment, in other words, is that team members can use e-mail in a substantive way to communicate with each other in the completion of group projects.

Mc Duff, Inc.

MEMORANDUM

DATE: September 5, 1996
TO: Danielle Firestein
FROM: Barbara Ralston *BR*
SUBJECT: Recommendation for AIM 500 Fax

INTRODUCTORY SUMMARY

This memo presents my evaluation of the AIM 500 facsimile (fax) machine by Simko, Inc. The AIM 500 has served our department well for the past two years. If other departments need a fax machine, I highly recommend this model because it is easy to operate, has many useful features, and has been quite dependable.

EASE OF OPERATION

The AIM 500 is so easy to operate that a novice can learn to transmit a document to another location in about two minutes. Here's the basic procedure:

1. Press the button marked TEL on the face of the fax machine. You then hear a dial tone.
2. Press the telephone number of the person receiving the fax on the number pad on the face of the machine.
3. Lay the document facedown on the tray at the back of the machine.

At this point, just wait for the document to be transmitted—about 18 seconds per page to transmit. The fax machine will even signal the user with a beep and a message on its LCD display when the document has been transmitted. Other more advanced operations are equally simple to use and require little training. Provided with the machine are two different charts that illustrate the machine's main functions.

The size of the AIM 500 makes it easy to set up almost anywhere in an office. The dimensions are 13 inches in width, 15 inches in length, and 9.5 inches in height. The narrow width, in particular, allows the machine to fit on most desks, file cabinets, or shelves.

FEATURES OF THE AIM 500

The AIM 500 has many features that will be beneficial to our employees. In the two years of use in our department, the following features were found to be most helpful:

Automatic redial
Last number redial memory
LCD display

MODEL 3–1
ABC format in whole document

Preset dialing
Group dialing
Use as a phone

Automatic Redial. Often when sending a fax, the sender finds the receiving line busy. The redial feature will automatically redial the busy number at 30-second intervals until the busy line is reached, saving the sender considerable time.

Last Number Redial Memory. Occasionally there may be interference on the telephone line or some other technical problem with the transmissions. The last number memory feature allows the user to press one button to automatically trigger the machine to retry the number.

LCD Display. This display feature clearly shows pertinent information, such as error messages that tell a user exactly why a transmission was not completed.

Preset Dialing. The AIM 500 can store 16 preset numbers that can be engaged with one-touch dialing. This feature makes the unit as fast and efficient as a sophisticated telephone.

Group Dialing. Upon selecting two or more of the preset telephone numbers, the user can transmit a document to all of the preset numbers at once.

Use as a Phone. The AIM 500 can also be used as a telephone, providing the user with more flexibility and convenience.

DEPENDABILITY OF THE AIM 500

Over the entire two years our department has used this machine, there have been no complaints. We always receive clear copies from the machine, and we never hear complaints about the documents we send out. This record is all the more impressive in light of the fact that we average 32 outgoing and 15 incoming transmissions a day. Obviously, we depend heavily on this machine.

So far, the only required maintenance has been to change the paper and dust the cover.

CONCLUSION

The success our department has enjoyed with the AIM 500 compels me to recommend it highly. The ease of operation, many exceptional features, and record of dependability are all good reasons to purchase additional units. If you have further questions about the AIM 500, please contact me at extension 3646.

MODEL 3–1
continued

ADDITIONAL FEATURES OF MAGCAD

This report has presented two main advantages of the MagCad Drawing System: ease of correction and multiple use of drawings. However, there are two other features that make this sytem a wise purchase for McDuff's Boston office: the selective print feature and the cost.

Selective Printing

When printing a MagCad drawing, you can "turn off" specific objects that are in the drawing with a series of keystrokes. The excluded items will not appear in the printout of the drawing. That is, the printed drawing will reflect exactly what you have temporarily left on the screen, after the deletions. Yet the drawing that remains in the memory of the machine is complete and ready to be reconstructed for another printout.

The selective print feature is especially useful on jobs where different groups have different needs. For example, in a drawing of a construction project intended only for the builder, one drawing may contain only land contours and the building structures. If the same drawing is going to the paving company, we may need to include only land contours and parking lots. In each case, we will have used the selective print feature to tailor the drawing to the specific needs of each reader.

This feature improves our service to the client. In the past, we either had to complete several different drawings or we had to clutter one drawing with details sufficient for the needs of all clients.

Cost of MagCad

When we started this inquiry, we set a project cost limit of $12,000. The MagCad system stays well within this budget, even considering the five stations that we need to purchase.

The main cost savings occurs because we have to buy only one copy of the MagCad program. For additional work stations, we need pay only a $400 licensing fee per station. The complete costs quoted by the MagCad representative are listed below:

1. MagCad Version 5	$5,000
2. Licenses for five additional systems	1,500
3. Plotter	2,000
4. Installation	1,000
TOTAL	$9,500

With the $2,500 difference between the budgeted amount and the projected cost of the system, we could purchase additional work stations or other peripheral equipment. The next section suggests some add-ons we might want to purchase later, once we see how the MagCad can improve our responsiveness to client needs.

MODEL 3–2
ABC format in document section

Conversion to a partial solar heating and cooling system would upgrade the hospital building considerably. In fact, the use of modern solar equipment could decrease your utility bills by up to 50%, using the formula explained in Appendix B. As you may know, state-of-the-art solar systems are much more efficient than earlier models. In addition, equipment now being installed around the country is much more pleasing to the eye than was the equipment of ten years ago. The overall effect will be to enhance the appearance of the building, as well as to save on utility costs.

We also believe that changes in landscaping would be a useful improvement to the hospital's physical plant. Specifically, planting shade trees in front of the windows on the eastern side of the complex would block sun and wind. The result would be a decrease in utility costs and enhancement of the appearance of the building. Of course, shade trees will have to grow for about five years before they begin to affect utility bills. Once they have reached adequate height, however, they will be a permanent change with low maintenance. In addition, your employees, visitors, and patients alike will notice the way that trees cut down on glare from the building walls and add "green space" to the hospital grounds.

MODEL 3–3
ABC format in paragraphs

4 Page Design

This McDuff manager reviews his report draft "on-screen." At this stage he performs tasks such as adding white space, revising headings, positioning graphics, changing fonts, and transforming text to lists.

*T*he four chapters in Part 1 cover basics you need to know before moving to the applications in Parts 2 and 3. The first chapter describes the technical writing process, with emphasis on writing for your reader. The second introduces McDuff, Inc., the fictional company used throughout the book, and the third deals with organizing information. This chapter covers page design, another basic building block in technical writing. Here's an operating definition:

Page design: a term that refers to formatting options used to create clear, readable, and visually interesting documents. Some of these options include judicious use of white space, headings, lists, and varied fonts. The term *page design* became an integral part of technical writing with the advent of word processing and desktop publishing (DTP). DTP refers to sophisticated hardware and software systems that individuals can use to write, edit, design, and print both text and graphics.

This chapter starts with brief sections on the history, benefits, and potential drawbacks of using computers to design pages. The rest of the chapter presents guidelines and examples for page design. As you read the material, remember that you can use this chapter during all three stages of the writing process: planning, drafting, and editing.

BRIEF HISTORY OF COMPUTERS AND WRITING

Personal computers provide the tools to write, edit, design, and print every part of a document. Today we take these tools for granted, but it was not long ago that legal pads and typewriters were all we had. Have you talked with anyone who wrote reports before the word processor? Let's take a brief look at the changes that have taken place, through the eyes of one person who lived and worked through it at the company used throughout this book, McDuff, Inc. As it happens, the origin and growth of McDuff, Inc., have paralleled the origin and growth of the use of computer technology in writing. (See Figure 4–1.)

Rob McDuff can well remember the precomputer era. Reports in the early days of the firm contained look-alike pages of text. Writers concentrated their efforts on producing accurate, readable technical writing, with little concern for devices like bulleted lists, white space, and graphics. The drafting staff supplied necessary engineering drawings, but these graphics were drawn by hand and usually separated from the text at the end of the report.

In those days, engineers and other professionals at McDuff wrote most first drafts in longhand. Then a secretary would type a first draft for editing. When final changes were made by the writer, the secretary would type a final draft for one last review by the writers. Woe be to the engineers who made changes after this point, for the secretary would have to type a completely new draft. Remember—this was before word processing, and even before typewriters with correction keys.

Time Period	Technologies Used at McDuff	Capabilities
Late 1940s	Basic typewriters	Straight typing—nothing fancy
Late 1950s	Advanced typewriters—with changeable font elements	Faster action, ability to switch fonts within document
Late 1960s	Advanced typewriters—with limited memory	Limited ability to save text for future printing on typewriter
Early 1970s	Advanced typewriters—with "daisy wheel" feature	Faster printing and wider range of font selection
Late 1970s	Basic word processors	Ability to change, save, and print text
Mid 1980s	Advanced word processors with laser printers	Sophisticated features and professional printing available at individual work station
Mid 1990s	Advanced word processors—networked within and among McDuff offices	Ability to design and print sophisticated documents *and* to communicate on-line among all McDuff offices

FIGURE 4–1
From typewriters to word processing at McDuff

What a difference a few decades have made. Figure 4–1 shows the transformation first brought about by advanced typewriters that kept text in a memory for later editing. Then word-processing systems allowed users to write and edit text on the screen. Finally, many firms graduated to systems that could produce features like these:

- Varied type fonts and type sizes
- Varied heading styles
- Multiple columns
- Innovative graphics incorporated into the text

Basic word processing—the use of computers to type and edit text—had been transformed into desktop publishing. That is, computers now could be used to produce text, design visuals, and prepare camera-ready copy without need of outside graphics shops.

This chapter shows the broad array of choices that access to the computer has brought to the business of page design. You'll learn how such writing techniques can add to the persuasive power of your text. The merging of message and design gives you a powerful tool for writing. The section that follows highlights the benefits of this tool, while also noting problems to avoid.

COMPUTERS IN THE WRITING PROCESS

Using a computer can speed up all three stages of writing: planning, drafting, and revising. Two main advantages are that (1) you can change text and graphics continuously and easily and (2) you have many typographical choices. Such choices give you the freedom to communicate your message in the most convincing way. Here are suggestions for using computers during all three writing stages.

Using Computers to Plan

As noted in chapter 1, the planning stage of writing requires that you determine your purpose, consider your readers' needs, collect information, and construct an outline. Computers are especially useful during the last two steps, collecting information and outlining.

Word processing can speed up the collection of information on your topic. The research procedure, detailed in chapter 13, may require that you assemble information from many sources. If you are taking notes next to your computer, you can enter them directly into your system. Each one can be placed on a separate "page" and then indexed and organized by topic, in preparation for writing the first draft. Of course, such computerized note taking is practical only if you are reading sources next to a terminal. Some software programs are more helpful than others in making such note-taking functions easy to use.

You can also use computers to place ideas in outline form. Words and phrases in your outline can be added and moved quickly—without the constant scratching out and rewriting necessary with handwritten outlines. Clustering ideas and arranging points in logical order become as simple as touching the keyboard. Some software programs provide the hierarchal outline format on the screen, just awaiting your insertion of wording. For extensive outlines, you can set up a separate file for each main topic and, again, use the keyboard to shift back and forth among files as you build the underlying structure of your document.

In summary, the ability to write and edit on screen can help you collect information and construct outlines. Yet many writers prefer to complete research notes and outlines by hand. The old-fashioned approach still offers the advantage of writing nonlinear (i.e., messy) outlines. Outlined points and research notes can be stretched all over paper of any size or even pinned to the walls, giving you a "big picture" effect that small, ever-changing screens may not. Choose the best method for you, but at least be aware of what options computers offer.

Using Computers to Draft

Though helpful during the planning process, word processing shows its main strength as you write early drafts. Whether you touch-type or plunk away with two fingers, the word processor will keep you writing faster. For example, the common "word-wrap" feature automatically moves you from line to line without need of carriage returns. Most importantly, you add and delete text very quickly. You simply "scroll" forward or backward on the screen to the point where you want to make changes. Here are some other advantages of writing early drafts on the computer:

- Systems with multiple windows may keep your outline on the screen while you write the related draft section.
- When you cannot think of a word or phrase, you can type in an easily recognizable symbol and then return later to insert the word(s).
- When several alternative passages are possible, you can type in all of them, with brackets or other associated symbols. Then during the revision stage, you can make your final choice.

As noted in the chapter 1 discussion on collaborative writing, the computer helps you combine your work with that of others in team-writing efforts. Individual writers in the group can produce draft material at their separate terminals, which are part of one network. At that point, individual files can be "pulled up" on the screens of other group members, for revision and commentary. Later, separate files can be merged into one draft for revision. Thus both groups and individuals benefit from the computer at the drafting stage of writing.

Using Computers to Revise

Drafting requires that you get ideas onto paper (or screen) as quickly as possible, to avoid writer's block. When you shift to the revising stage, the aim is to select options and change text in whatever way best meets the readers' needs. As shown in Figure 4–2, computer systems offer these sorts of tools for revision:

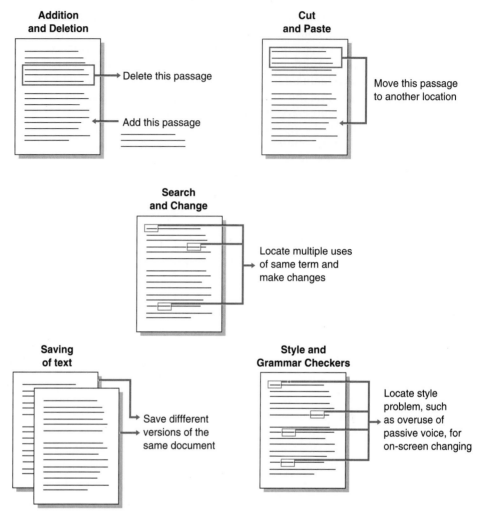

FIGURE 4–2
Sample changes during revising

- **Addition and deletion:** You can add or delete text by placing the cursor—an icon that shows where you are in the text—at the appropriate point. This technique eliminates the time-consuming process of scribbling changes into margins by hand, deleting words, and then retyping drafts.
- **Cut-and-paste:** This feature allows you to move sentences, paragraphs, graphics, or entire sections within one document, or among several. No longer must you literally cut and paste sections of typed or handwritten copy. Cut-and-paste allows you easily to revise text to produce the most logical arrangement of material.
- **Search and change:** Used correctly, this feature can save considerable time during revision. It helps you locate every instance of a particular word or phrase

throughout the document. For example, assume that you want to check your draft to make certain that you used *data* consistently as a plural noun, not a singular noun. Simply enter the word *data* on the keyboard so that your system will scroll to each section of the text where the word is used. Then you can make necessary changes.

- **Saving of text:** Often you may be uncertain what version of a paragraph or section is most appropriate for the final draft. In this case you can save multiple versions in a file for later reference. A note or an asterisk on your screen will trigger your memory that another version of the text is available. Later you can select the best option and delete the others.

- **Style and grammar checkers:** Now there are editing programs that use the "search and change" function to locate awkward or incorrect passages in your writing. Once you see the highlighted passage, you can decide whether to change it. This software is sophisticated enough to identify errors or constructions like these: split infinitives ("to randomly select"), passive voice ("the recommendations were made"), clichés ("skyrocketing costs"), sexist pronouns ("an engineer should complete his reports on time"), and overuse of "to be" verbs (such as "is," "are," "was," and "were"). Another useful feature can analyze the "readability" of your style by, for example, determining the average number of words per sentence.

    Interactive software also helps you locate grammar, proofreading, and spelling errors. Examples include double words ("and and"), incorrect capitalization ("THey"), wrong spacing, incorrect punctuation, and subject-verb agreement errors. Another feature is a thesaurus. It can suggest alternative word choices and even give the etymology of words. Some programs allow you to add particular grammar or style rules that you want applied to your writing.

    Computers allow changes as quickly as you can touch the keyboard. Besides speed, there is the advantage of convenience. Copy can be corrected until the last moment before printing. If errors are found, another draft can be printed. Ironically, it is the very ease of editing during word processing that can lead to misuse and inefficiency of computers during the writing process. The next section notes several problems and ways to avoid them.

Problems to Avoid

The following actual case typifies problems that can arise with computers during the writing process. At one engineering firm in the Southwest a few years ago, engineers usually produced their own report drafts in longhand or by cutting and pasting typed copy from previous reports. This hard copy was delivered to a central word-processing department, where operators produced first drafts for later editing. In theory, the operators were to see each report only two or three times—once during the initial inputting of information and another time or two when changes were incorporated into the final draft. In fact, however, writers constantly made changes that required multiple printing of the reports—often five or six times instead of two or three. As a result, productivity decreased, and word-processing expenses increased. The very ease of word processing had led to inefficiency in the writing process.

The company solved its productivity problem by forming a review committee of both users and operators, which resulted in the adoption of some new procedures. For example, the group agreed to limit the number of revision cycles, requiring writers to give more attention to each draft. In the same way, you can save time and take full advantage of computer technology in writing by following these guidelines:

- *Work in stages.* Note the suggestions in chapter 1 for completing stylistic, grammatical, and mechanical editing in stages—so that errors are caught at the appropriate time.
- *Limit number of printings.* Print as often as you need to print, but don't be wasteful. In other words, make sure you have edited enough to justify another printing. One hidden cost of writing today is the proliferation of word-processing drafts. Resources are squandered, and time is added to the writing process.
- *Use the buddy system.* Ask a colleague to help with the editing process so that another pair of eyes sees your work. Your closeness to the project may keep you from spotting errors, no matter how much technology is at your command.
- *Know the limitations of style programs.* Remember that software programs to correct spelling and other mechanical errors will not eliminate all errors. You still need to watch for problems with words like *effect/affect*, *complement/compliment*, and *principal/principle*, as well as misspellings of personal names and other proper nouns. You might want to use the "search and change" feature of your system to locate trouble spots.

If used with common sense, computers can be a powerful tool as you plan, draft, and revise documents. You will spend more time preparing the content of writing and less time on mechanics.

However, there is one more hazard brought about by this new technology. Computers allow far more typographical variations than most readers want or need. For example, systems give you the option of using one or all of the following techniques for typographical emphasis: underlining, bold, full caps, italics, and increased type size. Too much variety in one document can confuse rather than clarify a passage. The next two sections provide guidelines for effective page design.

GUIDELINES FOR PAGE DESIGN

As one expert says, often you will write for readers who are "in a hurry, frustrated, and bored, and who would prefer to get the information needed from text *in any other way but reading*" (my emphasis) [Schriver, K. A. Fourth Quarter, 1989. Document design from 1980 to 1989: Challenges that remain. *Technical Communication*, p. 319]. Most readers dislike solid text. Your challenge is to respond to this prejudice by making pages interesting to the eye.

Good organization, as pointed out in the last chapter, can fight readers' indifference by giving information when and where they want it. But to keep readers interested, you must use effective page design—that is, the physical appearance of each page in your document. Each page needs the right combination of visual elements to match the needs of readers and the purpose of the document.

This section briefly describes these elements of page design: (1) white space, (2) headings, (3) lists, and (4) in-text emphasis. Computers have made these features and others easy to introduce into documents. The next section covers aspects of document design dealing with type selection and font size. Together these two parts of the chapter give you the guidelines and examples you need to make text visually appealing to your readers.

White Space

The term *white space* simply means the open places on the page with no text or graphics—literally, the *white* space. Experts have learned that readers are attracted to text because of the white space that surrounds it, as with a newspaper ad that includes a few lines of copy in the middle of a white page. Readers connect white space with important information.

In technical writing you should use white space in a way that (1) attracts attention, (2) guides the eye to important information on the page, (3) relieves the boredom of reading text, and (4) helps readers organize information. Here are some opportunities for using white space effectively:

1. Margins: Most readers appreciate generous use of white space around the edges of text. Marginal space tends to "frame" your document, so the text doesn't appear to push the boundaries of the page. Good practice is to use 1" to $1\frac{1}{2}$" margins, with more space on the bottom margin. When the document is bound on the left, as in Figure 4–3, also place more space in the left margin than at the bottom—to account for space lost in the binding process.

FIGURE 4–3
Use of white space: margins

FIGURE 4–4
Use of white space: columns

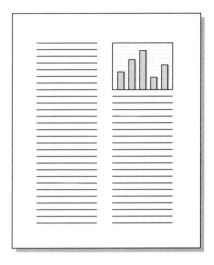

2. Columns: Long lines can be an obstacle to keeping the readers' attention. Eyes get weary of overly long lines, so some writers add double columns to their design options. This "book look," as shown in Figure 4–4, uses white space between columns to break up text and thus reduce line length.

3. Line space: When choosing single, double, or $1\frac{1}{2}$ line spacing, consider the document's length and degree of formality. Letters, memos, short reports, and other documents read in one sitting are usually single spaced, with one line space between paragraphs. Longer documents, especially if they are formal, are usually $1\frac{1}{2}$-space or double-spaced, usually without, but sometimes with, extra spacing between paragraphs. (See Figure 4–5.)

4. Right-justified versus ragged edge: To justify or not to justify lines is often the question. In right-justified copy, all lines are the same length—as on this textbook page. In ragged-edge copy, lines are variable length. Some readers prefer ragged-edge copy because it adds variation to the page, making reading less predictable for the eye. Yet many readers like the professional appearance of right-justified lines, especially in formal documents. Both views have merit.

As a rule, (1) use ragged edge on densely packed, single-spaced documents and (2) use either ragged or justified margins on $1\frac{1}{2}$-space and double-spaced documents, depending on reader preference or company style (see Figure 4–5). However, only use justified margins if your word-processing software maintains uniform spacing between words and between letters within words. It is unnerving to read justified text with inconsistent spacing at these points.

5. Paragraph length: New paragraphs give readers a chance to regroup, as one topic ends and another begins. These shifts also have a visual impact. The amount of white space produced by paragraph lengths can shape reader expectations. For example, two long paragraphs suggest a heavier reading burden than do three or four paragraphs of differing lengths. Most readers skip long paragraphs, so vary paragraph lengths and avoid putting more than 10 lines in any one paragraph (see Figure 4–6).

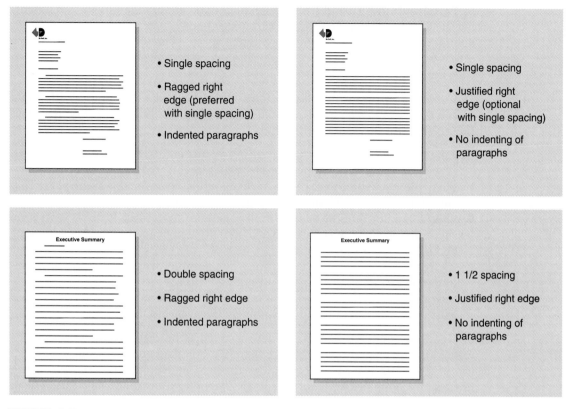

- Single spacing

- Ragged right
  edge (preferred
  with single spacing)

- Indented paragraphs

- Single spacing

- Justified right
  edge (optional
  with single spacing)

- No indenting of
  paragraphs

- Double spacing

- Ragged right edge

- Indented paragraphs

- 1 1/2 spacing

- Justified right edge

- No indenting of
  paragraphs

FIGURE 4–5
Use of white space: lines

FIGURE 4–6
Use of white space: paragraphs

Poor Format: One long
paragraph on page

Better Format: Several
paragraphs on page

6. Paragraph indenting: The argument goes on about indenting or not indenting the first lines of paragraphs. As with ragged-edge copy, most readers prefer indented paragraphs because the extra white space creates visual variety. Reading text is hard work for the eye. You should take advantage of any opportunity to snag the reader (see Figure 4–5).

7. In-text graphics: Any illustration within the text needs special attention. Chapter 11 provides a complete discussion of graphics, but this section discusses their placement for visual appeal. Here are some pointers:

- Make sure there is ample white space between any in-text graphic and the text. If the figure is too large to permit adequate margins, reduce its size.
- When you have the choice, place in-text graphics near the top of the page. That position gives them the most attention.
- When a graphic doesn't fit well on a page with text, place it on its own page where there will be adequate space. Normally it appears on the page following the first reference to it.
- Pay special attention to page balance when graphics will be included on multi-column pages, two-page spreads, or both.
- Draw rough sketches of the layout for the entire document so that you can use white space consistently and persuasively from start to finish.

8. Heading space and lines: White space helps the reader connect related information immediately. Always have slightly more space above a heading than below it. That extra space visually connects the heading with the material into which it leads. In a double-spaced document, for example, you would add a third line of space between the heading and the text that came before it.

In addition, some writers add a horizontal line across the page above headings, to emphasize the visual break. The next section will cover other aspects of headings.

In summary, well-used white space can add to the persuasive power of your text. As with any design element, however, it can be overused and abused. Make sure there is a *reason* for every decision you make with regard to white space on your pages.

Headings

Headings are brief labels used to introduce each new section or subsection of text. They serve as (1) a signpost for the reader who wants to know the content, (2) a "grabber" to entice readers to read documents, and (3) a visual "oasis" of white space where the reader gets relief from text.

As a general rule, every page of any document over one page should have at least one heading. Readers need these markers to find their way through your writing. Models throughout this text show how headings can be used in short and long documents. Of course, heading formats differ greatly from company to company and even from writer to writer. With all the typographical possibilities of word processing, there is incredible variety in typeface, type size, and the use of bold, underlining, and capitals. Here are some general guidelines that apply:

1. Use your outline to create headings and subheadings. A well-organized outline lists major and minor topics. With little or no change in wording, they can be converted to headings and subheadings within the document. As with outlines, you need to follow basic principles of organization.

- First, if you have one subheading, you must have at least one more at that same level—anything that is divided has at least two parts.
- Second, the number of subheadings should be one indication of the relative length or importance of the section. Be consistent with your approach to headings throughout the document.

2. Use substantive wording. Headings give readers an overview of what content will follow. They entice readers into your document; they can determine whether readers—especially those who are hurried and impatient—will read or skip over the text. Strive to use concrete rather than abstract nouns, even if the heading must be a bit longer. Note the improvements in the following revised headings:

Original:	"Background"
Revised:	"How the Simmons Road Project Got Started" or "Background on Simmons Road Project"
Original:	"Discussion"
Revised:	"Procedure for Measuring Toxicity" or "How to Measure Toxicity"
Original:	"Costs"
Revised:	"Production Costs of the FastCopy 800" or "Producing the FastCopy 800: How Much?"

3. Maintain parallel form in wording. Headings of equal value and degree should have the same grammatical form, as shown in the following:

A) *Headings with Parallel Form*
    Scope of Services
    Schedule for Fieldwork
    Conditions of Contract
B) *Headings That Lack Parallel Form*
    Scope of Services
    How Will Fieldwork Be Scheduled?
    Establish Contract Conditions

You don't have to be a grammar expert to see that the three headings in "B" are in different forms. The first is a noun phrase, the second is a question, and the third is an action phrase beginning with a verb. Because such inconsistencies distract the reader, you should make headings in each section uniform in wording.

4. Establish clear hierarchy in headings. Whatever typographical techniques you choose for headings, your readers must be able to distinguish one heading level from another. Visual features should be increasingly more striking as you move up the ranking of levels. Figure 4–7 shows several heading options that reflect such distinctions. Here are specific guidelines for using such typographical distinctions:

1. Four levels,
formal report

LEVEL-1 HEADING

LEVEL-2 HEADING

Level-3 Heading

Level-4 Heading.

2. Three levels,
formal report:
Option A

Level-1 Heading

Level-2 Heading

Level-3 Heading.

3. Three levels,
formal report:
Option B

LEVEL-1 HEADING

LEVEL-2 HEADING

Level-3 Heading

FIGURE 4–7
Some heading options

4. Three levels, informal (letter or memo) report

5. Two levels, informal (letter or memo) report: Option A

6. Two levels, informal (letter or memo) report: Option B

7. One level, informal (letter or memo) report: Option A

8. One level, informal (letter or memo) report: Option B

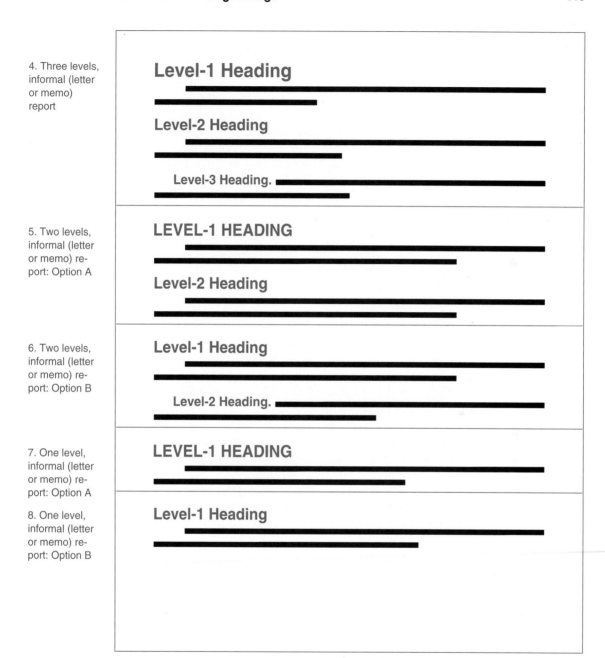

FIGURE 4–7
continued

- *Use larger type size for higher-level headings.* You want readers to grasp quickly the relative importance of heading levels as they read your document. Type size fixes this relative importance in their minds so that they can easily find their way through your material both the first time and upon rereading it. The examples in Figure 4–7 reflect two and sometimes three different type sizes in some of the examples. The incremental upgrading of type size helps readers determine the relative importance of the information.
- *Use heading position to show ranking.* In formal documents, your high-level headings can be centered. The next two or three levels of headings are at or off the left margin, as shown in Figure 4–7. Be sure these lower-level headings also use other typographical techniques, such as size, to help the reader distinguish levels.
- *Use typographical techniques to accomplish your purpose.* Besides type size and position, previously mentioned, you can vary heading type with features such as these:

  Uppercase and lowercase
  Bold type
  Underlining
  Changes in type font

  With this embarrassment of riches, writers must be careful not to overdo it and create "busy" pages of print. Use only those features that will look good on the page and provide an easy-to-grasp hierarchy of levels for the reader.
- *Consider using decimal headings for long documents.* Decimal headings include a hierarchy of numbers for every heading and subheading listed in the table of contents. Many an argument has been waged over their use. People who like them say that they help readers find their way through documents and refer to subsections in later discussions. People who dislike them say that they are cumbersome and give the appearance of "bureaucratic" writing.

  Unless decimal headings are expected by your reader, use them only with formal documents that are fairly long. Include at least three heading levels. Following is the normal progression of numbering in decimal headings for a three-level document:

```
1.0    xxxxxxxxxxxxx
       1.1    xxxxxxxxxxx
              1.1.1    xxxxxxxxxx
              1.1.2    xxxxxxxxxx
       1.2    xxxxxxxxxxx
              1.2.1    xxxxxxxxxx
              1.2.2    xxxxxxxxxx
2.0    xxxxxxxxxxxxx
       2.1    xxxxxxxxxxx
              2.1.1    xxxxxxxxxx
              2.1.2    xxxxxxxxxx
       2.2    xxxxxxxxxxx
3.0    xxxxxxxxxxxxx
```

Listings

Technical writing benefits from the use of lists. Readers welcome your efforts to cluster items into lists for easy reading. In fact, almost any group of three or more related points can be made into a bulleted or numbered listing. Here are some points to consider as you apply this important feature of page design:

1. **Typical uses:** Lists emphasize important points and provide a welcome change in format. Because they attract more attention than text surrounding them, they are usually reserved for these uses:

     Examples

     Reasons for a decision

     Conclusions

     Recommendations

     Steps in a process

     Cautions or warnings about a product

     Limitations or restrictions on conclusions

2. **Number of items:** The best lists are those that subscribe to the rule of short-term memory. That is, people can retain no more than five to nine items in their short-term memory. A listing over nine items may confuse rather than clarify an issue. Consider placing 10 or more items in two or three groupings, or grouped lists, as you would in an outline. This format gives the reader a way to grasp information being presented.

3. **Use of bullets and numbers:** The most common visual clues for listings are numbers and bullets (enlarged dots or squares like those used in the following listing). Here are a few pointers for choosing one or the other:

     ▪ *Bullets:* Best in lists of five or fewer items, unless there is a special reason for using numbers.
     ▪ *Numbers:* Best in lists of over five items *or* when needed to indicate an ordering of steps, procedures, or ranked alternatives. Remember that your readers sometimes will *infer* sequence or ranking in a numbered list.

4. **Format on page:** Every listing should be easy to read and pleasing to the eye. These specific guidelines cover practices preferred by most readers:

     ▪ *Indent the listing.* Although there is no standard list format, readers prefer lists that are indented farther than the standard left margin. Five spaces is adequate.
     ▪ *Hang your numbers and bullets.* Visual appeal is enhanced by placing numbers or bullets to the left of the margin used for the list, as done with the items here.
     ▪ *Use line spaces for easier reading.* When one or more listed items contain over a line of text, an extra line space between listed items can enhance readability.
     ▪ *Keep items as short as possible.* Depending on purpose and substance, lists can consist of words, phrases, or sentences—like the list you are reading. Whichever format you choose, pare down the wording as much as possible to retain the impact of the list format.

5. **Parallelism and lead-ins:** Make the listing easy to read by keeping all points grammatically parallel and by including a smooth transition from the lead-in to the listing itself. (The term *lead-in* refers to the sentence or fragment preceding the listing.) "Parallel" means that each point in the list is in the same grammatical form, whether a complete sentence, verb phrase, or noun phrase. If you change form in the midst of a listing, you take the chance of upsetting the flow of information.

EXAMPLE:
"To complete this project, we plan to do the following:

- Survey the site
- Take samples from the three boring locations
- Test selected samples in our lab
- Report on the results of the study"

The listed items are in verb form (note introductory words "survey," "take," "test," "report"). An alternative would be to put them in noun form, with a slightly different lead-in.

EXAMPLE:
"To complete the project, we will perform the following activities:

- Surveying the site
- Taking samples from the three boring locations
- Testing selected samples in our lab
- Reporting on the results of the study"

6. **Punctuation and capitalization:** Although there are acceptable variations on the punctuation of lists, preferred usage includes a colon before a listing, no punctuation after any of the items, and capitalization of the first letter of the first word of each item. Refer to the alphabetized Handbook under "Punctuation: Lists" for alternative ways to punctuate lists.

7. **Overuse:** With listings it *is* possible to have too much of a good thing. Too many lists on one page can create a distracting, fragmented effect. One rule of thumb is to use no more than one or two lists per page. Too many lists on the same page force the reader to decide which one deserves attention first.

In-Text Emphasis

Sometimes you want to emphasize an important word or phrase within a sentence. Computers give you these options: underlining, boldface, italics, and caps. The least effective are FULL CAPS and *italics,* for both are difficult to read within a paragraph and distracting to the eye. The most effective highlighting techniques are <u>underlining</u> or **boldface;** they add emphasis without distracting the reader. This writer's preference is <u>underlining</u>, which draws attention to the word without the overstatedness of bold copy (which can also be hard to read).

Whatever typographical techniques you select, use them sparingly. They can create a "busy" page that leaves the reader confused about what to read. Excessive in-text emphasis also detracts from the impact of headings and subheadings, which should be receiving significant attention.

SELECTION OF FONTS

Besides page format, you have something else in your word-processing bag of tricks: changes in the size and type of font you use in the text itself.

Size of Type

Traditionally, type size has been measured in "points" (72 points to an inch). When you go to your font-selection menu on your computer screen, the sizes may be listed as such: 9, 10, 12, 14, 18, and 24. Other features of your software will allow you to expand type even farther, for specialty uses.

Despite these many options, most technical writing is printed off the desktop in 10- or 12-point type. When you are choosing type size, however, be aware that the actual size of letters varies among font types. Some 12-point type appears larger than other 12-point type. Differences stem from the fact that your selection of a font affects (1) the thickness of the letters, (2) the size of lowercase letters, and (3) the length and style of the parts of letters that extend above and below the line. The following examples show the differences in three common fonts. Note that the typeface used in setting the text of this book is 10-point Meridien.

New Century Schoolbook
9 point
10 point
12 point
14 point
18 point
24 point

Times Roman
9 point
10 point
12 point
14 point
18 point
24 point

<u>Helvetica</u>
9 point
10 point
12 point
14 point

18 point
24 point

Before selecting your type size, run samples on your printer so that you are certain of how your copy will appear in final form.

Font Types

Font types vary tremendously. Most word-processing systems give you more choices than you will ever use. Generally, these types are classified into two groups:

- Serif fonts: Characters have "tails" at the ends of the letterlines.
- Sans serif fonts: Characters do not have tails. (See Figure 4–8.)

If you are able to choose your font, the obvious advice is to use the one that you know is preferred by your readers. A phone call or a look at documents generated by your reader may help you. If you have no reader-specific guidelines, here are three general rules to follow:

1. *Use serif fonts for regular text in your documents.* The tails on letters make letters and entire words more visually interesting to the reader's eye. In this sense, they serve the same purpose as ragged-edge copy—helping your reader move smoothly through the document.

2. *Consider using another typeface—sans serif—for headings.* Headings benefit from a clean look that emphasizes the white space around letters. Sans serif type helps attract attention to these elements of organization within your text.

3. *Avoid too many font variations in the same document.* There is a fine line between interesting font variations and busy and distracting text. But there *is* a line. Your rule of thumb might be to use no more than two fonts per document, one for text and another for headings and subheadings.

FIGURE 4–8
Font types   Serif Type

Nn > extra lines (serifs)

Sans Serif Type   Nn

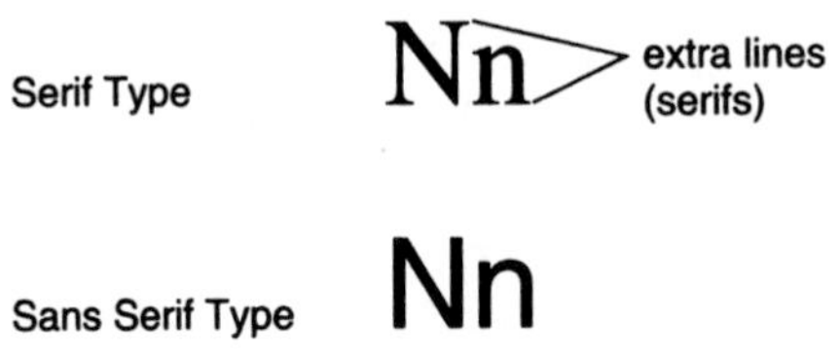

COMMUNICATION CHALLENGE

"The St. Paul Format Guide: Trouble in River City"

Frustrated by inconsistency in report formats, Elaine Johnson, a department manager at McDuff's St. Paul office, decided to take action. After collecting examples of office reports with diverse page designs, she met with her friend and branch manager, Randall DiSalvo, to complain. "Enough is enough, Randall," Elaine said as the meeting started. "The technical staff produces all kinds of formats, the word-processing staff doesn't know what designs are approved, and the clients get a fragmented image of the firm. Let's decide on one page design for reports and stay with it."

After an hour's talk, Elaine and Randall agreed that the office needed a style sheet to describe the required format for each document type written at the St. Paul branch. Busy with many other tasks, Randall told Elaine that he didn't have time to supervise the project. So he gave Elaine the authority to design what he wanted to be called the "Format Guide." However, first she had to meet with all department managers and a few other employees about the project. Also, he asked that her first version of the guide be a modest one that covered only brief letter reports. Later the guide could be expanded.

What follows are details about (1) Elaine's process of gathering information, (2) some actual guidelines she decided to include in the Format Guide, and (3) some problems that arose with the project.

Soliciting Opinions from Around the Office

The same morning she met with Randall, Elaine met with all five of her fellow department managers in the St. Paul office. Gathering in a meeting room overlooking the Mississippi River, they agreed immediately that the format problem needed to be solved.

The managers then concurred with the branch manager's idea about starting small—i.e., covering only short letter reports now but later adding formal reports, proposals, manuals, letters, and memos, along with suggestions on style and grammar. Knowing that Elaine was one of the best writers and editors in the office, the managers said they were comfortable with her writing the manual herself. She could draw from whatever information she gathered from around the office and whatever guidelines she collected from her research on the subject. When the draft was complete, she would run it by them for their comments. Then it would go to Randall for final approval before distribution to all branch employees.

Elaine could hardly believe it. In one morning, five department managers and the branch manager had reached consensus about the nature of the format problem and its solution. Buoyed by her success, Elaine was almost able to look beyond the fact that she had been given the job of writing the manual. Always the one to get a job done quickly, however, she moved to the following steps in the next few days:

- Notepad in hand, she interviewed all seven word processors and secretaries about their preferences in page design.
- She e-mailed all members of the professional staff, asking them to respond in writing in three days if they had specific preferences about the "look" they wanted to achieve in their letter reports.
- She called a local chapter of the Society for Technical Communication (STC), asking for references on page design.
- She located the four sources she received from STC and read them cover to cover.

By the end of the following week, Elaine was ready to begin writing the first draft of what would become the Format Guide for McDuff's St. Paul office.

Elaine's Format for Short Reports

Elaine quickly developed a clear idea of what features should be part of McDuff's short reports. To be sure, some of what she heard from department managers and other employees was at odds with her own views. For example, her preference for ragged-right margins in letter reports differed from that of many colleagues. When there were differences of opinion, she made decisions on the basis on her research and the level of response from those employees she surveyed. The following information summarizes some of the guidelines included in her draft:

1. Font choice should be 12-point New Century Schoolbook.
2. There should be 1.2" margins on the sides, a $\frac{1}{2}$" margin on the top, and a 1" margin on the bottom (except for the first page where letterhead requires the use of a top margin of 2" and a bottom margin of 1").
3. Paragraphs should be block style without indenting of the first line.
4. Text should have ragged-right margins, not justified-right margins.
5. Text should be single spaced, with double spacing between paragraphs.
6. Arrangement of date, inside address, and report title, should be the same as that used in Model 8–6 in this text.
7. Every page after the first page should include a header. Placed in the top right corner (see margin guideline above), the header should include three single-spaced items: the company name (McDuff, Inc.—St. Paul), the project number (e.g., McDuff Project #134), and the date (e.g., July 29, 1997).
8. The heading system should follow the pattern shown in example #4 in Figure 4–7 of this chapter.
9. Bulleted and numbered lists should be indented $\frac{1}{2}$" from the left margin, with double spacing before and after the list and between items in the list.

Once her draft was approved by the branch manager, Elaine had 95 copies printed and distributed to all employees of the St. Paul office. In a cover memo with the Format Guide, she indicated that (1) the guide should be considered the new model for all letter reports leaving the office but that (2) it was a pilot draft that the office would review after six months. Further, she noted that the guide would be expanded later to include other documents.

Problems and Questions

Having finished her project by her deadline, Elaine was pleased. There would be clear guidelines for the staff, and the office would reap the rewards of a more efficient process of producing letter reports. As you look back on Elaine's activities and the guidelines she developed, consider the following questions and comments for discussion:

1. Elaine did a good job of seeking opinions of branch employees before she began her draft. Would it have been useful to consult with McDuff customers while the guide was being developed? Why or why not?

2. Should Elaine have "tested" the usefulness of the Format Guide before it was issued to all employees or was her "pilot draft" approach adequate? If you think further testing was needed, what specifically would you have suggested?

3. Elaine chose to issue the final Format Guide through the office mail, with a cover memo. Was this strategy ideal? If so, why? If not, in what other way might she have introduced the manual?

4. Using Elaine's nine format guidelines, edit the letter report included in Model 8-6 in this textbook. Do you think the revision is in a better format than the original? Why or why not?

5. Elaine's manual provides a fairly rigid set of guidelines, as shown by the guidelines excerpt included in this case. Do you think a company should require employees to follow such a narrowly prescribed format? Why or why not? Give the advantages and disadvantages of each point of view.

6. One engineer called Elaine to complain that the new guidelines did not allow him to use decimal numbered headings and subheadings in his short report. He said that he preferred such headings, and he suspected that his clients did as well. If you were in Elaine's position, how would you respond to this complaint?

7. If you were designing a McDuff Format Guide for short reports, what are some of the guidelines you would include, considering your own personal preferences?

CHAPTER SUMMARY

This chapter shows you how to apply principles of page design to your assignments in this class and your on-the-job writing. The term *page design* refers to the array of formatting options you can use to improve the visual effect of your document.

The last several decades have seen an incredible change in the way documents are produced. Today individual writers working at their personal computers write, edit, design, and print sophisticated documents. Used judiciously, computers are an effective tool during the planning, drafting, and revising stages.

Effective page design requires that you use specific elements such as white space, headings, listings, and in-text emphasis. White space draws attention to adjacent items. Headings quickly lead the reader to important points and sub-points. Listings emphasize related groups of points. And conservative use of in-text emphasis, like underlining and bold print, can draw attention to items within sentences and paragraphs.

Another strategy for page design is to change the size and type of fonts in your documents. Like other strategies, this one must be used with care so that your document does not become too "busy." Page design remains a technique for highlighting content, not a substitute for careful organization and editing.

ASSIGNMENTS

1. **Group Evaluation of Page Design.** Working in small groups, analyze the effectiveness of the page design of the document in Model 4–1 on pages 124–125. Your instructor will indicate whether you should prepare a written or an oral report of your findings. Give specific support for your praise or criticism. (Assignment 4 uses this same memorandum for a writing exercise.)

2. **Individual Evaluation of Page Design.**
   Option A. Visit your library and locate an example of technical writing, such as a government document or a company's annual report. Use the guidelines in this chapter to analyze the document's page design. Your instructor will indicate whether your report should be oral or written.
   Option B. Use the guidelines in this chapter to evaluate the page design of one of the color inserts in chapter 2 of this textbook. What works well? What could be improved? Be specific in your comments.

3. **Individual Practice in Page Design.** As a manager at McDuff, you have just finished a major report to a client. It gives recommendations for transporting a variety of hazardous materials by sea, land, and air. The body of your report contains a section that defines the term *stowage plan* and describes its use. Given your mixed technical and nontechnical audience, this basic information is much needed. What follows is the *text* of that section. Revise the passage by applying any of this chapter's principles of page design that seem appropriate—such as adding headings, graphics, lists, and white space. If you wish, you also can make changes in organization and style. *Optional:* If your class has access to e-mail, transmit your version to another student to receive his or her response.

In the chemical shipping industry, a stowage plan is a kind of blueprint for a vessel. It lists all stowage tanks and provides information about tank volume, tank coating, stowed product, weight of product, loading port, and discharging port. A stowage plan is made out for each vessel on each voyage and records all chemicals loaded. The following information concerns cargo considerations (chemical properties and tank features) and some specific uses of the stowage plan in industry.

The three main cargo considerations in planning stowage are temperature, compatibility, and safety. Chemicals have physical properties that distinguish them from one another. To maintain the natural state of chemicals and to prevent alteration of their physical properties, a controlled environment becomes necessary. Some chemicals, for example, require firm temperature controls to maintain their physical characteristics and degree of viscosity (thickness) and to prevent contamination of the chemicals by any moisture in the tanks. In addition, some chemicals, like acids, react violently with each other and should not be stowed in adjoining, or even neighboring, tanks. In shipping, this relationship is known as chemical compatibility.

The controlled environment and compatibility of chemicals have resulted in safety regulations for the handling and transporting of these chemicals. These regulations originate with the federal government, which bases them on research done by the private manufacturers. Location and size of tanks also determine the placement of cargo. A ship's tanks are arranged with all smaller tanks around the periphery of the tank grouping and all larger tanks in the center. These tanks, made of heavy steel and coated with zinc or epoxy, are highly resistant to most chemicals, thereby reducing the chance of cargo contamination. Each tank has a maximum cargo capacity, and the amounts of each chemical are matched with the tanks. Often chemicals to be discharged at the same port are staggered in the stowage plan layout so that after they are discharged the ship maintains its equilibrium.

The stowage plan is finalized after considering the cargo and tank characteristics. In its final form, the plan is used as a reference document with all information relevant to the loading/discharging voyage recorded. If an accident occurs involving a ship, or when questions arise involving discharging operations, this document serves as a visual reference and brings about quick decisions.

---

4. **Group Practice in Page Design.** Working in small groups, prepare a redesigned version of the memorandum in Model 4–1 (pp. 124–125). If your class is being held in a computer lab, present your group's version on-screen. If you are not using a lab, present your version on an overhead transparency.

5. **Group Practice in Page Design: Using Computer Communication.** This assignment is feasible only if you and your classmates have access to software that will allow you to post messages to team members, edit on screen, and send edited copy back and forth. Your task is to add appropriate page design features to either (a) the "stowage plan" excerpt in assignment 3 or (b) any other piece of straight text permitted for use by your instructor. Choose a team leader who will collect and collate the individual edits. Choose another group member to type or scan the excerpt into the computer and then "mail" the passage to other group members. Then each person should add the features desired and mail the edited document to the team leader, who will collate the revisions and mail the new version to team members for a final edit. Throughout this process, participants may conduct e-mail "conversations" about the draft and resolve differences, if possible, before sending drafts to the leader. The group may need one or two short meetings in person, but most business should be conducted via the computer. The goal is to arrive at one final version for your group.

Mc Duff, Inc.

MEMORANDUM

DATE: August 19, 1996
TO: Randall Demorest, Dean
FROM: Kenneth Payne, Professor and Head *KP*
SUBJECT: BSTW Advisory Board

What? Lunch meetings between Advisory Board members and me
Why? To get more Board support for the BSTW degree program
Who? Each individual member at a separate luncheon
When? Fall 1996
How? Allocation of $360 to pay for the lunches

Rationale

When we seek support for the college, we have to (1) make people feel that they will get something in return and (2) make them feel comfortable about us and our organization. As businesses have demonstrated, one way we can accomplish these goals is by taking potential donors to lunch.

As you and I have discussed, the B.S. in Technical Writing degree program (BSTW) needs to strengthen ties to its Advisory Board. We must ask Board participants to provide tangible support for the program *and* give them meaningful involvement in the work we are doing.

Method

The immediate need is to involve members of the Advisory Board in the coming year's program. I want to do this in two ways:

1. Plan carefully for a fall Board meeting
2. Discuss with each of them individually what we want to accomplish this year

Cost

To do the second item mentioned. I request an allocation of $360 so that I can take each member to lunch for an extended one-on-one discussion. I plan to discuss the needs of our program and each member's capabilities to support it.

MODEL 4–1
Page design in memorandum

Specifics

Each member of the Board will be asked individually to consider the following ways to contribute:

1. Continuing support for the internship program
2. Participation in the research project we began a year ago
3. Cooperative work experiences for BSTW faculty, possibly during the summer of 1997
4. Financial support for the following items:
   • The college's membership as a sponsoring organization in the Society for Technical Communication
   • Contributions——financial or otherwise——to library holdings in technical writing
   • Usability testing laboratory
   • A workshop series bringing to the campus some outstanding technical communicators (for example, Edward Tufte, expert in graphics; JoAnn Hackos, expert in quality management; and William Horton, expert in online documentation)

Benefits

What are Board members going to get from this?

Long range: A better BSTW program, which will produce better technical writers for them to hire

Immediately: Meaningful involvement in the program

Specifically: Training opportunities for their personnel through the workshops mentioned

My tentative plan for those workshops is to provide a one-day seminar for our students and a second seminar for employees of Advisory Board members. (We will allow them a number of participants based on how much they contribute to the workshops.)

Response Needed

Please let me know as soon as possible if money is available for the lunches. I hope to begin scheduling meetings within a week.

MODEL 4–1
continued

PART II

5 Patterns of Organization

Definition, description, and other patterns of organization form the body of technical documents. These patterns must be clearly presented to a diverse audience, including hands-on technicians and supervisors.

*P*art 1 gave you some basic background on technical writing and on McDuff, Inc., the example company used throughout this book. Building on that foundation, Part 2 focuses on specific types of technical writing. This chapter and the next one cover seven common patterns for organizing information. Then chapters 7–10 discuss the following formats for entire documents: letters and memos, short reports, long reports, and proposals and feasibility studies.

If you have already taken a basic composition course, you will see similarities between patterns studied in that course and those described in this chapter. Indeed, technical writing uses the same building blocks as all other good writing. What follows are separate sections on five of these main patterns: argument, definition, description, classification/division, and comparison/contrast. They are roughly arranged by the frequency with which they are used in technical writing, starting with the most common pattern. Each section contains these four parts:

1. Introduction about the pattern
2. Short case studies from McDuff
3. Writing guidelines
4. Extended example at the end of the chapter, with marginal comments

Then the assignments challenge you to use the chapter's five patterns in the context of some short letter or memo reports.

ARGUMENT

Good argument forms the basis for *all* technical writing. Some people have the mistaken impression that only recommendation reports and proposals argue their case to the reader, and that all other writing should be objective rather than argumentative. The fact is, every time you commit words to paper you are "arguing" your point. This text uses the following broad-based definition for argument:

> **Argument:** the strategies you use in presenting evidence to support your point *and* to support your professional credibility, while still keeping the reader's goodwill.

Thus even the most uncontroversial document, like a trip report, involves argument in the sense defined here. That is, a trip report would present information to support the fact that you accomplished certain objectives on a business trip. It also would show the reader, usually your boss, that you worked hard to accomplish your objectives. In fact, you hope that every document you write becomes a written argument for your own conscientiousness as a professional.

The strongest form of argument—called "persuasion"—tries to convince your reader to adopt a certain point of view or pursue a certain line of action (see chapter 10, "Proposals and Feasibility Studies"). In other words, persuasion seeks obvious *changes* in opinions or actions, whereas argument only presents evidence or logic to support a point of view. To help you use argument correctly, the next section provides you with some short case studies from McDuff, guidelines for applying argument, and an annotated example.

Short Cases from McDuff: Argument

Under the definition just given, many in-house and external documents could be considered argument. Here are three McDuff examples:

■ *Argument Case 1: Fire Control in the Everglades*

As a fire-control expert in McDuff's Atlanta office, you just completed a project for the state of Florida. You spent two weeks in the Everglades examining the likelihood for major fires this season. Last season, major fires and westerly winds caused soot and smoke to drift to Florida's tourist area. Your investigation suggests that fires are likely and, in fact, necessary this season. Regular, contained swamp fires help keep down underbrush and thus reduce the chance for much bigger fires. Limited fires will not damage wildlife or major trees, whereas major fires will. Now you must write a report to Florida authorities arguing that controlled fires in the Everglades are desirable, despite the general feeling that all fires should be prevented.

■ *Argument Case 2: Back Pain in the Boston Office*

The engineers, programmers, scientists, and other office workers in McDuff's Boston branch spend a lot of time in their chairs. Although all the office furniture is new and expensive, you and your Boston branch colleagues have experienced regular back pain since the new chairs arrived. Unfortunately, the furniture was ordered through the corporate office, so your complaint cannot be handled in a routine, informal way in your own office. As the branch manager, you have mentioned the problem to your boss, the vice president for domestic operations. Predictably, he asked you to "put it in writing." Although this memo report must explain the problem, you do not want to convey a complaining attitude. Instead, you must thoroughly and objectively document the problems associated with the arrival of the new chairs.

■ *Argument Case 3: Quality Control in the Labs*

As McDuff's quality-control manager, you operate out of the corporate office in Baltimore. Though friendly with all the branch managers, you have the sensitive job of making sure that the quality of McDuff's products and services remains high. During a recent road trip to every office, you noticed problems at the labs. In particular, testing procedures were not being followed exactly, equipment was sometimes not properly cleaned, and samples from the field were not always labeled clearly. Now you must write a memo report to all lab supervisors noting these lapses.

All three cases involve argument as defined in this chapter. That is, you must collect evidence to support your point, while still keeping the goodwill of your readers.

Guidelines for Writing Argument

Argumentative writing has a long tradition, from the rhetoric of ancient times to the political debate of today. This section describes five guidelines about argument that apply to your on-the-job writing.

■ *Argument Guideline 1: Use Evidence Correctly*

Whether writing a proposal to a customer or a memo to your boss, you often move from specific evidence toward a general conclusion supported by the evidence. Called "inductive reasoning," this approach to argument requires that you follow some accepted guidelines. Here are three, along with brief examples:

■ **Use points the reader can grasp.** For example, as the fire-control expert in Case 1, you would need to educate readers about how limited fires can benefit swamp ecosystems. Your report must use evidence that could be understood by a mixed audience of park technicians and bureaucrats.

- **Seed-tree cutting** (removal in one cutting of all but a few trees, which are left to regenerate the forest)
- **Clearcutting** (removal of all trees in an area in one cutting)*

These three cases all require well-placed definitions for their readers. When in doubt, insert definitions! Readers can always skip over ones they do not need.

Guidelines for Writing Definitions

Once you know definitions are needed, you must decide on their format and location. Again, consider your readers. How much information do they need? Where is this information best placed within the document? To answer these and other questions, here are five working guidelines for writing good definitions.

■ Definition Guideline 1: Keep It Simple

Occasionally the sole purpose of a report is to define a term. Most times, however, a definition just clarifies a term in a document with a larger purpose. Your definitions should be as simple and unobtrusive as possible. Always present the simplest possible definition, with only that level of detail needed by the reader.

For example, in writing to a client on your land survey of her farm, you might briefly define a transit as "the instrument used by land surveyors to measure horizontal and vertical angles." The report's main purpose is to present property lines and total acreage, not to give a lesson in surveying, so this sentence definition is adequate. Choose from these three main formats (listed from least to most complex) in deciding the form and length of definitions:

- **Informal definition:** a word or brief phrase, often in parentheses, that gives only a synonym or other minimal information about the term
- **Formal definition:** a full sentence that distinguishes the term from other similar terms and that includes these three parts: the term itself, a class to which the term belongs, and distinguishing features of the term
- **Expanded definition:** a lengthy explanation that begins with a formal definition and is developed into several paragraphs or more

Guidelines 2–4 show you when to use these three options and where to put them in your document.

■ Definition Guideline 2: Use Informal Definitions for Simple Terms Most Readers Understand

Informal definitions appear right after the terms being defined, often as one-word synonyms in parentheses. They give just enough information to keep the reader

---

*Adapted from ENVIRONMENTAL SCIENCE: AN INTRODUCTION, 2/E by G. Tyler Miller, Jr. © 1988 by Wadsworth, Inc. Reprinted by permission of the publisher.

moving quickly. As such, they are best used with simple terms that can be adequately defined without much detail.

Here is a situation in which an informal definition would apply. McDuff has been hired to examine a possible shopping-mall site. The buyers, a group of physicians, want a list of previous owners and an opinion about the suitability of the site. As legal assistant at McDuff, you must assemble a list of owners in your part of the group-written report. You want your report to agree with court records, so you decide to include real-estate jargon such as "grantor" and "grantee." For your nontechnical readers, you include parenthetical definitions like these:

> All **grantors** (persons from whom the property was obtained) and **grantees** (persons who purchased the property) are listed on the following chart, by year of ownership.

This same McDuff report has a section describing creosote pollution found at the site. The chemist writing the contamination section also uses an informal definition for the readers' benefit:

> At the southwest corner of the mall site, we found 16 barrels of **creosote** (a coal tar derivative) buried under about three feet of sand.

The readers do not need a fancy chemical explanation of creosote. They only need enough information to keep them from getting lost in the terminology. Informal definitions perform this task nicely.

■ *Definition Guideline 3: Use Formal Definitions for More Complex Terms*

A formal definition appears in the form of a sentence that lists (1) the **term** to be defined, (2) the **class** to which it belongs, and (3) the **features** that distinguish the term from others in the same class. Use it when your reader needs more background than an informal definition provides. Formal definitions define in two stages:

- First, they place the term into a *class* (group) of similar items.
- Second, they list *features* (characteristics) of the term that separate it from all others in that same class.

In the list of sample definitions that follows, note that some terms are tangible (like "pumper") and others are intangible (like "arrest"). Yet all can be defined by first choosing a class and then selecting features that distinguish the term from others in the same class.

Term	Class	Features
An arrest is	restraint of persons	that deprives them of freedom of movement and binds them to the will and control of the arresting officer.

A financial statement is	a historical report about a business	and is prepared by an accountant to provide information useful in making economic decisions, particularly for owners and creditors.
A triaxial compression test is	a soils lab test	that determines the amount of force needed to cause a shear failure in a soil sample.
A pumper	is a fire-fighting apparatus	used to provide adequate pressure to propel streams of water toward a fire.

This list demonstrates three important points about formal definitions. First, the definition itself must not contain terms that are confusing to your readers. The definition of "triaxial compression test," for example, assumes readers will understand the term "shear failure" that is used to describe features. If this assumption were incorrect, then the term would need to be defined. Second, formal definitions may be so long that they create a major distraction in the text. (See Guideline 5 for alternative locations.) Third, the class must be narrow enough so that you will not have to list too many distinguishing features.

■ *Definition Guideline 4: Use Expanded Definitions for Supporting Information*

Sometimes a parenthetical phrase or formal sentence definition is not enough. If readers need more information, use an expanded definition with this three-part structure:

- **An overview at the beginning**—including a formal sentence definition and a description of the ways you will expand the definition
- **Supporting information in the middle**—using headings and lists as helpful format devices for the reader
- **Brief closing remarks at the end**—reminding the reader of the definition's relevance to the whole document

Here are seven ways to expand a definition, along with brief examples:

1. **Background and/or history of term**—expand the definition of "triaxial compression test" by giving a dictionary definition of "triaxial" and a brief history of the origin of the test
2. **Applications**—expand the definition of "financial statement" to include a description of the use of such a statement by a company about to purchase controlling interest in another
3. **List of parts**—expand the definition of "pumper" by listing the parts of the device, such as the compressor, the hose compartment, and the water tank
4. **Graphics**—expand the description of the triaxial compression test with an illustration showing the laboratory test apparatus

5. **Comparison/contrast**—expand the definition of a term like "management by objectives" (a technique for motivating and assessing the performance of employees) by pointing out similarities and differences between it and other management techniques

6. **Basic principle**—expand the definition of "ohm" (a unit of electrical resistance equal to that of a conductor in which a current of one ampere is produced by a potential of one volt across its terminals) by explaining the principle of Ohm's Law (that for any circuit the electric current is directly proportional to the voltage and inversely proportional to the resistance)

7. **Illustration**—expand the definition of CAD/CAM (Computer-Aided Design/Computer-Aided Manufacturing—computerized techniques to automate the design and manufacture of products) by giving examples of how CAD/CAM is changing methods of manufacturing many items, from blue jeans to airplanes

Obviously, long definitions might seem unwieldy within the text of a report, or even within a footnote. For this reason, they often appear in appendices, as noted in the next guideline. Readers who want additional information can seek them out, whereas other readers will not be distracted by digressions in the text.

■ *Definition Guideline 5: Choose the Right Location for Your Definition*

Short definitions are likely to be in the main text; long ones are often relegated to footnotes or appendices. However, length is not the main consideration. Think first about the *importance* of the definition to your reader. If you know that decision-makers reading your report will need the definition, then place it in the text—even if it is fairly lengthy. If the definition only provides supplementary information, then it can go elsewhere. You have these five choices for locating a definition:

1. **In the same sentence as the term,** as with an informal, parenthetical definition

2. **In a separate sentence,** as with a formal sentence definition occurring right after a term is mentioned

3. **In a footnote,** as with a formal or expanded definition listed at the bottom of the page on which the term is first mentioned

4. **In a glossary at the beginning or end of the document,** along with all other terms needing definition in that document

5. **In an appendix at the end of the document,** as with an expanded definition that would otherwise clutter the text of the document

Example of Expanded Definition

Expanded definitions are especially useful in reports from technical experts to nontechnical readers. McDuff's report writers, for example, often must explain environmental, structural, or geological problems to concerned citizens or non-technical decision-makers. Figure 5–1 gives a definition that might appear in a report to a county government about the placement of a landfill.

Starts with formal sentence definition—including term, class, and features.

Indicates way definition will be developed (description of acute and chronic types).

Gives examples of first type.

Gives examples of second type.

A **toxic substance** is a chemical that is harmful to people or other living organisms. The effects from exposure to a toxic substance may be acute or chronic. Acute effects are those that appear shortly after exposure, usually to a large concentration or dose over a short time. Examples are skin burns or rashes, eye irritation, chest pains, kidney damage, headache, convulsions, and death.

Effects that are delayed and usually long-lasting are called "chronic" effects. They may not appear for months or years after exposure and usually last for years. Examples are cancer, lung and heart disease, birth defects, genetic defects, and nerve and behavioral disorders. Chronic effects often occur as a result of prolonged exposure to fairly low concentrations or doses of a toxin. However, they may occur as the delayed effects of short-term exposure to high doses.

FIGURE 5–1
Definitions in a report
Excerpted from LIVING IN THE ENVIRONMENT: AN INTRODUCTION TO ENVIRONMENTAL SCIENCE, 6/E by G. Tyler Miller, Jr. © 1990 by Wadsworth, Inc. Reprinted by permission of the publisher.

DESCRIPTION

Technical descriptions, like expanded definitions, require that you pay special attention to *details*. In fact, you can consider a description to be a special type of definition that focuses on parts, functions, or other features. It emphasizes *physical* details. Descriptions can appear in any part of a document, from the introduction to the appendix. As a rule, however, detailed descriptions tend to be placed in the technical sections.

To help you write accurate descriptions, this section describes case studies, offers guidelines for writing descriptions, and introduces two annotated examples of equipment descriptions.

Short Cases from McDuff: Descriptions

Descriptions often appear as supporting information in the document body or in appendices. Here are three situations from McDuff in which a detailed description would add to the effectiveness of the complete document.

■ *Description Case 1: Possible Harbors*

McDuff's San Francisco office has been hired to recommend possible locations for a new swimming and surfing park in northern California. Written to a county commission (five laypersons who will make the decision), your report gives three possible locations and your reasons for selecting them. Then it refers to appendices that give brief physical descriptions of the sites.

Specifically, your appendices to the report describe (1) surface features, (2) current structures, (3) types of soils gathered from the surface, (4) water quality, and (5) aesthetic features, such as quality of the ocean views. Language is kept nontechnical, considering the lay background of the commissioners.

■ *Description Case 2: Sonar Testing Equipment*

A potential McDuff client, Rebecca Stern, calls you in your capacity as a geologist at McDuff's Baltimore office. She wants information about the kind of sonar equipment McDuff uses to map geological features on the seafloor.

This client has a strong technical background, so you write a letter with a detailed technical description of the McDuff system. The body of the letter describes the locations and functions of (1) the seismic source (a device, towed behind a boat, that sends the sound waves) and (2) the receiver (a unit, also towed behind the boat, that receives the signals).

■ *Description Case 3: Asbestos Site*

McDuff's Cleveland office was hired to examine asbestos contamination in a large high school built in 1949. As a member of the investigating team, you found asbestos throughout the basement in old pipe coverings. Your final report to the school board provides conclusions about the level of contamination and recommendations for removal. An appendix gives a detailed technical description of the entire basement, including a map with a layout of the plumbing system.

Guidelines for Writing Descriptions

Now that you know how descriptions fit into entire documents, here are some simple guidelines for writing accurate, detailed descriptions. Follow them carefully as you prepare assignments in this class and on the job.

■ *Description Guideline 1: Remember Your Readers' Needs*

The level of detail in a technical description depends on the purpose a description serves. Give readers precisely what they need—but no more. In the harbor description in Case 1, the commissioners do not want a detailed description of soil samples taken from borings. That level of detail will be reserved for a few sites selected later for further study. Instead, they want only surface descriptions. Always know just how much detail will get the job done.

■ *Description Guideline 2: Be Accurate and Objective*

More than anything else, readers expect accuracy in descriptions. Pay close attention to details. (As noted previously, the *degree* of detail in a description depends on the *purpose* of the document.) In the building-floor description in Case 3, for example, you would want to describe every possible location of asbestos in the school basement. Because the description will become the basis for a cost proposal to remove the material, accuracy is crucial.

Along with accuracy should come objectivity. This term is more difficult to pin down, however. Some writers assume that an objective description leaves out all opinion. This is not the case. Instead, an objective description may very well include opinions that have these features:

- They are based on your professional background.
- They can be justified by the time you have had to complete the description.
- They can be supported by details from the site or object being described.

For example, your description of the basement pipes mentioned in Case 3 might include a statement like this: "Because there is asbestos wrapping on the exposed pipes above the boiler, my experience suggests that asbestos wrapping probably also exists around the pipes above the ceiling—in areas that we were not able to view." This opinion does not reduce the objectivity of your description; it is simply a logical conclusion based on your experience.

■ *Description Guideline 3: Choose an Overall Organization Plan*

Like other patterns discussed in this chapter, technical descriptions usually make up only parts of documents. Nevertheless, they must have an organization plan that permits them to be read as self-contained, stand-alone sections. Indeed, a description may be excerpted later for separate use.

Following are three common ways to describe physical objects and events. In all three cases, a description should move from general to specific. That is, you begin with a view of the entire object or event. Then in the rest of the description, you focus on specifics. Headings may be used, depending on the format of the larger document.

1. **Description of the parts:** For many physical objects, like the basement floor and coastal scene in the previous cases, you will simply organize the description by moving from part to part.
2. **Description of the functions:** Often the most appropriate overall plan relies on how things work, not on how they look. In the sonar example, the reader was more interested in the way that the sender and receiver worked together to provide a map of the seafloor. This function-oriented description would include only a brief description of the parts.
3. **Description of the sequence:** If your description involves events, as in a police officer's description of an accident investigation, you can organize ideas around the major actions that occurred, in their correct sequence. As with any list, it is best to place a series of many activities into just a few groups. Four groups of 5 events each is much easier for readers to comprehend than a single list of 20 events.

■ *Description Guideline 4: Use "Helpers"
   Like Graphics and Analogies*

The words of a technical description need to come alive. Because your readers may be unfamiliar with the item, you must search for ways to connect with their experience and with their senses. Two effective tools are graphics and analogies.

Graphics respond to the desire of most readers to see pictures along with words. As readers move through your part-by-part or functional breakdown of a mechanism, they can refer to your graphic aid for assistance. The illustration helps you too, of course, in that you need not be as detailed in describing locations and dimensions of parts when you know the reader has easy access to a visual. Note how the diagrams in Models 5–2 and 5–3 on pages 165–169 give meaning to the technical details in the verbal descriptions.

Analogies, like illustrations, give readers a convenient handle for understanding your description. Put simply, an analogy allows you to describe something unknown or uncommon in terms of something that is known or more common. A brief analogy can sometimes save you hundreds of words of technical description. This paragraph description contains three analogies:

> McDuff, Inc., is equipped to help clean up oil spills with its patented product, SeaClean. This highly absorbent chemical is spread over the entire spill by means of
First analogy
> a helicopter, which makes passes over the spill much like a lawn mower would cover the complete surface area of a lawn. When the chemical contacts the oil, it acts like
Second analogy
> sawdust coming in contact with oil on a garage floor. That is, the oil is immediately absorbed into the chemical and physically transformed into a product that is easily collected. Then our nearby ship can collect the product, using a machine that oper-
Third analogy
> ates much like a vacuum cleaner. This machine sucks the SeaClean (now full of oil) off the surface of the water and into a sealed container in the ship's hold.

■ *Description Guideline 5: Give Your
   Description the "Visualizing Test"*

After completing a description, test its effectiveness by reading it to someone unfamiliar with the material—someone with about the same level of knowledge as your intended reader. If this person can draw a rough sketch of the object or events while listening to your description, then you have done a good job. If not, ask your listener for suggestions to improve the description. If you are too close to the subject yourself, sometimes an outside point of view will help refine your technical description.

Examples of Description

This section introduces two descriptions from McDuff documents, one written at a U.S. office and the other produced overseas. The descriptions themselves are at the end of the chapter. The first example includes a description of physical parts and a brief operating procedure. (For a thorough discussion of process descriptions and instructions, see chapter 6.) The second includes only a description of physical parts. Both show the importance of graphics in technical descriptions.

■ *Description 1: Blueprint Machine*

Donna Millsly, human resources coordinator at McDuff's St. Paul office, has been asked to assemble an orientation guide for new secretaries, office assistants, and other members of the office staff. The manual will contain descriptions and locations of the most common pieces of equipment in the office, sometimes with brief instructions for their use.

One section of her manual includes a series of short equipment descriptions organized by general purpose of the equipment. Model 5–2 on pages 165–166 includes a description of the office blueprint machine, which gets used by a wide variety of employees. Because the blueprint machine has an operating procedure that is not self-evident, the description includes a brief procedure that shows the manner in which the machine should be used.

■ *Description 2: Bunsen Burner*

Fahdi Ahmad, the director of procurement at McDuff's office in Saudi Arabia, is changing his buying procedures. He has decided to purchase some basic lab supplies from companies in nearby developing nations, rather than from firms in industrialized countries. For one thing, he thinks this move may save some money. For another, he believes it will help the company get more projects from these nations, for McDuff will become known as a firm that pumps back some of its profits into the local economies.

As a first step in this process, Fahdi is providing potential suppliers with descriptions of some basic lab equipment used at McDuff, such as pH meters, laboratory scales, glass beakers, and burners. Model 5–3 on pages 167–169 presents a moderately detailed description of one such piece of equipment—a Bunsen burner. Fahdi selected a burner model that is being successfully used at many McDuff offices in the United States. The Model 5–3 description can serve as a starting point for suppliers. However, McDuff and the suppliers realize that burners will have slightly different features, depending on the manufacturer.

CLASSIFICATION/DIVISION

In technical writing, you often perform these related tasks: (1) grouping lists of items into categories, a process called "classification," or (2) separating an individual item into its parts, a process called "division." In practice, the patterns usually work together. So that you can see classification and division in action, this section starts with some case studies from McDuff. Then it presents basic guidelines and an example for classification, followed by basic guidelines and an example for division.

Short Cases from McDuff: Classification/Division

The first case shows how you might use both classification and division in the same context. The other cases show only one pattern at work.

■ *Classification/Division Case 1: Civil-Engineering Projects*

A major client needs some detailed information before deciding between McDuff and a competitor for a big project. Specifically, the firm wants a detailed description of the civil-engineering projects completed by the Caracas office over the last 10 years.

- First, you *divide* the office's civil-engineering capabilities into these five groupings, based on type of project: (1) city planning, (2) construction, (3) transportation, (4) sanitation, and (5) hydraulics. (In each case, you describe the type of work done. For example, hydraulics projects concern the use of water.)
- Second, you collect descriptions of the 214 projects completed.
- Third, you *classify* the 214 projects into the five groupings mentioned. Thus the combined process of division and classification gives you a way to organize details for the client.

■ *Classification/Division Case 2: Birds Near a Sub Base*

The federal government wants to expand a submarine base off the U.S. southeastern coast. Plans went along fine until last year, when a major environmental group raised questions about the effect the expansion would have on bird nesting areas.

　　　The concerned organization, BirdWatch, hired McDuff to determine the environmental impact of increased base traffic on the bird populations of a nearby national seashore. As project director, you determine that 61 species of birds on the island could be affected by the expansion. For the purposes of your report, you classify the 61 species by physical features into the following groupings: (1) loons; (2) grebes; (3) gulls and terns; (4) cranes, rails, and coots; and (5) ducks, geese, and swans. These classifications, often used in ornithological work, will help readers understand the significance of your environmental impact statement.

■ *Classification/Division Case 3: Employee Grievances*

Rob McDuff wants to change the procedure by which employees can register grievances. He prefers that a committee be appointed to hear all grievances. Before he makes his final decision, however, he wants you to submit a summary of the types of grievances filed since the company was founded in 1954. Your painstaking research uncovers 116 separate grievances for which there is paperwork. For easier reading, your report to the company president classifies the 116 incidents into four main categories, by type: (1) firing or discharge from the firm; (2) the use of seniority in layoffs, promotions, or transfers; (3) yearly performance evaluations; and (4) overtime pay and the issue of required overtime at some offices.

Guidelines for Classification

Classification helps you (and of course your reader) make sense out of diverse but related items. The process of outlining a writing assignment requires the use of classification. Outlining (as described in chapter 1) forces you to apply both classification and division to organize diverse information into manageable "chunks." The guidelines presented here provide a three-step procedure for classifying any group of related items.

■ *Classification Guideline 1: Find a Common Basis*

Classification requires that you establish your groupings on one main basis. This basis can relate to size, function, purpose, or any other factor that serves to produce logical groupings. For example, here are the bases for groupings established in the three cases cited:

> **Case 1 basis:** the *type of work* being done in the civil-engineering field at McDuff (such as sanitation or city planning)
>
> **Case 2 basis:** the *physical features* of the marsh or ocean birds found at the site (note that the classifications in this case are not original but rather are ones commonly used in ornithology)
>
> **Case 3 basis:** the *purpose for the grievance* (that is, the grievances can be grouped under four main reasons why the employees made formal complaints to the company)

■ *Classification Guideline 2: Limit the Number of Groups*

In chapter 4, you learned that readers prefer groupings of under nine items—the fewer the better. This principle of organization, as well as the appropriateness of the basis, should guide your use of classification. Strive to select a basis that will result in a limited number of groupings.

In Case 1, another basis for classifying the 214 civil-engineering projects would be by country in which the project was located, rather than type of work. Assume that after applying this project-site basis, you end up with 18 different classifications (that is, countries) for the 214 projects. Given this unwieldy number of groupings, however, you should either (1) avoid using this basis or (2) reduce the number of classifications by grouping countries together, perhaps by continent. In other words, the number of classifications affects the degree to which this pattern of organization succeeds with the reader.

■ *Classification Guideline 3: Carefully Classify Each Item*

The final step is to place each item in its appropriate classification. If you have chosen classifications carefully, this step is no problem. For example, assume that as McDuff's finance expert, you want to identify sources for funding new projects. Therefore, you need to collect the names of all commercial banks started in Pennsylvania last year. A reference librarian gives you the names of 42 banks. To impose some order, you decide to classify them by charter. The resulting groups are as follows:

1. National banks (those chartered in all states)
2. Non-Federal Reserve state banks (exclusively Pennsylvania banks that are not members of the Federal Reserve System)
3. Federal Reserve state banks (exclusively Pennsylvania banks that are members of the Federal Reserve System)

With three such classifications that do not overlap, you can put each of the 42 banks in one of the three classifications.

Example of Classification

Now apply the three-part classification strategy to a detailed problem at McDuff. You are on a committee to write an outline summary of McDuff's safety practices. Since much of the company's work involves hazardous materials, you want to place special emphasis on techniques used to protect workers from toxic chemicals, polluted air, asbestos fibers, and so forth. This outline will be used as an attachment to sales letters and proposals sent to potential clients, such as the federal government and various state governments. Good organization is crucial so that the reader can locate information quickly. At its first meeting, your committee comes up with this list of topics to be included in the outline:

1. Headgear provided by company
2. Complete physicals done yearly
3. Partial physicals done at six-month intervals
4. Blood monitoring throughout work at hazardous sites
5. State-of-the-art face masks and oxygen equipment
6. Twenty-hour safety program during employment orientation
7. Certified safety official on-site during hazardous projects
8. Pre-employment drug testing
9. Random drug testing of all workers in dangerous jobs
10. State-of-the-art hand and body protection equipment
11. Biweekly training sessions on safety-related topics
12. Pre-employment complete physical
13. Monthly in-house newsletter with safety column
14. Incentive awards for employees with safety suggestions
15. Company membership in national safety organizations

Next the committee (1) selects an appropriate basis (the *time* at which these safety precautions should take place), (2) establishes three main groupings, (3) classifies each of the 15 items into one of the groups, and (4) assembles the following outline for use in McDuff sales literature. (Numbers in parentheses refer to the topics just listed.)

   I. Procedures before employment
      A. Twenty-hour safety program during orientation (6)
      B. Pre-employment drug testing (8)
      C. Pre-employment complete physical (12)

II. Procedures during a project
   A. Headgear provided by company (1)
   B. Blood monitoring throughout work at hazardous sites (4)
   C. State-of-the-art face masks and oxygen equipment (5)
   D. Certified safety official on-site during hazardous projects (7)
   E. State-of-the-art hand and body protection equipment (10)
III. Procedures that take place periodically during one's employment at McDuff
   A. Complete physicals done yearly (2)
   B. Partial physicals done at six-month intervals (3)
   C. Random drug testing of all workers in dangerous jobs (9)
   D. Biweekly training sessions on safety-related topics (11)
   E. Monthly in-house newsletter with safety column (13)
   F. Incentive awards for employees with safety suggestions (14)
   G. Company membership in national safety organizations (15)

Guidelines for Division

Division begins with an entire item that must be *broken down* or *partitioned* into its parts, whereas classification begins with a series of items that must be *grouped* into related categories. Division is especially useful when you need to explain a complicated piece of equipment to an audience unfamiliar with it. Follow these three guidelines for applying this pattern:

■ Division Guideline 1: Choose the Right Basis for Dividing

Like classification, division means you must find a logical reason for establishing groups or parts. Assume, for example, that you are planning to teach a McDuff training seminar in project management. In dividing this four-day training seminar into appropriate segments, it seems clear to you that each day should cover one of these crucial parts of managing projects: meeting budgets, scheduling staff, completing written reports, and seeking follow-up work from the client. In this case, the principle of division seems easy to employ.

Yet other cases present you with choices. If, for example, you were planning a training seminar on report writing, you could divide it in these three ways, among others: (1) by *purpose of the report* (for example, progress, trip, recommendation), (2) by *parts of the writing process* (for example, brainstorming, outlining, drafting, revising), or (3) by *report format* (for example, letter report, informal report, formal report). Here you would have to choose the basis most appropriate for your purpose and audience.

■ Division Guideline 2: Subdivide Parts When Necessary

As with classification, the division pattern of organization can suffer from the "laundry list" syndrome. Specifically, any particular level of groupings should have from three to seven partitions—the number that most readers find they can absorb. When you go over that number, consider reorganizing information or subdividing it.

Assume that you want to partition a short manual on writing formal proposals. Your first effort to divide the topic results in nine segments: cover page, letter of transmittal, table of contents, executive summary, introduction, discussion, conclusions, recommendations, appendices. You would prefer fewer groupings, so you then establish three main divisions: front matter, discussion, and back matter, with breakdowns of each. In other words, your effort to partition was guided by every reader's preference for a limited number of groupings.

■ *Division Guideline 3: Describe Each Part with Care*

This last step may seem obvious. Make sure to give equal treatment to each part of the item or process you have partitioned. Readers expect this sort of parallelism, just as they prefer the limited number of parts mentioned in Guideline 2.

Example of Division

You are a McDuff manager helping to prepare a client's report. The main task is to describe major types of offshore oil rigs. You decide to partition the subject on the basis of *environmental application,* which gives you five main types. In the following list, notice that each of the five is described in a parallel fashion: the rig's purpose, type of structure, and design with respect to wave strength.

Five Main Types of Offshore Oil Rigs

1. **Platform rig:** Generally for drilling at water depths of less than 1000 ft/ Permanent structure supported by steel and concrete legs driven into ocean floor/ Designed to withstand waves of about 50 ft
2. **Submersible rig:** Generally for drilling at water depths of less than 100 ft/ Temporary structure supported by large tanks that, when filled, go to the ocean floor and thus form the foundation for the columns extending to the deck structure above/ Designed to withstand waves of about 30 ft
3. **Semisubmersible rig:** Generally for drilling in extreme water depths of 1000 ft or more/ Temporary structure with large water-filled pontoons that keep it suspended just below the water surface, with anchors or cables extending to the ocean bottom/ Designed to withstand extreme wave heights of 90 ft or more
4. **Drillship:** Generally for drilling at water depths between 100 and 1000 ft/ Drilling operations take place through opening in the middle of the ship/ Designed to operate in relatively low wave heights of less than 30 ft
5. **Jack-up rig:** Generally for drilling at water depths between 25 and 500 ft/ Temporary structure with platformlike legs that can be jacked up and down to rest on the ocean surface, much like the jacking system used to elevate a car when changing a tire/ Designed to withstand hurricane-force winds that produce waves of over 50 ft

COMPARISON/CONTRAST

Many writing projects obligate you to show similarities or differences between ideas or objects. (For our purposes, the word *comparison* emphasizes similarities, whereas the word *contrast* emphasizes differences.) In the real world of career writing, this technique especially applies to situations wherein readers are making buying decisions. To help you write effective comparisons, this section presents several cases from McDuff, puts forth some simple guidelines, and introduces an annotated example that you will find at the end of the chapter.

Short Cases from McDuff: Comparison/Contrast

One of the most common patterns at McDuff, comparison/contrast is used in many in-house and external reports. Examples of each are noted here.

■ Comparison/Contrast Case 1: Jamaica Hotels

As an architect for McDuff, you have had the good fortune of traveling to Jamaica three times on business in the last year. Each time you stayed at a different hotel on Montego Bay. Now your boss, Byron Scarsdale, is going there for an extended business trip. Before making his travel arrangements, he asks you for a memorandum that compares and contrasts main features of the three hotels. Presumably, he will use the information to decide where he will stay.

■ Comparison/Contrast Case 2: Security Systems

One of your jobs as McDuff's corporate purchasing agent is to advise managers. The manager of the London branch has asked that you send him a summary of similarities and differences among five high-quality infrared detectors. He wants to install several in a new computer lab, to detect movement of any after-hours intruders and then to send a signal to local police.

■ Comparison/Contrast Case 3: Poisons

Your job in McDuff's toxicology laboratory brings you in contact with dozens of poisons. One client has asked you to compare and contrast the relative dangers of five poisonous chemicals found in the well water at the site where the client firm wants to build a warehouse. Your report will be used in making the decision to build or not to build.

Guidelines for Comparison/Contrast

The three cases just cited show you real contexts in which you will use the comparison/contrast pattern of organization. Now here are guidelines for writing effective comparisons and contrasts.

■ *Comparison/Contrast Guideline 1: Remember Your Purpose*

When using comparison/contrast in on-the-job writing, your purpose usually falls into one of these two categories:

1. **Objective:** essentially an unbiased presentation of features wherein you have no real "axe to grind"
2. **Persuasive:** an approach wherein you compare features in such a way as to recommend a preference

You must constantly remember your main purpose. You will either provide raw data that someone else will use to make decisions *or* you will urge someone toward your preference. In either case, the comparison must show fairness in dealing with all alternatives. Only in this way can you establish credibility in the eyes of the reader.

■ *Comparison/Contrast Guideline 2: Establish Clear Criteria and Use Them Consistently*

In any technical comparison, you must set clear standards of comparison and then apply them uniformly. Otherwise, your reader will not understand the evaluation or accept your recommendation (if there is one).

For example, assume you are a McDuff field supervisor who must recommend the purchase of a bulldozer for construction sites. You have been asked to recommend just *one* of these models: Cannon-D, Foley-G, or Koso-L. After background reading and field tests, you decide upon three main criteria for your comparison: (1) pushing capacity, (2) purchase details, and (3) dependability. These three factors, in your view, are most relevant to McDuff's needs. Having made this decision about criteria, you then must discuss all three criteria with regard to *each* of the three bulldozers. Only in this way can readers get the data needed for an informed decision.

■ *Comparison/Contrast Guideline 3: Choose the "Whole-by-Whole" Approach for Short Comparison/Contrasts*

This strategy requires that you discuss one item in full, then another item in full, and so on. Using the bulldozer example, you might first discuss all features of the Cannon, then all features of the Foley, and finally all features of the Koso. This strategy works best if individual descriptions are quite short so readers can remember points made about the Cannon bulldozer as they proceed to read sections on the Foley and then the Koso machines.

Keep these two points in mind if you select the whole-by-whole approach:

■ Discuss subpoints in the same order—that is, if you start the Cannon description with information about dependability, begin the Foley and Koso discussions in the same way.

- If you are making a recommendation, move from least important to most important, or vice versa, depending on what approach will be most effective with your reader. Busy readers usually prefer that you start with the recommended item, followed by the others in descending order of importance.

■ *Comparison/Contrast Guideline 4: Choose the "Part-by-Part" Approach for Long Comparison/Contrasts*

Longer comparison/contrasts require readers to remember much information. Thus readers usually prefer that you organize the comparison around major criteria, *not* around the whole items. Using the bulldozer example, your text would follow this outline:

   I. Pushing Capacity
      A. Cannon
      B. Foley
      C. Koso
  II. Purchase Details
      A. Cannon
      B. Foley
      C. Koso
 III. Dependability
      A. Cannon
      B. Foley
      C. Koso

Note that the bulldozers are discussed in the same order within each major section. As with the whole-by-whole approach, the order of the items can go either from most important to least important or vice versa—depending on what strategy you believe would be most effective with your audience.

■ *Comparison/Contrast Guideline 5: Use Illustrations*

Comparison/contrasts of all kinds benefit from accompanying graphics. In particular, tables are an effective way to present comparative data. For example, your report on the bulldozers might present some pushing-capacity data you found in company brochures.

Example of Comparison/Contrast

Using the bulldozer example, Model 5–4 on pages 170–171 presents a sample of the part-by-part pattern. Remember that such a comparison would be only part of a final report—in this case, one that recommends the Cannon-D. The complete report would include an introductory summary at the beginning and a list of conclusions and recommendations at the end (see chapter 8). This example could be written in either a whole-by-whole or part-by-part manner. The latter is used here to emphasize the importance of the three criteria for comparison.

COMMUNICATION CHALLENGE

"A Dome Gone South: Argument in Action"

When McDuff finished its project of managing construction of the Nevada Gold Dome (see Project #4 on color insert in chapter 2), all was well. The company more than met its completion deadline and saved its client, the stadium owners, about $100,000. Now, two years later (and a year after the comprehensive warranty expired), a number of problems have surfaced. The following sections (1) present the four main complaints McDuff has heard, (2) analyze the problem from the points of view of both the dome owners and McDuff, and (3) list questions and comments for you to consider in evaluating this "breakdown." The focus will be opportunities for using patterns of organization discussed in this chapter.

Problems with the Dome

Over the last few months, the Gold Dome owners have alerted McDuff to four problems they believe may have resulted from construction or material problems:

1. **Artificial Turf:** The turf has pulled up at several spots around the edge of the field. Although dome maintenance staff tried a quick fix, the turf has pulled back up again and again.
2. **Ramp Cracks:** Several one-inch cracks have developed in concrete ramps that lead from the team locker rooms to the field. Just last week two football players tripped on the cracks as they entered the field in front of TV cameras covering the start of a game. The embarrassment, as well as the possible danger to high-priced players, has the dome management fuming.
3. **Roof Leak:** Leaks developed in the dome roof, caused by the ponding of rainwater on a sunken roof section near one of the spectator decks.
4. **Equipment Damage:** Water entered one of the dome's control rooms, damaging three TV monitors and causing carpeting to mildew.

What brought the problems to a head was an incident before last Sunday's game. While team co-owners, Ted Burner and Jane Honda, were getting settled into their luxury box near the upper deck, a roof panel broke loose near the area of the leak and crashed onto their balcony, spilling wine and cheese on Ted and Jane. Needless to say, that event generated a meeting this week between McDuff and dome management.

McDuff and the Dome Management: Different Analyses

With all its training in Total Quality Management, McDuff believes that satisfying the customer is a crucial corporate objective. Besides being the ethical high road, this goal also generally leads to the company getting repeat business from the same client or good recommendations to be used with new clients. In either case, good service helps business.

Yet the firm has not reached its current level of success ·by admitting error every time a client expresses dissatisfaction with a job. Sometimes other parties are at fault. Indeed, at the end of the meeting between McDuff and the dome management, McDuff representatives had clear disagreements about the possible causes of the four problems. Here are the main differences that arose from preliminary analyses by both parties.

■ **Artificial Turf**
Dome: The dome managers believe that artificial turf was installed improperly, without adequate drying time allowed for the adhesive.
McDuff: McDuff expects that the problem was caused wholly or in part by the dome's home team, the Nevada Gamblers. Two years ago the team began practicing on the surface before the end of the two-week curing period recommended by the installers.

■ **Ramp Cracks**
Dome: Dome managers remember McDuff, Inc.'s, comments on a construction progress report, indicating that several trucks arrived late when concrete was being poured for the ramps. Thus there were longer than usual delays between truck pours for the ramps.
McDuff: Despite the truck delays, McDuff satisfied the minimum professional standards for timeliness during the concrete pour. Unrelated to this timing problem, McDuff had recommended additional reinforcing bars for the ramp concrete during construction. However, dome management had only approved the minimum amount required by applicable standards.

■ **Roof Leak**
Dome: Dome managers believe that a structural flaw in the roof support system caused water to pool on one small section of the roof, instead of rolling off into the drainage canals.
McDuff: After observing the roof area, McDuff suspects that a major hailstorm two months ago damaged the roof panels, which caused ponding of rainwater and led to the subsequent leak.

■ **Equipment Damage**
Dome: The route of the water suggests that it may have come through wall spacings from the area of the roof leak.
McDuff: Another possibility is that the damage resulted from a custodial worker failing to turn off a faucet located above the control room in a maintenance area. When the open faucet was discovered, the maintenance room was cleaned up without anyone observing seepage into other rooms or wall space, but such seepage seems just as likely as seepage from the region of the roof leak.

Although the dome's comprehensive warranty has ended, McDuff and key contractors remain partially liable for five years from construction for problems that can be linked to defects in construction or materials. Even if this warranty were not in force, however, McDuff would want to go above and beyond the call to satisfy the client—if there were some reason for doubt or if corrections were not too expensive. At this point, McDuff has not decided how to proceed.

Questions and Comments for Response

In responding to the following questions and comments, use information previously supplied as well as any other rationale you think applies.

1. *Argument:* Cyndy Perlman, a member of McDuff's dome project team, believes that McDuff should correct all four problems. What arguments, from strongest to weakest, should she use to convince her skeptical boss of this path of action?

2. *Argument:* Mason Hunter, another member of the McDuff project team, believes that McDuff should bear *no* financial responsibility for correcting any of the four problems. What arguments, from strongest to weakest, should he use to convince his skeptical boss of this path of action?

3. *Argument:* In the case presentation, find one example each of what could be considered *non sequitur* and *post hoc ergo propter hoc* argumentative fallacies.

4. *Definition:* Do some research to provide formal sentence definitions for some or all of the following terms mentioned in the Gold Dome case study:

Warranty

Dome stadium

Artificial turf

Concrete

TV monitor

Total Quality Management

Progress report

Reinforcing bars

Hailstorm

5. *Description:* Provide an outline of what you would include in a technical description of a domed athletic stadium.

6. *Classification/Division:* Separate into groups established by your instructor. Then brainstorm to come up with a list of at least 30 additional construction- or materials-related problems that could have occurred with a stadium like the Gold Dome. Finally, perform a classification exercise like the one presented in this chapter regarding McDuff's safety practices.

7. *Comparison/Contrast:* In the "McDuff and the Dome Management" section of this case study, a comparison/contrast is presented in a "part-by-part" format. Convert it to a "whole-by-whole" format. Which of the two organizational strategies do you consider most effective in this case?

CHAPTER SUMMARY

This chapter examines five common patterns of organization that make up reports, proposals, and correspondence. By studying these patterns, you will be better prepared to write the documents covered later in this book.

Argument is used when the writer needs to support points with evidence. (Persuasion, the strongest form of argument, occurs when the writer seeks to change the reader's opinions or actions.) To write effective arguments, follow these guidelines:

1. Use evidence correctly.
2. Choose the most convincing order for points.
3. Be logical.
4. Use only appropriate authorities.
5. Avoid argumentative fallacies.

Definitions occur in technical writing in one of three forms: informal (in parentheses), formal (in sentence form with term, class, and features), and expanded (in a paragraph or more). These main guidelines apply:

1. Keep it simple.
2. Use informal definitions for simple terms most readers understand.
3. Use formal definitions for more complex terms.
4. Use expanded definitions for supporting information.
5. Choose the right location for your definition.

Description, like definition, depends on detail and accuracy for its effect. Careful descriptions usually include a lengthy itemizing of the parts of a mechanism or the functions of a term. Follow these basic guidelines for producing effective descriptions:

1. Remember your readers' needs.
2. Be accurate and objective.
3. Choose an overall organization plan.
4. Use "helpers" like graphics and analogies.
5. Give your description the "visualizing test."

Classification/division patterns help you organize groups of related items (classification) and break down an item into its parts (division). The guidelines for classification are as follows:

1. Find a common basis (for grouping diverse items).
2. Limit the number of groups.
3. Carefully classify each item.

Similarly, the guidelines for division are as follows:

1. Choose the right basis for dividing.
2. Subdivide parts when necessary.
3. Describe each part with care.

Comparison/contrast gives you an organized way to highlight similarities and differences in related items—whether you are simply presenting data or are attempting to argue a point. These main writing rules apply:

1. Remember your purpose.
2. Establish clear criteria and use them consistently.
3. Choose the "whole-by-whole" approach for short comparison/contrasts.
4. Choose the "part-by-part" approach for long comparison/contrasts.
5. Use illustrations.

ASSIGNMENTS

Part 1: Short Assignments

The following short assignments can be completed either orally or in writing. Unless a group project is specifically indicated, an assignment can be either a group or an individual effort. Your instructor will give you specific directions.

1. **All Patterns of Organization—Recognition Exercise.** For this group assignment, your instructor will provide each group with a different packet of "junk mail" (catalogs, sales letters, promotions, etc.) and perhaps other documents such as memos or product information sheets. Your group will search for and evaluate examples of various patterns of organization in the documents. Then it will report its findings to the whole class.
2. **Argument.** Analyze the argumentative effectiveness, or lack thereof, in the following passage:

After a good deal of thought, I have decided not to accept the committee's recommendation to allow employees up to two weeks of unpaid vacation leave (in addition to whatever paid vacation leave the employee receives). My reasons are as follows:

a. The proposal obviously would cause the company to lose many customers, for we definitely would not have the staff to cover our daily operations in the office and in the field.

b. Just as the policy of flextime hours has caused some companies to fail to respond adequately to phone calls early in the morning, the leave plan would keep the office uncovered during days when an excessive number of employees were taking leave.

c. The salary of employees using unpaid vacation leave would decrease, and they would be less able to pay their bills. In effect, then, the leave time policy would hurt their families.

d. Unpaid vacation leave has been supported by some members of the state legislature, and we all know how little that organization knows about how to operate business. In fact, I heard the other day that our local state senator, who supports the idea of unpaid vacation leave, bounced 17 checks during the statehouse banking scandal several years ago. That will tell you something about his knowledge of business activities.

e. One of our competitors, Jonquil Engineering, adopted an unpaid vacation leave policy two years ago, and I have just learned that the firm's stock dropped 10% recently.

f. Unpaid leave has been supported by the Americans for Family, an organization whose president is Arlin Thomas. And we all know about his antics in the media. In the last few years, he has supported any cause that has come his way.

---

3. **Argument: McDuff Project.** For this assignment, use points from Project #7 (on the color insert in chapter 2) to complete one of the options below. Each option will also require that you create additional information that could relate to McDuff's technical writing seminar in Germany.

   Option A: Creating an Effective Argument. Assume you were one of the individuals attending the seminar. Create an argument you would present to your boss to justify offering another seminar for some members of your department.

   Option B: Creating Argumentative Fallacies. Assume you attended the seminar and are presenting an evaluation of it to your supervisor. Create an example of each of the argumentative fallacies included in this chapter. Your seven answers can be in support of the seminar, against it, or both.

4. **Definition.** Using the guidelines in this chapter, discuss the relative effectiveness of the following short definitions. Speculate on the likely audience the definitions are addressing. [Excerpted from Turner, R. S., R. B. Cook, H. Van Miegroet, D. W. Johnson, J. W. Elwood, O. P. Bricker, S. E. Lindberg, and G. M. Hornberger. September 1990. Watershed and lake processes affecting surface water acid-base chemistry (NAPAP Report 10). In *Acidic Deposition: State of Science and Technology.* National Acid Precipitation Assessment Program, 722 Jackson Place, NW, Washington, D.C.]

---

   a. Watershed—the geographic area from which surface water drains into a particular lake or point along a stream.

   b. Acid mine drainage—runoff having high concentrations of metals and sulfate and high levels of acidity resulting from the oxidation of sulfide minerals that have been exposed to air and water by mining activities.

   c. Steady-state model—a model in which the variables under investigation are assumed to reach equilibrium and are independent of time.

   d. Acidic lake or stream—a lake or stream in which the acid neutralizing capacity is less than or equal to zero.

   e. Biomass—the total quantity of organic matter in units of weight or mass.

   f. Detritus—dead and decaying organic matter originating from plants and animals.

   g. Hydrology—the science that deals with the waters of the earth—their occurrence, circulation, and distribution; their chemical and physical properties; and their relationship to living things.

   h. Plankton—plant or animal species that spend part or all of their lives carried passively by water currents.

   i. Mineral weathering—dissolution of rocks and minerals by chemical and physical processes.

---

5. **Definition: McDuff Projects.** This assignment can be completed as an individual or a group project. Select one of the projects in the color insert in chapter 2. Using the outline of information on the project as a starting point, do the following:

   - Conduct some research on the technical field reflected in the project.
   - Select some terms related to the field.
   - Write *either* short formal definitions *or* expanded definitions of the terms.

In assigning this project, your instructor will indicate (a) how many terms you should select and (b) whether you should write formal or expanded definitions.

6. **Description.** Write a description of a piece of equipment or furniture located in your classroom or brought to class by your instructor—for example, a classroom chair, an overhead projector, a screen, a three-hole punch, a mechanical pencil, or a computer floppy disk. Write the description for a reader totally unfamiliar with the item.

7. **Description: McDuff Project.** For this project put yourself in the position of someone who worked on the Grant Hospital project (Project #3 in color insert in chapter 2). Write a description of a piece of equipment that either (a) could have been used in the construction of the hospital or (b) could be housed in any modern medical facility such as Grant Hospital. This assignment may require a visit to a local hospital, construction company, or library with resources in the fields of construction or medical care.

8. **Classification/Division.** Divide into groups of eight or ten as selected by your instructor. Then, as a group, take an inventory of the career plans of each member of your group. Finally, using career plans as your basis, classify the group participants into a limited number of groupings. Be sure to adjust the size and focus of categories so that you have at least two students in each grouping. Present the group results to the entire class.

9. **Classification/Division: McDuff Projects.** For this assignment you will use the 33 "main technical tasks" listed on the seven projects on the color insert in chapter 2. Perform a classification exercise by finding a common basis, selecting an appropriate number of groups, and placing each of the 33 technical tasks into one of the groups.

10. **Comparison/Contrast.** Divide into groups of three to five students, as determined by your instructor. Select two members who will give the other group members information about their (a) academic career, (b) extracurricular activities, and (c) work experience. Using the information gathered during this exercise, develop an outline of either a whole-by-whole or part-by-part comparison/contrast.

11. **Comparison/Contrast: McDuff Projects.** Select two or three of the McDuff projects from the color insert in chapter 2. Perform a "part-by-part" comparison/contrast of the two or three projects. Use some or all of the information on the projects. If necessary, create some of your own information to supply adequate detail for your response.

Part 2: Longer Assignments

These assignments test your ability to use patterns of organization covered in this chapter. To lend realism, they are placed in the context of short reports within McDuff, Inc. Follow these guidelines for each assignment:

- Write each exercise in the form of a *memo report* (if it is directed within McDuff, Inc.) or a *letter report* (if it is directed to an outside reader).
- Follow organization and design guidelines given in chapters 3 and 4, especially with regard to the ABC format (**A**bstract/**B**ody/**C**onclusion) and the use of headings. Chapter 8 gives thorough format guidelines for short reports, but such detail is not necessary to complete the assignments here.
- For each assignment, fill out a copy of the Planning Form at the end of the book. Invent any audience analysis information not included in the following so that you have a "real" person to whom you are writing.

12. **Argument for New Wastewater Specialist.** You are a wastewater specialist and manager of a four-person crew with McDuff's Houston office. Recently you have become concerned about the amount of overtime worked by you and your group. Here are your main concerns, from most to least important. First, you are worried that excessive overtime might lead to errors by exhausted workers. The four employees on your crew often work at dangerous sites with poisonous chemicals and polluted water. Mistakes could lead to worker exposure to chemicals or errors in recording data or collecting samples. Second, three of your four field-workers have complained about their 50–55-hour weeks and the excessive time spent out of town on projects. Although they like the overtime pay, they would prefer to average just an extra five hours a week. You are concerned that they may quit to work at a competing firm. Third, you are convinced that there is enough work to support a fifth field employee, and still have three or four hours of overtime per employee per week. (Of course, you realize that there is always the risk that a future work slowdown would mean laying off an additional worker.)

    Given these concerns, you want to write a short report to the branch manager, Elmore Lindley, describing the problems. You also want to suggest that McDuff hire another field-worker, or at least give the matter some study. Present this information to Lindley, using the argumentative strategies described in this chapter.

13. **Technical Definitions in Your Field.** Select a technical area in which you have taken course work or in which you have technical experience. Now assume that you are employed as an outside consulting expert, acting as a resource in your particular area to a McDuff manager not familiar with your specialty. For example, a food-science expert might provide information related to the dietary needs of oil workers working on an offshore rig for three months; a business or management expert might report on a new management technique; an electronics expert might explain the operation of some new piece of equipment that McDuff is considering buying; a computer programmer might explain some new piece of hardware that could provide supporting services to McDuff; and a legal expert might define "sexism in the workplace" for the benefit of McDuff's human resources professionals.

    For the purpose of this report, develop a context in which you would have to define terms for an uninformed reader. Incorporate *one expanded definition* and *at least one sentence definition* into your report.

14. **Description of Equipment in Your Field.** Select a common piece of laboratory, office, or field equipment with which you are familiar. Now assume that you must write a short report to your McDuff supervisor, who wants this report to contain a thorough physical description of the equipment. Later he or she plans to incorporate your description into a training manual for those who need to know how to use, and perform minor repairs on, the equipment. For the body of your description, choose either a part-by-part physical description or a thorough description of functions.

15. **Description of Position in Your Field.** Interview a friend or colleague about the specific job that person holds. Make certain it is a job that you yourself have *not* had. On the basis of data collected in the interview, write a thorough description of the person's position—including major responsibilities, reporting relationships, educational preparation, experience required, etc.

    Now place this description in the context of a letter report to the manager of human resources at McDuff. Assume she has hired you, a technical consultant to McDuff, to submit a letter report that contains the description. She is preparing to advertise such an opening at McDuff but needs your report to write the job description and the advertisement. Because she has little firsthand knowledge of the position about which you are writing, you should avoid technical jargon.

16. **Classification/Division in Technical Courses.** For this assignment, you will need a catalog from your college or university or that of another school. First, select a number of courses that have not yet been classified except perhaps by academic department. Using course descriptions in the catalog or any other information you can find, *classify* the courses using an appropriate basis (for example, the course level, topic, purpose in the department, prerequisites, etc.). Also *partition* one of the courses by using information gathered from a course syllabus or an interview with someone familiar with the course.

    The context for this exercise is a memo report written by you, a technical training specialist at McDuff's St. Louis office. Assume that the courses are taught at St. Louis Tech, a nearby college. A group of McDuff's St. Louis employees has expressed interest in further education in the area you have investigated. Your classification of the courses and your in-depth partition of one particular course will help these employees decide whether to consider enrolling.

17. **Comparison/Contrast for the Purchasing Agent.** For this memo report, select a category in the list following or another category approved by your instructor. Then choose three specific types or brand-name products that fit within the category and for which you can find data. Write either a whole-by-whole or a part-by-part comparison/contrast. Place this comparison/contrast pattern within the context of a short report from you, as a McDuff employee, to the company purchasing agent. You may or may not include a preference for one item or the other. However, understand that the purpose of your report is to give the reader the information needed to order one of the items in your comparison/contrast.

Categories

1. Briefcases
2. Calculators
3. Compact discs
4. Credit cards
5. Electric pencil sharpeners
6. Electric sanders or saws
7. Lawn mowers
8. Mortgages
9. Personal computers
10. Photocopiers
11. Pickup trucks
12. Professional journals in a technical field
13. Refrigerators
14. Software programs
15. Retirement plans
16. Surveying methods
17. Telephone systems or companies
18. Types of savings accounts
19. Vacuum cleaners
20. VCRs

Mc Duff, Inc.

MEMORANDUM

DATE: February 25, 1996
TO: Kerry F. Camp, Vice President of Domestic Operations
FROM: Your Name, Boston Branch Manager
SUBJECT: Problems with Office Chairs

Approaches problem tactfully.

Mentions points of agreement—before moving toward argumentative issues.

Presents evidence clearly—including statistic.

Cites reliable authority.

States supporting statistic.

Gives basis for statistical information.

I enjoyed talking to you yesterday and look forward to seeing you at the Environmental Science Convention in New York. In the meantime, I am writing to ask your help with the chair problem I mentioned in our conversation. This memo will give you some background on our difficulties with the chairs. Also, I have presented a solution for you to consider.

SPECIFIC PROBLEMS WITH OFFICE CHAIRS

About six months ago, we received new office furniture ordered by the corporate office. In many ways, it has been a considerable improvement over the 20-year-old furniture it replaced. The desks, cabinets, and credenzas have been especially well received. Besides being quite practical, they give a much more professional appearance to our office.

As I mentioned in our conversation, the chairs (Model 223) that accompany the new desks have not worked out as well as the other furniture. Here are the two main problems.

Increased Employee Illness

Starting about a month after the chairs arrived, I received complaints from ten employees about back pains they claimed were related to the new chairs. Taking a wait-and-see approach, I asked managers to have chairs adjusted and to give the furniture more break-in time. In the second month, however, I heard from a dozen additional employees about the chairs and noticed a 25 percent increase in sick days. Upon further inquiry, I learned that most managers attributed the increased sick time to back problems related to the office chairs.

Decreased Productivity

The increased sick leave presented a serious enough concern. Adding to the problem, however, was roughly a 10 percent decrease in productivity last month among employees who were not sick. I measured this decrease by three criteria:

- Number of pages produced by the word-processing staff
- Number of billable hours logged by the professional staff
- Number of client calls made by the marketing staff

In my seven years managing this office, I have never witnessed so large a drop with no clear cause.

continues

MODEL 5–1
Memo report—example using argument

Sidebar notes (left margin):

Cites authority and gives her credentials.

Mentions this expert's opinion *last*, because it is the strongest evidence in this short report.

Gives *specific* points to support expert's views.

Sets up clear contrast between two chair types, to support chair exchange.

Describes alternative clearly— giving necessary details about cost, etc.

Ends with request for action.

Closes with tone that encourages agreement on *mutual* problem.

CONFIRMATION OF PROBLEM

Concerned about the health problems and lower productivity, I sought a recognized consultant in the area of workplace health and office design. Dr. Stacy Y. Stephens, professor of ergonomics at East Boston College, was referred to me when I called the local office of the Occupational Safety and Health Administration.

Dr. Stephens visited our office on January 17. She spent two days (1) interviewing and observing users of the new chairs, (2) examining the chairs in detail, and (3) meeting with me to offer her conclusions. At her suggestion, I called the supplier, Jones Office Furniture, to ask about the availability of other Jones chairs with different features. According to Dr. Stephens, the Jones Model 623 is much better suited to normal office use. Specifically, the Model 623 has these advantages:

- Excellent lower-lumbar support, compared to the inadequate support in the straight-backed Model 223
- Twelve inches of vertical adjustment, as opposed to the six inches available in Model 223
- Ball casters for easier rolling, as opposed to the Model 223 casters that move with difficulty on our office carpeting
- Adjustable back spring that provides limited movement backward, as opposed to the rigid Model 223

Considering Dr. Stephens' suggestions, I decided to seek more information from Jones Office Furniture Company.

PROPOSED SOLUTION

Last week, I met twice with Mr. Dan McCartney, the Boston sales representative for Jones Office Furniture. In response to our problem, he has offered this proposal. Jones will trade our 45 Model 223 chairs for 45 new Model 623s, for only an extra $2000 from us. Under this arrangement, he would be (1) crediting us for the full purchase of our four-month old Model 223s and (2) discounting the new chairs about $3000. I believe Jones is making this offer because it truly wants to retain our goodwill—and our future business.

CONCLUSION

As noted, this problem affects our employees' well-being and our office productivity. Would you please present my proposed solution to Ben Garner, vice president of business and marketing, so that he can approve the $2000 funding? We could have the new chairs within a week after approval.

Thanks for your help, Kerry. With relatively small investment, we should be able to solve our medical and productivity problems.

MODEL 5–1
continued

TECHNICAL DESCRIPTION: BLUEPRINT MACHINE

A blueprint machine is a piece of office equipment used to make photographic reproductions of architectural plans, technical drawings, and other types of figures. The blueprint shows as white lines on blue paper. This description covers the physical parts of the machine and a brief operation procedure.

PHYSICAL DESCRIPTION

The blueprint machine is contained in a metal cabinet measuring 36" wide, 10" tall, and 18" deep. Typically, the machine is placed on a cabinet containing blueprint supplies. The most evident features of the machine are the controls and the paper path.

Blueprint Machine

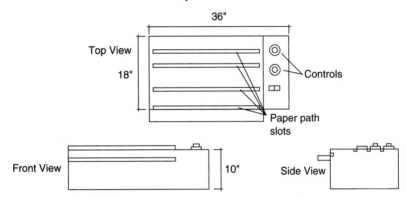

Controls: The controls for the machine are located on the top right-hand side of the case, as shown in the illustration below.

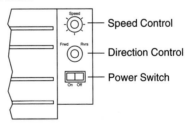

There are two knobs and one power switch. The topmost knob controls the speed of the paper feed. The lower knob changes the direction of the paper. The power switch turns the machine on and off.

MODEL 5–2
Detailed description

continues

Paper Path: The top of the machine has four horizontal slots. These slots are the openings to the paper path, as shown in the illustration below.

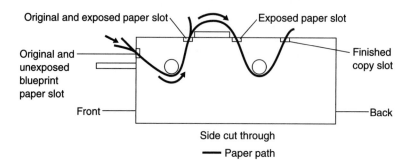

The first slot, beginning at the front of the machine, is the feed slot for the original and the unexposed blueprint paper. The second slot is the discharge for the original and the exposed print paper. The third slot is the feed for developing the exposed blueprint paper. The fourth slot is the discharge for the finished blueprint copy.

OPERATION OF THE BLUEPRINT MACHINE

Operating the blueprint machine involves setting the controls and making copies.

Setting the Controls:
1. Turn on the machine.
2. Set the paper path to forward.
3. Set the speed for the type of paper used.

Making Copies:
1. Place the original, face side up, on top of the blueprint paper, yellow side up.
2. Feed the two pieces of paper into the original feed slot.
3. Separate the original from the copy as they emerge from the discharge slot.
4. Feed the exposed blueprint paper into the developer slot.
5. Collect the copy as it emerges from the discharge slot.
6. Turn power off when desired copies have been made.

CONCLUSION

Blueprint machines are found in all McDuff offices and are used frequently. If a wide variety of employees understands how these machines function, our office will continue to run smoothly.

MODEL 5–2
continued

Notes burner's main parts and sections that follow.

McDuff uses Bunsen burners in all its laboratories. Following some background information, this technical description provides details about three main parts of a typical burner:

- Base
- Gas valve
- Pipe

The conclusion lists some standards for the burner's performance.

Background

Gives formal sentence definition and general information for nontechnical readers.

The Bunsen burner is a basic piece of laboratory equipment used to produce a continuous flame at relatively low temperatures. Originally designed by Robert W. Bunsen in the late 1800s, the "Bunsen burner" has become a generic term for basic lab burners made by many firms.

Most burners look and perform alike, though burners from different companies do include slightly different features. What follows is a description of the Model 03–962 Bunsen-style burner manufactured by the Fisher Scientific Company. It runs on natural gas.

Base

The heavy die-cast base of the Fisher burner is very stable. It is made from nonferrous metal and has a nickel finish. Here are its main features and dimensions:

Uses bullets for technical detail.

- Hexagonal-shaped foundation that is 2 3/4″ in diameter and 2″ high

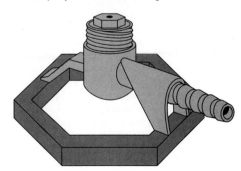

continues

MODEL 5–3
Technical description: "bunsen" burner

167

- A 3/4″-diameter threaded cylinder at the top of the base
- A 1/2″-diameter hexagonal brass nut at the top of the cylinder, with a small hole in the center from which gas is emitted into the pipe

Jutting out from the side of the cylinder, parallel to the surface on which the base of the burner rests, is a tapered gas inlet 2 1/2″ long. The inlet has a grooved surface that holds the gas tube securely to the burner.

Gas Valve

A valve is threaded vertically up into the bottom center of the base of the burner. It allows the user to adjust the volume of gas that flows from the gas inlet up through the base cylinder.

The valve looks like a car axle with only one wheel attached. The 2″-long stem, or "axle," rests on a round 3/4″-diameter base, or "wheel." Actually, this base is about the diameter and thickness of a U.S. nickel coin. It has serrated edges so that it can be twisted with ease. The 1/8″-diameter stem is threaded and screws vertically into the base of the burner.

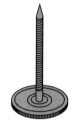

When twisted clockwise, the valve closes and decreases gas flow. When twisted counterclockwise, it opens and increases gas flow.

Pipe

A 4 1/2″-long pipe extends straight up from the top of the base of the burner. Except for its flared ends, the pipe is 1/2″ in diameter. The combining of gas and air at the bottom of the pipe produces a flame that emerges at the top.

The pipe threads on to the cylinder at the top of the burner base. The bottom of the pipe flares out to form an end piece with eight 3/16″ holes drilled around its circumference. The holes let in air that mixes with gas entering from the base. When the pipe is turned clockwise, the amount of air entering the holes is reduced and the temperature of the flame is lowered. When the pipe is turned counterclockwise, the amount of air entering the holes is increased and the temperature of the flame is raised.

The flared top end of the pipe looks much like a socket piece for a socket wrench. Called a "flame retainer" by the manufacturer, it helps keep the flame from going out. Viewed vertically from above the burner, the top of the retainer is shaped like a wagon wheel with short spokes. The "spokes" are actually eight ports that open to the pipe hole but close off before they reach the circumference of the pipe. Spaced evenly on the circumference, these ports help control the flame.

MODEL 5–3
continued

Uses analogies such as wheel, axle, and nickel coin.

Describes movement to help reader understand purpose of part.

Includes common visual terms like "flared."

Reveals purpose of parts through description.

Employs two more analogies to help less technical readers.

Performance Specifications

The Fisher version of the Bunsen burner offers the following performance standards:

- Produces flame that is adjustable from 3/4″ to 12″
- Has heat output of over 1465w (5000 BTU/hr.)
- Consumes 5 cu ft hr. of natural gas
- Meets U.S., NIST, USTM, and ASTM standards

Uses bullets for technical detail.

MODEL 5–3
continued

PART-BY-PART PATTERN COMPARISON OF BULLDOZERS

This is a comparison of the Cannon-D, Foley-G, and Koso-L bulldozers. The major criteria considered are pushing capacity, purchase details, and dependability.

Pushing Capacity

Both the Cannon-D and Foley-G have an excellent pushing capacity that is more than adequate for our U.S. construction projects. The Cannon has a pushing capacity of 1300 tons per hour (TPH) over 500 ft, whereas the Foley has a pushing capacity of 1100 TPH over 500 ft. Both figures are mentioned in brochures from their respective companies. Furthermore, they are confirmed by recent tests reported in the trade journal, *Bulldozer Unlimited.*

The Koso-L, however, lags behind its two competitors, being able to push only 1000 TPH over 500 ft. Furthermore, this figure was found only in the company's sales brochures, with no verification available in the trade journals I researched.

Purchase Details

The main elements of the purchase—price, warranty, and cost of extended warranty—vary considerably among the three machines. The basic purchase prices are as follows:

1. $250,000 for the Cannon-D
2. $300,000 for the Foley-G
3. $310,000 for the Koso-L

Concerning warranties, Cannon provides a complete parts-and-service warranty for 90 days, with an additional parts warranty on the drivetrain for another 12 months. Foley offers the same initial parts-and-service warranty, but it has a longer parts warranty on the drivetrain—18 months. Koso has a complete parts-and-service warranty for six months, with no additional parts warranty on the drivetrain.

Beyond these warranties that come with the machines, all three companies offer the same option of an additional two-year warranty that covers parts in the drivetrain. This additional warranty must be acquired at time of purchase and costs $4,000 for the Cannon, $4,000 for the Foley, and $7,000 for the Koso.

Dependability

Bulldozer downtime can cost the firm a good deal of money, either in project delays or in the added expense of renting another bulldozer, so dependability is an important criterion in comparing the three models. Although the trade journals I consulted contained no model-by-model comparison of dependability of the three bulldozers, I did find occasional references to features that affect reliability. In

MODEL 5–4
Part-by-part comparison/contrast: three bulldozers

addition, I sought out anecdotal evidence from nearby construction firms that have used the machines. Here is what I discovered.

Cannon-D. This machine is an established commercial bulldozer with a good reputation for reliability in the field. The "D" model is the latest version of a machine that began with the "A" model in 1954, so the company has had years to refine its technology. Interestingly, several years ago Cannon decided not to add sealed tracks to its list of features, even though this sealed approach is one of the newest track innovations in the industry. Even so, the Cannon-D generally will operate for 10,000 hours without major maintenance in the tracks. It remains to be seen if the decision about sealed tracks was the correct one.

Foley-G. While the Foley also has a good reputation for reliability in the field, the firm began making bulldozers only in 1970—16 years after Cannon started. Foley has the general reputation of being quicker than Cannon to introduce new technology into its bulldozer line. For example, two years ago it started using sealed tracks that lubricate themselves automatically. The track assembly should not need major maintenance for 15,000 hours, a 5000-hour improvement over Cannon. Of course, the newness of this advance suggests that there hasn't yet been enough time to judge the long-term effectiveness of sealed tracks.

Koso-L. This machine is definitely the "new guy on the block." Unlike the American-made Cannon and Foley, the Koso is produced in Korea by a company that got into business rather recently—1986. The Koso-L uses fairly traditional technology, not having incorporated sealed tracks into its design, for example. Despite the recent entry into the market, Koso has already built a strong reputation for reliability on projects in other countries. However, there are not yet enough data about performance on construction projects in the United States.

Uses subheadings because of large amount of information to relate.

Introduces Foley's main feature (technical innovation).

But reinforces Cannon preference by noting that sealed tracks are not fully tested.

Keeps option open for buying Koso later—but makes it clear that more data are needed.

MODEL 5–4
continued

6 Process Descriptions and Instructions

This vendor depends on clearly written instructions to repair the photocopying machine at McDuff's Atlanta office.

*L*ike other McDuff offices, McDuff's Denver office installed an electronic-mail system in the last few years. It permits employees to send and receive messages on their computer terminals. The idea seems to have pleased everyone. Messages are conveyed faster, and less paper is generated in the office. As office services manager, you met with a representative of the company that would install the system, shortly before the installation date. Your boss, Leonard Schwartz, expected a memo from you summarizing the installation process (see Model 6–1 on page 196). You also wrote a memo to all employees, giving them instructions about how to read electronic-mail messages (see Model 6–2, pp.197–198).

This brief McDuff case study demonstrates two types of technical writing you will often face—process descriptions and instructions. Both are important patterns, but instructions will play the greater role in your career. As noted in one essay, "The field of technical writing has expanded greatly in the last ten years, and the new work is in writing *instructions*. . . . Many graduates of technical programs now find themselves writing *instructions* more often than they write descriptions and reports"[1] (italics mine). For this reason, instructions receive the most emphasis in this chapter.

Instructions and process descriptions share an important common bond. Both must accurately describe a series of steps leading toward a specific result. Yet they differ in purpose, audience, and format. This chapter (1) explores these similarities and differences, with specific reference to McDuff applications, (2) gives specific guidelines for developing both types, and (3) provides models to use in your own writing.

---

[1]Reprinted by permission of the Modern Language Association of America from Janice C. Redish and David A. Schell, "Writing and Testing Usability Instructions," in *Technical Writing: Theory and Practice*, ed. Bertie E. Fearing and W. Keats Sparrow (New York: Modern Language Association of America, 1989), 63.

PROCESS DESCRIPTIONS VERSUS INSTRUCTIONS

In the McDuff example just given, the memo to your boss (Model 6–1, p. 196) explained the process by which the vendor installed electronic mail. The other memo (Model 6–2, pp. 197-198) gave users the directions needed to read on-line mail. In other words, you write a process description to help readers *understand* what has been, is being, or will be done, whereas you write instructions to show readers how to perform the *process* themselves.

Process descriptions are appropriate when the reader needs to be informed about the action but does not need to perform it. If you suspect a reader may in fact be a "user" (that is, someone who uses your document to perform the process), always write instructions. Figure 6–1 provides a list of contrasting features of process descriptions and instructions; the two subsections that follow give these features some realism by briefly describing some McDuff contexts.

Process Descriptions at McDuff

Process descriptions provide information for interested readers who do not need instructional details. At times, describing a process may be the sole purpose of your document, as in Model 6–1. More often, however, you use process description only as a pattern of organization within a document with a larger purpose. The

---

PROCESS DESCRIPTIONS

Purpose: Explain a sequence of steps in such a way that the reader understands a process

Format: Use paragraph descriptions, listed steps, or some combination of the two

Style: Use "objective" point of view ("2. The operator started the engine..."), as opposed to "command" point of view ("2. Start the engine...")

INSTRUCTIONS

Purpose: Describe a sequence of steps in such a way that the reader can *perform* the sequence of steps

Format: Employ numbered or bulleted lists, organized into subgroups of easily understandable units of information

Style: Use "command" point of view ("3. Plug the phone jack into the recorder unit"), as opposed to "objective" point of view ("3. The phone jack was plugged into the recorder unit")

FIGURE 6–1
Process descriptions versus instructions

following McDuff examples (1) show the supporting purpose of process descriptions and (2) reinforce the difference between process descriptions and instructions.

- **Accounting:** As an accountant at McDuff's corporate office, you have just finished auditing the firm's books. Now you must write a report to the vice president for business and marketing on the state of the firm's finances. Along with your findings, the vice president wants an overview of the procedure you followed to arrive at your conclusions.
- **Maintenance:** As a maintenance supervisor at McDuff's Saudi Arabian branch, you traveled to a construction site to repair a machine that tests the strength of concrete. The procedure requires billing the client for additional charges. Along with your bill, you send an attachment that summarizes the procedure you followed.
- **Laboratory work:** As lab supervisor at the St. Louis office, you spent all day Saturday in the lab assembling a new gas chromatograph needed to analyze gases. To justify the overtime hours, you write a memo to your manager describing the assembly process.
- **Welding inspection:** As an NDT (nondestructive testing) expert at McDuff's San Francisco office, you were hired by a California state agency to x-ray all welds at a bridge damaged by an earthquake. The text of your report gives test results; the appendices describe the procedures you followed.
- **Marketing:** As McDuff's marketing manager, you have devised a new procedure for tracking contacts with prospective clients (from first sales call to getting the job). You must write a memo to McDuff's two vice presidents for operations, briefly describing the process. Their approval is needed before the new marketing technique can be introduced at the 15 branch offices.

In each case, you are writing for a reader who wants to know what has happened or will happen, but who does *not* need to perform the process.

Instructions at McDuff

Think of instructions this way: They must provide users with a road map to *do* the procedure, not just understand it. That is, someone must complete a task on the basis of words and pictures you provide. Clearly, instructions present you, the writer, with a much greater challenge *and* risk. The reader must be able to replicate the procedure without error and, most importantly, with full knowledge of any dangers. The McDuff situations that follow reflect this challenge. Note that they parallel the case studies presented for process descriptions.

- **Accounting:** As McDuff's lead accountant for the last 20 years, you have always been responsible for auditing the firm's books. Because you developed the procedure yourself over many years, there is no comprehensive set of instructions for completing it. Now you want to record the steps so that other company accountants besides you can perform them.
- **Maintenance:** As a maintenance supervisor at McDuff's branch in Saudi Arabia, you must repair a piece of equipment for testing concrete. You have

never disassembled this particular machine, and there are no manufacturer's instructions available. Therefore, the job takes you three full days. To help other employees perform this task in the future, you write a set of detailed instructions for making the repair.

- **Laboratory work:** As lab supervisor for McDuff's St. Louis office, you have assembled one of the two new gas chromatographs just purchased by the company. You are supposed to send the other unit to the Tokyo branch, where it will be put together by Japanese technicians. Unfortunately, the manufacturer's instructions are poorly written, so you plan to rewrite them for the English-speaking technicians at the Tokyo office.

- **Welding inspection:** As McDuff's NDT (nondestructive testing) expert at the San Francisco office, you have seen a large increase in NDT projects. Given California's aging bridges and constant earthquake activity, you persuaded your branch manager to hire several NDT technicians. Now you must write a training manual that will instruct these new employees on methods for inspecting bridge welds.

- **Marketing:** As McDuff's marketing manager, you have suggested a new approach for tracking sales leads. Having had your proposal approved by the corporate staff, you now need to explain the marketing procedure to technical professionals at all 15 offices. Your written set of instructions must be understood by technical experts in many fields, who have little if any marketing experience.

In each case, your instructions must describe steps so thoroughly that the reader will be able to replicate the process, *without* having to speak in person with the writer of the instructions. The next two sections give rules for preparing both process descriptions and sets of instructions.

GUIDELINES AND MODELS FOR PROCESS DESCRIPTIONS

You have already learned that process descriptions are aimed at persons who need to understand the process, not perform it. Process descriptions often have these purposes:

- Describing an experiment
- Explaining how a machine works
- Recording steps in developing a new product
- Describing what happened during a field test

In each case, follow these guidelines for creating first-rate process descriptions:

Process Guideline 1: Know Your Purpose and Audience

Your intended purpose and expected audience influence every detail of your description. Here are some preliminary questions to answer before writing:

- Are you supposed to give just an overview or are details needed?
- Do readers understand the technical subject or are they laypersons?
- Do readers have mixed technical backgrounds?
- Does the process description supply supporting information (perhaps in an appendix) or is it the main part of the document?

Process descriptions are most challenging when directed to a mixed audience. In this case, write for the lowest common denominator—that is, for your least technical readers. It is better to write below the level of your most technical readers than to write above the level of your nontechnical readers.

For example, the process description in Model 6–3 on page 199 is directed to a mixed audience of city officials—some technical staff and some nontechnical political officials. It is contained in an appendix to a long McDuff report that recommends immediate cleanup of a toxic-waste dump. Note that the writer either uses nontechnical language or defines any technical terms used.

■ *Process Guideline 2: Follow the ABC Format*

In chapter 3 you learned about the ABC format (**A**bstract/**B**ody/**C**onclusion), which applies to all documents. The abstract gives a summary, the body supplies details, and the conclusion provides a wrap-up or leads to the next step in the communication process. Whether a process description forms all or part of a document, it usually subscribes to the following version of the three-part ABC plan:

- The **Abstract** component includes three background items:

  1. Purpose statement
  2. Overview or list of the main steps that follow
  3. List of equipment or materials used in the process

Model 6–3 on page 199 includes all three, with a separate heading for equipment. First, the purpose statement places the description in the context of the entire document. Then the list of main steps gives readers a framework for interpreting details that follow. Finally, the list of equipment or materials provides a central reference point as readers work through all the steps.

- The **Body** component of the process description moves logically through the steps of the process. By definition, all process descriptions follow a chronological, or step-by-step, pattern of organization. These steps can be conveyed in two ways:

  1. Paragraphs: This approach weaves steps of the process into the fabric of typical paragraphs, with appropriate transitions between sentences. Use paragraphs when your readers would prefer a smooth explanation of the entire process, rather than emphasis on individual steps.
  2. List of steps: This approach includes a list of steps, usually with numbers or bullets. Much like instructions, a listing emphasizes the individual parts of the process. Readers prefer it when they will need to refer to specific steps later on.

Both paragraph and list formats have their places in process descriptions. In fact, most descriptions can be written in either format. See Figure 6–2 for a McDuff example showing both a paragraph and list description for the same process of laying a concrete patio. As a public-service gesture, McDuff, Inc., has written a pamphlet that briefly describes simple home improvements. It is intended for owners of small homes who complete renovations with little or no help from contractors. If home owners are interested in one of the projects, they can write for detailed instructions to an address listed in the pamphlet.

Building a concrete patio is one project covered; the process description contains a subsection about constructing the wooden form into which concrete is poured.

■ The **Conclusion** component of a process description keeps the process from ending abruptly with the last step. Here you should help the reader put the steps together into a coherent whole. When the process description is part of a larger document, you can show how the process fits into a larger context (see Model 6–3, p. 199).

■ *Process Guideline 3: Use an Objective Point of View*

Process descriptions explain a process rather than direct how it is to be done. Thus they are written from an objective point of view—*not* from the personal "you" or "command" point of view common to instructions. Note the difference in these examples:

Steps of process are embedded in paragraph.

After brief lead-in, steps of process are placed in list format.

A. PARAGRAPH OPTION

The home owner should select rough-grade 2 x 4s for building the wooden form for the patio. The form is just a box, with an open top and with the ground for the bottom, into which concrete will be poured. First the four sides are nailed together, and then the form is leveled with a standard carpenter's level. Finally, 2 x 4 stakes are driven into the ground about every 2 or 3 ft on the outside of the form, to keep it in place during the pouring of the concrete.

B. LIST OPTION

Building a wooden form for a home concrete patio can be accomplished with some rough-grade 2 x 4s. This form is just a box with an open top and the ground for the bottom. Building involves three basic steps:

1. Nailing 2 x 4s into the intended shape of the patio
2. Leveling the box-shaped form with a standard carpenter's level
3. Nailing stakes (made from 2 x 4 lumber) every 2 or 3 ft at the outside edge of the form, to keep it in place during the pouring of the concrete

---

FIGURE 6–2
Two options for process description: (A) paragraph option; (B) list option

Process:	The concrete is poured into the two-by-four frame.
	or
	The technician pours the concrete into the two-by-four frame.
Instructions:	Pour the concrete into the two-by-four frame.

The process excerpts *explain* the step, whereas the instructions excerpt *gives a command* for completing the instructions.

■ *Process Guideline 4: Choose the Right Amount of Detail*

Only a thorough audience analysis will tell you how much detail to include. Model 6–3 (p. 199), for example, could have contained much more technical detail about the substeps for testing air quality at the site. The writer, however, decided that the city officials would not need more scientific and technical detail.

In supplying specifics, be sure to subdivide information for easy reading. In paragraph format, headings and subheadings can be used to make the process easier to grasp. In list format, an outline arrangement of points and subpoints may be appropriate. When such detail is necessary, remember this general rule of thumb: *place related steps into groups of from three to seven points.* Readers find it easier to remember several groupings with subpoints, as opposed to one long list. Following are two rough outlines for a process description. The second is preferred in that it groups the many steps into three easily grasped categories.

Employment Interview Process

1. Interviewer reviews job description
2. Interviewer analyzes candidate's application
3. Candidate and interviewer engage in "small talk"
4. Interviewer asks open-ended questions related to candidate's resume and completed application form
5. Interviewer expands topic to include matters of personal interest and the candidate's long-term career plans
6. Interviewer provides candidate with information about the position (salary, benefits, location, etc.)
7. Candidate is encouraged to ask questions about the position
8. Interviewer asks candidate about her or his general interest, at this point, in the position
9. Interviewer informs candidate about next step in hiring process

Employment Interview Process

■ **Preinterview Phase**

1. Interviewer reviews job description
2. Interviewer analyzes candidate's application

▪ **Interview**

3. Candidate and interviewer engage in "small talk"
4. Interviewer asks open-ended questions related to candidate's resume and completed application form
5. Interviewer expands topic to include matters of personal interest and the candidate's long-term career plans
6. Interviewer provides candidate with information about the position (salary, benefits, location, etc.)
7. Candidate is encouraged to ask questions about the position

▪ **Closure**

8. Interviewer asks candidate about his or her general interest, at this point, in the position
9. Interviewer informs candidate about next step in hiring process

■ *Process Guideline 5: Use Flowcharts for Complex Processes*

Some process descriptions contain steps that are occurring at the same time. In this case, you may want to supplement a paragraph or list description with a flowchart. Such charts use boxes, circles, and other geometric shapes to show progression and relationships among various steps.

Model 6–4 on page 200, for example, shows a flowchart and an accompanying process description at McDuff. Both denote services that McDuff's London branch provides for oil companies in the North Sea. The chart helps to demonstrate that the geophysical study (mapping by sonar equipment) and the engineering study (securing and testing of seafloor samples) take place at the same time. Such simultaneous steps are difficult to show in a list of sequential steps.

GUIDELINES AND MODELS FOR INSTRUCTIONS

Rules change considerably when moving from process descriptions to instructions. Although both patterns are organized by time, the similarity stops there. Instructions walk readers through the process so that they can *do* it, not just understand it. It is one thing to explain the process by which a word-processing program works; it is quite another to write a set of instructions for using that word-processing program. This section explores the challenge of writing instructions by giving you some basic writing and design guidelines.

These guidelines for instructions also apply to complete operating *manuals,* a document type that many technical professionals will help to write during their careers. Those manuals include the instructions themselves, as well as related information such as (1) features, (2) physical parts, and (3) troubleshooting tips.

In other words, manuals are complete documents, whereas instructions can be part of a larger piece.

■ *Instructions Guideline 1:*
Select the Correct Technical Level

This guideline is just another way of saying you need to know *exactly* who will be reading your instructions. Are your readers technicians, engineers, managers, general users, or some combination of these groups? Once you answer this question, select language that every reader can understand. If, for example, the instructions include technical terms or names of objects that may not be understood, use the techniques of definition and description discussed in the previous chapter.

■ *Instructions Guideline 2:*
Provide Introductory Information

Like process descriptions, instructions follow the ABC format (**A**bstract/ **B**ody/**C**onclusion) described in chapter 3. The introductory (or abstract) information should include (1) a purpose statement, (2) a summary of the main steps, and (3) a list or an illustration giving the equipment or materials needed (or a reference to an attachment with this information). These three items set the scene for the procedure itself.

Besides these three "musts," you should consider whether some additional items might help set the scene for your user:

- Pointers that will help with installation
- Definitions of terms
- Theory of how something works
- Notes, cautions, warnings, or dangers that apply to all steps

■ *Instructions Guideline 3:*
Use Numbered Lists in the Body

A simple format is crucial to the body of the instructions—that is, the steps themselves. Most users constantly go back and forth between these steps and the project to which they apply. Thus you should avoid paragraph format and instead use a simple numbering system. Model 6–5 on pages 201–202 shows a "before and after" example. The original version is written in paragraphs that are difficult to follow; the revised version includes nine separate, numbered steps.

■ *Instructions Guideline 4:*
Group Steps under Task Headings

Readers prefer that you group together related steps under headings, rather than present an uninterrupted "laundry list" of steps. Model 6–6 on pages 203–205 shows how this technique has been used in a fairly long set of instructions for operating an answering machine. Given the number of steps in this case, the writer has used a separate numbering system within each grouping.

Groupings provide two main benefits. First, they divide fragmented information into manageable "chunks" that readers find easier to read. Second, they give readers a sense of accomplishment as they complete each task, on the way to finishing the whole activity.

■ *Instructions Guideline 5: Place One Action in a Step*

A common error is to "bury" several actions in a single step. This approach can confuse and irritate readers. Instead, break up complex steps into discrete units, as shown here:

■ **Original:**

> **Step 3:** Fill in your name and address on the coupon, send it to the manufacturer within two weeks, return to the retail merchant when your letter of approval arrives from the manufacturer, and pick up your free toaster oven.

■ **Revision:**

> **Step 3:** Fill in your name and address on the coupon.
> **Step 4:** Send the coupon to the manufacturer within two weeks.
> **Step 5:** Show your retail merchant the letter of approval after it arrives from the manufacturer.
> **Step 6:** Pick up your free toaster oven.

■ *Instructions Guideline 6:*
Lead Off Each Action Step with a Verb

Instructions should include the "command" form of a verb at the start of each step. This style best conveys a sense of action to your readers. Model 6–5 on pages 201–202 and Model 6–6 on pages 203–205 consistently use command verbs for all steps throughout the procedures.

■ *Instructions Guideline 7:*
Remove Extra Information from the Step

Sometimes you may want to follow the command sentence with an explanatory sentence or two. In this case, distinguish such helpful information from actions by giving it a label, such as "Note" or "Result" (for example, see Model 6–2, pp. 197–198).

■ *Instructions Guideline 8:*
Use Bullets or Letters for Emphasis

Sometimes you may need to highlight information, especially within a particular step. Avoid using numbers for this purpose, since you are already using them to signify steps. Bullets work best if there are just a few items; letters are best if there are many, especially if they are in a sequence. The revised version in Model 6–5 on pages 201–202 shows the appropriate use of letters, and Model 6–6 (pp. 203–205) shows the use of bullets.

In particular, consider using bullets at any point at which users have an *option* as to how they will respond. The following example uses bullets in this way; it also eliminates the problem of too many actions being embedded in one step.

Part of Procedure for Firing Clay in a Kiln

(*Note:* A pyrometric "cone" is a piece of test clay used in a kiln, an oven for baking pottery. The melting of the small cone helps the operator determine that the clay piece has completed the firing process.)

■ **Original:**

> **Step 6:** Check the cone frequently as the kiln reaches its maximum temperature of 1850 degrees. If the cone retains its shape, continue firing the clay and checking the cone frequently. When the cone begins to bend, turn off the kiln. Then let the kiln cool overnight before opening it and removing the pottery.

■ **Revision:**

> **Step 6:** Check the cone frequently as the kiln reaches its maximum temperature of 1850 degrees.
>
> **Step 7:** Has the cone started to bend?
> - If *no,* continue firing the piece of pottery and checking the cone frequently to see if it has bent.
> - If *yes,* turn off the kiln.
>
> **Step 8:** Let the kiln cool overnight after turning it off.
>
> **Step 9:** Open the kiln and remove the pottery.

■ *Instructions Guideline 9: Emphasize Cautions, Warnings, and Dangers*

Instructions often require drawing attention to risks in using products and equipment. Your most important obligation is to highlight such information. Generally, the following three terms are used as "red flags" to the reader. The level of risk increases as you move from 1 to 3:

1. **Caution:** possibility of damage to equipment or materials
2. **Warning:** possibility of injury to people
3. **Danger:** probability of injury or death to people

If you are not certain that these distinctions will be understood by your readers, define the terms *caution, warning,* and *danger* in a prominent place before you begin your instructions.

As for placement of the actual cautions, warnings, or danger messages, here are your options:

■ **Option 1:** *In a separate section right before the instructions begin.* This approach is most appropriate when you have a list of general warnings that apply to much of the procedure *or* when one special warning should be heeded throughout the instructions—for example, "DANGER: Keep main breaker on 'off' during entire installation procedure." Figure 6–3 shows such a warning at the start of instructions to install a security keypad.

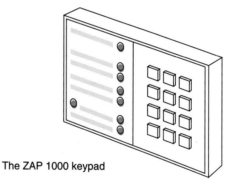

INTRODUCTION

You have purchased one of the most sophisticated security systems available for home, business, or industry use. The ZAP 1000 provides a multi-zoned blanket of protection for your family, your home, or your business. The ZAP 1000 will alert you to intrusions, fire, and smoke by sounding an alarm, calling the proper authorities, or both.

The ZAP 1000 keypad

Before installing or using the ZAP 1000, you should read this manual from front to back. Pay close attention to all SAFETY MESSAGES, such as the one below.

 DANGER! You can be injured or killed by improper or careless use of this equipment. Consult a qualified electrician if you have any doubts about installation or use.

FIGURE 6–3
Example of "danger" message

- **Option 2:** *In the text of the instructions.* This approach works best if the caution, warning, or danger message applies to the step that immediately follows it. Thus users are warned about a problem *before* they read the step to which it applies. For an example, see the following:

    CAUTION: Use 220-grade sandpaper, to avoid scratching the surface of furniture.

In other words, give information about potential risks *before* the operator has the chance to make the mistake. Also, the caution, warning, or danger message can be made visually prominent by the following techniques:

- Underlining:	<u>Warning</u>
- Bold:	**Warning**
- Full Caps:	WARNING
- Italics:	*Warning*
- Oversized Print:	Warning
- Boxing:	Warning
- Color:	Warning
- Combined Methods:	<u>*Warning*</u>
	<u>WARNING</u>
	WARNING

■ *Instructions Guideline 10: Keep a Simple Style*

Perhaps more than any other type of technical writing, instructions must be easy to read. Readers expect a no-nonsense approach to writing that gives them required information without fanfare. Here are some techniques to use:

- Keep sentences short, with an average length of under 10 words.
- Use informal definitions (parenthetical, like this one) to define any terms not understood by all readers.
- Never use a long word when a short one will do.
- Be specific and avoid words with multiple interpretations (*frequently, seldom, occasionally,* etc.).

■ *Instructions Guideline 11: Use Graphics*

Illustrations are essential for instructions that involve equipment. Place an illustration next to every major step when (1) the instructions or equipment is quite complicated or (2) the audience may contain poor readers or people who are in a hurry. Such word-picture associations create a page design that is easy to follow.

In other cases, just one or two diagrams may suffice for the entire set of instructions. The one reference illustration in Model 6–6 (pp. 203–205) helps the user of a message recorder locate parts mentioned throughout the instructions.

Another useful graphic in instructions is the table. Sometimes within a step you need to show correspondence between related data. For example, the instructions that follow would benefit from a list.

■ **Original:**

    Step 3: Use pyrometric cones to determine when a kiln has reached the proper temperature to fire pottery. Common cone ratings are as follows: a Cone 018 corresponds to 1200°F; a Cone 07 corresponds to 1814°F; a Cone 06 corresponds to 1859°F; and a Cone 04 corresponds to 1940°F.

■ **Revision:**

    Step 3: Use pyrometric cones to determine when a kiln has reached the proper temperature for firing pottery. Common cone ratings are as follows:

Cone 018	1200°F
Cone 07	1814°F
Cone 06	1859°F
Cone 04	1940°F

■ *Instructions Guideline 12: Test Your Instructions*

Professional writers often test their instructions on potential users before completing the final draft. The most sophisticated technique for such testing involves a "usability laboratory." Here test subjects are asked to use the instructions or manual to perform the process, often while speaking their observations and frustrations (if any). The writers or lab personnel unobtrusively observe the process from behind a one-way mirror. Later they may review audiotaped or videotaped observations of the test subjects or they may interview these persons. This complex process helps writers to anticipate and then eliminate problems that users will confront when they follow written instructions.

Of course, you probably will not have access to a usability laboratory to test your instructions. However, you can adapt the following user-based approach to testing assignments in this class and projects in your career. Specifically, follow these four steps:

1. Team up with another class member (or a colleague on the job). This person should be unfamiliar with the process and should approximate the technical level of your intended audience.

2. Give this person a draft of your instructions and provide any equipment or materials necessary to complete the process. Of course, for the purposes of a class assignment, this approach would work only for a simple process with little equipment or few materials.

3. Observe your colleague following the instructions you have provided. You should record both your observations and any responses this person makes while moving through the steps.

4. Revise your instructions to solve problems your user encountered during the test.

COMMUNICATION CHALLENGE

"McDuff's Home of Hope: The Good, the Bad, and the Ugly?"

This year McDuff's Atlanta office decided to change its approach to charitable giving at the branch. Instead of supporting various regional charities, employees could participate in a local project of their own—converting an abandoned building into a homeless shelter called "Home of Hope." The idea seemed to be a creative way to make a personal contribution to the community. What follows is a description of the stages of the project and some questions and comments for discussion.

Project Planning

The process of making "Home of Hope" a reality began at McDuff-Atlanta's annual employee meeting last year. The human resources manager suggested that the office try a new approach to annual giving, and the office supervisors agreed to investigate. Eventually the office decided to purchase an abandoned brick building on an acre lot in downtown Atlanta, in an area where homeless people often congregated.

McDuff conducted a preliminary study of the land and building, calculating that the project would cost about $100,000. Management developed a formula whereby the company would pay a 20% mortgage down payment from its savings and carry the monthly mortgage note. Then over a one-year period, the employees—through their annual financial contributions and personal labor—would renovate the house and add landscaping. The managers developed a suggested sliding scale for what money employees should contribute, based on their salaries. Managers and supervisors also were asked to meet individually with each employee to encourage contributions.

Once McDuff bought the land, the firm began benefiting from excellent publicity on local radio and in the papers. The media championed this effort by an Atlanta employer.

Site Problems

It appeared that nothing could go wrong—but it did. Ironically, considering that McDuff itself does environmental work, the firm found an environmental problem with the land that had not been detected before purchase. Apparently, part of the site had been used as a dumping ground for old car batteries and for chemicals from a nearby dry cleaners. Both the batteries and a large portion of soil would have to be removed, adding $10,000 to the cost of the project.

Just as bad, there were environmental surprises in the building itself. The company found some asbestos and lead paint that had not been detected before purchase. Removal would cost about $5,000. The increase in the total project cost irritated many employees, some of whom had been skeptical about the project from the start.

Employee Involvement

What did seem to go well were the weekend work groups that the company set up for the coming year. A group of 5 to 10 employees worked a half day on each Saturday, meaning that most employees would end up working three or four Saturdays during the entire year-long project. Employees were strongly encouraged to participate, and about 85% of them signed up for the groups.

As noted previously, through meetings with managers and other means, employees were encouraged to contribute the amount suggested on the sliding scale. About 75% agreed to the amount suggested, 10% pledged more, 10% pledged less, and 5% pledged nothing. Pledges were drawn from paychecks over the one-year period.

Community Involvement

Once the lot was purchased and the renovation designed, McDuff worked with groups in the surrounding community, making sure that local people were informed about the project. One home-owners group from this working-class neighborhood raised questions about the project attracting even more homeless people to the area. The group worried that the possibility of increasing crime would lower the value of their homes. McDuff decided that an open community meeting was in order.

At the meeting at a local school, McDuff produced speakers who suggested that the home would actually help decrease crime by giving shelter, meals, and activities to people who otherwise would be vagrants. Although the answers seemed to satisfy many, McDuff officials were on the defensive and wished they had done more networking with local residents.

Final Preparations

Once the home and yard were finished, McDuff hired two permanent staff members and set up a group of volunteers from the community. Retired people were especially active as volunteers. The company also asked for, and received, an ongoing commitment of $15,000 a year from the city to pay half the salary of the Home of Hope director.

With these details handled, the home took in its first 25 residents on January 1, 1997. McDuff arranged for media coverage of the opening celebration, inviting a diverse group of company leaders. Of course, the company also made sure the event was covered in the McDuff corporate newsletter and by *EnviroNews*, a national news magazine in engineering and science.

Questions and Comments for Discussion

1. The McDuff corporate managers have expressed interest in the charity "model" developed by the Atlanta office. Specifically, they want the Atlanta human resources director to write a **process description** for the Home of Hope project. The description will be reviewed by all McDuff branch managers. What

major points should be included in this process description? How will it differ from the way information is presented in the case just described?

2. Assume McDuff's corporate office has actually adopted a community-based charity option, such as that reflected by the Home of Hope project. Now it wants to provide project **instructions** for other urban offices that may want to build shelters. What major points will be emphasized in the instructions and in what order? What particular problems did the Atlanta office encounter, and how can the instructions be written to help other offices avoid such problems? In other words, how will the *ideal* set of instructions differ from the *actual* process that was performed?

3. Answer these questions first with regard to McDuff employees and second with regard to the community surrounding Home of Hope. What tactical mistakes, if any, were made by McDuff management in the process of promoting, communicating, and running this project? How could the problems have been avoided?

4. Are there any ethical problems revealed in the process described in this case? Specifically, how do you feel about the manner by which employees are encouraged to contribute to such causes?

5. Several large charity groups were disturbed that McDuff dropped them and instead involved employees in the Home of Hope. Give what you think would be the charities' point of view about the process described in this case.

CHAPTER SUMMARY

Both process descriptions and instructions share the same organization principle: time. That is, both relate a step-by-step description of events. Process descriptions address an audience that wants to be informed but does not need to perform the process itself. Instructions are geared specifically for persons who need to complete the procedure themselves.

In writing good process descriptions, follow these basic guidelines:

1. Know your purpose and audience.
2. Follow the ABC format.
3. Use an objective point of view.
4. Choose the right amount of detail.
5. Use flowcharts for complex processes.

For instructions, follow these twelve rules:

1. Select the correct technical level.
2. Provide introductory information.
3. Use numbered lists in the body.
4. Group similar steps under heads.
5. Place one action in a step.

6. Lead off each action step with a verb.
7. Remove extra information from the step.
8. Use bullets or letters for emphasis.
9. Emphasize cautions, warnings, and dangers.
10. Keep a simple style.
11. Use graphics.
12. Test your instructions.

ASSIGNMENTS

Part 1: Short Assignments

Assignments 1–5 can be completed either as individual exercises *or* as group projects, depending on the instructions you are given in class.

1. **Writing a Process Description—School-Related.** Your college or university has decided to evaluate the process by which students are advised about, and registered for, classes. As part of this evaluation, the registrar has asked a select group of students—you among them—to describe the actual process each of you went through individually during the last advising/registration cycle. These "case studies" collected from individual students, the customers, will be transmitted directly to a college-wide committee studying registration and advising problems.

   Your job is to give a detailed account of the process. Remain as objective as possible, without giving opinions. If you had problems during the process, the facts you relate will speak for themselves. Simply describe the process you personally experienced. Then let the committee members judge for themselves whether the steps you describe should or should not be part of the process.

2. **Writing a Process Description—McDuff Context.** Choose one of the projects from the color insert in chapter 2. For this assignment use (a) points listed in the "Main Technical Tasks" section of the project you have chosen or (b) related information you wish to supply from your own experience, reading, or imagination, or (c) both. Your assignment is to write a process description dealing with one or more of the bulleted points.

3. **Writing Instructions—McDuff Context.** Choose one of the projects from the color insert in chapter 2. For this assignment, conduct some research on either (a) one task or several related tasks in the "Main Technical Tasks" section or (b) a task that conceivably could be related to the project but is not specifically listed. Then write a set of numbered instructions for the task(s). Following are some sample tasks, with project references:

   - Project #1: Conducting a lab test to evaluate a soil sample
   - Project #2: Estimating the age of a geologic sample
   - Project #3: Inspecting all or part of a new building
   - Project #4: Running an effective meeting with subcontractors
   - Project #5: Testing soil or water for signs of pollution
   - Project #6: Evaluating the ergonometric features of a control panel
   - Project #7: Evaluating the effectiveness of a technical report

If you prefer to write about less specific tasks, select a general topic related to a project. For example, here are four general topics derived from specific ones above: conducting a lab test, running an effective meeting, evaluating the ergonometric features of any product, and evaluating the effectiveness of any document.

4. **Writing Instructions—McDuff Context.** As an employee at the corporate office of McDuff, you just received the job of writing a set of instructions for completing performance appraisal reviews (PARs). The instructions will be included in a memo that goes to all supervisors at all branches of the firm, along with related forms. To help you get started on the instructions, you have been given a narrative description of the process (see the following). Your task is to convert this narrative into a simple set of instructions to go into the memorandum to supervisors.

PARs are conducted annually for each employee, during the anniversary month in which the employee was originally hired. Several days before the month in which the PARs are to be conducted, the corporate office will send each supervisor a list of employees in that supervisor's group who should receive PARs. The main part of the PAR process is an interview between the supervisor and the employee receiving the PAR. Before this interview takes place, however, the supervisor should give the employee a copy of the "McDuff PAR Discussion Guide," which offers suggestions for the topics and tone of a PAR interview. The supervisor completes a "PAR Report Form" after each interview and then sends a copy to corporate and to the employee, with the original staying in the personnel files of that respective supervisor's branch. If for any reason a PAR interview and report form are not completed in the required month, the supervisor must send a memo of explanation to the corporate Human Resources Department, with a copy to the supervisor's branch manager.

---

5. **Writing Instructions—School-Related.** In either outline or final written form, provide a set of instructions for completing assignments in this class. Consider your audience to be another student who has been ill and missed much of the term. You have agreed to provide her with an overview that will help her to plan and then write any papers she has missed.

    Your instructions may include (1) highlights of the writing process from chapter 1 and (2) other assignment guidelines provided by your instructor in the syllabus or in class. Remember to present a generic procedure for all assignments in the class, not specific instructions for a particular assignment.

Part 2: Longer Assignments

These assignments test your ability to write and evaluate the two patterns covered in this chapter—process descriptions and instructions. Specifically, follow these guidelines:

- Write each exercise in the form of a letter report or memo report, as specified.
- Follow organization and design guidelines given in chapters 3 and 4, especially concerning the ABC format (**A**bstract/**B**ody/**C**onclusion) and the use of headings. Chapter 8 gives rules for short reports, but such detail is not necessary to complete the assignments here.
- Fill out a Planning Form (at the end of the book) for each assignment.

6. **Evaluating a Process Description.** Using a textbook in a technical subject area, find a description of a process. For example, a physics text might describe the process of waves developing and then breaking at a beach, an anatomy text might describe the

process of blood circulating, or a criminal justice text might describe the process of a criminal investigation.

Keeping in mind the author's purpose and audience, evaluate the effectiveness of the process description as presented in the textbook. Submit your evaluation in the form of a memo report to your instructor in this writing course, along with a copy of the textbook description.

For the purposes of this assignment, assume that your writing instructor has been asked by the publisher of the text you have chosen to review the book as an example of good or bad technical writing. Thus your instructor would incorporate comments from your memo report into his or her comprehensive evaluation.

7. **Writing a Process Description—School-Related.** Conduct a brief research project in your campus library. Specifically, use company directories, annual reports, or other library sources to find information about a company or other organization that could hire students from your college.

In a memo report to your instructor, (1) describe the process you followed in conducting the search and (2) provide an outline or paragraph summary of the information you found concerning the company or organization. Assume that your report will become part of a volume your college is assembling for juniors and seniors who are beginning their job search. These students will benefit both from information about the specific organization you chose and from a description of the process that you followed in getting the information—since they may want to conduct research on other companies.

8. **Writing a Process Description—McDuff Context.** As a project manager for McDuff's Atlanta office, you just found out that your office has been selected as one of the firms to help renovate Kiddieworld, a large amusement park in the Southeast. Before Kiddieworld officials sign the contract, however, they want you to report on the process McDuff uses to report and investigate accidents (since the project will involve some hazardous work). You found the following policy in your office manual, but you know it is not something you would want to send to a client. Take this stilted paragraph and convert it to a process description for your clients, in the form of a letter report. Remember: The readers will not be performing the process; they only want to understand it.

Accident reporting and investigation are an important phase of operating McDuff, Inc. The main purpose of an accident investigation and report is to gain an objective insight into facts surrounding the accident in order to improve future accident control measures and activities and to activate the protection provided by our insurance policies. It is therefore imperative that all losses, no matter how minor, be reported as soon as possible and preferably within 48 hours to the proper personnel. Specifically, all accidents must be reported orally to the immediate supervisor. For minor accidents that do not involve major loss of equipment or hospitalization, that supervisor has the responsibility of filling out a McDuff accident report form and then sending the form to the safety personnel at the appropriate branch office, who later sends it to the safety manager at the corporate office. For serious accidents that involve major loss of equipment or hospitalization of any individuals involved, the supervisor must call or telex the safety personnel at the appropriate branch office, who then should call or telex the safety manager at the corporate office. (A list of pertinent telephone numbers should be kept at every job site.) These oral reports will be followed up with a written report.

---

9. **Evaluation of Instructions.** Find a set of operating or assembly instructions for a VCR, microwave oven, CD player, computer, timing light, or other electronic device. Evaluate all or part of the document according to the criteria for instructions in this chapter.

    Write a memo report on your findings and send it, along with a copy of the instructions, to Natalie Bern. As a technical writer at the company that produced the electronic device, Natalie wrote the set of instructions. In your position as Natalie's supervisor, you are responsible for evaluating her work. Use your memo report either to compliment her on the instructions or to suggest modifications.

10. **User Test of Instructions.** Find a relatively simple set of instructions. Then ask another person to follow the instructions from beginning to end. Observe the person's activity, keeping notes on any problems she or he encounters.

    Use your notes to summarize the effectiveness of the instructions. Present your summary as a memo report to Natalie Bern, using the same situational context as described in assignment 7. That is, as Natalie's boss, you are to give her your evaluation of her efforts to produce the set of instructions.

11. **Writing Simple Instructions.** Choose a simple office procedure of 20 or fewer steps (for example, changing a printer ribbon, filling a mechanical pencil, adding dry ink to a copy machine, or adding paper to a laser printer). Then write a simple set of instructions for this process, in the form of a memo report. Your readers are assistants at the many offices of a large national firm. Consider them to be new employees who have no background or experience in office work and no education beyond high school. You are responsible for their training.

12. **Writing Complex Instructions, with Graphics—Group Project.** Complete this assignment as a group project (see the guidelines for group work in chapter 1). Choose a process connected with college life or courses—for example, completing a lab experiment, doing a field test, designing a model, writing a research paper, getting a parking sticker, paying fees, registering for classes, etc.

    Using memo report format, write a set of instructions for students who have never performed this task. Follow all the guidelines in this chapter. Include at least one illustration (along with warnings or cautions, if appropriate). If possible, conduct a user test before completing the final draft.

13. **Writing Instructions—McDuff Context.** McDuff does a good deal of environmental work around the country—cleaning up toxic-waste sites, building energy-efficient structures, removing asbestos from old buildings, and investigating construction sites to determine the most environmentally sound approach to design and construction. For business reasons—and also because of its sense of civic duty—the company encourages citizens to get directly involved in environmental action.

    As public relations manager for McDuff, you have just received an interesting assignment from the president, Rob McDuff. He wants you to prepare a set of instructions that will go out to citizen and school groups in the Baltimore-Washington area. In the form of a memo report, this document should give readers specific directions for recycling one or more types of waste. Your instructions should be directed toward a broad audience, of course. Moreover, they should give the kinds of details that allow someone to act without having to get more information.

    To get information for this report, you might consider (1) calling individuals in the waste-management department of your local government, (2) reading relevant articles from recent periodicals, or (3) checking an environmental science textbook at your college.

14. **Writing Instructions—Group Project with McDuff Context.** McDuff, Inc.'s, increasing international work has generated interest among the corporate staff in gaining ISO 9000 certification. (Based in Geneva, Switzerland, the International Organization for Standardization (ISO) helps organizations around the world develop standards in quality.) Your group will conduct some research on this topic of growing interest. Write a set of instructions for a company, like McDuff, that wishes to gain such certification. You may either (a) provide a generalized overview for completing the entire process or (b) focus on one limited, specific part of the process, such as the process for gaining certification for a particular product or service.

Mc Duff, Inc.

MEMORANDUM

DATE: May 29, 1996
TO: Leonard Schwartz
FROM: Your Name
SUBJECT: New Electronic-Mail System

Yesterday I met with Jane Ansel, the installation manager at BHG Electronics, about our new electronic-mail system. Ms. Ansel explained the process by which the system will be installed. As you requested, this memo summarizes what I learned about that process.

BHG technicians will be at our offices on June 18 to complete these five tasks:

1. Removing old cable from the building conduits
2. Laying cable to link remaining unconnected terminals with the central processing unit in the main frame
3. Installing software in the system that will give each terminal the capacity to operate the electronic-mail system
4. Testing each terminal to make sure that the system can operate from that location
5. Instructing selected managers on the use of the system

As you and I have agreed, next week I will send a memo to all office employees who will have access to electronic mail. That memo will mention the installation date and summarize the procedures for reading mail. Shortly thereafter, I will send another memo instructing them about sending electronic mail.

Let me know, Leonard, if you have further suggestions about how I can help make our transition to electronic mail as smooth as possible.

MODEL 6–1
McDuff process description; electronic mail

Mc Duff, Inc.

MEMORANDUM

DATE: June 5, 1996
TO: All Employees with Computer Terminals
FROM: Your Name
SUBJECT: Basic Instructions for Reading Electronic Mail

Gives clear purpose.

Last month, you attended a brief seminar on the features of the new electronic-mail system. We have just learned that the system will be installed on June 18. This memo provides some basic instructions for reading mail sent to you on this system. Soon you will receive another set of instructions for sending electronic mail.

Indicates what instructions do and do not cover.

NOTE: In these instructions, the messages or prompts on your terminal screen appear in *italics*. Any key you push or response you type is shown in **bold** print.

1. Turn on the computer terminal.
    NOTE: The on/off button is on the right front corner of the unit.

Provides information to help reader understand instructions that follow.

2. Type in your terminal's number when the system requests it.
    Example: *terminal number:* **23**

3. Respond with your initials when the system asks for "login."
    Example: *login:* **wsp**

Limits each step to one action.

4. Give your password at the next system prompt.
    Example: *password:* **Tex**
    RESULT: After the system has verified your password, it will respond with one of two messages: either *no mail* or *yes, you have mail.*

Separates action from results.

5. Respond to the message in one of these two ways:

If…	Then…
■ Screen reads "no mail"	■ Press "e" for "exit" ■ Begin another task on the terminal
■ Screen reads "yes, you have mail"	■ Press "r" for "read" ■ Continue with these instructions

Explains options clearly.

6. Read the first screen of your message.

7. Press the "**return**" key to discover whether there are additional screens with that message.

continues

MODEL 6–2
McDuff instructions: electronic mail

Memo to: Employees with Computer Terminals.   Page 2

8. Do you wish to return to other screens in that message?
    • If yes, press the "backspace".
    • If no, continue with these instructions.

9. Enter one of the abbreviations from the following list when you are finished with a message:

    s = save message
    d = delete message
    p = print message

10. Press "**m**" (for "**move**") to move on to next message.

11. Press "**e**" (for "**exit**") when the system indicates no more messages.

12. Turn off the machine or begin another activity with the terminal.

    As noted earlier, the system will be installed on June 18. Feel free to call me if you have any questions about the installation or the instructions for reading messages.

Uses list to show choices.

Restates important date and shows reader how to get more information.

MODEL 6–2
continued

ABC format begins with abstract–with purpose statement and summary of appendix in this paragraph.

Abstract ends with list of equipment used in process that follows.

Body section of this process uses paragraph format and is aimed at non-technical audience.

Listing is used to highlight locations for sampling.

Conclusion part of ABC format puts this process in larger context.

APPENDIX A: ON-SITE MONITORING

The purpose of monitoring the air is to determine the level of protective equipment needed for each day's work. This appendix gives an overview of the process for monitoring on-site air quality each day. Besides describing the main parts of the process, it notes other relevant information to be recorded and the manner in which data will be logged.

EQUIPMENT
This process requires the following equipment:

- Organic vapor analyzers (OVA)
- Combustible-gas instruments
- Personal sampling devices

PROCESS
The project manager at the site is responsible for supervising the technician who performs the air-quality tests. At the start of every day, a technician uses an OVA to check the quality of air at selected locations around the site. Throughout the workday (at times specified by the project manager), the technician monitors the air with combustible-gas instruments and personal sampling devices. This monitoring takes place at these locations:

1. Around the perimeter of the site
2. Downwind of the site (to determine the extent of migration of vapors and gases)
3. Generally throughout the site
4. At active work locations within the site

Then at the end of every workday, the technician uses the OVA to monitor the site for organic vapors and gases.

CONCLUSION
Besides the air-quality data, the following information is collected by the technician at each sampling time: percent relative humidity, wind direction and speed, temperature, and atmospheric pressure. The project manager keeps records of air quality and weather conditions in dated entries in a bound log.

MODEL 6–3
Process description

COMBINED SITE INVESTIGATION

In helping to select the site for an offshore oil platform, McDuff recommends a combined site investigation. This approach achieves the best results by integrating sophisticated geophysical work with traditional engineering activities.

As the accompanying flowchart shows, a combined site investigation consists of these main steps:

1. Planning the program, with McDuff's scientists and engineers and the client's representatives
2. Reviewing existing data
3. Completing a high-resolution geophysical survey of the site, followed by a preliminary analysis of the data
4. Collecting, testing, and analyzing soil samples
5. Combining geophysical and engineering information into one final report for the client

The report from this combined study will show how geological conditions at the site may affect the planned offshore oil platform.

Steps 1 and 2 are shown in top center portion of flowchart.

Steps 3 and 4 are shown in left and right portions of flowchart, respectively.

Step 5 is shown in bottom center portion of flowchart.

Flowchart shows relationship among steps occurring at the same time.

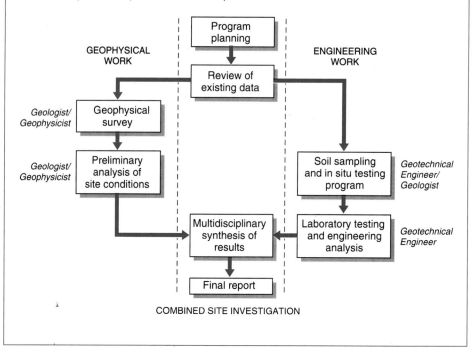

MODEL 6–4
A McDuff process description with a flowchart (Both are included in an appendix to a report to a client.)

200

MAKING TRAVEL ARRANGEMENTS
(Original Version)

Paragraph
format makes it
difficult for
reader to locate
individual steps.

When you're making travel arrangements, ask the person taking the trip to give you most of the details needed—dates, destinations, flight numbers, flight times, hotel requirements, rental car requirements, purpose of trip, and account number. Before proceeding, the first thing I do is confirm the flight information in the Official Airline Guide (OAG). You'll find the OAG on top of the credenza beside my typewriter. The next step is to call Turner Travel (566-0998). Although I've had great luck with all the people there, ask for Bonnie or Charlie—these two are most familiar with our firm. Turner Travel will handle reservations for flights, hotels, and rental cars. Remind them that we always use Avis midsize cars.

After you have confirmed the reservations information, fill out the McDuff travel form. Here's where you need to know the purpose of the trip and the traveler's McDuff account number. Blank forms are in the top drawer of my file cabinet in the folder labeled "Travel Forms—Blank." Once the form is complete, file the original in my "Travel Forms—Completed" folder, also in the top drawer of the file cabinet. Give the copy to the person taking the trip.

When you get the ticket in the mail from Turner Travel, check the flight information against the completed travel form. If everything checks out, give the ticket to the traveler. If there are errors, call Turner.

Also, when making any reservations for visitors to our office, call either the Warner Inn (566-7888) or the Hasker Hotel (567-9000). We have company accounts there, and they will bill us directly.

continues

MODEL 6–5
Instructions for making travel arrangements (McDuff's departed Baltimore travel coordinator left a narrative description of the procedure he followed [original version], which was then reformatted and edited [revised version].)

MAKING TRAVEL ARRANGEMENTS
(Revised Version)

Arranging Travel for Employees

To make travel arrangements for employees, follow these instructions:

Step	Action
1.	Obtain the following information from the traveler:

a. Dates
b. Destinations
c. Flight numbers
d. Flight times
e. Hotel requirements
f. Rental car requirements
g. Purpose of trip
h. Account number

| 2. | Confirm flight information in the Official Airline Guide (OAG). |

Note: The OAG is on the credenza beside my typewriter.

| 3. | Call Turner Travel (566-0998) to make reservations. |

Note: Ask for Bonnie or Charlie.
Note: For car rental, use Avis midsize cars.

| 4. | Complete the McDuff travel form. |

Note: Blank forms are in the folder labeled "Travel Forms—Blank," in the top drawer of my file cabinet.

| 5. | Make one copy of the completed travel form. |

| 6. | Place the original form in the folder labeled "Travel Forms—Completed," in the top drawer of my file cabinet. |

| 7. | Send the copy to the person taking the trip. |

| 8. | Check the ticket and the completed travel form after the ticket arrives from Turner Travel. |

| 9. | Do the ticket and the completed travel form agree? |

a. If *yes*, give the ticket to the traveler.
b. If *no*, call Turner Travel.

Arranging Hotel Reservations for Visitors

To make reservations for visitors, call the Warner Inn (566-7888) or the Hasker Hotel (567-9000). McDuff has company accounts there, and they will bill us.

Margin notes:

Action steps all begin with "command" form of verb.

Letters are used to show long list of subpoints, for easy reference.

Notes are used to provide reader with *extra* information, separate from action of steps.

Though closely related, Steps 5–7 are best separated—for convenient reference by reader.

As noted in Guideline 8, two subpoints can show reader the *options* that exist.

MODEL 6–5
continued

Mc Duff, Inc.

MEMORANDUM

DATE: June 23, 1996
TO: Employees Receiving New Message Recorders
FROM: Your Name, Purchasing Agent
SUBJECT: Instructions for new Message Recorders

INTRODUCTORY SUMMARY

We have just received the new phone message recorder you ordered. After processing, it will be delivered to your office within the week. The machine is one of the best on the market, but the instructions that accompany it are somewhat hard to follow. To help you begin using the recorder as soon as possible, I have simplified the instructions for setting up and operating the machine.

The illustration below labels the machine's parts. Following the illustration are seven easy steps you need to operate the recorder.

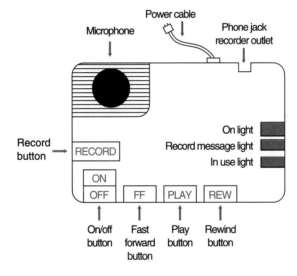

continues

MODEL 6–6
McDuff memo containing how-to instructions for a phone message recorder (rewritten from manufacturer's difficult-to-follow instructions)

Main steps are numbered 1 through 7.

For clarity, substeps under each main step have separate lettering.

Similar actions are separated into *two* different steps, to keep actions distinct.

Extra information is placed in note, *not* in step itself.

As with "notes," "results" should be *separated* from action in steps.

At point of decision, reader is given two clear options for action.

SETTING UP AND USING YOUR NEW RECORDER

If you devote about 15 minutes to these seven tasks, you can learn to operate your new message recorder.

1. Hooking Up Your Recorder

   a. Plug the recorder into any wall outlet using the *power cable.*
   b. Plug the *phone jack* into the *recorder outlet* located at the back of the unit.

2. Preparing Your Message

   a. Write down your:
      Greeting
      Name and department
      Time of return
   b. Write down the request you want to leave on the machine.
      NOTE: A sample request might be as follows: "Please leave your name, phone number, and a brief message after you hear the tone."

3. Recording Your Message

   a. Press the *ON* button.
      RESULT: The red *on* light will come on.
   b. Press and hold down the *RECORD* button, and keep holding it down for the entire time you record.
      RESULT: While the button is held down, the red *record/message* light will come on.
   c. Record your message directly into the *microphone.*
   d. Release the *RECORD* button when you are finished recording.
   e. Do you need to record the message again?
      If *yes,* repeat steps a through d (your previous message will be erased each time you record).
      If *no,* go on to the next step.

4. Turning On and Testing Your Recorder

   a. Press the *ON* button.
      RESULT: The red *on* light will come on.
   b. Press the *PLAY* button.
      RESULT: The red *in use* light will come on.
   c. Call in your message from another phone to make sure the unit is recording properly.

5. Playing Back Messages

   a. Look at the red *record/message* light to see if it is blinking.
      NOTE: The number of times the light blinks in succession indicates the number of messages you have received.

MODEL 6–6
continued

204

b. Press the *REW* (rewind) button.
NOTE: The tape will stop automatically when it is completely rewound.

Because of
potential dam-
age to equip-
ment, "caution"
appears *before*
steps to which it
applies.

> **CAUTION: Do not press *play* and *FF* (Fast Forward) at the same time! Doing so will break the tape. See the manufacturer's manual for process of replacing broken**

c. Press *play* and listen to the messages.
d. Do you want to replay messages?
   If *yes*, repeat steps b and c.
   If *no*, go on to next step.
e. Do you want to skip ahead to other messages?
   If *yes*, push the FF (fast forward) button.
   If *no*, go on to next step.

6. Erasing Received Messages
a. Press and continue holding down the *PLAY* and *REW* (rewind) buttons at the same time.
b. Release the buttons when you hear a click.
   NOTE: The tape automatically stops when the messages are erased.

7. Turning Off Your Recorder
a. Press the *OFF* button.
   RESULT: All red lights will go off.

Conclusion of
ABC format
wraps up memo
by telling read-
ers what to do if
they encounter
problems.

CONCLUSION

These new recorders are fully guaranteed for three years, so please report any problems right away. Paul Hansey (ext. 765) will be glad to help fix the machine or return the machine to the manufacturer for repair. In particular, you need to report these problems to Paul:

- Lost or incomplete messages
- Interference or noise on line
- Faulty equipment
- Inability to record

MODEL 6–6
continued

7 Letters and Memos

Good letters and memos are related to good oral communication with customers and colleagues. Both forms of discourse benefit from natural, clear, and tactful language.

*M*arie Stargill, McDuff's fire-science expert, just returned from a seminar that emphasized new techniques for preventing injuries from job-site fires. Within 24 hours of her return, she has already done three things:

1. Written her manager an electronic mail (e-mail) message over the office computer network
2. Sent a letter to a McDuff client suggesting use of fire-retardant gloves she learned about at the seminar
3. Sent the conference director a letter of appreciation about the meeting

Like Marie, you will write many letters and memos in your career. In fact, you probably will write more of them than any other type of document.

Both letters and memos are short documents written to accomplish a limited purpose. They are alike in most respects except one: Letters are directed outside your organization, whereas memos are directed within your organization. (Longer, more complicated letters and memos—called "letter reports" and "memo reports"—are covered in chapter 8.) Here are some working definitions:

Letter: document that conveys information to a member of one organization from someone outside that same organization. Also called "correspondence," letters usually cover one major point and go on one page. This chapter classifies letters into these four groups, according to type of message: (1) positive, (2) negative, (3) neutral, and (4) sales.

Memorandum: document written from a member of an organization to one or more members of the same organization. Abbreviated "memo," it usually covers just one main point and no more than a few. Readers prefer one-page memos.

As with other forms of technical writing, your ability to write good memos and letters depends on a clear sense of purpose, thorough understanding of reader needs and close attention to correct formats. This chapter prepares you for this challenge by presenting sections that cover (1) general rules that apply to both letters and memos and (2) specific formats for positive letters, negative letters, neutral letters, sales letters, and memoranda (printed memos and e-mail). Job letters and resumes are discussed in a separate chapter on the job search (chapter 14).

GENERAL GUIDELINES FOR LETTERS AND MEMOS

Letters convey your message to readers *outside* your organization, just as memos are an effective way to get things done *within* your own organization. By applying the guidelines in this chapter, you can master the craft of writing good letters and memos. You need to plan, draft, and revise each letter and memo as if your job depends on it—for it may.

Refer to Models 7–1 and 7–2 on pages 234 and 235–236 for McDuff examples that demonstrate the guidelines that follow. Later examples in this chapter show specific types of letters and additional memos.

■ *Letter/Memo Guideline 1: Know Your Purpose*

Before beginning your draft, write down your purpose in one clear sentence. This approach forces you to sift through details to find a main reason for writing every letter or memo. This "purpose sentence" often becomes one of the first sentences in the document. Here are some samples:

- **Letter purpose sentence:** "As you requested yesterday, I'm sending samples of the new candy brands you are considering placing in McDuff's office vending machines."
- **Memo purpose sentence:** "This memo will explain McDuff's new policy for selecting rental cars on business trips."

Some purpose statements are implied; other are stated. An implied purpose statement occurs in the second paragraph of Model 7–1 (p. 234). That paragraph shows that the writer wishes both to respond to requests for McDuff brochures and, just as important, to seek the professor's help in soliciting good graduates for McDuff's Atlanta office. In a sense, one purpose leads into the other. In Model 7–2 (pp. 235–236), you will find a more obvious purpose statement in the second sentence.

■ *Letter/Memo Guideline 2: Know Your Readers*

Whom are you trying to inform or influence? The answer to this question affects the vocabulary you choose, the arguments you make, and the tone you adopt. Pay particular attention when a letter or memo will be read by more than one person. If these readers are from different technical levels or different levels within an organization, the challenge increases. A complex audience compels you to either (1) reduce the level of technicality to that which can be understood by all readers or (2) write different parts of the document for different readers.

Model 7–1 (p. 234) is directed to a professor with whom the writer wants to develop a reciprocal relationship—that is, George Lux gives free guest lectures in civil-engineering classes, hoping the professor in turn will help him inform potential job applicants about McDuff. Model 7–2 (pp. 235–236), directed to an in-house technical audience, contains fairly general information about the new technical editor. This information would apply to, and be understood by, all readers.

■ *Letter/Memo Guideline 3: Follow Correct Format*

Most organizations adopt letter and memo formats that must be used uniformly by all employees. Here are the basic guidelines:

- **Letters:** There are three main letter formats—block, modified block, and simplified. Models 7–3, 7–4, and 7–5 on pages 237–239 show the basic page design of each; letter examples throughout the chapter use the three formats. As noted, you usually follow the preferred format of your own organization.
- **Memos:** With minor variations, all memos look much the same. The obligatory "date/to/from/subject" information hangs at the top left margin, in whatever order your organization requires. Model 7–6 on page 240 shows one basic format. These four lines allow you to dispense with lengthy introductory passages seen in more formal documents.

  Give the *subject line* special attention, for it telegraphs meaning to the audience immediately. In fact, readers use it to decide when, or if, they will read the complete memo. Be brief but also engage interest. For example, the subject line of the Model 7–2 memo could have been "Editing." Yet that brevity would have sacrificed reader interest. The actual subject line, "New Employee to Help with Technical Editing," conveys more information and shows readers that the contents of the memo will make their lives easier.

  Note that the sender signs his or her initials after or above the typed name in the "from" line.

- **Letters and Memos:** Several format conventions apply to letters and memos alike. Some of the more important features are listed here. See the models at the end of the chapter for details about spacing.

  Facsimile Reference: Readers often need to know—for convenience and for the record—when memos or letters have been sent by fax. Type FAX TRANSMISSION or FACSIMILE before the "date/to/from/subject" lines for a memo and between the date and inside address for a letter. This fax line also can be used for other similar notations such as CONFIDENTIAL or PERSONAL or REGISTERED.

  Reference Initials: If the document has been typed by someone other than the writer, place the typist's initials two lines below the signature block for letters and below the last paragraph for memos (example: jt). Some organizations prefer that the initials of the writer also be included, followed by those of the typist (example: GTY/jt).

Enclosure Notation: If attachments or enclosures accompany the letter or memo, type the singular or plural form of "Enclosure" or "Attachment" one or two lines below the reference initials. Some writers also list the item itself (example: Enclosure: Code of Ethics).

Copy Notation: If the memo or letter has been sent to anyone other than the recipient, type "Copy" or "Copies" one or two lines below the enclosure notation, followed by the name(s) of the person or persons receiving copies (example: Copy: Preston Hinkley). Some organizations prefer the initials "c" (for copy), "cc" (for carbon copy, even though carbons hardly exist anymore), or "pc" (for photocopy). If you are sending a copy but do not want the original letter or memo to include a reference to that copy, write "bc" (for blind copy) and the person's name only on the copy—not on the original (example: bc: Rob McDuff). Note: only send blind copies when you are certain it is appropriate and ethical to do so.

Postscripts: Items marked "PS" or "P.S." can appear occasionally in letters and rarely in memos. They are considered by many readers to be symbols of poor planning, so use them with caution. If used, they appear as the last item on the document (below the copy notation) and can be typed or written in longhand.

Multiple-Page Headings: Pages after the first page often have a heading that includes the name of the person or company receiving the letter or memo, the date, and the page number. Some organizations may prefer an abbreviated form such as "Jones to Bingham, 2," without the date.

■ *Letter/Memo Guideline 4: Follow the ABC Format for All Letters and Memos*

Letters and memos subscribe to the same three-part ABC (**A**bstract/**B**ody/-**C**onclusion) format used throughout this book. This approach responds to each reader's need to know "What does this document have to do with me?" According to the ABC format, your letter or memo comprises these three main sections:

- **Abstract:** The abstract introduces the purpose and usually gives a summary of main points to follow. It includes one or two short paragraphs.
- **Body:** The body contains supporting details and thus makes up the largest part of a letter or memo. You can help your readers by using techniques like these:

  Deductive patterns for paragraphs: In this general-to-specific plan, your first sentence should state the point that will help the reader understand the rest of the paragraph. This pattern avoids burying important points in the middle or end of the paragraph, where they might be missed. Fast readers tend to focus on paragraph beginnings and expect to find crucial information there. Note how most paragraphs in Model 7–2 (pp. 235–236) follow this format.

Personal names: If they know you, readers like to see their names in the body of the letter or memo. Your effort here shows concern for the reader's perspective, gives the letter a personal touch, and helps strengthen your personal relationship with the reader. (See the last paragraph in Model 7–1, page 234.) Of course, the same technique in direct mail can sometimes backfire, since it is an obvious ploy to create an artificially personal relationship.

Lists that break up the text: Listed points are a good strategy for highlighting details. Readers are especially attracted to groupings of three items, which create a certain rhythm, attract attention, and encourage recall. Use bullets, numbers, dashes, or other typographical techniques to signal the listed items. For example, the bulleted list in Model 7–1 (p. 234) draws attention to three important points about McDuff that the writer wants to emphasize.

Strongest points first or last: If your letter or memo presents support or makes an argument, include the most important points at the beginning and/or at the end—not in the middle. For example, Model 7–2 begins and ends with two crucial issues: the effect of poor editing on company productivity and the need to decide upon specific ways the new editor can improve McDuff writing.

Headings to divide information: Even one-page letters and memos sometimes benefit from the emphasis achieved by headings. The three headings in Model 7–2 (pp. 235–236) quickly steer the reader to main parts of the document.

- **Conclusion:** Readers remember first what they read last. The final paragraph of your letter or memo should leave the reader with an important piece of information—for example, (1) a summary of the main idea or (2) a clear statement of what will happen next. The Model 7–1 (p. 234) letter makes an offer that will help to continue the reader's association with the university, while the Model 7–2 (pp. 235–236) memo gives readers a specific task to accomplish before the next meeting.

■ *Letter/Memo Guideline 5: Use the 3Cs Strategy for Persuasive Messages*

The ABC format provides a way to organize all letters and memos. Another pattern of organization for you to employ is the "3Cs strategy"—especially when your letter or memo has a persuasive objective. This strategy has three main goals:

- **Capture** interest with a good opener, which tells the reader what the letter or memo can do for him or her.
- **Convince** the reader with supporting points, all of which confirm the opening point that this document will make life easier.
- **Control** the closing, with a statement that puts you in the position of following up on the letter or memo *and* solidifies your relationship with the reader.

Although neither Model 7–1 nor Model 7–2 is overtly persuasive, each has an underlying persuasive purpose. Note how both employ the 3Cs strategy.

■ *Letter/Memo Guideline 6: Stress the "You" Attitude*

As noted earlier, using the reader's name in the body helps convey interest. But your efforts to see things from the reader's perspective must go deeper than a name reference. For example, you should perform these tasks:

- **Anticipate questions** your reader might raise and then answer these questions. You can even follow an actual question ("And how will our new testing lab help your firm?") with an answer ("Now McDuff's labs can process samples in 24 hours").
- **Replace the pronouns "I," "me," and "we" with "you" and "your."** Of course, you have to use first-person pronouns at certain points in a letter, but many pronouns should be second-person. The technique is quite simple. You can change almost any sentence from writer-focused prose ("We feel that this new service will . . .") to reader-focused prose ("You'll find that this new service will . . .").

Model 7–1 (p. 234) shows this "you" attitude by emphasizing what McDuff and the writer himself can do for the professor and his students. Model 7–2 (pp. 235–236) shows it by emphasizing that the new editor will make the readers' job easier.

■ *Letter/Memo Guideline 7: Use Attachments for Details*

Keep text brief by placing details in attachments, which readers can examine later, rather than bogging down the middle of the letter or memo. In this way, the supporting facts are available for future reference, without distracting readers from the main message. The memo in Model 7–2 (pp. 235–236), for example, includes a list of possible job tasks for the new McDuff editor. The listing would only clutter the body of the memo, especially since its purpose is to stimulate discussion at the next meeting.

■ *Letter/Memo Guideline 8: Be Diplomatic*

Without a tactful tone, all your planning and drafting will be wasted. Choose words that will persuade and cajole, not demand. Be especially careful of memos written to subordinates. If you sound too authoritarian, your message may be ignored—even if it is clear that what you are suggesting will help the readers. Generally speaking, negative (or "bad news") letters often use the passive voice, whereas positive (or "good news") letters often use the active voice.

For example, the letter in Model 7–1 (p. 234) would fail in its purpose if it sounded too pushy and one-sided about McDuff's interest in hiring graduates. Similarly, the editing memo in Model 7–2 (pp. 235–236) would be poorly received if it used stuffy, condescending wording such as "Be advised that starting next month, you are to make use of proofreading services provided in-house by. . . ."

■ *Letter/Memo Guideline 9: Edit Carefully*

Because letters and memos are short, editing errors may be obvious to readers. Take special care to avoid the following errors:

- **Mechanics:**

- Misspelled words of any kind, but especially the reader's name
- Wrong job title (call the reader's office to double-check, if necessary)
- Old address (again, call the reader's office to check)

- **Grammar:**

- Subject-verb and pronoun non-agreement
- Misused commas

- **Style:**

- Stuffy phrases such as "per your request" and "enclosed herewith"
- Long sentences with more than one main and one dependent clause
- Presumptuous phrases such as "Thanking you in advance for . . ."
- Negative tone suggested by phrases such as "We cannot," "I won't," and "Please don't hesitate to"

The last point is crucial and gets more attention later in this chapter. Use the editing stage to rewrite any passage that could be phrased in a more positive tone. You must always keep the reader's goodwill, no matter what the message.

■ *Letter/Memo Guideline 10: Respond Quickly*

A letter or memo that comes too late will fail in its purpose, no matter how well written. Mail letters within 48 hours of your contact with, or request from, the reader. Send memos in plenty of time for your reader to make the appropriate adjustments in schedule, behavior, and so forth. This rule applies, for example, to letters and memos written in response to these situations:

- You want to write a follow-up letter after meeting or talking with a client.
- A customer requests information about a product or service.
- You discover that there will be a delay in your supply of a product or service to a customer.
- You select a candidate to interview for a position.
- You announce a change in company policy.
- You set the time for a company meeting.

The first sentence in the Model 7–1 (p. 234) letter, for example, shows that George Lux writes the day after his guest lecture. This responsiveness will help secure the goodwill of the professor.

SPECIFIC GUIDELINES FOR LETTERS AND MEMOS

Letters are to your clients and vendors what memos are to your colleagues. They relay information quickly and keep business flowing. This section gives you specific guidelines for these documents:

- Letters with a positive message
- Letters with a negative message
- Letters with a neutral message
- Letters with a sales message
- Memoranda

To be sure, many documents are hybrid forms that combine these patterns. As a technical sales expert for McDuff, for example, you may be writing to answer a customer question about a new piece of equipment just purchased from McDuff's Equipment Development group. Your main task is to solve a problem caused by a confusing passage in the owner's manual. At the same time, however, your concern for the customer's satisfaction can pave the way for purchase of a second machine later in the year. Thus the letter has both a positive message and a sales message. This example also points to a common thread that weaves all four letter types together: the need to maintain the reader's goodwill toward you and your organization.

The next five sections present (1) a pattern for each type of correspondence, based on the ABC (**A**bstract/**B**ody/**C**onclusion) format used throughout this text, and (2) one or more brief case studies in which the pattern might be used at McDuff.

Positive Letters

Everyone likes to give good news; fortunately, you will often be in the position of providing it when you write. Here are some sample situations:

- Replying to a question about products or services
- Acknowledging that an order has been received
- Recommending a colleague for a promotion or job
- Responding favorably to a routine request
- Responding favorably to a complaint or an adjustment
- Hiring an employee

The trick is to recognize the good-news potential of many situations. This section gives you an all-purpose format for positive letters, followed by a case study from McDuff.

ABC Format for Positive Letters.   All positive letters follow one overriding rule. You must always:

> ### State good news immediately!

Any delay gives readers the chance to wonder whether the news will be good or bad, thus causing momentary confusion. Here is a complete outline for positive letters that corresponds to the ABC format:

ABC Format: Positive Letter

Abstract

- Bridge between this letter and last communication with person
- Clear statement of good news you have to report

Body

- Supporting data for main point mentioned in abstract
- Clarification of any questions reader may have
- Qualification, if any, of the good news

Conclusion

- Statement of eagerness to continue relationship, complete project, etc.
- Clear statement, if appropriate, of what step should come next

---

McDuff Case Study for a Positive Letter.   As a project manager at McDuff's Houston office, Nancy Slade has agreed to complete a foundation investigation for a large church about 300 miles away. There are cracks in the basement floor slab and doors that do not close, so her crew will need a day to analyze the problem (observing the site, measuring walls, digging soil borings, taking samples, and so on). She took this small job on the condition that she could schedule it around several larger (and more profitable) projects in the same area during mid-August.

Yesterday Nancy received a letter from the minister (speaking for the church committee), who requested that McDuff change the date. He was just asked by the regional headquarters to host a three-day conference at the church during the same time that McDuff was originally scheduled to complete the project.

After checking her project schedule, Nancy determines that she can reschedule the church job. Model 7–7 on page 241 shows her response to the minister.

Negative Letters

It would be nice if all your letters could be as positive as those just described. Unfortunately, the real world does not work like that. You will have many opportunities to display both tact and clarity in relating negative information. Here are a few cases:

- Explaining delays in projects or delivery of services
- Declining invitations or requests
- Registering complaints about products or services
- Refusing to make adjustments based on complaints
- Denying credit
- Giving bad news about employment or performance
- Explaining changes from original orders

This section gives you a format to follow in writing sensitive letters with negative information. Then it provides one application at McDuff.

ABC Format for Negative Letters.   One main rule applies to all negative letters:

Buffer the bad news, but still be clear.

Despite the bad news, you want to keep the reader's goodwill. Spend time at the beginning building your relationship with the reader by introducing less controversial information—*before* you zero in on the main message. Here is an overall pattern to apply in each negative letter:

ABC Format: Negative Letter

Abstract

- Bridge between your letter and previous communication
- General statement of purpose or appreciation—in an effort to find common bond or area of agreement

Body

- Strong emphasis on what *can* be done, when possible
- Buffered yet clear statement of what cannot be done, with clear statement of reasons for negative news
- Facts that support your views

Conclusion

- Closing remarks that express interest in continued association
- Statement, if appropriate, of what will happen next

McDuff Case Study for a Negative Letter.   Reread the letter situation described in the section on positive letters. Now assume that instead of being able to comply with the minister's request, the writer is unable to complete the work on another date without changing the fee. This change would be necessary because Nancy would have to send a new crew the 300 miles to the site, rather than using a crew already working on a nearby project.

Nancy knows the church is on a tight budget, but she also knows that McDuff would not be in business too long by working for free. Most important, since the church is asking for a change in the original agreement, she believes it is fair to request a change in the fee. Model 7–8 on page 242 is the letter she sends. Note her effort to buffer the negative news.

Neutral Letters

Some letters express neither positive nor negative news. They are simply the routine correspondence written every day to keep businesses and other organizations operating. Some situations follow:

- Requesting information about a product or service
- Inviting the reader to an event
- Responding to an invitation or routine request
- Placing orders
- Providing a transmittal letter for fax transmissions
- Sending solicited or unsolicited items through the mail

Use the following outline in writing your neutral letters. Also, refer to the McDuff examples that follow the outline.

ABC Format for Neutral Letters.   Because the reader usually has no personal stake in the news, neutral letters require less emphasis on tone and tact than other types. Yet they still require careful planning. In particular, always abide by this main rule:

> Be absolutely clear about your inquiry or response.

Neutral letters operate a bit like good-news letters. You need to make your point early, without giving the reader time to wonder about your message. Neutral letters vary greatly in specific organization patterns. The "umbrella plan" suggested here emphasizes the main criterion of clarity.

ABC Format: Neutral Letters

Abstract

- Bridge or transition between letter and previous communication, if any
- Precise purpose of letter (request, invitation, response to invitation)

Body

- Details that support the purpose statement—for example,
    Description of item(s) requested
    Requirements related to the invitation
    Description of item(s) being sent

Conclusion

- Statement of appreciation
- Description of actions that should occur next

McDuff Case Studies for Neutral Letters. Letters with neutral messages get written by the hundreds each week at McDuff. Here are four situations that would require a neutral letter; items 2 and 4 provide the context for the examples in Model 7–9 on page 243 and Model 7–10 on page 244:

1. Zach Bowers, a lab assistant, writes a laboratory supply company for information about a new unbreakable beaker to use in testing.
2. Faron Abdullah, president of the Student Government Association at River College, asks representatives of McDuff's St. Louis office to attend a career fair.
3. Donna Martinich, a geologist, responds to the request of a past client for a copy of a report done three years ago.
4. Sarah Linkletter, a supply assistant with McDuff's San Francisco office, orders three new transits, making sure to emphasize that one is not to include a field case.

Sales Letters

Upon hearing the term *sales letter,* some people have visions of direct-mail requests for magazine subscriptions, vacation land, or diet plans. In this text, however, sales letters mean something quite different. They name all your correspondence with a customer—from the first contact letter through the last thank-you note. This list gives you some idea of the possibilities for sales letters:

- Starting a relationship ("I'll be calling you. . . .")
- Following a phone call ("Good talking to you. . . . Can we meet to discuss your needs regarding. . . .")
- Following a meeting ("You mentioned that you could use more information . . . so here's a brochure on. . . .")
- Following completion of sale or project ("We enjoyed working with you on. . . .")
- Seeking repeat business ("I'd like to know how the new machinery has been working. . . .")

Notice that sales letters almost always work together with personal contacts, such as meetings and phone calls. Your goal is to build a continuing relationship with the customer. Consult the following outline when writing sales letters for any context; the McDuff example shows the outline in action.

ABC Format for Sales Letters. The one main rule that governs all sales letters is as follows:

> Help readers solve their problems.

Customers are interested in your product or service only insofar as it can assist them. You must engage the readers' interest by showing that you understand their needs and can help fulfill them. Here is a plan for writing a successful sales letter.

Note reference to the 3Cs (Capture/Convince/Control) strategy mentioned earlier in the chapter:

ABC Format: Sales Letters

Abstract

(choose one or two to capture attention)

- Cite a surprising fact
- Announce a new product or service that client needs
- Ask a question
- Show understanding of a client's problem
- Show potential for solving a client's problem
- Present a testimonial
- Make a challenging claim
- Summarize results of a meeting
- Answer a question reader previously asked

Body

(choose one or two to convince the reader)

- Stress one main problem reader has concern about
- Stress one main selling point of your solution
- Emphasize what is unique about your solution
- Focus on value and quality, rather than price
- Put details in enclosures
- Briefly explain the value of any enclosures

Conclusion

(keep control of the next step in sales process)

- Leave the reader with one crucial point to remember
- Offer to call (first choice) or ask reader to call (last choice)

McDuff Case Study for a Sales Letter.   McDuff provides customers with professional services and equipment, so sales letters have an important place in the firm. Barbara Feinstein is one employee who writes them almost every day. As a first-year employee with a degree in industrial hygiene, Barbara works in the newly formed asbestos-abatement group. Basically, she helps clients find out if there is any asbestos that needs to be removed from structures, recommends a plan for removal, and has the work done by another division of McDuff.

Here is one series of sales contacts that involves several letters. First, Barbara sent "cold call" sales letters to 100 schools and small businesses in the St. Louis area, suggesting that they might want to have their structures checked for unsafe levels of asbestos. The letter contained a reply card. After calling and then meeting with a number of the respondents, she sent individualized follow-up letters that answered questions that came up in discussions and provided additional information. After another series of phone calls and meetings with some of the potential customers, she negotiated contracts with five of the businesses and completed the projects. Then within a few months of completion, she sent a final letter proposing additional McDuff services and began the cycle again. Model 7–11 on page 245 provides a sample sales letter that Barbara used at the beginning of the cycle.

Memoranda

Memoranda (also called *memos*) may be the single most common type of writing in business today. You will write them to peers, subordinates, and superiors in your organization—from the first days of your career until you retire. Even if you work in an organization with "electronic mail"—that is, the capacity to send and receive messages by computer—you still will have to compose messages that convey your point with brevity, clarity, and tact. The medium may change, but not the message. This section covers both types of memoranda: (1) the traditional printed memo and (2) the less formal e-mail message.

Printed Memos. Printed memos can contain all four types of messages discussed with respect to letters—positive, negative, neutral, and sales. Here are some situations that would require good memos in an organization.

Positive

- Announcing high bonuses for the fiscal year
- Commending an employee for performance on a project
- Informing employees about improved fringe benefits

Negative

- Reporting decreased quarterly revenues for the year
- Requesting closer attention to filling out time sheets
- Asking for volunteers to work on a holiday

Neutral

- Announcing a meeting
- Summarizing the results of a meeting with a client
- Explaining a new laboratory procedure

Sales

- Requesting funding for a training seminar
- Recommending another staff member for the proposals unit
- Suggesting changes in the performance evaluation system

Following is an ABC format for memos, along with several case studies from McDuff.

ABC Format for Printed Memoranda.   Abide by this one main rule in every memo-writing situation:

> Be clear, brief, and tactful.

Because many activities are competing for their time, readers expect information to be related as quickly and clearly as possible. Yet be sure not to sacrifice tact and sensitivity as you strive to achieve conciseness. This ABC format will help you accomplish both goals:

ABC Format: Memoranda

Abstract

- Clear statement of memo's purpose
- Outline of main parts of memo

Body

- Supporting points, with strong points at the beginning and/or end
- Frequent use of short paragraphs or listed items
- Absolute clarity about what memo has to do with reader
- Tactful presentation of any negative news
- Reference to attachments, when much detail is required

Conclusion

- Clear statement of what step should occur next
- Another effort to retain goodwill and cooperation of readers

---

McDuff Case Studies for Printed Memoranda.   At McDuff, memoranda are written to and from employees at all levels. To reflect this diversity, this section describes two different contexts for writing memoranda and shows accompanying examples.

In the first context, the lead secretary at McDuff's Baltimore office has chaired an office committee to improve efficiency in using the centralized word-processing center. The committee was formed when the branch manager realized that many technical staff members had not been trained to use the center. This lack of training led to sloppy habits and loss of productivity. Rather than issue a "dictum" from his office, the branch manager established a small committee to review the problem and issue guidelines to the office staff. The memorandum in Model 7–12 on page 246 resulted from the committee's meetings.

In the second McDuff case, the St. Louis personnel director, Timothy Fu, must announce several changes in benefits to the entire staff. Some changes are good news in that they expand employee benefits, and others are bad news in that they further limit benefits. Timothy has the difficult task of imparting both types of information in one memo to a broad audience. The memorandum in Model 7–13 on page 247 is a result of his efforts.

Electronic Mail (E-mail).   Though printed memoranda follow the ABC format, another form of in-house written communication is much less formal. Electronic mail—called *e-mail,* for short—allows you to communicate with others who are on your computer network. According to the Electronic Mail Association, about 30 to 50 million people use e-mail, with that number growing by at least 25% each year.*

E-mail is fast, accessible, and informal. These features can increase your productivity on a project when you don't have time to write memos and when you cannot reach (or do not want to reach) someone by phone.

Chapter 1, which mentions e-mail in the context of group writing, shows how electronic mail helps you collaborate with others during the writing process—especially the planning stage. Interestingly, the e-mail medium has produced a casual writing style similar to that of handwritten notes. It even has its own set of abbreviations and shortcut language (see Figure 7–1). Following is an e-mail message from one McDuff employee to another. Josh Bergen and Natalie Long are working together on a report wherein they must offer suggestions for designing an operator's control panel at a large dam. Josh has just learned about another control panel that McDuff designed and installed for a Russian nuclear power plant (see Project 6 in the color insert). Josh wrote this e-mail message to draw Natalie's attention to the related McDuff project:

> DATE: September 15, 1996
> TO: Natalie Long
> FROM: Josh Bergen
> SUBJECT: Zanger Dam Project
>
> Natalie—FWIW I've got an idea that might save us A LOT of time on the Zanger Dam project. Check out the company project sheet on the Russian nuclear plant job done last year. Should we look at that project report in order to get started on the job?
> Operators of hi-tech dams and nuke plants seem to face the same hassles—confusing displays, need to respond fast, distractions, etc. When either a dam or nuke operator messes up, there's often big-time trouble. IMHO, we'd save our time—and our client's money—if we could go right to some of the technical experts used in the nuke job. At least as a starting place. Maybe we'd even make our deadline on this project:-). That would be a change, considering the schedule delays this month on other jobs.
> What do ya think about this idea? TIA

This message displays some of the most common features of electronic mail. Although e-mail varies from company to company, group to group, and even person to person, the following suggestions are in wide use:

---

*Michael J. Legeros, "Etiquette and E-mail: Rules for Online Behavior," STC *INTERCOM,* Vol. 42, No. 6, July/August 1995, p. 10. Used by permission.

FIGURE 7–1

E-mail terms

Taken from Figures 2 and 3, Michael J. Legeros, "Etiquette and E-mail: Rules for Online Behavior," STC *INTERCOM*, July/August 1995, Vol. 42, No. 6, p. 10. Used by permission.

Commonly Used Acronyms

BTW	by the way
FWIW	for what it's worth
FYI	for your information
IMHO	in my humble opinion
IOW	in other words
ROTFL	rolling on the floor, laughing
TIA	thanks in advance
WRT	with respect to

Commonly Used Emoticons *

:-)	a smile; the sender is happy or making a joke
;-)	a wink, the sender is flirting or being sarcastic
:-(	a frown, the sender is upset or depressed
>:-<	a mean face, the sender is mad
>:->	a devilish remark
:-D	a laugh
:-@	a scream
%-)	the sender is confused
:-X	the sender's lips are sealed

1. Begin with standard "date/to/from/subject" information. The exact wording and order will depend on the particular e-mail system in your organization.

2. Focus on one main subject in a message, and state it as briefly as possible. When e-mail messages get too long or complicated, they lose their usefulness and impact.

3. Adopt a conversational style that resembles how you would talk to the recipient on the phone. Sentence fragments and slang are acceptable, as long as they contribute to your objectives and are in good taste.

4. Use abbreviations only if you know they'll be understood by the recipient.

**5. Only write in an e-mail message what you would not mind being made public. Remember—when you launch messages into cyberspace, you are never sure where they may land.

6. Don't write e-mail messages when you are upset. They cannot be retrieved, so cool down before you write.

7. Proofread and edit carefully. E-mail readers may not expect the same level of editing and page design as they do in print documents. Nevertheless, they prefer a message that is easy to read and free of obvious errors. Use white space, headings, and capitalization to help readers move through the message. Also, edit for grammar and proofread for spelling and other errors.

---

*Legeros defines "emoticons" as "combinations of punctuation symbols that, when viewed sideways, look like little faces. Emoticons help to prevent a message from being misunderstood because they can convey the expression on the sender's face or the inflection in the sender's voice."

**Points 5, 6, and 7 are paraphrased from pages 10–11 of the Legeros article from STC *INTERCOM*.

producing company project sheets, each of which uses one page to describe a specific project completed by McDuff and provides an accompanying graphic on the page. The color insert in this textbook shows seven examples of these project sheets. Write a memo to all 15 branch managers. Give them the information that follows: Beginning next month, project sheets will be written for every McDuff job that grosses $10,000 or more. Your office will have each sheet finished within 30 days of project completion and will then send each office the sheets for projects that were coordinated by that office. Then, as time permits, the public relations office will go back to significant previous projects, like the ones in the color insert, to do additional project sheets on previous work.

19. **Memo—Persuasive Message.** Assume you work at a McDuff office and have no undergraduate degree. You are not yet sure what degree program you want to enter, but you have decided to take one night course each term. Your McDuff office has agreed to pay 100 percent of your college expenses on two conditions. First, before taking each course, you must write a memo of request to your supervisor, justifying the value of the class to your specific job or to your future work with the company. Clearly, your boss wants to know that the course has specific application or that it will form the foundation for later courses. Second, you must receive a *C* or better in every class for which you want reimbursement.

   Write the persuasive memo just described. For the purposes of this assignment, choose one course that you actually have taken or are now taking. Yet in your simulated role for the assignment, write as if you have not taken the course.

20. **E-mail—Collaborative Project #1.** This assignment applies only if your campus offers students the use of electronic mail. Select one of the preceding memo assignments to complete as a group-writing project with two or three members of your class. Set up a plan of work that (1) involves the group in several face-to-face meetings and (2) requires each member of the group to send and receive at least one assignment-related e-mail message to and from every other member of the group.

21. **E-mail—International Communication.** E-mail messages can be sent around the world as easily as they can be sent to the next office. If you end up working for a company with international offices or clients, you probably will use e-mail to conduct business.

   Investigate the e-mail conventions of one or more countries outside your own. Search for any ways the format, content, or style of international e-mail may differ from e-mail in your country. Gather information by collecting hard copy of e-mail messages sent from other countries, interviewing people who use international e-mail, and/or consulting the library for information on international business communication. Write a memo to your instructor in which you (1) note differences you found and (2) explain why these differences exist. If possible, focus on any differences in culture that may affect e-mail transactions.

22. **E-mail—Collaborative Project #2.** Pair up with one or two members of your class. Assume your team has been asked to write a McDuff project sheet to add to the seven sheets in the color insert in chapter 2. Although you do not need to include a photo, hand in a description of what kind of photograph you would recommend for the sheet you are writing.

   After your group has one or two face-to-face meetings to agree on a topic and research agenda, conduct all further team communication by e-mail. One member will be responsible for e-mailing a draft of the project sheet to the others. Then other members will make all comments and suggestions by e-mail. Once the e-mail communication is complete, print and submit the project sheet along with hard copy of all e-mail correspondence within the group.

Mc Duff, Inc.

12 Peachtree Street
Atlanta, GA 30056
(404) 555-7524

August 2, 1996

Professor Willard R. Burton, Ph.D.
Department of Civil Engineering
Southern University of Technology
Paris, GA 30007

Dear Professor Burton:

Expresses appreciation *and* provides lead-in to body.

Thanks very much for your hospitality during my visit to your class yesterday. I appreciated the interest your students showed in my presentation on stress fractures in highway bridges. Their questions were very perceptive.

Responds to question that arose at class presentation.

You may recall that several students requested further information on McDuff, so I have enclosed a dozen brochures for any students who may be interested. As you know, job openings for civil-engineering graduates have increased markedly in the last five years. Some of the best opportunities lie in these three areas of the discipline:

Uses bulleted list to emphasize information of value to professor's students.

• Evaluation of environmental problems
• Renovation of the nation's infrastructure
• Management of construction projects

Adds unobtrusive reference to McDuff's needs.

These areas are three of McDuff's main interests. As a result, we are always searching for top-notch graduates from solid departments like yours.

Closes with offer to visit class again.

Again, I enjoyed my visit back to Southern last Friday, Professor Burton. Please call when you want additional guest lectures by me or other members of the McDuff staff.

Sincerely,

George F. Lux

George F. Lux, P.E.

Includes reference to enclosures.

Enclosures

MODEL 7–1
McDuff sample letter

Mc Duff, Inc.

MEMORANDUM

DATE: December 4, 1996
TO: Technical Staff
FROM: Ralph Simmons, Technical Manager RS
SUBJECT: New Employees to Help with Technical Editing

Uses informative
subject line.

Gives purpose
of memo and
highlights con-
tents.

Uses side head-
ings for easy
reading.

Shows that the
change arose
from *their* con-
cerns.

Adds evidence
from outside
observer.

Gives important
information
about Ron in
first sentence.

Establishes his
credibility.

Refers to attach-
ment.

Focuses on
benefit of
change to
reader. Restates
next action to
occur.

Last week we hired an editor to help you produce top-quality reports, proposals, and other documents. This memorandum gives you some background on this change, highlights the credentials of our new editor, and explains what the change will mean to you.

BACKGROUND

At September's staff meeting, many technical staff members noted the excessive time spent editing and proofreading. For example, some of you said that this final stage of writing takes from 15-30 percent of the billable time on an average report. Most important, editing often ends up being done by project managers—the employees with the highest billable time.

Despite these editing efforts, many errors still show up in documents that go out the door. Last month I asked a professional association, the Engineers Professional Society (EPS), to evaluate McDuff-Boston documents for editorial correctness. (EPS performs this service for members on a confidential basis.) The resulting report showed that our final reports and proposals need considerable editing work. Given your comments at September's meeting and the results of the EPS peer review, I began searching for a solution.

SOLUTION: IN-HOUSE EDITOR

To come to grips with this editing problem, the office just hired Ron Perez, an experienced technical editor. He'll start work January 3. For the last six years, Ron has worked as an editor at Jones Technical Services, a Toronto firm that does work similar to ours. Before that he completed a master's degree in technical writing at Sage University in Buffalo.

At next week's staff meeting, we'll discuss the best way to use Ron's skills to help us out. For now, he will be getting to know our work by reviewing recent reports and proposals. Also, the attached list of possible activities can serve as a springboard for our discussion.

CONCLUSION

By working together with Ron, we'll be able to improve the editorial quality of our documents, free up more of your time for technical tasks, and save the client and ourselves some money.

I look forward to meeting with you next week to discuss the best use of Ron's services.

Enclosure
Copy: Ron Perez

MODEL 7–2
McDuff sample letter

continues

POSSIBLE ACTIVITIES FOR IN-HOUSE EDITOR

1. Reviewing reports at all levels of production

2. Helping to coordinate the writing of proposals

3. Preparing a format manual for the word-processing operations and secretaries

4. Preparing a report/proposal guide for the technical staff

5. Teaching luncheon sessions on editing

6. Teaching writing seminars for the technical staff

7. Working with the graphics department to improve the page design of our documents

8. Helping to write and edit public-relations copy for the company

9. Visiting other offices to help produce consistency in the editing of documents throughout the company

MODEL 7–2
continued

Letterhead of your organization

Two or more blank lines (adjust space to center letter on page)

Date of letter

Two or more blank lines (adjust space to center letter on page)

Address of reader

One blank line

Greeting

One blank line

Paragraph: single-spaced (indenting optional)

One blank line

Paragraph: single-spaced (indenting optional)

One blank line

Paragraph: single-spaced (indenting optional)

One blank line

Complimentary close

Three blank lines (for signature)

Typed name and title

One blank line

Typist's initials (optional: Writer's initials before typist's initials)

Computer file # (if applicable)

One blank line (optional)

Enclosure notation

One blank line (optional)

Copy notation

MODEL 7–3
Block style for letters

Letterhead of your organization

Two or more blank lines (adjust space to center letter on page)

Date of letter

Two or more blank lines (adjust space to center letter on page)

Address of reader

One blank line

Greeting

One blank line

Paragraph: single-spaced, with first line indented 5 spaces

One blank line

Paragraph: single-spaced, with first line indented 5 spaces

One blank line

Paragraph: single-spaced, with first line indented 5 spaces

One blank line

Complimentary close

Three blank lines (for signature)

Typed name and title

One blank line

Typist's initials (optional: Writer's initials before typist's initials)

Computer file # (if applicable)

One blank line (optional)

Enclosure notation

One blank line (optional)

Copy notation

MODEL 7–4
Modified block style (with indented paragraphs) for letters

Letterhead of organization

Two or more blank lines (adjust space to center letter on page)

Date of letter

Two or more blank lines (adjust space to center letter on page)

Address of reader

Three blank lines

Short subject line

Three blank lines

Paragraph: single-spaced, no indenting

One blank line

Paragraph: single-spaced, no indenting

One blank line

Paragraph: single-spaced, no indenting

Five blank lines (for signature)

Typed name and title

One blank line (optional)

Typist's initials (optional: Writer's initials before typist's initials)

Computer file # (if applicable)

One blank line (optional)

Enclosure notation

One blank line (optional)

Copy notation

MODEL 7–5
Simplified style for letters

Facsimile reference

One or more blank lines

Date of memo

Reader's name (and position, if appropriate)

Writer's name (and position, if appropriate)

Subject of memo

Paragraph: Single–spaced (optional–first line indented)

One blank line

Paragraph: Single–spaced (optional–first line indented)

One blank line

Paragraph: Single–spaced (optional–first line indented)

One blank line

Typist's initials (optional–writer's initals before typist's initials)

One blank line

Enclosure notation

One blank line

Copy notation

MODEL 7–6
Memo style

Mc Duff, Inc.

12 Post Street
Houston, Texas 77000
(713) 555-9781

July 23, 1996

The Reverend Mr. John C. Davidson
Maxwell Street Church
Canyon Valley, Texas 79195

Dear Reverend Davidson:

Thanks for your letter asking to reschedule the church project from mid-August to another, more convenient time. Yes, we'll be able to do the project on one of two possible dates in September, as explained below.

As you know, McDuff originally planned to fit your foundation investigation between two other projects planned for the Canyon Valley area. In making every effort to lessen church costs, we would be saving money by having a crew already on site in your area—rather than having to charge you mobilization costs to and from Canyon Valley.

As it happens, we have just agreed to perform another large project in the Canyon Valley area beginning on September 18. We would be glad to schedule your project either before or after that job. Specifically, we could be at the church site for our one-day field investigation on either September 17 or September 25, whatever date you prefer.

Please call me by September 2 to let me know your scheduling preference for the project. In the meantime, have a productive and enjoyable conference at the church next month.

Sincerely,

Nancy Slade

Nancy Slade, P.E.
Project Manager

NS/mh
File #34678

Mentions letter that prompted this response. Gives good news *immediately.*

Reminds reader of rationale for original schedule—*cost savings.* Offers two options—both save the church money.

Shows McDuff's flexibility.

Makes clear what should happen next.

MODEL 7–7
Positive letter in block style

Mc Duff, Inc.

12 Post Street
Houston, Texas 77000
(713) 555-1381

July 23, 1996

The Reverend John C. Davidson
Maxwell Street Church
Canyon Valley, Texas 79195

Dear Reverend Davidson:

Thanks for your letter asking to reschedule the foundation project at your church from mid-August to late August, because of the regional conference. I am sure you are proud that Maxwell was chosen as the conference site.

One reason for our original schedule, as you may recall, was to save the travel costs for a project crew going back and forth between Houston and Canyon Valley. Because McDuff has several other jobs in the area, we had planned not to charge you for travel.

We can reschedule the project, as you request, to a more convenient date in late August, but the change will increase project costs from $1,500 to $1,800 to cover travel. At this point, we just don't have any other projects scheduled in your area in late August that would help defray the additional expenses. Given our low profit margin on such jobs, that additional $300 would make the difference between our firm making or losing money on the foundation investigation at your church.

I'll call you next week, Reverend Davidson, to select a new date that would be most suitable. McDuff welcomes its association with the Maxwell Street Church and looks forward to a successful project in late August.

Sincerely,

Nancy Slade

Nancy Slade, P.E.
Project Manager

NS/mh
File #34678

MODEL 7–8
Negative letter in modified block style (with indented paragraphs)

River College

January 4, 1996

Mr. Timothy Fu, Personnel Director
McDuff, Inc.
127 Rainbow Lane
St. Louis, MO 63103

Dear Mr. Fu:

McDuff, Inc., has hired 35 graduates of River College since 1975. To help continue that tradition, we would like to invite you to the college's first Career Fair, to be held February 21, 1996, from 8 a.m. until noon.

Sponsored by the Student Government Association, the Career Fair gives juniors and seniors the opportunity to get to know more about a number of potential employers. We give special attention to organizations, like McDuff, that have already had success in hiring River College graduates. Indeed, we have already had a number of inquiries about whether your firm will be represented at the fair.

Participating in the Career Fair is simple. We will provide you with a booth where one or two McDuff representatives can talk with students that come by to ask about your firm's career opportunities. Feel free to bring along whatever brochures or other written information that would help our students learn more about McDuff's products and services.

I will call you next week, Mr. Fu, to give more details about the fair and offer a specific booth location. We at River College look forward to building on our already strong association with McDuff.

Sincerely,

Faron G. Abdulla

Faron G. Abdullah, President
Student Government Association

Copy: Gene Abrams, Placement Director

56 New Lane
Bolt, Missouri
65101
(314) 555-0272

States purpose clearly.

Describes Career Fair and its importance.

Shows value of event to McDuff.

Gives clear instructions for participating.

States appreciation and indicates what will happen next.

MODEL 7–9
Neutral letter (invitation) in block style

Mc Duff, Inc.

345 Underwood Street
Belforth, California 90706
(713) 555-9781

April 2, 1996

Faraday Supply Company
34 State Street
San Francisco, CA 94987

ORDER FOR FIELD TRANSITS

Yesterday I called Ms. Gayle Nichols to ask what transits you had in current inventory. Having considered what you have in stock, I wish to order those listed below.

Please send us these items:

1. One Jordan #456 Transit, with special field case
2. One Smith-Beasley #101FR, with special field case
3. One Riggins #6NMG, without special field case

Note that we *do* want the special field cases with the Jordan and Smith-Beasley units, but do not want the case with the Riggins unit.

Please sent the units and the bill to my attention. As always, we appreciate doing business with Faraday.

Farah Linkletter

Farah Linkletter
Supply Assistant

gh

MODEL 7–10
Neutral letter (placing order) in simplified style

Mc Duff, Inc.

127 Rainbow Lane
St. Louis, Missouri 63103
(314) 555-8175

August 21, 1996

Mr. James Swartz, Safety Director
Jessup County School System
1111 Clay Street
Smiley, MO 64607

NEW ASBESTOS-ABATEMENT SERVICE NOW AVAILABLE

We enjoyed working with you last year, James, to update your entire fire alarm system.
Given the current concern in the country about another safety issue, asbestos, we wanted you
to know that our staff now does abatement work.

As you know, many of the state's school systems were constructed during years when
asbestos was used as a primary insulator. No one knew then, of course, that the material can
cause illness and even premature death for those who work in buildings where asbestos was
used in construction. Now we know that just a small portion of asbestos produces a major
health hazard.

Fortunately, there's a way to tell whether you have a problem: the asbestos survey. This
procedure, done by our certified asbestos-abatement professionals, results in a report that tells
whether or not your buildings are affected. And if we find asbestos, we can remove it for you.

Jessup showed real foresight in modernizing its alarm system last year, James. Your desire
for a thorough job on that project was matched, as you know, by the approach we take to our
business. Now we'd like to help give you the peace of mind that will come from knowing
that either (1) there is no asbestos problem in your 35 structures or (2) you have removed the
material.

The enclosed brochure outlines our asbestos services. I'll call you in a few days to see
whether McDuff can help you out.

Barbara Feinstein

Barbara H. Feinstein
Certified Industrial Hygienist

BHF/sg

MODEL 7–11
Sales letter in simplified style

Mc Duff, Inc.

MEMORANDUM

DATE: August 1, 1996
TO: Technical Staff
FROM: Gini Preston, Chair, Word-Processing Committee *GP*
SUBJECT: Word-Processing Suggestions

The Word Processing Committee has met for 6 weeks to consider changes in McDuff's Word Processing Center. This memo highlights the recommendations that have been approved by management.

Please note these changes in your daily use of the company's Word Processing Center.

1. **Document status:** Documents will be designated either "rush" or "regular" status, depending on what you request. If at all possible, rush documents will be returned within four hours. Regular documents will be returned within one working day.
2. **Draft stages:** Both users and operators should make every effort to produce no more than three hard-copy drafts of any document. Typically, these would include:

- **First typed draft** (typed from writer's handwritten or cut-and-paste copy)
- **Second typed draft** (produced after user has made editing corrections on first-draft copy)
- **Final typed draft** (produced after user makes final editing changes, after the proofreader makes a pass through the document, and after the operator incorporates final changes into the copy)

3. **New proofreader:** A company proofreader has been hired to improve the quality of our documents. This individual will have an office in the Word Processing Center and will review all documents produced by the word-processing operators.

These changes will all take effect August 15. Your efforts to implement them will help improve the efficiency of the center, the quality of your documents, and the productivity of the company.

Feel free to call me at ext. 567 if you have any questions.

Copy: Rob McDuff

MODEL 7–12
Memorandum: changes in procedures

Mc Duff, Inc.

DATE: May 3, 1996
TO: All Employees of Cleveland Office
FROM: Timothy Fu, Personnel Director TF
SUBJECT: New Cost Containment Measure for Health Care

The next fiscal year will bring several changes in the company's fringe benefit plan. Later this month, you'll receive a complete report on all adjustments to go into effect July 1. For now, this memo will outline one major change in health care. Specifically, McDuff will adopt a cost-containment program called PAC—intended to help you and the company get more health care for the dollar.

WHAT IS PAC AND HOW DOES IT WORK?

Health costs have risen dramatically in the last 10 years. The immediate effect on McDuff has been major increases in insurance premiums. Both you and the company have shared this burden. This year McDuff will fight this inflationary trend by introducing a new cost-containment program called PAC—Pre-Admission Check.

Started by Healthco, our company medical supplier, PAC changes the procedure by which you and your dependents will be recommended for hospitalization. Except in emergencies, you or your physician will need to call the PAC hotline before admission to the hospital. The PAC medical staff will do the following:

1. Review the length of stay recommended by your physician, to make sure it conforms to general practice
2. Request a second opinion if the PAC staff believes that such an opinion is warranted
3. Approve final plans for hospitalization

If your physician recommends that you stay in the hospital beyond the length originally planned, he or she will call PAC for authorization.

WILL PAC AFFECT THE LEVEL OR QUALITY OF HEALTH CARE?

No. PAC will in no way restrict your health care or increase your personal costs. Quite the contrary, it may reduce total costs considerably, leading to a stabilization of the employee contributions to premiums next year. The goal is to make sure physicians give careful scrutiny to the lengths of hospital stays, staying within the norms associated with a particular illness unless there is good reason to do otherwise.

Programs like PAC have worked well for many other firms around the country; there is a track record of lowering costs and working efficiently with physicians and hospitals. Also, you will be glad to know that Healthco has the firm support of its member physicians on this program.

WHAT WILL HAPPEN NEXT?

As mentioned earlier, this change goes into effect with the beginning of the new fiscal year on July 1. Soon you will receive a report about this and other changes in benefits. If you have any questions before that time, please call the Corporate Benefits Department at ext. 678.

MODEL 7–13
Memorandum: changes in benefits

8 Informal Reports

Two McDuff scientists review the draft of a recommendation report that they have written for a client.

*A*lan Murphy, a salesperson for McDuff's St. Paul office, has a full day ahead. Besides having to make some sales calls in the morning, he must complete two short reports back in the office. The first is a short progress report to Brasstown Bearings, a company that recently hired McDuff to train its technical staff in effective sales techniques. (As noted in chapter 2, McDuff works in the field of training as well as in technical areas.) As manager of the project, Alan has overseen the efforts of three McDuff trainers for the last three weeks. According to the contract, he must send a progress report to Brasstown every three weeks during the project. Alan's second report is internal. His boss wants a short report recommending ways that McDuff can pursue more training projects like the Brasstown job.

Like Alan Murphy, you will spend much of your time writing informal reports in your career. Though short and easy to read like letters and memos, informal reports have more substance, are longer, and thus require more organization skills than correspondence. A working definition follows:

> **Informal report:** this document contains about two to five pages of text, not including attachments. It has more substance than a simple letter or memo but less than a formal report. It can be directed to readers either outside or inside your organization. If *outside*, it may be called a letter report. If *inside*, it may be called a memo report. In either case, its purpose can be informative (to clarify or explain) or persuasive (to convince) or both.

This chapter has three sections. The first one shows you when to use informal reports in your career by describing some McDuff cases. The second provides 10 main writing guidelines that apply to both letter and memo reports. The third focuses on specific suggestions for writing five common types of informal reports.

At the end of the chapter are examples with marginal annotations. They will give you specific, real-life applications of the chapter's writing guidelines. As such, the models will help you complete chapter assignments and do actual reports on the job. During your career, you will write many types of informal reports other than those presented here. If you grasp this chapter's principles, however, you can adapt to other formats.

WHEN TO USE INFORMAL REPORTS

As noted in the definition just given, informal reports are clearly distinguished from both formal reports and routine letters and memos. Early in your career, however, you may have trouble deciding exactly where to draw the line. To help you decide, the two sections that follow briefly describe situations in which informal reports would be appropriate at McDuff.

Letter Reports at McDuff

Written to people outside your organization, letter reports use the format of a business letter because of their brevity. Yet they include more detail than a simple business letter. Here are some sample projects at McDuff that would require letter reports:

- **Training recommendation:** McDuff's corporate training staff recommends changes in the training program of a large construction company. Courses that are recommended include technical writing, interpersonal communication, and quality management.
- **Seafloor study:** McDuff's Nairobi staff writes a preliminary report on the stability of the seafloor where an oil rig might be located off the coast of Africa. This preliminary study includes only a survey of information on file about the site. The final report, involving fieldwork, will be longer and more formal.
- **Marketing report:** A marketing specialist at the corporate office completes a study on "New Markets Beyond 2000." The report has been solicited by a professional marketing association to which McDuff belongs.
- **Asbestos project:** McDuff's Houston staff reports to a suburban school board about possible asbestos contamination of an old elementary school. After two days on-site, the crew of two technicians determined that the structure had no asbestos in its walls, plumbing, floors, or storerooms.
- **Environmental study:** McDuff's San Francisco staff reports to the local Sierra Club chapter on possible environmental effects of an entertainment park, proposed for a rural area where eagles often nest. The project involved one site visit, interviews with a biologist, and some brief library research.
- **Equipment design project:** McDuff's equipment-development staff reports to a manufacturer on tentative designs for a computer-controlled device to cut plastic drainage pipe. The project involved several days' drafting work.

As these examples show, letter reports are the best format for projects with a limited scope. Also, this informal format is a good sales strategy when dealing with customers greatly concerned about the cost of your work. When reading letter reports, they realize—consciously or subconsciously—that these documents cost them less money than formal reports. Your use of letter reports for small jobs shows a sensitivity to their budget and may help gain their repeat work. See Model 8–1 on pages 276–277 for a letter report based on a small project at McDuff.

Memo Reports at McDuff

Memo reports are the informal reports that go back and forth among McDuff's own employees. Though in memorandum format, they include more technical detail and are longer than routine memos. These situations at McDuff show the varied contexts of memo reports:

- **Need for testing equipment:** Joan Watson, a lab technician in the Denver office, evaluates a new piece of chemical testing equipment for her department manager, Wes Powell. Powell discusses the report with his manager.
- **Personnel problem:** Werner Hoffman, a field engineer in the Munich office, writes to his project manager, Hans Schulman, about disciplinary problems with a field hand. Hoffman discusses the report with his manager and with the personnel manager.
- **Need for drafting tables:** Susan Gindle, an equipment-development technician in Baltimore, writes a report to the equipment-development manager, Ralph Peak. Gindle recommends the company purchase five drafting tables from Simulon, Inc., as opposed to similar tables from Sonet, Inc. Peak will discuss the report with the company's vice president for research and with the finance officer.
- **Progress in hiring minorities:** Scott Sampson, personnel manager, reports to Lynn Redmond, vice president of human resources, on the company's initial efforts to hire more minorities. Redmond will discuss Sampson's progress report with the company president and with all office managers.
- **Report on training session:** Pamela Martin, a field engineer in St. Louis, reports to her project manager, Mel Baron, on a one-week course she took in Omaha on new techniques for removing asbestos from buildings. Baron circulates the report to his office manager, Ramsey Pitt. Then Pitt sends copies to the manager of every company office, since asbestos projects are becoming common throughout the firm.

These five reports would require enough detail to justify writing memo reports, rather than simple memos. As for audience, each report would go directly to, or at least be discussed with, readers at *high* levels within the company. That means good memo reports can help advance your career. Model 8–2 on pages 278–279 provides an annotated example of a memo report about proposed computer software at McDuff.

GENERAL GUIDELINES FOR INFORMAL REPORTS

The following are 10 guidelines that focus mainly on report format.

■ *Informal Report Guideline 1: Plan Well Before You Write*

Like other chapters in this book, this section emphasizes the importance of the planning process. Complete the Planning Form at the end of the book for each assignment in this chapter, as well as for informal reports you write in your career. Before you begin writing a draft, use the Planning Form to record specific information about these points:

- The document's purpose
- The variety of readers who will receive the document
- The needs and expectations of readers, particularly decision-makers
- An outline of the main points to be covered in the body

■ *Informal Report Guideline 2: Use Letter or Memo Format*

Model 8–1 (pp. 276–277) shows that letter reports follow about the same format as typical business letters (see chapter 7). For example, both are produced on letterhead and both often include the reader's name, the date, and the page number on all pages after the first. Yet the format of letter reports differs from that of letters in these respects:

- The greeting is sometimes left out or replaced by an attention line, especially when your letter report will go to many readers in an organization.
- A report title often comes immediately after the inside address. It identifies the specific project covered in the report. You may have to use several lines because the project title should be described fully, in the same words that the reader would use.
- Spacing between lines might be single, one-and-one-half, or double, depending on the reader's preference.

Model 8–2 (pp. 278–279) shows the typical format for a memo report. Like most memos, it includes "date/to/from/subject" information at the top and has the reader's name, date, and page number on every page after the first. Also, both memos and memo reports have a subject line that should engage interest, give readers their first quick look at your topic, and be both specific and concise—for example, "Fracture Problems with Molds 43-D and 42-G" is preferable to "Problems with Molds."

There are, however, some format differences between memos and memo reports. Memo reports are longer and tend to contain more headings than routine memos. Also, spacing between lines varies from company to company, though one-and-one-half or double spacing is most common.

■ Informal Report Guideline 3: Make Text Visually Appealing

Your letter or memo report must compete with other documents for each reader's attention. Here are three visual devices that help get attention, maintain interest, and highlight important information:

- Bulleted points, for short lists like this one
- Numbered points, for lists that are longer or that include a list of ordered steps
- Frequent use of headings and subheadings

Headings are particularly useful in memo and letter reports. As Models 8–1 and 8–2 (pp. 276–279) show, they give readers much-needed visual breaks. Since informal reports have no table of contents, headings also help readers locate information quickly. (Chapter 4 gives more detail on headings and other features of page design.)

■ Informal Report Guideline 4: Use the ABC Format for Organization

Headings and lists attract attention, but these alone will not keep readers interested. You also need to organize information effectively. Most technical documents, including informal reports, follow what this book calls the ABC format. This approach to organization includes three parts: (1) **A**bstract, (2) **B**ody, and (3) **C**onclusion.

- **Abstract:** Start with a capsule version of the information most needed by decision-makers.
- **Body:** Give details in the body of the report, where technical readers are most likely to linger awhile to examine supporting evidence.
- **Conclusion:** Reserve the end of the report for a description or list of findings, conclusions, or recommendations.

"Abstract," "body," and "conclusion" are only generic terms. They indicate the *types* of information included at the beginning, middle, and end of your reports—*not* necessarily the exact headings you will use. The next three guidelines give details on the ABC format as applied to memo and letter reports.

■ Informal Report Guideline 5: Call the Abstract an Introductory Summary

Abstracts should give readers a summary, the "big picture." This text suggests that in informal reports, you label this overview as "Introductory Summary," a term that gives the reader a good idea of what the section contains. (You do have the option of leaving off a heading label. In this case, your first few paragraphs would contain the introductory summary information, followed by the first body heading of the report.)

In letter reports, the introductory summary comes immediately after the title. In memo reports, it comes after the subject line. Note that informal reports do not require long, drawn-out beginnings; just one or two paragraphs in this first section give readers three essential pieces of information:

1. **Purpose** for the report—why are you writing it?
2. **Scope** statement—what range of information does the report contain?
3. **Summary** of essentials—what main information does the reader most want or need to know?

■ *Informal Report Guideline 6: Put Important Details in the Body*

The body section provides details needed to expand upon the outline presented in the introductory summary. If your report goes to a diverse audience, managers often read the quick overview in the introductory summary and then skip to conclusions and recommendations. Technical readers, on the other hand, may look first to the body section(s), where they expect to find supporting details presented in a logical fashion. In other words, here is your chance to make your case and to explain points thoroughly.

Yet the discussion section is no place to ramble. Details must be organized so well and put forth so logically that the reader feels compelled to read on. Here are three main suggestions for organization:

- **Use headings generously.** Each time you change a major or minor point, consider whether a heading change would help the reader. Informal reports should include at least one heading per page.
- **Precede subheadings with a lead-in passage.** Here you mention the subsections to follow, before you launch into the first subheading. (For example, "This section covers these three phases of the field study: clearing the site, collecting samples, and classifying samples.") This passage does for the entire section exactly what the introductory summary does for the entire report—it sets the scene for what is to come by providing a "road map."
- **Move from general to specific in paragraphs.** Start each paragraph with a topic sentence that includes your main point. Then give supporting details. This approach always keeps your most important information at the beginnings of paragraphs, where readers tend to focus first while reading.

Another important consideration in organizing the report discussion is the way you handle facts versus opinions.

■ *Informal Report Guideline 7: Separate Fact from Opinion*

Some informal reports contain strong points of view. Others contain only subtle statements of opinion, if any. In either case, you must avoid any confusion about what constitutes fact or opinion. The safest approach in the report discussion is to move logically from findings to your conclusions and, finally, to your recommendations. Since these terms are often confused, here are some working definitions:

- **Findings:** Facts you uncover (for example, you observed severe cracks in the foundations of two adjacent homes in a subdivision).
- **Conclusions:** Ideas or beliefs you develop based on your findings (for example, you conclude that foundation cracks occurred because the two homes were built on soft fill, where original soil had been replaced by construction scraps). Opinion is clearly a part of conclusions.
- **Recommendations:** Suggestions or action items based on your conclusions (for example, you recommend that the foundation slab be supported by adding concrete posts below it). Recommendations are almost exclusively made up of opinions.

■ *Informal Report Guideline 8: Focus Attention in Your Conclusion*

Letter and memo reports end with a section labeled "Conclusion," "Closing," "Conclusions," or "Conclusions and Recommendations." Choose the wording that best fits the content of your report. In all cases, this section gives details about your major findings, your conclusions, and, if called for, your recommendations. People often remember best what they read last, so think hard about what you place at the end of a report.

The precise amount of detail in your conclusion depends on which of these two options you choose for your particular report:

Option 1: If your major conclusions or recommendations have already been stated in the discussion, then you only need to restate them briefly to reinforce their importance (see Model 8–2, pp. 278–279).

Option 2: If the discussion leads up to, but has not covered, these conclusions or recommendations, then you may want to give more detail in this final section (see Model 8–1, pp. 276–277).

As in Models 8–1 and 8–2, lists often are mixed with paragraphs in the conclusion. Use such lists if you believe they will help readers remember your main points.

■ *Informal Report Guideline 9: Use Attachments for Less Important Details*

The trend today is to avoid lengthy text in informal reports. Yet technical detail is often needed for support. One solution to this dilemma is to replace as much report text as possible with clearly labeled attachments that could include these items:

- **Tables and figures:** Illustrations in informal reports usually appear in attachments unless it is crucial that one is within the text. Memo and letter reports are so short that attached illustrations are easily accessible.

▪ **Costs:** It is best to list costs on a separate sheet. First, you do not want to bury important financial information within paragraphs. Second, readers often need to circulate cost information, and a separate cost attachment is easy to photo-copy and send.

▪ *Informal Report Guideline 10: Edit Carefully*

Many readers judge you on how well you edit a report. A few spelling errors or some careless punctuation makes you seem unprofessional. Your career and your firm's future can depend on your ability to write final drafts carefully. Chapter 15 and the Handbook at the end of this text give detailed information about editing. For now, remember these basic guidelines:

▪ Keep most sentences short and simple.
▪ Proofread several times for mechanical errors such as misspellings (particularly personal names).
▪ Triple-check all cost figures for accuracy.
▪ Make sure all attachments are included, are mentioned in the text, and are accurate.
▪ Check the format and wording of all headings and subheadings.
▪ Ask a colleague to check over the report.

These 10 guidelines help memo and letter reports accomplish their objectives. Remember—both your supervisors and your clients will judge you as much on communication skills as they do on technical ability. Consider each report to be part of your resume.

SPECIFIC GUIDELINES FOR FIVE INFORMAL REPORTS

Report types vary from company to company. The ones described here are only a sampling of what you will be asked to write on the job. These five types were cho-sen because they are common, they can be written as either memo reports or let-ter reports, and they incorporate the writing patterns described in chapters 5 and 6. If you master these five informal reports, you can probably handle other types that come your way.

The sections that follow include an ABC format for each report being dis-cussed, some brief case studies from McDuff, and report models based on the cases. Remember to consult chapters 5 and 6 if you need to review general patterns of organization used in short and long reports, such as cause-effect and technical description.

Problem Analyses

Every organization faces both routine and complex problems. The routine ones often get handled without much paperwork; they are discussed and then solved.

But other problems often need to be described in reports, particularly if they involve many people, are difficult to solve, or have been brewing for a long time. Use this working definition of a report that analyzes a problem:

> **Problem analysis:** this informal report presents readers with a detailed description of problems in areas such as personnel, equipment, products, services, and so forth. Its main goal is to provide *objective* information so that the readers can choose the next step. Any opinions must be well supported by facts.

Problem analyses, which can be either internal or external documents, should follow the pattern of organization described here.

ABC Format for Problem Analyses.   Like other informal reports, problem analyses fit the simple ABC (**A**bstract/**B**ody/**C**onclusion) format recommended throughout this text. The three sections contain some or all of the following information, depending on the specific report. Note that solutions to problems are not mentioned; this chapter deals separately with (1) problem analyses, whose main focus is problems, and (2) recommendation reports, whose main focus is solutions. Of course, be aware that during your career, you will be called on to write reports that combine both types.

ABC Format: Problem Analysis

Abstract

- Purpose of report
- Capsule summary of problems covered in report discussion

Body

- Background on source of problems
- Well-organized description of the problems observed
- Data that support your observations
- Consequences of the problems

Conclusion

- Brief restatement of main problems (unless report is so short that such restatement would seem repetitious)
- Degree of urgency required in handling problems
- Suggested next step

McDuff Case Study for a Problem Analysis.   Model 8–3 on pages 280–281 presents a sample problem analysis that follows this chapter's guidelines. Harold Marshal, a longtime McDuff employee, supervises all technical work aboard the *Seeker II,* a boat that McDuff leases during the summer. Staffed with several technicians and engineers, the boat is used to collect and test soil samples from the ocean floor. Different clients purchase these data, such as oil companies that need to place oil rigs safely and telecommunications companies that need to lay cable.

After a summer on the *Seeker II,* Harold has severe reservations about the safety and technical adequacy of the boat. Yet he knows that his supervisor, Jan Stillwright, will require detailed support of any complaints before she seriously considers negotiating a new boat contract next season. Given this critical audience, Harold focuses on specific problems that affect (1) the safety of the crew, (2) the accuracy of the technical work performed, and (3) the morale of the crew. He believes that this pragmatic approach, rather than an emotional appeal, will best persuade his boss that the problem is serious.

Recommendation Reports

Most problem analyses contain both facts and opinions. You as the writer must make special efforts to separate the two, for this reason: Most readers want the opportunity to draw their *own* conclusions about the problem. Also, support all opinions with facts. This guideline holds true especially with recommendation reports, for they include more personal views than other report types. Use the following working definition for recommendation reports:

> **Recommendation report:** this informal report presents readers with specific suggestions that affect personnel, equipment, procedures, products, services, and so on. Although the report's main purpose is to persuade, every recommendation must be supported by objective data.

Recommendation reports can be either internal or external documents. Both follow the ABC format suggested here.

ABC Format for Recommendation Reports.   Problem analyses and recommendation reports sometimes overlap in content. You may recommend solutions in a problem analysis, just as you may analyze problems in a recommendation report. The ABC format assumes that you want to mention the problem briefly before proceeding to discuss solutions.

ABC Format: Recommendation Report

Abstract

- Purpose of report
- Brief reference to problem to which recommendations respond
- Capsule summary of recommendations covered in report discussion

Body

- Details about problem, if necessary
- Well-organized description of recommendations
- Data that support your recommendations (with reference to attachments, if any)
- Main benefits of recommendations you put forth
- Any possible drawbacks

Conclusion

- Brief restatement of main recommendations (unless report is so short that restatement would seem repetitious)
- The main benefit of recommended change
- Your offer to help with next step

McDuff Case Study for a Recommendation Report.   Model 8–1 (pp. 276–277) shows a typical recommendation report written at McDuff. The reader is a client oil firm about to place an oil rig at an offshore site in the Gulf of Mexico. Given the potential for risk to human life and to the environment, Big Muddy Oil wants to take every precaution. Therefore, it has hired McDuff to determine whether the preferred site is safe.

This example presents an important problem you may face in writing recommendation reports. Occasionally you may be asked to deliver recommendations sooner than you would prefer if you were working under ideal circumstances. In such cases, assume the cautious approach taken by Bartley Hopkins, the McDuff writer of Model 8–1. That is, make sure to state that your report is preliminary and based on incomplete data. This approach is even more important in situations like this case study in which there is risk to human life. Take pains to qualify your recommendations so that they cannot possibly be misunderstood by your audience.

Equipment Evaluations

Every organization uses some kind of equipment, and someone has to help buy, maintain, or replace it. Because companies put so much money into this part of their business, evaluating equipment has become an important activity. Here is a working definition of evaluation reports:

> **Equipment evaluation:** this informal report provides objective data about how equipment has, or has not, functioned. The report may cover topics such as machinery, tools, vehicles, office supplies, computer hardware, and computer software.

Like a problem analysis, an equipment evaluation may just focus on problems. Or like a recommendation report, it may go on to suggest a change in equipment. Whatever its focus, an equipment evaluation *must* provide a well-documented review of the exact manner in which equipment has performed. Follow this ABC format in evaluating equipment.

ABC Format for Equipment Evaluations.   Equipment evaluations that are informal reports should include some or all of the points listed here. Remember that in this type of report, the discussion must include evaluation criteria most important to the *readers*, not you.

ABC Format: Equipment Evaluation

Abstract

- Purpose of report
- Capsule summary of what your report says about the equipment

Body

- Thorough description of the equipment being evaluated
- Well-organized critique, either analyzing the parts of one piece of equipment or contrasting several pieces of similar equipment according to selected criteria
- Additional supporting data, with reference to any attachments

Conclusion

- Brief restatement of major findings, conclusions, or recommendations

---

McDuff Case Study for an Equipment Evaluation.   Like other firms, McDuff relies on word processing for almost all internal and external documents. Model 8–2 (pp. 278–279) contains an evaluation of a new word-processing package used on a trial basis. Melanie Frank, office manager in San Francisco, conducted the trial in her office and wrote the report to the branch manager, Hank Worley. Note that she analyzes each of the software's five main features. Then she ends with a recommendation, much like a recommendation report.

Pay special attention to the tone and argumentative structure of this example. Frank shows restraint in her enthusiasm, knowing that facts will be more convincing than opinions. Indeed, every claim about Best Choice software is supported either by evidence from her trial or by a logical explanation. For example, her praise of the file-management feature is supported by the experience of a field engineer who used the system for three days. And her statement about the well-written user's guide is supported by the few calls made to the Best Choice support center during the trial.

Progress/Periodic Reports

Some short reports are intended to cover activities that occurred during a specific period of time. They can be directed inside or outside your organization and are defined in this way:

> **Progress report:** this informal report provides your manager or client with details about work on a specific project. Often you agree at the beginning of a project to submit a certain number of progress reports at certain intervals.

> **Periodic report:** this informal report, usually directed within your own organization, summarizes your work on diverse tasks over a specific time period. For example, as supervisor of company publications, you may be asked to submit periodic reports each month on McDuff's new brochures, public-relations releases, and product flyers.

Progress and periodic reports contain mostly objective data. Yet both of them, especially progress reports, sometimes may be written in a persuasive manner. (See chapter 5 for techniques of argumentation.) After all, you are trying to put forth the best case for the work you have completed. The next section provides an ABC format for these two report types.

ABC Format for Progress/Periodic Reports. Whether internal or external, progress and periodic reports follow a basic ABC format and contain some or all of these parts:

ABC Format: Progress/Periodic Report

Abstract

- Purpose of report
- Capsule summary of main project(s)
- Main progress to date or since last report

Body

- Description of work completed since last report, organized either by task or by time or by both
- Clear reference to any dead ends that may have taken considerable time but yielded no results
- Explanation of delays or incomplete work
- Description of work remaining on project(s), organized either by task or by time or by both
- Reference to attachments that may contain more specific information

Conclusion

- Brief restatement of work since last reporting period
- Expression of confidence, or concern, about overall work on project(s)
- Indication of your willingness to make any adjustments the reader may want to suggest

McDuff Case Study for a Progress Report. As Model 8–4 on pages 282–283 indicates, Scott Sampson, McDuff's personnel manager, is in the midst of an internal project being conducted for Kerry Camp, vice president of domestic operations. Sampson's goal is to find ways to improve the company's training for technical employees. Having completed two of three phases, he is reporting his progress to Camp. Note that Sampson organizes the body sections by task. This arrangement helps to focus the reader's attention on the two main accomplishments—the successful phone interviews and the potentially useful survey. If, instead, Sampson had completed many smaller tasks, he may have wanted to organize the body of the report by time, not tasks.

Also note that Sampson adopts a persuasive tone at the end of the report. That is, he uses his solid progress as a way to emphasize the importance of the project. In this sense, he is "selling" the project to his "internal customer," Kerry Camp, who ultimately will be in the position to make decisions about the future of technical training at McDuff.

McDuff Case Study for a Periodic Report. Model 8–5 on page 284 shows the rather routine nature of most periodic reports. Here Nancy Fairbanks is simply submitting her usual monthly report. The greatest challenge in such reports is to classify, divide, and label information in such a way that readers can quickly find what they need. Fairbanks selected the kind of substantive headings that help the reader locate information (for example, "Jones Fill Project" and "Performance Reviews").

Lab Reports

College students write lab reports for courses in science, engineering, psychology, and other subjects. Yet this report type also exists in technical organizations such as hospitals, engineering firms, and computer companies. Perhaps more than any other type of informal report, the lab report varies in format from organization to organization (and from instructor to instructor, in the case of college courses). This chapter will present a format to use when no other instructions have been given. A working definition follows:

> **Lab report:** this informal report describes work done in any laboratory—with emphasis on topics such as purpose of the work, procedures, equipment, problems, results, and implications. It may be directed to someone inside or outside your own organization. Also, it may stand on its own or it may become part of a larger report that uses the laboratory work as supporting detail.

The next section shows a typical ABC format for lab reports, with the types of information that might appear in the three main sections.

ABC Format for Lab Reports.   Whether simple or complicated, lab reports usually contain some or all of these parts:

ABC Format: Lab Report

Abstract

- Purpose of report
- Capsule summary of results

Body

- Purpose or hypothesis of lab work
- Equipment needed
- Procedures or methods used in the lab test
- Unusual problems or occurrences
- Results of the test with reference to your expectations (results may appear in conclusion, instead)

Conclusion

- Statement or restatement of main results
- Implications of lab test for further work

McDuff Case Study for a Lab Report.   Model 8–6 on pages 285–286 shows a McDuff lab report that is not part of a larger document. In this case, the client sent McDuff some soils taken from borings made into the earth. McDuff has analyzed the samples in its company laboratory and then drawn some conclusions about the kind of rock from which the samples were taken. The report writer, a geologist named Joseph Rappaport, uses the body of the report to provide background information, lab materials procedures, and problems encountered. Note that the report body uses process analysis, a main pattern of organization covered in chapter 6.

COMMUNICATION CHALLENGE

"A Nonprofit Job: Good Deed or Questionable Ethics?"

It all started with an innocent conversation. Velora Nescon, a project manager at McDuff's Houston branch, had lunch with her old college friend, Sibyl Sanders. As principal of Houston's Downtown Academy, Sibyl talked about her effort to keep the new private academy financially healthy and academically strong. Now she was busy with an expansion. What follows is a description of a problem she faced with the expansion, the help that Velora tried to offer, and some ethical and procedural questions raised by the situation.

A Working Lunch

Houston's Downtown Academy was established as a private elementary and middle school for bright inner-city kids who couldn't afford other private schools. Five years ago, business leaders had donated a renovated building for the new school and had raised money for a scholarship account. Now the academy had a respectable enrollment, a good academic reputation, and excellent morale among faculty and staff. All in all, the future looked good for the school. Recently a benefactor gave the school a piece of land adjacent to its campus, where a recreational area would be built.

In her conversation with Velora, Sibyl noted that although the school had some money to begin construction, the budget would be tight. At this point, Velora reminded her friend that McDuff, Inc., offered some of the technical services the project might require. She added that she could ask her branch manager if McDuff might handle the job just for cost, as its way of contributing to the growth of the school. Velora genuinely wanted to help her friend with this worthwhile venture, but in truth she also saw an opportunity to keep her technical staff busy during a slack period. By the end of lunch Sibyl and Velora had reached tentative agreement on McDuff doing the property study required before the land could be developed. Then back at the office, Velora got her boss to agree to allowing the job to be done for cost.

Velora's Lucky Find

The project involved a soil and environmental study. McDuff was to drill borings to determine what foundations would be needed for small structures in the recreation area. Also, soil samples would be taken from the site to check for contamination. These tasks were routine.

Before sending out her crew, Velora mentioned the project to a colleague, George Lightfoot, who thought he remembered doing some soil borings at the same location a couple years ago. Upon checking his files, George found a report that included two borings paid for by Ace Enterprises, a firm that had considered buying the property. Later Ace backed out of the purchase for reasons unrelated to the report. George loaned Velora the report and suggested she ask Ace for permission to use it, since she was trying to save the Downtown Academy money on the project. Velora thanked George for the report and said she'd call Ace.

Velora wanted to get on this no-profit job right away, while her crew wasn't busy, so she tried all afternoon to contact Ace Enterprises. There was no listing for the firm in Houston, and the McDuff librarian found no address in a quick search of her regional files. Velora assumed the firm had gone out of business, changed names, or left town. That being the case, she decided to move ahead in using information in the report—thus saving the Downtown Academy money for soil borings that would have been done. She assumed that Ace, if it still existed, would not mind contributing information for a nonprofit job like this one.

McDuff's Fieldwork

The next day the McDuff crew gathered soil samples from the surface and from shallow borings dug with a hand auger. Results of the lab tests on the samples showed there was an underground storage tank on the property. It had been used for kerosene, which had leaked into the surrounding soil. Both the tank and the soil would have to be removed.

Again trying to save her friend some money, Velora had the small tank and soil removed by a McDuff subcontractor working nearby later that week. The crew had been working for another McDuff client most of the day. Because that client had to pay for a full day's use of the crew and crane anyway, Velora didn't charge the Downtown Academy for the two hours it took to remove the tank and soil.

Questions and Comments for Discussion

Within a week, Velora handed Sibyl a complete report showing her fieldwork, lab tests, and conclusions. Sibyl was overjoyed that the study had come in even under the zero-profit budget she and Velora had first discussed. In thanking Velora, she assured her that McDuff would be a serious contender for the *profit* contracts that the Downtown Academy was sure to have in the future.

1. Do you think there are any ethical problems raised by this case study? If so, what are they and how would you have dealt with them? If not, explain your views.
2. Specifically, how do Sibyl's and Velora's actions either satisfy or violate the Equal Consideration of Interests principle described in chapter 2 of this text?
3. Putting aside the ethical issue, do you think Velora followed wise procedures in her handling of the Downtown Academy project? Why or why not?

CHAPTER SUMMARY

This chapter deals exclusively with the short, informal reports you will write throughout your career. On the job, you will write them for readers inside your organization (as **memo reports**) and outside your organization (as **letter reports**). In both cases, follow these 10 basic guidelines:

1. Plan well before you write.
2. Use letter or memo format.
3. Make text visually appealing.
4. Use the ABC format for organizing information.
5. Start with an introductory summary.
6. Put detailed support in the body.
7. Separate fact from opinion.
8. Focus attention in your conclusion.
9. Use attachments for details.
10. Edit carefully.

Although letter and memo reports come in many varieties, this chapter conveys only five common types: problem analyses, recommendation reports, equipment evaluations, progress/periodic reports, and lab reports. Each follows its own type of three-part ABC format for organizing information.

ASSIGNMENTS

This chapter includes both short and long assignments. The short assignments in Part 1 are designed to be used for in-class exercises and short homework assignments. The assignments in Part 2 generally require more time to complete.

Part 1: Short Assignments

1. **Problem Analysis—Critiquing a Report** Using the guidelines in this chapter, analyze the level of effectiveness of the following McDuff problem analysis.

April 16, 1996

Mr. Jay Henderson
Christ Church
10 Smith Dr.
Jar, Georgia 30060

PROBLEM ANALYSIS
NEW CHURCH BUILDING SITE

Introductory Summary

Last week your church hired our firm to study problems caused by the recent incorporation of the church's new building site into the city limits. Having reviewed the city's planning and zoning requirements, we have found some problems with your original site design—which initially was designed to meet the county's requirements only. My report focuses on problems with four areas on the site:

1. Landscaping screen
2. Church sign
3. Detention pond
4. Fire truck access

Attached to this report is a site plan to illustrate these problems as you review the report. The plan was drawn from an aerial viewpoint.

Landscaping Screen

The city zoning code requires a landscaping screen along the west property line, as shown on the attached site illustration sheet. The former design does not call for a screen in this area. The screen will act as a natural barrier between the church parking lot and the private residence adjoining the church property. The code requires that the trees for this screen be a minimum height of 8 feet with a height maturity level of at least 20 feet. The trees should be an aesthetically pleasing barrier for all parties, including the resident on the adjoining property.

Church Sign

After the site was incorporated into the city, the Department of Transportation decided to widen Woodstock Road and increase the setback to 50 feet, as illustrated on our site plan. With this change, the original location of the sign fell into the road setback. Its new location must be out of the setback and moved closer to the new church building.

Detention Pond

The city's civil engineers reviewed the original site drawing and found that the detention pond was too small. If the detention pond is not increased, rainwater may build up and overflow into the building, causing a considerable amount of flood damage to property in the building and to the building itself. There is a sufficient amount of land in the rear of the site to enlarge and deepen the pond to handle all expected rainfall.

Fire Truck Access

On the original site plan, the slope of the ground along the back side of the new building is so steep that a city fire truck would not be able to gain access to the rear of the building in the event of a fire. This area is shown on our site illustration around the north and east sides of the building. The zoning office enforces a code that is required by the fire marshal's office. This code states that all buildings within the city limits must provide a flat and unobstructed access path around the buildings. If the access is not provided, the safety of the church building and its members would be in jeopardy.

Conclusion

The just-stated problems are significant, yet they can be solved with minimal additional cost to the church. Once the problems are remedied and documented, the revised site plan must be approved by the zoning board before a building permit can be issued to the contractor.

I look forward to meeting with you and the church building committee next week to discuss any features of this study and its ramifications.

Sincerely,

Thomas K. Jones
Senior Landscape Engineer

Enclosure

---

2. **Problem Analysis—Group Project.** Divide into three- or four-person teams, as your instructor directs. In your group, share information about any problems that team members have encountered with services or facilities at the college or university you attend. Then select a problem substantive enough to be described in a short report. As a group, write a problem analysis in the format put forth in this chapter. Assume that your group represents a McDuff technical team that has been hired to investigate, and then write a series of reports on, problems at the school. Your report is one in the series. Select as your audience the appropriate administrators at the college or university.

3. **Recommendation Report—Critiquing a Report.** Using the guidelines in this chapter, analyze the level of effectiveness of the following McDuff recommendation report.

April 20, 1996

Kenman Aircraft Company
76 Jonesboro Road
Sinman, Colorado 87885

Attention: Mr. Ben Randall, Facilities Manager

EMERGENCY EXIT STUDY

Introductory Summary

As you requested, I have just completed a study of the emergency exits in your accounting office at the plant. My study indicates that you have two main problems: (1) easier access to exits is needed and (2) more exit signs and better visibility of these signs are needed. This report contains recommendations for rearranging the floor plan and improving signage.

Problems with Current Floor Plan

Two main problems cause the accounting office to fail to meet the county's guidelines for access to fire exits. First, the file cabinets on the north wall of the office are partially blocking the Reynolds Lane exit. Second, the office photocopier partially blocks the exit to the east hallway. In the first case, the file cabinets are so heavy that they could not be moved by one person. In the second case, the photocopier could be rolled out of the way only by a very strong individual. Obviously, both situations are unacceptable and violate the current code.

The other problem is signage. The Reynolds Lane exit has an exit sign, but it is not easily seen. The east hallway exit has no sign at all. In addition, the rest of the office lacks any maps that show people the location of the two fire exits.

Recommendations for Solving Exit Problem

Fortunately, the existing problems can be corrected with only minor cost to the company. The following recommendations should be implemented immediately upon your receipt of this report.

1. Move the file cabinets on the north wall to the east wall so that they no longer block the Reynolds Street exit.
2. Relocate the photocopier to the office supply room or the cubicle adjacent to it.
3. Remove the undersized exit sign from the Reynolds Street exit.
4. Purchase and install two county-approved exit signs above the two fire exits.
5. Draw up an emergency plan map and post a copy in every cubicle within the accounting office.

When you implement these recommendations, you will be in accordance with the county's current fire regulations.

Conclusion

I strongly suggest that my recommendations be put into action as soon as possible. By doing so you will greatly reduce the risk to your employees and your associated liability.

If you have any questions or need additional information, please call me at your convenience.

Sincerely,

Howard B. Manwell
Field Engineer

---

4. **Writing a Recommendation Report.** Divide into groups of three or four students, as your instructor directs. Consider your group to be a technical team from McDuff. Assume that the facilities director of your college or university has hired your team to recommend changes that would improve your classroom. Write a group report that includes the recommendations agreed to by your group. For example, you may want to consider structural changes of any kind, additions of equipment, changes in the type and arrangement of seating, and so forth.

5. **Writing an Equipment Evaluation.** Assume you are a supervisor at McDuff's Equipment Development shop, located in Baltimore. The Procurement Office routinely asks you to write evaluations of new pieces of equipment being used in the shop. Such evaluations help the director of procurement, Brenda Seymour, decide on future purchases.

Write a brief memo to Seymour, evaluating the Brakoh cordless drills that your staff began using in the shop about a year ago. The Brakoh brand replaced a more expensive brand that the shop had used for the 10 previous years. In the last few months, your technicians have reported that the cheaper models have been falling apart after six or eight months of use. Information coming to you suggests that there are two main problems: (1) a grinding noise can be heard in the housing, resulting in the failure of the chuck (the piece that holds the drill bit) to rotate; and (2) drilling time between rechargings tends to decrease as the drill gets older. You believe that the manufacturer, in order to cut the cost of the drill, has substituted poorly made components in high-wear locations. For example, the gears responsible for turning the chuck are made of plastic. With a little wear, the gears tend to slip, which produces the grinding sound and the rotation failure. As for the recharging problem, the power cell just seems to hold less charge than the previous drill. In summary, the drill has broken down four times faster than the other model, causing many repair bills and a loss in productivity.

In writing your memo, remember that in this case your main job is provide information to the director of procurement, *not* to make recommendations one way or the other. After receiving your memo, she probably will complete a cost analysis to determine if the problems with the cheaper drill outweigh the advantage of the initial cost savings.

Part 2: Longer Assignments—Individual or Group Work

While planning some of these assignments—especially assignment 6—you may need to review information in chapter 2 about McDuff, Inc. Also, for each assignment you should complete a copy of the Planning Form (included at the end of the book). These assignments can be completed as individual or group projects.

6. **Report Based on Color Insert.** The color insert included in this book contains summaries of seven McDuff projects, in various topic areas. These summaries were written for marketing purposes, after the jobs were completed.

   Using the information on one of these sheets, write a brief informal report that summarizes the project for the client. If necessary, add details that are not on the sheet. *Caution:* Remember that marketing sheets may *not* be organized as reports are organized. Consider your purpose and audience carefully before writing.

7. **Report Based on Internet "Surfing."** Use the Internet to collect actual information, and/or a list of sources that may contain information, about a topic that relates to your academic major. Then write an informal equipment evaluation in which you analyze (1) the ease with which the Internet allowed you to collect information on your topic and (2) the quality of the sources or information you received. Your audience is your instructor, who will let you know the degree of knowledge you can assume he or she has on this topic.

8. **Problem Analysis.** Assume you are a McDuff field engineer working at the construction site of a nuclear power plant in Jentsen, Missouri. For the past three weeks, your job has been to observe the construction of a water cooling tower, a large cylindrical structure. As consultants to the plant's construction firm, you and your McDuff crew were hired to make sure that work proceeds properly and on schedule. As the field engineer, you are supposed to report any problems in writing to your project manager, John Raines, back at your St. Louis office. Then he will contact the construction firm's office, if necessary.

Write a short problem analysis in the form of a memo report to Raines. (Follow the guidelines in the "Problem Analyses" section of this chapter.) Take the following randomly organized information and present it in a clear, well-organized fashion. If you wish, add information of your own that might fit the context.

- Three cement pourings for the tower wall were delayed an hour each on April 21 because of light rain.
- Cement-truck drivers need to slow down while driving through the site. Other workers complain about the excessive dust raised by the trucks.
- Mary Powell, a McDuff safety inspector on the crew, has cited 12 workers for not wearing their hard hats.
- You just heard from one subcontractor, Allis Wire, Inc., that there will be a two-day delay in delivering some steel reinforcing wires that go into the concrete walls. That delay will throw off next week's schedule. Last Monday's hard rain and flooding kept everyone home that day.
- It is probably time once again to get all the subcontractors together to discuss safety at the tower site. Recently two field hands had bad cuts from machinery.
- Although there have not been any major thefts at the site, some miscellaneous boards and masonry pieces are missing each day—probably because nearby residents (doing small home projects) think that whatever they find at the site has been discarded. Are additional "No trespassing" signs needed?
- Construction is only two days behind schedule, despite the problems that have occurred.

9. **Problem Analysis.** As a landscape engineer for McDuff, one of your jobs is to examine problems associated with the design of walkways, the location of trees and garden beds, the grading of land around buildings, and any other topographical features. Assume that you have been hired by a specific college, community, or company with which you are familiar. Your objective is to evaluate one or more landscaping problems at the site.

Write an informal report that describes the problem(s) in detail. (Follow the guidelines in the "Problem Analyses" section of this chapter.) Be specific about how the problem affects people—the employees, inhabitants, students, etc. Here are some sample problems that could be evaluated:

- Poorly landscaped entrance to a major subdivision
- Muddy, unpaved walkway between dormitories and academic buildings on a college campus
- Unpaved parking lot far from main campus buildings
- Soil runoff into the streets from several steep, muddy subdivision lots that have not yet been sold
- City tennis courts with poor drainage
- Lack of adequate flowers or bushes around a new office building
- Need for a landscaped common area within a subdivision or campus
- Need to save some large trees that may be doomed because of proposed construction

10. **Recommendation Report.** For this paper, choose a design problem at your college or company. Now put yourself in the position of a McDuff employee hired by your school or company to recommend solutions to the problem.

Your ideas must be in the form of a report that gives one or more recommendations resulting from your study. (Consult writing guidelines in the "Recommendation

Reports" section of this chapter.) Assume that the problem is well enough understood to require only a brief summary, before launching into your recommendations. Because this is a short report, it may not contain many technical details for implementing your recommendations. Also, you need to choose a limited-enough topic so that it can be covered in a short memo report. Here are some sample topics:

- Poor ventilation in an office or a classroom, such as one with sealed windows
- Inadequate space for quick exits during emergencies
- Poor visibility in a large auditorium
- Poor acoustics in a large classroom or training room
- Lack of, or improper placement of, lighting
- Energy inefficiency caused by structural flaws, such as poor insulation or high ceilings
- Rooms or walkways that are not handicap-accessible
- Failure to take advantage of solar heating
- Inefficient heating or air-conditioning systems

11. **Recommendation Report.** This project will require some research. Assume that your college plans either to embark on a major recycling effort or to expand a recycling program that has already started. Put yourself in the role of a McDuff environmental scientist or technician who has been asked to recommend these recycling changes.

    First, do some research about recycling programs that have worked in other organizations. A good place to start would be periodical indexes such as *Readers' Guide to Periodicals* or the *Environment Index,* which will lead you to some magazine articles of interest. Choose to discuss one or more recoverable resources such as paper, aluminum, cardboard, plastic, or glass bottles. Be specific about how your recommendations can be implemented by the organization or audience about which you are writing. (Consult the guidelines in the "Recommendation Reports" section of this chapter.)

12. **Equipment Evaluation.** For six months you have driven a new Ford 150 company truck at remote job sites. As lead field hand for McDuff's Boston office, you have been asked to write an evaluation of the vehicle for Brenda Seymour, director of procurement at the corporate office in Baltimore. Seymour will use your report to decide whether to recommend ordering five more F-150s for other offices. She has told you that you need to discuss only major positive or negative features, not every detail. If she needs more information after reading your report, she will let you know.

    Consider the list below to be your random notes. Use all this information to write a memo report that evaluates the truck. Make sure to follow the guidelines in this chapter.

    - My 150 has been very reliable—it never failed to start, even during subzero ice storms last winter.
    - The 302 engine, Ford's small V-8, has provided plenty of power to handle any hauling I have done. No need to order the more expensive and less fuel-efficient 350 V-8.
    - Have been to 18 job sites with the truck, from marshes in Maine to mountains in New Hampshire. Have put about 12,000 miles on it, on all kinds of roads and in all conditions.
    - Tires that came with the truck did not work well in muddy locations, even with four-wheel drive. Suggest we buy all-terrain tires for future vehicles. Continue to order four-wheel drive—it is necessary at over half our job sites.
    - The short bed (6 ft) did not provide enough hauling room, once I put my toolbox across the truck bed near the back window. Suggest company buy long-bed trucks with the added 2 ft of room.

- Given what I know now, I give the truck a good to excellent rating.
- Automatic transmission worked great. Am told by other owners that the automatic is better than the manual for construction jobs because the manual tends to burn out clutches, especially when the truck needs to be "rocked" back and forth to get out of mud holes. My automatic has taken a lot of abuse without problems.
- Have had some problems with front-end handling on rough roads. Suggest that future trucks be ordered with special handling package, which includes two shock absorbers—not just one—on each front wheel.
- Have had no major repairs, just the regular maintenance checks at the dealer.
- There was one recall from the manufacturer concerning an exhaust pipe hanger that might bend, but the dealer fixed the problem in 20 minutes.
- Really need to have another six months to see how well truck holds up.

13. **Equipment Evaluation.** McDuff, Inc., has decided to make a bulk purchase of 20 typewriters or word processors. (For the purposes of this assignment, choose a typewriter or word processor with which you are familiar.) The machinery will go in a new department being set up in several months.

    Assume that McDuff now uses five different types of machines (again, remember you can choose typewriters or word-processing systems). In the interests of a fair comparison/contrast, Brenda Seymour, director of McDuff's corporate Procurement Department, has asked you and several other employees to evaluate the effectiveness of your own system. Write Seymour a memo report that includes your evaluation. (Consult guidelines in the "Equipment Evaluations" section of this chapter.) She will use the data and opinions in all the equipment evaluations she receives to make her choice for the bulk purchase. Your criteria for evaluation might include topics such as one or more of these:

    - Physical design of the equipment
    - Ease with which system can be learned
    - Quality of the written instructions
    - Frequency and cost of maintenance
    - Availability of appropriate software
    - Length of coverage of warranty
    - Nearness to a service center
    - Reputation of the manufacturer

14. **Progress or Periodic Report.** Assume that you have worked as a field hand at McDuff's Atlanta office for 15 years. Because of your reliability, good judgment, and intelligence, the company is paying for your enrollment at a local college. Also, you get half time off, with pay. Because of its investment in you, McDuff expects you to report periodically on your college work. Choose one of these two options for this assignment:

    Progress report: Select a major project you are now completing in any college course. Following the guidelines in the "Progress/Periodic Reports" section of this chapter, write a progress report on this project. Direct the memo report to the Atlanta office's manager of engineering, Wade Simkins. Sample topics might include a major paper, laboratory experiment, field project, or design studio.

    Periodic report: Assume that McDuff requires that you submit periodic reports on your schooling every few weeks. Following the guidelines in the

"Progress/Periodic Reports" section of this chapter, write a periodic report on your recent course work (completed or ongoing classes or both). Direct the memo report to the manager of engineering, Wade Simkins. Organize the report by class, and then give specific updates on each one.

15. **Lab Report.** For this assignment, you must be taking a lab course now or have taken such a course recently. As in assignment 14, assume you work as a field hand with McDuff's Atlanta office. The company is sponsoring your schooling and has requested that you report on a specific college lab.

Following the guidelines in this chapter's "Lab Reports" section, write a report to Wade Simkins, manager of engineering. The quality of your report may affect whether or not McDuff continues to fund your schooling. Be specific about the goals, procedures, and results of your laboratory—just as you would in an actual college lab report.

16. **Informal Report—International Context.** Investigate features such as style, format, structure, and organization of short reports written in another country. For this assignment, it would be best to interview someone who does business in another country and, if possible, to get an actual report that you can submit. Write a memo report to your instructor that reports on the results of your research.

12 Post Street
Houston, Texas 77000
(713) 555-9781

April 22, 1996

Big Muddy Oil Company, Inc.
12 Rankin St.
Abilene, TX 79224

ATTENTION: Mr. James Smith, Engineering Manager

SHARK PASS STUDY
BLOCK 15, AREA 43-B
GULF OF MEXICO

INTRODUCTORY SUMMARY

You recently asked our firm to complete a preliminary soils investigation at an offshore rig site. This report presents the tentative results of our study, including major conclusions and recommendations. A longer, formal report will follow at the end of the project.

On the basis of what we have learned so far, it is our opinion that you can safely place an oil platform at the Shark Pass site. To limit the chance of a rig leg punching into the seafloor, however, we suggest you follow the recommendations in this report.

WORK AT THE PROJECT SITE

On April 16 and 17, 1996, McDuff's engineers and technicians worked at the Block 15 site in the Shark Pass region of the gulf. Using McDuff's leased drill ship, *Seeker II*, as a base of operations, our crew performed these main tasks:

- Seismic survey of the project study area
- Two soil borings of 40 feet each

Both seismic data and soil samples were brought to our Houston office the next day for laboratory analysis.

LABORATORY ANALYSIS

On April 18 and 19, our lab staff examined the soil samples, completed bearing capacity tests, and evaluated seismic data. Here are the results of that analysis.

Soil Layers

Our initial evaluation of the soil samples reveals a 7-9 ft layer of weak clay starting a few feet below the seafloor. Other than that layer, the composition of the soils seems fairly typical of other sites nearby.

Marginal notes (left column):

Includes specific title.

Uses *optional* heading for abstract part of ABC format.

Draws attention to *main point* of report.

Gives on-site details of project—dates, location, tasks.

Uses *lead-in* to subsections that follow.

Highlights most important point about soil layer—that is the *weak clay*.

MODEL 8–1
Recommendation report (letter format)

Notes *why* this method was chosen (that is, reliability).

Bearing Capacity

We used the most reliable procedure available, the XYZ method, to determine the soil's bearing capacity (that is, its ability to withstand the weight of a loaded oil rig). That method required that we apply the following formula:

Q	=	cNv + tY, where
Q	=	ultimate bearing capacity
c	=	average cohesive shear strength
Nv	=	the dimensionless bearing capacity factor
t	=	footing displacement
Y	=	weight of the soil unit

The final bearing capacity figure will be submitted in the final report, after we repeat the tests.

Explains both *how* the mapping procedure was done and *what results* it produced.

Seafloor Surface

By pulling our underwater seismometer back and forth across the project site, we developed a seismic "map" of the seafloor surface. That map seems typical of the flat floor expected in that area of the gulf. The only exception is the presence of what appears to be a small sunken boat. This wreck, however, is not in the immediate area of the proposed platform site.

Leads off section with major conclusion, for emphasis.

Restates points (made in body) that support conclusion.

CONCLUSIONS AND RECOMMENDATIONS

Based on our analysis, we conclude that there is only a slight risk of instability at the site. Though unlikely, it is possible that a rig leg could punch through the seafloor, either during or after loading. We base this opinion on (1) the existence of the weak clay layer, noted earlier, and (2) the marginal bearing capacity.

Nevertheless, we believe you can still place your platform if you follow careful rig-loading procedures. Specifically, take these precautions to reduce your risk:

Uses list to emphasize recommendations to *reduce risk*.

1. Load the rig in 10-ton increments, waiting one hour between loadings.
2. Allow the rig to stand 24 hours after the loading and before placement of workers on board.
3. Have a soils specialist observe the entire loading process, to assist with any emergency decisions if problems arise.

Again mentions tentative nature of information, to prevent mis-use of report.

As noted at the outset, these conclusions and recommendations are based on preliminary data and analysis. We will complete our final study in three weeks and submit a formal report shortly thereafter.

Maintains control and shows initiative by offering to *call* client.

McDuff, Inc., enjoyed working once again for Big Muddy Oil at its Gulf of Mexico lease holdings. I will phone you this week to see if you have any questions about our study. If you need information before then, please give me a call.

Sincerely,

Bartley Hopkins, Project Manager
McDuff, Inc.

hg

MODEL 8–1
continued

Mc Duff, Inc.

MEMORANDUM

DATE: July 26, 1996
TO: Melanie Frank, Office Manager
FROM: Hank Worley, Project Manager *HW*
SUBJECT: Evaluation of Best Choice Software

INTRODUCTORY SUMMARY

When the office purchased one copy of Best Choice Software last month, you suggested I send you an evaluation after 30 days' use. Having now used Best Choice for a month, I have concluded that it meets all our performance expectations. This memo presents our evaluation of the main features of Best Choice.

HOW BEST CHOICE HAS HELPED US

Best Choice provides five primary features: word processing, file management, spreadsheet, graphics, and a user's guide. Here is my critique of all five.

Word Processing

The system contains an excellent word-processing package that the engineers as well as the secretaries have been able to learn easily. This package can handle both our routine correspondence and the lengthy reports that our group generates. Of particular help is the system's 90,000-word dictionary, which can be updated at any time. The spelling correction feature has already saved much effort that was previously devoted to mechanical editing.

File Management

The file-manager function allows the user to enter information and then to manipulate it quickly. During one three-day site visit, for example, a field engineer recorded a series of problems observed in the field. Then she rearranged the data to highlight specific points I asked her to study, such as I-beam welds and concrete cracks.

Spreadsheet

Like the system's word-processing package, the spreadsheet is efficient and quickly learned. Because Best Choice is a multipurpose software package, spreadsheet data can be incorporated into letter or report format. In other words, spreadsheet information can be merged with our document format to create a final draft for submission to clients or supervisors, with a real savings in time. For example, the memo I sent you last week on budget projections for field equipment took me only an hour to complete; last quarter, the identical project took four hours.

MODEL 8–2
Equipment evaluation (memo format)

Uses optional first heading for abstract section of ABC format. Gives background, main points, and scope statement.

Notes five main points to be covered.

Begins paragraph with most important point. Supports claim with evidence.

Uses specific example to document opinion.

Gives simple explanation of how spreadsheet works.

278

Graphics

The graphics package permits visuals to be drawn from the data contained in the spreadsheet. For example, a pie chart that shows the breakdown of a project budget can be created easily by merging spreadsheet data with the graphics software. With visuals becoming such an important part of reports, we have used this feature of Best Choice quite frequently.

User's Guide

Eight employees in my group have now used the Best Choice user's guide. All have found it well laid out and thorough. Perhaps the best indication of this fact is that in 30 days of daily use, we have placed only three calls to the Best Choice customer-service number.

CONCLUSION

Best Choice seems to contain just the right combination of tools to help us do our job, both in the field and in the office. These are the system's main benefits:

- Versatility—it has diverse functions
- Simplicity—it is easy to master

The people in our group have been very pleased with the package during this 30-day trial. If you like, we would be glad to evaluate Best Choice for a longer period.

Shows relevance of graphics to current work.

Supplies strong supporting statistic.

Wraps up report by restating main points.

Offers follow-up effort.

MODEL 8–2
continued

Mc Duff, Inc.

MEMORANDUM

DATE: October 15, 1996
TO: Jan Stillwright, Vice President of Research and Training
FROM: Harold Marshal, Technical Supervisor HW
SUBJECT: Boat Problems During Summer Season

INTRODUCTORY SUMMARY

We have just completed a one-month project aboard the leased ship, *Seeker II*, in the Pacific Ocean. All work went just about as planned, with very few delays caused by weather or equipment failure.

However, there were some boat problems that need to be solved before we lease *Seeker II* again this season. This report highlights the problems so that they can be brought to the owner's attention. My comments focus on four areas of the boat: drill rig, engineering lab, main engine, and crew quarters.

DRILL RIG

Thus far the rig has operated without incident. Yet on one occasion, I noticed that the elevator for lifting pipe up the derrick swung too close to the derrick itself. A quick gust of wind or a sudden increase in sea height caused these shifts. If the elevator were to hit the derrick, causing the elevator door to open, pipe sections might fall to the deck below.

I believe the whole rig assembly needs to be checked over by someone knowledgeable about its design. Before we put men near that rig again, we need to know that their safety would not be jeopardized by the possibility of falling pipe.

ENGINEERING LAB

Quite frankly, it is a tribute to our technicians that they were able to complete all lab tests with *Seeker II's* limited facilities. Several weeks into the voyage, these four main problems became apparent:

1. Ceiling leaks
2. Poor water pressure in the cleanup sink
3. Leaks around the window near the electronics corner
4. Two broken outlet plugs

Although we were able to devise a solution to the window leaks, the other problems stayed with us for the entire trip.

MODEL 8–3
Problem analysis (memo format)

280

Uses *simple language* to describe technical problems.

MAIN ENGINE

On this trip, we had three valve failures on three different cylinder heads. From our experience on other ships, it is very unusual to have one valve fail, let alone three. Fortunately for us, these failures occurred between projects, so we did not lose time on a job. And fortunately for the owner, the broken valve parts did not destroy the engine's expensive turbocharger.

Closes section with opinion that flows from facts presented.

Only an expert will be able to tell whether these engine problems were flukes or if the entire motor needs to be rebuilt. In my opinion, the most prudent course of action is to have the engine checked over carefully before the next voyage.

Gives lead-in to three sections that follow.

CREW QUARTERS

When 15 men live in one room for three months, it is important that basic facilities work. On *Seeker II* we experienced problems with the bedroom, bathroom, and laundry room that caused some tension.

Describes three problem areas in great detail—knowing the owner will want facts to support complaints.

Bedroom

Three of the top bunks had such poor springs that the occupants sank 6 to 12 in. toward the bottom bunks. More important, five of the bunks are not structurally sound enough to keep from swaying in medium to high seas. Finally, most of the locker handles are either broken or about to break.

Bathroom

Poor pressure in three of the commodes made them almost unusable during the last two weeks. Our amateur repairs did not solve the problem, so I think the plumbing leading to the holding tank might be defective.

Laundry Room

We discovered early that the filtering system could not screen the large amount of rust in the old 10,000-gallon tank. Consequently, undergarments and other white clothes turned a yellow-red color and were ruined.

Briefly restates problem, with emphasis on *safety* and *profits*.

CONCLUSION

As noted at the outset, none of these problems kept us from accomplishing the major goals of this voyage. But they did make the trip much more uncomfortable than it had to be. Moreover, in the case of the rig and engine problems, we were fortunate that injuries and downtime did not occur.

Ends with specific recommendation.

I strongly urge that the owner be asked to correct these deficiencies before we consider using *Seeker II* for additional projects this season.

MODEL 8–3
continued

Mc Duff, Inc.

MEMORANDUM

DATE: June 11, 1996
TO: Kerry Camp, Vice President of Domestic Operations
FROM: Scott Sampson, Manager of Personnel *SS*
SUBJECT: Progress Report on Training Project

INTRODUCTORY SUMMARY

Summarizes project, to refresh reader's memory and establish common ground.

On May 21 you asked that I study ways our firm can improve training for technical employees in all domestic offices. We agreed that the project would take about six or seven weeks and involve three phases:

Phase 1: Make phone inquiries to competing firms
Phase 2: Send a survey to our technical people
Phase 3: Interview a cross section of our technical employees

Gives *overview* of report.

I have now completed Phase 1 and part of Phase 2. My observation thus far is that the project will offer many new directions to consider for our technical training program.

WORK COMPLETED

Summarizes two main tasks, as lead-in to subsections.

In the first week of the project, I had extensive phone conversations with people at three competing firms about their training programs. Then in the second week, I wrote and sent out a training survey to all technical employees in McDuff's domestic offices.

Phone Interviews

I contacted three firms for whom we have done similar favors in the past: Simkins Consultants, Judd & Associates, and ABG Engineering. Here is a summary of my conversations:

Organizes this section by the companies consulted.

1. Simkins Consultants
   Talked with Harry Roland, training director, on May 23. Harry said that his firm has most success with internal training seminars. Each technical person completes several one- or two-day seminars every year. These courses are conducted by in-house experts or external consultants, depending on the specialty.

Creates parallel form in organization of all three points.

2. Judd & Associates
   Talked with Jan Tyler, manager of engineering, on May 24. Jan said that Judd, like Simkins, depends mostly on internal seminars. But Judd spreads these seminars over one or two weeks, rather than teaching intensive courses in one or two days. Judd also offers short "technical awareness" sessions at the lunch hour every two weeks. In-house technical experts give informal presentations on some aspect of their research or fieldwork.

MODEL 8–4
Progress report (memo format)

3. ABG Engineering

Talked with Newt Mosely, personnel coordinator, on May 27. According to Newt, ABG's training program is much as it was two decades ago. Most technical people at high levels go to one seminar a year, usually sponsored by professional societies or local colleges. Other technical people get little training beyond what is provided on the job. In-house training has not worked well, mainly because of schedule conflicts with engineering jobs.

Internal Survey

After completing the phone interviews noted, I began the survey phase of the project. Last week, I finished writing the survey, had it reproduced, and sent it with cover memo to all 450 technical employees in domestic offices. The deadline for returning it to me is June 17.

WORK PLANNED

With phone interviews finished and the survey mailed, I foresee the following schedule for completing the project:

June 17:	Surveys returned
June 18-21:	Surveys evaluated
June 24-28:	Trips taken to all domestic offices to interview a cross section of technical employees
July 3:	Submission of final project report to you

CONCLUSION

My interviews with competitors gave me a good feel for what technical training might be appropriate for our staff. Now I am hoping for a high-percentage return on the internal survey. That phase will prepare a good foundation for my on-site interviews later this month. I believe this major corporate effort will upgrade our technical training considerably.

I would be glad to hear any suggestions you may have about my work on the rest of the project. For example, please call if you have any particular questions you want asked during the on-site interviews (ext. 348).

Side annotations:

Gives important details about the survey.

Organizes section chronologically, making sure to stay within a six or seven week schedule.

Looks to future tasks.

Emphasizes major benefit, to "sell" the project internally.

Indicates flexibility and encourages response from reader.

MODEL 8–4
continued

Mc Duff, Inc.

MEMORANDUM

DATE: August 2, 1996
TO: Ralph Buzby, Manager of Engineering
FROM: Nancy Fairbanks, Project Manager *NF*
SUBJECT: Activity Report for July 1996

Begins with overview of entire report.

July has been a busy month in our group. Besides starting and finishing many smaller jobs, we completed the Jones Fill project. Also, the John Lewis Dam borings began just a week ago. Finally, I did some marketing work and several performance reviews.

SMALL PROJECTS

Gives summary of small projects.

Last month, my group completed nine small projects, each with a budget under $20,000 and each lasting only a few days. These jobs were in three main areas:

Uses list to highlight main types.

1. Surveying subdivisions—five jobs
2. Taking samples from toxic sites—two jobs
3. Doing nearby soil borings—two jobs

Indicates reasons for delays.

All nine were completed within budget. Eight of the nine projects were completed on time. The Campbell County survey, however, was delayed for a day because of storms on July 12.

JONES FILL PROJECT

Again, gives *reasons* for delay.

Our written report on this 12-month job was finally submitted to Trunk Engineering, Inc., on July 23. The delay was caused by Trunk's decision to change the scope of the project again. The firm wanted another soil boring, which we completed on July 22.

JONES LEWIS DAM PROJECT

As you know, we had hoped to start work at the dam site last month. However, the client decided to make a lot of design changes that had to be approved by subcontractors. The final approval to start came just last week; thus our first day on site was July 29.

MARKETING

Supports section with *specifics*—for example, the exact number of meetings.

During July, my main marketing effort was to meet with some previous clients, acquainting them with some of our new services. I met with eight different clients at their offices, with two meetings occurring on each of these dates: July 15, 16, 22, and 23. There's a good possibility that several of these meetings will lead to additional waste-management work in the next few months.

PERFORMANCE REVIEWS

As we discussed last month, I fell behind on my staff's performance reviews in June. In July, I completed the three delayed reviews, as well as the four that were due in July. Copies of the paperwork were sent to your office and to the Personnel Department on July 19. This brings us up to date on all performance reviews.

Ralph Buzby
August 2, 1996
Page 2

Lays foundation for *next* meeting.

CONCLUSION

July was a busy month in almost all phases of my job. Because of this pace, I haven't had time to work on the in-house training course you asked me to develop. In fact, I'm concerned that time I devote to that project will take me away from my ongoing client jobs. At our next meeting, perhaps we should brainstorm about some solutions to this problem.

MODEL 8–5
Periodic report (memo format)

Mc Duff, Inc.

105 Halsey Street
Baltimore, Maryland 21212
(301) 555-7588

December 12, 1996

Mr. Andrew Hawkes
Monson Coal Company
2139 Lasiter Dr.
Baltimore, MD 21222

LABORATORY REPORT
BOREHOLE FOSSIL SAMPLES
BRAINTREE CREEK SITE, WEST VIRGINIA

INTRODUCTORY SUMMARY

Last week you sent us six fossilized samples from the Braintree Creek site. Having analyzed the samples in our lab, we believe they suggest the presence of coal-bearing rock. As you requested, this report will give a summary of the materials and procedures we used in this project, along with any problems we had.

As you know, our methodology in this kind of job is to identify microfossils in the samples, estimate the age of the rock by when the microfossils existed, and then make assumptions about whether the surrounding rock might contain coal.

LAB MATERIALS

Our lab analysis relies on only one piece of specialized equipment: a Piketon electron microscope. Besides the Piketon, we use a simple 400-power manual microscope. Other equipment is similar to that included in any basic geology lab, such as filtering screens and burners.

LAB PROCEDURE

Once we receive a sample, we first try to identify the exact kinds of microfossils that the rocks contain. Our specific lab procedure for your samples consisted of these two steps:

Step 1

We used a 400-power microscope to visually classify the microfossils that were present. Upon inspection of the samples, we concluded that there were two main types of microfossils: nannoplankton and foraminifera.

Gives *overview* of results.

Outlines *procedure* to be detailed in following paragraph.

Describes main equipment, in layperson's language.

Breaks down procedure into easy-to-read "chunks."

MODEL 8–6
Lab report (letter format)

continues

Step 2

Next, we had to extract the microfossils from the core samples you provided. We used two different techniques:

Nannoplankton Extraction Technique

a. Selected a pebble-size piece of the sample
b. Thoroughly crushed the piece under water
c. Used a dropper to remove some of the material that floats to the surface (it contains the nannoplankton)
d. Dried the nannoplankton-water combination
e. Placed the nannoplankton on a slide

Foraminifera Extraction Technique

a. Boiled a small portion of the sample
b. Used a microscreen to remove clay and other unwanted material
c. Dried remaining material (foraminifera)
d. Placed foraminifera on slide

PROBLEMS ENCOUNTERED

The entire lab procedure went as planned. The only problem was minor and occurred when we removed one of the samples from the container in which it was shipped. As the bag was taken from the shipping box, it broke open. The sample shattered when it fell onto the lab table. Fortunately, we had an extra sample from the same location.

CONCLUSION

Judging by the types of fossils present in the sample, they come from rock of an age that might contain coal. This conclusion is based on limited testing, so we suggest you test more samples at the site. We would be glad to help you with this additional sampling and testing.

I will call you this week to discuss our study and any possible follow-up you may wish us to do.

Sincerely,

Joseph Rappaport

Joseph Rappaport
Senior Geologist

Provides smooth transitions.

Itemizes steps because of their importance in procedure.

Uses *parallel form* in describing this process.

Does not bury sampling error— gives it proper treatment.

Ends with wrap-up that reinforces main point of report.

Offers follow-up services.

MODEL 8–6
continued

286

9 Formal Reports

An excellent formal report reflects well on you, the writer, and on your organization.

*T*oby West, McDuff's director of marketing, was given an interesting assignment two months ago. Rob McDuff asked him to take a long, hard look at the company's clients. Are they satisfied with the service they received? Do they routinely reward McDuff with additional work? Are there any features of the company, its employees, or its services that frustrate them? What do they want to see changed? In other words, Toby West was asked to step back from daily events and evaluate the company's level of service. He attacked the project in four stages:

1. He designed and sent out a survey to all recent and current clients.
2. He followed up on some of the returned surveys with phone and personal interviews.
3. He evaluated the data he collected.
4. He wrote a *formal report* on the results of his study. Besides going to all corporate and branch managers, West's report later served as a basis for some in-house training sessions called "Quality at McDuff."

Like Toby West, you will write a number of long, formal reports during your career. Most will be written collaboratively with colleagues; others will be just your creations. All of them will require major efforts at planning, organizing, drafting, and revising. Though informal reports are the most common report in business writing, formal reports become a larger part of your writing as you move along in your career. This text uses the following working definition:

> **Formal report:** this report covers complex projects and is directed to readers at different technical levels. Although not defined by length, a formal report usually contains at least 6 to 10 pages of text, not including appendices. It can be directed to readers either inside or outside your organization. Often bound, it usually includes these separate parts: cover/title page, letter/memo of transmittal, table of contents, list of illustrations, executive summary, introduction, discussion sections, and conclusions and recommendations. (Appendices often appear after the report text.)

To prepare you to write excellent formal reports, this chapter includes three main sections. The first section briefly describes four situations that would require formal reports—two are in-house (to readers *within* McDuff) and two are external (to readers *outside* McDuff). The second section provides guidelines for writing the main parts of a long report. The third section includes a complete long report from McDuff that follows this chapter's guidelines.

WHEN TO USE FORMAL REPORTS

Like most people, you probably associate formal reports with important projects. What else would justify all that time and effort? In comparison to informal reports, formal reports usually (1) cover more complicated projects and (2) are longer than their informal counterparts.

While complexity of subject matter and length are the main differences between formal and informal reports, sometimes there is another distinction. Formal reports may have a more diverse set of readers. In this case, readers who want just a quick overview can turn to the executive summary at the beginning or the conclusions and recommendations at the end. Technical readers who want to check your facts and figures can turn to discussion sections or appendices. And all readers can flip to the table of contents for a quick outline of what sections the report contains. You need to think about the needs of all these readers as you plan and write your formal reports.

The intended audience for formal reports can be inside or outside, though the latter is more common in formal reports. Here are four situations at McDuff for which formal reports would be appropriate:

- **Salary study and recommendations (internal):** Mary Kennelworth, a supervisor at McDuff's San Francisco office, has just completed a study of technicians' salaries among McDuff's competitors on the West Coast. What prompted the study was the problem she has had hiring technicians to assist environmental engineers and geologists. Lately some top applicants have been choosing other firms. Because the salary scales of her office are set by McDuff's corporate headquarters, she wants to give the main office some data showing that San Francisco starting salaries should be higher. Mary decides to submit a formal report, complete with data and recommendations for adjustments. Her main audience includes the branch manager and the vice president of human resources (the company's top decision-maker about salaries and other personnel matters).

- **Analysis of marketing problems (internal):** For several years, Jim Springer, engineering manager at McDuff's Houston office, has watched profits decline in onshore soils work. (In this type of work, engineers and technicians investigate the geological and surface features of a construction site and then recommend foundation designs and construction practices.) One problem has been the "soft" construction market in parts of Texas. But the slump in work has continued despite the recent surge in construction. In other words, some other company is getting the work. Jim and his staff have analyzed past marketing errors, with a view toward developing a new strategy for gaining new clients and winning back old ones. He plans to present the problem analysis and preliminary suggestions in a formal report. The main readers will be his manager, the corporate marketing manager in Baltimore, and managers at other domestic offices who have positions that correspond to his.

- **Waste-management survey (external):** For the last several years, the city of Belton, Georgia, has noticed increased fish kills on the Channel River, which flows through the city and serves as the city's main source of drinking water. Pollution has always been fairly well monitored on the river, so city officials are puzzled by the kills. McDuff's Atlanta office was hired to analyze the problem and present its opinion about the cause. A team of chemists, environmental engineers, and field technicians has just completed a study and will present its formal report. The audience will be quite diverse—from the technical experts in the city's water department to the members of a special citizens' panel representing the residents.

- **Collapse of oil rig (external):** A 10-year-old rig in the North Sea recently collapsed during a mild storm. Several rig workers died, and several million dollars' worth of equipment was lost. Also, the accident created an oil spill that destroyed a significant amount of fish and wildlife before it was finally contained. McDuff's London office was hired to examine the cause of the collapse of this structure, which supposedly was able to withstand hurricanes. After three months of on-site analysis and laboratory work, McDuff's experts are ready to submit their report. It will be read by corporate managers of the firm, agencies of the Norwegian government, and members of several major wildlife organizations. Also, it will be used as the basis for some articles in magazines and newspapers throughout the world.

As these four situations show, formal reports are among the most difficult on-the-job writing assignments you face in your career. You will write some yourself; you will write others as a member of a team of technical and professional people. In all cases, you need to (1) understand your purpose, (2) grasp the needs of your readers, and (3) design a report that responds to these needs. Guidelines in the next two sections will help you meet these goals.

STRATEGY FOR ORGANIZING FORMAL REPORTS

You will encounter different report formats in your career, depending on your profession and your specific employer. Whatever format you choose, however, there is a universal approach to good organization that always applies. This approach is based on these main principles, discussed in detail in chapter 3:

Principle 1: Write different parts for different readers.
Principle 2: Place important information first.
Principle 3: Repeat key points when necessary.

These principles apply to formal reports even more than they do to short documents, for these reasons:

1. A formal report often has a very mixed audience—from laypersons to highly technical specialists to executives.
2. The majority of readers of long reports focus on specific sections that interest them most, reading selectively each time they pick up the report.
3. Few readers have time to wade through a lot of introductory information before reaching the main point. They will get easily frustrated if you do not place important information first.

This chapter responds to these facts about readers of formal reports by following the ABC format (for **A**bstract, **B**ody, **C**onclusion). As noted in chapter 3, the three main rules are that you should (1) start with an abstract for decision-makers, (2) put supporting details in the body, and (3) use the conclusion to produce action. This simple ABC format should be evident in *all* formal reports, despite their complexity. Here is how the particular sections of formal reports fit within the ABC format:

ABC Format: Formal Report

Abstract

- Cover/title page
- Letter or memo of transmittal
- Table of contents
- List of illustrations
- Executive summary
- Introduction

Body

- Discussion sections
- [Appendices—appear after text but support Body section]

Conclusion

- Conclusions
- Recommendations

Several features of this structure deserve special mention. First, note that the generic abstract section includes five different parts of the report that help give readers a capsule version of the entire report. As you will learn shortly, the executive summary is by far the most important section for providing this "big picture" of the report. Second, appendices are placed within the body part of the outline, even though sequentially they come at the end of the report. The reason for this outline placement is that both appendices and body sections provide supporting details for the report. Third, remember that the generic conclusion section in the ABC format can contain conclusions or recommendations or both, depending on the nature of the report.

Before moving to a discussion of the specific sections that make up the ABC format, take note of the use of main headings in complex formal reports. (See Figure 4–7 pp. 110–114.) Much like chapter titles, these headings are often centered, in full caps, in bold type, and oversized. Also, they usually begin a new page. In this way, each major section of the formal report seems to exist on its own. Then you have three remaining heading levels for use within each section.

GUIDELINES FOR THE EIGHT PARTS OF FORMAL REPORTS

What follows is a description of eight parts of the formal report:

1. Cover/title page
2. Letter of transmittal
3. Table of contents
4. List of illustrations
5. Executive summary
6. Introduction
7. Discussion sections
8. Conclusions and recommendations

What could be considered a ninth part, appendices, is mentioned in the context of the discussion section.

Because formal reports can cover such a broad range of material, the guidelines here are rather general. For specific application of these guidelines, see the formal report in Model 9–9 on page 316–331.

Cover/Title Page

Formal reports are normally bound, usually with a cover used for all reports in the writer's organization. (Reports prepared for college courses, however, are often placed in a three-tab folder, the outside of which serves as the report cover.) Since the cover is the first item seen by the reader, it should be attractive and informative. Usually it contains the same four pieces of information mentioned in the following list with regard to the title page; sometimes it may have only one or two of these items.

Inside the cover is the title page, which should include these four pieces of information:

- Project title (exactly as it appears on the letter/memo of transmittal)
- Your client's name ("Prepared for . . .")
- Your name and/or the name of your organization ("Prepared by . . .")
- Date of submission

To make your title page or cover distinctive, you might want to place a simple illustration on it. Do not clutter the page, of course. Use a visual only if it reinforces a main point and if it can be simply and tastefully done. For example, assume that McDuff, Inc., has submitted a formal report to a coastal city in California, concluding that an industrial park can be built near the city's bird sanctuary without harming the habitat—if stringent guidelines are followed. The report writer decides to place the picture of a nesting bird on the title page, punctuating the report's point about the industrial part, as in Model 9–1 on page 308.

Letter/Memo of Transmittal

Letters or memos of transmittal are like an appetizer—they give the readers a taste of what is ahead. If your formal report is to readers outside your own organization, write a letter of transmittal. If it is to readers inside your organization, write a memo of transmittal. Models 9–2 and 9–3 on pages 309–310 show examples of both. Follow these guidelines for constructing this part of your report:

■ *Transmittal Guideline 1: Place Letter/Memo Immediately after Title Page*

This placement means that the letter/memo is bound with the document, to keep it from becoming separated. Some organizations paper-clip this letter or memo to the front of the report, making it a cover letter or memo. In so doing, however, they risk having it become separated from the report.

■ *Transmittal Guideline 2: Include a Major Point from Report*

Remember that readers are heavily influenced by what they read first in reports. Therefore, take advantage of the position of this section by including a major finding, conclusion, or recommendation from the report—besides supplying necessary transmittal information.

■ *Transmittal Guideline 3: Follow Letter and Memo Conventions*

Like other letters and memos, letters and memos of transmittal should be easy to read, inviting readers into the rest of the report. Keep introductory and concluding paragraphs relatively short—no more than three to five lines each. Also, write in a conversational style free of technical jargon and stuffy phrases such as "per your request" or "enclosed herewith." See the models at the end of chapter 7 for more details concerning letter/memo format. For now, here are some highlights about the mechanics of format:

Letters and Memos

- Use single spacing and ragged-edge copy, even if the rest of the report is doubled-spaced and right-justified.
- Use only one page.

Letters

- Include company project number with the letter date.
- Correctly spell the reader's name.
- Be sure the inside address includes the mailing address to appear on the envelope.
- Use the reader's last name ("Dear Mr. Jamison:") in the salutation or attention line because of the formality of the report—unless your close association with the reader would make it more appropriate to use first names ("Dear Bill:").
- Usually include a project title, as with letter reports. It is treated like a main heading. Use concise wording that matches wording on the title page.
- Use "Sincerely" as your closing.
- Include a line to indicate those who will receive copies of the report ("cc" for carbon copy, "pc" for photocopy, or just "c" or "copy" for copy).

Memos

- Give a clear description of the project in the subject line of the memo, including a project number if there is one.
- Include a distribution list to indicate those who will receive copies.

Table of Contents

Your contents page acts as an outline. Many readers go there right away to grasp the structure of the report, and then return again and again to locate report sections of most interest to them. Guidelines follow for assembling this important component of your report. See Model 9–4 on page 311 for an example.

■ Table of Contents Guideline 1: Make It Very Readable

The table of contents must be pleasing to the eye so that readers can find sections quickly and see their relationship to each other. Be sure to:

- Space items well on the page
- Use indenting to draw attention to subheadings
- Include page numbers for every heading and subheading, unless there are many headings in a relatively short report, in which case you can delete page numbers for all of the lowest-level headings listed in the table of contents

■ Table of Contents Guideline 2: Use the Contents Page to Reveal Report Emphases

Choose the wording of headings and subheadings with care. Be specific yet concise so that each heading listed in the table of contents gives the reader a good indication of what the section contains.

Readers associate the importance of report sections with the number of headings and subheadings listed in the table of contents. If, for example, a discussion section called "Description of the Problem" contains many more heading breakdowns than other sections, you are telling the reader that the section is more important. When possible, it is best to have about the same number of breakdowns for report sections of about the same importance. In short, the table of contents should be balanced.

■ Table of Contents Guideline 3: Consider Leaving Out Low-Level Headings

In very long reports, you may want to unclutter the table of contents by removing low-level headings. As always, the needs of the readers are the most important criterion to use in making this decision. If you think readers need access to all levels of headings on the contents page, keep them there. If you think they would prefer a simple contents page instead of a comprehensive one, delete all the lowest-level headings from the table of contents (see Model 9–5 on page 312 compared to Model 9–4 on page 311).

■ Table of Contents Guideline 4: List Appendices

Appendices include items such as tables of data or descriptions of procedures that are inserted at the end of the report. Typically, they are listed at the end of the table of contents. Often no page numbers are given, since many appendices contain "off-the-shelf" material and are thus individually paged (for example, Appendix A might be paged A-1, A-2, A-3, etc.). Tabs on the edges of pages can help the reader locate these sections.

■ Table of Contents Guideline 5: Use Parallel Form in All Entries

All headings in one section, and sometimes even all headings and subheadings in the report, have parallel grammatical form. Readers find mixed forms distracting. For example, "Subgrade Preparation" and "Fill Placement" are parallel, in that they are both the same type of phrase. However, if you were to switch the wording of the first item to "Preparing the Subgrade" or "How to Prepare the Subgrade," parallel structure would be lost.

■ Table of Contents Guideline 6: Proofread Carefully

The table of contents is one of the last report sections to be assembled; thus it often contains errors. Wrong page numbers and incorrect heading wording are two common mistakes. Another is the failure to show the correct relationship of headings and subheadings. Obviously, errors in the table of contents can confuse the reader and prove embarrassing to the writer. Proofread the section carefully.

List of Illustrations

Illustrations within the body of the report are usually listed on a separate page right after the table of contents. When there are few illustrations, another option is to list them at the bottom of the table of contents page rather than on a separate page. In either case, this list should include the *number, title,* and *page number* of every table and figure within the body of the report. If there are many illustrations, separate the list into tables and figures. See the example in Model 9–6 on page 313. (For more information on illustrations, see chapter 11.)

Executive Summary

No formal report would be complete without an executive summary. This short section provides decision-makers with a capsule version of the report. Consider it a stand-alone section that should be free of technical jargon. See Model 9–7 on page 314 for an example. Follow these basic guidelines in preparing this important section of your formal reports:

■ *Executive Summary Guideline 1: Put It on One Page*

The best reason to hold the summary to one page is that most readers expect and prefer this length. It is a comfort to know that somewhere within a long report there is one page to which one can turn for an easy-to-read overview. Moreover, a one-page length permits easy distribution at meetings. When the executive summary begins to crowd your page, it is acceptable to switch to single spacing if such a change helps keep the summary on one page—even though the rest of the report may be space-and-a-half or double-spaced.

Some extremely long formal reports may require that you write an executive summary of several pages or longer. In this case, you still need to provide the reader with a section that summarizes the report in less than a page. The answer to this dilemma is to write a brief "abstract," which is placed right before the executive summary. Consider the abstract to be a condensed version of the executive summary, directed to the highest-level decision-makers. (See chapter 13 for further discussion of abstracts.)

■ *Executive Summary Guideline 2: Avoid Technical Jargon*

Include only that level of technical language the decision-makers will comprehend. It makes no sense to talk over the heads of the most important readers.

■ *Executive Summary Guideline 3: Include Only Important Conclusions and Recommendations*

The executive summary mentions only major points of the report. An exhaustive list of findings, conclusions, and recommendations can come later at the end of the report. If you have trouble deciding what is most important, put yourself in the position of the readers. What information is most essential for them? If you want to leave them with one, two, or three points about the report, what would these points be? *That* is the information that belongs in the executive summary.

■ Executive Summary Guideline 4: Avoid References to the Report Body

Avoid the tendency to say that the report provides additional information. It is understood that the executive summary is only a generalized account of the report's contents. References to later sections do not provide the busy reader with further understanding.

An exception is those instances when you are discussing issues that involve danger or liability. Here you may need to add qualifiers in your summary—for example, "As noted in this report, further study will be necessary." Such statements protect you and the client in the event the executive summary is removed from the report and used as a separate stand-alone document.

■ Executive Summary Guideline 5: Use Paragraph Format

Whereas lists are often appropriate for body sections of a report, they can give executive summaries a fragmented effect. Instead, the best summaries create unity with a series of fairly short paragraphs that flow together well. Within a paragraph, there can be a short listing of a few points for emphasis (see Model 9–7 on page 314), but the listing should not be the main structural element of the summary.

Occasionally, you may be convinced that the paragraph approach is not desirable. For example, a project may involve a series of isolated topics that would not mesh into unified paragraphs. In this case, use a modified list. Start the summary with a brief introductory paragraph, followed by a numbered list of three to nine points. Each numbered point should include a brief explanation (for example, "3. *Sewer Construction:* We believe that seepage influx can be controlled by. . . . 4. *Geologic Fault Evaluation:* We found no evidence of surficial. . . .").

■ Executive Summary Guideline 6: Write the Executive Summary Last

Only after finishing the report do you have the perspective to write a summary. Approach the task this way. First, sit back and review the report from beginning to end. Then ask yourself, "What would my readers really need to know if they had only a minute or two to read?" The answer to that question becomes the core of your executive summary.

Introduction

View this section as your chance to prepare both technical and nontechnical readers for the discussion ahead. You do not need to summarize the report, for your executive summary has accomplished that goal. Instead, give information on the report's purpose, scope, and format, as well as a project description. Follow these basic guidelines, which are reflected in the Model 9–8 example on page 315:

■ *Introduction Guideline 1: State Your Purpose and Lead-in to Subsections*

The purpose statement for the document should appear immediately after the main introduction heading ("This report presents McDuff's foundation design recommendations for the new Hilltop Building in Franklin, Maine"). Follow it with a sentence that mentions the introduction subdivisions to follow ("This introduction provides a description of the project site and explains the scope of activities we conducted").

■ *Introduction Guideline 2: Include a Project Description*

Here you need to be precise about the project. Depending on the type of project, you may be describing a physical setting, a set of problems that prompted the report study, or some other data. The information may have been provided to you or you may have collected it yourself. Accuracy in this section will help prevent any later misunderstandings between you and the reader. (When the project description would be too long for the introduction, sometimes it is placed in the body of the report.)

■ *Introduction Guideline 3: Include Scope Information*

This section must outline the precise objectives of the study. Include all necessary details, using bulleted or numbered lists when appropriate. Your listing or description should parallel the order of the information presented in the body of the report. Like the project description, this subsection must be accurate in every detail. Careful, thorough writing here can prevent later misunderstanding about the tasks you were hired to perform.

■ *Introduction Guideline 4: Consider Including Information on Report Format*

Often the scope section lists information as it is presented in the report. If this is not the case, end the introduction with a short subsection on the report format. Here you can give readers a brief preview of the main sections that follow. In effect, the section acts as a condensed table of contents and may list the report's major sections and appendices.

Discussion Sections

Discussion sections compose the longest part of formal reports. In general, they are written for the most technically oriented members of your audience. You can focus on facts and opinions, demonstrating the technical expertise that the reader expects from you. General guidelines for writing the report discussion are listed here. For a complete example of the discussion component, see the formal-report example in Model 9–9 on pages 316–331.

■ *Discussion Guideline 1: Move from Facts to Opinions*

As you have learned, the ABC format requires that you start your formal report with a summary of the most important information. That is, you skip right to essential conclusions and recommendations the reader needs and wants to know. Once into the discussion section, however, you back up and adopt a strategy that parallels the stages of the technical project itself. You begin with hard data and move toward conclusions and recommendations (that is, those parts that involve more opinion).

One way to view the discussion is that it should follow the order of a typical technical project, which usually involves these stages:

First, you collect data (samples, interviews, records, etc.).

Second, you subject these data to verification or testing (lab tests or computer analyses, for example).

Third, you analyze all the information, using your professional experience and skills to form conclusions (or convictions based on the data).

Fourth, you develop recommendations that flow directly from the conclusions you have formed.

Thus, the body of your report gives technical readers the same movement from fact toward opinion that you experience during the project itself. There are two reasons for this approach, one ethical and the other practical. First, as a professional, you are obligated to draw clear distinctions between what you have observed and what you have concluded or recommended. Second, your reports will usually be more persuasive if you give readers the chance to draw conclusions for themselves. If you move carefully through the four-stage process just described, readers will be more likely to reach the same conclusions that you have drawn.

■ *Discussion Guideline 2: Use Frequent Headings and Subheadings*

Headings give readers handles by which to grasp the content of your report. They are especially needed in the report body, which presents technical details. Your readers will view headings, collectively, as a sort of outline by which they can make their way easily through the report.

■ *Discussion Guideline 3: Use Listings to Break Up Long Paragraphs*

Long paragraphs full of technical details irritate readers. Use paragraphs for brief explanations, not for descriptions of processes or other details that could be listed.

■ *Discussion Guideline 4: Use Illustrations for Clarification and Persuasion*

A simple table or figure can sometimes be just the right complement to a technical discussion in the text. Incorporate illustrations into the report body to make technical information accessible and easier to digest.

■ *Discussion Guideline 5: Place Excessive Detail in Appendices*

Today's trend is to place cumbersome detail in appendices that are attached to formal reports, rather than weighing down the discussion with this detail. In other words, you give readers access to supporting information without cluttering up the text of the formal report. Of course, you need to refer to appendices in the body of the report and label appendices clearly so that readers can locate them easily.

Tabbed sheets are a good way to make all report sections, including appendices, very accessible to the reader. Consider starting each section with a tabbed sheet so that the reader can "thumb" to it easily.

Conclusions and Recommendations

This final section of the report should give readers a place to turn to for a *comprehensive* description—sometimes in the form of a *listing*—of all conclusions and recommendations. The points may or may not have been mentioned in the body of the report, depending on the length and complexity of the document. Conclusions, on the one hand, are convictions or beliefs based on the findings of your study. Recommendations, on the other hand, are actions you are suggesting based on your conclusions. For example, your conclusion may be that there is a dangerous level of toxic chemicals in a town's water supply. Your recommendation may be that the toxic site near the reservoir should be immediately cleaned.

What distinguishes this last section of the report text from the executive summary is the level of detail and the audience. The conclusions and recommendations section provides an *exhaustive* list of conclusions and recommendations for technical and management readers. The executive summary provides a *selected* list or description of the most important conclusions and recommendations for decision-makers, who may not have technical knowledge.

In other words, view the conclusions and recommendations section as an expanded version of the executive summary. It usually assumes one of these three headings, depending of course on the content:

1. Conclusions
2. Recommendations
3. Conclusions and Recommendations

Another option for reports that contain many conclusions and recommendations is to separate this last section into two sections: (1) Conclusions and (2) Recommendations.

FORMAL REPORT EXAMPLE

Model 9–9 (pp. 316–331) provides a long, formal technical report from McDuff, Inc. It contains the main sections discussed previously, including the list of illustrations. Marginal annotations indicate how the model reflects proper use of this chapter's guidelines for format and organization.

The report results from a study that McDuff completed for the city of Winslow, Georgia. Members of the audience come from both technical and non-technical backgrounds. Some are full-time professionals hired by the city, whereas others are part-time, nonpaid citizens appointed by the mayor to explore environmental problems. The paid professionals include engineers, environmental specialists, accountants, city planners, managers, lawyers, real estate experts, and public-relations specialists. The part-time appointees include citizens who work in a variety of blue-collar and white-collar professions or who are homemakers.

COMMUNICATION CHALLENGE

"The Ethics of Clients Reviewing Report Drafts"

Last week Hank Wallace of McDuff's Kenya office completed the draft of an ocean exploration project for the Republic of Cameroon (see Project #2 on the color insert in chapter 2). As is routine with major reports, Hank showed the client a draft before the final draft was submitted. For the first time in his career, he was asked by the client to make changes he thinks are difficult to justify by project data. What follows is an explanation of why McDuff shares report drafts with some clients, some background on the ocean exploration project, and questions and comments for discussion.

Sharing Drafts with Clients

In McDuff's business, some of the firm's reports must be submitted both to the paying client and to regulatory agencies of the government. This dual audience has created a review procedure common in the industry. Client firms have an opportunity to review a draft and make suggestions before both they and the regulatory agencies are sent final drafts.

For example, a U.S. mining company hired McDuff to examine a Siberian site to determine if gold reserves could be mined without damaging the delicate permafrost surface of the tundra. Because the Russian government regulates development of the region, it received a final copy of the report. But before the final copy was submitted to the government, McDuff shared a draft with engineers and executives from the mining company. These client representatives questioned several technical assumptions McDuff made about the site, but McDuff had adequate justifications for its work. In the end, McDuff made no change in its original draft recommendation—that is, that further study was needed before mining is permitted in the permafrost region.

In another case, however, a client's review of a report on a dam in the Midwest prompted McDuff to adjust its report before submission of the final draft to the state's Department of Natural Resources, which regulates high-hazard dams. The owners of the dam—who paid for the study—convinced McDuff that the report should emphasize the fact that poor installation of a guardrail over the dam created a drainage problem. When heavy rains came, soil washed out an embankment near the dam's spillway. The first draft had failed to mention that the state's transportation group bore some responsibility for the dam's problems.

The Ocean Exploration Report Review

The draft review of the ocean exploration report did not go as smoothly as the two reviews just described. Major differences of opinion were evident between the McDuff project manager and the client, Worldwide Energy, Inc.

As indicated on the project sheet in the chapter 2 color insert, McDuff engineers developed conclusions and recommendations for the Cameroon coastal site. For the most part, they found that the offshore environment where they did the study would be too environmentally sensitive to drill offshore wells or run pipelines. There were two locations where a pipeline might be safely placed, but even in this case some environmental damage was likely. When Worldwide Energy got the draft report, the company asked for a meeting.

At the meeting the following week, McDuff engineers reviewed their findings, conclusions, and recommendations with the client. Ultimately, McDuff managers were asked to change the wording in the report to present a more favorable view of oil exploration at the site because, in the client's opinion, McDuff was being too conservative in its conclusions. If McDuff would just adjust some wording so as not to emphasize what is, after all, only *possible* environmental damage, then the Cameroon government might be provided the support it needs to develop this potentially rich oil field. Cameroon, the client argued, needs oil revenues to improve its economy and assist poor farmers with the transition to a modern economy. McDuff is not being asked to alter the facts—only to adjust the tone of the language.

Back at the office, the McDuff project manager met with the branch manager and later with corporate staff via teleconference. The project manager presented the facts of the project and a summary of the meeting. To all present, it was clear that the relationship with a long-term client was at stake.

Questions and Comments for Discussion

1. How should McDuff, Inc., respond to the client's request?
2. Generally, do you think McDuff's procedure for reviewing report drafts with clients is *ethically* sound? Support your answer.
3. If you answered "yes" to question 2, do you have any suggestions to improve the *procedure* for this client report review? That is, how might the process be adjusted to reduce the potential for misunderstandings and abuse?

4. If you answered "no" to question 2, is there any circumstance in which you would support the review of a report draft by a client before final submission to the client and its regulatory agency?
5. It is often said, in this text and elsewhere, that collaboration is essential in the workplace. Describe the kinds of on-the-job situations wherein you think collaboration between writer and reader would be useful, appropriate, and ethical.

CHAPTER SUMMARY

In your career you will write formal reports for large, complex projects—either inside or outside your organization. In both cases, you will be sending the report to people with different technical backgrounds. This complex audience will respond best to reports that subscribe to the ABC format, for its organizes information so that different readers can read different sections of the report. Although long-report formats vary according to company and profession, most will have these eight basic parts: cover/title page, letter/memo of transmittal, table of contents, list of illustrations, executive summary, introduction, discussion sections, and conclusions and recommendations. Follow the specific guidelines in this chapter for these sections. The annotated model can serve as your reference.

ASSIGNMENTS

Part 1 assignments ask you to evaluate a whole report, to write an individual section, or to evaluate an individual section. Part 2 assignments ask you to write complete formal reports. Remember to submit Planning Forms with the Part 2 assignments.

Part 1: Short Assignments

These assignments can be completed by individuals or by teams. If you are instructed to use teams, first review guidelines in chapter 1 on group writing.

1. **Evaluation—A Formal Report.** Use Model 9–9 on pages 316–331, the complete formal report example in this chapter, for this assignment. The audience for the report is described in the chapter section entitled "Formal Report Example." Although the writer directed the report to a mixed technical and nontechnical audience, some sections clearly are more technical than others.

   - Evaluate the likely audience for each section of the report.
   - Discuss ways that the writer did, or did not, address the needs of specific audience types.
   - Offer suggestions for improving the manner in which the report meets the needs of its intended audience.

2. **Evaluation—A Formal Report.** Locate a formal report written by a private firm or government agency *OR* use a long report provided by your instructor. Determine the degree to which the example follows the guidelines in this chapter. Depending on the instructions given by your teacher, choose between these options:

   - Present your findings orally *or* in writing.
   - Select part of the report *or* all of the report.

3. **Executive Summary.** Choose one of the seven project sheets included in the color insert in chapter 2. Write a brief executive summary for the project. If necessary, provide additional information or transitional wording not included on the sheet, but do not change the nature of the information already provided.

4. **Evaluation—An Introduction.** Review the chapter guidelines for writing an effective introduction to a formal report. Then evaluate the degree to which the following example follows or does not follow the guidelines presented.

INTRODUCTION

McDuff, Inc., has completed a three-week study of the manufacturing and servicing processes at King Radio Company. As requested, we have developed a blueprint for ways in which Computer-Aided Testing (CAT) can be used to improve the company's productivity and quality.

Project Description

M. Dan Mahoney familiarized our project team with the problems that prompted this study of computer-aided testing. According to Mr. Mahoney, the main areas of concern are as follows:

- Too many units on the production line are failing postproduction testing and thus returning to the repair line.
- Production bottlenecks are occurring throughout the plant because of the testing difficulties.
- Technicians in the servicing center are having trouble repairing faulty units because of their complexity.
- Customers' complaints have been increasing, both for new units under warranty and repaired units.

Scope

From May 3–5, 1996, McDuff, Inc., had a three-person team of experts working at the King Radio Company plant. This team interviewed many personnel, observed all the production processes, and acquired data needed to develop recommendations.

Upon returning to the McDuff office, team members met to share their observations and develop the master plan included in this report.

Report Format

This report is largely organized around the two ways that CAT can improve operation at the King Radio plant. Based on the detailed examination of the plant's problems in this regard, the report covers two areas for improvement and ends with a section that lists main conclusions and recommendations. The main report sections are as follows:

- Production and Servicing Problems at King Radio
- CAT and the Manufacturing Process

- CAT and the Servicing Process
- Major Conclusions and Recommendations

The report ends with two appendices. Appendix A offers detailed information on several pieces of equipment we recommend that you purchase. Appendix B provides three recent articles from the journal *CAT Today.* All three deal with the application of CAT to production and service problems similar to those you are experiencing.

Part 2: Longer Assignments

This section contains assignments for writing entire formal reports. Remember to complete the Planning Form for each assignment.

These assignments can be written by individual writers or by group-writing teams. If your instructor has made this a team assignment, review the chapter 1 guidelines on group writing.

5. **Research-Based Formal Report.** Complete the following procedure for writing a research-based report:

- Conduct either a computer-assisted search or a traditional library search on a general topic in a field that interests you. Do some preliminary reading to screen possible specific topics.
- Choose three to five specific topics that would require further research and for which you can locate information.
- Work with your instructor to select the one topic that would best fit this assignment, given your interests and the criteria set forth here.
- Develop a simulated context for the report topic, whereby you select a *purpose* for the report, a specific *audience* to whom it could be addressed (as if it were a "real" report), and a specific *role* for you as a writer.

   For example, assume you have selected "earth-sheltered homes" as your topic. You might be writing a report to the manager of a local design firm on the features and construction techniques of such structures. As a newly hired engineer or designer, you are presenting information so that your manager can decide whether the firm might want to begin building and marketing such homes. This report might present only data, or it could present data and recommendations.
- Write the report according to the format guidelines in this chapter and in consideration of the specific context you have chosen.
- Document your sources appropriately (see chapter 13).

6. **Work-Based Formal Report.** This assignment is based on the work experience that you may have had in the past or that you may be experiencing now.

- Choose 5 or 10 report topics that are based on your current or past work experience. For example, you could choose "warehouse design" if you stock parts, "check-out procedure" if you work behind the counter at a video-rental store, "report-production procedures" if you work as a secretary at an engineering firm, etc. In other words, find a subject that you know about or about which you can find more information, especially through interviews.
- Work with your instructor to select the one topic that holds out the best possibilities for a successful report, on the basis of the criteria given here.

- Develop a context for the report in which you give yourself a *role* in the company where you work(ed). This role should be one in which you would actually write a formal in-house or external report about the topic you have chosen, but the role does not have to be the exact one you had or have. Then select a precise *purpose* for which you might be writing the report and finally a set of *readers* that might read such a report within or outside the organization. Your report can be a presentation of data and conclusions *or* a presentation of data, conclusions, and recommendations.
- Follow the guidelines included in this chapter for format and organization.

7. **School-Based Formal Report.** This assignment can be completed as an individual project or as a group project. As an individual project, it will rely on observations you have made during the time you spent at a high school, college, or university—either the one where you are taking this course or another you attended previously. As a group project, it will rely on either (1) group members from diverse majors using their varied backgrounds to examine a common campus problem, or (2) group members majoring in the same field or working in the same department exploring a problem they have in common.

   Whether you write an individual or a group report, follow this general procedure:

- Assemble a list of 5 or 10 problems that you have observed at your school. These problems might concern (1) the physical campus (as in poor design of parking lots or inadequate lab space), (2) the curriculum (as in the need to update certain courses), (3) extracurricular activities (as in the need for more cultural or athletic events), or (4) difficulties with campus support services (as in red tape during registration).
- Work with your instructor to choose the one topic for which you can find the most information and for which you can develop the context described here.
- Collect information in whatever ways seem useful—for example, site observations, surveys to students, follow-up phone calls, or interviews.
- Submit progress reports at intervals requested by your instructor. (Consult guidelines in the "Progress/Periodic Reports" section of chapter 8.)
- Consider your *role* to be the one that you, in fact, have—a student or a group of students at the school. Then select as your *reader(s)* the school officials who would actually be in charge of solving the problem you have identified. (You may or may not end up sending the report. Follow the advice of your instructor in this matter.) The *purpose* of this report will be to explain, in great detail, all aspects of the problem *and* to form conclusions as to its cause. If it seems appropriate, you may take one further step to suggest recommendations for a solution—*if* your research has taken you this far. In any case, detail and also tact are important criteria.

8. **McDuff-Based Formal Report.** For this assignment you will place yourself into a role of your choosing at McDuff, Inc. Use the following procedure, which may be modified by your instructor:

- Review the section at the beginning of this chapter that lists McDuff cases for formal reports to get a sense of when formal reports are used at companies like McDuff.
- Review the McDuff information in chapter 2, especially with regard to the kinds of jobs people hold at the company and the kinds of projects that are undertaken.
- Choose a specific job that *you* could assume at McDuff—based on your academic background, your work experience, or your career interests.

- Choose a specific project that (a) could conceivably be completed at McDuff by someone in the role you have chosen, (b) would result in a formal report directed either inside or outside the company, and (c) would be addressed to a complex audience at two or three of the levels indicated on the Planning Form at the end of the book.
- Be sure you have access to information that will be used in this simulated report—for example, from work experience, from a term paper or class project in another course, or from your interviews of individuals already in the field. (For this assignment, you may want to talk with a professional, such as a recent graduate in your major.)
- Prepare a copy of the Planning Form at the end of the book for your instructor's approval—*before* proceeding further with the project.
- Complete the formal report, following the guidelines in this chapter.

Oceanside's New Industrial Park

Prepared for: City Council
                           Oceanside, California

Prepared by: McDuff, Inc.
                           San Francisco, California

Date: March 3, 1996

MODEL 9–1
Title page with illustration

Mc Duff, Inc.

12 Post Street
Houston, Texas 77000
(713) 555-9781

Report #82-651

July 19, 1996

Belton Oil Corporation
P.O. Box 301
Huff, Texas 77704

Attention: Mr. Paul A. Jones

GEOTECHNICAL INVESTIGATION
DREDGE DISPOSAL AREA F
BELTON OIL REFINERY
HUFF, TEXAS

This is the second volume of a three-volume report on our geotechnical investigation concerning dredge materials at your Huff refinery. This study was authorized by Term Contract No. 604 and Term Contract Release No. 20-6 dated May 6, 1996.

This report includes our findings and recommendations for Dredge Disposal Area F. Preliminary results were discussed with Mr. Jones on July 16, 1996. We consider the soil conditions at the site suitable for limited dike enlargements. However, we recommend that an embankment test section be constructed and monitored before dike design is finalized.

We appreciate the opportunity to work with you on this project. We look forward to assisting you with the final design and providing materials-testing services.

Sincerely,

George Fursten

George H. Fursten
Geotechnical/Environmental Engineer

GHF/dnn

MODEL 9–2
Letter of transmittal

Mc Duff, Inc.

MEMORANDUM

DATE: March 18, 1996
TO: Lynn Redmond, Vice President of Human Resources
FROM: Abe Andrews, Personnel Assistant   *aa*
SUBJECT: Report on Flextime Pilot Program at Boston Office

As you requested, I have examined the results of the six-month pilot program to introduce flextime to the Boston office. This report presents my data and conclusions about the use of flexible work schedules.

To determine the results of the pilot program, I asked all employees to complete a written survey. Then I followed up by interviewing every fifth person off an alphabetical list of office personnel. Overall, it appears that flextime has met with clear approval by employees at all levels. Productivity has increased and morale has soared. This report uses the survey and interview data to suggest why these results have occurred and where we might go from here.

I enjoyed working on this personnel study because of its potential impact on the way McDuff conducts business. Please give me a call if you would like additional details about the study.

MODEL 9–3
Memo of transmittal

TABLE OF CONTENTS

MODEL 9–4
Table of contents (all subheadings included)

311

TABLE OF CONTENTS

MODEL 9–5
Table of contents (third-level subheadings omitted)

LIST OF ILLUSTRATIONS

MODEL 9–6

List of illustrations—formal report

313

EXECUTIVE SUMMARY

Quarterly monitoring of groundwater showed the presence of nickel in Well M–17 at the Hennessey Electric facility in Jones, Georgia. Nickel was not detected in any other wells on the site. Hennessey then retained McDuff's environmental group to determine the source of the nickel.

The project consisted of four main parts. First, we collected and tested 20 soil samples within a 50-yard radius of the well. Second, we collected groundwater samples from the well itself. Third, we removed the stainless steel well screen and casing and submitted them for metallurgical analysis. Finally, we installed a replacement screen and casing built with teflon.

The findings from this project are as follows:

- The soil samples contained *no* nickel
- We found *significant* corrosion and pitting in the stainless steel screen and casing that we removed.
- We detected *no* nickel in water samples retrieved from the well after replacement of the screen and casing.

Our study concluded that the source of the nickel in the groundwater was corrosion on the stainless steel casing and screen.

MODEL 9–7
Executive summary—formal report

INTRODUCTION

This document examines the need for a McDuff, Inc., <u>Human Resources Manual</u>. Such a manual would apply to all U.S. offices of the firm. As background for your reading of this report, I have included (1) a brief description of the project, (2) the scope of my activities during the study, and (3) an overview of the report format.

Project Description

Three months ago, Rob McDuff met with the senior staff to discuss diverse human resources issues, such as performance appraisals and fringe benefits. After several meetings, the group agreed that the company greatly needed a manual to give guidance to managers and their employees. Shortly thereafter, I was asked to study and then report on three main topics: (1) the points that should be included in a manual, (2) the schedule for completing the document, and (3) the number of employees that should be involved in writing and reviewing policies.

Scope of Activities

This project involved seeking information from many McDuff employees and completing some outside research. Specifically, the project scope involved:

- Sending a survey to employees at every level at every domestic office
- Tabulating the results of the survey
- Interviewing some of the survey respondents
- Completing library research on the topic of human resource manuals
- Developing conclusions and recommendations that were based on the research completed

Report Format

To fulfill the report's purpose of examining the need for a McDuff <u>Human Resources Manual</u>, this report includes these main sections:

Section 1: Research Methods
Section 2: Findings of the Survey and Interviews
Section 3: Findings of the Library Research
Section 4: Conclusions and Recommendations

Appendices at the end of the text contain the survey form, interview questions, sample survey responses, and several journal articles of most use in my research.

MODEL 9–8
Introduction—formal report

STUDY OF WILDWOOD CREEK

WINSLOW GEORGIA

Prepared for:

The City of Winslow

Prepared by:

Christopher S. Rice, Hydro/Environmental Engineer
McDuff, Inc.

November 30, 1996

Uses graphic on title page to reinforce theme of environmental protection.

MODEL 9–9
Formal report

Mc Duff, Inc.

12 Peachtree Street
Atlanta, GA 30056
(404) 555-7524

McDuff Project #96-119
November 30, 1996

Adopt-a-Stream Program
City of Winslow
300 Lawrence Street
Winslow, Georgia 30000

Attention : Ms Elaine Sykes, Director

STUDY OF WILDWOOD CREEK
WINSLOW, GEORGIA

We have completed our seven-month project on the pollution study of Wildwood Creek. This project was authorized on May 18, 1996. We performed the study in accordance with our original proposal No. 14-P72, dated April 24, 1996.

This report mentions all completed tests and discusses the test results. Wildwood Creek scored well on many of the tests, but we are concerned about several problems—such as the level of phosphates in the stream. The few problems we observed during our study have led us to recommend that several additional tests should be completed.

Thank you for the opportunity to complete this project. We look forward to working with you on further tests for Wildwood Creek and other waterways in Winslow.

Sincerely,

Christopher S. Rice, P.E.

Christopher S. Rice, P.E.
Hydro/Environmental Engineer

Margin notes:

Lists project title as it appears on title page.

Gives brief statement of project information.

Provides major point from report.

MODEL 9–9
continued

continues

TABLE OF CONTENTS

Uses white space, indenting, and bold to accent organization of report.

i

MODEL 9–9
continued

318

LIST OF ILLUSTRATIONS

FIGURES

TABLES

Includes illustration titles as they appear in text.

ii

MODEL 9–9
continued

continues

EXECUTIVE SUMMARY

The City of Winslow hired McDuff, Inc., to perform a pollution study of Wildwood Creek. The section of the creek that was studied is a one-mile-long area in Burns Nature Park, from Newell College to U.S. Highway 42. The study lasted seven months.

McDuff completed 13 tests on four different test dates. Wildwood scored fairly well on many of the tests, but there were some problem areas. For example, high levels of phosphates were uncovered in the water. The phosphates were derived either from fertilizer or from animal and plant matter and waste. Also uncovered were small amounts of undesirable water organisms that are tolerant to pollutants and can survive in harsh environments.

McDuff recommends that (1) the tests done in this study be conducted two more times, through spring, 1997, (2) other environmental tests be conducted, as listed in the conclusions and recommendations section, and (3) a voluntary cleanup of the creek be scheduled. With these steps, we can better analyze the environmental integrity of Wildwood Creek.

Summarizes purpose and scope of report.

Describes major findings and conclusions.

Includes main recommendation from report text.

MODEL 9–9
continued

INTRODUCTION

Gives lead-in to Introduction.

McDuff, Inc., has completed a follow-up to a study completed in 1990 by Ware County on the health of Wildwood Creek. This introduction describes the project site, scope of our study, and format for this report.

PROJECT DESCRIPTION

Briefly describes project.

By law, all states must clean up their waterways. The State of Georgia shares this responsibility with its counties. Ware County has certain waterways that are threatened and must be cleaned. Wildwood Creek is one of the more endangered waterways. The portion of the creek that was studied for this report is a one-mile stretch in the Burns Nature Park between Newell College and U.S. Highway 42.

SCOPE OF STUDY

The purpose of this project was to determine whether the health of the creek has changed since the previous study in 1990. Both physical and chemical tests were completed. The nine physical tests were as follows:

Uses bulleted list to emphasize scope of activities.

- Air temperature
- Water temperature
- Water flow
- Water appearance
- Habitat description
- Algae appearance
- Algae location
- Visible litter
- Bug count

The four chemical tests were as follows:

- pH
- Dissolved oxygen (DO)
- Turbidity
- Phosphate

REPORT FORMAT

This report includes three main sections:

Provides "map" of main sections in report.

1. Field Investigation: a complete discussion of all the tests that were performed for the project
2. Test Comparison: charts of the test results and comparisons
3. Conclusions and Recommendations

2

MODEL 9–9
continued

continues

FIELD INVESTIGATION

Wildwood Creek has been cited repeatedly for environmental violations in the pollution of its water. Many factors can generate pollution and affect the overall health of the creek. In 1990, the creek was studied in the context of a study of all water systems in Ware County. Wildwood Creek was determined to be one of the more threatened creeks in the county.

The city needed to learn if much has changed in the past six years, so McDuff was hired to perform a variety of tests on the creek. Our effort involved a more in-depth study than that done in 1990. Tests were conducted four times over a seven-month period. The 1990 study lasted only one day.

The field investigation included two categories of tests: physical tests and chemical tests.

PHYSICAL TESTS

The physical tests covered a broad range of environmental features. This section will discuss the importance of the tests and some major findings. The Test Comparison section on page 8 includes a table that lists results of the tests and the completion dates. The test types were as follows: air temperature, water temperature, water flow, water appearance, habitat description, algae appearance, algae location, visible litter, and bug count.

Air Temperature

The temperature of the air surrounding the creek will affect life in the water. Unusual air temperature for the seasons will determine if life can grow in or out of the water.

Three of the four tests were performed in the warmer months. Only one was completed on a cool day. The difference in temperature from the warmest to coolest day was 10.5°C, an acceptable range.

Water Temperature

The temperature of the water determines which species will be present. Also affected are the feeding, reproduction, and metabolism of these species. If there are one or two weeks of high temperature, the stream is unsuitable for most species. If water temperature changes more than 1° to 2°C in 24 hours, thermal stress and shock can occur, killing much of the life in the creek.

During our study, the temperature of the water averaged 1°C cooler than the temperature of the air. The water temperature did not get above 23°C or below 13°C. These ranges are acceptable by law.

3

Amplifies information presented later in report.

MODEL 9–9
continued

Incorporates
graphic into
page of text.

Water Flow

The flow of the water will influence the type of life in the stream. Periods of high flow can cause erosion to occur on the banks and sediment to cover the streambed. Low water flow can decrease the living space and deplete the oxygen supply.

The flow of water was at the correct level for the times of year the tests were done—except for June, which had a high rainfall. With continual rain and sudden flash floods, the creek was almost too dangerous for the study to be performed that month.

In fact, in June we witnessed the aftermath of one flash flood. Figure 1 shows the creek with an average flow of water, and Figure 2 shows the creek during the flood. The water's average depth is 10 inches. During the flash flood, the water level rose and fell 10 feet in about one hour. Much dirt and debris were washing into the creek, while some small fish were left on dry land as the water receded.

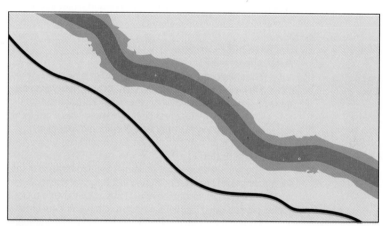

KEY

water
stream bed
running track

FIGURE 1 Wildwood Creek—Normal Water Level

4

MODEL 9–9
continued

continues

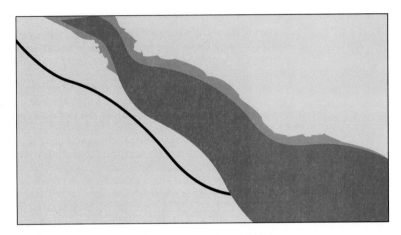

FIGURE 2 Wildwood Creek—Flash Flood Water Level

Elaborates on
importance of
information
shown in Table 1.
Description
parallels five
items in table.

Water Appearance

The color of the water gives a quick but fairly accurate view of the health of the creek. If the water is brown or dirty, then silt or human waste may be present. Black areas of water may contain oil or other chemical products.

On each of the four test days, the water was always clear. Thus the appearance of the creek water was considered excellent.

Habitat Description

The habitat description concerns the appearance of the stream and its surroundings. An important criterion is the number of pools and the number of ripples—that is, points where water flows quickly over a rocky area. Both pools and ripples provide good locations for fish and other stream creatures to live and breed.

In describing habitat, McDuff also evaluates the amount of sediment at the bottom of the stream. Too much sediment tends to cover up areas where aquatic life lays eggs and hides them from predators. We also evaluate the stability of the stream banks; a stable bank indicates that erosion has not damaged the habitat. Finally, we observe the amount of stream cover. Such vegetation helps keep soil in place on the banks.

5

MODEL 9–9
continued

Wildwood Creek tested fairly well for habitat. The number of pools and ripples was about average for such creeks. Stream deposits and stream bank stability were average to good, and stream cover was good to excellent. For more detail about test results, see the chart in the Test Comparison section on page 8.

Algae Appearance and Location

Algae is naturally present in any creek. The amount of algae can be a warning of pollution in the water. If algae is growing out of control, disproportionate amounts of nutrients such as nitrogen or phosphate could be present. These chemicals could come from fertilizer washed into the creek. Excessive amounts of algae cause the oxygen level to drop when they die and decompose.

During the four studies, algae was everywhere, but it was especially heavy on the rocks in the ripples of the creek. The algae was always brown and sometimes hairy.

Visible Litter

Litter can affect the habitat of a creek. While some litter has chemicals that can pollute the water, other litter can cover nesting areas and suffocate small animals. Whether the litter is harmful or not, it is always an eyesore.

Gives specific details that support the report's conclusions and recommendations, which come later.

On all four test dates, the litter we saw was heavy and ranged from tires to plastic bags. Some of the same trash that was at the site on the first visit was still there seven months later.

Bug Count

The bug count is a procedure that begins by washing dirt and water onto a screen. As water drains, the dirt with organisms is left on the screen. The bugs are removed and classified. Generally, the lower the bug count, the higher the pollution levels. Bug counts were considered low to average.

Two types of aquatic worms were discovered every time during our count, but in relatively small amounts. In addition, the worms we observed are very tolerant of pollution and can live in most conditions. Finally, we observed only two crayfish, animals that are somewhat sensitive to pollution.

CHEMICAL TESTS

While physical tests cover areas seen with the naked eye, chemical tests can uncover pollutants that are not so recognizable. Certain chemicals can wipe out all life in a creek. Other chemicals can cause an overabundance of one life-form, which in turn could kill more sensitive animals.

A chart of results of chemical tests is included in the Test Comparison section on page 8. The chemical tests that McDuff performed were pH, dissolved oxygen (DO), turbidity, and phosphate.

6

continues

MODEL 9–9
continued

pH

The pH test is a measure of active hydrogen ions in a sample. The range of the pH test is 0-14. If the sample is in the range of 0-7.0, it is acidic; but if the sample is in the range of 7.0-14, it is basic. By law, the pH of a water sample must be within the range of 6.0 to 8.5.

For the tests we completed, the water sample was always 7.0, which is very good for a creek.

Dissolved Oxygen (DO)

Normally, oxygen dissolves readily into water from surface air. Once dissolved, it diffuses slowly in the water and is distributed throughout the creek. The amount of DO depends on different circumstances. Oxygen is always highest in choppy water, just after noon, and in cooler temperatures.

In many streams, the level of DO can become critically low during the summer months. When the temperature is warm, organisms are highly active and consume the oxygen supply. If the amount of DO drops below 3.0 ppm (parts per million), the area can become stressful for the organisms. An amount of oxygen that is 2.0 ppm or below will not support fish. DO that is 5.0 ppm to 6.0 ppm is usually required for growth and activity of organisms in the water.

According to the Water Quality Criteria for Georgia, average daily amounts of DO should be 5.0 ppm with a minimum of 4.0 ppm. Wildwood Creek scored well on this test. The average amount of DO in the water was 6.9 ppm, with the highest amount being 9.0 ppm on November 11, 1996.

Turbidity

Turbidity is the discoloration of water due to sediment, microscopic organisms, and other matter. One major factor of turbidity is the level of rainfall before a test.

Three of our tests were performed on clear days with little rainfall. On these dates, the turbidity of Wildwood Creek was always 1.0, the best that creek water can score on the test. The fourth test, which scored worse, occurred during a rainy period.

Phosphate

Phosphorus occurs naturally as phosphates—for example, orthophosphates and organically bound phosphates. Orthophosphates are phosphates that are formed in fertilizer, while organically bound phosphates can form in plant and animal matter and waste.

Phosphate levels higher than .03 ppm contribute to an increase in plant growth. If phosphate levels are above 0.1 ppm, plants may be stimulated to grow out of control. The phosphate level of Wildwood was always 0.5 ppm, considerably higher than is desirable.

7

MODEL 9–9
continued

TEST COMPARISON

There was little change from each of the four test dates. The only tests that varied greatly from one test to another were air temperature, water temperature, water flow, and DO. On the basis of these results, it would appear that Wildwood Creek is a relatively stable environment.

Brings together test results for easy reference.

TABLE 1 Physical Tests

TEST DATES	5/26/96	6/25/96	9/24/96	11/19/96
Air Temperature in °C	21.5	23.0	24.0	13.5
Water Temperature in °C	20.0	22.0	23.0	13.0
Water Flow	Normal	High	Normal	Normal
Water Appearance	Clear	Clear	Clear	Clear
Habitat Description				
Number of Pools	2.0	3.0	2.0	5.0
Number of Ripples	1.0	2.0	2.0	2.0
Amount of Sediment Deposit	Average	Average	Good	Average
Stream Bank Stability	Average	Good	Good	Good
Stream Cover	Excellent	Good	Excellent	Good
Algae Appearance	Brown	Brown/hairy	Brown	Brown
Algae Location	Everywhere	Everywhere	Attached	Everywhere
Visible Litter	Heavy	Heavy	Heavy	Heavy
Bug Count	Low	Average	Low	Average

TABLE 2 Chemical Tests

Test	5/26/96	6/25/96	9/24/96	11/19/96
pH	7.0	7.0	7.0	7.0
Dissolved Oxygen (DO)	6.8	6.0	5.6	9.0
Turbidity	1.0	3.0	1.0	1.0
Phosphate	.50	.50	.50	.50

8

continues

MODEL 9–9
continued

CONCLUSIONS AND RECOMMENDATIONS

This section includes the major conclusions and recommendations from our study of Wildwood Creek.

CONCLUSIONS

Draws conclusions that flow from data in body of report.

Generally, we were pleased with the health of the stream bank and its floodplain. The area studied has large amounts of vegetation along the stream, and the banks seem to be sturdy. The floodplain has been turned into a park, which handles floods in a natural way. Floodwater in this area comes in contact with vegetation and some dirt. Floodwater also drains quickly, which keeps sediment from building up in the creek.

Uses paragraph format instead of lists because of lengthy explanations needed.

However, we are concerned with the number and types of animals uncovered in our bug counts. Only two bug types were discovered, and these were types quite tolerant to pollutants. The time of year these tests were performed could affect the discovery of some animals. However, the low count still should be considered a possible warning sign about water quality. Phosphate levels were also high and probably are the cause of the large amount of algae.

We believe something in the water is keeping sensitive animals from developing. One factor that affects the number of animals discovered is the pollutant problems in the past (see Appendix A). The creek may still be in a redevelopment stage, thus explaining the small numbers of animals.

RECOMMENDATIONS

On the basis of these conclusions, we recommend the following actions for Wildwood Creek:

Gives numbered list of recommendations for easy reference.

1. Conduct the current tests two more times, through spring 1997. Spring is the time of year that most aquatic insects are hatched. If sensitive organisms are found then, the health of the creek could be considered to have improved.
2. Add testing for nitrogen. With the phosphate level being so high, nitrogen might also be present. If it is, then fertilizer could be in the water.
3. Add testing for human waste. Some contamination may still be occurring.
4. Add testing for metals, such as mercury, that can pollute the water.
5. Add testing for runoff water from drainage pipes that flow into the creek.
6. Schedule a volunteer cleanup of the creek.

With a full year of study and additional tests, the problems of Wildwood Creek can be better understood.

9

MODEL 9–9
continued

APPENDIX A

Background on Wildwood Creek

Wildwood Creek begins from tributaries on the northeast side of the city of Winslow. From this point, the creek flows southwest to the Chattahoochee River. Winslow Wastewater Treatment Plant has severely polluted the creek in the past with discharge of wastewater directly into the creek. Wildwood became so contaminated that signs warning of excessive pollution were posted along the creek to alert the public.

Today, all known wastewater discharge has been removed. The stream's condition has dramatically improved, but nonpoint contamination sources continue to lower the creek's water quality. Nonpoint contamination includes sewer breaks, chemical dumping, and storm sewers.

Another problem for Wildwood Creek is siltration. Rainfall combines with bank erosion and habitat destruction to wash excess dirt into the creek. This harsh action destroys most of the macroinvertebrates. At the present time, Wildwood Creek may be one of the more threatened creeks in Ware County.

10

continues

MODEL 9–9
continued

APPENDIX B

Water Quality Criteria for Georgia

All waterways in Georgia are classified in one of the following categories: fishing, recreation, drinking, and wild and scenic. Different protection levels apply to the different uses. For example, the protection level for dissolved oxygen is stricter in drinking water than fishing water. All water is supposed to be free from all types of waste and sewage that can settle and form sludge deposits.

In Ware County, all waterways are classified as "fishing," according to Chapter 391-3-6.03 of "Water Use Classifications and Water Quality Standards" in the Georgia Department of Natural Resources *Rules and Regulations for Water Quality Control.* The only exception is the Chattahoochee River, which is classified as "drinking water supply" and "recreational."

11

MODEL 9–9
continued

Proposals: documents written to convince your readers to adopt an idea, a product, or a service. They can be directed to colleagues inside your own organization (*in-house proposals*), to clients outside your organization (*sales proposals*), or to organizations that fund research and other activities (*grant proposals*).

In all three cases, proposals can be presented in either a short, simple format (*informal proposal*) or a longer, more complicated format (*formal proposal*). Also, proposals can be either requested by the reader (*solicited*) or submitted without a request (*unsolicited*).

Feasibility studies: documents written to show the *practicality* of a proposed policy, product, service, or other change within an organization. Often prompted by ideas suggested in a *proposal,* they examine details such as costs, alternatives, and likely effects. Though they must reflect the objectivity of a report, most feasibility studies also try to convince readers either (1) to adopt or reject the one idea discussed or (2) to adopt one of several alternatives presented in the study.

Feasibility studies can be *in-house* (written to decision-makers in your own organization) or *external* (requested by clients from outside your organization).

There are four main sections in this chapter. The first gives specific situations in which you might write proposals and feasibility studies at McDuff. The second and third sections discuss informal and formal proposal formats, while also denoting differences between in-house and sales versions of these formats. The fourth section covers feasibility studies. All chapter guidelines are followed by annotated examples to use as models for your own writing.

PROPOSALS AND FEASIBILITY STUDIES AT MCDUFF

As the Alamo example shows, proposals and feasibility studies often work together. The proposal may suggest a topic upon which a feasibility study is then written. The flowchart in Figure 10–1 shows another possible communication cycle that would involve both a proposal and a feasibility study. Note that the diagram includes the term *RFP,* which stands for "request for proposal":

> **Request for proposal (RFP):** documents sometimes sent out by organizations that want to receive proposals for a product or service. The RFP gives guidelines on (1) what the proposal should cover, (2) when it should be submitted, and (3) to whom it should be sent. As writer, you should follow the RFP religiously in planning and drafting your proposal.
>   RFPs generally are *not* used in these situations:
>
> - When the proposal is solicited from within your own organization
> - When the proposal is requested less formally, as through a letter, phone call, or memo
> - When the proposal is unsolicited, meaning that you are writing it without a request from the person who will read it

FIGURE 10–1

Flowchart showing the main documents involved in one possible construction project

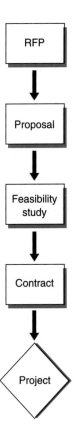

Sent by real estate developer to a number of construction design firms. This request for proposal (RFP) gives details about the kind of building the developers want built.

Sent by interested construction design firms to the developer, in response to the RFP.

Done in-house by the developer, to determine which of two top designs is the most practical, given the funds available and needs of potential building inhabitants.

Agreed upon by construction design firm and developer.

The sections that follow describe additional situations in which proposals and feasibility studies would be written at McDuff. Reading through these brief cases will show you the varied contexts for persuasive writing within just one company.

McDuff Proposals

Like many organizations, McDuff depends on (1) in-house proposals to breathe new life into its internal operations, (2) sales proposals to request work from clients, and (3) occasional grant proposals to seek research funds from outside organizations. Proposals are a main activity in healthy, growing organizations like McDuff.

Of the five cases described here, the first and second are internal, requiring in-house proposals; the third and fourth are external, requiring sales proposals; and the fifth is external, requiring a grant proposal.

- **In-house proposal for computer drafting equipment:** Meg Stevens, a graphics expert at the Denver office, writes an in-house proposal to the drafting manager, Elvin Lipkowsky, in which she proposes that the company purchase a new computer-drafting system. Her proposal includes a schedule whereby the department can shift entirely to computer drafting in the next five years.
- **In-house proposal for retaining legal counsel:** Jake Washington, an employment specialist in the Human Resources Department in the Baltimore office, writes an in-house proposal to Lynn Redmond, vice president of human resources. In it he proposes that the company retain legal counsel on a half-time basis (20 hours a week). In his position at McDuff, Jake uses outside legal advice in dealing with new hiring laws, unemployment compensation cases, affirmative action regulations, and occasional lawsuits by employees who have been fired. He is proposing that the firm retain regular half-time counsel, rather than dealing with different lawyers as is done now.
- **Sales proposal for asbestos removal:** Jane Wiltshire, asbestos department manager at McDuff's St. Paul office, regularly talks with owners of buildings that may contain asbestos. After an initial discussion with the head minister of First Street Church, she writes an informal sales proposal in which she offers McDuff's services in performing an asbestos survey of the church building. Specifically, she explains how McDuff will examine the structure for possible asbestos, gives a schedule for completing the survey and writing the final report, and proposes a lump-sum price for the project.
- **Sales proposal for work on wind turbine project:** A utility company in California plans to build 10 giant turbines in a desert valley in the southern part of the state. The "free" power that is generated will help offset the large increases in fuel costs for the company's other plants. Although the firm has selected a turbine design and purchased the units, it needs to decide where to place them and what kind of foundations to use. Thus it sent out a request for proposal to companies that have experience with foundation and environmental engineering. Louis Bergen, engineering manager at McDuff's San Francisco office, writes a

proposal that offers to test the soils at the site, pinpoint the best locations for the heavy turbines, and design the most effective foundations.

- **Grant proposal for new equipment design:** Oilarus, Ltd., a British oil company, sometimes gives research and development funds to small companies. Such funding usually goes toward development of new technology or products in the field of petroleum engineering. Angela Issam, who works in McDuff's Equipment Development group, decides to apply for some of the funding. Her proposed project, if successful, would provide a new piece of oil drilling safety equipment that would reduce the chance of offshore oil spills at production sites.

McDuff Feasibility Studies

The next two examples show that feasibility studies often flow from proposals. They can be internal, to managers who need facts before making a decision, or they can be external, to clients who request a service.

- **In-house feasibility study about legal counsel:** Lynn Redmond, the vice president of human resources, recently received Jake Washington's proposal that McDuff retain half-time legal counsel (see second case in previous section). The idea interests her, but she is not convinced of its practicality. She calls a meeting with Jake Washington and Scott Sampson, the personnel manager, who also uses legal counsel on a part-time basis. Because Lynn will have to sell her boss on this idea, she asks Jake and Scott to write a feasibility study on it.

  This study, unlike the proposal, must include a detailed comparison of the present mode of operating versus the proposed strategy of retaining a lawyer for 20 hours per week on a regular basis. The study must examine criteria such as current costs versus projected costs, current level of satisfaction versus projected level of satisfaction, and current level of services provided versus projected level of services provided. Lynn asks that the report include a clear recommendation, made on the basis of the data.

- **External feasibility study on plant site:** Tarnak, Inc., a large furniture manufacturing company in North Carolina, has decided to build a new plant in northern Georgia. After getting proposals from many cities that want the plant, the company has narrowed its choices to three spots that are about equal in cost of living, access to workers, standard of living, construction costs, transportation facilities, and access to raw materials. Yet the firm has not studied any site with respect to waste management.

  Specifically, Tarnak needs to know which of the three cities is best prepared to handle the solid and chemical wastes from the plant in a safe and economical manner. It hires McDuff's Atlanta office to write a feasibility study. The first goal of the study is to determine what sites, if any, meet Tarnak's criteria for waste management. If the first objective yields more than one site, McDuff then must compare the sites and recommend the best one.

GUIDELINES FOR INFORMAL PROPOSALS

Like informal reports, informal proposals are short documents that cover projects with a limited scope. But how short is short? And just what does "limited" mean? Following are some specific guidelines that you can use if your employer or client has not provided others:

Use Informal Proposals When:

- The text of the proposal (excluding attachments) is no more than 5 pages
- The size of the proposed project is such that a long, formal proposal would appear to be inappropriate
- The client has expressed a preference for a leaner, less formal document

Use Formal Proposals When:

- The text of the proposal (excluding attachments) is 10 pages or more
- The size and importance of the project is such that a formal proposal would be appropriate
- The client has expressed a preference for a more formal document

These two formats can be used for proposals that are either *in-house* (to readers within your own organization) or *external* (to readers outside your organization). The rest of this section provides writing guidelines and an annotated model for informal proposals, the type of persuasive writing you will do most often in your career.

Informal proposals have two formats: (1) memos (for in-house proposals) and (2) letters (for external proposals). The guidelines recommended apply to both. With some variations, they are essentially the guidelines suggested in chapter 8 for informal reports. The formats are much the same, though the content and tone are different. Reports explain, whereas proposals persuade.

◼ *Informal Proposal Guideline 1: Plan Well Before You Write*

Complete the Planning Form at the end of the book for all proposal assignments in class, as well as for proposals you write on the job. Carefully consider your purpose, audience, and organization. Two factors make this task especially difficult in sales-proposal writing:

1. You may know nothing more about the client than what is written on the RFP.
2. Proposals almost always are on a tight schedule that limits your planning time.

Despite these limitations, try to find out exactly who will be making the decision about your proposal. Many clients will tell you if you give them a call. In fact, they may be pleased that you care enough about the project to target the audience. Once you identify the decision-makers, spend time brainstorming about their needs *before* you begin writing. Proposals that betray an ignorance of client needs often do so because the writer began writing too soon about the product or service.

■ *Informal Proposal Guideline 2: Use Letter or Memo Format*

Letter proposals, such as the example shown in Model 10–1 on pages 363–365 basically follow the format of routine business letters (see chapter 7). This casual style gives readers the immediate impression that your document will be "approachable"—that is, easy to get through and limited in scope. Memo proposals, such as the example shown in Model 10–2 on pages 366–367, follow the format of an internal memorandum (see chapter 7). Here are a few highlights:

- Line spacing is usually single, but it may be $1\frac{1}{2}$ or double, depending on the reader's or company's preference.
- The recipient's name, date, and page number appear on sheets after the first.
- Most readers prefer an uneven or "ragged-edge" right margin, as opposed to an even or "right-justified" margin.

Your subject line in a memo proposal (if you choose to use one) gives readers the first impression of the proposal's purpose. Choose concise yet accurate wording. Furthermore, the wording must match that which you have used in the proposal text. See Model 10–2 on pages 366–367 for wording that gives the appropriate information and tries to engage the reader's interest.

■ *Informal Proposal Guideline 3: Make Text Visually Appealing*

The page design of informal proposals must draw readers into the document. Remember—you are trying to *sell* a product, a service, or an idea. If the layout is unappealing, then you will lose readers before they even get to your message. Also, remember that your proposal may be competing with others. Put yourself in the place of the reader who is wondering which one to pick up first. How the text looks on the page can make a big difference. Here are a few techniques to follow to help make your proposal visually appealing:

- Use lists (with bullets or numbered points) to highlight main ideas.
- Follow your readers' preferences as to font size, type, line spacing, and so forth. Proposals written in the preferred format of the reader will gain a competitive edge.
- Use headings and subheadings to break up blocks of text.

These and other techniques help to reveal the proposal's structure and lead readers through the informal proposal. Given that there is no table of contents, you need to take advantage of such strategies.

■ *Informal Proposal Guideline 4:*
Use the ABC Format for Organization

With its "hook" to gain the reader's attention, this structure makes good sense in proposal writing. Here are the main parts:

- **Abstract:** Gives the summary or "big picture" for those who will make decisions about your proposal. Usually includes some kind of "hook" or "grabber"—a point that will interest the audience in reading further.
- **Body:** Gives the details about exactly what you are proposing to do.
- **Conclusion:** Drives home the main benefit and makes clear the next step.

Note: Beginning and ending sections should be easy to read and stress just a few points. They provide a short "buffer" on both ends of the longer, more technical body section in the middle. The next three guidelines give more specific advice for writing the main parts of an informal proposal.

■ *Informal Proposal Guideline 5: Use the*
Heading "Introductory Summary"
for the Generic Abstract Section

Here you capture the client's attention with a capsule summary of the entire proposal. This one-paragraph or two-paragraph starting section permits space only for what the reader *really* needs to know at the outset, such as the following:

- Purpose of proposal
- Reader's main *need*
- Main *features* you offer and related *benefits*
- Overview of proposal sections to follow

As Models 10–1 and 10–2 on pages 363–367 show, the introductory summary appears immediately after the subject line of the memo proposal or salutation of the letter proposal. As with informal reports, you have the option of actually labeling the section "Introductory Summary" or simply leaving off the heading. In either case, keep this overview very brief. Answer the one question clients are thinking: "Why should we hire this firm instead of another?" If you find yourself starting to give too much detail, move background information into the first section of the discussion.

■ *Informal Proposal Guideline 6:*
Put Important Details in the Body

The discussion of your proposal should address these basic questions:

1. What problem are you trying to solve, and why?
2. What are the technical details of your approach?
3. Who will do the work, and with what?
4. When will it be done?
5. How much will it cost?

Discussion formats vary from proposal to proposal, but here are some sections commonly used to respond to these questions:

1. Description of problem or project and its significance. Give a precise technical description, along with any assumptions that you have made on the basis of previous contact with the reader. Explain the importance or significance of the problem, especially to the reader of the proposal.

2. Proposed solution or approach. Describe the specific tasks you propose in a manner that is clear and well organized. If you are presenting several options, discuss each one separately—making it as easy as possible for the reader to compare and contrast information.

3. Personnel. If the proposal involves people performing tasks, it may be appropriate to explain qualifications of participants.

4. Schedule. Even the simplest proposals usually require some sort of information about the schedule for delivering goods, performing tasks, and so on. Be both clear and realistic in this portion of the proposal. Use graphics when appropriate (see chapter 11 for guidelines on Gantt and milestone charts).

5. Costs. Place complete cost information in the body of the proposal unless you have a table that would be more appropriately placed in an attachment. Above all, do not bury dollar figures in paragraph format. Instead, highlight these figures with indented or bulleted lists, or at least place them at the beginnings of paragraphs. Because your reader will be looking for cost data, it is to your advantage to make that information easy to find.

■ *Informal Proposal Guideline 7: Give Special Attention to Establishing Need in the Body*

A common complaint about proposals is that writers fail to establish the need for what is being proposed. As any good salesperson knows, customers must feel that they need your product, service, or idea before they can be convinced to purchase or support it. In other words, do not simply try to dazzle readers with the good sense and quality of what you are proposing. Instead, lay the groundwork for acceptance by first showing the readers that a strong need exists.

Establishing need is most crucial in unsolicited proposals, of course, when readers may not be psychologically prepared to accept a change that will cost them money. Even in proposals that have been solicited, however, you should give some attention to restating the basic needs of the readers. If nothing else, this special attention shows your understanding of the problem.

■ *Informal Proposal Guideline 8: Focus Attention in Your Conclusion*

Called "conclusion" or "closing," this section gives you the opportunity to control the readers' last impression. It also helps you avoid the awkwardness of ending proposals with the statement of costs, which is usually the last section in the discussion. In this closing section you can:

- Emphasize a main benefit or feature of your proposal
- Restate your interest in doing the work
- Indicate what should happen next

Regarding the last point, sometimes you may ask readers to call if they have questions. In other situations, however, it is appropriate to say that you will follow up the proposal with a phone call. This approach leaves you in control of the next step.

Incidentally, for informal sales proposals, there is a special technique that can push the proposal one step closer to approval. After the signature section, place an "acceptance block." As shown in the following example, this item makes it as easy as a signature for the reader to accept your proposal, rather than his or her having to write a return letter.

ACCEPTED BY LMN DEVELOPMENT, INC.

By: _____

Title: _____

Date: _____

■ *Informal Proposal Guideline 9: Use Attachments for Less Important Details*

Remember that the text of informal proposals is usually less than 10 pages. That being the case, you may have to put supporting data or illustrations in attachments that follow the conclusion. Cost and schedule information, in particular, is best placed at the end in well-labeled sections.

Make sure that the proposal text includes clear references to these visuals. If you have more than one attachment, give each one a letter and a title (for example, "Attachment A: Project Costs"). If you have only one attachment, include the title but no letter (for example, "Attachment: Resumes").

■ *Informal Proposal Guideline 10: Edit Carefully*

In the rush of completing proposals, some writers fail to edit carefully. That is a big mistake. Make sure to build in enough time for a series of editing passes, preferably by different readers. There are two reasons why proposals of all kinds deserve this special attention.

1. They can be considered contracts in a court of law. If you make editing mistakes that alter meaning (such as an incorrect price figure), you could be bound to the error.

2. Proposals often present readers with their first impression of you. If the document is sloppy, they can make assumptions about your professional abilities as well.

GUIDELINES FOR FORMAL PROPOSALS

Sometimes the complexity of the proposal may be such that a formal response is best. As always, the final decision about format should depend upon the needs of your readers. Ask yourself questions like these in deciding whether to write an informal or a formal proposal:

- Is there too much detail for a letter or memo?
- Is a table of contents needed so that sections can be found quickly?
- Will the professional look of a formal document lend support to the cause?
- Are there so many attachments that a series of lengthy appendices would be useful?
- Are there many different readers with varying needs, such that there should be different sections for different people?

If you answer yes to one or more of these questions, give careful consideration to writing a formal proposal. This long format is most common in external sales proposals; however, important in-house proposals may sometimes require the same approach—especially in large organizations in which you may be writing to unknown persons in distant departments. Both in-house and sales examples follow the writing guidelines given next.

Formal proposals can be long and complex, so this part of the chapter treats each proposal section separately—from title page through conclusion. Two points will become evident as you use these guidelines. First, formal reports and formal proposals are a lot alike. A quick look at the last chapter will show you the similarities in format. Second, a formal proposal—like *all* technical writing described in this text—follows the basic ABC format described in chapter 3. Specifically, the parts of the formal proposal fit the pattern in this way:

ABC Format: Formal Proposal
Abstract

- Cover/Title Page
- Letter of Transmittal
- Table of Contents
- List of Illustrations
- Executive Summary
- Introduction

Body

- Technical information
- Management information
- Cost information
- [Appendices—appear after text but support Body section]

Conclusion

- Conclusion

As you read through and apply these guidelines, refer to Model 10–3 on pages 368–376 and Model 10–4 on pages 377–387 for annotated examples of the formal proposal. Note that each major section in the model proposals starts on a new page. Another alternative is to run most sections together, changing pages only at the end of the letter of transmittal and executive summary. Minor format variations abound, of course, but this chapter's guidelines will stand you in good stead throughout your career.

Cover/Title Page

Like formal reports, formal proposals usually are bound documents with a cover. The cover will include one or more of the items listed here for inclusion on the title page. Just as important, the cover should be designed to attract the reader's interest—with good page layout and perhaps even a graphic. Remember—proposals are sales documents. No one *has* to read them.

Inside the cover is the title page, which contains these four pieces of information:

- **Project title,** preceded by "Proposal for" or similar wording
- **Your reader's name** ("Prepared for . . .")
- **Your name or the name of your organization** spelled out in full ("Prepared by . . .")
- **Date of submission**

The title page gives clients their first impression of you. For that reason, consider using some tasteful graphics to make the proposal stand out from those of your competitors. For sales proposals, a particularly persuasive technique is to place the logo of the *client's company* on the cover or title page. In this way, you imply your interest in linking up with that firm *and* your interest in satisfying its needs, rather than simply selling your products or services.

Letter/Memo of Transmittal

Internal proposals have memos of transmittal; external sales proposals have letters of transmittal. These letters or memos must grab the reader's interest. The guidelines for format and organization presented here will help you write attention-getting prose. In particular, note that the letter or memo should be in single-spaced, ragged-right-edge format, even if the rest of the proposal is double-spaced copy with right-justified margins.

For details of letter and memo format, see chapter 7. The guidelines for the letter/memo of transmittal for formal reports also apply to formal proposals (see Transmittal Guideline 3 in chapter 9). For now, here are some highlights of format and content that apply especially to letters and memos of transmittal:

1. Use short beginning and ending paragraphs (about three to five lines each).
2. Use a conversational style, with little or no technical jargon. Avoid stuffy phrases such as "per your request."

3. Use the first paragraph for introductory information, mentioning what your proposal responds to (for example, a formal RFP, a conversation with the client, or your perception of a need).
4. Use the middle of the letter to emphasize one main benefit of your proposal, though the executive summary and proposal proper will mention benefits in detail. Stress what you can do to solve a problem, using the words "you" and "your" as much as possible (rather than "I" and "we").
5. Use the last paragraph to retain control by orchestrating the next step in the proposal process. When appropriate, indicate that you will call the client soon to follow up on the proposal.
6. Follow one of the letter formats described in chapter 7. Following are some exceptions, additions, or restrictions:

   - Use single-spaced, ragged-right-edge copy, which will make your letter stand out from the proposal proper.
   - Keep the letter on one page—a two-page letter loses that crisp, concise impact you want a letter to make.
   - Place the company proposal number (if there is one) at the top, above the date. Exact placement of both number and date depends on your letter style.
   - Include the client's company name or personal name on the first line of the inside address, followed by the mailing address that will be on the envelope. If you use a company name, place an "attention" line below the inside address. Include the full name (and title, if appropriate) of your contact person at the client firm. If you use a personal name, follow the last line of the inside address with a conventional greeting ("Dear Mr. Adams:").
   - (Optional) Include the project title below the attention line, using the exact wording that appears on the title page.
   - Close with "Sincerely" and your name at the bottom of the page. Also include your company affiliation.

Table of Contents

Create a very readable table of contents by spacing items well on the page. List all proposal sections, subsections, and their page references. At the end, list any appendices that may accompany the proposal.

Given the tight schedule on which most proposals are produced, errors can be introduced at the last minute because of additions or revisions. Therefore, take time to proofread the table of contents carefully. In particular, make sure to follow these guidelines:

- Wording of headings should match within the proposal text.
- Page references should be correct.
- All headings of the same order should be parallel in grammatical form.

List of Illustrations

When there are many illustrations, the list of illustrations appears on a separate page after the table of contents. When there are few entries, however, the illustrations may be listed at the end of the table of contents page. In either case, the list should include the number, title, and page number of every illustration appearing in the body of the text. (If there is only one illustration, a number need not be included.) You may divide the list into tables and figures if many of both appear in your proposal.

Executive Summary

Executive summaries are the most frequently read parts of proposals. That fact should govern the time and energy you put into their preparation. Often read by decision-makers in an organization, the summary should present a concise one-page overview of the proposal's most important points. It should also accomplish these objectives:

- Avoid technical language
- Be as self-contained as possible
- Make brief mention of the problem, proposed solution, and cost
- Emphasize the main benefits of your proposal

Start the summary with one or two sentences that command reader's attention and engage their interest. Then focus on just a few main selling points (three to five is best). You might even want to highlight these benefits with indented lead-ins such as "Benefit 1, Benefit 2." When possible, use the statement of benefits to emphasize what is unique about your company or your approach so that your proposal will attract special attention. Finally, remember to write the summary after you have completed the rest of the proposal. Only at this point do you have the perspective to sit back and develop a reader-oriented overview.

Introduction

The introduction provides background information for both nontechnical and technical readers. Although the content will vary from proposal to proposal, some general guidelines apply. Basically, you should include information on the (1) purpose, (2) description of the problem to which you are responding, (3) scope of the proposed study, and (4) format of the proposal. (A *lengthy* problem or project statement should be placed in the first discussion section of the proposal, not in the introduction.)

- Use subheadings if the introduction goes over a page. In this case, begin the section with a lead-in sentence or two that mention the sections to follow.
- Start with a purpose statement that concisely states the reason you are writing the proposal.
- Include a description of the problem or need to which your proposal is responding. Use language directly from the request for proposal or other document the reader may have given you so that there is no misunderstanding. For longer problem or need descriptions, adopt the alternative approach of including a separate needs section or problem description after the introduction.

- Include a scope section in which you briefly describe the range of proposed activities covered in the proposal, along with any research or preproposal tasks that have already been completed.
- Include a proposal format section if you feel the reader would benefit from a listing of the major proposal sections that will follow.

Discussion Sections

Aim the discussion or body toward readers who need supporting information. Traditionally, the discussion of a formal sales proposal contains three basic types of information: (1) technical, (2) management, and (3) cost. Here are some general guidelines for presenting each type. Remember that the exact wording of headings and subheadings will vary, depending on proposal content.

1. Technical Sections

- Respond thoroughly to the client's concerns, as expressed in writing or meetings.
- Follow whatever organization plan that can be inferred from the request for proposal.
- Use frequent subheadings with specific wording.
- Back up all claims with facts.

2. Management Sections

- Describe who will do the work.
- Explain when the work will be done.
- Display schedule information graphically.
- Highlight personnel qualifications (but put resumes in appendices).

3. Cost Section

- Make costs extremely easy to find.
- Use formal or informal tables when possible.
- Emphasize value received for costs.
- Be clear about add-on costs or options.
- Always total your costs.

Conclusion

Formal proposals should always end with a section labeled "Conclusion" or "Closing." This final section of the text gives you the chance to restate a main benefit, summarize the work to be done, and assure clients that you plan to work with them closely to satisfy their needs. Just as important, this brief section helps you end on a positive note. You come back full circle to what you stressed at the beginning of the document—benefits to the client and the importance of a strong personal relationship. (Without the conclusion, the client's last impression would be made by the cost section in the discussion.)

Appendices

Because formal proposals are so long, readers sometimes have trouble locating information they need. Headings help, but they are not the whole answer. Another way you can help readers is by transferring technical details from the proposal text into appendices. The proposal still will contain detail—for technical readers who want it—but detail will not intrude into the text. This technique can save you or your employer considerable time by permitting you to develop standard appendices (also called *boilerplate*) to be used in later proposals.

Any supporting information can be placed in appendices, but here are some common items included there:

- Resumes
- Organization charts
- Company histories
- Detailed schedule charts
- Contracts
- Cost tables
- Detailed options for technical work
- Summaries of related projects already completed
- Questionnaire samples

Boilerplate is often taken right off the shelf and thus is not paged in sequence with your text. Instead, it is best to use individual paging within each appendix. For example, pages in an Appendix B would be numbered B-1, B-2, B-3.

GUIDELINES FOR FEASIBILITY STUDIES

Much like recommendation reports (see chapter 8), feasibility studies guide readers toward a certain line of action. Another similarity is that both report types can be either in-house or external. Yet most feasibility studies have these five distinctive features that justify their being considered separately here:

1. They *always* are solicited by the reader, usually for the purpose of deciding on the best course of action.
2. They *always* assume one of these two patterns of organization:

   - An analysis of the advantages and disadvantages of one course of action, product, or idea
   - A comparison of two or more courses of action, products, or ideas

3. They *always* are intended to help managers and other decision-makers vote for or against an idea or select among several alternatives.
4. They *usually* "nudge" (as opposed to "urge" or "push") the reader toward a decision. That is, they are supposed to be written in such a way that the facts speak for themselves.
5. They *often* are preceded by a proposal.

In some ways, feasibility studies could be viewed as a cross between technical reports and proposals. As a writer you are expected to deal with the topic objectively and honestly, yet you are also expected to express your point of view. The *American Heritage Dictionary* defines "feasible" in this way: "capable of being accomplished or brought about." Thus a feasibility study determines if some course of action is practical. For example, it may be *desirable* for a student to quit work and return to college full-time. Yet if that same student has hefty car and apartment payments, the only *feasible* alternative may be part-time course work.

The following guidelines will help you prepare the kinds of feasibility studies requested by your boss (if the study is in-house) or by your client (if the study is external). In either case, your study may be used as the basis for a major decision. Refer to Model 10–5 on pages 388–389 as you read and apply these guidelines to your own writing.

■ *Feasibility Study Guideline 1: Choose Format Carefully*

In deciding whether to use the format of an informal (letter or memo) or formal document, use the same criteria mentioned earlier in the chapter with regard to proposals. As always, the central questions concern your readers:

- What format will give them easiest access to the data, conclusions, and recommendations of your study?
- Are there enough pages to suggest need of a table of contents (that is, a formal report)?
- What is the format preference of your readers?
- What has been the format of previous feasibility studies written for the same organization?

■ *Feasibility Study Guideline 2: Use the ABC Format*

Like other forms of technical writing, good feasibility studies have this basic three-part structure: **A**bstract, **B**ody, and **C**onclusion. As in other documents, the exact side headings you choose may vary from report to report. Yet, the overall structure should be as follows:

ABC Format: Feasibility Study

- **Abstract:** Capsule summary of information for the most important readers (that is, the decision-makers)
- **Body:** Details that support whatever conclusions and recommendations the study contains, working logically from fact toward opinion
- **Conclusion:** Wrap-up in which you state conclusions and recommendations resulting from study

The following guidelines examine specific sections of feasibility studies, along with details of content and tone.

■ *Feasibility Study Guideline 3: Call Your Abstract an Introductory Summary*

This section provides information that the most important readers would want if they were in a rush to read your study. With that criterion in mind, consider including these items:

- Brief statement about who has authorized the study and for what purpose
- Brief mention of the criteria used during the evaluation
- Brief reference to your recommendation

   The last item is important, for it saves readers the frustration of having to wade through the whole document in search of the answers to the questions "Is this a practical idea?" or "Which alternative is best?" It is best to mention the recommendation up front, giving readers a frame through which to see the entire report.

■ *Feasibility Study Guideline 4: Organize the Body Well*

More than anything else, readers of feasibility studies expect an unbiased presentation. That means the midsection of your report must clearly and logically work from facts toward recommendations. Here is one approach that works:

1. **Describe evaluation criteria used during your study,** if readers need more detail than was presented in the introductory summary.
2. **Describe exactly WHAT was evaluated and HOW,** especially if you are comparing several items.
3. **Choose criteria that are most meaningful to the readers,** such as:

   - Cost
   - Practicality of implementing idea
   - Changes that may be needed in personnel
   - Effect on growth of organization
   - Effects on day-to-day operations

      Of course, exact criteria will depend upon the precise topic you are investigating.

4. **Discuss both advantages and disadvantages** when you are evaluating just one item. Move from advantages to disadvantages. The conclusion will allow you to come back around to supporting points.
5. **Follow organization guidelines for comparisons** when evaluating several alternatives (see chapter 5). You can discuss one item at a time OR you can discuss one criterion at a time.

■ *Feasibility Study Guideline 5: Use the Conclusion for Detailed Conclusions and Recommendations*

Here you get the opportunity to state (or restate) the conclusions evident from data you have presented in the discussion. First state conclusions, and then state your recommendations. Use listings for three or more points, to make this last section of the study as easy as possible to read.

■ *Feasibility Study Guideline 6: Use Graphics for Comparisons*

When comparing several items, you need to consider most readers' preference for tabulated information. Tables can appear either in the discussion section or in attachments. In both cases, follow graphics guidelines explained in chapter 11.

■ *Feasibility Study Guideline 7: Offer to Meet with the Readers*

Most readers have many questions after reading a feasibility study, even if that study has been quite thorough. You score points for eagerness and professionalism if you anticipate needs and express your willingness to meet with readers later. Such meetings give you another opportunity to demonstrate your understanding of the topic.

COMMUNICATION CHALLENGE

"The Black Forest Proposal: Good Marketing or Bad Business?"

To strengthen its proposals, McDuff hired a new proposal writer at the corporate office in Baltimore. Ben Sadler came well recommended, having both advertising and marketing experience with technical firms. After he finished his first major proposal at McDuff, some disagreements arose during an internal review of his draft by one of the firm's technical experts. What follows is background information on the project, an overview of decisions Ben made in writing the proposal, and some questions and comments related to the review.

Background on Black Forest Project

Rob McDuff and his staff hired Ben Sadler for a specific reason. Although business was going fairly well, they felt the company needed new direction and energy in its marketing. Staff members seemed to be taking for granted that clients would always return and that word-of-mouth would keep new clients coming through the doors. Company leaders knew such an attitude was dangerous. Because they wanted to venture into new types of work, they believed the time was right for a new marketing expert. Ben Sadler seemed to be the catalyst the firm needed.

Just after arriving, Ben learned about a request for proposal recently issued for a large construction job—building a new university campus in southern Germany. The project at Black Forest University included four buildings, for a total of $35 million in construction. It would become the centerpiece of the new campus. McDuff had thus far done no major construction work in Germany, nor had it done much work at colleges and universities anywhere in the world. Yet Ben felt the firm had the technical tools and the personnel to be a contender. After convincing his immediate boss, the vice president for business and marketing, that the proposal was worth writing, Ben went to work.

Proposal Strategy

Although Ben had research assistance from McDuff employees in the United States and Germany, he wrote the draft himself. Here are parts of the writing and marketing strategy he planned to use:

- *Experience:* He emphasized the large construction jobs McDuff had done for other types of government-related agencies in Germany and around the world. Although McDuff had done no major college or university construction, Ben felt that including work for government agencies would be an adequate substitute.
- *Technical Experts:* Although McDuff's London and Munich offices had no experts to coordinate large-scale construction, Ben knew the company could bring in experts from the United States. Admittedly, it would be more expensive to import talent. Plus these high-salary individuals would be able to visit the site only periodically. Yet this arrangement satisfied the minimum technical requirements in the industry. Ben felt comfortable including the experts' resumes in the proposal and highlighting their experience, without mentioning the fact that they did not work out of the German office. That fact seemed to him to be an internal matter.
- *Costs:* When Ben calculated the tentative cost for the project, he was surprised that the figure was so high. The extra personnel costs previously noted were apparently part of the problem. But Ben also thought some costs may have been overstated because McDuff was not used to bidding on such jobs in Germany. (McDuff's corporate accounting manager had done the tentative cost estimate.) Believing the figures were inflated, Ben cut about 10 percent from personnel costs mentioned in the draft. He thought McDuff would perform more efficiently than the accounting manager had estimated.
- *Proposal Strategy:* Ben wanted to come on strong in the executive summary with what he saw as the benefits McDuff could offer. He focused on three main selling points: (a) availability of a nearby office and lab in Munich for project coordination, (b) experience with other large construction jobs in the United States, and (c) McDuff's history of good working relationships in Germany and the rest of Europe.

- *Personal Contacts:* Ben happened to have a close friend at a former firm (not a competitor of McDuff's) who went to college with an official now on the Black Forest University board of directors. Ben wanted to use this "friend of a friend" connection to get a meeting with the board member, perhaps to find out more about the project. He might then get the chance to give part of the "McDuff story" that was not revealed in the proposal.

Questions and Comments for Discussion

After Ben completed the draft, it was reviewed first by J. R. Link, one of the top technical experts at the Baltimore branch and an old-timer with McDuff. J. R. met with Ben and expressed reservations about the project and about the proposal. The questions that follow reflect their conversation, as well as some other concerns about the proposal:

1. J. R. Link first wondered why Sadler proposed on the job in the first place. Given that such proposals cost McDuff $10,000 or $15,000 to write, why did he bother with the Black Forest job when McDuff doesn't have experience on large construction jobs in Germany? Most projects out of the Munich office are environmental studies. Wouldn't it be a long shot to get the work? And shouldn't McDuff managers have some ethical concern about trying to get a job when they know they don't have the experience other competing firms probably have (or at least *should* have)?

    What is your view of the practical and ethical concerns raised by J. R.?

2. J. R. also questioned whether Ben was being deceptive about the way in which technical experts would be provided for the project. If the resumes were to be included in the proposal, shouldn't McDuff also mention that these experts reside in the United States? This matter didn't seem to be an "internal" one, as Ben stated.

    What's your view of the way Ben handled the issue of outside experts from the United States? How much of this sort of information has to be put forth in a competitive proposal?

3. Ben had an honest disagreement about the calculation of costs by the accounting manager. He may have been right or wrong in his reservations about the accountant's estimate. Putting this point aside, was it procedurally correct for him, as project manager, to make changes in the costs submitted by an advisor? Why or why not? Was it ethical?

4. Ben chose a "direct" approach to proposal content by placing main selling points first (in the executive summary). Do you think this strategy is appropriate in all cultures? Why or why not? (If possible, do some research on technical communication in Germany, Japan, or China before answering the question.)

5. As noted earlier, Ben decided to pursue a connection he had on the board of directors of Black Forest University. Is this strategy ethical? Would it work? What are some possible results of such a strategy?

6. Have two students in the class conduct a role-play of the conversation between J. R. Link and Ben Sadler. The students can use the information just presented and any additional points that conceivably could be put forth by these two men, considering the sketches provided of them.

CHAPTER SUMMARY

Proposals and feasibility studies stand out as documents that aim to *convince* readers. In the case of proposals, you are writing to convince someone inside or outside your organization to adopt an idea, a product, or a service. In the case of feasibility studies, you are marshalling facts to support the practicality of one approach to a problem—sometimes in comparison with other approaches. Both documents can be either informal or formal, depending on length, complexity, or reader preference.

This chapter includes lists of writing guidelines for informal proposals, formal proposals, and feasibility studies. For informal proposals, follow these basic guidelines:

1. Plan well before you write.
2. Use letter or memo format.
3. Make text visually appealing.
4. Use the ABC format for organization.
5. Use the heading "Introductory Summary" for the generic abstract section.
6. Put important details in the body.
7. Give special attention to establishing need in the body.
8. Focus attention in your conclusion.
9. Use attachments for less important details.
10. Edit carefully.

In formal proposals, abide by the same general format presented in chapter 9 for formal reports. To be sure, formal proposals have a different tone and substance because of their more persuasive purpose. Yet they do have the same basic parts, with minor variations: cover/title page, letter/memo of transmittal, table of contents, list of illustrations, executive summary, introduction, discussion sections, conclusion, and appendices.

Feasibility studies demonstrate that an idea is or is not practical. Also, they may compare several alternatives. Follow these basic writing guidelines:

1. Choose format carefully.
2. Use the ABC format.
3. Call your abstract an introductory summary.
4. Organize the body well.
5. Use the conclusion for detailed conclusions and recommendations.
6. Use graphics for comparisons.
7. Offer to meet with the readers.

ASSIGNMENTS

The assignments in Part 1 and Part 2 can be completed either as individual projects or as group-writing projects. If your instructor assigns group projects, review the information in chapter 1 on group writing.

Part 1: Short Assignments

These short assignments require either that you write parts of informal or formal proposals *or* that you evaluate the effectiveness of an informal proposal included here.

1. **Introductory Summary.** For this assignment, select one of the seven projects in the color insert. Now assume that you were responsible for writing the proposal that resulted in the project. In other words, work backwards from the project to the informal proposal that McDuff used to get the work. Write a short introductory summary for the original proposal. Focus on the main reason you think the client would have for hiring McDuff. If necessary, invent additional information to complete this assignment successfully.

2. **Needs Section.** As this chapter suggests, informal proposals—especially those that are unsolicited—must make a special effort to establish the need for the product or service being proposed. Assume that you are writing an informal proposal to suggest a change in procedures or equipment at your college. Keep the proposal limited to a small change; you may even see a need in the classroom where you attend class (audiovisual equipment? lighting? heating or air systems? aesthetics? soundproofing?). Write the needs section that would appear in the body of the informal proposal.

3. **Conclusion or Closing.** For this assignment, as with assignment 1, select a project from the color insert. Assume that you were the McDuff employee responsible for writing the informal proposal that resulted in the work described in the project. Write an effective conclusion or closing for the proposal.

4. **Evaluation—Informal Proposal.** Review the informal proposal that follows, submitted by MainAlert Security Systems to the McDuff, Inc., office in Atlanta. Evaluate the effectiveness of every section of the proposal.

---

200 Roswell Road
Marietta, Georgia 30062
(404) 555-2000

September 15, 1996

Mr. Bob Montrose
Operations Manager
McDuff, Inc.
3295 Peachtree Road
Atlanta, Georgia 30324

Dear Bob,

Thank you for giving MainAlert Security Systems an opportunity to submit a proposal for installation of an alarm system at your new office. The tour of your nearly completed office in Atlanta last week showed me all I need to know to provide you with burglary and fire protection. After reading this proposal, I think you will agree with me that my plan for your security system is perfectly suited to your needs.

This proposal describes the burglary and fire protection system I've designed for you. This proposal also describes various features of the alarm system that should be of great value. To provide you with a comprehensive description of my plan, I have assembled this proposal in several main sections:

1. Burglary Protection System
2. Fire Protection System
3. Arm/Disarm Monitoring
4. Installation Schedule
5. Installation and Monitoring Costs

BURGLARY PROTECTION SYSTEM

The burglary protection system would consist of a 46-zone MainAlert alarm control set, perimeter protection devices, and interior protection devices. The alarm system would have a strobe light and a siren to alert anyone nearby of a burglary in progress. Our system also includes a two-line dialer to alert our central station personnel of alarm and trouble conditions.

Alarm Control Set

The MainAlert alarm control set offers many features that make it well suited for your purposes. Some of these features are as follows:

1. Customer-programmable keypad codes
2. Customer-programmable entry/exit delays
3. Zone bypass option
4. Automatic reset feature
5. Point-to-point annunciation

I would like to explain the point-to-point annunciation feature, since the terminology is not as self-explanatory as the other features are. Point-to-point annunciation is a feature that enables the keypad to display the zone number of the point of protection that caused the alarm. This feature also transmits alarm-point information to our central station. Having alarm-point information available for you and the police can help prevent an unexpected confrontation with a burglar.

Interior and Perimeter Protection

The alarm system I have designed for you uses both interior and perimeter protection. For the interior protection, I plan to use motion detectors in the hallways. The perimeter protection will use glass-break detectors on the windows and door contacts on the doors.

There are some good reasons for using both interior and perimeter protection:

1. Interior and perimeter protection used together provide you with two lines of defense against intrusion.
2. A temporarily bypassed point of protection will not leave your office vulnerable to an undetected intrusion.
3. An employee who may be working late can still enjoy the security of the perimeter protection while leaving the interior protection off.

Although some people select only perimeter protection, it is becoming more common to add interior protection for the reasons I have given. Interior motion detection, placed at carefully selected locations, is a wise investment.

Local Alarm Signaling
The local alarm-signaling equipment consists of a 40-watt siren and a powerful strobe light. The siren and strobe will get the attention of any passerby and unnerve the most brazen burglar.

Remote Alarm Signaling
Remote alarm signaling is performed by a two-line dialer that alerts our central station to alarm and trouble conditions. The dialer uses two telephone lines so that a second line is available if one of the lines is out. Any two existing phone lines in your office can be used for the alarm system. Phone lines dedicated for alarm use are not required.

FIRE PROTECTION SYSTEM
My plan for the fire protection system includes the following equipment:

1. Ten-zone fire alarm panel
2. Eight smoke detectors
3. Water flow switch
4. Water cutoff switch
5. Four Klaxon horns

The ten-zone fire alarm panel will monitor one detection device per zone. Because each smoke detector, the water flow switch, and the water cutoff switch have a separate zone, the source of a fire alarm can be determined immediately.

To provide adequate local fire alarm signaling, this system is designed with four horns. Remote signaling for the fire alarm system is provided by the MainAlert control panel. The fire alarm would report alarm and trouble conditions to the MainAlert control panel. The MainAlert alarm control panel would, in turn, report fire alarm and fire trouble signals to our central station. The MainAlert alarm panel would not have to be set to transmit fire alarm and fire trouble signals to our central station.

ARM/DISARM MONITORING
Since 20 of your employees would have alarm codes, it is important to keep track of who enters and leaves the office outside of office hours. When an employee would arm or disarm the alarm system, the alarm would send a closing or opening signal to our central station. The central station would keep a record of the employee's identity and the time the signal was received. With the arm/disarm monitoring service, our central station would send you opening/closing reports on a semi-monthly basis.

INSTALLATION SCHEDULE
Given the size of your new office, our personnel could install your alarm in three days. We could start the day after we receive approval from you. The building is now complete enough for us to start anytime. If you would prefer for the construction to be completed before we start, that would not present any problems for us. To give you an idea of how the alarm system would be laid out, I have included an attachment to this proposal showing the locations of the alarm devices.

INSTALLATION AND MONITORING COSTS

Installation and monitoring costs for your burglary and fire alarm systems as I have described them in this proposal will be as follows:

- $8,200 for installation of all equipment
- $75 a month for monitoring of burglary, fire, and opening/closing signals under a two-year monitoring agreement

The $8,200 figure covers the installation of all the equipment I have mentioned in this proposal. The $75-a-month monitoring fee also includes opening/closing reports.

CONCLUSION

The MainAlert control panel, as the heart of your alarm system, is an excellent electronic security value. The MainAlert control panel is unsurpassed in its ability to report alarm status information to our central station. The perimeter and interior protection offers complete building coverage that will give you peace of mind.

The fire alarm system monitors both sprinkler flow and smoke conditions. The fire alarm system I have designed for you can provide sufficient warning to allow the fire department to save your building from catastrophic damage.

The arm/disarm reporting can help you keep track of employees who come and go outside of office hours. It's not always apparent how valuable this service can be until you need the information it can provide.

I'll call you early next week, Bob, in case you have any questions about this proposal. We will be able to start the installation as soon as you return a copy of this letter with your signature in the acceptance block.

Sincerely,

Anne Rodriguez Evans

Anne Rodriguez Evans
Commercial Sales

Enc.

ACCEPTED by McDuff, Inc.

By: _____

Title: _____

Date: _____

ALARM SYSTEM LAYOUT FOR
McDUFF INC. – ATLANTA, GA

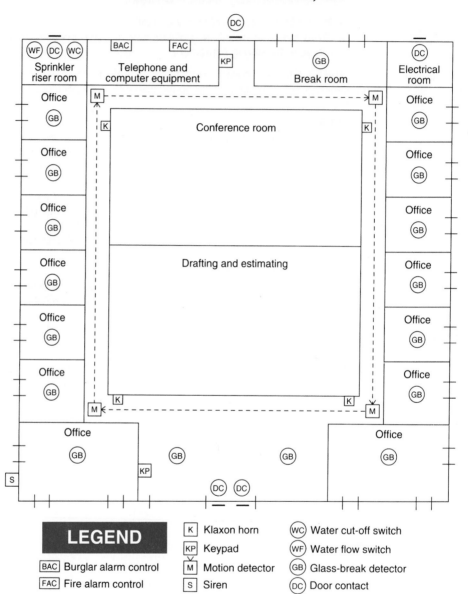

Part 2: Longer Assignments

For each of these assignments, complete a copy of the Planning Form included at the end of the book.

5. **Informal Proposal—McDuff.** Choose Option A or Option B. Remember that informal proposals should be fairly limited in scope, given their length and format.

Option A: In-House

- Use your past or present work experience to write a memo proposal suggesting a change at McDuff, Inc. Possible topic areas include changes in operating procedures, revisions to company policies, additions to the work force, alterations of the physical plant, or purchase of products or services.
- Place yourself in the role of an employee of McDuff. The proposal may be solicited or unsolicited, whatever best fits your situation.
- Make sure that your proposal topic is limited enough in scope to be covered fully in an informal proposal with memo format.
- Choose at least two levels of readers who could conceivably be decision-makers about a proposal such as the one you are writing—for example, branch or corporate managers. Review chapter 2 if necessary.

Option B: Sales

- Select a product or service (1) with which you are reasonably familiar (on the basis of your work experience, research, or other interests) and (2) that could conceivably be purchased by a company like McDuff.
- Put yourself in the role of someone representing the company that makes the product or provides the service.
- Write an informal sales proposal in which you propose purchase of the product or service by a representative of McDuff.

6. **Formal Proposal—McDuff.** Choose Option A, B, or C. Make sure that your topic is more complex than the one you would choose for the preceding informal-proposal assignments.

Option A: Community-Related

- Write a formal proposal in which you propose a change in (1) the services offered by a city or town (for example, mass transit or waste management) or (2) the structure or design of a building, garden, parking lot, shopping area, school, or other civic property.
- Select a topic that is reasonably complex and yet one about which you can locate information.
- Place yourself in the role of an outside consultant with a division of McDuff, Inc., who is proposing the change.
- Choose either an unsolicited or a solicited context.
- Write to an audience that could actually be the readers. Do enough research to identify at least two levels of audience.

Option B: School-Related

- Write a proposal in which you propose a change in some feature of a school you attend or have attended.

- Choose from topics such as operating procedures, personnel, curricula, activities, and physical plant.
- Select an audience that would actually make decisions on such a proposal.
- Give yourself the role of an outside consultant working for McDuff, Inc.

Option C: Word-Related

- Write a proposal in which you, as a representative of McDuff, propose purchase of a product or service by another firm.
- Choose a topic about which you have work experience, research knowledge, or keen interest—and one that could conceivably be offered in one of McDuff's project areas. Make sure you have good sources of information.
- Choose either a solicited or an unsolicited context.

7. Informal or Formal Proposal—International Context.

- Assume you are a consultant asked to propose a one-week training course to one of McDuff's offices outside the United States. (See the map on the color insert in chapter 2 for a list of these six locations.) Most or all seminar participants will be residents native to the country you choose—not U.S. citizens working overseas.
- Choose a seminar topic familiar to you—for example, from college courses, work experience, or hobbies—or one that you are willing to learn about quickly through some study.
- Research work habits, learning preferences, social customs, and other relevant topics concerning the country where the McDuff office you have chosen is located.
- Write McDuff, Inc., an informal or a formal proposal that reflects your understanding of the topic, your study of the country, and your grasp of the proposal-writing techniques presented in this chapter.

    Optional Group Approach: If this assignment is done by groups within your class, assume that members of your team work for a company proposing training seminars at McDuff offices around the world. Each group member has responsibility for one of McDuff's non-U.S. offices.

    Different sections of the proposal will be written by different group members, who may be proposing the same seminar for all offices or different seminars. Whatever the case, the document as a whole should be unified in structure, format, and tone. It will be read by (1) the vice president for international operations at the corporate office, (2) the vice president for research and training at the corporate office, and (3) all six branch managers in Venezuela, England, Saudi Arabia, Kenya, Germany, and Japan.

8. Feasibility Study—McDuff.

- Choose any one of the proposal assignments that you completed as part of the preceding assignments. (Or for this assignment, you can use a proposal completed by one of your classmates.)
- Take yourself out of the role of proposal writer. Instead, consider yourself to be someone assigned (or hired) to complete the task of evaluating the practicality of the proposal, after it has been received.
- If appropriate, choose several alternatives to evaluate.

Professional
Documentation, Inc.

3450 Jones Mill Road, Neming, Georgia 30092
(404) 555-8438

January 15, 1996

Mr. David Barker
Technical Communication Manager
Real Big Professional Software
P.O. Box 123456
Atlanta, Georgia 30339

Dear David:

Shows under-
standing of
client's main
concern—
scheduling.

I enjoyed meeting with you and learning about your new General Ledger software product. Because you require a March release, I can understand why you want to choose an approach to documentation and get the project started.

Asserts ability to
meet scheduling
need.

Gives helpful
overview of sec-
tions to follow.

This proposal describes a strategy for completing the documentation in the 10 weeks between now and your March deadline. Included are these main sections:

1. Selection of the Best Format
2. Adoption of a Publication Plan
3. Control of Costs
4. Conclusion

SELECTION OF THE BEST FORMAT

Uses list to
itemize
important
points—that is,
the *basis* for his
assessment.

I think your customers will be best served by a combined installation and user's guide. It uses a functional approach to show how General Ledger works. My assessment results from these completed steps:

- Interviews with support staffers responsible for providing technical support to customers using the company's other accounting products
- Interviews with programmers developing General Ledger, who have an intimate knowledge of how it works
- Conversations with you that clarified your organization's general expectations for the documentation

The assessment is also based on my experience developing documentation for other products. I strive to use clear, concise prose and ample white space to provide a visually appealing text. The text will be enhanced and supplemented with graphics depicting General Ledger's feature screens. The screens themselves will be captured directly

continues

MODEL 10–1
Letter proposal

from the program and inserted into the text by your staff using your in-house publishing system.

This approach will yield a thorough and easy-to-use document that will allow your customers to take full advantage of General Ledger's many innovative features.

As you know, writing documentation is a cooperative effort. Each member of the General Ledger product team will play key roles during the development process. To keep us all on track, I have put together a publication plan that shows how the project will progress from beginning to end.

ADOPTION OF A PUBLICATION PLAN

The publication plan shows how we can have the documentation ready for General Ledger's March unveiling. The four major steps are described here.

Define the Project

Much of this work has already been accomplished as a result of doing the research for this proposal. As a preliminary step, we will meet and review the project's scope and priority within the organization. We will detail the resources that will be available to complete the project. Most important, we will look at expectations: management's, yours, and the customers'.

Develop a Schedule

This step is the key to the publication process and ensures a common understanding of what has to be done and in what period of time. It has three basic steps:

- We define the tasks that are part of the project.
- We define the resources we have available to deal with the identified task.
- We assign tasks to the most appropriate individuals.

Manage the Project

What is good project management? In this plan, good management is essentially good communications. In the first three steps, we define the information that project members must have to understand how the document will be produced and their roles in that process. Ongoing management of the project will be a matter of keeping the channels of communication open.

Perform a Postmortem

The last step is an evaluation of the effectiveness of the publication plan. It provides the opportunity for us to learn how to do future documentation better. It is important to look back at what went right and what went wrong during a project and to share this information with the others. You will get a complete postmortem report from me after the project is completed.

MODEL 10–1
continued

Continues emphasis on benefits to reader.

Leads in smoothly to next section.

Starts with *overview* of sections to follow.

Organizes paragraph around three *main points*.

Uses bulleted list for primary *steps* in project.

Introduces section with *question* to attract attention to passage.

Shows interest
in *following
through*.

Throughout the project, this management system will guide us in completing General Ledger's documentation on time and within budget.

CONTROL OF COSTS

Places benefit in
heading.

Good documentation helps to sell software. By working smart, we can develop documentation that will enhance General Ledger's appeal, and we can do it at a reasonable cost.

Shows he can
meet project
criteria—but
also *clarifies* the
assumptions he
is making.

My experience in this area and the management system described here will reduce waste and duplication of effort, two factors that affect cost. This savings means I can bring the project in within the 200-hour cap you mentioned.

This estimate assumes that three of the program's four main features are in a complete, or "fixed," state and that the fourth main feature is about 50 percent complete. This estimate also assumes that all programming will be finished by March 5, which will allow time to put the guide through final review and production.

CONCLUSION

Returns to *main
concern* of
reader—
scheduling.

Retains *control*
of next step.

The functional approach, which describes a product in terms of its operations, is the documentation format that will best serve General Ledger customers. Your goal of having the documentation ready by March will be aided by adopting a four-step publication plan. The plan will define the strategy for writing the documentation and will help keep costs down.

I'll call you in a few days, David, to answer any questions you might have about this proposal. I can begin work on the documentation as soon as you sign the acceptance block and return a copy of this letter to me.

Sincerely,

Steven Nickels

Steven Nickels
Documentation Specialist

Enclosure

ACCEPTED by Real Big Professional Software

Includes accep-
tance block to
simplify approval
process.

By: _____

Title: _____

Date: _____

MODEL 10–1
continued

continues

DATE: October 4, 1996
TO: Gary Lane
FROM: Jeff Bilstrom *JB*
SUBJECT: Creation of Logo for Montrose Service Center

Part of my job as director of public relations is to get the Montrose name firmly entrenched in the minds of metro Atlanta residents. Having recently reviewed the contacts we have with the public, I believe we are sending a confusing message about the many services we offer retired citizens in this area.

To remedy the problem, I propose we adopt a logo to serve as an umbrella for all services and agencies supported by the Montrose Service Center. This proposal gives details about the problem and the proposed solution, including costs.

The Problem

The lack of a logo presents a number of problems related to marketing the center's services and informing the public. Here are a few:

- The letterhead mentions the organization's name in small type, with none of the impact that an accompanying logo would have.

- The current brochure needs the flair that could be provided by a logo on the cover page, rather than just the page of text and headings that we now have.

- Our 14 vehicles are difficult to identify because there is only the lettered organization name on the sides without any readily identifiable graphic.

- The sign in front of our campus, a main piece of free advertising, could better spread the word about Montrose if it contained a catchy logo.

- Other signs around campus could display the logo, as a way of reinforcing our identity and labeling buildings.

It's clear that without a logo, the Montrose Service Center misses an excellent opportunity to educate the public about its services.

The Solution

I believe a professionally designed logo could give the Montrose Service Center a more distinct identity. Helping to tie together all branches of our operation, it would give the public an easy-to-recognize symbol. As a result, there would be a stronger awareness of the center on the part of potential users and financial contributors.

MODEL 10–2
Memo proposal

The new logo could be used immediately to do the following:

- Design and print letterhead, envelopes, business cards, and a new brochure.
- Develop a decal for all company vehicles that would identify them as belonging to Montrose.
- Develop new signs for the entire campus, to include a new sign for the entrance to the campus, one sign at the entrance to the Blane Workshop, and one sign at the entrance to the Administration Building.

Cost

Developing a new logo can be quite expensive. However, I have been able to get the name of a well-respected graphic artist in Atlanta who is willing to donate his services in the creation of a new logo. All that we must do is give him some general guidelines to follow and then choose among eight to ten rough sketches. Once a decision is made, the artist will provide a camera-ready copy of the new logo.

• Design charge	$0.00
• Charge for new letterhead, envelopes, business cards, and brochures (min. order)	545.65
• Decal for vehicles 14 @ $50.00 + 4%	728.00
• Signs for campus	415.28
Total Cost	$1,688.93

Conclusion

As the retirement population of Atlanta increases in the next few years, there will be a much greater need for the services of the Montrose Service Center. Because of that need, it's in our best interests to keep this growing market informed about the organization.

I'll stop by later this week to discuss any questions you might have about this proposal.

MODEL 10–2
continued

PROPOSAL FOR SUPPLYING
TEAK CAM CLEAT SPACERS

Prepared by
Totally Teak, Inc.

Prepared for
John L. Riggini
Bosun's Locker Marine Supply

August 22, 1996

MODEL 10–3
Formal proposal (external)

Totally Teak, Inc.
6543 Amster Avenue, N.W.
Atlanta, Georgia 30308
(404) 555-9425

In this example, the letter of transmittal appears immediately following the title page. It can also appear before the title page (see Model 10–4).

Established *link* with previous client contact.

Stresses two main benefits.

Says he will *call* (rather than asking client to call).

August 22, 1996

John L. Riggini, President
Bosun's Locker Marine Supply
38 Oakdale Parkway
Norcross, OH 43293

Dear Mr. Riggini:

I enjoyed talking with you last week about inventory needs at the 10 Bosun's stores. In response to your interest in our products, I'm submitting this proposal to supply your store with our Teak Cam Cleat Spacers.

This proposal outlines the benefits of adding Teak Cam Cleat Spacers to your line of sailing accessories. The potential for high sales volume stems from the fact that the product satisfies two main criteria for any boat owner:

1. It enhances the appearance of the boat.
2. It makes the boat easier to handle.

Your store managers will share my enthusiasm for this product when they see the response of their customers.

I'll give you a call next week to answer any questions you have about this proposal.

Sincerely,

William G. Rugg

William G. Rugg
President
Totally Teak, Inc.

WR/rr

MODEL 10–3
continued

continues

TABLE OF CONTENTS

Organizes entire proposal around *benefits*.

LIST OF ILLUSTRATIONS

MODEL 10–3
continued

Briefly mentions
main *need* to
which proposal
responds.

Reinforces main
points men-
tioned in *letter*
(selective repeti-
tion of crucial
information is
acceptable).

EXECUTIVE SUMMARY

This proposal outlines features of a custom-made accessory designed for today's sailors—whether they be racers, cruisers, or single-handed skippers. The product, Teak Cam Cleat Spacers, has been developed for use primarily on the Catalina 22, a boat owned by many customers of the 10 Bosun's stores. However, it can also be used on other sailboats in the same class.

The predictable success of Teak Cam Cleat Spacers is based on two important questions asked by today's sailboat owners:

- Will the accessory enhance the boat's appearance?
- Will it make the boat easier to handle and, therefore, more enjoyable to sail?

This proposal answers both questions with a resounding affirmative by describing the benefits of teak spacers to thousands of people in your territory who own boats for which the product is designed. This potential market, along with the product's high profit margin, will make Teak Cam Cleat Spacers a good addition to your line of sailing accessories.

2

MODEL 10–3
continued

continues

INTRODUCTION

The purpose of this proposal is to show that Teak Cam Cleat Spacers will be a practical addition to the product line at the Bosun's Locker Marine Supply stores. This introduction highlights the need for the product, as well as the scope and format of the proposal.

Background

Sailing has gained much popularity in recent years. The high number of inland impoundment lakes, as well as the vitality of boating on the Great Lakes, has spread the popularity of the sport. With this increased interest, more and more sailors have become customers for a variety of boating accessories.

What kinds of accessories will these sailors be looking for? Accessories that (1) enhance the appearance of their sailboats and (2) make their sailboats easier to handle and, consequently, more enjoyable to sail. With these customer criteria in mind, it is easy to understand the running joke among boat owners (and a profitable joke among marine supply dealers): "A boat is just a hole in the water that you pour your money into."

The development of this particular product originated from our designers' firsthand sailing experiences on the Catalina 22 and knowledge obtained during manufacture (and testing) of the first prototype. In addition, we conducted a survey of owners of boats in this general class. The results showed that winch and cam cleat designs are major concerns.

Proposal Scope and Format

The proposal focuses on the main advantages that Teak Cam Cleat Spacers will provide your customers. These six sections follow:

1. Practicality
2. Suitability for a Variety of Sailors
3. High-Quality Construction and Appearance
4. Dealer Benefits
5. Sizable Potential Market
6. Affordable Price

3

MODEL 10–3
continued

FEATURES AND BENEFITS

Teak Cam Cleat Spacers offer Bosun's Locker Marine Supply the best of both worlds. On the one hand, the product solves a nagging problem for sailors. On the other, it offers your store managers a good opportunity for profitability. Described here are six main benefits for you to consider.

Practicality

This product is both functional and practical. When installed in the typical arrangement shown in the figure below, the Teak Cam Cleat Spacer raises the height of the cam cleat, thereby reducing the angle between the deck and the sheet as it feeds downward from the winch. As a result of this increased height, a crewmember is able to cleat a sheet with one hand instead of two.

SIDE VIEWS OF CLEATING ARRANGEMENT

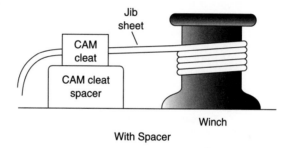

With Spacer

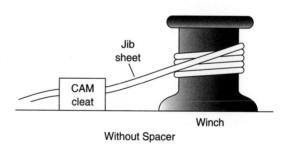

Without Spacer

4

MODEL 10–3
continued

continues

Such an arrangement allows a skipper to maintain steerage of the boat, keeping one hand on the helm while cleating the sheet with the other. Securing a sheet in this manner can be done more quickly and securely. Also, this installation reduces the likelihood of a sheet "popping out" of the cam cleat during a sudden gust of wind.

Suitability for a Variety of Sailors

For the racer, cruiser, and single-handed sailor, sailing enjoyment is increased as sheets and lines become easier to handle and more secure. In a tight racing situation, these benefits can be a deciding factor. The sudden loss of sail tension at the wrong moment as a result of a sheet popping out of the cam cleat could make the difference in a close race.

A cruising sailor is primarily concerned with relaxation and pleasure. A skipper in this situation wants to reduce his or her workload as much as possible. In the instance of a sheet popping loose, the sudden chaos of a sail flapping wildly interrupts an otherwise tranquil atmosphere. Teak Cam Cleat Spacers reduce the chance of this happening.

A cruising sailor often has guests aboard. In this situation, as well as in a race, the skipper wants to maintain a high level of seamanship, especially where the control of the boat and the trim of its sails are concerned.

The single-handed sailor derives the greatest benefit from installing Teak Cam Cleat Spacers. Without crew nearby to assist with handling lines or sheets, anything that makes work easier for this skipper is welcome.

High-Quality Construction and Appearance

The teakwood frame from which this product is manufactured is well suited for use around water, since teak will not rot. It also looks nice when oiled or varnished.

The deck of most sailboats is made primarily of fiberglass. The appearance of such a boat can be significantly enhanced by the addition of some teak brightwork.

Each spacer is individually handcrafted by Totally Teak, Inc., to guarantee a consistent level of high quality.

Dealer Benefits

Teak Cam Cleat Spacers make a valuable addition to the dealer's product line. They complement existing sailing accessories as well as provide the customer with the convenience of a readily available prefabricated product.

A customer who comes in to buy a cam cleat is a ready prospect for the companion spacer. Such a customer will likely want to buy mounting hardware as well.

With this unique teak product readily available, a dealer can save the customer the time and trouble of fabricating makeshift spacers.

5

MODEL 10–3
continued

Includes number of owners to emphasize *potential sales.*

Keeps price information *short* and *clear.*

Sizable Potential Market

These Teak Cam Cleat Spacers are designed with a large and growing potential market in mind. They are custom-made for the Catalina 22, one of the most popular sailboats in use today. Over 13,000 of these sailboats have been manufactured to date. These spacers are also well suited for other similar-class sailboats.

Affordable Price

The Teak Cam Cleat Spacers made by Totally Teak, Inc., wholesale for $3.95/pair. Suggested retail is $6.95/pair. This low price is easy on the skipper's wallet and should help this product move well. And, of course, the obviously high profit margin should provide an incentive to your store managers.

6

MODEL 10–3
continued

continues

CONCLUSION

Why should a marine supply dealer consider carrying Teak Cam Cleat Spacers? This product satisfies two common criteria of sailboat owners today: it enhances the appearance of any sailboat, and it makes the boat easier to handle. The potential success of this product is based on its ability to meet these criteria and the following features and benefits:

1. It is practical, allowing quick, one-handed cleating.

2. It is ideally suited for a variety of sailors, whether they are racing, cruising, or sailing single-handedly.

3. It is a high-quality, handcrafted product that enhances the appearance of any sailboat.

4. It is a product that benefits the dealer by making a valuable addition to her or his product. It complements existing sail accessories and satisfies a customer need.

5. It is geared toward a sizable potential market. Today there are thousands of sailboats in the class for which this accessory is designed.

6. It is affordably priced and provides a good profit margin.

7

Links list of *benefits* with order of same in discussion— drives home advantages of product to *user* and *dealer*.

MODEL 10–3
continued

NAVAL
AIR ■●■
STATION

There is no slack....in light Attack!

Marietta, North Carolina 27456
(919) 555-1050

February 24, 1996

Lt. Dennis Smoot
Maintenance Officer
ATKRON Two Zero Five
Naval Air Station
Marietta, NC 27456

Dear Lt. Smoot:

Emphasizes major *benefits*.

    My five years' work at the Naval Air Station has shown me that we have a very professional maintenance staff. I believe we can further increase the professionalism by starting an incentive awards program.

    The Silver Wrench Award program proposed here will offer many benefits for our operation, with a very low cost. Possible benefits include better aircraft availability, a more professional atmosphere, and increased morale in the maintenance department.

Retains control by stating he will *call* the reader.

    Please review the enclosed proposal at your convenience. I will call you next week to discuss the prospects for starting this program.

Sincerely,

Jim Barnes

AEC (AW) Jim Barnes
Maintenance Coordinator

MODEL 10–4
Formal proposal (internal)

continues

THE SILVER WRENCH AWARD
INCENTIVE PROGRAM

Prepared for
LT Dennis Smoot
Maintenance Officer
ATKRON Two Zero Five

by
AEC (AW) Jim Barnes

February 24, 1996

MODEL 10–4
continued

TABLE OF CONTENTS

LIST OF ILLUSTRATIONS

Reveals *organization* of entire proposal through table of contents.

Lists table numbers *and* titles.

MODEL 10–4
continued

continues

EXECUTIVE SUMMARY

Maintenance personnel are often required to work long hours with little or no reward for excellent performance. The constant tempo of flight operations demands that our aircraft and their electronic systems be maintained in top condition. Without the efforts of our dedicated maintenance workers, mission objectives could not be achieved. To keep their momentum going, I have developed this proposal for a program that will reward a superior work center each quarter.

You may ask, "How will the squadron benefit?" The answer is that for a minimum investment, we will accomplish these objectives:

- Increase our productivity by making more aircraft available
- Promote a professional atmosphere
- Improve morale

In short, the Silver Wrench Award will encourage maintenance employees to be their best at all times.

As you know, meeting our production goals is much easier if maintenance troops take pride in their work and willingly perform arduous assignments. We have many objectives to achieve this year, so we must act now to take full advantage of this proposed program. With your support, we will be recognized as the finest attack squadron in both the navy and the naval reserve.

2

MODEL 10–4
continued

INTRODUCTION

Today's high-tech navy requires optimum performance from all personnel to maintain a high state of readiness and achieve its objectives. This fact is especially true in naval aviation where complex aircraft systems must be kept in superior condition. Our squadron is no exception to this requirement.

Our maintenance personnel have received excellent training and have demonstrated on many occasions that they can get the job done. However, the rigors of maintaining an ever-increasing flight program can sometimes tax the professional capabilities of top-notch maintenance personnel. The Silver Wrench Award program would induce personnel to be their best at all times.

Purpose

This proposed program aims to increase production at the work center, instill pride among maintenance personnel, and encourage high levels of professionalism throughout the maintenance department.

Scope

This idea has been adapted from the COMNAVAIRESFOR Golden Wrench Award program. The Golden Wrench Award program permits formal, yearly recognition of an individual squadron type (such as fighter, attack, or patrol) for maintenance excellence. As this proposal will show, the Silver Wrench Award program would formally recognize an individual work center each quarter. To choose a winner, information would be gathered from these sources:

- Maintenance data reporting
- Work-center audits
- Monitor programs
- Maintenance CPO

Proposal Format

This proposal is organized into three main sections, as follows:

The management section assigns the responsibilities for program operations to the maintenance officer, quality-assurance supervisor, and data analyst. Also, it sets up specific guidelines for collecting data and maintaining the plaque.

Detailed information about point assignments is presented in the data-compilation section. Quality-assurance analyst and maintenance CPO data are fully explained and then rated on a point scale.

The financial section gives all cost and staffing requirements for program support. For your convenience, two tables are provided for easy interpretation of data. In addition, several sources of financial support for the award program are listed.

3

Gives brief background statement.

Concisely states why the proposal has been written.

Acknowledges debt to similar program.

Outlines scope of program.

Summarizes content of three main sections to follow in discussion.

MODEL 10–4
continued

continues

PROGRAM MANAGEMENT

The maintenance officer (MO) will oversee the Silver Wrench Award program, and the quality-assurance/analysis (QA/A) supervisor will have main responsibility for collecting all data.

Maintenance Officer

The primary responsibilities of the maintenance officer are to ensure that award guidelines (see Appendix) are strictly followed and that the award is presented on time. The Silver Wrench should be presented during the months of January, April, July, and October.

The MO will carefully review all point totals and select a winning work center. However, he or she should be careful not to select the work center with the most points if that shop has been involved in a recent malpractice incident: lost tool, improper maintenance procedures, low work standards, and so forth.

Quality-Assurance/Analysis Supervisor

The QA/A supervisor is ultimately responsible for collecting all point totals. These totals will be recorded on a data-collection form and presented to the maintenance officer for work-center selection.

Data collection should begin at least 15 days before the close of the award period. This date will coincide with the delivery of the monthly data reports. After the selection is made, the QA/A supervisor will have a brass plate engraved with the appropriate information:

- Work-center name
- Supervisor name
- Year and quarter selected
- Maintenance CPO

The QA/A supervisor has the responsibility for maintaining the plaque.

4

MODEL 10–4
continued

COMPILATION OF AWARD DATA

The main data for award selection will be obtained from the Quality-Assurance/ Analysis Division and the individual maintenance chief petty officers. Although the MO and the maintenance CPO ultimately decide the award winners, they must have access to accurate and carefully tabulated data to ensure fairness in the selection process.

Quality-Assurance Information

Quality-assurance workers will provide most of the required data for this award. This information will be obtained from work-center audits and monitor programs. Collected data will be passed to the quality-assurance supervisor and placed on the data-collection form.

Work-Center Audits. Quality-assurance personnel will review the audits from the previous quarter and select the top four work centers. Every work center is audited once each quarter to ensure compliance with the maintenance standards established by OPNAVINST 4790.2D. These audits provide a thorough review of all work centers and indicate any shortcomings that exist. Each of the top work centers will receive four points.

Monitor Programs. Monitor-program forms from the previous quarter will be reviewed for both good and poor performance. Programs that will be checked include the following:

- Tool control
- Hydraulic contamination
- Nitrogen servicing
- Oxygen servicing
- Corrosion control
- Foreign object damage
- Nondestructive testing
- Safety
- Calibration
- Oil analysis
- Fuel contamination
- Training
- Ejection seat safety

Each good report will receive plus one point, and each poor report will receive minus one point.

Analyst Information

The squadron analyst will provide data on the documentation habits of each work center. The areas to be examined by the analyst are as follows:

- Documentation accuracy
- Corrosion documentation
- End-of-month closeouts

Point totals shall be presented to the quality-assurance supervisor for tabulation.

5

continues

MODEL 10–4
continued

Uses readable scheme of *headings* and *subheadings* to *guide reader* through section.

Uses bullets to list *supporting details.*

Gives thorough analysis of *proposed procedure.*

MDR Documentation. The analyst will select the four work centers with the lowest documentation error rate during the past quarter. Each work center will receive one point. If complete reports are unavailable, the three latest reports will be used.

Corrosion Documentation. The analyst will review the MDR-4 report and determine which work centers will receive credit for documenting corrosion prevention and treatment. Work centers will get one point per month for each month of prevention documented and one point per month for each month of treatment.

Closeouts. Each work center that does not submit or is late in submitting its end-of-month closeouts will be penalized two points per month per quarter.

Maintenance CPO Information

Every maintenance chief petty officer stays informed of the events that occur throughout the squadron. Many times, a maintenance CPO will see top performers doing their jobs above and beyond normal expectations. This performance is often undocumented and requires some method of accountability.

To fill this need, the quality-assurance supervisor will solicit data from each maintenance CPO. These data will be rated at two points each. This information will be added to the collection form and submitted to the maintenance chief and maintenance officer.

6

MODEL 10–4
continued

continues

Emphasizes *economy* of proposed plan.

Employs informal table for *clarity*.

Keeps two tables in text rather than appendix, because of their *simplicity* and *relevance to text*.

Offers suggestions for funding, to make program seem as *feasible* as possible.

FINANCIAL REQUIREMENTS

The Silver Wrench Award program is an inexpensive method of increasing productivity. Table 1 and Table 2 indicate the low program costs and small staffing requirements.

After the initial outlay of nine staffing hours and $34.15, program upkeep will involve about six staffing hours and $5.00 a quarter. This cost equates to five minutes and three cents a day for a two-year period to promote a program that will reap many benefits to the squadron.

TABLE 1: EXPENSES

ITEM	COST
Plaque	$18.00
Brass Plates	4.50
Engraving (initial)	5.45
Engraving (quarterly)	5.00
Wrench	1.20
Total (initial)	$34.15
Total (quarterly)	$ 5.00

TABLE 2: STAFFING REQUIREMENTS

ITEM	MAN-HOURS
Purchase materials	1.0
Engrave plates	1.0
Assemble plaque	2.0
Compile data	4.0
Select winner	1.0
Total (initial)	9.0
Total (quarterly)	6.0

Financial backing can be provided from several sources:

- Squadron coffee mess
- Officer fund
- CPO fund
- Personal donations

The plaque suggested here is designed to cover a two-year period. However, larger and more expensive plaques can be purchased to cover longer periods.

7

MODEL 10–4
continued

CONCLUSION

The Silver Wrench Award should become a valuable part of our maintenance program. This award can produce many benefits for the squadron at a very low cost. These benefits consist of the following:

Returns to major benefits.

- Reduced aircraft downtime
- More personal professionalism
- Higher morale
- Increased work-center production
- Reduced audit discrepancies
- Increased attention to details
- Safer maintenance practices
- Improved control of aircraft corrosion

Leaves reader with impression that everyone will benefit from program.

Extreme importance is placed on a squadron's ability to exceed its flight-hour program and to complete every mission. With the start of the Silver Wrench Award program, our squadron is sure to advance to its highest potential.

8

MODEL 10–4
continued

Puts guidelines in text *appendix,* since they are supporting information that would "clutter" the discussion part of proposal.

APPENDIX: SILVER WRENCH AWARD GUIDELINES

The maintenance officer (MO) and the maintenance chief will select one work center per quarter for the Silver Wrench Award. Their selection will be based on the following information:

Quality-Assurance/Analysis

Audits. Select the four best work centers based on audit performance. Each will be rated at four points each.

Monitor Programs. Provide data based on the monitor-program forms from the past quarter. Each will be rated at PLUS one point for every satisfactory monitor and MINUS one point for every unsatisfactory monitor.

MDR Documentation. Select the four work centers that have submitted the most accurate documentation of MDR data during the last 3 months of available MDR-2 reports. Each work center will receive one point per work center per quarter.

Corrosion Documentation. Provide information on preventing and treating corrosion at work centers. This information will be scored at the following rates:

    Corrosion Prevention. (code A-04 series). Data will be rated at one point per month per quarter of documentation.

    Corrosion Treatment. (code Z-170 series). Data will be rated at one point per month per quarter of documentation.

MDR Closeouts. Provide information on delinquent, or nonsubmission of, MDR closeouts, to be rated at MINUS two points per month per quarter.

Maintenance Department CPOs

Have each CPO select one work center with the best performance during the past quarter (to be rated at two points).

MO and Maintenance Chief

Collect information from QA/A and maintenance chiefs and select the winner of the Silver Wrench Award. A high score should not be a substitute for sound judgment during the selection process.

9

MODEL 10–4
continued

Mc Duff, Inc.

MEMORANDUM

DATE: July 22, 1996
TO: Greg Bass
FROM: Mike Tran *MT*
SUBJECT: Replacement of In-House File Server

INTRODUCTORY SUMMARY

The purpose of this feasibility study is to determine if the NTR PC905 would make a practical replacement for our in-house file server. As we agreed in our weekly staff meeting, our current file-serving computer is damaged beyond repair and must be replaced by the end of the week. This study shows that the NTR PC905 is a suitable replacement that we can purchase within our budget and install by Friday afternoon.

FEASIBILITY CRITERIA

There are three major criteria that I addressed. First, the computer we buy must be able to perform the tasks of a file-serving computer on our in-house network. Second, it must be priced within our $4,000 budget for the project. Third, it must be delivered and installed by Friday afternoon.

Performance

As a file server, the computer we buy must be able to satisfy these criteria:

- Store all program used by network computers
- Store the source code and customer-specific files for Xtracheck
- Provide fast transfer of files between computers while serving as host to the network
- Serve as the printing station for the network laser printer

The NTR PC905 comes with a 120MB hard drive. This capacity will provide an adequate amount of storage for all programs that will reside on the file server. Our requirements are for 30MB of storage for programs used by network computers and 35MB of storage for source code and customer-specific programs. The 120MB drive will leave us with 55MB of storage for future growth and work space.

The PC905 can transfer files and execute programs across our network. It can perform these tasks at speeds up to five times faster than our current file server. Productivity should increase because the time spent waiting for transfer will decrease.

MODEL 10–5
Feasibility study (one alternative)

The computer we choose as the file server must also serve as the printing station for our network laser printer. The PC905 is compatible with our Hewy Packer laser printer. It also has 2.0MB more memory than our current server. As a result, it can store larger documents in memory and print them with greater speed.

Budget

The budget for the new file server is $4,000. The cost of the PC905 is as follows:

PC905 with 120MB Hard Drive	$2,910
Keyboard	112
Monitor	159
Total	$3,181

No new network boards need to be purchased because we can use those that are in the current server. We also have all additional hardware and cables that will be required for installation. Thus the PC905 can be purchased for $800 under budget.

Time Frame

Our sales representative at NTR guarantees that we can have delivery of the system by Friday morning. Given this assurance, we can have the system in operation by Friday afternoon.

Additional Benefits

We are currently using NTR PCs at our customer sites. I am very familiar with the setup and installation of these machines. By purchasing a brand of computer currently in use, we will not have to worry about additional time spent learning new installation and operation procedures. In addition, we know that all our software is fully compatible with NTR products.

The warranty on the PC905 is for one year. After the warranty period, the equipment is covered by the service plan that we have for all our other computers and printers.

CONCLUSION

I recommend that we purchase the NTR PC905 as the replacement computer for our file server. It meets or exceeds all criteria for performance, price, and installation.

MODEL 10–5
continued

PART

III

11 Graphics

McDuff employees like these often use computers to produce logos, charts, designs, and other graphics.

*T*echnology has radically changed the world of graphics. Now, almost anyone with a computer and the right software can quickly produce illustrations that used to take hours to construct. As a result, today there are sophisticated graphics in every medium—newspapers, magazines, television, and, of course, technical communication.

Because readers *expect* graphics to accompany text, you as a technical professional must respond to this need. Well-designed and well-placed graphics will keep you competitive. Your graphics do not have to be fancy, however. Nor is it true that adding graphics will necessarily improve a document. Readers are impressed by visuals *only* when they are well done and appropriate.

Fortunately, you do not have to be an expert to understand and use the fundamentals of graphics. In fact, the availability of high-tech graphics has made it even more important that technical professionals first understand the basics of graphics before applying sophisticated techniques. To emphasize these basics, this chapter (1) defines some common graphics terms, (2) explains the main reasons to use graphics and gives some general guidelines, (3) lists specific guidelines for eight common graphics, and (4) shows you how to avoid graphics misuse. Although the chapter does include some production tips, the main emphasis is on *why* and *when* to use graphics.

TERMS IN GRAPHICS

Terminology for graphics is not uniform in the professions. That fact can lead to some confusion. For the purposes of this chapter, however, some common definitions are adopted and listed here:

- **Graphics:** This generic term refers to any nontextual portion of documents or oral presentations. It can be used in two ways: (1) to designate the field (for example, "Graphics is an area in which he showed great interest") or (2) to name individual graphical items ("She placed three graphics in her report").
- **Illustrations, visual aids:** Used synonymously with "graphics," these terms also can refer to all nontextual parts of a document. The term *visual aids,* however, often is limited to the context of oral presentations.
- **Tables and figures:** These terms name the two subsets of graphics.
  Tables refers to illustrations that place numbers or words in columns or rows or both.
  Figures refers to all graphics other than tables. Examples include charts (pie, bar, line, flow, and organization), engineering drawings, maps, and photographs.
- **Charts, graphs:** A subset of "figures," these synonymous terms refer to a type of graphic that displays data in visual form—as with bars, pie shapes, or lines on graphs. Chart is the term used most often in this text.
- **Technical drawing:** Another subset of "figures," a technical drawing is a representation of a physical object. Such illustrations can be drawn from many perspectives and can include "exploded" views.

Of course, you may see other graphics terms. For example, some technical companies use the word *plates* for figures. Be sure to know the terms your readers understand and the types of graphics they use.

BACKGROUND

Although the technology for producing graphics continuously gets more complex, the reasons for using them remain the same. Before exploring specific types of illustrations, this section covers some fundamentals. Why do readers like graphics to accompany text? What basic guidelines should you follow with all illustrations?

Reasons for Using Graphics

Before deciding whether to use a pie chart, table, or any other graphic, you need to know what graphics do for your writing. Here are four main reasons for using them.

■ Reason 1: Graphics Simplify Ideas

Readers usually know less about the subject than you. Graphics can help them cut through technical details and grasp basic ideas. For example, a simple illustration of a laboratory instrument, such as a Bunsen burner, makes the description of a lab procedure much easier to understand. In a more complex example, Figure 11–1 uses a group of four different charts to convey the one main point—that McDuff's new Equipment Development group lags behind the company's other

Problems in McDuff's E.D. Group

1995 McDuff Sales (for 7 project areas)

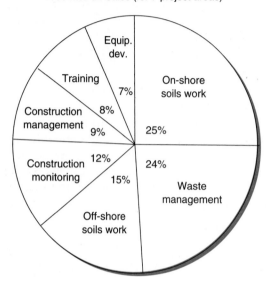

1993-1995 Profits for
Equipment Development (ED)

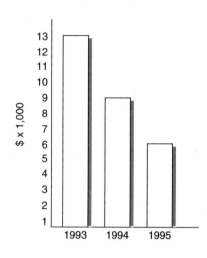

$ Value of ED Contracts

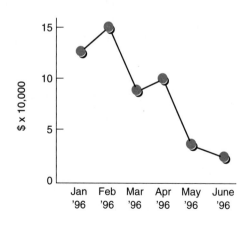

Billable vs. Non-billable Time
(average employee/based on 40 hr week)

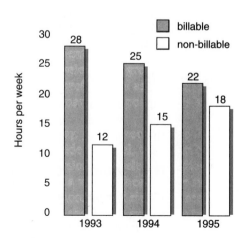

FIGURE 11–1
Graphics used to simplify ideas

profit centers. A quick look at the charts tells the story of the group's difficulties much better than would several hundred words of text.

■ *Reason 2: Graphics Reinforce Ideas*

When a point really needs emphasis, create a graphic. For example, you might draw a map to show where computer terminals will be located within a building, or use a pie chart to show how a budget will be spent, or include a drawing that indicates how to operate a VCR. In all three cases, the graphic would reinforce points made in the accompanying text.

■ *Reason 3: Graphics Create Interest*

Graphics are "grabbers." They can be used to entice readers into the text, just as they engage readers' interest in magazines and journals. If your customers have three reports on their desks and must quickly decide which one to read first, they probably will pick up the one with an engaging picture or chart on the cover page. It may be something as simple as (1) a map outline of the state, county, or city where you will be doing a project, (2) a picture of the product or service you are providing, or (3) a symbol of the purpose of your writing project. Whether on the cover or in the text, graphics attract attention.

Figure 11–2 shows how an outside consultant used a well-known Leonardo da Vinci drawing to attract attention to his proposal to McDuff. The drawing helps to (1) add a classical touch to the cover, (2) focus on the human side of employee testing, and (3) associate the innovation of Infinite Vision, Inc., with the creativity of da Vinci.

■ *Reason 4: Graphics Are Universal*

Some people wrongly associate the growing importance of graphics with today's reliance on television and other popular media—as if graphics pander to less-intellectual instincts. While visual media such as television obviously rely on pictures, the fact is that graphics have been mankind's universal language since cave drawings. A picture, drawing, or chart makes an immediate emotional impact that can help or hurt your case. Advertisers know the power of images, but few writers of technical documents have learned to merge the force of graphics with their text.

General Guidelines

A few basic guidelines apply to all graphics. Keep these fundamentals in mind as you move from one type of illustration to another.

■ *Graphics Guideline 1: Refer to All Graphics in the Text*

With a few exceptions—such as cover illustrations used to grab attention—graphics should be accompanied by clear references within your text. Specifically, you should follow these rules:

Improving Productivity at McDuff, Inc.
An Innovative Approach to Employee Testing

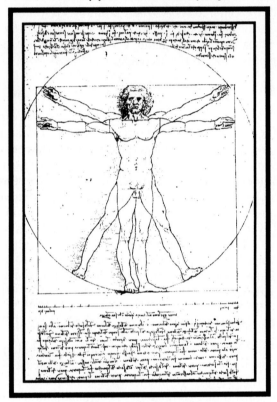

Prepared for Robert S. McDuff
President, McDuff, Inc.
by
James H. Stephens
Infinite Vision, Inc.

February 22, 1996

FIGURE 11–2
Graphics used to create interest

- Include the graphic number in Arabic, not Roman, when you are using more than one graphic.
- Include the title, and sometimes the page number, if either is needed for clarity or emphasis.
- Incorporate the reference smoothly into text wording.

Here are two ways to phrase and position a graphics reference. In Example 1, there is the additional emphasis of the graphics title, whereas in Example 2, the title is left out. Also, note that you can draw more attention to the graphic by placing the reference at the start of the sentence in a separate clause. Or you can relegate the reference to a parenthetical expression at the end or middle of the passage. Choose the option that best suits your purposes.

- **Example 1:** In the past five years, 56 businesses in the county have started in-house recycling programs. The result has been a dramatic shift in the amount of property the county has bought for new waste sites, as shown in Figure 5 ("Landfill Purchases, 1985–1990").
- **Example 2:** As shown in Figure 5, the county has purchased much less land for landfills during the last five years. This dramatic reduction results from the fact that 56 businesses have started in-house recycling programs.

Graphics Guideline 2: Think About Where to Put Graphics

In most cases, locate a graphic close to the text in which it is mentioned. This immediate reinforcement of text by an illustration gives graphics their greatest strength. Variations of this option, as well as several other possibilities, are presented here:

- **Same page as text reference:** A simple visual, such as an informal table, should go on the same page as the text reference if you think it too small for a separate page.
- **Page opposite text reference:** A complex graphic, such as a long table, that accompanies a specific page of text can go on the page opposite the text—that is, on the opposite page of a two-page spread. Usually this option is exercised *only* in documents that are printed on both sides of the paper throughout.
- **Page following first text reference:** Most text graphics appear on the page after the first reference. If the graphic is referred to throughout the text, it can be repeated at later points. (Note: Readers prefer to have graphics positioned exactly where they need them, rather than their having to refer to another part of the document.)
- **Attachments or appendices:** Graphics can go at the end of the document in two cases: first, if the text contains so many references to the graphic that placement in a central location, such as an appendix, would make it more accessible; and second, if the graphic contains less important supporting material that would only interrupt the text.

■ *Graphics Guideline 3: Position Graphics Vertically When Possible*

Readers prefer graphics they can view without having to turn the document sideways. However, if the table or figure cannot fit vertically on a standard 8 1/2″ × 11″ page, either use a foldout or place the graphic horizontally on the page. In the latter case, position the illustration so that the top is on the left margin. (In other words, the page must be turned clockwise to be viewed.)

■ *Graphics Guideline 4: Avoid Clutter*

Let simplicity be your guide. Readers go to graphics for relief from, or reinforcement of, the text. They do not want to be bombarded by visual clutter. Omit information that is not relevant to your purpose, while still making the illustration clear and self-contained. Also, use enough white space so that the readers' eyes are drawn to the graphic. The final section of this chapter discusses graphics clutter in more detail.

■ *Graphics Guideline 5: Provide Titles, Notes, Keys, and Source Data*

Graphics should be as self-contained and self-explanatory as possible. Moreover, they must note any borrowed information. Follow these basic rules for format and acknowledgement of sources:

- **Title:** Follow the graphic number with a short, precise title—either on the line below the number *or* on the same line after a colon (for example, "Figure 3: Salary Scales").
- **Tables:** the number and title go at the top. (As noted in Table Guideline 1 on page 420, one exception is informal tables. They have no table number or title.)
- **Figures:** the number and title can go either above or below the illustration. Center titles or place them flush with the left margin.
- **Notes for explanation:** When introductory information for the graphic is needed, place a note directly underneath the title *or* at the bottom of the graphic.
- **Keys or legends for simplicity:** If a graphic needs many labels, consider using a legend or key, which lists the labels and corresponding symbols on the graphic. For example, a pie chart might have the letters *A, B, C, D,* and *E* printed on the pie pieces, while a legend at the top, bottom, or side of the figure would list what the letters represent.
- **Source information at the bottom:** You have a moral, and sometimes legal, obligation to cite the person, organization, or publication from which you borrowed information for the figure. Either (1) precede the description with the word "Source" and a colon, or (2) if you borrowed just part of a graphic, introduce the citation with "Adapted from."

Besides citing the source, it is sometimes necessary to request permission to use copyrighted or proprietary information, depending on your use and the amount you are borrowing. (A prominent exception is most information provided by the federal government. Most government publications are not copyrighted.) Consult a reference librarian for details about seeking permission.

SPECIFIC GUIDELINES FOR EIGHT GRAPHICS

Illustrations come in many forms; almost any nontextual part of your document can be placed under the umbrella term *graphic*. Among the many types, these eight are often used in technical writing: (1) pie charts, (2) bar charts, (3) line charts, (4) schedule charts, (5) flowcharts, (6) organization charts, (7) technical drawings, and (8) tables. This section of the chapter highlights their different purposes and gives guidelines for using each type.

Pie Charts

Familiar to most readers, pie charts show relationships between the parts and the whole—when just approximate information is needed. Their simple circles with clear labels can provide comforting simplicity within even the most complicated report. Yet the simple form keeps them from being useful when you need to reveal detailed information. Here are specific guidelines for constructing pie charts.

■ ***Pie Chart Guideline 1: Use No More Than 10 Divisions***

To make pie charts work well, limit the number of pie pieces to no more than 10. In fact, the fewer the better. This approach lets the reader grasp major relationships, without having to wade through the clutter of tiny divisions that are difficult to read. In Figure 11–3, for example, McDuff's client can readily see that the project staff will come from the three McDuff offices closest to the project site.

■ ***Pie Chart Guideline 2: Move Clockwise from 12:00, from Largest to Smallest Wedge***

Readers prefer pie charts oriented like a clock—with the first wedge starting at 12:00. Move from largest to smallest wedge to provide a convenient organizing principle.

Make exceptions to this design only for good reason. In Figure 11–3, for example, the last wedge represents a greater percentage than the previous wedge. In this way, it does not break up the sequence the writer wants to establish by grouping the three McDuff offices with the three largest percentages of project workers.

■ ***Pie Chart Guideline 3: Use Pie Charts Especially for Percentages and Money***

Pie charts catch the reader's eye best when they represent items divisible by 100, as with percentages and dollars. Figure 11–3 shows percentages; Figure 11–4

FIGURE 11–3
Pie chart with as few pieces as possible. (Chart shows McDuff work force breakdown for the offshore Atlantic project. McDuff can draw most project workers from its East Coast offices.)

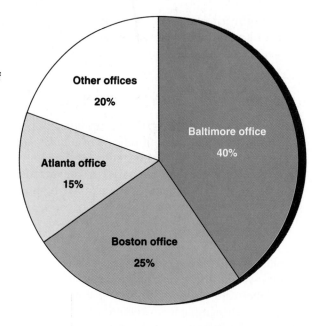

FIGURE 11–4
Pie chart showing money breakdown for average deductions from a McDuff paycheck

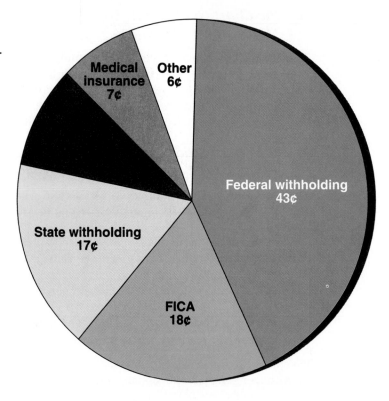

shows money. Using the pie chart for money breakdowns is made even more appropriate by the coinlike shape of the chart.

■ *Pie Chart Guideline 4: Be Creative, But Stay Simple*

Figure 11–5 shows that you can emphasize one piece of the pie by:

1. Shading a wedge
2. Removing a wedge from the main pie
3. Placing related pie charts in a three-dimensional drawing

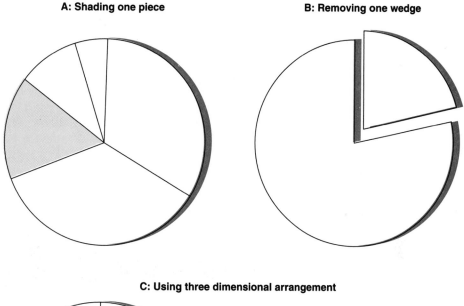

A: Shading one piece   B: Removing one wedge

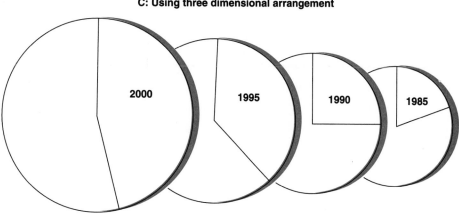

C: Using three dimensional arrangement

FIGURE 11–5
Techniques for emphasis in pie charts
Source: William S. Pfeiffer, *Proposal Writing* (Columbus, Ohio: Merrill, 1989), 145.

Today there are graphics software packages that can create these and other variations for you, so experiment a bit. Of course, always make sure to keep your charts from becoming too detailed. Pie charts should stay simple.

■ *Pie Chart Guideline 5: Draw and Label Carefully*

The most common pie chart errors are (1) wedge sizes that do not correspond correctly to percentages or money amounts and (2) pie sizes that are too small to accommodate the information placed in them. Here are some suggestions for avoiding these mistakes:

- **Pie size:** Make sure the chart occupies enough of the page. On a standard $8\frac{1}{2}$" × 11" sheet with only one pie chart, your circle should be from 3" to 6" in diameter—large enough not to be dwarfed by labels and small enough to leave sufficient white space in the margins.
- **Labels:** Place the wedge labels either inside the pie or outside, depending on the number of wedges, the number of wedge labels, or the length of the labels. Choose the option that produces the cleanest-looking chart.
- **Conversion of percentages:** If you are drawing the pie chart by hand, not using a computer program, use a protractor or similar device. One percent of the pie equals 3.6 degrees (3.6 × 100% = 360 degrees in a circle). With that formula as your guide, you can convert percentages or cents to degrees.

Remember, however, that a pie chart does not reveal fine distinctions very well; it is best used for showing larger differences.

Bar Charts

Like pie charts, bar charts are easily recognized, for they are seen every day in newspapers and magazines. Unlike pie charts, however, bar charts can accommodate a good deal of technical detail. Comparisons are provided by means of two or more bars running either horizontally or vertically on the page. Follow these five guidelines to create effective bar charts.

■ *Bar Chart Guideline 1: Use a Limited Number of Bars*

Though bar charts can show more information than pie charts, both types of illustrations have their limits. Bar charts begin to break down when there are so many bars that information is not easily grasped. The maximum bar number can vary according to chart size, of course. Figure 11–6 shows several multibar charts. The impact of the charts is enhanced by the limited number of bars.

■ *Bar Chart Guideline 2: Show Comparisons Clearly*

Bar lengths should be varied enough to show comparisons quickly and clearly. Avoid using bars that are too close in length, for then readers must study the chart before understanding it. Such a chart lacks immediate visual impact.

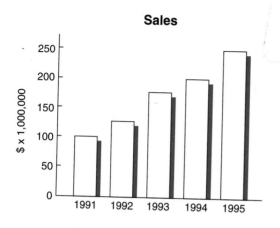

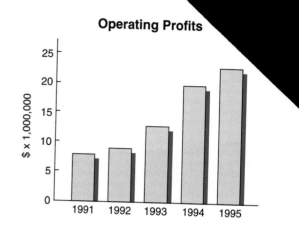

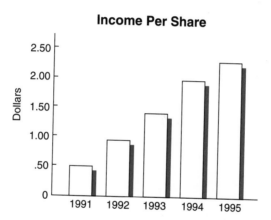

FIGURE 11–6
Bar charts

Also, avoid the opposite tendency of using bar charts to show data that are much different in magnitude. To relate such differences, some writers resort to the dubious technique of inserting "break lines" (two parallel lines) on an axis to reflect breaks in scale (see Figure 11–7). Although this approach at least reminds readers of the breaks, it is still deceptive. For example, note that Figure 11–7 provides no *visual* demonstration of the relationship between 50 and 2800. The reader must think about these differences before making sense out of the chart. In other words, the use of hash marks runs counter to a main goal of graphics—creating an immediate and accurate visual impact.

–7
s on bar charts—
e that can lead to
anding
m William S. Pfeiffer,
ting (Columbus, Ohio:
39), 147.

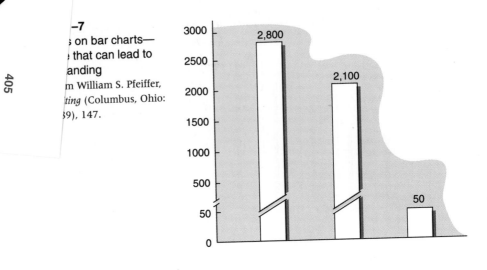

FIGURE 11–8
Bar chart variations
Source: William S. Pfeiffer,
Proposal Writing (Columbus,
Ohio: Merrill, 1989), 148.

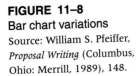

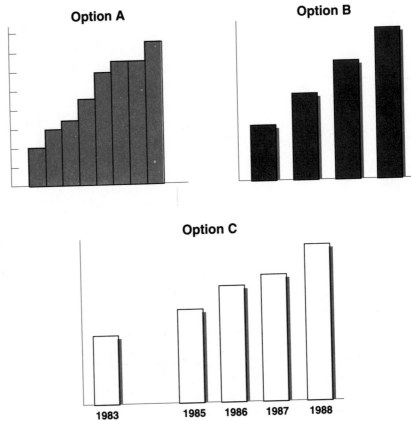

■ *Bar Chart Guideline 3: Keep Bar Widths Equal and Adjust Space Between Bars Carefully*

While bar length varies, bar width must remain constant. As for distance between the bars, following are three options (along with examples in Figure 11–8):

- **Option A: Use no space** when there are close comparisons or many bars, so that differences are easier to grasp.
- **Option B: Use equal space, but less than bar width** when bar height differences are great enough to be seen in spite of the distance between bars.
- **Option C: Use variable space** when gaps between some bars are needed to reflect gaps in the data.

■ *Bar Chart Guideline 4: Carefully Arrange the Order of Bars*

The arrangement of bars is what reveals meaning to readers. Here are two common approaches:

- **Sequential:** used when the progress of the bars shows a trend—for example, McDuff's increasing number of environmental projects in the last five years
- **Ascending or descending order:** used when you want to make a point by the rising or falling of the bars—for example, the 1996 profits of McDuff's six international offices, from lowest to highest

■ *Bar Chart Guideline 5: Be Creative*

Figure 11–9 shows two bar chart variations that help display multiple trends. The *segmented bars* in Option A produce four types of information: the total sales (A + B + C) and the individual sales for A, B, and C. The *grouped bars* in Option B show the individual sales trends for D, F, and G, along with a comparison of all three by year. Note that the amounts are written on the bars to highlight comparisons.

Although these and other bar chart variations may be useful, remember to retain the basic simplicity of the chart.

Line Charts

Line charts are a common graphic. Almost every newspaper contains a few charts covering topics such as stock trends, car prices, or weather. More than other graphics, line charts telegraph complex trends immediately.

They work by using vertical and horizontal axes to reflect quantities of two different variables. The vertical (or *y*) axis usually plots the dependent variable; the horizontal (or *x*) axis usually plots the independent variable. (The dependent variable is affected by changes in the independent variable.) Lines then connect points that have been plotted on the chart. When drawing line charts, follow these five main guidelines:

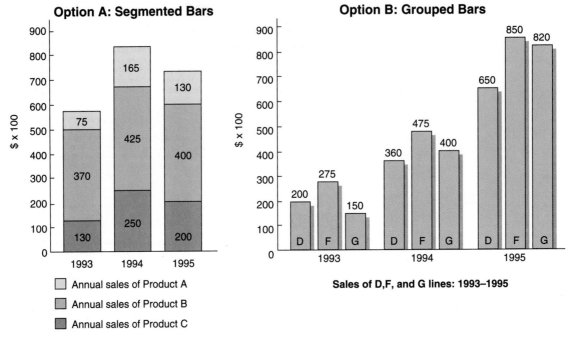

FIGURE 11–9
Bar chart variations for multiple trends
Adapted from William S. Pfeiffer, *Proposal Writing* (Columbus, Ohio: Merrill, 1989), 150.

■ *Line Chart Guideline 1: Use Line Charts for Trends*

Readers are affected by the direction and angle of the chart's line(s), so take advantage of this persuasive potential. In Figure 11–10, for example, the writer wants to show the feasibility of adopting a new medical plan for McDuff. Including a line chart in the study gives immediate emphasis to the most important issue—the effect the new plan would have on stabilizing the firm's medical costs.

■ *Line Chart Guideline 2: Locate Line Charts with Care*

Given their strong impact, line charts can be especially useful as attention-grabbers. Consider placing them (1) on cover pages (to engage reader interest in the document), (2) at the beginning of sections that describe trends, and (3) in conclusions (to reinforce a major point of your document).

■ *Line Chart Guideline 3: Strive for Accuracy and Clarity*

Like bar charts, line charts can be misused or just poorly constructed. Be sure that the line or lines on the graph truly reflect the data from which you have drawn.

Also, select a scale that does not mislead readers with visual gimmicks. Here are some specific suggestions to keep your line charts accurate and clear:

- Start all scales from zero to eliminate the possible confusion of breaks in amounts (see Bar Chart Guideline 2).
- Select a vertical-to-horizontal ratio for axis lengths that is pleasing to the eye (three vertical to four horizontal is common).
- Make chart lines as thick as or thicker than the axis lines.
- Use shading under the line when it will make the chart more readable.

■ *Line Chart Guideline 4: Do Not Place Numbers on the Chart Itself*

Line charts derive their main effect from the simplicity of lines that show trends. Avoid cluttering the chart with a lot of numbers that only detract from the visual impact.

■ *Line Chart Guideline 5: Use Multiple Lines with Care*

Like bar charts, line charts can show multiple trends. Simply add another line or two. If you place too many lines on one chart, however, you run the risk of confusing the reader with too much data. Use no more than four or five lines on a single chart (see Figure 11–11).

FIGURE 11–10
Line chart used to show effect of proposed medical plan on McDuff health costs
Adapted from William S. Pfeiffer, *Proposal Writing* (Columbus, Ohio: Merrill, 1989), 151.

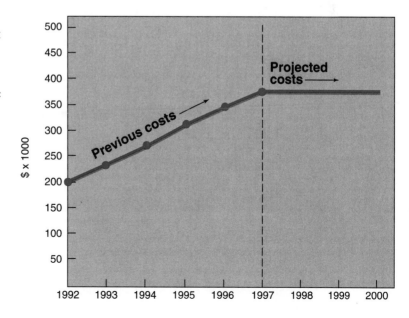

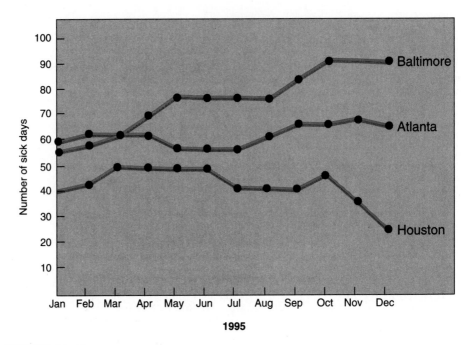

FIGURE 11–11
Line chart using multiple lines to show number of sick days taken at four McDuff offices: 1995
Adapted from William S. Pfeiffer, *Proposal Writing* (Columbus, Ohio: Merrill, 1989), 152.

Schedule Charts

Many documents, especially proposals and feasibility studies, include a special kind of chart that shows readers when certain activities will be accomplished. This kind of chart usually highlights tasks and times already mentioned in the text. Often called a milestone or Gantt chart (after Henry Laurence Gantt, 1861–1919), it usually includes these parts (see Figure 11–12):

- **Vertical axis,** which lists the various parts of the project, in sequential order
- **Horizontal axis,** which registers the appropriate time units
- **Horizontal bar lines** (Gantt) or separate markers (milestone), which show the starting and ending times for each task

Follow these basic guidelines for constructing effective schedule charts in your proposals, feasibility studies, or other documents.

■ Schedule Chart Guideline 1: Include Only Main Activities

Keep readers focused on no more than 10 or 15 main activities. If more detail is needed, construct a series of schedule charts linked to the main "overview" chart.

FIGURE 11–12
Gantt and milestone schedule charts
Source: William S. Pfeiffer, *Proposal Writing* (Columbus, Ohio: Merrill, 1989), 153.

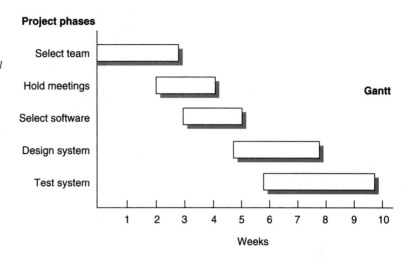

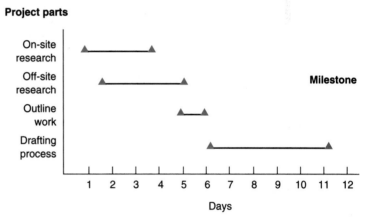

■ *Schedule Chart Guideline 2: List Activities in Sequence, Starting at the Top of the Chart*

As shown in Figure 11–12, the convention is to list activities from the top to the bottom of the vertical axis. Thus the reader's eye moves from the top left to the bottom right of the page, the most natural flow for most readers.

■ *Schedule Chart Guideline 3: Run Labels in the Same Direction*

If readers have to turn the chart sideways to read labels, they may lose interest.

■ *Schedule Chart Guideline 4: Create New Formats When Needed*

Figure 11–12 shows only two common types of schedule charts; you should devise your own hybrid form when it suits your purposes. Your goal is to find the simplest

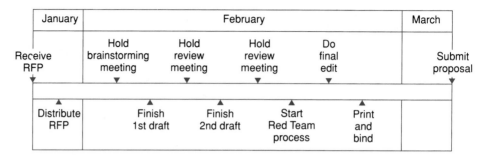

FIGURE 11–13
Schedule chart variation

format for telling your reader when a product will be delivered, a service completed, and so forth. Figure 11–13 includes one such variation.

■ *Schedule Chart Guideline 5: Be Realistic About the Schedule*

Schedule charts can come back to haunt you if you do not include feasible deadlines. As you set dates for activities, be realistic about the likely time something can be accomplished. Your managers and clients understand delays caused by weather, equipment breakdowns, and other unforeseen events. However, they will be less charitable about schedule errors that result from sloppy planning.

Flowcharts

Flowcharts tell a story about a process, usually by stringing together a series of boxes and other shapes that represent separate activities (see Figure 11–14). Because they have a reputation for being hard to read, you need to take extra care in designing them. These five guidelines will help.

■ *Flowchart Guideline 1: Present Only Overviews*

Readers usually want flowcharts to give them only a capsule version of the process, not all the details. Reserve your list of particulars for the text or the appendices, where readers expect it.

■ *Flowchart Guideline 2: Limit the Number of Shapes*

Flowcharts rely on rectangles and other shapes to relate a process—in effect, to tell a story. Different shapes represent different types of activities. This variety helps in describing a complex process, but it can also produce confusion. For the sake of clarity and simplicity, limit the number of different shapes in your flowcharts. Figure 11–15 includes a flowchart that is complex but still readable. Note that the writer has modified geometric shapes to match what they represent (for example, note the tractor-feed holes on the sides of the "printout" block).

FIGURE 11–14
Flowchart for basic McDuff
project
Adapted from William S. Pfeiffer,
Proposal Writing (Columbus, Ohio:
Merrill, 1989), 155.

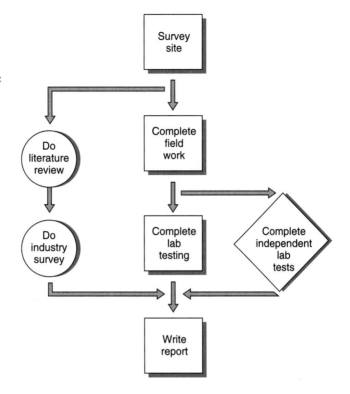

■ *Flowchart Guideline 3: Provide a Legend When Necessary*

Simple flowcharts often need no legend. The few shapes on the chart may already be labeled by their specific steps. When charts get more complex, however, include a legend that identifies the meaning of each shape used.

■ *Flowchart Guideline 4: Run the Sequence from Top to Bottom or from Left to Right*

Long flowcharts like the one in Figure 11–15 may cover the page with several columns or rows. Yet they should always show some degree of uniformity by assuming either a basically vertical or horizontal direction.

■ *Flowchart Guideline 5: Label All Shapes Clearly*

Besides a legend that defines meanings of different shapes, the chart usually includes a label for each individual shape or step. Follow one of these approaches:

■ Place the label inside the shape.
■ Place the label immediately outside the shape.

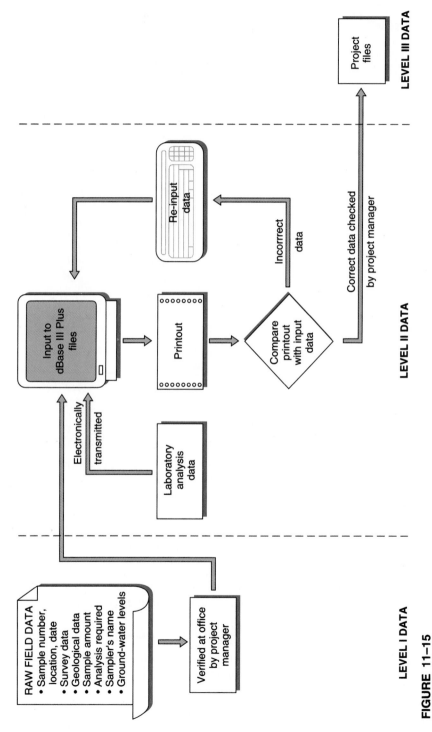

FIGURE 11–15

Flowchart for complex McDuff project

■ Put a number in each shape and place a legend for all numbers in another location (preferably on the same page).

Organization Charts

Organization charts reveal the structure of a company or other organization—the people, positions, or work units. The challenge in producing this graphic is to make sure that the arrangement of information accurately reflects the organization.

■ Organization Chart Guideline 1: Use the Linear "Boxes" Approach to Emphasize High-Level Positions

This traditional format uses rectangles connected by lines to represent some or all of the positions in an organization (see Figure 11–16). Because high-level positions usually appear at the top of the chart, where the attention of most readers is focused, this design tends to emphasize upper management.

■ Organization Chart Guideline 2: Connect Boxes with Solid or Dotted Lines

Solid lines show direct reporting relationships; dotted lines show indirect or staff relationships (see Figure 11–16).

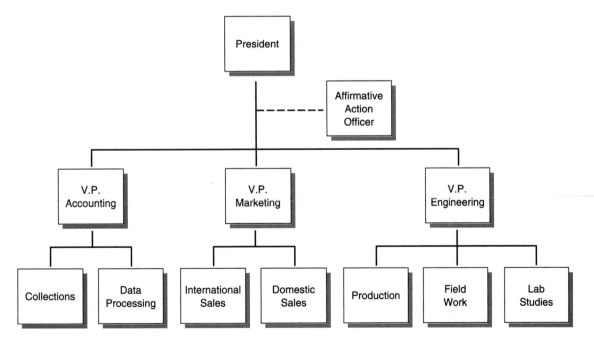

FIGURE 11–16
Basic organization chart
Adapted from William S. Pfeiffer, *Proposal Writing* (Columbus, Ohio: Merrill, 1989), 157.

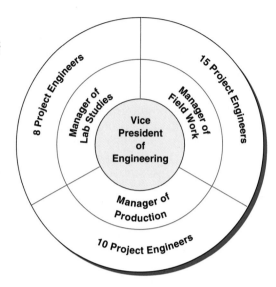

FIGURE 11–17
Concentric organization chart
Source: William S. Pfeiffer, *Proposal Writing* (Columbus, Ohio: Merrill, 1989), 158.

■ *Organization Chart Guideline 3: Use a Circular Design to Emphasize Mid- and Low-Level Positions*

This arrangement of concentric circles gives more visibility to workers outside upper management. These are often the technical workers most deeply involved in the details of a project. For example, Figure 11–17 draws attention to the project engineers perched on the chart's outer ring.

■ *Organization Chart Guideline 4: Use Varied Shapes Carefully*

Like flowcharts, organization charts can use different shapes to indicate different levels or types of jobs. However, beware of introducing more complexity than you need. Use more than one shape only if you are convinced this approach is needed to convey meaning to the reader.

■ *Organization Chart Guideline 5: Be Creative*

When standard forms will not work, create new ones. For example, Figure 11–18 uses an organization chart as the vehicle for showing the lines of responsibility in a specific project.

Technical Drawings

Technical drawings are important tools of companies that produce or use technical products. These drawings can accompany documents such as instructions, reports, sales orders, and proposals. They are preferred over photographs when

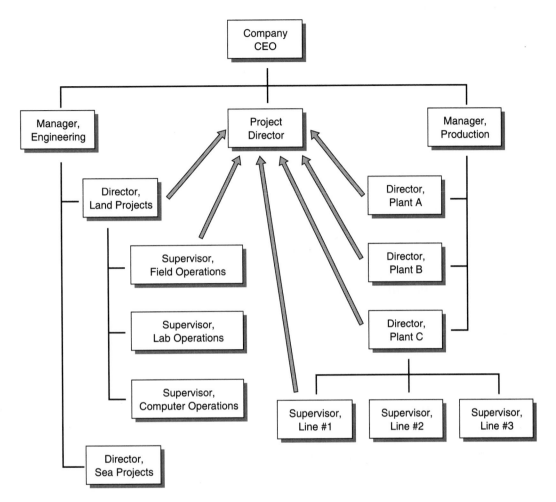

FIGURE 11–18
Organization chart focusing on project (indicates individuals most involved with upcoming project)
Source: William S. Pfeiffer, *Proposal Writing* (Columbus, Ohio: Merrill, 1989), 159.

specific views are more important than photographic detail. Whereas all drawings used to be produced mainly by hand, now they are usually created by CAD (computer-assisted design) systems. Follow these guidelines for producing technical drawings that complement your text.

■ *Drawing Guideline 1: Choose the Right Amount of Detail*

Keep drawings as simple as possible. Use only that level of detail that serves the purpose of your document and satisfies your reader's needs. For example,

Figure 11–19 will be used in a McDuff brochure on maintaining home heating systems. Its intention is to focus on one part of the thermostat—the lever and attached roller. Completed on a CAD system, this drawing presents an exploded view so that the location of the arm can be easily seen.

■ *Drawing Guideline 2: Label Parts Well*

A common complaint of drawings is that parts included in the illustration are not carefully or clearly labeled. Place labels on every part you want your reader to see. (Conversely, you can choose *not* to label those parts that are irrelevant to your purpose.)

When you label parts, use a typeface large enough for easy reading. Also, arrange labels so that (1) they are as easy as possible for your reader to locate and (2) they do not detract from the importance of the drawing itself. The simple labeling in Figure 11–19 fulfills these objectives.

■ *Drawing Guideline 3: Choose the Most Appropriate View*

As already noted, illustrations—unlike photographs—permit you to choose the level of detail needed. In addition, drawings offer you a number of options for perspective or view:

FIGURE 11–19
Technical drawing (exploded view) of home thermostat

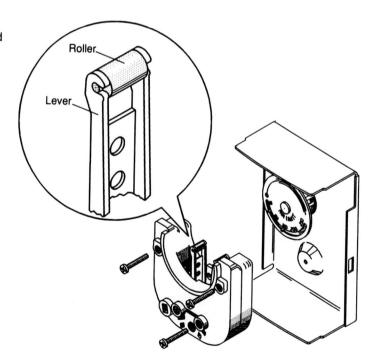

- **Exterior view** (shows surface features with either a two- or three-dimensional appearance—see Figure 11–20)
- **Cross-section view** (shows a "slice" of the object so that interiors can be viewed)
- **Exploded view** (shows relationship of parts to each other by "exploding" the mechanism—see Figure 11–19)

■ *Drawing Guideline 4: Use Legends When There Are Many Parts*

In complex drawings, avoid cluttering the illustration with many labels. Figure 11–20, for example, places all labels in one easy-to-find spot, rather than leaving them on the drawing.

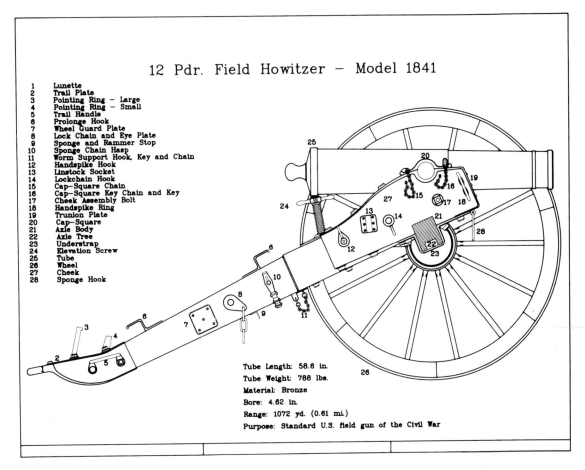

FIGURE 11–20
Technical drawing using CAD system

Assume that Figure 11–20 is part of a McDuff report to the National Park System. A group of specialists just completed a restoration project at a Civil War battlefield. Among many other tasks, the company (1) stopped erosion that had been destroying several hilly sites, (2) moved five howitzer cannon to permanent sites on a mountain ridge, where they were located during the war, and (3) built walking paths that would allow some public access to the battle locations, without damaging the terrain. Given the importance of the cannon to the project, a McDuff CAD draftsperson completed a technical illustration. The complete drawing, with labels, appears in the text of the report. A reduced-size version appears on the cover of the report.

Tables

Tables present readers with raw data, usually in the form of numbers but sometimes in the form of words. Tables are classified as either formal or informal:

- **Informal tables:** limited data arranged in the form of either rows or columns
- **Formal tables:** data arranged in a grid, always with both horizontal rows and vertical columns

These five guidelines will help you design and position tables within the text of your documents.

■ *Table Guideline 1: Use Informal Tables as Extensions of Text*

Informal tables are usually merged with the text on a page, rather than isolated on a separate page or attachment. As such, an informal table usually has (1) no table number or title, (2) no listing in the list of illustrations in a formal report or proposal, and (3) few if any headings for rows or columns.

Example:
Our project in Alberta, Canada, will involve engineers, technicians, and salespeople from three offices, in these numbers:

San Francisco Office	45
St. Louis Office	34
London Office	6
Total	85

■ *Table Guideline 2: Use Formal Tables for Complex Data Separated from Text*

Formal tables may appear on the page of text that includes the table reference, on the page following the first text reference, or in an attachment or appendix. In any case, you should:

- Extract important data from the table and highlight them in the text
- Make every formal table as clear and visually appealing as possible

■ Table Guideline 3: Use Plenty of White Space

Used around and within tables, white space guides the eye through a table much better than do black lines. Avoid putting complete boxes around tables. Instead, leave one inch more of white space than you would normally leave around text.

■ Table Guideline 4: Follow Usual Conventions for Dividing and Explaining Data

Figure 11–21 shows a typical formal table. It satisfies the overriding goal of being clear and self-contained. To achieve that objective in your tables, follow these guidelines:

1. **Titles and numberings:** Give a title to each formal table, and place title and number above the table. Number each table if the document contains two or more tables.
2. **Headings:** Create short, clear headings for all columns and rows.
3. **Abbreviations:** Include in the headings any necessary abbreviations or symbols, such as lb or %. Spell out abbreviations and define terms in a key or footnote if any reader may need such assistance.
4. **Numbers:** Round off numbers when possible, for ease of reading. Also, align multidigit numbers on the right edge, or at the decimal when shown.
5. **Notes:** Place any necessary explanatory headnotes either between the title and the table (if the notes are short) *or* at the bottom of the table.
6. **Footnotes:** Place any necessary footnotes below the table.
7. **Sources:** Place any necessary source references below the footnotes.
8. **Caps:** Use uppercase and lowercase letters, rather than full caps.

TABLE 6: McDuff's Employee Retirement Fund

Investment Type	Book Value	Market Value	% of Total Market Value
Temporary Securities	$ 434,084	434,084	5.9%
Bonds	3,679,081	3,842,056	52.4
Common Stocks	2,508,146	3,039,350	41.4
Mortgages	18,063	18,063	.3
Real Estate	1,939	1,939	nil
Totals	$6,641,313	$7,335,492	100.0%

Note: This table contrasts the book value versus the market value of the McDuff Employee Retirement Fund, as of December 31, 1995.

FIGURE 11–21
Example of formal table
Source: McDuff's accounting firm of Bumble and Bumble, Inc.

■   *Table Guideline 5: Pay Special Attention to Cost Data*

Most readers prefer to have complicated financial information placed in tabular form. Given the importance of such data, edit cost tables with great care. Devote extra attention to these two issues:

- Placement of decimals in costs
- Correct totals of figures

Documents like proposals can be considered contracts in some courts of law, so there is no room for error in relating costs.

MISUSE OF GRAPHICS

Technology has revolutionized the world of graphics by placing sophisticated tools in the hands of many writers. Yet this largely positive event has its dark side. You will see many graphics that—in spite of their slickness—distort data and misinform the reader. The previous sections of this chapter have established principles and guidelines to help writers avoid such distortion and misinformation. This last section shows what can happen to graphics when sound design principles are *not* applied.

Description of the Problem

The popular media give a good glimpse into the problem of faulty graphics. One observer has used newspaper reports about the October 19, 1987, stock market plunge as one indication of the problem. Writing in *Aldus Magazine,* Daryl Moen noted that 60 percent of U.S. newspapers included charts and other graphics about the market drop the day after it occurred.[1] Moen's study revealed that one out of eight had data errors, and one out of three distorted the facts with visual effects. That startling statistic suggests that faulty illustrations are a genuine problem.

Edward R. Tufte analyzes graphics errors in more detail in his excellent work, *The Visual Display of Quantitative Information.* In setting forth his main principles, Tufte notes that "graphical excellence is the well designed presentation of interesting data—a matter of *substance* of *statistics,* and of *design.*" He further contends that graphics must "give to the viewer the greatest number of ideas in the shortest time with the least ink in the smallest space."[2]

One of Tufte's main criticisms is that charts are often disproportional to the actual differences in the data represented. The next subsection shows some specific ways that this error has worked its way into contemporary graphics.

---

[1] Daryl Moen, "Misinformation Graphics," *Aldus Magazine* (January/February 1990), 64.
[2] Edward R. Tufte, *The Visual Display of Quantitative Information* (Cheshire, Conn.: Graphics Press, 1983), 51.

Examples of Distorted Graphics

There are probably as many ways to distort graphics as there are graphical types. This section gets at the problem of misrepresentation by showing several examples and describing the errors involved. None of the examples commits major errors, yet each one fails to represent the data accurately.

■ Example 1: Faulty Comparisons on Modified Bar Chart

Figure 11–22 accompanied a newspaper article about changes in mailing costs and service. The problem here is that the chart's decoration—the mailboxes—inhibits rather than promotes clear communication. Although the writer intends to use mailbox symbolism in lieu of precise bars, the height of the mailboxes does not correspond to the *actual* increase in second-class postage rates.

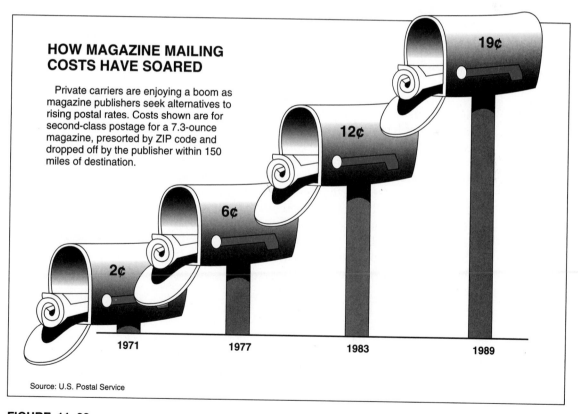

FIGURE 11–22

Faulty comparisons on modified bar chart

Source: *Atlanta Constitution,* 30 Nov. 1989, p. H–1. Used by permission.

A revised graph should include either (1) mailboxes that correctly approximate the actual differences in second-class rates or (2) a traditional bar chart without the mailboxes.

■ *Example 2: "Chartjunk" That Confuses the Reader*

Figure 11–23 concludes a report from a county government to its citizens. Whereas the dollar backdrop is meant to reinforce the topic—that is, the use to which tax funds are put—in fact, it impedes communication. Readers cannot quickly see comparisons. Instead, they must read the entire list below the illustration, mentally rearranging the items into some order.

At the very least, the expenditures should have been placed in sequence, from least to greatest percentage or vice versa. Even with this order, however, one could argue that the dollar bill is a piece of "chartjunk" that fails to display the data effectively.

■ *Example 3: Confusing Pie Charts*

The pie chart in Figure 11–24 (1) omits percentages that should be attached to each of the budgetary expenditures, (2) fails to move in a largest-to-smallest, clock-wise sequence, (3) includes too many divisions, many of which are about the same size and thus difficult to distinguish, and (4) introduces a third dimension that adds no value to the graphic.

Figure 11–25 attempts the visual strategy of alternating shades, but it only succeeds in overloading the chart with too many small percentage divisions in uncertain order. Moreover, the reader cannot easily see how the pie slices would be grouped under the four headings listed below the chart. A grouped bar chart would have better served the purpose, with "Southeast," "New England," "Mid-Atlantic," and "Other" providing the groupings.

Figure 11–26 negates the value of the pie chart by assuming an oblong shape, rather than a circle. This distortion can make it difficult for the reader to distinguish among sections that are similar in size, such as Sections 1 and 2 in Figure 11–26. The pie chart should be a perfect circle, should have percentages on the circle, and should move in large-to-small sequence from the 12:00 position.

WHAT YOUR GENERAL FUND TAX DOLLAR PROVIDES

The General fund is the county's primary operating fund, used to account for the revenues and expenditures necessary to carry out the basic governmental activities of the county. Revenues are derived primarily from taxes, license and permit fees, and service charges. The expenditures incurred are for current day-to-day expenses and operating equipment.

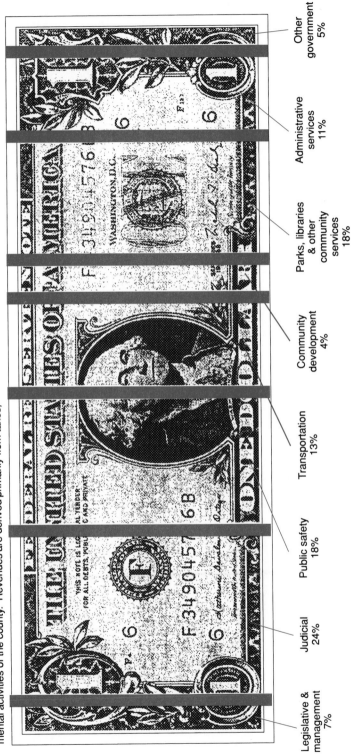

Other government 5%

Administrative services 11%

Parks, libraries & other community services 18%

Community development 4%

Transportation 13%

Public safety 18%

Judicial 24%

Legislative & management 7%

FIGURE 11–23

"Chartjunk" that confuses the reader

Source: Cobb County 1988–1989 Annual Report (Cobb County, GA.). Used by permission.

425

	FUND NAME	DESCRIPTION	FY '89 BUDGET
A	General Fund	Basic government activities	$112,895,822
B	Transit Fund	Implementation of bus system	10,812,522
C	Fire District Fund	Operation of Fire Department	21,253,523
D	Bond Funds	General obligation bond issue proceeds	11,073,371
E	Road Sales Tax Fund	1% special purpose sales tax for road improvements	116,869,904
F	Water & Pollution Control Fund	Daily water system operation	60,572,506
G	Debt Service Fund	Principal & interest payments for general obligation bonds	8,240,313
H	Water RE&I Fund	Maintenance of existing facilities	27,365,744
I	Solid Waste RE&I Fund	Maintenance of existing facilities	1,111,237
J	Solid Waste Disposal Facilities	Landfill operations	6,003,367
K	Water Construction Fund	Construction of new facilities	110,884,507
L	Other Uses*		18,384,364
		SUB-TOTAL	$505,467,180
		LESS INTERFUND ACTIVITY	− 23,393,042
		TOTAL EXPENDITURES	**$482,074,138**

*Other Uses includes: Community Service Block Grants, Law Library, Claims Fund, Capital Projects, Senior Services, Community Development Block Grant, Grant Fund

In addition to the General Fund, the county budgets a number of other specialized funds. These include the Fire District Fund, Transit Fund, Road Sales Tax Fund, and enterprise funds such as Water and Pollution Control, and Solid Waste Disposal Facilities.

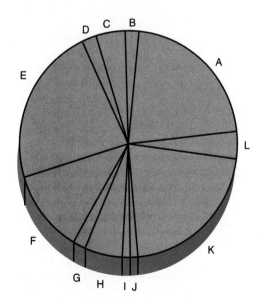

FIGURE 11–24
Confusing pie chart
Source: Cobb County 1988–89 Annual Report (Cobb County, GA.), 14. Used by permission.

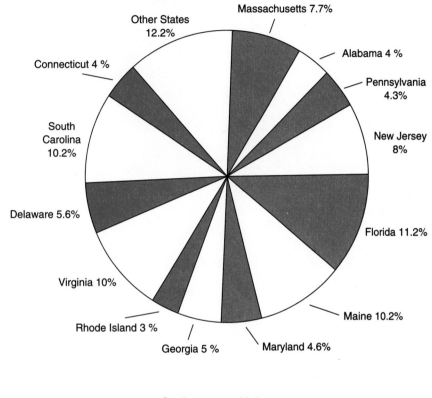

Location of All Ding-Dong Convenience Stores

Southeast	30.4
New England	24.9
Mid-Atlantic	32.5
Other	12.2
	100%

FIGURE 11–25
Confusing pie chart

ASSETS OF JONES RETIREMENT FUND

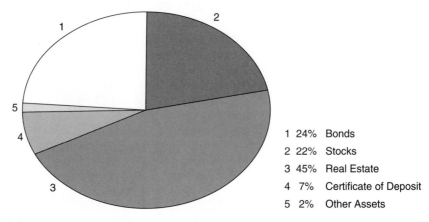

1 24% Bonds
2 22% Stocks
3 45% Real Estate
4 7% Certificate of Deposit
5 2% Other Assets

FIGURE 11–26
Confusing pie chart

COMMUNICATION CHALLENGE

"Massaging McDuff's Annual Report"

Just about everyone considered McDuff's 1995 annual report a boring piece of work. It contained pages of text with only a few tables for visual relief. Wanting to spice up the next annual report, the company hired a graphics firm to create a more appealing design and graphics. GeeWhiz Graphics is completing the 1996 annual report draft for review by McDuff's corporate staff. What follows are highlights of the graphical challenge, along with some questions and comments for discussion.

Beth's Part of the Project

When GeeWhiz got the McDuff job, Beth Chang and Rick Ford were assigned the account. They were to take text and data provided by McDuff's PR department and create a graphically interesting format for readers of the annual report—who are mostly stockholders, McDuff employees, or clients. Beth and Rick have been asked to make data as appealing as possible, especially in light of criticism the company received for its previous annual report. Beth is creating graphics for four pieces of information that McDuff wants emphasized in the report:

1. **International Sales:** McDuff has become a more international firm. Beth was asked to create some graphics that reflect this shift. In 1996 the international offices accounted for 35% of the total $96 million sales. Of that 35%, the Tokyo office was highest with $12 million in sales, Munich was next with $10 million, and the other four international offices shared the rest.
2. **Total Sales:** Over the last 10 years, total sales have gone up steadily. Figures for 1987 through 1996 are, in millions: $65, 70, 73, 74, 80, 83.5, 87, 90, 90.5, 96.

3. **Number of Employees:** Except for one year, when there was a minor lay-off to reduce costs, the number of employees has risen over the last five years, as follows: 1,800 (in 1992), 1,950 (in 1993), 1,925 (in 1994), 2,200 (in 1995), 2,500 (in 1996).

4. **Corporate Overhead:** Of the six service areas covered by the corporate office in Baltimore (see pages 54–57 in chapter 2), the corporate budget spends 40% on human resources, 20% on research, 15% on computer operations, 10% on training, 10% on project management, and 5% on marketing. The company wants to emphasize that the employee-related portion of overhead grew since last year—for example, training went from 5% to 10%, and human resources went from 35% to 40%.

Rick's Part of the Project

Beth's colleague at GeeWhiz Graphics, Rick Ford, was given a similar assignment—that is, to create interesting graphical representations of data about the company. He produced three graphics in his initial work on the report:

1. **Bar Chart:** Rick drew a bar chart to reflect the growth of the international offices in the last five years.

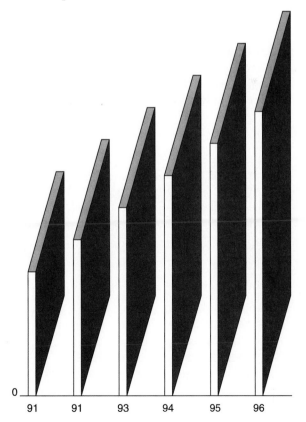

2. **Pie Chart:** To show the investment portfolio of McDuff's retirement plan, Rick produced a pie chart.

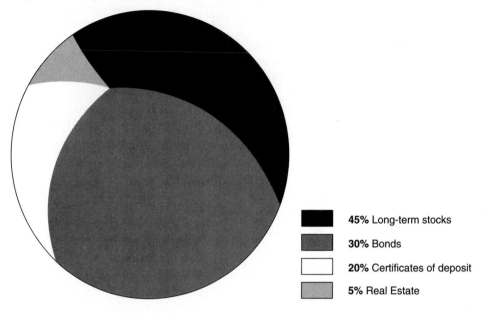

45% Long-term stocks

30% Bonds

20% Certificates of deposit

5% Real Estate

3. **Bar Chart without Bars:** In the past five years, McDuff has made a concerted effort to emphasize preventive medical care and "wellness" programs among its employees. A variation on a bar chart was meant to show this progress in a more visually appealing manner than a conventional bar chart.

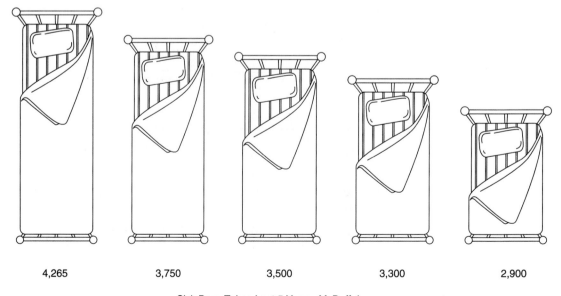

4,265   3,750   3,500   3,300   2,900

Sick Days Taken Last 5 Years: McDuff, Inc.

Questions and Comments for Discussion

1. Separate into groups and discuss the kinds of graphics that would be most effective, appropriate, and clear for the four assignments given to Beth Chang. Report the results of your discussion to the entire class.
2. Are there any ethical implications Beth should consider in producing her graphics? If so, what are they?
3. Separate into groups and discuss any ethical or clarity issues suggested by the graphics produced by Rick Ford. Should these graphics be included in McDuff's annual report? If so, why? If not, why not and what would you change? If useful, refer to the ECI (Equal Consideration of Interests) principle discussed on pages 62–64.

CHAPTER SUMMARY

More than ever before, readers of technical documents expect good graphics to accompany text. Graphics (also called illustrations or visual aids) can be in the form of (1) tables (rows and/or columns of data) or (2) figures (a catchall term for all nontable illustrations). Both types are used to simplify ideas, reinforce points made in the text, generate interest, and create a universal appeal.

Eight common graphics used in technical writing are pie charts, bar charts, line charts, schedule charts, flowcharts, organization charts, technical drawings, and tables. As detailed in this chapter, you should follow specific guidelines in constructing each type. These basic guidelines apply to all graphics:

1. Refer to all graphics in the text.
2. Think about where to put graphics.
3. Position graphics vertically when possible.
4. Avoid clutter.
5. Provide titles, notes, keys, and source data.

ASSIGNMENTS

Your instructor may want you to practice graphics in the context of some of the writing assignments in this textbook, especially in chapters 8, 9, and 10. Here are a few additional exercises.

1. **Pie, Bar, and Line Charts.** Figure 11–27 shows total energy production and consumption from 1960 through 1987, while also breaking down both into the four categories of coal, petroleum, natural gas, and "other." Use those data to complete the following charts:

   - A pie chart that shows the four groupings of energy consumption in 1987
   - A bar chart that shows the trend in total consumption during these six years: 1960, 1965, 1970, 1975, 1980, and 1985
   - A segmented bar chart that shows the total energy production, and the four percent-of-production subtotals, for 1960 and 1980
   - A single-line chart showing energy production from 1965 through 1975

NO. **926.** ENERGY PRODUCTION AND CONSUMPTION, BY MAJOR SOURCE: 1960 TO 1987

[Btu = British thermal unit. For Btu conversion factors, see text, section 19. See also *Historical Statistics, Colonial Times to 1970*, series M 76–92]

YEAR	Total production (quad. Btu)	PERCENT OF PRODUCTION				Total consumption (quad. Btu)	PERCENT OF CONSUMPTION				Consumption/production ratio
		Coal	Petroleum [1]	Natural gas [2]	Other [3]		Coal	Petroleum [1]	Natural gas [2]	Other [3]	
1960	41.5	26.1	36.0	34.0	3.9	43.8	22.5	45.5	28.3	3.8	1.06
1961	42.0	24.9	36.2	34.9	4.0	44.5	21.6	45.5	29.1	3.8	1.06
1962	43.6	25.0	35.6	35.1	4.2	46.5	21.3	45.2	29.5	4.0	1.07
1963	45.9	25.8	34.8	35.4	4.0	48.3	21.5	44.9	29.8	3.7	1.05
1964	47.7	26.2	33.9	35.8	4.0	50.5	21.7	44.2	30.3	3.8	1.06
1965	49.3	26.5	33.5	35.8	4.3	52.7	22.0	44.1	29.9	4.0	1.07
1966	52.2	25.8	33.7	36.4	4.1	55.7	21.8	43.8	30.5	3.8	1.07
1967	55.0	25.1	33.9	36.5	4.4	57.6	20.7	43.9	31.2	4.2	1.05
1968	56.8	24.0	34.0	37.6	4.4	61.0	20.2	44.2	31.5	4.1	1.07
1969	59.1	23.5	33.1	38.7	4.8	64.2	19.3	44.1	32.2	4.4	1.09
1970	62.1	23.5	32.9	38.9	4.7	66.4	18.5	44.4	32.8	4.3	1.07
1971	61.3	21.5	32.7	40.5	5.3	67.9	17.1	45.0	33.1	4.8	1.11
1972	62.4	22.6	32.1	39.7	5.6	71.3	16.9	46.2	31.9	5.0	1.14
1973	62.1	22.5	31.4	39.9	6.2	74.3	17.5	46.9	30.3	5.3	1.20
1974	60.8	23.1	30.5	38.9	7.4	72.5	17.5	46.1	30.0	6.5	1.19
1975	59.9	25.0	29.6	36.8	8.6	70.5	17.9	46.4	28.3	7.4	1.18
1976	59.9	26.1	28.8	36.4	8.6	74.4	18.3	47.3	27.4	7.1	1.24
1977	60.2	26.2	29.0	36.4	8.5	76.3	18.2	48.7	26.1	7.0	1.27
1978	61.1	24.4	30.2	35.6	9.9	78.1	17.6	48.6	25.6	8.1	1.28
1979	63.8	27.5	28.4	35.0	9.1	[4] 78.9	19.1	47.1	26.2	7.7	1.24
1980	64.8	28.7	28.2	34.2	8.9	76.0	20.3	45.0	26.8	7.8	1.17
1981	64.4	28.5	28.2	34.2	9.1	74.0	21.5	43.2	26.9	8.4	1.15
1982	63.9	29.2	28.7	32.0	10.2	70.8	21.6	42.7	26.1	9.6	1.11
1983	61.2	28.2	30.1	30.6	11.2	70.5	22.6	42.6	24.6	10.2	1.15
1984	[5] 65.8	30.0	28.6	30.7	10.7	74.1	23.0	41.9	25.0	10.0	1.13
1985	64.8	29.8	29.3	29.6	11.3	74.0	23.6	41.8	24.1	10.4	1.14
1986	64.3	30.4	28.6	29.0	12.0	74.3	23.2	43.4	22.5	10.9	1.16
1987	64.6	31.2	27.3	29.5	12.0	76.0	23.7	42.9	22.6	10.8	1.18

[1] Production includes crude oil and lease condensate. Consumption includes domestically produced crude oil, natural gas liquids, and lease condensate, plus imported crude oil and products.   [2] Production includes natural gas liquids; consumption excludes natural gas liquids.   [3] Comprised of hydropower, nuclear power, geothermal energy and other.   [4] Represents peak year for U.S. energy consumption.   [5] Represents peak year for U.S. energy production.

Source: U.S. Energy Information Administration, *Annual Energy Review*, and unpublished data.

FIGURE 11–27

Reference for Assignment 1

Source: U.S. Department of Commerce, Bureau of the Census, *Statistical Abstract of the United States, 1989* (Washington, 1989), 554.

- A multiple-line chart that contrasts the coal, petroleum, and natural gas percent of production for any 10-year span on the table

2. **Schedule Charts.** Using any options discussed in this chapter, draw a schedule chart that reflects your work on one of the following:

- A project at work
- A laboratory course at school
- A lengthy project in a course such as this one

3. **Flowcharts.** Select a process with which you are familiar because of work, school, home, or other interests. Then draw a flowchart that outlines the main activities involved in this process.

4. **Organization Chart.** Select an organization with which you are familiar, or one about which you can find information. Then construct a linear flowchart that would help an outsider understand the management structure of all or part of the organization.
5. **Technical Drawing.** Drawing freehand or using computer-assisted design, produce a simple technical drawing of an object with which you are familiar through work, school, or home use.
6. **Table.** Using the map in Figure 11–28, draw an informal table correlating the five main groupings with the number of states in each.

Hazardous Waste Sites—June 1988

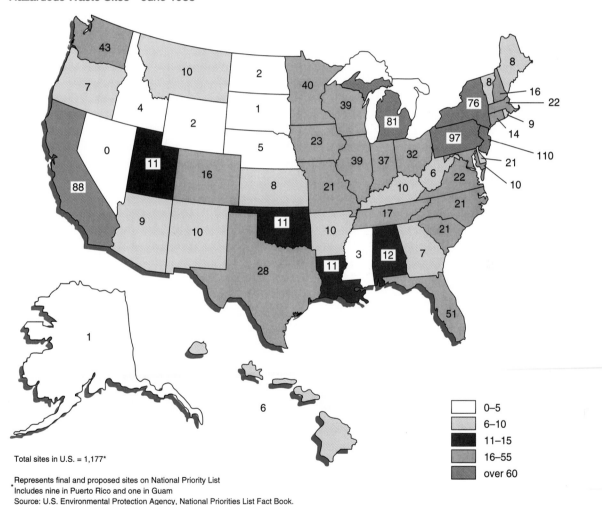

Total sites in U.S. = 1,177*

Represents final and proposed sites on National Priority List
*Includes nine in Puerto Rico and one in Guam
Source: U.S. Environmental Protection Agency, National Priorities List Fact Book.

FIGURE 11–28
Reference for Assignment 6
Source: U.S. Department of Commerce, Bureau of the Census, *Statistical Abstract of the United States, 1989* (Washington, 1989), 220.

7. **Misuse of Graphics.** Find three deficient graphics in newspapers, magazines, reports, or other technical documents. Submit copies of the graphics along with a written critique that (1) describes in detail the deficiencies of the graphics and (2) offers suggestions for improving them.

8. **Misuse of Graphics.** Analyze the graphics in Figures 11–29, 11–30, and 11–31. Describe any deficiencies and offer suggestions for improvement.

FIGURE 11–29

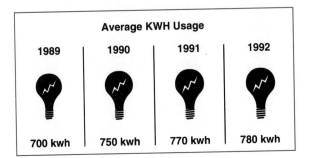

FIGURE 11–30

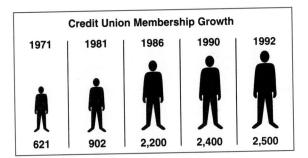

FIGURE 11–31

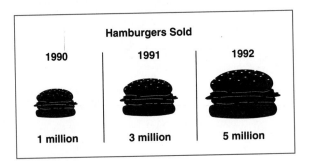

12 Oral Communication

A manager at McDuff's Munich office presents an overview of the firm to some prospective clients.

Your career will present you with many opportunities for oral presentations, both formal and informal. At the time they arise, however, you may not consider them to be "opportunities." They may seem to loom on the horizon as stressful obstacles. That response is normal. The purpose of this chapter is to provide the tools that will help oral presentations contribute to your self-esteem and career success. You will find guidelines for preparation and delivery, techniques for dealing with anxiety, and an example of a technical presentation. Also, the chapter addresses the related topic of running effective meetings.

The entire chapter is based on one simple principle: *Almost anyone can become an excellent speaker.* Put aside the myth that competent speakers are born with the talent, that "either they have it or they don't." Certainly some people have more natural talent at thinking on their feet or have a more resonant voice. But success at speaking can come to all speakers, whatever their talent, if they follow the "3 Ps":

Step 1: **P**repare carefully
Step 2: **P**ractice often
Step 3: **P**erform with enthusiasm

These steps form the foundation for all specific guidelines that follow. Before presenting these guidelines, this chapter examines specific ways that formal and informal presentations become part of your professional life.

PRESENTATIONS AND YOUR CAREER

Some oral presentations you will choose to give; others will be "command performances" thrust upon you. Using McDuff, Inc., as a backdrop, the following

■ Involve the usual risks that reliance on machinery always introduces into your presentation

■ *Presentation Guideline 5: Practice, Practice, Practice*

Many speakers prepare a well-organized speech but then fail to add the essential ingredient: practice. Constant practice distinguishes superior presentations from mediocre ones. It also helps to eliminate the nervousness that most speakers feel at one time or another.

In practicing your presentation, make use of four main techniques. They are listed here, from least effective to most effective:

■ **Practice before a mirror:** This old-fashioned approach allows you to hear and see yourself in action. The drawback, of course, is that it is difficult to evaluate your own performance while you are speaking. Nevertheless, such run-throughs definitely make you more comfortable with the material.

■ **Use of audiotape:** Most presenters have access to a tape player, so this approach is quite practical. The portability of the machines allows you to practice almost anywhere. Although taping a presentation will not improve gestures, it will help you discover and eliminate verbal distractions such as filler words (*uhhhh, um, ya know*).

■ **Use of live audience:** Groups of your colleagues, friends, or family—simulating a real audience—can provide the kinds of responses that approximate those of a real audience. In setting up this type of practice session, however, make certain that observers understand the criteria for a good presentation and are prepared to give an honest, forthright critique.

■ **Use of videotape:** This practice technique allows you to see and hear yourself as others do. Your careful review of the tape, particularly when done with another qualified observer, can help you identify and eliminate problems with posture, eye contact, vocal patterns, and gestures. At first it can be a chilling experience, but soon you will get over the awkwardness of seeing yourself on film.

■ *Presentation Guideline 6: Speak Vigorously and Deliberately*

"Vigorously" means with enthusiasm; "deliberately" means with care, attention, and appropriate emphasis on words and phrases. The importance of this guideline becomes clear when you think back to how you felt during the last speech you heard. At the very least, you expected the speaker to show interest in the subject and to demonstrate enthusiasm. Good information is not enough. You need to arouse the interest of the listeners.

You may wonder, "How much enthusiasm is enough?" The best way to answer this question is to hear or (preferably) watch yourself on tape. Your delivery should incorporate just enough enthusiasm so that it sounds and looks a bit unnatural to you. Few if any listeners ever complain about a speech being too enthusiastic or a speaker being too energetic. But many, many people complain about dull speakers who fail to show that they themselves are excited about the topic. Remember—every presentation is, in a sense, "show time."

■ *Presentation Guideline 7: Avoid Filler Words*

Avoiding filler words presents a tremendous challenge to most speakers. When they think about what comes next or encounter a break in the speech, they may tend to fill the gap with filler words and phrases such as these:

uhhhhh. . .

ya know. . .

okay. . .

well. . . uh. . .

like . . .

I mean. . .

umm. . .

These gap-fillers are a bit like spelling errors in written work: Once your listeners find a few, they start looking for more and are distracted from your presentation. To eliminate such distractions, follow these three steps:

Step 1: **Use pauses to your advantage.** Short gaps or pauses inform the listener that you are shifting from one point to another. In signaling a transition, a pause serves to draw attention to the point you make right after the pause. Note how listeners look at you when you pause. Do *not* fill these strategic pauses with filler words.

Step 2: **Practice with tape.** Tape is brutally honest: When you play it back, you will become instantly aware of fillers that occur more than once or twice. Keep a tally sheet of the fillers you use and their frequency. Your goal will be to reduce this frequency with every practice session.

Step 3: **Ask for help from others.** After working with tape machines in Step 2, give your speech to an individual who has been instructed to stop you after each filler. This technique gives immediate reinforcement.

■ *Presentation Guideline 8: Use Rhetorical Questions*

Enthusiasm, of course, is your best delivery technique for capturing the attention of the audience. Another technique is the use of rhetorical questions at pivotal points in your presentation.

Rhetorical questions are those you ask to get listeners thinking about a topic, not those that you would expect them to answer out loud. They prod listeners to think about your point and set up an expectation that important information will follow. Also, they break the monotony of standard declarative sentence patterns.

For example, here is a rhetorical question used by a computer salesperson in proposing a purchase by one of McDuff's small offices:

> I've discussed the three main advantages that a centralized word-processing center would provide your office staff. But is this an approach that you can afford at this point in the company's growth?

Then the speaker would follow the question with remarks supporting the position that the system is affordable.

"What if" scenarios provide another way to introduce rhetorical questions. They gain the listeners' attention by having them envision a situation that might occur. For example, a safety engineer could use this kind of rhetorical question in proposing McDuff's asbestos-removal services to a regional bank:

> What if you repossessed a building that contained dangerous levels of asbestos? Do you think that your bank would then be liable for removing all the asbestos?

Again, the question pattern heightens listener interest.

Rhetorical questions do not come naturally. You must make a conscious effort to insert them at points when it is most important to gain or redirect the attention of the audience. Three particularly effective uses follow:

1. **As a grabber at the beginning of a speech:** "Have you ever wondered how you might improve the productivity of your word-processing staff?"
2. **As a transition between major points:** "We've seen that centralized word processing can improve the speed of report production, but will it require any additions to your staff?"
3. **As an attention-getter right before your conclusion:** "Now that we've examined the features of centralized word processing, what's the next step you should make at McDuff?"

■ *Presentation Guideline 9: Maintain Eye Contact*

Your main goal—always—is to keep listeners interested in what you are saying. This goal requires that you maintain control, using whatever techniques you can employ to direct the attention of the audience. Frequent eye contact is one good strategy.

The simple truth is that listeners pay closer attention to what you are saying when you look at them. Think how you react when a speaker makes constant eye contact with you. If you are like most people, you feel as if the speaker is speaking to you personally—even if there are 100 people in the audience. Also, you tend to feel more obligated to listen when you know that the speaker's eyes will be meeting yours throughout the presentation. Here are some ways you can make eye contact a natural part of your own strategy for effective oral presentations:

- **With audiences of about 30 or less:** Make regular eye contact with everyone in the room. Be particularly careful not to ignore members of the audience who are seated to your far right and far left (see Figure 12–1). Many speakers tend to focus on the listeners within Section B. Instead, make wide sweeps so that listeners in Sections A and C get equal attention.

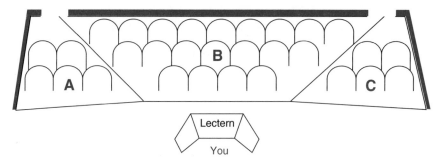

FIGURE 12–1
Audience sections

- **With large audiences:** There may be too many people or too large a room for you to make individual eye contact with all listeners. In this case, focus on just a few people in all three sections of the audience noted in Figure 12–1. This approach gives the appearance that you are making eye contact with the entire audience.
- **With any size audience:** Occasionally look away from the audience—either to your notes or toward a part of the room where there are no faces looking back. In this way, you avoid the appearance of staring too intensely at your audience. Also, these breaks give you the chance to collect your thoughts or check your notes.

■ *Presentation Guideline 10: Use Appropriate Gestures and Posture*

Speaking is only one part of giving a speech; another is adopting appropriate posture and using gestures that will reinforce what you are saying. Note that good speakers are much more than "talking heads" before a lectern. Instead, they:

1. Use their hands and fingers to emphasize major points
2. Stand straight, without leaning on or gripping the lectern
3. Step out from behind the lectern on occasion, to decrease the distance between them and the audience
4. Point toward visuals on screens or charts, without losing eye contact with the audience

The audience will judge you by what you say *and* what they see, a fact that again makes videotaping a crucial part of your preparation. With work on this facet of your presentation, you can avoid problems like keeping your hands constantly in your pockets, rustling change (remove pocket change and keys beforehand), tapping a pencil, scratching nervously, slouching over a lectern, and shifting from foot to foot.

GUIDELINES FOR PRESENTATION GRAPHICS

More than ever before, listeners expect good graphics during oral presentations. Much like gestures, graphics transform the words of your presentation into true communication with the audience. To emphasize the importance of speech graphics, here is an incident from industry once reported to the author:

> Several years ago the competitors for designing a large city's football stadium had been narrowed to three firms. Firm A, a large and respected company, had done some preliminary design work on the project and was expected to get the contract. Firm B, another large and respected firm, was competing fiercely for the job. And Firm C, a small and fairly new company, was considered by all concerned to be a genuine long shot. Yet it had submitted an interesting-enough proposal to be chosen as a finalist.
>
> All three firms were invited to make 10- or 15-minute presentations on their proposals. The presentations by Firms A and B were professional, conventional, and predictable. Firm C, however, took a different and riskier approach. Its presentation was barely 5 minutes long and was given simultaneously with a videotape. As expected, the speech itself stressed the benefits of Firm C's design for the stadium. The accompanying videotape, however, was quite unconventional. It interspersed drawings of Firm C's design with highlights of that city's football team scoring touchdowns, catching passes, and making game-winning tackles.
>
> Firm C's effort to associate the winning football team with its proposed design worked. Shortly after the presentations, the selection committee chose the dark horse, Firm C, to design the new stadium.

The lesson here is *not* that fancy visuals always win a contract. Instead, the point is that innovative graphics, in concert with a solid proposal presentation, can set you apart from the competition. Firm C had a sound stadium design reinforced by an unusual visual display. Granted, it walked the fine line between effective and manipulative graphics. Yet even the fanciest visuals cannot disguise a bad idea to a discerning audience. The Firm C presenters won because they found an effective way to present their proposal. They incorporated graphics into their presentation to reinforce main selling points.

■ *Graphics Guideline 1: Discover Listener Preferences*

Some professionals prefer simple speech graphics, such as a conventional flip chart. Others prefer more sophisticated equipment, such as video projectors connected to laptop computers. Your listeners are usually willing to indicate their preferences when you call on them. Contact the audience ahead of time and make some inquiries.

■ *Graphics Guideline 2: Think About Graphics Early*

Graphics done as an afterthought usually look "tacked on." Plan graphics while you prepare the text so that the final presentation will seem fluid. This guideline holds true especially if you rely upon specialists to prepare your visuals. These professionals need some lead time to do their best work. Also, they can often provide helpful insights about how visuals will enhance the presentation—*if* you consult them early enough and *if* you make them a part of your presentation team.

The goal is to use graphics of which you can be proud. Never, never put yourself in the position of having to apologize for the quality of your graphic material. If an illustration is not up to the quality your audience would expect, do *not* use it.

■ *Graphics Guideline 3: Keep the Message Simple*

Listeners can be suspicious of overly slick visual effects. Most people prefer the simplicity of simple overhead transparencies and flip charts, for example. If you decide to use more sophisticated techniques, make sure they fit your context. In the previous stadium example, Firm C took a risk by using videotaped football highlights to sell its stadium design. Complex graphics such as videotape can sometimes overshadow the proposal itself. In Firm C's case, however, the tape's purpose was kept quite simple. It simply associated the success of the team with the potential success of the proposed stadium design.

■ *Graphics Guideline 4: Make Any*
Wording Brief and Visible

The best graphics rely on visual image, not words. Avoid cluttering them with language. Instead, provide necessary explanations during the presentation. When you do need to put words in a visual—perhaps in a list of major points—pare them down to the bare minimum. Single words or phrases can then be elaborated on in your speech text.

Equally important, be certain that all wording is visible from the *back of the room.* Nothing is more irritating than a poster, an overhead, or a slide that cannot be read. Prevent this problem by asking beforehand about the room size and arrangement; then adjust letter size and thickness accordingly. Incidentally, standard type is too small to use effectively on overhead transparencies. When using overheads, have the originals typeset in large print or prepared on a word-processing system with oversized type.

■ *Graphics Guideline 5: Use Colors Carefully*

Colors can add flair to visuals. Follow these simple guidelines to make colors work for you:

- Have a good reason for using color (such as the need to highlight three different bars on a graph with three distinct colors).
- Use only dark, easily seen colors, and be sure that a color contrasts with its background (for example, yellow on white would not work well).
- Use no more than three or four colors in each graphic (to avoid a confused effect).
- For variety, consider using white on a black or dark green background.

■ *Graphics Guideline 6: Leave Graphics Up Long Enough*

Because graphics reinforce text, they should be shown only while you address the particular point at hand. For example, reveal a graph just as you are saying, "As you can see from the graph, the projected revenue reaches a peak in 1995." Then pause and leave the graph up a bit longer for the audience to absorb your point.

How long is *too* long? A graphic outlives its usefulness when it remains in sight after you have moved on to another topic. Listeners will continue to study it and ignore what you are now saying. If you use a graphic once and plan to return to it, take it down after its first use and show it again later.

■ *Graphics Guideline 7: Avoid Handouts*

Because timing is so important in your use of speech graphics, handouts are usually a bad idea. Readers move through a handout at their own pace, rather than at the pace the speaker might prefer. Thus handouts cause you to lose the attention of your audience. Use them only if (1) no other visual will do, (2) your listener has requested them, or (3) you distribute them as reference material *after* you have finished talking.

■ *Graphics Guideline 8: Maintain Eye Contact While Using Graphics*

Do not stare at your visuals while you speak. Maintain control of listeners' responses by looking back and forth from the visual to faces in the audience. To point to the graphic aid, use the hand closest to the visual. Using the opposite hand causes you to cross over your torso, forcing you to turn your neck and head away from the audience.

■ *Graphics Guideline 9: Include All Graphics in Your Practice Sessions*

Dry runs before the actual presentation should include every graphic you plan to use, in its final form. This is a good reason to prepare graphics as you prepare text, rather than as an afterthought. Running through a final practice without graphics would be much like doing a dress rehearsal for a play without costumes and props—you would be leaving out parts that require the greatest degree of timing and orchestration. Practicing with graphics helps you improve transitions.

■ *Graphics Guideline 10: Use Your Own Equipment*

Murphy's Law always seems to apply when you use another person's audiovisual equipment: Whatever can go wrong, will. For example, a new bulb burns out, there is no extra bulb in the equipment drawer, an extension cord is too short, the screen does not stay down, the overhead projector won't focus—all these problems the author has experienced, and more. Even if the equipment works, it often operates differently from what you are used to. The only sure way to put the odds in your favor is to carry your own equipment and set it up in advance.

However, most of us have to rely on someone else's equipment at least sometimes. Here are a few ways to ward off disaster:

- Find out exactly who will be responsible for providing the equipment and contact that person in advance.
- Have some easy-to-carry backup supplies in your car—an extension cord, an overhead projector bulb, felt-tip markers, and chalk, for example.
- Bring handout versions of your visuals, as a last resort.

In short, you want to avoid putting yourself in the position of having to apologize. Plan well.

OVERCOMING NERVOUSNESS

The problem of nervousness deserves special mention because it is so common. Virtually everyone who gives speeches feels some degree of nervousness before "the event." An instinctive "fight or flight" response kicks in for the many people who have an absolute dread of presentations. In fact, surveys have determined that most of us rate public speaking at the top of our list of fears, even above sickness and death! Given this common response, this chapter considers the problem and offers suggestions for overcoming it.

Why Do We Fear Presentations?

Most of us feel comfortable with informal conversations, when we can voice our views to friends and indulge in impromptu exchanges. We are used to this type of casual presenting of our ideas. Formal presentations, however, put us into a more structured, more awkward, and thus more tense environment. Despite the fact that we may know the audience is friendly and interested in our success, the formal context triggers nervousness that is sometimes difficult to control.

This nervous response is normal and, to some degree, useful. It gets you "up" for the speech. That adrenaline pumping through your body can generate a degree of enthusiasm that propels the presentation forward and creates a lively performance. Just as veteran actors admit to some nervousness helping to improve their performance, excellent speakers usually can benefit from the same effect.

The problem occurs when nervousness felt before or during a speech becomes so overwhelming that it affects the quality of the presentation. Since sympathy is the last feeling a speaker wants the audience to have, it is worth considering some techniques to combat nervousness.

A Strategy for Staying Calm

As the cliché goes, do not try to eliminate "butterflies" before a presentation—just get them to fly in formation. In other words, it is best to acknowledge that a certain degree of nervousness will always remain. Then go about the business of getting it to work for you. Here are a few suggestions:

■ *No Nerves Guideline 1: Know Your Speech*

The most obvious suggestion is also the most important one. If you prepare your speech well, your command of the material will help to conquer any queasiness you feel—particularly at the beginning of the speech, when nervousness is usually at its peak. Be so sure of the material that your listeners will overlook any initial discomfort you may feel.

■ *No Nerves Guideline 2: Prepare Yourself Physically*

Your physical well-being before the speech can have a direct bearing on anxiety. More than ever before, most cultures understand the essential connection between mental and physical well-being. This connection suggests you should take these precautions before your presentation:

- **Avoid caffeine or alcohol for at least several hours before you speak.** You do not need the additional jitters brought on by caffeine or the false sense of ease brought on by alcohol.
- **Eat a light, well-balanced meal within a few hours of speaking.** However, do not overdo it—particularly if a meal comes right before your speech. If you are convinced that any eating will increase your anxiety, wait to eat until after speaking.
- **Practice deep-breathing exercises before you speak.** Inhale and exhale slowly, making your body slow down to a pace you can control. If you can control your breathing, you can probably keep the butterflies flying in formation.
- **Exercise normally the same day of the presentation.** A good walk will help invigorate you and reduce nervousness. However, do not wear yourself out by exercising more than you would normally.

■ *No Nerves Guideline 3: Picture Yourself Giving a Great Presentation*

Many speakers become nervous because their imaginations are working overtime. They envision the kinds of failure that almost never occur. Instead, speakers should be constantly bombarding their psyches with images of success, not failure. Mentally take yourself through the following steps of the presentation:

- Arriving at the room
- Feeling comfortable at your chair
- Getting encouraging looks from your audience

- Giving an attention-getting introduction
- Presenting your supporting points with clarity and smoothness
- Ending with an effective wrap-up
- Fielding questions with confidence

Sometimes called "imaging," this technique helps to program success into your thinking and to control negative feelings that pass through the minds of even the best speakers.

■ No Nerves Guideline 4: Arrange the Room as You Want

To control your anxiety, assert some control over the physical environment as well. You need everything going for you if you are to feel at ease. Make sure that chairs are arranged to your satisfaction, that the lectern is positioned to your taste, that the lighting is adequate, and so on. These features of the setting can almost always be adjusted if you make the effort to ask. Again, it is a matter of your asserting control so that your overall confidence is increased.

■ No Nerves Guideline 5: Have a Glass of Water Nearby

Extreme thirst and a dry throat are physical symptoms of nervousness that can affect delivery. There is nothing to worry about as long as you have water available. Think about this need ahead of time so that you do not have to interrupt your presentation to pour a glass of water.

■ No Nerves Guideline 6: Engage in Casual Banter Before the Speech

If you have the opportunity, chat with members of the audience before the speech. This ice-breaking technique will reduce your nervousness and help start your relationship with the audience.

■ No Nerves Guideline 7: Remember That You Are the Expert

As a final "psyching up" exercise before you speak, remind yourself that you have been invited or hired to speak on a topic about which you have useful knowledge. Your listeners want to hear what you have to say and are eager for you to provide useful information to them. So tell yourself, "I'm the expert here!"

■ No Nerves Guideline 8: Do Not Admit Nervousness to the Audience

No matter how anxious you may feel, never admit it to others. First of all, you do not want listeners to feel sorry for you—that is not an emotion that will lead to a positive critique of your speech. Second, nervousness is almost never apparent to the audience. Your heart may be pounding, your knees may be shaking, and your throat may be dry, but few if any members of the audience can see these symptoms. Why draw attention to the problem by admitting to it? Third, you can best defeat initial anxiety by simply pushing right on through.

■ *No Nerves Guideline 9: Slow Down*

Some speakers who feel nervous tend to speed through their presentations. If you have prepared well and practiced the speech on tape, you are not likely to let this happen. Having heard yourself on tape, you will be better able to sense that the pace is too quick. As you speak, constantly remind yourself to maintain an appropriate pace. If you have had this problem before, you might even write "Slow down!" in the margin of your notes.

■ *No Nerves Guideline 10: Join a Speaking Organization*

The previous nine guidelines will help reduce your anxiety about a particular speech. To help solve the problem over the long term, however, consider joining an organization like Toastmasters International, which promotes the speaking skills of all its members. Like some other speech organizations, Toastmasters has chapters that meet at many companies and campuses. These meetings provide an excellent, supportive environment in which all members can refine their speaking skills.

EXAMPLE OF MCDUFF ORAL PRESENTATION

This section presents the text and visuals of a short presentation given by Kim Mason, an environmental expert for McDuff's Atlanta office. She has been invited to speak at the monthly lunch meeting of an organization of building owners in the Atlanta region. The agreed-upon topic is the problem of asbestos contamination.

The members of Kim's audience have an obvious interest in the problem: They own buildings that are at risk. Yet they know little more about asbestos than that it is a health issue they must consider when they renovate. Kim's job is to inform them and heighten their awareness. She needs to cover only the highlights, however, because the presentation will be followed by a detailed question-and-answer session. Although some of these owners have been, and will be, clients of McDuff, she has an ethical obligation to avoid promoting McDuff during her presentation.

> Good evening. My name is Kim Mason, and I work for the asbestos-abatement division of McDuff, Inc., in Atlanta. I've been asked to give a short presentation on the problem of asbestos and then to respond to your questions about the importance of removing it from buildings. I'll focus on three main reasons why you, as building

1. **Prevent Health Problems**

2. **Satisfy Regulatory Requirements**

3. **Give Yourself Peace of Mind**

Mc Duff, Inc.

FIGURE 12–2
Transparency 1 for sample presentation

owners, should be concerned about the asbestos problem: (TRANSPARENCY 1 [see Figure 12–2, p. 452])

1. To prevent future health problems of your tenants
2. To satisfy regulatory requirements of the government
3. To give yourself peace of mind for the future

Again, my comments will provide just an overview, serving as a basis for the question session that follows in a few minutes. (TRANSPARENCY 2 [see Figure 12–3, p. 453])

Question: What is the most important reason you need to be concerned about asbestos? Answer: The long-term health of the tenants, workers, and other people in buildings that contain asbestos. Research has clearly linked asbestos with a variety of diseases, including lung cancer, colon cancer, and asbestosis (a debilitating lung disease). Although this connection was first documented in the 1920s, it has only been taken seriously in the last few decades. Unfortunately, by that time asbestos had already been commonly used in many building materials that are part of many structures today.

FIGURE 12–3
Transparency 2 for sample presentation

Here's a list of some of the most common building products containing asbestos. (TRANSPARENCY 3 [see Figure 12–4, p. 454]) As you can see, asbestos was used in materials as varied as floor tiles, pipe wrap, roof felt, and insulation around heating systems. An abundant and naturally occurring mineral, asbestos was fashioned into construction materials through processes such as packing, weaving, and spraying. Its property of heat resistance, as well as its availability, was the main reason for such widespread use.

While still embedded in material, asbestos causes no real problems. However, when it deteriorates or is damaged, fibers may become airborne. In this state, they can enter the lungs and cause the health problems mentioned a minute ago. This risk prompted the Environmental Protection Agency in the mid-1970s to ban the use of certain asbestos products in most new construction. But today the decay and renovation of many asbestos-containing building materials may put many of our citizens at risk for years to come. (TRANSPARENCY 4 [see Figure 12–5, p. 455])

After your concern for occupants' health, what's the next best reason to learn more about asbestos? It's the *law.* Both the Occupational Safety and Health Administration (OSHA) and the Georgia Department of Natural Resources (DNR)

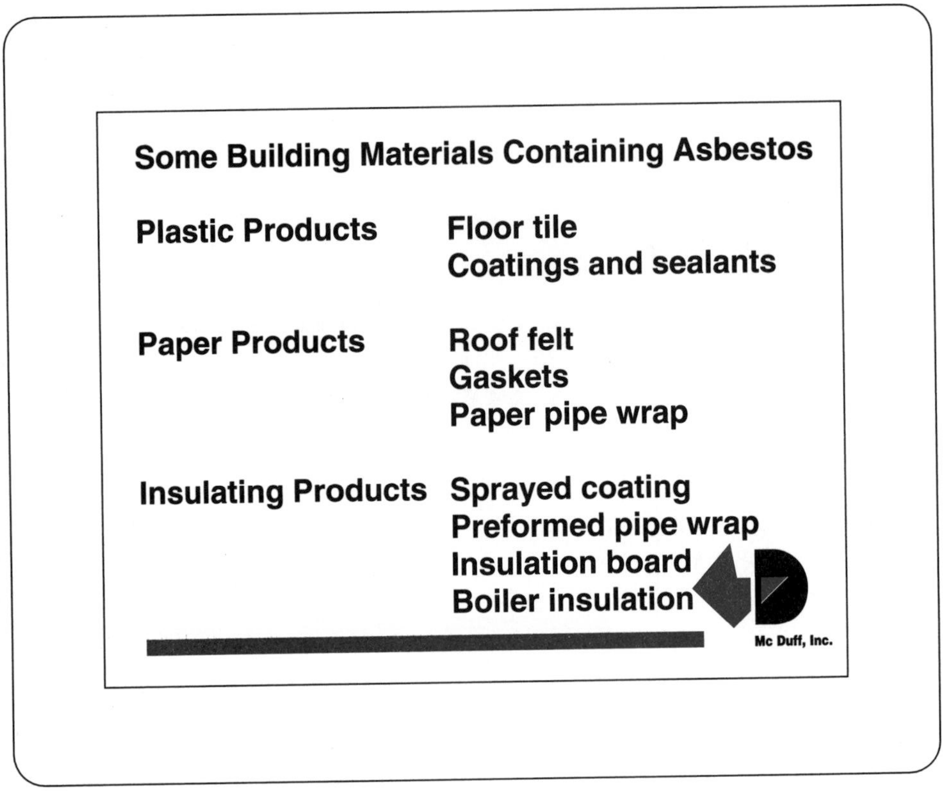

Some Building Materials Containing Asbestos

Plastic Products	Floor tile Coatings and sealants
Paper Products	Roof felt Gaskets Paper pipe wrap
Insulating Products	Sprayed coating Preformed pipe wrap Insulation board Boiler insulation

Mc Duff, Inc.

FIGURE 12–4
Transparency 3 for sample presentation

require that you follow certain procedures when structures you own could endanger tenants and asbestos-removal workers with contamination. For example, when a structure undergoes renovation that will involve any asbestos-containing material (ACM), the ACM must be removed by following approved engineering procedures. Also, the contaminated refuse must be disposed of in approved landfills. Considering the well-documented potential for health problems related to airborne asbestos, this legislative focus on asbestos contamination makes good sense.

By the way, both OSHA and DNR regulations require removal of asbestos by licensed contractors. These contractors, however, will assume liability only for what they have been told to remove. They may or may not have credentials and training in health and safety. Therefore, building owners should hire a firm with a professional who will (1) survey the building and present a professional report on the degree of asbestos contamination and (2) monitor the work of the contractor in removing the asbestos. By taking this approach, you as an owner stand a good chance of eliminating all problems with your asbestos.

Yes, it is *your* asbestos. As owner of a building, you also legally own the asbestos associated with that building—*forever.* For example, if a tenant claims to have been exposed to asbestos because of your abatement activity and then brings a lawsuit, you

FIGURE 12–5
Transparency 4 for sample presentation

must have documentation showing that you contracted to have the work performed in a "state-of-the-art" manner. If, as recommended, you have hired a qualified monitoring firm and a reputable contracting firm, liability will be focused on the contractor and the monitoring firm—*not* on you. (TRANSPARENCY 5 [see Figure 12–6, p. 456])

Which brings me to the last reason for concerning yourself with any potential asbestos problem: *peace of mind.* If you examine and then effectively deal with any asbestos contamination that exists in your buildings, you will sleep better at night. For one thing, you will have done your level best to preserve the health of your tenants. For another, as previously noted, you will have shifted any potential liability from you to the professionals you hired to solve the problem—assuming you hired professionals. Your monitoring firm will have continuously documented the contractor's operations and will have provided you with reports to keep in your files, in the event of later questions by lawyers or regulatory agencies.

In just these few minutes, I have given only highlights about asbestos. It poses a considerable challenge for all of us who own buildings or work in the abatement business. Yet the current diagnostic and cleanup methods are sophisticated enough to suggest that this problem, over time, *will* be solved. Now I would be glad to answer questions.

FIGURE 12–6
Transparency 5 for sample presentation

RUNNING EFFECTIVE MEETINGS

Like formal presentations, meetings are a form of spoken communication that goes hand in hand with written work. Important reports and proposals—even many routine ones—often are followed or preceded by a meeting. For example, you may meet with your colleagues to prepare a group-written report, with your clients to discuss a proposal, or with your department staff to outline recommendations to appear in a yearly report to management. This section will make you a first-class meeting leader by (1) highlighting some common problems with meetings, along with their associated costs to organizations, and (2) describing 10 guidelines for overcoming these problems.

Common Problems with Meetings

Here are six major complaints about meetings held in all types of organizations:

1. They start and end too late.
2. Their purpose is unclear.

3. Not everyone in the meeting really needs to be there.
4. Conversations get off track.
5. Some people dominate while others do not contribute at all.
6. Meetings end with no sense of accomplishment.

As a result of these frustrations, career professionals waste much of their time in poorly run meetings.

Because they waste participants' time, bad meetings also waste a lot of money. To find out what meetings cost an organization, do this rough calculation. Use information about an organization for which you work, or for which a friend or family member works.

1. Take the average weekly number of meetings in an office.
2. Multiply that number by the average length of each meeting, in hours.
3. Multiply the result of step 2 by the average number of participants in each meeting.
4. Multiply the result of step 3 by the average hourly salary or billable amount of the participants.

The result, which may surprise you, is the average weekly cost of meetings in the office that you investigated. With these heavy costs in mind, the next section presents some simple guidelines for running good meetings.

Guidelines for Good Meetings

When you choose (or are chosen) to run a meeting, your professional reputation is at stake—let alone the costs just mentioned. Therefore, it is in your own best interests to make sure meetings run well. When you are a meeting participant, you also have an obligation to speak up and help accomplish the goals of the meeting.

The guidelines that follow will help create successful meetings. They fall into three main stages:

> **Stage 1:** Before the meeting (Guidelines 1–4)
> **Stage 1:** During the meeting (Guidelines 5–9)
> **Stage 1:** After the meeting (Guideline 10)

These 10 guidelines apply to *working* meetings—that is, those in which participants use their talents to accomplish specific objectives. Such meetings usually involve a lot of conversation. The guidelines do not apply as well to *informational* meetings wherein a large number of people are assembled only to listen to announcements.

■ *Meeting Guideline 1: Involve Only Necessary People*

"Necessary" means those people who, because of their position or knowledge, can contribute to the meeting. Your goal should be a small working group—four to six people is ideal. If others need to know what occurs, send them a copy of the minutes after the meeting.

■ *Meeting Guideline 2: Distribute an Agenda Before the Meeting*

To be good participants, most people need to think before the meeting about the objectives of the session. The agenda also gives you, as leader, a way to keep the meeting on schedule. If you are worried about having time to cover the agenda items, consider attaching time limits to each item. That technique helps the meeting leader keep the discussion moving.

■ *Meeting Guideline 3: Distribute Readings Before the Meeting*

Jealously guard time at a meeting, making sure to use it for productive discussion. If any member has reading materials that committee members should review as a basis for these discussions, such readings should be handed out ahead of time. Do not use meeting time for reading. Even worse, do not refer to handouts that all members have not had the opportunity to go over.

■ *Meeting Guideline 4: Have Only One Meeting Leader*

To prevent confusion, one person should always be in charge. The meeting leader should be able to perform these tasks:

- **Listen carefully** so that all views get a fair hearing
- **Generalize accurately** so that earlier points can be brought back into the discussion when appropriate
- **Give credit to participants** so that they receive reinforcement for their efforts
- **Move toward consensus** so that the meeting does not involve endless discussion

■ *Meeting Guideline 5: Start and End on Time*

Nothing deadens a meeting more than a late start, particularly when it is caused by people arriving late. Tardy participants are given no incentive to arrive on time when a meeting leader waits for them. Even worse, prompt members become demoralized by such delays. Latecomers will mend their ways if you make a practice of starting right on time.

It is also important to set an ending time for meetings so that members have a clear view of the time available. Concerning meeting length, most people do their best work in the first hour. After that, productive discussion reaches a point of diminishing returns. If working meetings must last longer than an hour, make sure to build in short breaks and stay on the agenda.

■ *Meeting Guideline 6: Keep Meetings on Track*

By far the biggest challenge for a meeting leader is to encourage open discussion while still moving toward resolution of agenda items. As a leader, you need to be assertive, yet tactful, in your efforts to discourage these three main time-wasters:

to complete a project for Rob McDuff, the president of the firm. We'll observe Tanya as she gathers research.

Like Tanya, later you will have to apply the research process to a specific technical-writing task in college or on the job. It is one thing to read about doing research; it is quite another to dive into your project and work directly with bibliographies, books, periodicals, indexes, and other resources that may be in print or on-line format. Get firsthand research experience as soon as you can.

Finally, remember that the best research writing *smoothly* merges the writer's ideas with supporting data. Such writing should (1) impress readers with its clarity and simplicity and (2) avoid sounding like a strung-together series of quotations. These two goals present a challenge in research writing.

GETTING STARTED

In chapter 1, you learned about the three phases of any writing project: planning, drafting, and revising. Research can occur in the planning stage, right before you complete an outline, but it can also occur again and again throughout the project. Before starting your research, ask yourself questions like these, to give direction to your work:

1. What *questions* must be answered during the research phase?
2. What *information* might be most useful?
3. What *sources* would be most useful?
4. What *format* must be used to document material borrowed from sources?

Let's take a look at the way Tanya Grant answers these questions during her project.

Tanya has just been given an important task. The company president, Rob McDuff, wants her to examine the feasibility of the company publishing a newsletter on acid rain. McDuff believes the acid-rain problem is so important that a separate newsletter—written from a private company's perspective—will provide a service in reporting current research. Also, he hopes his firm becomes a major player in solving the acid-rain problem. In short, the newsletter could serve both as a public service and as a marketing device. Although at this point he wants a traditional print newsletter, he explained to Tanya that later it could become an on-line resource available through personal computers.

Rob McDuff told Tanya that the newsletter will seek two types of readers: (1) well-educated consumers who want more information and (2) current and prospective clients whose business interests compel them to learn more about acid rain, as well as other environmental issues.

Tanya must write a report on the practicality of starting the environmental newsletter McDuff proposed. Some of her report will investigate start-up costs, employee needs, and other in-house matters. Her other research effort, however, will be to (1) see what current journals cover the topic, and (2) find out what readers, especially clients, would want covered in a newsletter. The following outline shows how Tanya would probably answer the four questions previously noted, as she begins her research:

1. *Main question:* Is there a need for the acid-rain newsletter that her boss is considering?

2. *Main types of information needed:*

   - Number of acid-rain magazines published
   - Types of articles now published and magazines in which they are published
   - Types of government and nongovernment groups that now put out magazines containing acid-rain articles
   - Interest level and needs of potential readers

3. *Possible sources:*

   - Directories (of periodicals, newsletters, newspapers)
   - Periodicals (indexed)
   - Government documents
   - Newspapers (indexed)
   - Actual copies of environmental magazines
   - Questionnaire
   - Interviews with some potential readers, such as current clients
   - International e-mail

4. *Format for documentation:* Tanya will submit a short report to Rob McDuff, documenting her research using the author-date system of citing borrowed information (the same format used by McDuff engineers and scientists in their research reports).

With this basic plan in mind, Tanya can begin her work. She decides to start at a nearby university library—rather than the McDuff library, the local library, or the Internet—because she knows about the university's extensive holdings in science and technology. The next section outlines major types of library research and government sources, along with examples from Tanya Grant's project. Then the following section examines primary research that Tanya will pursue.

SECONDARY RESEARCH: LOCATING LIBRARY SOURCES

The library can seem like an intimidating place when you first start a project. Once you learn a few basics, however, you will become comfortable and even confident about using this amazing resource. The complexity and the automated nature of the modern library mean your *first* stop should be the reference librarian, who will explain what is available in the library.

This section includes descriptions of seven types of research materials for technical projects: (1) books; (2) periodicals; (3) newspapers; (4) company directories;

(5) dictionaries, encyclopedias, and other general references; (6) abstracts; and (7) the Internet and World Wide Web. Though brief, the descriptions will help you "divide and conquer" your research task by learning about one type of resource at a time.

■ *Resource 1: Books*

Books provide well-supported, tested information about a topic, but, by definition, the information is often dated. Even a book just published has information that is one or two years old, given the time it takes to put a book-length manuscript into print. Keep this limitation in mind as you work in the library.

Despite its somewhat dated information, the book collection remains the most used part of the library. Most college libraries organize their collections by the Library of Congress (LC) system (see Figure 13–1) or the Dewey Decimal System (see Figure 13–2). Some still offer the card catalog or microfiche as the road map to the library collection. However, the majority of college and university libraries offer sophisticated on-line catalogs to their book and periodical collections. If your library is automated, the on-line catalog will have "help screens" to assist you. See Figure 13–3 for instructions similar to what you would encounter on an on-line catalog. Here are some basic search guidelines, whether you are using catalog cards, a microfiche catalog, or on-line information:

1. If you know specific titles of potentially useful books, consult the title entries for catalog numbers and other information.
2. If you know of authors who may have written books in the field, start with author entries.
3. If you do not know specific authors/titles or wish to view the library's range of books on a topic, consult the subject entries to build a list of available sources.

In practice, defining your subject can cause some confusion. For example, your term for a subject might be different from subject headings used in the catalog, or books on your topic might be grouped under several headings in the Library of Congress classification system. In this case, consult the Library of Congress *Subject Headings*. Often kept near the library's catalog, this three-volume set is your key to the LC system. Upon looking up your subject, you will discover if there is other phrasing under which information might be listed in the catalog.

Tanya Grant's McDuff Project

Tanya Grant, for example, rightly thinks that books will not be her main source of information about acid-rain periodicals, since the field has developed so recently. Yet she at least wants to see what range of sources the catalog offers, just as a starting point. Upon looking up "acid rain" in *Subject Headings*, she locates the information in Figure 13–4. Thus her quick inquiry has yielded several additional subject headings under which sources might be listed in the library catalog.

In automated libraries, however, the Library of Congress *Subject Headings* is considered out of date. Instead, the on-line catalog automatically leads you from one possible subject to another, in an effort to help you scan the library collection library.

Library of Congress Cataloging System: A General Breakdown

A	Collections, Encyclopedias, Indexes, Yearbooks, Directories, etc.
B	Philosophy, Psychology, Religion
C	History of Civilization and Culture
D	History – General and Old World – Europe, etc.
E-F	American History
G-GF	Geography, Maps, Oceanography, Human Ecology
GN-GT	Anthropology and Related Subjects
GV	Recreation
H	Social Sciences – General
HA	Statistics
HB-HJ	Economics
HM-HX	Sociology
J	Political Science
K	Law
L	Education
M	Music
N	Art and Architecture (Architectural Design)
P	Language and Literature, Philology
PN-PX	Literary History, Literature
PR, PS, PZ	English and American Literature
Q	Science – General
QA	Math
QB	Astronomy
QC	Physics
QD	Chemistry
QE	Geology
QH	Natural History
QK	Botany
QL	Zoology
QM	Human Anatomy
QP	Physiology
QR	Microbiology
R	Medicine
S	Agriculture, Plant and Animal Culture, Hunting Sports
T	General Technology

FIGURE 13–1
General categories from LC system

General Engineering and Civil Engineering

TA	Engineering - General, Civil Engineering - General
TC	Hydraulic Engineering
TD	Environmental Technology, Sanitary Engineering
TE	Highway Engineering, Roads and Pavements
TF	Railroad Engineering and Operation
TG	Bridge Engineering
TH	Building Construction

Mechanical Group

TJ	Mechanical Engineering and Machinery
TK	Electrical Engineering, Electronics, Nuclear Engineering
TL	Motor Vehicles, Aeronautics, Astronautics

Chemical Group

TN	Mining Engineering, Metallurgy
TP	Chemical Technology
TR	Photography

Composite Group

TS	Manufactures
TT	Handicrafts, Arts and Crafts
TX	Home Economics
U	Military Science
V	Naval Science
Z	Bibliography

FIGURE 13–1
continued

FIGURE 13–2
Dewey decimal system

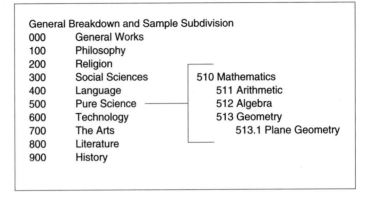

General Breakdown and Sample Subdivision
000   General Works
100   Philosophy
200   Religion
300   Social Sciences
400   Language   510 Mathematics
500   Pure Science ————   511 Arithmetic
600   Technology   512 Algebra
700   The Arts   513 Geometry
800   Literature   513.1 Plane Geometry
900   History

FIGURE 13–3
Author, title, and subject
cards for same book

This catalog allows you to search the Library collection by computer. Although the catalog mainly covers the book collection, it also gives you titles of periodicals (though it does not index particular articles). Use the following basic commands for your search.

Search by Subject Area
Type SU followed by work or term you want searched
Example: SU acid rain
Select item(s) of interest from screen
Type LI and call number to see if item is available for checkout

Search by Individual Title
Type TI followed by title of book or periodical
Note: delete "a," "an" or "the" at beginning
Example: TI Acid Rain Controversy
Type LI and call number to see if item is available for checkout

Search by Author
Type AU followed by author's name, last name first
Example: AU Regens, James L.
Select works of interest from screen
Type LI and call number to see if an item is available

Search by Author and Title
Type AT followed by author's last name and first main word of title
Example: AT Regens Acid
Type LI and call number to see if item is available for checkout

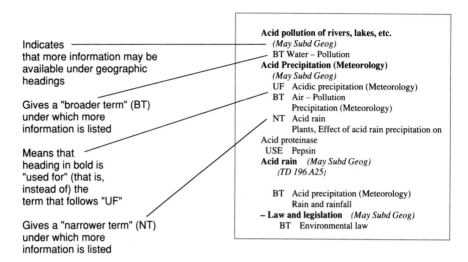

Indicates that more information may be available under geographic headings

Gives a "broader term" (BT) under which more information is listed

Means that heading in bold is "used for" (that is, instead of) the term that follows "UF"

Gives a "narrower term" (NT) under which more information is listed

Acid pollution of rivers, lakes, etc.
  (May Subd Geog)
  BT Water – Pollution
Acid Precipitation (Meteorology)
  (May Subd Geog)
  UF Acidic precipitation (Meteorology)
  BT Air – Pollution
      Precipitation (Meteorology)
  NT Acid rain
      Plants, Effect of acid rain precipitation on
Acid proteinase
  USE Pepsin
Acid rain *(May Subd Geog)*
  [TD 196.A25]

  BT Acid precipitation (Meteorology)
      Rain and rainfall
 – Law and legislation *(May Subd Geog)*
   BT Environmental law

FIGURE 13–4
Sample entries from subject headings (Library of Congress)
Source: Library of Congress, *Subject Headings,* 12th ed., vol. 1 (A–E) (Washington, D.C.: Cataloging Distribution Service, Library of Congress, 1989), 20.

■ *Resource 2: Periodicals*

The *American Heritage Dictionary* defines periodical as a publication issued at "regular intervals of more than one day." The term encompasses:

- Popular magazines that take commercial advertising, such as *Time, Science,* and *National Geographic*
- Professional journals, such as *IEEE Transactions on Professional Communication*

Most library visitors are familiar with the section that houses current periodicals, either in alphabetical order or by subject area. Yet they are less familiar with the part of the library containing back issues. Libraries keep back issues of the periodicals considered most important to its users. They may be in the form of bound volumes of actual issues, microfilm, CDs, or even full texts of articles available through a computerized periodical index format.

Your key to information in periodicals is a periodical index. By looking up a subject area in an index, you can find articles listed that could provide the information you need. Some indexes, like the familiar *Readers' Guide to Periodical Literature,* deal with popular periodicals. Others, like the *Engineering Index,* deal with a broad range of technical information. Still others, like the *Society of Mechanical Engineers Technical Digest,* focus on periodicals, books, and papers in specialized technical fields. In all cases, periodicals covered in an index will be listed in the volume, along with the inclusive dates of the issues indexed in that volume.

A growing trend is to use computerized indexes, which, as noted previously, may include access to the full texts of articles on-line. When working in a library for the first time, ask a reference librarian about available indexes. Many libraries have handouts that list common indexes and their fields. Here are a few well-known technical indexes, available in both print and computer form:

Applied Science and Technology Index

Business Periodicals Index

Computer Literature Index

Energy Index

Engineering Index

Microcomputer Index

Monthly Catalogue of U.S. Government Publications

Tanya Grant's McDuff Project

Tanya decides to (1) consult some traditional print periodical indexes and (2) use electronic databases. Here are the three steps she takes, based on suggestions from a reference librarian:

1. She looks through a print source called *The Environment Index,* which indexes journal articles, conference papers, reports, and other documents. (Figure 13–5 shows some acid-rain entries contained in one yearly volume.) The index contains a list of environmental periodicals. Scanning the list, she sees none devoted exclusively to acid rain.

2. Next she consults a periodical index connected to the World Wide Web. This particular index, which covers 10 years, has several search options. She selects one that includes abstracts of some entries and types "acid rain" in the subject search box (see Figure 13–6 for a page that includes 10 of the 464 entries). Bullets indicate the items for which the index has on-line abstracts. For Entry #8 in Figure 13–6, she calls up the text of an abstract (see Figure 13–7), just to see if the piece might interest her.

3. Finally, Tanya consults the *Ei Tech Index,* a stand-alone CD-ROM index produced by Engineering Information, Inc. The reference librarian tells her that this index may contain information not included in the more general Internet index. Indeed, one screen notes that *Ei* includes citations to 40 journals in engineering and technology, conference articles, and some abstracts. When she types "acid rain" for the search, she finds no separate subject listing for the topic. However, the index locates 267 citations to articles or papers that mention acid rain. Figure 13–8 shows the index entry for one item, followed by the abstract and other source information. Note that the abbreviations (for example, TI for title), would all be explained in the CD-ROM directions.

■ *Resource 3: Newspapers*

If your research topic demands the most current information, newspapers provide an excellent source. One disadvantage is that newspaper information has not "stood the test of time"—that is, it is not validated to the same extent as information in journals and books. Another disadvantage is that many newspapers either

ACID RAIN

Atmospheric Deposition in Fenno-Scandia: Characteristics and Trends (Proceedings of the International Symposium on Acidic Precipitation, Muskoka, Ontario, September 15-20, 1985), Water Air & Soil Pollution, Sep 86, v30, n1-2, p5(12)   *01-87-00411

Pollutant Wet Deposition Mechanisms in Precipitation and Fog Water (Proceedings of the International Symposium on Acidic Precipitation, Muskoka, Ontario, September 15-20, 1985), Water Air & Soil Pollution, Sep 86, v30 , n1-2, p91(14)   *01-87-00413

Acidic Precipitation in Western North America: Trends, Sources, and Altitude Effects in New Mexico, 1979-1985 (Proceedings of the International Symposium on Acidic Precipitation, Muskoka, Ontario, September 15-20, 1985), Water Air & Soil Pollution, Sep 86, v30, n1-2, p125(9)   *01-87-00418

Alkaline Materials Flux from Unpaved Roads: Source Strength, Chemistry and Potential for Acid Rain Neutralization (Proceedings of the International Symposium on Acidic Precipitation, Muskoka, Ontario, September 15-20, 1985), Water Air & Soil Pollution, Sep 86, v30, n1-2, p285(9)   *01-87-00423

Overview of Historical and Paleoecological Studies of Acidic Air Pollution and its Effects (Proceedings of the International Symposium on Acidic Precipitation, Muskoka, Ontario, September 15-20, 1985) Water Air & Soil Pollution, Sep 86, v30, n1-2, p311(8)   *01-87-00425

A Review of the Chemical Record in Lake Sediment of Energy Related Air Pollution and its Effects on Lakes (Proceedings of the International Symposium on Acidic Precipitation, Muskoka, Ontario, September 15-20, 1985), Water Air & Soil Pollution, Sep 86, v30, n1-2, p331(15)   *02-87-00512

Application of Conceptual Environmental Model to Assess the Impact of Acid Precipitation on Drinking Water Quality II — Studies of Chemical Thermodynamic Equilbria in Water, Water Quality B, Jul 86, v11, n3, p152(9)   *19-87-00516

Bone Concentration of Manganese in White Sucker (Catostomus commersoni) from Acid, Circumneutral and Metal-Stressed Lakes (Proceedings of the International Symposium on Acidic Precipitation, Muskoka, Ontario, September 15-20, 1985), Water Air & Soil Pollution, Sep 86, v30, n1-2, p515(7)   *0287-00518

Issues in Environmental Science (Environmental Quality), CEQ Report 15, 1985, p433(44)   *07-87-00620

Gardsjon Project: Lake Acidification, Chemistry in Catchment Runoff, Lake Liming and Microcatchment Manipulations (Proceedings of the International Symposium on Acidic Precipitation, Muskoka, Ontario, September 15-20, 1985), Water Air & Soil Pollution, Sep 86, v30, n1-2, p31(16)   *19-87-00873

Changes in Fish Populations in Southernmost Norway During the Last Decade (Proceedings of the International Symposium on Acidic Precipitation, Muskoka, Ontario, September 15-20, 1985), Water Air & Soil Pollution, Sep 86, v30, n1-2, p381(6)   *19-87-00874

Evidence for Recent Acidification of Lentic Soft Waters in the Netherlands (Proceedings of the International Symposium on Acidic Precipitation, Muskoka, Ontario, September 15-20, 1985), Water Air & Soil Pollution, Sep 86, v30, n1-2, p387(6)   *19-87-00875

Ecological Effects of Acidification on Primary Producers in Aquatic Systems (Proceedings of the International Symposium on Acidic Precipitation, Muskoka, Ontario, September 15-20, 1985), Water Air & Soil Pollution, Sep 86, v30, n1-2, p421(18)   *19-87-00876

Ecological Effects of Acidification on Tertiary Consumers. Fish Population Responses (Proceedings of the International Symposium on Acidic Precipitation, Muskoka, Ontario, September 15-20, 1985), Water Air & Soil Pollution, Sep 86, v30, n1-2, p451(10)   *19-87-00877

FIGURE 13–5

"Acid rain" entries from *The Environment Index*

Source: *The Environment Index: 1987 in Retrospect,* vol. 17 (New York: EIC/Intelligence, Inc., 1988), 10.

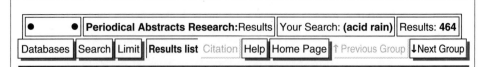

FIGURE 13–6

Sample periodical index listing from the World Wide Web

Source: Adapted from screens accessed through the Georgia Library Learning Online (GALILEO) system, September, 1995.

are not indexed or are only indexed by local libraries or other agencies. Without an index, your only option would be to pore over each issue in search of information.

Fortunately, there are indexes—the *New York Times Index* and the *Wall Street Journal Index*—for two well-known newspapers. Consult the *New York Times* for general research topics; consult the *Wall Street Journal* for business-related topics, especially those dealing with specific corporations. Also, as an alternative to print indexes, you will find on-line access to newspapers through sources such as NEXUS and Newsbank.

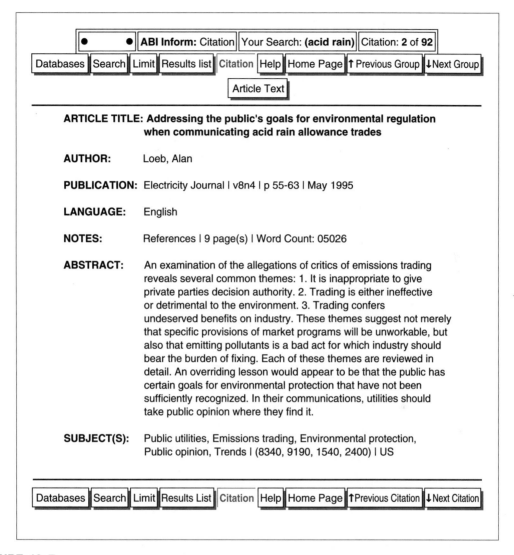

FIGURE 13–7

Online abstract of technical article

Source: Adapted from screens accessed through the Georgia Library Learning Online (GALILEO) system, September, 1995.

Tanya Grant's McDuff Project

As an aside in her research, Tanya decides to see what kinds of general articles might be available in the *New York Times.* First she checks the CD-ROM database called Proquest, produced by UMI, a Bell and Howell Information Company. This particular database covers 1993 to the present and yields a number of entries that mention acid rain. Figure 13–9 shows a page of the entries she found. Then she went on to call up a few article abstracts, available in the same database. To check articles before

TI: Needed a national renewable energy strategy
AU: Kozloff, -K.
SO: Environmental Science and Technology v 28 n 4 Apr 1994. p 196A-197A
SN: 0013-936X
LA: English
AN: EIX95181606199

PC-SPIRS 3.30   Ei Tech Index (TM) 1987-7/95

Ei Tech Index (TM) 1987-7/95 usage is subject to the terms and conditions of the
Subscription and License Agreement and the applicable Copyright and intellectual
property protection as dictated by the appropriate laws of your country and/or by
International Convention.   1 of 1
                                                        Marked Record

TI: Needed a national renewable energy strategy
AU: Kozloff, -K.
AF: World Resources Inst, Washington, DC, USA
SO: Environmental Science and Technology v 28 n 4 Apr 1994. p 196A-197A
ST: Environmental-Science-and-Technology
SN: 0013-936X
CO: ESTHAG
AB: Renewable energy sources now supply only 8% of U.S. energy, and that share
will not reach 9 in 20 years if current government policy and market trends persist. It is
in the nation's interest to spur the growth of solar, wind, biomass, geothermal and hydro
energy technologies. Besides slowing down climate change, a shift towards renewables
would mean less pollution and acid rain. Besides fueling economic development
forever, renewables can minimize regional energy development disparities and end the
boom-and-bust cycles associated with fossil fuel production.
DE: Renewable-energy-resources
DE: Public-policy; Solar-energy; Geothermal-energy; Wind-power; Water-power;
Technology- ; Environmental-protection
 ID: Strategy- ; Private-sector; Regulatory-reforms
CC: Energy-Resources (525.1); Energy-Policy (525.6); Wind-Power (615.8);
Geothermal-Energy (615.1); Solar-Power (615.2); Environmental-Impact-and-
Protection (454.2)
PY: 1994
LA: English
DT: JA (Journal-Article)
TR: G (General-Review); M (Management-Aspects)
UD: 9518
AN: EIX95181606199

FIGURE 13–8
Index entry and abstract from Ei Tech Index
Source: Adapted from Ei Tech Index, a stand-alone CD-ROM index produced by Engineering
Information, Inc.

Date: Thursday Apr 13, 1995 Sec: D Financial Desk p: 2 Length: Medium (620 words)
Subjects: AIR POLLUTION; INTERNET (COMPUTER NETWORK); ELECTRONIC INFORMATION SYSTEMS
Companies: CALIFORNIA INSTITUTE OF TECHNOLOGY; CANTOR FITZGERALD LP; PACIFIC STOCK EXCHANGE; BANK OF AMERICA

Access No: 9300116571 ProQuest - The New York Times (R) Ondisc
Title: MOUNTAIN BIKES CARVE UP FRAGILE PARK TERRAIN
Source: The New York Times, Late Edition - Final
Date: Monday Apr 10, 1995 Sec: A Editorial Desk p: 14 Length: Medium (303 words) Type LETTER
Subjects: BICYCLES & BICYCLING; HIKING

Access No: 9300112719 ProQuest - The New York Times (R) Ondisc
Title: LAW STUDENTS BUY AND HOLD POLLUTION RIGHTS
Authors: DAVIDSON GOLDIN
Source: The New York Times, Late Edition - Final
Date: Friday Mar 31, 1995 Sec: A National Desk p: 28 Length: Medium (333)
Subjects: AIR POLLUTION; LAW SCHOOLS; LICENSES; SULFUR DIOXIDE

Access No: 9300112433 ProQuest - The New York Times (R) Ondisc
Title: ECONOMIC SCENE; ILLINOIS IS LOOKING TO MARKET FORCES TO HELP REDUCE ITS SMOG.
Authors: Peter Passell
Source: The New York Times, Late Edition - Final
Date: Thursday Mar 30, 1995 Sec: D Financial Desk p: 2 Length: Long (802 words) Illus: Drawing
Subjects: AIR POLLUTION; REGULATION & DEREGULATION OF INDUSTRY; SMOG; FINANCES; STATES (US); ILLINOIS; ECONOMIC SCENE (TIMES COLUMN)

Access No: 9300109946 ProQuest - The New York Times (R) Ondisc
Title: IN WEST, WILDFLOWERS HAVE JUMP ON SPRING AND THE TOURISTS GLOW
Authors: ANNE RAVER
Source: The New York Times, Late Edition - Final
Date: Monday Mar 20, 1995 Sec B National Desk p: 7 Length: Long (1349 words) Illus: Photo
Subjects: FLOWERS & PLANTS; DESERTS; WEATHER; NYTRAVEL; SONORAN DESERT; ARIZONA

Access No: 9300109931 ProQuest - The New York Times (R) Ondisc
Title: WORK & IMAGE; BEYOND THE SHROUD
Authors: MAX FRANKEL
Source: The New York Times, Late Edition - Final
Date: Sunday Mar 19, 1995 Sec: 6 Magazine Desk p: 30 Length: Long (1222 words)
Subjects: UNITED STATES INTERNATIONAL RELATIONS; NEWS & NEWS MEDIA

FIGURE 13-9

Sample screen from Proquest

Source: Adapted from Proquest, a CD-ROM database produced by UMI, a Bell and Howell Information Company.

1993, she found the hardcopy version of the index. Figure 13–10 shows one entry, which includes citation and summary.

■ Resource 4: Company Directories

Often your research needs may require that you find detailed information about specific firms. For example, you could be completing research about a company that may hire you, or you may seek information about companies that compete with your own. Following are some useful directories. Consult them individually to discover each one's particular focus.

Corporate Technology Directory

D & B Million Dollar Directory

Moody's Industrial Manual

Standard and Poor's Register of Corporations and Executives

Try Us: National Minority Business Directory

Ward's Directory of 51,000 U.S. Corporations

Ward's Directory of Major U.S. Private Companies

Who's Who in Engineering

Who's Who in Technology

World Business Directory

Gives summary of article – along with date, section, and page number.

ACID RAIN

Huge federal study finds acid rain has turned many lakes and streams acidic, not only in Northeast but also in other areas of East and parts of Midwest - - including northern Florida, Appalachians and New Jersey Pine Barrens - - but that overall acidification has been less extensive than was feared when research began a decade ago; findings in six areas across US discussed; map (M), Ja 16,C,4:1

Teachers and students at about a dozen schools in Connecticut and one in Massachusetts are taking part in project intended to involve students in science and provide much-needed information about acid rain in Connecticut; project is also pilot for Thames Science Center in New London, which is developing environmental science curriculum for state schools; photos (M), Ja 28,XII-CN,21:1

Editorial holds that preliminary results of National Acid Precipitation Assessment Program, 10-year Federal study on acid rain, lends urgency to proposals now before Congress that coal-burning utilities sharply cut sulfur dioxide emissions, Ja 29,A,22:1

FIGURE 13–10
"Acid rain" entry from the *New York Times Index*

Source: *New York Times Index*, vol. 78, no. 2, January 16–31, 1990 (semimonthly edition), 2–3. Copyright © 1990 by the New York Times Company. Reprinted by permission.

■ *Resource 5: Dictionaries, Encyclopedias, and Other General References*

Sometimes you may need some general information to help you get started on a research project. In this case, consult one of the specialized dictionaries or encyclopedias listed here. You can also use any number of general encyclopedias available in most libraries.

Cowles' Encyclopedia of Science, Industry, and Technology

Dictionary of Business and Economics

Encyclopedia of Business Information Sources

Encyclopedia of Engineering Materials and Processes

Encyclopedia of Physical Science and Technology

Engineering Encyclopedia

McGraw-Hill Dictionary of Science and Engineering

McGraw-Hill Encyclopedia of Engineering

McGraw-Hill Encyclopedia of Science and Technology

Van Nostrand's Scientific Encyclopedia

Of course, you should consider explaining the nature of your project to a librarian, who may refer you to a general reference book that could help you in the early stages of your research. Note the help that Tanya Grant received in her search.

Tanya Grant's McDuff Project

At this point, Tanya has spent a few hours on her own examining the library catalog (with the help of the *Subject Headings*), periodical indexes, and newspaper indexes. Although she suspects that there are no acid-rain periodicals published by environmental-science firms, she wants to pursue her research further.

Upon consulting a librarian at her local university library, Tanya learns about several specialized reference books that list magazines and journals from around the world. In one, called *Ulrich's International Periodicals Directory,* she turns to the subject heading of "Environmental Studies" and finds an alphabetical listing of periodicals. A quick look under "acid rain" reveals several publications associated with government and nonprofit agencies, such as *Acid Magazine, Acid Precipitation,* and *Acid Rain Update.* However, there are no newsletters, journals, magazines, or other periodicals published by corporations involved in environmental work.

A similar publication, the annual *Gale Directory of Publications and Broadcast Media,* lists broadcast stations and publications, such as newsletters, magazines, journals, and trade publications. There Tanya finds some of the same entries as in *Ulrich's* as well as at least one other, *Acid Precipitation Digest.* Nevertheless, she still does not find a newsletter of the kind being considered by McDuff—one published by a private firm in the environmental business.

■ *Resource 6: Abstracts*

Periodical indexes tell you where to find articles, but they do not indicate whether an article will provide the needed information. For this purpose, you can consult any number of periodical abstracts. Abstracts give you brief descriptions of articles so that you can decide whether or not an entire article is worth finding. They are especially useful when the article being summarized is not available in your library. The abstract can help you decide whether to (1) visit another library, (2) order an article through an interlibrary loan service, or (3) disregard an article altogether. Here are some common technical abstracts:

Abstracts of Health Care
Agricultural Index
Biological Abstracts
Chemical Abstracts
Energy Information Abstracts
Engineering Abstracts
Engineering Index
Geological Abstracts
Management Studies
Mineralogical Abstracts
Transportation Research Abstracts
World Textile Abstracts

As with other sources mentioned in this chapter, abstracts can be found on CD-ROM and on-line databases. In fact, sometimes you can print not only the abstract but the entire article as well. Once again, you should consult a reference librarian to find out exactly what tools are available at the library where you are working.

The last section of this chapter will show you how to write abstracts yourself, for times when you may be called upon to summarize research items.

■ *Resource 7: Internet and World Wide Web*

Throughout this chapter you have seen references to the Internet and World Wide Web. These networks are crucial to the modern researcher. Although some features of good research remain the same—such as asking the right questions and formulating a plan of attack—the Internet and World Wide Web have changed the manner and speed with which we can gather information during the search.

Already we have seen how parts of a library search can involve networks. Here are some other sources on the Internet and World Wide Web for gathering information:

- On-line "bulletin boards" made up of people who may have the same research interest as you
- "Home Pages" for companies and other organizations that can provide information on your research topic
- Informal "chat" groups whose members can provide you with leads for your research

In other words, the Internet and World Wide Web serve both as a vehicle for finding sources and as an actual source themselves for research information.

■ *Step 5: Write the Draft from the Outline and the Cards*

This step poses the greatest challenge. Here you must incorporate borrowed information with your own ideas to create fluid prose. Your goal should be to demonstrate (a) a smooth transition between your ideas and those you have borrowed and (b) absolute clarity about when borrowed ideas and quotations start and end.

SELECTING AND FOLLOWING A DOCUMENTATION SYSTEM

"Documentation" refers to the mechanical system you use to cite sources from which you borrow information. This section first highlights the main approaches to documentation and then outlines one common approach. For details about a particular documentation system you are using, consult one of the manuals in the list that follows. Pay special attention to new guidelines these manuals may provide for documenting information from on-line databases.

Varieties of Documentation

There are almost as many systems as there are professional organizations. Yet all have the same goal of showing readers the sources from which you gathered information. Here are just a few documentation manuals commonly used in business, industry, and the professions:

The Chicago Manual of Style

Council of Biology Editors Style Manual

MLA Handbook for Writers of Research Papers

Publication Manual of the American Psychological Association

Style Manual for Engineering Authors and Editors

U.S. Government Printing Office Style Manual

These and other approaches to documentation can be grouped into three main categories, with these features:

1. Footnotes at the bottom of pages, with an alphabetical list of sources at the end of the document
2. Endnotes collected on a page at the end of the document, followed by an alphabetical list of all sources
3. Parenthetical references in the text of the paper, with an alphabetical list of sources at the end of the document

Most professions have adopted some form of the third system—parenthetical documentation. It is the simplest one for writers to use and the easiest one for readers to decipher. Source information is given right within the text, rather than at the bottom of the page or the end of the document. Then a list of works cited occurs at the end of the document. The next section gives guidelines for one such form of parenthetical documentation.

Author-Date System with Pages

Often used in scientific and technical fields, the author-date system closely resembles systems recommended by the Modern Language Association (for the humanities), the American Psychological Association (for behavioral sciences), and the *Chicago Manual of Style* (for a variety of fields). The version described here includes the page number as well as author and date, giving it enough versatility to be used in many professional fields.

Citations within the Text.   Follow these six guidelines for acknowledging borrowed information within the text. Remember that you must note *any* quotations, paraphrases, or summaries that are not considered common knowledge.

1. *Immediately after the borrowed information occurs in the text, place the author's last name, publication date, and page number in parentheses.* As always, your main goal is to consider the reader's needs. EXAMPLE: "Aerial photos made at this site in 1965 revealed geomorphic features indicative of fault activity (Spears 1966, 76–77)." Note that the parenthetical citation is placed *inside* the punctuation for the sentence and that there is no comma between author and year.
2. *To show where borrowed information starts, or just to vary your style, you also have the option of placing the author's name at the beginning of the text passage.* In this case, remove the author's name from the parenthetical citation. EXAMPLE: "As Spears has shown, aerial photos made at the site in 1965 revealed geomorphic features indicative of fault activity (1966, 76–77)."
3. *When a source has no author or editor, use a short form of the title.* EXAMPLE: (Faults today 1981, 12). Make sure that the first word of your short title is also the first word under which the title is alphabetized in the list of references.
4. *For works with two authors, list both.* EXAMPLE: (Hobbs and Smith 1989, 52). For works with three or more authors, list the first author's name followed by *et al.*, Latin for "and others." EXAMPLE: (Munson et al. 1967).
5. *When your references contain two or more works with the same author and with the same date, distinguish them from each other by placing letters after the date.* EXAMPLE: (Jones 1987a) versus (Jones 1987b). Then you will make this same distinction in the list of references (Works Cited).
6. *If you need to mention several sources in the same citation, separate them by semicolons.* EXAMPLE: (Barns 1945, 34; Timm 1956, 12).

List of References.   Like other forms of parenthetical documentation, the author-date system requires that you place a list of references at the end of the document. This alphabetized listing includes all sources you cited in the document text. However, it does *not* include references you may have consulted but did not cite. View the list as the spot to which readers turn for complete bibliographical information on sources mentioned in the text, in case they want to find the sources themselves in a library. A sample list of references is shown in Figure 13–13. When assembling such a list, follow these basic rules:

1. *Arrange the sources alphabetically according to author.* When there is no author, list a source by its title.
2. *For books, give (a) the author (last name first, followed by initials or by first name and middle initial), (b) year, (c) book title (underlined or in italic with only the first word and proper nouns in initial caps), (d) edition (if any), (e) city of publication (along with state if city is not well known), and (f) publisher.* Note punctuation of examples in Figure 13–13. For additional authors, place names in last-name-last order, after the first author's name.
3. *For articles, give the (a) author, (b) year, (c) article title (no quotation marks, and with only first word and proper nouns in caps), (d) periodical title (underlined or in italic with main words in initial caps), (e) volume number in arabic numbers, and (f) inclusive page numbers on which the article appears.*

Figure 13–13 shows additional details about books and article citations and about other specialized sources.

On-Line Documentation

Because information found in on-line sources is also borrowed, it deserves the same level of care in documentation as you apply to print sources. After all, borrowed information is borrowed information, whatever the source.

However, documenting on-line data presents some special problems. Most important and perhaps most obvious, you do not have the assurance with on-line information—as you do with print sources—that material will stay the same each time it is used. Thus the documentation format must include information that clearly notes the time of access and location. Generally, your entry should include the same kind of source data used for print sources, with the addition of the following items:

- Reference to the publication medium (*On-line*)
- Name of the computer network, database, or computer service
- Date you used the on-line source

Some databases will include information that is only in the databases, and others will reproduce information from print sources. In the latter case, your entry must include reference to the original source of publication (see Figure 13–3).

Of course, there are many on-line sources. A reference book that lists available on-line publications is the *Gale Guide to Internet Databases.*

WRITING RESEARCH ABSTRACTS

The term *abstract* has been used throughout this book to describe the summary component of any technical document. As the first part of the ABC pattern, it gives

Book with two or more authors: Note that the second author's name is given in normal order, with a comma between the two authors' names.

Andrews, T.S., and L. Kelly. 1965a. *Geography of central Oregon.* 4th ed. New York: Jones and Caliber Press.

Book by same authors: Note that the blank line indicates another source by same authors. The "b" is used because the same authors published two cited books in the same year. Also, the state abbreviation is used for clarity, since Hiram is a small town.

____. 1965b. *Geography today.* Hiram, OH.: Pixie Publishers.

Journal article: Note that there are no spaces between the first page number of this journal article and the colon that follows the volume number. Also, there is only a space, but no punctuation, between the journal title and the volume number.

Cranberg, E. V. 1986. Fossils are fun: The life of a geologist in the 1980s. *Geology Issues* 34:233–344

Article in collection: This entry is for an article that appears in a collection, with a general editor. Note the comma and "ed." (for "edited by") after the collection title. This same format would be used in other cases where you were referring to a piece from a collection, such as a paper in a conference proceedings.

Fandell, C. N., L. Guest, H. M. Smith, and Z. H. Taylor. 1976. Achieving purity in your sampling techniques. In *Geotechnical Engineering Practices*, ed. J. Schwartz, 23–67. Cleveland: Hapsburg Press.

Interview: Refer to yourself in the third person as the "author."

Iris, J. G. 1988. Resident of Summer Hills Subdivision. Interview with the author at site of toxic-waste dump, 23 March.

Newspaper article: This reference includes the day, section, and page number of the article. If no author had been listed, the entry would have begun with the article title.

Mongo, G. P. 1989. Sinkhole psychology: The ground is falling, Chicken Little. *Dayton Gazette,* 12 July, sec. D, 5.

Article from popular magazine: This reference is handled like a journal article except that the date of the particular issue is also included, after the volume number. Note that there is no extra spacing around the parentheses.

Runyon, D. G., and L. P. Goss. 1967. Sinkholes are coming to your area soon. *Timely News* 123(15 July):65–66.

Article from Online Database: For this reference we will use the article listed above, assuming that you found it in a database instead of in its print version.

Runyon, D.G. and L.P. Moss. 1967. Sinkholes are coming to your area soon. *Timely News* 123 (15 July):65-66. Online Southern Tech Library. Internet. 5 August 1996.

FIGURE 13–13
Sample list of references

decision-makers the most important information they need. However, here we use abstract for a narrower purpose. It is a stand-alone summary that provides readers with a capsule version of a piece of research, such as an article or a book. This section (1) describes the two main types of research abstracts, with examples of each, and (2) gives five guidelines for writing research abstracts.

Types of Abstracts

There are two types of abstracts: informational and descriptive. As the following definitions indicate, informational abstracts include more detail than descriptive abstracts:

Informational Abstract.

- **Format:** This type of abstract includes the major points from the original document.
- **Purpose:** Given their level of detail, informational abstracts give readers enough information to grasp the main findings, conclusions, and recommendations of the original document.
- **Length:** Though longer than descriptive abstracts, informational abstracts are still best kept to one to three paragraphs.
- **Example:** A sentence from such an abstract might read, "The article notes that functional resumes should include a career objective, academic experience, and a list of the applicant's skills." (See corresponding example in definition of a descriptive abstract.)

Descriptive Abstract.

- **Format:** This type of abstract gives only main topics of the document, without supplying supporting details such as findings, conclusions, or recommendations.
- **Purpose:** Given their lack of detail, descriptive abstracts can only help readers decide whether they want to read the original document.
- **Length:** Their lack of detail usually ensures that descriptive abstracts are no more than one paragraph.
- **Example:** A sentence from such an abstract might read, "The article lists the main parts of the functional resume." (See corresponding example in definition of an informational abstract.)

You may wonder when you'll need to write abstracts during your career. First, your boss may ask you to summarize some research, perhaps because he or she lacks your technical background. Second, you may want to collect abstracts as part of your own research project. In either case, you need to write abstracts that accurately reflect the tone and content of the original document.

Assume, for example, that your McDuff supervisor has asked you to read some current research on strategies for negotiating. Later your boss plans to use your abstracts to get an overview of the field and to decide which, if any, of the original full-length documents should be read in full. The examples that follow show both informational and descriptive abstracts of the section of chapter 14 that covers negotiating (pp. 523–527). Note that the informational abstract actually lists the guidelines contained in the chapter, whereas the descriptive abstract notes only that the article includes the guidelines.

> *Informational Abstract: "Guidelines for Negotiating"*
> This article suggests that modern negotiations should replace "I win, you lose" thinking with a "we can both win" attitude. To achieve this change, these six main guidelines are prescribed: (1) think long-term, (2) explore many options, (3) find the shared interests, (4) listen carefully, (5) be patient, and (6) DO look back. Although this strategy applies to all types of negotiation, this article focuses on a business context. It includes an extended example that involves establishing an appropriate entry salary for a job applicant in computer systems engineering.

> *Descriptive Abstract: "Guidelines for Negotiating"*
> This article describes six main guidelines that apply to all types of negotiations. The emphasis is on strategies to be used in the context of business. All the suggestions in the article support the need for a "we both win" attitude in negotiating, rather than an "I win, you lose" approach.

Guidelines for Writing Research Abstracts

The guidelines given here will help you (1) locate the important information in a document written by you or someone else and (2) present it with clarity and precision in an abstract. In every case, you must present a capsule version of the document in language the reader can understand. The ultimate goal is to save the readers time.

■ Abstracting Guideline 1: Highlight the Main Points

This guideline applies whether you are abstracting a document written by you or someone else. To extract information that will be used in your abstract, follow these steps:

- Find a purpose statement in the first few paragraphs.
- Skim the entire piece quickly, getting a sense of its organization.
- Read the piece more carefully, underlining main points and placing comments in margins.
- Pay special attention to information gained from headings, first sentences of paragraphs, listings, graphics, and beginning and ending sections.

■ Abstracting Guideline 2: Sketch Out an Outline

From the notes and marginal comments gathered in Abstracting Guideline 1, write a brief outline that contains the main points of the piece. If you are dealing with a well-organized piece of writing, it will be an easy task. If you are not, it will be a challenge. Here is an outline for the negotiation section of chapter 14, as abstracted in the previous examples.

Outline for "Guidelines for Negotiating"
Purpose: to provide rules that help readers adopt a "we both win" strategy

I. Think long term
  A. Focus on building mutual trust
  B. Project the long-term attitude into every part of the negotiation process

II. Explore many options
  A. Get away from thinking there are only two choices
  B. Put diverse options on the table early in the negotiation

III. Find the shared interests
  A. Stress points of agreement, rather than conflict
  B. Use mutual concerns to defuse contentious issues

IV. Listen carefully
  A. Ask questions and listen, rather than talk
  B. Use probing questions to move discussion along in salary discussion
    1. Break out of attack/counterattack cycle
    2. Uncover motivations
    3. Expose careless logic and unsupported demands
    4. Move both sides closer to objective standards

V. Be patient
  A. Avoid the mistakes that come from hasty decisions
  B. Avoid the bad feeling that results when people feel pressured

VI. DO look back
  A. Keep a journal in which you reflect on your negotiations
  B. Analyze the degree to which you followed the previous five guidelines

■ Abstracting Guideline 3: Begin with a Short Purpose Statement

Both descriptive and informational abstracts should start with a concise overview sentence. This sentence acquaints the reader with the document's main purpose. Stylistically, it should include an action verb and a clear subject. Here are three options that can be adapted to any abstract:

- The article "Recycle Now!" states that Georgia must intensify its effort to recycle all types of waste.
- In "Recycle Now!" Laurie Hellman claims that Georgia must intensify its effort to recycle all types of waste.
- According to "Recycle Now!" Georgians must intensify their efforts to recycle all types of waste.

■ *Abstracting Guideline 4: Maintain a Fluid Style*

One potential hazard of the abstracting process is that you may produce disjointed, awkward paragraphs. You can reduce the possibility of this stylistic flaw by following these steps:

- Writing in complete sentences, without deleting articles (*a, an, the*)
- Using transitional words and phrases between sentences
- Following the natural logic and flow of the original document itself

■ *Abstracting Guideline 5: Avoid Technical Terms Readers May Not Know*

Another potential hazard is that the abstract writer, in pursuit of brevity, will use terms unfamiliar to the readers of the abstract. This flaw is especially bothersome to readers who do not have access to the original document. As a general rule, use no technical terms that may be unclear to your intended audience. If a term or two are needed, provide a brief definition in the abstract itself.

Note, also, that abstracts that might become separated from the original document should include a bibliographical citation (see the previous examples).

COMMUNICATION CHALLENGE

"To Cite or Not To Cite"

Dan Gibbs works as a benefits and finance specialist at McDuff's corporate office in Baltimore. As the number of McDuff employees has grown, he has received many inquiries about ways to save for retirement. Recently he wrote and distributed a four-page flyer on the topic, using materials from print and on-line sources. The response was so positive that his boss wants to send the flyer to clients as a "freebie"—both to help clients' employees and to create "good will" in marketing. This use of the flyer has made Dan re-think how he developed the piece. His research process, his results, and some questions for discussion follow.

Background of Retirement Booklet

Unlike Tanya Grant in the acid-rain project described in this chapter, Dan didn't have time or interest in pursuing a full-scale library search about retirement strategies. Besides, he has personnel magazines in the office with data that would support his points. In addition, he is connected to the Internet, a series of loosely connected databases that might provide information directly to him at his office computer.

Like many companies, McDuff has a retirement plan largely in the form of what is called a 401K program. It allows employees to contribute a percentage of their salaries into a tax-deferred retirement account, a portion of which is matched by the employer. Even though McDuff has a generous matching arrangement, many employees do not take full advantage of the program. Therefore, Dan wrote the retirement flyer to remind them that it is never too early to plan for retirement. As it happens, he learned that many U.S. workers are failing to put away enough money for their retirement years.

The Research Process

After outlining his goals for the booklet, Dan began "surfing" through related information on the Internet. He made use of four pieces of information from an *Atlanta-Journal Constitution* article found on an Internet database called "Human Resources Retrieval." Following are three of the themes he stressed, along with related information he used from the newspaper article.

1. *Theme #1: We're living longer past retirement.* The following changes occurred in years of life expected after age 65: for men, 12.8 in 1960, 13.1 in 1970, 14.1 in 1980, and 15.1 in 1990; for women, 15.8 in 1960, 17.0 in 1970, 18.3 in 1980, and 18.9 in 1990.
2. *Theme #2: We cannot depend exclusively on Social Security.* As many more people retire from the "Baby Boom" generation born between 1946 and 1964, fewer and fewer workers paying Social Security are supporting each person getting it. The following numbers are actual and projected number of workers supporting each retiree: 41.9 in 1945, 8.6 in 1955, 4.0 in 1965, 3.2 in 1975, 3.3 in 1985, 3.3 in 1995, 3.1 in 2005, 2.7 in 2015, 2.2 in 2025, and 2.0 in 2035.
3. *Theme #3: We should begin saving when we're young.* If you start at age 25 saving $3,000 yearly in a tax-deferred account, with a 9% annual return, you'll accumulate $166,971 by age 45, $457,685 by age 55, and $1,170,330 by age 65. If you start at age 35, you'll have $48,378 by 45, $166,971 by 55, and $457,685 by 65. If you start at age 45, you'll have $48,378 by 55 and $166,971 by 65.

Questions and Comments for Discussion

1. If you were presenting the data above in a research report, what format would you choose? Why? (See chapter 11.)
2. Considering the four data sets Dan took from the newspaper article/Internet sources, which ones need documentation and which, if any, do not? Explain your answer.
3. Does the fact that the flyer will be sent to clients have any effect on your answer to question #2?
4. Do a "works cited" reference for the data in Theme #1 above. See the footnote to this Communication Challenge for actual source information. Assume that Dan found the piece on the Internet on March 4, 1996.

---

*The database is a fictional one created just for this case. However, the data are real and included in the following source: "A Special Report: The Rocky Road to Retirement," by Hank Ezell, *Atlanta Journal-Constitution,* September 25, 1995, pp. E1, E4–6. The article cites these sources for data listed: the Rand Corporation, National Vital Statistics System, and Ibbotson Associates for item #1; the Social Security Administration for item #2; and Hewitt Associates for item #3.

CHAPTER SUMMARY

This chapter highlights the process of conducting technical research and writing about the results. Much of the information is presented within the context of a research project conducted at McDuff.

Before starting your search for information, you need to decide what main question you are trying to answer. Also, think about the types of information you need (secondary and/or primary), the types of sources that would be useful, and the format required for the final document. Once in the library, you have many sources available to you: books, periodicals, newspapers, company directories, general references such as dictionaries and encyclopedias, abstracts—both on-line and in print. You can also use the Internet, World Wide Web, questionnaires, and interviews.

As you begin to locate sources, follow this five-step research process: (1) write complete bibliography cards, (2) develop a rough outline, (3) take careful notes on large note cards, (4) organize research in an outline, and (5) write the draft from the outline and the cards. For the final paper, choose a documentation system appropriate for your field or organization. Today the preferred approach is to use some form of parenthetical citations, such as the author-date system outlined in this chapter.

Another research skill is writing research abstracts (summaries) of articles, books, or other sources of information. Abstracts can be either descriptive (quite brief) or informational (somewhat more detailed).

ASSIGNMENTS

If your instructor considers it appropriate, use a copy of the Planning Form at the end of the book for completing these assignments.

1. **General Research Paper.** Using a topic approved by your instructor, follow the procedure suggested in this chapter for writing a paper that results from some technical research. Be sure that your topic (1) relates to a technical field in which you have an interest, by virtue of your career or academic experience, and (2) is in a field about which you can find information in nearby libraries.

2. **Research Paper—Your Major Field.** Write a research paper on your major field. Consider some of these questions in arriving at your thesis for the paper: What is the history of your major? What types of jobs do majors in your discipline pursue? Do their job responsibilities change after 5, 10, or 15 years in the field? What kinds of professional organizations exist to support your field?

3. **Research Paper—McDuff.** As a McDuff engineer or scientist, you have been asked to write a research paper for McDuff's upper management. Choose your topic from one of the technical fields listed here. Assume that your readers are gathering information about the topic because they may want to conduct consulting work for companies or government agencies involved in these fields. Focus on advantages and

disadvantages associated with the particular technology you choose. Follow the procedure outlined in this chapter.

- Artificial intelligence
- Chemical hazards in the home
- Fiber optics
- Forestry management
- Geothermal energy
- Human-powered vehicles
- Lignite-coal mining
- Organic farming
- Satellite surveying
- Solar power
- Wind power

4. **Abstract—One Article or Several Articles.**
   Option A. Visit your college library and find a magazine or journal in a technical area, perhaps your major field. Then photocopy a short article (about five pages) that does not already contain a separate abstract or summary at the beginning of the article. Using the guidelines in this chapter, write both an informative and a descriptive abstract for a nontechnical audience. Submit the two abstracts, along with the copy of the article.
   Option B. Follow the instructions in Option A, but use a short article that has been selected or provided by your instructor.
   Option C. Read 3–5 current articles in your major field. Write an abstract that summarizes *all* of them on one page.

5. **Questionnaire—Analysis.** Using the guidelines in this chapter for questionnaires, point out problems posed by the following questions:
   a. Is the poor economy affecting your opinion about the current Congress?
   b. Do you think the company's severe morale problem is being caused by excessive layoffs?
   c. Was the response of our salespeople both courteous and efficient?
   d. Of all the computer consultants you have used in the last 15 years, which category most accurately reflects your ranking of our firm: (a) the top 5%, (b) the top 10%, (c) the top 25%, (d) the top 50%, or (e) the bottom 50%?
   e. In choosing your next writing consultant, would you consider seeking the advice of a professional association such as the STC or the CPTSC?
   f. Besides the position just filled, how many job openings at your firm have been handled by Dowry Personnel Services?

6. **Questionnaire—Writing.** Design a brief questionnaire to be completed by students on your campus. Select a topic of general interest, such as the special needs of evening students or the level of satisfaction with certain college facilities or services. Administer the questionnaire to at least 20 individuals (in classes, at the student union, in dormitories, etc.). After you analyze the results, write a brief report that summarizes your findings. NOTE: Before completing this exercise, make sure that you gain any necessary approvals of college officials, if required.

7. **Interviews—Simulation and Analysis.** Divide into groups of three or four students, as your instructor directs. Two members of the group will take part in a simulated interview between a placement specialist at your school and a personnel

representative from an area company. Assume that the firm might have a number of openings for your school's graduates in the next few years.

As a group, create some questions that would be useful during the simulated interview. Then have the two members perform the role-playing exercise for 15–20 minutes. Finally, as a group, critique the interview according to the suggestions in this chapter and share your findings with the entire class.

8. **Interview—Real-World.** Select a simple research project that would benefit from information gained from an interview. (Your project may or may not be associated with a written assignment in this course.) Using the suggestions in this chapter, conduct the interview with the appropriate official.

9. **Library Search.** Use your library skills to find the answers to the following questions. Be sure that you can explain exactly how you found the answers.

   a. Largest corporate employer in your state
   b. Number of companies on the New York Stock Exchange
   c. Number of doctors in the American Medical Association
   d. Largest university in New Zealand
   e. Average pay of secondary schoolteachers in your state last year
   f. Percentage of children below the poverty line in the United States
   g. Year that *Huckleberry Finn* was first published
   h. Last names of the nine justices of the U.S. Supreme Court
   i. Average starting salary of chemical engineers in 1994
   j. Number of nuclear power plants in operation
   k. Address of the STC (Society for Technical Communication)
   l. Contrast of ABS and Kevlar, two materials for constructing canoes
   m. Current head of the USGS (United States Geological Survey)
   n. Median age of a new mother in 1994
   o. Month and year that the Berlin Wall came down
   p. Last 10 presidents of the United States
   q. Number of members in the president's cabinet
   r. Greek island that is largest in land mass
   s. Number of novels published by Isaac Asimov
   t. Year in which Fidel Castro came to power in Cuba
   u. Names of two "grammar-checker" computer packages
   v. Brief biography of Gunning (of *Gunning Fog Index* fame)
   w. Last five locations of the summer Olympics
   x. Three most popular dog breeds in a recent year of your choice
   y. Brief description of what a micropaleontologist does
   z. Name of the organization in Utah that supplies genealogical information

14 | The Job Search

The job search tests *all* your communication skills: researching career opportunities, writing letters and resumes, interviewing with potential employers, and negotiating for a contract.

*I*n applying for a job, you are selling yourself. It is no time for either self-delu-
sion or false modesty. You must first assess your abilities, then find an appropriate job match, and finally persuade a potential employer that you are the right
one for the job.

This chapter offers suggestions for landing a job in your profession. You'll
find information on these main activities:

- Researching occupations and companies
- Writing job letters and resumes
- Succeeding in job interviews
- Negotiating with current and potential employers

RESEARCHING OCCUPATIONS AND COMPANIES

Before writing a job letter and resume, you may need information about (1) career
fields that interest you (if you have not already chosen one), (2) specific companies that hire graduates in your field, and, obviously, (3) specific jobs that are
available. Here are some pointers for finding such information—both from traditional sources and from your computer.

Do Basic Research in Your College Library or Placement Office

Libraries and placement centers offer one good starting point for getting information about professions. Following are a few well-known handbooks and bibliographies found in reference collections. They either give information about occupations or provide names of other books that supply such information:

Career Choices Encyclopedia: Guide to Entry-Level Jobs

Dictionary of Occupational Titles

Directory of Career Training and Development Programs

Encyclopedia of Business Information Sources

Encyclopedia of Careers and Vocational Guidance

High-Technology Careers

Occupational Outlook Handbook

Professional Careers Sourcebook: An Information Guide for Career Planning

■ *Interview Someone in Your Field of Interest*

To get the most current information, arrange an interview with someone working in an occupation that interests you. This abundant source of information often goes untapped by college students, who mistakenly think such interviews are difficult to arrange. In fact, usually you can locate people to interview through (1) your college placement office, (2) your college alumni association, or (3) your own network of family and friends. Another possibility is to call a reputable firm in the field and explain that you wish to interview someone in a certain occupation. Make it clear, however, that you are not looking for a job—only information about a profession.

Once you set up the interview, prepare well by listing your questions in a notebook or on a clipboard that you take with you to the interview. This preparation will keep you on track and show persons being interviewed that you value their time and information. Here are some questions to ask:

- How did you prepare for the career or position you now have?
- What college course work or other training was most useful?
- What types of activities fill your typical working day?
- What features of your career do you like the most? The least?
- What personality characteristics are most useful to someone in your career?
- How would you describe the long-term outlook of your field?
- How do you expect your career to develop in the next 5 years, 10 years, or 15 years?
- Do you know any books or periodicals that might help me find out more about your field?
- Do you know any individuals who, like you, might permit themselves to be interviewed about their choice of a profession?

Although this interview *may* lead to a discussion about job openings in the interviewer's organization, the main purpose of the conversation is to retrieve information about an occupation.

■ *Find Information on Companies in Your Field*

With your focus on a profession, you can begin screening companies that employ people in the field chosen. First, determine the types of information you want to find. Examples might include location, net worth, number of employees, number of workers in your specific field, number of divisions, types of products or services, financial rating, and names and titles of company officers. The following are some sources that might include such information. They can be found in the reference sections of libraries and in college placement centers:

> *Business Bankings Annual* contains ranked lists related to business and industry, such as "Largest Data Communication Companies."

> *The Career Guide* gives overviews of many American companies and includes information such as types of employees hired, training opportunities, and fringe benefits.

> *Corporate Technology Directory* profiles high-tech firms and covers topics such as sales figures, number of employees, locations, and names of executives.

> *Dun's Million Dollar Directory: America's Leading Public and Private Companies* lists information about 160,000 U.S. businesses with net worth over $500,000.

> *Facts on File Directory of Major Public Corporations* gives essential information on 5,700 of the largest U.S. companies listed on major stock exchanges.

> *Job Choices in Science and Engineering,* an annual magazine published by the College Placement Council, includes helpful articles and information about hundreds of companies that hire technical graduates.

> *Peterson's Business and Management Jobs* provides background on employers of business, management, and liberal-arts graduates.

> *Peterson's Engineering, Science and Computer Jobs* provides background information on employers of technical graduates.

> *Standard and Poor's Register of Corporations, Directors, and Executives* lists names and titles of officials at 55,000 public and private U.S. corporations.

■ *Do Intensive Research on a Selected List of Potential Employers*

The previous steps help get you started finding information on occupations and firms. Ultimately, you will develop a selected list of firms that interest you. Your research may have led you to these companies, or your college placement office may have told you that openings exist there. Now you need to conduct an intensive search to learn as much as you can about the firms. Here are a few sources of information, along with the kinds of questions each source will help to answer.

- **Annual reports** (often available in your library or placement office): How does the firm describe its year's activities to stockholders? What are its products or services?
- **Media or press kits** (available from public relations offices): How does the firm portray itself to the public?
- **Personnel manuals and other policy guidelines:** What are features of the firm's "corporate culture"? How committed is the firm to training? What are the

benefits and retirement programs? Where are its branches? What are its customary career paths?

- **Graduates of your college or university now working for the firm:** What sort of reputation does your school have among decision-makers at the firm?
- **Company newsletters and in-house magazines:** How open and informative is the firm's internal communication?
- **Business sections of newspapers and magazines:** What kind of news gets generated about the firm?
- **Professional organizations or associations:** Is the firm active within its profession?
- **Stock reports:** Is the firm making money? How has it done in the past five years?
- **Accrediting agencies or organizations:** How has the firm fared during peer evaluations?
- **Former employees of the company:** Why have people left the firm?
- **Current employees of the company:** What do employees like, or dislike, about the company? Why do they stay?

Other good sources include the Better Business Bureau, Chamber of Commerce, and local newspapers. In other words, you should thoroughly examine an organization from the outside. The information you gather will help you decide where to apply and, if you later receive a job offer, where to begin or continue your career.

■ *Use Your Computer to Gather Data*

Besides traditional sources, you can use computers to find information about professions, organizations, graduate schools, and job openings. No doubt between the time this book is written and then published, the names and number of on-line resources will change dramatically. Generally, are some of the kinds of information available:

- College and university catalogs
- "Home page" documents on companies, organizations, and schools
- Employment listings from local and national sources
- On-line discussion forums involving recent graduates of colleges and universities

In other words, the Internet will help you locate a variety of information during your job search. Moreover, you can use your computer to search for openings and respond to job ads, as mentioned in the next section.

JOB CORRESPONDENCE

Job letters and resumes must grab the attention of busy readers, who may spend only 60 seconds deciding whether to consider you further. This section gives you the tools to write a successful letter and resume. "Successful," of course, means a letter and resume that will get you an interview. After that, your interpersonal skills will help you land the job. The letter and resume only aim to get you to the next step—the personal interview.

Most job letters and resumes still get sent through the mail. However, a growing number of applicants use the Internet to apply for jobs.

For example, on-line services can place resumes into a bank used by hundreds, perhaps thousands, of companies. The resumes will be scanned with the use of software, which searches for key words that reflect abilities needed for specific jobs and then sends selected resumes to companies. If you use this kind of service, remember one point: when you send credentials into cyberspace, you cannot be sure where they will land. Do not expect the level of confidentiality and security that you have with personal mail.

Whether you use on-line techniques like e-mail and resume services or stick with the traditional approach, the same basic writing guidelines apply. Your letter, no longer than one page, should be specific about the job you seek and your main selling points. Then the resume—one page or two at most—should simply, specifically, and neatly highlight your background.

Job Letters

In preparing to write a job letter, take the point of view of the persons to whom you are writing. What criteria will they use to evaluate your credentials? How much or how little do they want in the letter? What main points will they be hunting for as they scan your resume? Accordingly, this section first examines the needs of these readers and then gives guidelines for you, the writer. Models 14–1 and 14–2 on pages 533–536 include sample job letters and resumes.

The Readers' Needs.   You probably will not know personally the readers of your job letter, so you must think hard about what they may want. Your task is complicated by the fact that often there are several readers of your letter and resume, who may have quite different backgrounds.

Here is one possible scenario:

Step 1: The letter may go first to the personnel office, where a staff member specializing in employment selects letters and resumes that meet the criteria stated in the position announcement. (In some large employers, letters and resumes may even be stored in a computer where they are scanned for key words that relate to specific jobs.)

Step 2: Applications that pass this screening are sent to the department manager who will supervise the employee that is hired. This manager will interview applicants and ultimately hire the employee. The manager may then select a group to be interviewed.

One variation of this process has the personnel department doing an interview as well as screening letters and resumes—before the department manager even hears about any applications. Another variation, as noted earlier, has the employer relying on an on-line resume service for the initial screening.

Yet sooner or later, a real human being will read your letter and resume. And most readers, whatever their professional background, have these five characteristics in common:

■ *Feature 1: They Read Job Letters in Stacks*

Most search-and-screen processes are such that letters get filed until there are many to evaluate. Your reader faces this intimidating pile of paper, from which you want your letter to emerge as victor.

■ *Feature 2: They Are Tired*

Some employment specialists may save job letters for their fresher moments, but many people who do the hiring get to job letters at the end of a busy day or at home in the evening. So they have even less patience than usual for flowery wording or hard-to-read print.

■ *Feature 3: They Are Impatient*

Your readers expect major points to jump right out at them. In most cases, they will not dig for information that cannot be found quickly.

■ *Feature 4: They Become Picky Grammarians*

Readers of all professional and academic backgrounds expect good writing when they read job letters. There is an unspoken assumption that a letter asking for a chance at a career should reflect solid use of the language. Furthermore, it should have no typographical errors. If the letter does contain a typo or grammar error, the reader may wonder about the quality of writing you will produce on the job.

■ *Feature 5: They Want Attention-Grabbers but Not Slickness*

You want your letter and resume to stand out without the use of gimmicks. Most readers prefer a tasteful, reserved format that does not draw too much attention to itself. For example, white or off-white stationary is still the standard, along with traditional fonts with lots of white space for easy reading. If you want to attract attention in a professional manner, consider attaching a business card to your letter so that the reader has your name and number handy. Students can design and print business cards with software available in many college computer labs.

Of course, likes and dislikes vary. An advertising director, who works all day with graphics, would probably want a bolder format design than an engineering manager, who works with documents that are less flashy. If you cannot decide, it is best to use a conservative format and style.

The Letter's Organization.   The job-letter guidelines that follow relate to the features mentioned about readers. Your one and only goal is to tantalize the reader enough to want to interview you. That is all. With that goal and the reader's needs in mind, your job letter should follow this ABC format:

ABC Format: Job Letters

Abstract

- Apply for a specific job
- Refer to ad, mutual friend, or other source of information about the job
- (Optional) Briefly state how you can meet the main need of your potential employer

Body

- Specify your understanding of the reader's main needs
- Provide main qualifications that satisfy these needs (but only *highlight* points from resume—do NOT simply repeat all resume information)
- Avoid mentioning weak points or deficiencies
- Keep body paragraphs to six or fewer lines
- Use a bulleted or numbered list if it helps draw attention to three or four main points
- Maintain the "you" attitude throughout (see chapter 7, p. 213)

Conclusion

- Tie the letter together with one main theme or selling point, as you would a sales letter
- Refer to your resume
- Explain how and when the reader can contact you for an interview

---

This pattern gives you a starting point, but it is not the whole story. There is one feature of application letters that cannot be placed easily in a formula. That feature is style. Work hard with your draft to develop a unity and flow that, by itself, will set you apart from the crowd. Your attention-grabber will engage interest. But the clarity of your prose will keep readers attentive and persuade them that you are an applicant who should be interviewed.

Resumes

Resumes usually accompany application letters. Three points make writing resumes a challenge:

1. **Emphasis:** You should select just a *few major points of emphasis* from your personal and professional life. Avoid the tendency to include college and employment details best left for the interview.
2. **Length:** You usually should use only *one page*. For individuals with extensive experience, a two-page resume is acceptable—if it is arranged evenly over both pages.

3. **Arrangement:** You should arrange information so that it is *pleasing to the eye and easy to scan.* (Prospective employers spend less than a minute assessing your application.) You may even want to include an appropriate, simple illustration. (See the innovative format of Model 14–7 on pages 543–544.)

There is no easy formula for writing excellent resumes. Stylistic preferences vary greatly. This section distills the best qualities of many formats into three basic patterns: (1) the chronological resume, which emphasizes employment history, (2) the functional resume, which emphasizes the skills you have developed, and (3) the combined resume, which merges features of both the chronological and functional formats. See the "Experience" section that follows to learn when to use each format. Choose the pattern that best demonstrates your strengths.

The following paragraphs describe the main parts of the resume. The "Experience" section explains the differences between chronological, functional, and combined resumes. Refer to the following models on pages 533–545 for resume examples:

Model 14–1: Job Letter and Chronological Resume

Model 14–2: Job Letter and Chronological Resume

Model 14–3: Job Letter and Functional Resume

Model 14–4: Job Letter and Functional Resume

Model 14–5: Combined Resume

Model 14–6: Combined Resume

Model 14–7: Resume with Innovative Format

Model 14–8: Resume with Innovative Format

Objective.   Personnel directors and other people in the employment cycle often sort resumes by the "Objective" statement. Writing a good one is hard work, especially for new graduates, who often just want a chance to start working at a firm at any level. Despite this eagerness to please, do not make the mistake of writing an all-encompassing statement such as "Seeking challenging position in innovative firm in civil-engineering field." Your reader will find such a general statement of little use in sorting your application. It gives the impression that you have not set clear professional goals.

Most objectives should be short, preferably one sentence. Also, they should be detailed enough to show that you have prepared for, and are interested in, a specific career, yet open-ended enough to reflect a degree of flexibility. If you have several quite different career options, you might want to design a different resume for each job description, rather than trying to write a job objective that takes in too much territory. Word processing allows you to tailor resume objectives to the particular employer to whom you are writing.

Note: Some employers prefer that you *not* include an objective. For example, you may be applying for an entry-level job for which an objective would be inappropriate. As always, consider your reader's needs as you make decisions about objectives.

Education.   Whether you follow the objective with the "Education" or "Experience" section depends on the answer to one question: Which topic is most important to the reader? Most recent college graduates lead off with "Education," particularly if the completion of the degree prompted the job search.

This section seems simple at the outset. Obligatory information includes your school, school location, degree, and date of graduation. It is what you include beyond the bare details, however, that most interests employers. Here are some possibilities:

- **Grade point average:** Include it if you are proud of it; do not if it fails to help your case.
- **Honors:** List anything that sets you apart from the crowd—such as dean's list or individual awards in your major department. If you have many, include a separate "Recognitions" heading toward the end of the resume.
- **Minors:** Highlight any minors or degree options, whether they are inside or outside your major field. Employers place value on this specialized training, even if (and sometimes *especially* if) it is outside your major field.
- **Key courses:** When there is room, provide a short list of courses you consider most appropriate for the kind of position you are seeking. Because the employer probably will not look at your transcripts until a later stage of the hiring process, use this brief listing as an attention-grabber.

Experience.   This section poses a problem for many applicants just graduating from college. Students often comment that experience is what they are *looking* for, *not* what they have yet. Depending on the amount of work experience you have gained, consider three options for completing this section of the resume: (1) emphasize specific positions you have held (chronological resume), (2) emphasize specific skills you have developed in your experience (functional resume), or (3) emphasize both experience and skills (combined resume).

Option 1: Chronological Format. This option works best if your job experience has led logically toward the job you now seek. Follow these guidelines:

- List relevant full-time or part-time experience, including co-op work, in *reverse* chronological order.
- Be specific about your job responsibilities, while still being brief.
- Be selective if you have had more jobs than can fit on a one-page resume.
- Include nonprofessional tasks (such as working on the campus custodial staff) *if* it will help your case (for example, the employer might want to know that you worked your way through college).
- Remember that if you leave out some jobs, the interview will give you the chance to elaborate upon your work experience.
- Select a readable format, with appropriate white space.

- Use action verbs and lists to emphasize what you did or what you learned at jobs—for example, "Provided telephone support to users of System/23." Use parallel form in each list.

Option 2: Functional Format. This approach works best if (1) you wish to emphasize the skills and strengths you have developed in your career, rather than specific jobs you have had, or (2) you have had "gaps" in your work history, which would be obvious if you used the chronological format. Although it is sometimes used by those whose job experience is not a selling point, this is not always the case. Sometimes your skills built up over time may be the best argument for your being considered for a position, even if your job experience also is strong. For example, you may have five years' experience in responsible positions at four different retailers. You then decide to write a functional resume focused on the three skill areas you developed: sales, inventory control, and management.

If you write a functional resume that stresses skills, you may still want to follow this section with a brief employment history (see Option 3). Most potential employers want to know where and when you worked, even though this issue is not a high priority. Note: If you decide to leave out the history, bring it with you to the interview on a separate sheet.

Option 3: Combined Format. The combined format uses features of both chronological and functional formats. This format works best when you want to emphasize the skills you have developed, while still giving limited information on the chronology of your employment.

Models 14–5 and 14–6 on pages 541–542 show two variations of the combined format. In Model 14–5, the experience section looks exactly as it would in a functional resume, with subheadings giving the names of skills. However, the writer adds a brief skeleton work history near the end of the page; he believes the reader will want some sort of chronological work history, even if it is not the writer's strength. Model 14–6 integrates chronological information into the skills section. The positions held may not be prestigious, but together they show that the applicant has considerable experience developing the two sets of skills listed: Editing/Writing and Teaching/Research.

Activities, Recognitions, Interests.   Most resumes use one or two of these headings to provide the reader with additional background information. The choice of which ones, if any, to use depends on what you think will best support your job objective. Here are some possibilities:

- **Activities:** selected items that show your involvement in your college or your community or both.
- **Recognitions:** awards and other specific honors that set you apart from other applicants. (Do not include awards that might appear obscure, meaningless, or dated to the reader, such as most high-school honors.)
- **Interests:** hobbies or other interests that give the reader a brief look at the "other" you.

However you handle these sections, they should be fairly brief and should not detract from the longer, more significant sections described previously.

References.   Your resume opens the door to the job interview and later stages of the job process, when references will be called. There are two main approaches to the reference section of the resume:

1. Writing "Available upon request" at the end of the page
2. Listing names, addresses, and phone numbers at the end of the resume

The first approach assumes that the reader prefers the intermediate step of contacting you before references are sent or solicited. The second approach assumes that the reader prefers to call or write references directly, without having to contact you first. Use the format most commonly used in your field or, most important, the one most likely to meet the needs of a particular employer. As always, be ready to tailor your letter and resume each time you put it in the mail.

Your goal is to write an honest resume that emphasizes your good points and minimizes your deficiencies. To repeat a point made at the outset, you want your resume and job letter to open the door for later stages of the application process. Look upon this writing task as your greatest persuasive challenge. Indeed, it is the ultimate sales letter, for what you are selling is the potential you offer to change an organization and, perhaps, the world as well. Considering such heady possibilities, make sure to spend the time necessary to produce first-rate results.

JOB INTERVIEWS

Your job letter and resume have only one purpose: to secure a personal interview by the personnel director or other official who screens applicants for a position.

Much has been written about job interviews. Fortunately, most of the good advice about interviewing goes back to just plain common sense about dealing with people. Following are some suggestions to show you how to prepare for a job interview, perform at your best, and send a follow-up letter.

Preparation

■ *Do Your Homework on the Organization*

You have learned how to locate data about specific companies. Once you have been selected for an interview, review whatever information you have already gathered about the employer. Then go one step further by searching for the *most current* information you can find. Your last source may be someone you know at the organization, or a "friend of a friend."

When you don't have personal contacts, use your research skills again. For large firms, locate recent periodical or newspaper articles by consulting general indexes—such as the *Business Periodicals Index, Wall Street Journal Index, Readers' Guide to Periodicals, New York Times Index,* or the index for any newspaper in a large metropolitan area. For smaller firms, consult recent issues of local newspapers for announcements about the company. Being aware of current company issues will demonstrate your initiative and show your interest in the firm.

As noted earlier in the chapter, the Internet and World Wide Web can also be a good source of current information about an organization.

■ *Write Out Answers to the Questions You Consider Likely*

You probably would not take written answers with you to the interview. But writing them out will give you a level of confidence unmatched by candidates who only ponder possible questions that might come their way. This technique resembles the manner in which some people prepare for oral presentations: First they write out a speech, then they commit it to notes, and finally they give an extemporaneous presentation that reflects confidence in themselves and knowledge of the material. This degree of preparation will place you ahead of the competition.

There are few, if any, original questions asked in job interviews. Most interviewers simply select from some standard questions to help them find out more about you and your background. Here are some typical questions, along with tips for responses in parentheses:

1. **Tell me a little about yourself.** (Keep your answer brief and relate it to the position and company—do *not* wander off into unrelated issues, like hobbies, unless asked to do so.)

2. **Why did you choose your college or university?** (Be sure your main reasons relate to academics—for example, the academic standing of the department, the reputation of the faculty, or the job placement statistics in your field.)

3. **What are your strengths?** (Focus on two or three qualities that would directly or indirectly lead to success in the position for which you are applying.)

4. **What are your weaknesses?** (Choose weaknesses that, if viewed from another perspective, could be considered strengths—for example, your perfectionism or overattention to detail.)

5. **Why do you think you would fit into this company?** (Using your research on the firm, cite several points about the company that correspond to your own professional interests—for example, the firm may offer services in three fields that relate to your academic or work experience.)

6. **What jobs have you held?** (Use this question as a way to show that each previous position, no matter how modest, has helped prepare you for this position—for example, part-time employment in a fast-food restaurant developed teamwork and interpersonal skills.)

7. **What are your long-term goals?** (Be ready to give a 5- or 10-year plan that, preferably, fits within the corporate goals and structure of the firm to

which you are applying—for example, you may want to move from the position of technical field engineer into the role of a project manager, to develop your management skills.)

8. **What salary range are you considering?** (Avoid discussing salary if you can. Instead, note that you are most interested in criteria such as job satisfaction and professional growth. If pushed, give a salary range that is in line with the research you did on the career field in general and this company in particular; see the last section of this chapter on negotiating.)

9. **Do you like working in groups or prefer working alone?** (Most employers want to know that you have interest and experience in group work—whether in college courses or previous jobs. But they also admire and reward individual accomplishment. In deciding what part of your background to emphasize, consider the "corporate culture" of the organization interviewing you.)

10. **Do you have any questions of me?** (*Always* be ready with questions that reinforce your interest in the organization and your knowledge of the position—for example, "Given the recent opening of your Tucson warehouse, do you plan other expansions in the Southwest?" or "What types of in-house or off-site training do you offer new engineers who are moving toward project management?" Other questions can concern issues such as (a) benefits, (b) promotions, (c) availability of personal computers, and (d) travel requirements.)

■ *Do Mock Interviews*

You can improve your chances considerably by practicing for job interviews. One of the easiest and best techniques is role-playing. Ask a friend to serve as the interviewer, and give him or her a list of questions from which to choose. Also, inform that person about the company so that he or she can improvise during the session. In this way you will be prepared for the real thing.

You can get additional information about your interviewing abilities by videotaping your role-playing session. Reviewing the videotape will help you highlight (1) questions that pose special problems for you and for which you need further preparation and (2) mannerisms that need correction. This preparation technique is especially useful if you are one of the growing number of applicants who take part in a video interview with a recruiter.

■ *Be Physically Prepared for the Interview*

Like oral presentations, job interviews work best when you are physically at your best. Thus all the old standbys apply:

- Get a good night's rest before the interview.
- Avoid caffeine or other stimulants.
- Eat about an hour beforehand so that you are not distracted by hunger pangs during the session.
- Take a brisk walk to dispel nervous energy.

Performance

Good planning is your best assurance of a successful interview. Of course, there are always surprises that may catch you. Remember, however, that most interviewers are seriously interested in your application and want you to succeed. Help them by selling *yourself* and thus giving them a reason to hire you. Here are some guidelines for the interview.

■ *Dress Appropriately*

Much has been written on the topic of appropriate attire for interviews. Here are some practical suggestions that are often emphasized:

- Dress conservatively and thus avoid drawing attention to your dress—for example, do not use the interview as an opportunity to break in a garment in the newest style.
- Consider the organization—for example, a brokerage-firm interview may require a dark suit for a man and a tailored suit for a woman, whereas an interview at a construction firm may require less formal attire.
- Avoid excessive jewelry.
- Pay attention to the fine points—for example, wear shined shoes and carry a tasteful briefcase or notebook.

■ *Take an Assertive Approach*

Either directly or indirectly, use everything you say to make the case for your hiring. Be positive, direct, and unflappable. Use every question as a springboard to show your capabilities and interest, rather than waiting for point-blank questions about your qualifications. To be sure, the degree to which you assert yourself partly depends on your interpretations of the interviewer's preference and style. Although you do not want to appear "pushy," you should take the right opportunities to sell yourself and your abilities.

■ *Use the First Few Minutes to Set the Tone*

What you have heard about first impressions is true: Interviewers draw conclusions quickly. Having given many interviews, they are looking for an applicant who injects vitality into the interview and makes their job easier. Within a minute or two, establish the themes and the tone that will be reinforced throughout the conversation—that is, your relevant background, your promising future, and your eagerness (*not* pushiness). In this sense, the interview subscribes to the Preacher's Maxim mentioned in chapter 12: "First you tell 'em what you're going to tell 'em, then you tell 'em, and then you tell 'em what you told 'em."

■ *Maintain Eye Contact While You Speak*

Although you may want to look away occasionally, much of the time your eyes should remain fixed on the person interviewing you. In this way you show interest in what she or he is saying.

If you are being interviewed by several people, make eye contact with *all* of them throughout the interview. No one should feel ignored. You are never quite certain exactly who may be the decision-maker in your case.

■ *Be Specific in the Body of the Interview*

In every question you should see the opportunity to say something specific about you and your background. For example, rather than simply stating that your degree program in computer science prepared you for the open position, cite three specific courses and briefly summarize their relevance to the job.

■ *Do Not Hesitate*

A job interview is no time to hesitate, unless you are convinced the job is not for you. If the interviewer notes that the position involves 40 percent travel, quickly respond that the prospect of working around the country excites you. The question is this: Do you want the job or not? If you do, then accept the requirements of the position and show excitement about the possibilities. You can always turn down the job if you receive an offer and decide later that some restrictions, like travel, are too demanding.

■ *Reinforce Main Points*

The interviewer has no text for the session other than your resume. Therefore, you should drive home main points by injecting short summaries into the conversation. After a five-minute discussion of your recent work experience, take 15 seconds to present a capsule version of relevant employment. Similarly, orchestrate the end of the interview so that you have the chance to summarize your interest in the position and your qualifications. Here is your chance to follow through on the "tell 'em what you told 'em" part of the Preacher's Maxim.

Follow-Up Letters

Follow *every* personal contact with a letter to the person with whom you spoke. Send it within 24 hours of the interview or meeting so that it immediately reinforces the person's recollection of you. This simple strategy gives you a powerful tool for showing interest in a job.

Follow-up letters abide by the same basic letter pattern discussed in chapter 7. In particular, follow these guidelines:

- Write no more than one page.
- Use a short first paragraph to express appreciation for the interview.
- Use the middle paragraph(s) to (a) reinforce a few reasons why you would be the right choice for the position or (b) express interest in something specific about the organization.
- Use a short last paragraph to restate your interest in the job and to provide a hopeful closing.

See chapter 7 for the various formats appropriate for all types of business letters. Here is sample text of a thank-you letter:

Dear Ms. Ferguson:

I enjoyed meeting with you yesterday about the career possibilities at Klub Kola's district headquarters. The growth that you are experiencing makes Klub an especially exciting company to join.

As I mentioned, my marketing background at Seville College has prepared me for the challenge of working in your new Business Development Department. Several courses last semester focused specifically on sales strategies for consumer goods. In addition, an internship this semester has given me the chance to try out marketing strategies in the context of a local firm.

Again, thank you for the chance to learn about your firm's current success and promising future. I remain very interested in joining the Klub Kola team.

Sincerely,

Marcia B Mahoney

Marcia B. Mahoney

When your audience might appreciate a less formal response, consider writing your interviewer a personal note instead of a typed letter. This sort of note is most appropriate when you plan a short message.

NEGOTIATING

All of us negotiate every day of our lives. Both on the job and in our personal lives, we constantly find ourselves in give-and-take discussions to negotiate issues as diverse as those that follow:

- Major and minor purchases
- Relationships with spouses and friends
- Performance evaluations—with bosses and with subordinates
- Salaries—with those to whom we report and with those who report to us

Because negotiating will become an important part of your career, it receives attention in this final section. After some brief background information, the chapter focuses on six guidelines that will steer you toward successful negotiations—when you are hired and also at other points in your career. The main example used in this section is a salary negotiation for an entry-level position.

How has the art of negotiating changed recently? In the past, the process was often characterized by words like *trickery, intimidation,* and *manipulation.* In this game's lexicon there were "winners" and "losers" and lots of warlike imagery. Participants, seen as battlefield adversaries, took up extreme positions, defended and attacked each other's flanks, finally agreed reluctantly to some middle ground, and then departed wounded and usually uncertain of who had won the battle.

Today, the trend is away from this war-zone approach with its "I win, you lose" mentality. As a negotiator, you must enter the process searching for common ground for a very practical reason: Long-term relationships are at stake. In later negotiations, you are much more likely to achieve success if the present negotiation helps both parties. This goal—"we both win"—requires a new set of practices at the negotiation table.

Specifically, six guidelines should drive the negotiation process. All of them embody the viewpoint that successful negotiations involve honest communication wherein both parties benefit. Try to weave these six guidelines into the style of negotiating that you develop.

■ *Negotiating Guideline 1: Think Long Term*

Enter every negotiation with a long-term strategy for success. You need to establish and nurture a continuing relationship with the person on the other side of the table. Later dealings might depend on mutual understandings and goodwill that result from your first meeting. First impressions *do* count.

How might such long-term thinking apply to actual contract discussions for jobs, especially for your first position after graduating? If you are fortunate enough to be in demand in the job market, you will have the leverage to discuss salary expectations and other benefits during an interview. Such discussions often are characterized by you and the employer sharing details about your expectations and the employer's offer. You should enter such sessions with a realistic idea of what you can command in the marketplace. Neither sell yourself short nor harbor inflated ideas of your worth. Your college or university placement office should be able to provide information about salary ranges and benefit options for graduates in your field and organizations in your region.

Of course, the "real world" of the job hunt is such that the supply of new talent may overshadow the demand. You may be so glad to receive a good offer that you hesitate to jeopardize it by attempting to negotiate. Yet, ironically, you can damage your long-term interests in an organization by being overly timid before accepting an offer. Even if there is little or no room for salary negotiation, you should engage in a wide-ranging discussion that allows you to explore options for your contract and learn about features of the position. This dialogue helps you learn about the organization. It also gives the employer a healthy respect for your ability to ask serious questions about your career.

Whatever your bargaining position, take advantage of the opportunity to discuss features of your job and the organization. Questions like those that follow may yield important information for you *and* show your interest in developing a long-term relationship with the employer:

- What philosophy underlies the firm's approach to management?
- What is the general timetable for career advancement?
- Where will your specific job lead?
- What opportunities exist for company-sponsored training?
- How will you be evaluated and how often?

Employers respect applicants who have done enough homework to ask informed questions about the firm's employment practices. Both parties benefit from a frank, detailed discussion. You get what you need to make an informed decision about the firm; and your potential employer can showcase the organization and observe your ability to ask perceptive questions.

■ *Negotiating Guideline 2: Explore Many Options*

The negotiation process sometimes begins with only two options—your salary objective and the employer's offer—with seemingly little room for movement. You can escape this "either/or" trap by working to explore many options in the early stages of contract negotiation. This technique opens both parties to a variety of possible solutions and keeps the discussion rolling.

For example, assume that McDuff recently decided to add a new computer systems engineer to the staff at the corporate office in Baltimore. As a college senior about to graduate with a degree in computer science, you have applied for the job and have had a good first interview. The next week you are called back for a second interview and are offered a job, with a starting salary of $29,000. You are told this firm offer reflects the standard salary for new engineers with no experience. However, your research suggests that entry-level jobs in your field should pay closer to $32,000 a year, a full $3,000 more than the McDuff offer. While this difference concerns you, you have heard good things about the working environment at McDuff and would like to join the firm.

If you immediately were to state your need for a $32,000 starting salary, the negotiation might be thrown into the "either/or" trap that leaves little room for agreement. Instead, you should keep the conversation going by putting additional options on the table and asking open-ended questions (that is, questions that require more than a "yes" or "no" answer). For example, you could temporarily put aside your salary objective and ask how McDuff arrived at the offer figure. While giving the McDuff representative the chance to get facts on the table, this strategy also gives you opportunities to develop and then offer alternatives other than the two salary figures. The discussion might lead to options like these: (1) starting at $29,000 but moving to a higher figure after a successful 90-day trial period, (2) starting at the $29,000 figure but receiving an enhanced stock-option package upon being hired, or (3) starting at $31,000 but giving up the standard $2,000 moving allowance offered to entry-level employees.

The point is that you must be careful to avoid rigidity. Consider possibilities other than the two ideal goals both parties brought to the negotiation table.

■ *Negotiating Guideline 3: Find the Shared Interests*

If you succeed in keeping options open during the negotiation process, you will discover points on which you agree. Psychologically, it is to your advantage to draw attention to these points rather than to points of conflict. Finding shared interests helps establish a friendship that, in turn, makes your counterpart more willing to compromise.

Let's go back to the preceding McDuff example. Assume you are continuing to discuss a number of salary options but have reached no agreement. Chances for closure may increase if you temporarily stop discussing salary and instead search for points, however minor, upon which you agree. For example, you could ask about job tasks in the position. When you learn that new engineers spend about 25 percent of their workday writing reports, you comment that your college training included two electives in technical writing, along with a senior-level research report. The McDuff representative praises the extra effort you made to prepare for the communication tasks in a technical profession.

This discussion about writing, though brief, has highlighted information that may have been missed during McDuff's early reviews of your application. The company's interest in good writing overlaps with the extra effort you gave to this discipline in college. That shared interest may motivate the company to offer a salary figure closer to what you desire. At the very least, you will have reinforced the decision McDuff officials made to offer you the job over three other finalists.

■ *Negotiating Guideline 4: Listen Carefully*

Despite shared interests, negotiations often return to basic differences. An effective technique at this point is to seek information on the rationale behind your counterpart's views. It furthers the negotiation and, in fact, your own case to ask questions and then listen carefully to the answers coming from the other side of the table.

How are we helped by asking questions? Let's return to the McDuff example. When you are confronted with the salary offer, ask how McDuff arrived at that figure. Your question may uncover what is really behind the offer. Did McDuff recently make similar offers to other applicants? Is McDuff aware of national salary surveys that tend to support your request? Asking such questions benefits both you and the entire negotiation process in four ways:

- You give your counterparts the opportunity to explain their views (thus breaking out of the either/or cycle).
- You discover what motivates them (making it more likely that you will reach consensus).
- You expose careless logic and unsupported demands.
- You move closer to objective standards on which to base negotiations.

From your persistent questioning, careful listening, and occasional responses, information may emerge that would otherwise have remained buried. You may discover, for example, that McDuff is basing its salary offer on data pertaining to another part of the country, where both salaries and costs of living are lower. That would give you the opportunity to argue for a higher starting salary, on the basis of regional differences in compensation.

■ *Negotiation Guideline 5: Be Patient*

In the old hard-sell negotiations, participants frequently pushed for quick decisions, often to the regret of at least one of the parties. The better approach is to

Option: Include a third member in your group. Have this person serve as a recorder, providing an oral critique of each interview at the end of the exercise. Then collaborate among the three of you in producing a written critique of the role-playing exercise. Specifically, explain what the exercise taught you about the main challenges of the job interview.

3. **Follow-Up Letter.** Write a follow-up letter to the interview that resulted from assignment 2.

4. **Follow-Up Letter—McDuff Projects.** Last month you submitted a job letter and resume for a position with the Barlow Group in Dallas, Texas. Now the firm has written to express interest in your application. It wants to know more about some summer employment you mentioned on your resume—the project you worked on was similar to some of Barlow's projects.

   Assume the summer work in question was as "student-in-training" on one of the projects described in the color insert in chapter 2. Write a letter that briefly describes the project and your participation in it. Use information from the project, along with invented details about the activities you completed as an assistant. Even if your tasks were not especially glorified—manual labor or office support, for example—strive to describe learning experiences that would be meaningful to your reader. You are writing Daniel C. Yates, Barlow Consulting Group, 600 Industrial Way, Dallas, TX 75221.

5. **Negotiation for Entry-Level Job.** As in assignment 2, pair up with another student. Assume that the letters, resumes, interviews, and follow-up letters from the preceding assignments have resulted in a second interview for one of you. (That is, select one of the positions, with one of you acting as applicant and the other as interviewer.)

   The topic of this second interview is the position being offered to you. After talking with your team member about the context of this simulated interview, conduct a negotiation session wherein the two of you discuss one or more aspects of the position being offered (salary, benefits, travel schedule, employee orientation, training arrangement, career development, etc.).

6. **Negotiation with McDuff Client.** In this exercise, you and a classmate will simulate a negotiation session between Sharon Gibbon, a McDuff training manager at the Cleveland office, and Bernard Claxton, training director of Cleveland's Mercy Hospital. Study the following details before beginning your 10- or 15-minute discussion.

   Option: Collaborate with your teammate in writing an evaluation of this role-playing exercise. Explain the major obstacles encountered by both Gibbon and Claxton, and describe the techniques attempted by both parties to overcome these obstacles.

   General Background: Gibbon recently submitted a proposal to Claxton, offering to have McDuff conduct three hazardous-waste seminars for the plant staff at Mercy Hospital. Claxton calls Gibbon to say that he wants to go ahead with the seminars, contingent on some final negotiations between the two. Claxton and Gibbon agree to meet in a few days, presumably to iron out a final agreement. Gibbon wants the contract, and Claxton's staff needs the training. Yet the deal won't be sealed until they have their discussion and resolve several issues. Following are their respective points of view.

   Gibbon's Viewpoint: Sharon Gibbon has offered to have McDuff teach five one-day seminars for a fee of $15,000 ($3,000 per seminar). Each seminar will be team-taught by two of McDuff's certified industrial hygienists, Tom Rusher and Susan Sontack. They are expert trainers with much field experience in the identification and safe use of hazardous chemicals and other wastes. The $3,000 course fee is standard for McDuff's hazardous-waste seminars, though the company has on rare occasions given 10 percent discounts for any of the same seminars after the first one for the same client. Gibbon is interested in picking up Mercy Hospital as a client, but she also recognizes that the two instructors she has committed for the seminars may be needed for jobs the company has not yet scheduled. She is leery of cutting fees for Mercy Hospital when there may be other full-fee work right around the corner.

Claxton's Viewpoint. Claxton knows that the hospital staff must have hazardous-waste training to conform to new county and city regulations, and he has heard from other hospitals that McDuff has the best training in the business. Yet he has real problems spending $15,000 on five seminars. Proposals from other firms were in the $9,000 to $12,000 range for the five seminars, and Claxton's training budget is modest. Though the other firms that submitted proposals did not share McDuff's reputation, they too offered team-taught seminars by certified industrial hygienists. Although Claxton would prefer to hire McDuff and although he knows that good training is worth the money, he is hoping to get Gibbon to lower McDuff's fee when they meet for their negotiation session. He knows that one benefit he can offer McDuff is continued training contracts from the hospital, since the high employee turnover will necessitate frequent training in hazardous waste. In addition, there may be other training opportunities for McDuff at the hospital, once Claxton completes his upcoming needs assessment of the staff training program.

201 Edge Drive
Norcross, PA 17001
March 15, 1997

Mr. James Vernon, Personnel Director
McDuff, Inc.
105 Halsey Street
Baltimore, MD 21212

Dear Mr. Vernon:

My academic advisor, Professor Sam Singleton, informed me about an electrical-engineering opening at McDuff, where he worked until last year. I am writing to apply for the job.

I understand that McDuff is making a major effort to build a full-scale equipment development laboratory. That prospect interests me greatly, because of my academic background in electrical engineering. At Northern Tech, I took courses in several subjects that might be useful in the lab's work—for example, microprocessor applications, artificial intelligence, and fiber optics.

Also, related work at two firms has given me experience building and developing new electronics systems. In particular, more than two years' work as an assembler taught me the importance of precision and quality control. I'd like the opportunity to apply this knowledge at McDuff.

Personal business will take me to Baltimore April 8-10. Could you meet with me on one of those days to discuss how McDuff might use my skills? Please let me know if an interview would be convenient at that time.

Enclosed is a resume that highlights my credentials. I hope to be talking with you in June.

Sincerely,

Donald Vizano

Donald Vizano

Enclosure: Resume

MODEL 14–1
Job letter and chronological resume

continues

Donald Vizano
201 Edge Drive
Norcross, PA 17001
(300) 555-7861

OBJECTIVE: A full-time position in electrical engineering, with emphasis on designing new equipment in automation and microprocessing

EDUCATION: 1991-1997 Bachelor of Science in Electrical Engineering (expected June 1997)
Northern College of Technology, Shipley, PA
3.5 GPA (out of 4.0 scale)

Major Courses:

Fiber Optics	Artificial Machine Intelligence
Robotic Systems	Communication Control Systems
Microprocessor Control	Microcomputer Applications
Microcomputer Systems	Digital Control Systems
	Semiconductor Circuits & Devices

Related Courses:

BASIC Programming	FORTRAN
Business Communication	Engineering Economy
Industrial Psychology	Technical Communication

ACTIVITIES AND HONORS: Institute of Electrical and Electronic Engineering (IEEE)
Dean's List, 8 quarters.

EMPLOYMENT:

1993-1997 Electronic Assembler (part-time)
Jones Energy & Automation, Inc.
Banner, PA

1992-1993 Lab Monitor (part-time)
Computer Services
Northern College of Technology
Shipley, PA

1991-1992 Electronic Assembler (part-time)
Jones Energy & Automation, Inc.
Banner, PA

1989-1992 Electronic Assembler (full-time)
Jones Energy & Automation, Inc.
Banner, PA

PERSONAL: Willing to travel, fluent in Spanish

REFERENCES: Available upon request

MODEL 14–1
continued

534

1523 River Lane
Worthville, OH 43804
August 6, 1996

Mr. Willard Yancy
Director, Automotive Systems
XYZ Motor Company, Product Development Division
Charlotte, NC 28202

Dear Mr. Yancy:

Recently I have been researching the leading national companies in automotive computer systems. Your job ad in the July 6 *National Business Employment Weekly* caught my eye because of XYZ's innovations in computer-controlled safety systems. I would like to apply for the automotive computer engineer job.

Your advertisement notes that experience in computer systems for machinery or robotic systems would be a plus. I have had extensive experience in the military with computer systems, ranging from a digital communications computer to an air traffic control training simulator. In addition, my college experience includes courses in computer engineering that have broadened my experience. I am eager to apply what I have learned to your company.

My mechanical knowledge was gained from growing up on my family's dairy farm. After watching and learning from my father, I learned to repair internal combustion engines, diesel engines, and hydraulic systems. Then for five years I managed the entire dairy operation.

With my training and hands-on experience, I believe I can contribute to your company. Please contact me at 614/882-2731 if you wish to arrange an interview.

Sincerely,

James M. Sistrunk

James M. Sistrunk

Enclosure: Resume

MODEL 14–2
Job letter and chronological resume

continues

James M. Sistrunk
1523 River Lane
Worthville, OH 43804
(614) 882-2731

Professional Objective:

To contribute to the research, design, and development of automotive computer control systems

Education:

B.S., Computer Engineering, 1993-present
Columbus College, Columbus, Ohio
Major concentration in Control Systems with minor in Industrial Engineering. Courses included Microcomputer Systems, Digital Control Systems, and several different programming courses.

Computer Repair Technician Certification Training, 1990-1991
U.S. Air Force Technical Training Center, Keesler Air Force Base,
Biloxi, MS.
General Computer Systems Option with emphasis on mainframe computers. Student leader in charge of processing and orientation for new students from basic training.

Career Development:

Computer Repair Technician, U.S. Air Force, 1990-1993
Secret Clearance

Responsibilities and duties included:
- Repair of computer systems
- Documentation of work accomplished
- Preventative maintenance inspections
- Diagnostics and troubleshooting of equipment

Accomplishments include:
- "Excellent" score during skills evaluation
- Award of an Air Force Specialty Code "5" skill level

Assistant Manager, Spring Farm, Wootan, Ohio, 1984-1989
Responsible for dairy operations on this 500-acre farm. Developed the management and technical skills; learned to repair sophisticated farm equipment.

Special Skills:

Macintosh desk-top publishing
IBM - MS DOS
Assembly Language
C++ Programming

References:

Available upon request

MODEL 14–2
continued

456 Cantor Way, #245
Gallop, Minnesota 55002
September 3, 1996

Ms. Judith R. Gonzalez
American Hospital Systems
3023 Center Avenue
Randolf, Minnesota 55440

Dear Ms. Gonzalez:

My placement center recently informed me about the Management Trainee opening with Mercy Hospital. As a business major with experience working in hospitals, I wish to apply for the position.

Your job advertisement notes that you seek candidates with a broad academic background in business and an interest in hospital management. At Central State College, I've taken extensive coursework in three major areas in business: finance, marketing, and personnel management. This broad-based academic curriculum has provided a solid foundation for a wide variety of management tasks at Mercy Hospital.

My summer and part-time employment also matches the needs of your position. While attending Central State, I've worked part-time and summers as an assistant in the Business Office at Grady Hospital. That experience has acquainted me with the basics of business management within the context of a mid-sized hospital, much like Mercy.

The enclosed resume highlights the skills that match your Management Trainee opening. I would like the opportunity to talk with you in person and can be reached at 612-111-1111 for an interview.

Sincerely,

Denise Ware Sanborn

Denise Ware Sanborn

MODEL 14–3
Job letter and functional resume

continues

Denise Ware Sanborn
456 Cantor Way, #245
Gallop, Minnesota 55002
612-111-1111

Objective

Entry-level management position in the health care industry. Seek position that includes exposure to a wide variety of management and business-related tasks.

Education

Bachelor of Arts Degree, June 1996
Central State College
Gallop, Minnesota

Major: Business Administration
Grade Point Average: 3.26 of possible 4.0, with 3.56 in all major courses
All college expenses financed by part-time and summer work at Grady Hospital in
St. Paul, Minnesota.

Skills and Experience

Finance
   Helped with research for three fiscal year budgets
   Developed new spreadsheet for monthly budget reports
   Wrote accounts payable correspondence
   Called on collections from insurance companies
Marketing
   Solicited copy from managers for new brochure
   Designed and edited new brochure
   Participated in team visits to ten area physicians
   Wrote copy for one-page flyer
Personnel
   Designed new performance appraisal form for secretarial staff
   Interviewed applicants for Maintenance Department jobs
   Coordinated annual training program for nursing staff

Awards

1993 Arden Award for best senior project in the Business Administration Department (paper that examined latest developments in Total Quality Management)

Dean's list for six semesters.

References

Academic and work references available upon request.

MODEL 14–3
continued

2389 Jenson Court
Gulfton, MS 39200
(601) 111-1111
February 17, 1996

Mr. Nigel Pierce, Personnel Director
Structural Systems, Inc.
105 Paisley Way
Jackson, MS 39236

Dear Mr. Pierce:

I am writing in response to your ad for a technical representative in the February 13 (Sunday) edition of the *Jackson Journal*. I believe my experience and education make me an excellent candidate for this position.

I am very familiar with your products for the wood construction market. The laminated beams and floor joists your company manufactures were specified by many of the architects I have worked with during my co-op experience at Mississippi College. Work I have done in the residential and small commercial construction industry convinced me of the advantages
of your products over nominal lumber.

Enclosed is my resume, which focuses on the skills gained from my co-op work that would transfer to your firm. I look forward to meeting you and discussing my future with your company.

Sincerely,

Todd L. Fisher

Todd L. Fisher

Enclosure: Resume

MODEL 14–4
Job letter and functional resume

continues

Todd L. Fisher
2389 Jenson Court
Gulfton, MS 39200
(601) 111-1111

PROFESSIONAL OBJECTIVE	Use my education in civil engineering and my construction experience to assume a technical advisory position.
EDUCATION	Mississippi College Hart, Mississippi; Bachelor of Science, Civil Engineering Technology June 1995, GPA: 3.00 (out of 4.00)
PROFESSIONAL EXPERIENCE	Financed education by working as co-op student for two Jackson construction firms for 18 months.
Design Skills	Assisted with the layout and design of wall panels for Ridge Development condominium project.
	Created layout and design for complete roof and floor systems for numerous churches and small commercial projects.
Computer skills	Introduced computerization to the design offices of a major construction company (HP hardware in HPbasic operating system).
	Designed trusses on Sun workstations in the UNIX operating system. Operated as the system administrator for the office.
	Learned DOS operating system and the Windows environment (on IBM hardware and its clones).
Leadership skills	Instructed new CAD (computer-assisted design) operators on the operation of design software for panel layout and design.
	Designed and implemented management system for tracking jobs in plant.
INTERESTS	Family, gardening, sailing, travel
REFERENCES	References and transcripts available upon request.

MODEL 14–4
continued

SUSAN A. MARTIN

PRESENT ADDRESS	**PERMANENT ADDRESS**
540 Wood Drive	30 Avon Place
Bama, CA 90012	Atlas, CA 90000
(901) 666-2222	(901) 555-6074

PROFESSIONAL OBJECTIVE: Analyze and solve problems involving natural and pollution control systems as an Environmental Scientist.

EDUCATION:
Pierce College, Bama, California
Bachelor of Science, Environmental Science
May 1996, GPA: 3.15 (out of 4.00)

Pleasant Valley College, Barnes, Nevada
Associate in Applied Science, Engineering Science
May 1994, GPA: 3.15 (out of 4.00)

PROFESSIONAL EXPERIENCE:

Research Skills:
- Worked as lab assistant in a research project to analyze the effect of acid rain on frog reproduction in Lake Lane.
- Designed Pierce College computer program to analyze data on ozone depletion.

Leadership Skills:
- Taught inventory procedures to new employees of Zane's Office Supply.
- Helped incoming freshmen and transfer students adjust to Pierce College (as dormitory resident assistant).

Organizational Skills:
- Maintained academic department files as student assistant in Environmental Science Department.
- Organized field trips for Pierce College Mountaineering Club.

HONORS AND ACTIVITIES:
Dean's List (five semesters)
President of Cycling Club

INTERESTS: Photography, camping, biking, traveling

EMPLOYMENT HISTORY:
Dormitory Resident Assistant, Pierce College, Bama, CA, 1995-1996
Trainer, Zane's Office Supply, Bama, CA, 1994-1995

REFERENCES: References and transcripts available upon request

MODEL 14–5
Combined resume

Karen S. Patel
300 Park Drive
Burtingdale, New York 20092

Home: (210) 400-2112   **Messages:** (210) 400-0111

OBJECTIVE	Position as in-house technical writer and as trainer in communication skills
EDUCATION	**Sumpter College, Marist, Vermont** M. S. in Technical Communication, GPA: 4.0 December 1995
	Warren College, Aurora, New York M.A. in English, Cum Laude, June 1992
	University of Bombay, India B.A. in English, First Class Honors, June 1989
EMPLOYMENT *Editing/* *Writing*	**Public Relations Office, Sumpter College, 1995-present** Administrative Assistant: Write press releases and conduct interviews. Publish news stories in local newspapers and in *Sumpter Express*. Edit daily campus newsletter.
	Hawk Newspapers, Albany, New York, 1990-1991 Warren College Internship: Covered and reported special events; conducted interviews; assisted with proofreading, layout, headline count. Scanned newspapers for current events; conducted research for stories. Published feature stories.
Teaching/ *Research*	**Sumpter College, Marist, Vermont, 1994-1995** Teaching Assistant: Tutored English at the Writing Center, answered "Grammar Hotline" phone questions, edited and critiqued student papers, taught English to non-English speakers and helped students prepare for Regents exams.
	Warren College, Aurora, New York, 1991-1992 Teaching Assistant: Taught business writing, supervised peer editing and in-class discussions, held student conferences, and graded student papers.
	Research Assistant: Verified material by checking facts, wrote brief reports related to research, researched information and bibliographies.
COMPUTER SKILLS	Wordperfect, Microsoft Word, Pagemaker, Unix, Excel
REFERENCES	Available upon request

MODEL 14–6
Combined resume

EXPERIENCE

12/95 to Present
DataCorp, Atlanta, Georgia
Administrative/Document Manager
Created and edited marketing documents. Also hired and supervised sales support staff.

3/95-12/95
Sunvie Corporation, Atlanta, Georgia
Director of Client Support Services
Edited various reports, graphics, and publications developed from research data. Indexed information for a reference library. Managed office activities and functions.

12/93-2/95
ComKing, Atlanta, Georgia
National Accounts Coordinator
Set up account-tracking system. Initiated all paperwork involved with opening a new account and the follow up, including invoicing. Handled client requests. Proofed and edited print materials before being sent to press. Developed charts and data for presentations.

9/93-12/93
Self-Employed Consultant
Editorial Assistant/Administrative Assistant
Proofed and edited materials for brochures and booklets.

EXPERIENCE

8/92-8/93
Lidgate Press Ltd., Craftrends Magazine, Norcross, Georgia
Advertising Coordinator
Called advertisers monthly for ad material. Generated reader service and sales reports. Proofed boards and chromalins before they went to the printers. Arranged photography shoots for advertising material.

3/88-7/92
Capstone Channels, Inc.
Atlanta, Georgia
Marketing Assistant
Coordinated research projects to acquire new magazines, tabulated in-house and outside studies, and ran individual research projects for company personnel. Provided reports for various departments and outside firms.

10/84-3/88
Genuine Parts, Inc.,
Charlotte, North Carolina
Administrative Assistant
Maintained sales records and created sales charts. Coordinated sales activities and general support duties.
Typed manuscripts and correspondence for 16 editors. Assisted promotion director in writing and organizing promotions.

EDUCATION

Currently working on *Master of Science, Technical and Professional Communication*
Southern College of Technology, Marietta, Georgia
Estimated completion date-January 1997

1/83-8/84
Bachelor of Arts, Journalism
University of Georgia, Athens, Georgia
School of Journalism

9/80-8/82
Associate in Journalism
Abraham Baldwin Junior College, Tifton, Georgia

SKILLS

Writing, editing, proofreading.
Working knowledge of Windows 95, Ventura Windows, PageMaker IBM, Excel 5.0, Charisma 2.1, Scan Gallery, HP Paintbrush, Zybuild/ZyFind, Lotus 2.2, 2.3, and 5, WordPerfect 5.1, Microsoft Word, Grammatik, Q & A, Paradox, Filepro database, Harvard Graphics 3.0, Freelance 3.0, the HP Plotter, HP LaserJet III, and IBM ExecJet.

INTERESTS

Writing, computer graphics, desktop publishing, racquetball, guitar, oil painting.

MODEL 14-7
Resume with innovative format

continues

RESUME

of

Becky Dacnell

Becky Dacnell
39 Rock Drive
Marietta, Georgia
30062
(770) 000-6000

MODEL 14–7
continued

Leslie Highland
997 Simmons Drive
Boise, Idaho 88822

OBJECTIVE:	A full-time position in architectural design with emphasis on model-making and renderings for future buildings.
EDUCATION:	**Boise Architectural College** Boise, Idaho Bachelor of Science Architectural Engineering Technology June 1996
	Harvard University Cambridge, Massachusetts Certificate in Advance Architectural Delineation August 1990
ACTIVITIES AND HONORS:	**Boise Architectural College** Winner of Senior Design Project Architectural Engineering Technology
	Charter Member of American Society of Architectural Perspectives
EMPLOYMENT:	
1990-1996	**Architectural Designer and Delineator** Dorsey-Hudson, Architects Boise, Idaho
1988-1990	**Architectural Designer and Renderer** Windsor and Associates, Architects St. Lake, Utah
1985-1988	**Architectural Renderer and Drafter** Sanders and Associates, Architects Provo, Utah
1983-1985	**Architectural Drafter** Brown Engineering St. Lake, Utah
REFERENCES:	References and portfolio available upon request.

MODEL 14–8

15 Style in Technical Writing

Alone with his thoughts and his computer, this McDuff manager puts finishing touches on a report written by his group.

*T*his chapter, as well as the Handbook that follows, focuses on the last stage of the writing process— revising. As you may already have discovered, revision sometimes gets short shrift during the rush to finish documents on time. That's a big mistake. Your writing must be clear, concise, and correct if you expect the reader to pay attention to your message. Toward that end, this chapter offers a few basic guidelines on style. The Handbook contains alphabetized entries on grammar and mechanics.

After defining style and its importance, this chapter gives suggestions for achieving five main stylistic goals:

- Writing clear sentences
- Being concise
- Being accurate in wording
- Using the active voice
- Using nonsexist language

STYLE OVERVIEW

Just as all writers have distinct personalities, they also display distinct features in their writing. Writing style can be defined in this way:

> **Style:** the features of one's writing that show its individuality, separating it from the writing of another. Style results from the conscious and subconscious decisions each writer makes in matters like word choice, word order, sentence length, and active and passive voice. These decisions are different from the "right and wrong" matters of grammar and mechanics (see the Handbook). Instead, they comprise choices writers make in deciding how to transmit ideas to others.

Style is largely a series of personal decisions you make when you write. As noted in chapter 1, however, much writing is being done these days by teams of writers. Collaborative writing requires individual writers to combine their efforts to produce a consensus style, usually a compromise of stylistic preferences of the individuals involved. Thus personal style becomes absorbed into a jointly produced product.

Similarly, many companies tend to develop a company style in documents like reports and proposals. The reports at McDuff, Inc., for example, tend to be formal, objective, and "scientific" in tone. In the last few years, the company has tried to change its technical and scientific style to one that is more informal, readable, and reflective of the speech of average readers. You might very well be hired by an organization that is making this same shift toward a more readable style.

Despite the need to make style conform to group or company guidelines, each individual remains the final arbiter of her or his own style in technical writing. Most of us will be our own stylists, even in firms in which in-house editors help "clean up" writing errors. This chapter will help such writers deal with everyday decisions of sentence arrangement, word choice, and the like. But in seeing style as a personal statement, you should not presume that "anything goes." Certain fundamentals are part of all good technical style in the professional world. Let's take a look at these basics.

WRITING CLEAR SENTENCES

Each writer has his or her own approach to sentence style. Yet everyone has the same tools with which to work: words, phrases, and clauses. This section defines some basic terminology in sentence structure. Then it provides simple stylistic guidelines for writing clear sentences.

Sentence Terms

The most important sentence parts are the subject and verb. The *subject* names the person doing the action or the thing being discussed (*He* completed the study/ The *figure* shows that); the *verb* conveys action or state of being (She *visited* the site/ He *was* the manager).

Whether they are subjects, verbs, or other parts of speech, words are used in two main units: phrases and clauses. A *phrase* lacks a subject or verb or both and it thus must always relate to or modify another part of the sentence (She went *to the office./As project manager,* he had to write the report). A *clause,* on the other hand, has both a subject and a verb. Either it stands by itself as a *main clause (He talked to the group)* or it relies on another part of the sentence for its meaning and is thus a *dependent clause (After she left the site,* she went home).

Beyond these basic terms for sentence parts, you also should know the four main types of sentences:

- A *simple sentence* contains one main clause *(He completed his work).*
- A *compound sentence* contains two or more main clauses connected by conjunctions *(He completed his work, but she stayed at the office to begin another job).*
- A *complex sentence* includes one main clause and at least one dependent clause *(After he finished the project, he headed for home).*
- A *compound-complex sentence* contains at least two main clauses and at least one dependent clause *(After they studied the maps, they left the fault line, but they were unable to travel much farther that night).*

Guidelines for Sentence Style

Knowing the basic terms of sentence structure makes it easier to apply stylistic guidelines. Here are a few fundamental ones that form the underpinnings for good technical writing. As you review and edit your own writing or that of others, put these principles into practice.

■ Guideline 1: Place the Main Point Near the Beginning

One way to satisfy this criterion for good style is to avoid excessive use of the passive voice (see "Using the Active Voice" on pages 558–559). Another way is to avoid lengthy introductory phrases or clauses at the beginnings of sentences. Remember that the reader usually wants the most important information first.

> **Original:** "After reviewing the growth of the Cleveland office, it was decided by the corporate staff that an additional lab should be constructed at the Cleveland location."
>
> **Revision:** "The corporate staff decided to build a new lab in Cleveland after reviewing the growth of the office there."

■ Guideline 2: Focus on One Main Clause in Each Sentence

When you string together too many clauses with "and" or "but," you dilute the meaning of your text. However, an occasional compound or compound-complex sentence is acceptable, just for variety.

> **Original:** "The McDuff hiring committee planned to interview Jim Steinway today, but bad weather delayed his plane departure, and the committee had to reschedule the interview for tomorrow."
>
> **Revision:** "The McDuff hiring committee had to change Jim Steinway's interview from today to tomorrow because bad weather delayed his flight."

■ Guideline 3: Vary Sentence Length but Seek an Average Length of 15–20 Words

Of course, do not inhibit your writing process by counting words while you write. Instead, analyze one of your previous reports to see how you fare. If your sentences are too long, make an effort to shorten them, such as by making two sentences out of one compound sentence connected by an "and" or a "but."

You should also vary the length of sentences. Such variety keeps your reader's attention engaged. Make an effort to place important points in short, emphatic sentences. Reserve longer sentences for supporting main points.

> **Original:** "Our field trip for the project required that we conduct research on Cumberland Island, a national wilderness area off the Georgia Coast, where we observed a number of species that we had not seen on previous field trips. Armadillos were common in the campgrounds, along with raccoons that were so aggressive that they would come out toward the campfire for a handout while we were still eating. We saw the wild horses that are fairly common on the island and were introduced there by explorers centuries ago, as well as a few bobcats that were introduced fairly recently in hopes of checking the expanding population of armadillos."
>
> **Revision:** "Our field trip required that we complete research on Cumberland Island, a wilderness area off the Georgia Coast. There we observed many species we had not seen on previous field trips. Both armadillos and raccoons were common in the campgrounds. Whereas the armadillos were docile, the raccoons were quite aggressive. They would approach the campfire for a handout while we were still eating. We also encountered Cumberland's famous wild horses, introduced centuries ago by explorers. Another interesting sighting was a pair of bobcats. They were brought to the island recently to check the expanding armadillo population."

BEING CONCISE

Some experts believe that careful attention to conciseness would shorten technical documents by 10 percent to 15 percent. As a result, reports and proposals would take less time to read and cost less to produce. This section on conciseness offers several techniques for reducing verbiage without changing meaning.

■ *Guideline 1: Replace Abstract Nouns with Verbs*

Concise writing depends more on verbs than it does on nouns. Sentences that contain abstract nouns, especially ones with more than two syllables, can be shortened by focusing on strong verbs instead. By converting abstract nouns to action verbs, you can eliminate wordiness, as the following sentences illustrate:

Wordy:	"The *acquisition* of the property was accomplished through long and hard negotiations."
Concise:	"The property was *acquired* through long and hard negotiations."
Wordy:	"*Confirmation* of the contract occurred yesterday."
Concise:	"The contract was *confirmed* yesterday."
Wordy:	"*Exploration* of the region had to be effected before the end of the year."
Concise:	"The region had to be *explored* before the end of the year."
Wordy:	"*Replacement* of the transmission was achieved only three hours before the race."
Concise:	"The transmission was *replaced* only three hours before the race."

As the examples show, abstract nouns often end with "-tion" or "-ment" and are often followed by the preposition "of." These words are not always "bad" words; they cause problems only when they replace action verbs from which they are derived. The following examples show some noun phrases along with the preferred verb substitutes:

assessment of	assess
classification of	classify
computation of	compute
delegation of	delegate
development of	develop
disbursement of	disburse
documentation of	document
elimination of	eliminate
establishment of	establish
negotiation of	negotiate
observation of	observe
requirement of	require
verification of	verify

■ *Guideline 2: Shorten Wordy Phrases*

Many wordy phrases have become common in business and technical writing. Weighty expressions add unnecessary words and rob prose of clarity. Here are some of the culprits, along with their concise substitutes:

afford an opportunity to	permit
along the lines of	like
an additional	another
at a later date	later
at this point in time	now
by means of	by
come to an end	end
due to the fact that	because
during the course of	during
for the purpose of	for
give consideration to	consider
in advance of	before
in the amount of	of
in the event that	if
in the final analysis	finally
in the proximity of	near
prior to	before
subsequent to	after
with regard to	about

■ *Guideline 3: Replace Long Words with Short Ones*

In grade school, most students are taught to experiment with long words. Although this effort helps build vocabularies, it also can lead to a lifelong tendency to use long words when short ones will do. Of course, sometimes you want to use longer words just for variety—for example, using an occasional "approximately" for the preferred "about." As a rule, however, the following long words in the left column routinely should be replaced by the short words in the right column:

advantageous	helpful
alleviate	lessen, lighten
approximately	about
cognizant	aware
commence	start, begin

demonstrate	show
discontinue	end, stop
endeavor	try
finalize	end, complete
implement	carry out
initiate	start, begin
inquire	ask
modification	change
prioritize	rank, rate
procure	buy
terminate	end, fire
transport	move
undertake	try, attempt
utilize	use

■ *Guideline 4: Leave Out Clichés*

Clichés are worn-out expressions that add words to your writing. Though they once were fresh phrases, they became clichés when they no longer conveyed their original meaning. You can make writing more concise by replacing clichés with a good adjective or two. Here are some clichés to avoid:

as plain as day

ballpark figure

efficient and effective

few and far between

last but not least

leaps and bounds

needless to say

reinvent the wheel

skyrocketing costs

step in the right direction

■ *Guideline 5: Make Writing More Direct by Reading It Aloud*

Much wordiness results from talking around a topic. Sometimes called "circumlo-cution," this stylistic flaw arises from a tendency to write indirectly. It can be avoided by reading passages aloud. Hearing the sound of the words makes problems of wordiness quite apparent. It helps condense all kinds of inflated language, including the wordy expressions mentioned earlier. Remember, however, that direct writing must also retain a tactful, diplomatic tone when it conveys negative or sensitive information.

Indirect: "We would like to suggest that you consider directing your attention toward completing the project before the commencement of the seasonal monsoon rains in the region of the project area."

Direct: "We suggest you complete the project before the monsoons begin."

Indirect: "At the close of the last phase of the project, a bill for your services should be expedited to our central office for payment."

Direct: "After the project ends, please send your bill immediately to our central office."

Indirect: "It is possible that the well-water samples collected during our investigation of the well on the site of the subdivision could possibly contain some chemicals in concentrations higher than is allowable according to the state laws now in effect."

Direct: "Our samples from the subdivision's well might contain chemical concentrations beyond those permitted by the state."

■ *Guideline 6: Avoid "There Are,"*
"It Is," and Similar Constructions

"There are" and "it is" should not be substituted for concrete subjects and action verbs, which are preferable in good writing. Such constructions delay the delivery of information about who or what is doing something. They tend to make your writing lifeless and abstract. Avoid them by creating (1) main subjects that are concrete nouns and (2) main verbs that are action words. Note that the following revised passages give readers a clear idea of who is doing what in the subject and verb positions.

Original: "There are many McDuff projects that could be considered for design awards."

Revision: "Many McDuff projects could be considered for design awards."

Original: "It is clear to the hiring committee that writing skills are an important criterion for every technical position."

Revision: "The hiring committee believes that writing skills are an important criterion for every technical position."

Original: "There were 15 people who attended the meeting at the client's office in Charlotte."

Revision: "Fifteen people attended the meeting at the client's office in Charlotte."

■ Guideline 7: Cut Out Extra Words

This guideline covers all wordiness errors not mentioned earlier. You need to keep a vigilant eye for *any* extra words or redundant phrasing. Sometimes the problem comes in the form of needless connecting words, like *to be* or *that.* Other times it appears as redundant points—that is, those that have been made earlier in a sentence, paragraph, or section and do not need repeating.

Delete extra words when their use (1) does not add a necessary transition between ideas or (2) does not provide new information to the reader. (One important exception is the intentional repetition of main points for emphasis, as in repeating important conclusions in different parts of a report.) The examples in Figure 15–1 display a variety of wordy or redundant writing, with corrections made in longhand.

BEING ACCURATE IN WORDING

Good technical writing also demands accuracy in phrasing. Technical professionals place their reputations and financial futures on the line with every document that goes out the door. That fact shows the importance of taking your time on editing that deals with the accuracy of phrasing. Accuracy often demands more words, not fewer. The main rule is this:

> Never sacrifice clarity for conciseness.

Careful writing helps to limit liability that your organization may incur. Your goal is very simple: Make sure words convey the meaning you intend—no more, no less. Here are some basic guidelines to follow:

■ Guideline 1: Distinguish Facts from Opinions

In practice, this guideline means you must identify opinions and judgments as such by using phrases like "we recommend," "we believe," "we suggest," or "in our opinion." EXAMPLE: "In our opinion, spread footings would be an acceptable foundation for the building you plan at the site." If you want to avoid repetitious use of such phrases, group your opinions into listings or report sections. Thus a single lead-in can show the reader that opinions, not facts, are forthcoming. EXAMPLE: "On the basis of our site visit and our experience at similar sites, we believe that (1) _____, (2) _____, and (3) _____."

■ Guideline 2: Include Obvious Qualifying Statements When Needed

This guideline does not mean you have to be overly defensive in every part of the report. It does mean that you must be wary of possible misinterpretations. EXAMPLE: "Our summary of soil conditions is based only on information obtained during a brief visit to the site. We did not drill any soil borings."

Example 1: Preparing the client's final bill involves ~~the~~ checking ~~of~~ all
project ʌinvoices ~~for the project.~~

Example 2: The report examined what the McDuff project manager
considered ~~to be~~ a technically acceptable risk.

Example 3: During ~~the course of~~ its field work, the McDuff team will ~~be~~
~~engaged in the process of~~ reviewing all ~~of the~~ notes ~~that have~~
~~been~~ accumulated in previous studies.

Example 4: ~~Because of his position~~ as head of ~~the~~ McDuff public relations group, ~~at~~
~~McDuff,~~ he planned ~~such that he would be able~~ to attend the
meeting.

Example 5: She believed ~~that the~~ recruiting ~~of~~ more minorities for the
technical staff is essential.

Example 6: The department must determine its ~~aims and~~ goals so that
they can be included in the McDuff's 1995 annual strategic plan ~~produced by~~
~~McDuff for the year of 1995.~~

Example 7: Most McDuff managers ~~generally~~ agree that all ~~of the~~
company~~'s~~ employees ~~at all the offices~~ deserve ~~at least~~ some
~~degree of~~ training each year ~~that they work for the firm.~~

FIGURE 15–1
Editing of wordy or redundant writing

■ *Guideline 3: Use Absolute Words Carefully*

Avoid words that convey an absolute meaning or that convey a stronger meaning than you intend. One notable example is "minimize," which means to reduce to the lowest possible level or amount. If a report claims that a piece of equipment will "minimize" breakdowns on the assembly line, the passage could be interpreted as an absolute commitment. The reader could consider any breakdown at all to be a violation of the report's implications. If instead the writer had used the verb "limit" or "reduce," the wording would have been more accurate and less open to misunderstanding.

USING THE ACTIVE VOICE

Striving to use the active voice can greatly improve your technical writing style. This section defines the active and passive voices and then gives examples of each. It also lists some practical guidelines for using both voices.

What Do Active and Passive Mean?

Active-voice sentences emphasize the person (or thing) performing the action—that is, somebody (or something) does something ("Matt completed the field study yesterday"). Passive-voice sentences emphasize the recipient of the action itself—that is, something is being done to something by somebody ("The field study was completed [by Matt] yesterday"). Here are some other examples of the same thoughts being expressed in first the active and then the passive voice:

■ EXAMPLES: Active-Voice Sentences:

1. "We *reviewed* aerial photographs in our initial assessment of possible fault activity at the site."
2. "The study *revealed* that three underground storage tanks had leaked unleaded gasoline into the soil."
3. "We *recommend* that you use a minimum concrete thickness of 6 in. for residential subdivision streets."

■ EXAMPLES: Passive-Voice Sentences:

1. "Aerial photographs *were reviewed* [by us] in our initial assessment of possible fault activity at the site."
2. "The fact that three underground storage tanks had been leaking unleaded gasoline into the soil *was revealed* in the study."
3. "*It is recommended* that you use a minimum concrete thickness of 6 in. for residential subdivision streets."

Just reading through these examples gives the sense that passive constructions are wordier than active ones. Also, passives tend to leave out the person or thing doing the action. Although occasionally this impersonal approach is appropriate, the reader can become frustrated by writing that fails to say who or what is doing something.

When Should Actives and Passives Be Used?

Both the active and passive voices have a place in your writing. Knowing when to use each is the key. Here are a few guidelines that will help:

- *Use the active voice when you want to:*

  1. Emphasize who is responsible for an action (*"We recommend* that you consider . . . "*)
  2. Stress the name of a company, whether yours or the reader's (*"PineBluff Contracting has expressed* interest in receiving bids to perform work at . . . "*)
  3. Rewrite a top-heavy sentence so that the person or thing doing the action is up front (*"Figure 1 shows* the approximate locations of . . . "*)
  4. Pare down the verbiage in your writing, since the active voice is usually a shorter construction

- *Use the passive voice when you want to:*

  1. Emphasize the receiver of the action or the action itself rather than the person performing the action (*"Samples will be sent* directly from the site to our laboratory in Sacramento"*)
  2. Avoid the kind of egocentric tone that results from repetitious use of "I," "we," and the name of your company (*"The project will be directed* by two programmers from our Boston office"*)
  3. Break the monotony of writing that relies too heavily on active-voice sentences

Although the passive voice has its place, it is far too common in business and technical writing. This stylistic error results from the common misperception that passive writing is more objective. In fact, excessive use of the passive voice only makes writing more tedious to read. In modern business and technical writing, strive to use the active voice.

USING NONSEXIST LANGUAGE

Language usually *follows* changes in culture, rather than *anticipating* such changes. A case in point is today's shift away from sexist language in business and technical writing—indeed, in all writing and speaking. The change reflects the increasing number of women entering previously male-dominated professions such as engineering, management, medicine, and law. It also reflects the fact that many men have taken previously female-dominated positions as nurses and flight attendants.

This section on style defines sexist and nonsexist language. Then it suggests ways to avoid using gender-offensive language in your writing.

Sexism and Language

Sexist language is the use of wording, especially masculine pronouns like "he" or "him," to represent positions or individuals who could be either men or women. For many years, it was perfectly appropriate to use "he," "his," "him," or other masculine words in sentences such as these:

- "The operations specialist should check page 5 of his manual before flipping the switch."
- "Every physician was asked to renew his membership in the medical association before next month."
- "Each new student at the military academy was asked to leave most of his personal possessions in the front hallway of the administration building."

The masculine pronoun was understood to represent any person—male or female. Such usage came under attack for several reasons:

1. As already mentioned, the entry of many more women into male-dominated professions has called attention to the inappropriate generic use of masculine pronouns.
2. Many people believe the use of masculine pronouns in a context that could include both genders constrains women from achieving equal status in the professions and in the culture. That is, the use of masculine pronouns encourages sexism in society as a whole.

Either point supplies a good enough reason to avoid sexist language. Many women in positions of responsibility may read your on-the-job writing. If you fail to rid your writing of sexism, you risk drawing attention toward sexist language and away from your ideas. Common sense argues for following some basic style techniques to avoid this problem.

Techniques for Nonsexist Language

This section offers techniques for shifting from sexist to nonsexist language. Not all these strategies will suit your taste in writing style; use the ones that work for you.

■ Technique 1: Avoid Personal Pronouns Altogether

One easy way to avoid sexist language is to delete or replace unnecessary pronouns:

Example:

Sexist Language: "During *his* first day on the job, any new employee in the toxic-waste laboratory must report to the company doctor for *his* employment physical."

Nonsexist Language: "During *the* first day on the job, each new employee in the toxic-waste laboratory must report to the company doctor for *a* physical."

■ *Technique 2: Use Plural Pronouns Instead of Singular*

In most contexts you can shift from singular to plural pronouns without altering meaning. The plural usage avoids the problem of using masculine pronouns.

Example:

Sexist Language: *"Each* geologist should submit *his* time sheet by noon on the Thursday before checks are issued."

Nonsexist Language: *"All* geologists should submit *their* time sheets on the Thursday before checks are issued."

Interestingly, you may encounter sexist language that uses generic female pronouns inappropriately. For example, "Each nurse should make every effort to complete *her* rounds each hour." As in the preceding case, a shift to plural pronouns is appropriate: "Nurses should make every effort to complete *their* rounds each hour."

■ *Technique 3: Alternate Masculine and Feminine Pronouns*

Writers who prefer singular pronouns can avoid sexist use by alternating "he" and "him" with "she" and "her." Using this technique usually avoids the unsettling practice of switching pronoun use within too brief a passage, such as a paragraph or page. Instead, writers may switch every few pages, or every section or chapter.

Although this technique is not yet in common usage, its appeal is growing. It gives writers the linguistic flexibility to continue to use masculine and feminine pronouns in a generic fashion. However, one problem is that the alternating use of masculine and feminine pronouns tends to draw attention to itself. Also, the writer must work to balance the use of masculine and feminine pronouns, in a sense to give "equal treatment."

■ *Technique 4: Use Forms Like "He or She," "Hers or His," and "Him or Her"*

This solution requires the writer to include pronouns for both genders.

Example:

Sexist Language: "The president made it clear that each McDuff branch manager will be responsible for the balance sheet of *his* respective office."

Nonsexist Language: "The president made it clear that each McDuff branch manager will be responsible for the balance sheet of *his or her* respective office."

This stylistic correction of sexist language may bother some readers. They feel that the doublet structure, "her or his," is wordy and awkward. Many readers are bothered even more by the slash formations "he/she," "his/her," and "her/him." Avoid this usage.

■ *Technique 5: Shift to Second-Person Pronouns*

Consider shifting to the use of "you" and "your," words without any sexual bias. This technique is effective only with documents in which it is appropriate to use an instructions-related "command" tone associated with the use of "you."

Example:

> **Sexist Language:** "After selecting *her* insurance option in the benefit plan, each new nurse should submit *her* paperwork to the Human Resources Department."

> **Nonsexist Language:** "Submit *your* paperwork to the Human Resources Department after selecting *your* insurance option in the benefit plan."

■ *Technique 6: Be Especially Careful of Titles and Letter Salutations*

When you do not know how a woman you are writing prefers to be addressed, use "Ms." Even better, call the person's employer and ask if the recipient goes by "Miss," "Mrs.," "Ms.," or some other title. (When calling, also check on the correct spelling of the person's name and her current job title.) Receptionists and secretaries expect to receive such inquiries.

When you do not know who will read your letter, never use "Dear Sir" or "Gentlemen" as a generic greeting. Such a mistake may offend women reading the letter and may even cost you some business. "Dear Sir or Madam" is also inappropriate. It shows you do not know your audience, and it includes the archaic form "madam." Instead, call the organization for the name of a particular person to whom you can direct your letter. If you must write to a group of people, replace the generic greeting with an "Attention" line that denotes the name of the group.

Examples:

> **Sexist Language:** Dear Miss Finnegan: [to a single woman for whom you can determine no title preference]

> **Nonsexist Language:** Dear Ms. Finnegan:

> **Sexist Language:** Dear Sir: or Gentlemen:

> **Nonsexist Language:** Attention: Admissions Committee

No doubt the coming years will bring additional suggestions for solving the problem of sexist language. Whatever the culture finally settles on, it is clear that good technical writing style will no longer tolerate the use of such language.

COMMUNICATION CHALLENGE

"An Editorial Adjustment"

McDuff, Inc., has hired a technical writer/editor at its Cleveland office, the smallest branch in the company. The office finally generates enough reports and proposals to justify the addition, and Evelyn Tobin started the job a month ago. Some of the Cleveland employees, who were comfortable with the old system, are now having trouble adjusting to having an editor. What follows is some background on the hiring of Evelyn, the changes that she is making in office writing, and some questions and comments for discussion.

Winds of Change

For years the staff at McDuff's Cleveland office handled all its own writing and editing. Managers, engineers, scientists, accountants, trainers, and others had to draft and edit their own copy. Because they could depend on no one else to help, they gave great attention to the process and prided themselves on the quality of their writing. With the aid of several good secretaries, who often corrected grammar while they typed, the documents produced seemed adequate.

The growth of the office, however, increased the number and complexity of the reports and proposals that went out the door. The quality of editing began to decline. Those who observed the trend tied it to the following changes:

- Each writer simply had a higher volume of reports and proposals to complete, to keep the office competitive with similar firms.
- A new mobility in the workforce meant that fewer employees had received on-the-job training from old-timers at the office. In fact, over half the positions requiring a college degree had been filled in the last three years.
- This new workforce came from many different academic backgrounds and from other firms, making it harder than it used to be to impose a set "style" at the office.
- The experienced secretaries, who had been expert editors, had now retired. Most of the replacements were excellent keyboard operators but did not have the same editorial skills as their predecessors. They assumed their job was to type exactly what writers gave them.

The branch manager had observed these changes. Perhaps the last straw came when one long-time client returned a report with corrections made in red ink, along with this note: "You guys used to turn out good reports. What's happened?" With that embarrassment, the branch manager quickly hired an in-house technical writer/editor.

New Editor Takes Charge

When Evelyn Tobin started work a month ago, she met with all the staff to discuss her duties. At that meeting, there was general agreement that Evelyn would

(1) provide writing advice, (2) perform a style edit for some reports, (3) be the lead writer for key proposals, (4) help with training in the office, and (5) do a quick grammar edit on as many reports as she had time to review.

With a B.S. in Technical Communication and two years of editing experience with a government agency, Evelyn was used to simplifying writing that was confusing, convoluted, or too technical. Although she had not worked with technical firms like McDuff, she assumed all her experience would translate to the new job. As it happened, most of her initial work involved style edits of reports that were to be sent to a mixed readership—some readers had a technical background, but others did not. Following are several changes Evelyn made in the reports, along with the original passages:

1. *Original:* The purpose of the new well is to allow Tank, Inc., to perform monthly water-level monitoring at three locations at the oil field so that the results can be sent to the Water Quality Control Board.

   Evelyn's Revision: The new well will allow Tank, Inc., to monitor water levels at the oil field. Then the data will be sent to the Water Quality Control Board.

2. *Original:* During the drilling of the boring, some soil sampling was performed by our technicians for the purpose of determining the exact location of the water table at the site.

   Evelyn's Revision: While drilling the boring, the technicians sampled soils to locate the water table.

3. *Original:* This letter proposal has been prepared by us for use by whatever attorney you select so that he can present a ballpark figure of costs to the college governing board.

   Evelyn's Revision: We prepared this proposal for whatever attorney you select. Then she can present a cost estimate to the college governing board.

4. *Original:* At this point in time, it is our belief that you should give equal consideration to both alternatives, for both can afford you the opportunity to complete expansion of the office complex prior to summer.

   Evelyn's Revision: At this point, we believe you should consider both alternatives. Either one will allow you to expand the office by next summer.

5. *Original:* There are a total of two ways we are recommending that you consider changing the plans in order to minimize the chance for earthquake damage.

   Evelyn's Revision: We recommend two changes to reduce the chance for earthquake damage.

Questions and Comments for Discussion

1. Study the before and after versions carefully.

   ■ Explain the rationale you think Evelyn would have for each of the changes she made.

- Given the audience for the documents, was she right to make the changes?
- Can you see changes in content that the original writer may find unacceptable?
- Are there any cases where you need more context surrounding the passage to provide adequate answers to the two previous questions? Explain.

2. Would your answers to any of the previous questions change if the only audience for the report had been a group of technical experts?
3. Are there any alternative revisions that you think would be as effective as, or more effective than, the revisions Evelyn made?
4. Suggest what you think would be the best way for Evelyn to convey her revisions to the writer. Would this method change or stay the same as she gains more experience at the office?
5. One employee has come to Evelyn for advice on some grammar-checking software. He noted that his software stopped at every passive-voice sentence and suggested an active-voice replacement, and he wondered if he should always make the change. If you were in Evelyn's position, what answer would you give?
6. Discuss the effect that hiring a technical writer/editor might have on an office like McDuff-Cleveland. That is, how might the change affect the "corporate culture" of a such a company, where the professional staff spends from 25% to 50% of its time writing and editing documents?
7. If you were working at the Cleveland office, how would you feel about having your documents reviewed for style? for grammar?

CHAPTER SUMMARY

Style is an important part of technical writing. During the editing process, writers make the kinds of changes that place their personal stamp on a document. Style can also be shaped (1) by a group, in that writing done collaboratively can acquire features of its diverse contributors, or (2) by an organization, in that an organization may require writers to adopt a particular writing style. Yet the decision-making process of individual writers remains the most important influence on the style of technical documents.

This chapter offers five basic suggestions for achieving good technical writing style. First, sentences should be clear, with main ideas at the beginning and with one main clause in most sentences. Although sentences should average only 15–20 words, you should vary sentence patterns in every document. Second, technical writing should be concise. You can achieve this goal by reading prose aloud as you rewrite and edit. Third, wording should be accurate. Fourth, the active voice should be dominant, though the passive voice also has a place in good technical writing. And fifth, the language of technical documents should be free of sexual bias.

ASSIGNMENTS

1. **Conciseness—Abstract Words.** Make the following sentences more concise by replacing abstract nouns with verbs. Other minor changes in wording may be necessary.
   a. Verification of the agreement was indicated by the signing of the contract by members of the McDuff corporate staff.
   b. The inspectors indicated that observation of the site occurred on July 16, 1996.
   c. Negotiation of the final contract was to happen on the day after their arrival.
   d. After three hours of discussion, the branch managers agreed that establishment of a new McDuff mission statement should take place in the next fiscal year.
   e. Assessment of the firm's progress will happen during the annual meeting of the McDuff Board of Directors.
   f. The entire company agreed that classification of employees according to level of education was inappropriate.
   g. Documentation of the results of the lab test appeared in the final report.
   h. Unlike the previous year, this year the disbursement of stock dividends will occur after the annual meeting.
   i. In analyzing the managerial style of the manager, the outside evaluators determined that delegation of authority appeared to be a problem for her.
   j. The financial statement showed that computation of the annual revenues had been done properly.

2. **Conciseness—Wordy Phrases and Long Words.** Condense the following sentences by replacing long phrases and words with shorter substitutes.
   a. In the final analysis, we decided to place the new pumping station in the proximity of the old one.
   b. Prior to commencing the project, they met to prioritize their objectives.
   c. Endeavoring to complete the study on time, Sheila transported the supplies immediately from the field location to the McDuff lab.
   d. During the course of his career, he planned to utilize the experience he had gained in the ambulance business.
   e. His work with the firm terminated due to the fact that he took a job with another competing firm.
   f. In the event that two clients need a crew in Austin next week, we can give consideration to using the same crew for both projects and lowering travel costs for both clients.
   g. Rob McDuff was not cognizant of the fact that younger employees felt differently than older employees about the expansion of their office building.
   h. To implement the Phoenix asbestos project, we made adjustments in the workload of two engineers so that they could be available to undertake the project in Phoenix.
   i. Subsequent to the announcement he made, he held a news conference for approximately one hour of time.
   j. At this point in time, she had every hope that her annual bonus would afford her family the opportunity to take an additional family vacation.

3. **Conciseness—Clichés and "There Are/It Is" Constructions.** Rewrite the following sentences by eliminating clichés and the wordy constructions "there are" and "it is."

   a. They all agreed that the issue had been discussed repeatedly for the last 10 years; thus they did not want to reinvent the wheel during the current study.

   b. There are many examples of skyrocketing equipment costs affecting the final budget for a project.

   c. It is a fact that most employees at McDuff believe the company has taken a step in the right direction by adding international offices.

   d. Needless to say, it is clear that Karen is looking forward to the three-week vacation.

   e. She explained to her staff that it was as plain as day that they would have to decrease their labor costs.

   f. The prospective client asked for a ballpark figure of the project costs.

   g. Last but not least, there was the issue of quality control that he wanted to emphasize in his speech.

   h. In these modern times today, there are new approaches that college graduates should take to the job search.

   i. Susan ended the meeting by concluding that there were a number of mutually agreeable solutions that could be explored so that the new departments in conflict could peacefully coexist.

   j. It is a fact that our boss ended the meeting about a loss of profits by noting that we are all in the same boat.

4. Sentence Clarity. Improve the clarity of the following sentences by changing sentence structures or by splitting long sentences into several shorter ones.

   a. Therefore, to collect a sample from above the water table, and thus to follow the directions provided by the client, the initial boring was abandoned and the drill rig was repositioned about two feet away and a new boring was drilled.

   b. After capping the soil sample ring with PVC end caps and then notifying all members of the project team, we placed it in a cooler for storage on-site and transportation later to a chemical analytical laboratory.

   c. Based on the geotechnical data obtained from the subsurface exploration program, the results of the percolation testing, and the planned plumbing fixtures, the feasibility of installing a leachfield-type on-site sewage-disposal system was evaluated.

   d. Percolation test #1 was performed approximately 40 feet east of the existing pump house and percolation test #2 was performed near the base of the slope approximately 65 feet west of the pump house, and then the results were submitted to the builder.

   e. We appreciate the opportunity to provide our services on this project and look forward to continuing our relationship with XYZ Trading and Transportation Company when we begin the Zanter Project with your Finance Department next spring.

   f. All of the earth materials encountered in our exploration can be used for trench backfill above manhole and pipe bedding, provided they are free of organic material, debris, and other deleterious materials, and they are screened to remove particles greater than six inches in diameter.

   g. This study was conducted to identify, to the extent possible, based on available information from the city files and the criteria described in our proposal of June 18, 1996, whether activities near the site may have involved the use, storage, disposal, or release of hazardous or potentially hazardous substances to the environment.

    h. The properties consist of approximately 5,000 acres, including those parcels of Heron Ranch owned by American Axis Insurance Company, the unsold Jones Ranch parcels, the village commercial area, the mobile home subdivisions, two condominium complexes, a contractor's storage area, an RV storage area, a sales office, a gatehouse, open space parcels, and the undeveloped areas for future Buildings 1666, 1503, 1990, and 1910.

    i. Having already requested permits for the construction of the bathhouse, medical center, maintenance building, boat dock, swimming pool, community building, and an addition to the community building, we still need to apply for the storeroom permit.

    j. A report dated May 25, 1996, for the ABC Corporation confirmed that the updated business plan had been completed the previous month, but a new plan had to be submitted by May 25, 1997.

5. Active and Passive Voice Verbs. Make changes in active and passive voice verbs, where appropriate. Refer to the guidelines in the chapter. Be able to supply a rationale for any change you make.

    a. It was recommended by the personnel committee that you consider changing the requirements for promotion.

    b. No formal report about assets was reported by the corporation before it announced the merger.

    c. The graphs showing the differences in depreciation and interest and the net loss on the investment are shown in Appendix A.

    d. It has been noted by the Department of Environmental Services that the laundry business was storing toxic chemicals in an unsafe location.

    e. The samples from the Scottish Highlands will be sent to McDuff's engineering lab in London.

    f. The violation of ethical guidelines was reported by the commissioner to the president of the association.

    g. No complete equipment inventory has been made by McDuff's Boston office.

    h. It was concluded by the employee committee that McDuff's retirement program needed to be revised.

    i. Dirt brought to the site should be evaluated by the engineer on-site before it is placed in the foundation.

    j. Due to presence of a good deal of sand at the location, excavations are anticipated by us to be relatively unstable.

6. Sexist Language. Revise the following sentences to eliminate sexist language.

    a. The department decided to advertise for a department chairman in three national newspapers.

    b. Although each manager was responsible for his own budget, some managers obviously had better accounting skills than others.

    c. The company policy manual states that each secretary should submit her time card twice a month.

    d. If an hourly worker misses no work for sickness during a calendar year, he will receive a $500 bonus at year's end.

    e. Each flight attendant is required to meet special work standards as long as she is employed by an international airline.

    f. Typically, a new engineer at McDuff receives his first promotion after about a year.

    g. Every worker wonders whether he is saving enough for retirement.

    h. If a pilot senses danger, she should abort the takeoff.

    i. Upon arriving at the site, a McDuff scientist should make immediate contact with his client representative.

    j. [greeting section of a letter] Gentlemen:

7. Advanced Exercise—Conciseness. The following sentences contain more words than necessary. Rewrite each passage more concisely, without changing the meaning. If appropriate, make two sentences out of one.

    a. The disbursement of the funds from the estate will occur on the day that the proceedings concerning the estate are finalized in court.

    b. During the course of the project that we conducted for Acme Pipe, several members of our project team were in the unfortunate position of having to perform their fieldwork at the same time that torrential rains hit the area, totaling three inches of rain in one afternoon.

    c. At a later date we plan to begin the process of prioritizing our responsibilities on the project so that we will have a clear idea of which activities deserve the most attention from the project personnel.

    d. Needless to say, we do not plan to add our participation to the project if we conclude that the skyrocketing costs of the project will prohibit our earning what could be considered to be a fair profit from the venture.

    e. The government at this point in time plans to discontinue its testing of every item but will undertake to implement testing again in approximately five months.

    f. Hazerd, Inc., will endeavor to finalize the modifications of the blueprints for a ballpark figure of about $850.

    g. For us to supply the additional supplies that the client wishes to procure from us, the client will have to initiate a change order that permits additional funds to be transferred into the project account.

    h. Upon further analysis of the many and varied options that we are cognizant of at this time, it is our opinion that the long-term interests of our firm would be best served by reducing the size of the production staff by 300 workers.

    i. Prior to the implementation of the state law with regard to the use of asbestos as a building material, it was common practice to utilize this naturally occurring mineral in all kinds of facilities, some of which became health hazards subsequently.

    j. In the event that we are given permission to undertake the research, be sure to make certain to perform an efficient and effective search of available literature in a research facility so that we do not end up, in the final analysis, reinventing the wheel with regard to knowledge of superconductors.

8. Advanced Exercise—General Style Rules. Revise the following sentences by applying all guidelines mentioned in this chapter. When you change passive verbs to active, you may need to make some assumptions about the agent of the action, since the sentences are taken out of context.

a. Based on our review of the available records, conversations with the various agencies involved, including the Fire Department and the Police Department, and a thorough survey of the site where the spill occurred, it was determined that the site contained chemicals that were hazardous to human health.

b. After seven hours at the negotiation table, the union representatives and management decided that the issues they were discussing could not be resolved that evening, so they met the next day at the hotel complex, at which point they agreed on a new contract that would increase job security and benefits.

c. It is recommended by us that your mainframe computer system be replaced immediately by a newer model.

d. After the study was completed by the research team and the results were published in the company newsletter the following month, the president decided to call a meeting of all senior-level managers to discuss strategies for addressing problems highlighted by the research team.

e. Our project activities can be generally described in this way. The samples were retrieved from the site and then were transported to the testing lab in the containers made especially for this project, and at the lab they were tested to determine their soil properties; the data were analyzed by all the members of the team before findings and conclusions were arrived at.

f. First the old asbestos tile was removed. Then the black adhesive was scraped off. Later the floor was sanded smooth. The wood arrived shortly. Then the floor was installed.

g. The figures on the firm's profit margins in July and August, along with sales commissions for the last six months of the previous year and the top 10 salespersons in the firm, are included in the Appendix.

h. It was suggested by the team that the company needs to invest in modern equipment.

i. It is the opinion of this writer that the company's health plan is adequate.

j. Shortly after the last change in leadership, and during the time that the board of directors was expressing strong views about the direction that the company was taking, it became clear to me and other members of the senior staff that the company was in trouble.

k. Each manager should complete and submit his monthly report by the second Tuesday of every month.

l. After completing our engineering analysis, it is clear that metal fatigue caused the structure to fail.

m. Upon hearing the captain's signal, each flight attendant should complete her checklist of preflight procedures.

n. Our weed-spraying procedure will have minimal impact on shrubbery that surrounds the building site.

o. It was reported today from the corporate headquarters that the health-care plan has been approved by the president.

9. **Editing Paper of Classmate.** For this assignment, exchange papers with a member of your class. Use either the draft of a current assignment *or* a paper that was completed earlier in the term. Edit your classmate's work in accordance with this chapter's guidelines on style. Then explain your changes to the writer.

10. **Editing Sample Memo.** Using the guidelines in this chapter, edit the following memorandum.

DATE: January 12, 1996
TO: All Employees of Denver Branch
FROM: Leonard Schwartz, Branch Manager
SUBJECT: New Loss-Prevention System

As you may have recently heard, lately we received news from the corporate headquarters of the company that it would be in the best interest of the entire company to pay more attention to matters of preventing accidents and any other safety-related measures that affect the workplace, including both office and field activities related to all types of jobs that we complete. Every single employee in each office at every branch needs to be ever mindful in this regard so that he is most efficient and effective in the daily performance of his everyday tasks that relate to his job responsibilities such that safety is always of paramount concern.

With this goal of safety ever present in our minds, I believe the bottom line of the emphasis on safety could be considered to be the training that each of us receives in his first, initial weeks on the job as well as the training provided on a regular basis throughout each year of our employment with McDuff, so that we are always aware of how to operate in a safe manner. The training vehicle gives the company the mechanism to provide each of you with the means to become aware of the elements of safety that relate to the specific needs and requirements of your own particular job. Therefore, at this point in time I have come to the conclusion in the process of contemplating the relevance of the new corporate emphasis on safety to our particular branch that we need, as a branch, to give much greater scrutiny and analysis to the way we can prevent accidents and emphasize the concern of safety at every stage of our operation for every employee. Toward this end, I have asked the training coordinator, Kendra Jones, to assemble a written training program that will involve every single employee and that can be implemented beginning no later than June of this year. When the plan has been written and approved at the various levels within the office, I will conduct a meeting with every department in order to emphasize the major and minor components of this upcoming safety program.

It is my great pleasure to announce to all of you that effective in the next month (February) I will give a monthly safety award of $100 to the individual branch employee at any level of the branch who comes up with the best, most useful suggestion related to safety in any part of the branch activities. Today I will take the action of placing a suggestion box on the wall of the lunchroom so that all of you will have easy access to a way to get your suggestions for safety into the pipeline and to be considered. As an attachment to the memo you are now reading from me I have provided you with a copy of the form that you are to use in making any suggestions that are then to be placed in the suggestion box. On the last day of each month that we work, the box will be emptied of the completed forms for that month, and before the end of the following week a winner will be selected by me for the previous month's suggestion program and an announcement will be placed by me to that effect on the bulletin board in the company workroom.

If you have any questions in regard to the corporate safety program as it affects our branch or about the suggestion program that is being implemented here at the Denver office at McDuff, please do not hesitate to make your comments known either in memorandum form or by way of telephonic response to this memorandum.

Handbook

*T*his handbook includes entries on the basics of writing. Here you will find three main types of information:

1. **Grammar:** the rules by which we edit sentence elements. Examples include rules for the placement of punctuation, the agreement of subjects and verbs, and the placement of modifiers.
2. **Mechanics:** the rules by which we make final proofreading changes. Examples include the rules for abbreviations and the use of numbers. This handbook also includes a list of commonly misspelled words.
3. **Usage:** information on the correct use of particular words, especially pairs of words that are often confused. Examples include problem words like "affect/effect," "complement/compliment," and "who/whom."

Another editing concern, technical style, is the topic of chapter 15. In that chapter are guidelines for sentence structure, conciseness, accuracy of wording, active and passive voice, and nonsexist language. Together, chapter 15 and this handbook will help you turn unedited drafts into final revised documents.

This handbook is presented in alphabetized fashion for easy reference during the editing process. A table of contents follows. Grammar and mechanics entries are in caps; usage entries are in lowercase. Several exercises follow the entries.

"continually" should be used with activities that are intermittent, or repeated at intervals. If you think your reader may not understand the difference, you should either (1) use synonyms that will be clearer (such as "uninterrupted" for "continuous," and "intermittent" for "continual") or (2) define each word at the point you first use it in the document. EXAMPLES:

- "We *continually* checked the water pressure for three hours before the equipment arrived, while also using the time to set up the next day's tests."
- "Because it rained *continuously* from 10:00 A.M. until noon, we were unable to move our equipment onto the utility easement."

Data/Datum

Coming as it does from the Latin, the word "data" is the plural form of "datum." Although many writers now accept "data" as singular or plural, traditionalists in the technical and scientific community still consider "data" exclusively a plural form. Therefore, you should maintain the plural usage. EXAMPLES:

- "These *data* show that there is a strong case for building the dam at the other location."
- "This particular *datum* shows that we need to reconsider recommendations put forth in the original report."

If you consider the traditional singular form of "datum" to be awkward, use substitutes such as "This item in the data shows" or "One of the data shows that." Singular subjects like "one" or "item" allow you to keep your original meaning without using the word "datum."

Definite/Definitive

Though similar in meaning, these words have slightly different contexts. "Definite" refers to that which is precise, explicit, or final. "Definitive" has the more restrictive meaning of "authoritative" or "final." EXAMPLES:

- "It is now *definite* that he will be assigned to the London office for six months."
- "He received the *definitive* study on the effect of the oil spill on the marine ecology."

Discrete/Discreet/Discretion

The adjective "discrete" suggests something that is separate, or something that is made up of many separate parts. The adjective "discreet" is associated with actions that require caution, modesty, or reserve. The noun "discretion" refers to the quality of being "discreet" or the freedom a person has to act on her or his own. EXAMPLES:

- "The orientation program at McDuff includes a writing seminar, which is a *discrete* training unit offered for one full day."
- "The orientation program at McDuff includes five *discrete* units."

- "As a counselor in McDuff's Human Resources Office, Sharon was *discreet* in her handling of personal information about employees."
- "Every employee in the Human Resources Office was instructed to show *discretion* in handling personal information about employees."
- "By starting a flextime program, McDuff, Inc., will give employees a good deal of *discretion* in selecting the time to start and end their workday."

Disinterested/Uninterested

In contemporary business use, these words have quite different meanings. Because errors can cause confusion for the reader, make sure not to use the words as synonyms. "Disinterested" means "without prejudice or bias," whereas "uninterested" means "showing no interest." EXAMPLES:

- "The agency sought a *disinterested* observer who had no stake in the outcome of the trial."
- "They spent several days talking to officials from Iceland, but they still remain *uninterested* in performing work in that country."

Due to/Because of

Besides irritating those who expect proper English, mixing these two phrases can also cause confusion. "Due to" is an adjective phrase meaning "attributable to" and almost always follows a "to be" verb (such as "is," "was," or "were"). It should not be used in place of prepositional phrases such as "because of," "owing to," or "as a result of." EXAMPLES:

- "The cracked walls were *due to* the lack of proper foundation fill being used during construction."
- "We won the contract *because of* [not *due to*] our thorough understanding of the client's needs."

e.g./i.e.

The abbreviation "e.g." means "for example," whereas "i.e." means "that is." These two Latin abbreviations are often confused, a fact that should give you pause before using them. Many writers prefer to write them out, rather than risk confusion on the part of the reader. EXAMPLES:

- "During the trip, he visited 12 cities where McDuff is considering opening offices—*e.g.*, [or, preferably, *for example*] Kansas City, New Orleans, and Seattle."
- "A spot along the Zayante Fault was the earthquake's epicenter—*i.e.*, [or, preferably, *that is*] the focal point for seismic activity."

Fewer/Less

The adjective "fewer" is used before items that can be counted, whereas the adjective "less" is used before mass quantities. When errors occur, they usually result from "less" being used with countable items, as in this *incorrect* sentence: "We can complete the job with less men at the site." EXAMPLES:

- "The newly certified industrial hygienist signed with us because the other firm in which he was interested offered *fewer* [not *less*] benefits."
- "There was *less* sand in the sample taken from 15 ft than in the one taken from 10 ft."

Flammable/Inflammable/Nonflammable

Given the importance of these words in avoiding injury and death, make sure to use them correctly—especially in instructions. "Flammable" means "capable of burning quickly" and is acceptable usage. "Inflammable" has the same meaning, but it is *not* acceptable usage for this reason: Some readers confuse it with "non-flammable." The word "nonflammable," then, means "not capable of burning" and is accepted usage. EXAMPLES:

- "They marked the package *flammable* because its contents could be easily ignited by a spark." (Note that *flammable* is preferred here over its synonym, *inflammable*.)
- "The foreman felt comfortable placing the crates near the heating unit, since all the crates' contents were *nonflammable*."

Fortuitous/Fortunate

The word "fortuitous" is an adjective that refers to an unexpected action, without regard to whether it is desirable or not. The word "fortunate" is an adjective that indicates an action that is clearly desired. The common usage error with this pair is the wrong assumption that "fortuitous" events must also be "fortunate." EXAMPLES:

- "Seeing McDuff's London manager at the conference was quite *fortuitous*, since I had not been told that he also was attending."
- "It was indeed *fortunate* that I encountered the London manager, for it gave us the chance to talk about an upcoming project involving both our offices."

Generally/Typically/Usually

Words like these can be useful qualifiers in your reports. They indicate to the reader that what you have stated is often, but not always, the case. Make certain to place these adverb modifiers as close as possible to the words they modify. In the first example here, it would be inaccurate to write "were typically sampled," in that the adverb modifies the entire verb phrase "were sampled." EXAMPLES:

- "Cohesionless soils *typically* were sampled by driving a 2-in. diameter, split-barrel sampler." (Active-voice alternative: "*Typically*, we sampled cohesionless soils by driving a 2-in. diameter, split-barrel sampler.")

- "For projects like the one you propose, the technician *usually* will clean the equipment before returning to the office."
- "It is *generally* known that sites for dumping waste should be equipped with appropriate liners."

Good/Well

Though similar in meaning, "good" is used as an adjective and "well" is used as an adverb. A common usage error occurs when writers use the adjective when the adverb is required. EXAMPLES:

- "It is *good* practice to submit three-year plans on time."
- "He did *well* to complete the three-year plan on time, considering the many reports he had to finish that same week."

Imply/Infer

Remember that the person doing the speaking or writing implies, whereas the person hearing or reading the words infers. In other words, the word "imply" requires an active role; the word "infer" requires a passive role. When you imply a point, your words suggest rather than state a point. When you infer a point, you form a conclusion or deduce meaning from someone else's words or actions. EXAMPLES:

- "The contracts officer *implied* that there would be stiff competition for that $20 million waste-treatment project."
- "We *inferred* from her remarks that any firm hoping to secure the work must have completed similar projects recently."

Its/It's

These words are often confused. You can avoid error by remembering that "it's" with the apostrophe is used *only* as a contraction for "it is" or "it has." The other form—"its"—is a possessive pronoun. EXAMPLES:

- "Because of the rain, *it's* [or *it is*] going to be difficult to move the equipment to the site."
- "*It's* [or *it has*] been a long time since we submitted the proposal."
- "The company completed *its* part of the agreement on time."

Loose/Lose

"Loose," which rhymes with "goose," is an adjective that means "unfastened, flexible, or unconfined." "Lose," which rhymes with "ooze," is a verb that means "to misplace." EXAMPLES:

- "The power failure was linked to a *loose* connection at the switchbox."
- "Because of poor service, the photocopy machine company may *lose* its contract with McDuff's San Francisco office."

Modifiers: Dangling and Misplaced

This section includes guidelines for avoiding the most common modification errors—dangling modifiers and misplaced modifiers. But first we need to define the term "modifier." Words, phrases, and even dependent clauses can serve as modifiers. They serve to qualify, or add meaning to, other elements in the sentence. For our purposes here, the most important point is that modifiers need to be clearly connected to what they modify.

Modification errors occur most often with verbal phrases. A phrase is a group of words that lacks either a subject or predicate. The term "verbal" refers to (1) gerunds (*-ing* form of verbs used as nouns, such as "He likes skiing"), (2) participles (*-ing* form of verbs used as adjectives, such as "Skiing down the hill, he lost a glove"), or (3) infinitives (the word "to" plus the verb root, such as "To attend the opera was his favorite pastime"). Now let's look at the two main modification errors.

Dangling Modifiers.   When a verbal phrase "dangles," the sentence in which it is used contains no specific word for the phrase to modify. As a result, the meaning of the sentence can be confusing to the reader. For example, "In designing the foundation, several alternatives were discussed." It is not at all clear exactly who is doing the "designing." The phrase dangles because it does not modify a specific word. The modifier does not dangle in this version of the sentence: "In designing the foundation, we discussed several alternatives."

Misplaced Modifiers.   When a verbal phrase is misplaced, it may appear to refer to a word that it, in fact, does not modify. EXAMPLE: "Floating peacefully near the oil rig, we saw two humpback whales." Obviously, the whales are doing the floating, and the rig workers are doing the seeing here. Yet because the verbal phrase is placed at the beginning of the sentence, rather than at the end immediately after the word it modifies, the sentence presents some momentary confusion.

Misplaced modifiers can lead to confusion about the agent of action in technical tasks. EXAMPLE: "Before beginning to dig the observation trenches, we recommend that the contractors submit their proposed excavation program for our review." On quick reading, the reader is not certain about who will be "beginning to dig"—the contractors or the "we" in the sentence. The answer is the contractors. Thus a correct placement of the modifier would be "We recommend the following: Before the contractors begin digging observation trenches, they should submit their proposed excavation for our review."

Solving Modifier Problems.   At best, dangling and misplaced modifiers produce a momentary misreading by the audience. At worst, they can lead to confusion that results in disgruntled readers, lost customers, or liability problems. To prevent modification problems, place all verbal phrases—indeed, all modifiers—as close as possible to the word they modify. If you spot a modification error while you are editing, correct it in one of two ways:

1. Leave the modifier as it is and rework the rest of the sentence. Thus you would change "Using an angle of friction of 20 degrees and a vertical weight of 300 tons, the sliding resistance would be . . . " to the following: "Using an angle of friction of 20 degrees and a vertical weight of 300 tons, we computed a sliding resistance of. . . . "

2. Rephrase the modifier as a complete clause. Thus you would change the previous original sentence to "If the angle of friction is 20 degrees and the vertical weight is 300 tons, the sliding resistance should be. . . . "

In either case, your goal is to link the modifier clearly and smoothly with the word or phrase it modifies.

Numbers

Like rules for abbreviations, those for numbers vary from profession to profession and even from company to company. Most technical writing subscribes to the approach that numbers are best expressed in figures (45) rather than words (forty-five). Note that this style may differ from that used in other types of writing, such as this textbook. Unless the preferences of a particular reader suggest that you do otherwise, follow these common rules for use of numbers in writing your technical documents:

■ *Rule 1: Follow the 10-or-Over Rule*

In general, use figures for numbers of 10 or more, words for numbers below 10. EXAMPLES: three technicians at the site/15 reports submitted last month/one rig contracted for the job.

■ *Rule 2: Do Not Start Sentences with Figures*

Begin sentences with the word form of numbers, not with figures. EXAMPLE: "Forty-five containers were shipped back to the lab."

■ *Rule 3: Use Figures as Modifiers*

Whether above or below 10, numbers are usually expressed as figures when used as modifiers with units of measurement, time, and money, especially when these units are abbreviated. EXAMPLES: 4 in., 7 hr, 17 ft, $5 per hr. Exceptions can be made when the unit is not abbreviated. EXAMPLE: five years.

■ *Rule 4: Use Figures in a Group of Mixed Numbers*

Use only figures when the numbers grouped together in a passage (usually *one* sentence) are both above and below 10. EXAMPLE: "For that project they assembled 15 samplers, 4 rigs, and 25 containers." In other words, this rule argues for consistency within a writing unit.

■ *Rule 5: Use the Figure Form in Illustration Titles*

Use the numeric form when labeling specific tables and figures in your reports. EXAMPLES: Figure 3, Table 14-B.

■ *Rule 6: Be Careful with Fractions*

Express fractions as words when they stand alone, but as figures when they are used as a modifier or are joined to whole numbers. EXAMPLE: "We have completed two-thirds of the project using the 2 1/2 in. pipe."

■ *Rule 7: Use Figures and Words with Numbers in Succession*

When two numbers appear in succession in the same unit, write the first as a word and the second as a figure. EXAMPLE: "We found fifteen 2-ft pieces of pipe in the machinery."

■ *Rule 8: Only Rarely Use Numbers in Parentheses*

Except in legal documents, avoid the practice of placing figures in parentheses after their word equivalents. EXAMPLE: "The second party will send the first party forty-five (45) barrels on or before the first of each month." Note that the parenthetical amount is placed immediately after the figure, not after the unit of measurement.

■ *Rule 9: Use Figures with Dollars*

Use figures with all dollar amounts, with the exception of the context noted in Rule 8. Avoid cents columns unless exactness to the penny is necessary.

■ *Rule 10: Use Commas in Four-Digit Figures*

To prevent possible misreading, use commas in figures of four digits or more. EXAMPLES: 15,000; 1,247; 6,003.

■ *Rule 11: Use Words for Ordinals*

Usually spell out the ordinal form of numbers. EXAMPLE: "The government informed all parties of the first, second, and third [not 1st, 2nd, and 3rd] choices in the design competition." A notable exception is tables and figures, where space limitations could argue for the abbreviated form.

Oral/Verbal

"Oral" refers to words that are spoken, as in "oral presentation." The term "verbal" refers to spoken or written language. To prevent confusion, avoid the word "verbal" and instead specify your meaning with the words "oral" and "written." EXAMPLES:

- "In its international operations, McDuff, Inc., has learned that some countries still rely upon *oral* [not *verbal*] contracts."
- "Their *oral* agreement last month was followed by a *written* [not *verbal*] contract this month."

Parts of Speech

This term refers to the eight main groups of words in English grammar. A word's placement in one of these groups is based upon its function within the sentence.

Noun.   Words in this group name persons, places, objects, or ideas. The two major categories are (1) proper nouns and (2) common nouns. Proper nouns name specific persons, places, objects, or ideas, and they are capitalized. EXAMPLES: Cleveland; Mississippi River; McDuff, Inc.; Student Government Association; Susan Jones; Existentialism. Common nouns name general groups of persons, places, objects, and ideas, and they are not capitalized. EXAMPLES: trucks, farmers, engineers, assembly lines, philosophy.

Verb.   A verb expresses action or state of being. Verbs give movement to sentences and form the core of meaning in your writing. EXAMPLES: explore, grasp, write, develop, is, has.

Pronoun.   A pronoun is a substitute for a noun. Some sample pronoun categories include (1) personal pronouns (I, we, you, she, he), (2) relative pronouns (who, whom, that, which), (3) reflexive and intensive pronouns (myself, yourself, itself), (4) demonstrative pronouns (this, that, these, those), and (5) indefinite pronouns (all, any, each, anyone).

Adjective.   An adjective modifies a noun. EXAMPLES: horizontal, stationary, green, large, simple.

Adverb.   An adverb modifies a verb, an adjective, another adverb, or a whole statement. EXAMPLES: soon, generally, well, very, too, greatly.

Preposition.   A preposition shows the relationship between a noun or pronoun (the object of a preposition) and another element of the sentence. Forming a prepositional phrase, the preposition and its object can reveal relationships such as location ("They went *over the hill*"), time ("He left *after the meeting*"), and direction ("She walked *toward the office*").

Conjunction.   A conjunction is a connecting word that links words, phrases, or clauses. EXAMPLES: and, but, for, nor, although, after, because, since.

Interjection.   As an expression of emotion, an interjection can stand alone ("Look out!") or can be inserted into another sentence.

Per Cent/Percent/Percentage

"Per cent" and "percent" have basically the same usage and are used with exact numbers. The one word "percent" is preferred. Even more common in technical writing, however, is the use of the percent sign (%) after numbers. The word "percentage" is only used to express general amounts, not exact numbers. EXAMPLES:

- "After completing a marketing survey, McDuff, Inc., discovered that 83 *percent* [or 83%] of its current clients have hired McDuff for previous projects."
- "A large *percentage* of the defects can be linked to the loss of two experienced quality-control inspectors."

Principal/Principle

When these two words are misused, the careful reader will notice. Keep them straight by remembering this simple distinction: "Principle" is always a noun that means "basic truth, belief, or theorem." EXAMPLE: "He believed in the principle of free speech." "Principal" can be either a noun or an adjective and has three basic uses:

- **As a noun meaning "head official" or "person who plays a major role."** EXAMPLE: "We asked that a *principal* in the firm sign the contract."
- **As a noun meaning "the main portion of a financial account upon which interest is paid."** EXAMPLE: "If we deposit $5,000 in *principal,* we will earn 9 percent interest."
- **As an adjective meaning "main or primary."** EXAMPLE: "We believe that the *principal* reason for contamination at the site is the leaky underground storage tank."

Pronouns: Agreement and Reference

A pronoun is a word that replaces a noun, which is called the "antecedent" of the pronoun. EXAMPLES: this, it, he, she, they. Pronouns, as such, provide you with a useful strategy for varying your style by avoiding repetition of nouns. Here are some rules to prevent pronoun errors:

■ *Rule 1: Make Pronouns Agree with Antecedents*

Check every pronoun to make certain it agrees with its antecedent in number. That is, both noun and pronoun must be singular, or both must be plural. Of special concern are the pronouns "it" and "they." EXAMPLES:

- Change "McDuff, Inc., plans to complete their Argentina project next month" to this sentence: "McDuff, Inc., plans to complete its Argentina project next month."

- Change "The committee released their recommendations to all departments" to this sentence: "The committee released its recommendations to all departments."

■ Rule 2: Be Clear About the Antecedent of Every Pronoun

There must be no question about what noun a pronoun replaces. Any confusion about the antecedent of a pronoun can change the entire meaning of a sentence. To avoid such reference problems, you may need to rewrite a sentence or even use a noun rather than a pronoun. Do whatever is necessary to prevent misunderstanding by your reader. EXAMPLE: Change "The gas filters for these tanks are so dirty that they should not be used" to this sentence: "These filters are so dirty that they should not be used."

■ Rule 3: Avoid Using "This" as the Subject Unless a Noun Follows It

A common stylistic error is the vague use of "this," especially as the subject of a sentence. Sometimes the reference is not clear at all; sometimes the reference may be clear after several readings. In almost all cases, however, the use of "this" as a pronoun reflects poor technical style and tends to make the reader want to ask, "This what?" Instead, make the subject of your sentences concrete, either by adding a noun after the "this" or by recasting the sentence. EXAMPLE: Change "He talked constantly about the project to be completed at the Olympics. This made his office-mates irritable" to the following: "His constant talk about the Olympics project irritated his office-mates."

Punctuation: General

Commas.   Most writers struggle with commas, so you are not alone. The problem is basically threefold. First, the teaching of punctuation has been approached in different, and sometimes quite contradictory, ways. Second, comma rules themselves are subject to various interpretations. And third, problems with comma placement often mask more fundamental problems with the structure of a sentence itself.

You need to start by knowing the basic rules of comma use. The rules that follow are fairly simple. If you learn them now, you will save yourself a good deal of time later in that you will not be constantly questioning usage. In other words, the main benefit of learning the basics of comma use is increased confidence in your own ability to handle the mechanics of editing. (If you do not understand some of the grammatical terms that follow, such as "compound sentence," refer to the section on sentence structure.)

■ Rule 1: Commas in a Series

Use commas to separate words, phrases, and short clauses written in a series of three or more items. EXAMPLE: "The samples contained gray sand, sandy clay, and silty sand." According to current U.S. usage, a comma always comes before the "and" in a series. (In the United Kingdom, the comma is left out.)

■ *Rule 2: Commas in Compound Sentences*

Use a comma before the conjunction that joins main clauses in a compound sentence. EXAMPLE: "We completed the drilling at the Smith Industries location, and then we grouted the holes with Sakrete." The comma is needed here because it separates two complete clauses, each with its own subject and verb ("we completed" and "we grouted"). If the second "we" had been deleted, there would be only one clause containing one subject and two verbs ("we completed and grouted"). Thus no comma would be needed. Of course, it may be that a sentence following this comma rule is far too long; do not use the rule to string together intolerably long sentences.

■ *Rule 3: Commas with Nonessential Modifiers*

Set off nonessential modifiers with commas—either at the beginning, middle, or end of sentences. Nonessential modifiers are usually phrases that add more information to a sentence, rather than greatly changing its meaning. When you speak, often there is a pause between this kind of modifier and the main part of the sentence, giving you a clue that a comma break is needed. EXAMPLE: "The report, which we submitted three weeks ago, indicated that the company would not be responsible for transporting hazardous wastes." But—"The report that we submitted three weeks ago indicated that the company would not be responsible for transporting hazardous wastes." The first example includes a nonessential modifier, would be spoken with pauses, and therefore uses separating commas. The second example includes an *essential* modifier, would be spoken *without* pauses, and therefore includes *no* separating commas.

■ *Rule 4: Commas with Adjectives in a Series*

Use a comma to separate two or more adjectives that modify the same noun. To help you decide if adjectives modify the same noun, use this test: If you can reverse their positions and still retain the same meaning, then the adjectives modify the same word and should be separated by a comma. EXAMPLE: "Jason opened the two containers in a clean, well-lighted place."

■ *Rule 5: Commas with Introductory Elements*

Use a comma after introductory phrases or clauses of about five words or more. EXAMPLE: "After completing the topographic survey of the area, the crew returned to headquarters for its weekly project meeting." Commas like the one after "area" help readers separate secondary or modifying points from your main idea, which of course should be in the main clause. Without these commas, there may be difficulty reading such sentences properly.

■ *Rule 6: Commas in Dates, Titles, Etc.*

Abide by the conventions of comma usage in punctuating dates, titles, geographic place names, and addresses. EXAMPLES:

- "May 3, 1996, is the projected date of completion." (But note the change in the "military" form of dates: "We will complete the project on 3 May 1996.")
- "John F. Dunwoody, Ph.D., has been hired to assist on the project."
- "McDuff, Inc., has been selected for the project."
- "He listed Dayton, Ohio, as his permanent residence."

Note the need for commas after the year "1996," the title "Ph.D.," the designation "Inc.," and the state name "Ohio." Also note that if the day had not been in the first example, there would be *no* comma between the month and year and no comma after the year.

Semicolons.   The semicolon is easy to use if you remember that it, like a period, indicates the end of a complete thought. Its most frequent use is in situations where grammar rules would allow you to use a period but where your stylistic preference is for a less abrupt connector. EXAMPLE: "Five engineers left the convention hotel after dinner; only two returned by midnight."

One of the most common punctuation errors, the comma splice, occurs when a comma is used instead of a semicolon or period in compound sentences connected by words such as "however," "therefore," "thus," and "then." When you see that these connectors separate two main clauses, make sure either to use a semicolon or to start a new sentence. EXAMPLE: "We made it to the project site by the agreed-upon time; however, [or " . . . time. However, . . .] the rain forced us to stay in our trucks for two hours."

As noted in the "Lists" entry, there is another instance in which you might use semicolons. Place them after the items in a list when you are treating the list like a sentence and when any one of the items contains internal commas.

Colons.   As mentioned in the "Lists" entry, you should place a colon immediately after the last word in the lead-in before a formal list of bulleted or numbered items. EXAMPLE: "Our field study involved these three steps:" or "In our field study we were asked to:" The colon may come after a complete clause, as in the first example, or it may split a grammatical construction, as in the second example. However, it is preferable to use a complete clause before a formal list.

The colon can also be used in sentences in which you want a formal break before a point of clarification or elaboration. EXAMPLE: "They were interested in just one result: quality construction." In addition, use the colon in sentences in which you want a formal break before a series that is not part of a listing. EXAMPLE: "They agreed to perform all on-site work required in these four cities: Houston, Austin, Laredo, and Abilene." But note that there is no colon before a sentence series without a break in thought. EXAMPLE: "They agreed to perform all the on-site work required in Houston, Austin, Laredo, and Abilene."

Apostrophes.   The apostrophe can be used for contractions, for some plurals, and for possessives. Only the latter two uses cause confusion. Use an apostrophe to indicate the plural form of a word as a word. EXAMPLE: "That redundant paragraph contained seven *area's* and three *factor's* in only five sentences." Although some writers also use apostrophes to form the plurals of numbers and full-cap abbreviations, the current tendency is to include only the "s." EXAMPLES: 7s, ABCs, PCBs, P.E.s.

As for possessives, you probably already know that the grammar rules seem to vary, depending on the reference book you are reading. Here are some simple guidelines:

■ *Possessive Rule 1*

Form the possessive of multisyllabic nouns that end in "s" by adding just an apostrophe, whether the nouns are singular or plural. EXAMPLES: actress' costume, genius' test score, the three technicians' samples, Jesus' parables, the companies' joint project.

■ *Possessive Rule 2*

Form the possessive of one-syllable, singular nouns ending in "s" or an "s" sound by adding an apostrophe plus "s." EXAMPLES: Hoss's horse, Tex's song, the boss's progress report.

■ *Possessive Rule 3*

Form the possessive of all plural nouns ending in "s" or an "s" sound by adding just an apostrophe. EXAMPLES: the cars' engines, the ducks' flight path, the trees' roots.

■ *Possessive Rule 4*

Form the possessive of all singular and plural nouns not ending in "s" by adding an apostrophe plus "s." EXAMPLES: the man's hat, the men's team, the company's policy.

■ *Possessive Rule 5*

Form the possessive of paired nouns by first determining whether there is joint ownership or individual ownership. For joint ownership, make only the last noun possessive. For individual ownership, make both nouns possessive. EXAMPLE: "Susan and Terry's project was entered in the science fair; but Tom's and Scott's projects were not."

Quotation Marks.   In technical writing, you may want to use this form of punctuation to draw attention to particular words, to indicate passages taken directly from another source, or to enclose the titles of short documents such as reports or book chapters. The rule to remember is this: Periods and commas go inside quotation marks; semicolons and colons go outside quotation marks.

Parentheses.   Use parentheses carefully, since long parenthetical expressions can cause the reader to lose the train of thought. This form of punctuation can be used when you (1) place an abbreviation after a complete term, (2) add a brief explanation within the text, or (3) include reference citations within the document text (as explained in chapter 13). The period goes after the close parenthesis when the parenthetical information is part of the sentence, as in the previous sentence. (However, it goes inside the close parenthesis when the parenthetical information forms its own sentence, as in the sentence you are reading.)

Brackets.   Use a pair of brackets for these purposes: (1) to set off parenthetical material already contained within another parenthetical statement and (2) to draw attention to a comment you are making within a quoted passage. EXAMPLE: "Two McDuff studies have shown that the Colony Dam is up to safety standards. (See Figure 4-3 [Dam Safety Record] for a complete record of our findings.) In addition, the county engineer has a letter on file that will give further assurance to prospective homeowners on the lake. His letter notes that 'After finishing my three-month study [he completed the study in July 1993], I conclude that the Colony Dam meets all safety standards set by the county and state governments.' "

Hyphens.   The hyphen is used to form certain word compounds in English. Although the rules for its use sometimes seem to change from handbook to handbook, those that follow are the most common.

■ *Hyphen Rule 1*

Use hyphens with compound numerals. EXAMPLE: twenty-one through ninety-nine.

■ *Hyphen Rule 2*

Use hyphens with most compounds that begin with "self." EXAMPLES: self-defense, self-image, self-pity. Other "self" compounds, like "selfhood" and "selfsame," are written as unhyphenated words.

■ *Hyphen Rule 3*

Use hyphens with group modifiers when they precede the noun but not when they follow the noun. EXAMPLES: A well-organized paper, a paper that was well organized, twentieth-century geotechnical technology, bluish-gray shale, fire-tested material, thin-bedded limestone.

However, remember that when the first word of the modifier is an adverb ending in "-ly," place no hyphen between the words. EXAMPLES: carefully drawn plate, frightfully ignorant teacher.

■ *Hyphen Rule 4*

Place hyphens between prefixes and root words in the following cases: (a) between a prefix and a proper name (ex-Republican, pre-Sputnik); (b) between some prefixes that end with a vowel and root words beginning with a vowel, particularly if the use of a hyphen would prevent an odd spelling (semi-independent, re-enter, re-elect); and (c) between a prefix and a root when the hyphen helps to prevent confusion (re-sent, not resent; re-form, not reform; re-cover, not recover).

Punctuation: Lists

As noted in chapter 4 ("Page Design"), listings draw attention to parallel pieces of information whose importance would be harder to grasp in paragraph format. In other words, employ lists as an attention-getting strategy. Following are some general pointers for punctuating lists. (See pages 115-116 in chapter 4 for other rules for lists.)

You have three main options for punctuating a listing. The common denominators for all three are that you (1) always place a colon after the last word of the lead-in and (2) always capitalize the first letter of the first word of each listed item.

Option A: Place no punctuation after listed items. This style is appropriate when the list includes only short phrases. More and more writers are choosing this option, as opposed to Option B. EXAMPLE:

"In this study, we will develop recommendations that address these six concerns in your project:

- Site preparation
- Foundation design
- Sanitary-sewer design
- Storm-sewer design
- Geologic surface faulting
- Projections for regional land subsidence"

Option B: Treat the list like a sentence series. In this case, you place commas or semicolons between items and a period at the end of the series. Whether you choose Option A or B largely depends on your own style or that of your employer. EXAMPLE:

"In this study, we developed recommendations that dealt with four topics:

- Site preparation,
- Foundation design,
- Sewer construction, and
- Geologic faulting."

Note that this option requires you to place an "and" after the comma that appears before the last item. Another variation of Option B occurs when you have internal commas within one or more of the items. In this case, you need to change the commas that follow the listed items into semicolons. Yet you still keep the "and" before the last item. EXAMPLE:

"Last month we completed environmental assessments at three locations:

- A gas refinery in Dallas, Texas;
- The site of a former chemical plant in Little Rock, Arkansas; and
- A waste pit outside of Baton Rouge, Louisiana."

Option C: Treat each item like a separate sentence. When items in a list are complete sentences, you may want to punctuate each one like a separate sentence, placing a period at the end of each. You *must* choose this option when one or more of your listed items contain more than one sentence. EXAMPLE:

"The main conclusions of our preliminary assessment are summarized here:

- At five of the six borehole locations, petroleum hydrocarbons were detected at concentrations greater than a background concentration of 10 mg/kg.
- No PCB concentrations were detected in the subsurface soils we analyzed. We will continue the testing, as discussed in our proposal.
- Sampling and testing should be restarted three weeks from the date of this report."

Sic

Latin for "thus," this word is most often used when a quoted passage contains an error or other point that might be questioned by the reader. Inserted within brackets, "sic" shows the reader that the error was included in the original passage—and that it was not introduced by you. EXAMPLE: "The customer's letter to our sales department claimed that 'there are too [sic] or three main flaws in the product.' "

Spelling

All writers find at least some words difficult to spell, and some writers have major problems with spelling. Automatic spell-checking software helps solve the problem. Yet you still need to remain vigilant during the proofreading stage. One or more misspelled words in an otherwise well-written document may cause readers to question professionalism in other areas.

This entry includes a list of commonly misspelled words. However, you should keep your own list of words you most frequently have trouble spelling. Like most writers, you probably have a relatively short list of words that give you repeated difficulty.

absence	acquaintance	arctic	bulletin
accessible	admittance	athlete	calendar
accommodate	advisable	athletic	career
accumulate	aisle	awful	changeable
accustomed	allotting	basically	channel
achievement	analysis	believable	column
acknowledgment	analyze	benefited	commitment

committee	foresee	lightning	profession
compatible	forfeit	likely	professor
compelled	forty	loneliness	pronunciation
conscience	fourth	maintenance	publicly
conscientious	genius	manageable	quantity
conscious	government	maneuver	questionnaire
controlled	guarantee	mathematics	recession
convenient	guidance	medieval	reference
definitely	handicapped	mileage	safety
dependable	harass	miscellaneous	similar
descend	height	misspelled	sincerely
dilemma	illogical	mortgage	specifically
disappear	incidentally	movable	subtle
disappoint	independence	necessary	temperament
disaster	indispensable	noticeable	temperature
disastrous	ingenious	nuisance	thorough
efficient	initially	numerous	tolerance
eligible	initiative	occasionally	transferred
embarrass	insistence	occurred	truly
endurance	interfered	occurrence	undoubtedly
environment	interference	omission	unmistakably
equipment	interrupt	pamphlet	until
equipped	irrelevant	parallel	useful
essential	judgment	pastime	usually
exaggerate	knowledge	peculiar	valuable
existence	later	possess	various
experience	latter	practically	vehicle
familiar	liable	preference	wholly
favorite	liaison	preferred	writing
February	library	privilege	written
foreign			

Subject-Verb Agreement

Subject-verb agreement errors are quite common in technical writing. They occur when writers fail to make the subject of a clause agree in number with the verb. EXAMPLE: "The nature of the diverse geological deposits are explained in the report." (The verb should be "is," since the singular subject is "nature.")

Writers who tend to make these errors should devote special attention to them. Specifically, isolate the subjects and verbs of all the clauses in a document and make certain that they agree. Here are seven specific rules for making subjects agree with verbs:

■ *Rule 1: Subjects Connected by "And" Take Plural Verbs*

This rule applies to two or more words or phrases that, together, form one subject phrase. EXAMPLE: "The site preparation section and the foundation design portion of the report are to be written by the same person."

■ *Rule 2: Verbs After "Either/Or" Agree with the Nearest Subject*

Subject words connected by "either" or "or" confuse many writers, but the rule is very clear. Your verb choice depends on the subject nearest the verb. EXAMPLE: "He told his group that neither the three reports nor the proposal was to be sent to the client that week."

■ *Rule 3: Verbs Agree with the Subject, Not with the Subjective Complement*

Sometimes called a predicate noun or adjective, a subjective complement renames the subject and occurs after verbs such as "is," "was," "are," and "were." EXAMPLE: "The theme of our proposal is our successful projects in that region of the state." But the same rule would permit this usage: "Successful projects in that part of the state are the theme we intend to emphasize in the proposal."

■ *Rule 4: Prepositional Phrases Do Not Affect Matters of Agreement*

"As long as," "in addition to," "as well as," and "along with" are prepositions, not conjunctions. A verb agrees with its subject, not with the object of a prepositional phrase. EXAMPLE: "The manager of human resources, along with the personnel director, is supposed to meet with the three applicants."

■ *Rule 5: Collective Nouns Usually Take Singular Verbs*

Collective nouns have singular form but usually refer to a group of persons or things (for example, "team," "committee," or "crew"). When a collective noun refers to a group as a whole, use a singular verb. EXAMPLE: "The project crew was ready to complete the assignment." Occasionally, a collective noun refers to the members of the group acting in their separate capacities. In this case, either use a plural verb or, to avoid awkwardness, reword the sentence. EXAMPLE: "The crew were not in agreement about the site locations." Or, "Members of the crew were not in agreement about the site locations."

■ *Rule 6: Foreign Plurals Usually Take Plural Verbs*

Although usage is gradually changing, most careful writers still use plural verbs with "data," "strata," "phenomena," "media," and other irregular plurals. EXAMPLE: "The data he asked for in the request for proposal are incorporated into the three tables."

■ *Rule 7: Indefinite Pronouns Like "Each" and "Anyone" Take Singular Verbs*

Writers often fail to follow this rule when they make the verb agree with the object of a prepositional phrase, instead of with the subject. EXAMPLE: "Each of the committee members are ready to adjourn" (incorrect). "Each of the committee members is ready to adjourn" (correct).

To/Too/Two

"To" is part of the infinitive verb form *or* is a preposition in a prepositional phrase. "Too" is an adverb that suggests an excessive amount *or* that means "also." "Two" .is a noun or an adjective that stands for the numeral "2." EXAMPLES:

- "He volunteered *to* go [infinitive verb] *to* Alaska [prepositional phrase] *to* work [another infinitive verb form] on the project."
- "Stephanie explained that the proposed hazardous-waste dump would pose *too* many risks *to* the water supply. Scott made this point, *too.*"

Utilize/Use

"Utilize" is simply a long form for the preferred verb "use." Although some verbs that end in "-ize" are useful words, most are simply wordy substitutes for shorter forms. As some writing teachers say, "Why use 'utilize' when you can use 'use.' "

Who/Whom

These two words give writers (and speakers) fits, but the importance of their correct use probably has been exaggerated. If you want to be one who uses them properly, remember this basic point: "Who" is a subjective form that can only be used in the subject slot of a clause; "whom" is an objective form that can only be used as a direct object or other nonsubject noun form of a sentence. EXAMPLES:

- "The man *who* you said called me yesterday is a good customer of the firm." (The clause "who . . . called me yesterday" modifies "man." Within this clause, "who" is the subject of the verb "called." Note that the subject role of "who" is not affected by the two words "you said," which interrupt the clause.)
- "They could not remember the name of the person *whom* they interviewed." (The clause "whom they interviewed" modifies "person." Within this clause, "whom" is the direct object of the verb "interviewed.")

EXERCISE 1: GRAMMAR AND MECHANICS

The following passages contain a variety of grammatical and mechanical errors covered in the handbook. The major focus is punctuation. Rewrite each passage.

1. Some concerns regarding plumbing design are mentioned in our report, however, no unusual design problems are expected.
2. An estimate of the total charges for an audit and for three site visits are based on our standard fee schedules.
3. The drill bit was efficient cheap and available.
4. The plan unless we have completely misjudged it, will increase sales markedly.
5. Our proposal contains design information for these two parts of the project; Phase 1 (evaluating the 3 computers) and Phase 2 (installing the computer selected).
6. If conditions require the use of all-terrain equipment to reach the construction locations, this will increase the cost of the project slightly.
7. An asbestos survey was beyond the scope of this project, if you want one, we would be happy to submit a proposal.
8. Jones-Simon Company, the owners of the new building, were informed of the problem with the foundation.
9. Also provided is the number and type of tests to be given at the office.
10. Calculating the standard usages by the current purchase order prices result in a downward adjustment of $.065.
11. Data showing the standard uses of the steel, including allowances for scrap, waste and end pieces of the tube rolls, are included for your convenience at the end of this report in Table 7.
12. This equipment has not been in operation for 3 months, and therefore, its condition could not be determined by a quick visual inspection.
13. Arthur Jones Manager of the Atlanta branch wrote that three proposals had been accepted.
14. The generator that broke yesterday has been shipped to Tampa already by Harry Thompson.
15. The first computer lasted eight years the second two years.
16. He wants one thing out of their work speed.
17. On 25 September 1993 the papers were signed.
18. On March 23 1993 the proposal was accepted.
19. The meeting was held in Columbus the Capital of Ohio.
20. McDuff, Inc. completed its Indonesia project in record time.
21. He decided to write for the brochure then he changed his mind.
22. Interest by the Kettering Hospital staff in the development of a masterplan for the new building wings have been expressed.
23. However much he wants to work for Gasion engineering he will turn the job down if he has to move to another state.
24. 35 computer scientists attended the convention, but only eleven of them were from private industry.
25. Working at a high salary gives him some satisfaction still he would like more emotional satisfaction from his job.
26. His handwriting is almost unreadable therefore his secretary asked him to dictate letters.
27. Any major city especially one that is as large as Chicago is bound to have problems with mass transit.

Limited Use License Agreement

This is the John Wiley and Sons, Inc. (Wiley) limited use License Agreement, which governs your use of any Wiley proprietary software products (Licensed Program) and User Manual (s) delivered with it.

Your use of the Licensed Program indicates your acceptance of the terms and conditions of this Agreement. If you do not accept or agree with them, you must return the Licensed Program unused within 30 days of receipt or, if purchased, within 30 days, as evidenced by a copy of your receipt, in which case, the purchase price will b[...]

License: Wiley hereby grants you, and you accept, a non-exclusive and [...] ensed Program and User Manual (s) on the following terms and conditions only:

a. The Licensed Program and User Manual(s) are for your personal use only.
b. You may use the Licensed Program on a single computer, or on its temporary replacement, or on a subsequent computer only.
c. The Licensed Program may be copied to a single computer hard drive for playing.
d. A backup copy or copies may be made only as provided by the User Manual(s), except as expressly permitted by this Agreement.
e. You may not use the Licensed Program on more than one computer system, make or distribute unauthorized copies of the Licensed Program or User Manual(s), create by decompilation or otherwise the source code of the Licensed Program or use, copy, modify, or transfer the Licensed Program, in whole or in part, or User Manual(s), except as expressly permitted by this Agreement. If you transfer possession of any copy or modification of the Licensed Program to any third party, your license is automatically terminated. Such termination shall be in addition to and not in lieu of any equitable, civil, or other remedies available to Wiley.

Term: This License Agreement is effective until terminated. You may terminate it at any time by destroying the Licensed Program and User Manual together with all copies made (with or without authorization).
This Agreement will also terminate upon the conditions discussed elsewhere in this Agreement, or if you fail to comply with any term or condition of this Agreement. Upon such termination, you agree to destroy the Licensed Program, User Manual (s), and any copies made (with or without authorization) of either.

Wiley's Rights: You acknowledge that all rights (including without limitation, copyrights, patents and trade secrets) in the Licensed Program (including without limitation, the structure, sequence, organization, flow, logic, source code, object code and all means and forms of operation of the Licensed Program) are the sole and exclusive property of Wiley. By accepting this Agreement, you do not become the owner of the Licensed Program, but you do have the right to use it in accordance with the provisions of this Agreement. You agree to protect the Licensed Program from unauthorized use, reproduction, or distribution. You further acknowledge that the Licensed Program contains valuable trade secrets and confidential information belonging to Wiley. You may not disclose any component of the Licensed Program, whether or not in machine readable form, except as expressly provided in this Agreement.

WARRANTY: TO THE ORIGINAL LICENSEE ONLY, WILEY WARRANTS THAT THE MEDIA ON WHICH THE LICENSED PROGRAM IS FURNISHED ARE FREE FROM DEFECTS IN THE MATERIAL AND WORKMANSHIP UNDER NORMAL USE FOR A PERIOD OF NINETY (90) DAYS FROM THE DATE OF PURCHASE OR RECEIPT AS EVIDENCED BY A COPY OF YOUR RECEIPT. IF DURING THE 90 DAY PERIOD, A DEFECT IN ANY MEDIA OCCURS, YOU MAY RETURN IT. WILEY WILL REPLACE THE DEFECTIVE MEDIA WITHOUT CHARGE TO YOU. YOUR SOLE AND EXCLUSIVE REMEDY IN THE EVENT OF A DEFECT IS EXPRESSLY LIMITED TO REPLACEMENT OF THE DEFECTIVE MEDIA AT NO ADDITIONAL CHARGE. THIS WARRANTY DOES NOT APPLY TO DAMAGE OR DEFECTS DUE TO IMPROPER USE OR NEGLIGENCE. THIS LIMITED WARRANTY IS IN LIEU OF ALL OTHER WARRANTIES, EXPRESSED OR IMPLIED, INCLUDING, WITHOUT LIMITATION, ANY WARRANTIES OF MERCHANTABILITY OR FITNESS FOR A PARTICULAR PURPOSE.
EXCEPT AS SPECIFIED ABOVE, THE LICENSED PROGRAM AND USER MANUAL(S) ARE FURNISHED BY WILEY ON AN "AS IS" BASIS AND WITHOUT WARRANTY AS TO THE PERFORMANCE OR RESULTS YOU MAY OBTAIN BY USING THE LICENSED PROGRAM AND USER MANUAL(S). THE ENTIRE RISK AS TO THE RESULTS OR PERFORMANCE, AND THE COST OF ALL NECESSARY SERVICING, REPAIR, OR CORRECTION OF THE LICENSED PROGRAM AND USER MANUAL(S) IS ASSUMED BY YOU.
IN NO EVENT WILL WILEY OR THE AUTHOR, BE LIABLE TO YOU FOR ANY DAMAGES, INCLUDING LOST PROFITS, LOST SAVINGS, OR OTHER INCIDENTAL OR CONSEQUENTIAL DAMAGES ARISING OUT OF THE USE OR INABILITY TO USE THE LICENSED PROGRAM OR USER MANUAL(S), EVEN IF WILEY OR AN AUTHORIZED WILEY DEALER HAS BEEN ADVISED OF THE POSSIBILITY OF SUCH DAMAGES.

General: This Limited Warranty gives you specific legal rights. You may have others by operation of law which varies from state to state. If any of the provisions of this Agreement are invalid under any applicable statute or rule of law, they are to that extent deemed omitted. This Agreement represents the entire agreement between us and supersedes any proposals or prior Agreements, oral or written, and any other communication between us relating to the subject matter of this Agreement.
This Agreement will be governed and construed as if wholly entered into and performed within the State of New York. You acknowledge that you have read this Agreement, and agree to be bound by its terms and conditions.

A Brief Introduction to Fluid Mechanics

Second Edition

DONALD F. YOUNG
BRUCE R. MUNSON

Department of Aerospace Engineering
and Engineering Mechanics

THEODORE H. OKIISHI

Department of Mechanical Engineering
Iowa State University
Ames, Iowa, USA

JOHN WILEY & SONS, INC.

New York   **Chichester**   **Brisbane**   **Toronto**   **Singapore**   **Weinheim**

ASSISTANT EDITOR   Penny Perrotto

ACQUISITIONS EDITOR   Wayne Anderson

MARKETING MANAGER   Katherine Hepburn

PRODUCTION SERVICES MANAGER   Jeanine Furino

COVER DESIGNER   Lynn Rogan

COVER PHOTO   Steve Gettle/ENP Images

ILLUSTRATION EDITOR   Gene Aiello

PHOTO EDITOR   Nicole Horlacher

PRODUCTION MANAGEMENT SERVICES   York Production Services

This book was set in Times Roman by York Graphic Services and printed and bound by R.R. Donnelley & Sons. The cover was printed by Phoenix Color Corp.

This book was printed on acid-free paper. ∞

Library of Congress Cataloging in Publication Data:
Young, Donald F.
  A brief introduction to fluid mechanics / Donald F. Young, Bruce R. Munson, Theodore
H. Okiishi—2nd ed.
    p. cm.
  Includes bibliographical references.
  ISBN 0-471-36243-3 (alk. paper)
    1. Fluid mechanics. I. Munson, Bruce Roy, 1940– II. Okiishi, T. H. (Theodore Hisao),
1939– III. Title.

TA357.Y68 2000
620.1′06–dc21   00-025726

Printed in the United States of America

10 9 8 7 6 5 4 3 2 1

About the Authors

Donald F. Young, Anson Marston Distinguished Professor Emeritus in Engineering, is a faculty member in the Department of Aerospace Engineering and Engineering Mechanics at Iowa State University. Dr. Young received his B.S. degree in mechanical engineering, his M.S. and Ph.D. degrees in theoretical and applied mechanics from Iowa State, and has taught both undergraduate and graduate courses in fluid mechanics for many years. In addition to being named a Distinguished Professor in the College of Engineering, Dr. Young has also received the Standard Oil Foundation Outstanding Teacher Award and the Iowa State University Alumni Association Faculty Citation. He has been engaged in fluid mechanics research for more than 45 years, with special interests in similitude and modeling and the interdisciplinary field of biomedical fluid mechanics. Dr. Young has contributed to many technical publications and is the author or coauthor of two textbooks on applied mechanics. He is a Fellow of The American Society of Mechanical Engineers.

Bruce R. Munson, Professor of Engineering Mechanics at Iowa State University since 1974, received his B.S. and M.S. degrees from Purdue University and his Ph.D. degree from the Aerospace Engineering and Mechanics Department of the University of Minnesota in 1970.

From 1970 to 1974, Dr. Munson was on the mechanical engineering faculty of Duke University. From 1964 to 1966, he worked as an engineer in the jet engine fuel control department of Bendix Aerospace Corporation, South Bend, Indiana.

Dr. Munson's main professional activity has been in the area of fluid mechanics education and research. He has been responsible for the development of many fluid mechanics courses for studies in civil engineering, mechanical engineering, engineering science, and agricultural engineering and is the recipient of an Iowa State University Superior Engineering Teacher Award and the Iowa State University Alumni Association Faculty Citation.

He has authored and coauthored many theoretical and experimental technical papers on hydrodynamic stability, low Reynolds number flow, secondary flow, and the applications of viscous incompressible flow. He is a member of The American Society of Mechanical Engineers, The American Physical Society, and The American Society for Engineering Education.

Theodore H. Okiishi, Associate Dean of Engineering and past Chair of Mechanical Engineering at Iowa State University, has taught fluid mechanics courses there since 1967. He received his undergraduate and graduate degrees at Iowa State.

From 1965 to 1967, Dr. Okiishi served as a U.S. Army officer with duty assignments at the National Aeronautics and Space Administration Lewis Research Center, Cleveland, Ohio, where he participated in rocket nozzle heat transfer research, and at the Combined Intelligence Center, Saigon, Republic of South Vietnam, where he studied seasonal river flooding problems.

Professor Okiishi is active in research on turbomachinery fluid dynamics. He and his graduate students and other colleagues have written a number of journal articles based on their studies. Some of these projects have involved significant collaboration with government and industrial laboratory researchers with one technical paper winning the ASME Melville Medal.

Dr. Okiishi has received several awards for teaching. He has developed undergraduate and graduate courses in classical fluid dynamics as well as the fluid dynamics of turbomachines.

He is a licensed professional engineer. His technical society activities include having been chair of the board of directors of The American Society of Mechanical Engineers (ASME) International Gas Turbine Institute. He is a fellow member of the ASME and the technical editor of the *Journal of Turbomachinery*.

Preface

A Brief Introduction to Fluid Mechanics, second edition, is an abridged version of a more comprehensive treatment found in *Fundamentals of Fluid Mechanics* by Munson, Young, and Okiishi. Although this latter work continues to be successfully received by students and colleagues, it is a large volume containing much more material than can be covered in a typical one-semester undergraduate fluid mechanics course. A consideration of the numerous fluid mechanics texts that have been written during the past several decades reveals that there is a definite trend toward larger and larger books. This trend is understandable because the knowledge base in fluid mechanics has increased, along with the desire to include a broader scope of topics in an undergraduate course. Unfortunately, one of the dangers in this trend is that these large books can become intimidating to students who may have difficulty, in a beginning course, focusing on basic principles without getting lost in peripheral material. It is with this background in mind that the authors felt that a shorter but comprehensive text, covering the basic concepts and principles of fluid mechanics in a modern style, was needed. In this abridged version there is still more than ample material for a one-semester undergraduate fluid mechanics course. We have made every effort to retain the principal features of the original book while presenting the essential material in a more concise and focused manner that will be helpful to the beginning student.

This second edition has been prepared by the authors after several years of using the first edition for an introductory course in fluid mechanics. Based on this experience, along with suggestions from reviewers, colleagues, and students, we have made a number of changes in this new edition. Many of these are minor and have been made to simply clarify or expand certain ideas or concepts. Major changes include the addition of many new problems, the addition of a concise chapter on turbomachines, and a supplement in the form of a

CD containing short video segments that illustrate various aspects of "real-world" fluid mechanics.

One of our aims remains to represent fluid mechanics as it really is—an exciting and useful discipline. To this end, we include analyses of numerous everyday examples of fluid flow phenomena to which students and faculty can easily relate. One hundred examples are presented that provide detailed solutions to a variety of problems. Also, a generous set of homework problems in each chapter stresses the practical application of principles. Those problems that can best be worked with a programmable calculator or a computer are also identified. In addition, several open-ended problems that do not provide all the information required to solve the problem are included in most chapters. Students are thus required to make reasonable estimates or obtain additional information outside the classroom. These open-ended problems are clearly identified. Another feature is the inclusion of extended, laboratory-type problems in most chapters. Actual experimental data are included in these problems, and the student is asked to perform a detailed analysis of the problem similar to that required for a typical laboratory. It is believed that this type of problem will be particularly useful for fluid mechanics courses where a laboratory is not part of the course. These laboratory-type problems are located at the end of the problems section in most chapters and can be easily recognized.

Two systems of units continue to be used throughout the text: the British Gravitational System (pounds, slugs, feet, and seconds) and the International System of Units (newtons, kilograms, meters, and seconds).

In the first four chapters, the student is made aware of some fundamental aspects of fluid mechanics, including important fluid properties, regimes of flow, pressure variations in fluids at rest and in motion, fluid kinematics, and methods of flow description and analysis. The Bernoulli equation is introduced in Chapter 3 to draw attention, early on, to some of the interesting effects of fluid motion on the distribution of pressure in a flow field.

Chapters 5, 6, and 7 expand on the basic analysis methods generally used to solve or to begin solving fluid mechanics problems. Emphasis is placed on understanding how flow phenomena are described mathematically and on when and how to use infinitesimal and finite control volumes. Experiments or tests must be relied on when mathematical analysis alone is inadequate to solve a problem. The advantages of using dimensional analysis and similitude for organizing test data and for planning experiments and the basic techniques involved are featured in Chapter 7.

Chapters 8, 9, and 10 offer students opportunities for further application of the principles learned early in the text. These include practical concerns such as pipe flow, open-channel flow, flow measurement, drag and lift. Also, where appropriate, additional important notions such as boundary layers, transition from laminar to turbulent flow, and flow separation are introduced. **A major new feature of the second edition is the addition of Chapter 11—Turbomachines.** This new chapter, in keeping with the general philosophy of the rest of the book, is presented in a concise fashion with emphasis on the fluid mechanics fundamentals associated with turbomachines, particularly pumps and turbines.

A new supplement for the second edition is the *Fluid Mechanics Phenomena* **CD containing seventy-five short video segments that illustrate various aspects of fluid mechanics.** Many of the segments show how fluid mechanics is related to familiar devices and everyday experiences. A short text included with each segment indicates the key fluid mechanics topic being demonstrated and provides a brief description of the content. Each video segment is identified in the textbook by an icon of the type shown in the margin. These icons

V2.3 Hoover dam

are located so that the various video segments are associated with the fluid mechanics concepts and theory discussed in the textbook at that location. The number with the icon identifies the segment, e.g., V2.3 refers to video segment number 3 in Chapter 2, and the video title is also included. Many of the new problems that have been added refer to the video segments so that the student can more closely associate a specific problem with actual fluid mechanics phenomena. These "video-related" problems are clearly identified.

An Instructor's Manual containing complete, detailed solutions to all the problems in the text is available to professors who adopt this book for classroom use.

We express our thanks to the many colleagues who have helped in the development of this text. We are indebted to the following reviewers for their comments and suggestions: Professors Frank Chambers, Oklahoma State University; Robert Medrow, University of Missouri-Rolla; Ronald Flack, University of Virginia; Dick Desautel, San Jose State University; Doyle Knight, Rutgers University; and Young Cho, Drexel University. We also thank our families for their continued support and encouragement during the writing of this second edition.

We hope that this new, concise introduction to fluid mechanics will be appealing to students and will make the material more readily accessible to them. Our goal has been to develop a unique, user-friendly, introductory text that clearly focuses on the essential aspects of the subject. Any suggestions for improvements from you, the user, are certainly welcome.

Donald F. Young
Bruce R. Munson
Theodore H. Okiishi

Contents

*I*ntroduction

*F*luid mechanics is that discipline within the broad field of applied mechanics concerned with the behavior of liquids and gases at rest or in motion. This field of mechanics obviously encompasses a vast array of problems that may vary from the study of blood flow in the capillaries (which are only a few microns in diameter) to the flow of crude oil across Alaska through an 800-mile-long, 4-ft-diameter pipe. Fluid mechanics principles are needed to explain why airplanes are made streamlined with smooth surfaces for the most efficient flight, whereas golf balls are made with rough surfaces (dimpled) to increase their efficiency. It is very likely that during your career as an engineer you will be involved in the analysis and design of systems that require a good understanding of fluid mechanics. It is hoped that this introductory text will provide a sound foundation of the fundamental aspects of fluid mechanics.

1.1   Some Characteristics of Fluids

One of the first questions we need to explore is—what is a fluid? Or we might ask—what is the difference between a solid and a fluid? We have a general, vague idea of the difference. A solid is "hard" and not easily deformed, whereas a fluid is "soft" and is easily deformed

Viscous shear stresses between a moving layer of fluid and fluid within a cavity produce a swirl motion within the cavity. (Particles in oil; time exposure.) (Photograph by B. R. Munson.)

(we can readily move through air). Although quite descriptive, these casual observations of the differences between solids and fluids are not very satisfactory from a scientific or engineering point of view. A more specific distinction is based on how materials deform under the action of an external load. *A fluid is defined as a substance that deforms continuously when acted on by a shearing stress of any magnitude.* A shearing stress (force per unit area) is created whenever a tangential force acts on a surface. When common solids such as steel or other metals are acted on by a shearing stress, they will initially deform (usually a very small deformation), but they will not continuously deform (flow). However, common fluids such as water, oil, and air satisfy the definition of a fluid—that is, they will flow when acted on by a shearing stress. Some materials, such as slurries, tar, putty, toothpaste, and so on, are not easily classified since they will behave as a solid if the applied shearing stress is small, but if the stress exceeds some critical value, the substance will flow. The study of such materials is called *rheology,* and does not fall within the province of classical fluid mechanics.

Although the molecular structure of fluids is important in distinguishing one fluid from another, it is not possible to study the behavior of individual molecules when trying to describe the behavior of fluids at rest or in motion. Rather, we characterize the behavior by considering the average, or macroscopic, value of the quantity of interest, where the average is evaluated over a small volume containing a large number of molecules.

We thus assume that all the fluid characteristics we are interested in (pressure, velocity, etc) vary continuously throughout the fluid—that is, we treat the fluid as a *continuum.* This concept will certainly be valid for all the circumstances considered in this text.

1.2   Dimensions, Dimensional Homogeneity, and Units

Since in our study of fluid mechanics we will be dealing with a variety of fluid characteristics, it is necessary to develop a system for describing these characteristics both *qualitatively* and *quantitatively.* The qualitative aspect serves to identify the nature, or type, of the characteristics (such as length, time, stress, and velocity), whereas the quantitative aspect provides a numerical measure of the characteristics. The quantitative description requires both a number and a standard by which various quantities can be compared. A standard for length might be a meter or foot, for time an hour or second, and for mass a slug or kilogram. Such standards are called *units,* and several systems of units are in common use as described in the following section. The qualitative description is conveniently given in terms of certain *primary quantities*, such as length, L, time, T, mass, M, and temperature, Θ. These primary quantities can then be used to provide a qualitative description of any other *secondary quantity*, for example, area $\doteq L^2$, velocity $\doteq LT^{-1}$, density $\doteq ML^{-3}$, and so on, where the symbol $\doteq$ is used to indicate the *dimensions* of the secondary quantity in terms of the primary quantities. Thus, to describe qualitatively a velocity, V, we would write

$$V \doteq LT^{-1}$$

and say that "the dimensions of a velocity equal length divided by time." The primary quantities are also referred to as *basic dimensions.*

For a wide variety of problems involving fluid mechanics, only the three basic dimensions, L, T, and M are required. Alternatively, L, T, and F could be used, where F is the basic dimension of force. Since Newton's law states that force is equal to mass times acceleration, it follows that $F \doteq MLT^{-2}$ or $M \doteq FL^{-1}T^2$. Thus, secondary quantities expressed in terms of M can be expressed in terms of F through the relationship above. For example, stress, σ, is a force per unit area, so that $\sigma \doteq FL^{-2}$, but an equivalent dimensional equation is $\sigma \doteq ML^{-1}T^{-2}$. Table 1.1 provides a list of dimensions for a number of common physical quantities.

All theoretically derived equations are *dimensionally homogeneous*—that is, the dimensions of the left side of the equation must be the same as those on the right side, and all additive separate terms must have the same dimensions. We accept as a fundamental premise

■ **TABLE 1.1**
Dimensions Associated with Common Physical Quantities

	FLT System	MLT System
Acceleration	LT^{-2}	LT^{-2}
Angle	$F^0L^0T^0$	$M^0L^0T^0$
Angular acceleration	T^{-2}	T^{-2}
Angular velocity	T^{-1}	T^{-1}
Area	L^2	L^2
Density	$FL^{-4}T^2$	ML^{-3}
Energy	FL	ML^2T^{-2}
Force	F	MLT^{-2}
Frequency	T^{-1}	T^{-1}
Heat	FL	ML^2T^{-2}
Length	L	L
Mass	$FL^{-1}T^2$	M
Modulus of elasticity	FL^{-2}	$ML^{-1}T^{-2}$
Moment of a force	FL	ML^2T^{-2}
Moment of inertia (area)	L^4	L^4
Moment of inertia (mass)	FLT^2	ML^2
Momentum	FT	MLT^{-1}
Power	FLT^{-1}	ML^2T^{-3}
Pressure	FL^{-2}	$ML^{-1}T^{-2}$
Specific heat	$L^2T^{-2}\Theta^{-1}$	$L^2T^{-2}\Theta^{-1}$
Specific weight	FL^{-3}	$ML^{-2}T^{-2}$
Strain	$F^0L^0T^0$	$M^0L^0T^0$
Stress	FL^{-2}	$ML^{-1}T^{-2}$
Surface tension	FL^{-1}	MT^{-2}
Temperature	Θ	Θ
Time	T	T
Torque	FL	ML^2T^{-2}
Velocity	LT^{-1}	LT^{-1}
Viscosity (dynamic)	$FL^{-2}T$	$ML^{-1}T^{-1}$
Viscosity (kinematic)	L^2T^{-1}	L^2T^{-1}
Volume	L^3	L^3
Work	FL	ML^2T^{-2}

that all equations describing physical phenomena must be dimensionally homogeneous. For example, the equation for the velocity, V, of a uniformly accelerated body is

$$V = V_0 + at \tag{1.1}$$

where V_0 is the initial velocity, a the acceleration, and t the time interval. In terms of dimensions the equation is

$$LT^{-1} \doteq LT^{-1} + LT^{-1}$$

and thus Eq. 1.1 is dimensionally homogeneous.

Some equations that are known to be valid contain constants having dimensions. The equation for the distance, d, traveled by a freely falling body can be written as

$$d = 16.1t^2 \tag{1.2}$$

and a check of the dimensions reveals that the constant must have the dimensions of LT^{-2} if the equation is to be dimensionally homogeneous. Actually, Eq. 1.2 is a special form of the well-known equation from physics for freely falling bodies,

$$d = \frac{gt^2}{2} \tag{1.3}$$

in which g is the acceleration of gravity. Equation 1.3 is dimensionally homogeneous and valid in any system of units. For $g = 32.2\,\text{ft/s}^2$ the equation reduces to Eq. 1.2 and thus Eq. 1.2 is valid only for the system of units using feet and seconds. Equations that are restricted to a particular system of units can be denoted as *restricted homogeneous equations,* as opposed to equations valid in any system of units, which are *general homogeneous equations.* The concept of dimensions also forms the basis for the powerful tool of *dimensional analysis,* which is considered in detail in Chapter 7.

*E*XAMPLE 1.1

A commonly used equation for determining the volume rate of flow, Q, of a liquid through an orifice located in the side of a tank is

$$Q = 0.61\,A\sqrt{2gh}$$

where A is the area of the orifice, g is the acceleration of gravity, and h is the height of the liquid above the orifice. Investigate the dimensional homogeneity of this formula.

*S*OLUTION

The dimensions of the various terms in the equation are

$$Q = \text{volume/time} \doteq L^3 T^{-1}$$
$$A = \text{area} \doteq L^2$$
$$g = \text{acceleration of gravity} \doteq LT^{-2}$$
$$h = \text{height} \doteq L$$

These terms, when substituted into the equation, yield the dimensional form:

$$(L^3T^{-1}) \doteq (0.61)(L^2)(\sqrt{2})(LT^{-2})^{1/2}(L)^{1/2}$$

or

$$(L^3T^{-1}) \doteq [(0.61)\sqrt{2}](L^3T^{-1})$$

It is clear from this result that the equation is dimensionally homogeneous (both sides of the formula have the same dimensions of L^3T^{-1}), and the numbers (0.61 and $\sqrt{2}$) are dimensionless.

If we were going to use this relationship repeatedly we might be tempted to simplify it by replacing g with its standard value of 32.2 ft/s^2 and rewriting the formula as

$$Q = 4.90\,A\sqrt{h} \tag{1}$$

A quick check of the dimensions reveals that

$$L^3T^{-1} \doteq (4.90)(L^{5/2})$$

and, therefore, the equation expressed as Eq. 1 can only be dimensionally correct if the number, 4.90, has the dimensions of $L^{1/2}T^{-1}$. Whenever a number appearing in an equation or formula has dimensions, it means that the specific value of the number will depend on the system of units used. Thus, for the case being considered with feet and seconds used as units, the number 4.90 has units of ft$^{1/2}$/s. Equation 1 will only give the correct value for Q (in ft^3/s) when A is expressed in square feet and h in feet. Thus, Eq. 1 is a *restricted* homogeneous equation, whereas the original equation is a *general* homogeneous equation that would be valid for any consistent system of units. A quick check of the dimensions of the various terms in an equation is a useful practice and will often be helpful in eliminating errors—that is, as noted previously, all physically meaningful equations must be dimensionally homogeneous. We have briefly alluded to units in this example, and this important topic will be considered in more detail in the next section.

1.2.1 Systems of Units

In addition to the qualitative description of the various quantities of interest, it is generally necessary to have a quantitative measure of any given quantity. For example, if we measure the width of this page in the book and say that it is 10 units wide, the statement has no meaning until the unit of length is defined. If we indicate that the unit of length is a meter, and define the meter as some standard length, a unit system for length has been established (and a numerical value can be given to the page width). In addition to length, a unit must be established for each of the remaining basic quantities (force, mass, time, and temperature). There are several systems of units in use and we shall consider two systems that are commonly used in engineering.

British Gravitational (BG) System. In the BG system the unit of length is the foot (ft), the time unit is the second (s), the force unit is the pound (lb), and the temperature unit is the degree Fahrenheit (°F), or the absolute temperature unit is the degree Rankine (°R), where

$$°R = °F + 459.67$$

The mass unit, called the *slug,* is defined from Newton's second law (force = mass ×
acceleration) as

$$1 \text{ lb} = (1 \text{ slug})(1 \text{ ft/s}^2)$$

This relationship indicates that a 1-lb force acting on a mass of 1 slug will give the mass an
acceleration of 1 ft/s^2.

The weight, $\mathcal{W}$ (which is the force due to gravity, g) of a mass, m, is given by the
equation

$$\mathcal{W} = mg$$

and in BG units

$$\mathcal{W} \text{ (lb)} = m \text{ (slugs) } g \text{ (ft/s}^2)$$

Since the earth's standard gravity is taken as $g = 32.174$ ft/s^2 (commonly approximated as
32.2 ft/s^2), it follows that a mass of 1 slug weighs 32.2 lb under standard gravity.

International System (SI).   In 1960 the Eleventh General Conference on Weights
and Measures, the international organization responsible for maintaining precise uniform
standards of measurements, formally adopted the *International System of Units* as the international standard. This system, commonly termed SI, has been widely adopted worldwide
and is widely used (although certainly not exclusively) in the United States. It is expected
that the long-term trend will be for all countries to accept SI as the accepted standard and it
is imperative that engineering students become familiar with this system. In SI the unit of
length is the meter (m), the time unit is the second (s), the mass unit is the kilogram (kg),
and the temperature unit is the kelvin (K). Note that there is no degree symbol used when
expressing a temperature in kelvin units. The Kelvin temperature scale is an absolute scale
and is related to the Celsius (centigrade) scale (°C) through the relationship

$$K = {}^\circ C + 273.15$$

Although the Celsius scale is not in itself part of SI, it is common practice to specify temperatures in degrees Celsius when using SI units.

The force unit, called the newton (N), is defined from Newton's second law as

$$1 \text{ N} = (1 \text{ kg})(1 \text{ m/s}^2)$$

Thus, a 1-N force acting on a 1-kg mass will give the mass an acceleration of 1 m/s^2. Standard gravity in SI is 9.807 m/s^2 (commonly approximated as 9.81 m/s^2) so that a 1-kg mass
weighs 9.81 N under standard gravity. Note that weight and mass are different, both qualitatively and quantitatively! The unit of *work* in SI is the joule (J), which is the work done
when the point of application of a 1-N force is displaced through a 1-m distance in the direction of the force. Thus,

$$1 \text{ J} = 1 \text{ N} \cdot \text{m}$$

The unit of *power* is the watt (W) defined as a joule per second. Thus,

$$1 \text{ W} = 1 \text{ J/s} = 1 \text{ N} \cdot \text{m/s}$$

Prefixes for forming multiples and fractions of SI units are commonly used. For example, the notation kN would be read as "kilonewtons" and stands for 10^{3}N. Similarly, mm
would be read as "millimeters" and stands for 10^{-3}m. The centimeter is not an accepted unit

■ **TABLE 1.2**
Conversion Factors from BG Units to SI Units

(See inside of back cover.)

■ **TABLE 1.3**
Conversion Factors from SI Units to BG Units

(See inside of back cover.)

of length in the SI system, and for most problems in fluid mechanics in which SI units are used, lengths will be expressed in millimeters or meters.

In this text we will use the BG system and SI for units. Approximately one-half the problems and examples are given in BG units and one-half in SI units. Tables 1.2 and 1.3 provide conversion factors for some quantities that are commonly encountered in fluid mechanics, and these tables are located on the inside of the back cover. Note that in these tables (and others) the numbers are expressed by using computer exponential notation. For example, the number 5.154 E + 2 is equivalent to 5.154×10^2 in scientific notation, and the number 2.832 E − 2 is equivalent to 2.832×10^{-2}. More extensive tables of conversion factors for a large variety of unit systems can be found in Appendix A.

1.3 Analysis of Fluid Behavior

The study of fluid mechanics involves the same fundamental laws you have encountered in physics and other mechanics courses. These laws include Newton's laws of motion, conservation of mass, and the first and second laws of thermodynamics. Thus, there are strong similarities between the general approach to fluid mechanics and to rigid-body and deformable-body solid mechanics.

The broad subject of fluid mechanics can be generally subdivided into *fluid statics,* in which the fluid is at rest, and *fluid dynamics,* in which the fluid is moving. In subsequent chapters we will consider both of these areas in detail. Before we can proceed, however, it will be necessary to define and discuss certain fluid *properties* that are intimately related to fluid behavior. In the following several sections, the properties that play an important role in the analysis of fluid behavior are considered.

1.4 Measures of Fluid Mass and Weight

1.4.1 Density

The *density* of a fluid, designated by the Greek symbol ρ (rho), is defined as its mass per unit volume. Density is typically used to characterize the mass of a fluid system. In the BG system ρ has units of slugs/ft^3 and in SI the units are kg/m^3.

The value of density can vary widely between different fluids, but for liquids, variations in pressure and temperature generally have only a small effect on the value of ρ. The

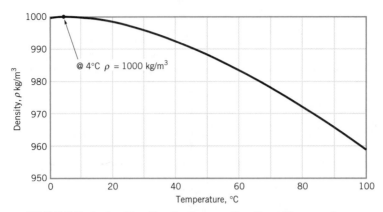

@ 4°C ρ = 1000 kg/m³

■ FIGURE 1.1   **Density of water as a function of temperature.**

small change in the density of water with large variations in temperature is illustrated in Fig. 1.1. Tables 1.4 and 1.5 list values of density for several common liquids. The density of water at 60°F is 1.94 slugs/ft³ or 999 kg/m³. The large difference between those two values illustrates the importance of paying attention to units! Unlike liquids, the density of a gas is strongly influenced by both pressure and temperature, and this difference will be discussed in the next section.

The *specific volume, v,* is the *volume* per unit mass and is therefore the reciprocal of the density—that is,

$$v = \frac{1}{\rho} \tag{1.4}$$

This property is not commonly used in fluid mechanics but is used in thermodynamics.

1.4.2   Specific Weight

The *specific weight* of a fluid, designated by the Greek symbol γ (gamma), is defined as its *weight* per unit volume. Thus, specific weight is related to density through the equation

$$\gamma = \rho g \tag{1.5}$$

where g is the local acceleration of gravity. Just as density is used to characterize the mass of a fluid system, the specific weight is used to characterize the weight of the system. In the

■ **TABLE 1.4**
Approximate Physical Properties of Some Common Liquids (BG Units)

(See inside of front cover.)

■ **TABLE 1.5**
Approximate Physical Properties of Some Common Liquids (SI Units)

(See inside of front cover.)

BG system γ has units of lb/ft^3 and in SI the units are N/m^3. Under conditions of standard gravity ($g = 32.174$ ft/s^2 = 9.807 m/s^2), water at 60 °F has a specific weight of 62.4 lb/ft^3 and 9.80 kN/m^3. Tables 1.4 and 1.5 list values of specific weight for several common liquids (based on standard gravity). More complete tables for water can be found in Appendix B (Tables B.1 and B.2).

1.4.3   Specific Gravity

The *specific gravity* of a fluid, designated as *SG*, is defined as the ratio of the density of the fluid to the density of water at some specified temperature. Usually the specified temperature is taken as 4 °C (39.2 °F), and at this temperature the density of water is 1.94 slugs/ft^3 or 1000 kg/m^3. In equation form specific gravity is expressed as

$$SG = \frac{\rho}{\rho_{H_2O@4°C}} \qquad (1.6)$$

and since it is the *ratio* of densities, the value of *SG* does not depend on the system of units used. For example, the specific gravity of mercury at 20 °C is 13.55 and the density of mercury can thus be readily calculated in either BG or SI units through the use of Eq. 1.6 as

$$\rho_{Hg} = (13.55)(1.94 \text{ slugs/ft}^3) = 26.3 \text{ slugs/ft}^3$$

or

$$\rho_{Hg} = (13.55)(1000 \text{ kg/m}^3) = 13.6 \times 10^3 \text{ kg/m}^3$$

It is clear that density, specific weight, and specific gravity are all interrelated, and from a knowledge of any one of the three the others can be calculated.

1.5   Ideal Gas Law

Gases are highly compressible in comparison to liquids, with changes in gas density directly related to changes in pressure and temperature through the equation

$$p = \rho RT \qquad (1.7)$$

where p is the absolute pressure, ρ the density, T the absolute temperature,[1] and R is a gas constant. Equation 1.7 is commonly termed the *ideal* or *perfect gas law,* or the *equation of state* for an ideal gas. It is known to closely approximate the behavior of real gases under normal conditions when the gases are not approaching liquefaction.

Pressure in a fluid at rest is defined as the normal force per unit area exerted on a plane surface (real or imaginary) immersed in a fluid, and is created by the bombardment of the surface with the fluid molecules. From the definition, pressure has the dimension of FL^{-2}, and in BG units is expressed as lb/ft^2 (psf) or lb/in.^{2} (psi) and in SI units as N/m^2. In SI, 1 N/m^2 is defined as a *pascal,* abbreviated as Pa, and pressures are commonly specified in pascals. The pressure in the ideal gas law must be expressed as an *absolute* pressure, which means that it is measured relative to absolute zero pressure (a pressure that would only occur in a perfect vacuum). Standard sea-level atmospheric pressure (by international agreement) is

---

[1]We will use T to represent temperature in thermodynamic relationships although T is also used to denote the basic dimension of time.

■ **TABLE 1.6**
Approximate Physical Properties of Some Common Gases at Standard Atmospheric Pressure (BG Units)

(See inside of front cover.)

■ **TABLE 1.7**
Approximate Physical Properties of Some Common Gases at Standard Atmospheric Pressure (SI Units)

(See inside of front cover.)

14.696 psi (abs) or 101.33 kPa (abs). For most calculations these pressures can be rounded to 14.7 psi and 101 kPa, respectively. In engineering it is common practice to measure pressure relative to the local atmospheric pressure, and when measured in this fashion it is called *gage* pressure. Thus, the absolute pressure can be obtained from the gage pressure by adding the value of the atmospheric pressure. For example, a pressure of 30 psi (gage) in a tire is equal to 44.7 psi (abs) at standard atmospheric pressure. Pressure is a particularly important fluid characteristic and it will be discussed more fully in the next chapter.

The gas constant, R, which appears in Eq. 1.7, depends on the particular gas and is related to the molecular weight of the gas. Values of the gas constant for several common gases are listed in Tables 1.6 and 1.7. Also in these tables the gas density and specific weight are given for standard atmospheric pressure and gravity and for the temperature listed. More complete tables for air at standard atmospheric pressure can be found in Appendix B (Tables B.3 and B.4).

EXAMPLE 1.2

A compressed air tank has a volume of 0.84 ft³. When the tank is filled with air at a gage pressure of 50 psi, determine the density of the air and the weight of air in the tank. Assume the temperature is 70°F and the atmospheric pressure is 14.7 psi (abs).

SOLUTION

The air density can be obtained from the ideal gas law (Eq. 1.7) expressed as

$$\rho = \frac{p}{RT}$$

so that

$$\rho = \frac{(50 \text{ lb/in.}^2 + 14.7 \text{ lb/in.}^2)(144 \text{ in.}^2/\text{ft}^2)}{(1716 \text{ ft·lb/slug·°R})[(70 + 460)\text{°R}]} = 0.0102 \text{ slugs/ft}^3 \qquad \textbf{(Ans)}$$

Note that both the pressure and temperature were changed to absolute values.

The weight, $\mathcal{W}$, of the air is equal to

$$\mathcal{W} = \rho g \times (\text{volume})$$
$$= (0.0102 \text{ slugs/ft}^3)(32.2 \text{ ft/s}^2)(0.84 \text{ ft}^3)$$

so that

$$\mathcal{W} = 0.276 \text{ lb} \qquad \text{(Ans)}$$

since $1 \text{ lb} = 1 \text{ slug·ft/s}^2$.

1.6 Viscosity

V1.1 Viscous fluids

The properties of density and specific weight are measures of the "heaviness" of a fluid. It is clear, however, that these properties are not sufficient to uniquely characterize how fluids behave since two fluids (such as water and oil) can have approximately the same value of density but behave quite differently when flowing. There is apparently some additional property that is needed to describe the "fluidity" of the fluid.

To determine this additional property, consider a hypothetical experiment in which a material is placed between two very wide parallel plates as shown in Fig. 1.2. The bottom plate is rigidly fixed, but the upper plate is free to move.

When the force P is applied to the upper plate, it will move continuously with a velocity U (after the initial transient motion has died out) as illustrated in Fig. 1.2. This behavior is consistent with the definition of a fluid—that is, if a shearing stress is applied to a fluid it will deform continuously. A closer inspection of the fluid motion between the two plates would reveal that the fluid in contact with the upper plate moves with the plate velocity, U, and the fluid in contact with the bottom fixed plate has a zero velocity. The fluid between the two plates moves with velocity $u = u(y)$ that would be found to vary linearly, $u = Uy/b$, as illustrated in Fig. 1.2. Thus, a *velocity gradient, du/dy*, is developed in the fluid between the plates. In this particular case the velocity gradient is a constant since $du/dy = U/b$, but in more complex flow situations this would not be true. The experimental observation that the fluid "sticks" to the solid boundaries is a very important one in fluid mechanics and is usually referred to as the *no-slip condition*. All fluids, both liquids and gases, satisfy this condition.

V1.2 No-slip condition

In a small time increment, δt, an imaginary vertical line AB in the fluid (see Fig. 1.2) would rotate through an angle, $\delta\beta$, so that

$$\tan \delta\beta \approx \delta\beta = \frac{\delta a}{b}$$

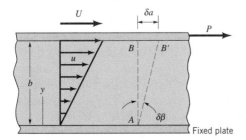

■ **FIGURE 1.2** **Behavior of a fluid placed between two parallel plates.**

Since $\delta a = U \, \delta t$ follows that

$$\delta\beta = \frac{U \, \delta t}{b}$$

Note that in this case, $\delta\beta$ is a function not only of the force P (which governs U) but also of time. We consider the *rate* at which $\delta\beta$ is changing, and define the *rate of shearing strain,* $\dot{\gamma}$, as

$$\dot{\gamma} = \lim_{\delta t \to 0} \frac{\delta\beta}{\delta t}$$

which in this instance is equal to

$$\dot{\gamma} = \frac{U}{b} = \frac{du}{dy}$$

A continuation of this experiment would reveal that as the shearing stress, τ, is increased by increasing P (recall that $\tau = P/A$), the rate of shearing strain is increased in direct proportion—that is

$$\tau \propto \dot{\gamma}$$

or

$$\tau \propto \frac{du}{dy}$$

This result indicates that for common fluids such as water, oil, gasoline, and air the shearing stress and rate of shearing strain (velocity gradient) can be related with a relationship of the form

$$\tau = \mu \frac{du}{dy} \tag{1.8}$$

where the constant of proportionality is designated by the Greek symbol μ (mu) and is called the *absolute viscosity, dynamic viscosity,* or simply the *viscosity* of the fluid. In accordance with Eq. 1.8, plots of τ versus du/dy should be linear with the slope equal to the viscosity as illustrated in Fig. 1.3. The actual value of the viscosity depends on the particular fluid, and for a particular fluid the viscosity is also highly dependent on temperature as illustrated in Fig. 1.3 with the two curves for water. Fluids for which the shearing stress is *linearly* related to the rate of shearing strain (also referred to as rate of angular deformation) are designated as *Newtonian fluids.* Fortunately most common fluids, both liquids and gases, are Newtonian. A more general formulation of Eq. 1.8 which applies to more complex flows of Newtonian fluids, is given in Section 6.8.1.

V1.3 Capillary tube viscometer

Fluids for which the shearing stress is not linearly related to the rate of shearing strain are designated as *non-Newtonian fluids.* It is beyond the scope of this book to consider the behavior of such fluids, and we will only be concerned with Newtonian fluids.

From Eq. 1.8 it can be readily deduced that the dimensions of viscosity are FTL^{-2}. Thus, in BG units viscosity is given as $lb{\cdot}s/ft^2$ and in SI units as $N{\cdot}s/m^2$. Values of viscosity for several common liquids and gases are listed in Tables 1.4 through 1.7. A quick glance at these tables reveals the wide variation in viscosity among fluids. Viscosity is only mildly dependent on pressure and the effect of pressure is usually neglected. However, as previously mentioned, and as illustrated in Appendix B (Figs. B.1 and B.2), viscosity is very sensitive to temperature.

V1.4 Non-Newtonian behavior

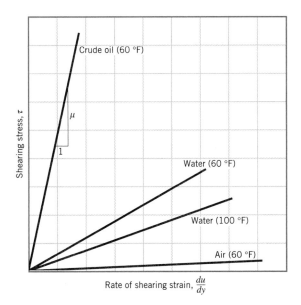

■ **FIGURE 1.3** **Linear variation of shearing stress with rate of shearing strain for common fluids.**

Quite often viscosity appears in fluid flow problems combined with the density in the form

$$\nu = \frac{\mu}{\rho}$$

This ratio is called the *kinematic viscosity* and is denoted with the Greek symbol ν (nu). The dimensions of kinematic viscosity are L^2/T, and the BG units are ft^2/s and SI units are m^2/s. Values of kinematic viscosity for some common liquids and gases are given in Table 1.4 through 1.7. More extensive tables giving both the dynamic and kinematic viscosities for water and air can be found in Appendix B (Tables B.1 through B.4), and graphs showing the variation in both dynamic and kinematic viscosity with temperature for a variety of fluids are also provided in Appendix B (Figs. B.1 and B.2).

Although in this text we are primarily using BG and SI units, dynamic viscosity is often expressed in the metric CGS (centimeter-gram-second) system with units of dyne·s/cm^2. This combination is called a *poise,* abbreviated P. In the CGS system, kinematic viscosity has units of cm^2/s, and this combination is called a *stoke,* abbreviated St.

EXAMPLE 1.3

A dimensionless combination of variables that is important in the study of viscous flow through pipes is called the *Reynolds number,* Re, defined as $\rho V D/\mu$ where ρ is the fluid density, V the mean fluid velocity, D the pipe diameter, and μ the fluid viscosity. A Newtonian fluid having a viscosity of 0.38 N·s/m^2 and a specific gravity of 0.91 flows through a 25-mm-diameter pipe with a velocity of 2.6 m/s. Determine the value of the Reynolds number using (a) SI units, and (b) BG units.

SOLUTION

(a)   The fluid density is calculated from the specific gravity as

$$\rho = SG \, \rho_{H_2O@4°C} = 0.91 \, (1000 \text{ kg/m}^3) = 910 \text{ kg/m}^3$$

and from the definition of the Reynolds number

$$\text{Re} = \frac{\rho VD}{\mu} = \frac{(910 \text{ kg/m}^3)(2.6 \text{ m/s})(25 \text{ mm})(10^{-3} \text{ m/mm})}{0.38 \text{ N·s/m}^2}$$

$$= 156 (\text{kg·m/s}^2)/\text{N}$$

However, since $1 \text{ N} = 1 \text{ kg·m/s}^2$ it follows that the Reynolds number is unitless—that is,

$$\text{Re} = 156 \qquad \text{(Ans)}$$

The value of any dimensionless quantity does not depend on the system of units used if all variables that make up the quantity are expressed in a consistent set of units. To check this we will calculate the Reynolds number using BG units.

(b)   We first convert all the SI values of the variables appearing in the Reynolds number to BG values by using the conversion factors from Table 1.3. Thus,

$$\rho = (910 \text{ kg/m}^3)(1.940 \times 10^{-3}) = 1.77 \text{ slugs/ft}^3$$
$$V = (2.6 \text{ m/s})(3.281) = 8.53 \text{ ft/s}$$
$$D = (0.025 \text{ m})(3.281) = 8.20 \times 10^{-2} \text{ ft}$$
$$\mu = (0.38 \text{ N·s/m}^2)(2.089 \times 10^{-2}) = 7.94 \times 10^{-3} \text{ lb·s/ft}^2$$

and the value of the Reynolds number is

$$\text{Re} = \frac{(1.77 \text{ slugs/ft}^3)(8.53 \text{ ft/s})(8.20 \times 10^{-2} \text{ ft})}{7.94 \times 10^{-3} \text{ lb·s/ft}^2}$$

$$= 156 (\text{slug·ft/s}^2)/\text{lb} = 156 \qquad \text{(Ans)}$$

since $1 \text{ lb} = 1 \text{ slug·ft/s}^2$. The values from part (a) and part (b) are the same, as expected. Dimensionless quantities play an important role in fluid mechanics and the significance of the Reynolds number as well as other important dimensionless combinations will be discussed in detail in Chapter 7. It should be noted that in the Reynolds number it is actually the ratio μ/ρ that is important, and this is the property that we have defined as the kinematic viscosity.

EXAMPLE 1.4

The velocity distribution for the flow of a Newtonian fluid between two wide, parallel plates (see Fig. E1.4) is given by the equation

$$u = \frac{3V}{2}\left[1 - \left(\frac{y}{h}\right)^2\right]$$

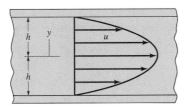

■ FIGURE E1.4

where V is the mean velocity. The fluid has a viscosity of 0.04 lb·s/ft^2. When $V = 2$ ft/s and $h = 0.2$ in. determine: (a) the shearing stress acting on the bottom wall, and (b) the shearing stress acting on a plane parallel to the walls and passing through the centerline (midplane).

SOLUTION

For this type of parallel flow the shearing stress is obtained from Eq. 1.8.

$$\tau = \mu \frac{du}{dy} \tag{1}$$

Thus, if the velocity distribution, $u = u(y)$ is known, the shearing stress can be determined at all points by evaluating the velocity gradient, du/dy. For the distribution given

$$\frac{du}{dy} = -\frac{3Vy}{h^2} \tag{2}$$

(a) Along the bottom wall $y = -h$ so that (from Eq. 2)

$$\frac{du}{dy} = \frac{3V}{h}$$

and therefore the shearing stress is

$$\tau_{\text{bottom wall}} = \mu\left(\frac{3V}{h}\right) = \frac{(0.04 \text{ lb·s/ft}^2)(3)(2 \text{ ft/s})}{(0.2 \text{ in.})(1 \text{ ft}/12 \text{ in.})}$$

$$= 14.4 \text{ lb/ft}^2 \text{ (in direction of flow)} \tag{Ans}$$

This stress creates a drag on the wall. Since the velocity distribution is symmetrical, the shearing stress along the upper wall would have the same magnitude and direction.

(b) Along the midplane where $y = 0$ it follows from Eq. 2 that

$$\frac{du}{dy} = 0$$

and thus the shearing stress is

$$\tau_{\text{midplane}} = 0 \tag{Ans}$$

From Eq. 2 we see that the velocity gradient (and therefore the shearing stress) varies linearly with y and in this particular example varies from 0 at the center of the channel to 14.4 lb/ft^2 at the walls. For the more general case the actual variation will, of course, depend on the nature of the velocity distribution.

1.7   Compressibility of Fluids

1.7.1   Bulk Modulus

An important question to answer when considering the behavior of a particular fluid is how easily can the volume (and thus the density) of a given mass of the fluid be changed when there is a change in pressure? That is, how compressible is the fluid? A property that is commonly used to characterize compressibility is the *bulk modulus, E_v,* defined as

$$E_v = -\frac{dp}{d\forall/\forall} \tag{1.9}$$

where dp is the differential change in pressure needed to create a differential change in volume, $d\forall$, of a volume $\forall$. The negative sign is included since an increase in pressure will cause a decrease in volume. Since a decrease in volume of a given mass, $m = \rho\forall$, will result in an increase in density, Eq. 1.9 can also be expressed as

$$E_v = \frac{dp}{d\rho/\rho} \tag{1.10}$$

The bulk modulus (also referred to as the *bulk modulus of elasticity*) has dimensions of pressure, FL^{-2}. In BG units values for E_v are usually given as lb/in.^{2} (psi) and in SI units as N/m^2 (Pa). Large values for the bulk modulus indicate that the fluid is relatively incompressible— that is, it takes a large pressure change to create a small change in volume. As expected, values of E_v for common liquids are large (see Tables 1.4 and 1.5).

Since such large pressures are required to effect a change in volume, we conclude that liquids can be considered as *incompressible* for most practical engineering applications. As liquids are compressed the bulk modulus increases, but the bulk modulus near atmospheric pressure is usually the one of interest. The use of bulk modulus as a property describing compressibility is most prevalent when dealing with liquids, although the bulk modulus can also be determined for gases.

1.7.2   Compression and Expansion of Gases

When gases are compressed (or expanded) the relationship between pressure and density depends on the nature of the process. If the compression or expansion takes place under constant temperature conditions (*isothermal process*), then from Eq. 1.7

$$\frac{p}{\rho} = \text{constant} \tag{1.11}$$

If the compression or expansion is frictionless and no heat is exchanged with the surroundings (*isentropic process*), then

$$\frac{p}{\rho^k} = \text{constant} \tag{1.12}$$

where k is the ratio of the specific heat at constant pressure, c_p, to the specific heat at constant volume, c_v (i.e., $k = c_p/c_v$). The two specific heats are related to the gas constant, R, through the equation $R = c_p - c_v$. As was the case for the ideal gas law, the pressure in both or in terms of the bulk modulus defined by Eq. 1.10

$$c = \sqrt{\frac{E_v}{\rho}} \qquad (1.14)$$

Since the disturbance is small, there is negligible heat transfer and the process is assumed to be isentropic. Thus, the pressure-density relationship used in Eq. 1.13 is that for an isentropic process.

For gases undergoing an isentropic process, $E_v = kp$, so that

$$c = \sqrt{\frac{kp}{\rho}}$$

and making use of the ideal gas law, it follows that

$$c = \sqrt{kRT} \qquad (1.15)$$

Thus, for ideal gases the speed of sound is proportional to the square root of the absolute temperature. The speed of sound in air at various temperatures can be found in Appendix B (Tables B.3 and B.4). Equation 1.14 is also valid for liquids, and values of E_v can be used to determine the speed of sound in liquids. Note that the speed of sound in water is much higher than in air. If a fluid were truly incompressible ($E_v = \infty$) the speed of sound would be infinite. The speed of sound in water for various temperatures can be found in Appendix B (Tables B.1 and B.2).

EXAMPLE 1.6

A jet aircraft flies at a speed of 550 mph at an altitude of 35,000 ft, where the temperature is $-66\,°F$. Determine the ratio of the speed of the aircraft, V, to that of the speed of sound, c, at the specified altitude. Assume $k = 1.40$.

SOLUTION

From Eq. 1.15 the speed of sound can be calculated as

$$c = \sqrt{kRT} = \sqrt{(1.40)(1716 \text{ ft·lb/slug·°R})(-66 + 460)\,°R}$$
$$= 973 \text{ ft/s}$$

Since the air speed is

$$V = \frac{(550 \text{ mi/hr})(5280 \text{ ft/mi})}{(3600 \text{ s/hr})} = 807 \text{ ft/s}$$

the ratio is

$$\frac{V}{c} = \frac{807 \text{ ft/s}}{973 \text{ ft/s}} = 0.829 \qquad \text{(Ans)}$$

Eqs. 1.11 and 1.12 must be expressed as an absolute pressure. Values of k for some comn gases are given in Tables 1.6 and 1.7, and for air over a range of temperatures, in Appen B (Tables B.3 and B.4). It is clear that in dealing with gases greater attention will need be given to the effect of compressibility on fluid behavior. However, as discussed in Secti 3.8, gases can often be treated as incompressible fluids if the changes in pressure are sma

EXAMPLE 1.5

A cubic foot of helium at an absolute pressure of 14.7 psi is compressed isentropically to $\frac{1}{2}$ ft³. What is the final pressure?

SOLUTION

For an isentropic compression

$$\frac{p_i}{\rho_i^k} = \frac{p_f}{\rho_f^k}$$

where the subscripts i and f refer to initial and final states, respectively. Since we are interested in the final pressure, p_f, it follows that

$$p_f = \left(\frac{\rho_f}{\rho_i}\right)^k p_i$$

As the volume is reduced by one half, the density must double, since the mass of the gas remains constant. Thus,

$$p_f = (2)^{1.66}(14.7 \text{ psi}) = 46.5 \text{psi (abs)} \qquad \text{(Ans)}$$

1.7.3   Speed of Sound

Another important consequence of the compressibility of fluids is that disturbances introduced at some point in the fluid propagate at a finite velocity. For example, if a fluid is flowing in a pipe and a valve at the outlet is suddenly closed (thereby creating a localized disturbance) the effect of the valve closure is not felt instantaneously upstream. It takes a finite time for the increased pressure created by the valve closure to propagate to an upstream location. Similarly, a loud speaker diaphragm causes a localized disturbance as it vibrates, and the small change in pressure created by the motion of the diaphragm is propagated through the air with a finite velocity. The velocity at which these small disturbances propagate is called the *acoustic velocity* or the *speed of sound, c.* It can be shown that the speed of sound is related to changes in pressure and density of the fluid medium through the equation

$$c = \sqrt{\frac{dp}{d\rho}} \qquad \text{(1.13)}$$

This ratio is called the *Mach number,* Ma. If Ma $<$ 1.0 the aircraft is flying at *subsonic* speeds, whereas for Ma $>$ 1.0 it is flying at *supersonic* speeds. The Mach number is an important dimensionless parameter used in the study of the flow of gases at high speeds and will be further discussed in Chapters 7 and 9.

1.8   Vapor Pressure

It is a common observation that liquids such as water and gasoline will evaporate if they are simply placed in a container open to the atmosphere. Evaporation takes place because some liquid molecules at the surface have sufficient momentum to overcome the intermolecular cohesive forces and escape into the atmosphere. If the container is closed with a small air space left above the surface, and this space evacuated to form a vacuum, a pressure will develop in the space as a result of the vapor that is formed by the escaping molecules. When an equilibrium condition is reached so that the number of molecules leaving the surface is equal to the number entering, the vapor is said to be saturated and the pressure the vapor exerts on the liquid surface is termed the *vapor pressure.*

Since the development of a vapor pressure is closely associated with molecular activity, the value of vapor pressure for a particular liquid depends on temperature. Values of vapor pressure for water at various temperatures can be found in Appendix B (Tables B.1 and B.2), and the values of vapor pressure for several common liquids at room temperatures are given in Tables 1.4 and 1.5. *Boiling,* which is the formation of vapor bubbles within a fluid mass, is initiated when the absolute pressure in the fluid reaches the vapor pressure.

An important reason for our interest in vapor pressure and boiling lies in the common observation that in flowing fluids it is possible to develop very low pressure due to the fluid motion, and if the pressure is lowered to the vapor pressure, boiling will occur. For example, this phenomenon may occur in flow through the irregular, narrowed passages of a valve or pump. When vapor bubbles are formed in a flowing fluid they are swept along into regions of higher pressure where they suddenly collapse with sufficient intensity to actually cause structural damage. The formation and subsequent collapse of vapor bubbles in a flowing fluid, called *cavitation,* is an important fluid flow phenomenon to be given further attention in Chapters 3 and 7.

1.9   Surface Tension

At the interface between a liquid and a gas, or between two immiscible liquids, forces develop in the liquid surface that cause the surface to behave as if it were a "skin" or "membrane" stretched over the fluid mass. Although such a skin is not actually present, this conceptual analogy allows us to explain several commonly observed phenomena. For example, a steel needle will float on water if placed gently on the surface because the tension developed in the hypothetical skin supports the needle. Small droplets of mercury will form into spheres when placed on a smooth surface because the cohesive forces in the surface tend to hold all the molecules together in a compact shape. Similarly, discrete water droplets will form when placed on a newly waxed surface.

V1.5 Floating razor blade

These various types of surface phenomena are due to the unbalanced cohesive forces acting on the liquid molecules at the fluid surface. Molecules in the interior of the fluid mass are surrounded by molecules that are attracted to each other equally. However, molecules along the surface are subjected to a net force toward the interior. The apparent physical consequence of this unbalanced force along the surface is to create the hypothetical skin or membrane. A tensile force may be considered to be acting in the plane of the surface along any line in the surface. The intensity of the molecular attraction per unit length along any line in the surface is called the *surface tension* and is designated by the Greek symbol σ (sigma). Surface tension is a property of the liquid and depends on temperature as well as the other fluid it is in contact with at the interface. The dimensions of surface tension are FL^{-1} with BG units of lb/ft and SI units of N/m. Values of surface tension for some common liquids (in contact with air) are given in Tables 1.4 and 1.5 and in Appendix B (Tables B.1 and B.2) for water at various temperatures. The value of the surface tension decreases as the temperature increases.

Among common phenomena associated with surface tension is the rise (or fall) of a liquid in a capillary tube. If a small open tube is inserted into water, the water level in the tube will rise above the water level outside the tube as is illustrated in Fig. 1.4a. In this situation we have a liquid–gas–solid interface. For the case illustrated there is an attraction (adhesion) between the wall of the tube and liquid molecules, which is strong enough to overcome the mutual attraction (cohesion) of the molecules and pull them up to the wall. Hence, the liquid is said to *wet* the solid surface.

The height, h, is governed by the value of the surface tension, σ, the tube radius, R, the specific weight of the liquid, γ, and the *angle of contact, θ*, between the fluid and tube. From the free-body diagram of Fig. 1.4b we see that the vertical force due to the surface tension is equal to $2\pi R\sigma \cos\theta$ and the weight is $\gamma\pi R^2 h$ and these two forces must balance for equilibrium. Thus,

$$\gamma\pi R^2 h = 2\pi R\sigma \cos\theta$$

so that the height is given by the relationship

$$h = \frac{2\sigma \cos\theta}{\gamma R} \tag{1.16}$$

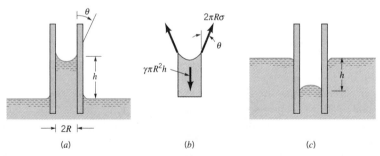

■ **FIGURE 1.4** **Effect of capillary action in small tubes. (*a*) Rise of column for a liquid that wets the tube. (*b*) Free-body diagram for calculating column height. (*c*) Depression of column for a nonwetting liquid.**

The angle of contact is a function of both the liquid and the surface. For water in contact with clean glass $\theta \approx 0°$. It is clear from Eq. 1.16 that the height is inversely proportional to the tube radius, and therefore the rise of a liquid in a tube as a result of capillary action becomes increasingly pronounced as the tube radius is decreased.

EXAMPLE 1.7

Pressures are sometimes determined by measuring the height of a column of liquid in a vertical tube. What diameter of clean glass tubing is required so that the rise of water at 20 °C in a tube due to a capillary action (as opposed to pressure in the tube) is less than 1.0 mm?

SOLUTION

From Eq. 1.16

$$h = \frac{2\sigma \cos \theta}{\gamma R}$$

so that

$$R = \frac{2\sigma \cos \theta}{\gamma h}$$

For water at 20 °C (from Table B.2), $\sigma = 0.0728$ N/m and $\gamma = 9.789$ kN/m³. Since $\theta \approx 0°$ it follows that for $h = 1.0$ mm,

$$R = \frac{2(0.0728 \text{ N/m})(1)}{(9.789 \times 10^3 \text{ N/m}^3)(1.0 \text{ mm})(10^{-3} \text{ m/mm})} = 0.0149 \text{ m}$$

and the minimum required tube diameter, D, is

$$D = 2R = 0.0298 \text{ m} = 29.8 \text{ mm} \qquad \text{(Ans)}$$

If adhesion of molecules to the solid surface is weak compared to the cohesion between molecules, the liquid will not wet the surface and the level in a tube placed in a nonwetting liquid will actually be depressed as shown in Fig. 1.4c. Mercury is a good example of a nonwetting liquid when it is in contact with a glass tube. For nonwetting liquids the angle of contact is greater than 90°, and for mercury in contact with clean glass $\theta \approx 130°$.

Surface tension effects play a role in many mechanics problems including the movement of liquids through soil and other porous media, flow of thin films, formation of drops and bubbles, and the breakup of liquid jets. Surface phenomena associated with liquid-gas, liquid-liquid, liquid–gas–solid interfaces are exceedingly complex, and more detailed and rigorous discussion of them is beyond the scope of this text. Fortunately, in many fluid mechanics problems, surface phenomena, as characterized by surface tension, are not important, since inertial, gravitational, and viscous forces are much more dominant.

Problems

Note: Unless specific values of required fluid properties are given in the statement of the problem, use the values found in the tables on the inside of the front cover. Problems designated with an (*) are intended to be solved with the aid of a programmable calculator or a computer. Problems designated with a (†) are "open-ended" problems and require critical thinking in that to work them one must make various assumptions and provide the necessary data. There is not a unique answer to these problems.

1.1   Determine the dimensions, in both the *FLT* system and the *MLT* system, for (a) the product of mass times velocity, (b) the product of force times volume, and (c) kinetic energy divided by area.

1.2   Verify the dimensions, in both the *FLT* system and the *MLT* system, of the following quantities which appear in Table 1.1: (a) acceleration, (b) stress, (c) moment of a force, (d) volume, and (e) work.

1.3   If P is a force and x a length, what are the dimensions (in the *FLT* system) of (a) dP/dx, (b) d^3P/dx^3, and (c) $\int P\,dx$?

1.4   Dimensionless combinations of quantities (commonly called dimensionless parameters) play an important role in fluid mechanics. Make up five possible dimensionless parameters by using combinations of some of the quantities listed in Table 1.1.

1.5   The force, P, that is exerted on a spherical particle moving slowly through a liquid is given by the equation

$$P = 3\pi\mu DV$$

where μ is a fluid property (viscosity) having dimensions of $FL^{-2}T$, D is the particle diameter, and V is the particle velocity. What are the dimensions of the constant, 3π? Would you classify this equation as a general homogeneous equation?

1.6   The pressure difference, Δp, across a partial blockage in an artery (called a *stenosis*) is approximated by the equation

$$\Delta p = K_v\frac{\mu V}{D} + K_u\left(\frac{A_0}{A_1} - 1\right)^2\rho V^2$$

where V is the blood velocity, μ the blood viscosity ($FL^{-2}T$), ρ the blood density (ML^{-3}), D the artery diameter, A_0 the area of the unobstructed artery, and A_1 the area of the stenosis. Determine the dimensions of the constants K_v and K_u. Would this equation be valid in any system of units?

1.7   According to information found in an old hydraulics book, the energy loss per unit weight of fluid flowing through a nozzle connected to a hose can be estimated by the formula

$$h = (0.04 \text{ to } 0.09)(D/d)^4V^2/2g$$

where h is the energy loss per unit weight, D the hose diameter, d the nozzle tip diameter, V the fluid velocity in the hose, and g the acceleration of gravity. Do you think this equation is valid in any system of units? Explain.

†1.8   Cite an example of a restricted homogeneous equation contained in a technical article found in an engineering journal in your field of interest. Define all terms in the equation, explain why it is a restricted equation, and provide a complete journal citation (title, date, etc.).

1.9   Make use of Table 1.2 to express the following quantities in SI units: (a) 10.2 in./min, (b) 4.81 slugs, (c) 3.02 lb, (d) 73.1 ft/s², (e) 0.0234 lb·s/ft².

1.10   Make use of Table 1.3 to express the following quantities in BG units: (a) 14.2 km, (b) 8.14 N/m³, (c) 1.61 kg/m³, (d) 0.0320 N·m/s, (e) 5.67 mm/hr.

1.11   Water flows from a large drainage pipe at a rate of 1500 gal/min. What is this volume rate of flow in m³/s and in liters/min?

1.12   An important dimensionless parameter in certain types of fluid flow problems is the *Froude number* defined as $V/\sqrt{g\ell}$, where V is a velocity, g the acceleration of gravity, and ℓ a length. Determine the value of the Froude number for $V = 10$ ft/s, $g = 32.2$ ft/s², and $\ell = 2$ ft. Recalculate the Froude number using SI units for V, g, and ℓ. Explain the significance of the results of these calculations.

1.13   The specific weight of a certain liquid is 85.3 lb/ft³. Determine its density and specific gravity.

1.14   The density of a certain type of jet fuel is 805 kg/m³. Determine its specific gravity and specific weight.

†1.15   Estimate the number of pounds of mercury it would take to fill your bath tub. List all assumptions and show all calculations.

1.16   A liquid when poured into a graduated cylinder is found to weigh 6 N when occupying a volume of 500 ml (milliliters). Determine its specific weight, density, and specific gravity.

*1.17   The variation in the density of water, ρ, with temperature, T, in the range of $20\,°C \le T \le 60\,°C$, is given in the following table.

Density (kg/m³)	998.2	997.1	995.7	994.1	992.2	990.2	998.1
Temperature (°C)	20	25	30	35	40	45	50

Use these data to determine an empirical equation of the form $\rho = c_1 + c_2T + c_3T^2$ which can be used to predict the density over the range indicated. Compare the predicted values with the data given. What is the density of water at 42.1 °C?

†**1.18** Estimate the number of kilograms of water consumed per day for household purposes in your city. List all assumptions and show all calculations.

1.19 The density of oxygen contained in a tank is 2.0 kg/m^3 when the temperature is 25 °C. Determine the gage pressure of the gas if the atmospheric pressure is 97 kPa.

1.20 A closed tank having a volume of 2 ft^3 is filled with 0.30 lb of a gas. A pressure gage attached to the tank reads 12 psi when the gas temperature is 80 °F. There is some question as to whether the gas in the tank is oxygen or helium. Which do you think it is? Explain how you arrived at your answer.

†**1.21** Estimate the volume of car exhaust produced per day by automobiles in the United States. List all assumptions and show calculations.

1.22 A compressed air tank contains 8 kg of air at a temperature of 80 °C. A gage on the tank reads 300 kPa. Determine the volume of the tank.

1.23 Determine the ratio of the dynamic viscosity of water to air at a temperature of 70 °C. Compare this value with the corresponding ratio of kinematic viscosities. Assume the air is at standard atmospheric pressure.

1.24 The kinematic viscosity and specific gravity of a liquid are 3.5×10^{-4} m^2/s and 0.79, respectively. What is the dynamic viscosity of the liquid in SI units?

1.25 The time, t, it takes to pour a liquid from a container depends on several factors, including the kinematic viscosity, ν, of the liquid. (See **Video V1.1**.) In some laboratory tests various oils having the same density but different viscosities were poured at a fixed tipping rate from small 150 ml beakers. The time required to pour 100 ml of the oil was measured, and it was found that an approximate equation for the pouring time in seconds was $t = 1 + 9 \times 10^2 \nu + 8 \times 10^3 \nu^2$ with ν in m^2/s. **(a)** Is this a general homogeneous equation? Explain. **(b)** Compare the time it would take to pour 100 ml of SAE 30 oil from a 150 ml beaker at 0 °C to the corresponding time at a temperature of 60 °C. Make use of Fig. B.2 in Appendix B for viscosity data.

1.26 SAE 30 oil at 60 °F flows through a 2-in.-diameter pipe with a mean velocity of 5 ft/s. Determine the value of the Reynolds number (see Example 1.3).

1.27 Calculate the Reynolds number for the flow of water and for air through a 3-mm-diameter tube, if the mean velocity is 2 m/s and the temperature is 30 °C in both cases (see Example 1.3). Assume the air is at standard atmospheric pressure.

1.28 A Newtonian fluid having a specific gravity of 0.92 and a kinematic viscosity of 4×10^{-4} m^2/s flows past a fixed surface. Due to the no-slip condition, the velocity at

the fixed surface is zero (as shown in **Video V1.2**), and the velocity profile near the surface is shown in Fig. P1.28. Determine the magnitude and direction of the shearing stress developed on the plate. Express your answer in terms of U and δ, with U and δ expressed in units of meters per second and meters, respectively.

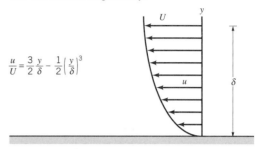

$$\frac{u}{U} = \frac{3}{2}\frac{y}{\delta} - \frac{1}{2}\left(\frac{y}{\delta}\right)^3$$

■ **FIGURE P1.28**

1.29 Solve Problem 1.28 if the velocity profile is given by the equation

$$\frac{u}{U} = \sin\left(\frac{\pi}{2}\frac{y}{\delta}\right)$$

1.30 When a viscous fluid flows past a thin sharp-edged plate, a thin layer adjacent to the plate surface develops in which the velocity, u, changes rapidly from zero to the approach velocity, U, in a small distance, δ. This layer is called a *boundary layer*. The thickness of this layer increases with the distance x along the plate as shown in Fig. P1.30. Assume that $u = Uy/\delta$ and $\delta = 3.5\sqrt{\nu x/U}$ where ν is the kinematic viscosity of the fluid. Determine an expression for the force (drag) that would be developed on one side of the plate of length l and width b. Express your answer in terms of l, b, ν, and ρ, where ρ is the fluid density.

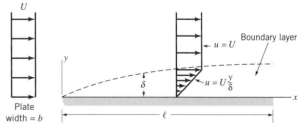

■ **FIGURE P1.30**

1.31 A 10-kg block slides down a smooth inclined surface as shown in Fig. P1.31. Determine the terminal velocity of the block if the 0.1-mm gap between the block and the surface contains SAE 30 oil at 60 °F. Assume velocity distribution in the gap is linear, and the area of the block in contact with the oil is 0.2 m^2.

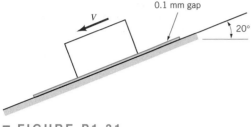

■ **FIGURE P1.31**

1.32 A solid cube measuring 0.5 ft per side and weighing 100 lb slides down a smooth surface, which is inclined 30° from the horizontal. The block slides on a film of oil having a viscosity of 1.71×10^{-2} lb·s/ft². If the terminal velocity of the block is 1.2 ft/s, what is the film thickness? Assume a linear velocity distribution in the film.

1.33 A layer of water flows down an inclined fixed surface with the velocity profile shown in Fig. P1.33. Determine the magnitude and direction of the shearing stress that the water exerts on the fixed surface for $U = 3$ m/s and $h = 0.1$ m.

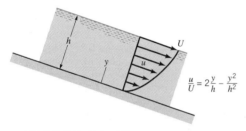

$$\frac{u}{U} = 2\frac{y}{h} - \frac{y^2}{h^2}$$

■ **FIGURE P1.33**

*1.34 Standard air flows past a flat surface and velocity measurements near the surface indicate the following distribution:

y (ft)	0.005	0.01	0.02	0.04	0.06	0.08
u (ft/s)	0.74	1.51	3.03	6.37	10.21	14.43

The coordinate y is measured normal to the surface and u is the velocity parallel to the surface. **(a)** Assume the velocity distribution is of the form

$$u = C_1 y + C_2 y^3$$

and use a standard curve-fitting technique to determine the constants C_1 and C_2. **(b)** Make use of the results of part (a) to determine the magnitude of the shearing stress at the wall ($y = 0$) and at $y = 0.05$ ft.

1.35 The viscosity of liquids can be measured through the use of a *rotating cylinder viscometer* of the type illustrated in Fig. P1.35. In this device the outer cylinder is fixed and the inner cylinder is rotated with an angular velocity, ω. The torque $\mathcal{T}$ required to develop ω is measured and the

viscosity is calculated from these two measurements. Develop an equation relating μ, ω, $\mathcal{T}$, ℓ, R_o and R_i. Neglect end effects and assume the velocity distribution in the gap is linear.

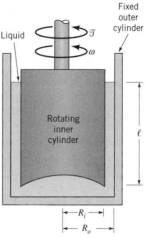

■ **FIGURE P1.35**

1.36 One type of *capillary-tube viscometer* is shown in Video V1.3 and in Fig. P1.36. For this device the liquid to be tested is drawn into the tube to a level above the top etched line. The time is then obtained for the liquid to drain to the bottom etched line. The kinematic viscosity, ν, in m²/s is then obtained from the equation $\nu = KR^4 t$ where K is a constant, R is the radius of the capillary tube in mm, and t is the drain time in seconds. When glycerin at 20°C is used as a calibration fluid in a particular viscometer the drain time is 1,430 s. When a liquid having a density of 970 kg/m³ is tested in the same viscometer the drain time is 900 s. What is the dynamic viscosity of this liquid?

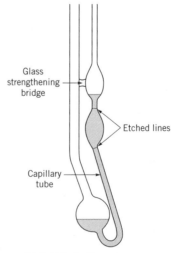

■ **FIGURE P1.36**

1.37 One type of rotating cylinder viscometer, called a *Stormer viscometer*, uses a falling weight, $\mathcal{W}$, to cause the cylinder to rotate with an angular velocity, ω, as illustrated in Fig. P1.37. For this device the viscosity, μ, of the liquid is related to $\mathcal{W}$ and ω through the equation $\mathcal{W} = K\mu\omega$, where K is a constant that depends only on the geometry (including the liquid depth) of the viscometer. The value of K is usually determined by using a calibration liquid (a liquid of known viscosity).

(a) Some data for a particular Stormer viscometer, obtained using glycerin at $20\,^\circ$C as a calibration liquid, are given below. Plot values of the weight as ordinates and values of the angular velocity as abscissae. Draw the best curve through the plotted points and determine K for the viscometer.

$\mathcal{W}$ (lb)	0.22	0.66	1.10	1.54	2.20
ω (rev/s)	0.53	1.59	2.79	3.83	5.49

(b) A liquid of unknown viscosity is placed in the same viscometer used in part (a), and the data given below are obtained. Determine the viscosity of this liquid.

$\mathcal{W}$ (lb)	0.04	0.11	0.22	0.33	0.44
ω (rev/s)	0.72	1.89	3.73	5.44	7.42

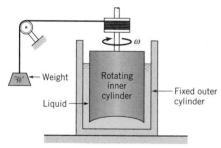

■ **FIGURE P1.37**

1.38 A 25-mm-diameter shaft is pulled through a cylindrical bearing as shown in Fig. P1.38. The lubricant that fills the 0.3-mm gap between the shaft and bearing is an oil having a kinematic viscosity of $8.0 \times 10^{-4}\,\mathrm{m^2/s}$ and a specific gravity of 0.91. Determine the force P required to pull the shaft at a velocity of 3 m/s. Assume the velocity distribution in the gap is linear.

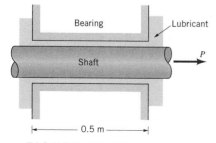

■ **FIGURE P1.38**

1.39 There are many fluids that exhibit non-Newtonian behavior (see for example **Video V1.4**). For a given fluid the distinction between Newtonian and non-Newtonian behavior is usually based on measurements of shear stress and rate of shearing strain. Assume that the viscosity of blood is to be determined by measurements of shear stress, τ, and rate of shearing strain, du/dy, obtained from a small blood sample tested in a suitable viscometer. Based on the data given below determine if the blood is a Newtonian or non-Newtonian fluid. Explain how you arrived at your answer.

$\tau\ (\mathrm{N/m^2})$	0.04	0.06	0.12	0.18	0.30	0.52	1.12	2.10
$du/dy\ (s^{-1})$	2.25	4.50	11.25	22.5	45.0	90.0	225	450

1.40 Calculate the speed of sound in m/s for **(a)** gasoline, **(b)** mercury, and **(c)** seawater.

1.41 Often the assumption is made that the flow of a certain fluid can be considered as incompressible flow if the density of the fluid changes by less than 2%. If air is flowing through a tube such that the air pressure at one section is 9.0 psi and at a downstream section it is 8.6 psi at the same temperature, do you think that this flow could be considered an incompressible flow? Support your answer with the necessary calculations. Assume standard atmospheric pressure.

1.42 Natural gas at $70\,^\circ$F and standard atmospheric pressure of 14.7 psi is compressed isentropically to a new absolute pressure of 60 psi. Determine the final density and temperature of the gas.

1.43 When water at $90\,^\circ$C flows through a converging section of pipe, the pressure is reduced in the direction of flow. Estimate the minimum absolute pressure that can develop without causing cavitation. Express your answer in both BG and SI units.

1.44 Estimate the minimum absolute pressure (in pascals) that can be developed at the inlet of a pump to avoid cavitation if the fluid is ethyl alcohol at $20\,^\circ$C.

1.45 At what atmospheric pressure will water boil at $35\,^\circ$C? Express your answer in both SI and BG units.

1.46 Estimate the excess pressure inside a raindrop having a diameter of 3 mm.

1.47 Two vertical, parallel, clean glass plates are spaced a distance of 2 mm apart. If the plates are placed in water, how high will the water rise between the plates due to capillary action?

1.48 An open, clean glass tube, having a diameter of 3 mm, is inserted vertically into a dish of mercury at $20\,^\circ$C. How far will the column of mercury in the tube be depressed?

1.49 As shown in **Video V1.5**, surface tension forces can be strong enough to allow a double-edge steel razor blade to "float" on water, but a single-edge blade will sink.

Assume that the surface tension forces act at an angle θ relative to the water surface as shown in Fig. P1.49. **(a)** The mass of the double-edge blade is 0.64×10^{-3} kg, and the total length of its sides is 206 mm. Determine the value of θ required to maintain equilibrium between the blade weight and the resultant surface tension force. **(b)** The mass of the single-edge blade is 2.61×10^{-3} kg, and the total length of its sides is 154 mm. Explain why this blade sinks. Support your answer with the necessary calculations.

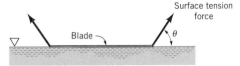

■ **FIGURE P1.49**

1.50 The capillary rise in a tube depends on the cleanliness of both the fluid and the tube. Typically, values of h are less than those predicted by Eq. 1.16 using values of σ and θ for clean fluids and tubes. Some measurements of the height, h, a water column rises in a vertical open tube of diameter d are given below. The water was tap water at a temperature of 60°F and no particular effort was made to clean the glass tube. Fit a curve to these data and estimate the value of the product $\sigma \cos \theta$. If it is assumed that σ has the value given in Table 1.4, what is the value of θ? If it is assumed that θ is equal to 0°, what is the value of σ?

d (in.)	0.3	0.25	0.20	0.15	0.10	0.05
h (in.)	0.133	0.165	0.198	0.273	0.421	0.796

1.51 The capillary tube viscometer device shown in Fig. P1.51 can be used to determine the kinematic viscosity, $\nu = \mu/\rho$, of a liquid. The volume flowrate, Q cubic feet per second or mℓ per second, at which a viscous liquid flows through a small diameter tube (i.e., a capillary tube) depends upon many parameters including the diameter and length of the tube, the acceleration of gravity, the density and viscosity of the liquid, and the head (height) of the liquid above the top of the tube. An advanced analysis of this situation would show that with other parameters held constant, the kinematic viscosity is related to the flowrate as $\nu = K/Q$,

where K is a constant. The value of the constant K can be determined by measuring Q for a fluid of known viscosity, in this case water. The flowrate is given by $Q = \mathcal{V}/t$, where $\mathcal{V}$ is the volume of water collected in a graduated cylinder in the time period t.

Values of $\mathcal{V}$ and t determined experimentally when using water at different temperatures are shown in the table below. For each temperature, use the book value of the viscosity of water and the given data to determine the constant K.

It is assumed that the value of K is constant, independent of the viscosity of the fluid used. Do your results support this? Discuss some possible reasons for this not being true.

$\mathcal{V}$ (mℓ)	t(s)	T (°C)
9.50	15.4	26.3
9.30	17.0	21.3
9.05	20.4	12.3
9.25	13.3	34.3
9.40	9.9	50.4
9.10	8.9	58.0

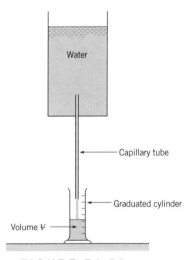

■ **FIGURE P1.51**

Fluid Statics

*I*n this chapter we will consider an important class of problems in which the fluid is either at rest or moving in such a manner that there is no relative motion between adjacent particles. In both instances there will be no shearing stresses in the fluid, and the only forces that develop on the surfaces of the particles will be due to the pressure. Thus, our principal concern is to investigate pressure and its variation throughout a fluid, and the effect of pressure on submerged surfaces.

2.1 Pressure at a Point

As we briefly discussed in Chapter 1, the term pressure is used to indicate the normal force per unit area at a given point acting on a given plane within the fluid mass of interest. A question that immediately arises is how the pressure at a point varies with the orientation of the plane passing through the point. To answer this question, consider the free-body diagram, illustrated in Fig. 2.1, that was obtained by removing a small triangular wedge of fluid from some arbitrary location within a fluid mass. Since we are considering the situation in which

An image of hurricane Allen viewed via satellite: although there is considerable motion and structure to a hurricane, the pressure variation in the vertical direction is approximated by the pressure-depth relationship for a static fluid. (Visible and infrared image pair from a NOAA satellite using a technique developed at NASA/GSPC.) (Photograph courtesy of A. F. Hasler, [Ref. 3].)

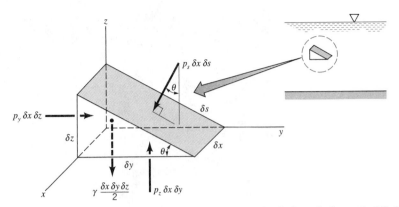

■ FIGURE 2.1 Forces on an arbitrary wedged-shaped element of fluid.

there are no shearing stresses, the only external forces acting on the wedge are due to the pressure and the weight. For simplicity the forces in the x direction are not shown, and the z axis is taken as the vertical axis so the weight acts in the negative z direction. Although we are primarily interested in fluids at rest, to make the analysis as general as possible, we will allow the fluid element to have accelerated motion. The assumption of zero shearing stresses will still be valid so long as the fluid element moves as a rigid body; that is, there is no relative motion between adjacent elements.

The equations of motion (Newton's second law, $\mathbf{F} = m\mathbf{a}$) in the y and z directions are, respectively,

$$\Sigma F_y = p_y \, \delta x \, \delta z - p_s \, \delta x \, \delta s \sin \theta = \rho \frac{\delta x \, \delta y \, \delta z}{2} a_y$$

$$\Sigma F_z = p_z \, \delta x \, \delta y - p_s \, \delta x \, \delta s \cos \theta - \gamma \frac{\delta x \, \delta y \, \delta z}{2} = \rho \frac{\delta x \, \delta y \, \delta z}{2} a_z$$

where p_x, p_y, and p_z are the average pressures on the faces, γ and ρ are the fluid specific weight and density, respectively, and a_y, a_z the accelerations. It follows from the geometry that

$$\delta y = \delta s \cos \theta \qquad \delta z = \delta s \sin \theta$$

so that the equations of motion can be rewritten as

$$p_y - p_s = \rho a_y \frac{\delta y}{2}$$

$$p_z - p_s = (\rho a_z + \gamma) \frac{\delta z}{2}$$

Since we are really interested in what is happening at a point, we take the limit as δx, δy, and δz approach zero (while maintaining the angle θ), and it follows that

$$p_y = p_s \qquad p_z = p_s$$

or $p_s = p_y = p_z$. The angle θ was arbitrarily chosen so we can conclude that *the pressure at a point in a fluid at rest, or in motion, is independent of direction as long as there are no shearing stresses present.* This important result is known as *Pascal's law.*

In Chapter 6 it will be shown that for moving fluids in which there is relative motion between particles (so that shearing stresses develop) the normal stress at a point, which corresponds to pressure in fluids at rest, is not necessarily the same in all directions. In such cases the pressure is defined as the *average* of any three mutually perpendicular normal stresses at the point.

2.2   Basic Equation for Pressure Field

Although we have answered the question of how the pressure at a point varies with direction, we are now faced with an equally important question—how does the pressure in a fluid in which there are no shearing stresses vary from point to point? To answer this question consider a small rectangular element of fluid removed from some arbitrary position within the mass of fluid of interest as illustrated in Fig. 2.2. There are two types of forces acting on this element: *surface forces* due to the pressure, and a *body force* equal to the weight of the element.

If we let the pressure at the center of the element be designated as p, then the average pressure on the various faces can be expressed in terms of p and its derivatives as shown in Fig. 2.2. For simplicity the surface forces in the x direction are not shown. The resultant surface force in the y direction is

$$\delta F_y = \left(p - \frac{\partial p}{\partial y} \frac{\delta y}{2} \right) \delta x\, \delta z - \left(p + \frac{\partial p}{\partial y} \frac{\delta y}{2} \right) \delta x\, \delta z$$

or

$$\delta F_y = -\frac{\partial p}{\partial y}\, \delta x\, \delta y\, \delta z$$

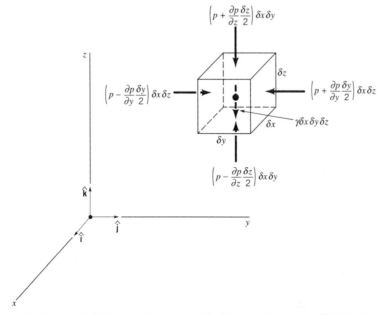

■ FIGURE 2.2   Surface and body forces acting on small fluid element.

Similarly, for the x and z directions the resultant surface forces are

$$\delta F_x = -\frac{\partial p}{\partial x}\, \delta x\, \delta y\, \delta z \qquad \delta F_z = -\frac{\partial p}{\partial z}\, \delta x\, \delta y\, \delta z$$

The resultant surface force acting on the element can be expressed in vector form as

$$\delta \mathbf{F}_s = \delta F_x \hat{\mathbf{i}} + \delta F_y \hat{\mathbf{j}} + \delta F_z \hat{\mathbf{k}}$$

or

$$\delta \mathbf{F}_s = -\left(\frac{\partial p}{\partial x}\, \hat{\mathbf{i}} + \frac{\partial p}{\partial y}\, \hat{\mathbf{j}} + \frac{\partial p}{\partial z}\, \hat{\mathbf{k}}\right) \delta x\, \delta y\, \delta z \tag{2.1}$$

where $\hat{\mathbf{i}}$, $\hat{\mathbf{j}}$, and $\hat{\mathbf{k}}$ are the unit vectors along the coordinate axes shown in Fig. 2.2. The group of terms in parentheses in Eq. 2.1 represents in vector form the *pressure gradient* and can be written as

$$\frac{\partial p}{\partial x}\, \hat{\mathbf{i}} + \frac{\partial p}{\partial y}\, \hat{\mathbf{j}} + \frac{\partial p}{\partial z}\, \hat{\mathbf{k}} = \nabla p$$

where

$$\nabla(\ ) = \frac{\partial(\ )}{\partial x}\, \hat{\mathbf{i}} + \frac{\partial(\ )}{\partial y}\, \hat{\mathbf{j}} + \frac{\partial(\ )}{\partial z}\, \hat{\mathbf{k}}$$

and the symbol ∇ is the *gradient* or "del" vector operator. Thus, the resultant surface force per unit volume can be expressed as

$$\frac{\delta \mathbf{F}_s}{\delta x\, \delta y\, \delta z} = -\nabla p$$

Since the z axis is vertical, the weight of the element is

$$-\delta \mathcal{W}\hat{\mathbf{k}} = -\gamma\, \delta x\, \delta y\, \delta z\, \hat{\mathbf{k}}$$

where the negative sign indicates that the force due to the weight is downward (in the negative z direction). Newton's second law, applied to the fluid element, can be expressed as

$$\Sigma\, \delta \mathbf{F} = \delta m\, \mathbf{a}$$

where $\Sigma\, \delta \mathbf{F}$ represents the resultant force acting on the element, $\mathbf{a}$ is the acceleration of the element, and δm is the element mass, which can be written as $\rho\, \delta x\, \delta y\, \delta z$. It follows that

$$\Sigma\, \delta \mathbf{F} = \delta \mathbf{F}_s - \delta \mathcal{W}\hat{\mathbf{k}} = \delta m\, \mathbf{a}$$

or

$$-\nabla p\, \delta x\, \delta y\, \delta z - \gamma\, \delta x\, \delta y\, \delta z\, \hat{\mathbf{k}} = \rho\, \delta x\, \delta y\, \delta z\, \mathbf{a}$$

and, therefore,

$$-\nabla p - \gamma \hat{\mathbf{k}} = \rho \mathbf{a} \tag{2.2}$$

Equation 2.2 is the general equation of motion for a fluid in which there are no shearing stresses. Although Eq. 2.2 applies to both fluids at rest and moving fluids, we will primarily restrict our attention to fluids at rest.

2.3   Pressure Variation in a Fluid at Rest

For a fluid at rest $\mathbf{a} = 0$ and Eq. 2.2 reduces to

$$\nabla p + \gamma \hat{\mathbf{k}} = 0$$

or in component form

$$\frac{\partial p}{\partial x} = 0 \qquad \frac{\partial p}{\partial y} = 0 \qquad \frac{\partial p}{\partial z} = -\gamma \tag{2.3}$$

These equations show that the pressure does not depend on x or y. Thus, as we move from point to point in a horizontal plane (any plane parallel to the $x - y$ plane), the pressure does not change. Since p depends only on z, the last of Eqs. 2.3 can be written as the ordinary differential equation

$$\boxed{\frac{dp}{dz} = -\gamma} \tag{2.4}$$

Equation 2.4 is the fundamental equation for fluids at rest and can be used to determine how pressure changes with elevation. This equation indicates that the pressure gradient in the vertical direction is negative; that is, the pressure decreases as we move upward in a fluid at rest. There is no requirement that γ be a constant. Thus, it is valid for fluids with constant specific weight, such as liquids, as well as fluids whose specific weight may vary with elevation, such as air or other gases. However, to proceed with the integration of Eq. 2.4 it is necessary to stipulate how the specific weight varies with z.

2.3.1   Incompressible Fluid

Since the specific weight is equal to the product of fluid density and acceleration of gravity ($\gamma = \rho g$), changes in γ are caused either by a change in ρ or g. For most engineering applications the variation in g is negligible, so our main concern is with the possible variation in the fluid density. For liquids the variation in density is usually negligible, even over large vertical distances, so that the assumption of constant specific weight when dealing with liquids is a good one. For this instance, Eq. 2.4 can be directly integrated

$$\int_{p_1}^{p_2} dp = -\gamma \int_{z_1}^{z_2} dz$$

to yield

$$p_1 - p_2 = \gamma(z_2 - z_1) \tag{2.5}$$

where p_1 and p_2 are pressures at the vertical elevations z_1 and z_2, as is illustrated in Fig. 2.3. Equation 2.5 can be written in the compact form

$$p_1 - p_2 = \gamma h \tag{2.6}$$

or

$$p_1 = \gamma h + p_2 \tag{2.7}$$

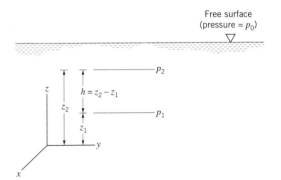

Free surface
(pressure = p_0)

p_2

$h = z_2 - z_1$

p_1

■ **FIGURE 2.3**   **Notation for pressure variation in a fluid at rest with a free surface.**

where h is the distance, $z_2 - z_1$, which is the depth of fluid measured downward from the location of p_2. This type of pressure distribution is commonly called a *hydrostatic distribution,* and Eq. 2.7 shows that in an incompressible fluid at rest the pressure varies linearly with depth. The pressure must increase with depth to "hold up" the fluid above it.

It can also be observed from Eq. 2.6 that the pressure difference between two points can be specified by the distance h since

$$h = \frac{p_1 - p_2}{\gamma}$$

In this case h is called the *pressure head* and is interpreted as the height of a column of fluid of specific weight γ required to give a pressure difference $p_1 - p_2$. For example, a pressure difference of 10 psi can be specified in terms of pressure head as 23.1 ft of water ($\gamma = 62.4$ lb/ft^3), or 518 mm of Hg ($\gamma = 133$ kN/m^3).

When one works with liquids there is often a free surface, as is illustrated in Fig. 2.3, and it is convenient to use this surface as a reference plane. The reference pressure p_0 would correspond to the pressure acting on the free surface (which would frequently be atmospheric pressure), and thus if we let $p_2 = p_0$ in Eq. 2.7 it follows that the pressure p at any depth h below the free surface is given by the equation:

$$p = \gamma h + p_0 \tag{2.8}$$

As is demonstrated by Eq. 2.7 or 2.8, the pressure in a homogeneous, incompressible fluid at rest depends on the depth of the fluid relative to some reference plane, and it is *not* influenced by the *size* or *shape* of the tank or container in which the fluid is held.

EXAMPLE 2.1

Because of a leak in a buried gasoline storage tank, water has seeped in to the depth shown in Fig. E2.1. If the specific gravity of the gasoline is $SG = 0.68$, determine the pressure at the gasoline-water interface, and at the bottom of the tank. Express the pressure in units of lb/ft^2, lb/in.^{2}, and as a pressure head in feet of water.

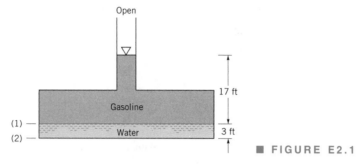

Open

17 ft

Gasoline

(1) ———

(2) ———

Water

3 ft

■ **FIGURE E2.1**

Solution

Since we are dealing with liquids at rest, the pressure distribution will be hydrostatic, and therefore the pressure variation can be found from the equation:

$$p = \gamma h + p_0$$

With p_0 corresponding to the pressure at the free surface of the gasoline, then the pressure at the interface is

$$
\begin{aligned}
p_1 &= SG\gamma_{H_2O}h + p_0 \\
&= (0.68)(62.4 \text{ lb/ft}^3)(17 \text{ ft}) + p_0 \\
&= 721 + p_0 \,(\text{lb/ft}^2)
\end{aligned}
$$

If we measure the pressure relative to atmospheric pressure (gage pressure), it follows that $p_0 = 0$, and therefore

$$p_1 = 721 \text{ lb/ft}^2 \tag{Ans}$$

$$p_1 = \frac{721 \text{ lb/ft}^2}{144 \text{ in.}^2/\text{ft}^2} = 5.01 \text{ lb/in.}^2 \tag{Ans}$$

$$\frac{p_1}{\gamma_{H_2O}} = \frac{721 \text{ lb/ft}^2}{62.4 \text{ lb/ft}^3} = 11.6 \text{ ft} \tag{Ans}$$

It is noted that a rectangular column of water 11.6 ft tall and 1 ft^2 in cross section weighs 721 lb. A similar column with a 1-in.^{2} cross section weighs 5.01 lb.

We can now apply the same relationship to determine the pressure at the tank bottom; that is,

$$
\begin{aligned}
p_2 &= \gamma_{H_2O}h_{H_2O} + p_1 \\
&= (62.4 \text{ lb/ft}^3)(3 \text{ ft}) + 721 \text{ lb/ft}^2 \\
&= 908 \text{ lb/ft}^2 \tag{Ans}
\end{aligned}
$$

$$p_2 = \frac{908 \text{ lb/ft}^2}{144 \text{ in.}^2/\text{ft}^2} = 6.31 \text{ lb/in.}^2 \tag{Ans}$$

$$\frac{p_2}{\gamma_{H_2O}} = \frac{908 \text{ lb/ft}^2}{62.4 \text{ lb/ft}^3} = 14.6 \text{ ft} \tag{Ans}$$

Observe that if we wish to express these pressures in terms of *absolute* pressure, we would have to add the local atmospheric pressure (in appropriate units) to the previous results. A further discussion of gage and absolute pressure is given in Section 2.5.

2.3.2   Compressible Fluid

We normally think of gases such as air, oxygen, and nitrogen as being compressible fluids since the density of the gas can change significantly with changes in pressure and temperature. Thus, although Eq. 2.4 applies at a point in a gas, it is necessary to consider the possible variation in γ before the equation can be integrated. However, as we discussed in Chapter 1, the specific weights of common gases are small when compared with those of liquids. For example, the specific weight of air at sea level and 60 °F is 0.0763 lb/ft^3, whereas the specific weight of water under the same conditions is 62.4 lb/ft^3. Since the specific weights of gases are comparatively small, it follows from Eq. 2.4 that the pressure gradient in the vertical direction is correspondingly small, and even over distances of several hundred feet the pressure will remain essentially constant for a gas. This means we can neglect the effect of elevation changes on the pressure in gases in tanks, pipes, and so forth in which the distances involved are small.

For those situations in which the variations in heights are large, on the order of thousands of feet, attention must be given to the variation in the specific weight. As is described in Chapter 1, the equation of state for an ideal (or perfect) gas is

$$p = \rho R T$$

where p is the absolute pressure, R is the gas constant, and T is the absolute temperature. This relationship can be combined with Eq. 2.4 to give

$$\frac{dp}{dz} = -\frac{gp}{RT}$$

and by separating variables

$$\int_{p_1}^{p_2} \frac{dp}{p} = \ln\frac{p_2}{p_1} = -\frac{g}{R}\int_{z_1}^{z_2}\frac{dz}{T} \tag{2.9}$$

where g and R are assumed to be constant over the elevation change from z_1 to z_2.

Before completing the integration, one must specify the nature of the variation of temperature with elevation. For example, if we assume that the temperature has a constant value T_0 over the range z_1 to z_2 (*isothermal* conditions), it then follows from Eq. 2.9 that

$$p_2 = p_1 \exp\left[-\frac{g(z_2 - z_1)}{RT_0}\right] \tag{2.10}$$

This equation provides the desired pressure-elevation relationship for an isothermal layer. For nonisothermal conditions a similar procedure can be followed if the temperature-elevation relationship is known.

2.4   Standard Atmosphere

An important application of Eq. 2.9 relates to the variation in pressure in the earth's atmosphere. Ideally, we would like to have measurements of pressure versus altitude over the specific range for the specific conditions (temperature, reference pressure) for which the pressure is to be determined. However, this type of information is usually not available. Thus, a

■ **TABLE 2.1**
Properties of U.S. Standard Atmosphere at Sea Level[a]

Property	SI Units	BG Units
Temperature, T	288.15 K (15 °C)	518.67 °R (59.00 °F)
Pressure, p	101.33 kPa (abs)	2116.2 lb/ft^2 (abs) [14.696 lb/in.^{2} (abs)]
Density, ρ	1.225 kg/m^3	0.002377 slugs/ft^3
Specific weight, γ	12.014 N/m^3	0.07647 lb/ft^3
Viscosity, μ	1.789×10^{-5} N·s/m^2	3.737×10^{-7} lb·s/ft^2

[a]Acceleration of gravity at sea level = 9.807 m/s^2 = 32.174 ft/s^2.

"standard atmosphere" has been determined that can be used in the design of aircraft, missiles, and spacecraft, and in comparing their performance under standard conditions.

The currently accepted standard atmosphere is based on a report published in 1962 and updated in 1976 (see Refs. 1 and 2), defining the so-called *U.S. standard atmosphere,* which is an idealized representation of middle-latitude, year-round mean conditions of the earth's atmosphere. Several important properties for standard atmospheric conditions at *sea level* are listed in Table 2.1.

Tabulated values for temperature, acceleration of gravity, pressure, density, and viscosity for the U.S. standard atmosphere are given in Tables C.1 and C.2 in Appendix C.

2.5   Measurement of Pressure

Since pressure is a very important characteristic of a fluid field, it is not surprising that numerous devices and techniques are used in its measurement. As is noted briefly in Chapter 1, the pressure at a point within a fluid mass will be designated as either an *absolute* pressure or a *gage* pressure. Absolute pressure is measured relative to a perfect vacuum (absolute zero pressure), whereas gage pressure is measured relative to the local atmospheric pressure. Thus, a gage pressure of zero corresponds to a pressure that is equal to the local atmospheric pressure. Absolute pressures are always positive, but gage pressure can be either positive or negative depending on whether the pressure is above atmospheric pressure (a positive value) or below atmospheric pressure (a negative value). A negative gage pressure is also referred to as a *suction* or *vacuum* pressure. For example, 10 psi (abs) could be expressed as −4.7 psi (gage), if the local atmospheric pressure is 14.7 psi, or alternatively 4.7 psi suction or 4.7 psi vacuum. The concept of gage and absolute pressure is illustrated graphically in Fig. 2.4 for two typical pressures located at points 1 and 2.

In addition to the reference used for the pressure measurement, the *units* used to express the value are obviously of importance. As is described in Section 1.5, pressure is a force per unit area, and the units in the BG system are lb/ft^2 or lb/in.^{2}, commonly abbreviated psf or psi, respectively. In the SI system the units are N/m^2; this combination is called the pascal and written as Pa (1 N/m^2 = 1 Pa). As noted earlier, pressure can also be expressed as the height of a column of liquid. Then, the units will refer to the height of the column (in., ft, mm, m, etc.), and in addition, the liquid in the column must be specified (H_2O, Hg,

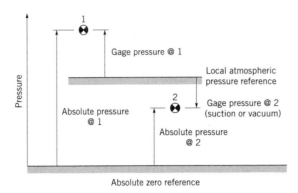

■ FIGURE 2.4 **Graphical representation of gage and absolute pressure.**

etc.). For example, standard atmospheric pressure can be expressed as 760 mm Hg (abs). *In this text, pressures will be assumed to be gage pressures unless specifically designated absolute.* For example, 10 psi or 100 kPa would be gage pressures, whereas 10 psia or 100 kPa (abs) would refer to absolute pressures. It is to be noted that *pressure differences* are independent of the reference, so that no special notation is required in this case.

The measurement of atmospheric pressure is usually accomplished with a mercury *barometer,* which in its simplest form consists of a glass tube closed at one end with the open end immersed in a container of mercury as shown in Fig. 2.5. The tube is initially filled with mercury (inverted with its open end up) and then turned upside down (open end down) with the open end in the container of mercury. The column of mercury will come to an equilibrium position where its weight plus the force due to the vapor pressure (which develops in the space above the column) balances the force due to the atmospheric pressure. Thus,

$$p_{atm} = \gamma h + p_{vapor} \tag{2.11}$$

where γ is the specific weight of mercury. For most practical purposes the contribution of the vapor pressure can be neglected since it is very small [for mercury, $p_{vapor} = 0.000023$ lb/in.^{2} (abs) at a temperature of 68 °F] so that $p_{atm} \approx \gamma h$. It is convenient to specify atmospheric pressure in terms of the height, h, in millimeters or inches of mercury.

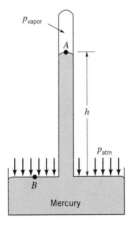

■ FIGURE 2.5 **Mercury barometer.**

2.6   Manometry

A standard technique for measuring pressure involves the use of liquid columns in vertical or inclined tubes. Pressure measuring devices based on this technique are called *manometers*. The mercury barometer is an example of one type of manometer, but there are many other configurations possible, depending on the particular application. Three common types of manometers include the piezometer tube, the U-tube manometer, and the inclined-tube manometer.

2.6.1   Piezometer Tube

The simplest type of manometer consists of a vertical tube, open at the top, and attached to the container in which the pressure is desired, as illustrated in Fig. 2.6. Since manometers involve columns of fluids at rest, the fundamental equation describing their use is Eq. 2.8

$$p = \gamma h + p_0$$

which gives the pressure at any elevation within a homogeneous fluid in terms of a reference pressure p_0 and the vertical distance h between p and p_0. Remember that in a fluid at rest pressure will *increase* as we move *downward,* and will decrease as we move *upward.* Application of this equation to the piezometer tube of Fig. 2.6 indicates that the pressure p_A can be determined by a measurement of h_1 through the relationship

$$p_A = \gamma_1 h_1$$

where γ_1 is the specific weight of the liquid in the container. Note that since the tube is open at the top, the pressure p_0 can be set equal to zero (we are now using gage pressure), with the height h_1 measured from the meniscus at the upper surface to point (1). Since point (1) and point A within the container are at the same elevation, $p_A = p_1$.

Although the piezometer tube is a very simple and accurate pressure measuring device, it has several disadvantages. It is only suitable if the pressure in the container is greater than atmospheric pressure (otherwise air would be sucked into the system), and the pressure to be measured must be relatively small so the required height of the column is reasonable. Also, the fluid in the container in which the pressure is to be measured must be a liquid rather than a gas.

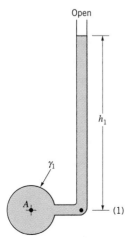

■ **FIGURE 2.6**   **Piezometer tube.**

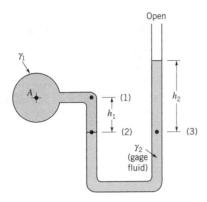

■ FIGURE 2.7 Simple U-tube manometer.

2.6.2   U-Tube Manometer

V2.1 Blood pressure measurement

To overcome the difficulties noted previously, another type of manometer that is widely used consists of a tube formed into the shape of a U as is shown in Fig. 2.7. The fluid in the manometer is called the *gage fluid*. To find the pressure p_A in terms of the various column heights, we start at one end of the system and work our way around to the other end, simply utilizing Eq. 2.8. Thus, for the U-tube manometer shown in Fig. 2.7, we will start at point A and work around to the open end. The pressure at points A and (1) are the same, and as we move from point (1) to (2) the pressure will increase by $\gamma_1 h_1$. The pressure at point (2) is equal to the pressure at point (3), since the pressures at equal elevations in a continuous mass of fluid at rest must be the same. Note that we could not simply "jump across" from point (1) to a point at the same elevation in the right-hand tube since these would not be points within the same continuous mass of fluid. With the pressure at point (3) specified we now move to the open end where the pressure is zero. As we move vertically upward the pressure decreases by an amount $\gamma_2 h_2$. In equation form these various steps can be expressed as

$$p_A + \gamma_1 h_1 - \gamma_2 h_2 = 0$$

and, therefore, the pressure p_A can be written in terms of the column heights as

$$p_A = \gamma_2 h_2 - \gamma_1 h_1 \tag{2.12}$$

A major advantage of the U-tube manometer lies in the fact that the gage fluid can be different from the fluid in the container in which the pressure is to be determined. For example, the fluid in A in Fig. 2.7 can be either a liquid or a gas. If A does contain a gas, the contribution of the gas column, $\gamma_1 h_1$, is almost always negligible so that $p_A \approx p_2$ and in this instance Eq. 2.12 becomes

$$p_A = \gamma_2 h_2$$

EXAMPLE 2.2

A closed tank contains compressed air and oil ($SG_{\text{oil}} = 0.90$) as is shown in Fig. E2.2. A U-tube manometer using mercury ($SG_{\text{Hg}} = 13.6$) is connected to the tank as shown. For column heights $h_1 = 36$ in., $h_2 = 6$ in., and $h_3 = 9$ in., determine the pressure reading (in psi) of the gage.

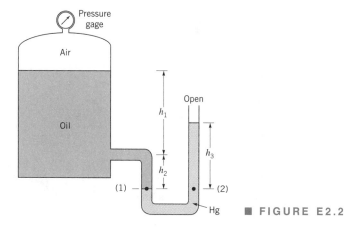

■ FIGURE E2.2

SOLUTION

Following the general procedure of starting at one end of the manometer system and work-ing around to the other, we will start at the air–oil interface in the tank and proceed to the open end where the pressure is zero. The pressure at level (1) is

$$p_1 = p_{air} + \gamma_{oil}(h_1 + h_2)$$

This pressure is equal to the pressure at level (2), since these two points are at the same el-evation in a homogeneous fluid at rest. As we move from level (2) to the open end, the pres-sure must decrease by $\gamma_{Hg}h_3$, and at the open end the pressure is zero. Thus, the manometer equation can be expressed as

$$p_{air} + \gamma_{oil}(h_1 + h_2) - \gamma_{Hg}h_3 = 0$$

or

$$p_{air} + (SG_{oil})(\gamma_{H_2O})(h_1 + h_2) - (SG_{Hg})(\gamma_{H_2O})h_3 = 0$$

For the values given

$$p_{air} = -(0.9)(62.4 \text{ lb/ft}^3)\left(\frac{36 + 6}{12} \text{ ft}\right) + (13.6)(62.4 \text{ lb/ft}^3)\left(\frac{9}{12} \text{ ft}\right)$$

so that

$$p_{air} = 440 \text{ lb/ft}^2$$

Since the specific weight of the air above the oil is much smaller than the specific weight of the oil, the gage should read the pressure we have calculated; that is,

$$p_{gage} = \frac{440 \text{ lb/ft}^2}{144 \text{ in.}^2/\text{ft}^2} = 3.06 \text{ psi} \qquad \text{(Ans)}$$

The U-tube manometer is also widely used to measure the *difference* in pressure be-tween two containers or two points in a given system. Consider a manometer connected be-tween containers A and B as is shown in Fig. 2.8. The difference in pressure between A and B can be found by again starting at one end of the system and working around to the other

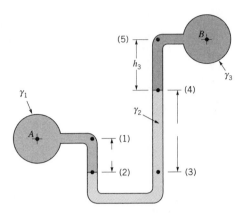

■ FIGURE 2.8   **Differential U-tube manometer.**

end. For example, at A the pressure is p_A, which is equal to p_1, and as we move to point (2) the pressure increases by $\gamma_1 h_1$. The pressure at p_2 is equal to p_3, and as we move upward to point (4) the pressure decreases by $\gamma_2 h_2$. Similarly, as we continue to move upward from point (4) to (5) the pressure decreases by $\gamma_3 h_3$. Finally, $p_5 = p_B$, since they are at equal elevations. Thus,

$$p_A + \gamma_1 h_1 - \gamma_2 h_2 - \gamma_3 h_3 = p_B$$

and the pressure difference is

$$p_A - p_B = \gamma_2 h_2 + \gamma_3 h_3 - \gamma_1 h_1$$

EXAMPLE 2.3

As will be discussed in Chapter 3, the volume rate of flow, Q, through a pipe can be determined by a means of a flow nozzle located in the pipe as illustrated in Fig. E2.3. The nozzle creates a pressure drop, $p_A - p_B$, along the pipe which is related to the flow through the equation, $Q = K\sqrt{p_A - p_B}$, where K is a constant depending on the pipe and nozzle size. The pressure drop is frequently measured with a differential U-tube manometer of the type illustrated. (a) Determine an equation for $p_A - p_B$ in terms of the specific weight of the flowing fluid, γ_1, the specific weight of the gage fluid, γ_2, and the various heights indicated. (b) For $\gamma_1 = 9.80$ kN/m^3, $\gamma_2 = 15.6$ kN/m^3, $h_1 = 1.0$ m, and $h_2 = 0.5$ m, what is the value of the pressure drop, $p_A - p_B$?

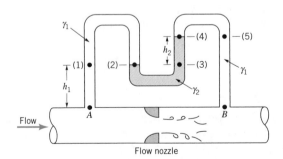

Flow nozzle

■ FIGURE E2.3

SOLUTION

(a) Although the fluid in the pipe is moving, the fluids in the columns of the manometer are at rest so that the pressure variation in the manometer tubes is hydrostatic. If we start at point A and move vertically upward to level (1), the pressure will decrease by $\gamma_1 h_1$ and will be equal to the pressure at (2) and at (3). We can now move from (3) to (4) where the pressure has been further reduced by $\gamma_2 h_2$. The pressures at levels (4) and (5) are equal, and as we move from (5) to B the pressure will increase by $\gamma_1(h_1 + h_2)$. Thus, in equation form

$$p_A - \gamma_1 h_1 - \gamma_2 h_2 + \gamma_1(h_1 + h_2) = p_B$$

or

$$p_A - p_B = h_2(\gamma_2 - \gamma_1) \qquad \text{(Ans)}$$

It is to be noted that the only column height of importance is the differential reading, h_2. The differential manometer could be placed 0.5 or 5.0 m above the pipe ($h_1 = 0.5$ m or $h_1 = 5.0$ m) and the value of h_2 would remain the same. Relatively large values for the differential reading h_2 can be obtained for small pressure differences, $p_A - p_B$, if the difference between γ_1 and γ_2 is small.

(b) The specific value of the pressure drop for the data given is

$$p_A - p_B = (0.5 \text{ m})(15.6 \text{ kN/m}^3 - 9.80 \text{ kN/m}^3)$$
$$= 2.90 \text{ kPa} \qquad \text{(Ans)}$$

2.6.3 Inclined-Tube Manometer

To measure small pressure changes, a manometer of the type shown in Fig. 2.9 is frequently used. One leg of the manometer is inclined at an angle θ, and the differential reading ℓ_2 is measured along the inclined tube. The difference in pressure $p_A - p_B$ can be expressed as

$$p_A + \gamma_1 h_1 - \gamma_2 \ell_2 \sin \theta - \gamma_3 h_3 = p_B$$

or

$$p_A - p_B = \gamma_2 \ell_2 \sin \theta + \gamma_3 h_3 - \gamma_1 h_1 \qquad \textbf{(2.13)}$$

where it is to be noted the pressure difference between points (1) and (2) is due to the *vertical* distance between the points, which can be expressed as $\ell_2 \sin \theta$. Thus, for relatively

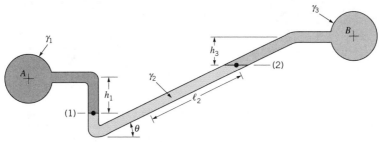

■ **FIGURE 2.9**   **Inclined-tube manometer.**

small angles the differential reading along the inclined tube can be made large even for small pressure differences. The inclined-tube manometer is often used to measure small differences in gas pressures so that if pipes A and B contain a gas then

$$p_A - p_B = \gamma_2 \ell_2 \sin \theta$$

or

$$\ell_2 = \frac{p_A - p_B}{\gamma_2 \sin \theta} \tag{2.14}$$

where the contributions of the gas columns h_1 and h_3 have been neglected. Equation 2.14 shows that the differential reading ℓ_2 (for a given pressure difference) of the inclined-tube manometer can be increased over that obtained with a conventional U-tube manometer by the factor $1/\sin \theta$. Recall that $\sin \theta \rightarrow 0$ as $\theta \rightarrow 0$.

2.7   Mechanical and Electronic Pressure Measuring Devices

V2.2 Bourdon gage

Although manometers are widely used, they are not well suited for measuring very high pressures, or pressures that are changing rapidly with time. In addition, they require the measurement of one or more column heights, which, although not particularly difficult, can be time consuming. To overcome some of these problems numerous other types of pressure-measuring instruments have been developed. Most of these make use of the idea that when a pressure acts on an elastic structure the structure will deform, and this deformation can be related to the magnitude of the pressure. Probably the most familiar device of this kind is the *Bourdon* pressure gage, which is shown in Fig. 2.10*a*. The essential mechanical element in this gage is the hollow, elastic curved tube (Bourdon tube), which is connected to the pressure source as shown in Fig. 2.10*b*. As the pressure within the tube increases the tube tends to straighten, and although the deformation is small, it can be translated into the motion of a pointer on a dial as illustrated. Since it is the difference in pressure between the outside of the tube (atmospheric pressure) and the inside of the tube that causes the movement of the tube, the indicated pressure is gage pressure. The Bourdon gage must be calibrated so that the dial reading can directly

■ FIGURE 2.10   *(a)* Liquid-filled Bourdon pressure gages for various pressure ranges. *(b)* Internal elements of Bourdon gages. The "C-shaped" Bourdon tube is shown on the left, and the "coiled spring" Bourdon tube for high pressures of 1000 psi and above is shown on the right. (Photographs courtesy of Weiss Instruments, Inc.)

indicate the pressure in suitable units such as psi, psf, or pascals. A zero reading on the gage indicates that the measured pressure is equal to the local atmospheric pressure. This type of gage can be used to measure a negative gage pressure (vacuum) as well as positive pressures.

For many applications in which pressure measurements are required, the pressure must be measured with a device that converts the pressure into an electrical output. For example, it may be desirable to continuously monitor a pressure that is changing with time. This type of pressure measuring device is called a *pressure transducer,* and many different designs are used.

2.8 Hydrostatic Force on a Plane Surface

V2.3 Hoover
dam

When a surface is submerged in a fluid, forces develop on the surface due to the fluid. The determination of these forces is important in the design of storage tanks, ships, dams, and other hydraulic structures. For fluids at rest we know that the force must be *perpendicular* to the surface since there are no shearing stresses present. We also know that the pressure will vary linearly with depth if the fluid is incompressible. For a horizontal surface, such as the bottom of a liquid-filled tank (Fig. 2.11), the magnitude of the resultant force is simply $F_R = pA$, where p is the uniform pressure on the bottom and A is the area of the bottom. For the open tank shown, $p = \gamma h$. Note that if atmospheric pressure acts on both sides of the bottom, as is illustrated, the *resultant* force on the bottom is simply due to the liquid in the tank. Since the pressure is constant and uniformly distributed over the bottom, the resultant force acts through the centroid of the area as shown in Fig. 2.11.

For the more general case in which a submerged plane surface is inclined, as is illustrated in Fig. 2.12, the determination of the resultant force acting on the surface is more involved. For the present we will assume that the fluid surface is open to the atmosphere. Let the plane in which the surface lies intersect the free surface at 0 and make an angle θ with this surface as in Fig. 2.12. The *x-y* coordinate system is defined so that 0 is the origin and y is directed along the surface as shown. The area can have an arbitrary shape as shown. We wish to determine the direction, location, and magnitude of the resultant force acting on one side of this area due to the liquid in contact with the area. At any given depth, h, the force acting on dA (the differential area of Fig. 2.12) is $dF = \gamma h\, dA$ and is perpendicular to the surface. Thus, the magnitude of the resultant force can be found by summing these differential forces over the entire surface. In equation form

$$F_R = \int_A \gamma h\, dA = \int_A \gamma y \sin\theta\, dA$$

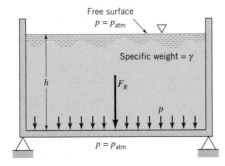

■ **FIGURE 2.11** **Pressure and resultant hydrostatic force developed on the bottom of an open tank.**

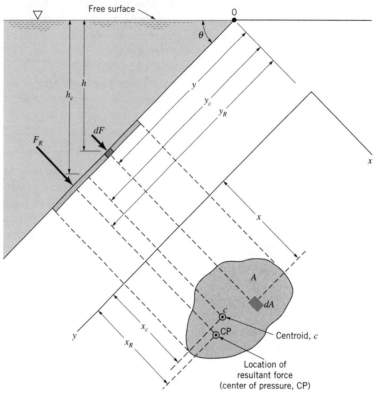

■ **FIGURE 2.12** **Notation for hydrostatic force on an inclined plane surface of arbitrary shape.**

where $h = y \sin \theta$. For constant γ and θ

$$F_R = y \sin \theta \int_A y \, dA \qquad (2.15)$$

The integral appearing in Eq. 2.15 is the *first moment of the area* with respect to the *x* axis, so we can write

$$\int_A y \, dA = y_c A$$

where y_c is the *y* coordinate of the centroid measured from the *x* axis, which passes through 0. Equation 2.15 can thus be written as

$$F_R = \gamma A y_c \sin \theta$$

or more simply as

$$\boxed{F_R = \gamma h_c A} \qquad (2.16)$$

where h_c is the vertical distance from the fluid surface to the centroid of the area. Note that the magnitude of the force is independent of the angle θ and depends only on the specific weight of the fluid, the total area, and the depth of the centroid of the area below the surface. In effect, Eq. 2.16 indicates that the magnitude of the resultant force is equal to the pressure at the centroid of the area multiplied by the total area. Since all the differential forces that were summed to obtain F_R are perpendicular to the surface, the resultant F_R must also be perpendicular to the surface.

Although our intuition might suggest that the resultant force should pass through the centroid of the area, this is not actually the case. The y coordinate, y_R, of the resultant force can be determined by summation of moments around the x axis. That is, the moment of the resultant force must equal the moment of the distributed pressure force, or

$$F_R y_R = \int_A y \, dF = \int_A \gamma \sin \theta \, y^2 \, dA$$

and, therefore, since $F_R = \gamma A y_c \sin \theta$

$$y_R = \frac{\displaystyle\int_A y^2 \, dA}{y_c A}$$

The integral in the numerator is the *second moment of the area (moment of inertia)*, I_x, with respect to an axis formed by the intersection of the plane containing the surface and the free surface (x axis). Thus, we can write

$$y_R = \frac{I_x}{y_c A}$$

Use can now be made of the parallel axis theorem to express I_x as

$$I_x = I_{xc} + A y_c^2$$

where I_{xc} is the second moment of the area with respect to an axis passing through its *centroid* and parallel to the x axis. Thus,

$$\boxed{y_R = \frac{I_{xc}}{y_c A} + y_c} \tag{2.17}$$

Equation 2.17 clearly shows that the resultant force does not pass through the centroid but is always *below* it, since $I_{xc}/y_c A > 0$.

The x coordinate, x_R, for the resultant force can be determined in a similar manner by summing moments about the y axis. It follows that

$$\boxed{x_R = \frac{I_{xyc}}{y_c A} + x_c} \tag{2.18}$$

where I_{xyc} is the product of inertia with respect to an orthogonal coordinate system passing through the *centroid* of the area and formed by a translation of the *x-y* coordinate system. If the submerged area is symmetrical with respect to an axis passing through the centroid and parallel to either the x or y axes, the resultant force must lie along the line $x = x_c$, since I_{xyc} is identically zero in this case. The point through which the resultant force acts is called the

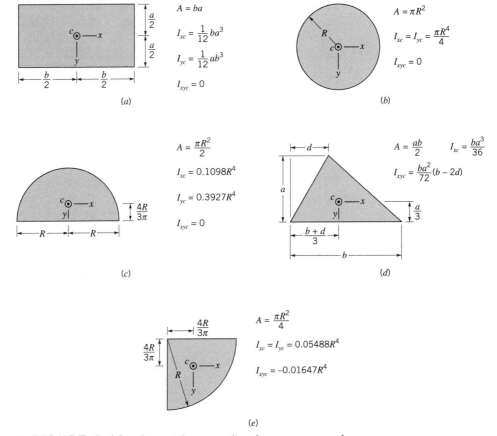

■ **FIGURE 2.13**   **Geometric properties of some common shapes.**

center of pressure. It is to be noted from Eqs. 2.17 and 2.18 that as y_c increases the center of pressure moves closer to the centroid of the area. Since $y_c = h_c/\sin\theta$, the distance y_c will increase if the depth of submergence, h_c, increases, or, for a given depth, the area is rotated so that the angle, θ, decreases. Centroidal coordinates and moments of inertia for some common areas are given in Fig. 2.13.

EXAMPLE 2.4

The 4-m-diameter circular gate of Fig. E2.4a is located in the inclined wall of a large reservoir containing water ($\gamma = 9.80$ kN/m³). The gate is mounted on a shaft along its horizontal diameter. For a water depth of 10 m above the shaft determine: (a) the magnitude and location of the resultant force exerted on the gate by the water, and (b) the moment that would have to be applied to the shaft to open the gate.

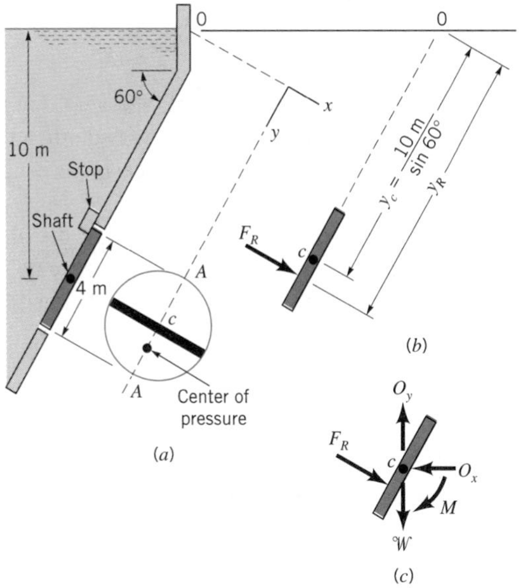

■ FIGURE E2.4

SOLUTION

(a) To find the magnitude of the force of the water we can apply Eq. 2.16,

$$F_R = \gamma h_c A$$

and since the vertical distance from the fluid surface to the centroid of the area is 10 m it follows that

$$F_R = (9.80 \times 10^3 \text{ N/m}^3)(10 \text{ m})(4\pi \text{ m}^2)$$
$$= 1230 \times 10^3 \text{ N} = 1.23 \text{ MN} \qquad \text{(Ans)}$$

To locate the point (center of pressure) through which F_R acts, we use Eqs. 2.17 and 2.18,

$$x_R = \frac{I_{xyc}}{y_c A} + x_c \qquad y_R = \frac{I_{xc}}{y_c A} + y_c$$

For the coordinate system shown, $x_R = 0$ since the area is symmetrical, and the center of pressure must lie along the diameter A-A. To obtain y_R, we have from Fig. 2.13

$$I_{xc} = \frac{\pi R^4}{4}$$

and y_c is shown in Fig. E2.4b. Thus,

$$y_R = \frac{(\pi/4)(2 \text{ m})^4}{(10 \text{ m}/\sin 60°)(4\pi \text{ m}^2)} + \frac{10 \text{ m}}{\sin 60°}$$
$$= 0.0866 \text{ m} + 11.55 \text{ m} = 11.6 \text{ m}$$

and the distance (along the gate) below the shaft to the center of pressure is

$$y_R - y_c = 0.0866 \text{ m} \tag{Ans}$$

We can conclude from this analysis that the force on the gate due to the water has a magnitude of 1.23 MN and acts through a point along its diameter A-A at a distance of 0.0866 m (along the gate) below the shaft. The force is perpendicular to the gate surface as shown.

(b) The moment required to open the gate can be obtained with the aid of the free-body diagram of Fig. E2.4c. In this diagram $\mathcal{W}$ is the weight of the gate and O_x and O_y are the horizontal and vertical reactions of the shaft on the gate. We can now sum moments about the shaft

$$\Sigma M_c = 0$$

and, therefore,

$$\begin{aligned} M &= F_R(y_R - y_c) \\ &= (1230 \times 10^3 \text{ N})(0.0866 \text{ m}) \\ &= 1.07 \times 10^5 \text{ N·m} \end{aligned} \tag{Ans}$$

2.9   Pressure Prism

An informative and useful graphical interpretation can be made for the force developed by a fluid acting on a plane area. Consider the pressure distribution along a vertical wall of a tank of width b, which contains a liquid having a specific weight γ. Since the pressure must vary linearly with depth, we can represent the variation as is shown in Fig. 2.14a, where the pressure is equal to zero at the upper surface and equal to γh at the bottom. It is apparent from this diagram that the average pressure occurs at the depth $h/2$, and therefore the resultant force acting on the rectangular area $A = bh$ is

$$F_R = p_{av}A = \gamma \left(\frac{h}{2}\right)A$$

which is the same result as obtained from Eq. 2.16. The pressure distribution shown in Fig. 2.14a applies across the vertical surface so we can draw the three-dimensional representation

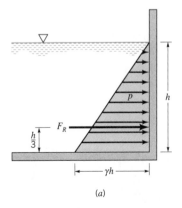

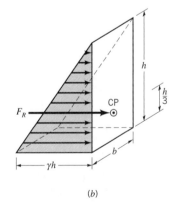

■ **FIGURE 2.14**
Pressure prism for vertical rectangular area.

of the pressure distribution as shown in Fig. 2.14*b*. The base of this "volume" in pressure-area space is the plane surface of interest, and its altitude at each point is the pressure. This volume is called the *pressure prism,* and it is clear that the magnitude of the resultant force acting on the surface is equal to the volume of the pressure prism. Thus, for the prism of Fig. 2.14*b* the fluid force is

$$F_R = \text{volume} = \frac{1}{2}(\gamma h)(bh) = \gamma\left(\frac{h}{2}\right)A$$

where *bh* is the area of the rectangular surface, *A.*

The resultant force must pass through the *centroid* of the pressure prism. For the volume under consideration the centroid is located along the vertical axis of symmetry of the surface, and at a distance of *h*/3 above the base (since the centroid of a triangle is located at *h*/3 above its base). This result can readily be shown to be consistent with that obtained from Eqs. 2.17 and 2.18.

If the surface pressure of the liquid is different from atmospheric pressure (such as might occur in a closed tank), the resultant force acting on a submerged area, *A,* will be changed in magnitude from that caused simply by hydrostatic pressure by an amount $p_s A$, where p_s is the gage pressure at the liquid surface (the outside surface is assumed to be exposed to atmospheric pressure).

EXAMPLE 2.5

A pressurized tank contains oil (*SG* = 0.90) and has a square, 0.6-m by 0.6-m plate bolted to its side, as is illustrated in Fig. E2.5*a*. When the pressure gage on the top of the tank reads 50 kPa, what is the magnitude and location of the resultant force on the attached plate? The outside of the tank is at atmospheric pressure.

SOLUTION

The pressure distribution acting on the inside surface of the plate is shown in Fig. E2.5*b*. The pressure at a given point on the plate is due to the air pressure, p_s, at the oil surface, and the pressure due to the oil, which varies linearly with depth as is shown in the figure. The resultant force on the plate (having an area *A*) is due to the components, F_1 and F_2, with

$$
\begin{aligned}
F_1 &= (p_s + \gamma h_1)A \\
&= [50 \times 10^3 \text{ N/m}^2 + (0.90)(9.81 \times 10^3 \text{ N/m}^3)(2 \text{ m})](0.36 \text{ m}^2) \\
&= 24.4 \times 10^3 \text{ N}
\end{aligned}
$$

and

$$
\begin{aligned}
F_2 &= \gamma\left(\frac{h_2 - h_1}{2}\right)A \\
&= (0.90)(9.81 \times 10^3 \text{ N/m}^3)\left(\frac{0.6 \text{ m}}{2}\right)(0.36 \text{ m}^2) \\
&= 0.954 \times 10^3 \text{ N}
\end{aligned}
$$

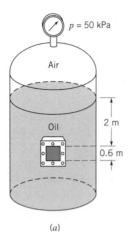

(a)

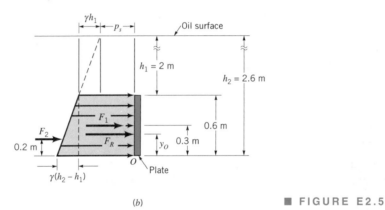

(b)

■ **FIGURE E2.5**

The magnitude of the resultant force, F_R, is therefore

$$F_R = F_1 + F_2 = 25.4 \times 10^3 \text{ N} = 25.4 \text{ kN} \qquad \text{(Ans)}$$

The vertical location of F_R can be obtained by summing moments around an axis through point O so that

$$F_R y_O = F_1(0.3 \text{ m}) + F_2(0.2 \text{ m})$$

or

$$(25.4 \times 10^3 \text{ N})y_O = (24.4 \times 10^3 \text{ N})(0.3 \text{ m}) + (0.954 \times 10^3 \text{ N})(0.2 \text{ m})$$
$$y_O = 0.296 \text{ m} \qquad \text{(Ans)}$$

Thus, the force acts at a distance of 0.296 m above the bottom of the plate along the vertical axis of symmetry.

Note that the air pressure used in the calculation of the force was gage pressure. Atmospheric pressure does not affect the resultant force (magnitude or location), since it acts on both sides of the plate, thereby canceling its effect.

2.10 Hydrostatic Force on a Curved Surface

The equations developed in Section 2.8 for the magnitude and location of the resultant force acting on a submerged surface only apply to plane surfaces. However, many surfaces of interest (such as those associated with dams, pipes, and tanks) are nonplanar. Although the resultant fluid force can be determined by integration, as was done for the plane surfaces, this is generally a rather tedious process and no simple, general formulas can be developed. As an alternative approach we will consider the equilibrium of the fluid volume enclosed by the curved surface of interest and the horizontal and vertical projections of this surface.

V2.4 Pop bottle

For example, consider the curved section BC of the open tank of Fig. 2.15a. We wish to find the resultant fluid force acting on this section, which has a unit length perpendicular to the plane of the paper. We first isolate a volume of fluid that is bounded by the surface of interest, in this instance section BC, and the horizontal plane surface AB and the vertical plane surface AC. The free-body diagram for this volume is shown in Fig. 2.15b. The magnitude and location of forces F_1 and F_2 can be determined from the relationships for planar surfaces. The weight, $\mathcal{W}$, is simply the specific weight of the fluid times the enclosed volume and acts through the center of gravity (CG) of the mass of fluid contained within the volume. The forces F_H and F_V represent the components of the force that the tank *exerts on the fluid*.

In order for this force system to be in equilibrium, the horizontal component F_H must be equal in magnitude and collinear with F_2, and the vertical component F_V equal in magnitude and collinear with the resultant of the vertical forces F_1 and $\mathcal{W}$. This follows since the three forces acting on the fluid mass (F_2, the resultant of F_1 and $\mathcal{W}$, and the resultant force that the tank exerts on the mass) must form a *concurrent* force system. That is, from the principles of statics, it is known that when a body is held in equilibrium by three non-parallel forces they must be concurrent (their lines of action intersect at a common point), and coplanar. Thus,

$$F_H = F_2$$
$$F_V = F_1 + \mathcal{W}$$

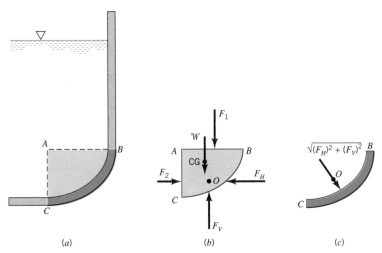

(a) (b) (c)

■ FIGURE 2.15 Hydrostatic force on a curved surface.

and the magnitude of the resultant is obtained from the equation

$$F_R = \sqrt{(F_H)^2 + (F_V)^2}$$

The resultant F_R passes through the point O, which can be located by summing moments about an appropriate axis. The resultant force of the fluid acting *on the curved surface BC* is equal and opposite in direction to that obtained from the free-body diagram of Fig. 2.15b. The desired fluid force is shown in Fig. 2.15c.

EXAMPLE 2.6

The 6-ft-diameter drainage conduit of Fig. E2.6a is half full of water at rest. Determine the magnitude and line of action of the resultant force that the water exerts on a 1-ft-width of the curved section *BC* of the conduit wall.

SOLUTION

We first isolate a volume of fluid bounded by the curved section *BC*, the horizontal surface *AB*, and the vertical surface *AC*, as shown in Fig. E2.6b. The volume has a length of 1 ft. The forces acting on the volume are the horizontal force, F_1, which acts on the vertical surface *AC*, the weight, $\mathcal{W}$, of the fluid contained within the volume, and the horizontal and vertical components of the force of the conduit wall on the fluid, F_H and F_V, respectively.

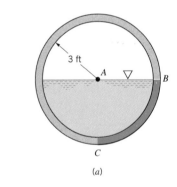

(a)

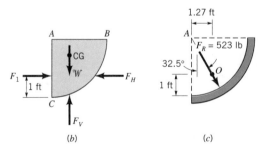

(b)   (c)   ■ FIGURE E2.6

The magnitude of F_1 is found from the equation

$$F_1 = \gamma h_c A = (62.4 \text{ lb/ft}^3)(\tfrac{3}{2} \text{ ft})(3 \text{ ft}^2) = 281 \text{ lb}$$

and this force acts 1 ft above C as shown. The weight, $\mathscr{W}$, is

$$\mathscr{W} = \gamma \text{ vol} = (62.4 \text{ lb/ft}^3)(9\pi/4 \text{ ft}^2)(1 \text{ ft}) = 441 \text{ lb}$$

and acts through the center of gravity of the mass of fluid, which according to Fig. 2.13 is located 1.27 ft to the right of AC as shown. Therefore, to satisfy equilibrium

$$F_H = F_1 = 281 \text{ lb}$$
$$F_V = \mathscr{W} = 441 \text{ lb}$$

and the magnitude of the resultant force is

$$F_R = \sqrt{(F_H)^2 + (F_V)^2}$$
$$= \sqrt{(281 \text{ lb})^2 + (441 \text{ lb})^2} = 523 \text{ lb} \qquad \text{(Ans)}$$

The force the water exerts *on* the conduit wall is equal, but *opposite in direction,* to the forces F_H and F_V shown in Fig. E2.6b. Thus, the resultant force *on the conduit wall* is shown in Fig. E2.6c. This force acts through the point O at the angle shown.

An inspection of this result will show that the line of action of the resultant force passes through the center of the conduit. In retrospect, this is not a surprising result since at each point on the curved surface of the conduit the elemental force due to the pressure is normal to the surface, and each line of action must pass through the center of the conduit. It therefore follows that the resultant of this concurrent force system must also pass through the center of concurrence of the elemental forces that make up the system.

This same general approach can also be used for determining the force on curved surfaces of pressurized, closed tanks. If these tanks contain a gas, the weight of the gas is usually negligible in comparison with the forces developed by the pressure. Thus, the forces (such as F_1 and F_2 in Fig. 2.15b) on horizontal and vertical projections of the curved surface of interest can simply be expressed as the internal pressure times the appropriate projected area.

2.11 Buoyancy, Flotation, and Stability

2.11.1 Archimedes' Principle

When a body is completely submerged in a fluid, or floating so that it is only partially submerged, the resultant fluid force acting on the body is called the *buoyant force.* A net upward vertical force results because pressure increases with depth and the pressure forces acting from below are larger than the pressure forces acting from above.

It is well known from elementary physics that the buoyant force, F_B, is given by the equation

V2.5 Cartesian Diver

$$\boxed{F_B = \gamma \mathcal{V}} \qquad \qquad \textbf{(2.19)}$$

where γ is the specific weight of the fluid and $\mathcal{V}$ is the volume of the body. Thus, the buoyant force has a magnitude equal to the weight of the fluid displaced by the body, and is directed vertically upward. This result is commonly referred to as *Archimedes' principle.* It is easily derived by using the principles discussed in Section 2.10. The *buoyant force passes through the centroid of the displaced volume,* and the point through which the buoyant force acts is called the *center of buoyancy.*

V2.6 Hydro-
meter

These same results apply to floating bodies which are only partially submerged, if the specific weight of the fluid above the liquid surface is very small compared with the liquid in which the body floats. Since the fluid above the surface is usually air, for practical purposes this condition is satisfied.

EXAMPLE 2.7

A spherical buoy has a diameter of 1.5 m, weighs 8.50 kN, and is anchored to the sea floor with a cable as is shown in Fig. E2.7a. Although the buoy normally floats on the surface, at certain times the water depth increases so that the buoy is completely immersed as illustrated. For this condition what is the tension of the cable?

SOLUTION

We first draw a free-body diagram of the buoy as shown in Fig. E2.7b, where F_B is the buoyant force acting on the buoy, $\mathcal{W}$ is the weight of the buoy, and T is the tension in the cable. For equilibrium it follows that

$$T = F_B - \mathcal{W}$$

From Eq. 2.19

$$F_B = \gamma \mathcal{V}$$

and for seawater with $\gamma = 10.1$ kN/m³ and $\mathcal{V} = \pi d^3/6$, then

$$F_B = (10.1 \times 10^3 \text{ N/m}^3)[(\pi/6)(1.5 \text{ m})^3] = 1.785 \times 10^4 \text{ N}$$

The tension in the cable can now be calculated as

$$T = 1.785 \times 10^4 \text{ N} - 0.850 \times 10^4 \text{ N} = 9.35 \text{ kN} \qquad \text{(Ans)}$$

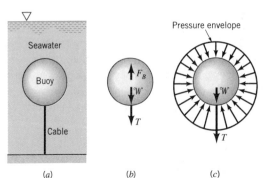

■ FIGURE E2.7

Note that we replaced the effect of the hydrostatic pressure force on the body by the buoyant force, F_B. Another correct free-body diagram of the buoy is shown in Fig. E2.7c. The net effect of the pressure forces on the surface of the buoy is equal to the upward force of magnitude F_B (the buoyant force). Do not include both the buoyant force and the hydrostatic pressure effects in your calculations—use one or the other.

2.11.2   Stability

Another interesting and important problem associated with submerged or floating bodies is concerned with the stability of the bodies. A body is said to be in a *stable equilibrium* position if, when displaced, it returns to its equilibrium position. Conversely, it is in an *unstable equilibrium* position if, when displaced (even slightly), it moves to a new equilibrium position. Stability considerations are particularly important for submerged or floating bodies since the centers of buoyancy and gravity do not necessarily coincide. A small rotation can result in either a restoring or overturning couple.

For example, for a *completely* submerged body with a center of gravity below the center of buoyancy, a rotation from its equilibrium position will create a restoring couple formed by the weight, W, and the buoyant force, F_B, which causes the body to rotate back to its original position. Thus, for this configuration the body is stable. It is to be noted that as long as the center of gravity falls *below* the center of buoyancy, this will always be true; that is, the body is in a *stable equilibrium* position with respect to small rotations. However, if the center of gravity is above the center of buoyancy, the resulting couple formed by the weight and the buoyant force will cause the body to overturn and move to a new equilibrium position. Thus, a completely submerged body with its center of gravity *above* its center of buoyancy is in an *unstable equilibrium* position.

For *floating* bodies the stability problem is more complicated, since as the body rotates the location of the center of buoyancy (which passes through the centroid of the displaced volume) may change. As is shown in Fig. 2.16, a floating body such as a barge that rides low in the water can be stable even though the center of gravity lies above the center of buoyancy. This is true since as the body rotates the buoyant force, F_B, shifts to pass through the centroid of the newly formed displaced volume and, as illustrated, combines with the weight, W, to form a couple, which will cause the body to return to its original equilibrium position. However, for the relatively tall, slender body shown in Fig. 2.17, a small rotational displacement can cause the buoyant force and the weight to form an overturning couple as illustrated.

V2.7 Stability of a model barge

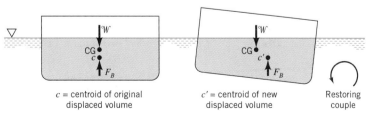

c = centroid of original displaced volume

c' = centroid of new displaced volume

Restoring couple

Stable

■ **FIGURE 2.16**   **Stability of a floating body—stable configuration.**

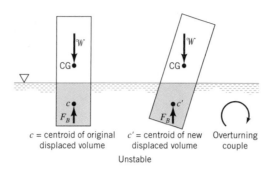

c = centroid of original   c′ = centroid of new   Overturning
displaced volume   displaced volume   couple

Unstable

■ FIGURE 2.17 **Stability of a floating body—unstable configuration.**

It is clear from these simple examples that the determination of the stability of submerged or floating bodies can be difficult since the analysis depends in a complicated fashion on the particular geometry and weight distribution of the body. The problem can be further complicated by the necessary inclusion of other types of external forces such as those induced by wind gusts or currents. Stability considerations are obviously of great importance in the design of ships, submarines, bathyscaphes, and so forth, and such considerations play a significant role in the work of naval architects.

2.12 Pressure Variation in a Fluid with Rigid-Body Motion

Although in this chapter we have been primarily concerned with fluids at rest, the general equation of motion (Eq. 2.2)

$$-\nabla p - \gamma \hat{\mathbf{k}} = \rho \mathbf{a}$$

was developed for both fluids at rest and fluids in motion, with the only stipulation being that there were no shearing stresses present.

A general class of problems involving fluid motion in which there are no shearing stresses occurs when a mass of fluid undergoes rigid-body motion. For example, if a container of fluid accelerates along a straight path, the fluid will move as a rigid mass (after the initial sloshing motion has died out) with each particle having the same acceleration. Since there is no deformation, there will be no shearing stresses and, therefore, Eq. 2.2 applies. Similarly, if a fluid is contained in a tank that rotates about a fixed axis, the fluid will simply rotate with the tank as a rigid body, and again Eq. 2.2 can be applied to obtain the pressure distribution throughout the moving fluid.

References

1. *The U.S. Standard Atmosphere, 1962.* U.S. Government Printing Office, Washington, D.C., 1962.
2. *The U.S. Standard Atmosphere, 1976.* U.S. Government Printing Office, Washington, D.C., 1976.
3. Hasler, A. F., Pierce, H., Morris, K. R., and Dodge, J., "Meteorological Data Fields 'In Perspective'." *Bulletin of the American Meteorological Society,* Vol. 66, No. 7, July 1985.

Problems

Note: Unless otherwise indicated use the values of fluid properties found in the tables on the inside of the front cover. Problems designated with an (*) are intended to be solved with the aid of a programmable calculator or a computer. Problems designated with a (†) are "open-ended" problems and require critical thinking in that to work them one must make various assumptions and provide the necessary data. There is not a unique answer to these problems.

2.1   The water level in an open standpipe is 90 ft above the ground. What is the static pressure at a fire hydrant that is connected to the standpipe and located at ground level? Express your answer in psi.

2.2   How high a column of SAE 30 oil would be required to give the same pressure as 700 mm Hg?

2.3   The closed tank of Fig. P2.3 is filled with water and is 5 ft long. The pressure gage on the tank reads 7 psi. Determine: **(a)** the height, h, in the open water column, **(b)** the gage pressure acting on the bottom tank surface AB, and **(c)** the absolute pressure of the air in the top of the tank if the local atmospheric pressure is 14.7 psia.

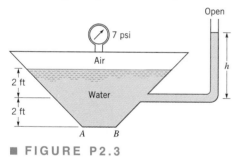

■ **FIGURE P2.3**

2.4   Bathyscaphes are capable of submerging to great depths in the ocean. What is the pressure at a depth of 6 km, assuming that seawater has a constant specific weight of 10.1 kN/m³? Express your answer in pascals and psi.

2.5   Blood pressure is usually given as a ratio of the maximum pressure (systolic pressure) to the minimum pressure (diastolic pressure). As shown in **Video V2.1**, such pressures are commonly measured with a mercury manometer. A typical value for this ratio for a human would be 120/70, where the pressures are in mm Hg. **(a)** What would these pressures be in pascals? **(b)** If your car tire was inflated to 120 mm Hg, would it be sufficient for normal driving?

*2.6   In a certain liquid at rest, measurements of the specific weight at various depths show the following variation:

h (ft)	γ (lb/ft³)
0	70
10	76
20	84
30	91
40	97
50	102
60	107
70	110
80	112
90	114
100	115

The depth $h = 0$ corresponds to a free surface at atmospheric pressure. Determine, through numerical integration of Eq. 2.4, the corresponding variation in pressure and show the results on a plot of pressure (in psf) versus depth (in feet).

2.7   A barometric pressure of 29.4 in. Hg corresponds to what value of atmospheric pressure in psia, and in pascals?

2.8   What would be the barometric pressure reading, in mm Hg, at an elevation of 4 km in the U.S. standard atmosphere? (Refer to Table C.2 in Appendix C.)

2.9   An absolute pressure of 7 psia corresponds to what gage pressure for standard atmospheric pressure of 14.7 psia?

2.10   Bourdon gages (see **Video V2.2** and Fig. 2.10) are commonly used to measure pressure. When such a gage is attached to the closed water tank of Fig. P2.10 the gage reads 5 psi. What is the absolute air pressure in the tank? Assume standard atmospheric pressure of 14.7 psi.

2.11   On the suction side of a pump a Bourdon pressure gage reads 40-kPa vacuum. What is the corresponding absolute pressure if the local atmospheric pressure is 100 kPa (abs)?

*2.12   Under normal conditions the temperature of the atmosphere decreases with increasing elevation. In some situations, however, a temperature inversion may exist so that the air temperature increases with elevation. A series of temperature probes on a mountain give the elevation–temperature data shown in the table on page 58. If the barometric pressure at the base of the mountain is 12.1 psia, determine by means of numerical integration the pressure at the top of the mountain.

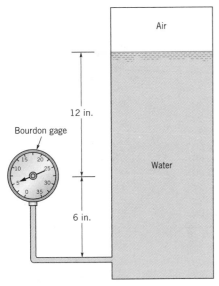

■ **FIGURE P2.10**

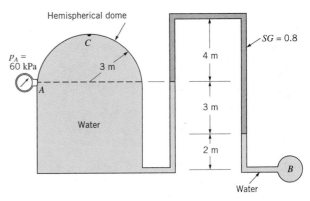

■ **FIGURE P2.13**

Elevation (ft)	Temperature (°F)
5000	50.1 (base)
5500	55.2
6000	60.3
6400	62.6
7100	67.0
7400	68.4
8200	70.0
8600	69.5
9200	68.0
9900	67.1 (top)

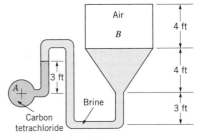

■ **FIGURE P2.14**

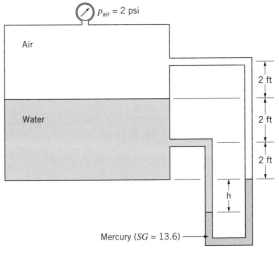

■ **FIGURE P2.15**

2.13   A closed cylindrical tank filled with water has a hemispherical dome and is connected to an inverted piping system as shown in Fig. P2.13. The liquid in the top part of the piping system has a specific gravity of 0.8, and the remaining parts of the system are filled with water. If the pressure gage reading at A is 60 kPa, determine: **(a)** the pressure in pipe B, and **(b)** the pressure head, in millimeters of mercury, at the top of the dome (point C).

2.14   In Fig. P2.14 pipe A contains carbon tetrachloride ($SG = 1.60$) and the closed storage tank B contains a salt brine ($SG = 1.15$). Determine the air pressure in tank B if the pressure in pipe A is 25 psi.

2.15   A U-tube mercury manometer is connected to a closed pressurized tank as illustrated in Fig. P2.15. If the air pressure is 2 psi, determine the differential reading, h. The specific weight of the air is negligible.

2.16   Water, oil, and an unknown fluid are contained in the vertical tubes shown in Fig. P2.16. Determine the density of the unknown fluid.

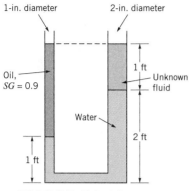

■ FIGURE P2.16

†2.17   Although it is difficult to compress water, the density of water at the bottom of the ocean is greater than that at the surface because the pressure increases with depth. Estimate how much higher the ocean's surface would be if the density of seawater were instantly changed to a uniform density equal to that at the surface.

2.18   For the inclined-tube manometer of Fig. P2.18 the pressure in pipe A is 0.8 psi. The fluid in both pipes A and B is water, and the gage fluid in the manometer has a specific gravity of 2.6. What is the pressure in pipe B corresponding to the differential reading shown?

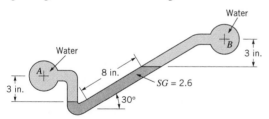

■ FIGURE P2.18

2.19   The mercury manometer of Fig. P2.19 indicates a differential reading of 0.30 m when the pressure in pipe A is 30-mm Hg vacuum. Determine the pressure in pipe B.

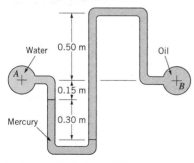

■ FIGURE P2.19

2.20   Compartments A and B of the tank shown in Fig. P2.20 are closed and filled with air and a liquid with a specific gravity equal to 0.6. Determine the manometer reading, h, if the barometric pressure is 14.7 psia and the pressure gage reads 0.5 psi. The effect of the weight of the air is negligible.

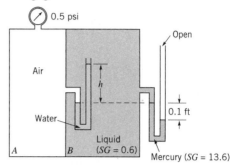

■ FIGURE P2.20

2.21   Three different liquids with properties as indicated fill the tank and manometer tubes as shown in Fig. P2.21. Determine the specific gravity of Fluid 3.

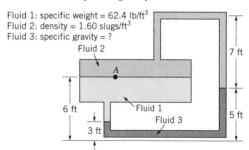

■ FIGURE P2.21

2.22   Determine the angle θ of the inclined tube shown in Fig. P2.22 if the pressure at A is 2 psi greater than that at B.

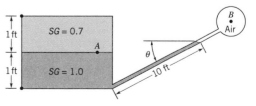

■ FIGURE P2.22

2.23　Water, oil, and saltwater fill a tube as shown in Fig. P2.23. Determine the pressure at point 1 (inside the closed tube).

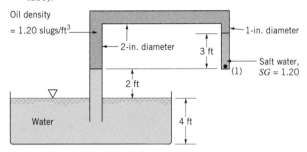

■ **FIGURE P2.23**

2.24　In Fig. P2.24 pipe A contains gasoline ($SG = 0.7$), pipe B contains oil ($SG = 0.9$), and the manometer fluid is mercury. Determine the new differential reading if the pressure in pipe A is decreased 25 kPa, and the pressure in pipe B remains constant. The initial differential reading is 0.30 m as shown.

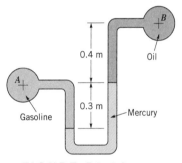

■ **FIGURE P2.24**

2.25　A 6-in.-diameter piston is located within a cylinder, which is connected to a $\frac{1}{2}$-in.-diameter inclined-tube manometer as shown in Fig. P2.25. The fluid in the cylinder and the manometer is oil (specific weight = 59 lb/ft³). When a weight $\mathcal{W}$ is placed on the top of the cylinder the fluid level in the manometer tube rises from point (1) to (2). How heavy is the weight? Assume that the change in position of the piston is negligible.

2.26　Determine the ratio of areas, A_1/A_2, of the two manometer legs of Fig. P2.26 if a change in pressure in pipe B of 0.5 psi gives a corresponding change of 1 in. in the level of the mercury in the right leg. The pressure in pipe A does not change.

2.27　Concrete is poured into the forms as shown in Fig. P2.27 to produce a set of steps. Determine the weight of the sandbag needed to keep the bottomless forms from lifting

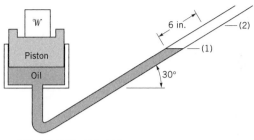

■ **FIGURE P2.25**

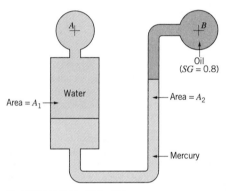

■ **FIGURE P2.26**

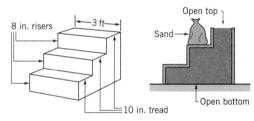

■ **FIGURE P2.27**

off the ground. The weight of the forms is 85 lb, and the specific weight of the concrete is 150 lb/ft³.

2.28　A square gate (4 m by 4 m) is located on the 45° face of a dam. The top edge of the gate lies 8 m below the water surface. Determine the force of the water on the gate and the point through which it acts.

2.29　A large, open tank contains water and is connected to a 6-ft diameter conduit as shown in Fig. P2.29. A circular plug is used to seal the conduit. Determine the magnitude, direction, and location of the force of the water on the plug.

2.30　A homogeneous, 4-ft-wide, 8-ft-long rectangular gate weighing 800 lb is held in place by a horizontal flexible

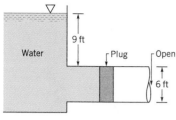

■ FIGURE P2.29

cable as shown in Fig. P2.30. Water acts against the gate, which is hinged at point *A*. Friction in the hinge is negligible. Determine the tension in the cable.

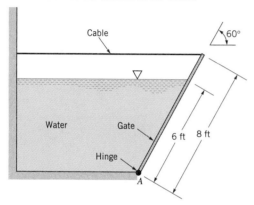

■ FIGURE P2.30

†2.31   A rubber stopper covers the drain in your bathtub. Estimate the force that the water exerts on the stopper. List all assumptions and show all calculations. Is this the force that is actually needed to lift the stopper? Explain.

2.32   An area in the form of an isosceles triangle with a base width of 6 ft and an altitude of 8 ft lies in the plane forming one wall of a tank that contains a liquid having a specific weight of 79.8 lb/ft³. The side slopes upward making an angle of 60° with the horizontal. The base of the triangle is horizontal and the vertex is above the base. Determine the resultant force the fluid exerts on the area when the fluid depth is 20 ft above the base of the triangular area. Show, with the aid of a sketch, where the center of pressure is located.

2.33   Solve Problem 2.32 if the isosceles triangle is replaced with a right triangle having the same base width and altitude.

2.34   Two square gates close two openings in a conduit connected to an open tank of water as shown in Fig. P2.34. When the water depth, *h*, reaches 5 m it is desired that both gates open at the same time. Determine the weight of the homogeneous horizontal gate and the horizontal force, *R*,

acting on the vertical gate that is required to keep the gates closed until this depth is reached. The weight of the vertical gate is negligible, and both gates are hinged at one end as shown. Friction in the hinges is negligible.

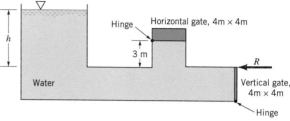

■ FIGURE P2.34

2.35   The massless, 4-ft-wide gate shown in Fig. P2.35 pivots about the frictionless hinge *O*. It is held in place by the 2000 lb counterweight, *W*. Determine the water depth, *h*.

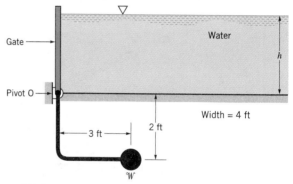

■ FIGURE P2.35

2.36   The rigid gate, *OAB*, of Fig. P2.36 is hinged at *O* and rests against a rigid support at *B*. What minimum horizontal force, *P*, is required to hold the gate closed if its width is 3 m? Neglect the weight of the gate and friction in the hinge. The back of the gate is exposed to the atmosphere.

*2.37   A 200-lb homogeneous gate of 10-ft width and 5-ft length is hinged at point *A* and held in place by a 12-ft-long brace as shown in Fig. P2.37. As the bottom of the brace is moved to the right, the water level remains at the top of the gate. The line of action of the force that the brace exerts on the gate is along the brace. (a) Plot the magnitude of the force exerted on the gate by the brace as a function of the angle of the gate, *θ*, for 0 ≤ *θ* ≤ 90°. (b) Repeat the calculations for the case in which the weight of the gate is negligible. Comment on the results as *θ* → 0.

2.38   An open rectangular tank is 3 m wide and 4 m long. The tank contains water to a depth of 2 m and oil (*SG* = 0.8)

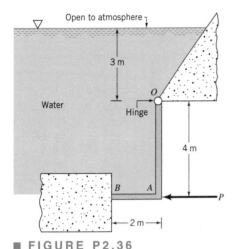

■ FIGURE P2.36

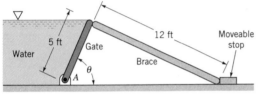

■ FIGURE P2.37

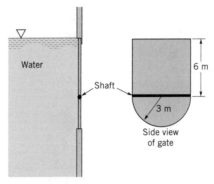

■ FIGURE P2.39

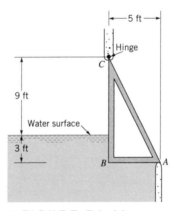

■ FIGURE P2.40

on top of the water to a depth of 1 m. Determine the magnitude and location of the resultant fluid force acting on one end of the tank.

2.39 A gate having the shape shown in Fig. P2.39 is located in the vertical side of an open tank containing water. The gate is mounted on a horizontal shaft. (a) When the water level is at the top of the gate, determine the magnitude of the fluid force on the rectangular portion of the gate above the shaft and the magnitude of the fluid force on the semicircular portion of the gate below the shaft. (b) For this same fluid depth determine the moment of the force acting on the semicircular portion of the gate with respect to an axis that coincides with the shaft.

2.40 A gate having the cross section shown in Fig. P2.40 is 4 ft wide and is hinged at C. The gate weighs 18,000 lb, and its mass center is 1.67 ft to the right of the plane BC. Determine the vertical reaction at A on the gate when the water level is 3 ft above the base. All contact surfaces are smooth.

*2.41 An open rectangular settling tank contains a liquid suspension that at a given time has a specific weight that varies approximately with depth according to the following data:

h (m)	γ (kN/m^3)
0	10.0
0.4	10.1
0.8	10.2
1.2	10.6
1.6	11.3
2.0	12.3
2.4	12.7
2.8	12.9
3.2	13.0
3.6	13.1

The depth $h = 0$ corresponds to the free surface. Determine, by means of numerical integration, the magnitude and location of the resultant force that the liquid suspension exerts on a vertical wall of the tank that is 6 m wide. The depth of fluid in the tank is 3.6 m.

2.42 The concrete dam of Fig. P2.42 weighs 23.6 kN/m^3 and rests on a solid foundation. Determine the minimum coefficient of friction between the dam and the foundation required to keep the dam from sliding at the water depth shown. Assume no fluid uplift pressure along the base. Base your analysis on a unit length of the dam.

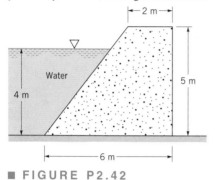

■ FIGURE P2.42

*2.43   Water backs up behind a concrete dam as shown in Fig. P2.43. Leakage under the foundation gives a pressure distribution under the dam as indicated. If the water depth, h, is too great, the dam will topple over about its toe (point A). For the dimensions given, determine the maximum water depth for the following widths of the dam: $\ell = 20, 30, 40, 50$, and 60 ft. Base your analysis on a unit length of the dam. The specific weight of the concrete is 150 lb/ft^3.

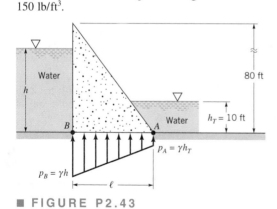

■ FIGURE P2.43

2.44   A 3-m-long curved gate is located in the side of a reservoir containing water as shown in Fig. P2.44. Determine the magnitude of the horizontal and vertical components of the force of the water on the gate. Will this force pass through point A? Explain.

2.45   A 3-m-diameter open cylindrical tank contains water and has a hemispherical bottom as shown in Fig. P2.45. Determine the magnitude, line of action, and direction of the force of the water on the curved bottom.

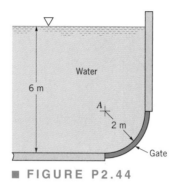

■ FIGURE P2.44

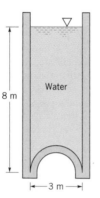

■ FIGURE P2.45

2.46   The 20-ft-long gate of Fig. P2.46 is a quarter circle and is hinged at H. Determine the horizontal force, P, required to hold the gate in place. Neglect friction at the hinge and the weight of the gate.

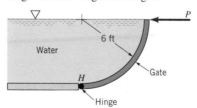

■ FIGURE P2.46

2.47   A plug in the bottom of a pressurized tank is conical in shape as shown in Fig. P2.47. The air pressure is 50 kPa and the liquid in the tank has a specific weight of 27 kN/m^3. Determine the magnitude, direction, and line of action of the force exerted on the curved surface of the cone within the tank due to the 50-kPa pressure and the liquid.

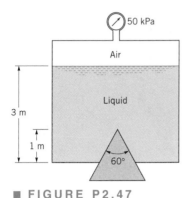

■ FIGURE P2.47

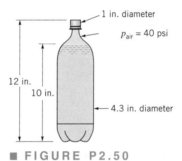

■ FIGURE P2.49

2.48 Hoover Dam (see Video 2.3) is the highest arch-gravity type of dam in the United States. A plan view and cross section of the dam are shown in Fig. P2.48(a). The walls of the canyon in which the dam is located are sloped, and just upstream of the dam the vertical plane shown in Fig. P2.48(b) approximately represents the cross section of the water acting on the dam. Use this vertical cross section to estimate the resultant horizontal force of the water on the dam, and show where this force acts.

2.49 A tank wall has the shape shown in Fig. P2.49. Determine the horizontal and vertical components of the force of the water on a 1-ft-width of the curved section AB.

2.50 The air pressure in the top of the two liter pop bottle shown in Video V2.4 and Fig. P2.50 is 40 psi, and the pop depth is 10 in. The bottom of the bottle has an irregular shape with a diameter of 4.3 in. **(a)** If the bottle cap has a diameter of 1 in. what is magnitude of the axial force required to hold the cap in place? **(b)** Determine the force needed to secure the bottom 2 inches of the bottle to its cylindrical sides. For this calculation assume the effect of

■ FIGURE P2.50

the weight of the pop is negligible. **(c)** By how much does the weight of the pop increase the pressure 2 inches above the bottom? Assume the pop has the same specific weight as that of water.

2.51 A solid cube floats in water with a 0.5-ft thick oil layer on top as shown in Fig. P2.51. Determine the weight of the cube.

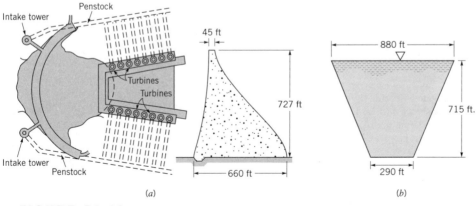

(a)   (b)

■ FIGURE P2.48

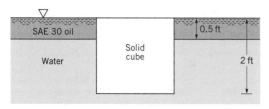

■ **FIGURE P2.51**

2.52 The homogeneous timber *AB* of Fig. P2.52 is 0.15 m by 0.35 m in cross section. Determine the specific weight of the timber and the tension in the rope.

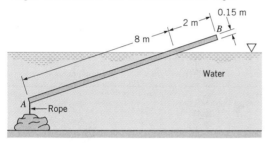

■ **FIGURE P2.52**

2.53 A cube, 4 ft on a side, weighs 3000 lb and floats half-submerged in an open tank as shown in Fig. P2.53. For a liquid depth of 10 ft, determine the force of the liquid on the inclined section *AB* of the tank wall. The width of the wall is 6 ft. Show the magnitude, direction, and location of the force on a sketch.

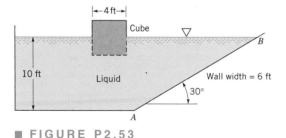

■ **FIGURE P2.53**

†**2.54** Estimate the minimum water depth needed to float a canoe carrying two people and their camping gear. List all assumptions and show all calculations.

2.55 An inverted test tube partially filled with air floats in a plastic water-filled soft drink bottle as shown in Video V2.5 and Fig. P2.55. The amount of air in the tube has been adjusted so that it just floats. The bottle cap is securely fastened. A slight squeezing of the plastic bottle will cause the test tube to sink to the bottom of the bottle. Explain this phenomenon.

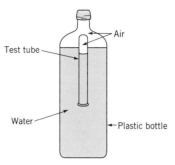

■ **FIGURE P2.55**

2.56 A 1-ft-diameter, 2-ft-long cylinder floats in an open tank containing a liquid having a specific weight γ. A U-tube manometer is connected to the tank as shown in Fig. P2.56. When the pressure in pipe *A* is 0.1 psi below atmospheric pressure, the various fluid levels are as shown. Determine the weight of the cylinder. Note that the top of the cylinder is flush with the fluid surface.

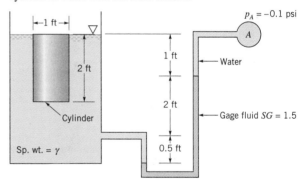

■ **FIGURE P2.56**

2.57 A plate of negligible weight closes a 1-ft diameter hole in a tank containing air and water as shown in Fig. P2.57. A block of concrete (specific weight = 150 lb/ft³), having a volume of 1.5 ft³, is suspended from the plate and is completely immersed in the water. As the air pressure is increased the differential reading, Δh, on the inclined-tube mercury manometer increases. Determine Δh just before the plate starts to lift off the hole. The weight of the air has a negligible effect on the manometer reading.

2.58 The hydrometer shown in Video V2.6 and Fig. P2.58 has a mass of 0.045 kg and the cross-sectional area of its stem is 290 mm². Determine the distance between graduations (on the stem) for specific gravities of 1.00 and 0.90.

2.59 A 5-gal, cylindrical open container with a bottom area of 120 in.² is filled with glycerin and rests on the floor

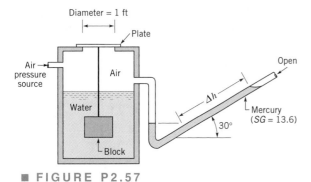

■ **FIGURE P2.57**

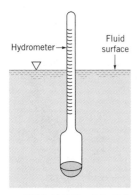

■ **FIGURE P2.58**

weight, W, is attached to the beam as shown, and the water depth, h, to the bottom of the rectangular surface is adjusted until the beam is again horizontal.

Values of W and h obtained experimentally are shown in the table below. Use these results to plot a graph of weight as a function of water depth. On the same graph plot the theoretical curve obtained by equating the moment that the weight produces about the pivot point to the moment produced by the hydrostatic force on the rectangular end of the block. Note that the pressure forces on the circular curved sides of the block do not produce a moment about the pivot because the line of action of these forces is through the pivot.

Compare the experimental and theoretical results and discuss some possible reasons for any differences between them.

W (lb)	h (in.)
0	0
0.044	1.11
0.132	1.92
0.264	2.76
0.352	3.20
0.440	3.60
0.573	4.17
0.663	4.51
0.882	5.39
1.101	6.27
1.211	6.70

of an elevator. **(a)** Determine the fluid pressure at the bottom of the container when the elevator has an upward acceleration of 3 ft/s². **(b)** What resultant force does the container exert on the floor of the elevator during this acceleration? The weight of the container is negligible. (Note: 1 gal = 231 in.³)

2.60　A closed cylindrical tank that is 8 ft in diameter and 24 ft long is completely filled with gasoline. The tank, with its long axis horizontal, is pulled by a truck along a horizontal surface. Determine the pressure difference between the ends (along the long axis of the tank) when the truck undergoes an acceleration of 5 ft/s².

2.61　The device shown in Fig. P2.61 is used to investigate the hydrostatic force on a plane rectangular surface. With no water in the tank the balance beam is horizontal. A

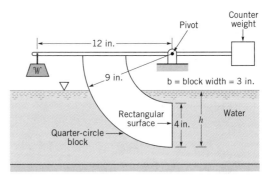

■ **FIGURE P2.61**

3

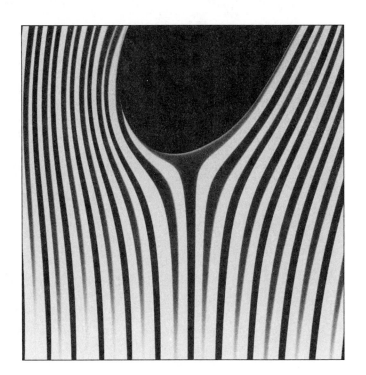

Elementary Fluid Dynamics— The Bernoulli Equation

*I*n this chapter we investigate some typical fluid motions (fluid dynamics) in an elementary way. We will discuss in some detail the use of Newton's second law ($\mathbf{F} = m\mathbf{a}$) as it is applied to fluid particle motion that is "ideal" in some sense. We will obtain the celebrated Bernoulli equation and apply it to various flows. Although this equation is one of the oldest in fluid mechanics and the assumptions involved in its derivation are numerous, it can be effectively used to predict and analyze a variety of flow situations.

3.1 Newton's Second Law

According to Newton's second law of motion, the net force acting on the fluid particle under consideration must equal its mass times its acceleration,

$$\mathbf{F} = m\mathbf{a}$$

In this chapter we consider the motion of inviscid fluids. That is, the fluid is assumed to have zero viscosity.

Flow past a blunt body: On any object placed in a moving fluid there is a stagnation point on the front of the object where the velocity is zero. This location has a relatively large pressure and divides the flow field into two portions—one flowing over the body, and one flowing under the body. (Dye in water) (Photograph by B. R. Munson).

67

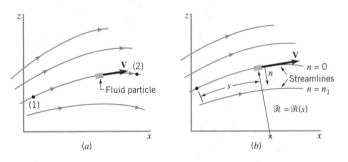

■ **FIGURE 3.1**
(*a*) **Flow in the** $x - z$
plane. (*b*) **Flow in terms
of streamline and normal
coordinates.**

We assume that the fluid motion is governed by pressure and gravity forces only and examine Newton's second law as it applies to a fluid particle in the form:

(Net pressure force on a particle) + (net gravity force on particle) =

(particle mass) × (particle acceleration)

The results of the interaction between the pressure, gravity, and acceleration provide numerous applications in fluid mechanics.

We consider two-dimensional motion like that confined to the x–z plane as is shown in Fig. 3.1*a*. The motion of each fluid particle is described in terms of its velocity vector, **V,** which is defined as the time rate of change of the position of the particle. The particle's velocity is a vector quantity with a magnitude (the speed, $V = |\mathbf{V}|$) and direction. As the particle moves about, it follows a particular path, the shape of which is governed by the velocity of the particle.

If the flow is *steady* (i.e., nothing changes with time at a given location in the flow field), each particle slides along its path, and its velocity vector is everywhere tangent to the path. The lines that are tangent to the velocity vectors throughout the flow field are called *streamlines.* The particle motion is described in terms of its distance, $s = s(t)$, along the streamline from some convenient origin and the local radius of curvature of the streamline, $\mathcal{R} = \mathcal{R}(s)$. The distance along the streamline is related to the particle's speed by $V = ds/dt$, and the radius of curvature is related to shape of the streamline. In addition to the coordinate along the streamline, s, the coordinate normal to the streamline, n, as is shown in Fig. 3.1*b*, will be of use.

By definition, the acceleration is the time rate of change of the velocity of the particle, $\mathbf{a} = d\mathbf{V}/dt$. The acceleration has two components—one along the streamline, a_s, the streamwise acceleration, and one normal to the streamline, a_n, the normal acceleration.

By use of the chain rule of differentiation, the s component of the acceleration is given by $a_s = dV/dt = (\partial V/\partial s)(ds/dt) = (\partial V/\partial s)V$. We have used the fact that $V = ds/dt$. The normal component of acceleration, the centrifugal acceleration, is given in terms of the particle speed and the radius of curvature of its path as $a_n = V^2/\mathcal{R}$. Thus, the components of acceleration in the s and n directions, a_s and a_n, for steady flow are given by

$$a_s = V\frac{\partial V}{\partial s}, \qquad a_n = \frac{V^2}{\mathcal{R}} \qquad (3.1)$$

3.2   F = ma Along a Streamline

We consider the free-body diagram of a small fluid particle as is shown in Fig. 3.2. The small fluid particle is of size δs by δn in the plane of the figure and δy normal to the figure as shown in the free-body diagram of Fig. 3.3. Unit vectors along and normal to the streamline

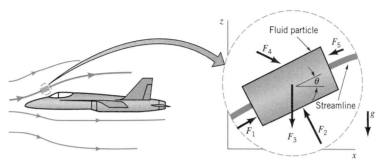

■ **FIGURE 3.2**   **Isolation of a small fluid particle in a flow field.**

are denoted by $\hat{\mathbf{s}}$ and $\hat{\mathbf{n}}$, respectively. For steady flow, the component of Newton's second law along the streamline direction, s, can be written as

$$\sum \delta F_s = \delta m\, a_s = \delta m\, V \frac{\partial V}{\partial s} = \rho\, \delta \Psi\, V \frac{\partial V}{\partial s} \tag{3.2}$$

where $\sum \delta F_s$ represents the sum of the s components of all the forces acting on the particle, which has mass $\delta m = \rho\, \delta \Psi$, and $V \partial V / \partial s$ is the acceleration in the s direction. Here, $\delta \Psi = \delta s\, \delta n\, \delta y$ is the particle volume.

The gravity force (weight) on the particle can be written as $\delta \mathcal{W} = \gamma\, \delta \Psi$, where $\gamma = \rho g$ is the specific weight of the fluid (lb/ft^3 or N/m^3). Hence, the component of the weight force in the direction of the streamline is

$$\delta \mathcal{W}_s = -\delta \mathcal{W} \sin \theta = -\gamma\, \delta \Psi \sin \theta$$

If the streamline is horizontal at the point of interest, then $\theta = 0$, and there is no component of the particle weight along the streamline to contribute to its acceleration in that direction.

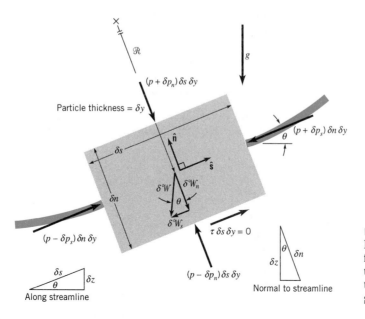

■ **FIGURE 3.3**

Free-body diagram of a fluid particle for which the important forces are those due to pressure and gravity.

If the pressure at the center of the particle shown in Fig. 3.3 is denoted as p, then its average value on the two end faces that are perpendicular to the streamline are $p + \delta p_s$ and $p - \delta p_s$. Since the particle is "small," we can use a one-term Taylor series expansion for the pressure field to obtain

$$\delta p_s \approx \frac{\partial p}{\partial s} \frac{\delta s}{2}$$

Thus, if δF_{ps} is the net pressure force on the particle in the streamline direction, it follows that

$$\delta F_{ps} = (p - \delta p_s)\delta n\,\delta y - (p + \delta p_s)\delta n\,\delta y = -2\delta p_s \delta n\,\delta y$$

$$= -\frac{\partial p}{\partial s}\delta s\,\delta n\,\delta y = -\frac{\partial p}{\partial s}\delta\!\!\!\!\!-\,$$

Thus, the net force acting in the streamline direction on the particle shown in Fig. 3.3 is given by

$$\sum \delta F_s = \delta \mathcal{W}_s + \delta F_{ps} = \left(-\gamma\sin\theta - \frac{\partial p}{\partial s}\right)\delta\!\!\!\!\!-\, \qquad (3.3)$$

By combining Eqs. 3.2 and 3.3 we obtain the following equation of motion along the streamline direction:

$$-\gamma\sin\theta - \frac{\partial p}{\partial s} = \rho V \frac{\partial V}{\partial s} \qquad (3.4)$$

The physical interpretation of Eq. 3.4 is that a change in fluid particle speed is accomplished by the appropriate combination of pressure and particle weight along the streamline.

EXAMPLE 3.1

Consider the inviscid, incompressible, steady flow along the horizontal streamline A–B in front of the sphere of radius a as shown in Fig. E3.1a. From a more advanced theory of flow past a sphere, the fluid velocity along this streamline is

$$V = V_0\left(1 + \frac{a^3}{x^3}\right)$$

Determine the pressure variation along the streamline from point A far in front of the sphere ($x_A = -\infty$ and $V_A = V_0$) to point B on the sphere ($x_B = -a$ and $V_B = 0$).

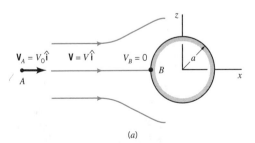

(a)

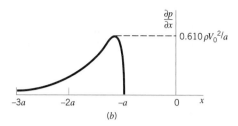

(b)

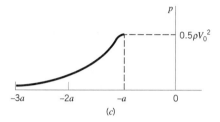

(c)   ■ FIGURE E3.1

SOLUTION

Since the flow is steady and inviscid, Eq. 3.4 is valid. In addition, since the streamline is horizontal, $\sin \theta = \sin 0° = 0$ and the equation of motion along the streamline reduces to

$$\frac{\partial p}{\partial s} = -\rho V \frac{\partial V}{\partial s} \tag{1}$$

With the given velocity variation along the streamline, the acceleration term is

$$V \frac{\partial V}{\partial s} = V \frac{\partial V}{\partial x} = V_0 \left(1 + \frac{a^3}{x^3}\right)\left(-\frac{3V_0 a^3}{x^4}\right)$$

$$= -3V_0^2 \left(1 + \frac{a^3}{x^3}\right)\frac{a^3}{x^4}$$

where we have replaced s by x since the two coordinates are identical (within an additive constant) along streamline A–B. It follows that $V \partial V/\partial s < 0$ along the streamline. The fluid slows down from V_0 far ahead of the sphere to zero velocity on the "nose" of the sphere ($x = -a$).

Thus, according to Eq. 1, to produce the given motion the pressure gradient along the streamline is

$$\frac{\partial p}{\partial x} = \frac{3\rho a^3 V_0^2 (1 + a^3/x^3)}{x^4} \tag{2}$$

This variation is indicated in Fig. E3.1*b*. It is seen that the pressure increases in the direction of flow ($\partial p/\partial x > 0$) from point A to point B. The maximum pressure gradient ($0.610 \rho V_0^2/a$) occurs just slightly ahead of the sphere ($x = -1.205a$). It is the pressure gradient that slows the fluid down from $V_A = V_0$ to $V_B = 0$.

The pressure distribution along the streamline can be obtained by integrating Eq. 2 from $p = 0$ (gage) at $x = -\infty$ to pressure p at location x. The result, plotted in Fig. E3.1*c*, is

$$p = -\rho V_0^2 \left[\left(\frac{a}{x}\right)^3 + \frac{(a/x)^6}{2}\right] \tag{Ans}$$

The pressure at B, a stagnation point since $V_B = 0$, is the highest pressure along the streamline ($p_B = \rho V_0^2/2$). As shown in Chapter 9, this excess pressure on the front of the sphere (i.e., $p_B > 0$) contributes to the net drag force on the sphere. Note that the pressure gradient and pressure are directly proportional to the density of the fluid, a representation of the fact that the fluid inertia is proportional to its mass.

Equation 3.4 can be rearranged and integrated as follows. First, we note from Fig. 3.3 that along the streamline $\sin \theta = dz/ds$. Also, we can write $V dV/ds = \frac{1}{2}d(V^2)/ds$. Finally, along the streamline $\partial p/\partial s = dp/ds$. These ideas combined with Eq. 3.4 give the following result valid along a streamline

$$-\gamma \frac{dz}{ds} - \frac{dp}{ds} = \frac{1}{2}\rho \frac{d(V^2)}{ds}$$

This simplifies to

$$dp + \frac{1}{2}\rho d(V^2) + \gamma\, dz = 0 \qquad \text{(along a streamline)} \tag{3.5}$$

which, for constant density, can be integrated to give

$$\boxed{p + \tfrac{1}{2}\rho V^2 + \gamma z = \text{constant along streamline}} \tag{3.6}$$

V3.1 Balancing ball

This is the celebrated *Bernoulli Equation*—a very powerful tool in fluid mechanics.

EXAMPLE 3.2

Consider the flow of air around a bicyclist moving through still air with velocity V_0 as is shown in Fig. E3.2. Determine the difference in the pressure between points (1) and (2).

SOLUTION

In a coordinate system fixed to the bike, it appears as though the air is flowing steadily toward the bicyclist with speed V_0. If the assumptions of Bernoulli's equation are valid (steady,

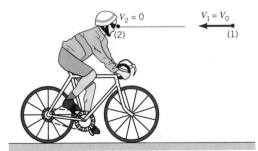

■ FIGURE E3.2

incompressible, inviscid flow), Eq. 3.6 can be applied as follows along the streamline that passes through (1) and (2).

$$p_1 + \tfrac{1}{2}\rho V_1^2 + \gamma z_1 = p_2 + \tfrac{1}{2}\rho V_2^2 + \gamma z_2$$

We consider (1) to be in the free stream so that $V_1 = V_0$ and (2) to be at the tip of the bicyclist's nose and assume that $z_1 = z_2$ and $V_2 = 0$ (both of which, as is discussed in Section 3.5, are reasonable assumptions). It follows that the pressure of (2) is greater than that at (1) by an amount

$$p_2 - p_1 = \tfrac{1}{2}\rho V_1^2 = \tfrac{1}{2}\rho V_0^2 \qquad \text{(Ans)}$$

A similar result was obtained in Example 3.1 by integrating the pressure gradient, which was known because the velocity distribution along the streamline, $V(s)$, was known. The Bernoulli equation is a general integration of $\mathbf{F} = m\mathbf{a}$. To determine $p_2 - p_1$, knowledge of the detailed velocity distribution is not needed—only the "boundary conditions" at (1) and (2) are required. Of course, knowledge of the value of V along the streamline is needed to determine the pressure at points between (1) and (2). Note that if we measure $p_2 - p_1$ we can determine the speed, V_0. As discussed in Section 3.5, this is the principle upon which many velocity measuring devices are based.

If the bicyclist were accelerating or decelerating, the flow would be unsteady (i.e., $V_0 \neq$ constant) and the above analysis would be incorrect since Eq. 3.6 is restricted to steady flow.

3.3   F = _m_a Normal to a Streamline

We again consider the force balance on the fluid particle shown in Fig. 3.3. This time, however, we consider components in the normal direction, $\hat{\mathbf{n}}$, and write Newton's second law in this direction as

$$\sum \delta F_n = \frac{\delta m V^2}{\mathcal{R}} = \frac{\rho\, \delta\mathit{V}\, V^2}{\mathcal{R}} \qquad (3.7)$$

where $\sum \delta F_n$ represents the sum of n components of all the forces acting on the particle. We assume the flow is steady with a normal acceleration $a_n = V^2/\mathcal{R}$, where $\mathcal{R}$ is the local radius of curvature of the streamlines.

We again assume that the only forces of importance are pressure and gravity. Using the method of Section 3.2 for determining forces along the streamline, the net force acting in the normal direction on the particle shown in Fig. 3.3 is determined to be

$$\sum \delta F_n = \delta W_n + \delta F_{pn} = \left(-\gamma \cos\theta - \frac{\partial p}{\partial n} \right) \delta\mathit{V} \qquad (3.8)$$

where $\partial p/\partial n$ is the pressure gradient normal to the streamline. By combining Eqs. 3.7 and 3.8 and using the fact that along a line normal to the streamline $\cos\theta = dz/dn$ (see Fig. 3.3), we obtain the following equation of motion along the normal direction

$$-\gamma \frac{dz}{dn} - \frac{\partial p}{\partial n} = \frac{\rho V^2}{\mathcal{R}} \qquad (3.9)$$

The physical interpretation of Eq. 3.9 is that a change in the direction of flow of a fluid particle (i.e., a curved path, $\mathcal{R} < \infty$) is accomplished by the appropriate combination of pressure gradient and particle weight normal to the streamline. By integration of Eq. 3.9, the final form of Newton's second law applied across the streamlines for steady, inviscid, incompressible flow is obtained as

$$p + \rho \int \frac{V^2}{\mathcal{R}} \, dn + \gamma z = \text{constant across the streamline} \qquad (3.10)$$

EXAMPLE 3.3

Shown in Figs. E3.3a,b are two flow fields with circular streamlines. The velocity distributions are

$$V(r) = C_1 r \qquad \text{for case } (a)$$

and

$$V(r) = \frac{C_2}{r} \qquad \text{for case } (b)$$

where C_1 and C_2 are constant. Determine the pressure distributions, $p = p(r)$, for each, given that $p = p_0$ at $r = r_0$.

SOLUTION

We assume the flows are steady, inviscid, and incompressible with streamlines in the horizontal plane ($dz/dn = 0$). Since the streamlines are circles, the coordinate n points in a

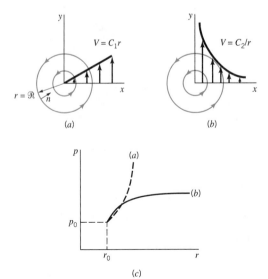

(a)

(b)

(c)

■ FIGURE E3.3

direction opposite of that of the radial coordinate, $\partial/\partial n = -\partial/\partial r$, and the radius of curvature is given by $\mathcal{R} = r$. Hence, Eq. 3.9 becomes

$$\frac{\partial p}{\partial r} = \frac{\rho V^2}{r}$$

For case (a) this gives

$$\frac{\partial p}{\partial r} = \rho C_1^2 r$$

while for case (b) it gives

$$\frac{\partial p}{\partial r} = \frac{\rho C_2^2}{r^3}$$

For either case the pressure increases as r increases since $\partial p/\partial r > 0$. Integration of these equations with respect to r, starting with a known pressure $p = p_0$ at $r = r_0$, gives

$$p = \frac{1}{2}\rho C_1^2(r^2 - r_0^2) + p_0 \qquad \text{(Ans)}$$

for case (a) and

$$p = \frac{1}{2}\rho C_2^2\left(\frac{1}{r_0^2} - \frac{1}{r^2}\right) + p_0 \qquad \text{(Ans)}$$

for case (b). These pressure distributions are sketched in Fig. E3.3c. The pressure distributions needed to balance the centrifugal accelerations in cases (a) and (b) are not the same because the velocity distributions are different. In fact for case (a) the pressure increases without bound as $r \to \infty$, while for case (b) the pressure approaches a finite value as $r \to \infty$. The streamline patterns are the same for each case, however.

Physically, case (a) represents rigid body rotation (as obtained in a can of water on a turntable after it has been "spun up") and case (b) represents a free vortex (an approximation to a tornado or the swirl of water in a drain, the "bathtub vortex").

V3.2 Free vortex

3.4   Physical Interpretation

An alternate but equivalent form of the Bernoulli equation is obtained by dividing each term of Eq. 3.6 by the specific weight, γ, to obtain

$$\frac{p}{\gamma} + \frac{V^2}{2g} + z = \text{constant on a streamline} \qquad \text{(3.11)}$$

Each of the terms in this equation has the units of length and represents a certain type of head.

The elevation term, z, is related to the potential energy of the particle and is called the *elevation head*. The pressure term p/γ, is called the *pressure head* and represents the height of a column of the fluid that is needed to produce the pressure p. The velocity term, $V^2/2g$, is the *velocity head* and represents the vertical distance needed for the fluid to fall freely (neglecting friction) if it is to reach velocity V from rest. The Bernoulli equation states that the sum of the pressure head, the velocity head, and the elevation head is constant along a streamline.

EXAMPLE 3.4

Consider the flow of water from the syringe shown in Fig. E3.4. A force applied to the plunger will produce a pressure greater than atmospheric at point (1) within the syringe. The water flows from the needle, point (2), with relatively high velocity and coasts up to point (3) at the top of its trajectory. Discuss the energy of the fluid at points (1), (2), and (3) by using the Bernoulli equation.

SOLUTION

If the assumptions (steady, inviscid, incompressible flow) of the Bernoulli equation are approximately valid, it then follows that the flow can be explained in terms of the partition of the total energy of the water. According to Eq. 3.11 the sum of the three types of energy (kinetic, potential, and pressure) or heads (velocity, elevation, and pressure) must remain constant. The following table indicates the relative magnitude of each of these energies at the three points shown in the figure.

| | Energy Type | | |
Point	Kinetic $\rho V^2/2$	Potential γz	Pressure p
1	Small	Zero	Large
2	Large	Small	Zero
3	Zero	Large	Zero

(Ans)

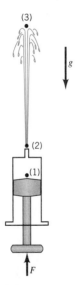

■ FIGURE E3.4

The motion results in (or is due to) a change in the magnitude of each type of energy as the fluid flows from one location to another. An alternate way to consider this flow is as follows. The pressure gradient between (1) and (2) produces an acceleration to eject the water from the needle. Gravity acting on the particle between (2) and (3) produces a deceleration to cause the water to come to a momentary stop at the top of its flight.

If friction (viscous) effects were important, there would be an energy loss between (1) and (3) and for the given p_1 the water would not be able to reach the height indicated in the figure. Such friction may arise in the needle (see Chapter 8, pipe flow) or between the water stream and the surrounding air (see Chapter 9, external flow).

When a fluid particle travels along a curved path, a net force directed toward the center of curvature is required. Under the assumptions valid for Eq. 3.10 this force may be either gravity or pressure, or a combination of both. In many instances the streamlines are nearly straight ($\mathcal{R} = \infty$) so that centrifugal effects are negligible and the pressure variation across the streamlines is merely hydrostatic (because of gravity alone), even though the fluid is in motion.

EXAMPLE 3.5

Consider the inviscid, incompressible, steady flow shown in Fig. E3.5. From section A to B the streamlines are straight, while from C to D they follow circular paths. Describe the pressure variation between points (1) and (2) and points (3) and (4).

SOLUTION

With the above assumptions and the fact that $\mathcal{R} = \infty$ for the portion from A to B, Eq. 3.10 becomes

$$p + \gamma z = \text{constant}$$

The constant can be determined by evaluating the known variables at the two locations using $p_2 = 0$ (gage), $z_1 = 0$, and $z_2 = h_{2-1}$ to give

$$p_1 = p_2 + \gamma(z_2 - z_1) = p_2 + \gamma h_{2-1} \qquad \text{(Ans)}$$

Note that since the radius of curvature of the streamline is infinite, the pressure variation in the vertical direction is the same as if the fluid were stationary.

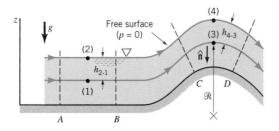

■ FIGURE E3.5

However, if we apply Eq. 3.10 between points (3) and (4) we obtain (using $dn = -dz$)

$$p_4 + \rho \int_{z_3}^{z_4} \frac{V^2}{\mathcal{R}} (-dz) + \gamma z_4 = p_3 + \gamma z_3$$

With $p_4 = 0$ and $z_4 - z_3 = h_{4-3}$ this becomes

$$p_3 = \gamma h_{4-3} - \rho \int_{z_3}^{z_4} \frac{V^2}{\mathcal{R}} \, dz \qquad \text{(Ans)}$$

To evaluate the integral we must know the variation of V and $\mathcal{R}$ with z. Even without this detailed information we note that the integral has a positive value. Thus, the pressure at (3) is less than the hydrostatic value, γh_{4-3}, by an amount equal to $\rho \int_{z_3}^{z_4} (V^2/\mathcal{R}) \, dz$. This lower pressure, caused by the curved streamline, is necessary in order to accelerate (centrifugal acceleration) the fluid around the curved path.

3.5 Static, Stagnation, Dynamic, and Total Pressure

Each term of the Bernoulli equation, Eq. 3.6, has the dimensions of force per unit area—psi, lb/ft^2, N/m^2. The first term, p, is the actual thermodynamic pressure of the fluid as it flows. To measure its value, one could move along with the fluid, thus being "static" relative to the moving fluid. Hence, it is normally termed the *static pressure*. Another way to measure the static pressure would be to drill a hole in a flat surface and fasten a piezometer tube as indicated by the location of point (3) in Fig. 3.4.

The third term in Eq. 3.5, γz, is termed the *hydrostatic pressure,* in obvious regard to the hydrostatic pressure variation discussed in Chapter 2. It is not actually a pressure, but does represent the change in pressure possible due to potential energy variations of the fluid as a result of elevation changes.

V3.3 Stagnation point flow

The second term in the Bernoulli equation, $\rho V^2/2$, is termed the *dynamic pressure*. Its interpretation can be seen in Fig. 3.4 by considering the pressure at the end of a small tube inserted into the flow and pointing upstream. After the initial transient motion has died out, the liquid will fill the tube to a height of H as shown. The fluid in the tube, including that at its tip, (2), will be stationary. That is, $V_2 = 0$, or point (2) is a *stagnation point.*

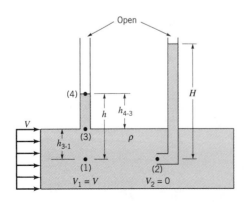

■ **FIGURE 3.4** **Measurement of static and stagnation pressures.**

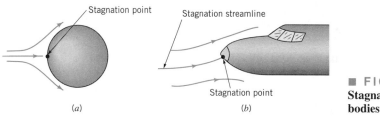

■ **FIGURE 3.5**
Stagnation points on bodies in flowing fluids.

If we apply the Bernoulli equation between points (1) and (2), using $V_2 = 0$ and assuming that $z_1 = z_2$, we find that

$$p_2 = p_1 + \tfrac{1}{2}\rho V_1^2$$

Hence, the pressure at the stagnation point is greater than the static pressure, p_1, by an amount $\rho V_1^2/2$, the dynamic pressure. It can be shown that there is a stagnation point on any stationary body that is placed into a flowing fluid (see Fig. 3.5).

The sum of the static pressure, hydrostatic pressure, and dynamic pressure is termed the *total pressure, p_T*. The Bernoulli equation is a statement that the total pressure remains constant along a streamline. That is,

$$p + \tfrac{1}{2}\rho V^2 + \gamma z = p_T = \text{constant along a streamline} \tag{3.12}$$

Knowledge of the values of the static and stagnation pressures in a fluid implies that the fluid speed can be calculated. This is the principle on which the *Pitot-static tube* is based. As shown in Fig. 3.6, two concentric tubes are attached to two pressure gages. The center tube measures the stagnation pressure at its open tip. If elevation changes are negligible,

$$p_3 = p + \tfrac{1}{2}\rho V^2$$

V3.4 Airspeed indicator

where p and V are the pressure and velocity of the fluid upstream of point (2). The outer tube is made with several small holes at an appropriate distance from the tip so that they measure the static pressure. If the elevation difference between (1) and (4) is negligible, then

$$p_4 = p_1 = p$$

These two equations can be rearranged to give

$$V = \sqrt{2(p_3 - p_4)/\rho} \tag{3.13}$$

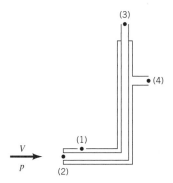

■ **FIGURE 3.6** **The Pitot-static tube.**

EXAMPLE 3.6

An airplane flies 100 mi/hr at an elevation of 10,000 ft in a standard atmosphere as shown in Fig. E3.6. Determine the pressure at point (1) far ahead of the airplane, the pressure at the stagnation point on the nose of the airplane, point (2), and the pressure difference indicated by a Pitot-static probe attached to the fuselage.

SOLUTION

From Table C.1 we find that the static pressure at the altitude given is

$$p_1 = 1456 \text{ lb/ft}^2 \text{ (abs)} = 10.11 \text{ psia} \qquad \text{(Ans)}$$

Also, the density is $\rho = 0.001756 \text{ slug/ft}^3$.

If the flow is steady, inviscid, and incompressible and elevation changes are neglected, Eq. 3.6 becomes

$$p_2 = p_1 + \frac{\rho V_1^2}{2}$$

With $V_1 = 100$ mi/hr = 146.7 ft/s and $V_2 = 0$ (since the coordinate system is fixed to the airplane) we obtain

$$p_2 = 1456 \text{ lb/ft}^2 + (0.001756 \text{ slugs/ft}^3)(146.7 \text{ ft/s})^2/2$$
$$= (1456 + 18.9) \text{ lb/ft}^2 \text{ (abs)}$$

Hence, in terms of gage pressure

$$p_2 = 18.9 \text{ lb/ft}^2 = 0.1313 \text{ psi} \qquad \text{(Ans)}$$

Thus, the pressure difference indicated by the Pitot-static tube is

$$p_2 - p_1 = \frac{\rho V_1^2}{2} = 0.1313 \text{ psi} \qquad \text{(Ans)}$$

Note that it is very easy to obtain incorrect results by using improper units. Do not add lb/in.^{2} and lb/ft^2. Note that $(\text{slug/ft}^3)(\text{ft}^2/\text{s}^2) = (\text{slug·ft/s}^2)/(\text{ft}^2) = \text{lb/ft}^2$.

It was assumed that the flow is incompressible—the density remains constant from (1) to (2). However, since $\rho = p/RT$, a change in pressure (or temperature) will cause a change in density. For this relatively low speed, the ratio of the absolute pressures is nearly unity [i.e., $p_1/p_2 = (10.11 \text{ psia})/(10.11 + 0.1313 \text{ psia}) = 0.987$], so that the density change is negligible. However, at high speed it is necessary to use compressible flow concepts to obtain accurate results.

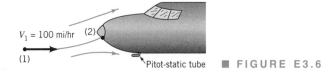

$V_1 = 100$ mi/hr (2)

(1)

Pitot-static tube   ■ FIGURE E3.6

3.6   Examples of Use of the Bernoulli Equation

Between any two points, (1) and (2), on a streamline in steady, inviscid, incompressible flow the Bernoulli equation (Eq. 3.6) can be applied in the form

$$p_1 + \tfrac{1}{2}\rho V_1^2 + \gamma z_1 = p_2 + \tfrac{1}{2}\rho V_2^2 + \gamma z_2 \tag{3.14}$$

The use of this equation is discussed in this section.

3.6.1   Free Jets

Consider flow of a liquid from a large reservoir as is shown in Fig. 3.7. A jet of liquid of diameter d flows from the nozzle with velocity V. Application of Eq. 3.14 between points (1) and (2) on the streamline shown gives

$$\gamma h = \tfrac{1}{2}\rho V^2$$

We have used the facts that $z_1 = h$, $z_2 = 0$, the reservoir is large ($V_1 = 0$), open to the atmosphere ($p_1 = 0$ gage), and the fluid leaves as a "free jet" ($p_2 = 0$). Thus, we obtain

$$V = \sqrt{2\frac{\gamma h}{\rho}} = \sqrt{2gh} \tag{3.15}$$

Once outside the nozzle, the stream continues to fall as a free jet with zero pressure throughout ($p_5 = 0$) and as seen by applying Eq. 3.14 between points (1) and (5), the speed increases according to

$$V = \sqrt{2g(h + H)}$$

where H is the distance the fluid has fallen outside the nozzle.

Equation 3.15 could also be obtained by writing the Bernoulli equation between points (3) and (4) using the fact that $z_4 = 0$, $z_3 = \ell$. Also, $V_3 = 0$ since it is far from the nozzle, and from hydrostatics, $p_3 = \gamma(h - \ell)$.

If the exit of the tank shown in Fig. 3.7 is not a smooth, well-contoured nozzle, the diameter of the jet, d_j, will be less than the diameter of the hole, d_h. This phenomenon, called a *vena contracta* effect, is a result of the inability of the fluid to turn a sharp 90° corner.

V3.5 Flow
from a tank

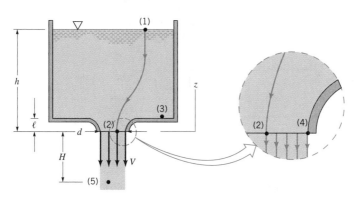

■ FIGURE 3.7
Vertical flow from a tank.

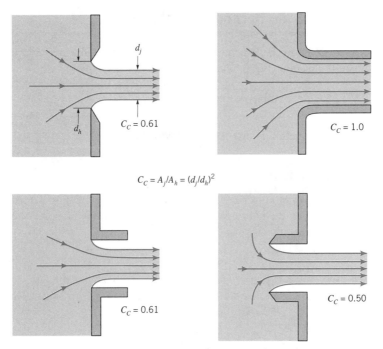

$$C_C = A_j/A_h = (d_j/d_h)^2$$

■ **FIGURE 3.8** Typical flow patterns and contraction coefficients for various round exit configurations.

Shown in Fig. 3.8 are typical values of the experimentally obtained *contraction coefficient*, $C_c = A_j/A_h$, where A_j and A_h are the areas of the jet at the vena contracta and the area of the hole, respectively.

3.6.2 Confined Flows

In many cases the fluid is physically constrained within a device so that its pressure cannot be prescribed a priori as was done for the free jet examples above. For these situations it is necessary to use the concept of conservation of mass (the continuity equation) along with the Bernoulli equation.

Consider a fluid flowing through a fixed volume (such as a tank) that has one inlet and one outlet as shown in Fig. 3.9. If the flow is steady so that there is no additional accumulation of fluid within the volume, the rate at which the fluid flows into the volume must equal the rate at which it flows out of the volume (otherwise mass would not be conserved).

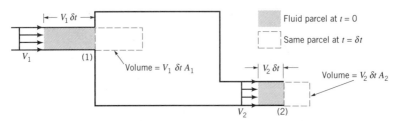

■ **FIGURE 3.9** Steady flow into and out of a tank.

The *mass flowrate* from an outlet, m (slugs/s or kg/s), is given by $\dot{m} = \rho Q$, where Q (ft^3/s or m^3/s) is the *volume flowrate*. If the outlet area is A and the fluid flows across this area (normal to the area) with an average velocity V, then the volume of the fluid crossing this area in a time interval δt is $VA\,\delta t$, equal to that in a volume of length $V\,\delta t$ and cross-sectional area A (see Fig. 3.9). Hence, the volume flowrate (volume per unit time) is $Q = VA$. Thus, $\dot{m} = \rho VA$. To conserve mass, the inflow rate must equal the outflow rate. If the inlet is designated as (1) and the outlet as (2), it follows that $\dot{m}_1 = \dot{m}_2$. Thus, conservation of mass requires

$$\rho_1 A_1 V_1 = \rho_2 A_2 V_2$$

If the density remains constant, then $\rho_1 = \rho_2$ and the above becomes the *continuity equation* for incompressible flow

$$A_1 V_1 = A_2 V_2, \text{ or } Q_1 = Q_2 \qquad\qquad (3.16)$$

EXAMPLE 3.7

A stream of water of diameter $d = 0.1\,$m flows steadily from a tank of diameter $D = 1.0\,$m as shown in Fig. E3.7a. Determine the flow rate, Q, needed from the inflow pipe if the water depth remains constant, $h = 2.0\,$m.

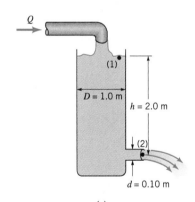

(a)

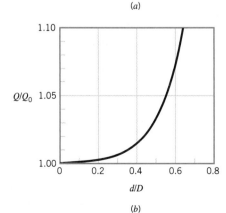

(b)

■ FIGURE E3.7

SOLUTION

For steady, inviscid, incompressible flow the Bernoulli equation applied between points (1) and (2) is

$$p_1 + \tfrac{1}{2}\rho V_1^2 + \gamma z_1 = p_2 + \tfrac{1}{2}\rho V_2^2 + \gamma z_2 \qquad (1)$$

With the assumptions that $p_1 = p_2 = 0$, $z_1 = h$, and $z_2 = 0$, Eq. 1 becomes

$$\tfrac{1}{2}V_1^2 + gh = \tfrac{1}{2}V_2^2 \qquad (2)$$

Although the water level remains constant ($h = $ constant), there is an average velocity, V_1, across section (1) because of the flow from the tank. From Eq. 3.16 for steady incompressible flow, conservation of mass requires $Q_1 = Q_2$, where $Q = AV$. Thus, $A_1V_1 = A_2V_2$, or

$$\frac{\pi}{4}D^2V_1 = \frac{\pi}{4}d^2V_2$$

Hence,

$$V_1 = \left(\frac{d}{D}\right)^2 V_2 \qquad (3)$$

Equations 1 and 3 can be combined to give

$$V_2 = \sqrt{\frac{2gh}{1 - (d/D)^4}}$$

Thus, with the given data

$$V_2 = \sqrt{\frac{2(9.81\,\text{m/s}^2)(2.0\,\text{m})}{1 - (0.1\,\text{m}/1\,\text{m})^4}} = 6.26\,\text{m/s}$$

and

$$Q = A_1V_1 = A_2V_2 = \frac{\pi}{4}(0.1\,\text{m})^2(6.26\,\text{m/s}) = 0.0492\,\text{m}^3/\text{s} \qquad \text{(Ans)}$$

In this example we have not neglected the kinetic energy of the water in the tank ($V_1 \neq 0$). If the tank diameter is large compared to the jet diameter ($D \gg d$), Eq. 3 indicates that $V_1 \ll V_2$ and the assumption that $V_1 \approx 0$ would be reasonable. The error associated with this assumption can be seen by calculating the ratio of the flowrate assuming $V_1 \neq 0$, denoted Q, to that assuming $V_1 = 0$, denoted Q_0. This ratio, written as

$$\frac{Q}{Q_0} = \frac{V_2}{V_2|_{D=\infty}} = \frac{\sqrt{2gh/[1 - (d/D)^4]}}{\sqrt{2gh}} = \frac{1}{\sqrt{1 - (d/D)^4}}$$

is plotted in Fig. E3.7b. With $0 < d/D < 0.4$ it follows that $1 < Q/Q_0 \leq 1.01$, and the error in assuming $V_1 = 0$ is less than 1%. Thus, it is often reasonable to assume $V_1 = 0$.

The fact that a kinetic energy change is often accompanied by a change in pressure is shown by Example 3.8.

EXAMPLE 3.8

Air flows steadily from a tank, through a hose of diameter $D = 0.03$ m and exits to the atmosphere from a nozzle of diameter $d = 0.01$ m as shown in Fig. E3.8. The pressure in the tank remains constant at 3.0 kPa (gage) and the atmospheric conditions are standard temperature and pressure. Determine the flowrate and the pressure in the hose.

SOLUTION

If the flow is assumed steady, inviscid, and incompressible, we can apply the Bernoulli equation along the streamline shown as

$$p_1 + \tfrac{1}{2}\rho V_1^2 + \gamma z_1 = p_2 + \tfrac{1}{2}\rho V_2^2 + \gamma z_2$$
$$= p_3 + \tfrac{1}{2}\rho V_3^2 + \gamma z_3$$

With the assumption that $z_1 = z_2 = z_3$ (horizontal hose), $V_1 = 0$ (large tank), and $p_3 = 0$ (free jet) this becomes

$$V_3 = \sqrt{\frac{2p_1}{\rho}}$$

and

$$p_2 = p_1 - \tfrac{1}{2}\rho V_2^2 \tag{1}$$

The density of the air in the tank is obtained from the perfect gas law, using standard absolute pressure and temperature, as

$$\rho = \frac{p_1}{RT_1}$$
$$= [(3.0 + 101)\ \text{kN/m}^2]$$
$$\times \frac{10^3\ \text{N/kN}}{(286.9\ \text{N·m/kg·K})(15 + 273)\text{K}}$$
$$= 1.26\ \text{kg/m}^3$$

Thus, we find that

$$V_3 = \sqrt{\frac{2(3.0 \times 10^3\ \text{N/m}^2)}{1.26\ \text{kg/m}^3}} = 69.0\ \text{m/s}$$

or

$$Q = A_3 V_3 = \frac{\pi}{4}d^2 V_3 = \frac{\pi}{4}(0.01\ \text{m})^2(69.0\ \text{m/s})$$
$$= 0.00542\ \text{m}^3/\text{s} \tag{Ans}$$

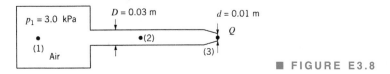

$p_1 = 3.0$ kPa $D = 0.03$ m $d = 0.01$ m

•(2) Q

(1)   (3)

Air

■ FIGURE E3.8

Note that the value of V_3 is determined strictly by the value of p_1 (and the assumptions involved in the Bernoulli equation), independent of the "shape" of the nozzle. The pressure head within the tank, $p_1/\gamma = (3.0 \text{ kPa})/(9.81 \text{ m/s}^2)(1.26 \text{ kg/m}^3) = 243 \text{ m}$, is converted to the velocity head at the exit, $V_2^2/2g = (69.0 \text{ m/s})^2/(2 \times 9.81 \text{ m/s}^2) = 243 \text{ m}$. Although we used gage pressure in the Bernoulli equation ($p_3 = 0$), we had to use absolute pressure in the perfect gas law when calculating the density.

The pressure within the hose can be obtained from Eq. 1 and the continuity equation (Eq. 3.16)

$$A_2V_2 = A_3V_3$$

Hence,

$$V_2 = A_3V_3/A_2 = \left(\frac{d}{D}\right)^2 V_3 = \left(\frac{0.01 \text{ m}}{0.03 \text{ m}}\right)^2 (69.0 \text{ m/s})$$

$$= 7.67 \text{ m/s}$$

and from Eq. 1

$$p_2 = 3.0 \times 10^3 \text{ N/m}^2 - \tfrac{1}{2}(1.26 \text{ kg/m}^3)(7.67 \text{ m/s})^2$$
$$= (3000 - 37.1)\text{N/m}^2 = 2963 \text{ N/m}^2 \qquad \text{(Ans)}$$

In the absence of viscous effects the pressure throughout the hose is constant and equal to p_2. Physically, the decreases in pressure from p_1 to p_2 to p_3 accelerate the air and increase its kinetic energy from zero in the tank to an intermediate value in the hose and finally to its maximum value at the nozzle exit. Since the air velocity in the nozzle exit is nine times that in the hose, most of the pressure drop occurs across the nozzle ($p_1 = 3000 \text{ N/m}^2$, $p_2 = 2963 \text{ N/m}^2$ and $p_3 = 0$).

Since the pressure change from (1) to (3) is not too great [that is, in terms of absolute pressure $(p_1 - p_3)/p_1 = 3.0/101 = 0.03$], it follows from the perfect gas law that the density change is also not significant. Hence, the incompressibility assumption is reasonable for this problem. If the tank pressure were considerably larger or if viscous effects were important, the above results would be incorrect.

In many situations the combined effects of kinetic energy, pressure, and gravity are important. Example 3.9 illustrates this.

EXAMPLE 3.9

Water flows through a pipe reducer as is shown in Fig. E3.9. The static pressures at (1) and (2) are measured by the inverted U-tube manometer containing oil of specific gravity, SG, less than one. Determine the manometer reading, h.

SOLUTION

With the assumptions of steady, inviscid, incompressible flow, the Bernoulli equation can be written as

$$p_1 + \tfrac{1}{2}\rho V_1^2 + \gamma z_1 = p_2 + \tfrac{1}{2}\rho V_2^2 + \gamma z_2$$

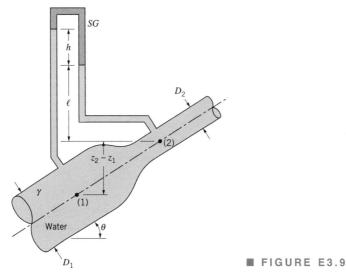

The continuity equation (Eq. 3.16) provides a second relationship between V_1 and V_2 if we assume the velocity profiles are uniform at those two locations and the fluid incompressible:

$$Q = A_1V_1 = A_2V_2$$

By combining these two equations we obtain

$$p_1 - p_2 = \gamma(z_2 - z_1) + \tfrac{1}{2}\rho V_2^2[1 - (A_2/A_1)^2] \tag{1}$$

This pressure difference is measured by the manometer and can be determined by using the pressure-depth ideas developed in Chapter 2. Thus,

$$p_1 - \gamma(z_2 - z_1) - \gamma\ell - \gamma h + SG\ \gamma h + \gamma\ell = p_2$$

or

$$p_1 - p_2 = \gamma(z_2 - z_1) + (1 - SG)\gamma h \tag{2}$$

As discussed in Chapter 2, this pressure difference is neither merely γh nor $\gamma(h + z_1 - z_2)$. Equations 1 and 2 can be combined to give the desired result as follows

$$(1 - SG)\gamma h = \frac{1}{2}\rho V_2^2\left[1 - \left(\frac{A_2}{A_1}\right)^2\right]$$

or since $V_2 = Q/A_2$

$$h = (Q/A_2)^2\frac{1 - (A_2/A_1)^2}{2g(1 - SG)} \tag{Ans}$$

The difference in elevation, $z_1 - z_2$, was not needed because the change in elevation term in the Bernoulli equation exactly cancels the elevation term in the manometer equation. However, the pressure difference, $p_1 - p_2$, depends on the angle θ, because of the elevation, $z_1 - z_2$, in Eq. 1. Thus, for a given flowrate, the pressure difference, $p_1 - p_2$, as measured by a pressure gage would vary with θ, but the manometer reading, h, would be independent of θ.

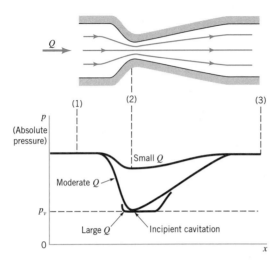

■ **FIGURE 3.10** **Pressure variation and cavitation in a variable area pipe.**

In general, an increase in velocity is accompanied by a decrease in pressure. If the differences in velocity are considerable, the differences in pressure can also be considerable. For flows of liquids, this may result in cavitation, a potentially dangerous situation that results when the liquid pressure is reduced to the vapor pressure and the liquid "boils."

V3.6 Venturi
channel

One way to produce cavitation in a flowing liquid is noted from the Bernoulli equation. If the fluid velocity is increased (for example, by a reduction in flow area as shown in Fig. 3.10) the pressure will decrease. This pressure decrease (needed to accelerate the fluid through the constriction) can be large enough so that the pressure in the liquid is reduced to its vapor pressure.

_E_ XAMPLE 3.10

Water at 60 °F is siphoned from a large tank through a constant diameter hose as shown in Fig. E3.10. Determine the maximum height of the hill, H, over which the water can be siphoned without cavitation occurring. The end of the siphon is 5 ft below the bottom of the tank. Atmospheric pressure is 14.7 psia.

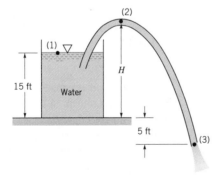

■ FIGURE E3.10

SOLUTION

If the flow is steady, inviscid, and incompressible, we can apply the Bernoulli equation along the streamline from (1) to (2) to (3) as follows

$$p_1 + \tfrac{1}{2}\rho V_1^2 + \gamma z_1 = p_2 + \tfrac{1}{2}\rho V_2^2 + \gamma z_2 = p_3 + \tfrac{1}{2}\rho V_3^2 + \gamma z_3 \tag{1}$$

With the tank bottom as the datum, we have $z_1 = 15\,\text{ft}$, $z_2 = H$, and $z_3 = -5\,\text{ft}$. Also, $V_1 = 0$ (large tank), $p_1 = 0$ (open tank), $p_3 = 0$ (free jet), and from the continuity equation $A_2 V_2 = A_3 V_3$, or because the hose is constant diameter, $V_2 = V_3$. Thus, the speed of the fluid in the hose is determined from Eq. 1 to be

$$V_3 = \sqrt{2g(z_1 - z_3)} = \sqrt{2(32.2\ \text{ft/s}^2)[15 - (-5)]\,\text{ft}}$$
$$= 35.9\ \text{ft/s} = V_2$$

Use of Eq. 1 between points (1) and (2) then gives the pressure p_2 at the top of the hill as

$$p_2 = p_1 + \tfrac{1}{2}\rho V_1^2 + \gamma z_1 - \tfrac{1}{2}\rho V_2^2 - \gamma z_2 = \gamma(z_1 - z_2) - \tfrac{1}{2}\rho V_2^2 \tag{2}$$

From Table B.1, the vapor pressure of water at 60 °F is 0.256 psia. Hence, for incipient cavitation the lowest pressure in the system will be $p = 0.256$ psia. Careful consideration of Eq. 2 and Fig. E3.10 will show that this lowest pressure will occur at the top of the hill. Since we have used gage pressure at point (1) ($p_1 = 0$), we must use gage pressure at point (2) also. Thus, $p_2 = 0.256 - 14.7 = -14.4$ psi and Eq. 2 gives

$$(-14.4\ \text{lb/in.}^2)(144\ \text{in.}^2/\text{ft}^2) = (62.4\ \text{lb/ft}^3)(15 - H)\text{ft} - \tfrac{1}{2}(1.94\ \text{slugs/ft}^3)(35.9\ \text{ft/s})^2$$

or

$$H = 28.2\ \text{ft} \qquad\qquad\qquad \text{(Ans)}$$

For larger values of H, vapor bubbles will form at point (2) and the siphon action may stop.

Note that we could have used absolute pressure throughout ($p_2 = 0.256$ psia and $p_1 = 14.7$ psia) and obtained the same result. The lower the elevation of point (3), the larger the flowrate and, therefore, the smaller the value of H allowed.

We could also have used the Bernoulli equation between (2) and (3), with $V_2 = V_3$, to obtain the same value of H. In this case it would not have been necessary to determine V_2 by use of the Bernoulli equation between (1) and (3).

The above results are independent of the diameter and length of the hose (provided viscous effects are not important). Proper design of the hose (or pipe) is needed to ensure that it will not collapse due to the large pressure difference (vacuum) between the inside and the outside of the hose.

3.6.3   Flowrate Measurement

Many types of devices using principles involved in the Bernoulli equation have been developed to measure fluid velocities and flowrates.

An effective way to measure the flowrate through a pipe is to place some type of restriction within the pipe as shown in Fig. 3.11 and to measure the pressure difference between the low-velocity, high-pressure upstream section (1), and the high-velocity, low-pressure

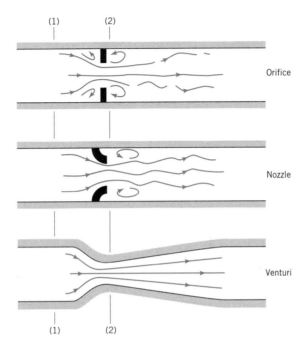

■ **FIGURE 3.11** **Typical devices for measuring flowrate in pipes.**

downstream section (2). Three commonly used types of flowmeters are illustrated: the *orifice meter,* the *nozzle meter,* and the *Venturi meter.* The operation of each is based on the same physical principles—an increase in velocity causes a decrease in pressure.

We assume the flow is horizontal ($z_1 = z_2$), steady, inviscid, and incompressible between points (1) and (2). The Bernoulli equation becomes

$$p_1 + \tfrac{1}{2}\rho V_1^2 = p_2 + \tfrac{1}{2}\rho V_2^2$$

In addition, the continuity equation (Eq. 3.16) can be written as

$$Q = A_1 V_1 = A_2 V_2$$

where A_2 is the small ($A_2 < A_1$) flow area at section (2). Combination of these two equations results in the following theoretical flowrate

$$Q = A_2 \sqrt{\frac{2(p_1 - p_2)}{\rho[1 - (A_2/A_1)^2]}} \tag{3.17}$$

The actual measured flowrate, Q_{actual}, will be smaller than this theoretical result because of various differences between the "real world" and the assumptions used in the derivation of Eq. 3.17. These differences (which are quite consistent and may be as small as 1 to 2% or as large as 40% depending on the geometry used) are discussed in Chapter 8.

EXAMPLE 3.11

Kerosene ($SG = 0.85$) flows through the Venturi meter shown in Fig. E3.11 with flowrates between 0.005 and 0.050 m³/s. Determine the range in pressure difference, $p_1 - p_2$, needed to measure these flowrates.

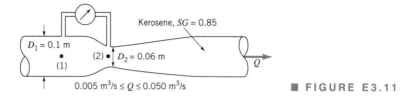

Kerosene, $SG = 0.85$

$D_1 = 0.1$ m

(2) • $D_2 = 0.06$ m

(1)

Q

0.005 m³/s $\leq Q \leq 0.050$ m³/s

■ **FIGURE E3.11**

SOLUTION

If the flow is assumed to be steady, inviscid, and incompressible, the relationship between flowrate and pressure is given by Eq. 3.17. This can be rearranged to give

$$p_1 - p_2 = \frac{Q^2 \rho [1 - (A_2/A_1)^2]}{2A_2^2}$$

With a density of the flowing fluid of

$$\rho = SG \, \rho_{H_2O} = 0.85(1000 \text{ kg/m}^3) = 850 \text{ kg/m}^3$$

the pressure difference for the smallest flowrate is

$$p_1 - p_2 = (0.005 \text{ m}^3/\text{s})^2(850 \text{ kg/m}^3)\frac{[1 - (0.06 \text{ m}/0.10 \text{ m})^4]}{2[(\pi/4)(0.06 \text{ m})^2]^2}$$

$$= 1160 \text{ N/m}^2 = 1.16 \text{ kPa}$$

Likewise, the pressure difference for the largest flowrate is

$$p_1 - p_2 = (0.05)^2(850)\frac{[1 - (0.06/0.10)^4]}{2[(\pi/4)(0.06)^2]^2}$$

$$= 1.16 \, 10^5 \text{ N/m}^2$$

$$= 116 \text{ kPa}$$

Thus,

$$1.16 \text{ kPa} \leq p_1 - p_2 \leq 116 \text{ kPa} \qquad \text{(Ans)}$$

These values represent the pressure differences for inviscid, steady, incompressible conditions. The ideal results presented here are independent of the particular flowmeter geometry—an orifice, nozzle, or Venturi meter (see Fig. 3.11).

It is seen from Eq. 3.17 that the flowrate varies as the square root of the pressure difference. Hence, as indicated by the numerical results, a tenfold increase in flowrate requires a one-hundredfold increase in pressure difference. This nonlinear relationship can cause difficulties when measuring flowrates over a wide range of values. Such measurements would require pressure transducers with a wide range of operation. An alternative is to use two flowmeters in parallel—one for the larger and one for the smaller flowrate ranges.

Other flowmeters based on the Bernoulli equation are used to measure flowrates in open channels such as flumes and irrigation ditches. The *sluice gate* as shown in Fig. 3.12 is an example.

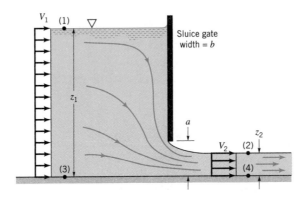

■ **FIGURE 3.12** **Sluice gate geometry.**

We apply the Bernoulli and continuity equations between points on the free surfaces at (1) and (2) to give

$$p_1 + \tfrac{1}{2}\rho V_1^2 + \gamma z_1 = p_2 + \tfrac{1}{2}\rho V_2^2 + \gamma z_2$$

and

$$Q = A_1 V_1 = b V_1 z_1 = A_2 V_2 = b V_2 z_2$$

With the fact that $p_1 = p_2 = 0$, these equations can be combined to give the flowrate as

$$Q = z_2 b \sqrt{\frac{2g(z_1 - z_2)}{1 - (z_2/z_1)^2}} \tag{3.18}$$

The downstream depth, z_2, not the gate opening, a, was used to obtain the result of Eq. 3.18 since a vena contracta results with a contraction coefficient, $C_c = z_2/a$, less than 1. Typically C_c is approximately 0.61 over the depth ratio range of $0 < a/z_1 < 0.2$. For larger values of a/z_1 the value of C_c increases rapidly.

EXAMPLE 3.12

Water flows under the sluice gate shown in Fig. E3.12. Determine the approximate flowrate per unit width of the channel.

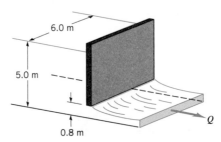

■ **FIGURE E3.12**

SOLUTION

Under the assumptions of steady, inviscid, incompressible flow, we can apply Eq. 3.18 to obtain Q/b, the flowrate per unit width, as

$$\frac{Q}{b} = z_2 \sqrt{\frac{2g(z_1 - z_2)}{1 - (z_2/z_1)^2}}$$

In this instance $z_1 = 5.0$ m and $a = 0.80$ m so the ratio $a/z_1 = 0.16 < 0.20$, and we can assume that the contraction coefficient is approximately $C_c = 0.61$. Thus, $z_2 = C_c a = 0.61$ (0.80 m) $= 0.488$ m and we obtain the flowrate

$$\frac{Q}{b} = (0.488 \text{ m}) \sqrt{\frac{2(9.81 \text{ m/s}^2)(5.0 \text{ m} - 0.488 \text{ m})}{1 - (0.488 \text{ m}/5.0 \text{ m})^2}}$$

$$= 4.61 \text{ m}^2/\text{s} \tag{Ans}$$

If we consider $z_1 \gg z_2$ and neglect the kinetic energy of the upstream fluid, we would have

$$\frac{Q}{b} = z_2 \sqrt{2gz_1} = 0.488 \text{ m} \sqrt{2(9.81 \text{ m/s}^2)(5.0 \text{ m})} = 4.83 \text{ m}^2/\text{s}$$

In this case the difference in Q with or without including V_1 is not too significant because the depth ratio is fairly large ($z_1/z_2 = 5.0/0.488 = 10.2$). Thus, it is often reasonable to neglect the kinetic energy upstream from the gate compared to that downstream of it.

3.7   The Energy Line and the Hydraulic Grade Line

A useful interpretation of the Bernoulli equation can be obtained through the use of the concepts of the *hydraulic grade line* (HGL) and the *energy line* (EL). These ideas represent a geometrical interpretation of a flow.

For steady, inviscid, incompressible flow the Bernoulli equation states that the sum of the pressure head, the velocity head, and the elevation head is constant along a streamline. This constant is called the *total head, H*.

$$\frac{p}{\gamma} + \frac{V^2}{2g} + z = \text{constant on a streamline} = H \tag{3.19}$$

The energy line is a line that represents the total head available to the fluid. As shown in Fig. 3.13, the elevation of the energy line can be obtained by measuring the stagnation pressure with a Pitot tube. The stagnation point at the end of the Pitot tube provides a measurement of the total head (or energy) of the flow. The static pressure tap connected to the piezometer tube shown, on the other hand, measures the sum of the pressure head and the elevation head, $p/\gamma + z$. This sum is often called the *piezometric head*.

A Pitot tube at another location in the flow will measure the same total head, as is shown in the figure. The elevation head, velocity head, and pressure head may vary along the streamline, however.

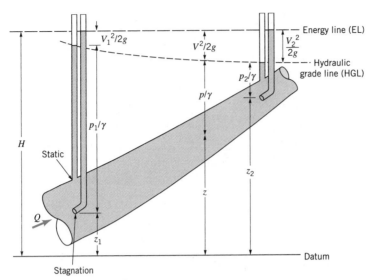

■ **FIGURE 3.13** **Representation of the energy line and the hydraulic grade line.**

The locus of elevations provided by a series of Pitot tubes is termed the energy line, EL. That provided by a series of piezometer taps is termed the hydraulic grade line, HGL. Under the assumptions of the Bernoulli equation, the energy line is horizontal. If the fluid velocity changes along the streamline, the hydraulic grade line will not be horizontal.

The energy line and hydraulic grade line for flow from a large tank are shown in Fig. 3.14. If the flow is steady, incompressible, and inviscid, the energy line is horizontal and at the elevation of the liquid in the tank. The hydraulic grade line lies a distance of one velocity head, $V^2/2g$, below the energy line.

The distance from the pipe to the hydraulic grade line indicates the pressure within the pipe as is shown in Fig. 3.15. If the pipe lies below the hydraulic grade line the pressure within the pipe is positive (above atmospheric). If the pipe lies above the hydraulic grade line the pressure is negative (below atmospheric).

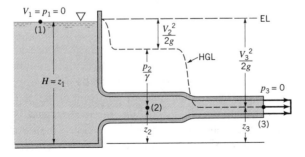

■ **FIGURE 3.14** **The energy line and hydraulic grade line for flow from a tank.**

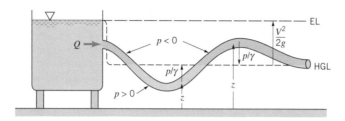

■ **FIGURE 3.15** **Use of the energy line and the hydraulic grade line.**

EXAMPLE 3.13

Water is siphoned from the tank shown in Fig. E3.13 through a hose of constant diameter. A small hole is found in the hose at location (1) as indicated. When the siphon is used, will water leak out of the hose, or will air leak into the hose, thereby possibly causing the siphon to malfunction?

SOLUTION

Whether air will leak into or water will leak out of the hose depends on whether the pressure within the hose at (1) is less than or greater than atmospheric. Which happens can be easily determined by using the energy line and hydraulic grade line concepts as follows. With the assumption of steady, incompressible, inviscid flow it follows that the total head is constant—thus, the energy line is horizontal.

Since the hose diameter is constant, it follow from the continuity equation (AV = constant) that the water velocity in the hose is constant throughout. Thus, the hydraulic grade line is a constant distance, $V^2/2g$, below the energy line as shown in Fig. E3.13. Since the pressure at the end of the hose is atmospheric, it follows that the hydraulic grade line is at the same elevation as the end of the hose outlet. The fluid within the hose at any point above the hydraulic grade line will be at less than atmospheric pressure.

Thus, air will leak into the hose through the hole at point (1). **(Ans)**

In practice, viscous effects may be quite important, making this simple analysis (horizontal energy line) incorrect. However, if the hose is "not too small diameter," "not too long,"

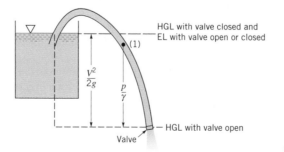

■ **FIGURE E3.13**

the fluid "not too viscous," and the flowrate "not too large," the above result may be very accurate. If any of these assumptions are relaxed, a more detailed analysis is required (see Chapter 8). If the end of the hose were closed so the flowrate were zero, the hydraulic grade line would coincide with the energy line ($V^2/2g = 0$ throughout), the pressure at (1) would be greater than atmospheric, and water would leak through the hole at (1).

3.8   Restrictions on the Use of the Bernoulli Equation

One of the main assumptions in deriving the Bernoulli equation is that the fluid is incompressible. Although this is reasonable for most liquid flows, it can, in certain instances, introduce considerable errors for gases.

In the previous section we saw that the stagnation pressure is greater than the static pressure by an amount $\rho V^2/2$, provided that the density remains constant. If this dynamic pressure is not too large compared with the static pressure, the density change between two points is not very large and the flow can be considered incompressible. However, since the dynamic pressure varies as V^2, the error associated with the assumption that a fluid is incompressible increases with the square of the velocity of the fluid.

A "rule of thumb" is that the flow of a perfect gas may be considered as incompressible provided the Mach number is less than about 0.3. The Mach number, Ma $= V/c$, is the ratio of the fluid speed, V, to the speed of sound in the fluid, c. In standard air ($T_1 = 59°F$, $c_1 = \sqrt{kRT_1} = 1117$ ft/s) this corresponds to a speed of $V_1 = c_1 \text{Ma}_1 = 0.3 (1117 \text{ ft/s}) = 335$ ft/s $= 228$ mi/hr. At higher speeds, compressibility may become important.

Another restriction of the Bernoulli equation (Eq. 3.6) is the assumption that the flow is steady. For such flows, on a given streamline the velocity is a function of only s, the location along the streamline. That is, along a streamline $V = V(s)$. For unsteady flows the velocity is also a function of time, so that along a streamline $V = V(s,t)$. Thus, when taking the time derivative of the velocity to obtain the streamwise acceleration, we obtain $a_s = \partial V/\partial t + V\partial V/\partial s$ rather than just $a_s = V\partial V/\partial s$ as is true for steady flow. The unsteady term, $\partial V/\partial t$, does not allow the equation of motion to be easily integrated (as was done to obtain the Bernoulli equation) unless additional assumptions are made.

Another restriction on the Bernoulli equation is that the flow is inviscid. Recall that the Bernoulli equation is actually a first integral of Newton's second law along a streamline. This general integration was possible because, in the absence of viscous effects, the fluid system considered was a conservative system. The total energy of the system remains constant. If viscous effects are important, the system is nonconservative and energy losses occur. A more detailed analysis is needed for these cases. Such material is presented in Chapter 8.

The final basic restriction on use of the Bernoulli equation is that there are no mechanical devices (pumps or turbines) in the system between the two points along the streamline for which the equation is applied. These devices represent sources or sinks of energy. Since the Bernoulli equation is actually one form of the energy equation, it must be altered to include pumps or turbines, if these are present. The inclusion of pumps and turbines is covered in Chapter 5.

Problems

Note: Unless otherwise indicated use the values of fluid properties found in the tables on the inside of the front cover. Problems designated with an (*) are intended to be solved with the aid of a programmable calculator or a computer. Problems designated with a (†) are "open-ended" problems and require critical thinking in that to work them one must make various assumptions and provide the necessary data. There is not a unique answer to these problems.

3.1   Water flows steadily through the variable area horizontal pipe shown in Fig. P3.1. The centerline velocity is given by $\mathbf{V} = 10(1 + x)\hat{\mathbf{i}}$ ft/s, where x is in feet. Viscous effects are neglected. **(a)** Determine the pressure gradient, $\partial p/\partial x$ (as a function of x) needed to produce this flow. **(b)** If the pressure at section (1) is 50 psi, determine the pressure at (2) by (i) integration of the pressure gradient obtained in **(a)**, (ii) application of the Bernoulli equation.

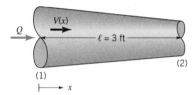

■ FIGURE P3.1

3.2   Repeat Problem 3.1 if the pipe is vertical with the flow upward.

3.3   An incompressible fluid with density ρ flows steadily past the object shown in **Video V3.3** and Fig. P3.3. The fluid velocity along the horizontal dividing streamline $(-\infty \le x \le -a)$ is found to be $V = V_0(1 + a/x)$, where a is the radius of curvature of the front of the object and V_0 is the upstream velocity. **(a)** Determine the pressure gradient along this streamline. **(b)** If the upstream pressure is p_0, integrate the pressure gradient to obtain the pressure $p(x)$ for

$-\infty \le x \le -a$. **(c)** Show from the result of part **(b)** that the pressure at the stagnation point $(x = -a)$ is $p_0 + \rho V_0^2/2$, as expected from the Bernoulli equation.

3.4   What pressure gradient along the streamline, dp/ds, is required to accelerate water in a horizontal pipe at a rate of 10 m/s^2?

3.5   What pressure gradient along the streamline, dp/ds, is required to accelerate water upward in a vertical pipe at a rate of 30 ft/s^2? What is the answer if the flow is downward?

3.6   Water in a container and air in a tornado flow in horizontal circular streamlines of radius r and speed V as shown in **Video V3.2** and Fig. P3.6. Determine the radial pressure gradient, $\partial p/\partial r$, needed for the following situations: **(a)** The fluid is water with $r = 3$ in. and $V = 0.8$ ft/s. **(b)** The fluid is air with $r = 300$ ft and $V = 200$ mph.

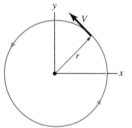

■ FIGURE P3.6

3.7   Water flows around the vertical two-dimensional bend with circular streamlines and constant velocity as shown in Fig. P3.7. If the pressure is 40 kPa at point (1), determine the pressures at points (2) and (3). Assume that the velocity profile is uniform as indicated.

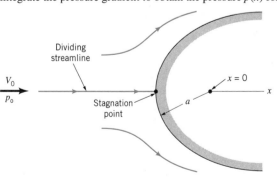

■ FIGURE P3.3

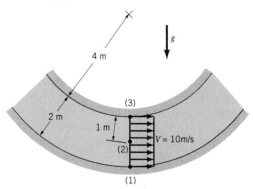

■ FIGURE P3.7

†**3.8**   Air flows smoothly past your face as you ride your bike, but bugs and particles or dust pelt your face and get into your eyes. Explain why this is so.

3.9   Some animals have learned to take advantage of the Bernoulli effect without having read a fluid mechanics book. For example, a typical prairie dog burrow contains two entrances—a flat front door, and a mounded back door as shown in Fig. P3.9. When the wind blows with velocity V_0 across the front door, the average velocity across the back door is greater than V_0 because of the mound. Assume the air velocity across the back door is $1.07 V_0$. For a wind velocity of 6 m/s, what pressure difference, $p_1 - p_2$, is generated to provide a fresh air flow within the burrow?

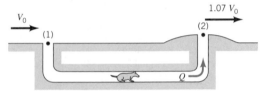

■ FIGURE P3.9

3.10   Water flows from a pop bottle that has holes in it as shown in **Video V3.5** and Fig. P3.10. Two streams coming from holes located distances h_1 and h_2 below the free surface intersect at a distance L from the side of the bottle. If viscous effects are negligible and the flow is quasi-steady, show that $L = 2(h_1 h_2)^{1/2}$. Compare this result with experimental data measured from the paused video for which the holes are 2 inches apart.

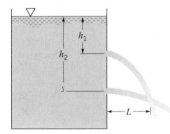

■ FIGURE P3.10

†**3.11**   Estimate the pressure needed at the pumper truck in order to shoot water from the street level onto a fire on the roof of a five-story building. List all assumptions and show all calculations.

3.12   A fire hose nozzle has a diameter of $1\frac{1}{8}$ in. According to some fire codes, the nozzle must be capable of delivering at least 300 gal/min. If the nozzle is attached to a 3-in.-diameter hose, what pressure must be maintained just upstream of the nozzle to deliver this flowrate?

3.13   Water flowing from the 0.75-in.-diameter outlet shown in **Video V8.6** and Fig. P3.13 rises 2.8 inches above the outlet. Determine the flowrate.

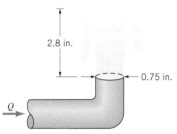

■ FIGURE P3.13

3.14   A person holds her hand out of an open car window while the car drives through still air at 65 mph. Under standard atmospheric conditions, what is the maximum pressure on her hand? What would be the maximum pressure if the "car" were an Indy 500 racer traveling 200 mph?

3.15   A 100 ft/s jet of air flows past a ball as shown in **Video V3.1** and Fig. P3.15. When the ball is not centered in the jet, the air velocity is greater on the side of the ball near the jet center [point (1)] than it is on the other side of the ball [point (2)]. Determine the pressure difference, $p_2 - p_1$, across the ball if $V_1 = 140$ ft/s and $V_2 = 110$ ft/s. Neglect gravity and viscous effects.

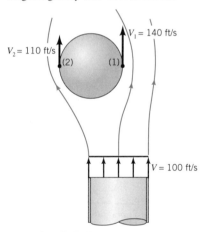

■ FIGURE P3.15

3.16   A 4-in.-diameter pipe carries 300 gal/min of water at a pressure of 60 psi. Determine **(a)** the pressure head in feet of water, **(b)** the velocity head, and **(c)** the total head with reference to a datum plane 20 ft below the pipe.

3.17   Air is drawn into a small open-circuit wind tunnel as shown in Fig. P3.17. Atmospheric pressure is 98.7 kPa (abs) and the temperature is 27 °C. If viscous effects are negligible, determine the pressure at the stagnation point on the nose of the airplane. Also determine the manometer reading, h, for the manometer attached to the static pressure tap within the test section of the wind tunnel if the air velocity within the test section is 60 m/s.

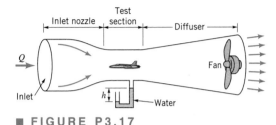

■ **FIGURE P3.17**

3.18 Water flows through the pipe contraction shown in Fig. P3.18. For the given 0.2-m difference in the manometer level, determine the flowrate as a function of the diameter of the small pipe, D.

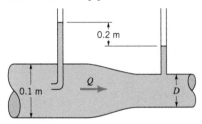

■ **FIGURE P3.18**

3.19 Water flows through the pipe contraction shown in Fig. P3.19. Determine the difference in manometer level, h, for a flowrate of 0.10 m^3/s.

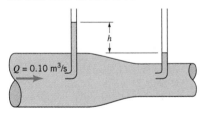

■ **FIGURE P3.19**

3.20 The speed of an airplane through the air is obtained by use of a Pitot-static tube that measures the difference between the stagnation and static pressures. (See **Video V3.4**.) Rather than indicating this pressure difference (psi or N/m^2) directly, the indicator is calibrated in speed (mph or knots). This calibration is done using the density of standard sea level air. Thus, the air speed displayed (termed the indicated air speed) is the actual air speed only at standard sea level conditions. If the aircraft is flying at an altitude of 20,000 ft and the indicated air speed is 220 knots, what is the actual air speed?

3.21 Carbon tetrachloride flows in a pipe of variable diameter with negligible viscous effects. At point A in the pipe the pressure and velocity are 20 psi and 30 ft/s, respectively. At location B the pressure and velocity are 23 psi and 14 ft/s. Which point is at the higher elevation and by how much?

3.22 A loon is a diving bird equally at home "flying" in the air or water. What swimming velocity under water will produce a dynamic pressure equal to that when it flies in the air at 40 mph?

3.23 Water flows steadily from the pipe shown in Fig. P3.23 with negligible viscous effects. Determine the maximum flowrate if the water is not to flow from the open vertical tube at A.

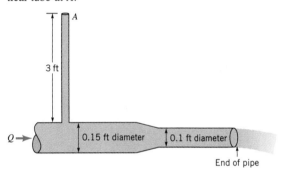

■ **FIGURE P3.23**

3.24 The circular stream of water from a faucet is observed to taper from a diameter of 20 mm to 10 mm in a distance of 50 cm. Determine the flowrate.

3.25 Water is siphoned from the tank shown in Fig. P3.25. The water barometer indicates a reading of 30.2 ft. Determine the maximum value of h allowed without cavitation occurring. Note that the pressure of the vapor in the closed end of the barometer equals the vapor pressure.

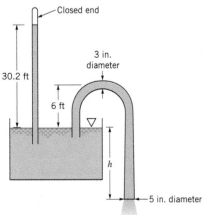

■ **FIGURE P3.25**

3.26   An inviscid fluid flows steadily through the contraction shown in Fig. P3.26. Derive an expression for the fluid velocity at (2) in terms of D_1, D_2, ρ, ρ_m, and h if the flow is assumed incompressible.

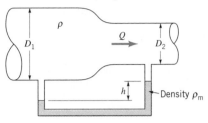

■ **FIGURE P3.26**

3.27   A plastic tube of 50-mm diameter is used to siphon water from the large tank shown in Fig. P3.27. If the pressure on the outside of the tube is more than 30 kPa greater than the pressure within the tube, the tube will collapse and the siphon will stop. If viscous effects are negligible, determine the minimum value of h allowed without the siphon stopping.

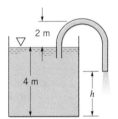

■ **FIGURE P3.27**

3.28   A smooth plastic, 10-m-long garden hose with an inside diameter of 15 mm is used to drain a wading pool as is shown in Fig. P3.28. If viscous effects are neglected, what is the flowrate from the pool?

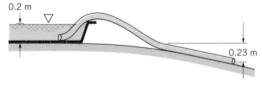

■ **FIGURE P3.28**

3.29   Carbon dioxide flows at a rate of 1.5 ft³/s from a 3-in. pipe in which the pressure and temperature are 20 psi (gage) and 120°F into a 1.5-in. pipe. If viscous effects are neglected and incompressible conditions are assumed, determine the pressure in the smaller pipe.

3.30   Determine the flowrate through the pipe in Fig. P3.30.

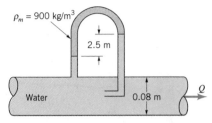

■ **FIGURE P3.30**

3.31   Water flows without viscous effects from the nozzle shown in Fig. P3.31. Determine the flowrate and the height, h, to which the water can flow.

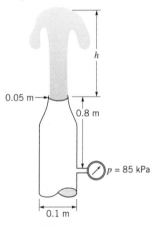

■ **FIGURE P3.31**

3.32   For the pipe enlargement shown in Fig. P3.32, the pressures at sections (1) and (2) are 56.3 and 58.2 psi, respectively. Determine the weight flowrate (lb/s) of the gasoline in the pipe.

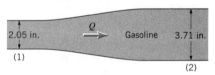

■ **FIGURE P3.32**

3.33   Water is pumped from a lake through an 8-in. pipe at a rate of 10 ft³/s. If viscous effects are negligible, what is the pressure in the suction pipe (the pipe between the lake and the pump) at an elevation 6 ft above the lake?

3.34   Air flows through a Venturi channel of rectangular cross section as shown in **Video V3.6** and Fig. P3.34. The constant width of the channel is 0.06 m and the height at the exit is 0.04 m. Compressibility and viscous effects are negligible. **(a)** Determine the flowrate when water is drawn up 0.10 m in a small tube attached to the static pressure tap at the throat where the channel height is 0.02 m. **(b)** Determine the channel height, h_2, at section (2) where, for the same flowrate as in part **(a)**, the water is drawn up 0.05 m. **(c)** Determine the pressure needed at section (1) to produce this flow.

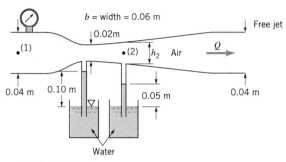

■ **FIGURE P3.34**

3.35 The center pivot irrigation system shown in Fig. P3.35 is to provide uniform watering of the entire circular field. Water flows through the common supply pipe and out through 10 evenly spaced nozzles. Water from each nozzle is to cover a strip 30 feet wide as indicated. If viscous effects are negligible, determine the diameter of each nozzle, d_i, $i = 1$ to 10, in terms of the diameter, d_{10}, of the nozzle at the outer end of the arm.

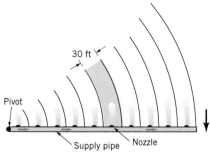

■ **FIGURE P3.35**

3.36 The vent on the tank shown in Fig. P3.36 is closed and the tank pressurized to increase the flowrate. What pressure, p_1, is needed to produce twice the flowrate of that when the vent is open?

3.37 Water flows steadily through the large tanks shown in Fig. P3.37. Determine the water depth, h_A.

3.38 Water flows from a large tank as shown in Fig. P3.38. Atmospheric pressure is 14.5 psia and the vapor pressure is 2.88 psia. If viscous effects are neglected, at what

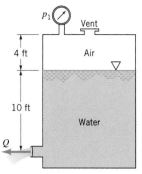

■ **FIGURE P3.36**

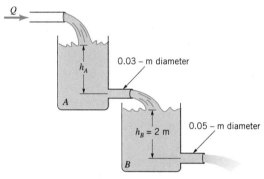

■ **FIGURE P3.37**

height, h, will cavitation begin? To avoid cavitation should the value of D_1 be increased or decreased? To avoid cavitation should the value of D_2 be increased or decreased? Explain.

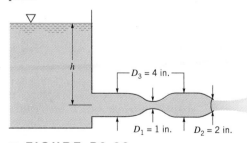

■ **FIGURE P3.38**

3.39 If viscous effects are neglected and the tank is large, determine the flowrate from the tank shown in Fig. P3.39.

3.40 Laboratories containing dangerous materials are often kept at a pressure slightly less than ambient pressure so that contaminants can be filtered through an exhaust

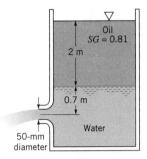

■ **FIGURE P3.39**

system rather than leaked through cracks around doors, etc. If the pressure in such a room is 0.1 in. of water below that of the surrounding rooms, with what velocity will air enter the room through an opening? Assume viscous effects are negligible.

3.41   Water is siphoned from the tank shown in Fig. P3.41. Determine the flowrate from the tank and the pressure at points (1), (2), and (3) if viscous effects are negligible.

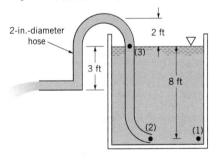

■ **FIGURE P3.41**

3.42   Redo Problem 3.41 if a 1-in.-diameter nozzle is placed at the end of the tube.

3.43   The specific gravity of the manometer fluid shown in Fig. P3.43 is 1.07. Determine the volume flowrate, Q, if the flow is inviscid and incompressible and the flowing fluid is (**a**) water, (**b**) gasoline, or (**c**) air at standard conditions.

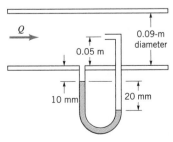

■ **FIGURE P3.43**

3.44   JP-4 fuel ($SG = 0.77$) flows through the Venturi meter shown in Fig. P3.44 with a velocity of 15 ft/s in the 6-in. pipe. If viscous effects are negligible, determine the elevation, h, of the fuel in the open tube connected to the throat of the Venturi meter.

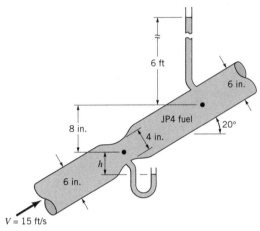

■ **FIGURE P3.44**

3.45   Air at standard conditions flows through the cylindrical drying stack shown in Fig. P3.45. If viscous effects are negligible and the inclined water-filled manometer reading is 20 mm as indicated, determine the flowrate.

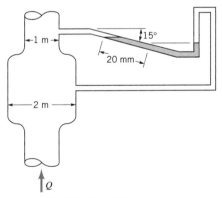

■ **FIGURE P3.45**

3.46   Determine the flowrate through the Venturi meter shown in Fig. P3.46 if ideal conditions exist.

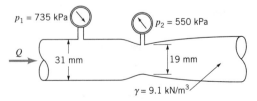

■ **FIGURE P3.46**

3.47 What diameter orifice hole, d, is needed if under ideal conditions the flowrate through the orifice meter of Fig. P3.47 is to be 30 gal/min of seawater with $p_1 - p_2 = 2.37$ lb/in.^{2}? The contraction coefficient is assumed to be 0.63.

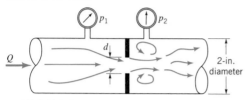

■ **FIGURE P3.47**

*3.48 A spherical tank of diameter D has a drain hole of diameter d at its bottom. A vent at the top of the tank maintains atmospheric pressure at the liquid surface within the tank. The flow is quasi-steady and inviscid and the tank is full of water initially. Determine the water depth as a function of time, $h = h(t)$, and plot graphs of $h(t)$ for tank diameters of 1, 5, 10, and 20 ft if $d = 1$ in.

3.49 Water flows through the branching pipe shown in Fig. P3.49. If viscous effects are negligible, determine the pressure at section (2) and the pressure at section (3).

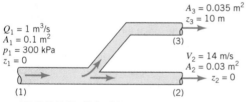

■ **FIGURE P3.49**

3.50 Water flows from a pipe shown in Fig. P3.50 as a free jet and strikes a circular flat plate. The flow geometry shown is axisymmetrical. Determine the flowrate and the manometer reading, H.

3.51 A conical plug is used to regulate the air flow from the pipe shown in Fig. P3.51. The air leaves the edge of the cone with a uniform thickness of 0.02 m. If viscous effects are negligible and the flowrate is 0.50 m^3/s, determine the pressure within the pipe.

*3.52 The surface area, A, of the pond shown in Fig. P3.52 varies with the water depth, h, as shown in the table. At time $t = 0$ a valve is opened and the pond is allowed to drain through a pipe of diameter D. If viscous effects are negligible and quasi-steady conditions are assumed, plot the water depth as a function of time from when the valve is opened ($t = 0$) until the pond is drained for pipe diameters of $D = 0.5$, 1.0, 1.5, 2.0, 2.5, and 3.0 ft. Assume $h = 18$ ft at $t = 0$.

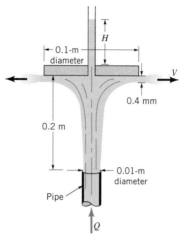

■ **FIGURE P3.50**

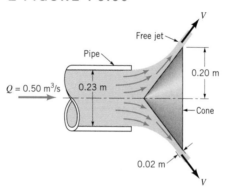

■ **FIGURE P3.51**

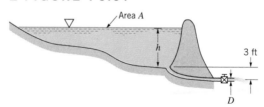

■ **FIGURE P3.52**

h (ft)	A [acres (1 acre = 43,560 ft^2)]
0	0
2	0.3
4	0.5
6	0.8
8	0.9
10	1.1
12	1.5
14	1.8
16	2.4
18	2.8

3.53   Water flows over the spillway shown in Fig. P3.53. If the velocity is uniform at sections (1) and (2) and viscous effects are negligible, determine the flowrate per unit width of the spillway.

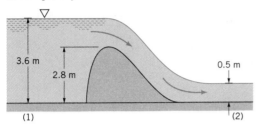

■ **FIGURE P3.53**

3.54   Water flows down the sloping ramp shown in Fig. P3.54 with negligible viscous effects. The flow is uniform at sections (1) and (2). For the conditions given, show that three solutions for the downstream depth, h_2, are obtained by use of the Bernoulli and continuity equations. However, show that only two of these solutions are realistic. Determine these values.

■ **FIGURE P3.54**

3.55   Water flows under the inclined sluice gate shown in Fig. P3.55. Determine the flowrate if the gate is 8 ft wide.

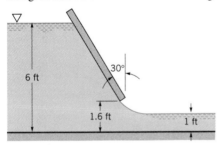

■ **FIGURE P3.55**

3.56   Water flows in a vertical pipe of 0.15-m diameter at a rate of 0.2 m^3/s and a pressure of 200 kPa at an elevation of 25 m. Determine the velocity head and pressure head at elevations of 20 and 55 m.

3.57   Draw the energy line and the hydraulic grade line for the flow of Problem 3.38.

3.58   Draw the energy line and hydraulic grade line for the flow shown in Problem 3.41.

3.59   Draw the energy line and hydraulic grade line for the flow shown in Problem 3.42.

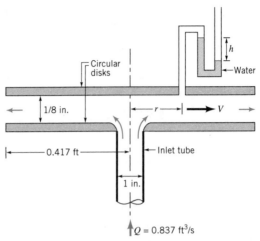

■ **FIGURE P3.60**

3.60   The device shown in Fig. P3.60 is used to investigate the flow in a radial diffuser—radial flow between two parallel circular disks. Air at a temperature of 83 °F and an absolute pressure of 29.09 in. of mercury flows at a rate of $Q = 0.837$ cfs through the inlet tube and radially out in the gap between the parallel disks as shown. The static pressure, p, as a function of radial location, r, is determined from the manometer reading, h. Since the velocity, V, decreases as r increases, it follows from the Bernoulli equation that the pressure increases in the radial direction. At the edge of the disks (the exit) the gage pressure is zero.

Experimental values of the manometer reading as a function of the radial distance are given in the table below. Use these results to plot a graph of the pressure head (feet of air) as a function of the radial location. On the same graph plot a theoretical curve obtained by using the Bernoulli equation and the given flowrate to calculate the pressure head.

Compare the experimental and theoretical results and discuss some possible reasons for any differences between them.

h (in.)	r (ft)
−2.79	0
−1.75	0.026
0.50	0.036
9.05	0.061
6.02	0.083
2.02	0.125
0.96	0.167
0.48	0.208
0.24	0.250
0.13	0.292
0.03	0.333
0.01	0.375
0.00	0.417

4

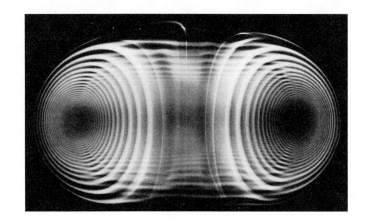

*F*luid Kinematics

*I*n this chapter we will discuss various aspects of fluid motion without being concerned with the actual forces necessary to produce the motion. That is, we will consider the *kinematics* of the motion—the velocity and acceleration of the fluid, and the description and visualization of its motion.

4.1 The Velocity Field

The infinitesimal particles of a fluid are tightly packed together (as is implied by the continuum assumption). Thus, at a given instant in time, a description of any fluid property (such as density, pressure, velocity, and acceleration) may be given as a function of the fluid's location. This representation of fluid parameters as functions of the spatial coordinates is termed a *field representation* of the flow. Of course, the specific field representation may be different at different times, so that to describe a fluid flow we must determine the various parameters not only as a function of the spatial coordinates (x, y, z, for example) but also as a function of time, t.

A vortex ring: The complex, three-dimensional structure of a smoke ring is indicated in this cross-sectional view. (Smoke in air.) (Photograph courtesy of R. H. Magarvey and C. S. MacLatchy, Ref. 3.)

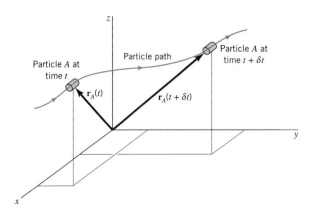

■ **FIGURE 4.1** **Particle location in terms of its position vector.**

V4.1 Velocity field

One of the most important fluid variables is the *velocity field,*

$$\mathbf{V} = u(x, y, z, t)\hat{\mathbf{i}} + v(x, y, z, t)\hat{\mathbf{j}} + w(x, y, z, t)\hat{\mathbf{k}}$$

where u, v, and w are the x, y, and z components of the velocity vector. By definition, the velocity of a particle is the time rate of change of the position vector for that particle. As is illustrated in Fig. 4.1, the position of particle A relative to the coordinate system is given by its *position vector,* $\mathbf{r}_A$, which (if the particle is moving) is a function of time. The time derivative of this position gives the *velocity* of the particle, $d\mathbf{r}_A/dt = \mathbf{V}_A$.

EXAMPLE 4.1

A velocity field is given by $\mathbf{V} = (V_0/\ell)(x\hat{\mathbf{i}} - y\hat{\mathbf{j}})$, where V_0 and ℓ are constants. At what location in the flow field is the speed equal to V_0? Make a sketch of the velocity field in the first quadrant ($x \geq 0$, $y \geq 0$) by drawing arrows representing the fluid velocity at representative locations.

SOLUTION

The x, y, and z components of the velocity are given by $u = V_0 x/\ell$, $v = -V_0 y/\ell$, and $w = 0$ so that the fluid speed, V, is

$$V = (u^2 + v^2 + w^2)^{1/2} = \frac{V_0}{\ell}(x^2 + y^2)^{1/2} \qquad (1)$$

The speed is $V = V_0$ at any location on the circle of radius ℓ centered at the origin $[(x^2 + y^2)^{1/2} = \ell]$ as shown in Fig. E4.1a. **(Ans)**

The direction of the fluid velocity relative to the x axis is given in terms of $\theta = \arctan(v/u)$ as shown in Fig. E4.1b. For this flow

$$\tan \theta = \frac{v}{u} = \frac{-V_0 y/\ell}{V_0 x/\ell} = \frac{-y}{x}$$

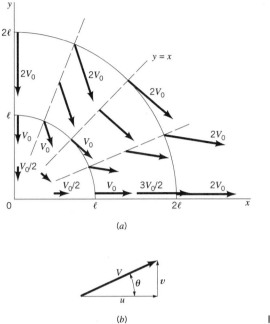

(a)

(b)

Thus, along the axis ($y = 0$) we see that $\tan \theta = 0$, so that $\theta = 0°$ or $\theta = 180°$. Similarly, along the y axis ($x = 0$) we obtain $\tan \theta = \pm\infty$ so that $\theta = 90°$ or $\theta = 270°$. Also, for $y = 0$ we find $\mathbf{V} = (V_0 x/\ell)\hat{\mathbf{i}}$, while for $x = 0$ we have $\mathbf{V} = (-V_0 y/\ell)\hat{\mathbf{j}}$, indicating (if $V_0 > 0$) that the flow is directed toward the origin along the y axis and away from the origin along the x axis as shown in Fig. E4.1a.

By determining $\mathbf{V}$ and θ for other locations in the x–y plane, the velocity field can be sketched as shown in the figure. For example, on the line $y = x$ the velocity is at a $-45°$ angle relative to the x axis ($\tan \theta = v/u = -y/x = -1$). At the origin $x = y = 0$ so that $\mathbf{V} = 0$. This point is a stagnation point. The farther from the origin the fluid is, the faster it is flowing (as seen from Eq. 1). By careful consideration of the velocity field it is possible to determine considerable information about the flow.

4.1.1   Eulerian and Lagrangian Flow Descriptions

There are two general approaches in analyzing fluid mechanics problems. The first method, called the *Eulerian method,* uses the field concept introduced above. In this case, the fluid motion is given by completely prescribing the necessary properties (pressure, density, velocity, etc.) as functions of space and time. From this method we obtain information about the flow in terms of what happens at fixed points in space as the fluid flows past those points.

The second method, called the *Lagrangian method,* involves following individual fluid particles as they move about and determining how the fluid properties associated with these particles change as a function of time. That is, the fluid particles are "tagged" or identified, and their properties determined as they move.

The difference between the two methods of analyzing fluid problems can be seen in the example of smoke discharging from a chimney, as is shown in Fig. 4.2. In the Eulerian method one may attach a temperature-measuring device to the top of the chimney (point 0) and record the temperature at that point as a function of time. That is, $T = T(x_0, y_0, z_0, t)$. The use of numerous temperature-measuring devices fixed at various locations would provide the temperature field, $T = T(x, y, z, t)$.

In the Lagrangian method, one would attach the temperature-measuring device to a particular fluid particle (particle A) and record that particle's temperature as it moves about. Thus, one would obtain that particle's temperature as a function of time, $T_A = T_A(t)$. The use of many such measuring devices moving with various fluid particles would provide the temperature of these fluid particles as a function of time. In fluid mechanics it is usually easier to use the Eulerian method to describe a flow.

Example 4.1 provides an Eulerian description of the flow. For a Lagrangian description we would need to determine the velocity as a function of time for each particle as it flows along from one point to another.

4.1.2 One-, Two-, and Three-Dimensional Flows

V4.2 Flow
past a wing

In almost any flow situation, the velocity field actually contains all three velocity components (u, v, and w, for example). In many situations the *three-dimensional flow* characteristics are important in terms of the physical effects they produce. A feel for the three-dimensional structure of such flows can be obtained by studying Fig. 4.3, which is a photograph of the flow past a model airfoil.

In many situations one of the velocity components may be small (in some sense) relative to the two other components. In situations of this kind it may be reasonable to neglect the smaller component and assume *two-dimensional flow*. That is, $\mathbf{V} = u\hat{\mathbf{i}} + v\hat{\mathbf{j}}$, where u and v are functions of x and y (and possibly time, t).

It is sometimes possible to further simplify a flow analysis by assuming that two of the velocity components are negligible, leaving the velocity field to be approximated as a *one-dimensional flow* field. That is, $\mathbf{V} = u\hat{\mathbf{i}}$. There are many flow fields for which the one-dimensional flow assumption provides a reasonable approximation. There are also many flow situations for which use of a one-dimensional flow field assumption will give completely erroneous results.

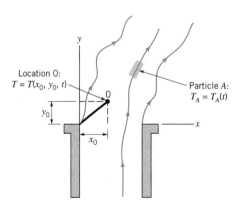

■ FIGURE 4.2 Eulerian and Lagrangian description of temperature of a flowing fluid.

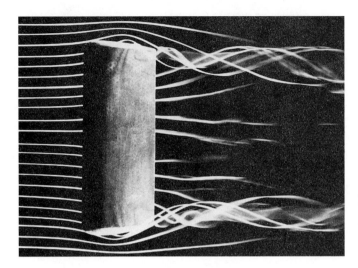

■ **FIGURE 4.3**
**Flow visualization of the
complex three-dimensional
flow past a model airfoil.
(Photograph by M. R.
Head)**

4.1.3   Steady and Unsteady Flows

V4.3 Flow
types

For *steady flow* the velocity at a given point in space does not vary with time, $\partial \mathbf{V}/\partial t = 0$. In reality, almost all flows are unsteady in some sense. That is, the velocity does vary with time. An example of a nonperiodic, unsteady flow is that produced by turning off a faucet to stop the flow of water. In other flows the unsteady effects may be periodic, occurring time after time in basically the same manner. The periodic injection of the air-gasoline mixture into the cylinder of an automobile engine is such an example.

V4.4 Jupiter
red spot

In many situations the unsteady character of a flow is quite random. That is, there is no repeatable sequence or regular variation to the unsteadiness. This behavior occurs in *turbulent flow* and is absent from *laminar flow.* The "smooth" flow of highly viscous syrup onto a pancake represents a "deterministic" laminar flow. It is quite different from the turbulent flow observed in the "irregular" splashing of water from a faucet onto the sink below it. The "irregular" gustiness of the wind represents another random turbulent flow.

4.1.4   Streamlines, Streaklines, and Pathlines

A *streamline* is a line that is everywhere tangent to the velocity field. If the flow is steady, nothing at a fixed point (including the velocity direction) changes with time, so the streamlines are fixed lines in space.

V4.5 Stream-
lines

For two-dimensional flows the slope of the streamline, dy/dx, must be equal to the tangent of the angle that the velocity vector makes with the x axis or

$$\frac{dy}{dx} = \frac{v}{u} \tag{4.1}$$

If the velocity field is known as a function of x and y (and t if the flow is unsteady), this equation can be integrated to give the equation of the streamlines.

EXAMPLE 4.2

Determine the streamlines for the two-dimensional steady flow discussed in Example 4.1, $\mathbf{V} = (V_0/\ell)(x\hat{\mathbf{i}} - y\hat{\mathbf{j}})$.

SOLUTION

Since $u = (V_0/\ell)x$ and $v = -(V_0/\ell)y$ it follows that streamlines are given by solution of the equation

$$\frac{dy}{dx} = \frac{v}{u} = \frac{-(V_0/\ell)y}{(V_0/\ell)x} = -\frac{y}{x}$$

in which variables can be separated and the equation integrated to give

$$\int \frac{dy}{y} = -\int \frac{dx}{x}$$

or

$$\ln y = -\ln x + \text{constant}$$

Thus, along the streamline

$$xy = C, \qquad \text{where } C \text{ is a constant} \qquad \text{(Ans)}$$

By using different values of the constant C, we can plot various lines in the x–y plane—the streamlines. The usual notation for a streamline is $\psi = $ constant on a streamline. Thus, the equation for the streamlines of this flow are

$$\psi = xy$$

As is discussed more fully in Chapter 6, the function $\psi = \psi(x, y)$ is called the *stream function*. The streamlines in the first quadrant are plotted in Fig. E4.2. A comparison of this figure with Fig. E4.1a illustrates the fact that streamlines are lines parallel to the velocity field.

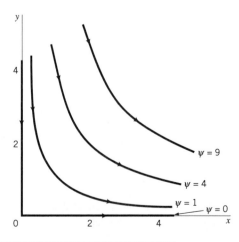

■ FIGURE E4.2

A *streakline* consists of all particles in a flow that have previously passed through a common point. Streaklines are more of a laboratory tool than an analytical tool. They can be obtained by taking instantaneous photographs of marked particles that all passed through a given location in the flow field at some earlier time. Such a line can be produced by continuously injecting marked fluid (neutrally buoyant smoke in air, or dye in water) at a given location (Ref. 1).

A *pathline* is the line traced out by a given particle as it flows from one point to another. The pathline is a Lagrangian concept that can be produced in the laboratory by marking a fluid particle (dying a small fluid element) and taking a time exposure photograph of its motion.

V4.6 Pathlines

Pathlines, streamlines, and streaklines are the same for steady flows. For unsteady flows none of these three types of lines need be the same (Ref. 2). Often one sees pictures of "streamlines" made visible by the injection of smoke or dye into a flow as is shown in Fig. 4.3. Actually, such pictures show streaklines rather than streamlines. However, for steady flows the two are identical; only the nomenclature is incorrectly used.

EXAMPLE 4.3

Water flowing from the oscillating slit shown in Fig. E4.3a produces a velocity field given by $\mathbf{V} = u_0 \sin[\omega(t - y/v_0)]\hat{\mathbf{i}} + v_0\hat{\mathbf{j}}$, where u_0, v_0, and ω are constants. Thus, the y component of velocity remains constant ($v = v_0$) and the x component of velocity at $y = 0$ coincides with the velocity of the oscillating sprinkler head [$u = u_0 \sin(\omega t)$ at $y = 0$].

(a) Determine the streamline that passes through the origin at $t = 0$; at $t = \pi/2\omega$. (b) Determine the pathline of the particle that was at the origin at $t = 0$; at $t = \pi/2\omega$. (c) Discuss the shape of the streakline that passes through the origin.

SOLUTION

(a) Since $u = u_0 \sin[\omega(t - y/v_0)]$ and $v = v_0$ it follows from Eq. 4.1 that streamlines are given by the solution of

$$\frac{dy}{dx} = \frac{v}{u} = \frac{v_0}{u_0 \sin[\omega(t - y/v_0)]}$$

in which the variables can be separated and the equation integrated (for any given time t) to give

$$u_0 \int \sin\left[\omega\left(t - \frac{y}{v_0}\right)\right] dy = v_0 \int dx,$$

or

$$u_0(v_0/\omega) \cos\left[\omega\left(t - \frac{y}{v_0}\right)\right] = v_0 x + C \tag{1}$$

where C is a constant. For the streamline at $t = 0$ that passes through the origin ($x = y = 0$), the value of C is obtained from Eq. 1 as $C = u_0 v_0/\omega$. Hence, the equation for this streamline is

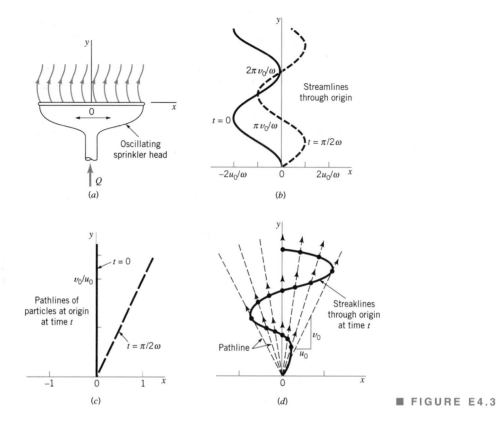

■ **FIGURE E4.3**

$$x = \frac{u_0}{\omega} \left[\cos\left(\frac{\omega y}{v_0}\right) - 1 \right]$$ (2) (Ans)

Similarly, for the streamline at $t = \pi/2\omega$ that passes through the origin, Eq. 1 gives $C = 0$. Thus, the equation for this streamline is

$$x = \frac{u_0}{\omega} \cos\left[\omega\left(\frac{\pi}{2\omega} - \frac{y}{v_0}\right)\right] = \frac{u_0}{\omega} \cos\left(\frac{\pi}{2} - \frac{\omega y}{v_0}\right)$$

or

$$x = \frac{u_0}{\omega} \sin\left(\frac{\omega y}{v_0}\right)$$ (3) (Ans)

These two streamlines, plotted in Figure E4.3b, are not the same because the flow is unsteady. For example, at the origin $(x = y = 0)$ the velocity is $\mathbf{V} = v_0\hat{\mathbf{j}}$ at $t = 0$ and $\mathbf{V} = u_0\hat{\mathbf{i}} + v_0\hat{\mathbf{j}}$ at $t = \pi/2\omega$. Thus, the angle of the streamline passing through the origin changes with time. Similarly, the shape of the entire streamline is a function of time.

(b) The pathline of a particle (the location of the particle as a function of time) can be obtained from the velocity field and the definition of the velocity. Since $u = dx/dt$ and $v = dy/dt$ we obtain

$$\frac{dx}{dt} = u_0 \sin \left[\omega \left(t - \frac{y}{v_0} \right) \right] \quad \text{and} \quad \frac{dy}{dt} = v_0$$

The y equation can be integrated (since v_0 = constant) to give the y coordinate of the pathline as

$$y = v_0 t + C_1 \tag{4}$$

where C_1 is a constant. With this known $y = y(t)$ dependence, the x equation for the pathline becomes

$$\frac{dx}{dt} = u_0 \sin \left[\omega \left(t - \frac{v_0 t + C_1}{v_0} \right) \right] = -u_0 \sin \left(\frac{C_1 \omega}{v_0} \right)$$

This can be integrated to give the x component of the pathline as

$$x = - \left[u_0 \sin \left(\frac{C_1 \omega}{v_0} \right) \right] t + C_2 \tag{5}$$

where C_2 is a constant. For the particle that was at the origin ($x = y = 0$) at time $t = 0$, Eqs. 4 and 5 give $C_1 = C_2 = 0$. Thus, the pathline is

$$x = 0 \quad \text{and} \quad y = v_0 t \tag{6} \quad \text{(Ans)}$$

Similarly, for the particle that was at the origin at $t = \pi/2\omega$, Eqs. 4 and 5 give $C_1 = -\pi v_0/2\omega$ and $C_2 = -\pi u_0/2\omega$. Thus, the pathline for this particle is

$$x = u_0 \left(t - \frac{\pi}{2\omega} \right) \quad \text{and} \quad y = v_0 \left(t - \frac{\pi}{2\omega} \right) \tag{7}$$

The pathline can be drawn by plotting the locus of x(t), y(t) values for $t \geq 0$ or by eliminating the parameter t from Eq. 7 to give

$$y = \frac{v_0}{u_0} x \tag{8} \quad \text{(Ans)}$$

The pathlines given by Eqs. 6 and 8, shown in Fig. E4.3c, are straight lines from the origin (rays). The pathlines and streamlines do not coincide because the flow is unsteady.

(c) The streakline through the origin at time $t = 0$ is the locus of particles at $t = 0$ that previously ($t < 0$) passed through the origin. The general shape of the streaklines can be seen as follows. Each particle that flows through the origin travels in a straight line (pathlines are rays from the origin), the slope of which lies between $\pm v_0/u_0$ as shown in Fig. E4.3d. Particles passing through the origin at different times are located on different rays from the origin and at different distances from the origin. The net result is that a stream of dye continually injected at the origin (a streakline) would have the shape shown in Fig. E4.3d. Because of the unsteadiness, the streakline will vary with time, although it will always have the oscillating, sinuous character shown. Similar streaklines are given by the stream of water from a garden hose nozzle that oscillates back and forth in a direction normal to the axis of the nozzle.

In this example neither the streamlines, pathlines, nor streaklines coincide. If the flow were steady, all of these lines would be the same.

4.2 The Acceleration Field

To apply Newton's second law ($\mathbf{F} = m\mathbf{a}$) we must be able to describe the particle acceleration in an appropriate fashion. For the infrequently used Lagrangian method, we describe the fluid acceleration just as is done in solid body dynamics—$\mathbf{a} = \mathbf{a}(t)$ for each particle. For the Eulerian description we describe the *acceleration field* as a function of position and time without actually following any particular particle. This is analogous to describing the flow in terms of the velocity field, $\mathbf{V} = \mathbf{V}(x, y, z, t)$, rather than the velocity for particular particles.

4.2.1 The Material Derivative

Consider a fluid particle moving along its pathline as is shown in Fig. 4.4. In general, the particle's velocity, denoted $\mathbf{V}_A$ for particle A, is a function of its location and the time.

$$\mathbf{V}_A = \mathbf{V}_A(\mathbf{r}_A, t) = \mathbf{V}_A[x_A(t), y_A(t), z_A(t), t]$$

where $x_A = x_A(t)$, $y_A = y_A(t)$, and $z_A = z_A(t)$ define the location of the moving particle. By definition, the acceleration of a particle is the time rate of change of its velocity. Thus, we use the chain rule of differentiation to obtain the acceleration of particle A, $\mathbf{a}_A$, as

$$\mathbf{a}_A(t) = \frac{d\mathbf{V}_A}{dt} = \frac{\partial \mathbf{V}_A}{\partial t} + \frac{\partial \mathbf{V}_A}{\partial x}\frac{dx_A}{dt} + \frac{\partial \mathbf{V}_A}{\partial y}\frac{dy_A}{dt} + \frac{\partial \mathbf{V}_A}{\partial z}\frac{dz_A}{dt} \quad \textbf{(4.2)}$$

Using the fact that the particle velocity components are given by $u_A = dx_A/dt$, $v_A = dy_A/dt$, and $w_A = dz_A/dt$, Eq. 4.2 becomes

$$\mathbf{a}_A = \frac{\partial \mathbf{V}_A}{\partial t} + u_A \frac{\partial \mathbf{V}_A}{\partial x} + v_A \frac{\partial \mathbf{V}_A}{\partial y} + w_A \frac{\partial \mathbf{V}_A}{\partial z}$$

Since the above is valid for any particle, we can drop the reference to particle A and obtain the acceleration field from the velocity field as

$$\mathbf{a} = \frac{\partial \mathbf{V}}{\partial t} + u \frac{\partial \mathbf{V}}{\partial x} + v \frac{\partial \mathbf{V}}{\partial y} + w \frac{\partial \mathbf{V}}{\partial z} \quad \textbf{(4.3)}$$

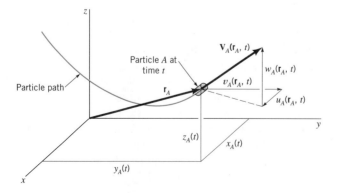

■ **FIGURE 4.4** Velocity and position of particle A at time t.

This is a vector result whose scalar components can be written as

$$a_x = \frac{\partial u}{\partial t} + u\frac{\partial u}{\partial x} + v\frac{\partial u}{\partial y} + w\frac{\partial u}{\partial z}$$

$$a_y = \frac{\partial v}{\partial t} + u\frac{\partial v}{\partial x} + v\frac{\partial v}{\partial y} + w\frac{\partial v}{\partial z} \tag{4.4}$$

and

$$a_z = \frac{\partial w}{\partial t} + u\frac{\partial w}{\partial x} + v\frac{\partial w}{\partial y} + w\frac{\partial w}{\partial z}$$

The above result is often written in shorthand notation as

$$\mathbf{a} = \frac{D\mathbf{V}}{Dt}$$

where the operator

$$\frac{D(\ )}{Dt} \equiv \frac{\partial(\ )}{\partial t} + u\frac{\partial(\ )}{\partial x} + v\frac{\partial(\ )}{\partial y} + w\frac{\partial(\ )}{\partial z} \tag{4.5}$$

is termed the *material derivative* or *substantial derivative*. An often-used shorthand notation for the material derivative operator is

$$\frac{D(\ )}{Dt} = \frac{\partial(\ )}{\partial t} + (\mathbf{V} \cdot \nabla)(\ ) \tag{4.6}$$

The dot product of the velocity vector, $\mathbf{V}$, and the gradient operator, $\nabla(\ ) = \partial(\ )/\partial x\,\hat{\mathbf{i}} + \partial(\ )/\partial y\,\hat{\mathbf{j}} + \partial(\ )/\partial z\,\hat{\mathbf{k}}$ (a vector operator) provides a convenient notation for the spatial derivative terms appearing in the Cartesian coordinate representation of the material derivative. Note that the notation $\mathbf{V} \cdot \nabla$ represents the operator $\mathbf{V} \cdot \nabla(\ ) = u\partial(\ )/\partial x + v\partial(\ )/\partial y + w\partial(\ )/\partial z$.

EXAMPLE 4.4

An incompressible, inviscid fluid flows steadily past a sphere of radius a as shown in Fig. E4.4a. According to a more advanced analysis of the flow, the fluid velocity along streamline $A-B$ is given by

$$\mathbf{V} = u(x)\hat{\mathbf{i}} = V_0\left(1 + \frac{a^3}{x^3}\right)\hat{\mathbf{i}}$$

where V_0 is the upstream velocity far ahead of the sphere. Determine the acceleration experienced by fluid particles as they flow along this streamline.

SOLUTION

Along streamline $A-B$ there is only one component of velocity ($v = w = 0$) so that from Eq. 4.3

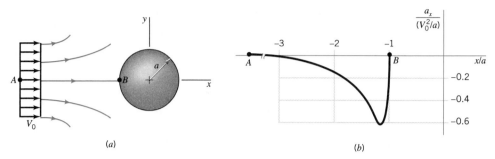

■ **FIGURE E4.4**

$$\mathbf{a} = \frac{\partial \mathbf{V}}{\partial t} + u \frac{\partial \mathbf{V}}{\partial x} = \left(\frac{\partial u}{\partial t} + u \frac{\partial u}{\partial x} \right) \hat{\mathbf{i}}$$

or

$$a_x = \frac{\partial u}{\partial t} + u \frac{\partial u}{\partial x}, \qquad a_y = 0, \qquad a_z = 0$$

Since the flow is steady, the velocity at a given point in space does not change with time. Thus, $\partial u / \partial t = 0$. With the given velocity distribution along the streamline, the acceleration becomes

$$a_x = u \frac{\partial u}{\partial x} = V_0 \left(1 + \frac{a^3}{x^3} \right) V_0 [a^3 (-3 x^{-4})]$$

or

$$a_x = -3 (V_0^2 / a) \frac{1 + (a/x)^3}{(x/a)^4} \qquad \text{(Ans)}$$

Along streamline A–B ($-\infty \leq x \leq -a$ and $y = 0$) the acceleration has only an x component and it is negative (a deceleration). Thus, the fluid slows down from its upstream velocity of $\mathbf{V} = V_0 \hat{\mathbf{i}}$ at $x = -\infty$ to its stagnation point velocity of $\mathbf{V} = 0$ at $x = -a$, the "nose" of the sphere. The variation of a_x along streamline A–B is shown in Fig. E4.4b. It is the same result as is obtained in Example 3.1 by using the streamwise component of the acceleration, $a_x = V \partial V / \partial s$. The maximum deceleration occurs at $x = -1.205a$ and has a value of $a_x = -0.610 V_0^2 / a$.

In general, for fluid particles on streamlines other than A–B, all three components of the acceleration (a_x, a_y, and a_z) will be nonzero.

4.2.2 Unsteady Effects

As is seen from Eq. 4.5, the material derivative formula contains two types of terms—those involving the time derivative $[\partial (\ ) / \partial t]$ and those involving spatial derivatives $[\partial (\ ) / \partial x, \partial (\ ) / \partial y,$ and $\partial (\ ) / \partial z]$. The time derivative portions are denoted as the *local derivative*. They represent effects of the unsteadiness of the flow. If the parameter involved is the acceleration, that portion given by $\partial \mathbf{V} / \partial t$ is termed the *local acceleration*. For steady flow the time derivative is zero throughout the flow field $[\partial (\ ) / \partial t \equiv 0]$, and the local effect vanishes. Physically, there is no change in flow parameters at a fixed point in space if the flow is steady.

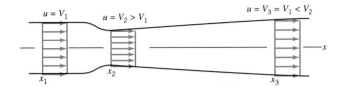

■ **FIGURE 4.5** Uniform, steady flow in a variable area pipe.

4.2.3   Convective Effects

The portion of the material derivative (Eq. 4.5) represented by the spatial derivatives is termed the *convective derivative.* It represents the fact that a flow property associated with a fluid particle may vary because of the motion of the particle from one point in space where the parameter has one value to another point in space where its value is different. This contribution is due to the convection, or motion, of the particle through space in which there is a gradient $[\nabla(\ ) = \partial(\ )/\partial x\,\hat{\mathbf{i}} + \partial(\ )/\partial y\,\hat{\mathbf{j}} + \partial(\ )/\partial z\,\hat{\mathbf{k}}]$ in the parameter value. That portion of the acceleration given by the term $(\mathbf{V}\cdot\nabla)\mathbf{V}$ is termed the *convective acceleration.*

Consider flow in a variable area pipe as shown in Fig. 4.5. It is assumed that the flow is steady and one-dimensional with velocity that increases and decreases in the flow direction as indicated. As the fluid flows from section (1) to section (2), its velocity increases from V_1 to V_2. Thus, even though $\partial\mathbf{V}/\partial t = 0$, fluid particles experience an acceleration given by $a_x = u\,\partial u/\partial x$. For $x_1 < x < x_2$, it is seen that $\partial u/\partial x > 0$ so that $a_x > 0$—the fluid accelerates. For $x_2 < x < x_3$, it is seen that $\partial u/\partial x < 0$ so that $a_x < 0$—the fluid decelerates.

*E*XAMPLE 4.5

Consider the steady, two-dimensional flow field discussed in Example 4.2. Determine the acceleration field for this flow.

*S*OLUTION

In general, the acceleration is given by

$$\mathbf{a} = \frac{D\mathbf{V}}{Dt} = \frac{\partial\mathbf{V}}{\partial t} + (\mathbf{V}\cdot\nabla)(\mathbf{V}) = \frac{\partial\mathbf{V}}{\partial t} + u\frac{\partial\mathbf{V}}{\partial x} + v\frac{\partial\mathbf{V}}{\partial y} + w\frac{\partial\mathbf{V}}{\partial z} \tag{1}$$

where the velocity is given by $\mathbf{V} = (V_0/\ell)(x\hat{\mathbf{i}} - y\hat{\mathbf{j}})$ so that $u = (V_0/\ell)x$ and $v = -(V_0/\ell)y$. For steady $[\partial(\ )/\partial t = 0]$, two-dimensional $[w = 0$ and $\partial(\ )/\partial z = 0]$ flow, Eq. 1 becomes

$$\mathbf{a} = u\frac{\partial\mathbf{V}}{\partial x} + v\frac{\partial\mathbf{V}}{\partial y} = \left(u\frac{\partial u}{\partial x} + v\frac{\partial u}{\partial y}\right)\hat{\mathbf{i}} + \left(u\frac{\partial v}{\partial x} + v\frac{\partial v}{\partial y}\right)\hat{\mathbf{j}}$$

Hence, for this flow the acceleration is given by

$$\mathbf{a} = \left[\left(\frac{V_0}{\ell}\right)(x)\left(\frac{V_0}{\ell}\right) + \left(\frac{V_0}{\ell}\right)(y)(0)\right]\hat{\mathbf{i}} + \left[\left(\frac{V_0}{\ell}\right)(x)(0) + \left(\frac{-V_0}{\ell}\right)(y)\left(\frac{-V_0}{\ell}\right)\right]\hat{\mathbf{j}}$$

or

$$a_x = \frac{V_0^2 x}{\ell^2}, \qquad a_y = \frac{V_0^2 y}{\ell^2} \qquad \text{(Ans)}$$

The fluid experiences an acceleration in both the x and y directions. Since the flow is steady, there is no local acceleration—the fluid velocity at any given point is constant in time. However, there is a convective acceleration due to the change in velocity from one point on the particle's pathline to another. Recall that the velocity is a vector—it has both a magnitude and a direction. In this flow both the fluid speed (magnitude) and flow direction change with location (see Fig. E4.1a).

For this flow the magnitude of the acceleration is constant on circles centered at the origin, as is seen from the fact that

$$|\mathbf{a}| = (a_x^2 + a_y^2 + a_z^2)^{1/2} = \left(\frac{V_0}{\ell}\right)^2 (x^2 + y^2)^{1/2} \qquad (2)$$

Also, the acceleration vector is oriented at an angle θ from the x axis, where

$$\tan \theta = \frac{a_y}{a_x} = \frac{y}{x}$$

This is the same angle as that formed by a ray from the origin to point (x, y). Thus, the acceleration is directed along rays from the origin and has a magnitude proportional to the distance from the origin. Typical acceleration vectors (from Eq. 2) and velocity vectors (from Example 4.1) are shown in Fig. E4.5 for the flow in the first quadrant. Note that $\mathbf{a}$ and $\mathbf{V}$ are not parallel except along the x and y axes (a fact that is responsible for the curved pathlines of the flow), and that both the acceleration and velocity are zero at the origin ($x = y = 0$). An infinitesimal fluid particle placed precisely at the origin will remain there, but its neighbors (no matter how close they are to the origin) will drift away.

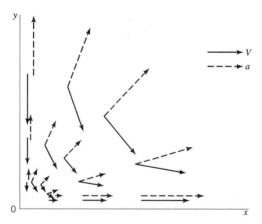

■ FIGURE E4.5

4.2.4 Streamline Coordinates

In many flow situations it is convenient to use a coordinate system defined in terms of the streamlines of the flow. An example for steady, two-dimensional flows is illustrated in Fig. 4.6. Such flows can be described in terms of the streamline coordinates involving one coordinate

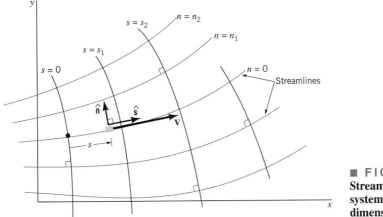

■ **FIGURE 4.6**
**Streamline coordinate
system for two-
dimensional flow.**

along the streamlines, denoted s, and the second coordinate normal to the streamlines, denoted n. Unit vectors in these two directions are denoted by $\hat{s}$ and $\hat{n}$ as shown in the figure.

One of the major advantages of using the streamline coordinate system is that the velocity is always tangent to the s direction. That is,

$$\mathbf{V} = V\hat{s}$$

For steady, two-dimensional flow we can determine the acceleration as (see Eq. 3.1)

$$\mathbf{a} = V\frac{\partial V}{\partial s}\hat{s} + \frac{V^2}{\mathcal{R}}\hat{n} \quad \text{or} \quad a_s = V\frac{\partial V}{\partial s}, \quad a_n = \frac{V^2}{\mathcal{R}} \tag{4.7}$$

The first term, $a_s = V\,\partial V/\partial s$, represents the convective acceleration along the streamline and the second term, $a_n = V^2/\mathcal{R}$, represents centrifugal acceleration (one type of convective acceleration) normal to the fluid motion. These forms of the acceleration are probably familiar from previous dynamics or physics considerations.

4.3   Control Volume and System Representations

A fluid's behavior is governed by a set of fundamental physical laws which are approximated by an appropriate set of equations. The application of laws such as the conservation of mass, Newton's laws of motion, and the laws of thermodynamics form the foundation of fluid mechanics analyses. There are various ways that these governing laws can be applied to a fluid, including the system approach and the control volume approach. By definition, a *system* is a collection of matter of fixed identity (always the same atoms or fluid particles), which may move, flow, and interact with its surroundings. A *control volume,* on the other hand, is a volume in space (a geometric entity, independent of mass) through which fluid may flow.

We may often be more interested in determining the forces put on a fan, airplane, or automobile by air flowing past the object than we are in the information obtained by following a given portion of the air (a system) as it flows along. For these situations we often use the control volume approach. We identify a specific volume in space (a volume associated with the fan, airplane, or automobile, for example) and analyze the fluid flow within, through, or around that volume.

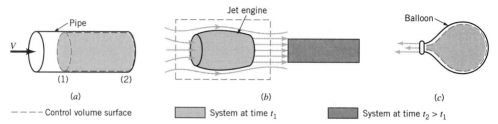

■ **FIGURE 4.7** **Typical control volumes: (a) fixed control volume, (b) fixed or moving control volume, (c) deforming control volume.**

Examples of control volumes and *control surfaces* (the surface of the control volume) are shown in Fig. 4.7. For case (*a*), fluid flows through a pipe. The fixed control surface consists of the inside surface of the pipe, the outlet end at section (2), and a section across the pipe at (1). Fluid flows across part of the control surface, but not across all of it.

Another control volume is the rectangular volume surrounding the jet engine shown in Fig. 4.7*b*. The air that was within the engine itself at time $t = t_1$ (a system) has passed through the engine and is outside of the control volume at a later time $t = t_2$ as indicated. At this later time other air (a different system) is within the engine.

The deflating balloon shown in Fig. 4.7*c* provides an example of a deforming control volume. As time increases, the control volume (whose surface is the inner surface of the balloon) decreases in size.

All of the laws governing the motion of a fluid are stated in their basic form in terms of a system approach. For example, "the mass of a system remains constant," or "the time rate of change of momentum of a system is equal to the sum of all the forces acting on the system." Note the word system, not control volume, in these statements. To use the governing equations in a control volume approach to problem solving, we must rephrase the laws in an appropriate manner. To this end we introduce the Reynolds transport theorem.

4.4   The Reynolds Transport Theorem

We need to describe the laws governing fluid motion using both system concepts (consider a given mass of the fluid) and control volume concepts (consider a given volume). To do this we need an analytical tool to shift from one representation to the other. The *Reynolds transport theorem* provides this tool.

All physical laws are stated in terms of various physical parameters such as velocity, acceleration, mass, temperature, and momentum. Let B represent any of these (or other) fluid parameters and b represent the amount of that parameter per unit mass. That is,

$$B = mb$$

where m is the mass of the portion of fluid of interest. If $B = mV^2/2$, the kinetic energy of the mass, then $b = V^2/2$, the kinetic energy per unit mass. The parameters B and b may be scalars or vectors. Thus, if $\mathbf{B} = m\mathbf{V}$, the momentum of the mass, then $\mathbf{b} = \mathbf{V}$. (The momentum per unit mass is the velocity.) The parameter B is termed an *extensive property* and the parameter b is termed an *intensive property*.

The amount of an extensive property that a system possesses at a given instant, B_{sys}, can be determined by adding up the amount associated with each fluid particle in the system. For infinitesimal fluid particles of size δV and mass $\rho \, \delta V$, this summation (in the limit of $\delta V \to 0$) takes the form of an integration over all the particles in the system and can be written as

$$B_{sys} = \lim_{\delta V \to 0} \sum_i b_i (\rho_i \, \delta V_i) = \int_{sys} \rho b \, dV$$

The limits of integration cover the entire system—a (usually) moving volume.

4.4.1   Derivation of the Reynolds Transport Theorem

A simple version of the Reynolds transport theorem relating system concepts to control volume concepts can be obtained easily for the one-dimensional flow through a fixed control volume as is shown in Fig. 4.8a. We consider the control volume to be that stationary volume within the pipe or duct between sections (1) and (2) as indicated. The system that we consider is that fluid occupying the control volume at some initial time t. A short time later, at time $t + \delta t$, the system has moved slightly to the right. The fluid particles that coincided with section (2) of the control surface at time t have moved a distance $\delta \ell_2 = V_2 \, \delta t$ to the right, where V_2 is the velocity of the fluid as it passes section (2). Similarly, the fluid initially at section (1) has moved a distance $\delta \ell_1 = V_1 \delta t$, where V_1 is the fluid velocity at section (1). We assume the fluid flows across sections (1) and (2) in a direction normal to these surfaces and that V_1 and V_2 are constant across sections (1) and (2).

As is shown in Fig. 4.8b, the outflow from the control volume from time t to $t + \delta t$ is denoted as volume II, the inflow as volume I, and the control volume itself as CV. Thus, the system at time t consists of the fluid in section CV ("SYS = CV" at time t), while at time $t + \delta t$ the system consists of the same fluid that now occupies sections (CV − I) + II. That is, "SYS = CV − I + II" at time $t + \delta t$. The control volume remains as section CV for all time.

If B is an extensive parameter of the system, then the value of it for the system at time t is the same as that for the control volume B_{cv},

$$B_{sys}(t) = B_{cv}(t)$$

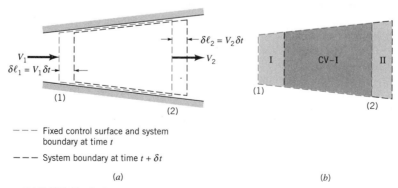

— — — Fixed control surface and system
boundary at time t

— — — System boundary at time $t + \delta t$

(a)   (b)

■ **FIGURE 4.8**   **Control volume and system for flow through a variable area pipe.**

since the system and the fluid within the control volume coincide at this time. Its value at time $t + \delta t$ is

$$B_{\text{sys}}(t + \delta t) = B_{\text{cv}}(t + \delta t) - B_{\text{I}}(t + \delta t) + B_{\text{II}}(t + \delta t)$$

Thus, the change in the amount of B in the system in the time interval δt divided by this time interval is given by

$$\frac{\delta B_{\text{sys}}}{\delta t} = \frac{B_{\text{sys}}(t + \delta t) - B_{\text{sys}}(t)}{\delta t} = \frac{B_{\text{cv}}(t + \delta t) - B_{\text{I}}(t + \delta t) + B_{\text{II}}(t + \delta t) - B_{\text{sys}}(t)}{\delta t}$$

By using the fact that at the initial time t we have $B_{\text{sys}}(t) = B_{\text{cv}}(t)$, this ungainly expression may be rearranged as follows.

$$\frac{\delta B_{\text{sys}}}{\delta t} = \frac{B_{\text{cv}}(t + \delta t) - B_{\text{cv}}(t)}{\delta t} - \frac{B_{\text{I}}(t + \delta t)}{\delta t} + \frac{B_{\text{II}}(t + \delta t)}{\delta t} \tag{4.8}$$

In the limit $\delta t \to 0$, the left-hand side of Eq. 4.8 is equal to the time rate of change of B for the system and is denoted as DB_{sys}/Dt.

In the limit $\delta t \to 0$, the first term on the right-hand side of Eq. 4.8 is seen to be the time rate of change of the amount of B within the control volume

$$\lim_{\delta t \to 0} \frac{B_{\text{cv}}(t + \delta t) - B_{\text{cv}}(t)}{\delta t} = \frac{\partial B_{\text{cv}}}{\partial t} = \frac{\partial \left(\int_{\text{cv}} \rho b \, d\mkern-1mu V \right)}{\delta t} \tag{4.9}$$

The third term on the right-hand side of Eq. 4.8 represents the rate at which the extensive parameter B flows from the control volume, across the control surface. This can be seen from the fact that the amount of B within region II, the outflow region, is its amount per unit volume, ρb, times the volume $\delta V_{\text{II}} = A_2 \, \delta \ell_2 = A_2(V_2 \, \delta t)$. Hence,

$$B_{\text{II}}(t + \delta t) = (\rho_2 b_2)(\delta V_{\text{II}}) = \rho_2 b_2 A_2 V_2 \, \delta t$$

where b_2 and ρ_2 are the constant values of b and ρ across section (2). Thus, the rate at which this property flows from the control volume, $\dot{B}_{\text{out}}$, is given by

$$\dot{B}_{\text{out}} = \lim_{\delta t \to 0} \frac{B_{\text{II}}(t + \delta t)}{\delta t} = \rho_2 A_2 V_2 b_2 \tag{4.10}$$

Similarly, the inflow of B into the control volume across section (1) during the time interval δt corresponds to that in region I and is given by the amount per unit volume times the volume, $\delta V_{\text{I}} = A_1 \, \delta \ell_1 = A_1(V_1 \, \delta t)$. Hence,

$$B_{\text{I}}(t + \delta t) = (\rho_1 b_1)(\delta V_{\text{I}}) = \rho_1 b_1 A_1 V_1 \, \delta t$$

where b_1 and ρ_1 are the constant values of b and ρ across section (1). Thus, the rate of inflow of property B into the control volume, $\dot{B}_{\text{in}}$, is given by

$$\dot{B}_{\text{in}} = \lim_{\delta t \to 0} \frac{B_{\text{I}}(t + \delta t)}{\delta t} = \rho_1 A_1 V_1 b_1 \tag{4.11}$$

If we combine Eqs. 4.8, 4.9, 4.10, and 4.11 we see that the relationship between the time rate of change of B for the system and that for the control volume is given by

$$\frac{DB_{sys}}{Dt} = \frac{\partial B_{cv}}{\partial t} + \dot{B}_{out} - \dot{B}_{in} \tag{4.12}$$

or

$$\frac{DB_{sys}}{Dt} = \frac{\partial B_{cv}}{\delta t} + \rho_2 A_2 V_2 b_2 - \rho_1 A_1 V_1 b_1 \tag{4.13}$$

This is a version of the Reynolds transport theorem valid under the restrictive assumptions associated with the flow shown in Fig. 4.8—fixed control volume with one inlet and one outlet having uniform properties (density, velocity, and the parameter b) across the inlet and outlet with the velocity normal to sections (1) and (2). Note that the time rate of change of B for the system (the left-hand side of Eq. 4.13) is not necessarily the same as the rate of change of B within the control volume (the first term on the right-hand side of Eq. 4.13). This is true because the inflow rate $(b_1 \rho_1 V_1 A_1)$ and the outflow rate $(b_2 \rho_2 V_2 A_2)$ of the property B for the control volume need not be the same.

EXAMPLE 4.6

Consider the flow from the fire extinguisher shown in Fig. E4.6. Let the extensive property of interest be the system mass ($B = m$, the system mass, or $b = 1$), and write the appropriate form of the Reynolds transport theorem for this flow.

SOLUTION

We take the control volume to be the fire extinguisher, and the system to be the fluid within it at time $t = 0$. For this case there is no inlet, section (1), across which the fluid flows into the control volume ($A_1 = 0$). There is, however, an outlet, section (2). Thus, the Reynolds transport theorem, Eq. 4.13, along with Eq. 4.9 with $b = 1$ can be written as

$$\frac{Dm_{sys}}{Dt} = \frac{\partial \left(\int_{cv} \rho \, d\forall \right)}{\partial t} + \rho_2 A_2 V_2 \tag{1} \quad \text{(Ans)}$$

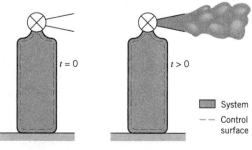

System
—— Control surface

(a)   (b)   ■ **FIGURE E4.6**

If we proceed one step further and use the basic law of conservation of mass, we may set the left-hand side of this equation equal to zero (the amount of mass in a system is constant) and rewrite Eq. 1 in the form:

$$\frac{\partial\left(\displaystyle\int_{cv} \rho \, d\forall\right)}{\partial t} = -\rho_2 A_2 V_2 \tag{2}$$

The physical interpretation of this result is that the rate at which the mass in the tank decreases in time is equal in magnitude but opposite to the rate of flow of mass from the exit, $\rho_2 A_2 V_2$. Note the units for the two terms of Eq. 2 (kg/s or slugs/s). Note that if there were both an inlet and an outlet to the control volume shown in Fig. E4.6, Eq. 2 would become

$$\frac{\partial\left(\displaystyle\int_{cv} \rho \, d\forall\right)}{\partial t} = \rho_1 A_1 V_1 - \rho_2 A_2 V_2 \tag{3}$$

In addition, if the flow were steady, the left-hand side of Eq. 3 would be zero (the amount of mass in the control would be constant in time) and Eq. 3 would become

$$\rho_1 A_1 V_1 = \rho_2 A_2 V_2$$

This is one form of the conservation of mass principle—the mass flowrates into and out of the control volume are equal. Other more general forms are discussed in Chapter 5.

Equation 4.13 is a simplified version of the Reynolds transport theorem. We will now derive it for much more general conditions. A general, fixed control volume with fluid flowing through it is shown in Fig. 4.9. We again consider the system to be the fluid within the control volume at the initial time t. A short time later a portion of the fluid (region II) has exited from the control volume and additional fluid (region I, not part of the original system) has entered the control volume.

We consider an extensive fluid property B and seek to determine how the rate of change of B associated with the system is related to the rate of change of B within the control

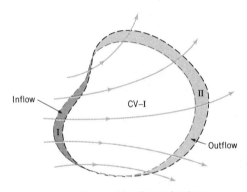

- - - Fixed control surface and system
        boundary at time t

- - - System boundary at time $t + \delta t$

■ **FIGURE 4.9** **Control volume and system for flow through an arbitrary, fixed control volume.**

volume at any instant. By repeating the exact steps that we did for the simplified control volume shown in Fig. 4.8, we see that Eq. 4.12 is valid for the general case also, provided that we give the correct interpretation to the terms $\dot{B}_{out}$ and $\dot{B}_{in}$.

The term $\dot{B}_{out}$ represents the net flowrate of the property B from the control volume. Its value can be thought of as arising from the addition (integration) of the contributions through each infinitesimal area element of size δA on the portion of the control surface dividing region II and the control volume. This surface is denoted CS_{out}. As is indicated in Fig. 4.10, in time δt the volume of fluid that passes across each area element is given by $\delta V = \delta \ell_n \, \delta A$, where $\delta \ell_n = \delta \ell \cos \theta$ is the height (normal to the base, δA) of the small volume element, and θ is the angle between the velocity vector and the outward pointing normal to the surface, $\hat{\mathbf{n}}$. Thus, since $\delta \ell = V \, \delta t$, the amount of the property B carried across the area element δA in the time interval δt is given by

$$\delta B = b\rho \, \delta V = b\rho(V \cos \theta \, \delta t) \, \delta A$$

The rate at which B is carried out of the control volume across the small area element δA, denoted $\delta \dot{B}_{out}$, is

$$\delta \dot{B}_{out} = \lim_{\delta t \to 0} \frac{\rho b \, \delta V}{\delta t} = \lim_{\delta t \to 0} \frac{(\rho b V \cos \theta \, \delta t) \delta A}{\delta t} = \rho b V \cos \theta \, \delta A$$

By integrating over the entire outflow portion of the control surface, CS_{out}, we obtain

$$\dot{B}_{out} = \int_{cs_{out}} d\dot{B}_{out} = \int_{cs_{out}} \rho b V \cos \theta \, dA$$

The quantity $V \cos \theta$ is the component of the velocity normal to the area element δA. From the definition of the dot product, this can be written as $V \cos \theta = \mathbf{V} \cdot \hat{\mathbf{n}}$. Hence, an alternate form of the outflow rate is

$$\dot{B}_{out} = \int_{cs_{out}} \rho b \mathbf{V} \cdot \hat{\mathbf{n}} \, dA \tag{4.14}$$

In a similar fashion, by considering the inflow portion of the control surface, CS_{in}, as shown in Fig. 4.11, we find that the inflow rate of B into the control volume is

$$\dot{B}_{in} = -\int_{cs_{in}} \rho b V \cos \theta \, dA = -\int_{cs_{in}} \rho b \mathbf{V} \cdot \hat{\mathbf{n}} \, dA \tag{4.15}$$

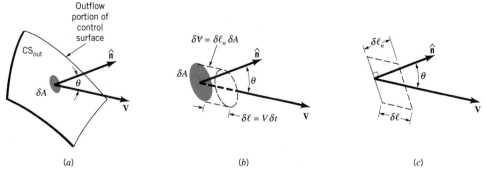

(a)   (b)   (c)

■ **FIGURE 4.10**   **Outflow across a typical portion of the control surface.**

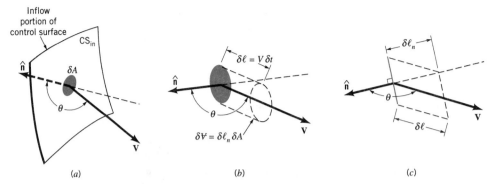

■ **FIGURE 4.11** **Inflow across a typical portion of the control surface.**

Therefore, the net flux (flowrate) of parameter B across the entire control surface is

$$\dot{B}_{\text{out}} - \dot{B}_{\text{in}} = \int_{\text{cs}_{\text{out}}} \rho b \mathbf{V} \cdot \hat{\mathbf{n}} \, dA - \left(-\int_{\text{cs}_{\text{in}}} \rho b \mathbf{V} \cdot \hat{\mathbf{n}} \, dA \right)$$

$$= \int_{\text{cs}} \rho b \mathbf{V} \cdot \hat{\mathbf{n}} \, dA \tag{4.16}$$

where the integration is over the entire control surface.

By combining Eqs. 4.12 and 4.16 we obtain

$$\frac{DB_{\text{sys}}}{Dt} = \frac{\partial B_{\text{cv}}}{\partial t} + \int_{\text{cs}} \rho b \mathbf{V} \cdot \hat{\mathbf{n}} \, dA$$

This can be written in a slightly different form by using $B_{\text{cv}} = \int_{\text{cv}} \rho b \, d\mathcal{V}$ so that

$$\boxed{\frac{DB_{\text{sys}}}{Dt} = \frac{\partial}{\partial t} \int_{\text{cv}} \rho b \, d\mathcal{V} + \int_{\text{cs}} \rho b \, \mathbf{V} \cdot \hat{\mathbf{n}} \, dA} \tag{4.17}$$

Equation 4.17 is the general form of the Reynolds transport theorem for a fixed, nonde-forming control volume. Its interpretation and use are discussed in the following sections.

4.4.2 Physical Interpretation

The left side of Eq. 4.17 is the time rate of change of an arbitrary extensive parameter of a system. This may represent the rate of change of mass, momentum, energy, or angular momentum of the system, depending on the choice of the parameter B.

The first term on the right side of Eq. 4.17 represents the rate of change of B within the control volume as the fluid flows through it. Recall that b is the amount of B per unit mass, so that $\rho b \, d\mathcal{V}$ is the amount of B in a small volume $d\mathcal{V}$. Thus, the time derivative of the integral of ρb throughout the control volume is the time rate of change of B within the control volume at a given time.

The last term in Eq. 4.17 (an integral over the control surface) represents the net flowrate of the parameter B across the entire control surface. Over a portion of the control surface

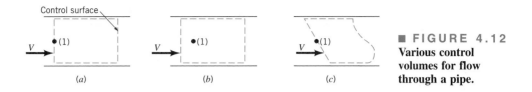

FIGURE 4.12
Various control
volumes for flow
through a pipe.

(a)   *(b)*   *(c)*

this property is being carried out of the control volume ($\mathbf{V} \cdot \hat{\mathbf{n}} > 0$); over other portions it is being carried into the control volume ($\mathbf{V} \cdot \hat{\mathbf{n}} < 0$). Over the remainder of the control surface there is no transport of B across the surface since $b\mathbf{V} \cdot \hat{\mathbf{n}} = 0$, because either $b = 0$, $\mathbf{V} = 0$, or $\mathbf{V}$ is parallel to the surface at those locations.

4.4.3   Selection of a Control Volume

Any volume in space can be considered as a control volume. The ease of solving a given fluid mechanics problem is often very dependent upon the choice of the control volume used. Only by practice can we develop skill at selecting the "best" control volume. None are "wrong," but some are "much better" than others.

Figure 4.12 illustrates three possible control volumes associated with flow through a pipe. If the problem is to determine the pressure at point (1), the selection of the control volume (*a*) is better than that of (*b*) because point (1) lies on the control surface. Similarly, control volume (*a*) is better than (*c*) because the flow is normal to the inlet and exit portions of the control volume. None of these control volumes are wrong—(*a*) will be easier to use. Proper control volume selection will become much clearer in Chapter 5 where the Reynolds transport theorem is used to transform the governing equations from the system formulation into the control volume formulation, and numerous examples using control volume ideas are discussed.

References

1. Goldstein, R. J., *Fluid Mechanics Measurements,* Hemisphere, New York, 1983.

2. Homsy, G. M., et. al., *Multimedia Fluid Mechanics* CD-ROM, Cambridge University Press, New York, 2000.

3. Magarvey, R. H., and MacLatchy, C. S., The Formation and Structure of Vortex Rings, *Canadian Journal of Physics,* Vol. 42, 1964.

Problems

Note: Unless otherwise indicated use the values of fluid properties found in the tables on the inside of the front cover. Problems designated with an (*) are intended to be solved with the aid of a programmable calculator or a computer. Problems designated with a (†) are "open-ended" problems and require critical thinking in that to work them one must make various assumptions and provide the necessary data. There is not a unique answer to these problems.

4.1   The velocity field of a flow is given by $\mathbf{V} = (3y + 2)\hat{\mathbf{i}} + (x - 8)\hat{\mathbf{j}} + 5z\hat{\mathbf{k}}$ ft/s, where x, y, and z are in feet. Determine the fluid speed at the origin ($x = y = z = 0$) and on the y axis ($x = z = 0$).

4.2   A flow can be visualized by plotting the velocity field as velocity vectors at representative locations in the flow as shown in **Video V4.1** and Fig. E4.1. Consider the velocity field given in polar coordinates by $v_r = -10/r$ and $v_\theta = 10/r$. This flow approximates a fluid swirling into a sink as shown in Fig. P4.2. Plot the velocity field at locations given by $r = 1$, 2, and 3 with $\theta = 0$, 30, 60, and 90 deg.

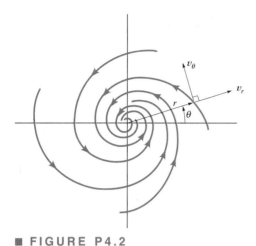

■ **FIGURE P4.2**

4.3   The x and y components of velocity for a two-dimensional flow are $u = 4$ ft/s and $v = 6x$ ft/s, where x is in feet. Determine the equation for the streamline and sketch representative streamlines in the upper half plane.

4.4   A velocity field is given by $\mathbf{V} = x\hat{\mathbf{i}} + x(x - 1)(y + 1)\hat{\mathbf{j}}$, where u and v are in ft/s and x and y are in feet. Plot the streamline that passes through $x = 0$ and $y = 0$. Compare this streamline with the streakline through the origin.

4.5   Water flows from a rotating lawn sprinkler as shown in **Video V4.6** and Figure P4.5. The end of the sprinkler arm moves with a speed of ωR, where $\omega = 10$ rad/s is the angular velocity of the sprinkler arm and $R = 0.5$ ft is its radius. The water exits the nozzle with a speed of $V = 10$ ft/s

relative to the rotating arm. Gravity and the interaction between the air and the water are negligible. **(a)** Show that the pathlines for this flow are straight radial lines. Hint: Consider the direction of flow (relative to the stationary ground) as the water leaves the sprinkler arm. **(b)** Show that at any given instant the stream of water that came from the sprinkler forms an arc given by $r = R + (V_a/\omega)\theta$, where the angle θ is as indicated in the figure and V_a is the water speed relative to the ground. Plot this curve for the data given.

4.6   In addition to the customary horizontal velocity components of the air in the atmosphere (the "wind"), there often are vertical air currents (thermals) caused by buoyant effects due to uneven heating of the air as indicated in Fig. P4.6. Assume that the velocity field in a certain region is approximated by $u = u_0$, $v = v_0(1 - y/h)$ for $0 < y < h$, and $u = u_0$, $v = 0$ for $y > h$. Determine the equation for the streamlines and plot the streamline that passes through the origin for values of $u_0/v_0 = 0.5$, 1, and 2.

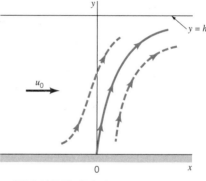

■ **FIGURE P4.6**

*4.7   Repeat Problem 4.6 using the same information except that $u = u_0 y/h$ for $0 \leq y \leq h$ rather than $u = u_0$. Use values of $u_0/v_0 = 0$, 0.1, 0.2, 0.4, 0.6, 0.8, and 1.0.

4.8   A velocity field is given by $u = cx^2$ and $v = cy^2$, where c is a constant. Determine the x and y components of the acceleration. At what point (points) in the flow field is the acceleration zero?

†**4.9**   Estimate the average acceleration of water as it travels through the nozzle on your garden hose. List all assumptions and show all calculations.

4.10   The velocity of air in the diverging pipe shown in Fig. P4.10 is given by $V_1 = 4t$ ft/s and $V_2 = 2t$ ft/s, where t is in seconds. **(a)** Determine the local acceleration at points (1) and (2). **(b)** Is the average convective acceleration between these two points negative, zero, or positive? Explain.

4.11   A fluid particle flowing along a stagnation streamline, as shown in **Video V4.5** and Fig. P4.11, slows down as it approaches the stagnation point. Measurements of the

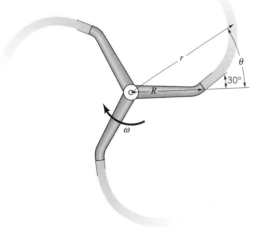

■ **FIGURE P4.5**

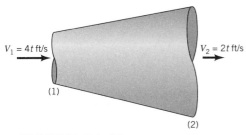

$V_1 = 4t$ ft/s $V_2 = 2t$ ft/s

(1)

(2)

■ FIGURE P4.10

dye flow in the video indicate that the location of a particle starting on the stagnation streamline a distance $s = 0.6$ ft upstream of the stagnation point at $t = 0$ is given approximately by $s = 0.6e^{-0.5t}$, where t is in seconds and s is in ft. **(a)** Determine the speed of a fluid particle as a function of time, $V_{particle}(t)$, as it flows along the streamline. **(b)** Determine the speed of the fluid as a function of position along the streamline, $V = V(s)$. **(c)** Determine the fluid acceleration along the streamline as a function of position, $a_s = a_s(s)$.

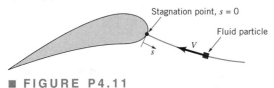

Stagnation point, $s = 0$

Fluid particle

s V

■ FIGURE P4.11

4.12   The fluid velocity along the x axis shown in Fig. P4.12 changes from 12 m/s at point A to 36 m/s at point B. It is also known that the velocity is a linear function of distance along the streamline. Determine the acceleration at points A, B, and C. Assume steady flow.

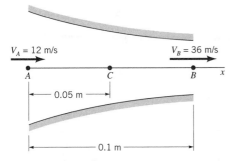

$V_A = 12$ m/s $V_B = 36$ m/s

A C B x

|← 0.05 m →|

|← 0.1 m →|

■ FIGURE P4.12

4.13   As shown in **Video V4.2** and Fig. P4.13, a flying airplane produces swirling flow near the end of its wings. In certain circumstances this flow can be approximated by the velocity field $u = -Ky/(x^2 + y^2)$ and $v = Kx/(x^2 + y^2)$,

where K is a constant depending on various parameters associated with the airplane (i.e., its weight, speed, etc.) and x and y are measured from the center of the swirl. **(a)** Show that for this flow the velocity is inversely proportional to the distance from the origin. That is, $V = K/(x^2 + y^2)^{1/2}$. **(b)** Show that the streamlines are circles.

y v u

x

■ FIGURE P4.13

4.14   A fluid flows along the x axis with a velocity given by $\mathbf{V} = (x/t)\hat{\mathbf{i}}$, where x is in feet and t is in seconds. **(a)** Plot the speed for $0 \le x \le 10$ ft and $t = 3$ s. **(b)** Plot the speed for $x = 7$ ft and $2 \le t \le 4$ s. **(c)** Determine the local and convective acceleration. **(d)** Show that the acceleration of any fluid particle in the flow is zero. **(e)** Explain physically how the velocity of a particle in this unsteady flow remains constant throughout its motion.

4.15   A hydraulic jump is a rather sudden change in depth of a liquid layer as it flows in an open channel as shown in Fig. P4.15. In a relatively short distance (thickness $= \ell$) the liquid depth changes from z_1 to z_2, with a corresponding change in velocity from V_1 to V_2. If $V_1 = 5$ m/s, $V_2 = 1$ m/s, and $\ell = 0.2$ m, estimate the average deceleration of the liquid as it flows across the hydraulic jump. How many g's deceleration does this represent?

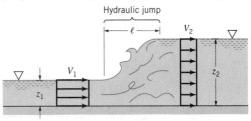

Hydraulic jump

|← ℓ →| V_2

V_1 z_2

z_1

■ FIGURE P4.15

4.16   A nozzle is designed to accelerate the fluid from V_1 to V_2 in a linear fashion. That is, $V = ax + b$, where a and b are constants. If the flow is constant with $V_1 = 10$ m/s at $x_1 = 0$ and $V_2 = 25$ m/s at $x_2 = 1$ m, determine the local acceleration, the convective acceleration, and the acceleration of the fluid at points (1) and (2).

4.17   Assume the temperature of the exhaust in an exhaust pipe can be approximated by $T = T_0(1 + ae^{-bx})$ $[1 + c \cos(\omega t)]$, where $T_0 = 100$ °C, $a = 3$, $b = 0.03$ m^{-1}, $c = 0.05$, and $\omega = 100$ rad/s. If the exhaust speed is a constant 3 m/s, determine the time rate of change of temperature of the fluid particles at $x = 0$ and $x = 4$ m when $t = 0$.

4.18 The temperature distribution in a fluid is given by $T = 10x + 5y$, where x and y are the horizontal and vertical coordinates in meters and T is in degrees centigrade. Determine the time rate of change of temperature of a fluid particle traveling **(a)** horizontally with $u = 20$ m/s, $v = 0$ or **(b)** vertically with $u = 0$, $v = 20$ m/s.

4.19 A fluid flows past a sphere with an upstream velocity of $V_0 = 40$ m/s as shown in Fig. P4.19. From a more advanced theory it is found that the speed of the fluid along the front part of the sphere is $V = \frac{3}{2}V_0 \sin \theta$. Determine the streamwise and normal components of acceleration at point A if the radius of the sphere is $a = 0.20$ m.

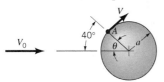

■ **FIGURE P4.19**

4.20 Water flows through the curved hose shown in Fig. P4.20 with an increasing speed of $V = 10t$ ft/s, where t is in seconds. For $t = 2$ s determine **(a)** the component of acceleration along the streamline, **(b)** the component of acceleration normal to the streamline, and **(c)** the net acceleration (magnitude and direction).

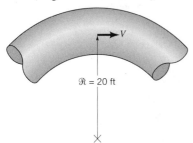

■ **FIGURE P4.20**

4.21 Water flows steadily through the funnel shown in Fig. P4.21. Throughout most of the funnel the flow is approximately radial (along rays from O) with a velocity of $V = c/r^2$, where r is the radial coordinate and c is a constant. If the velocity is 0.4 m/s when $r = 0.1$ m, determine the acceleration at points A and B.

4.22 Air flows from a pipe into the region between two parallel circular disks as shown in Fig. P4.22. The fluid velocity in the gap between the disks is closely approximated by $V = V_0R/r$, where R is the radius of the disk, r is the radial coordinate, and V_0 is the fluid velocity at the edge of the disk. Determine the acceleration for $r = 1$, 2, or 3 ft if $V_0 = 5$ ft/s and $R = 3$ ft.

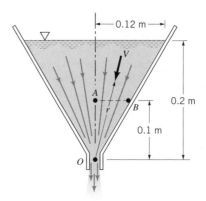

■ **FIGURE P4.21**

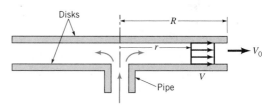

■ **FIGURE P4.22**

4.23 Water flows through a duct of square cross section as shown in Fig. P4.23 with a constant, uniform velocity of $V = 20$ m/s. Consider fluid particles that lie along line A–B at time $t = 0$. Determine the position of these particles, denoted by line A'–B', when $t = 0.20$ s. Use the volume of fluid in the region between lines A–B and A'–B' to determine the flowrate in the duct. Repeat the problem for fluid particles originally along line C–D; along line E–F. Compare your three answers.

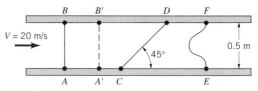

■ **FIGURE P4.23**

4.24 At time $t = 0$ the valve on an initially empty (perfect vacuum, $\rho = 0$) tank is opened and air rushes in. If the tank has a volume of V_0 and the density of air within the tank increases as $\rho = \rho_\infty(1 - e^{-bt})$, where b is a constant, determine the time rate of change of mass within the tank.

4.25 Air enters an elbow with a uniform speed of 10 m/s as shown in Fig. P4.25. At the exit of the elbow the velocity profile is not uniform. In fact, there is a region of separation or reverse flow. The fixed control volume *ABCD* coincides with the system at time $t = 0$. Make a sketch to indicate (**a**) the system at time $t = 0.01$ s and (**b**) the fluid that has entered and exited the control volume in that time period.

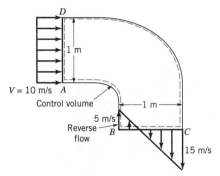

■ **FIGURE P4.25**

4.26 Water flows in the branching pipe shown in Fig. P4.26 with uniform velocity at each inlet and outlet. The fixed control volume indicated coincides with the system at time $t = 20$ s. Make a sketch to indicate (**a**) the boundary of the system at time $t = 20.2$ s, (**b**) the fluid that left the control volume during that 0.2-s interval, and (**c**) the fluid that entered the control volume during that time interval.

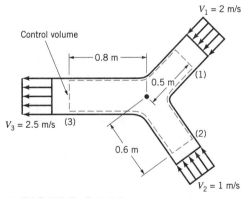

■ **FIGURE P4.26**

4.27 Two plates are pulled in opposite directions with speeds of 1.0 ft/s as shown in Fig. P4.27. The oil between the plates moves with a velocity given by $\mathbf{V} = 10y\hat{\mathbf{i}}$ ft/s, where y is in feet. The fixed control volume *ABCD* coincides with the system at time $t = 0$. Make a sketch to indicate (**a**) the system at time $t = 0.2$ s and (**b**) the fluid that has entered and exited the control volume in that time period.

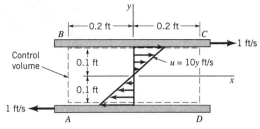

■ **FIGURE P4.27**

4.28 The wind blows across a field with an approximate velocity profile as shown in Fig. P4.28. Use Eq. 4.14 with the parameter b equal to the velocity to determine the momentum flowrate across the vertical surface A–B, which is of unit depth into the paper.

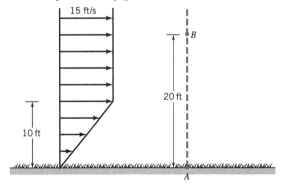

■ **FIGURE P4.28**

4.29 Water flows through the 2-m-wide rectangular channel shown in Fig. P4.29 with a uniform velocity of 3 m/s. (**a**) Directly integrate Eq. 4.14 with $b = 1$ to determine the mass flowrate (kg/s) across section *CD* of the control volume. (**b**) Repeat part (a) with $b = 1/\rho$, where ρ is the density. Explain the physical interpretation of the answer to part (b).

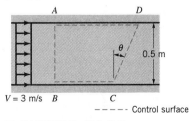

■ **FIGURE P4.29**

CHAPTER

5

Finite Control Volume Analysis

Many practical problems in fluid mechanics require analysis of the behavior of the contents of a finite region in space (a control volume). For example, we may be asked to calculate the anchoring force required to hold a jet engine in place during a test. Important questions can be answered readily with finite control volume analyses. The bases of this analysis method are some fundamental principles of physics, namely, conservation of mass, Newton's second law of motion, and the laws of thermodynamics. Thus, as one might expect, the resultant techniques are powerful and applicable to a wide variety of fluid mechanical circumstances that require engineering judgment. Furthermore, the finite control volume formulas are easy to interpret physically and not difficult to use.

5.1   Conservation of Mass—The Continuity Equation

5.1.1   Derivation of the Continuity Equation

A system is defined as a collection of unchanging contents, so the conservation of mass principle for a system is simply stated as

A jet of water injected into stationary water: Upon emerging from the slit at the left, the jet of fluid loses some of its momentum to the surrounding fluid. This causes the jet to slow down and its width to increase (air bubbles in water). (Photograph courtesy of ONERA, France)

$$\text{time rate of change of the system mass} = 0$$

or

$$\frac{DM_{sys}}{Dt} = 0 \tag{5.1}$$

where the system mass, M_{sys}, is more generally expressed as

$$M_{sys} = \int_{sys} \rho \, d\mathcal{V} \tag{5.2}$$

and the integration is over the volume of the system.

For a system and a fixed, nondeforming control volume that are coincident at an instant of time, as are illustrated in Fig. 5.1, the Reynolds transport theorem (Eq. 4.17) allows us to state that

$$\frac{D}{Dt} \int_{sys} \rho \, d\mathcal{V} = \frac{\partial}{\partial t} \int_{cv} \rho \, d\mathcal{V} + \int_{cs} \rho \mathbf{V} \cdot \hat{\mathbf{n}} \, dA \tag{5.3}$$

or

| time rate of change of the mass of the coincident system | = | time rate of change of the mass of the contents of the coincident control volume | + | net rate of flow of mass through the control surface |

When a flow is steady, all field properties (i.e., properties at any specified point) including density remain constant with time and the time rate of change of the mass of the contents of the control volume is zero. That is,

$$\frac{\partial}{\partial t} \int_{cv} \rho \, d\mathcal{V} = 0$$

The integrand, $\mathbf{V} \cdot \hat{\mathbf{n}} \, dA$, in the mass flowrate integral represents the product of the component of velocity, $\mathbf{V}$, perpendicular to the small portion of control surface and the differential area, dA. Thus, $\mathbf{V} \cdot \hat{\mathbf{n}} \, dA$ is the volume flowrate through dA and $\rho \mathbf{V} \cdot \hat{\mathbf{n}} \, dA$ is the mass flowrate through dA. Furthermore, the sign of the dot product $\mathbf{V} \cdot \hat{\mathbf{n}}$ is "+" for flow

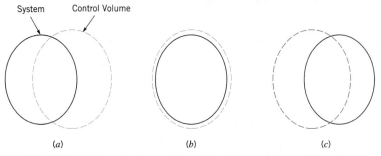

■ **FIGURE 5.1** **System and control volume at three different instances of time. (*a*) System and control at time $t - \delta t$. (*b*) System and control volume at t, coincident condition. (*c*) System and control volume at $t + \delta t$.**

out of the control volume and "−" for flow *into* the control volume since $\hat{\mathbf{n}}$ is considered positive when it points out of the control volume. When all of the differential quantities, $\rho\mathbf{V} \cdot \hat{\mathbf{n}} \, dA$, are summed over the entire control surface, the result is the net mass flowrate through the control surface, or

$$\int_{cs} \rho\mathbf{V} \cdot \hat{\mathbf{n}} \, dA = \sum \dot{m}_{out} - \sum \dot{m}_{in} \tag{5.4}$$

where $\dot{m}$ is the mass flowrate (slugs/s or kg/s).

The control volume expression for *conservation of mass,* which is commonly called the *continuity equation,* for a fixed, nondeforming control volume is obtained by combining Eqs. 5.1, 5.2, and 5.3 to obtain

$$\boxed{\frac{\partial}{\partial t} \int_{cv} \rho \, d\mathcal{V} + \int_{cs} \rho\mathbf{V} \cdot \hat{\mathbf{n}} \, dA = 0} \tag{5.5}$$

In words, Eq. 5.5 states that to conserve mass the time rate of change of the mass of the contents of the control volume plus the net rate of mass flow through the control surface must equal zero.

An often-used expression for mass flowrate, $\dot{m}$, through a section of control surface having area A is

$$\boxed{\dot{m} = \rho Q = \rho A V} \tag{5.6}$$

where ρ is the fluid density, Q is the volume flowrate (ft³/s or m³/s), and V is the component of fluid velocity perpendicular to area A. The appropriate fluid velocity to use in Eq. 5.6 is the average value of the component of velocity normal to the section area involved. This average value, $\overline{V}$, is defined as

$$\boxed{\overline{V} = \frac{\displaystyle\int_A \rho\mathbf{V} \cdot \hat{\mathbf{n}} \, dA}{\rho A}} \tag{5.7}$$

If the velocity is considered uniformly distributed (one-dimensional flow) over the section area, A, then $\overline{V} = V$ and the bar notation is not necessary.

5.1.2   Fixed, Nondeforming Control Volume

V5.1 Sink
flow

Several example problems that involve the continuity equation for fixed, nondeforming control volumes (Eq. 5.5) follow.

EXAMPLE 5.1

Seawater flows steadily through a simple conical shaped nozzle at the end of a fire hose as illustrated in Fig. E5.1. If the nozzle exit velocity must be at least 20 m/s, determine the minimum pumping capacity required in m³/s.

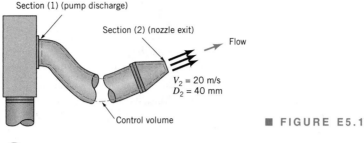

Section (1) (pump discharge)

Section (2) (nozzle exit)

Flow

$V_2 = 20$ m/s
$D_2 = 40$ mm

Control volume

■ **FIGURE E5.1**

SOLUTION

The pumping capacity sought is the volume flowrate delivered by the fire pump to the hose and nozzle. Since we desire knowledge about the pump discharge flowrate and we have information about the nozzle exit flowrate, we link these two flowrates with the control volume designated with the dashed line in Fig. E5.1. This control volume contains, at any instant, seawater that is within the hose and nozzle from the pump discharge to the nozzle exit plane.

Equation 5.5 is applied to the contents of this control volume to give

$$\overset{\displaystyle 0 \text{ (flow is steady)}}{\frac{\partial}{\partial t} \int_{cv} \rho \, d\forall} + \int_{cs} \rho \mathbf{V} \cdot \hat{\mathbf{n}} \, dA = 0 \tag{1}$$

The time rate of change of the mass of the contents of this control volume is zero because the flow is steady. From Eq. 5.4, we see that the control surface integral in Eq. 1 involves mass flowrates at the pump discharge, section (1), and at the nozzle exit, section (2), or

$$\int_{cs} \rho \mathbf{V} \cdot \hat{\mathbf{n}} \, dA = \dot{m}_2 - \dot{m}_1 = 0$$

so that

$$\dot{m}_2 = \dot{m}_1 \tag{2}$$

Since the mass flowrate is equal to the product of fluid density, ρ, and volume flowrate, Q, (see Eq. 5.6) we obtain from Eq. 2

$$\rho_2 Q_2 = \rho_1 Q_1 \tag{3}$$

Liquid flow at low speeds, as in this example, may be considered incompressible. Therefore

$$\rho_2 = \rho_1 \tag{4}$$

and from Eqs. 3 and 4

$$Q_2 = Q_1 \tag{5}$$

The pumping capacity is equal to the volume flowrate at the nozzle exit. If, for simplicity, the velocity distribution at the nozzle exit plane, section (2), is considered uniform (one-dimensional), then from Eqs. 5 and 5.6

$$Q_1 = Q_2 = V_2 A_2$$
$$= V_2 \frac{\pi}{4} D_2^2 = (20 \text{ m/s}) \frac{\pi}{4} \left(\frac{40 \text{ mm}}{1000 \text{ mm/m}} \right)^2 = 0.0251 \text{ m}^3\text{/s} \tag{Ans}$$

EXAMPLE 5.2

Incompressible, laminar water flow develops in a straight pipe having radius R as indicated in Fig. E5.2. At section (1), the velocity profile is uniform; the velocity is equal to a constant value U and is parallel to the pipe axis everywhere. At section (2), the velocity profile is axisymmetric and parabolic, with zero velocity at the pipe wall and a maximum value of u_{max} at the centerline. How are U and u_{max} related? How are the average velocity at section (2), $\overline{V}_2$, and u_{max} related?

SOLUTION

An appropriate control volume is sketched (dashed lines) in Fig. E5.2. The application of Eq. 5.5 to the contents of this control volume yields

$$\int_{cs} \rho \mathbf{V} \cdot \hat{\mathbf{n}} \, dA = 0$$

The surface integral is evaluated at sections (1) and (2) to give

$$-\rho_1 A_1 U + \int_{A_2} \rho \mathbf{V} \cdot \hat{\mathbf{n}} \, dA_2 = 0 \tag{1}$$

or, since the component of velocity, $\mathbf{V}$, perpendicular to the area at section (2) is u_2, and the element cross-sectional area, dA_2, is equal to $2\pi r \, dr$ (see shaded area element in Fig. E5.2), Eq. 1 becomes

$$-\rho_1 A_1 U + \rho_2 \int_0^R u_2 2\pi r \, dr = 0 \tag{2}$$

Since the flow is considered incompressible, $\rho_1 = \rho_2$. The parabolic velocity relationship for flow through section (2) is used in Eq. 2 to yield

$$-A_1 U + 2\pi u_{max} \int_0^R \left[1 - \left(\frac{r}{R}\right)^2 \right] r \, dr = 0 \tag{3}$$

Integrating, we get from Eq. 3

$$-\pi R^2 U + 2\pi u_{max} \left(\frac{r^2}{2} - \frac{r^4}{4R^2} \right)_0^R = 0$$

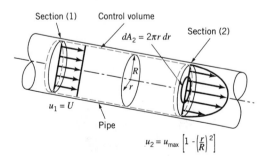

Section (1)   Control volume

$dA_2 = 2\pi r \, dr$ Section (2)

R

r

$u_1 = U$

Pipe

$u_2 = u_{max}\left[1 - \left(\frac{r}{R}\right)^2\right]$

■ FIGURE E5.2

or

$$u_{max} = 2U \tag{Ans}$$

Since this flow is incompressible, we conclude from Eq. 5.7 that U is the average velocity at all sections of the control volume. Thus, the average velocity at section (2), $\overline{V}_2$, is one-half the maximum velocity, u_{max}, there, or

$$\overline{V}_2 = \frac{u_{max}}{2} \tag{Ans}$$

EXAMPLE 5.3

A bathtub is being filled with water from a faucet. The rate of flow from the faucet is steady at 9 gal/min. The tub volume is approximated by a rectangular space as indicated in Fig. E5.3. Estimate the time rate of change of the depth of water in the tub, $\partial h/\partial t$, in in./min at any instant.

SOLUTION

We use the fixed, nondeforming control volume outlined with a dashed line in Fig. E5.3. This control volume includes in it, at any instant, the water accumulated in the tub, some of the water flowing from the faucet into the tub, and some air. Application of Eqs. 5.4 and 5.5 to these contents of the control volume results in

$$\frac{\partial}{\partial t} \int_{\substack{air \\ volume}} \rho_{air} \, d\mathcal{V}_{air} + \frac{\partial}{\partial t} \int_{\substack{water \\ volume}} \rho_{water} \, d\mathcal{V}_{water} - \dot{m}_{water} + \dot{m}_{air} = 0$$

Note that the time rate of change of air mass and water mass are each not zero. Recognizing, however, that the air mass must be conserved, we know that the time rate of change of the mass of air in the control volume must be equal to the rate of air mass flow out of the control volume. For simplicity, we disregard any water evaporation that occurs. Thus, applying Eqs. 5.4 and 5.5 to the air only and to the water only, we obtain

$$\frac{\partial}{\partial t} \int_{\substack{air \\ volume}} \rho_{air} \, d\mathcal{V}_{air} + \dot{m}_{air} = 0$$

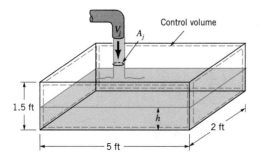

■ FIGURE E5.3

for air, and

$$\frac{\partial}{\partial t} \int_{\substack{\text{water} \\ \text{volume}}} \rho_{\text{water}} \, dV_{\text{water}} = \dot{m}_{\text{water}} \tag{1}$$

for water. For the water,

$$\int_{\substack{\text{water} \\ \text{volume}}} \rho_{\text{water}} \, dV_{\text{water}} = \rho_{\text{water}} \left[h(2 \text{ ft})(5 \text{ ft}) + (1.5 \text{ ft} - h)A_j \right] \tag{2}$$

where A_j is the cross-sectional area of the water flowing from the faucet into the tub. Combining Eqs. 1 and 2, we obtain

$$\rho_{\text{water}} \left(10 \text{ ft}^2 - A_j\right) \frac{\partial h}{\partial t} = \dot{m}_{\text{water}}$$

and, thus

$$\frac{\partial h}{\partial t} = \frac{Q_{\text{water}}}{\left(10 \text{ ft}^2 - A_j\right)}$$

For $A_j \ll 10 \text{ ft}^2$ we can conclude that

$$\frac{\partial h}{\partial t} = \frac{Q_{\text{water}}}{\left(10 \text{ ft}^2\right)}$$

or

$$\frac{\partial h}{\partial t} = \frac{(9 \text{ gal/min})(12 \text{ in./ft})}{(7.48 \text{ gal/ft}^3)(10 \text{ ft}^2)} = 1.44 \text{ in./min} \tag{Ans}$$

The preceding example problems illustrate that when the flow is steady, the time rate of change of the mass of the contents of the control volume is zero and the net amount of mass flowrate, $\dot{m}$, through the control surface is therefore also zero

$$\sum \dot{m}_{\text{out}} - \sum \dot{m}_{\text{in}} = 0 \tag{5.8}$$

If the steady flow is also incompressible, the net amount of volume flowrate, Q, through the control surface is also zero

$$\sum Q_{\text{out}} - \sum Q_{\text{in}} = 0 \tag{5.9}$$

When the flow is unsteady, the instantaneous time rate of change of the mass of the contents of the control volume is not necessarily zero.

For steady flow involving only one stream of a specific fluid flowing through the control volume at sections (1) and (2),

$$\dot{m} = \rho_1 A_1 \overline{V}_1 = \rho_2 A_2 \overline{V}_2 \tag{5.10}$$

V5.2 Shop vac filter

and for incompressible flow,

$$Q = A_1 \overline{V}_1 = A_2 \overline{V}_2 \tag{5.11}$$

5.1.3 Moving, Nondeforming Control Volume

When a moving control volume is used, the velocity relative to the moving control volume (relative velocity) is an important flow field variable. The relative velocity, $\mathbf{W}$, is the fluid velocity seen by an observer moving with the control volume. The control volume velocity, $\mathbf{V}_{cv}$, is the velocity of the control volume as seen from a fixed coordinate system. The absolute velocity, $\mathbf{V}$, is the fluid velocity seen by a stationary observer in a fixed coordinate system. These velocities are related to each other by the vector equation

$$\mathbf{V} = \mathbf{W} + \mathbf{V}_{cv} \tag{5.12}$$

The control volume expression for conservation of the mass (the continuity equation) for a moving, nondeforming control volume is the same as that for a stationary control volume, provided the absolute velocity is replaced by the relative velocity. Thus,

$$\boxed{\frac{\partial}{\partial t}\int_{cv} \rho \, d\forall + \int_{cs} \rho \mathbf{W} \cdot \hat{\mathbf{n}} \, dA = 0} \tag{5.13}$$

EXAMPLE 5.4

Water enters a rotating lawn sprinkler through its base at the steady rate of 1000 ml/s as sketched in Figure E5.4. If the exit area of each of the two nozzles is 30 mm², determine the average speed of the water leaving the nozzle, relative to the nozzle, if **(a)** the rotary sprinkler head is stationary, **(b)** the sprinkler head rotates at 600 rpm, **(c)** the sprinkler head accelerates from 0 to 600 rpm.

SOLUTION

We specify a control volume that contains the water in the rotary sprinkler head at any instant. This control volume is nondeforming, but it moves (rotates) with the sprinkler head.

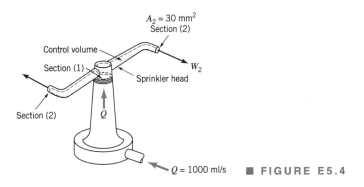

FIGURE E5.4

The application of Eq. 5.13 to the contents of this control volume for situation **(a)**, **(b)**, or **(c)** of the problem results in the same expression, namely,

$$\frac{\partial}{\partial t}\overset{\nearrow 0 \text{ flow is steady or the}}{\int_{cv} \rho \, dV} + \int_{cs} \rho \mathbf{W} \cdot \hat{\mathbf{n}} \, dA = 0$$

flow is steady or the control volume is filled with an incompressible fluid

The flow is steady in the control volume reference frame when the control volume is stationary [part **(a)**] and when it moves [parts **(b)** and **(c)**]. Also, the control volume is filled with water. Thus, the time rate of change of the mass of the water in the control volume is zero. The control surface integral has a nonzero value only where water enters and leaves the control volume; thus,

$$\int_{cv} \rho \mathbf{W} \cdot \mathbf{n} \, dA = -\dot{m}_{in} + \dot{m}_{out} = 0$$

or

$$\dot{m}_{out} = \dot{m}_{in} \tag{1}$$

Since

$$\dot{m}_{out} = 2\rho A_2 W_2$$

and

$$\dot{m}_{in} = \rho Q$$

it follows from Eq. 1 that

$$W_2 = \frac{Q}{2A_2}$$

or

$$W_2 = \frac{(1000 \text{ ml/s})(0.001 \text{ m}^3/\text{liter})(10^6 \text{ mm}^2/\text{m}^2)}{(1000 \text{ ml/liter})(2)(30 \text{ mm}^2)} = 16.7 \text{ m/s} \tag{Ans}$$

The value of W_2 is independent of the speed of rotation of the sprinkler head and represents the average velocity of the water exiting from each nozzle with respect to the nozzle for cases **(a)**, **(b)**, **(c)**. The velocity of water discharging from each nozzle, when viewed from a stationary reference (i.e., V_2), will vary as the rotation speed of the sprinkler head varies since from Eq. 5.12,

$$V_2 = W_2 - U$$

where $U = \omega R$ is the speed of the nozzle and ω and R are the angular velocity and radius of the sprinkler head, respectively.

5.2 Newton's Second Law—The Linear Momentum and Moment-of-Momentum Equations

5.2.1 Derivation of the Linear Momentum Equation

Newton's second law of motion for a system is

$$
\begin{array}{c}
\text{time rate of change of the} \\
\text{linear momentum of the system}
\end{array}
=
\begin{array}{c}
\text{sum of external forces} \\
\text{acting on the system}
\end{array}
$$

Since momentum is mass times velocity, the momentum of a small particle of mass $\rho d\mathcal{V}$ is $\mathbf{V}\rho d\mathcal{V}$. Thus, the momentum of the entire system is $\int_{sys}\mathbf{V}\rho d\mathcal{V}$ and Newton's law becomes

$$\frac{D}{Dt}\int_{sys}\mathbf{V}\rho\, d\mathcal{V} = \sum\mathbf{F}_{sys} \tag{5.14}$$

V5.3 Smoke-stack plume momentum

When a control volume is coincident with a system at an instant of time, the forces acting on the system and the forces acting on the contents of the coincident control volume (see Fig. 5.2) are instantaneously identical, that is,

$$\sum\mathbf{F}_{sys} = \sum\mathbf{F}_{\substack{\text{contents of the} \\ \text{coincident control volume}}} \tag{5.15}$$

Furthermore, for a system and the contents of a coincident control volume that is fixed and nondeforming, the Reynolds transport theorem (Eq. 4.17 with b set equal to the velocity, and B_{sys} being the system momentum) allows us to conclude that

$$\frac{D}{Dt}\int_{sys}\mathbf{V}\rho\, d\mathcal{V} = \frac{\partial}{\partial t}\int_{cv}\mathbf{V}\rho\, d\mathcal{V} + \int_{cs}\mathbf{V}\rho\mathbf{V}\cdot\hat{\mathbf{n}}\, dA \tag{5.16}$$

or

$$
\begin{array}{c}
\text{time rate of change} \\
\text{of the linear} \\
\text{momentum of the} \\
\text{system}
\end{array}
=
\begin{array}{c}
\text{time rate of change} \\
\text{of the linear} \\
\text{momentum of the} \\
\text{contents of the} \\
\text{control volume}
\end{array}
+
\begin{array}{c}
\text{net rate of flow} \\
\text{of linear momentum} \\
\text{through the} \\
\text{control surface}
\end{array}
$$

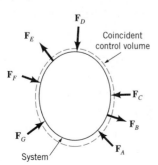

■ **FIGURE 5.2** **External forces acting on system and coincident control volume.**

Equation 5.16 states that the time rate of change of system linear momentum is expressed as the sum of the two control volume quantities: the time rate of change of the *linear momentum of the contents of the control volume,* and the net rate of *linear momentum flow through the control surface.* As particles of mass move into or out of a control volume through the control surface, they carry linear momentum in or out. Thus, linear momentum flow should seem no more unusual than mass flow.

For a control volume that is fixed (inertial) and nondeforming, Eqs. 5.14, 5.15, and 5.16 suggest that an appropriate mathematical statement of Newton's second law of motion is

$$\frac{\partial}{\partial t} \int_{cv} \mathbf{V} \rho \, d\mathbf{V} + \int_{cs} \mathbf{V} \rho \mathbf{V} \cdot \hat{\mathbf{n}} \, dA = \sum \mathbf{F}_{\substack{\text{contents of the} \\ \text{control volume}}} \tag{5.17}$$

We call Eq. 5.17 the *linear momentum equation.*

The forces involved in Eq. 5.17 are body and surface forces that act on what is contained in the control volume. The only body force we consider in this chapter is the one associated with the action of gravity. We experience this body force as weight. The surface forces are basically exerted on the contents of the control volume by material just outside the control volume in contact with material just inside the control volume. For example, a wall in contact with fluid can exert a reaction surface force on the fluid it bounds. Similarly, fluid just outside the control volume can push on fluid just inside the control volume at a common interface, usually an opening in the control surface through which fluid flow occurs.

V5.4 Force
due to a
water jet

5.2.2   Application of the Linear Momentum Equation

The linear momentum equation for the inertial control volume is a vector equation (Eq. 5.17). In engineering applications, components of this vector equation resolved along orthogonal coordinates, for example, x, y, and z (rectangular coordinate system) or r, θ, and x (cylindrical coordinate system), will normally be used. A simple example involving one-dimensional, steady, incompressible flow is considered first.

EXAMPLE 5.5

As shown in Fig. E5.5a, a horizontal jet of water exits a nozzle with a uniform speed of $V_1 = 10$ ft/s, strikes a vane, and is turned through an angle θ. Determine the anchoring force needed to hold the vane stationary. Neglect gravity and viscous effects.

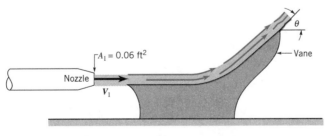

(a)

■ FIGURE E5.5a

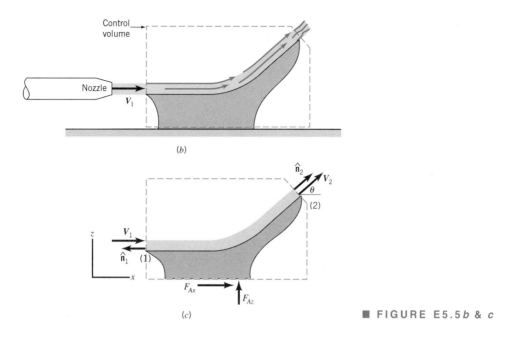

■ FIGURE E5.5*b* & *c*

SOLUTION

We select a control volume that includes the vane and a portion of the water (see Figs. E5.5*b*, *c*) and apply the linear momentum equation to this fixed control volume. The *x*- and *z*-components of Eq.5.17 become

$$\overset{\nearrow 0 \text{ (flow is steady)}}{\frac{\partial}{\partial t} \int_{cv} u \rho \, d\mathcal{V}} + \int_{cs} u \rho \mathbf{V} \cdot \hat{\mathbf{n}} \, dA = \sum F_x \tag{1}$$

and

$$\overset{\nearrow 0 \text{ (flow is steady)}}{\frac{\partial}{\partial t} \int_{cv} w \rho \, dV} + \int_{cs} w \rho \mathbf{V} \cdot \hat{\mathbf{n}} \, dA = \sum F_z \tag{2}$$

where $\mathbf{V} = u\,\hat{\mathbf{i}} + w\,\hat{\mathbf{k}}$, and $\sum F_x$ and $\sum F_z$ are the net *x*- and *z*-components of force acting on the contents of the control volume.

The water enters and leaves the control volume as a free jet at atmospheric pressure. Hence, there is atmospheric pressure surrounding the entire control volume, and the net pressure force on the control volume surface is zero. If we neglect the weight of the water and vane, the only forces applied to the control volume contents are the horizontal and vertical components of the anchoring force, F_{Ax} and F_{Az}, respectively.

The only portions of the control surface across which fluid flows are section 1 (the entrance) where $\mathbf{V} \cdot \hat{\mathbf{n}} = -V_1$ and section 2 (the exit) where $\mathbf{V} \cdot \hat{\mathbf{n}} = +V_2$. (Recall that the unit normal vector is directed out from the control surface.) Also, with negligible gravity and viscous effects, and since $p_1 = p_2$, the speed of the fluid remains constant, so that $V_1 = V_2 =$

10 ft/s (see the Bernoulli equation, Eq. 3.6). Hence, at section 1, $u = V_1$, $w = 0$, and at section 2, $u = V_1 \cos \theta$, $w = V_1 \sin \theta$.

By using the above information, Eqs. 1 and 2 can be written as

$$V_1 \rho(-V_1)A_1 + V_1 \cos \theta \rho(V_1)A_2 = F_{Ax} \qquad (3)$$

and

$$(0)\rho(-V_1)A_1 + V_1 \sin \theta \rho(V_1)A_2 = F_{Az} \qquad (4)$$

Note that since the flow is uniform across the inlet and exit, the integrals simply reduce to multiplications. Equations 3 and 4 can be simplified by using conservation of mass, which states that for this incompressible flow $A_1 V_1 = A_2 V_2$, or $A_1 = A_2$ since $V_1 = V_2$. Thus

$$F_{Ax} = -\rho A_1 V_1^2 + \rho A_1 V_1^2 \cos \theta = -\rho A_1 V_1^2 (1 - \cos \theta) \qquad (5)$$

and

$$F_{Az} = \rho A_1 V_1^2 \sin \theta \qquad (6)$$

With the given data we obtain

$$F_{Ax} = -(1.94 \text{ slugs/ft}^3)(0.06 \text{ ft}^2)(10 \text{ ft/s})^2(1 - \cos \theta)$$
$$= -11.64(1 - \cos \theta) \text{ slugs·ft/s}^2 = -11.64(1 - \cos \theta) \text{ lb} \qquad \textbf{(Ans)}$$

and

$$F_{Az} = (1.94 \text{ slugs/ft}^3)(0.06 \text{ ft}^2)(10 \text{ ft/s})^2 \sin \theta$$
$$= 11.64 \sin \theta \text{ lb} \qquad \textbf{(Ans)}$$

Note that if $\theta = 0$ (i.e., the vane does not turn the water), the anchoring force is zero. The inviscid fluid merely slides along the vane without putting any force on it. If $\theta = 90°$, then $F_{Ax} = -11.64$ lb and $F_{Az} = 11.64$ lb. It is necessary to push on the vane (and, hence, for the vane to push on the water) to the left (F_{Ax} is negative) and up in order to change the direction of flow of the water from horizontal to vertical. A momentum change requires a force. If $\theta = 180°$, the water jet is turned back on itself. This requires no vertical force ($F_{Az} = 0$), but the horizontal force ($F_{Ax} = -23.3$ lb) is two times that required if $\theta = 90°$. This force must eliminate the incoming fluid momentum and create the outgoing momentum.

Note that the anchoring force (Eqs. 5, 6) can be written in terms of the mass flowrate, $\dot{m} = \rho A_1 V_1$, as

$$F_{Ax} = -\dot{m} V_1(1 - \cos \theta)$$

and

$$F_{Az} = \dot{m} V_1 \sin \theta$$

In this example the anchoring force is needed to produce the nonzero net momentum flowrate (mass flowrate times the change in x- or z-component of velocity) across the control surface.

EXAMPLE 5.6

Determine the anchoring force required to hold in place a conical nozzle attached to the end of a laboratory sink faucet (see Fig. E5.6a) when the water flowrate is 0.6 liter/s. The nozzle mass is 0.1 kg. The nozzle inlet and exit diameters are 16 mm and 5 mm, respectively.

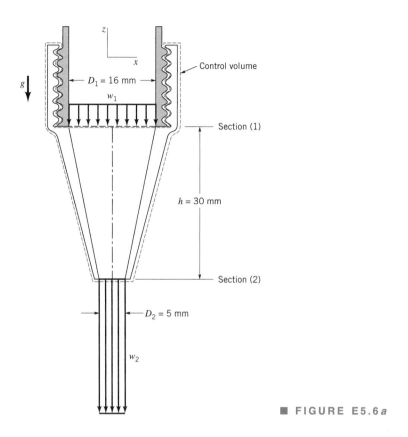

■ **FIGURE E5.6** *a*

The nozzle axis is vertical and the axial distance between sections (1) and (2) is 30 mm. The pressure at section (1) is 464 kPa.

SOLUTION

The anchoring force sought is the reaction between the faucet and nozzle threads. To evaluate this force we select a control volume that includes the entire nozzle and the water contained in the nozzle at an instant, as is indicated in Figs. E5.6*a* and E5.6*b*. All of the vertical forces acting on the contents of this control volume are identified in Fig. E5.6*b*. The action of atmospheric pressure cancels out in every direction and is not shown. Gage pressure forces do not cancel out in the vertical direction and are shown. Application of the vertical or *z* direction component of Eq. 5.17 to the contents of this control volume leads to

$$\underbrace{\frac{\partial}{\partial t} \int_{cv} w\rho \, d\forall}_{0 \text{ (flow is steady)}} + \int_{cs} w\rho \mathbf{V} \cdot \hat{\mathbf{n}} \, dA = F_A - \mathcal{W}_n - p_1 A_1 - \mathcal{W}_w + p_2 A_2 \tag{1}$$

where *w* is the *z* direction component of fluid velocity, and the various parameters are identified in the figure.

Note that the positive direction is considered "up" for the forces. We will use this same sign convention for the fluid velocity, *w*, in Eq. 1. In Eq. 1, the dot product, $\mathbf{V} \cdot \hat{\mathbf{n}}$, is "+"

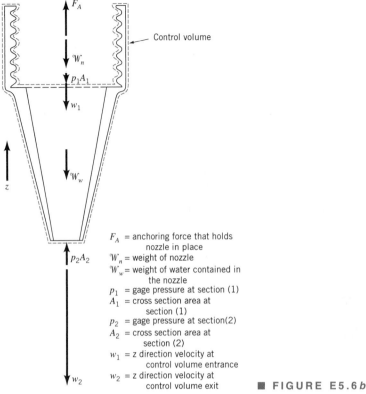

F_A = anchoring force that holds
nozzle in place
$\mathcal{W}_n$ = weight of nozzle
$\mathcal{W}_w$ = weight of water contained in
the nozzle
p_1 = gage pressure at section (1)
A_1 = cross section area at
section (1)
p_2 = gage pressure at section(2)
A_2 = cross section area at
section (2)
w_1 = z direction velocity at
control volume entrance
w_2 = z direction velocity at
control volume exit

■ **FIGURE E5.6***b*

for flow out of the control volume and "−" for flow into the control volume. For this particular example

$$\mathbf{V} \cdot \hat{\mathbf{n}}\, dA = \pm |w|\, dA \tag{2}$$

with the "+" used for flow out of the control volume and "−" used for flow in. To evaluate the control surface integral in Eq. 1, we need to assume a distribution for fluid velocity, w, and fluid density, ρ. For simplicity, we assume that w is uniformly distributed or constant, with magnitudes of w_1 and w_2 over cross-sectional areas A_1 and A_2. Also, this flow is incompressible so the fluid density, ρ, is constant throughout. Proceeding further we obtain for Eq. 1

$$\begin{aligned}(-\dot{m}_1)(-w_1) &+ \dot{m}_2(-w_2) \\ = F_A - \mathcal{W}_n &- p_1 A_1 - \mathcal{W}_w + p_2 A_2\end{aligned} \tag{3}$$

where $\dot{m} = \rho A V$ is the mass flowrate.

Note that $-w_1$ and $-w_2$ are used because both of these velocities are "down." Also, $-\dot{m}_1$ is used because it is associated with flow into the control volume. Similarly, $+\dot{m}_2$ is used because it is associated with flow out of the control volume. Solving Eq. 3 for the anchoring force, F_A, we obtain

$$F_A = \dot{m}_1 w_1 - \dot{m}_2 w_2 + \mathcal{W}_n + p_1 A_1 + \mathcal{W}_w - p_2 A_2 \tag{4}$$

From the conservation of mass equation, Eq. 5.10, we obtain

$$\dot{m}_1 = \dot{m}_2 = \dot{m} \tag{5}$$

which when combined with Eq. 4 gives

$$F_A = \dot{m}(w_1 - w_2) + \mathcal{W}_n + p_1 A_1 + \mathcal{W}_w - p_2 A_2 \tag{6}$$

It is instructive to note how the anchoring force is affected by the different actions involved. As expected, the nozzle weight, $\mathcal{W}_n$, the water weight, $\mathcal{W}_w$, and gage pressure force at section (1), $p_1 A_1$, all increase the anchoring force, while the gage pressure force at section (2), $p_2 A_2$, acts to decrease the anchoring force. The change in the vertical momentum flowrate, $\dot{m}(w_1 - w_2)$, will, in this instance, decrease the anchoring force because this change is negative ($w_2 > w_1$).

To complete this example we use quantities given in the problem statement to quantify the terms on the right-hand side of Eq. 6. From Eq. 5.6,

$$\dot{m} = \rho w_1 A_1 = \rho Q = (999 \text{ kg/m}^3)(0.6 \text{ liter/s})(10^{-3} \text{ m}^3/\text{liter}) = 0.599 \text{ kg/s} \tag{7}$$

and

$$w_1 = \frac{Q}{A_1} = \frac{Q}{\pi(D_1^2/4)} = \frac{(0.6 \text{ liter/s})(10^{-3} \text{ m}^3/\text{liter})}{\pi(16 \text{ mm})^2/4(1000^2 \text{ mm}^2/\text{m}^2)} = 2.98 \text{ m/s} \tag{8}$$

Also from Eq. 5.6,

$$w_2 = \frac{Q}{A_2} = \frac{Q}{\pi(D_2^2/4)} = \frac{(0.6 \text{ liter/s})(10^{-3} \text{ m}^3/\text{liter})}{\pi(5 \text{ mm})^2/4(1000^2 \text{ mm}^2/\text{m}^2)} = 30.6 \text{ m/s} \tag{9}$$

The weight of the nozzle, $\mathcal{W}_n$, can be obtained from the nozzle mass, m_n, with

$$\mathcal{W}_n = m_n g = (0.1 \text{ kg})(9.81 \text{ m/s}^2) = 0.981 \text{ N} \tag{10}$$

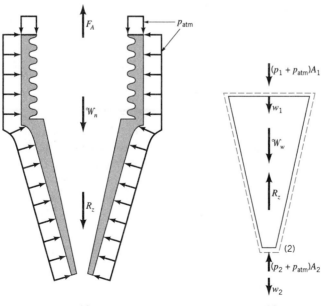

(c)   (d)   ■ FIGURE E5.6 *c* & *d*

The weight of the water in the control volume, $\mathcal{W}_w$, can be obtained from the water density, ρ, and the volume of water, $\mathcal{V}_w$, in the truncated cone of height h. That is,

$$\mathcal{W}_w = \rho \mathcal{V}_w g = \rho \tfrac{1}{12}\pi h(D_1^2 + D_2^2 + D_1 D_2)g$$

Thus,

$$\mathcal{W}_w = (999 \text{ kg/m}^3)\frac{1}{12}\pi\frac{(30 \text{ mm})}{(1000 \text{ mm/m})}$$
$$\times \left[\frac{(16 \text{ mm})^2 + (5 \text{ mm})^2 + (16 \text{ mm})(5 \text{ mm})}{(1000^2 \text{ mm}^2/\text{m}^2)}\right](9.81 \text{ m/s}^2) = 0.0278 \text{ N} \qquad \textbf{(11)}$$

The gage pressure at section (2), p_2, is zero since, as discussed in Section 3.6.1, when a subsonic flow discharges to the atmosphere as in the present situation, the discharge pressure is essentially atmospheric. The anchoring force, F_A, can now be determined from Eqs. 6 through 11 with

$$F_A = (0.599 \text{ kg/s})(2.98 \text{ m/s} - 30.6 \text{ m/s}) + 0.981 \text{ N}$$
$$+ (464 \text{ kPa})(1000 \text{ Pa/kPa})\frac{\pi(16 \text{ mm})^2}{4(1000^2 \text{ mm}^2/\text{m}^2)}$$
$$+ 0.0278 \text{ N} - 0$$

or

$$F_A = -16.5 \text{ N} + 0.981 \text{ N} + 93.3 \text{ N} + 0.0278 \text{ N} = 77.8 \text{ N} \qquad \textbf{(Ans)}$$

Since the anchoring force, F_A, is positive, it acts upward in the z direction. The nozzle would be pushed off the pipe if it were not fastened securely.

The control volume selected above to solve problems such as this is not unique. The following is an alternate solution that involves two other control volumes—one containing only the nozzle and the other containing only the water in the nozzle. These control volumes are shown in Figs. E5.6c and E5.6d along with the vertical forces acting on the contents of each control volume. The new force involved, R_z, represents the interaction between the water and the conical inside surface of the nozzle. It includes the net pressure and viscous forces at this interface.

Application of Eq. 5.17 to the contents of the control volume of Fig. E5.6c leads to

$$F_A = \mathcal{W}_n + R_z - p_{\text{atm}}(A_1 - A_2) \qquad \textbf{(12)}$$

The term $p_{\text{atm}}(A_1 - A_2)$ is the resultant force from the atmospheric pressure acting upon the exterior surface of the nozzle (i.e., that portion of the surface of the nozzle that is not in contact with the water). Recall that the pressure force on a curved surface (such as the exterior surface of the nozzle) is equal to the pressure times the projection of the surface area on a plane perpendicular to the axis of the nozzle. The projection of this area on a plane perpendicular to the z direction is $A_1 - A_2$. The effect of the atmospheric pressure on the internal area (between the nozzle and the water) is already included in R_z which represents the net force on this area.

Similarly, for the control volume of Fig. E5.6d we obtain

$$R_z = \dot{m}(w_1 - w_2) + \mathcal{W}_w + (p_1 + p_{\text{atm}})A_1 - (p_2 + p_{\text{atm}})A_2 \qquad \textbf{(13)}$$

where p_1 and p_2 are gage pressures. From Eq. 13 it is clear that the value of R_z depends on the value of the atmospheric pressure, p_{atm}, since $A_1 \neq A_2$. That is, we must use absolute pressure, not gage pressure, to obtain the correct value of R_z.

By combining Eqs. 12 and 13 we obtain the same result as before (Eq. 6) for F_A:

$$F_A = \dot{m}(w_1 - w_2) + \mathcal{W}_n + p_1 A_1 + \mathcal{W}_w - p_2 A_2$$

Note that although the force between the fluid and the nozzle wall, R_z, is a function of p_{atm}, the anchoring force, F_A, is not. That is, we were correct in using gage pressure when solving for F_A by means of the original control volume shown in Fig. E5.6b.

Several important generalities about the application of the linear momentum equation (Eq. 5.17) are apparent in the example just considered.

1. When the flow is uniformly distributed over a section of the control surface where flow into or out of the control volume occurs, the integral operations are simplified. Thus, one-dimensional flows are easier to work with than flows involving nonuniform velocity distributions.

2. Linear momentum is directional; it can have components in as many as three orthogonal coordinate directions. Furthermore, along any one coordinate, the linear momentum of a fluid particle can be in the positive or negative direction and thus be considered as a positive or a negative quantity. In Example 5.6, only the linear momentum in the z direction was considered (all of it was in the negative z direction and was hence treated as being negative).

3. The flow of positive or negative linear momentum *into* a control volume involves a negative $\mathbf{V} \cdot \hat{\mathbf{n}}$ product. Momentum flow *out* of the control volume involves a positive $\mathbf{V} \cdot \hat{\mathbf{n}}$ product. The correct algebraic sign ($+$ or $-$) to assign to momentum flow ($\mathbf{V}\rho\mathbf{V} \cdot \hat{\mathbf{n}} \, dA$) will depend on the sense of the velocity ($+$ in positive coordinate direction, $-$ in negative coordinate direction) and the $\mathbf{V} \cdot \hat{\mathbf{n}}$ product ($+$ for flow out of the control volume, $-$ for flow into the control volume). In Example 5.6, the momentum flow into the control volume past section (1) was a positive ($+$) quantity while the momentum flow out of the control volume at section (2) was a negative ($-$) quantity.

4. The time rate of change of the linear momentum of the contents of a nondeforming control volume (i.e., $\partial/\partial t \int_{cv} \mathbf{V}\rho \, d\mathcal{V}$) is zero for steady flow. The momentum problems considered in this text all involve steady flow.

5. If the control surface is selected so that it is perpendicular to the flow where fluid enters or leaves the control volume, the surface force exerted at these locations by fluid outside the control volume on fluid inside will be due to pressure. Furthermore, when subsonic flow exits from a control volume into the atmosphere, atmospheric pressure prevails at the exit cross section. In Example 5.6, the flow was subsonic and so we set the exit flow pressure at the atmospheric level. The continuity equation (Eq. 5.10) allowed us to evaluate the fluid flow velocities w_1 and w_2 at sections (1) and (2).

6. The forces due to atmospheric pressure acting on the control surface may need consideration as indicated by Eq. 13 for the reaction force between the nozzle and the fluid. When calculating the anchoring force, F_A, the forces due to atmospheric pressure on the control surface cancel each other (for example, after combining Eqs. 12 and 13 the atmospheric pressure forces are no longer involved) and gage pressures may be used.

7. The external forces have an algebraic sign, positive if the force is in the assigned positive coordinate direction and negative otherwise.

8. Only external forces acting on the contents of the control volume are considered in the linear momentum equation (Eq. 5.17). If the fluid alone is included in a control volume, reaction forces between the fluid and the surface or surfaces in contact with the fluid [wetted surface(s)] will need to be in Eq. 5.17. If the fluid and the wetted surface or surfaces are within the control volume, the reaction forces between fluid and wetted surface(s) do not appear in the linear momentum equation (Eq. 5.17) because they are internal, not external forces. The anchoring force that holds the wetted surface(s) in place is an external force, however, and must therefore be in Eq. 5.17.

9. The force required to anchor an object will generally exist in response to surface pressure and/or shear forces acting on the control surface, to a change in linear momentum flow through the control volume containing the object, and to the weight of the object and the fluid contained in the control volume. In Example 5.6 the nozzle anchoring force was required mainly because of pressure forces and partly because of a change in linear momentum flow associated with accelerating the fluid in the nozzle. The weight of the water and the nozzle contained in the control volume influenced the size of the anchoring force only slightly.

EXAMPLE 5.7

Water flows through a horizontal, 180° pipe bend as illustrated in Fig. E5.7a. The flow cross-sectional area is constant at a value of 0.1 ft^2 through the bend. The flow velocity everywhere in the bend is axial and 50 ft/s. The absolute pressures at the entrance and exit of the bend are 30 psia and 24 psia, respectively. Calculate the horizontal (x and y) components of the anchoring force required to hold the bend in place.

SOLUTION

Since we want to evaluate components of the anchoring force to hold the pipe bend in place, an appropriate control volume (see dashed line in Fig. E5.7a) contains the bend and the water in the bend at an instant. The horizontal forces acting on the contents of this control volume are identified in Fig. E5.7b. Note that the weight of the water is vertical (in the negative z direction) and does not contribute to the x and y components of the anchoring force. All of the horizontal normal and tangential forces exerted on the fluid and the pipe bend are resolved and combined into the two resultant components, F_{Ax} and F_{Ay}. These two forces act on the control volume contents, and thus for the x direction, Eq. 5.17 leads to

$$\int_{cs} u\rho \mathbf{V} \cdot \hat{\mathbf{n}} \, dA = F_{Ax} \tag{1}$$

At sections (1) and (2), the flow is in the y direction and therefore $u = 0$ at both cross sections. There is no x direction momentum flow into or out of the control volume and we conclude from Eq. 1 that $F_{Ax} = 0$.

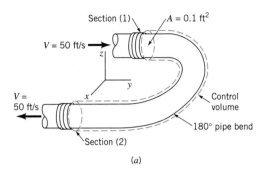

(a)

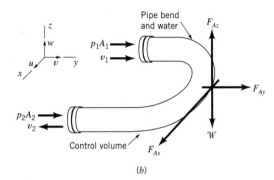

(b)

■ **FIGURE E5.7a & b**

For the y direction, we get from Eq. 5.17

$$\int_{cs} u\rho \mathbf{V} \cdot \hat{\mathbf{n}} \, dA = F_{Ay} + p_1 A_1 + p_2 A_2 \tag{2}$$

For one-dimensional flow, the surface integral in Eq. 2 is easy to evaluate and Eq. 2 becomes

$$(+v_1)(-\dot{m}_1) + (-v_2)(+\dot{m}_2) = F_{Ay} + p_1 A_1 + p_2 A_2 \tag{3}$$

Note that the y component of velocity is positive at section (1) but is negative at section (2). Also, the mass flowrate term is negative at section (1) (flow in) and is positive at section (2) (flow out). From the continuity equation (Eq. 5.10), we get

$$\dot{m} = \dot{m}_1 = \dot{m}_2 \tag{4}$$

and thus Eq. 3 can be written as

$$-\dot{m}(v_1 + v_2) = F_{Ay} + p_1 A_1 + p_2 A_2 \tag{5}$$

Solving Eq. 5 for F_{Ay} we obtain

$$F_{Ay} = -\dot{m}(v_1 + v_2) - p_1 A_1 - p_2 A_2 \tag{6}$$

From the given data we can calculate $\dot{m}$ from Eq. 5.6 as

$$\dot{m} = \rho_1 A_1 v_1 = (1.94 \text{ slugs/ft}^3)(0.1 \text{ ft}^2)(50 \text{ ft/s}) = 9.70 \text{ slugs/s}$$

For determining the anchoring force, F_{Ay}, the effects of atmospheric pressure cancel and thus gage pressures for p_1 and p_2 are appropriate. By substituting numerical values of variables into Eq. 6, we get

$$F_{Ay} = -(9.70 \text{ slugs/s})(50 \text{ ft/s} + 50 \text{ ft/s})\{1 \text{ lb}/[\text{slug}\cdot(\text{ft/s}^2)]\}$$
$$-(30 \text{ psia} - 14.7 \text{ psia})(144 \text{ in.}^2/\text{ft}^2)(0.1 \text{ ft}^2)$$
$$-(24 \text{ psia} - 14.7 \text{ psia})(144 \text{ in.}^2/\text{ft}^2)(0.1 \text{ ft}^2)$$
$$F_{Ay} = -970 \text{ lb} - 220 \text{ lb} - 134 \text{ lb} = -1324 \text{ lb} \qquad \text{(Ans)}$$

The negative sign for F_{Ay} is interpreted as meaning that the y component of the anchoring force is actually in the negative y direction, not the positive y direction as originally indicated in Fig. E5.7b.

As with Example 5.6, the anchoring force for the pipe bend is independent of the atmospheric pressure. However, the force that the bend puts on the fluid inside of it, R_y, depends on the atmospheric pressure. We can see this by using a control volume that surrounds only the fluid within the bend as shown in Fig. E5.7c. Application of the momentum equation to this situation gives

$$R_y = -\dot{m}(v_1 + v_2) - p_1 A_1 - p_2 A_2$$

where p_1 and p_2 must be in terms of absolute pressure because the force between the fluid and the pipe wall, R_y, is the complete pressure effect (i.e., absolute pressure).

Thus, we obtain

$$R_y = -(9.70 \text{ slugs/s})(50 \text{ ft/s} + 50 \text{ ft/s}) - (30 \text{ psia})(144 \text{ in.}^2/\text{ft}^2)(0.1 \text{ ft}^2)$$
$$-(24 \text{ psia})(144 \text{ in.}^2/\text{ft}^2)(0.1 \text{ ft}^2) \qquad \text{(7)}$$
$$= -1748 \text{ lb}$$

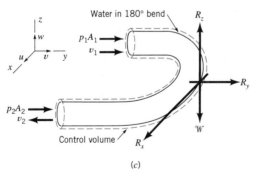

(c)

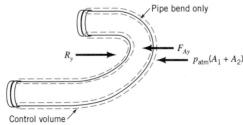

(d)

■ FIGURE E5.7c & d

We can use the control volume that includes just the pipe bend (without the fluid inside it) as shown in Fig. E5.7d to determine F_{Ay}, the anchoring force component in the y direction necessary to hold the bend stationary. The y component of the momentum equation applied to this control volume gives

$$F_{Ay} = R_y + p_{atm} (A_1 + A_2) \tag{8}$$

where R_y is given by Eq. 7. The $p_{atm} (A_1 + A_2)$ term represents the net pressure force on the outside portion of the control volume. Recall that the pressure force on the inside of the bend is accounted for by R_y. By combining Eqs. 7 and 8 we obtain

$$F_{Ay} = -1748 \text{ lb} + 14.7 \text{ lb/in.}^2 (0.1 \text{ ft}^2 + 0.1 \text{ ft}^2)(144 \text{ in.}^2/\text{ft}^2)$$
$$= -1324 \text{ lb}$$

in agreement with the original answer obtained using the control volume of Fig. E5.7b.

From Examples 5.5, 5.6, and 5.7 we see that changes in flow speed and/or direction result in a reaction force. Other types of problems that can be solved with the linear momentum equation (Eq. 5.17) are illustrated in the following examples.

EXAMPLE 5.8

If the flow of Example 5.2 is vertically upward, develop an expression for the fluid pressure drop that occurs between section (1) and section (2).

SOLUTION

A control volume (see dashed lines in Fig. E5.2) that includes only fluid from section (1) to section (2) is selected. The forces acting on the fluid in this control volume are identified in Fig. E5.8. The application of the axial component of Eq. 5.17 to the fluid in this control volume results in

$$\int_{cs} w\rho \mathbf{V} \cdot \hat{\mathbf{n}} \, dA = p_1 A_1 - R_z - \mathcal{W} - p_2 A_2 \tag{1}$$

where R_z is the resultant force of the wetted pipe wall on the fluid. Further, for uniform flow at section (1), and because the flow at section (2) is out of the control volume, Eq. 1 becomes

$$(+w_1)(-\dot{m}_1) + \int_{A_2} (+w_2)\rho(+w_2 \, dA_2) = p_1 A_1 - R_z - \mathcal{W} - p_2 A_2 \tag{2}$$

The positive direction is considered up. The surface integral over the cross-sectional area at section (2), A_2, is evaluated by using the parabolic velocity profile obtained in Example 5.2, $w_2 = 2w_1[1 - (r/R)^2]$, as

$$\int_{A_2} w_2 \rho w_2 \, dA_2 = \rho \int_0^R w_2^2 \, 2 \, \pi \, r \, dr = 2\pi\rho \int_0^R (2w_1)^2 \left[1 - \left(\frac{r}{R} \right)^2 \right]^2 r \, dr$$

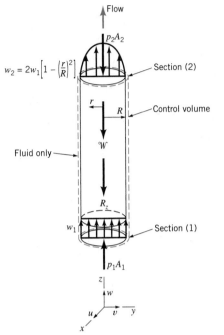

■ **FIGURE E5.8**

or

$$\int_{A_2} w_2 \rho w_2 \, dA_2 = 4 \, \pi \rho w_1^2 \frac{R^2}{3} \tag{3}$$

Combining Eqs. 2 and 3 we obtain

$$-w_1^2 \rho \pi R^2 + \tfrac{4}{3} w_1^2 \rho \pi R^2 = p_1 A_1 - R_z - \mathcal{W} - p_2 A_2 \tag{4}$$

Solving Eq. 4 for the pressure drop from section (1) to section (2), $p_1 - p_2$, we obtain

$$p_1 - p_2 = \frac{\rho w_1^2}{3} + \frac{R_z}{A_1} + \frac{\mathcal{W}}{A_1} \tag{Ans}$$

We see that the drop in pressure from section (1) to section (2) occurs because of the following:

1. The change in momentum flow between the two sections associated with going from a uniform velocity profile to a parabolic velocity profile.
2. Pipe wall friction.
3. The weight of the water column; a hydrostatic pressure effect.

 If the velocity profiles had been identically parabolic at sections (1) and (2), the momentum flowrate at each section would have been identical, a condition we call "fully developed" flow. Then, the pressure drop, $p_1 - p_2$, would be due only to pipe wall friction and the weight of the water column. If in addition to being fully developed, the flow involved negligible weight effects (for example, horizontal flow of liquids or the flow of gases in any direction) the drop in pressure between any two sections, $p_1 - p_2$, would be a result of pipe wall friction only.

EXAMPLE 5.9

A sluice gate across a channel of width b is shown in the closed and open positions in Figs. E5.9a and E5.9b. Is the anchoring force required to hold the gate in place larger when the gate is closed or when it is open?

SOLUTION

We will answer this question by comparing expressions for the horizontal reaction force, R_x, between the gate and the water when the gate is closed and when the gate is open. The control volume used in each case is indicated with dashed lines in Figs. E5.9a and E5.9b.

When the gate is closed, the horizontal forces acting on the contents of the control volume are identified in Fig. E5.9c. Application of Eq. 5.17 to the contents of this control volume yields

$$\int_{cs} u\rho \mathbf{V} \cdot \hat{\mathbf{n}} \, dA \overset{\nearrow 0 \text{ (no flow)}}{=} \tfrac{1}{2}\gamma H^2 b - R_x \tag{1}$$

Note that the hydrostatic pressure force, $\gamma H^2 b/2$, is used. From Eq. 1, the force exerted on the water by the gate (which is equal to the force necessary to hold the gate stationary) is

$$R_x = \tfrac{1}{2}\gamma H^2 b \tag{2}$$

which is equal in magnitude to the hydrostatic force exerted on the gate by the water.

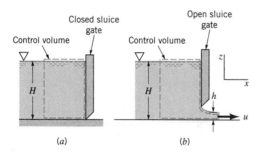

(a)   (b)

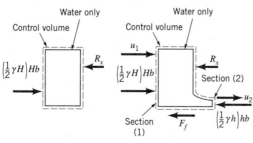

(c)   (d)

■ **FIGURE E5.9**

When the gate is open, the horizontal forces acting on the contents of the control volume are shown in Fig. E5.9d. Application of Eq. 5.17 to the contents of this control volume leads to

$$\int_{cs} u\rho \mathbf{V} \cdot \hat{\mathbf{n}} \, dA = \tfrac{1}{2}\gamma H^2 b - R_x - \tfrac{1}{2}\gamma h^2 b - F_f \tag{3}$$

Note that we have assumed that the pressure distribution is hydrostatic in the water at sections (1) and (2). (See Section 3.4.) Also, the frictional force between the channel bottom and the water is specified as F_f. The surface integral in Eq. 3 is nonzero only where there is flow across the control surface. With the assumption of uniform velocity distributions

$$\int_{cs} u\rho \mathbf{V} \cdot \hat{\mathbf{n}} \, dA = (u_1)\rho(-u_1)Hb + (+u_2)\rho(+u_2)hb \tag{4}$$

With $H \gg h$, the upstream velocity, u_1, is much less than u_2 so that the contribution of the incoming momentum flow to the control surface integral can be neglected. Thus, Eqs. 3 and 4 combine to form

$$\rho u_2^2 hb = \tfrac{1}{2}\gamma H^2 b - R_x - \tfrac{1}{2}\gamma h^2 b - F_f \tag{5}$$

Solving Eq. 5 for the reaction force, R_x, we obtain

$$R_x = \tfrac{1}{2}\gamma H^2 b - \tfrac{1}{2}\gamma h^2 b - F_f - \rho u_2^2 hb \tag{6}$$

Comparing the expressions for R_x (Eqs. 2 and 6) we conclude that the reaction force between the gate and the water (and therefore the anchoring force required to hold the gate in place) is smaller when the gate is open than when it is closed.   (Ans)

It should be clear from the preceding examples that fluid flows can lead to a reaction force in the following ways:

1. Linear momentum flow variation in direction and/or magnitude.
2. Fluid pressure forces.
3. Fluid friction forces.
4. Fluid weight.

The selection of a control volume is an important matter. An appropriate control volume can make a problem solution straightforward.

5.2.3 Derivation of the Moment-of-Momentum Equation

In many engineering problems, the moment of a force with respect to an axis, namely, *torque*, is important. Newton's second law of motion has already led to a useful relationship between forces and linear momentum flow. The linear momentum equation can also be used to solve problems involving torques. However, by forming the moment of the linear momentum and the resultant force associated with each particle of fluid with respect to a point in an inertial coordinate system, we obtain a *moment-of-momentum equation* that relates *torques* and *angular momentum flow* for the contents of a control volume.

We define $\mathbf{r}$ as the position vector from the origin of the inertial coordinate system to the fluid particle (Fig. 5.3) and form the moment of each side of Eq. 5.14 with respect to the origin of an inertial coordinate system. The result is

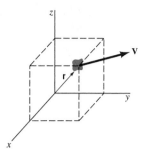

■ **FIGURE 5.3**   **Inertial coordinate system.**

$$\frac{D}{Dt}\int_{\text{sys}}(\mathbf{r}\times\mathbf{V})\rho\,d\mathcal{V} = \sum(\mathbf{r}\times\mathbf{F})_{\text{sys}} \tag{5.18}$$

or

the time rate of change of the $\quad$ = $\quad$ sum of the external torques
moment-of-momentum of the system $\qquad$ acting on the system

For a control volume that is instantaneously coincident with the system, the torques acting on the system and on the control volume contents will be identical:

$$\sum(\mathbf{r}\times\mathbf{F})_{\text{sys}} = \sum(\mathbf{r}\times\mathbf{F})_{\text{cv}} \tag{5.19}$$

Further, for the system and the contents of the coincident control volume that is fixed and nondeforming, the Reynolds transport theorem (Eq. 4.17) leads to

$$\frac{D}{Dt}\int_{\text{sys}}(\mathbf{r}\times\mathbf{V})\rho\,d\mathcal{V} = \frac{\partial}{\partial t}\int_{\text{cv}}(\mathbf{r}\times\mathbf{V})\rho\,d\mathcal{V} + \int_{\text{cs}}(\mathbf{r}\times\mathbf{V})\rho\mathbf{V}\cdot\hat{\mathbf{n}}\,dA \tag{5.20}$$

or

time rate of change		time rate of change		net rate of flow
of the moment-of-		of the moment-of-		of the moment-of-
momentum of the	=	momentum of the	+	momentum through
system		contents of the		the control
		control volume		surface

For a control volume that is fixed (and therefore inertial) and nondeforming, we combine Eqs. 5.18, 5.19, and 5.20 to obtain the moment-of-momentum equation:

$$\boxed{\frac{\partial}{\partial t}\int_{\text{cv}}(\mathbf{r}\times\mathbf{V})\rho\,d\mathcal{V} + \int_{\text{cs}}(\mathbf{r}\times\mathbf{V})\rho\mathbf{V}\cdot\hat{\mathbf{n}}\,dA = \sum(\mathbf{r}\times\mathbf{F})_{\substack{\text{contents of the}\\ \text{control volume}}}} \tag{5.21}$$

5.2.4   Application of the Moment-of-Momentum Equation

We simplify our use of Eq. 5.21 in several ways:

1. We assume that flows considered are one-dimensional (uniform distributions of average velocity at any section).
2. We confine ourselves to steady or steady-in-the-mean cyclical flows.
3. We work only with the component of Eq. 5.21 resolved along the axis of rotation.

Consider the rotating sprinkler sketched in Fig. 5.4. Because the direction and magnitude of the flow through the sprinkler from the inlet [section (1)] to the outlet [section (2)] of the arm changes, the water exerts a torque on the sprinkler head causing it to tend to rotate or to actually rotate in the direction shown, much like a turbine rotor. In applying the moment-of-momentum equation (Eq. 5.21) to this flow situation, we elect to use the fixed and non-deforming control volume shown in Fig. 5.4. The disk-shaped control volume contains within its boundaries the spinning or stationary sprinkler head and the portion of the water flowing through the sprinkler contained in the control volume at an instant. The control surface cuts through the sprinkler head's solid material so that the shaft torque that resists motion can be clearly identified. When the sprinkler is rotating, the flow field in the stationary control

V5.5 Rotating lawn sprinkler

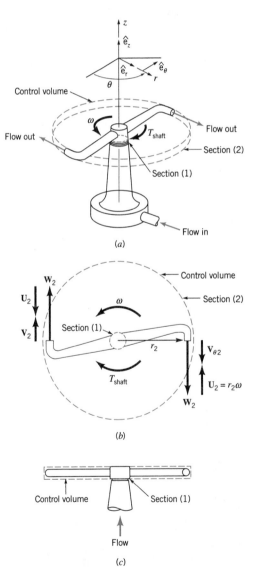

■ FIGURE 5.4 (*a*) Rotary water sprinkler. (*b*) Rotary water sprinkler, plan view. (*c*) Rotary water sprinkler, side view.

volume is cyclical and unsteady, but steady in the mean. We proceed to use the axial component of the moment-of-momentum equation (Eq. 5.21) to analyze this flow.

The integrand of the moment-of-momentum flow term in Eq. 5.21,

$$\int_{cs} (\mathbf{r} \times \mathbf{V})\rho \mathbf{V} \cdot \hat{\mathbf{n}} \, dA$$

can be nonzero only where fluid is crossing the control surface. Everywhere else on the control surface this term will be zero because $\mathbf{V} \cdot \hat{\mathbf{n}} = 0$. Water enters the control volume axially through the hollow stem of the sprinkler at section (1). At this portion of the control surface, the component of $\mathbf{r} \times \mathbf{V}$ resolved along the axis of rotation is zero because $\mathbf{r} \times \mathbf{V}$ and the axis of rotation are perpendicular. Thus, there is no axial moment-of-momentum flow in at section (1). Water leaves the control volume through each of the two nozzle openings at section (2). For the exiting flow, the magnitude of the axial component of $\mathbf{r} \times \mathbf{V}$ is $r_2 V_{\theta 2}$, where r_2 is the radius from the axis of rotation to the nozzle centerline and $V_{\theta 2}$ is the value of the tangential component of the velocity of the flow exiting each nozzle as observed from a frame of reference attached to the fixed and nondeforming control volume. The fluid velocity measured relative to a fixed control surface is an absolute velocity, $\mathbf{V}$. The velocity of the nozzle exit flow as viewed from the nozzle is called the relative velocity, $\mathbf{W}$. The absolute and relative velocities, $\mathbf{V}$ and $\mathbf{W}$, are related by the vector relationship

$$\mathbf{V} = \mathbf{W} + \mathbf{U} \tag{5.22}$$

where $\mathbf{U}$ is the velocity of the moving nozzle as measured relative to the fixed control surface.

The cross product and the dot product involved in the moment-of-momentum flow term of Eq. 5.21,

$$\int_{cs} (\mathbf{r} \times \mathbf{V})\rho \mathbf{V} \cdot \hat{\mathbf{n}} \, dA$$

can each result in a positive or negative value. For flow into the control volume, $\mathbf{V} \cdot \hat{\mathbf{n}}$ is negative. For flow out, $\mathbf{V} \cdot \hat{\mathbf{n}}$ is positive. The correct algebraic sign to assign the axis component of $\mathbf{r} \times \mathbf{V}$ can be ascertained by using the right-hand rule. The positive direction along the axis of rotation is the direction the thumb of the right hand points when it is extended and the remaining fingers are curled around the rotation axis in the positive direction of rotation as illustrated in Fig. 5.5. The direction of the axial component of $\mathbf{r} \times \mathbf{V}$ is similarly ascertained by noting the direction of the cross product of the radius from the axis of rotation, $r\hat{\mathbf{e}}_r$, and the tangential component of absolute velocity, $V_\theta \hat{\mathbf{e}}_\theta$. Thus, for the sprinkler of Fig. 5.4, we can state that

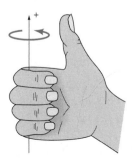

■ FIGURE 5.5   **Right-hand rule convention.**

$$\left[\int_{cs} (\mathbf{r} \times \mathbf{V})\rho \mathbf{V} \cdot \hat{\mathbf{n}} \, dA\right]_{axial} = (-r_2 V_{\theta 2})(+\dot{m}) \tag{5.23}$$

where, because of mass conservation, $\dot{m}$ is the total mass flowrate through both nozzles. As was demonstrated in Example 5.4, the mass flowrate is the same whether the sprinkler rotates or not. The correct algebraic sign of the axial component of $\mathbf{r} \times \mathbf{V}$ can be easily remembered in the following way: if $\mathbf{V}_\theta$ and $\mathbf{U}$ are in the same direction, use $+$; if $\mathbf{V}_\theta$ and $\mathbf{U}$ are in opposite directions, use $-$. For the sprinkler of Fig. 5.4

$$\sum \left[(\mathbf{r} \times \mathbf{F})_{\substack{\text{contents of the} \\ \text{control volume}}}\right]_{axial} = T_{shaft} \tag{5.24}$$

Note that we have entered T_{shaft} as a positive quantity in Eq. 5.24. This is equivalent to assuming that T_{shaft} is in the same direction as rotation.

For the sprinkler of Fig. 5.4, the axial component of the moment-of-momentum equation (Eq. 5.21) is, from Eqs. 5.23 and 5.24

$$-r_2 V_{\theta 2}\dot{m} = T_{shaft} \tag{5.25}$$

We interpret T_{shaft} being a negative quantity from Eq. 5.25 to mean that the shaft torque actually opposes the rotation of the sprinkler arms as shown in Fig. 5.4. The shaft torque, T_{shaft}, opposes rotation in all turbine devices.

We could evaluate the shaft power, $\dot{W}_{shaft}$, associated with shaft torque, T_{shaft}, by forming the product T_{shaft} and the rotational speed of the shaft, ω. Thus, from Eq. 5.25 we get

$$\dot{W}_{shaft} = T_{shaft}\omega = -r_2 V_{\theta 2}\dot{m}\omega \tag{5.26}$$

Since $r_2 \omega$ is the speed of each sprinkler nozzle, U, we can also state Eq. 5.26 in the form

$$\dot{W}_{shaft} = -U_2 V_{\theta 2}\dot{m} \tag{5.27}$$

Shaft work per unit mass, w_{shaft}, is equal to $\dot{W}_{shaft}/\dot{m}$. Dividing Eq. 5.27 by the mass flowrate, $\dot{m}$, we obtain

$$w_{shaft} = -U_2 V_{\theta 2} \tag{5.28}$$

V5.6 Impulse-type lawn sprinkler

Negative shaft work as in Eqs. 5.26, 5.27, and 5.28 is work out of the control volume, i.e., work done by the fluid on the rotor and thus its shaft.

EXAMPLE 5.10

Water enters a rotating lawn sprinkler through its base at the steady rate of 1000 ml/s as sketched in Fig. E5.10. The exit area of each of the two nozzles is 30 mm² and the flow leaving each nozzle is in the tangential direction. The radius from the axis of rotation to the centerline of each nozzle is 200 mm.

(a) Determine the resisting torque required to hold the sprinkler head stationary.
(b) Determine the resisting torque associated with the sprinkler rotating with a constant speed of 500 rev/min.
(c) Determine the speed of the sprinkler if no resisting torque is applied.

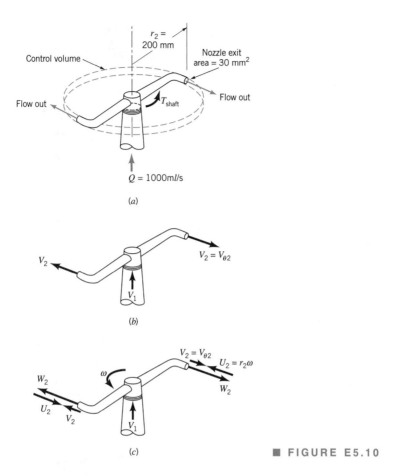

■ FIGURE E5.10

SOLUTION

To solve parts **(a)**, **(b)**, and **(c)** of this example we can use the same fixed and nondeforming, disk shaped control volume illustrated in Fig. 5.4. As is indicated in Fig. E5.10*a*, the only axial torque considered is the one resisting motion, T_{shaft}.

When the sprinkler head is held stationary as specified in part **(a)** of this example problem, the velocities of the fluid entering and leaving the control volume are shown in Fig. E5.10*b*. Equation 5.25 applies to the contents of this control volume. Thus

$$T_{shaft} = -r_2 V_{\theta 2} \dot{m} \tag{1}$$

Since the control volume is fixed and nondeforming and the flow exiting from each nozzle is tangential,

$$V_{\theta 2} = V_2 \tag{2}$$

Equations 1 and 2 give

$$T_{shaft} = -r_2 V_2 \dot{m} \tag{3}$$

In Example 5.4, we ascertained that $V_2 = 16.7$ m/s. Thus, from Eq. 3,

$$T_{shaft} = -\frac{(200 \text{ mm})(16.7 \text{ m/s})(1000 \text{ ml/s})(10^{-3} \text{ m}^3/\text{liter})(999 \text{ kg/m}^3)[1 (\text{N/kg})/(\text{m/s}^2)]}{(1000 \text{ mm/m})(1000 \text{ ml/liter})}$$

or

$$T_{shaft} = -3.34 \text{ N·m} \qquad \text{(Ans)}$$

When the sprinkler is rotating at a constant speed of 500 rpm, the flow field in the control volume is unsteady but cyclical. Thus, the flow field is steady in the mean. The velocities of the flow entering and leaving the control volume are as indicated in Fig. E5.10c. The absolute velocity of the fluid leaving each nozzle, V_2, is, from Eq. 5.22,

$$V_2 = W_2 - U_2 \qquad \text{(4)}$$

where

$$W_2 = 16.7 \text{ m/s}$$

as determined in Example 5.4. The speed of the nozzle, U_2, is obtained from

$$U_2 = r_2\omega \qquad \text{(5)}$$

Application of the axial component of the moment-of-momentum equation (Eq. 5.25) leads again to Eq. 3. From Eqs. 4 and 5,

$$V_2 = 16.7 \text{ m/s} - r_2\omega = 16.7 \text{ m/s} - \frac{(200 \text{ mm})(500 \text{ rev/min})(2\pi \text{ rad/rev})}{(1000 \text{ mm/m})(60 \text{ s/min})}$$

or

$$V_2 = 16.7 \text{ m/s} - 10.5 \text{ m/s} = 6.2 \text{ m/s}$$

Thus, using Eq. 3, we get

$$T_{shaft} = -\frac{(200 \text{ mm})(6.2 \text{ m/s})(1000 \text{ ml/s})(10^{-3} \text{ m}^3/\text{liter})(999 \text{ kg/m}^3)[1 (\text{N/kg})/(\text{m/s}^2)]}{(1000 \text{ mm/m})(1000 \text{ ml/liter})}$$

or

$$T_{shaft} = -1.24 \text{ N·m} \qquad \text{(Ans)}$$

Note that the resisting torque associated with sprinkler head rotation is much less than the resisting torque that is required to hold the sprinkler stationary.

When no resisting torque is applied to the rotating sprinkler head, a maximum constant speed of rotation will occur as demonstrated below. Application of Eqs. 3, 4, and 5 to the contents of the control volume results in

$$T_{shaft} = -r_2(W_2 - r_2\omega)\dot{m} \qquad \text{(6)}$$

For no resisting torque, Eq. 6 yields

$$0 = -r_2(W_2 - r_2\omega)\dot{m}$$

Thus,

$$\omega = \frac{W_2}{r_2} \qquad \text{(7)}$$

In Example 5.4, we learned that the relative velocity of the fluid leaving each nozzle, W_2, is the same regardless of the speed of rotation of the sprinkler head, ω, as long as the mass flowrate of the fluid, $\dot{m}$, remains constant. Thus, by using Eq. 7 we obtain

$$\omega = \frac{W_2}{r_2} = \frac{(16.7 \text{ m/s})(1000 \text{ mm/m})}{(200 \text{ mm})} = 83.5 \text{ rad/s}$$

or

$$\omega = \frac{(83.5 \text{ rad/s})(60 \text{ s/min})}{2 \pi \text{ rad/rev}} = 797 \text{ rpm} \qquad \text{(Ans)}$$

For this condition ($T_{shaft} = 0$), the water both enters and leaves the control volume with zero angular momentum.

In summary, we observe that the resisting torque associated with rotation is less than the torque required to hold a rotor stationary. Even in the absence of a resisting torque, the rotor maximum speed is finite.

When the moment-of-momentum equation (Eq. 5.21) is applied to a more general, one-dimensional flow through a rotating machine, we obtain

$$\boxed{T_{shaft} = (-\dot{m}_{in})(\pm r_{in}V_{\theta in}) + \dot{m}_{out}(\pm r_{out}V_{\theta out})} \qquad \textbf{(5.29)}$$

by applying the same kind of analysis used with the sprinkler of Fig. 5.4. The "−" is used with mass flowrate into the control volume, $\dot{m}_{in}$, and the "+" is used with the mass flowrate out of the control volume, $\dot{m}_{out}$, to account for the sign of the dot product, $\mathbf{V} \cdot \hat{\mathbf{n}}$, involved. Whether "+" or "−" is used with the rV_θ product depends on the direction of $(\mathbf{r} \times \mathbf{V})_{axial}$. A simple way to determine the sign of the rV_θ product is to compare the direction of the V_θ and the blade speed, U. If V_θ and U are in the same direction, then the rV_θ product is positive. If V_θ and U are in opposite directions, the rV_θ product is negative. The sign of the shaft torque is "+" if T_{shaft} is in the same direction along the axis of rotation as ω, and "−" otherwise.

The shaft power, $\dot{W}_{shaft}$, is related to shaft torque, T_{shaft}, by

$$\dot{W}_{shaft} = T_{shaft}\omega \qquad \textbf{(5.30)}$$

Thus, using Eq. 5.29 and 5.30 with a "+" for T_{shaft} in Eq. 5.29, we obtain

$$\dot{W}_{shaft} = (-\dot{m}_{in})(\pm r_{in}\omega V_{\theta in}) + \dot{m}_{out}(\pm r_{out}\omega V_{\theta out}) \qquad \textbf{(5.31)}$$

or since $r\omega = U$

$$\boxed{\dot{W}_{shaft} = (-\dot{m}_{in})(\pm U_{in} V_{\theta in}) + \dot{m}_{out}(\pm U_{out} V_{\theta out})} \qquad \textbf{(5.32)}$$

The "+" is used for the UV_θ product when U and V_θ are in the same direction; the "−" is used when U and V_θ are in opposite directions. Also, since $+T_{shaft}$ was used to obtain Eq. 5.32, when $\dot{W}_{shaft}$ is positive, power is into the control volume (e.g., pump), and when $\dot{W}_{shaft}$ is negative, power is out of the control volume (e.g., turbine).

The shaft work per unit mass, w_{shaft}, can be obtained from the shaft power, $\dot{W}_{\text{shaft}}$, by dividing Eq. 5.32 by the mass flowrate, $\dot{m}$. By conservation of mass,

$$\dot{m} = \dot{m}_{\text{in}} = \dot{m}_{\text{out}}$$

From Eq. 5.32, we obtain

$$w_{\text{shaft}} = -(\pm U_{\text{in}}V_{\theta\text{in}}) + (\pm U_{\text{out}}V_{\theta\text{out}}) \tag{5.33}$$

EXAMPLE 5.11

An air fan has a bladed rotor of 12-in. outside diameter and 10-in. inside diameter as illustrated in Fig. E5.11a. The height of each rotor blade is constant at 1 in. from blade inlet to outlet. The flowrate is steady, on a time-average basis, at 230 ft³/min and the absolute velocity of the air at blade inlet, $\mathbf{V}_1$, is radial. The blade discharge angle is 30° from the tangential direction. If the rotor rotates at a constant speed of 1725 rpm, estimate the power required to run the fan.

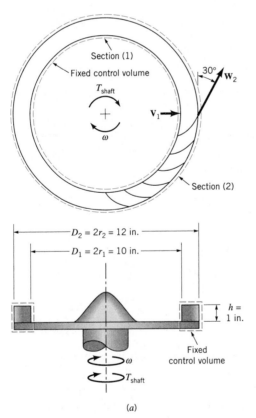

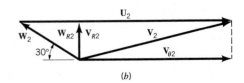

(a) (b)

■ **FIGURE E5.11**

SOLUTION

We select a fixed and nondeforming control volume that includes the rotating blades and the fluid within the blade row at an instant, as shown with a dashed line in Fig. E5.11a. The flow within this control volume is cyclical, but steady in the mean. The only torque we consider is the driving shaft torque, T_{shaft}. This torque is provided by a motor. We assume that the entering and leaving flows are each represented by uniformly distributed velocities and flow properties. Since shaft power is sought, Eq. 5.32 is appropriate. Application of Eq. 5.32 to the contents of the control volume in Fig. E5.11 gives

$$\dot{W}_{\text{shaft}} = (-\dot{m}_1)(\pm U_1 V_{\theta 1})^{\nearrow 0 \ (\mathbf{V}_1 \text{ is radial})} + \dot{m}_2(\pm U_2 V_{\theta 2}) \tag{1}$$

From Eq. 1 we see that to calculate fan power, we need mass flowrate, $\dot{m}$, rotor exit blade velocity, U_2, and fluid tangential velocity at blade exit, $V_{\theta 2}$. The mass flowrate, $\dot{m}$, is easily obtained from Eq. 5.6 as

$$\dot{m} = \rho Q = \frac{(2.38 \times 10^{-3} \text{ slug/ft}^3)(230 \text{ ft}^3/\text{min})}{(60 \text{ s/min})} = 0.00912 \text{ slug/s} \tag{2}$$

The rotor exit blade speed, U_2, is

$$U_2 = r_2 \omega = \frac{(6 \text{ in.})(1725 \text{ rpm})(2\pi \text{ rad/rev})}{(12 \text{ in./ft})(60 \text{ s/min})} = 90.3 \text{ ft/s} \tag{3}$$

To determine the fluid tangential speed at the fan rotor exit, $V_{\theta 2}$, we use Eq. 5.22 to get

$$\mathbf{V}_2 = \mathbf{W}_2 + \mathbf{U}_2 \tag{4}$$

The vector addition of Eq. 4 is shown in the form of a "velocity triangle" in Fig. E5.11b. From Fig. E5.11b, we can see that

$$V_{\theta 2} = U_2 - W_2 \cos 30° \tag{5}$$

To solve Eq. 5 for $V_{\theta 2}$ we need a value of W_2, in addition to the value of U_2 already determined (Eq. 3). To get W_2, we recognize that

$$W_2 \sin 30° = V_{R2} \tag{6}$$

where V_{R2} is the radial component of either $\mathbf{W}_2$ or $\mathbf{V}_2$. Also, using Eq. 5.6, we obtain

$$\dot{m} = \rho A_2 V_{R2} \tag{7}$$

or since

$$A_2 = 2\pi r_2 h \tag{8}$$

where h is the blade height, Eqs. 7 and 8 combine to form

$$\dot{m} = \rho 2\pi r_2 h V_{R2} \tag{9}$$

Taking Eqs. 6 and 9 together we get

$$W_2 = \frac{\dot{m}}{\rho 2\pi r_2 h \sin 30°} \tag{10}$$

Substituting known values into Eq. 10, we obtain

$$W_2 = \frac{(0.00912 \text{ slugs/s})(12 \text{ in./ft})(12 \text{ in./ft})}{(2.38 \times 10^{-3} \text{ slugs/ft}^3)2\pi(6 \text{ in.})(1 \text{ in.}) \sin 30°} = 29.3 \text{ ft/s}$$

By using this value of W_2 in Eq. 5 we get

$$V_{\theta 2} = U_2 - W_2 \cos 30°$$
$$= 90.3 \text{ ft/s} - (29.3 \text{ ft/s})(0.866) = 64.9 \text{ ft/s}$$

Equation 1 can now be used to obtain

$$\dot{W}_{\text{shaft}} = \dot{m}U_2 V_{\theta 2} = \frac{(0.00912 \text{ slug/s})(90.3 \text{ ft/s})(64.9 \text{ ft/s})}{[1(\text{slug·ft/s}^2)/\text{lb}][550(\text{ft·lb})/(\text{hp·s})]}$$

or

$$\dot{W}_{\text{shaft}} = 0.0972 \text{ hp} \tag{Ans}$$

Note that the "+" was used with the $U_2 V_{\theta 2}$ product because U_2 and $V_{\theta 2}$ are in the same direction. This result, 0.0972 hp, is the power that needs to be delivered through the fan shaft for the given conditions. Ideally, all of this power would go into the flowing air. However, because of fluid friction, only some of this power will produce a useful effect (e.g., pressure rise) in the air. How much useful effect depends on the efficiency of the energy transfer between the fan blades and the fluid.

5.3 First Law of Thermodynamics—The Energy Equation

5.3.1 Derivation of the Energy Equation

The first law of thermodynamics for a system is, in words

time rate of increase of the total stored energy of the system	=	net time rate of energy addition by heat transfer into the system	+	net time rate of energy addition by work transfer into the system

In symbolic form, this statement is

$$\frac{D}{Dt} \int_{\text{sys}} e\rho \, dV = \left(\sum \dot{Q}_{\text{in}} - \sum \dot{Q}_{\text{out}} \right)_{\text{sys}} + \left(\sum \dot{W}_{\text{in}} - \sum \dot{W}_{\text{out}} \right)_{\text{sys}}$$

or

$$\frac{D}{Dt} \int_{\text{sys}} e\rho \, dV = (\dot{Q}_{\text{net}}_{\text{in}} + \dot{W}_{\text{net}}_{\text{in}})_{\text{sys}} \tag{5.34}$$

Some of these variables deserve a brief explanation before proceeding further. The total stored energy per unit mass for each particle in the system, e, is related to the internal energy per unit mass, $\check{u}$, the kinetic energy per unit mass, $V^2/2$, and the potential energy per unit mass, gz, by the equation

$$e = \breve{u} + \frac{V^2}{2} + gz \tag{5.35}$$

The net rate of heat transfer into the system is denoted with $\dot{Q}_{net\ in}$, and the net rate of work transfer into the system is labeled $\dot{W}_{net\ in}$. Heat transfer and work transfer are considered "$+$" going into the system and "$-$" coming out.

For the control volume that is coincident with the system at an instant of time

$$(\dot{Q}_{net} + \dot{W}_{net})_{sys} = (\dot{Q}_{net} + \dot{W}_{net})_{coincident} \tag{5.36}$$
$$\quad\ {}_{in}\qquad {}_{in}\qquad\qquad {}_{in}\qquad\ {}_{in\ \ control}$$
$$\qquad\qquad\qquad\qquad\qquad\qquad\qquad\ {}_{volume}$$

Furthermore, for the system and the contents of the coincident control volume that is fixed and nondeforming, the Reynolds transport theorem (Eq. 4.17 with the parameter b set equal to e) allows us to conclude that

$$\frac{D}{Dt} \int_{sys} e\rho\, dV = \frac{\partial}{\partial t} \int_{cv} e\rho\, dV + \int_{cs} e\rho \mathbf{V} \cdot \hat{\mathbf{n}}\, dA \tag{5.37}$$

or in words,

the time rate of increase of the total stored energy of the system	=	the time rate of increase of the total stored energy of the contents of the control volume	+	the net rate of flow of the total stored energy out of the control volume through the control surface

Combining Eqs. 5.34, 5.36, and 5.37 we get the control volume formula for the first law of thermodynamics:

$$\boxed{\frac{\partial}{\partial t} \int_{cv} e\rho\, dV + \int_{cs} e\rho \mathbf{V} \cdot \hat{\mathbf{n}}\, dA = (\dot{Q}_{net} + \dot{W}_{net})_{cv}} \tag{5.38}$$
$$\qquad\qquad\qquad\qquad\qquad\qquad\qquad\qquad\qquad\ \ {}_{in}\qquad\ {}_{in}$$

The heat transfer rate, $\dot{Q}$, represents all of the ways in which energy is exchanged between the control volume contents and surroundings because of a temperature difference. Thus, radiation, conduction, and/or convection are possible. Heat transfer into the control volume is considered positive, heat transfer out is negative. In many engineering applications, the process is *adiabatic*; the heat transfer rate, $\dot{Q}$, is zero. The net heat transfer rate, $\dot{Q}_{net\ in}$, can also be zero when $\Sigma \dot{Q}_{in} - \Sigma \dot{Q}_{out} = 0$.

The work transfer rate, $\dot{W}$, also called *power*, is positive when work is done on the contents of the control volume by the surroundings. Otherwise, it is considered negative.

In many instances, work is transferred across the control surface by a moving shaft. In rotary devices such as turbines, fans, and propellers, a rotating shaft transfers work across that portion of the control surface that slices through the shaft. Since work is the dot product of force and related displacement, rate of work (or power) is the dot product of force and related displacement per unit time. For a rotating shaft, the power transfer, $\dot{W}_{shaft}$, is related to the shaft torque that causes the rotation, T_{shaft}, and the angular velocity of the shaft, ω, by the relationship

$$\dot{W}_{shaft} = T_{shaft}\omega$$

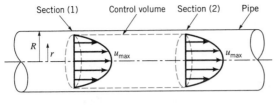

Section (1)   Control volume   Section (2)   Pipe

$$u_1 = u_{max}\left[1 - \left(\tfrac{r}{R}\right)^2\right] \qquad u_2 = u_{max}\left[1 - \left(\tfrac{r}{R}\right)^2\right]$$

■ **FIGURE 5.6** **Simple fully developed pipe flow.**

When the control surface cuts through the shaft material, the shaft torque is exerted by shaft material at the control surface. To allow for consideration of problems involving more than one shaft we use the notation

$$\dot{W}_{\substack{\text{shaft} \\ \text{net in}}} = \sum \dot{W}_{\substack{\text{shaft} \\ \text{in}}} - \sum \dot{W}_{\substack{\text{shaft} \\ \text{out}}} \tag{5.39}$$

Work transfer can also occur at the control surface when a force associated with fluid normal stress acts over a distance. Consider the simple pipe flow illustrated in Fig. 5.6 and the control volume shown. For this situation, the fluid normal stress, σ, is simply equal to the negative of fluid pressure, p, in all directions; that is, $\sigma = -p$.

The power transfer associated with normal stresses acting on a single fluid particle, $\delta\dot{W}_{\text{normal stress}}$, can be evaluated as the dot product of the normal stress force, $\delta\mathbf{F}_{\text{normal stress}}$, and the fluid particle velocity, $\mathbf{V}$, as

$$\delta\dot{W}_{\text{normal stress}} = \delta\mathbf{F}_{\text{normal stress}} \cdot \mathbf{V}$$

If the normal stress force is expressed as the product of local normal stress, $\sigma = -p$, and fluid particle surface area, $\hat{\mathbf{n}}\,\delta A$, the result is

$$\delta\dot{W}_{\text{normal stress}} = \sigma\hat{\mathbf{n}}\,\delta A \cdot \mathbf{V} = -p\hat{\mathbf{n}}\,\delta A \cdot \mathbf{V} = -p\mathbf{V} \cdot \hat{\mathbf{n}}\,\delta A$$

For all fluid particles on the control surface of Fig. 5.6 at the instant considered, power transfer due to fluid normal stress, $\dot{W}_{\text{normal stress}}$, is

$$\dot{W}_{\substack{\text{normal} \\ \text{stress}}} = \int_{cs} \sigma\mathbf{V} \cdot \hat{\mathbf{n}}\,dA = \int_{cs} -p\mathbf{V} \cdot \hat{\mathbf{n}}\,dA \tag{5.40}$$

Note that the value of $\dot{W}_{\text{normal stress}}$ for particles on the wetted inside surface of the pipe is zero because $\mathbf{V} \cdot \hat{\mathbf{n}}$ is zero there. Thus, $\dot{W}_{\text{normal stress}}$ can be nonzero only where fluid enters and leaves the control volume.

Work transfer can also occur at the control surface because of tangential stress forces. Rotating shaft work is transferred by tangential stresses in the shaft material. For a fluid particle, shear stress force power, $\delta\dot{W}_{\text{tangential stress}}$, can be evaluated as the dot product of tangential stress force, $\delta\mathbf{F}_{\text{tangential stress}}$, and the fluid particle velocity, $\mathbf{V}$. That is,

$$\delta\dot{W}_{\text{tangential stress}} = \delta\mathbf{F}_{\text{tangential stress}} \cdot \mathbf{V}$$

For the control volume of Fig. 5.6, the fluid particle velocity is zero everywhere on the wetted inside surface of the pipe. Thus, no tangential stress work is transferred across that portion of the control surface. Furthermore, where fluid crosses the control surface, the tangential stress force is perpendicular to the fluid particle velocity and therefore tangential stress work transfer is also zero there. In general, we select control volumes like the one of Fig. 5.6 and consider fluid tangential stress power transfer to be negligibly small.

Using the information we have developed about power, we can express the first law of thermodynamics for the contents of a control volume by combining Eqs. 5.38, 5.39, and 5.40 to obtain

$$\frac{\partial}{\partial t} \int_{cv} e\rho \, d\mathcal{V} + \int_{cs} e\rho \mathbf{V} \cdot \hat{\mathbf{n}} \, dA = \dot{Q}_{\substack{net \\ in}} + \dot{W}_{\substack{shaft \\ net \, in}} - \int_{cs} p\mathbf{V} \cdot \hat{\mathbf{n}} \, dA \qquad (5.41)$$

When the equation for total stored energy (Eq. 5.35) is considered with Eq. 5.41, we obtain the energy equation:

$$\frac{\partial}{\partial t} \int_{cv} e\rho \, d\mathcal{V} + \int_{cs} \left(\check{u} + \frac{p}{\rho} + \frac{V^2}{2} + gz \right) \rho \mathbf{V} \cdot \hat{\mathbf{n}} \, dA = \dot{Q}_{\substack{net \\ in}} + \dot{W}_{\substack{shaft \\ net \, in}} \qquad (5.42)$$

5.3.2 Application of the Energy Equation

For many applications, Eq. 5.42 can be simplified. For example, the term $\partial/\partial t \int_{cv} e\rho \, d\mathcal{V}$ represents the time rate of change of the total stored energy, e, of the contents of the control volume. This term is zero when the flow is steady. This term is also zero in the mean when the flow is steady in the mean (cyclical). Furthermore, if there is only one stream entering and leaving the control volume, and if the properties are all assumed to be uniformly distributed over the flow cross-sectional areas involved, the integration becomes simple and gives

$$\int_{cs} \left(\check{u} + \frac{p}{\rho} + \frac{V^2}{2} + gz \right) \rho \mathbf{V} \cdot \hat{\mathbf{n}} \, dA =$$

$$\left(\check{u} + \frac{p}{\rho} + \frac{V^2}{2} + gz \right)_{out} \dot{m}_{out} - \left(\check{u} + \frac{p}{\rho} + \frac{V^2}{2} + gz \right)_{in} \dot{m}_{in} \quad (5.43)$$

Uniform flow as described above will occur in an infinitesimally small diameter streamtube as illustrated in Fig. 5.7. This kind of streamtube flow is representative of the steady flow of a particle of fluid along a pathline.

Thus, Eq. 5.42 can be simplified with the help of Eqs. 5.8 and 5.43 to form

$$\dot{m} \left[\check{u}_{out} - \check{u}_{in} + \left(\frac{p}{\rho} \right)_{out} - \left(\frac{p}{\rho} \right)_{in} + \frac{V_{out}^2 - V_{in}^2}{2} + g(z_{out} - z_{in}) \right] = \dot{Q}_{\substack{net \\ in}} + \dot{W}_{\substack{shaft \\ net \, in}} \quad (5.44)$$

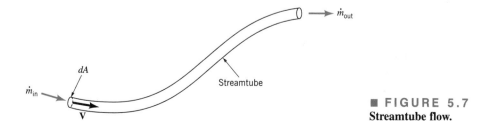

■ FIGURE 5.7
Streamtube flow.

We call Eq. 5.44 the *one-dimensional energy equation for steady-in-the-mean flow*. Note that Eq. 5.44 is valid for incompressible and compressible flows. Often, the fluid property called *enthalpy, $\check{h}$*, where

$$\check{h} = \check{u} + \frac{p}{\rho} \tag{5.45}$$

is used in Eq. 5.44. With enthalpy, the one-dimensional energy equation for steady-in-the-mean flow (Eq. 5.44) is

$$\dot{m}\left[\check{h}_{\text{out}} - \check{h}_{\text{in}} + \frac{V_{\text{out}}^2 - V_{\text{in}}^2}{2} + g(z_{\text{out}} - z_{\text{in}}) \right] = \dot{Q}_{\substack{\text{net} \\ \text{in}}} + \dot{W}_{\substack{\text{shaft} \\ \text{net in}}} \tag{5.46}$$

Equation 5.46 is often used for solving compressible flow problems.

EXAMPLE 5.12

A pump delivers water at a steady rate of 300 gal/min as shown in Fig. E5.12. Just upstream of the pump [section (1)] where the pipe diameter is 3.5 in., the pressure is 18 psi. Just downstream of the pump [section (2)] where the pipe diameter is 1 in., the pressure is 60 psi. The change in water elevation across the pump is zero. The rise in internal energy of water, $\check{u}_2 - \check{u}_1$, associated with a temperature rise across the pump is 3000 ft·lb/slug. If the pumping process is considered to be adiabatic, determine the power (hp) required by the pump.

SOLUTION

We include in our control volume the water contained in the pump between its entrance and exit sections. Application of Eq. 5.44 to the contents of this control volume on a time-average basis yields

$$\dot{m}\left[\check{u}_2 - \check{u}_1 + \left(\frac{p}{\rho}\right)_2 - \left(\frac{p}{\rho}\right)_1 + \frac{V_2^2 - V_1^2}{2} + \overset{\nearrow 0 \text{ (no elevation change)}}{g(z_2 - z_1)} \right]$$

$$= \overset{\nearrow 0 \text{ (adiabatic flow)}}{\dot{Q}_{\substack{\text{net} \\ \text{in}}}} + \dot{W}_{\substack{\text{shaft} \\ \text{net in}}} \tag{1}$$

We can solve directly for the power required by the pump, $\dot{W}_{\text{shaft net in}}$, from Eq. 1, after we first determine the mass flowrate, $\dot{m}$, the speed of flow into the pump, V_1, and the speed of the flow out of the pump, V_2. All other quantities in Eq. 1 are given in the problem statement. From Eq. 5.6, we get

$$\dot{m} = \rho Q = \frac{(1.94 \text{ slugs/ft}^3)(300 \text{ gal/min})}{(7.48 \text{ gal/ft}^3)(60 \text{ s/min})} = 1.30 \text{ slugs/s} \tag{2}$$

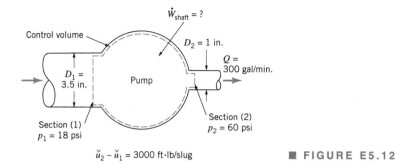

■ FIGURE E5.12

Also from Eq. 5.6,

$$V = \frac{Q}{A} = \frac{Q}{\pi D^2/4}$$

so

$$V_1 = \frac{Q}{A_1} = \frac{(300 \text{ gal/min})4(12 \text{ in./ft})^2}{(7.48 \text{ gal/ft}^3)(60 \text{ s/min})\pi(3.5 \text{ in.})^2} = 10.0 \text{ ft/s} \qquad (3)$$

and

$$V_2 = \frac{Q}{A_2} = \frac{(300 \text{ gal/min})4(12 \text{ in./ft})^2}{(7.48 \text{ gal/ft}^3)(60 \text{ s/min})\pi(1 \text{ in.})^2} = 123 \text{ ft/s} \qquad (4)$$

Substituting the values of Eqs. 2, 3, and 4 and values from the problem statement into Eq. 1 we obtain

$$\dot{W}_{\substack{\text{shaft} \\ \text{net in}}} = (1.30 \text{ slugs/s})\left[(3000 \text{ ft·lb/slug}) + \frac{(60 \text{ psi})(144 \text{ in.}^2/\text{ft}^2)}{(1.94 \text{ slugs/ft}^3)} \right.$$
$$\left. - \frac{(18 \text{ psi})(144 \text{ in.}^2/\text{ft}^2)}{(1.94 \text{ slugs/ft}^3)} + \frac{(123 \text{ ft/s})^2 - (10.0 \text{ ft/s})^2}{2[1 \text{ (slug·ft)/(lb·s}^2)]} \right]$$
$$\times \frac{1}{[550(\text{ft·lb/s})/\text{hp}]} = 32.2 \text{ hp} \qquad \text{(Ans)}$$

Of the total 32.2 hp, internal energy change accounts for 7.09 hp, the pressure rise accounts for 7.37 hp, and the kinetic energy increase accounts for 17.8 hp.

EXAMPLE 5.13

Steam enters a turbine with a velocity of 30 m/s and enthalpy, $\check{h}_1$, of 3348 kJ/kg (see Fig. E5.13). The steam leaves the turbine as a mixture of vapor and liquid having a velocity of 60 m/s and an enthalpy of 2550 kJ/kg. If the flow through the turbine is adiabatic and changes in elevation are negligible, determine the work output involved per unit mass of steam through-flow.

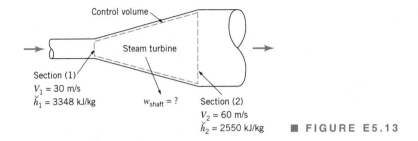

■ **FIGURE E5.13**

Solution

We use a control volume that includes the steam in the turbine from the entrance to the exit as shown in Fig. E5.13. Applying Eq. 5.46 to the steam in this control volume we get

$$\dot{m}\left[\check{h}_2 - \check{h}_1 + \frac{V_2^2 - V_1^2}{2} + g(z_2 - z_1)\right] = \dot{Q}_{\substack{net \\ in}} + \dot{W}_{\substack{shaft \\ net\ in}} \qquad (1)$$

with the annotations: "0 (elevation change is negligible)" pointing to $g(z_2 - z_1)$ and "0 (adiabatic flow)" pointing to $\dot{Q}_{net\ in}$.

The work output per unit mass of steam through-flow, $w_{shaft\ net\ in}$, can be obtained by dividing Eq. 1 by the mass flow rate, $\dot{m}$, to obtain

$$w_{\substack{shaft \\ net\ in}} = \frac{\dot{W}_{\substack{shaft \\ net\ in}}}{\dot{m}} = \check{h}_2 - \check{h}_1 + \frac{V_2^2 - V_1^2}{2} \qquad (2)$$

Since $w_{shaft\ net\ out} = -w_{shaft\ net\ in}$, we obtain

$$w_{\substack{shaft \\ net\ out}} = \check{h}_1 - \check{h}_2 + \frac{V_1^2 - V_2^2}{2}$$

or

$$w_{\substack{shaft \\ net\ out}} = 3348\ \text{kJ/kg} - 2550\ \text{kJ/kg}$$

$$+ \frac{[(30\ \text{m/s})^2 - (60\ \text{m/s})^2][1\ \text{J/(N·m)}]}{2[1(\text{kg·m})/(\text{N·s}^2)](1000\ \text{J/kJ})}$$

Thus

$$w_{\substack{shaft \\ net\ out}} = 3348\ \text{kJ/kg} - 2550\ \text{kJ/kg} - 1.35\ \text{kJ/kg} = 797\ \text{kJ/kg} \qquad \text{(Ans)}$$

Note that in this particular example, the change in kinetic energy is small in comparison to the difference in enthalpy involved. This is often true in applications involving steam turbines. To determine the power output, $\dot{W}_{shaft}$, we must know the mass flowrate, $\dot{m}$.

5.3.3 Comparison of the Energy Equation with the Bernoulli Equation

For steady, incompressible flow with zero shaft power, the energy equation (Eq. 5.44) becomes

$$\dot{m}\left[\breve{u}_{\text{out}} - \breve{u}_{\text{in}} + \frac{p_{\text{out}}}{\rho} - \frac{p_{\text{in}}}{\rho} + \frac{V_{\text{out}}^2 - V_{\text{in}}^2}{2} + g(z_{\text{out}} - z_{\text{in}})\right] = \dot{Q}_{\substack{\text{net}\\\text{in}}} \tag{5.47}$$

Dividing Eq. 5.47 by the mass flowrate, $\dot{m}$, and rearranging terms we obtain

$$\frac{p_{\text{out}}}{\rho} + \frac{V_{\text{out}}^2}{2} + gz_{\text{out}} = \frac{p_{\text{in}}}{\rho} + \frac{V_{\text{in}}^2}{2} + gz_{\text{in}} - (\breve{u}_{\text{out}} - \breve{u}_{\text{in}} - q_{\substack{\text{net}\\\text{in}}}) \tag{5.48}$$

where

$$q_{\substack{\text{net}\\\text{in}}} = \frac{\dot{Q}_{\text{net in}}}{\dot{m}}$$

is the heat transfer rate per mass flowrate, or heat transfer per unit mass. Note that Eq. 5.48 involves energy per unit mass and is applicable to one-dimensional flow of a single stream of fluid between two sections or flow along a streamline between two sections.

If the steady, incompressible flow we are considering also involves negligible viscous effects (frictionless flow), then the Bernoulli equation, Eq. 3.6, can be used to describe what happens between two sections in the flow as

$$p_{\text{out}} + \frac{\rho V_{\text{out}}^2}{2} + \gamma z_{\text{out}} = p_{\text{in}} + \frac{\rho V_{\text{in}}^2}{2} + \gamma z_{\text{in}} \tag{5.49}$$

where $\gamma = \rho g$ is the specific weight of the fluid. To get Eq. 5.49 in terms of energy per unit mass, so that it can be compared directly with Eq. 5.48, we divide Eq. 5.49 by density, ρ, and obtain

$$\frac{p_{\text{out}}}{\rho} + \frac{V_{\text{out}}^2}{2} + gz_{\text{out}} = \frac{p_{\text{in}}}{\rho} + \frac{V_{\text{in}}^2}{2} + gz_{\text{in}} \tag{5.50}$$

A comparison of Eqs. 5.48 and 5.50 prompts us to conclude that

$$\breve{u}_{\text{out}} - \breve{u}_{\text{in}} - q_{\substack{\text{net}\\\text{in}}} = 0 \tag{5.51}$$

when the steady, incompressible flow is frictionless. For steady, incompressible flow with friction, we learn from experience that

$$\breve{u}_{\text{out}} - \breve{u}_{\text{in}} - q_{\substack{\text{net}\\\text{in}}} > 0 \tag{5.52}$$

In Eqs. 5.48 and 5.50, we consider the combination of variables

$$\frac{p}{\rho} + \frac{V^2}{2} + gz$$

as equal to *useful* or *available energy*. Thus, from inspection of Eqs. 5.48 and 5.50, we can conclude that $\breve{u}_{\text{out}} - \breve{u}_{\text{in}} - q_{\text{net in}}$ represents the *loss* of useful or available energy that occurs in an incompressible fluid flow because of friction. In equation form we have

$$\breve{u}_{\text{out}} - \breve{u}_{\text{in}} - q_{\substack{\text{net}\\\text{in}}} = \text{loss} \tag{5.53}$$

For a frictionless flow, Eqs. 5.48 and 5.50 tell us that loss equals zero.

It is often convenient to express Eq. 5.48 in terms of loss as

$$\frac{p_{\text{out}}}{\rho} + \frac{V_{\text{out}}^2}{2} + gz_{\text{out}} = \frac{p_{\text{in}}}{\rho} + \frac{V_{\text{in}}^2}{2} + gz_{\text{in}} - \text{loss} \qquad \textbf{(5.54)}$$

V5.7 Energy transfer

An example of the application of Eq. 5.54 follows.

*E*XAMPLE 5.14

Compare the volume flowrates associated with two different vent configurations, a cylindrical hole in the wall having a diameter of 120 mm and the same diameter cylindrical hole in the wall but with a well-rounded entrance (see Fig. E5.14). The room pressure is held constant at 1.0 kPa above atmospheric pressure. Both vents exhaust into the atmosphere. As discussed in Section 8.4.2, the loss in available energy associated with flow through the cylindrical vent from the room to the vent exit is $0.5V_2^2/2$ where V_2 is the uniformly distributed exit velocity of air. The loss in available energy associated with flow through the rounded entrance vent from the room to the vent exit is $0.05V_2^2/2$, where V_2 is the uniformly distributed exit velocity of air.

*S*OLUTION

We use the control volume for each vent sketched in Fig. E5.14. What is sought is the flowrate, $Q = A_2V_2$, where A_2 is the vent exit cross-sectional area, and V_2 is the uniformly distributed exit velocity. For both vents, application of Eq. 5.54 leads to

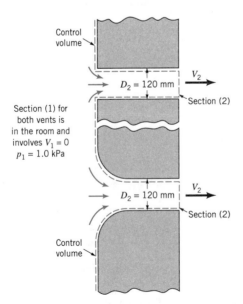

■ FIGURE E5.14

$$\frac{p_2}{\rho} + \frac{V_2^2}{2} + g\cancel{z_2} \overset{0 \text{ (no elevation change)}}{=} \frac{p_1}{\rho} + \cancel{\frac{V_1^2}{2}} + g\cancel{z_1} - {}_1\text{loss}_2$$
$$0(V_1 \approx 0)$$

(1)

where ${}_1\text{loss}_2$ is the loss between sections (1) and (2). Solving Eq. 1 for V_2 we get

$$V_2 = \sqrt{2\left[\left(\frac{p_1 - p_2}{\rho}\right) - {}_1\text{loss}_2\right]}$$

(2)

Since

$$_1\text{loss}_2 = K_L \frac{V_2^2}{2}$$

(3)

where K_L is the loss coefficient ($K_L = 0.5$ and 0.05 for the two vent configurations involved), we can combine Eqs. 2 and 3 to get

$$V_2 = \sqrt{2\left[\left(\frac{p_1 - p_2}{\rho}\right) - K_L \frac{V_2^2}{2}\right]}$$

(4)

Solving Eq. 4 for V_2 we obtain

$$V_2 = \sqrt{\frac{p_1 - p_2}{\rho[(1 + K_L)/2]}}$$

(5)

Therefore, for flowrate, Q, we obtain

$$Q = A_2 V_2 = \frac{\pi D_2^2}{4}\sqrt{\frac{p_1 - p_2}{\rho[(1 + K_L)/2]}}$$

(6)

For the rounded entrance cylindrical vent, Eq. 6 gives

$$Q = \frac{\pi (120 \text{ mm})^2}{4(1000 \text{ mm/m})^2}\sqrt{\frac{(1.0 \text{ kPa})(1000 \text{ Pa/kPa})[1(\text{N/m}^2)/(\text{Pa})]}{(1.23 \text{ kg/m}^3)[(1 + 0.05)/2][1(\text{N}\cdot\text{s}^2)/(\text{kg}\cdot\text{m})]}}$$

or

$$Q = 0.445 \text{ m}^3/\text{s}$$

(Ans)

For the cylindrical vent, Eq. 6 gives us

$$Q = \frac{\pi (120 \text{ mm})^2}{4(1000 \text{ mm/m})^2}\sqrt{\frac{(1.0 \text{ kPa})(1000 \text{ Pa/kPa})[1(\text{N/m}^2)/(\text{Pa})]}{(1.23 \text{ kg/m}^3)[(1 + 0.5)/2][1(\text{N}\cdot\text{s}^2)/(\text{kg}\cdot\text{m})]}}$$

or

$$Q = 0.372 \text{ m}^3/\text{s}$$

(Ans)

Note that the rounded entrance vent passes more air than the cylindrical vent because the loss associated with the rounded entrance vent is less than with the cylindrical vent.

An important group of fluid mechanics problems involves one-dimensional, incompressible, steady-in-the-mean flow with friction and shaft work. Included in this category are constant density flows through pumps, blowers, fans, and turbines. For this kind of flow, Eq. 5.44 becomes

$$\dot{m}\left[\check{u}_{\text{out}} - \check{u}_{\text{in}} + \frac{p_{\text{out}}}{\rho} - \frac{p_{\text{in}}}{\rho} + \frac{V_{\text{out}}^2 - V_{\text{in}}^2}{2} + g(z_{\text{out}} - z_{\text{in}})\right] = \dot{Q}_{\text{net}\atop\text{in}} + \dot{W}_{\text{shaft}\atop\text{net in}} \qquad (5.55)$$

We divide Eq. 5.55 by the mass flowrate, use the facts that loss $= \check{u}_{\text{out}} - \check{u}_{\text{in}} - q_{\text{net in}}$ and work per unit mass $= w_{\text{shaft net in}} = \dot{W}_{\text{shaft net in}}/\dot{m}$ to obtain

$$\frac{p_{\text{out}}}{\rho} + \frac{V_{\text{out}}^2}{2} + gz_{\text{out}} = \frac{p_{\text{in}}}{\rho} + \frac{V_{\text{in}}^2}{2} + gz_{\text{in}} + w_{\text{shaft}\atop\text{net in}} - \text{loss} \qquad (5.56)$$

This is a form of the energy equation for steady-in-the-mean flow that is often used for incompressible flow problems. It is sometimes called the *mechanical energy* equation or the *extended Bernoulli* equation. Note that Eq. 5.56 involves energy per unit mass (ft·lb/slug $=$ ft^2/s^2 or N·m/kg $=$ m^2/s^2).

If Eq. 5.56 is divided by the acceleration of gravity, g, we get

$$\frac{p_{\text{out}}}{\gamma} + \frac{V_{\text{out}}^2}{2g} + z_{\text{out}} = \frac{p_{\text{in}}}{\gamma} + \frac{V_{\text{in}}^2}{2g} + z_{\text{in}} + h_s - h_L \qquad (5.57)$$

where

$$h_s = w_{\text{shaft net in}}/g = \frac{\dot{W}_{\text{shaft}\atop\text{net in}}}{\dot{m}g} = \frac{\dot{W}_{\text{shaft}\atop\text{net in}}}{\gamma Q} \qquad (5.58)$$

V5.8 Water plant aerator

and $h_L = \text{loss}/g$. Equation 5.57 involves *energy per unit weight* (ft·lb/lb $=$ ft or N·m/N $=$ m). In Section 3.7, we introduced the notion of "head," which is energy per unit weight. Units of length (e.g., ft, m) are used to quantify the amount of head involved. If a turbine is in the control volume, the notation $h_s = -h_T$ (with $h_T > 0$) is sometimes used, particularly in the field of hydraulics. For a pump in the control volume, $h_s = h_P$. The quantity h_T is termed the *turbine head* and h_P is the *pump head*. The loss term, h_L, is often referred to as *head loss*.

EXAMPLE 5.15

An axial-flow ventilating fan driven by a motor that delivers 0.4 kW of power to the fan blades produces a 0.6-m-diameter axial stream of air having a speed of 12 m/s. The flow upstream of the fan involves negligible speed. Determine how much of the work to the air actually produces a useful effect, that is, a rise in available energy and estimate the fluid mechanical efficiency of this fan.

SOLUTION

We select a fixed and nondeforming control volume as is illustrated in Fig. E5.15. The application of Eq. 5.56 to the contents of this control volume leads to

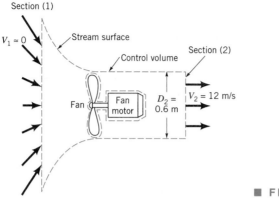

Section (1)

$V_1 \approx 0$

Stream surface

Control volume

Section (2)

Fan

Fan motor

$D_2 = 0.6$ m

$V_2 = 12$ m/s

■ FIGURE E5.15

$$w_{\substack{\text{shaft} \\ \text{net in}}} - \text{loss} = \overbrace{\left(\cancel{\frac{p_2}{\rho}} + \frac{V_2^2}{2} + \cancel{g z_2}\right)}^{0 \text{ (atmospheric pressures cancel)}} - \left(\cancel{\frac{p_1}{\rho}} + \cancel{\frac{V_1^2}{2}}^{\,0(V_1 \approx 0)} + \cancel{g z_1}\right) \tag{1}$$

0 (no elevation change)

where $w_{\text{shaft net in}} - \text{loss}$ is the amount of work added to the air that produces a useful effect. Equation 1 leads to

$$w_{\substack{\text{shaft} \\ \text{net in}}} - \text{loss} = \frac{V_2^2}{2} = \frac{(12 \text{ m/s})^2}{2[1(\text{kg·m})/(\text{N·s}^2)]} = 72.0 \text{ N·m/kg} \qquad \textbf{(2)} \quad \textbf{(Ans)}$$

A reasonable estimate of *efficiency*, η, would be the ratio of amount of work that produces a useful effect, Eq. 2, to the amount of work delivered to the fan blades. That is

$$\eta = \frac{w_{\substack{\text{shaft} \\ \text{net in}}} - \text{loss}}{w_{\substack{\text{shaft} \\ \text{net in}}}} \tag{3}$$

To calculate the efficiency we need a value of $w_{\text{shaft net in}}$, which is related to the power delivered to the blades, $\dot{W}_{\text{shaft net in}}$. We note that

$$w_{\substack{\text{shaft} \\ \text{net in}}} = \frac{\dot{W}_{\substack{\text{shaft} \\ \text{net in}}}}{\dot{m}} \tag{4}$$

where the mass flowrate, $\dot{m}$, is (from Eq. 5.6)

$$\dot{m} = \rho A V = \rho \frac{\pi D_2^2}{4} V_2 \tag{5}$$

For fluid density, ρ, we use 1.23 kg/m³ (standard air) and thus from Eqs. 4 and 5 we obtain

$$w_{\substack{\text{shaft} \\ \text{net in}}} = \frac{\dot{W}_{\substack{\text{shaft} \\ \text{net in}}}}{(\rho \pi D_2^2/4)V_2} = \frac{(0.4 \text{ kW})[1000 \text{ (N·m)/(s·kW)}]}{(1.23 \text{ kg/m}^3)[(\pi)(0.6 \text{ m})^2/4](12 \text{ m/s})}$$

or

$$w_{\substack{\text{shaft} \\ \text{net in}}} = 95.8 \text{ N·m/kg} \tag{6}$$

From Eqs. 2, 3, and 6 we obtain

$$\eta = \frac{72.0 \text{ N·m/kg}}{95.8 \text{ N·m/kg}} = 0.752 \quad \text{(Ans)}$$

Note that only 75% of the power that was delivered to the air resulted in a useful effect, and thus 25% of the shaft power is lost to air friction.

EXAMPLE 5.16

The pump shown in Fig. E5.16 adds 10 horsepower to the water as it pumps 2 ft^3/s from the lower lake to the upper lake. The elevation difference between the lake surfaces is 30 ft. Determine the head loss and power loss associated with this flow.

SOLUTION

The energy equation (Eq. 5.57) for this flow is

$$\frac{p_A}{\gamma} + \frac{V_A^2}{2g} + z_A = \frac{p_B}{\gamma} + \frac{V_B^2}{2g} + z_B + h_s - h_L \quad \text{(1)}$$

where points A and B (corresponding to "out" and "in" in Eq. 5.57) are located on the lake surfaces. Thus, $p_A = p_B = 0$ and $V_A = V_B = 0$ so that Eq. 1 becomes

$$h_L = h_s + z_B - z_A \quad \text{(2)}$$

where $z_B = 0$ and $z_A = 30$ ft. The pump head is obtained from Eq. 5.58 as

$$
\begin{aligned}
h_s &= \dot{W}_{\text{shaft net in}}/\gamma Q \\
&= (10 \text{ hp})(550 \text{ ft·lb/s/hp})/(62.4 \text{ lb/ft}^3)(2 \text{ ft}^3/\text{s}) \\
&= 44.1 \text{ ft}
\end{aligned}
$$

Hence, from Eq. 2,

$$h_L = 44.1 \text{ ft} - 30 \text{ ft} = 14.1 \text{ ft} \quad \text{(Ans)}$$

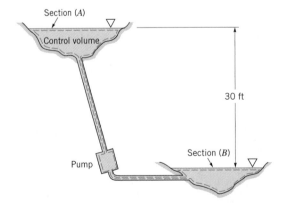

■ FIGURE E5.16

Note that in this example the purpose of the pump is to lift the water (a 30 ft head) and over-come the head loss (a 14.1 ft head); it does not, overall, alter the water's pressure or veloc-ity.

The power lost due to friction can be obtained from Eq. 5.58 as

$$\dot{W}_{loss} = \gamma Q h_L = (62.4 \text{ lb/ft}^3)(2 \text{ ft}^3/\text{s})(14.1 \text{ ft})$$
$$= 1760 \text{ ft·lb/s} \ (1 \text{ hp}/550 \text{ ft·lb/s}) \qquad \text{(Ans)}$$
$$= 3.20 \text{ hp}$$

The remaining 10 hp $-$ 3.20 hp $=$ 6.80 hp that the pump adds to the water is used to lift the water from the lower to the upper lake. This energy is not "lost," but is stored as potential energy.

5.3.4   Application of the Energy Equation to Nonuniform Flows

The forms of the energy equation discussed in Sections 5.3.2 and 5.3.3 are applicable to one-dimensional flows, flows that are approximated with uniform velocity distributions where fluid crosses the control surface.

If the velocity profile at any section where flow crosses the control surface is not uniform, inspection of the energy equation for a control volume, Eq. 5.42, suggests that the integral

$$\int_{cs} \frac{V^2}{2} \rho \mathbf{V} \cdot \hat{\mathbf{n}} \ dA$$

will require special attention. The result is that the kinetic energy term is slightly modified. For example, for nonuniform velocity profiles, the energy equation on an energy per unit mass basis (Eq. 5.56) is

$$\frac{p_{out}}{\rho} + \frac{\alpha_{out} \overline{V}_{out}^2}{2} + g z_{out} = \frac{p_{in}}{\rho} + \frac{\alpha_{in} \overline{V}_{in}^2}{2} + g z_{in} + w_{\substack{shaft \\ net \ in}} - \text{loss} \qquad \textbf{(5.59)}$$

where α is the *kinetic energy coefficient* and $\overline{V}$ is the average velocity (see Eq. 5.7). It can be shown that for any velocity profile, $\alpha \geq 1$, with $\alpha = 1$ only for uniform flow. However, for many practical applications $\alpha \approx 1.0$.

EXAMPLE 5.17

The small fan shown in Fig. E5.17 moves air at a mass flowrate of 0.1 kg/min. Upstream of the fan, the pipe diameter is 60 mm, the flow is laminar, the velocity distribution is para-bolic, and the kinetic energy coefficient, α_1, is equal to 2.0. Downstream of the fan, the pipe diameter is 30 mm, the flow is turbulent, the velocity profile is quite uniform, and the ki-netic energy coefficient, α_2, is equal to 1.08. If the rise in static pressure across the fan is 0.1 kPa and the fan motor draws 0.14 W, compare the value of loss calculated: (a) assuming uni-form velocity distributions, (b) considering actual velocity distributions.

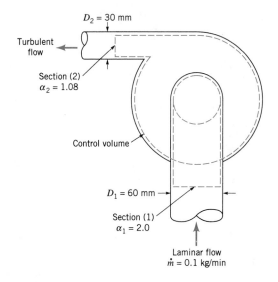

SOLUTION

Application of Eq. 5.59 to the contents of the control volume shown in Fig. E5.17 leads to

$$\frac{p_2}{\rho} + \frac{\alpha_2 \overline{V}_2^2}{2} + \cancel{gz_2}^{\text{0 (change in } gz \text{ is negligible)}} = \frac{p_1}{\rho} + \frac{\alpha_1 \overline{V}_1^2}{2} + \cancel{gz_1} - \text{loss} + w_{\substack{\text{shaft} \\ \text{net in}}} \qquad (1)$$

or solving Eq. 1 for loss we get

$$\text{loss} = w_{\substack{\text{shaft} \\ \text{net in}}} - \left(\frac{p_2 - p_1}{\rho}\right) + \frac{\alpha_1 \overline{V}_1^2}{2} - \frac{\alpha_2 \overline{V}_2^2}{2} \qquad (2)$$

To proceed further, we need values of $w_{\text{shaft net in}}$, $\overline{V}_1$, and $\overline{V}_2$. These quantities can be obtained as follows. For shaft work

$$w_{\substack{\text{shaft} \\ \text{net in}}} = \frac{\text{power to fan motor}}{\dot{m}}$$

or

$$w_{\substack{\text{shaft} \\ \text{net in}}} = \frac{(0.14 \text{ W})([1 \text{ (N·m/s)/W}]}{0.1 \text{ kg/min}} (60 \text{ s/min})[1 \text{ (kg·m)/(N·s}^2)]$$

so that

$$w_{\substack{\text{shaft} \\ \text{net in}}} = 84.0 \text{ N·m/kg} \qquad (3)$$

For the average velocity at section (1), $\overline{V}_1$, from Eq. 5.10 we obtain

$$\overline{V}_1 = \frac{\dot{m}}{\rho A_1}$$

or

$$\bar{V}_1 = \frac{\dot{m}}{\rho(\pi D_1^2/4)}$$

$$= \frac{(0.1 \text{ kg/min})}{(1.23 \text{ kg/m}^3)[\pi(60 \text{ mm})^2/4][(60 \text{ s/min})/(1000 \text{ mm/m})^2]} \qquad (4)$$

$$= 0.479 \text{ m/s}$$

For the average velocity at section (2), $\bar{V}_2$,

$$\bar{V}_2 = \frac{(0.1 \text{ kg/min})}{(1.23 \text{ kg/m}^3)[\pi(30 \text{ mm})^2/4][(60 \text{ s/min})/(1000 \text{ mm/m})^2]} = 1.92 \text{ m/s} \qquad (5)$$

(a)   For the assumed uniform velocity profiles ($\alpha_1 = \alpha_2 = 1.0$), Eq. 2 yields

$$\text{loss} = w_{\substack{\text{shaft} \\ \text{net in}}} - \left(\frac{p_2 - p_1}{\rho}\right) + \frac{\bar{V}_1^2}{2} - \frac{\bar{V}_2^2}{2} \qquad (6)$$

Using Eqs. 3, 4, and 5 and the pressure rise given in the problem statement, Eq. 6 gives

$$\text{loss} = 84.0 \frac{\text{N·m}}{\text{kg}} - \frac{(0.1 \text{ kPa})(1000 \text{ Pa/kPa})(1 \text{ N/m}^2/\text{Pa})}{1.23 \text{ kg/m}^3}$$
$$+ \frac{(0.479 \text{ m/s})^2}{2[1 \text{ (kg·m)/(N·s}^2)]}$$
$$- \frac{(1.92 \text{ m/s})^2}{2[1 \text{ (kg·m)/(N·s}^2)]}$$

or

$$\text{loss} = 84.0 \text{ N·m/kg} - 81.3 \text{ N·m/kg} + 0.115 \text{ N·m/kg} - 1.84 \text{ N·m/kg}$$
$$= 0.975 \text{ N·m/kg} \qquad \text{(Ans)}$$

(b)   For the actual velocity profiles ($\alpha_1 = 2$, $\alpha_2 = 1.08$), Eq. 1 gives

$$\text{loss} = w_{\substack{\text{shaft} \\ \text{net in}}} - \left(\frac{p_2 - p_1}{\rho}\right) + \alpha_1 \frac{\bar{V}_1^2}{2} - \alpha_2 \frac{\bar{V}_2^2}{2} \qquad (7)$$

If we use Eqs. 3, 4, and 5 and the given pressure rise, Eq. 7 yields

$$\text{loss} = 84 \text{ N·m/kg} - \frac{(0.1 \text{ kPa})(1000 \text{ Pa/kPa})(1 \text{ N/m}^2/\text{Pa})}{1.23 \text{ kg/m}^3}$$
$$+ \frac{2(0.479 \text{ m/s})^2}{2[1 \text{ (kg·m)/(N·s}^2)]}$$
$$- \frac{1.08(1.92 \text{ m/s})^2}{2[1 \text{ (kg·m)/(N·s}^2)]}$$

or

$$\text{loss} = 84.0 \text{ N·m/kg} - 81.3 \text{ N·m/kg} + 0.230 \text{ N·m/kg} - 1.99 \text{ N·m/kg}$$
$$= 0.940 \text{ N·m/kg} \qquad \text{(Ans)}$$

The difference in loss calculated assuming uniform velocity profiles and actual velocity profiles is not large compared to $w_{\text{shaft net in}}$ for this fluid flow situation.

Problems

Note: Unless otherwise indicated, use the values of fluid properties found in the tables on the inside of the front cover. Problems designated with an (*) are intended to be solved with the aid of a programmable calculator or a computer. Problems designated with a (†) are "open-ended" problems and require critical thinking in that to work them one must make various assumptions and provide the necessary data. There is not a unique answer to these problems.

5.1   A water flow situation is described by the velocity field equation

$$\mathbf{V} = (3x + 2)\hat{\mathbf{i}} + (2y - 4)\hat{\mathbf{j}} - 5z\hat{\mathbf{k}} \text{ ft/s}$$

where x, y, and z are in feet. **(a)** Determine the mass flow rate through the rectangular area in the plane corresponding to $z = 2$ ft having corners at $(x, y, z) = (0, 0, 2)$, $(5, 0, 2)$, $(5, 5, 2)$, and $(0, 5, 2)$ as shown in Fig. P5.1a. **(b)** Show that mass is conserved in the control volume having corners at $(x, y, z) = (0, 0, 2)$, $(5, 0, 2)$, $(5, 5, 2)$, $(0, 5, 2)$, $(0, 0, 0)$, $(5, 0, 0)$, $(5, 5, 0)$, and $(0, 5, 0)$ as shown in Fig. P5.1b.

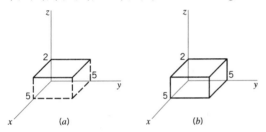

■ **FIGURE P5.1**

5.2   A hydroelectric turbine passes 2 million gal/min through its blades. If the average velocity of the flow in the circular cross-section conduit leading to the turbine is not to exceed 30 ft/s, determine the minimum allowable diameter of the conduit.

5.3   Air flows steadily between two cross sections in a long, straight section of 0.25-m inside diameter pipe. The static temperature and pressure at each section are indicated in Fig. P5.3. If the average air velocity at section (2) is 320 m/s, determine the average air velocity at section (1).

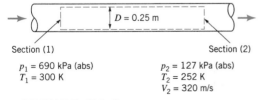

Section (1)   Section (2)

$p_1 = 690$ kPa (abs) $p_2 = 127$ kPa (abs)
$T_1 = 300$ K $T_2 = 252$ K
                             $V_2 = 320$ m/s

■ **FIGURE P5.3**

5.4   The wind blows through a 7 ft × 10 ft garage door with a speed of 2 ft/s as shown in Fig. P5.4. Determine the average speed, V, of the air through the two 3 ft × 4 ft windows.

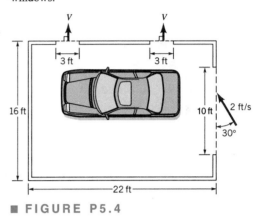

■ **FIGURE P5.4**

5.5   Water flows out through a set of thin, closely spaced blades as shown in Fig. P5.5 with a speed of $V = 10$ ft/s around the entire circumference of the outlet. Determine the mass flowrate through the inlet pipe.

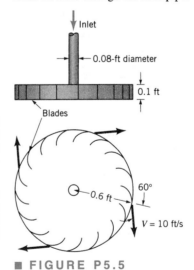

■ **FIGURE P5.5**

5.6   Water flows into a sink as shown in Video V5.1 and Fig. P5.6 at a rate of 2 gallons per minute. Determine the average velocity through each of the three 0.4 in. diameter overflow holes if the drain is closed and the water level in the sink remains constant.

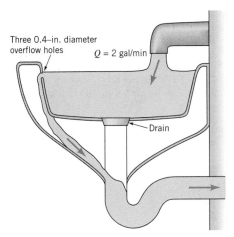

Three 0.4–in. diameter overflow holes

$Q = 2$ gal/min

Drain

■ **FIGURE P5.6**

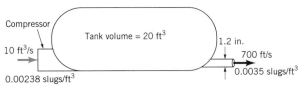

Compressor

Tank volume = 20 ft³

10 ft³/s

0.00238 slugs/ft³

1.2 in.

700 ft/s

0.0035 slugs/ft³

■ **FIGURE P5.8**

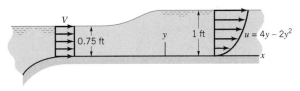

V

0.75 ft

y

1 ft

$u = 4y - 2y^2$

x

■ **FIGURE P5.9**

5.7 Various types of attachments can be used with the shop vac shown in **Video V5.2.** Two such attachments are shown in Fig. P5.7—a nozzle and a brush. The flowrate is 1 ft³/s. **(a)** Determine the average velocity through the nozzle entrance, V_n. **(b)** Assume the air enters the brush attachment in a radial direction all around the brush with a velocity profile that varies linearly from 0 to V_b along the length of the bristles as shown in the figure. Determine the value of V_b.

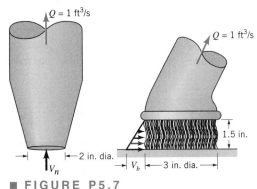

$Q = 1$ ft³/s

$Q = 1$ ft³/s

1.5 in.

2 in. dia.

V_n

V_b

3 in. dia.

■ **FIGURE P5.7**

5.8 Air at standard conditions enters the compressor shown in Fig. P5.8 at a rate of 10 ft³/s. It leaves the tank through a 1.2-in.-diameter pipe with a density of 0.0035 slugs/ft³ and a uniform speed of 700 ft/s. **(a)** Determine the rate (slugs/s) at which the mass of air in the tank is increasing or decreasing. **(b)** Determine the average time rate of change of air density within the tank.

5.9 As shown in Fig. P5.9, at the entrance to a 3-ft-wide channel the velocity distribution is uniform with a velocity

V. Further downstream the velocity profile is given by $u = 4y - 2y^2$, where u is in ft/s and y is in ft. Determine the value of V.

5.10 The flow in an open channel has a velocity distribution

$$\mathbf{V} = U(y/h)^{1/7}\hat{\mathbf{i}} \text{ ft/s}$$

where U = free-surface velocity, y = perpendicular distance from the channel bottom in feet, and h = depth of the channel in feet. Determine the average velocity of the channel stream as a fraction of U.

5.11 The Hoover Dam backs up the Colorado River and creates Lake Meade, which is approximately 115 miles long and has a surface area of approximately 225 square miles. (See **Video V2.3.**) If during flood conditions the Colorado River flows into the lake at a rate of 45,000 cfs and the outflow from the dam is 8,000 cfs, how many feet per 24-hour day will the lake level rise?

5.12 Storm sewer backup causes your basement to flood at the steady rate of 1 in. of depth per hour. The basement floor area is 1500 ft². What capacity (gal/min) pump would you rent to **(a)** keep the water accumulated in your basement at a constant level until the storm sewer is blocked off, **(b)** reduce the water accumulation in your basement at a rate of 3 in./hr even while the backup problem exists?

†5.13 Estimate the maximum flowrate of rainwater (during a heavy rain) that you would expect from the downspout connected to the gutters of your house. List all assumptions and show all calculations.

5.14 Two rivers merge to form a larger river as shown in Fig. P5.14. At a location downstream from the junction (before the two streams completely merge), the nonuniform velocity profile is as shown and the depth is 6 ft. Determine the value of V.

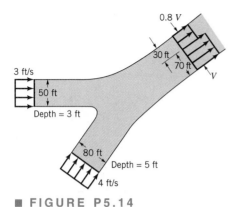

■ **FIGURE P5.14**

5.15 Exhaust (assumed to have the properties of standard air) leaves the 4-ft diameter chimney shown in **Video V5.3** and Fig. P5.15 with a speed of 6 ft/s. Because of the wind, after a few diameters downstream the exhaust flows in a horizontal direction with the speed of the wind, 15 ft/s. Determine the horizontal component of the force that the blowing wind puts on the exhaust gases.

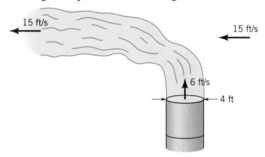

■ **FIGURE P5.15**

5.16 Water enters the horizontal, circular cross-sectional, sudden contraction nozzle sketched in Fig. P5.16 at section (1) with a uniformly distributed velocity of 25 ft/s and a pressure of 75 psi. The water exits from the nozzle into the atmosphere at section (2) where the uniformly distributed velocity is 100 ft/s. Determine the axial component of the anchoring force required to hold the contraction in place.

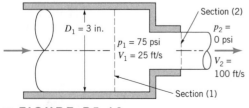

■ **FIGURE P5.16**

5.17 A nozzle is attached to a vertical pipe and discharges water into the atmosphere as shown in Fig. P5.17. When the discharge is 0.1 m³/s, the gage pressure at the flange is 40 kPa. Determine the vertical component of the anchoring force required to hold the nozzle in place. The nozzle has a weight of 200 N, and the volume of water in the nozzle is 0.012 m³. Is the anchoring force directed upward or downward?

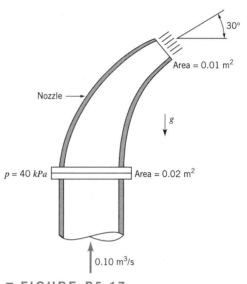

■ **FIGURE P5.17**

5.18 Determine the magnitude and direction of the x and y components of the anchoring force required to hold in place the horizontal 180° elbow and nozzle combination shown in Fig. P5.18. Neglect gravity.

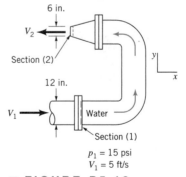

■ **FIGURE P5.18**

5.19 A converging elbow (see Fig. P5.19) turns water through an angle of 135° in a vertical plane. The flow cross-sectional diameter is 400 mm at the elbow inlet, section (1), and 200 mm at the elbow outlet, section (2). The elbow flow

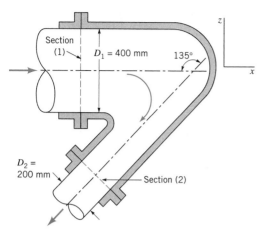

■ FIGURE P5.19

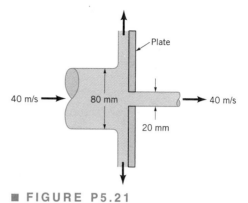

■ FIGURE P5.21

passage volume is 0.2 m³ between sections (1) and (2). The water volume flowrate is 0.4 m³/s and the elbow inlet and outlet pressures are 150 kPa and 90 kPa. The elbow mass is 12 kg. Calculate the horizontal (x direction) and vertical (z direction) anchoring forces required to hold the elbow in place.

5.20   Water is sprayed radially outward over 180° as indicated in Fig. P5.20. The jet sheet is in the horizontal plane. If the jet velocity at the nozzle exit is 30 ft/s, determine the direction and magnitude of the resultant horizontal anchoring force required to hold the nozzle in place.

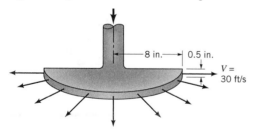

■ FIGURE P5.20

5.21   A circular plate having a diameter of 300 mm is held perpendicular to an axisymmetric horizontal jet of air having a velocity of 40 m/s and a diameter of 80 mm as shown in Fig. P5.21. A hole at the center of the plate results in a discharge jet of air having a velocity of 40 m/s and a diameter of 20 mm. Determine the horizontal component of force required to hold the plate stationary.

5.22   A sheet of water of uniform thickness ($h = 0.01$ m) flows from the device shown in Fig. P5.22. The water enters vertically through the inlet pipe and exits horizontally

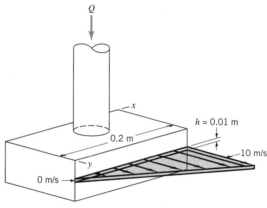

■ FIGURE P5.22

with a speed that varies linearly from 0 to 10 m/s along the 0.2 m length of the slit. Determine the y component of anchoring force necessary to hold this device stationary.

5.23   The results of a wind tunnel test to determine the drag on a body (see Fig. P5.23) are summarized below. The upstream [section (1)] velocity is uniform at 100 ft/s. The static pressures are given by $p_1 = p_2 = 14.7$ psia. The downstream velocity distribution, which is symmetrical about the centerline, is given by

$$u = 100 - 30\left(1 - \frac{|y|}{3}\right) \qquad |y| \le 3\,\text{ft}$$

$$u = 100 \qquad |y| > 3\,\text{ft}$$

where u is the velocity in ft/s and y is the distance on either side of the centerline in feet (see Fig. P5.23). Assume that the body shape does not change in the direction normal to the paper. Calculate the drag force (reaction force in x direction) exerted on the air by the body per unit length normal to the plane of the sketch.

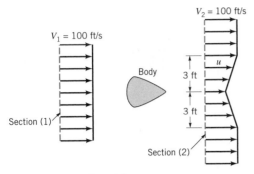

■ FIGURE P5.23

5.24 Water flows steadily from a tank mounted on a cart as shown in Fig. P5.24. After the water jet leaves the nozzle of the tank, it falls and strikes a vane attached to another cart. The carts' wheels are frictionless, and the fluid is inviscid. **(a)** Determine the speed of the water leaving the tank, V_1, and the water speed leaving the cart, V_2. **(b)** Determine the tension in rope A. **(c)** Determine the tension in rope B.

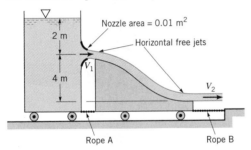

■ FIGURE P5.24

5.25 The thrust developed to propel the jet ski shown in **Video V9.7** and Fig. P5.25 is a result of water pumped through the vehicle and exiting as a high-speed water jet. For the conditions shown in the figure, what flowrate is needed to produce a 300 lb thrust? Assume the inlet and outlet jets of water are free jets.

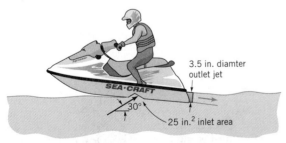

■ FIGURE P5.25

5.26 In a laminar pipe flow that is fully developed, the axial velocity profile is parabolic. That is,

$$u = u_c \left[1 - \left(\frac{r}{R} \right)^2 \right]$$

as is illustrated in Fig. P5.26. Compare the axial direction momentum flowrate calculated with the average velocity, $\bar{u}$, with the axial direction momentum flowrate calculated with the nonuniform velocity distribution taken into account.

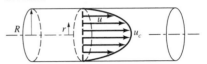

■ FIGURE P5.26

5.27 Determine the magnitude of the horizontal component of the anchoring force per unit width required to hold in place the sluice gate shown in Fig. P5.27. Compare this result with the size of the horizontal component of the anchoring force required to hold in place the sluice gate when it is closed and the depth of water upstream is 6 ft.

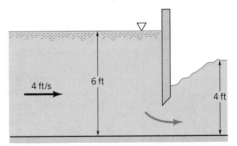

■ FIGURE P5.27

5.28 Water flows from a two-dimensional open channel and is diverted by an inclined plate as illustrated in Fig. P5.28. When the velocity at section (1) is 10 ft/s, what horizontal force (per unit width) is required to hold the plate in position? At section (1) the pressure distribution is hydrostatic, and the fluid acts as a free jet at section (2). Neglect friction.

5.29 A horizontal, circular cross-sectional jet of air having a diameter of 6 in. strikes a conical deflector as shown in Fig. P5.29. A horizontal anchoring force of 5 lb is required to hold the cone in place. Estimate the nozzle flowrate in ft³/s. The magnitude of the velocity of the air remains constant.

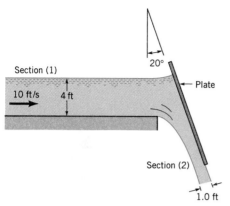

■ FIGURE P5.28

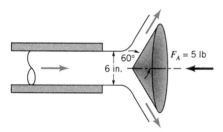

■ FIGURE P5.29

5.30 A 10-mm diameter jet of water is deflected by a homogeneous rectangular block (15 mm by 200 mm by 100 mm) that weighs 6 N as shown in Video V5.4 and Fig. P5.30. Determine the minimum volume flowrate needed to tip the block.

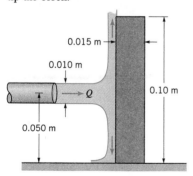

■ FIGURE P5.30

5.31 Air flows into the atmosphere from a nozzle and strikes a vertical plate as shown in Fig. P5.31. A horizontal force of 9 N is required to hold the plate in place. Determine the reading on the pressure gage. Assume the flow to be incompressible and frictionless.

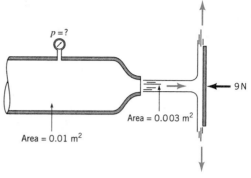

■ FIGURE P5.31

5.32 Two water jets of equal size and speed strike each other as shown in Fig. P5.32. Determine the speed, V, and direction, θ, of the resulting combined jet. Gravity is negligible.

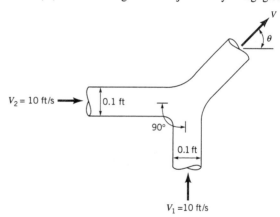

■ FIGURE P5.32

5.33 Water is added to the tank shown in Fig. P5.33 through a vertical pipe to maintain a constant (water) level. The tank is placed on a horizontal plane, which has a frictionless surface. Determine the horizontal force, F, required to hold the tank stationary. Neglect all losses.

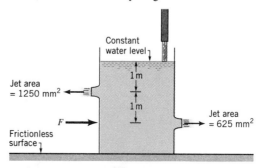

■ FIGURE P5.33

5.34   Water enters a rotating lawn sprinkler through its base at the steady rate of 16 gal/min as shown in Fig. P5.34. The exit cross-sectional area of each of the two nozzles is 0.04 in.^{2}, and the flow leaving each nozzle is tangential. The radius from the axis of rotation to the centerline of each nozzle is 8 in. **(a)** Determine the resisting torque required to hold the sprinkler head stationary. **(b)** Determine the resisting torque associated with the sprinkler rotating with a constant speed of 500 rev/min. **(c)** Determine the angular velocity of the sprinkler if no resisting torque is applied.

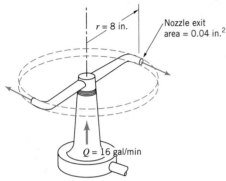

■ FIGURE P5.34

5.35   Five liters/s of water enters the rotor shown in Video V5.5 and Fig. P5.35 along the axis of rotation. The cross-sectional area of each of the three nozzle exits normal to the relative velocity is 18 mm^2. How large is the resisting torque required to hold the rotor stationary? How fast will the rotor spin steadily if the resisting torque is reduced to zero and **(a)** $\theta = 0°$, **(b)** $\theta = 30°$, **(c)** $\theta = 60°$?

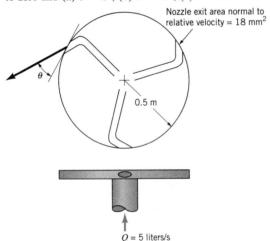

■ FIGURE P5.35

5.36   An inward flow radial turbine (see Fig. P5.36) involves a nozzle angle, α_1, of 60° and an inlet rotor tip speed,

U_1, of 6 m/s. The ratio of rotor inlet to outlet diameters is 2.0. The absolute velocity leaving the rotor at section (2) is radial with a magnitude of 12 m/s. Determine the energy transfer per unit of mass of fluid flowing through this turbine if the fluid is **(a)** air, **(b)** water.

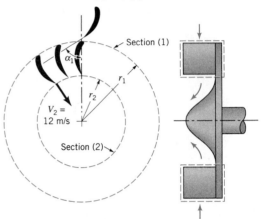

■ FIGURE P5.36

5.37   A water turbine wheel rotates at the rate of 50 rpm in the direction shown in Fig. P5.37. The inner radius, r_2, of the blade row is 2 ft, and the outer radius, r_1, is 4 ft. The absolute velocity vector at the turbine rotor entrance makes an angle of 20° with the tangential direction. The inlet blade angle is 60° relative to the tangential direction. The blade outlet angle is 120°. The flowrate is 20 ft^3/s. For the flow tangent to the rotor blade surface at inlet and outlet, determine an appropriate constant blade height, b, and the corresponding power available at the rotor shaft.

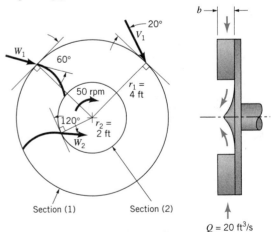

■ FIGURE P5.37

5.38   The radial component of velocity of water leaving the centrifugal pump sketched in Fig. P5.38 is 30 ft/s. The magnitude of the absolute velocity at the pump exit is 60 ft/s.

The fluid enters the pump rotor radially. Calculate the shaft work required per unit mass flowing through the pump.

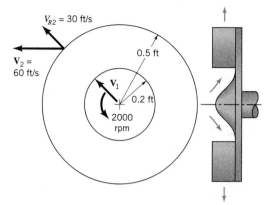

■ FIGURE P5.38

5.39   A fan (see Fig. P5.39) has a bladed rotor of 12-in. outside diameter and 5-in. inside diameter and runs at 1725 rpm. The width of each rotor blade is 1 in. from blade inlet to outlet. The volume flowrate is steady at 230 ft³/min, and the absolute velocity of the air at blade inlet, V_1, is purely radial. The blade discharge angle is 30° measured with respect to the tangential direction at the outside diameter of the rotor. **(a)** What would be a reasonable blade inlet angle (measured with respect to the tangential direction at the inside diameter of the rotor)? **(b)** Find the power required to run the fan.

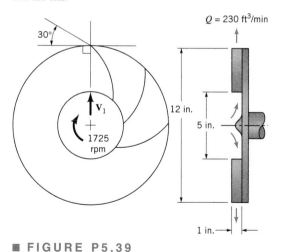

■ FIGURE P5.39

5.40   An axial flow gasoline pump (see Fig. P5.40) consists of a rotating row of blades (rotor) followed downstream by a stationary row of blades (stator). The gasoline enters the rotor axially (without any angular momentum) with an absolute velocity of 3 m/s. The rotor blade inlet and exit angles are 60° and 45° from axial directions. The pump annulus passage cross-sectional area is constant. Consider the flow as being tangent to the blades involved. Sketch velocity triangles for flow just upstream and downstream of the rotor and just downstream of the stator where the flow is axial. How much energy is added to each kilogram of gasoline?

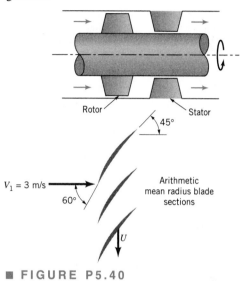

■ FIGURE P5.40

5.41   A sketch of the arithmetic mean radius blade sections of an axial-flow water turbine stage is shown in Fig. P5.41. The rotor speed is 1000 rpm. **(a)** Sketch and label velocity triangles for the flow entering and leaving the rotor row. Use **V** for absolute velocity, **W** for relative velocity, and **U** for blade velocity. Assume flow enters and leaves each blade row at the blade angles shown. **(b)** Calculate the work per unit mass delivered at the shaft.

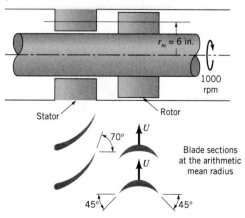

■ FIGURE P5.41

5.42   Water enters a pump impeller radially. It leaves the impeller with a tangential component of absolute velocity of 10 m/s. The impeller exit diameter is 60 mm and the impeller speed is 1800 rpm. If the stagnation pressure rise across the impeller is 45 kPa, determine the loss of available energy across the impeller and the hydraulic efficiency of the pump.

5.43   An axial-flow turbomachine rotor involves the upstream (1) and downstream (2) velocity triangles shown in Fig. P5.43. Is this turbomachine a turbine or a fan? Sketch an appropriate blade section and determine the energy transferred per unit mass of fluid.

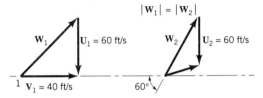

■ FIGURE P5.43

5.44   Water enters an axial-flow turbine rotor with an absolute velocity tangential component, V_θ, of 15 ft/s. The corresponding blade velocity, U, is 50 ft/s. The water leaves the rotor blade row with no angular momentum. If the stagnation pressure drop across the turbine is 12 psi, determine the hydraulic efficiency of the turbine.

5.45   For adiabatic flow through a turbomachine rotor, prove that the quantity

$$\check{h} + \frac{W^2}{2} - \frac{U^2}{2}$$

remains constant, where

$$\check{h} = \text{enthalpy}$$
$$W = \text{relative flow velocity}$$
$$U = \text{blade speed}$$

5.46   A 200-m-high waterfall involves steady flow from one large body to another. Determine the temperature rise associated with this flow.

5.47   Air flows past an object in a pipe of 2-m diameter and exits as a free jet as shown in Fig. P5.47. The velocity

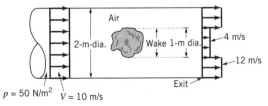

■ FIGURE P5.47

and pressure upstream are uniform at 10 m/s and 50 N/m², respectively. At the pipe exit the velocity is nonuniform as indicated. The shear stress along the pipe wall is negligible. **(a)** Determine the head loss associated with a particle as it flows from the uniform velocity upstream of the object to a location in the wake at the exit plane of the pipe. **(b)** Determine the force that the air puts on the object.

5.48   Oil $(SG = 0.9)$ flows downward through a vertical pipe contraction as shown in Fig. P5.48. If the mercury manometer reading, h, is 120 mm, determine the volume flowrate for frictionless flow. Is the actual flowrate more or less than the frictionless value? Explain.

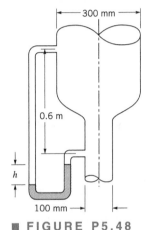

■ FIGURE P5.48

5.49   A water siphon having a constant inside diameter of 3 in. is arranged as shown in Fig. P5.49. If the friction loss between A and B is $0.6V^2/2$, where V is the velocity of flow in the siphon, determine the flowrate involved.

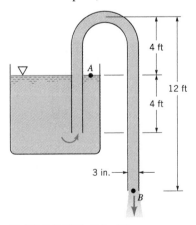

■ FIGURE P5.49

5.50   Water flows through a valve (see Fig. P5.50) at the rate of 1000 lb/s. The pressure just upstream of the valve is 90 psi and the pressure drop across the valve is 5 psi. The inside diameters of the valve inlet and exit pipes are 12 and 24 in. If the flow through the valve occurs in a horizontal plane, determine the loss in available energy across the valve.

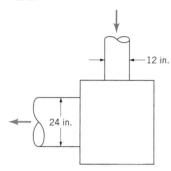

■ **FIGURE P5.50**

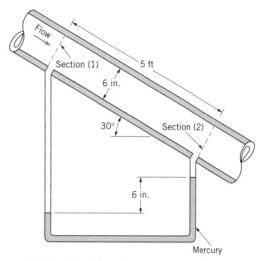

■ **FIGURE P5.53**

5.51   An incompressible liquid flows steadily along the pipe shown in Fig. P5.51. Determine the direction of flow and the head loss over the 6-m length of pipe.

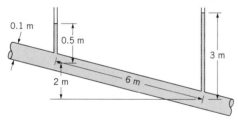

■ **FIGURE P5.51**

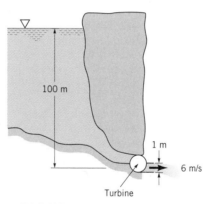

■ **FIGURE P5.54**

5.52   A fire hose nozzle is designed to deliver water that will rise 30 m vertically. Calculate the stagnation pressure required at the nozzle inlet if (a) no loss is assumed, (b) a loss of 30 N·m/kg is assumed.

5.53   Water flows steadily down the inclined pipe as indicated in Fig. P5.53. Determine the following: (a) the difference in pressure $p_1 - p_2$, (b) the loss between sections (1) and (2), (c) the net axial force exerted by the pipe wall on the flowing water between sections (1) and (2).

5.54   What is the maximum possible power output of the hydroelectric turbine shown in Fig. P5.54?

5.55   A hydroelectric turbine passes 4 million gal/min across a head of 100 ft of water. What is the maximum

amount of power output possible? Why will the actual amount be less?

5.56   A hydraulic turbine is provided with 4.25 m³/s of water at 415 kPa. A vacuum gage in the turbine discharge 3 m below the turbine inlet centerline reads 250 mm Hg vacuum. If the turbine shaft output power is 1100 kW, calculate the power loss through the turbine. The supply and discharge pipe inside diameters are identically 800 mm.

5.57   Water is supplied at 150 ft³/s and 60 psi to a hydraulic turbine through a 3-ft inside diameter inlet pipe as indicated in Fig. P5.57. The turbine discharge pipe has a 4-ft inside diameter. The static pressure at section (2), 10 ft below the turbine inlet, is 10 in. Hg vacuum. If the turbine develops 2500 hp, determine the rate of loss of available energy between sections (1) and (2).

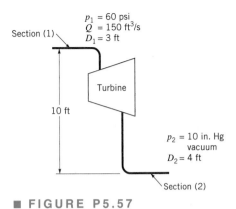

■ **FIGURE P5.57**

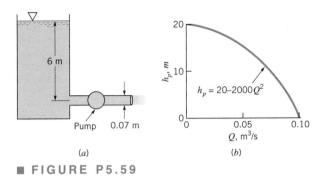

■ **FIGURE P5.59**

5.58   Water is pumped from a tank, point (1), to the top of a water plant aerator, point (2), as shown in **Video V5.8** and Fig. P5.58 at a rate of 3.0 ft³/s. **(a)** Determine the power that the pump adds to the water if the head loss from (1) to (2) where $V_2 = 0$ is 4 ft. **(b)** Determine the head loss from (2) to the bottom of the aerator column, point (3), if the average velocity at (3) is $V_3 = 2$ ft/s.

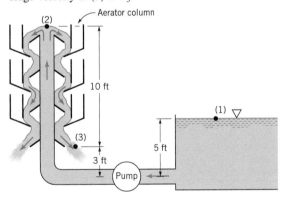

■ **FIGURE P5.58**

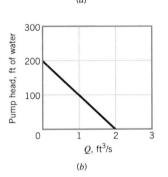

■ **FIGURE P5.60**

5.59   Water is pumped from the tank shown in Fig. P5.59a. The head loss is known to be 1.2 $V^2/2g$, where V is the average velocity in the pipe. According to the pump manufacturer, the relationship between the pump head and the flowrate is as shown in Fig. P5.59b: $h_p = 20 - 2000\,Q^2$, where h_p is in meters and Q is in m³/s. Determine the flowrate, Q.

5.60   A pump transfers water from the lower reservoir to the upper one as shown in Fig. P5.60a. The difference in elevation between the two reservoirs is 100 ft. The friction head loss in the piping is given by $K_L V^2/2g$, where V is the average fluid velocity in the pipe and K_L is the loss coeffi-

cient, which is considered constant. The relation between the head added to the water by the pump and the flowrate, Q, through the pump is given in Fig. 5.60b. If $K_L = 20$, and the pipe diameter is 4 in., what is the flowrate through the pump?

5.61   Water flows by gravity from one lake to another as sketched in Fig. P5.61 at the steady rate of 100 gpm. What is the loss in available energy associated with this flow? If this same amount of loss is associated with pumping the fluid from the lower lake to the higher one at the same flowrate, estimate the amount of pumping power required.

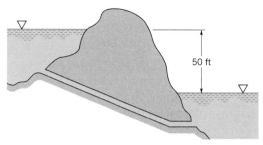

■ FIGURE P5.61

5.62 The turbine shown in Fig. P5.62 develops 100 hp when the flowrate of water is 20 ft³/s. If all losses are negligible, determine (**a**) the elevation h, (**b**) the pressure difference across the turbine, and (**c**) the flowrate expected if the turbine were removed.

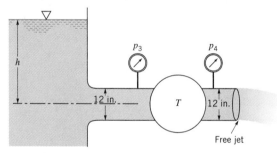

■ FIGURE P5.62

5.63 A pump moves water horizontally at a rate of 0.02 m³/s. Upstream of the pump where the pipe diameter is 90 mm, the pressure is 120 kPa. Downstream of the pump where the pipe diameter is 30 mm, the pressure is 400 kPa. If the loss in energy across the pump due to fluid friction effects is 170 N·m/kg, determine the hydraulic efficiency of the pump.

5.64 Oil ($SG = 0.88$) flows in an inclined pipe at a rate of 5 ft³/s as shown in Fig. P5.64. If the differential reading in the mercury manometer is 3 ft, calculate the power that the pump supplies to the oil if head losses are negligible.

5.65 Water is to be moved from one large reservoir to another at a higher elevation as indicated in Fig. P5.65. The loss in available energy associated with 2.5 ft³/s being pumped from sections (1) to (2) is $61\overline{V}^2/2$ ft²/s², where $\overline{V}$ is the average velocity of water in the 8-in. inside diameter piping involved. Determine the amount of shaft power required.

5.66 Water, contained in a large open tank, discharges steadily into the atmosphere from a curved pipe as shown in Fig. P5.66. The tank rests on a smooth surface, and to

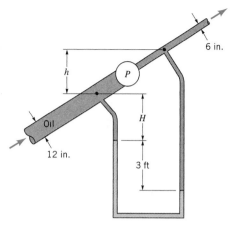

■ FIGURE P5.64

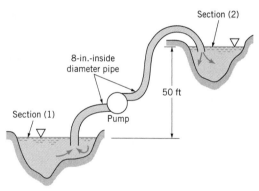

■ FIGURE P5.65

prevent it from sliding, a horizontal flexible cable is to be connected to hooks on either the right or left side of the tank. Assuming the cable can only support a tensile force, would you connect it to the right or left side? What tensile force does the cable have to support? Assume the flow to be frictionless.

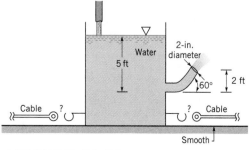

■ FIGURE P5.66

5.67 Assuming frictionless, incompressible, one-dimensional flow of water through the horizontal tee connection sketched in Fig. P5.67, estimate values of the x and y components of the force exerted by the tee on the water. Each pipe has an inside diameter of 1 m.

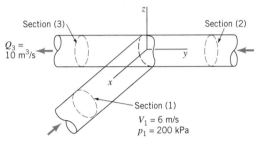

■ **FIGURE P5.67**

5.68 Water flows through a 2-ft-diameter pipe arranged horizontally in a circular arc as shown in Fig. P5.68. If the pipe discharges to the atmosphere ($p = 14.7$ psia), determine the x and y components of the resultant force needed to hold the piping between sections (1) and (2) stationary. The steady flowrate is 3000 ft³/min. The loss in pressure due to fluid friction between sections (1) and (2) is 25 psi.

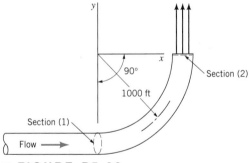

■ **FIGURE P5.68**

5.69 When fluid flows through an abrupt expansion as indicated in Fig. P5.69, the loss in available energy across the expansion, loss_{ex}, is often expressed as

$$\text{loss}_{ex} = \left(1 - \frac{A_1}{A_2}\right)^2 \frac{V_1^2}{2}$$

where A_1 = cross-sectional area upstream of expansion, A_2 = cross-sectional area downstream of expansion, and V_1 = velocity of flow upstream of expansion. Derive this relationship.

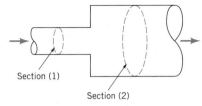

■ **FIGURE P5.69**

5.70 A vertical jet of water leaves a nozzle at a speed of 10 m/s and a diameter of 20 mm. It suspends a plate having a mass of 1.5 kg as indicated in Fig. P5.70. What is the vertical distance h?

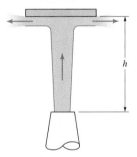

■ **FIGURE P5.70**

5.71 A vertical jet of water having a nozzle exit velocity of 10 ft/s with a diameter of 1 in. suspends a hollow hemisphere as indicated in Fig. P5.71. If the hemisphere is stationary at an elevation of 12 in., determine its weight.

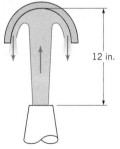

■ **FIGURE P5.71**

5.72 Two water jets collide and form one homogeneous jet as shown in Fig. P5.72. **(a)** Determine the speed, V, and direction, θ, of the combined jet. **(b)** Determine the loss for a fluid particle flowing from (1) to (3), from (2) to (3). Gravity is negligible.

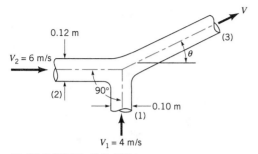

■ FIGURE P5.72

5.73   Air discharges from a 2-in.-diameter nozzle and strikes a curved vane, which is in a vertical plane as shown in Fig. P5.73. A stagnation tube connected to a water U-tube manometer is located in the free air jet. Determine the horizontal component of the force that the air jet exerts on the vane. Neglect the weight of the air and all friction.

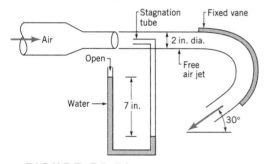

■ FIGURE P5.73

5.74   The device shown in Fig. P5.74 is used to investigate the force needed to deflect a jet of water. Water pumped from a tank at a given flowrate, Q, issues from a nozzle with speed V and is deflected through a known angle, θ, by means of a vane as shown. The vane is constrained from moving horizontally. The tension in the spring attached to the vane is adjusted to give a null reading on the position indicator when the flowrate is zero and $W = 0$. With a known weight, W, on the balance pan, the flowrate is adjusted to return the position indicator to its null position. The flowrate is determined by measuring the weight of water, W_w, that is pumped from the tank in a given time, t. That is, $Q = W_w/(\gamma t)$, where γ is the specific weight of water. Use the results in the table below for two values of θ to plot a graph of the force that

the water puts on the vane as a function of the speed of the water from the nozzle. There will be two curves, one for each value of θ. On the same graph plot the theoretical curves for the two cases tested.

Compare the experimental and theoretical results and discuss some possible reasons for any differences between them.

For $\theta = 90°$:

W (lb)	W_w (lb)	t (s)
0.044	7.71	26.8
0.154	8.66	18.2
0.264	8.92	12.6
0.374	8.78	10.0
0.485	9.96	10.6

For $\theta = 180°$:

W (lb)	W_w (lb)	t (s)
0.110	6.81	24.5
0.220	9.00	20.8
0.551	7.88	10.9
0.771	7.97	9.5
0.880	6.37	7.6

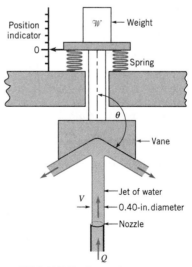

■ FIGURE P5.74

CHAPTER

6

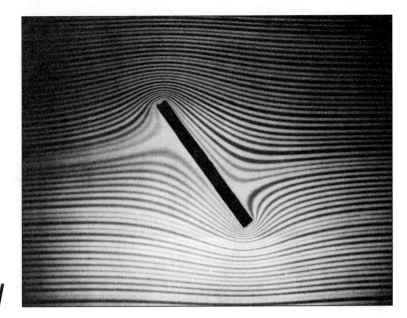

Differential Analysis of Fluid Flow

*I*n the previous chapter attention is focused on the use of finite control volumes for the solution of a variety of fluid mechanics problems. This approach is very practical and useful, since it does not generally require a detailed knowledge of the pressure and velocity variations within the control volume. Typically, we found that only conditions on the surface of the control volume entered the problem, and thus problems could be solved without a detailed knowledge of the flow field. Unfortunately, there are many situations that arise in which the details of the flow are important and the finite control volume approach will not yield the desired information. For example, we may need to know how the velocity varies over the cross section of a pipe, or how the pressure and shear stress vary along the surface of an airplane wing. In these circumstances we need to develop relationships that apply at a point, or at least in a very small region (infinitesimal volume) within a given flow field. This approach, which involves an *infinitesimal control volume,* as distinguished from a finite control volume, is commonly referred to as *differential analysis,* since (as we will soon discover) the governing equations are differential equations.

We begin our introduction to differential analysis by reviewing and extending some of the ideas associated with fluid kinematics that were introduced in Chapter 4. With this

Flow past an inclined plate: The streamlines of a viscous fluid flowing slowly past a two-dimensional object placed between two closely spaced plates (a Hele-Shaw cell) approximate inviscid, irrotational (potential) flow. (Dye in water between glass plates spaced 1 mm apart) (Photography courtesy of D. H. Peregrine).

background the remainder of the chapter will be devoted to the derivation of the basic differential equations (which will be based on the principle of conservation of mass and Newton's second law of motion) and to some applications.

6.1 Fluid Element Kinematics

In this section we will be concerned with the mathematical description of the motion of fluid elements moving in a flow field. A small fluid element in the shape of a cube, which is initially in one position, will move to another position during a short time interval δt as illustrated in Fig. 6.1. Because of the generally complex velocity variation within the field, we expect the element to not only translate from one position but to also have its volume changed (linear deformation), to rotate, and to undergo a change in shape (angular deformation). Although these movements and deformations occur simultaneously, we can consider each one separately as illustrated in Fig. 6.1. Since element motion and deformation is intimately related to the velocity and variation of velocity throughout the flow field, we will briefly review the manner in which velocity and acceleration fields can be described.

6.1.1 Velocity and Acceleration Fields Revisited

As discussed in detail in Section 4.1, the velocity field can be described by specifying the velocity **V** at all points, and at all times, within the flow field of interest. Thus, in terms of rectangular coordinates, the notation **V** (x, y, z, t) means that the velocity of a fluid particle depends on where it is located within the flow field (as determined by its coordinates x, y, and z) and when it occupies the particular point (as determined by the time, t). As is pointed out in Section 4.1.1, this method of describing the fluid motion is called the Eulerian method. It is also convenient to express the velocity in terms of three rectangular components so that

$$\mathbf{V} = u\hat{\mathbf{i}} + v\hat{\mathbf{j}} + w\hat{\mathbf{k}} \tag{6.1}$$

where u, v, and w are the velocity components in the x, y, and z directions, respectively, and $\hat{\mathbf{i}}$, $\hat{\mathbf{j}}$, and $\hat{\mathbf{k}}$ are the corresponding unit vectors. Of course, each of these components will, in general, be a function of x, y, z, and t. One of the goals of differential analysis is to determine how these velocity components specifically depend on x, y, z, and t for a particular problem.

With this description of the velocity field it was also shown in Section 4.2.1 that the acceleration of a fluid particle can be expressed as

$$\mathbf{a} = \frac{\partial \mathbf{V}}{\partial t} + u\frac{\partial \mathbf{V}}{\partial x} + v\frac{\partial \mathbf{V}}{\partial y} + w\frac{\partial \mathbf{V}}{\partial z} \tag{6.2}$$

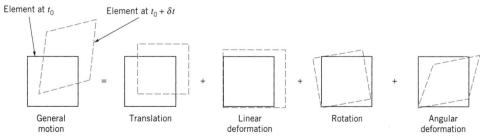

■ FIGURE 6.1 **Types of motion and deformation for a fluid element.**

and in component form:

$$a_x = \frac{\partial u}{\partial t} + u\frac{\partial u}{\partial x} + v\frac{\partial u}{\partial y} + w\frac{\partial u}{\partial z} \tag{6.3a}$$

$$a_y = \frac{\partial v}{\partial t} + u\frac{\partial v}{\partial x} + v\frac{\partial v}{\partial y} + w\frac{\partial v}{\partial z} \tag{6.3b}$$

$$a_z = \frac{\partial w}{\partial t} + u\frac{\partial w}{\partial x} + v\frac{\partial w}{\partial y} + w\frac{\partial w}{\partial z} \tag{6.3c}$$

The acceleration is also concisely expressed as

$$\mathbf{a} = \frac{D\mathbf{V}}{Dt} \tag{6.4}$$

where the operator

$$\frac{D(\ )}{Dt} = \frac{\partial(\ )}{\partial t} + u\frac{\partial(\ )}{\partial x} + v\frac{\partial(\ )}{\partial y} + w\frac{\partial(\ )}{\partial z} \tag{6.5}$$

is termed the *material derivative,* or *substantial derivative.* In vector notation

$$\frac{D(\ )}{Dt} = \frac{\partial(\ )}{\partial t} + (\mathbf{V} \cdot \boldsymbol{\nabla})(\ ) \tag{6.6}$$

where the gradient operator, $\boldsymbol{\nabla}(\ )$, is

$$\boldsymbol{\nabla}(\ ) = \frac{\partial(\ )}{\partial x}\hat{\mathbf{i}} + \frac{\partial(\ )}{\partial y}\hat{\mathbf{j}} + \frac{\partial(\ )}{\partial z}\hat{\mathbf{k}} \tag{6.7}$$

which was introduced in Chapter 2. As we will see in the following sections, the motion and deformation of a fluid element depend on the velocity field. The relationship between the motion and the forces causing the motion depends on the acceleration field.

6.1.2   Linear Motion and Deformation

The simplest type of motion that a fluid element can undergo is translation as illustrated in Fig. 6.2. In a small time interval δt a particle located at point O will move to point O' as is illustrated in the figure. If all points in the element have the same velocity (which is only true if there are no velocity gradients), then the element will simply translate from one position to another. However, because of the presence of velocity gradients, the element will

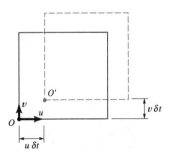

■ FIGURE 6.2   **Translation of a fluid element.**

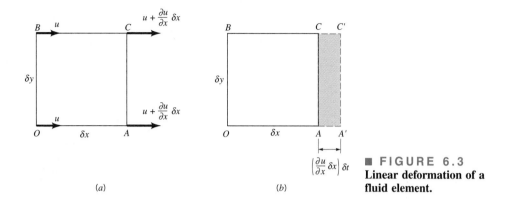

■ **FIGURE 6.3**
Linear deformation of a fluid element.

generally be deformed and rotated as it moves. For example, consider the effect of a single velocity gradient $\partial u/\partial x$, on a small cube having sides δx, δy, and δz. As is shown in Fig. 6.3a, if the x component of velocity of O and B is u, then at nearby points A and C the x component of the velocity can be expressed as $u + (\partial u/\partial x)\,\delta x$. This difference in velocity causes a "stretching" of the volume element by an amount $(\partial u/\partial x)(\delta x)(\delta t)$ during the short time interval δt in which line OA stretches to OA' and BC to BC' (Fig. 6.3b). The corresponding change in the original volume, $\delta V = \delta x\,\delta y\,\delta z$, would be

$$\text{Change in } \delta V = \left(\frac{\partial u}{\partial x}\,\delta x\right)(\delta y\,\delta z)(\delta t)$$

and the *rate* at which the volume δV is changing *per unit volume* due to the gradient $\partial u/\partial x$ is

$$\frac{1}{\delta V}\frac{d(\delta V)}{dt} = \lim_{\delta t \to 0}\left[\frac{(\partial u/\partial x)\,\delta t}{\delta t}\right] = \frac{\partial u}{\partial x} \tag{6.8}$$

If velocity gradients $\partial v/\partial y$ and $\partial w/\partial z$ are also present, then using a similar analysis it follows that, in the general case,

$$\frac{1}{\delta V}\frac{d(\delta V)}{dt} = \frac{\partial u}{\partial x} + \frac{\partial v}{\partial y} + \frac{\partial w}{\partial z} = \boldsymbol{\nabla} \cdot \mathbf{V} \tag{6.9}$$

This rate of change of the volume per unit volume is called the *volumetric dilatation rate*. Thus, we see that the volume of a fluid may change as the element moves from one location to another in the flow field. However, for an *incompressible fluid* the volumetric dilatation rate is zero, since the element volume cannot change without a change in fluid density (the element mass must be conserved). Variations in the velocity in the direction of the velocity, as represented by the derivatives $\partial u/\partial x$, $\partial v/\partial y$, and $\partial w/\partial z$, simply cause a *linear deformation* of the element in the sense that the shape of the element does not change. Cross derivatives, such as $\partial u/\partial y$ and $\partial v/\partial x$, will cause the element to rotate and generally to undergo an *angular deformation,* which changes the shape of the element.

6.1.3   Angular Motion and Deformation

For simplicity we will consider motion in the x–y plane, but the results can be readily extended to the more general case. The velocity variation that causes rotation and angular deformation is illustrated in Fig. 6.4a. In a short time interval δt the line segments OA and

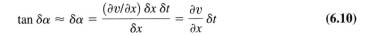

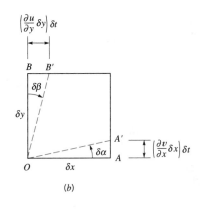

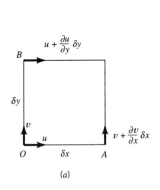

■ **FIGURE 6.4**
Angular motion and deformation of a fluid element.

(a)   (b)

OB will rotate through the angles $\delta\alpha$ and $\delta\beta$ to the new positions OA' and OB' as shown in Fig. 6.4b. The angular velocity of line OA, ω_{OA}, is

$$\omega_{OA} = \lim_{\delta t \to 0} \frac{\delta\alpha}{\delta t}$$

For small angles

$$\tan \delta\alpha \approx \delta\alpha = \frac{(\partial v/\partial x)\, \delta x\, \delta t}{\delta x} = \frac{\partial v}{\partial x}\, \delta t \tag{6.10}$$

so that

V6.1 Shear deformation

$$\omega_{OA} = \lim_{\delta t \to 0} \left[\frac{(\partial v/\partial x)\, \delta t}{\delta t} \right] = \frac{\partial v}{\partial x}$$

Note that if $\partial v/\partial x$ is positive, ω_{OA} will be counterclockwise. Similarly, the angular velocity of the line OB is

$$\omega_{OB} = \lim_{\delta t \to 0} \frac{\delta\beta}{\delta t}$$

and

$$\tan \delta\beta \approx \delta\beta = \frac{(\partial u/\partial y)\, \delta y\, \delta t}{\delta y} = \frac{\partial u}{\partial y}\, \delta t \tag{6.11}$$

so that

$$\omega_{OB} = \lim_{\delta t \to 0} \left[\frac{(\partial u/\partial y)\, \delta t}{\delta t} \right] = \frac{\partial u}{\partial y}$$

In this instance if $\partial u/\partial y$ is positive, ω_{OB} will be clockwise. The *rotation*, ω_z, of the element about the z axis is defined as the average of the angular velocities ω_{OA} and ω_{OB} of the two mutually perpendicular lines OA and OB.[1] Thus, if counterclockwise rotation is considered to be positive, it follows that

$$\omega_z = \frac{1}{2}\left(\frac{\partial v}{\partial x} - \frac{\partial u}{\partial y} \right) \tag{6.12}$$

Rotation of the fluid element about the other two coordinate axes can be obtained in a similar manner with the result that for rotation about the x axis

[1]With this definition ω_z can also be interpreted to be the angular velocity of the bisector of the angle between the lines OA and OB.

$$\omega_x = \frac{1}{2}\left(\frac{\partial w}{\partial y} - \frac{\partial v}{\partial z}\right) \tag{6.13}$$

and for rotation about the y axis

$$\omega_y = \frac{1}{2}\left(\frac{\partial u}{\partial z} - \frac{\partial w}{\partial x}\right) \tag{6.14}$$

The three components ω_x, ω_y, and ω_z can be combined to give the rotation vector, $\boldsymbol{\omega}$, in the form

$$\boldsymbol{\omega} = \omega_x\hat{\mathbf{i}} + \omega_y\hat{\mathbf{j}} + \omega_z\hat{\mathbf{k}} \tag{6.15}$$

An examination of this result reveals that $\boldsymbol{\omega}$ is equal to one-half the curl of the velocity vector. That is,

$$\boldsymbol{\omega} = \tfrac{1}{2}\,\text{curl }\mathbf{V} = \tfrac{1}{2}\boldsymbol{\nabla} \times \mathbf{V} \tag{6.16}$$

since by definition of the vector operator $\boldsymbol{\nabla} \times \mathbf{V}$

$$\frac{1}{2}\boldsymbol{\nabla} \times \mathbf{V} = \frac{1}{2}\begin{vmatrix} \hat{\mathbf{i}} & \hat{\mathbf{j}} & \hat{\mathbf{k}} \\ \dfrac{\partial}{\partial x} & \dfrac{\partial}{\partial y} & \dfrac{\partial}{\partial z} \\ u & v & w \end{vmatrix}$$

$$= \frac{1}{2}\left(\frac{\partial w}{\partial y} - \frac{\partial v}{\partial z}\right)\hat{\mathbf{i}} + \frac{1}{2}\left(\frac{\partial u}{\partial z} - \frac{\partial w}{\partial x}\right)\hat{\mathbf{j}} + \frac{1}{2}\left(\frac{\partial v}{\partial x} - \frac{\partial u}{\partial y}\right)\hat{\mathbf{k}}$$

The *vorticity*, $\boldsymbol{\zeta}$, is defined as a vector that is twice the rotation vector; that is,

$$\boldsymbol{\zeta} = 2\,\boldsymbol{\omega} = \boldsymbol{\nabla} \times \mathbf{V} \tag{6.17}$$

The use of the vorticity to describe the rotational characteristics of the fluid simply eliminates the $(\frac{1}{2})$ factor associated with the rotation vector.

We observe from Eq. 6.12 that the fluid element will rotate about the z axis as an *undeformed* block (i.e., $\omega_{OA} = -\omega_{OB}$) only when $\partial u/\partial y = -\partial v/\partial x$. Otherwise the rotation will be associated with an angular deformation. We also note from Eq. 6.12 that when $\partial u/\partial y = \partial v/\partial x$ the rotation around the z axis is zero. More generally if $\boldsymbol{\nabla} \times \mathbf{V} = 0$, then the rotation (and the vorticity) are zero, and flow fields for which this condition applies are termed *irrotational*. We will find in Section 6.4 that the condition of irrotationality often greatly simplifies the analysis of complex flow fields. However, it is probably not immediately obvious why some flow fields would be irrotational, and we will need to examine this concept more fully in Section 6.4.

EXAMPLE 6.1

For a certain two-dimensional flow field the velocity is given by the equation

$$\mathbf{V} = 4xy\hat{\mathbf{i}} + 2(x^2 - y^2)\hat{\mathbf{j}}$$

Is this flow irrotational?

SOLUTION

For an irrotational flow the rotation vector, **ω**, having the components given by Eqs. 6.12, 6.13, and 6.14 must be zero. For the prescribed velocity field

$$u = 4xy \qquad v = 2(x^2 - y^2) \qquad w = 0$$

and therefore

$$\omega_x = \frac{1}{2}\left(\frac{\partial w}{\partial y} - \frac{\partial v}{\partial z}\right) = 0$$

$$\omega_y = \frac{1}{2}\left(\frac{\partial u}{\partial z} - \frac{\partial w}{\partial x}\right) = 0$$

$$\omega_z = \frac{1}{2}\left(\frac{\partial v}{\partial x} - \frac{\partial u}{\partial y}\right) = \frac{1}{2}(4x - 4x) = 0$$

Thus, the flow is irrotational. (Ans)

It is to be noted that for a two-dimensional flow field (where the flow is in the x–y plane) ω_x and ω_y will always be zero, since by definition of two-dimensional flow u and v are not functions of z, and w is zero. In this instance the condition for irrotationality simply becomes $\omega_z = 0$ or $\partial v/\partial x = \partial u/\partial y$. (Lines OA and OB of Fig. 6.4 rotate with the same speed but in opposite directions so that there is no rotation of the fluid element.)

In addition to the rotation associated with the derivatives $\partial u/\partial y$ and $\partial v/\partial x$, it is observed from Fig. 6.4b that these derivatives can cause the fluid element to undergo an *angular deformation,* which results in a change in shape of the element. The change in the original right angle formed by the lines OA and OB is termed the shearing strain, $\delta\gamma$, and from Fig. 6.4b

$$\delta\gamma = \delta\alpha + \delta\beta$$

where $\delta\gamma$ is considered to be positive if the original right angle is decreasing. The rate of change of $\delta\gamma$ is called the *rate of shearing strain* or the *rate of angular deformation* and is commonly denoted with the symbol, $\dot{\gamma}$. The angles $\delta\alpha$ and $\delta\beta$ are related to the velocity gradients through Eqs. 6.10 and 6.11 so that

$$\dot{\gamma} = \lim_{\delta t \to 0}\frac{\delta\gamma}{\delta t} = \lim_{\delta t \to 0}\left[\frac{(\partial v/\partial x)\,\delta t + (\partial u/\partial y)\,\delta t}{\delta t}\right]$$

and, therefore,

$$\dot{\gamma} = \frac{\partial v}{\partial x} + \frac{\partial u}{\partial y} \tag{6.18}$$

As we will learn in Section 6.7, the rate of angular deformation is related to a corresponding shearing stress, which causes the fluid element to change in shape. From Eq. 6.18 we note that if $\partial u/\partial y = -\partial v/\partial x$, the rate of angular deformation is zero, and this condition corresponds to the case in which the element is simply rotating as an undeformed block (Eq. 6.12). In the remainder of this chapter we will see how the various kinematical relationships developed in this section play an important role in the development and subsequent analysis of the differential equations that govern fluid motion.

6.2 Conservation of Mass

As is discussed in Section 5.2, conservation of mass requires that the mass, M, of a system remain constant as the system moves through the flow field. In equation form this principle is expressed as

$$\frac{DM_{sys}}{Dt} = 0$$

We found it convenient to use the control volume approach for fluid flow problems, with the control volume representation of the conservation of mass written as

$$\frac{\partial}{\partial t}\int_{cv} \rho \, dV + \int_{cs} \rho \, \mathbf{V} \cdot \hat{\mathbf{n}} \, dA = 0 \qquad (6.19)$$

where the equation (commonly called the continuity equation) can be applied to a finite control volume (cv), which is bounded by a control surface (cs). The first integral on the left side of Eq. 6.19 represents the rate at which the mass within the control volume is increasing, and the second integral represents the net rate at which mass is flowing out through the control surface (rate of mass outflow − rate of mass inflow). To obtain the differential form of the continuity equation, Eq. 6.19 is applied to an infinitesimal control volume.

6.2.1 Differential Form of Continuity Equation

We will take as our control volume the small, stationary cubical element shown in Fig. 6.5a. At the center of the element the fluid density is ρ and the velocity has components u, v, and w. Since the element is small the volume integral in Eq. 6.19 can be expressed as

$$\frac{\partial}{\partial t}\int_{cv} \rho \, dV \approx \frac{\partial \rho}{\partial t}\, \delta x \, \delta y \, \delta z \qquad (6.20)$$

The rate of mass flow through the surfaces of the element can be obtained by considering the flow in each of the coordinate directions separately. For example, in Fig. 6.5b flow in

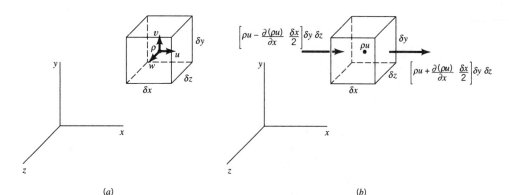

(a)   (b)

■ FIGURE 6.5 A differential element for the development of conservation of mass equation.

the x direction is depicted. If we let ρu represent the x component of the mass rate of flow per unit area at the center of the element, then on the right face

$$\rho u|_{x+(\delta x/2)} = \rho u + \frac{\partial(\rho u)}{\partial x}\frac{\delta x}{2} \tag{6.21}$$

and on the left face

$$\rho u|_{x-(\delta x/2)} = \rho u - \frac{\partial(\rho u)}{\partial x}\frac{\delta x}{2} \tag{6.22}$$

Note that we are really using a Taylor series expansion of ρu and neglecting higher order terms such as $(\delta x)^2$, $(\delta x)^3$, and so on. When the right-hand sides of Eqs. 6.21 and 6.22 are multiplied by the area $\delta y\,\delta z$, the rate at which mass is crossing the right and left sides of the element are obtained as illustrated in Fig. 6.5b. When these two expressions are combined, the net rate of mass flowing from the element through the two surfaces can be expressed as

$$\begin{aligned}\text{Net rate of mass} \atop \text{outflow in } x \text{ direction} = &\left[\rho u + \frac{\partial(\rho u)}{\partial x}\frac{\delta x}{2}\right]\delta y\,\delta z \\ &- \left[\rho u - \frac{\partial(\rho u)}{\partial x}\frac{\delta x}{2}\right]\delta y\,\delta z = \frac{\partial(\rho u)}{\partial x}\delta x\,\delta y\,\delta z\end{aligned} \tag{6.23}$$

For simplicity, only flow in the x direction has been considered in Fig. 6.5b, but, in general, there will also be flow in the y and z directions. An analysis similar to the one used for flow in the x direction shows that

$$\begin{aligned}\text{Net rate of mass} \atop \text{outflow in } y \text{ direction} = \frac{\partial(\rho v)}{\partial y}\delta x\,\delta y\,\delta z\end{aligned} \tag{6.24}$$

and

$$\begin{aligned}\text{Net rate of mass} \atop \text{outflow in } z \text{ direction} = \frac{\partial(\rho w)}{\partial z}\delta x\,\delta y\,\delta z\end{aligned} \tag{6.25}$$

Thus,

$$\begin{aligned}\text{Net rate of} \atop \text{mass outflow} = \left[\frac{\partial(\rho u)}{\partial x} + \frac{\partial(\rho v)}{\partial y} + \frac{\partial(\rho w)}{\partial z}\right]\delta x\,\delta y\,\delta z\end{aligned} \tag{6.26}$$

From Eqs. 6.19, 6.20, and 6.26 it now follows that the differential equation for conservation of mass is

$$\boxed{\frac{\partial\rho}{\partial t} + \frac{\partial(\rho u)}{\partial x} + \frac{\partial(\rho v)}{\partial y} + \frac{\partial(\rho w)}{\partial z} = 0} \tag{6.27}$$

As previously mentioned, this equation is also commonly referred to as the continuity equation.

The continuity equation is one of the fundamental equations of fluid mechanics and, as expressed in Eq. 6.27, is valid for steady or unsteady flow, and compressible or incompressible fluids. In vector notation Eq. 6.27 can be written as

$$\frac{\partial\rho}{\partial t} + \nabla\cdot\rho\mathbf{V} = 0 \tag{6.28}$$

Two special cases are of particular interest. For *steady* flow of *compressible* fluids

$$\nabla \cdot \rho \mathbf{V} = 0$$

or

$$\frac{\partial(\rho u)}{\partial x} + \frac{\partial(\rho v)}{\partial y} + \frac{\partial(\rho w)}{\partial z} = 0 \qquad \textbf{(6.29)}$$

This follows since by definition ρ is not a function of time for steady flow, but could be a function of position. For *incompressible* fluids the fluid density, ρ, is a constant throughout the flow field so that Eq. 6.28 becomes

$$\nabla \cdot \mathbf{V} = 0 \qquad \textbf{(6.30)}$$

or

$$\frac{\partial u}{\partial x} + \frac{\partial v}{\partial y} + \frac{\partial w}{\partial z} = 0 \qquad \textbf{(6.31)}$$

Equation 6.31 applies to both steady and unsteady flow of incompressible fluids. Note that Eq. 6.31 is the same as that obtained by setting the volumetric dilatation rate (Eq. 6.9) equal to zero. This result should not be surprising since both relationships are based on conservation of mass for incompressible fluids.

6.2.2   Cylindrical Polar Coordinates

For some problems it is more convenient to express the various differential relationships in cylindrical polar coordinates rather than Cartesian coordinates. As is shown in Fig. 6.6, with cylindrical coordinates a point is located by specifying the coordinates r, θ, and z. The coordinate r is the radial distance from the z axis, θ is the angle measured from a line parallel to the x axis (with counterclockwise taken as positive), and z is the coordinate along the z axis. The velocity components, as sketched in Fig. 6.6, are the radial velocity, v_r, the tangential velocity, v_θ, and the axial velocity, v_z. Thus, the velocity at some arbitrary point P can be expressed as

$$\mathbf{V} = v_r \hat{\mathbf{e}}_r + v_\theta \hat{\mathbf{e}}_\theta + v_z \hat{\mathbf{e}}_z \qquad \textbf{(6.32)}$$

where $\hat{\mathbf{e}}_r$, $\hat{\mathbf{e}}_\theta$, and $\hat{\mathbf{e}}_z$ are the unit vectors in the r, θ, and z directions, respectively, as illustrated in Fig. 6.6. The use of cylindrical coordinates is particularly convenient when the boundaries

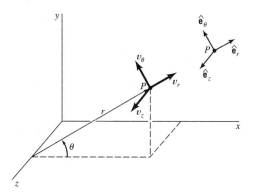

■ FIGURE 6.6   The representation of velocity components in cylindrical polar coordinates.

of the flow system are cylindrical. Several examples illustrating the use of cylindrical coordinates will be given in succeeding sections in this chapter.

The differential form of the continuity equation in cylindrical coordinates is

$$\frac{\partial \rho}{\partial t} + \frac{1}{r}\frac{\partial(r\rho v_r)}{\partial r} + \frac{1}{r}\frac{\partial(\rho v_\theta)}{\partial \theta} + \frac{\partial(\rho v_z)}{\partial z} = 0 \qquad (6.33)$$

This equation can be derived by following the same procedure used in the preceding section. For steady, compressible flow

$$\frac{1}{r}\frac{\partial(r\rho v_r)}{\partial r} + \frac{1}{r}\frac{\partial(\rho v_\theta)}{\partial \theta} + \frac{\partial(\rho v_z)}{\partial z} = 0 \qquad (6.34)$$

For incompressible fluids (for steady or unsteady flow)

$$\frac{1}{r}\frac{\partial(r v_r)}{\partial r} + \frac{1}{r}\frac{\partial v_\theta}{\partial \theta} + \frac{\partial v_z}{\partial z} = 0 \qquad (6.35)$$

6.2.3 The Stream Function

Steady, incompressible, plane, two-dimensional flow represents one of the simplest types of flow of practical importance. By plane, two-dimensional flow we mean that there are only two velocity components, such as u and v, when the flow is considered to be in the x–y plane. For this flow the continuity equation, Eq. 6.31, reduces to

$$\frac{\partial u}{\partial x} + \frac{\partial v}{\partial y} = 0 \qquad (6.36)$$

We still have two variables, u and v, to deal with, but they must be related in a special way as indicated by Eq. 6.36. This equation suggests that if we define a function $\psi(x, y)$, called the *stream function*, which relates the velocities as

$$u = \frac{\partial \psi}{\partial y} \qquad v = -\frac{\partial \psi}{\partial x} \qquad (6.37)$$

then the continuity equation is identically satisfied.

Thus, whenever the velocity components are defined in terms of the stream function we know that conservation of mass will be satisfied. Of course, we still do not know what $\psi(x, y)$ is for a particular problem, but at least we have simplified the analysis by having to determine only one unknown function, $\psi(x, y)$, rather than the two functions, $u(x, y)$ and $v(x, y)$.

Another particular advantage of using the stream function is related to the fact that *lines along which ψ is constant are streamlines.* Recall from Section 4.1.4 that streamlines are lines in the flow field that are everywhere tangent to the velocities, as illustrated in Fig. 6.7. It follows from the definition of the streamline that the slope at any point along a streamline is given by

$$\frac{dy}{dx} = \frac{v}{u}$$

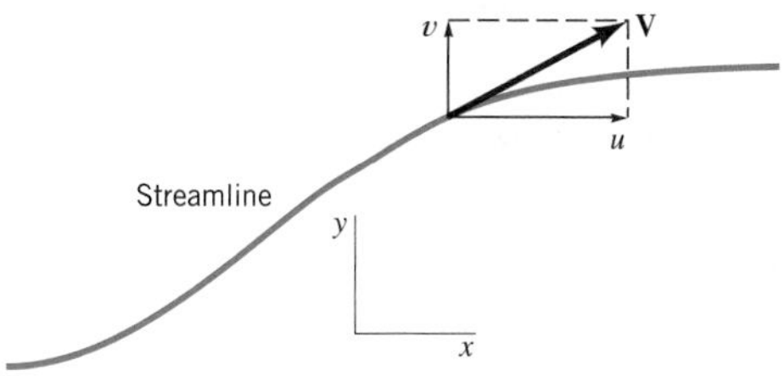

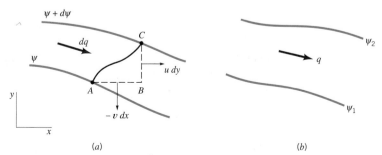

■ FIGURE 6.7 **Velocity and velocity components along a streamline.**

The change in the value of ψ as we move from one point (x, y) to a nearby point $(x + dx, y + dy)$ is given by the relationship:

$$d\psi = \frac{\partial \psi}{\partial x} dx + \frac{\partial \psi}{\partial y} dy = -v \, dx + u \, dy$$

Along a line of constant ψ we have $d\psi = 0$ so that

$$-v \, dx + u \, dy = 0$$

and, therefore, along a line of constant ψ

$$\frac{dy}{dx} = \frac{v}{u}$$

which is the defining equation for a streamline. Thus, if we know the function $\psi(x, y)$ we can plot lines of constant ψ to provide the family of streamlines that are helpful in visualizing the pattern of flow. There are an infinite number of streamlines that make up a particular flow field, since for each constant value assigned to ψ a streamline can be drawn.

The actual numerical value associated with a particular streamline is not of particular significance, but the change in the value of ψ is related to the volume rate of flow. Consider two closely spaced streamlines, as shown in Fig. 6.8a. The lower streamline is designated ψ and the upper one $\psi + d\psi$. Let dq represent the volume rate of flow (per unit width perpendicular to the x–y plane) passing between the two streamlines. Note that flow never crosses streamlines, since by definition the velocity is tangent to the streamline. From conservation of mass we know that the inflow, dq, crossing the arbitrary surface AC of Fig. 6.8a must equal the net outflow through surfaces AB and BC. Thus,

$$dq = u \, dy - v \, dx$$

■ FIGURE 6.8 **The flow between two streamlines.**

or in terms of the stream function

$$dq = \frac{\partial \psi}{\partial y} \, dy + \frac{\partial \psi}{\partial x} \, dx \qquad (6.38)$$

The right-hand side of Eq. 6.38 is equal to $d\psi$ so that

$$dq = d\psi \qquad (6.39)$$

Thus, the volume rate of flow, q, between two streamlines such as ψ_1 and ψ_2 of Fig. 6.8b can be determined by integrating Eq. 6.39 to yield

$$q = \int_{\psi_1}^{\psi_2} d\psi = \psi_2 - \psi_1 \qquad (6.40)$$

If the upper streamline, ψ_2, has a value greater than the lower streamline, ψ_1, then q is positive, which indicates that the flow is from left to right. For $\psi_1 > \psi_2$ the flow is from right to left.

In cylindrical coordinates the continuity equation (Eq. 6.35) for incompressible, plane, two-dimensional flow reduces to

$$\frac{1}{r} \frac{\partial (rv_r)}{\partial r} + \frac{1}{r} \frac{\partial v_\theta}{\partial \theta} = 0 \qquad (6.41)$$

and the velocity components, v_r and v_θ, can be related to the stream function, $\psi(r, \theta)$, through the equations

$$\boxed{v_r = \frac{1}{r} \frac{\partial \psi}{\partial \theta} \qquad v_\theta = -\frac{\partial \psi}{\partial r}} \qquad (6.42)$$

Substitution of these expressions for the velocity components into Eq. 6.41 shows that the continuity equation is identically satisfied. The stream function concept can be extended to axisymmetric flows, such as flow in pipes or flow around bodies of revolution, and to two-dimensional compressible flows. However, the concept is not applicable to general three-dimensional flows.

EXAMPLE 6.2

The velocity components in a steady, two-dimensional incompressible flow field are

$$u = 2y$$
$$v = 4x$$

Determine the corresponding stream function and show on a sketch several streamlines. Indicate the direction of flow along the streamlines.

SOLUTION

From the definition of the stream function (Eqs. 6.37)

$$u = \frac{\partial \psi}{\partial y} = 2y$$

and

$$v = -\frac{\partial \psi}{\partial x} = 4x$$

The first of these equations can be integrated to give

$$\psi = y^2 + f_1(x)$$

where $f_1(x)$ is an arbitrary function of x. Similarly from the second equation

$$\psi = -2x^2 + f_2(y)$$

where $f_2(y)$ is an arbitrary function of y. It now follows that in order to satisfy both expressions for the stream function

$$\psi = -2x^2 + y^2 + C \qquad\qquad \text{(Ans)}$$

where C is an arbitrary constant.

Since the velocities are related to the derivatives of the stream function, an arbitrary constant can always be added to the function, and the value of the constant is actually of no consequence. Usually, for simplicity, we set $C = 0$ so that for this particular example the simplest form for the stream function is

$$\psi = -2x^2 + y^2 \qquad\qquad \textbf{(1)} \quad \text{(Ans)}$$

Either answer indicated would be acceptable.

Streamlines can now be determined by setting ψ = constant and plotting the resulting curve. With the above expression for ψ (with $C = 0$) the value of ψ at the origin is zero so that the equation of the streamline passing through the origin (the $\psi = 0$ streamline) is

$$0 = -2x^2 + y^2$$

or

$$y = \pm\sqrt{2}x$$

Other streamlines can be obtained by setting ψ equal to various constants. It follows from Eq. 1 that the equations of these streamlines (for $\psi \neq 0$) can be expressed in the form

$$\frac{y^2}{\psi} - \frac{x^2}{\psi/2} = 1$$

which we recognize as the equation of a hyperbola. Thus, the streamlines are a family of hyperbolas with the $\psi = 0$ streamlines as asymptotes. Several of the streamlines are plotted in Fig. E6.2. Since the velocities can be calculated at any point, the direction of flow along a given streamline can be easily deduced. For example, $v = -\partial\psi/\partial x = 4x$ so that $v > 0$ if $x > 0$ and $v < 0$ if $x < 0$. The direction of flow is indicated on the figure.

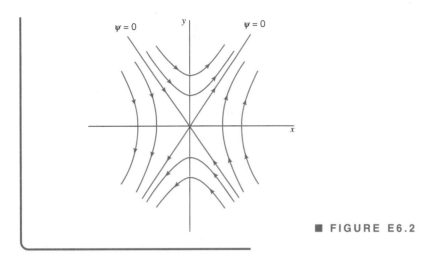

$\psi = 0$ y $\psi = 0$

x

■ FIGURE E6.2

6.3 Conservation of Linear Momentum

To develop the differential, linear momentum equations we can start with the linear momentum equation

$$\mathbf{F} = \left.\frac{D\mathbf{P}}{Dt}\right|_{\text{sys}} \tag{6.43}$$

where $\mathbf{F}$ is the resultant force acting on a fluid mass, $\mathbf{P}$ is the linear momentum defined as

$$\mathbf{P} = \int_{\text{sys}} \mathbf{V}\, dm$$

and the operator $D(\ )/Dt$ is the material derivative (see Section 4.2.1). In the last chapter it was demonstrated how Eq. 6.43 in the form

$$\Sigma\, \mathbf{F}_{\substack{\text{contents of the}\\\text{control volume}}} = \frac{\partial}{\partial t}\int_{\text{cv}} \mathbf{V}\rho\, d\forall + \int_{\text{cs}} \mathbf{V}\rho\mathbf{V}\cdot\hat{\mathbf{n}}\, dA \tag{6.44}$$

could be applied to a finite control volume to solve a variety of flow problems. To obtain the differential form of the linear momentum equation, we can either apply Eq. 6.43 to a differential system, consisting of a mass, δm, or apply Eq. 6.44 to an infinitesimal control volume, $\delta\forall$, which initially bounds the mass δm. It is probably simpler to use the system approach since application of Eq. 6.43 to the differential mass, δm, yields

$$\delta\mathbf{F} = \frac{D(\mathbf{V}\,\delta m)}{Dt}$$

where $\delta\mathbf{F}$ is the resultant force acting on δm. Using this system approach δm can be treated as a constant so that

$$\delta\mathbf{F} = \delta m\,\frac{D\mathbf{V}}{Dt}$$

But DV/Dt is the acceleration, **a**, of the element. Thus,

$$\delta\mathbf{F} = \delta m\,\mathbf{a} \tag{6.45}$$

which is simply Newton's second law applied to the mass, δm. This is the same result that would be obtained by applying Eq. 6.44 to an infinitesimal control volume (see Ref. 1). Before we can proceed, it is necessary to examine how the force, $\delta\mathbf{F}$, can be most conveniently expressed.

6.3.1   Description of Forces Acting on Differential Element

In general, two types of forces need to be considered: *surface forces,* which act on the surface of the differential element, and *body forces,* which are distributed throughout the element. For our purpose, the only body force, $\delta\mathbf{F}_b$, of interest is the weight of the element, which can be expressed as

$$\delta\mathbf{F}_b = \delta m\,\mathbf{g} \tag{6.46}$$

where **g** is the vector representation of the acceleration of gravity. In component form

$$\delta F_{bx} = \delta m\,g_x \tag{6.47a}$$

$$\delta F_{by} = \delta m\,g_y \tag{6.47b}$$

$$\delta F_{bz} = \delta m\,g_z \tag{6.47c}$$

where g_x, g_y, and g_z are the components of the acceleration of gravity vector in the x, y, and z directions, respectively.

Surface forces act on the element as a result of its interaction with its surroundings. At any arbitrary location within a fluid mass, the force acting on a small area, δA, which lies in an arbitrary surface can be represented by $\delta\mathbf{F}_s$, as shown in Fig. 6.9. In general, $\delta\mathbf{F}_s$ will be inclined with respect to the surface. The force $\delta\mathbf{F}_s$ can be resolved into three components, δF_n, δF_1, and δF_2, where δF_n is normal to the area, δA, and δF_1 and δF_2 are parallel to the area and orthogonal to each other. The *normal stress, σ_n* is defined as

$$\sigma_n = \lim_{\delta A \to 0} \frac{\delta F_n}{\delta A}$$

and the *shearing stresses* are defined as

$$\tau_1 = \lim_{\delta A \to 0} \frac{\delta F_1}{\delta A}$$

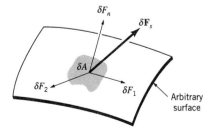

■ **FIGURE 6.9**   **Component of force acting on an arbitrary differential area.**

and

$$\tau_2 = \lim_{\delta A \to 0} \frac{\delta F_2}{\delta A}$$

We will use σ for normal stresses and τ for shearing stresses. The intensity of the force per unit area at a point in a body can thus be characterized by a normal stress and two shearing stresses, if the orientation of the area is specified. For purposes of analysis it is usually convenient to reference the area to the coordinate system. For example, for the rectangular coordinate system shown in Fig. 6.10 we choose to consider the stresses acting on planes parallel to the coordinate planes. On the plane $ABCD$ of Fig. 6.10a, which is parallel to the $y–z$ plane, the normal stress is denoted σ_{xx} and the shearing stresses are denoted as τ_{xy} and τ_{xz}. To easily identify the particular stress component we use a double subscript notation. The first subscript indicates the direction of the *normal* to the plane on which the stress acts, and the second subscript indicates the direction of the stress. Thus, normal stresses have repeated subscripts, whereas the subscripts for the shearing stresses are always different.

It is also necessary to establish a sign convention for the stresses. We define the positive direction for the stress as the positive coordinate direction on the surfaces for which the outward normal is in the positive coordinate direction. This is the case illustrated in Fig. 6.10a where the outward normal to the area $ABCD$ is in the positive x direction. The positive directions for σ_{xx}, τ_{xy}, and τ_{xz} are as shown in Fig. 6.10a. If the outward normal points in the negative coordinate direction, as in Fig. 6.10b for the area $A'B'C'D'$, then the stresses are considered positive if directed in the negative coordinate directions. Thus, the stresses shown in Fig. 6.10b are considered to be positive when directed as shown. Note that positive normal stresses are tensile stresses; that is, they tend to "stretch" the material.

It should be emphasized that the state of stress at a point in a material is not completely defined by simply three components of a "stress vector." This follows, since any particular stress vector depends on the orientation of the plane passing through the point. However, it can be shown that the normal and shearing stresses acting on *any* plane passing through a point can be expressed in terms of the stresses acting on three orthogonal planes passing through the point (Ref. 2).

We now can express the surface forces acting on a small cubical element of fluid in terms of the stresses acting on the faces of the element as shown in Fig. 6.11. It is expected

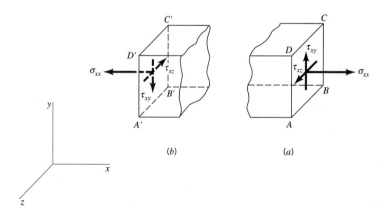

(b)　　　(a)

■ **FIGURE 6.10**
Double subscript notation for stresses.

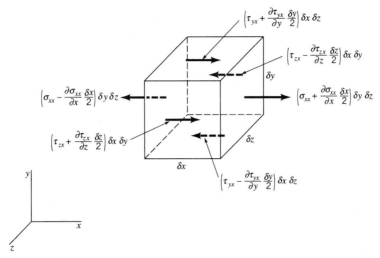

■ **FIGURE 6.11** **Surface forces in the x direction acting on a fluid element.**

that in general the stresses will vary from point to point within the flow field. Thus, we will express the stresses on the various faces in terms of the corresponding stresses at the center of the element of Fig. 6.11 and their gradients in the coordinate directions. For simplicity only the forces in the x direction are shown. Note that the stresses must be multiplied by the area on which they act to obtain the force. Summing all these forces in the x direction yields

$$\delta F_{sx} = \left(\frac{\partial \sigma_{xx}}{\partial x} + \frac{\partial \tau_{yx}}{\partial y} + \frac{\partial \tau_{zx}}{\partial z} \right) \delta x \, \delta y \, \delta z \tag{6.48a}$$

for the resultant surface force in the x direction. In a similar manner the resultant surface forces in the y and z direction can be obtained and expressed as

$$\delta F_{sy} = \left(\frac{\partial \tau_{xy}}{\partial x} + \frac{\partial \sigma_{yy}}{\partial y} + \frac{\partial \tau_{zy}}{\partial z} \right) \delta x \, \delta y \, \delta z \tag{6.48b}$$

and

$$\delta F_{sz} = \left(\frac{\partial \tau_{xz}}{\partial x} + \frac{\partial \tau_{yz}}{\partial y} + \frac{\partial \sigma_{zz}}{\partial z} \right) \delta x \, \delta y \, \delta z \tag{6.48c}$$

The resultant surface force can now be expressed as

$$\delta \mathbf{F}_s = \delta F_{sx} \hat{\mathbf{i}} + \delta F_{sy} \hat{\mathbf{j}} + \delta F_{sz} \hat{\mathbf{k}} \tag{6.49}$$

and this force combined with the body force, $\delta \mathbf{F}_b$, yields the resultant force, $\delta \mathbf{F}$, acting on the differential mass, δm. That is, $\delta \mathbf{F} = \delta \mathbf{F}_s + \delta \mathbf{F}_b$.

6.3.2 Equations of Motion

The expressions for the body and surface forces can now be used in conjunction with Eq. 6.45 to develop the equations of motion. In component form Eq. 6.45 can be written as

$$\delta F_x = \delta m\, a_x$$

$$\delta F_y = \delta m\, a_y$$

$$\delta F_z = \delta m\, a_z$$

where $\delta m = \rho\, \delta x\, \delta y\, \delta z$, and the acceleration components are given by Eq. 6.3. It now follows (using Eqs. 6.47 and 6.48 for the forces on the element) that

$$\rho g_x + \frac{\partial \sigma_{xx}}{\partial x} + \frac{\partial \tau_{yx}}{\partial y} + \frac{\partial \tau_{zx}}{\partial z} = \rho \left(\frac{\partial u}{\partial t} + u\frac{\partial u}{\partial x} + v\frac{\partial u}{\partial y} + w\frac{\partial u}{\partial z} \right) \qquad \text{(6.50a)}$$

$$\rho g_y + \frac{\partial \tau_{xy}}{\partial x} + \frac{\partial \sigma_{yy}}{\partial y} + \frac{\partial \tau_{zy}}{\partial z} = \rho \left(\frac{\partial v}{\partial t} + u\frac{\partial v}{\partial x} + v\frac{\partial v}{\partial y} + w\frac{\partial v}{\partial z} \right) \qquad \text{(6.50b)}$$

$$\rho g_z + \frac{\partial \tau_{xz}}{\partial x} + \frac{\partial \tau_{yz}}{\partial y} + \frac{\partial \sigma_{zz}}{\partial z} = \rho \left(\frac{\partial w}{\partial t} + u\frac{\partial w}{\partial x} + v\frac{\partial w}{\partial y} + w\frac{\partial w}{\partial z} \right) \qquad \text{(6.50c)}$$

where the element volume $\delta x\, \delta y\, \delta z$ cancels out.

Equations 6.50 are the general differential equations of motion for a fluid. In fact, they are applicable to any continuum (solid or fluid) in motion or at rest. However, before we can use the equations to solve specific problems, some additional information about the stresses must be obtained. Otherwise, we will have more unknowns (all of the stresses and velocities and the density) than equations. It should not be too surprising that the differential analysis of fluid motion is complicated. We are attempting to describe, in detail, complex fluid motion.

6.4 Inviscid Flow

As is discussed in Section 1.6, shearing stresses develop in a moving fluid because of the viscosity of the fluid. We know that for some common fluids, such as air and water, the viscosity is small, and therefore it seems reasonable to assume that under some circumstances we may be able to simply neglect the effect of viscosity (and thus shearing stresses). Flow fields in which the shearing stresses are assumed to be negligible are said to be *inviscid, nonviscous,* or *frictionless.* These terms are used interchangeably. As is discussed in Section 2.1, for fluids in which there are no shearing stresses the normal stress at a point is independent of direction—that is, $\sigma_{xx} = \sigma_{yy} = \sigma_{zz}$. In this instance we define the pressure, p, as the negative of the normal stress so that

$$-p = \sigma_{xx} = \sigma_{yy} = \sigma_{zz}$$

The negative sign is used so that a *compressive* normal stress (which is what we expect in a fluid) will give a *positive* value for p.

In Chapter 3 the inviscid flow concept was used in the development of the Bernoulli equation, and numerous applications of this important equation were considered. In this section we will again consider the Bernoulli equation and will show how it can be derived from the general equations of motion for inviscid flow.

6.4.1 Euler's Equations of Motion

For an inviscid flow in which all the shearing stresses are zero, and the normal stresses are replaced by $-p$, the general equations of motion (Eqs. 6.50) reduce to

$$\rho g_x - \frac{\partial p}{\partial x} = \rho\left(\frac{\partial u}{\partial t} + u\frac{\partial u}{\partial x} + v\frac{\partial u}{\partial y} + w\frac{\partial u}{\partial z}\right) \tag{6.51a}$$

$$\rho g_y - \frac{\partial p}{\partial y} = \rho\left(\frac{\partial v}{\partial t} + u\frac{\partial v}{\partial x} + v\frac{\partial v}{\partial y} + w\frac{\partial v}{\partial z}\right) \tag{6.51b}$$

$$\rho g_z - \frac{\partial p}{\partial z} = \rho\left(\frac{\partial w}{\partial t} + u\frac{\partial w}{\partial x} + v\frac{\partial w}{\partial y} + w\frac{\partial w}{\partial z}\right) \tag{6.51c}$$

These equations are commonly referred to as *Euler's equations of motion,* named in honor of Leonhard Euler, a famous Swiss mathematician who pioneered work on the relationship between pressure and flow. In vector notation Euler's equations can be expressed as

$$\rho\mathbf{g} - \nabla p = \rho\left[\frac{\partial \mathbf{V}}{\partial t} + (\mathbf{V}\cdot\nabla)\mathbf{V}\right] \tag{6.52}$$

Although Eqs. 6.51 are considerably simpler than the general equations of motion, they are still not amenable to a general analytical solution that would allow us to determine the pressure and velocity at all points within an inviscid flow field. The main difficulty arises from the nonlinear velocity terms (such as $u\,\partial u/\partial x$, $v\,\partial u/\partial y$, etc.), which appear in the convective acceleration. Because of these terms, Euler's equations are nonlinear partial differential equations for which we do not have a general method for solving. However, under some circumstances we can use them to obtain useful information about inviscid flow fields. For example, as shown in the following section we can integrate Eq. 6.52 to obtain a relationship (the Bernoulli equation) between elevation, pressure, and velocity along a streamline.

6.4.2 The Bernoulli Equation

In Section 3.2 the Bernoulli equation was derived by a direct application of Newton's second law to a fluid particle moving along a streamline. In this section we will again derive this important equation, starting from Euler's equations. Of course, we should obtain the same result since Euler's equations simply represent a statement of Newton's second law expressed in a general form that is useful for flow problems. We will restrict our attention to steady flow so Euler's equation in vector form becomes

$$\rho\mathbf{g} - \nabla p = \rho(\mathbf{V}\cdot\nabla)\mathbf{V} \tag{6.53}$$

We wish to integrate this differential equation along some arbitrary streamline (Fig. 6.12) and select the coordinate system with the z axis vertical (with "up" being positive) so that the acceleration of gravity vector can be expressed as

$$\mathbf{g} = -g\,\nabla z$$

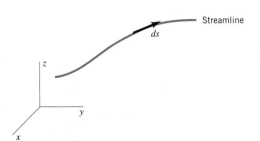

■ **FIGURE 6.12** The notation for differential length along a streamline.

where g is the magnitude of the acceleration of gravity vector. Also, it will be convenient to use the vector identity

$$(\mathbf{V} \cdot \nabla)\mathbf{V} = \tfrac{1}{2}\nabla(\mathbf{V} \cdot \mathbf{V}) - \mathbf{V} \times (\nabla \times \mathbf{V})$$

Equation 6.53 can now be written in the form

$$-\rho g\,\nabla z - \nabla p = \frac{\rho}{2}\,\nabla(\mathbf{V} \cdot \mathbf{V}) - \rho(\mathbf{V} \times \nabla \times \mathbf{V})$$

and this equation can be rearranged to yield

$$\frac{\nabla p}{\rho} + \frac{1}{2}\nabla(V^2) + g\nabla z = \mathbf{V} \times (\nabla \times \mathbf{V})$$

We next take the dot product of each term with a differential length $d\mathbf{s}$ along a streamline (Fig. 6.12). Thus,

$$\frac{\nabla p}{\rho} \cdot d\mathbf{s} + \frac{1}{2}\nabla(V^2) \cdot d\mathbf{s} + g\nabla z \cdot d\mathbf{s} = [\mathbf{V} \times (\nabla \times \mathbf{V})] \cdot d\mathbf{s} \qquad \textbf{(6.54)}$$

Since $d\mathbf{s}$ has a direction along the streamline, the vectors $d\mathbf{s}$ and $\mathbf{V}$ are parallel. However, the vector $\mathbf{V} \times (\nabla \times \mathbf{V})$ is perpendicular to $\mathbf{V}$ (why?), so it follows that

$$[\mathbf{V} \times (\nabla \times \mathbf{V})] \cdot d\mathbf{s} = 0$$

Recall also that the dot product of the gradient of a scalar and a differential length gives the differential change in the scalar in the direction of the differential length. That is, with $d\mathbf{s} = dx\,\hat{\mathbf{i}} + dy\,\hat{\mathbf{j}} + dz\,\hat{\mathbf{k}}$ we can write $\nabla p \cdot d\mathbf{s} = (\partial p/\partial x)\,dx + (\partial p/\partial y)\,dy + (\partial p/\partial z)\,dz = dp$. Thus, Eq. 6.54 becomes

$$\frac{dp}{\rho} + \frac{1}{2}d(V^2) + g\,dz = 0 \qquad \textbf{(6.55)}$$

where the change in p, V, and z is along the streamline. Equation 6.55 can now be integrated to give

$$\int\frac{dp}{\rho} + \frac{V^2}{2} + gz = \text{constant} \qquad \textbf{(6.56)}$$

which indicates that the sum of the three terms on the left side of the equation must remain a constant along a given streamline. Equation 6.56 is valid for both compressible and incompressible inviscid flows, but for compressible fluids the variation in ρ with p must be specified before the first term in Eq. 6.56 can be evaluated.

For inviscid, incompressible fluids (commonly called *ideal fluids*) Eq. 6.56 can be written as

$$\boxed{\frac{p}{\rho} + \frac{V^2}{2} + gz = \text{constant}} \qquad \textbf{(6.57)}$$

and this equation is the Bernoulli equation used extensively in Chapter 3. It is often convenient to write Eq. 6.57 between two points (1) and (2) along a streamline and to express the equation in the "head" form by dividing each term by g so that

$$\boxed{\frac{p_1}{\gamma} + \frac{V_1^2}{2g} + z_1 = \frac{p_2}{\gamma} + \frac{V_2^2}{2g} + z_2} \qquad (6.58)$$

It should be again emphasized that the Bernoulli equation, as expressed by Eqs. 6.57 and 6.58, is restricted to the following:

- inviscid flow
- steady flow
- incompressible flow
- flow along a streamline

You may want to go back and review some of the examples in Chapter 3 that illustrate the use of the Bernoulli equation.

6.4.3 Irrotational Flow

If we make one additional assumption—that the flow is *irrotational*—the analysis of inviscid flow problems is further simplified. Recall from Section 6.1.3 that the rotation of a fluid element is equal to $\frac{1}{2}(\nabla \times \mathbf{V})$, and an irrotational flow field is one for which $\nabla \times \mathbf{V} = 0$. Since the vorticity, ζ, is defined as $\nabla \times \mathbf{V}$, it also follows that in an irrotational flow field the vorticity is zero. The concept of irrotationality may seem to be a rather strange condition for a flow field. Why would a flow field be irrotational? To answer this question we note that if $\frac{1}{2}(\nabla \times \mathbf{V}) = 0$, then each of the components of this vector, as are given by Eqs. 6.12, 6.13, and 6.14, must be equal to zero. Since these components include the various velocity gradients in the flow field, the condition of irrotationality imposes specific relationships among these velocity gradients. For example, for rotation about the z axis to be zero, it follows from Eq. 6.12 that

$$\omega_z = \frac{1}{2}\left(\frac{\partial v}{\partial x} - \frac{\partial u}{\partial y}\right) = 0$$

and, therefore,

$$\frac{\partial v}{\partial x} = \frac{\partial u}{\partial y} \qquad (6.59)$$

Similarly from Eqs. 6.13 and 6.14

$$\frac{\partial w}{\partial y} = \frac{\partial v}{\partial z} \qquad (6.60)$$

and

$$\frac{\partial u}{\partial z} = \frac{\partial w}{\partial x} \qquad (6.61)$$

A general flow field would not satisfy these three equations. However, a uniform flow as is illustrated in Fig. 6.13 does. Since $u = U$ (a constant), $v = 0$, and $w = 0$, it follows that Eqs. 6.59, 6.60, and 6.61 are all satisfied. Therefore, a uniform flow field (in which there are no velocity gradients) is certainly an example of an irrotational flow.

For an inviscid fluid there are no shearing stresses—the only forces acting on a fluid element are its weight and pressure forces. Since the weight acts through the element center of gravity, and the pressure acts in a direction normal to the element surface, neither of these forces can cause the element to rotate. Therefore, for an inviscid fluid, if some part of the

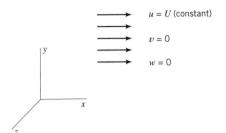

$u = U$ (constant)

$v = 0$

$w = 0$

■ **FIGURE 6.13** **Uniform flow in the x direction.**

flow field is irrotational, the fluid elements emanating from this region will not take on any rotation as they progress through the flow field.

6.4.4 The Bernoulli Equation for Irrotational Flow

In the development of the Bernoulli equation in Section 6.4.2, Eq. 6.54 was integrated along a streamline. This restriction was imposed so the right side of the equation could be set equal to zero; that is

$$(\mathbf{V} \times \nabla \times \mathbf{V}) \cdot d\mathbf{s} = 0$$

(since $d\mathbf{s}$ is parallel to $\mathbf{V}$). However, for irrotational flow, $\nabla \times \mathbf{V} = 0$, so the right side of Eq. 6.54 is zero regardless of the direction of $d\mathbf{s}$. We can now follow the same procedure used to obtain Eq. 6.55, where the differential changes dp, $d(V^2)$, and dz can be taken in any direction. Integration of Eq. 6.55 again yields

$$\int \frac{dp}{\rho} + \frac{V^2}{2} + gz = \text{constant} \tag{6.62}$$

but the constant is the same throughout the flow field. Thus, for incompressible, irrotational flow the Bernoulli equation can be written as

$$\boxed{\frac{p_1}{\gamma} + \frac{V_1^2}{2g} + z_1 = \frac{p_2}{\gamma} + \frac{V_2^2}{2g} + z_2} \tag{6.63}$$

between *any two points in the flow field.* Equation 6.63 is exactly the same form as Eq. 6.58 but is not limited to application along a streamline.

6.4.5 The Velocity Potential

For an irrotational flow the velocity gradients are related through Eqs. 6.59, 6.60, and 6.61. It follows that in this case the velocity components can be expressed in terms of a scalar function $\phi(x, y, z, t)$ as

$$u = \frac{\partial \phi}{\partial x} \qquad v = \frac{\partial \phi}{\partial y} \qquad w = \frac{\partial \phi}{\partial z} \tag{6.64}$$

where ϕ is called the *velocity potential.* Direct substitution of these expressions for the velocity components into Eqs. 6.59, 6.60, and 6.61 will verify that a velocity field defined by Eqs. 6.64 is indeed irrotational. In vector form, Eqs. 6.64 can be written as

$$\boxed{\mathbf{V} = \nabla\phi}$$ (6.65)

so that for an irrotational flow the velocity is expressible as the gradient of a scalar function ϕ.

The velocity potential is a consequence of the irrotationality of the flow field, whereas the stream function is a consequence of conservation of mass. It is to be noted, however, that the velocity potential can be defined for a general three-dimensional flow, whereas the stream function is restricted to two-dimensional flows.

For an incompressible fluid we know from conservation of mass that

$$\nabla \cdot \mathbf{V} = 0$$

and therefore for incompressible, irrotational flow (with $\mathbf{V} = \nabla\phi$) it follows that

$$\nabla^2\phi = 0$$ (6.66)

where $\nabla^2(\ ) = \nabla \cdot \nabla(\ )$ is the *Laplacian operator*. In Cartesian coordinates

$$\frac{\partial^2\phi}{\partial x^2} + \frac{\partial^2\phi}{\partial y^2} + \frac{\partial^2\phi}{\partial z^2} = 0$$

This differential equation arises in many different areas of engineering and physics and is called *Laplace's equation*. Thus, inviscid, incompressible, irrotational flow fields are governed by Laplace's equation. This type of flow is commonly called a *potential flow*. To complete the mathematical formulation of a given problem, boundary conditions have to be specified. These are usually velocities specified on the boundaries of the flow field of interest. It follows that if the potential function can be determined, then the velocity at all points in the flow field can be determined from Eq. 6.64, and the pressure at all points can be determined from the Bernoulli equation (Eq. 6.63). Although the concept of the velocity potential is applicable to both steady and unsteady flow, we will confine our attention to steady flow.

For some problems it will be convenient to use cylindrical coordinates, r, θ, and z. In this coordinate system the gradient operator is

$$\nabla(\ ) = \frac{\partial(\ )}{\partial r}\,\hat{\mathbf{e}}_r + \frac{1}{r}\frac{\partial(\ )}{\partial \theta}\,\hat{\mathbf{e}}_\theta + \frac{\partial(\ )}{\partial z}\,\hat{\mathbf{e}}_z$$ (6.67)

so that

$$\nabla\phi = \frac{\partial\phi}{\partial r}\,\hat{\mathbf{e}}_r + \frac{1}{r}\frac{\partial\phi}{\partial \theta}\,\hat{\mathbf{e}}_\theta + \frac{\partial\phi}{\partial z}\,\hat{\mathbf{e}}_z$$ (6.68)

where $\phi = \phi(r, \theta, z)$. Since

$$\mathbf{V} = v_r\hat{\mathbf{e}}_r + v_\theta\hat{\mathbf{e}}_\theta + v_z\hat{\mathbf{e}}_z$$ (6.69)

it follows for an irrotational flow (with $\mathbf{V} = \nabla\phi$)

$$v_r = \frac{\partial\phi}{\partial r} \qquad v_\theta = \frac{1}{r}\frac{\partial\phi}{\partial \theta} \qquad v_z = \frac{\partial\phi}{\partial z}$$ (6.70)

Also, Laplace's equation in cylindrical coordinates is

$$\frac{1}{r}\frac{\partial}{\partial r}\left(r\frac{\partial\phi}{\partial r}\right) + \frac{1}{r^2}\frac{\partial^2\phi}{\partial \theta^2} + \frac{\partial^2\phi}{\partial z^2} = 0$$ (6.71)

EXAMPLE 6.3

The two-dimensional flow of a nonviscous, incompressible fluid in the vicinity of the 90° corner of Fig. E6.3a is described by the stream function

$$\psi = 2r^2 \sin 2\theta$$

where ψ has units of m²/s when r is in meters. **(a)** Determine, if possible, the corresponding velocity potential. **(b)** If the pressure at point (1) on the wall is 30 kPa, what is the pressure at point (2)? Assume the fluid density is 10^3 kg/m³ and the x–y plane is horizontal—that is, there is no difference in elevation between points (1) and (2).

SOLUTION

(a)   The radial and tangential velocity components can be obtained from the stream function as (see Eq. 6.42)

$$v_r = \frac{1}{r}\frac{\partial \psi}{\partial \theta} = 4r \cos 2\theta$$

and

$$v_\theta = -\frac{\partial \psi}{\partial r} = -4r \sin 2\theta$$

Since

$$v_r = \frac{\partial \phi}{\partial r}$$

it follows that

$$\frac{\partial \phi}{\partial r} = 4r \cos 2\theta$$

and therefore by integration

$$\phi = 2r^2 \cos 2\theta + f_1(\theta) \tag{1}$$

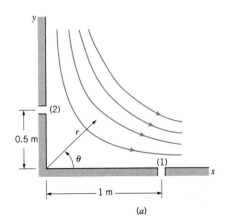

(a)   ■ FIGURE E6.3a

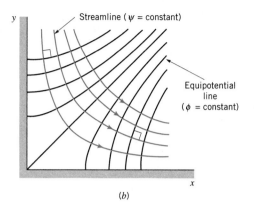

(b)

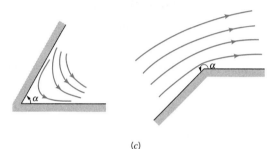

(c)

■ FIGURE E6.3*b, c*

where $f_1(\theta)$ is an arbitrary function of θ. Similarly

$$v_\theta = \frac{1}{r}\frac{\partial \phi}{\partial \theta} = -4r \sin 2\theta$$

and integration yields

$$\phi = 2r^2 \cos 2\theta + f_2(r) \qquad (2)$$

where $f_2(r)$ is an arbitrary function of r. To satisfy both Eqs. 1 and 2, the velocity potential must have the form

$$\phi = 2r^2 \cos 2\theta + C \qquad \text{(Ans)}$$

where C is an arbitrary constant. As is the case for stream functions, the specific value of C is not important, and it is customary to let $C = 0$ so that the velocity potential for this corner flow is

$$\phi = 2r^2 \cos 2\theta \qquad \text{(Ans)}$$

In the statement of this problem it was implied by the wording "if possible" that we might not be able to find a corresponding velocity potential. The reason for this concern is that we can always define a stream function for two-dimensional flow, but the flow must be *irrotational* if there is a corresponding velocity potential. Thus, the fact that we were able to determine a velocity potential means that the flow is irrotational. Several streamlines and lines of constant ϕ are plotted in Fig. E6.3*b*. These two sets of lines are *orthogonal*. The reason why streamlines and lines of constant ϕ are always orthogonal is explained in Section 6.5.

(b) Since we have an irrotational flow of a nonviscous, incompressible fluid, the Bernoulli equation can be applied between any two points. Thus, between points (1) and (2) with no elevation change

$$\frac{p_1}{\gamma} + \frac{V_1^2}{2g} = \frac{p_2}{\gamma} + \frac{V_2^2}{2g}$$

or

$$p_2 = p_1 + \frac{\rho}{2}(V_1^2 - V_2^2) \tag{3}$$

Since

$$V^2 = v_r^2 + v_\theta^2$$

it follows that for any point within the flow field

$$V^2 = (4r \cos 2\theta)^2 + (-4r \sin 2\theta)^2$$
$$= 16r^2(\cos^2 2\theta + \sin^2 2\theta)$$
$$= 16r^2$$

This result indicates that the square of the velocity at any point depends only on the radial distance, r, to the point. Note that the constant, 16, has units of s^{-2}. Thus,

$$V_1^2 = (16\ s^{-2})(1\ m)^2 = 16\ m^2/s^2$$

and

$$V_2^2 = (16\ s^{-2})(0.5\ m)^2 = 4\ m^2/s^2$$

Substitution of these velocities into Eq. 3 gives

$$p_2 = 30 \times 10^3\ N/m^2 + \frac{10^3\ kg/m^3}{2}(16\ m^2/s^2 - 4\ m^2/s^2) = 36\ kPa \tag{Ans}$$

The stream function used in this example could also be expressed in Cartesian coordinates as

$$\psi = 2r^2 \sin 2\theta = 4r^2 \sin\theta \cos\theta$$

or

$$\psi = 4xy$$

since $x = r \cos\theta$ and $y = r \sin\theta$. However, in the cylindrical polar form the results can be generalized to describe flow in the vicinity of a corner of angle α (see Fig. E6.3c) with the equations

$$\psi = Ar^{\pi/\alpha} \sin\frac{\pi\theta}{\alpha}$$

and

$$\phi = Ar^{\pi/\alpha} \cos\frac{\pi\theta}{\alpha}$$

where A is a constant.

6.5   Some Basic, Plane Potential Flows

A major advantage of Laplace's equation is that it is a linear partial differential equation. Since it is linear, various solutions can be added to obtain other solutions—that is, if $\phi_1(x, y, z)$ and $\phi_2(x, y, z)$ are two solutions to Laplace's equation, then $\phi_3 = \phi_1 + \phi_2$ is also a solution. The practical implication of this result is that if we have certain basic solutions we can combine them to obtain more complicated and interesting solutions. In this section several basic velocity potentials, which describe some relatively simple flows, will be determined. In the next section these basic potentials will be combined to represent more complicated flows.

For simplicity, only plane (two-dimensional) flows will be considered. In this case, by using Cartesian coordinates

$$u = \frac{\partial \phi}{\partial x} \qquad v = \frac{\partial \phi}{\partial y} \tag{6.72}$$

or by using cylindrical coordinates

$$v_r = \frac{\partial \phi}{\partial r} \qquad v_\theta = \frac{1}{r}\frac{\partial \phi}{\partial \theta} \tag{6.73}$$

Since we can define a stream function for plane flow, we can also let

$$u = \frac{\partial \psi}{\partial y} \qquad v = -\frac{\partial \psi}{\partial x} \tag{6.74}$$

or

$$v_r = \frac{1}{r}\frac{\partial \psi}{\partial \theta} \qquad v_\theta = -\frac{\partial \psi}{\partial r} \tag{6.75}$$

where the stream function was previously defined in Eqs. 6.37 and 6.42. We know that by defining the velocities in terms of the stream function, conservation of mass is identically satisfied. If we now impose the condition of irrotationality, it follows from Eq. 6.59 that

$$\frac{\partial u}{\partial y} = \frac{\partial v}{\partial x}$$

and in terms of the stream function

$$\frac{\partial}{\partial y}\left(\frac{\partial \psi}{\partial y}\right) = \frac{\partial}{\partial x}\left(-\frac{\partial \psi}{\partial x}\right)$$

or

$$\frac{\partial^2 \psi}{\partial x^2} + \frac{\partial^2 \psi}{\partial y^2} = 0$$

Thus, for a plane, irrotational flow we can use either the velocity potential or the stream function—both must satisfy Laplace's equation in two dimensions. It is apparent from these results that the velocity potential and the stream function are somehow related. We have previously shown that lines of constant ψ are streamlines; that is,

$$\left.\frac{dy}{dx}\right|_{\text{along } \psi = \text{constant}} = \frac{v}{u} \tag{6.76}$$

The change in ϕ as we move from one point (x, y) to a nearby point $(x + dx, y + dy)$ is given by the relationship:

$$d\phi = \frac{\partial \phi}{\partial x} dx + \frac{\partial \phi}{\partial y} dy = u \, dx + v \, dy$$

Along a line of constant ϕ we have $d\phi = 0$ so that

$$\left. \frac{dy}{dx} \right|_{\text{along } \phi = \text{constant}} = -\frac{u}{v} \tag{6.77}$$

A comparison of Eqs. 6.76 and 6.77 shows that lines of constant ϕ (called *equipotential lines*) are orthogonal to lines of constant ψ (streamlines) at all points where they intersect. (Recall that two lines are orthogonal if the product of their slopes is minus one.) For any potential flow field a "*flow net*" can be drawn that consists of a family of streamlines and equipotential lines. The flow net is useful in visualizing flow patterns and can be used to obtain graphical solutions by sketching in streamlines and equipotential lines and adjusting the lines until the lines are approximately orthogonal at all points where they intersect. An example of a flow net is shown in Fig. 6.14. Velocities can be estimated from the flow net, since the velocity is inversely proportional to the streamline spacing. Thus, for example, from Fig. 6.14 we can see that the velocity near the inside corner will be higher than the velocity along the outer part of the bend.

6.5.1 Uniform Flow

The simplest plane flow is one for which the streamlines are all straight and parallel, and the magnitude of the velocity is constant. This type of flow is called a *uniform flow*. For example, consider a uniform flow in the positive x direction as illustrated in Fig. 6.15a. In this instance, $u = U$ and $v = 0$, and in terms of the velocity potential

$$\frac{\partial \phi}{\partial x} = U \qquad \frac{\partial \phi}{\partial y} = 0$$

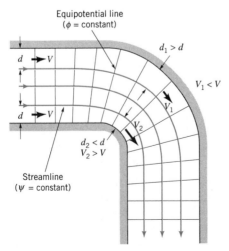

■ **FIGURE 6.14** **Flow net for a 90° bend. (From Ref. 3, used by permission.)**

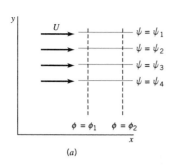 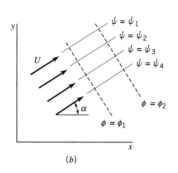

Uniform flow: (*a*) in the *x* direction; (*b*) in an arbitrary direction, *α*.

These two equations can be integrated to yield

$$\phi = Ux + C$$

where C is an arbitrary constant, which can be set equal to zero. Thus, for a uniform flow in the positive x direction

$$\phi = Ux \tag{6.78}$$

The corresponding stream function can be obtained in a similar manner, since

$$\frac{\partial \psi}{\partial y} = U \qquad \frac{\partial \psi}{\partial x} = 0$$

and, therefore,

$$\psi = Uy \tag{6.79}$$

These results can be generalized to provide the velocity potential and stream function for a uniform flow at an angle α with the x axis, as in Fig. 6.15*b*. For this case

$$\phi = U(x \cos \alpha + y \sin \alpha) \tag{6.80}$$

and

$$\psi = U(y \cos \alpha - x \sin \alpha) \tag{6.81}$$

6.5.2   Source and Sink

Consider a fluid flowing radially outward from a line through the origin perpendicular to the x–y plane as shown in Fig. 6.16. Let m be the volume rate of flow emanating from the line (per unit length), and therefore to satisfy conservation of mass

$$(2\pi r)v_r = m$$

or

$$v_r = \frac{m}{2\pi r}$$

Also, since the flow is a purely radial flow, $v_\theta = 0$, the corresponding velocity potential can be obtained by integrating the equations

$$\frac{\partial \phi}{\partial r} = \frac{m}{2\pi r} \qquad \frac{1}{r}\frac{\partial \phi}{\partial \theta} = 0$$

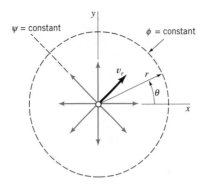

■ **FIGURE 6.16** **The streamline pattern for a source.**

It follows that

$$\phi = \frac{m}{2\pi} \ln r \qquad (6.82)$$

If m is positive, the flow is radially outward, and the flow is considered to be a *source* flow. If m is negative, the flow is toward the origin, and the flow is considered to be a *sink* flow. The flowrate, m, is the *strength* of the source or sink.

We note that at the origin where $r = 0$ the velocity becomes infinite, which is of course physically impossible. Thus, sources and sinks do not really exist in real flow fields, and the line representing the source or sink is a mathematical *singularity* in the flow field. However, some real flows can be approximated at points away from the origin by using sources or sinks. Also, the velocity potential representing this hypothetical flow can be combined with other basic velocity potentials to describe approximately some real flow fields. This idea is further discussed in Section 6.6.

The stream function for the source can be obtained by integrating the relationships

$$\frac{1}{r} \frac{\partial \psi}{\partial \theta} = \frac{m}{2\pi r} \qquad \frac{\partial \psi}{\partial r} = 0$$

to yield

$$\psi = \frac{m}{2\pi} \theta \qquad (6.83)$$

It is apparent from Eq. 6.83 that the streamlines (lines of $\psi = $ constant) are radial lines, and from Eq. 6.82 the equipotential lines (lines of $\phi = $ constant) are concentric circles centered at the origin.

EXAMPLE 6.4

A nonviscous, incompressible fluid flows between wedge-shaped walls into a small opening as shown in Fig. E6.4. The velocity potential (in ft²/s), which approximately describes this flow, is

$$\phi = -2 \ln r$$

Determine the volume rate of flow (per unit length) into the opening.

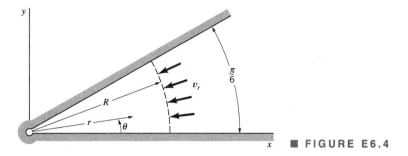

■ FIGURE E6.4

SOLUTION

The components of velocity are

$$v_r = \frac{\partial \phi}{\partial r} = -\frac{2}{r} \qquad v_\theta = \frac{1}{r} \frac{\partial \phi}{\partial \theta} = 0$$

which indicates we have a purely radial flow. The flowrate per unit width, q, crossing the arc of length $R\pi/6$ can thus be obtained by integrating the expression

$$q = \int_0^{\pi/6} v_r R \, d\theta = -\int_0^{\pi/6} \left(\frac{2}{R}\right) R \, d\theta = -\frac{\pi}{3} = -1.05 \text{ ft}^2/\text{s} \qquad \textbf{(Ans)}$$

Note that the radius R is arbitrary since the flowrate crossing any curve between the two walls must be the same. The negative sign indicates that the flow is toward the opening, that is, in the negative radial direction.

6.5.3   Vortex

We next consider a flow field in which the streamlines are concentric circles—that is, we interchange the velocity potential and stream function for the source. Thus, let

$$\phi = K\theta \tag{6.84}$$

and

$$\psi = -K \ln r \tag{6.85}$$

where K is a constant. In this case the streamlines are concentric circles as illustrated in Fig. 6.17, with $v_r = 0$ and

$$v_\theta = \frac{1}{r} \frac{\partial \phi}{\partial \theta} = -\frac{\partial \psi}{\partial r} = \frac{K}{r} \tag{6.86}$$

This result indicates that the tangential velocity varies inversely with the distance from the origin, with a singularity occurring at $r = 0$ (where the velocity becomes infinite).

It may seem strange that this *vortex* motion is irrotational (and it is since the flow field is described by a velocity potential). However, it must be recalled that rotation refers to the orientation of a fluid element and not the path followed by the element. Thus, for an irrotational vortex, if a pair of small sticks were placed in the flow field at location A, as indicated

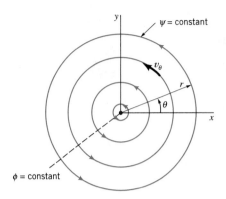

■ **FIGURE 6.17** **The streamline pattern for a vortex.**

in Fig. 6.18*a*, the sticks would rotate as they move to location *B*. One of the sticks, the one that is aligned along the streamline, would follow a circular path and rotate in a counterclockwise direction. The other stick would rotate in a clockwise direction due to the nature of the flow field—that is, the part of the stick nearest the origin moves faster than the opposite end. Although both sticks are rotating, the average angular velocity of the two sticks is zero since the flow is irrotational.

If the fluid were rotating as a rigid body, such that $v_\theta = K_1 r$ where K_1 is a constant, then sticks similarly placed in the flow field would rotate as is illustrated in Fig. 6.18*b*. This type of vortex motion is *rotational* and cannot be described with a velocity potential. The rotational vortex is commonly called a *forced vortex,* whereas the irrotational vortex is usually called a *free vortex.* The swirling motion of the water as it drains from a bathtub is similar to that of a free vortex, whereas the motion of a liquid contained in a tank that is rotated about its axis with angular velocity ω corresponds to a forced vortex.

A *combined vortex* is one with a forced vortex as a central core and a velocity distribution corresponding to that of a free vortex outside the core. Thus, for a combined vortex

$$v_\theta = \omega r \qquad r \leq r_0 \tag{6.87}$$

and

$$v_\theta = \frac{K}{r} \qquad r > r_0 \tag{6.88}$$

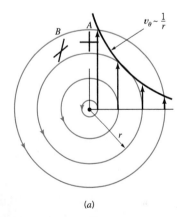

(*a*)

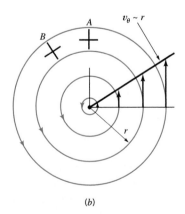

(*b*)

■ **FIGURE 6.18** **Motion of fluid element from *A* to *B:* (*a*) for irrotational (free) vortex; (*b*) for rotational (forced) vortex.**

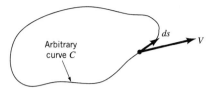

■ **FIGURE 6.19** **The notation for determining circulation around closed curve *C*.**

where K and ω are constants and r_0 corresponds to the radius of the central core. The pressure distribution in both the free and forced vortex was previously considered in Example 3.3.

A mathematical concept commonly associated with vortex motion is that of *circulation*. The circulation, Γ, is defined as the line integral of the tangential component of the velocity taken around a closed curve in the flow field. In equation form, Γ can be expressed as

$$\Gamma = \oint_C \mathbf{V} \cdot d\mathbf{s} \tag{6.89}$$

where the integral sign means that the integration is taken around a closed curve, C, in the counterclockwise direction, and $d\mathbf{s}$ is a differential length along the curve as illustrated in Fig. 6.19. For an irrotational flow, $\mathbf{V} = \nabla\phi$ so that $\mathbf{V} \cdot d\mathbf{s} = \nabla\phi \cdot d\mathbf{s} = d\phi$ and, therefore,

$$\Gamma = \oint_C d\phi = 0$$

This result indicates that for an irrotational flow the circulation will generally be zero. However, if there are singularities enclosed within the curve the circulation may not be zero. For example, for the free vortex with $v_\theta = K/r$ the circulation around the circular path of radius r shown in Fig. 6.20 is

$$\Gamma = \int_0^{2\pi} \frac{K}{r}(r\, d\theta) = 2\pi K$$

which shows that the circulation is nonzero and the constant $K = \Gamma/2\pi$. However, the circulation around any path that does not include the singular point at the origin will be zero. This can be easily confirmed by evaluating the circulation around a closed path such as *ABCD* of Fig. 6.20, which does not include the origin.

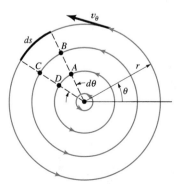

■ **FIGURE 6.20** **Circulation around various paths in a free vortex.**

The velocity potential and stream function for the free vortex are commonly expressed in terms of the circulation as

$$\phi = \frac{\Gamma}{2\pi}\theta \tag{6.90}$$

and

$$\psi = -\frac{\Gamma}{2\pi}\ln r \tag{6.91}$$

V6.2 Vortex in a beaker

The concept of circulation is often useful when evaluating the forces developed on bodies immersed in moving fluids. This application will be considered in Section 6.6.2.

EXAMPLE 6.5

A liquid drains from a large tank through a small opening as illustrated in Fig. E6.5. A vortex forms whose velocity distribution away from the tank opening can be approximated as that of a free vortex having a velocity potential

$$\phi = \frac{\Gamma}{2\pi}\theta$$

Determine an expression relating the surface shape to the strength of the vortex as specified by the circulation Γ.

SOLUTION

Since the free vortex represents an irrotational flow field, the Bernoulli equation

$$\frac{p_1}{\gamma} + \frac{V_1^2}{2g} + z_1 = \frac{p_2}{\gamma} + \frac{V_2^2}{2g} + z_2$$

can be written between any two points. If the points are selected at the free surface, $p_1 = p_2 = 0$, so that

$$\frac{V_1^2}{2g} = z_s + \frac{V_2^2}{2g} \tag{1}$$

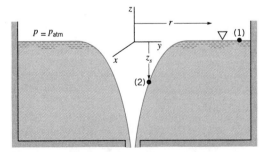

■ FIGURE E6.5

where the free surface elevation, z_s, is measured relative to a datum passing through point (1). The velocity is given by the equation

$$v_\theta = \frac{1}{r}\frac{\partial \phi}{\partial \theta} = \frac{\Gamma}{2\pi r}$$

We note that far from the origin at point (1) $V_1 = v_\theta \approx 0$ so that Eq. 1 becomes

$$z_s = -\frac{\Gamma 2}{8\pi^2 r^2 g} \qquad\qquad \text{(Ans)}$$

which is the desired equation for the surface profile. The negative sign indicates that the surface falls as the origin is approached as shown in Fig. E6.5. This solution is not valid very near the origin since the predicted velocity becomes excessively large as the origin is approached.

6.5.4 Doublet

The final, basic potential flow to be considered is one that is formed by combining a source and sink in a special way. Consider the equal strength, source-sink pair of Fig. 6.21. The combined stream function for the pair is

$$\psi = -\frac{m}{2\pi}(\theta_1 - \theta_2)$$

which can be rewritten as

$$\tan\left(-\frac{2\pi\psi}{m}\right) = \tan(\theta_1 - \theta_2) = \frac{\tan\theta_1 - \tan\theta_2}{1 + \tan\theta_1 \tan\theta_2} \qquad\qquad \textbf{(6.92)}$$

From Fig. 6.21 it follows that

$$\tan\theta_1 = \frac{r\sin\theta}{r\cos\theta - a}$$

and

$$\tan\theta_2 = \frac{r\sin\theta}{r\cos\theta + a}$$

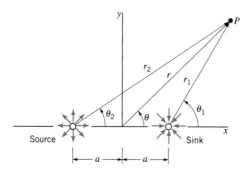

■ **FIGURE 6.21** **The combination of a source and sink of equal strength located along the x axis.**

These results substituted into Eq. 6.92 give

$$\tan\left(-\frac{2\pi\psi}{m}\right) = \frac{2ar\sin\theta}{r^2 - a^2}$$

so that

$$\psi = -\frac{m}{2\pi}\tan^{-1}\left(\frac{2ar\sin\theta}{r^2 - a^2}\right) \tag{6.93}$$

For small values of a

$$\psi = -\frac{m}{2\pi}\frac{2ar\sin\theta}{r^2 - a^2} = -\frac{mar\sin\theta}{\pi(r^2 - a^2)} \tag{6.94}$$

since the tangent of an angle approaches the value of the angle for small angles.

The so-called *doublet* is formed by letting the source and sink approach one another ($a \to 0$) while increasing the strength m ($m \to \infty$) so that the product ma/π remains constant. In this case, since $r/(r^2 - a^2) \to 1/r$, Eq. 6.94 reduces to

$$\psi = -\frac{K\sin\theta}{r} \tag{6.95}$$

where K, a constant equal to ma/π, is called the *strength* of the doublet. The corresponding velocity potential for the doublet is

$$\phi = \frac{K\cos\theta}{r} \tag{6.96}$$

Plots of lines of constant ψ reveal that the streamlines for a doublet are circles through the origin tangent to the x axis as shown in Fig. 6.22. Just as sources and sinks are not physically realistic entities, neither are doublets. However, the doublet when combined with other basic potential flows provides a useful representation of some flow fields of practical interest. For example, we will determine in Section 6.6.2 that the combination of a uniform flow and a doublet can be used to represent the flow around a circular cylinder. Table 6.1 provides a summary of the pertinent equations for the basic, plane potential flows considered in the preceding sections.

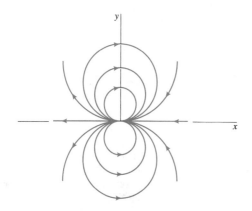

■ **FIGURE 6.22**   **Streamlines for a doublet.**

■ **TABLE 6.1**

Summary of Basic, Plane Potential Flows.

Description of Flow Field	Velocity Potential	Stream Function	Velocity Components[a]
Uniform flow at angle α with the x axis (see Fig. 6.15b)	$\phi = U(x \cos \alpha + y \sin \alpha)$	$\psi = U(y \cos \alpha - x \sin \alpha)$	$u = U \cos \alpha$ $v = U \sin \alpha$
Source or sink (see Fig. 6.16) $m > 0$ source $m < 0$ sink	$\phi = \dfrac{m}{2\pi} \ln r$	$\psi = \dfrac{m}{2\pi} \theta$	$v_r = \dfrac{m}{2\pi r}$ $v_\theta = 0$
Free vortex (see Fig. 6.17) $\Gamma > 0$ counterclockwise motion $\Gamma < 0$ clockwise motion	$\phi = \dfrac{\Gamma}{2\pi} \theta$	$\psi = -\dfrac{\Gamma}{2\pi} \ln r$	$v_r = 0$ $v_\theta = \dfrac{\Gamma}{2\pi r}$
Doublet (see Fig. 6.22)	$\phi = \dfrac{K \cos \theta}{r}$	$\psi = -\dfrac{K \sin \theta}{r}$	$v_r = -\dfrac{K \cos \theta}{r^2}$ $v_\theta = -\dfrac{K \sin \theta}{r^2}$

[a]Velocity components are related to the velocity potential and stream function through the relationships:
$$u = \frac{\partial \phi}{\partial x} = \frac{\partial \psi}{\partial y} \qquad v = \frac{\partial \phi}{\partial y} = -\frac{\partial \psi}{\partial x} \qquad v_r = \frac{\partial \phi}{\partial r} = \frac{1}{r}\frac{\partial \psi}{\partial \theta} \qquad v_\theta = \frac{1}{r}\frac{\partial \phi}{\partial \theta} = -\frac{\partial \psi}{\partial r}$$

6.6 Superposition of Basic, Plane Potential Flows

As was discussed in the previous section, potential flows are governed by Laplace's equation, which is a linear partial differential equation. It therefore follows that the various basic velocity potentials and stream functions can be combined to form new potentials and stream functions. (Why is this true?) Whether such combinations yield useful results remains to be seen. It is to be noted that *any streamline in an inviscid flow field can be considered as a solid boundary,* since the conditions along a solid boundary and a streamline are the same— that is, there is no flow through the boundary or the streamline. Thus, if we can combine some of the basic velocity potentials or stream functions to yield a streamline that corresponds to a particular body shape of interest, that combination can be used to describe in detail the flow around that body. This method of solving some interesting flow problems, commonly called the *method of superposition,* is illustrated in the following three sections.

6.6.1 Source in a Uniform Stream—Half-Body

Consider the superposition of a source and a uniform flow as shown in Fig. 6.23a. The resulting stream function is

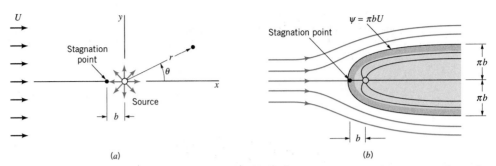

■ FIGURE 6.23 **The flow around a half-body: (a) superposition of a source and a uniform flow; (b) replacement of streamline $\psi = \pi bU$ with solid boundary to form half-body.**

$$\psi = \psi_{\text{uniform flow}} + \psi_{\text{source}}$$

$$= Ur \sin \theta + \frac{m}{2\pi} \theta \tag{6.97}$$

and the corresponding velocity potential is

$$\phi = Ur \cos \theta + \frac{m}{2\pi} \ln r \tag{6.98}$$

V6.3 Half-body

It is clear that at some point along the negative x axis the velocity due to the source will just cancel that due to the uniform flow and a stagnation point will be created. For the source alone

$$v_r = \frac{m}{2\pi r}$$

so that the stagnation point will occur at $x = -b$ where

$$U = \frac{m}{2\pi b}$$

or

$$b = \frac{m}{2\pi U} \tag{6.99}$$

The value of the stream function at the stagnation point can be obtained by evaluating ψ at $r = b$ and $\theta = \pi$, which yields from Eq. 6.97

$$\psi_{\text{stagnation}} = \frac{m}{2}$$

Since $m/2 = \pi bU$ (from Eq. 6.99) it follows that the equation of the streamline passing through the stagnation point is

$$\pi bU = Ur \sin \theta + bU\theta$$

or

$$r = \frac{b(\pi - \theta)}{\sin \theta} \tag{6.100}$$

where θ can vary between 0 and 2π. A plot of this streamline is shown in Fig. 6.23b. If we replace this streamline with a solid boundary, as indicated in the figure, then it is clear that this combination of a uniform flow and a source can be used to describe the flow around a streamlined body placed in a uniform stream. The body is open at the downstream end, and thus is called a *half-body*. Other streamlines in the flow field can be obtained by setting ψ = constant in Eq. 6.97 and plotting the resulting equation. A number of these streamlines is shown in Fig. 6.23b. Although the streamlines inside the body are shown, they are actually of no interest in this case, since we are concerned with the flow field outside the body. It should be noted that the singularity in the flow field (the source) occurs inside the body, and there are no singularities in the flow field of interest (outside the body).

The width of the half-body asymptotically approaches $2\pi b$. This follows from Eq. 6.100, which can be wrtten as

$$y = b(\pi - \theta)$$

so that as $\theta \to 0$ or $\theta \to 2\pi$ the half-width approaches $\pm b\pi$. With the stream function (or velocity potential) known, the velocity components at any point can be obtained. For the half-body, using the stream function given by Eq. 6.97,

$$v_r = \frac{1}{r} \frac{\partial \psi}{\partial \theta} = U \cos \theta + \frac{m}{2\pi r}$$

and

$$v_\theta = -\frac{\partial \psi}{\partial r} = -U \sin \theta$$

Thus, the square of the magnitude of the velocity, V, at any point is

$$V^2 = v_r^2 + v_\theta^2 = U^2 + \frac{Um \cos \theta}{\pi r} + \left(\frac{m}{2\pi r}\right)^2$$

and since $b = m/2\pi U$

$$V^2 = U^2\left(1 + 2\frac{b}{r} \cos \theta + \frac{b^2}{r^2}\right) \tag{6.101}$$

With the velocity known, the pressure at any point can be determined from the Bernoulli equation, which can be written between any two points in the flow field since the flow is irrotational. Thus, applying the Bernoulli equation between a point far from the body, where the pressure is p_0 and the velocity is U, and some arbitrary point with pressure p and velocity V, it follows that

$$p_0 + \tfrac{1}{2}\rho U^2 = p + \tfrac{1}{2}\rho V^2 \tag{6.102}$$

where elevation changes have been neglected. Equation 6.101 can now be substituted into Eq. 6.102 to obtain the pressure at any point in terms of the reference pressure, p_0, and velocity, U.

This relatively simple potential flow provides some useful information about the flow around the front part of a streamlined body, such as a bridge pier or strut placed in a uniform stream. An important point to be noted is that the velocity tangent to the surface of the body is not zero; that is, the fluid "slips" by the boundary. This result is a consequence of neglecting viscosity, the fluid property that causes real fluids to stick to the boundary, thus creating a "no-slip" condition. All potential flows differ from the flow of real fluids in this respect and do not accurately represent the velocity very near the boundary. However, outside this very thin boundary layer the velocity distribution will generally correspond to that predicted by potential flow theory if flow separation does not occur. Also, the pressure distribution along the surface will closely approximate that predicted from the potential flow theory, since the boundary layer is thin and there is little opportunity for the pressure to vary through the thin layer. In fact, as will be discussed in more detail in Chapter 9, the pressure distribution obtained from potential flow theory is used in conjunction with viscous flow theory to determine the nature of flow within the boundary layer.

EXAMPLE 6.6

The shape of a hill arising from a plain can be approximated with the top section of a half-body as illustrated in Fig. E6.6. The height of the hill approaches 200 ft as shown. **(a)** When a 40 mi/hr wind blows toward the hill, what is the magnitude of the air velocity at a point on the hill directly above the origin [point (2)]? **(b)** What is the elevation of point (2) above the plain and what is the difference in pressure between point (1) on the plain far from the hill and point (2)? Assume an air density of 0.00238 slugs/ft^3.

SOLUTION

(a) The velocity is given by Eq. 6.101 as

$$V^2 = U^2\left(1 + 2\frac{b}{r}\cos\theta + \frac{b^2}{r^2}\right)$$

At point (2), $\theta = \pi/2$, and since this point is on the surface (Eq. 6.100)

$$r = \frac{b(\pi - \theta)}{\sin\theta} = \frac{\pi b}{2} \tag{1}$$

Thus,

$$V_2^2 = U^2\left[1 + \frac{b^2}{(\pi b/2)^2}\right]$$

$$= U^2\left(1 + \frac{4}{\pi^2}\right)$$

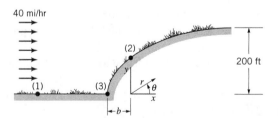

■ FIGURE E6.6

and the magnitude of the velocity at (2) for a 40 mi/hr approaching wind is

$$V_2 = \left(1 + \frac{4}{\pi^2}\right)^{1/2} (40 \text{ mi/hr}) = 47.4 \text{ mi/hr} \qquad \text{(Ans)}$$

(b) The elevation at (2) above the plain is given by Eq. 1 as

$$y_2 = \frac{\pi b}{2}$$

Since the height of the hill approaches 200 ft and this height is equal to πb, it follows that

$$y_2 = \frac{200 \text{ ft}}{2} = 100 \text{ ft} \qquad \text{(Ans)}$$

From the Bernoulli equation (with the y axis the vertical axis)

$$\frac{p_1}{\gamma} + \frac{V_1^2}{2g} + y_1 = \frac{p_2}{\gamma} + \frac{V_2^2}{2g} + y_2$$

so that

$$p_1 - p_2 = \frac{\rho}{2}(V_2^2 - V_1^2) + \gamma(y_2 - y_1)$$

and with

$$V_1 = (40 \text{ mi/hr})\left(\frac{5280 \text{ ft/mi}}{3600 \text{ s/hr}}\right) = 58.7 \text{ ft/s}$$

and

$$V_2 = (47.4 \text{ mi/hr})\left(\frac{5280 \text{ ft/mi}}{3600 \text{ s/hr}}\right) = 69.5 \text{ ft/s}$$

it follows that

$$p_1 - p_2 = \frac{(0.00238 \text{ slugs/ft}^3)}{2}[(69.5 \text{ ft/s})^2 - (58.7 \text{ ft/s})^2]$$
$$+ (0.00238 \text{ slugs/ft}^3)(32.2 \text{ ft/s}^2)(100 \text{ ft} - 0 \text{ ft})$$
$$= 93.1 \text{ lb/ft}^2 = 0.0647 \text{ psi} \qquad \text{(Ans)}$$

This result indicates that the pressure on the hill at point (2) is slightly lower than the pressure on the plain at some distance from the base of the hill with a 0.0533 psi difference due to the elevation increase and a 0.0114 psi difference due to the velocity increase.

The maximum velocity along the hill surface does not occur at point (2) but further up the hill at $\theta = 63°$. At this point $V_{\text{surface}} = 1.26U$ (Problem 6.32). The minimum velocity ($V = 0$) and maximum pressure occur at point (3), the stagnation point.

The half-body is a body that is "open" at one end. To study the flow around a closed body a source and a sink of equal strength can be combined with a uniform flow. These bodies have an oval shape and are termed *Rankine ovals*.

6.6.2 Flow Around a Circular Cylinder

A uniform flow in the positive x direction combined with a doublet can be used to represent flow around a circular cylinder. This combination gives for the stream function

$$\psi = Ur \sin \theta - \frac{K \sin \theta}{r} \tag{6.103}$$

and for the velocity potential

$$\phi = Ur \cos \theta + \frac{K \cos \theta}{r} \tag{6.104}$$

In order for the stream function to represent flow around a circular cylinder it is necessary that ψ = constant for $r = a$, where a is the radius of the cylinder. Since Eq. 6.103 can be written as

$$\psi = \left(U - \frac{K}{r^2} \right) r \sin \theta$$

it follows that $\psi = 0$ for $r = a$ if

$$U - \frac{K}{a^2} = 0$$

which indicates that the doublet strength, K, must be equal to Ua^2. Thus, the stream function for flow around a circular cylinder can be expressed as

$$\psi = Ur \left(1 - \frac{a^2}{r^2} \right) \sin \theta \tag{6.105}$$

and the corresponding velocity potential is

$$\phi = Ur \left(1 + \frac{a^2}{r^2} \right) \cos \theta \tag{6.106}$$

A sketch of the streamlines for this flow field is shown in Fig. 6.24.

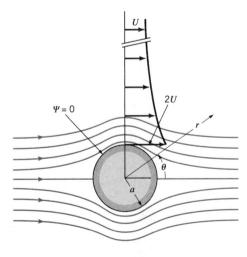

■ **FIGURE 6.24** The flow around a circular cylinder.

The velocity components can be obtained from either Eq. 6.105 or 6.106 as

$$v_r = \frac{\partial \phi}{\partial r} = \frac{1}{r}\frac{\partial \psi}{\partial \theta} = U\left(1 - \frac{a^2}{r^2}\right)\cos\theta \qquad \textbf{(6.107)}$$

and

$$v_\theta = \frac{1}{r}\frac{\partial \phi}{\partial \theta} = -\frac{\partial \psi}{\partial r} = -U\left(1 + \frac{a^2}{r^2}\right)\sin\theta \qquad \textbf{(6.108)}$$

On the surface of the cylinder $(r = a)$ it follows from Eqs. 6.107 and 6.108 that $v_r = 0$ and

$$v_{\theta s} = -2U\sin\theta$$

We observe from this result that the maximum velocity occurs at the top and bottom of the cylinder $(\theta = \pm\pi/2)$ and has a magnitude of twice the upstream velocity, U. As we move away from the cylinder along the ray $\theta = \pi/2$ the velocity varies as illustrated in Fig. 6.24.

The pressure distribution on the cylinder surface is obtained from the Bernoulli equation written from a point far from the cylinder where the pressure is p_0 and the velocity is U so that

$$p_0 + \tfrac{1}{2}\rho U^2 = p_s + \tfrac{1}{2}\rho v_{\theta s}^2$$

where p_s is the surface pressure. Elevation changes are neglected. Since $v_{\theta s} = -2U\sin\theta$, the surface pressure can be expressed as

$$p_s = p_0 + \tfrac{1}{2}\rho U^2(1 - 4\sin^2\theta) \qquad \textbf{(6.109)}$$

A comparison of this theoretical, symmetrical pressure distribution expressed in dimensionless form with a typical measured distribution is shown in Fig. 6.25. This figure clearly reveals that only on the upstream part of the cylinder is there approximate agreement between

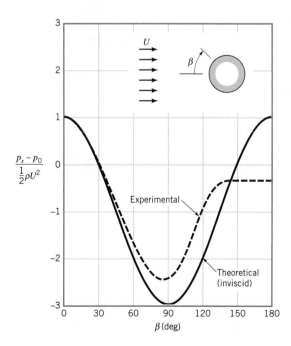

■ **FIGURE 6.25** A comparison of theoretical (inviscid) pressure distribution on the surface of a circular cylinder with typical experimental distribution.

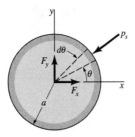

■ **FIGURE 6.26** **The notation for determining lift and drag on a circular cylinder.**

the potential flow and the experimental results. Because of the viscous boundary layer that develops on the cylinder, the main flow separates from the surface of the cylinder, leading to the large difference between the theoretical, frictionless fluid solution and the experimental results on the downstream side of the cylinder (see Chapter 9).

The resultant force (per unit length) developed on the cylinder can be determined by integrating the pressure over the surface. From Fig. 6.26 it can be seen that

$$F_x = -\int_0^{2\pi} p_s \cos \theta \, a \, d\theta \qquad \qquad \textbf{(6.110)}$$

and

$$F_y = -\int_0^{2\pi} p_s \sin \theta \, a \, d\theta \qquad \qquad \textbf{(6.111)}$$

where F_x is the *drag* (force parallel to direction of the uniform flow) and F_y is the *lift* (force perpendicular to the direction of the uniform flow). Substitution for p_s from Eq. 6.109 into these two equations, and subsequent integration, reveals that $F_x = 0$ and $F_y = 0$.

These results indicate that both the drag and lift as predicted by potential theory for a fixed cylinder in a uniform stream are zero. Since the pressure distribution is symmetrical around the cylinder, this is not really a surprising result. However, we know from experience that there is a significant drag developed on a cylinder when it is placed in a moving fluid. This discrepancy is known as d'Alembert's paradox.

EXAMPLE 6.7

When a circular cylinder is placed in a uniform stream, a stagnation point is created on the cylinder as shown in Fig. E6.7a. If a small hole is located at this point, the stagnation pressure, p_{stag}, can be measured and used to determine the approach velocity, U. **(a)** Show how p_{stag} and U are related. **(b)** If the cylinder is misaligned by an angle α (Figure E6.7b), but the measured pressure still interpreted as the stagnation pressure, determine an expression for the ratio of the true velocity, U, to the predicted velocity, U'. Plot this ratio as a function of α for the range $-20° \le \alpha \le 20°$.

SOLUTION

(a) The velocity at the stagnation point is zero so the Bernoulli equation written between a point on the stagnation streamline upstream from the cylinder and the stagnation point gives

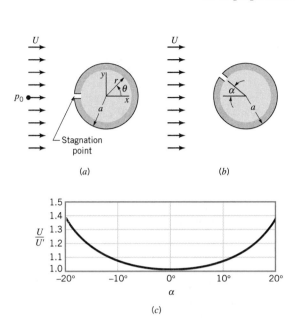

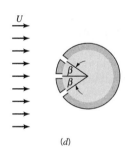

(d)   ■ FIGURE E6.7

$$\frac{p_0}{\gamma} + \frac{U^2}{2g} = \frac{p_{\text{stag}}}{\gamma}$$

Thus,

$$U = \left[\frac{2}{\rho}(p_{\text{stag}} - p_0)\right]^{1/2}$$ **(Ans)**

A measurement of the difference between the pressure at the stagnation point and the upstream pressure can be used to measure the approach velocity. This is, of course, the same result that was obtained in Section 3.5 for Pitot-static tubes.

(b) If the direction of the fluid approaching the cylinder is not known precisely, it is possible that the cylinder is misaligned by some angle, α. In this instance the pressure actually measured, p_α, will be different from the stagnation pressure, but if the misalignment is not recognized, the predicted approach velocity, U', would still be calculated as

$$U' = \left[\frac{2}{\rho}(p_\alpha - p_0)\right]^{1/2}$$

Thus,

$$\frac{U(\text{true})}{U'(\text{predicted})} = \left(\frac{p_{\text{stag}} - p_0}{p_\alpha - p_0}\right)^{1/2}$$ **(1)**

The velocity on the surface of the cylinder, v_θ, where $r = a$, is obtained from Eq. 6.108 as

$$v_\theta = -2U \sin \theta$$

If we now write the Bernoulli equation between a point upstream of the cylinder and the point on the cylinder where $r = a$, $\theta = \alpha$, it follows that

$$p_0 + \frac{1}{2} \rho U^2 = p_\alpha + \frac{1}{2} \rho(-2U \sin \alpha)^2$$

and, therefore,

$$p_\alpha - p_0 = \tfrac{1}{2}\rho U^2(1 - 4 \sin^2\alpha) \tag{2}$$

Since $p_{stag} - p_0 = \tfrac{1}{2}\rho U^2$ it follows from Eqs. 1 and 2 that

$$\frac{U(\text{true})}{U'(\text{predicted})} = (1 - 4\sin^2\alpha)^{-1/2} \tag{Ans}$$

This velocity ratio is plotted as a function of the misalignment angle α in Fig. E6.7c.

It is clear from these results that significant errors can arise if the stagnation pressure tap is not aligned with the stagnation streamline. If two additional, symmetrically located holes are drilled on the cylinder, as illustrated in Fig. E6.7d, the correct orientation of the cylinder can be determined. The cylinder is rotated until the pressures in the two symmetrically placed holes are equal, thus indicating that the center hole coincides with the stagnation streamline. For $\beta = 30°$ the pressure at the two holes theoretically corresponds to the upstream pressure, p_0. With this orientation a measurement of the difference in pressure between the center hole and the side holes can be used to determine U.

An additional, interesting potential flow can be developed by adding a free vortex to the stream function or velocity potential for the flow around a cylinder. In this case

$$\psi = Ur\left(1 - \frac{a^2}{r^2}\right)\sin \theta - \frac{\Gamma}{2\pi} \ln r \tag{6.112}$$

and

$$\phi = Ur\left(1 + \frac{a^2}{r^2}\right)\cos \theta + \frac{\Gamma}{2\pi} \theta \tag{6.113}$$

where Γ is the circulation. We note that the circle $r = a$ will still be a streamline (and thus can be replaced with a solid cylinder), since the streamlines for the added free vortex are all circular. However, the tangential velocity, v_θ, on the surface of the cylinder ($r = a$) now becomes

$$v_{\theta s} = -\frac{\partial \psi}{\partial r}\bigg|_{r=a} = -2U \sin \theta + \frac{\Gamma}{2\pi a} \tag{6.114}$$

This type of flow field could be approximately created by placing a rotating cylinder in a uniform stream. Because of the presence of viscosity in any real fluid, the fluid in contact with the rotating cylinder would rotate with the same velocity as the cylinder, and the resulting flow field would resemble that developed by the combination of a uniform flow past a cylinder and a free vortex.

A variety of streamline patterns can be developed, depending on the vortex strength, Γ. For example, from Eq. 6.114 we can determine the location of stagnation points on the surface of the cylinder. These points will occur at $\theta = \theta_{\text{stag}}$ where $v_\theta = 0$ and therefore from Eq. 6.114

$$\sin \theta_{\text{stag}} = \frac{\Gamma}{4\pi Ua} \tag{6.115}$$

If $\Gamma = 0$, then $\theta_{\text{stag}} = 0$ or π—that is, the stagnation points occur at the front and rear of the cylinder as are shown in Fig. 6.27a. However, for $-1 \leq \Gamma/4\pi Ua \leq 1$, the stagnation points will occur at some other location on the surface as illustrated in Figs. 6.27b, c. If the absolute value of the parameter $\Gamma/4\pi Ua$ exceeds 1, Eq. 6.115 cannot be satisfied, and the stagnation point is located away from the cylinder as shown in Fig. 6.27d.

The force per unit length developed on the cylinder can again be obtained by integrating the differential pressure forces around the circumference as in Eqs. 6.110 and 6.111. For the cylinder with circulation the surface pressure, p_s, is obtained from the Bernoulli equation (with the surface velocity given by Eq. 6.114)

$$p_0 + \frac{1}{2}\rho U^2 = p_s + \frac{1}{2}\rho\left(-2U \sin\theta + \frac{\Gamma}{2\pi a}\right)^2$$

or

$$p_s = p_0 + \frac{1}{2}\rho U^2\left(1 - 4\sin^2\theta + \frac{2\Gamma \sin\theta}{\pi aU} - \frac{\Gamma^2}{4\pi^2 a^2 U^2}\right) \tag{6.116}$$

Equation 6.116 substituted into Eq. 6.110 for the drag, and integrated, again yields

$$F_x = 0$$

That is, even for the rotating cylinder no force in the direction of the uniform flow is developed. However, use of Eq. 6.116 with the equation for the lift, F_y (Eq. 6.111), yields

$$F_y = -\rho U\Gamma \tag{6.117}$$

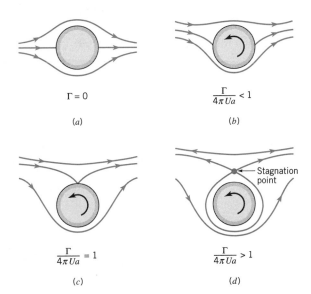

$\Gamma = 0$

(a)

$\dfrac{\Gamma}{4\pi Ua} < 1$

(b)

$\dfrac{\Gamma}{4\pi Ua} = 1$

(c)

$\dfrac{\Gamma}{4\pi Ua} > 1$

(d)

Stagnation point

■ **FIGURE 6.27** **The location of stagnation points on a circular cylinder: (a) without circulation; (b, c, d) with circulation.**

Thus, for the cylinder with circulation, lift is developed equal to the product of the fluid density, the upstream velocity, and the circulation. The negative sign means that if U is positive (in the positive x direction) and Γ is positive (a free vortex with counterclockwise rotation), the direction of the F_y is downward. Of course, if the cylinder is rotated in the clockwise direction ($\Gamma < 0$) the direction of F_y would be upward. It is this force acting in a direction perpendicular to the direction of the approach velocity that causes baseballs and golf balls to curve when they spin as they are propelled through the air. The development of this lift on rotating bodies is called the *Magnus effect*. (See Section 9.4 for further comments.) Although Eq. 6.117 was developed for a cylinder with circulation, it gives the lift per unit length for a right cylinder of any cross-sectional shape placed in a uniform, inviscid stream. The circulation is determined around any closed curve containing the body. The generalized equation relating lift to the fluid density, velocity, and circulation is called the *Kutta–Joukowski law,* and is commonly used to determine the lift on airfoils (see Section 9.4.2 and Refs. 2–6).

6.7   Other Aspects of Potential Flow Analysis

V6.4 Potential flow

In the preceding section the method of superposition of basic potentials has been used to obtain detailed descriptions of irrotational flow around certain body shapes immersed in a uniform stream. It is possible to extend the idea of superposition by considering a *distribution* of sources and sinks, or doublets, which when combined with a uniform flow can describe the flow around bodies of arbitrary shape. Techniques are available to determine the required distribution to give a prescribed body shape. Also, for plane, potential flow problems it can be shown that complex variable theory (the use of real and imaginary numbers) can be effectively used to obtain solutions to a great variety of important flow problems. There are, of course, numerical techniques that can be used to solve not only plane two-dimensional problems, but the more general three-dimensional problems. Since potential flow is governed by Laplace's equation, any procedure that is available for solving this equation can be applied to the analysis of irrotational flow of frictionless fluids. Potential flow theory is an old and well-established discipline within the general field of fluid mechanics. The interested reader can find many detailed references on this subject, including Refs. 2–6 given at the end of this chapter.

An important point to remember is that regardless of the particular technique used to obtain a solution to a potential flow problem, the solution remains approximate because of the fundamental assumption of a frictionless fluid. The general differential equations that describe viscous fluid behavior and some simple solutions to these equations are considered in the remaining sections of this chapter.

6.8   Viscous Flow

To incorporate viscous effects into the differential analysis of fluid motion we must return to the previously derived general equations of motion, Eqs. 6.50. Since these equations include both stresses and velocities, there are more unknowns than equations, and therefore before proceeding it is necessary to establish a relationship between the stresses and velocities.

6.8.1   Stress-Deformation Relationships

For incompressible, Newtonian fluids it is known that the stresses are linearly related to the rates of deformation and can be expressed in Cartesian coordinates as (for normal stresses)

$$\sigma_{xx} = -p + 2\mu \frac{\partial u}{\partial x} \tag{6.118a}$$

$$\sigma_{yy} = -p + 2\mu \frac{\partial v}{\partial y} \tag{6.118b}$$

$$\sigma_{zz} = -p + 2\mu \frac{\partial w}{\partial z} \tag{6.118c}$$

(for shearing stresses)

$$\tau_{xy} = \tau_{yx} = \mu \left(\frac{\partial u}{\partial y} + \frac{\partial v}{\partial x} \right) \tag{6.118d}$$

$$\tau_{yz} = \tau_{zy} = \mu \left(\frac{\partial v}{\partial z} + \frac{\partial w}{\partial y} \right) \tag{6.118e}$$

$$\tau_{zx} = \tau_{xz} = \mu \left(\frac{\partial w}{\partial x} + \frac{\partial u}{\partial z} \right) \tag{6.118f}$$

where p is the pressure, the negative of the average of the three normal stresses; that is $-p = (\frac{1}{3})(\sigma_{xx} + \sigma_{yy} + \sigma_{zz})$. For viscous fluids in motion the normal stresses are not necessarily the same in different directions, thus, the need to define the pressure as the average of the three normal stresses. For fluids at rest, or frictionless fluids, the normal stresses are equal in all directions. (We have made use of this fact in the chapter on fluid statics and in developing the equations for inviscid flow.) Detailed discussions of the development of these stress–velocity gradient relationships can be found in Refs. 3, 7, and 8. An important point to note is that whereas for elastic solids the stresses are linearly related to the deformation (or strain), for Newtonian fluids the stresses are linearly related to the rate of deformation (or rate of strain).

In cylindrical polar coordinates the stresses for Newtonian, incompressible fluids are expressed as (for normal stresses)

$$\sigma_{rr} = -p + 2\mu \frac{\partial v_r}{\partial r} \tag{6.119a}$$

$$\sigma_{\theta\theta} = -p + 2\mu \left(\frac{1}{r} \frac{\partial v_\theta}{\partial \theta} + \frac{v_r}{r} \right) \tag{6.119b}$$

$$\sigma_{zz} = -p + 2\mu \frac{\partial v_z}{\partial z} \tag{6.119c}$$

(for shearing stresses)

$$\tau_{r\theta} = \tau_{\theta r} = \mu \left[r \frac{\partial}{\partial r} \left(\frac{v_\theta}{r} \right) + \frac{1}{r} \frac{\partial v_r}{\partial \theta} \right] \tag{6.119d}$$

$$\tau_{\theta z} = \tau_{z\theta} = \mu \left(\frac{\partial v_\theta}{\partial z} + \frac{1}{r} \frac{\partial v_z}{\partial \theta} \right) \tag{6.119e}$$

$$\tau_{zr} = \tau_{rz} = \mu \left(\frac{\partial v_r}{\partial z} + \frac{\partial v_z}{\partial r} \right) \tag{6.119f}$$

The double subscript has a meaning similar to that of stresses expressed in Cartesian coordinates—that is, the first subscript indicates the plane on which the stress acts, and the second subscript the direction. Thus, for example, σ_{rr} refers to a stress acting on a plane perpendicular to the radial direction and in the radial direction (thus a normal stress). Similarly, $\tau_{r\theta}$ refers to a stress acting on a plane perpendicular to the radial direction but in the tangential (θ direction) and is therefore a shearing stress.

6.8.2   The Navier–Stokes Equations

The stresses as defined in the preceding section can be substituted into the differential equations of motion (Eqs. 6.50) and simplified by using the continuity equation (Eq. 6.31) to obtain (x direction)

$$\rho\left(\frac{\partial u}{\partial t} + u\frac{\partial u}{\partial x} + v\frac{\partial u}{\partial y} + w\frac{\partial u}{\partial z}\right) = -\frac{\partial p}{\partial x} + \rho g_x + \mu\left(\frac{\partial^2 u}{\partial x^2} + \frac{\partial^2 u}{\partial y^2} + \frac{\partial^2 u}{\partial z^2}\right) \quad \textbf{(6.120a)}$$

(y direction)

$$\rho\left(\frac{\partial v}{\partial t} + u\frac{\partial v}{\partial x} + v\frac{\partial v}{\partial y} + w\frac{\partial v}{\partial z}\right) = -\frac{\partial p}{\partial y} + \rho g_y + \mu\left(\frac{\partial^2 v}{\partial x^2} + \frac{\partial^2 v}{\partial y^2} + \frac{\partial^2 v}{\partial z^2}\right) \quad \textbf{(6.120b)}$$

(z direction)

$$\rho\left(\frac{\partial w}{\partial t} + u\frac{\partial w}{\partial x} + v\frac{\partial w}{\partial y} + w\frac{\partial w}{\partial z}\right) = -\frac{\partial p}{\partial z} + \rho g_z + \mu\left(\frac{\partial^2 w}{\partial x^2} + \frac{\partial^2 w}{\partial y^2} + \frac{\partial^2 w}{\partial z^2}\right) \quad \textbf{(6.120c)}$$

where we have rearranged the equations so the acceleration terms are on the left side and the force terms are on the right. These equations are commonly called the *Navier–Stokes* equations, named in honor of the French mathematician L. M. H. Navier and the English mechanician Sir G. G. Stokes, who were responsible for their formulation. These three equations of motion, when combined with the conservation of mass equation (Eq. 6.31), provide a complete mathematical description of the flow of incompressible, Newtonian fluids. We have four equations and four unknowns (u, v, w, and p), and therefore the problem is "well-posed" in mathematical terms. Unfortunately, because of the general complexity of the Navier–Stokes equations (they are nonlinear, second order, partial differential equations), they are not amenable to exact mathematical solutions except in a few instances. However, in those few instances in which solutions have been obtained and compared with experimental results, the results have been in close agreement. Thus, the Navier–Stokes equations are considered to be the governing differential equations of motion for incompressible, Newtonian fluids.

In terms of cylindrical polar coordinates (see Fig. 6.6) the Navier–Stokes equations can be written as (r direction)

$$\rho\left(\frac{\partial v_r}{\partial t} + v_r\frac{\partial v_r}{\partial r} + \frac{v_\theta}{r}\frac{\partial v_r}{\partial \theta} - \frac{v_\theta^2}{r} + v_z\frac{\partial v_r}{\partial z}\right)$$

$$= -\frac{\partial p}{\partial r} + \rho g_r + \mu\left[\frac{1}{r}\frac{\partial}{\partial r}\left(r\frac{\partial v_r}{\partial r}\right) - \frac{v_r}{r^2} + \frac{1}{r^2}\frac{\partial^2 v_r}{\partial \theta^2} - \frac{2}{r^2}\frac{\partial v_\theta}{\partial \theta} + \frac{\partial^2 v_r}{\partial z^2}\right] \quad \textbf{(6.121a)}$$

(θ direction)

$$\rho\left(\frac{\partial v_\theta}{\partial t} + v_r\frac{\partial v_\theta}{\partial r} + \frac{v_\theta}{r}\frac{\partial v_\theta}{\partial \theta} + \frac{v_r v_\theta}{r} + v_z\frac{\partial v_\theta}{\partial z}\right)$$

$$= -\frac{1}{r}\frac{\partial p}{\partial \theta} + \rho g_\theta + \mu\left[\frac{1}{r}\frac{\partial}{\partial r}\left(r\frac{\partial v_\theta}{\partial r}\right) - \frac{v_\theta}{r^2} + \frac{1}{r^2}\frac{\partial^2 v_\theta}{\partial \theta^2} + \frac{2}{r^2}\frac{\partial v_r}{\partial \theta} + \frac{\partial^2 v_\theta}{\partial z^2}\right] \quad \textbf{(6.121b)}$$

(z direction)

$$\rho\left(\frac{\partial v_z}{\partial t} + v_r\frac{\partial v_z}{\partial r} + \frac{v_\theta}{r}\frac{\partial v_z}{\partial \theta} + v_z\frac{\partial v_z}{\partial z}\right)$$

$$= -\frac{\partial p}{\partial z} + \rho g_z + \mu\left[\frac{1}{r}\frac{\partial}{\partial r}\left(r\frac{\partial v_z}{\partial r}\right) + \frac{1}{r^2}\frac{\partial^2 v_z}{\partial \theta^2} + \frac{\partial^2 v_z}{\partial z^2}\right] \quad \textbf{(6.121c)}$$

To provide a brief introduction to the use of the Navier–Stokes equations, a few of the simplest exact solutions are developed in the next section. Although these solutions will prove to be relatively simple, this is not the case in general. In fact, only a few other exact solutions have been obtained.

6.9   Some Simple Solutions for Viscous, Incompressible Fluids

A principal difficulty in solving the Navier–Stokes equations is because of their nonlinearity arising from the convective acceleration terms (i.e., $u\,\partial u/\partial x$, $w\,\partial v/\partial z$, etc.). There are no general analytical schemes for solving nonlinear partial differential equations (e.g., superposition of solutions cannot be used), and each problem must be considered individually. For most practical flow problems fluid particles do have accelerated motion as they move from one location to another in the flow field. Thus, the convective acceleration terms are usually important. However, there are a few special cases for which the convective acceleration vanishes because of the nature of the geometry of the flow system. In these cases exact solutions are usually possible. The Navier–Stokes equations apply to both laminar and turbulent flow, but for turbulent flow each velocity component fluctuates randomly with respect to time and this added complication makes an analytical solution intractable. Thus, the exact solutions referred to are for laminar flows in which the velocity is either independent of time (steady flow) or dependent on time (unsteady flow) in a well-defined manner.

6.9.1   Steady, Laminar Flow Between Fixed Parallel Plates

We first consider flow between the two horizontal, infinite parallel plates of Fig. 6.28a. For this geometry the fluid particles move in the x direction parallel to the plates, and there is no velocity in the y or z direction—that is, $v = 0$ and $w = 0$. In this case it follows from the continuity equation (Eq. 6.31) that $\partial u/\partial x = 0$. Furthermore, there would be no variation of u in the z direction for infinite plates, and for steady flow $\partial u/\partial t = 0$ so that $u = u(y)$. If these conditions are used in the Navier–Stokes equations (Eqs. 6.120), they reduce to

$$0 = -\frac{\partial p}{\partial x} + \mu\left(\frac{\partial^2 u}{\partial y^2}\right) \quad \textbf{(6.122)}$$

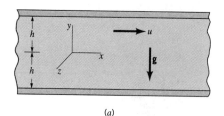
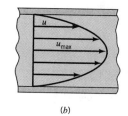

(a)

(b)

$$0 = -\frac{\partial p}{\partial y} - \rho g \qquad (6.123)$$

$$0 = -\frac{\partial p}{\partial z} \qquad (6.124)$$

where we have set $g_x = 0$, $g_y = -g$, and $g_z = 0$. That is, the y axis points up. We see that for
this particular problem the Navier–Stokes equations reduce to some rather simple equations.
Equations 6.123 and 6.124 can be integrated to yield

$$p = -\rho g y + f_1(x) \qquad (6.125)$$

which shows that the pressure varies hydrostatically in the y direction. Equation 6.122, rewritten as

$$\frac{d^2 u}{dy^2} = \frac{1}{\mu}\frac{\partial p}{\partial x}$$

can be integrated to give

$$\frac{du}{dy} = \frac{1}{\mu}\left(\frac{\partial p}{\partial x}\right) y + c_1$$

and integrated again to yield

$$u = \frac{1}{2\mu}\left(\frac{\partial p}{\partial x}\right) y^2 + c_1 y + c_2 \qquad (6.126)$$

V6.5 No-slip
boundary
condition

Note that for this simple flow the pressure gradient, $\partial p/\partial x$, is treated as constant as far as the
integration is concerned, since (as shown in Eq. 6.125) it is not a function of y. The two constants c_1 and c_2 must be determined from the boundary conditions. For example, if the two
plates are fixed, then $u = 0$ for $y = \pm h$ (because of the no-slip condition for viscous fluids).
To satisfy this condition $c_1 = 0$ and

$$c_2 = -\frac{1}{2\mu}\left(\frac{\partial p}{\partial x}\right) h^2$$

Thus, the velocity distribution becomes

$$u = \frac{1}{2\mu}\left(\frac{\partial p}{\partial x}\right)(y^2 - h^2) \qquad (6.127)$$

Equation 6.127 shows that the velocity profile between the two fixed plates is parabolic as
illustrated in Fig. 6.28*b*.

The volume rate of flow, q, passing between the plates (for a unit width in the z direction) is obtained from the relationship

$$q = \int_{-h}^{h} u \, dy = \int_{-h}^{h} \frac{1}{2\mu}\left(\frac{\partial p}{\partial x}\right)(y^2 - h^2) \, dy$$

or

$$q = -\frac{2h^3}{3\mu}\left(\frac{\partial p}{\partial x}\right) \tag{6.128}$$

The pressure gradient $\partial p/\partial x$ is negative, since the pressure decreases in the direction of flow. If we let Δp represent the pressure *drop* between two points a distance ℓ apart, then

$$\frac{\Delta p}{\ell} = -\frac{\partial p}{\partial x}$$

and Eq. 6.128 can be expressed as

$$q = \frac{2h^3 \, \Delta p}{3\mu\ell} \tag{6.129}$$

The flow is proportional to the pressure gradient, inversely proportional to the viscosity, and strongly dependent $(\sim h^3)$ on the gap width. In terms of the mean velocity, V, where $V = q/2h$, Eq. 6.129 becomes

$$V = \frac{h^2 \, \Delta p}{3\mu\ell} \tag{6.130}$$

Equations 6.129 and 6.130 provide convenient relationships for relating the pressure drop along a parallel-plate channel and the rate of flow or mean velocity. The maximum velocity, u_{max}, occurs midway $(y = 0)$ between the two plates so that from Eq. 6.127

$$u_{max} = -\frac{h^2}{2\mu}\left(\frac{\partial p}{\partial x}\right)$$

or

$$u_{max} = \tfrac{3}{2}V \tag{6.131}$$

The details of the steady, laminar flow between infinite parallel plates are completely predicted by this solution to the Navier–Stokes equations. For example, if the pressure gradient, viscosity, and plate spacing are specified, then from Eq. 6.127 the velocity profile can be determined, and from Eqs. 6.129 and 6.130 the corresponding flowrate and mean velocity determined. In addition, from Eq. 6.125 it follows that

$$f_1(x) = \left(\frac{\partial p}{\partial x}\right)x + p_0$$

where p_0 is a reference pressure at $x = y = 0$, and the pressure variation throughout the fluid can be obtained from

$$p = -\rho g y + \left(\frac{\partial p}{\partial x}\right)x + p_0 \tag{6.132}$$

For a given fluid and reference pressure, p_0, the pressure at any point can be predicted. This relatively simple example of an exact solution illustrates the detailed information about the flow field which can be obtained. The flow will be laminar if the Reynolds number, $Re = \rho V(2h)/\mu$, remains below about 1400. For flow with larger Reynolds numbers the flow becomes turbulent and the preceding analysis is not valid since the flow field is complex, three-dimensional, and unsteady.

6.9.2   Couette Flow

Another simple parallel-plate flow can be developed by fixing one plate and letting the other plate move with a constant velocity, U, as illustrated in Fig. 6.29a. The Navier–Stokes equations reduce to the same form as those in the preceding section and the solution for the pressure and velocity distribution are still given by Eqs. 6.125 and 6.126, respectively. However, for the moving plate problem the boundary conditions for the velocity are different. For this case we locate the origin of the coordinate system at the bottom plate and designate the distance between the two plates as b (see Fig. 6.29a). The two constants c_1 and c_2 in Eq. 6.126 can be determined from the boundary conditions, $u = 0$ at $y = 0$ and $u = U$ at $y = b$. It follows that

$$u = U\frac{y}{b} + \frac{1}{2\mu}\left(\frac{\partial p}{\partial x}\right)(y^2 - by) \tag{6.133}$$

or, in dimensionless form

$$\frac{u}{U} = \frac{y}{b} - \frac{b^2}{2\mu U}\left(\frac{\partial p}{\partial x}\right)\left(\frac{y}{b}\right)\left(1 - \frac{y}{b}\right) \tag{6.134}$$

The actual velocity profile will depend on the dimensionless parameter

$$P = -\frac{b^2}{2\mu U}\left(\frac{\partial p}{\partial x}\right)$$

Several profiles are shown in Fig. 6.29b. This type of flow is called *Couette flow*.

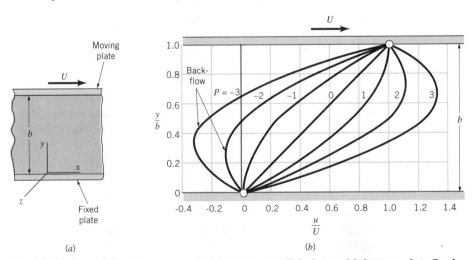

■ **FIGURE 6.29**   The viscous flow between parallel plates with bottom plate fixed and upper plate moving (Couette flow): (*a*) coordinate system and notation used in analysis; (*b*) velocity distribution as a function of parameter, *P*, where $P = -(b^2/2\mu U)\partial p/\partial x$. (From Ref. 8, used by permission.)

The simplest type of Couette flow is one for which the pressure gradient is zero; that is, the fluid motion is caused by the fluid being dragged along by the moving boundary. In this case, with $\partial p/\partial x = 0$, Eq. 6.133 simply reduces to

$$u = U\frac{y}{b} \tag{6.135}$$

which indicates that the velocity varies linearly between the two plates as shown in Fig. 6.29b for $P = 0$.

EXAMPLE 6.8

A wide moving belt passes through a container of a viscous liquid. The belt moves vertically upward with a constant velocity, V_0, as illustrated in Fig. E6.8. Because of viscous forces the belt picks up a film of fluid of thickness h. Gravity tends to make the fluid drain down the belt. Use the Navier–Stokes equations to determine an expression for the average velocity of the fluid film as it is dragged up the belt. Assume that the flow is laminar, steady, and fully developed.

SOLUTION

Since the flow is assumed to be uniform, the only velocity component is in the y direction (the v component) so that $u = w = 0$. It follows from the continuity equation that $\partial v/\partial y = 0$, and for steady flow $\partial v/\partial t = 0$, so that $v = v(x)$. Under these conditions the Navier–Stokes equations for the x direction (Eq. 6.120a) and the z direction (perpendicular to the paper) (Eq. 6.120c) simply reduce to

$$\frac{\partial p}{\partial x} = 0 \qquad \frac{\partial p}{\partial z} = 0$$

This result indicates that the pressure does not vary over a horizontal plane, and since the pressure on the surface of the film ($x = h$) is atmospheric, the pressure throughout the film

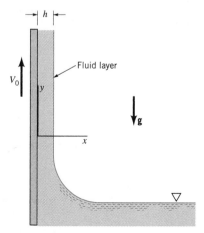

■ FIGURE E6.8

must be atmospheric (or zero gage pressure). The equation of motion in the y direction (Eq. 6.120b) thus reduces to

$$0 = -\rho g + \mu \frac{d^2 v}{dx^2}$$

or

$$\frac{d^2 v}{dx^2} = \frac{\gamma}{\mu} \tag{1}$$

Integration of Eq. 1 yields

$$\frac{dv}{dx} = \frac{\gamma}{\mu} x + c_1 \tag{2}$$

On the film surface ($x = h$) we assume the shearing stress is zero—that is, the drag of the air on the film is negligible. The shearing stress at the free surface (or any interior parallel surface) is designated as τ_{xy} where from Eq. 6.118d

$$\tau_{xy} = \mu \left(\frac{dv}{dx} \right)$$

Thus, if $\tau_{xy} = 0$ at $x = h$, it follows from Eq. 2 that

$$c_1 = -\frac{\gamma h}{\mu}$$

A second integration of Eq. 2 gives the velocity distribution in the film as

$$v = \frac{\gamma}{2\mu} x^2 - \frac{\gamma h}{\mu} x + c_2$$

At the belt ($x = 0$) the fluid velocity must match the belt velocity, V_0, so that

$$c_2 = V_0$$

and the velocity distribution is therefore

$$v = \frac{\gamma}{2\mu} x^2 - \frac{\gamma h}{\mu} x + V_0$$

With the velocity distribution known we can determine the flowrate per unit width, q, from the relationship

$$q = \int_0^h v \, dx = \int_0^h \left(\frac{\gamma}{2\mu} x^2 - \frac{\gamma h}{\mu} x + V_0 \right) dx$$

and thus

$$q = V_0 h - \frac{\gamma h^3}{3\mu}$$

The average film velocity, V (where $q = Vh$), is therefore

$$V = V_0 - \frac{\gamma h^2}{3\mu} \tag{Ans}$$

It is interesting to note from this result that there will be a net upward flow of liquid (positive V) only if $V_0 > \gamma h^2 / 3\mu$. It takes a relatively large belt speed to lift a small viscosity fluid.

6.9.3 Steady, Laminar Flow in Circular Tubes

Probably the best known exact solution to the Navier–Stokes equations is for steady, incompressible, laminar flow through a straight circular tube of constant cross section. This type of flow is commonly called *Hagen–Poiseuille flow,* or simply *Poiseuille flow.* It is named in honor of J. L. Poiseuille, a French physician, and G. H. L. Hagen, a German hydraulic engineer. Poiseuille was interested in blood flow through capillaries and deduced experimentally the resistance laws for laminar flow through circular tubes. Hagen's investigation of flow in tubes was also experimental. It was actually after the work of Hagen and Poiseuille that the theoretical results presented in this section were determined, but their names are commonly associated with the solution of this problem.

Consider the flow through a horizontal circular tube of radius R as shown in Fig. 6.30*a*. Because of the cylindrical geometry it is convenient to use cylindrical coordinates. We assume that the flow is parallel to the walls so that $v_r = 0$ and $v_\theta = 0$, and from the continuity equation (6.35) $\partial v_z / \partial z = 0$. Also, for steady, axisymmetric flow, v_z is not a function of t or θ so the velocity, v_z, is only a function of the radial position within the tube—that is, $v_z = v_z(r)$. Under these conditions the Navier–Stokes equations (Eqs. 6.121) reduce to

$$0 = -\rho g \sin \theta - \frac{\partial p}{\partial r} \tag{6.136}$$

$$0 = -\rho g \cos \theta - \frac{1}{r} \frac{\partial p}{\partial \theta} \tag{6.137}$$

$$0 = -\frac{\partial p}{\partial z} + \mu \left[\frac{1}{r} \frac{\partial}{\partial r} \left(r \frac{\partial v_z}{\partial r} \right) \right] \tag{6.138}$$

where we have used the relationships $g_r = -g \sin \theta$ and $g_\theta = -g \cos \theta$ (with θ measured from the horizontal plane).

Equations 6.136 and 6.137 can be integrated to give

$$p = -\rho g (r \sin \theta) + f_1(z)$$

or

$$p = -\rho g y + f_1(z) \tag{6.139}$$

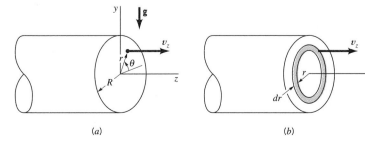

■ **FIGURE 6.30**
The viscous flow in a horizontal, circular tube: (*a*) coordinate system and notation used in analysis; (*b*) flow through differential annular ring.

(*a*)   (*b*)

Equation 6.139 indicates that the pressure is hydrostatically distributed at any particular cross section, and the z component of the pressure gradient, $\partial p / \partial z$, is not a function of r or θ.

The equation of motion in the z direction (Eq. 6.138) can be written in the form

$$\frac{1}{r} \frac{\partial}{\partial r}\left(r \frac{\partial v_z}{\partial r}\right) = \frac{1}{\mu} \frac{\partial p}{\partial z}$$

and integrated (using the fact that $\partial p / \partial z = $ constant) to give

$$r \frac{\partial v_z}{\partial r} = \frac{1}{2\mu}\left(\frac{\partial p}{\partial z}\right) r^2 + c_1$$

Integrating again we obtain

$$v_z = \frac{1}{4\mu}\left(\frac{\partial p}{\partial z}\right) r^2 + c_1 \ln r + c_2 \tag{6.140}$$

Since we wish v_z to be finite at the center of the tube ($r = 0$), it follows that $c_1 = 0$ [since $\ln (0) = -\infty$]. At the wall ($r = R$) the velocity must be zero so that

$$c_2 = -\frac{1}{4\mu}\left(\frac{\partial p}{\partial z}\right) R^2$$

and the velocity distribution becomes

$$v_z = \frac{1}{4\mu}\left(\frac{\partial p}{\partial z}\right)(r^2 - R^2) \tag{6.141}$$

V6.6 Laminar flow

Thus, at any cross section the velocity distribution is parabolic.

To obtain a relationship between the volume rate of flow, Q, passing through the tube and the pressure gradient, we consider the flow through the differential, washer-shaped ring of Fig. 6.30b. Since v_z is constant on this ring, the volume rate of flow through the differential area $dA = (2\pi r)\, dr$ is

$$dQ = v_z(2\pi r)\, dr$$

and therefore

$$Q = 2\pi \int_0^R v_z r\, dr \tag{6.142}$$

Equation 6.141 for v_z can be substituted into Eq. 6.142, and the resulting equation integrated to yield

$$Q = -\frac{\pi R^4}{8\mu}\left(\frac{\partial p}{\partial z}\right) \tag{6.143}$$

This relationship can be expressed in terms of the pressure *drop*, Δp, which occurs over a length, ℓ, along the tube, since

$$\frac{\Delta p}{\ell} = -\frac{\partial p}{\partial z}$$

and therefore

$$Q = \frac{\pi R^4 \Delta p}{8\mu\ell} \tag{6.144}$$

For a given pressure drop per unit length, the volume rate of flow is inversely proportional to the viscosity and proportional to the tube radius to the fourth power. A doubling of the tube radius produces a sixteenfold increase in flow! Equation 6.144 is commonly called *Poiseuille's law.*

In terms of the mean velocity, V, where $V = Q/\pi R^2$, Eq. 6.144 becomes

$$V = \frac{R^2\,\Delta p}{8\mu\ell} \tag{6.145}$$

The maximum velocity, v_{max}, occurs at the center of the tube, where from Eq. 6.141

$$v_{max} = -\frac{R^2}{4\mu}\left(\frac{\partial p}{\partial z}\right) = \frac{R^2\,\Delta p}{4\mu\ell} \tag{6.146}$$

so that

$$v_{max} = 2V$$

The velocity distribution can be written in terms of v_{max} as

$$\frac{v_z}{v_{max}} = 1 - \left(\frac{r}{R}\right)^2 \tag{6.147}$$

As was true for the similar case of flow between parallel plates (sometimes referred to as *plane Poiseuille flow*), a very detailed description of the pressure and velocity distribution in tube flow results from this solution to the Navier–Stokes equations. Numerous experiments performed to substantiate the theoretical results show that the theory and experiment are in agreement for the laminar flow of Newtonian fluids in circular tubes or pipes. The flow remains laminar for Reynolds numbers, $\text{Re} = \rho V(2R)/\mu$, below 2100. Turbulent flow in tubes is considered in Chapter 8.

6.10   Other Aspects of Differential Analysis

In this chapter the basic differential equations that govern the flow of fluids have been developed. The Navier–Stokes equations, which can be compactly expressed in vector notation as

$$\rho\left(\frac{\partial \mathbf{V}}{\partial t} + \mathbf{V}\cdot\nabla\mathbf{V}\right) = -\nabla p + \rho\mathbf{g} + \mu\,\nabla^2\mathbf{V} \tag{6.148}$$

along with the continuity equation

$$\nabla\cdot\mathbf{V} = 0 \tag{6.149}$$

are the general equations of motion for incompressible, Newtonian fluids. Although we have restricted our attention to incompressible fluids, these equations can be readily extended to include compressible fluids. It is well beyond the scope of this introductory text to consider in depth the variety of analytical and numerical techniques that can be used to obtain both exact and approximate solutions to the Navier–Stokes equations.

Numerical techniques using digital computers are, of course, commonly used to solve a wide variety of flow problems. Numerous laminar flow solutions based on the full Navier–Stokes equations have been obtained by using both finite element and finite difference methods. Flow characteristics of highly nonlinear problems can be obtained from numerical solutions. However, these solutions do typically require the use of powerful digital computers, and the nonlinearities in the equations represent a complication that challenges the ingenuity of the numerical analyst. Practical turbulent flow problems are not amenable to a completely numerical solution because of the extreme complexity of the motion. The solution of real turbulent flows usually involves the use of some type of empirical turbulence model.

The general field of computational fluid dynamics (CFD), in which computers and numerical analysis are combined to solve fluid flow problems, represents an extremely important subject area in advanced fluid mechanics. There is a vast, continually growing literature on CFD, and a few representative references are given at the end of this chapter (Refs. 9, 10, 11, 12).

V6.7 CFD example

References

1. White, F. M., *Fluid Mechanics,* Second Edition, McGraw-Hill, New York, 1986.
2. Street, V. L., *Fluid Dynamics,* McGraw-Hill, New York, 1948.
3. Rouse, H., *Advanced Mechanics of Fluids,* Wiley, New York, 1959.
4. Milne-Thomson, L. M., *Theoretical Hydrodynamics,* Fourth Edition, Macmillan, New York, 1960.
5. Robertson, J. M., *Hydrodynamics in Theory and Application,* Prentice-Hall, Englewood Cliffs, N.J., 1965.
6. Panton, R. L., *Incompressible Flow,* Wiley, New York, 1984.
7. Li, W. H., and Lam, S. H., *Principles of Fluid Mechanics,* Addison-Wesley, Reading, Mass., 1964.
8. Schlichting, H., *Boundary-Layer Theory,* Seventh Edition, McGraw-Hill, New York, 1979.
9. Baker, A. J., *Finite Element Computational Fluid Mechanics,* McGraw-Hill, New York, 1983.
10. Peyret, R., and Taylor, T. D., *Computational Methods for Fluid Flow,* Springer-Verlag, New York, 1983.
11. Anderson, D. A., Tannehill, J. C., and Pletcher, R. H., *Computational Fluid Mechanics and Heat Transfer,* McGraw-Hill, New York, 1984.
12. Carey, G. F., and Oden, J. T., *Finite Elements: Fluid Mechanics,* Prentice-Hall, Englewood Cliffs, N.J., 1986.

Problems

Note: Unless otherwise indicated, use the values of fluid properties found in the tables on the inside of the front cover. Problems designated with an (*) are intended to be solved with the aid of a programmable calculator or a computer.

6.1 The velocity in a certain two-dimensional flow field is given by the equation

$$\mathbf{V} = 2xt\hat{\mathbf{i}} - 2yt\hat{\mathbf{j}}$$

where the velocity is in ft/s when x, y, and t are in feet and seconds, respectively. Determine expressions for the local and convective components of acceleration in the x and y directions. What is the magnitude and direction of the velocity and the acceleration at the point $x = y = 1$ ft at the time $t = 0$?

6.2 The velocity in a certain flow field is given by the equation

$$\mathbf{V} = yz\hat{\mathbf{i}} + x^2z\hat{\mathbf{j}} + x\hat{\mathbf{k}}$$

Determine the expressions for the three rectangular components of acceleration.

6.3 The three components of velocity in a flow field are given by

$$u = x^2 + y^2 + z^2$$
$$v = xy + yz + z^2$$
$$w = -3xz - z^2/2 + 4$$

(a) Determine the volumetric dilatation rate and interpret the results. **(b)** Determine an expression for the rotation vector. Is this an irrotational flow field?

6.4 An incompressible viscous fluid is placed between two large parallel plates as shown in Fig. P6.4. The bottom plate is fixed and the upper plate moves with a constant velocity, U. For these conditions the velocity distribution between the plates is linear and can be expressed as

$$u = U\frac{y}{b}$$

Determine: **(a)** the volumetric dilatation rate, **(b)** the rotation vector, **(c)** the vorticity, and **(d)** the rate of angular deformation.

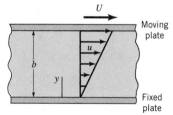

■ FIGURE P6.4

6.5 A viscous fluid is contained in the space between concentric cylinders. The inner wall is fixed and the outer wall rotates with an angular velocity ω. (See Fig. P6.5a and Video V6.1.) Assume that the velocity distribution in the gap is linear as illustrated in Fig. P6.5b. For the small rectangular element shown in Fig. P6.5b, determine the rate of change of the right angle γ due to the fluid motion. Express your answer in terms of r_0, r_i, and ω.

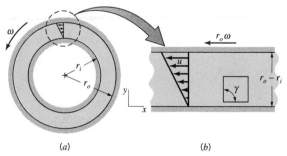

(a)   (b)

■ FIGURE P6.5

6.6 Some velocity measurements in a three-dimensional incompressible flow field indicate that $u = 6xy^2$ and $v = -4y^2z$. There is some conflicting data for the velocity

component in the z direction. One set of data indicates that $w = 4yz^2$ and the other set indicates that $w = 4yz^2 - 6y^2z$. Which set do you think is correct? Explain.

6.7 For incompressible fluids the volumetric dilatation rate must be zero; that is, $\nabla \cdot \mathbf{V} = 0$. For what combination of constants, a, b, c, and e can the velocity components

$$u = ax + by$$
$$v = cx + ey$$
$$w = 0$$

be used to describe an incompressible flow field?

6.8 For a certain two-dimensional flow field

$$u = 0$$
$$v = V$$

(a) What are the corresponding radial and tangential velocity components? **(b)** Determine the corresponding stream function expressed in Cartesian coordinates and in cylindrical polar coordinates.

6.9 The stream function for a certain incompressible flow field is given by the equation

$$\psi = 2x^2y - \tfrac{2}{3}y^3$$

Show that the velocity field represented by this stream function satisfies the continuity equation.

6.10 In a two-dimensional, incompressible flow field, the x component of velocity is given by the equation $u = 2x$. **(a)** Determine the corresponding equation for the y component of velocity if $v = 0$ along the x axis. **(b)** For this flow field, what is the magnitude of the average velocity of the fluid crossing the surface OA of Fig. P6.10? Assume that the velocities are in ft/s when x and y are in feet.

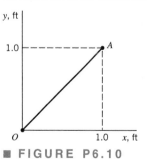

■ FIGURE P6.10

6.11 The radial velocity component in an incompressible, two-dimensional flow field ($v_z = 0$) is

$$v_r = 2r + 3r^2 \sin \theta$$

Determine the corresponding tangential velocity component, v_θ, required to satisfy conservation of mass.

6.12 The stream function for an incompressible flow field is given by the equation

$$\psi = 3x^2y - y^3$$

where the stream function has the units of m²/s with x and y in meters. (**a**) Sketch the streamline(s) passing through the origin. (**b**) Determine the rate of flow across the straight path AB shown in Fig. P6.12.

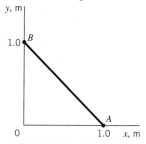

■ **FIGURE P6.12**

6.13 A two-dimensional flow field for a nonviscous, incompressible fluid is described by the velocity components

$$u = U_0 + 2y$$
$$v = 0$$

where U_0 is a constant. If the pressure at the origin (Fig. P6.13) is p_0, determine an expression for the pressure at (**a**) point A, and (**b**) point B. Explain clearly how you obtained your answer. Assume the units are consistent and body forces may be neglected.

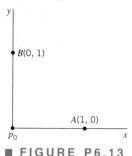

■ **FIGURE P6.13**

6.14 The velocity potential for a given two-dimensional flow field is

$$\phi = (\tfrac{5}{3})x^3 - 5xy^2$$

Show that the continuity equation is satisfied and determine the corresponding stream function.

6.15 A certain flow field is described by the velocity potential

$$\phi = A \ln r + Br \cos \theta$$

where A and B are positive constants. Determine the corresponding stream function and locate any stagnation points in this flow field.

6.16 It is known that the velocity distribution for two-dimensional flow of a viscous fluid between wide, fixed parallel plates (Fig. P6.16) is parabolic; that is

$$u = U_c \left[1 - \left(\frac{y}{h} \right)^2 \right]$$

with $v = 0$. Determine, if possible, the corresponding stream function and velocity potential.

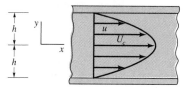

■ **FIGURE P6.16**

6.17 The velocity potential for a certain inviscid flow field is

$$\phi = -(3x^2y - y^3)$$

where ϕ has the units of ft²/s when x and y are in feet. Determine the pressure difference (in psi) between the points (1, 2) and (4, 4), where the coordinates are in feet, if the fluid is water and elevation changes are negligible.

6.18 Consider the incompressible, two-dimensional flow of a nonviscous fluid between the boundaries shown in Fig. P6.18. The velocity potential for this flow field is

$$\phi = x^2 - y^2$$

(**a**) Determine the corresponding stream function. (**b**) What is the relationship between the discharge, q (per unit width normal to plane of paper), passing between the walls and the coordinates x_i, y_i of any point on the curved wall? Neglect body forces.

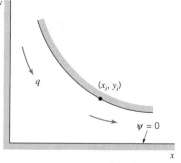

■ **FIGURE P6.18**

6.19 The velocity components in an ideal, two-dimensional velocity field are given by the equations

$$u = 3(x^2 - y^2)$$
$$v = -6xy$$

All body forces are negligible. **(a)** Does this velocity field satisfy the continuity equation? **(b)** Determine the equation for the pressure gradient in the y direction at any point in the field.

6.20 The streamlines for an incompressible, inviscid, two-dimensional flow field are all concentric circles and the velocity varies directly with the distance from the common center of the streamlines; that is

$$v_\theta = Kr$$

where K is a constant. **(a)** For this *rotational* flow, determine, if possible, the stream function. **(b)** Can the pressure difference between the origin and any other point be determined from the Bernoulli equation? Explain.

6.21 The stream function for the flow of a nonviscous, incompressible fluid in the vicinity of a corner (Fig. P6.21) is

$$\psi = 2r^{4/3} \sin \tfrac{4}{3}\theta$$

Determine an expression for the pressure *gradient* along the boundary $\theta = 0$.

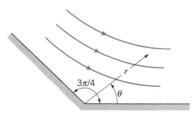

■ **FIGURE P6.21**

6.22 Water flows through a two-dimensional diffuser having a 20° expansion angle as shown in Fig. P6.22. Assume that the flow in the diffuser can be treated as a radial flow emanating from a source at the origin O. **(a)** If the velocity at the entrance is 20 m/s, determine an expression for the pressure gradient along the diffuser walls. **(b)** What is the pressure rise between the entrance and exit?

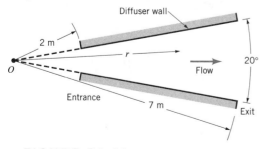

■ **FIGURE P6.22**

6.23 As illustrated in Fig. P6.23 a tornado can be approximated by a free vortex of strength Γ for $r > R_c$, where R_c is the radius of the core. Velocity measurements at points A and B indicate that $V_A = 125$ ft/s and $V_B = 75$ ft/s. Determine the distance from point A to the center of the tornado. Why can the free vortex model not be used to approximate the tornado throughout the flow field ($r \geq 0$)?

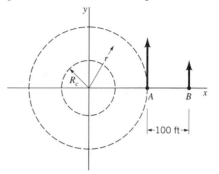

■ **FIGURE P6.23**

6.24 The velocity distribution in a horizontal, two-dimensional bend through which an ideal fluid flows can be approximated with a free vortex as shown in Fig. P6.24. Show how the discharge (per unit width normal to plane of paper) through the channel can be expressed as

$$q = C\sqrt{\frac{\Delta p}{\rho}}$$

where $\Delta p = p_B - p_A$. Determine the value of the constant C for the bend dimensions given.

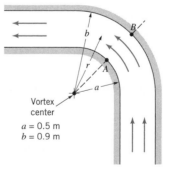

■ **FIGURE P6.24**

6.25 When water discharges from a tank through an opening in its bottom, a vortex may form with a curved surface profile as shown in Fig. P6.25 and **Video V6.2**. Assume that the velocity distribution in the vortex is the same as that for a free vortex. At the same time the water is being discharged from the tank at point A it is desired to discharge a small quantity of water through the pipe B. As the discharge through A is increased, the strength of the vortex, as indicated by its circulation, is increased. Determine the maximum strength that the vortex can have in order that no air is sucked in at B. Express your answer in terms of the circulation. Assume that the fluid level in the tank at a large distance from the opening at A remains constant and viscous effects are negligible.

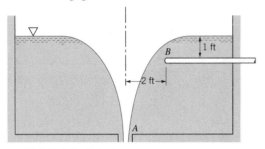

■ **FIGURE P6.25**

6.26   Water flows over a flat surface at 5 ft/s as shown in Fig. P6.26. A pump draws off water through a narrow slit at a volume rate of 0.1 ft³/s per foot length of the slit. Assume that the fluid is incompressible and inviscid and can be represented by the combination of a uniform flow and a sink. Locate the stagnation point on the wall (point A), and determine the equation for the stagnation streamline. How far above the surface, H, must the fluid be so that it does not get sucked into the slit?

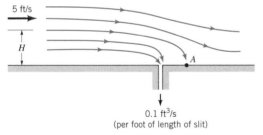

■ **FIGURE P6.26**

6.27   Consider a uniform flow in the positive x direction combined with a free vortex located at the origin of the coordinate system. The streamline $\psi = 0$ passes through the point $x = 4$, $y = 0$. Determine the equation of this streamline.

6.28   Potential flow against a flat plate (Fig. P6.28a) can be described with the stream function

$$\psi = Axy$$

where A is a constant. This type of flow is commonly called a "stagnation point" flow since it can be used to describe

the flow in the vicinity of the stagnation point at O. By adding a source of strength m at O, stagnation point flow against a flat plate with a "bump" is obtained as illustrated in Fig. P6.28b. Determine the relationship between the bump height, h, the constant, A, and the source strength, m.

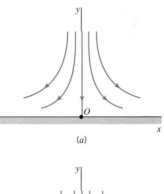

(a)

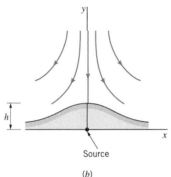

(b)

■ **FIGURE P6.28**

6.29   The combination of a uniform flow and a source can be used to describe flow around a streamlined body called a half-body. (See **Video V6.3**.) Assume that a certain body has the shape of a half-body with a thickness of 0.5 m. If this body is placed in an air stream moving at 15 m/s, what source strength is required to simulate flow around the body?

6.30   A body having the general shape of a half-body is placed in a stream of fluid. At a great distance upstream the velocity is U as shown in Fig. P6.30. Show how a mea-

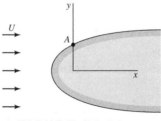

■ **FIGURE P6.30**

surement of the differential pressure between the stagnation point and point A can be used to predict the free-stream velocity, U. Express the pressure differential in terms of U and fluid density. Neglect body forces and assume that the fluid is nonviscous and incompressible.

6.31   One end of a pond has a shoreline that resembles a half-body as shown in Fig. P6.31. A vertical porous pipe is located near the end of the pond so that water can be pumped out. When water is pumped at the rate of 0.06 m³/s through a 3-m-long pipe, what will be the velocity at point A? *Hint:* Consider the flow *inside* a half-body.

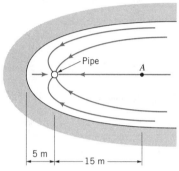

■ **FIGURE P6.31**

*6.32   For the half-body described in Section 6.6.1, show on a plot how the magnitude of the velocity on the surface, V_s, varies as a function of the distance, s (measured along the surface), from the stagnation point. Use the dimensionless variables V_s/U and s/b where U and b are defined in Fig. 6.23.

6.33   Assume that the flow around the long circular cylinder of Fig. P6.33 is nonviscous and incompressible. Two pressures, p_1 and p_2, are measured on the surface of the cylinder, as illustrated. It is proposed that the free-stream velocity, U, can be related to the pressure difference $\Delta p = p_1 - p_2$ by the equation

$$U = C\sqrt{\frac{\Delta p}{\rho}}$$

where ρ is the fluid density. Determine the value of the constant C. Neglect body forces.

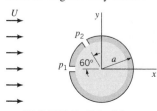

■ **FIGURE P6.33**

6.34   An ideal fluid flows past an infinitely long semicircular "hump" located along a plane boundary as shown in Fig. P6.34. Far from the hump the velocity field is uniform, and the pressure is p_0. **(a)** Determine expressions for the maximum and minimum values of the pressure along the hump, and indicate where these points are located. Express your answer in terms of ρ, U, and p_0. **(b)** If the solid surface is the $\psi = 0$ streamline, determine the equation of the streamline passing through the point $\theta = \pi/2$, $r = 2a$.

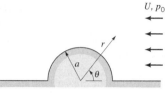

■ **FIGURE P6.34**

6.35   Water flows around a 6-ft-diameter bridge pier with a velocity of 12 ft/s. Estimate the force (per unit length) that the flowing water exerts on the front half of the pier. Assume that the flow can be approximated as ideal fluid around a circular cylinder.

*6.36   Consider the steady potential flow around the circular cylinder shown in Fig. 6.24. Show on a plot the variation of the magnitude of the dimensionless fluid velocity, V/U, along the positive y axis. At what distance, y/a (along the y axis), is the velocity within 1% of the free-stream velocity?

6.37   The velocity potential for a cylinder (Fig. P6.37) rotating in a uniform stream of fluid is

$$\phi = Ur\left(1 + \frac{a^2}{r^2}\right)\cos\theta + \frac{\Gamma}{2\pi}\theta$$

where Γ is the circulation. For what value of the circulation will the stagnation point be located at: **(a)** point A, **(b)** point B?

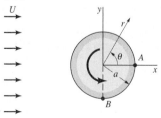

■ **FIGURE P6.37**

6.38   The two-dimensional velocity field for an incompressible, Newtonian fluid is described by the relationship

$$\mathbf{V} = (12xy^2 - 6x^3)\hat{\mathbf{i}} + (18x^2y - 4y^3)\hat{\mathbf{j}}$$

where the velocity has units of m/s when x and y are in meters. Determine the stresses σ_{xx}, σ_{yy}, and τ_{xy} at the point $x = 0.5$ m, $y = 1.0$ m if pressure at this point is 6 kPa and the fluid is glycerin at 20°C. Show these stresses on a sketch.

6.39 The stream function for a certain incompressible, two-dimensional flow field is

$$\psi = 3r^3 \sin 2\theta + 2\theta$$

where ψ is in ft^2/s when r is in feet and θ in radians. Determine the shearing stress, $\tau_{r\theta}$, at the point $r = 2$ ft, $\theta = \pi/3$ radians if the fluid is water.

6.40 Typical inviscid flow solutions for flow around bodies indicate that the fluid flows smoothly around the body, even for blunt bodies as shown in **Video V6.4**. However, experience reveals that due to the presence of viscosity, the main flow may actually separate from the body creating a wake behind the body. As discussed in a later section (Section 9.2.6), whether or not separation takes place depends on the pressure gradient along the surface of the body, as calculated by inviscid flow theory. If the pressure decreases in the direction of flow (a *favorable* pressure gradient), no separation will occur. However, if the pressure increases in the direction of flow (an *adverse* pressure gradient), separation may occur. For the circular cylinder of Fig. P6.40 placed in a uniform stream with velocity, U, determine an expression for the pressure gradient in the direction flow on the surface of the cylinder. For what range of values for the angle θ will an adverse pressure gradient occur?

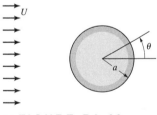

■ FIGURE P6.40

6.41 Two horizontal, infinite, parallel plates are spaced a distance b apart. A viscous liquid is contained between the plates. The bottom plate is fixed and the upper plate moves parallel to the bottom plate with a velocity U. Because of the no-slip boundary condition (see **Video V6.5**), the liquid motion is caused by the liquid being dragged along by the moving boundary. There is no pressure gradient in the direction of flow. Note that this is a so-called simple *Couette flow* discussed in Section 6.9.2. **(a)** Start with the Navier–Stokes equations and determine the velocity distribution between the plates. **(b)** Determine an expression for the flowrate passing between the plates (for a unit width). Express your answer in terms of b and U.

6.42 Two fixed, horizontal, parallel plates are spaced 0.2 in. apart. A viscous liquid ($\mu = 8 \times 10^{-3}$ lb·s/ft^2, $SG = 0.9$) flows between the plates with a mean velocity of 0.9 ft/s. Determine the pressure drop per unit length in the direction of flow. What is the maximum velocity in the channel?

6.43 A layer of viscous liquid of constant thickness (no velocity perpendicular to plate) flows steadily down an infinite, inclined plane. Determine, by means of the Navier–Stokes equations, the relationship between the thickness of the layer and the discharge per unit width. The flow is laminar, and assume air resistance is negligible so that the shearing stress at the free surface is zero.

6.44 For the problem described in Example 6.8 determine the equation for the velocity distribution in the fluid layer when the net upward flow is zero. Show this velocity distribution on a sketch.

6.45 An incompressible, viscous fluid is placed between horizontal, infinite, parallel plates as is shown in Fig. P6.45. The two plates move in opposite directions with constant velocities, U_1 and U_2, as shown. The pressure gradient in the x direction is zero and the only body force is due to the fluid weight. Use the Navier–Stokes equations to derive an expression for the velocity distribution between the plates. Assume laminar flow.

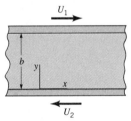

■ FIGURE P6.45

6.46 The viscous, incompressible flow between the parallel plates shown in Fig. P6.46 is caused by both the motion of the bottom plate and a pressure gradient, $\partial p / \partial x$. Determine the relationship between U and $\partial p / \partial x$ so that the shearing stress acting on the fixed plate is zero.

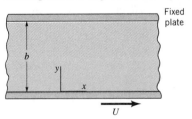

■ FIGURE P6.46

6.47 A viscous fluid (specific weight = 76 lb/ft³; viscosity = 0.02 lb·s/ft²) is contained between two infinite horizontal parallel plates as shown in Fig. P6.47. The fluid moves between the plates under the action of a pressure gradient, and the upper plate moves with a velocity U while the bottom plate is fixed. A U-tube manometer connected between two points along the bottom indicates a differential reading of 0.1 in. If the upper plate moves with a velocity of 0.02 ft/s, at what distance from the bottom plate does the maximum velocity in the gap between the two plates occur? Assume laminar flow.

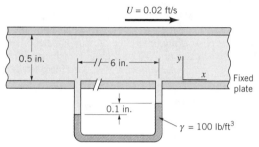

■ **FIGURE P6.47**

6.48 A vertical shaft passes through a bearing and is lubricated with an oil having a viscosity of 0.2 N·s/m² as shown in Fig. P6.48. Assume that the flow characteristics in the gap between the shaft and bearing are the same as those for laminar flow between infinite parallel plates with zero pressure gradient in the direction of flow. Estimate the torque required to overcome viscous resistance when the shaft is turning at 80 rev/min.

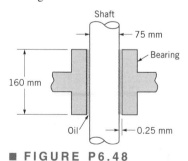

■ **FIGURE P6.48**

6.49 A viscous fluid is contained between two long concentric cylinders. The geometry of the system is such that the flow between the cylinders is approximately the same as the laminar flow between two infinite parallel plates. Determine an expression for the torque required to rotate the outer cylinder with an angular velocity ω. The inner cylinder is fixed. Express your answer in terms of the geometry of the system, the viscosity of the fluid, and the angular velocity.

*6.50 Oil (SAE 30) flows between parallel plates spaced 5 mm apart. The bottom plate is fixed but the upper plate moves with a velocity of 0.2 m/s in the positive x direction. The pressure gradient is 60 kPa/m, and is negative. Compute the velocity at various points across the channel and show the results on a plot. Assume laminar flow.

6.51 Consider a steady, laminar flow through a straight horizontal tube having the constant elliptical cross section given by the equation:

$$\frac{x^2}{a^2} + \frac{y^2}{b^2} = 1$$

The streamlines are all straight and parallel. Investigate the possibility of using an equation for the z component of velocity of the form

$$w = A\left(1 - \frac{x^2}{a^2} - \frac{y^2}{b^2}\right)$$

as an exact solution to this problem. With this velocity distribution, what is the relationship between the pressure gradient along the tube and the volume flowrate through the tube?

6.52 It is known that the velocity distribution for steady, laminar flow in circular tubes (either horizontal or vertical) is parabolic. (See **Video V6.6**.) Consider a 10-mm diameter horizontal tube through which ethyl alcohol is flowing with a steady mean velocity 0.15 m/s. **(a)** Would you expect the velocity distribution to be parabolic in this case? Explain. **(b)** What is the pressure drop per unit length along the tube?

6.53 A simple flow system to be used for steady flow tests consists of a constant head tank connected to a length of 4-mm-diameter tubing as shown in Fig. P6.53. The liquid has a viscosity of 0.015 N·s/m² and a density of 1200 kg/m³, and discharges into the atmosphere with a mean velocity of 1 m/s. **(a)** Verify that the flow will be laminar. **(b)** The flow is fully developed in the last 3 m of the tube. What is the pressure at the pressure gage? **(c)** What is the magnitude of the wall shearing stress, τ_{rz}, in the fully developed region?

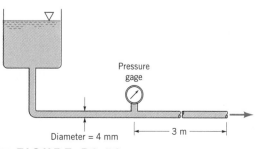

■ **FIGURE P6.53**

6.54 An infinitely long, solid, vertical cylinder of radius R is located in an infinite mass of an incompressible fluid. Start with the Navier–Stokes equation in the θ direction and derive an expression for the velocity distribution for the steady flow case in which the cylinder is rotating about a fixed axis with a constant angular velocity ω. You need not consider body forces. Assume that the flow is axisymmetric and the fluid is at rest at infinity.

6.55 A liquid (viscosity = 0.002 N·s/m²; density = 1000 kg/m³) is forced through the circular tube shown in Fig. P6.55. A differential manometer is connected to the tube as shown to measure the pressure drop along the tube. When the differential reading, Δh, is 9 mm, what is the mean velocity in the tube?

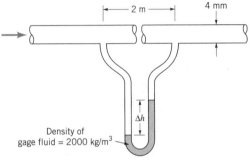

■ **FIGURE P6.55**

6.56 **(a)** Show that for Poiseuille flow in a tube of radius R the magnitude of the wall shearing stress, τ_{rz}, can be obtained from the relationship

$$|(\tau_{rz})_{\text{wall}}| = \frac{4\mu Q}{\pi R^3}$$

for a Newtonian fluid of viscosity μ. The volume rate of flow is Q. **(b)** Determine the magnitude of the wall shearing stress for a fluid having a viscosity of 0.003 N·s/m² flowing with an average velocity of 100 mm/s in a 2-mm-diameter tube.

*6.57 As is shown by Eq. 6.143 the pressure gradient for laminar flow through a tube of constant radius is given by the expression:

$$\frac{\partial p}{\partial z} = -\frac{8\mu Q}{\pi R^4}$$

For a tube whose radius is changing very gradually, such as the one illustrated in Fig. P6.57, it is expected that this equation can be used to approximate the pressure change along the tube if the actual radius, $R(z)$, is used at each cross section. The following measurements were obtained along a particular tube.

z/ℓ	0	0.1	0.2	0.3	0.4	0.5	0.6	0.7	0.8	0.9	1.0
$R(z)/R_o$	1.00	0.73	0.67	0.65	0.67	0.80	0.80	0.71	0.73	0.77	1.00

Compare the pressure drop over the length ℓ for this nonuniform tube with one having the constant radius R_o. *Hint:* To solve this problem you will need to numerically integrate the equation for the pressure gradient given above.

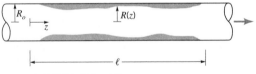

■ **FIGURE P6.57**

CHAPTER
7

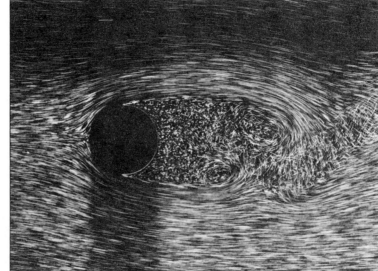

Similitude, Dimensional Analysis, and Modeling

Although many practical engineering problems involving fluid mechanics can be solved by using the equations and analytical procedures described in the preceding chapters, there remain a large number of problems that rely on experimentally obtained data for their solution. An obvious goal of any experiment is to make the results as widely applicable as possible. To achieve this end, the concept of *similitude* is often used so that measurements made on one system (for example, in the laboratory) can be used to describe the behavior of other similar systems (outside the laboratory). The laboratory systems are usually thought of as *models* and are used to study the phenomenon of interest under carefully controlled conditions. From these model studies, empirical formulations can be developed, or specific predictions of one or more characteristics of some other similar system can be made. To do this, it is necessary to establish the relationship between the laboratory model and the "other" system. In the following sections, we find out how this can be accomplished in a systematic manner.

7.1 Dimensional Analysis

To illustrate a typical fluid mechanics problem in which experimentation is required, consider the steady flow of an incompressible, Newtonian fluid through a long, smooth-walled,

Flow past a circular cylinder with Re = 2000: The streaklines of flow past any circular cylinder (regardless of size, velocity, or fluid) are as shown provided that the dimensionless parameter called the Reynolds number, Re, is equal to 2000. For other values of Re the flow pattern will be different. (air bubbles in water) (Photograph courtesy of ONERA, France.)

horizontal, circular pipe. An important characteristic of this system, which would be of interest to an engineer designing a pipeline, is the pressure drop per unit length that develops along the pipe as a result of friction. Although this would appear to be a relatively simple flow problem, it cannot generally be solved analytically (even with the aid of large computers) without the use of experimental data.

The first step in the planning of an experiment to study this problem would be to decide on the factors, or variables, that will have an effect on the pressure drop per unit length, Δp_ℓ. We expect the list to include the pipe diameter, D, the fluid density, ρ, and fluid viscosity, μ, and the mean velocity, V, at which the fluid is flowing through the pipe. Thus, we can express this relationship as

$$\Delta p_\ell = f(D, \rho, \mu, V) \tag{7.1}$$

which simply indicates mathematically that we expect the pressure drop per unit length to be some function of the factors contained within the parentheses. At this point the nature of the function is unknown and the objective of the experiments to be performed is to determine the nature of this function.

To perform the experiments in a meaningful and systematic manner, it would be necessary to change one of the variables, such as the velocity, while holding all others constant, and measure the corresponding pressure drop. This approach to determining the functional relationship between the pressure drop and the various factors that influence it, although logical in concept, is fraught with difficulties. Some of the experiments would be hard to carry out—for example, it would be necessary to vary fluid density while holding viscosity constant. How would you do this? Finally, once we obtained the various curves, how could we combine these data to obtain the desired general functional relationship between Δp_ℓ, D, ρ, μ, and V which would be valid for any similar pipe system?

Fortunately, there is a much simpler approach to this problem that will eliminate the difficulties described above. In the following sections we will show that rather than working with the original list of variables, as described in Eq. 7.1, we can collect these into two nondimensional combinations of variables (called *dimensionless products* or *dimensionless groups*) so that

$$\frac{D \, \Delta p_\ell}{\rho V^2} = \phi\left(\frac{\rho V D}{\mu}\right) \tag{7.2}$$

Thus, instead of having to work with five variables, we now have only two. The necessary experiment would simply consist of varying the dimensionless product $\rho V D / \mu$ and determining the corresponding value of $D \, \Delta p_\ell / \rho V^2$. The results of the experiment could then be represented by a single, universal curve.

The basis for this simplification lies in a consideration of the dimensions of the variables involved. As was discussed in Chapter 1, a qualitative description of physical quantities can be given in terms of basic dimensions such as mass, M, length, L, and time, T.[1] Alternatively, we could use force, F, L, and T as basic dimensions, since from Newton's second law

$$F \doteq MLT^{-2}$$

(Recall from Chapter 1 that the notation $\doteq$ is used to indicate dimensional equality.) The dimensions of the variables in the pipe flow example are $\Delta p_\ell \doteq FL^{-3}$, $D \doteq L$, $\rho \doteq FL^{-4}T^2$,

---

[1]As noted in Chapter 1, we will use T to represent the basic dimension of time, although T is also used for temperature in thermodynamic relationships (such as the ideal gas law).

$\mu \doteq FL^{-2}T$, and $V \doteq LT^{-1}$. A quick check of the dimensions of the two groups that appear in Eq. 7.2 shows that they are in fact *dimensionless* products; that is,

$$\frac{D\,\Delta p_\ell}{\rho V^2} \doteq \frac{L(F/L^3)}{(FL^{-4}T^2)(LT^{-1})^2} \doteq F^0 L^0 T^0$$

and

$$\frac{\rho VD}{\mu} \doteq \frac{(FL^{-4}T^2)(LT^{-1})(L)}{(FL^{-2}T)} \doteq F^0 L^0 T^0$$

Not only have we reduced the numbers of variables from five to two, but the new groups are dimensionless combinations of variables, which means that the results will be independent of the system of units we choose to use. This type of analysis is called *dimensional analysis,* and the basis for its application to a wide variety of problems is found in the *Buckingham pi theorem* described in the following section.

7.2 Buckingham Pi Theorem

A fundamental question we must answer is how many dimensionless products are required to replace the original list of variables? The answer to this question is supplied by the basic theorem of dimensional analysis that states the following:

> If an equation involving k variables is dimensionally homogeneous, it can be reduced to a relationship among $k - r$ independent dimensionless products, where r is the minimum number of reference dimensions required to describe the variables.

The dimensionless products are frequently referred to as "pi terms," and the theorem is called the Buckingham pi theorem. Buckingham used the symbol Π to represent a dimensionless product, and this notation is commonly used. Although the pi theorem is a simple one, its proof is not so simple and we will not include it here. Many entire books have been devoted to the subject of similitude and dimensional analysis, and a number of these are listed at the end of this chapter (Refs. 1–5). Students interested in pursuing the subject in more depth (including the proof of the pi theorem) can refer to one of these books.

The pi theorem is based on the idea of dimensional homogeneity which was introduced in Chapter 1. Essentially we assume that for any physically meaningful equation involving k variables, such as

$$u_1 = f(u_2, u_3, \ldots, u_k)$$

the dimensions of the variable on the left side of the equal sign must be equal to the dimensions of any term that stands by itself on the right side of the equal sign. It then follows that we can rearrange the equation into a set of dimensionless products (pi terms) so that

$$\Pi_1 = \phi(\Pi_2, \Pi_3, \ldots, \Pi_{k-r})$$

The required number of pi terms is fewer than the number of original variables by r, where r is determined by the minimum number of reference dimensions required to describe the original list of variables. Usually the reference dimensions required to describe the variables will be the basic dimensions M, L, and T or F, L, and T. However, in some instances perhaps only two dimensions, such as L and T, are required, or maybe just one, such as L. Also, in a few rare cases the variables may be described by some combination of basic dimensions, such as M/T^2, and L, and in this case r would be equal to two rather than three. Although the use of the pi theorem may appear to be a little mysterious and complicated, we can actually develop a simple, systematic procedure for developing the pi terms for a given problem.

7.3   Determination of Pi Terms

Several methods can be used to form the dimensionless products, or pi terms, that arise in a dimensional analysis. Essentially we are looking for a method that will allow us to systematically form the pi terms so that we are sure that they are dimensionless and independent, and that we have the right number. The method we will describe in detail in this section is called the *method of repeating variables*.

It will be helpful to break the repeating variable method down into a series of distinct steps that can be followed for any given problem. With a little practice you will be able to readily complete a dimensional analysis for your problem.

Step 1.   **List all the variables that are involved in the problem.** This step is the most difficult one and it is, of course, vitally important that all pertinent variables be included. Otherwise the dimensional analysis will not be correct! We are using the term "variable" to include any quantity, including dimensional and nondimensional constants, which play a role in the phenomenon under investigation. All such quantities should be included in the list of "variables" to be considered for the dimensional analysis. The determination of the variables must be accomplished by the experimenter's knowledge of the problem and the physical laws that govern the phenomenon. Typically the variables will include those that are necessary to describe the *geometry* of the system (such as a pipe diameter), to define any *fluid properties* (such as a fluid viscosity), and to indicate *external effects* that influence the system (such as a driving pressure). These general classes of variables are intended as broad categories that should be helpful in identifying variables. It is likely, however, that there will be variables that do not fit easily into one of these categories, and each problem needs to be carefully analyzed.

Since we wish to keep the number of variables to a minimum, so that we can minimize the amount of laboratory work, it is important that all variables be independent. For example, if in a certain problem the cross-sectional area of a pipe is an important variable, either the area or the pipe diameter could be used, but not both, since they are obviously not independent. Similarly, if both fluid density, ρ, and specific weight, γ, are important variables, we could list ρ and γ, or ρ and g (acceleration of gravity), or γ and g. However, it would be incorrect to use all three since $\gamma = \rho g$; that is, ρ, γ, and g are not independent. Note that although g would normally be constant in a given experiment, that fact is irrelevant as far as a dimensional analysis is concerned.

Step 2.   **Express each of the variables in terms of basic dimensions.** For the typical fluid mechanics problem the basic dimensions will be either M, L, and T or F, L, and T. Dimensionally these two sets are related through Newton's second law ($\mathbf{F} = m\mathbf{a}$) so that $F \doteq MLT^{-2}$. For example, $\rho \doteq ML^{-3}$ or $\rho \doteq FL^{-4}T^2$. Thus, either set can be used. The basic dimensions for typical variables found in fluid mechanics problems are listed in Table 1.1 in Chapter 1.

Step 3. **Determine the required number of pi terms.** This can be accomplished by means of the Buckingham pi theorem, which indicates that the number of pi terms is equal to $k - r$, where k is the number of variables in the problem (which is determined from Step 1) and r is the number of reference dimensions required to describe these variables (which is determined from Step 2). The reference dimensions usually correspond to the basic dimensions, and can be determined by an inspection of the dimensions of the variables obtained in Step 2. As previously noted, there may be occasions (usually rare) in which the basic dimensions appear in combinations so that the number of reference dimensions is less than the number of basic dimensions.

Step 4. **Select a number of repeating variables, where the number required is equal to the number of reference dimensions.** Essentially what we are doing here is selecting from the original list of variables several of which can be combined with each of the remaining variables to form a pi term. All of the required reference dimensions must be included within the group of repeating variables, and each repeating variable must be dimensionally independent of the others (i.e., the dimensions of one repeating variable cannot be reproduced by some combination of products of powers of the remaining repeating variables). This means that the repeating variables cannot themselves be combined to form a dimensionless product.

For any given problem we usually are interested in determining how one particular variable is influenced by the other variables. We would consider this variable to be the dependent variable, and we would want this to appear in only one pi term. Thus, do *not* choose the dependent variable as one of the repeating variables, since the repeating variables will generally appear in more than one pi term.

Step 5. **Form a pi term by multiplying one of the nonrepeating variables by the product of the repeating variables, each raised to an exponent that will make the combination dimensionless.** Essentially each pi term will be of the form $u_i u_1^{a_i} u_2^{b_i} u_3^{c_i}$ where u_i is one of the nonrepeating variables; u_1, u_2, and u_3 are the repeating variables; and the exponents a_i, b_i, and c_i are determined so that the combination is dimensionless.

Step 6. **Repeat Step 5 for each of the remaining nonrepeating variables.** The resulting set of pi terms will correspond to the required number obtained from Step 3. If not, check your work—you have made a mistake!

Step 7. **Check all the resulting pi terms to make sure they are dimensionless.** It is easy to make a mistake in forming the pi terms. However, this can be checked by simply substituting the dimensions of the variables into the pi terms to confirm that they are dimensionless. One good way to do this is to express the variables in terms of M, L, and T if the basic dimensions F, L, and T were initially, or vice versa, and then check to make sure the pi terms are dimensionless.

Step 8. **Express the final form as a relationship among the pi terms, and think about what it means.** Typically the final form can be written as

$$\Pi_1 = \phi(\Pi_2, \Pi_3, \dots, \Pi_{k-r})$$

where Π_1 would contain the dependent variable in the numerator. It should be emphasized that if you started out with the correct list of variables (and the other steps were completed correctly), then the relationship in terms of the pi terms can be used to describe the problem. You need only work with the pi terms—not with the individual variables. However, it should be clearly noted that this is as far as we can go with the dimensional analysis; that is, the actual functional relationship among the pi terms must be determined by experiment.

To illustrate these various steps we will again consider the problem discussed earlier in this chapter which was concerned with the steady flow of an incompressible, Newtonian fluid through a long, smooth-walled horizontal, circular pipe. We are interested in the pressure drop per unit length, Δp_ℓ, along the pipe. According to Step 1 we must list all of the pertinent variables that are involved based on the experimenter's knowledge of the problem. In this problem we assume that

$$\Delta p_\ell = f(D, \rho, \mu, V)$$

where D is the pipe diameter, ρ and μ are the fluid density and viscosity, respectively, and V is the mean velocity.

Next (Step 2) we express all the variables in terms of basic dimensions. Using F, L, and T as basic dimensions it follows that

$$\Delta p_\ell \doteq (FL^{-2})/L = FL^{-3}$$

$$D \doteq L$$

$$\rho \doteq FL^{-4}T^2$$

$$\mu \doteq FL^{-2}T$$

$$V \doteq LT^{-1}$$

We could also use M, L, and T as basic dimensions if desired—the final result will be the same! Note that for density, which is a mass per unit volume (ML^{-3}), we have used the relationship $F \doteq MLT^{-2}$ to express the density in terms of F, L, and T. Do not mix the basic dimensions; that is, use either F, L, and T or M, L, and T.

We can now apply the pi theorem to determine the required number of pi terms (Step 3). An inspection of the dimensions of the variables from Step 2 reveals that all three basic dimensions are required to describe the variables. Since there are five ($k = 5$) variables (do not forget to count the dependent variable, Δp_ℓ) and three required reference dimensions ($r = 3$), then according to the pi theorem there will be ($5 - 3$), or two pi terms required.

The repeating variables to be used to form the pi terms (Step 4) need to be selected from the list D, ρ, μ, and V. Remember, we do not want to use the dependent variable as one of the repeating variables. Since three reference dimensions are required, we will need to select three repeating variables. Generally, we would try to select for repeating variables those that are the simplest, dimensionally. For example, if one of the variables has the dimension of a length, choose it as one of the repeating variables. In this example we will use D, V, and ρ as repeating variables. Note that these are dimensionally independent, since D is a length, V involves both length and time, and ρ involves force, length, and time. This means that we cannot form a dimensionless product from this set.

We are now ready to form the two pi terms (Step 5). Typically, we would start with the dependent variable and combine it with the repeating variables to form the first pi term; that is,

$$\Pi_1 = \Delta p_\ell D^a V^b \rho^c$$

Since this combination is to be dimensionless, it follows that

$$(FL^{-3})(L)^a(LT^{-1})^b(FL^{-4}T^2)^c \doteq F^0 L^0 T^0$$

The exponents a, b, and c must be determined such that the resulting exponent for each of the basic dimensions—F, L, and T—must be zero (so that the resulting combination is di-mensionless). Thus, we can write

$$1 + c = 0 \quad \text{(for } F)$$
$$-3 + a + b - 4c = 0 \quad \text{(for } L)$$
$$-b + 2c = 0 \quad \text{(for } T)$$

The solution of this system of algebraic equations gives the desired values for a, b, and c. It follows that $a = 1$, $b = -2$, $c = -1$, and, therefore,

$$\Pi_1 = \frac{\Delta p_\ell D}{\rho V^2}$$

The process is now repeated for the remaining nonrepeating variables (Step 6). In this example there is only one additional variable (μ) so that

$$\Pi_2 = \mu D^a V^b \rho^c$$

or

$$(FL^{-2}T)(L)^a(LT^{-1})^b(FL^{-4}T^2)^c \doteq F^0 L^0 T^0$$

and, therefore,

$$1 + c = 0 \quad \text{(for } F)$$
$$-2 + a + b - 4c = 0 \quad \text{(for } L)$$
$$1 - b + 2c = 0 \quad \text{(for } T)$$

Solving these equations simultaneously it follows that $a = -1$, $b = -1$, $c = -1$ so that

$$\Pi_2 = \frac{\mu}{DV\rho}$$

Note that we end up with the correct number of pi terms as determined from Step 3.

At this point stop and check to make sure the pi terms are actually dimensionless (Step 7). Finally (Step 8), we can express the result of the dimensional analysis as

$$\frac{\Delta p_\ell D}{\rho V^2} = \tilde{\phi}\left(\frac{\mu}{DV\rho}\right)$$

This result indicates that this problem can be studied in terms of these two pi terms, rather than the original five variables we started with. However, dimensional analysis will *not* provide the form of the function $\tilde{\phi}$. This can only be obtained from a suitable set of experiments. If desired, the pi terms can be rearranged; that is, the reciprocal of $\mu/DV\rho$ could be used, and of course the order in which we write the variables can be changed. Thus, for example, Π_2 could be expressed as

$$\Pi_2 = \frac{\rho V D}{\mu}$$

and the relationship between Π_1 and Π_2 as

$$\frac{D \, \Delta p_\ell}{\rho V^2} = \phi\left(\frac{\rho V D}{\mu}\right)$$

This is the form we previously used in our initial discussion of this problem (Eq. 7.2). The dimensionless product, $\rho V D/\mu$, is a very famous one in fluid mechanics—the Reynolds number. This number has been briefly alluded to in Chapters 1 and 6 and will be further discussed in Section 7.6.

EXAMPLE 7.1

A thin rectangular plate having a width w and a height h is located so that it is normal to a moving stream of fluid. Assume the drag, $\mathcal{D}$, that the fluid exerts on the plate is a function of w and h, the fluid viscosity and density, μ and ρ, respectively, and the velocity V of the fluid approaching the plate. Determine a suitable set of pi terms to study this problem experimentally.

SOLUTION

From the statement of the problem we can write

$$\mathcal{D} = f(w, h, \mu, \rho, V)$$

where this equation expresses the general functional relationship between the drag and the several variables that will affect it. The dimensions of the variables (using the *MLT* system) are

$$\mathcal{D} \doteq MLT^{-2}$$
$$w \doteq L$$
$$h \doteq L$$
$$\mu \doteq ML^{-1}T^{-1}$$
$$\rho \doteq ML^{-3}$$
$$V \doteq LT^{-1}$$

We see that all three basic dimensions are required to define the six variables so that the Buckingham pi theorem tells us that three pi terms will be needed (six variables minus three reference dimensions, $k - r = 6 - 3$).

We will next select three repeating variables such as w, V, and ρ. A quick inspection of these three reveals that they are dimensionally independent, since each one contains a basic dimension not included in the others. Note that it would be incorrect to use both w and h as repeating variables since they have the same dimensions.

Starting with the dependent variable, $\mathcal{D}$, the first pi term can be formed by combining $\mathcal{D}$ with the repeating variables such that

$$\Pi_1 = \mathcal{D}w^a V^b \rho^c$$

and in terms of dimensions

$$(MLT^{-2})(L)^a(LT^{-1})^b(ML^{-3})^c \doteq M^0 L^0 T^0$$

Thus, for Π_1 to be dimensionless it follows that

$$1 + c = 0 \qquad \text{(for } M\text{)}$$
$$1 + a + b - 3c = 0 \qquad \text{(for } L\text{)}$$
$$-2 - b = 0 \qquad \text{(for } T\text{)}$$

and, therefore, $a = -2$, $b = -2$, and $c = -1$. The pi term then becomes

$$\Pi_1 = \frac{\mathcal{D}}{w^2 V^2 \rho}$$

Next the procedure is repeated with the second nonrepeating variable, h, so that

$$\Pi_2 = hw^a V^b \rho^c$$

It follows that

$$(L)(L)^a(LT^{-1})^b(ML^{-3})^c \doteq M^0 L^0 T^0$$

and

$$c = 0 \qquad \text{(for } M\text{)}$$
$$1 + a + b - 3c = 0 \qquad \text{(for } L\text{)}$$
$$b = 0 \qquad \text{(for } T\text{)}$$

so that $a = -1$, $b = 0$, $c = 0$, and therefore

$$\Pi_2 = \frac{h}{w}$$

The remaining nonrepeating variable is μ so that

$$\Pi_3 = \mu w^a V^b \rho^c$$

with

$$(ML^{-1}T^{-1})(L)^a(LT^{-1})^b(ML^{-3})^c \doteq M^0 L^0 T^0$$

and, therefore,

$$1 + c = 0 \qquad \text{(for } M\text{)}$$
$$-1 + a + b - 3c = 0 \qquad \text{(for } L\text{)}$$
$$-1 - b = 0 \qquad \text{(for } T\text{)}$$

Solving for the exponents we obtain $a = -1$, $b = -1$, $c = -1$ so that

$$\Pi_3 = \frac{\mu}{wV\rho}$$

Now that we have the three required pi terms we should check to make sure they are dimensionless. To make this check we use F, L, and T, which will also verify the correctness of the original dimensions used for the variables. Thus,

$$\Pi_1 = \frac{\mathcal{D}}{w^2 V^2 \rho} \doteq \frac{(F)}{(L)^2 (LT^{-1})^2 (FL^{-4}T^2)} \doteq F^0 L^0 T^0$$

$$\Pi_2 = \frac{h}{w} \doteq \frac{(L)}{(L)} \doteq F^0 L^0 T^0$$

$$\Pi_3 = \frac{\mu}{wV\rho} \doteq \frac{(FL^{-2}T)}{(L)(LT^{-1})(FL^{-4}T^2)} \doteq F^0 L^0 T^0$$

If these do not check, go back to the original list of variables and make sure you have the correct dimensions for each of the variables and then check the algebra you used to obtain the exponents a, b, and c.

Finally, we can express the results of the dimensional analysis in the form

$$\frac{\mathcal{D}}{w^2 V^2 \rho} = \tilde{\phi} \left(\frac{h}{w}, \frac{\mu}{wV\rho} \right) \qquad \text{(Ans)}$$

Since at this stage in the analysis the nature of the function $\tilde{\phi}$ is unknown, we could rearrange the pi terms if we so desire. For example, we could express the final result in the form

$$\frac{\mathcal{D}}{w^2 \rho V^2} = \phi \left(\frac{w}{h}, \frac{\rho V w}{\mu} \right) \qquad \text{(Ans)}$$

which would be more conventional, since the ratio of the plate width to height, w/h, is called the *aspect ratio*, and $\rho V w / \mu$ is the Reynolds number. To proceed, it would be necessary to perform a set of experiments to determine the nature of the function ϕ, as discussed in Section 7.7.

7.4   Some Additional Comments About Dimensional Analysis

The preceding section provides a systematic procedure for performing a dimensional analysis. Other methods could be used, although we think the method of repeating variables is the easiest for the beginning student to use. Pi terms can also be formed by inspection, as is discussed in Section 7.5. Regardless of the specific method used for the dimensional analysis, there are certain aspects of this important engineering tool that must seem a little baffling and mysterious to the student (and sometimes to the experienced investigator as well). In this section we will attempt to elaborate on some of the more subtle points that, based on our experience, can prove to be puzzling to students.

7.4.1   Selection of Variables

One of the most important, and difficult, steps in applying dimensional analysis to any given problem is the selection of the variables that are involved. As noted previously, for convenience we will use the term variable to indicate any quantity involved, including dimensional and nondimensional constants. There is no simple procedure whereby the variables can be easily identified. Generally, one must rely on a good understanding of the phenomenon involved and the governing physical laws.

For most engineering problems (including areas outside of fluid mechanics), pertinent variables can be classified into three general groups—geometry, material properties, and external effects.

Geometry. The geometric characteristics can usually be prescribed by a series of lengths and angles. In most problems the geometry of the system plays an important role, and a sufficient number of geometric variables must be included to describe the system. These variables can usually be readily identified.

Material Properties. Since the response of a system to applied external effects such as forces, pressures, and changes in temperature is dependent on the nature of the materials involved in the system, the material properties that relate the external effects and the responses must be included as variables. For example, for Newtonian fluids the viscosity of the fluid is the property that relates the applied forces to the rates of deformation of the fluid.

External Effects. This terminology is used to denote any variable that produces, or tends to produce, a change in the system. For example, in structural mechanics, forces (either concentrated or distributed) applied to a system tend to change its geometry, and such forces would need to be considered as pertinent variables. For fluid mechanics, variables in this class would be related to pressures, velocities, or gravity.

7.4.2 Determination of Reference Dimensions

For any given problem it is obviously desirable to reduce the number of pi terms to a minimum and, therefore, we wish to reduce the number of variables to a minimum; that is, we certainly do not want to include extraneous variables. It is also important to know how many reference dimensions are required to describe the variables. As we have seen in the preceding examples, F, L, and T appear to be a convenient set of basic dimensions for characterizing fluid-mechanical quantities. There is, however, really nothing "fundamental" about this set, and as previously noted M, L, and T would also be suitable. Of course, in some problems only one or two of these is required.

7.4.3 Uniqueness of Pi Terms

A little reflection on the process used to determine pi terms by the method of repeating variables reveals that the specific pi terms obtained depend on the somewhat arbitrary selection of repeating variables. For example, in the problem of studying the pressure drop in a pipe, we selected D, V, and ρ as repeating variables. This led to the formulation of the problem in terms of pi terms as

$$\frac{\Delta p_\ell D}{\rho V^2} = \phi\left(\frac{\rho V D}{\mu}\right) \tag{7.3}$$

What if we had selected D, V, and μ as repeating variables? A quick check will reveal that the pi term involving Δp_ℓ becomes

$$\frac{\Delta p_\ell D^2}{V \mu}$$

and the second pi term remains the same. Thus, we can express the final result as

$$\frac{\Delta p_\ell D^2}{V\mu} = \phi_1\left(\frac{\rho VD}{\mu}\right) \tag{7.4}$$

Both results are correct, and both would lead to the same final equation for Δp_ℓ. Note, however, that the functions ϕ and ϕ_1 in Eqs. 7.3 and 7.4 will be different because the dependent pi terms are different for the two relationships.

We can conclude from this illustration that there is *not* a unique set of pi terms which arises from a dimensional analysis. However, the required *number* of pi terms is fixed.

7.5 Determination of Pi Terms by Inspection

One method for forming pi terms has been presented in Section 7.3. This method provides a step-by-step procedure that if executed properly will provide a correct and complete set of pi terms. Although this method is simple and straightforward, it is rather tedious, particularly for problems in which large numbers of variables are involved. Since the only restrictions placed on the pi terms are that they be (1) correct in number, (2) dimensionless, and (3) independent, it is possible to simply form the pi terms by inspection, without resorting to the more formal procedure.

To illustrate this approach, we again consider the pressure drop per unit length along a smooth pipe. Regardless of the technique to be used, the starting point remains the same—determine the variables, which in this case are

$$\Delta p_\ell = f(D, \rho, \mu, V)$$

Next, the dimensions of the variables are listed:

$$\Delta p_\ell \doteq FL^{-3}$$

$$D \doteq L$$

$$\rho \doteq FL^{-4}T^2$$

$$\mu \doteq FL^{-2}T$$

$$V \doteq LT^{-1}$$

and subsequently the number of reference dimensions determined. The application of the pi theorem then tells us how many pi terms are required. In this problem, since there are five variables and three reference dimensions, two pi terms are needed. Thus, the required number of pi terms can be easily determined, and the determination of this number should always be done at the beginning of the analysis.

Once the number of pi terms is known, we can form each pi term by inspection, simply making use of the fact that each pi term must be dimensionless. We will always let Π_1 contain the dependent variable, which in this example is Δp_ℓ. Since this variable has the dimensions FL^{-3}, we need to combine it with other variables so that a nondimensional product will result. One possibility is

$$\Pi_1 = \frac{\Delta p_\ell D}{\rho V^2}$$

Next, we will form the second pi term by selecting the variable that was not used in Π_1, which in this case is μ. We simply combine μ with the other variables to make the combination dimensionless (but do not use Δp_ℓ in Π_2, since we want the dependent variable to appear only in Π_1). For example, divide μ by ρ (to eliminate F), then by V (to eliminate T), and finally by D (to eliminate L). Thus,

$$\Pi_2 = \frac{\mu}{\rho VD}$$

and, therefore,

$$\frac{\Delta p_\ell D}{\rho V^2} = \phi\left(\frac{\mu}{\rho VD}\right)$$

which is, of course, the same result we obtained by using the method of repeating variables.

Although forming pi terms by inspection is essentially equivalent to the repeating variable method, it is less structured. With a little practice the pi terms can be readily formed by inspection, and this method offers an alternative to the more formal procedure.

7.6 Common Dimensionless Groups in Fluid Mechanics

At the top of Table 7.1 is a list of variables that commonly arise in fluid mechanics problems. The list is obviously not exhaustive, but does indicate a broad range of variables likely to be found in a typical problem. Fortunately, not all of these variables would be encountered in each problem. However, when combinations of these variables are present, it is standard practice to combine them into some of the common dimensionless groups (pi terms) given in Table 7.1. These combinations appear so frequently that special names are associated with them as indicated in the table.

It is also often possible to provide a physical interpretation to the dimensionless groups which can be helpful in assessing their influence in a particular application. For example, the Froude number is an index of the ratio of the force due to the acceleration of a fluid particle (inertial force) to the force due to gravity (weight). A similar interpretation in terms of indices of force ratios can be given to the other dimensionless groups, as indicated in Table 7.1. The Reynolds number is undoubtedly the most famous dimensionless parameter in fluid mechanics. It is named in honor of Osborne Reynolds, a British engineer, who first demonstrated that this combination of variables could be used as a criterion to distinguish between laminar and turbulent flow. In most fluid flow problems there will be a characteristic length, ℓ, and a velocity, V, as well as the fluid properties of density, ρ, and viscosity, μ, which are relevant variables in the problem. Thus, with these variables the Reynolds number

V7.1 Reynolds number

$$\text{Re} = \frac{\rho V\ell}{\mu}$$

arises naturally from the dimensional analysis. The Reynolds number is a measure of the ratio of the inertia force on an element of fluid to the viscous force on an element. When these two types of forces are important in a given problem, the Reynolds number will play an important role.

■ **TABLE 7.1**

Some Common Variables and Dimensionless Groups in Fluid Mechanics

Variables: Acceleration of gravity, g; Bulk modulus, E_v; Characteristic length, ℓ; Density, ρ; Frequency of oscillating flow, ω; Pressure, p (or Δp); Speed of sound, c; Surface tension, σ; Velocity, V; Viscosity, μ

Dimensionless Groups	Name	Interpretation (Index of Force Ratio Indicated)	Types of Applications
$\dfrac{\rho V \ell}{\mu}$	Reynolds number, Re	$\dfrac{\text{inertia force}}{\text{viscous force}}$	Generally of importance in all types of fluid dynamics problems
$\dfrac{V}{\sqrt{g\ell}}$	Froude number, Fr	$\dfrac{\text{inertia force}}{\text{gravitational force}}$	Flow with a free surface
$\dfrac{p}{\rho V^2}$	Euler number, Eu	$\dfrac{\text{pressure force}}{\text{inertia force}}$	Problems in which pressure, or pressure differences, are of interest
$\dfrac{\rho V^2}{E_v}$	Cauchy number,[a] Ca	$\dfrac{\text{inertia force}}{\text{compressibility force}}$	Flows in which the compressibility of the fluid is important
$\dfrac{V}{c}$	Mach number,[a] Ma	$\dfrac{\text{inertia force}}{\text{compressibility force}}$	Flows in which the compressibility of the fluid is important
$\dfrac{\omega \ell}{V}$	Strouhal number, St	$\dfrac{\text{inertia (local) force}}{\text{inertia (convective) force}}$	Unsteady flow with a characteristic frequency of oscillation
$\dfrac{\rho V^2 \ell}{\sigma}$	Weber number, We	$\dfrac{\text{inertia force}}{\text{surface tension force}}$	Problems in which surface tension is important

[a]The Cauchy number and the Mach number are related and either can be used as an index of the relative effects of inertia and compressibility.

7.7 Correlation of Experimental Data

One of the most important uses of dimensional analysis is as an aid in the efficient handling, interpretation, and correlation of experimental data. Since the field of fluid mechanics relies heavily on empirical data, it is not surprising that dimensional analysis is such an important tool in this field. As noted previously, a dimensional analysis cannot provide a complete answer to any given problem, since the analysis only provides the dimensionless groups describing the phenomenon, and not the specific relationship among the groups. To determine this relationship, suitable experimental data must be obtained. The degree of difficulty involved in this process depends on the number of pi terms, and the nature of the experiments (How hard is it to obtain the measurements?). The simplest problems are obviously those involving the fewest pi terms, and the following sections indicate how the complexity of the analysis increases with the increasing number of pi terms.

7.7.1   Problems with One Pi Term

Application of the pi theorem indicates that if the number of variables minus the number of reference dimensions is equal to unity, then only *one* pi term is required to describe the phenomenon. The functional relationship that must exist for one pi term is

$$\Pi_1 = C$$

where C is a constant. This is one situation in which a dimensional analysis reveals the specific form of the relationship and, as is illustrated by the following example, shows how the individual variables are related. The value of the constant, however, must still be determined by experiment.

EXAMPLE 7.2

Assume that the drag, $\mathcal{D}$, acting on a spherical particle that falls very slowly through a viscous fluid is a function of the particle diameter, d, the particle velocity, V, and the fluid viscosity, μ. Determine, with the aid of dimensional analysis, how the drag depends on the particle velocity.

SOLUTION

From the information given, it follows that

$$\mathcal{D} = f(d, V, \mu)$$

and the dimensions of the variables are

$$\mathcal{D} \doteq F$$
$$d \doteq L$$
$$V \doteq LT^{-1}$$
$$\mu \doteq FL^{-2}T$$

We see that there are four variables and three reference dimensions (F, L, and T) required to describe the variables. Thus, according to the pi theorem, one pi term is required. This pi term can be easily formed by inspection and can be expressed as

$$\Pi_1 = \frac{\mathcal{D}}{\mu V d}$$

Since there is only one pi term, it follows that

$$\frac{\mathcal{D}}{\mu V d} = C$$

or

$$\mathcal{D} = C\mu V d$$

Thus, for a given particle and fluid, the drag varies directly with the velocity so that

$$\mathcal{D} \propto V \qquad \text{(Ans)}$$

Actually, the dimensional analysis reveals that the drag not only varies directly with the velocity, but it also varies directly with the particle diameter and the fluid viscosity. We could not, however, predict the value of the drag, since the constant, C, is unknown. An experiment would have to be performed in which the drag and the corresponding velocity are measured for a given particle and fluid. Although in principle we would only have to run a single test, we would certainly want to repeat it several times to obtain a reliable value for C. It should be emphasized that once the value of C is determined it is not necessary to run similar tests by using different spherical particles and fluids; that is, C is a universal constant so long as the drag is a function only of particle diameter, velocity, and fluid viscosity.

An approximate solution to this problem can also be obtained theoretically, from which it is found that $C = 3\pi$ so that

$$\mathscr{D} = 3\pi\mu Vd$$

This equation is commonly called *Stokes law* and is used in the study of the settling of particles. Our experiments would reveal that this result is only valid for small Reynolds numbers ($\rho Vd/\mu \ll 1$). This follows, since in the original list of variables, we have neglected inertial effects (fluid density is not included as a variable). The inclusion of an additional variable would lead to another pi term so that there would be two pi terms rather than one.

7.7.2   Problems with Two or More Pi Terms

If a given phenomenon can be described with two pi terms such that

$$\Pi_1 = \phi(\Pi_2)$$

the functional relationship among the variables can then be determined by varying Π_2 and measuring the corresponding values of Π_1. For this case the results can be conveniently presented in graphical form by plotting Π_1 versus Π_2. It should be emphasized that the resulting curve would be a "universal" one for the particular phenomenon studied. This means that if the variables and the resulting dimensional analysis are correct, then there is only a single relationship between Π_1 and Π_2.

In addition to presenting the data graphically, it may be possible (and desirable) to obtain an empirical equation relating Π_1 and Π_2 by using a standard curve fitting technique.

EXAMPLE 7.3

The relationship between the pressure drop per unit length along a smooth walled, horizontal pipe and the variables that affect the pressure drop is to be determined experimentally. In the laboratory the pressure drop was measured over a 5-ft length of smooth walled pipe having an inside diameter of 0.496 in. The fluid used was water at 60°F ($\mu = 2.34 \times 10^{-5}$ lb·s/ft², $\rho = 1.94$ slugs/ft³). Tests were run in which the velocity was varied and the corresponding pressure drop measured. The results of these tests are shown below:

Velocity (ft/s)	1.17	1.95	2.91	5.84	11.13	16.92	23.34	28.73
Pressure drop (lb/ft²) (for 5-ft length)	6.26	15.6	30.9	106	329	681	1200	1730

Make use of these data to obtain a general relationship between the pressure drop per unit length and the other variables.

SOLUTION

The first step is to perform a dimensional analysis during the planning stage *before* the experiments are actually run. As was discussed in Section 7.3, we will assume that the pressure drop per unit length, Δp_ℓ, is a function of the pipe diameter, D, fluid density, ρ, fluid viscosity, μ, and the velocity, V. Thus,

$$\Delta p_\ell = f(D, \rho, \mu, V)$$

and application of the pi theorem yields

$$\frac{D\,\Delta p_\ell}{\rho V^2} = \phi\left(\frac{\rho VD}{\mu}\right)$$

To determine the form of the relationship, we need to vary the Reynolds number, $\rho VD/\mu$, and to measure the corresponding values of $D\,\Delta p_\ell/\rho V^2$. The Reynolds number could be varied by changing any one of the variables, ρ, V, D, or μ, or any combination of them. However, the simplest way to do this is to vary the velocity, since this will allow us to use the same fluid and pipe. Based on the data given, values for the two pi terms can be computed with the result:

$D\,\Delta p_\ell/\rho V^2$	0.0195	0.0175	0.0155	0.0132
$\rho VD/\mu$	4.01×10^3	6.68×10^3	9.97×10^3	2.00×10^4
	0.0113	0.0101	0.00939	0.00893
	3.81×10^4	5.80×10^4	8.00×10^4	9.85×10^4

These are dimensionless groups so that their values are independent of the system of units used so long as a consistent system is used. For example, if the velocity is in ft/s, then the diameter should be in feet, not inches or meters.

A plot of these two pi terms can now be made with the results shown in Fig. E7.3a. The correlation appears to be quite good, and if it was not, this would suggest that either we had large experimental measurement errors, or that we had perhaps omitted an important variable. The curve shown in Fig. E7.3a represents the general relationship between the pressure drop and the other factors in the range of Reynolds numbers between 4.01×10^3 and 9.85×10^4. Thus, for this range of Reynolds numbers it is *not* necessary to repeat the tests for other pipe sizes or other fluids provided the assumed independent variables (D, ρ, μ, V) are the only important ones.

Since the relationship between Π_1 and Π_2 is nonlinear, it is not immediately obvious what form of empirical equation might be used to describe the relationship. If, however, the same data are plotted on logarithmic graph paper, as shown in Fig. E7.3b, the data form a straight line, suggesting that a suitable equation is of the form $\Pi_1 = A\Pi_2^n$ where A and n are empirical constants to be determined from the data by using a suitable curve fitting technique, such as a nonlinear regression program. For the data given in this example, a good fit of the data is obtained with the equation

$$\Pi_1 = 0.150\,\Pi_2^{-0.25} \qquad \text{(Ans)}$$

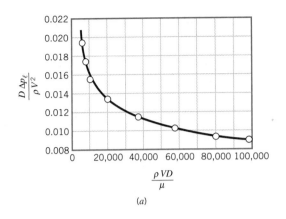

(a)

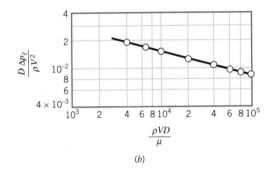

(b)

■ FIGURE E7.3

In 1911, H. Blasius, a German fluid mechanician, established a similar empirical equation that is used widely for predicting the pressure drop in smooth pipes in the range $4 \times 10^3 < \text{Re} < 10^5$. This equation can be expressed in the form

$$\frac{D\,\Delta p_\ell}{\rho V^2} = 0.1582 \left(\frac{\rho VD}{\mu} \right)^{-1/4}$$

The so-called Blasius formula is based on numerous experimental results of the type used in this example. Flow in pipes is discussed in more detail in the next chapter, where it is shown how pipe roughness (which introduces another variable) may affect the results given in this example (which is for smooth walled pipes).

As the number of required pi terms increases, it becomes more difficult to display the results in a convenient graphical form and to determine a specific empirical equation that describes the phenomenon. For problems involving three pi terms

$$\Pi_1 = \phi(\Pi_2, \Pi_3)$$

it is still possible to show data correlations on simple graphs by plotting families of curves. This is an informative and useful way of representing the data in a general way. It may also be possible to determine a suitable empirical equation relating the three pi terms. However, as the number of pi terms continues to increase, corresponding to an increase in the general complexity of the problem of interest, both the graphical presentation and the determination of a suitable empirical equation become intractable. For these more complicated problems, it is often more feasible to use models to predict specific characteristics of the system rather than to try to develop general correlations.

7.8 Modeling and Similitude

Models are widely used in fluid mechanics. Major engineering projects involving structures, aircraft, ships, rivers, harbors, dams, air and water pollution, and so on, frequently involve the use of models. Although the term "model" is used in many different contexts, the "engineering model" generally conforms to the following definition. *A model is a representation of a physical system that may be used to predict the behavior of the system in some desired respect.* The physical system for which the predictions are to be made is called the *prototype.* Although *mathematical* or *computer* models may also conform to this definition, our interest will be in physical models, that is, models that resemble the prototype but are generally of a different size, may involve different fluids, and often operate under different conditions (pressures, velocities, etc.). Usually a model is smaller than the prototype. Therefore, it is more easily handled in the laboratory and less expensive to construct and operate than a large prototype. With the successful development of a valid model, it is possible to predict the behavior of the prototype under a certain set of conditions.

In the following sections we will develop the procedures for designing models so that the model and prototype will behave in a similar fashion.

7.8.1 Theory of Models

The theory of models can be readily developed by using the principles of dimensional analysis. It has been shown that any given problem can be described in terms of a set of pi terms as

$$\Pi_1 = \phi(\Pi_2, \Pi_3, \ldots, \Pi_n) \tag{7.5}$$

In formulating this relationship, only a knowledge of the general nature of the physical phenomenon, and the variables involved, is required. Specific values for variables (size of components, fluid properties, and so on) are not needed to perform the dimensional analysis. Thus, Eq. 7.5 applies to any system that is governed by the same variables. If Eq. 7.5 describes the behavior of a particular prototype, a similar relationship can be written for a model of this prototype; that is,

$$\Pi_{1m} = \phi(\Pi_{2m}, \Pi_{3m}, \ldots, \Pi_{nm}) \tag{7.6}$$

where the form of the function will be the same as long as the same phenomenon is involved in both the prototype and the model. Variables, or pi terms, without a subscript will refer to the prototype, whereas the subscript m will be used to designate the model variables or pi terms.

The pi terms can be developed so that Π_1 contains the variable that is to be predicted from observations made on the model. Therefore, if the model is designed and operated under the following conditions

$$\Pi_{2m} = \Pi_2$$

$$\Pi_{3m} = \Pi_3 \tag{7.7}$$

$$\vdots$$

$$\Pi_{nm} = \Pi_n$$

then with the presumption that the form of ϕ is the same for model and prototype, it follows that

$$\Pi_1 = \Pi_{1m} \tag{7.8}$$

Equation 7.8 is the desired *prediction equation* and indicates that the measured value of Π_{1m} obtained with the model will be equal to the corresponding Π_1 for the prototype as long as the other pi terms are equal. The conditions specified by Eqs. 7.7 provide the *model design conditions,* also called *similarity requirements* or *modeling laws.*

As an example of the procedure, consider the problem of determining the drag, $\mathcal{D}$, on a thin rectangular plate ($w \times h$ in size) placed normal to a fluid with velocity, V. The dimensional analysis of this problem was performed in Example 7.1, where it was assumed that

$$\mathcal{D} = f(w, h, \mu, \rho, V)$$

Application of the pi theorem yielded

$$\frac{\mathcal{D}}{w^2 \rho V^2} = \phi\left(\frac{w}{h}, \frac{\rho V w}{\mu}\right) \tag{7.9}$$

We are now concerned with designing a model that could be used to predict the drag on a certain prototype (which presumably has a different size than the model). Since the relationship expressed by Eq. 7.9 applies to both prototype and model, Eq. 7.9 is assumed to govern the prototype, with a similar relationship

$$\frac{\mathcal{D}_m}{w_m^2 \rho_m V_m^2} = \phi\left(\frac{w_m}{h_m}, \frac{\rho_m V_m w_m}{\mu_m}\right) \tag{7.10}$$

for the model. The model design conditions, or similarity requirements, are therefore

$$\frac{w_m}{h_m} = \frac{w}{h} \qquad \frac{\rho_m V_m w_m}{\mu_m} = \frac{\rho V w}{\mu}$$

The size of the model is obtained from the first requirement which indicates that

$$w_m = \frac{h_m}{h} w \tag{7.11}$$

We are free to establish the height ratio h_m/h, but then the model plate width, w_m, is fixed in accordance with Eq. 7.11.

The second similarity requirement indicates that the model and prototype must be operated at the same Reynolds number. Thus, the required velocity for the model is obtained from the relationship

$$V_m = \frac{\mu_m}{\mu} \frac{\rho}{\rho_m} \frac{w}{w_m} V \tag{7.12}$$

Note that this model design requires not only geometric scaling, as specified by Eq. 7.11, but also the correct scaling of the velocity in accordance with Eq. 7.12. This result is typical of most model designs—there is more to the design that simply scaling the geometry!

With the foregoing similarity requirements satisfied, the prediction equation for the drag is

$$\frac{\mathcal{D}}{w^2 \rho V^2} = \frac{\mathcal{D}_m}{w_m^2 \rho_m V_m^2}$$

or

$$\mathcal{D} = \left(\frac{w}{w_m}\right)^2 \left(\frac{\rho}{\rho_m}\right) \left(\frac{V}{V_m}\right)^2 \mathcal{D}_m$$

Thus, a measured drag on the model, $\mathcal{D}_m$, must be multiplied by the ratio of the square of the plate widths, the ratio of the fluid densities, and the ratio of the square of the velocities to obtain the predicted value of the prototype drag, $\mathcal{D}$.

Generally, as is illustrated in this example, to achieve similarity between model and prototype behavior, *all the corresponding pi terms must be equated between model and prototype.* Usually, one or more of these pi terms will involve ratios of important lengths (such as *w/h* in the foregoing example); that is, they are purely geometrical. Thus, when we equate the pi terms involving length ratios we are requiring that there be complete *geometric similarity* between the model and prototype. This means that the model must be a scaled version of the prototype. Geometric scaling may extend to the finest features of the system, such as surface roughness, or small protuberances on a structure, since these kinds of geometric features may significantly influence the flow.

Another group of typical pi terms (such as the Reynolds number in the foregoing example) involves force ratios as noted in Table 7.1. The equality of these pi terms requires the ratio of like forces in model and prototype to be the same. Thus, for flows in which the Reynolds numbers are equal, the ratio of viscous forces in model and prototype is equal to the ratio of inertia forces. If other pi terms are involved, such as the Froude number or Weber number, a similar conclusion can be drawn; that is, the equality of these pi terms requires the ratio of like forces in model and prototype to be the same. Thus, when these types of pi terms are equal in model and prototype, we have *dynamic similarity* between model and prototype. It follows that with both geometric and dynamic similarity the streamline patterns will be the same and corresponding velocity ratios (V_m/V) and acceleration ratios (a_m/a) are constant throughout the flow field. Thus, *kinematic similarity* exists between model and prototype. To have complete similarity between model and prototype, we must maintain geometric, kinematic, and dynamic similarity between the two systems. This will automatically follow if all the important variables are included in the dimensional analysis, and if all the similarity requirements based on the resulting pi terms are satisfied.

V7.2 Environmental models

EXAMPLE 7.4

A long structural component of a bridge has the cross section shown in Fig. E7.4. It is known that when a steady wind blows past this type of bluff body, vortices may develop on the downwind side that are shed in a regular fashion at some definite frequency. Since these vortices can create harmful periodic forces acting on the structure, it is important to determine

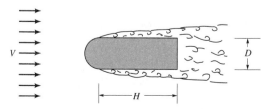

■ FIGURE E7.4

the shedding frequency. For the specific structure of interest, $D = 0.1$ m, $H = 0.3$ m, and a representative wind velocity is 50 km/hr. Standard air can be assumed. The shedding frequency is to be determined through the use of a small-scale model that is to be tested in a water tunnel. For the model $D_m = 20$ mm and the water temperature is 20°C. Determine the model dimension, H_m, and the velocity at which the test should be performed. If the shedding frequency for the model is found to be 49.9 Hz, what is the corresponding frequency for the prototype?

SOLUTION

We expect the shedding frequency, ω, to depend on the lengths D and H, the approach velocity, V, and the fluid density, ρ, and viscosity, μ. Thus,

$$\omega = f(D, H, V, \rho, \mu)$$

where

$$\omega \doteq T^{-1}$$
$$D \doteq L$$
$$H \doteq L$$
$$V \doteq LT^{-1}$$
$$\rho \doteq ML^{-3}$$
$$\mu \doteq ML^{-1}T^{-1}$$

Since there are six variables and three reference dimensions (MLT), three pi terms are required. Application of the pi theorem yields

$$\frac{\omega D}{V} = \phi\left(\frac{D}{H}, \frac{\rho VD}{\mu}\right)$$

We recognize the pi term on the left as the Strouhal number, and the dimensional analysis indicates that the Strouhal number is a function of the geometric parameter, D/H, and the Reynolds number. Thus, to maintain similarity between model and prototype

$$\frac{D_m}{H_m} = \frac{D}{H}$$

and

$$\frac{\rho_m V_m D_m}{\mu_m} = \frac{\rho VD}{\mu}$$

From the first similarity requirement

$$H_m = \frac{D_m}{D} H$$
$$= \frac{(20 \times 10^{-3} \text{ m})}{(0.1 \text{ m})} (0.3 \text{ m})$$
$$H_m = 60 \times 10^{-3} \text{ m} = 60 \text{ mm} \qquad \text{(Ans)}$$

The second similarity requirement indicates that the Reynolds number must be the same for model and prototype so that the model velocity must satisfy the condition

$$V_m = \frac{\mu_m}{\mu} \frac{\rho}{\rho_m} \frac{D}{D_m} V \tag{1}$$

For air at standard conditions, $\mu = 1.79 \times 10^{-5}$ kg/m·s, $\rho = 1.23$ kg/m³, and for water at 20°C, $\mu = 1.00 \times 10^{-3}$ kg/m·s, $\rho = 998$ kg/m³. The fluid velocity for the prototype is

$$V = \frac{(50 \times 10^3 \text{ m/hr})}{(3600 \text{ s/hr})} = 13.9 \text{ m/s}$$

The required velocity can now be calculated from Eq. 1 as

$$V_m = \frac{[1.00 \times 10^{-3} \text{ kg/(m·s)}](1.23 \text{ kg/m}^3)(0.1 \text{ m})}{[1.79 \times 10^{-5} \text{ kg/(m·s)}](998 \text{ kg/m}^3)(20 \times 10^{-3} \text{ m})} (13.9 \text{ m/s})$$

$$V_m = 4.79 \text{ m/s} \tag{Ans}$$

This is a reasonable velocity that could be readily achieved in a water tunnel.

With the two similarity requirements satisfied, it follows that the Strouhal numbers for prototype and model will be the same so that

$$\frac{\omega D}{V} = \frac{\omega_m D_m}{V_m}$$

and the predicted prototype vortex shedding frequency is

$$\omega = \frac{V}{V_m} \frac{D_m}{D} \omega_m$$

$$= \frac{(13.9 \text{ m/s})}{(4.79 \text{ m/s})} \frac{(20 \times 10^{-3} \text{ m})}{(0.1 \text{ m})} (49.9 \text{ Hz})$$

$$\omega = 29.0 \text{ Hz} \tag{Ans}$$

This same model could also be used to predict the drag per unit length, $\mathcal{D}_\ell$, on the prototype, since the drag would depend on the same variables as those used for the frequency. Thus, the similarity requirements would be the same and with these requirements satisfied it follows that the drag per unit length expressed in dimensionless form, such as $\mathcal{D}_\ell/D\rho V^2$, would be equal in model and prototype. The measured drag on the model could then be related to the corresponding drag on the prototype through the relationship

$$\mathcal{D}_\ell = \left(\frac{D}{D_m}\right)\left(\frac{\rho}{\rho_m}\right)\left(\frac{V}{V_m}\right)^2 \mathcal{D}_{\ell m}$$

7.8.2   Model Scales

It is clear from the preceding section that the ratio of like quantities for the model and prototype naturally arises from the similarity requirements. For example, if in a given problem there are two length variables ℓ_1 and ℓ_2, the resulting similarity requirement based on a pi term obtained from these variables is

$$\frac{\ell_1}{\ell_2} = \frac{\ell_{1m}}{\ell_{2m}}$$

so that

$$\frac{\ell_{1m}}{\ell_1} = \frac{\ell_{2m}}{\ell_2}$$

We define the ratio ℓ_{1m}/ℓ_1 or ℓ_{2m}/ℓ_2 as the *length scale*. For true models there will be only one length scale, and all lengths are fixed in accordance with this scale. There are, however, other scales such as the velocity scale, V_m/V, density scale, ρ_m/ρ, viscosity scale, μ_m/μ, and so on. In fact, we can define a scale for each of the variables in the problem. Thus, it is actually meaningless to talk about a "scale" of a model without specifying which scale.

We will designate the length scale as λ_ℓ, and other scales as λ_V, λ_ρ, λ_μ, and so on, where the subscript indicates the particular scale. Also, we will take the ratio of the model value to the prototype value as the scale (rather than the inverse). Length scales are often specified, for example, as 1 : 10 or as a $\frac{1}{10}$-scale model. The meaning of this specification is that the model is one-tenth the size of the prototype, and the tacit assumption is that all relevant lengths are scaled accordingly so the model is geometrically similar to the prototype.

7.8.3 Distorted Models

Although the general idea behind establishing similarity requirements for models is straightforward (we simply equate pi terms), it is not always possible to satisfy all the known requirements. If one or more of the similarity requirements are not met, for example, if $\Pi_{2m} \neq \Pi_2$, then it follows that the prediction equation $\Pi_1 = \Pi_{1m}$ is not true; that is, $\Pi_1 \neq \Pi_{1m}$. Models for which one or more of the similarity requirements are not satisfied are called *distorted models*.

Distorted models are rather commonplace, and they can arise for a variety of reasons. For example, perhaps a suitable fluid cannot be found for the model. The classic example of a distorted model occurs in the study of open channel or free-surface flows. Typically in these problems both the Reynolds number, $\rho V \ell/\mu$, and the Froude number, $V/\sqrt{g\ell}$, are involved.

Froude number similarity requires

$$\frac{V_m}{\sqrt{g_m \ell_m}} = \frac{V}{\sqrt{g\ell}}$$

If the model and prototype are operated in the same gravitational field, then the required velocity scale is

$$\frac{V_m}{V} = \sqrt{\frac{\ell_m}{\ell}} = \sqrt{\lambda_\ell}$$

Reynolds number similarity requires

$$\frac{\rho_m V_m \ell_m}{\mu_m} = \frac{\rho V \ell}{\mu}$$

and the velocity scale is

$$\frac{V_m}{V} = \frac{\mu_m}{\mu} \frac{\rho}{\rho_m} \frac{\ell}{\ell_m}$$

V7.3 Model
of fish hatch-
ery pond

Since the velocity scale must be equal to the square root of the length scale, it follows that

$$\frac{\mu_m/\rho_m}{\mu/\rho} = \frac{\nu_m}{\nu} = (\lambda_\ell)^{3/2} \tag{7.13}$$

where the ratio μ/ρ is the kinematic viscosity, ν. Although, in principle it may be possible to satisfy this design condition, it may be quite difficult, if not impossible, to find a suitable model fluid, particularly for small length scales. For problems involving rivers, spillways, and harbors, for which the prototype fluid is water, the models are also relatively large so that the only practical model fluid is water. However, in this case (with the kinematic viscosity scale equal to unity) Eq. 7.13 will not be satisfied, and a distorted model will result. Generally, hydraulic models of this type are distorted and are designed on the basis of the Froude number, with the Reynolds number different in model and prototype.

Distorted models can be successfully used, but the interpretation of results obtained with this type of model is obviously more difficult than the interpretation of results obtained with *true models* for which all similarity requirements are met.

7.9   Some Typical Model Studies

Models are used to investigate many different types of fluid mechanics problems, and it is difficult to characterize in a general way all necessary similarity requirements, since each problem is unique. We can, however, broadly classify many of the problems on the basis of the general nature of the flow, and subsequently develop some general characteristics of model designs in each of these classifications. In the following sections we will consider models for the study of (1) flow through closed circuits, (2) flow around immersed bodies, and (3) flow with a free surface. Turbomachine models are considered in Chapter 11.

7.9.1   Flow Through Closed Conduits

Common examples of this type of flow include pipe flow and flow through valves, fittings, and metering devices. Although the conduits are often circular, they could have other shapes as well and may contain expansions or contractions. Since there are no fluid interfaces or free surfaces, the dominant forces are inertial and viscous so that the Reynolds number is an important similarity parameter. For low Mach numbers (Ma $<$ 0.3), compressibility effects are negligible for both the flow of liquids or gases. For this class of problems, geometric similarity between model and prototype must be maintained. Generally the geometric characteristics can be described by a series of length terms, $\ell_1, \ell_2, \ell_3, \ldots, \ell_i,$ and ℓ, where ℓ is some particular length dimension for the system. Such a series of length terms leads to a set of pi terms of the form

$$\Pi_i = \frac{\ell_i}{\ell}$$

where $i = 1, 2, \ldots,$ and so on. In addition to the basic geometry of the system, the roughness of the internal surfaces in contact with the fluid may be important. If the average height of surface roughness elements is defined as ε, then the pi term representing roughness would be ε/ℓ. This parameter indicates that for complete geometric similarity, surface roughness would also have to be scaled.

It follows from this discussion that for flow in closed conduits at low Mach numbers, any dependent pi term (the one that contains the particular variable of interest, such as pressure drop) can be expressed as

$$\text{Dependent pi term} = \phi\left(\frac{\ell_i}{\ell}, \frac{\varepsilon}{\ell}, \frac{\rho V \ell}{\mu}\right) \tag{7.14}$$

This is a general formulation for this type of problem.

With the similarity requirements satisfied, it follows that the dependent pi term will be equal in model and prototype. For example, if the dependent variable of interest is the pressure differential, Δp, between two points along a closed conduit, then the dependent pi term could be expressed as

$$\Pi_1 = \frac{\Delta p}{\rho V^2}$$

The prototype pressure drop would then be obtained from the relationship

$$\Delta p = \frac{\rho}{\rho_m}\left(\frac{V}{V_m}\right)^2 \Delta p_m$$

so that from a measured pressure differential in the model, Δp_m, the corresponding pressure differential for the prototype could be predicted. Note that in general $\Delta p \neq \Delta p_m$.

EXAMPLE 7.5

Model tests are to be performed to study the flow through a large valve having a 2-ft-diameter inlet and carrying water at a flowrate of 30 cfs. The working fluid in the model is water at the same temperature as that in the prototype. Complete geometric similarity exists between model and prototype, and the model inlet diameter is 3 in. Determine the required flowrate in the model.

SOLUTION

To ensure dynamic similarity, the model tests should be run so that

$$\text{Re}_m = \text{Re}$$

or

$$\frac{V_m D_m}{\nu_m} = \frac{VD}{\nu}$$

where V and D correspond to the inlet velocity and diameter, respectively. Since the same fluid is to be used in model and prototype, $\nu = \nu_m$, and therefore

$$\frac{V_m}{V} = \frac{D}{D_m}$$

The discharge, Q, is equal to VA, where A is the inlet area, so

$$\frac{Q_m}{Q} = \frac{V_m A_m}{VA} = \left(\frac{D}{D_m}\right)\frac{[(\pi/4)D_m^2]}{[(\pi/4)D^2]}$$

$$= \frac{D_m}{D}$$

and for the data given

$$Q_m = \frac{(3/12 \text{ ft})}{(2 \text{ ft})}(30 \text{ ft}^3/\text{s})$$

$$Q_m = 3.75 \text{ cfs} \hspace{4cm} \textbf{(Ans)}$$

Although this is a large flowrate to be carried through a 3-in.-diameter pipe (the corresponding velocity is 76.4 ft/s), it could be attained in a laboratory facility. However, it is to be noted that if we tried to use a smaller model, say one with $D = 1$ in., the required model velocity is 229 ft/s, a very high velocity that would be difficult to achieve. These results are indicative of one of the difficulties encountered in maintaining Reynolds number similarity—the required model velocities may be impractical to obtain.

7.9.2   Flow Around Immersed Bodies

Models have been widely used to study the flow characteristics associated with bodies that are completely immersed in a moving fluid. Examples include flow around aircraft, automobiles, golf balls, and buildings. (These types of models are usually tested in wind tunnels as is illustrated in Fig. 7.1.) Modeling laws for these problems are similar to those described in the preceding section; that is, geometric and Reynolds number similarity is required. Since there are no fluid interfaces, surface tension (and therefore the Weber number) is not important. Also, gravity will not affect the flow patterns, so the Froude number need not be considered. The Mach number will be important for high-speed flows in which compressibility becomes an important factor, but for incompressible fluids (such as liquids or for gases at relatively low speeds) the Mach number can be omitted as a similarity requirement. In this case, a general formulation for these problems is

$$\text{Dependent pi term} = \phi\left(\frac{\ell_i}{\ell}, \frac{\varepsilon}{\ell}, \frac{\rho V \ell}{\mu}\right) \hspace{3cm} \textbf{(7.15)}$$

■ **FIGURE 7.1** **Model of the National Bank of Commerce, San Antonio, Texas, for measurement of peak, rms, and mean pressure distributions. The model is located in a long-test-section, meteorological wind tunnel. (Photograph courtesy of Cermak Peterka Petersen, Inc.)**

V7.4 Wind
engineering
models

where ℓ is some characteristic length of the system and ℓ_i represents other pertinent lengths, ε/ℓ is the relative roughness of the surface (or surfaces), and $\rho V\ell/\mu$ is the Reynolds number.

Frequently, the dependent variable of interest for this type of problem is the drag, $\mathscr{D}$, developed on the body, and in this situation the dependent pi term would usually be expressed in the form of a *drag coefficient, C_D*, where

$$C_D = \frac{\mathscr{D}}{\frac{1}{2}\rho V^2 \ell^2}$$

The numerical factor, $\frac{1}{2}$, is arbitrary but commonly included, and ℓ^2 is usually taken as some representative area of the object. Thus, drag studies can be undertaken with the formulation

$$\frac{\mathscr{D}}{\frac{1}{2}\rho V^2 \ell^2} = C_D = \phi\left(\frac{\ell_i}{\ell}, \frac{\varepsilon}{\ell}, \frac{\rho V\ell}{\mu}\right) \tag{7.16}$$

EXAMPLE 7.6

The drag on an airplane cruising at 240 mph in standard air is to be determined from tests on a 1:10 scale model placed in a pressurized wind tunnel. To minimize compressibility effects, the air speed in the wind tunnel is also to be 240 mph. Determine the required air pressure in the tunnel (assuming the same air temperature for model and prototype), and the drag on the prototype corresponding to a measured force of 1 lb on the model.

SOLUTION

From Eq. 7.16 it follows that drag can be predicted from a geometrically similar model if the Reynolds numbers in model and prototype are the same. Thus,

$$\frac{\rho_m V_m \ell_m}{\mu_m} = \frac{\rho V\ell}{\mu}$$

For this example, $V_m = V$ and $\ell_m/\ell = \frac{1}{10}$ so that

$$\frac{\rho_m}{\rho} = \frac{\mu_m}{\mu}\frac{V}{V_m}\frac{\ell}{\ell_m}$$

$$= \frac{\mu_m}{\mu}(1)(10)$$

and therefore

$$\frac{\rho_m}{\rho} = 10\frac{\mu_m}{\mu}$$

This result shows that the same fluid with $\rho_m = \rho$ and $\mu_m = \mu$ cannot be used if Reynolds number similarity is to be maintained. One possibility is to pressurize the wind tunnel to increase the density of the air. We assume that an increase in pressure does not significantly change the viscosity so that the required increase in density is given by the relationship

$$\frac{\rho_m}{\rho} = 10$$

For an ideal gas, $p = \rho RT$ so that

$$\frac{p_m}{p} = \frac{\rho_m}{\rho}$$

for constant temperature $(T = T_m)$. Therefore, the wind tunnel would need to be pressurized so that

$$\frac{p_m}{p} = 10$$

Since the prototype operates at standard atmospheric pressure, the required pressure in the wind tunnel is 10 atmospheres or

$$p_m = 10\,(14.7 \text{ psia})$$
$$= 147 \text{ psia} \qquad \textbf{(Ans)}$$

Thus, we see that a high pressure would be required and this could not be easily or inexpensively achieved. However, under these conditions Reynolds similarity would be attained and the drag could be obtained from Eq. 7.16 so that

$$\frac{\mathcal{D}}{\frac{1}{2}\rho V^2 \ell^2} = \frac{\mathcal{D}}{\frac{1}{2}\rho_m V_m^2 \ell_m^2}$$

or

$$\mathcal{D} = \frac{\rho}{\rho_m}\left(\frac{V}{V_m}\right)^2 \left(\frac{\ell}{\ell_m}\right)^2 \mathcal{D}_m$$
$$= \left(\frac{1}{10}\right)(1)^2(10)^2 \mathcal{D}_m$$
$$= 10\mathcal{D}_m$$

Thus, for a drag of 1 lb on the model the corresponding drag on the prototype is

$$\mathcal{D} = 10 \text{ lb} \qquad \textbf{(Ans)}$$

For problems involving high velocities in which the Mach number is greater than about 0.3, the influence of compressibility, and therefore the Mach number (or Cauchy number), becomes significant. In this case complete similarity requires not only geometric and Reynolds number similarity but also Mach number similarity so that

$$\frac{V_m}{c_m} = \frac{V}{c} \qquad (7.17)$$

This similarity requirement, when combined with that for Reynolds number similarity yields

$$\frac{c}{c_m} = \frac{\nu}{\nu_m}\frac{\ell_m}{\ell} \qquad (7.18)$$

V7.5 Wind
tunnel train
model

Clearly the same fluid with $c = c_m$ and $\nu = \nu_m$ cannot be used in model and prototype unless the length scale is unity (which means that we are running tests on the prototype). In high-speed aerodynamics the prototype fluid is usually air, and it is difficult to satisfy Eq. 7.18 for reasonable length scales. Thus, models involving high-speed flows are often distorted with respect to Reynolds number similarity, but Mach number similarity is maintained.

7.9.3 Flow with a Free Surface

Flows in canals, rivers, spillways, and stilling basins, as well as flow around ships, are all examples of flow phenomena involving a free surface. For this class of problems, both gravitational and inertial forces are important and, therefore, the Froude number becomes an important similarity parameter. Also, since there is a free surface with a liquid-air interface, forces due to surface tension may be significant, and the Weber number becomes another similarity parameter that needs to be considered along with the Reynolds number. Geometric variables will obviously still be important. Thus a general formulation for problems involving flow with a free surface can be expressed as

V7.6 River flow model

$$\text{Dependent pi term} = \phi\left(\frac{\ell_i}{\ell}, \frac{\varepsilon}{\ell}, \frac{\rho V \ell}{\mu}, \frac{V}{\sqrt{g\ell}}, \frac{\rho V^2 \ell}{\sigma}\right) \tag{7.19}$$

As discussed previously, ℓ is some characteristic length of the system, ℓ_i represents other pertinent lengths, and ε/ℓ is the relative roughness of the various surfaces. Since gravity is the driving force in these problems, Froude number similarity is definitely required so that

$$\frac{V_m}{\sqrt{g_m \ell_m}} = \frac{V}{\sqrt{g\ell}}$$

The model and prototype are expected to operate in the same gravitational field ($g_m = g$), and therefore it follows that

$$\frac{V_m}{V} = \sqrt{\frac{\ell_m}{\ell}} = \sqrt{\lambda_\ell} \tag{7.20}$$

Thus, when models are designed on the basis of Froude number similarity, the velocity scale is determined by the square root of the length scale. As is discussed in Section 7.8.3, to simultaneously have Reynolds and Froude number similarity it is necessary that the kinematic viscosity scale be related to the length scale as

$$\frac{\nu_m}{\nu} = (\lambda_\ell)^{3/2} \tag{7.21}$$

V7.7 Boat model

The working fluid for the prototype is normally either freshwater or seawater and the length scale is small. Under these circumstances it is virtually impossible to satisfy Eq. 7.21, so models involving free-surface flows are usually distorted. The problem is further complicated if an attempt is made to model surface tension effects, since this requires equality of Weber numbers. Fortunately, in many problems involving free-surface flows, both surface tension and viscous effects are small and consequently strict adherence to Weber and Reynolds number similarity is not required.

For large hydraulic structures, such as dam spillways, the Reynolds numbers are large so that viscous forces are small in comparison to the forces due to gravity and inertia. In this case Reynolds number similarity is not maintained and models are designed on the basis of Froude number similarity. Care must be taken to ensure that the model Reynolds numbers are also large, but they are not required to be equal to those of the prototype. This type of hydraulic model is usually made as large as possible so that the Reynolds number will be large. A spillway model is shown in Fig. 7.2.

■ FIGURE 7.2 A scale hydraulic model (1:197) of the Guri Dam in Venezuela which is used to simulate the characteristics of the flow over and below the spillway and the erosion below the spillway. (Photograph courtesy of St. Anthony Falls Hydraulic Laboratory.)

EXAMPLE 7.7

A certain spillway for a dam is 20 m wide and is designed to carry 125 m^3/s at flood stage. A 1 : 15 model is constructed to study the flow characteristics through the spillway. Determine the required model width and flowrate. What operating time for the model corresponds to a 24-hr period in the prototype? The effects of surface tension and viscosity are to be neglected.

SOLUTION

The width, w_m, of the model spillway is obtained from the length scale, λ_ℓ, so that

$$\frac{w_m}{w} = \lambda_\ell$$

$$= \frac{1}{15}$$

and

$$w_m = \frac{20 \text{ m}}{15} = 1.33 \text{ m} \qquad \text{(Ans)}$$

Of course, all other geometric features (including surface roughness) of the spillway must be scaled in accordance with the same length scale.

With the neglect of surface tension and viscosity, Eq. 7.19 indicates that dynamic similarity will be achieved if the Froude numbers are equal between model and prototype. Thus,

$$\frac{V_m}{\sqrt{g_m \ell_m}} = \frac{V}{\sqrt{g\ell}}$$

and for $g_m = g$

$$\frac{V_m}{V} = \sqrt{\frac{\ell_m}{\ell}}$$

Since the flowrate is given by $Q = VA$, where A is an appropriate cross-sectional area, it follows that

$$\frac{Q_m}{Q} = \frac{V_m A_m}{VA} = \sqrt{\frac{\ell_m}{\ell}} \left(\frac{\ell_m}{\ell}\right)^2$$
$$= (\lambda_\ell)^{5/2}$$

where we have made use of the relationship $A_m/A = (\ell_m/\ell)^2$. For $\lambda_\ell = \frac{1}{15}$ and $Q = 125$ m³/s

$$Q_m = \left(\tfrac{1}{15}\right)^{5/2} (125 \text{ m}^3/\text{s}) = 0.143 \text{ m}^3/\text{s} \qquad \text{(Ans)}$$

The time scale can be obtained from the velocity scale, since the velocity is distance divided by time ($V = \ell/t$), and therefore

$$\frac{V}{V_m} = \frac{\ell}{t} \frac{t_m}{\ell_m}$$

or

$$\frac{t_m}{t} = \frac{V}{V_m} \frac{\ell_m}{\ell} = \sqrt{\frac{\ell_m}{\ell}} = \sqrt{\lambda_\ell}$$

This result indicates that time intervals in the model will be smaller than the corresponding intervals in the prototype if $\lambda_\ell < 1$. For $\lambda_\ell = \frac{1}{15}$ and a prototype time interval of 24 hr

$$t_m = \sqrt{\tfrac{1}{15}} (24 \text{ hr}) = 6.20 \text{ hr} \qquad \text{(Ans)}$$

The ability to scale times may be very useful, since it is possible to "speed up" events in the model which may occur over a relatively long time in the prototype.

References

1. Bridgman, P. W., *Dimensional Analysis,* Yale University Press, New Haven, Conn., 1922.
2. Murphy, G., *Similitude in Engineering,* Ronald Press, New York, 1950.
3. Langhaar, H. L., *Dimensional Analysis and Theory of Models,* Wiley, New York, 1951.
4. Ipsen, D. C., *Units, Dimensions, and Dimensionless Numbers,* McGraw-Hill, New York, 1960.
5. Isaacson, E. de St. Q., and Isaacson, M. de St. Q., *Dimensional Methods in Engineering and Physics,* Wiley, New York, 1975.

Problems

Note: Unless otherwise indicated use the values of fluid properties found in the tables on the inside of the front cover. Problems designated with an (*) are intended to be solved with the aid of a programmable calculator or a computer. Problems designated with a (†) are "open ended" problems and require critical thinking in that to work them one must make various assumptions and provide the necessary data. There is not a unique answer to these problems.

7.1 The Reynolds number, $\rho VD/\mu$, is a very important parameter in fluid mechanics. Verify that the Reynolds number is dimensionless, using both the *FLT* system and the

MLT system for basic dimensions, and determine its value for water (at 70°C) flowing at a velocity of 2 m/s through a 1-in.-diameter pipe.

7.2   Some common variables in fluid mechanics include: volume flowrate, Q, acceleration of gravity, g, viscosity, μ, density, ρ, and a length, ℓ. Which of the following combinations of these variables are dimensionless? (a) $Q^2/g\ell^2$. (b) $\rho Q/\mu\ell$. (c) $g\ell^2/Q$. (d) $\rho Q\ell/\mu$.

7.3   For the flow of a thin film of a liquid with a depth h and a free surface, two important dimensionless parameters are the Froude number, $V/\sqrt{gh}$, and the Weber number, $\rho V^2 h/\sigma$. Determine the value of these two parameters for glycerin (at 20°C) flowing with a velocity of 0.5 m/s at a depth of 2 mm.

7.4   At a sudden contraction in a pipe the diameter changes from D_1 to D_2. The pressure drop, Δp, which develops across the contraction is a function of D_1 and D_2, as well as the velocity, V, in the larger pipe, and the fluid density, ρ, and viscosity, μ. Use D_1, V, and μ as repeating variables to determine a suitable set of dimensionless parameters. Why would it be incorrect to include the velocity in the smaller pipe as an additional variable?

7.5   Assume that the power, $\mathcal{P}$, required to drive a fan is a function of the fan diameter, D, the fluid density, ρ, the rotational speed, ω, and the flowrate, Q. Use D, ω, and ρ as repeating variables to determine a suitable set of pi terms.

7.6   It is desired to determine the wave height when wind blows across a lake. The wave height, H, is assumed to be a function of the wind speed, V, the water density, ρ, the air density, ρ_a, the water depth, d, the distance from the shore, ℓ, and the acceleration of gravity, g, as shown in Fig. P7.6. Use d, V, and ρ as repeating variables to determine a suitable set of pi terms that could be used to describe this problem.

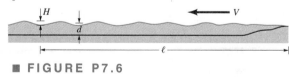

■ **FIGURE P7.6**

7.7   The pressure rise, Δp, across a pump can be expressed as

$$\Delta p = f(D, \rho, \omega, Q)$$

where D is the impeller diameter, ρ the fluid density, ω the rotational speed, and Q the flowrate. Determine a suitable set of dimensionless parameters.

7.8   The drag, $\mathcal{D}$, on a washer shaped plate placed normal to a stream of fluid can be expressed as

$$\mathcal{D} = f(d_1, d_2, V, \mu, \rho)$$

where d_1 is the outer diameter, d_2 the inner diameter, V the fluid velocity, μ the fluid viscosity, and ρ the fluid density. Some experiments are to be performed in a wind tunnel to determine the drag. What dimensionless parameters would you use to organize these data?

7.9   The velocity, V, of a spherical particle falling slowly in a viscous liquid can be expressed as

$$V = f(d, \mu, \gamma, \gamma_s)$$

where d is the particle diameter, μ the liquid viscosity, and γ and γ_s the specific weight of the liquid and particle, respectively. Develop a set of dimensionless parameters that can be used to investigate this problem.

7.10   The velocity, c, at which pressure pulses travel through arteries (pulse-wave velocity) is a function of the artery diameter, D, and wall thickness, h, the density of blood, ρ, and the modulus of elasticity, E, of the arterial wall. Determine a set of nondimensional parameters that can be used to study experimentally the relationship between the pulse-wave velocity and the variables listed. Form the nondimensional parameters by inspection.

7.11   Assume that the drag, $\mathcal{D}$, on an aircraft flying at supersonic speeds is a function of its velocity, V, fluid density, ρ, speed of sound, c, and a series of lengths, $\ell_1, \ldots, \ell_i$, which describe the geometry of the aircraft. Develop a set of pi terms that could be used to investigate experimentally how the drag is affected by the various factors listed. Form the pi terms by inspection.

7.12   When a fluid flows slowly past a vertical plate of height h and width b (see Fig. P7.12), pressure develops on the face of the plate. Assume that the pressure, p, at the midpoint of the plate is a function of plate height and width, the approach velocity, V, and the fluid viscosity, μ. Make use of dimensional analysis to determine how the pressure, p, will change when the fluid velocity, V, is doubled.

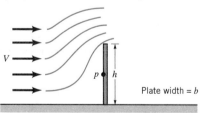

■ **FIGURE P7.12**

7.13   The buoyant force, F_B, acting on a body submerged in a fluid is a function of the specific weight, γ, of the fluid and the volume, $\mathcal{V}$, of the body. Show, by dimensional analysis, that the buoyant force must be directly proportional to the specific weight.

7.14   The viscosity, μ, of a liquid can be measured by determining the time, t, it takes for a sphere of diameter, d, to settle slowly through a distance, ℓ, in a vertical cylinder of diameter, D, containing the liquid (see Fig. P7.14). Assume that

$$t = f(\ell, d, D, \mu, \Delta\gamma)$$

where $\Delta\gamma$ is the difference in specific weights between the sphere and the liquid. Use dimensional analysis to show how t is related to μ, and describe how such an apparatus might be used to measure viscosity.

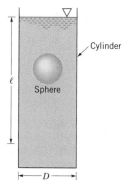

■ **FIGURE P7.14**

*7.15 The pressure drop across a short hollowed plug placed in a circular tube through which a liquid is flowing (see Fig. P7.15) can be expressed as

$$\Delta p = f(\rho, V, D, d)$$

where ρ is the fluid density, and V is the mean velocity in the tube. Some experimental data obtained with $D = 0.2$ ft, $\rho = 2.0$ slugs/ft^3, and $V = 2$ ft/s are given in the following table:

d (ft)	0.06	0.08	0.10	0.15
Δp (lb/ft^2)	493.8	156.2	64.0	12.6

Plot the results of these tests, using suitable dimensionless parameters, on log–log graph paper. Use a standard curve-fitting technique to determine a general equation for Δp. What are the limits of applicability of the equation?

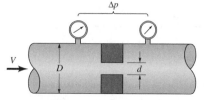

■ **FIGURE P7.15**

7.16 A liquid flows with a velocity V through a hole in the side of a large tank. Assume that

$$V = f(h, g, \rho, \sigma)$$

where h is the depth of fluid above the hole, g is the acceleration of gravity, ρ the fluid density, and σ the surface tension. The following data were obtained by changing h and measuring V, with a fluid having a density $= 10^3$ kg/m^3 and surface tension $= 0.074$ N/m.

V (m/s)	3.13	4.43	5.42	6.25	7.00
h (m)	0.50	1.00	1.50	2.00	2.50

Plot these data by using appropriate dimensionless variables. Could any of the original variables have been omitted?

*7.17 The concentric cylinder device of the type shown in Fig. P7.17 is commonly used to measure the viscosity, μ, of liquids by relating the angle of twist, θ, of the inner cylinder to the angular velocity, ω, of the outer cylinder. Assume that

$$\theta = f(\omega, \mu, K, D_1, D_2, \ell)$$

where K depends on the suspending wire properties and has the dimensions FL. The following data were obtained in a series of tests for which $\mu = 0.01$ lb·s/ft^2, $K = 10$ lb·ft, $\ell = 1$ ft, and D_1 and D_2 were constant.

θ (rad)	ω (rad/s)
0.89	0.30
1.50	0.50
2.51	0.82
3.05	1.05
4.28	1.43
5.52	1.86
6.40	2.14

Determine from these data, with the aid of dimensional analysis, the relationship between θ, ω, and μ for this

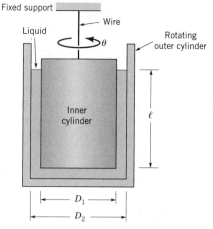

■ **FIGURE P7.17**

particular apparatus. *Hint:* Plot the data using appropriate dimensionless parameters, and determine the equation of the resulting curve using a standard curve-fitting technique. The equation should satisfy the condition that $\theta = 0$ for $\omega = 0$.

7.18   The pressure drop per unit length, Δp_ℓ, for the flow of blood through a horizontal small diameter tube is a function of the volume rate of flow, Q, the diameter, D, and the blood viscosity, μ. For a series of tests in which $D = 2$ mm and $\mu = 0.004$ N·s/m², the following data were obtained, where the Δp listed was measured over the length, $\ell = 300$ mm.

Q (m³/s)	Δp (N/m²)
3.6×10^{-6}	1.1×10^4
4.9×10^{-6}	1.5×10^4
6.3×10^{-6}	1.9×10^4
7.9×10^{-6}	2.4×10^4
9.8×10^{-6}	3.0×10^4

Perform a dimensional analysis for this problem, and make use of the data given to determine a general relationship between Δp_ℓ and Q (one that is valid for other values of D, ℓ, and μ).

7.19   The time, t, it takes to pour a certain volume of liquid from a cylindrical container depends on several factors, including the viscosity of the liquid. (See **Video V1.1**.) Assume that for very viscous liquids the time it takes to pour out 2/3 of the initial volume depends on the initial liquid depth, ℓ, the cylinder diameter, D, the liquid viscosity, μ, and the liquid specific weight, γ. The data shown in the following table were obtained in the laboratory. For these tests $\ell = 45$ mm, $D = 67$ mm, and $\gamma = 9.60$ kN/m³. **(a)** Perform a dimensional analysis and based on the data given, determine if variables used for this problem appear to be correct. Explain how you arrived at your answer. **(b)** If possible, determine an equation relating the pouring time and viscosity for the cylinder and liquids used in these tests. If it is not possible, indicate what additional information is needed.

μ (N·s/m²)	11	17	39	61	107
t(s)	15	23	53	83	145

7.20   SAE 30 oil at 60°F is pumped through a 3-ft-diameter pipeline at a rate of 5700 gal/min. A model of this pipeline is to be designed using a 2-in.-diameter pipe and water at 60°F as the working fluid. To maintain Reynolds number similarity between these two systems, what fluid velocity will be required in the model?

7.21   A liquid contained in a steadily rotating cylinder with a vertical axis moves as a rigid body. In this case, as shown in Fig. P7.21 and **Video V7.1**, the fluid velocity, V, varies directly with the radius r so that $V = r\omega$ where ω is

the angular velocity of the rotating cylinder. Assume that the characteristic Reynolds number for this system is based on the radius and velocity at the wall of the cylinder. **(a)** For a 12-in. diameter cylinder rotating with an angular velocity $\omega = 0.4$ rad/s calculate the Reynolds number if the liquid has a kinematic viscosity of (*i*) 0.33 ft²/s or (*ii*) 0.33 × 10^{-2} ft²/s. **(b)** If the cylinder were suddenly stopped, would you expect the motion of the liquids to be similar for the two liquids of part **(a)**? Explain. Do the results shown in the **Video V7.1** support your conclusions?

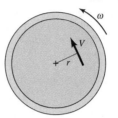

■ **FIGURE P7.21**

7.22   The design of a river model is to be based on Froude number similarity, and a river depth of 3 m is to correspond to a model depth of 100 mm. Under these conditions what is the prototype velocity corresponding to a model velocity of 2 m/s?

7.23   The fluid dynamic characteristics of an airplane flying at 240 mph at 10,000 ft are to be investigated with the aid of a 1:20 scale model. If the model tests are to be performed in a wind tunnel using standard air, what is the required air velocity in the wind tunnel? Is this a realistic velocity?

7.24   If an airplane travels at a speed of 1120 km/hr at an altitude of 15 km, what is the required speed at an altitude of 7 km to satisfy Mach number similarity? Assume the air properties correspond to those for the U.S. standard atmosphere.

7.25   The flowrate over the spillway of a dam is 27,000 ft³/min. Determine the required flowrate for a 1:30 scale model that is operated in accordance with Froude number similarity.

7.26   The lift and drag developed on a hydrofoil are to be determined through wind tunnel tests using standard air. If full scale tests are to be run, what is the required wind tunnel velocity corresponding to a hydrofoil velocity in seawater at 20 mph? Assume Reynolds number similarity is required.

7.27   The drag on a 2-m-diameter satellite dish due to an 80 km/hr wind is to be determined through a wind tunnel test using a geometrically similar 0.4-m-diameter model dish. Assume standard air for both model and prototype. **(a)** At what air speed should the model test be run? **(b)** With all similarity conditions satisfied, the measured drag on the model was determined to be 170 N. What is the predicted drag on the prototype dish?

7.28 As illustrated in **Video V7.2**, models are commonly used to study the dispersion of a gaseous pollutant from an exhaust stack located near a building complex. Similarity requirements for the pollutant source involve the following independent variables: the stack gas speed, V, the wind speed, U, the density of the atmospheric air, ρ, the difference in densities between the air and the stack gas, $\rho - \rho_s$, the acceleration of gravity, g, the kinematic viscosity of the stack gas, ν_s, and the stack diameter, D. **(a)** Based on these variables, determine a suitable set of similarity requirements for modeling the pollutant source. **(b)** For this type of model a typical length scale might be 1:200. If the same fluids were used in model and prototype, would the similarity requirements be satisfied? Explain and support your answer with the necessary calculations.

7.29 When small particles of diameter d are transported by a moving fluid having a velocity V they settle to the ground at some distance ℓ after starting from a height h as shown in Fig. P7.29. The variation in ℓ with various factors is to be studied with a model having a length scale of $\frac{1}{10}$. Assume that

$$\ell = f(h, d, V, \gamma, \mu)$$

where γ is the particle specific weight and μ is the fluid viscosity. The same fluid is to be used in both the model and the prototype, but γ (model) = 9 × γ (prototype). **(a)** If $V = 50$ mph, at what velocity should the model tests be run? **(b)** During a certain model test it was found that ℓ (model) = 0.8 ft. What would be the predicted ℓ for this test?

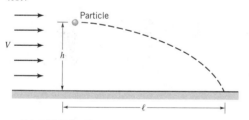

■ **FIGURE P7.29**

7.30 At a large fish hatchery the fish are reared in open, water-filled tanks. Each tank is approximately square in shape with curved corners, and the walls are smooth. To create motion in the tanks, water is supplied through a pipe at the edge of the tank. The water is drained from the tank through an opening at the center. (See **Video V7.3**.) A model with a length scale of 1:13 is to be used to determine the velocity, V, at various locations within the tank. Assume that $V = f(\ell, \ell_i, \rho, \mu, g, Q)$ where ℓ is some characteristic length such as the tank width, ℓ_i represents a series of other pertinent lengths, such as inlet pipe diameter, fluid depth, etc., ρ is the fluid density, μ is the fluid viscosity, g is the acceler-

ation of gravity, and Q is the discharge through the tank. **(a)** Determine a suitable set of dimensionless parameters for this problem and the prediction equation for the velocity. If water is to be used for the model, can all of the similarity requirements be satisfied? Explain and support your answer with the necessary calculations. **(b)** If the flowrate into the full-sized tank is 250 gpm, determine the required value for the model discharge assuming Froude number similarity. What model depth will correspond to a depth of 32 in. in the full-sized tank?

7.31 During snow storms, snow drifts commonly form behind bushes (see **Video V9.4**) and snow fences as shown in Fig. P7.31. Assume that the height of the drift, h, is a function of the number of inches of snow deposited by the storm, d, height of the fence, H, width of slats in the fence, b, wind speed, V, acceleration of gravity, g, air density, ρ, and specific weight of snow, γ_s. **(a)** If this problem is to be studied with a model, determine the similarity requirements for the model and the relationship between the drift depth for model and prototype (prediction equation). **(b)** A storm with winds of 30 mph deposits 16 in. of snow having a specific weight of 5.0 lb/ft³. A $\frac{1}{2}$-sized scale model is to be used to investigate the effectiveness of a proposed snow fence. If the air density is the same for the model and the storm, determine the required specific weight for the model snow and required wind speed for the model.

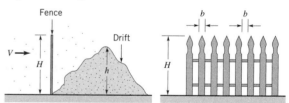

■ **FIGURE P7.31**

7.32 The drag on a sphere moving in a fluid is known to be a function of the sphere diameter, the velocity, and the fluid viscosity and density. Laboratory tests on a 4-in.-diameter sphere were performed in a water tunnel and some model data are plotted in Fig. P7.32. For these tests the vis-

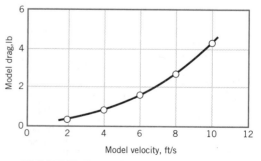

■ **FIGURE P7.32**

cosity of the water was 2.3×10^{-5} lb·s/ft^2 and the water density was 1.94 slugs/ft^3. Estimate the drag on an 8-ft-diameter balloon moving in air at a velocity of 3 ft/s. Assume the air to have a viscosity of 3.7×10^{-7} lb·s/ft^2 and a density of 2.38×10^{-3} slugs/ft^3.

7.33 The drag characteristics for a newly designed automobile having a maximum characteristic length of 20 ft are to be determined through a model study. The characteristics at both low speed (approximately 20 mph) and high speed (90 mph) are of interest. For a series of projected model tests an unpressurized wind tunnel that will accommodate a model with a maximum characteristic length of 4 ft is to be used. Determine the range of air velocities that would be required for the wind tunnel if Reynolds number similarity is desired. Are the velocities suitable? Explain.

7.34 As winds blow past buildings, complex flow patterns can develop due to various factors such as flow separation and interactions between adjacent buildings. (See Video V7.4.) Assume that the local gage pressure, p, at a particular location on a building is a function of the air density, ρ, the wind speed, V, some characteristic length, ℓ, and all other pertinent lengths, ℓ_i, needed to characterize the geometry of the building or building complex. **(a)** Determine a suitable set of dimensionless parameters that can be used to study the pressure distribution. **(b)** An eight-story building that is 100 ft tall is to be modeled in a wind tunnel. If a length scale of 1:300 is to be used, how tall should the model building be? **(c)** How will a measured pressure in the model be related to the corresponding prototype pressure? Assume the same air density in model and prototype. Based on the assumed variables, does the model wind speed have to be equal to the prototype wind speed? Explain.

7.35 Flow patterns that develop as winds blow past a vehicle, such as a train, are often studied in low-speed environmental (meteorological) wind tunnels. (See Video V7.5.) Typically, the air velocities in these tunnels are in the range of 0.1 m/s to 30 m/s. Consider a cross wind blowing past a train locomotive. Assume that the local wind velocity, V, is a function of the approaching wind velocity (at some distance from the locomotive), U, the locomotive length, ℓ, height, h, and width, b, the air density, ρ, and the air viscosity, μ. **(a)** Establish the similarity requirements and prediction equation for a model to be used in the wind tunnel to study the air velocity, V, around the locomotive. **(b)** If the model is to be used for cross winds gusting to $U = 25$ m/s, explain why it is not practical to maintain Reynolds number similarity for a typical length scale 1:50.

7.36 River models are used to study many different types of flow situations. (See, for example, Video V7.6.) A certain small river has an average width and depth of 60 ft and 4 ft, respectively, and carries water at a flowrate of 700 ft^3/s. A model is to be designed based on Froude number similarity so that the discharge scale is 1/250. At what depth and flowrate would the model operate?

†**7.37** If a large oil spill occurs from a tanker operating near a coastline, the time it would take for the oil to reach shore is of great concern. Design a model system that can be used to investigate this type of problem in the laboratory. Indicate all assumptions made in developing the design and discuss any difficulty that may arise in satisfying the similarity requirements arising from your model design.

7.38 A circular cylinder of diameter d is placed in a uniform stream of fluid as shown in Fig. P7.38a. Far from the cylinder the velocity is V and the pressure is atmospheric. The gage pressure, p, at point A on the cylinder surface is to be determined from a model study for an 18-in.-diameter prototype placed in an air stream having a speed of 8 ft/s. A 1:12 scale model is to be used with water as the working fluid. Some experimental data obtained from the model are shown in Fig. P7.38b. Predict the prototype pressure.

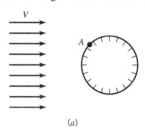

(a)

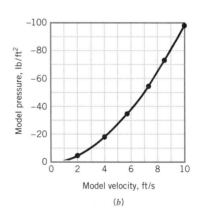

(b)

■ **FIGURE P7.38**

7.39 The pressure rise, Δp, across a centrifugal pump of a given shape (see Fig. P7.39a) can be expressed as

$$\Delta p = f(D, \omega, \rho, Q)$$

where D is the impeller diameter, ω the angular velocity of the impeller, ρ the fluid density, and Q the volume rate of flow through the pump. A model pump having a diameter of 8 in. is tested in the laboratory using water. When operated at an angular velocity of 40π rad/s the model pressure rise as a function of Q is shown in Fig. P7.39b. Use this curve to predict the pressure rise across a geometrically similar pump (prototype) for a prototype flowrate of 6 ft³/s. The prototype has a diameter of 12 in. and operates at an angular velocity of 60 π rad/s. The prototype fluid is also water.

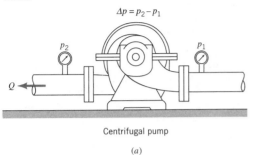

$$\Delta p = p_2 - p_1$$

p_2 p_1

Q

Centrifugal pump

(a)

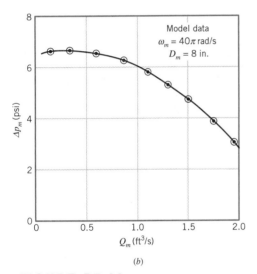

Model data
$\omega_m = 40\pi$ rad/s
$D_m = 8$ in.

Δp_m (psi)

Q_m (ft³/s)

(b)

■ **FIGURE P7.39**

7.40 A 1/50 scale model is to be used in a towing tank to study the water motion near the bottom of a shallow channel as a large barge passes over. (See **Video V7.7**.) Assume that the model is operated in accordance with the Froude number criteria for dynamic similitude. The prototype barge moves at a typical speed of 15 knots. **(a)** At what speed (in ft/s) should the model be towed? **(b)** Near the bottom of the model channel a small particle is found to move 0.15 ft in one second so that the fluid velocity at that point is approximately 0.15 ft/s. Determine the velocity at the corresponding point in the prototype channel.

7.41 A very viscous fluid flows slowly past the submerged rectangular plate of Fig. P7.41. The drag, $\mathscr{D}$, is known to be a function of the plate height, h, plate width,

b, fluid velocity, V, and fluid viscosity, μ. A model is to be used to predict the drag and during a certain model test using glycerin ($\mu_m = 0.03$ lb·s/ft²), with $h_m = 1$ in. and $b_m = 3$ in., it was found that $\mathscr{D}_m = 0.2$ lb when $V_m = 0.5$ ft/s. If possible, predict the drag on a geometrically similar larger plate with $h = 4$ in. and $b = 12$ in. immersed in the same glycerin moving with a velocity of 2 ft/s. If it is *not* possible, explain why.

Plate width = b

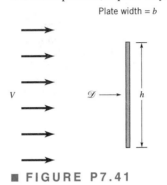

V $\mathscr{D} \longrightarrow$ h

■ **FIGURE P7.41**

7.42 A square parking lot of width w is bounded on all sides by a curb of height d with only one opening of width b as shown in Fig. P7.42. During a heavy rain the lot fills with water and it is of interest to determine the time, t, it takes for the water to completely drain from the lot after the rain stops. A scale model is to be used to study this problem, and it is assumed that

$$t = f(w, b, d, g, \mu, \rho)$$

where g is the acceleration of gravity, μ is the fluid viscosity, and ρ is the fluid density. **(a)** A dimensional analysis indicates that two important dimensionless parameters are b/w and d/w. What additional dimensionless parameters are required? **(b)** For a geometrically similar model having a length scale of 1/10, what is the relationship between the drain time for the model and the corresponding drain time for the actual parking lot? Assume all similarity requirements are satisfied. Can water be used as the model fluid? Explain and justify your answer.

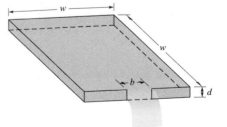

■ **FIGURE P7.42**

7.43 As a liquid drains from an open cylindrical tank through a small orifice in its bottom, the liquid depth, h, decreases with time (see Fig. P7.43). This change in depth as a function of time, t, is to be studied with a one-half scale model. The liquid in the prototype tank has an initial depth, H, of 16 in., a diameter, D, equal to 4.0 in., and an orifice diameter, d, of 0.25 in. The fluid is water at 20 °C. Develop a suitable set of dimensionless parameters for this problem assuming that

$$h = f(H, D, d, \gamma, \rho, t)$$

where γ and ρ are the specific weight and density of the liquid, respectively. Based on these dimensionless parameters, establish the similarity requirements for the model and the prediction equation relating the model depth to the prototype depth.

Some experimental data obtained from a geometrically similar model ($D_m = 2.0$ in., $d_m = 0.125$ in., and $H_m = 8.0$ in.) using water at 20 °C are given in the following table. On a graph, plot the values of the water depth, h_m, as a function of time, t_m. On another graph, plot these data in dimensionless form.

Some prototype data are also given in the following table. On the same graphs used for the model, plot the corresponding prototype data. Based on a comparison of the model data with the prototype data, does the model design seem correct? Explain. The effect of viscosity has been neglected in this experiment. Does this appear to be a reasonable assumption? If viscosity is included as an important variable, how would the model design be affected? Explain.

Model Data		Prototype Data	
h_m (in.)	t_m (s)	h (in.)	t (s)
8.0	0.0	16.0	0.0
7.0	3.1	14.0	4.5
6.0	6.2	12.0	8.9
5.0	9.9	10.0	14.0
4.0	13.5	8.0	20.2
3.0	18.1	6.0	25.9
2.0	24.0	4.0	32.8
1.0	32.5	2.0	45.7
0.0	43.0	0.0	59.8

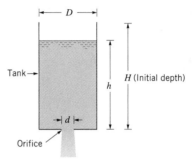

■ **FIGURE P7.43**

CHAPTER

8

Viscous Flow in Pipes

*I*n this chapter we will apply the basic principles concerning mass, momentum, and energy to a specific, important topic—the flow of viscous incompressible fluids in pipes and ducts. Some of the basic components of a typical *pipe system* are shown in Fig. 8.1. They include the pipes themselves (perhaps of more than one diameter), the various fittings used to connect the individual pipes to form the desired system, the flowrate control devices (valves), and the pumps or turbines that add energy to or remove energy from the fluid.

8.1 General Characteristics of Pipe Flow

Before we apply the various governing equations to pipe flow examples, we will discuss some of the basic concepts of pipe flow. Unless otherwise specified, we will assume that the conduit is round, although we will show how to account for other shapes. For all flows involved in this chapter, we assume that the pipe is completely filled with the fluid being transported.

Turbulent jet: The jet of water from the pipe is turbulent. The complex, irregular, unsteady structure typical of turbulent flows is apparent. (Laser-induced fluorescence of dye in water.) (Photography by P. E. Dimotakis, R. C. Lye, and D. Z. Papantoniou.)

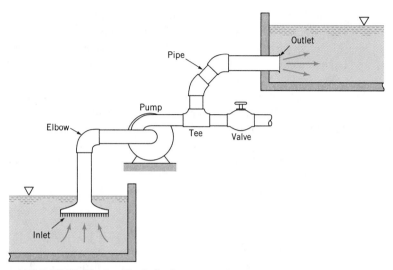

■ **FIGURE 8.1** **Typical pipe system components.**

8.1.1 Laminar or Turbulent Flow

The flow of a fluid in a pipe may be laminar flow or it may be turbulent flow. Osborne Reynolds, a British scientist and mathematician, was the first to distinguish the difference between these two classifications of flow by using a simple apparatus as shown in Fig. 8.2a. For "small enough flowrates" the dye streak (a streakline) will remain as a well-defined line as it flows along, with only slight blurring due to molecular diffusion of the dye into the surrounding water. For a somewhat larger "intermediate flowrate" the dye streak fluctuates in time and space, and intermittent bursts of irregular behavior appear along the streak. On the other hand, for "large enough flowrates" the dye streak almost immediately becomes blurred and spreads across the entire pipe in a random fashion. These three characteristics, denoted as *laminar, transitional,* and *turbulent* flow, respectively, are illustrated in Fig. 8.2b.

V8.1 Laminar/turbulent pipe flow

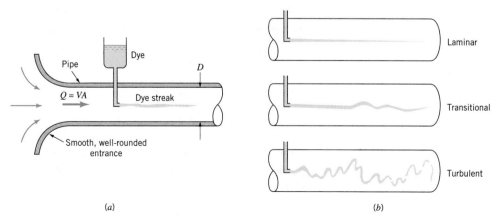

(a) (b)

■ **FIGURE 8.2** *(a)* **Experiment to illustrate type of flow.** *(b)* **Typical dye streaks.**

In the previous paragraph the term flowrate should be replaced by Reynolds number, Re $= \rho VD/\mu$, where V is the average velocity in the pipe. That is, the flow in a pipe is laminar, transitional, or turbulent provided the Reynolds number is "small enough," "intermediate," or "large enough." It is not only the fluid velocity that determines the character of the flow—its density, viscosity, and the pipe size are of equal importance. These parameters combine to produce the Reynolds number. For general engineering purposes (i.e., without undue precautions to eliminate disturbances), the following values are appropriate: The flow in a round pipe is laminar if the Reynolds number is less than approximately 2100. The flow in a round pipe is turbulent if the Reynolds number is greater than approximately 4000. For Reynolds numbers between these two limits, the flow may switch between laminar and turbulent conditions in an apparently random fashion (transitional flow).

EXAMPLE 8.1

Water at a temperature of 50 °F flows through a pipe of diameter $D = 0.73$ in. **(a)** Determine the minimum time taken to fill a 12-oz glass (volume $= 0.0125$ ft^3) with water if the flow in the pipe is to be laminar. **(b)** Determine the maximum time taken to fill the glass if the flow is to be turbulent. Repeat the calculations if the water temperature is 140 °F.

SOLUTION

(a) If the flow in the pipe is to remain laminar, the minimum time to fill the glass will occur if the Reynolds number is the maximum allowed for laminar flow, typically Re $= \rho VD/\mu = 2100$. Thus, $V = 2100\,\mu/\rho D$, where from Table B.1, $\rho = 1.94$ slugs/ft^3 and $\mu = 2.73 \times 10^{-5}$ lb·s/ft^2 at 50 °F, while $\rho = 1.91$ slugs/ft^3 and $\mu = 0.974 \times 10^{-5}$ lb·s/ft^2 at 140 °F. Thus, the maximum average velocity for laminar flow in the pipe is

$$V = \frac{2100\mu}{\rho D} = \frac{2100(2.73 \times 10^{-5}\ \text{lb·s/ft}^2)}{(1.94\ \text{slugs/ft}^3)(0.73/12\ \text{ft})} = 0.486\ \text{lb·s/slug}$$

$$= 0.486\ \text{ft/s}$$

Similarly, $V = 0.176$ ft/s at 140 °F. With $\mathcal{V} =$ volume of glass and $\mathcal{V} = Qt$ we obtain

$$t = \frac{\mathcal{V}}{Q} = \frac{\mathcal{V}}{(\pi/4)D^2 V} = \frac{4(0.0125\ \text{ft}^3)}{(\pi[0.73/12]^2\text{ft}^2)(0.486\ \text{ft/s})}$$

$$= 8.85\ \text{s at}\ T = 50\ °\text{F}$$ \hfill **(Ans)**

Similarly, $t = 24.4$ s at 140 °F. To maintain laminar flow, the less viscous hot water requires a lower flowrate than the cold water.

(b) If the flow in the pipe is to be turbulent, the maximum time to fill the glass will occur if the Reynolds number is the minimum allowed for turbulent flow, Re $= 4000$. Thus, $V = 4000\mu/\rho D = 0.925$ ft/s and $t = 4.65$ s at 50 °F, while $V = 0.335$ ft/s and $t = 12.8$ s at 140°F. \hfill **(Ans)**

Note that because water is "not very viscous," the velocity must be "fairly small" to maintain laminar flow. In general, turbulent flows are encountered more often than laminar flows because of the relatively small viscosity of most common fluids (water, gasoline, air). If the flowing fluid had been honey with a kinematic viscosity ($v = \mu/\rho$) 3000 times greater than that of water, the above velocities would be increased by a factor of 3000 and the times reduced by the same factor. As we will see in the following sections, the pressure needed to force a very viscous fluid through a pipe at such a high velocity may be unreasonably large.

8.1.2 Entrance Region and Fully Developed Flow

Any fluid flowing in a pipe had to enter the pipe at some location. The region of flow near where the fluid enters the pipe is termed the *entrance region* and is illustrated in Fig. 8.3. As shown, the fluid typically enters the pipe with a nearly uniform velocity profile at section (1). As the fluid moves through the pipe, viscous effects cause it to stick to the pipe wall (the no-slip boundary condition). This is true whether the fluid is relatively inviscid air or a very viscous oil. Thus, a *boundary layer* in which viscous effects are important is produced along the pipe wall such that the initial velocity profile changes with distance along the pipe, x, until the fluid reaches the end of the entrance length, section (2), beyond which the velocity profile does not vary with x. The boundary layer has grown in thickness to completely fill the pipe.

The shape of the velocity profile in the pipe depends on whether the flow is laminar or turbulent, as does the *entrance length, ℓ_e.* Typical entrance lengths are given by

$$\frac{\ell_e}{D} = 0.06 \text{ Re for laminar flow} \tag{8.1}$$

and

$$\frac{\ell_e}{D} = 4.4 \, (\text{Re})^{1/6} \text{ for turbulent flow} \tag{8.2}$$

Once the fluid reaches the end of the entrance region, section (2) of Fig. 8.3, the flow is simpler to describe because the velocity is a function of only the distance from the pipe

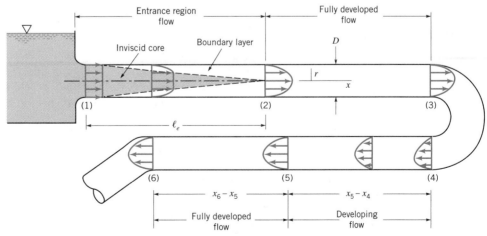

■ **FIGURE 8.3** **Entrance region, developing flow, and fully developed flow in a pipe system.**

centerline, r, and independent of x. This is true until the character of the pipe changes in some way, such as a change in diameter, or the fluid flows through a bend, valve, or some other component at section (3). The flow between (2) and (3) is termed *fully developed*. Beyond the interruption of the fully developed flow [at section (4)], the flow gradually begins its return to its fully developed character [section (5)] and continues with this profile until the next pipe system component is reached [section (6)].

8.2 Fully Developed Laminar Flow

Knowledge of the velocity profile can lead directly to other useful information such as pressure drop, head loss, flowrate, and the like. Thus, we begin by developing the equation for the velocity profile in fully developed laminar flow. If the flow is not fully developed, a theoretical analysis becomes much more complex and is outside the scope of this text. If the flow is turbulent, a rigorous theoretical analysis is as yet not possible.

8.2.1 From F = ma Applied Directly to a Fluid Element

We consider the fluid element at time t as is shown in Fig. 8.4. It is a circular cylinder of fluid of length ℓ and radius r centered on the axis of a horizontal pipe of diameter D. Because the velocity is not uniform across the pipe, the initially flat ends of the cylinder of fluid at time t become distorted at tine $t + \delta t$ when the fluid element has moved to its new location along the pipe as shown in the figure. If the flow is fully developed and steady, the distortion on each end of the fluid element is the same, and no part of the fluid experiences any acceleration as it flows. Every part of the fluid merely flows along its pathline parallel to the pipe walls with constant velocity, although neighboring particles have slightly different velocities. The velocity varies from one pathline to the next. This velocity variation, combined with the fluid viscosity, produces the shear stress.

If gravitational effects are neglected, the pressure is constant across any vertical cross section of the pipe, although it varies along the pipe from one section to the next. Thus, if the pressure is $p = p_1$ at section (1), it is $p_2 = p_1 - \Delta p$ at section (2). We anticipate the fact that the pressure decreases in the direction of flow so that $\Delta p > 0$. A shear stress, τ, acts on the surface of the cylinder of fluid. This viscous stress is a function of the radius of the cylinder, $\tau = \tau(r)$.

As was done in fluid statics analysis (Chapter 2), we isolate the cylinder of fluid as is shown in Fig. 8.5 and apply Newton's second law, $F_x = ma_x$. In this case even though the fluid is moving, it is not accelerating, so that $a_x = 0$. Thus, fully developed horizontal pipe flow is merely a balance between pressure and viscous forces. This can be written as

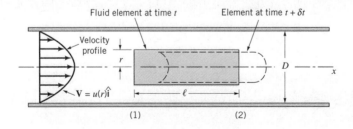

■ FIGURE 8.4
Motion of a cylindrical fluid element within a pipe.

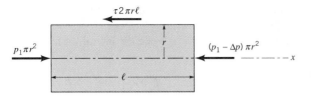

■ **FIGURE 8.5** **Free-body diagram of a cylinder of fluid.**

$$(p_1)\pi r^2 - (p_1 - \Delta p)\pi r^2 - (\tau)2\pi r\ell = 0$$

and simplified to give

$$\frac{\Delta p}{\ell} = \frac{2\tau}{r} \tag{8.3}$$

Since neither Δp nor ℓ are functions of the radial coordinate, r, it follows that $2\tau/r$ must also be independent of r. That is, $\tau = Cr$, where C is a constant. At $r = 0$ (the centerline of the pipe) there is no shear stress ($\tau = 0$). At $r = D/2$ (the pipe wall) the shear stress is a maximum, denoted τ_w, the *wall shear stress*. Hence, $C = 2\tau_w/D$ and the shear stress distribution throughout the pipe is a linear function of the radial coordinate

$$\tau = \frac{2\tau_w r}{D} \tag{8.4}$$

as is indicated in Fig. 8.6. As is seen from Eqs. 8.3 and 8.4, the pressure drop and wall shear stress are related by

$$\Delta p = \frac{4\ell\tau_w}{D} \tag{8.5}$$

To carry the analysis further we must prescribe how the shear stress is related to the velocity. This is the critical step that separates the analysis of laminar from that of turbulent flow—from being able to solve for the laminar flow properties and not being able to solve for the turbulent flow properties without additional ad hoc assumptions. As is discussed in Section 8.3, the shear stress dependence for turbulent flow is very complex. However, for laminar flow of a Newtonian fluid, the shear stress is simply proportional to the velocity gradient, "$\tau = \mu \, du/dy$" (see Section 1.6). In the notation associated with our pipe flow, this becomes

$$\tau = -\mu \frac{du}{dr} \tag{8.6}$$

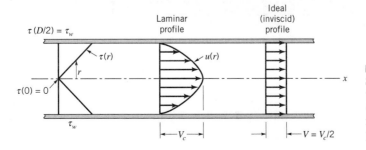

■ **FIGURE 8.6**
Shear stress distribution within the fluid in a pipe (laminar or turbulent flow) and typical velocity profiles.

The negative sign is indicated to give $\tau > 0$ with $du/dr < 0$ (the velocity decreases from the pipe centerline to the pipe wall).

By combining Equations 8.3 (Newton's second law of motion) and 8.6 (the definition of a Newtonian fluid) we obtain

$$\frac{du}{dr} = -\left(\frac{\Delta p}{2\mu\ell}\right) r$$

which can be integrated to give the velocity profile as follows:

$$\int du = -\frac{\Delta p}{2\mu\ell} \int r\, dr$$

or

$$u = -\left(\frac{\Delta p}{4\mu\ell}\right) r^2 + C_1$$

where C_1 is a constant. Because the fluid is viscous it sticks to the pipe wall so that $u = 0$ at $r = D/2$. Hence, $C_1 = (\Delta p/16\mu\ell)D^2$ and the velocity profile can be written as

$$u(r) = \left(\frac{\Delta p D^2}{16\mu\ell}\right)\left[1 - \left(\frac{2r}{D}\right)^2\right] = V_c\left[1 - \left(\frac{2r}{D}\right)^2\right] \tag{8.7}$$

where $V_c = \Delta p D^2/(16\mu\ell)$ is the centerline velocity.

This velocity profile, plotted in Fig. 8.6, is parabolic in the radial coordinate, r, has a maximum velocity, V_c, at the pipe centerline, and a minimum velocity (zero) at the pipe wall. The volume flowrate through the pipe can be obtained by integrating the velocity profile across the pipe. Since the flow is axisymmetric about the centerline, the velocity is constant on small area elements consisting of rings of radius r and thickness dr. Thus,

$$Q = \int u\, dA = \int_{r=0}^{r=R} u(r)2\pi r\, dr = 2\pi V_c \int_0^R \left[1 - \left(\frac{r}{R}\right)^2\right] r\, dr$$

or

$$Q = \frac{\pi R^2 V_c}{2}$$

By definition, the average velocity is the flowrate divided by the cross-sectional area, $V = Q/A = Q/\pi R^2$, so that for this flow

$$V = \frac{\pi R^2 V_c}{2\pi R^2} = \frac{V_c}{2} = \frac{\Delta p D^2}{32\mu\ell} \tag{8.8}$$

and

$$\boxed{Q = \frac{\pi D^4\, \Delta p}{128\mu\ell}} \tag{8.9}$$

This flow is termed *Hagen–Poiseuille flow*. Equation 8.9 is commonly referred to as Poiseuille's law. Recall that all of these results are restricted to laminar flow (those with Reynolds numbers less than approximately 2100) in a horizontal pipe.

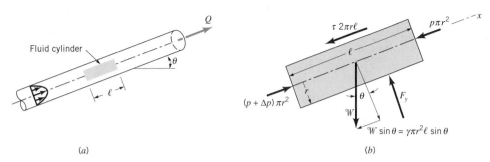

■ **FIGURE 8.7**   **Free-body diagram of a fluid cylinder for flow in a nonhorizontal pipe.**

The adjustment necessary to account for nonhorizontal pipes, as shown in Fig. 8.7, can be easily included by replacing the pressure drop, Δp, by the combined effect of pressure and gravity, $\Delta p - \gamma \ell \sin \theta$, where θ is the angle between the pipe and the horizontal. This can be shown from a force balance in the x direction (along the pipe axis) on the cylinder of fluid. The method is exactly analogous to that used to obtain the Bernoulli equation (Eq. 3.6) when the streamline is not horizontal. Thus, all of the results for the horizontal pipe are valid provided the pressure gradient is adjusted for the elevation term. That is, Δp is replaced by $\Delta p - \gamma \ell \sin \theta$ so that

$$V = \frac{(\Delta p - \gamma \ell \sin \theta)D^2}{32\mu\ell} \tag{8.10}$$

and

$$Q = \frac{\pi(\Delta p - \gamma \ell \sin \theta)D^4}{128\mu\ell} \tag{8.11}$$

It is seen that the driving force for pipe flow can be either a pressure drop in the flow direction, Δp, or the component of weight in the flow direction, $-\gamma \ell \sin \theta$.

EXAMPLE 8.2

An oil with a viscosity of $\mu = 0.40$ N·s/m^2 and density $\rho = 900$ kg/m^3 flows in a pipe of diameter $D = 0.020$ m. **(a)** What pressure drop, $p_1 - p_2$, is needed to produce a flowrate of $Q = 2.0 \times 10^{-5}$ m^3/s if the pipe is horizontal with $x_1 = 0$ and $x_2 = 10$ m? **(b)** How steep a hill, θ, must the pipe be on if the oil is to flow through the pipe at the same rate as in part **(a)**, but with $p_1 = p_2$? **(c)** For the conditions of part **(b)**, if $p_1 = 200$ kPa, what is the pressure at section $x_3 = 5$ m, where x is measured along the pipe?

SOLUTION

(a)   If the Reynolds number is less than 2100 the flow is laminar and the equations derived in this section are valid. Since the average velocity is $V = Q/A = 2.0 \times 10^{-5}$ m^3/s/ $[\pi(0.020)^2\text{m}^2/4] = 0.0637$ m/s, the Reynolds number is Re $= \rho VD/\mu = 2.87 < 2100$.

Hence, the flow is laminar and from Eq. 8.9 with $\ell = x_2 - x_1 = 10$ m, the pressure drop is

$$\Delta p = p_1 - p_2 = \frac{128\mu\ell Q}{\pi D^4}$$

$$= \frac{128(0.40 \text{ N·s/m}^2)(10.0 \text{ m})(2.0 \times 10^{-5} \text{ m}^3/\text{s})}{\pi(0.020 \text{ m})^4}$$

or

$$\Delta p = 20{,}400 \text{ N/m}^2 = 20.4 \text{ kPa} \qquad\qquad \text{(Ans)}$$

(b)   If the pipe is on a hill of angle θ such that $\Delta p = p_1 - p_2 = 0$, Eq. 8.11 gives

$$\sin\theta = -\frac{128\mu Q}{\pi\rho g D^4} \qquad\qquad (1)$$

or

$$\sin\theta = \frac{-128(0.40 \text{ N·s/m}^2)(2.0 \times 10^{-5} \text{ m}^3/\text{s})}{\pi(900 \text{ kg/m}^3)(9.81 \text{ m/s}^2)(0.020 \text{ m})^4}$$

Thus, $\theta = -13.34°$. $\qquad\qquad$ (Ans)
This checks with the previous horizontal result as is seen from the fact that a change in elevation of $\Delta z = \ell \sin\theta = (10 \text{ m}) \sin(-13.34°) = -2.31$ m is equivalent to a pressure change of $\Delta p = \rho g\, \Delta z = (900 \text{ kg/m}^3)(9.81 \text{ m/s}^2)(2.31 \text{ m}) = 20{,}400 \text{ N/m}^2$, which is equivalent to that needed for the horizontal pipe. For the horizontal pipe it is the work done by the pressure forces that overcomes the viscous dissipation. For the zero pressure drop pipe on the hill, it is the change in potential energy of the fluid "falling" down the hill that is converted to the energy lost by viscous dissipation. Note that if it is desired to increase the flowrate to $Q = 1.0 \times 10^{-4}$ m^3/s with $p_1 = p_2$, the value of θ given by Eq. 1 is $\sin\theta = -1.15$. Since the sine of an angle cannot be greater than 1, this flow would not be possible. The weight of the fluid would not be large enough to offset the viscous force generated for the flowrate desired. A larger diameter pipe would be needed.

(c)   With $p_1 = p_2$ the length of the pipe, ℓ, does not appear in the flowrate equation (Eq. 1). This is a statement of the fact that for such cases the pressure is constant all along the pipe (provided the pipe lies on a hill of constant slope). This can be seen by substituting the values of Q and θ from case **(b)** into Eq. 8.11 and noting that $\Delta p = 0$ for any ℓ. For example, $\Delta p = p_1 - p_3 = 0$ if $\ell = x_3 - x_1 = 5$ m. Thus, $p_1 = p_2 = p_3$ so that

$$p_3 = 200 \text{ kPa} \qquad\qquad \text{(Ans)}$$

Note that if the fluid were gasoline ($\mu = 3.1 \times 10^{-4}$ N·s/m^2 and $\rho = 680$ kg/m^3), the Reynolds number would be Re = 2790, the flow would probably not be laminar, and use of Eqs. 8.9 and 8.11 would give incorrect results. Also note from Eq. 1 that the kinematic viscosity, $v = \mu/\rho$, is the important viscous parameter. This is a statement of the fact that with constant pressure along the pipe, it is the ratio of the viscous force ($\sim\mu$) to the weight force ($\sim\gamma = \rho g$) that determines the value of θ.

8.2.2   From the Navier–Stokes Equations

In the previous section we obtained results for fully developed laminar pipe flow by applying Newton's second law and the assumption of a Newtonian fluid to a specific portion of the fluid—a cylinder of fluid centered on the axis of a long round pipe. When this governing law and assumptions are applied to a general fluid flow (not restricted to pipe flow), the result is the Navier–Stokes equations as discussed in Chapter 6. In Section 6.9.3 these equations were solved for the specific geometry of fully developed laminar flow in a round pipe. The results are the same as those given in Eq. 8.7.

8.3   Fully Developed Turbulent Flow

In the previous section various properties of fully developed laminar pipe flow were discussed. Since turbulent pipe flow is actually more likely to occur than laminar flow in practical situations, it is necessary to obtain similar information for turbulent pipe flow. However, turbulent flow is a very complex process. Numerous persons have devoted considerable effort in attempting to understand the variety of baffling aspects of turbulence. Although a considerable amount of knowledge about the topic has been developed, the field of turbulent flow still remains the least understood area of fluid mechanics.

8.3.1   Transition from Laminar to Turbulent Flow

Flows are classified as laminar or turbulent. For any flow geometry, there is one (or more) dimensionless parameter such that with this parameter value below a particular value the flow is laminar, whereas with the parameter value larger than a certain value it is turbulent. For pipe flow this parameter is the Reynolds number. The value of the Reynolds number must be less than approximately 2100 for laminar flow and greater than approximately 4000 for turbulent flow.

A typical trace of the axial component of velocity, $u = u(t)$, measured at a given location in turbulent pipe flow is shown in Fig. 8.8. Its irregular, random nature is the distinguishing feature of turbulent flows. The character of many of the important properties of the

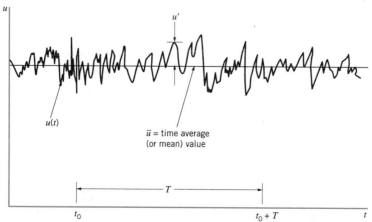

■ **FIGURE 8.8**   **The time averaged, $\bar{u}$, and fluctuating, u', description of a parameter for turbulent flow.**

flow (pressure drop, heat transfer, etc.) depends strongly on the existence and nature of the turbulent fluctuations or randomness indicated.

For example, mixing processes and heat and mass transfer processes are considerably enhanced in turbulent flow compared to laminar flow. This is due to the macroscopic scale of the randomness in turbulent flow. We are all familiar with the "rolling," vigorous eddy type motion of the water in a pan being heated on the stove (even if it is not heated to boiling). Such finite-sized random mixing is very effective in transporting energy and mass throughout the flow field, thereby increasing the various rate processes involved. Laminar flow, on the other hand, can be thought of as very small but finite-sized fluid particles flowing smoothly in layers, one over another. The only randomness and mixing take place on the molecular scale and result in relatively small heat, mass, and momentum transfer rates.

V8.2 Turbulence in a bowl

8.3.2 Turbulent Shear Stress

The fundamental difference between laminar and turbulent flow lies in the chaotic, random behavior of the various fluid parameters. As is indicated in Fig. 8.8, such flows can be described in terms of their mean values (denoted with an overbar) on which are superimposed the fluctuations (denoted with a prime). Thus, if $u = u(x, y, z, t)$ is the x component of instantaneous velocity, then its time mean (or *time average*) value, $\bar{u}$, is

$$\bar{u} = \frac{1}{T} \int_{t_0}^{t_0 + T} u(x, y, z, t) \, dt \tag{8.12}$$

where the time interval, T, is considerably longer than the period of the longest fluctuations, but considerably shorter than any unsteadiness of the average velocity. This is illustrated in Fig. 8.8.

It is tempting to extend the concept of viscous shear stress for laminar flow ($\tau = \mu \, du/dy$) to that of turbulent flow by replacing u, the instantaneous velocity, by $\bar{u}$, the time-average velocity. However, numerous experimental and theoretical studies have shown that such an approach leads to completely incorrect results.

That is, the shear stress in turbulent flow is not merely proportional to the gradient of the time-average velocity: $\tau \neq \mu \, d\bar{u}/dy$. It also contains a contribution due to the random fluctuations of the components of velocity. One could express the shear stress for turbulent flow in terms of a new parameter called the *eddy viscosity*, η, where

$$\tau = \eta \frac{d\bar{u}}{dy} \tag{8.13}$$

Although the concept of an eddy viscosity is intriguing, in practice it is not an easy parameter to use. Unlike the absolute viscosity, μ, which is a known value for a given fluid, the eddy viscosity is a function of both the fluid and the flow conditions. That is, the eddy viscosity of water cannot be looked up in handbooks—its value changes from one turbulent flow condition to another and from one point in a turbulent flow to another.

Several semiempirical theories have been proposed (Ref. 1) to determine approximate values of η. For example, the turbulent process could be viewed as the random transport of bundles of fluid particles over a certain distance, ℓ_m, the *mixing length*, from a region of one velocity to another region of a different velocity. By the use of some ad hoc assumptions and physical reasoning, the eddy viscosity is then given by

$$\eta = \rho \ell_m^2 \left| \frac{d\bar{u}}{dy} \right|$$

Thus, the turbulent shear stress is

$$\tau_{\text{turb}} = \rho \ell_m^2 \left(\frac{d\bar{u}}{dy} \right)^2 \tag{8.14}$$

The problem is thus shifted to that of determining the mixing length, ℓ_m. Further considerations indicate that ℓ_m is not a constant throughout the flow field. Near a solid surface the turbulence is dependent on the distance from the surface. Thus, additional assumptions are made regarding how the mixing length varies throughout the flow.

The net result is that as yet there is no general, all-encompassing, useful model that can accurately predict the shear stress throughout a general incompressible, viscous turbulent flow. Without such information it is impossible to integrate the force balance equation to obtain the turbulent velocity profile and other useful information, as was done for laminar flow.

8.3.3 Turbulent Velocity Profile

Although considerable information concerning turbulent velocity profiles has been obtained through the use of dimensional analysis, experimentation, and semiempirical theoretical efforts, there is still no general accurate expression for turbulent velocity profiles.

An often-used (and relatively easy to use) correlation is the empirical *power-law velocity profile*

$$\frac{\bar{u}}{V_c} = \left(1 - \frac{r}{R} \right)^{1/n} \tag{8.15}$$

V8.3 Laminar/ turbulent velocity profiles

In this representation, the value of n is a function of the Reynolds number, with typical values between $n = 6$ and $n = 10$. Typical turbulent velocity profiles based on this power-law representation are shown in Fig. 8.9. Note that the turbulent profiles are much "flatter" than the laminar profile.

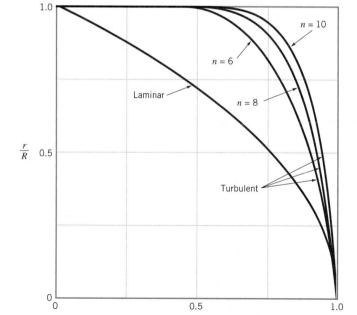

■ FIGURE 8.9
Typical laminar flow and turbulent flow velocity profiles.

A closer examination of Eq. 8.15 shows that the power-law profile cannot be valid near the wall, since according to this equation the velocity gradient is infinite there. In addition, Eq. 8.15 cannot be precisely valid near the centerline because it does not give $d\bar{u}/dr = 0$ at $r = 0$. However, it does provide a reasonable approximation to the measured velocity profiles across most of the pipe.

8.4 Dimensional Analysis of Pipe Flow

As previously noted, turbulent flow can be a very complex, difficult topic—one that as yet has defied a rigorous theoretical treatment. Thus, most turbulent pipe flow analyses are based on experimental data and semiempirical formulas. These data are conveniently expressed in dimensionless form.

8.4.1 The Moody Chart

A dimensional analysis treatment of pipe flow provides the most convenient base from which to consider turbulent, fully developed pipe flow. The pressure drop and head loss in a pipe are dependent on the wall shear stress, τ_w, between the fluid and the pipe surface. A fundamental difference between laminar and turbulent flow is that the shear stress for turbulent flow is a function of the density of the fluid, ρ. For laminar flow, the shear stress is independent of the density, leaving the viscosity, μ, as the only important fluid property.

Thus, the pressure drop, Δp, for steady, incompressible turbulent flow in a horizontal round pipe of diameter D can be written in functional form as

$$\Delta p = F(V, D, \ell, \varepsilon, \mu, \rho) \tag{8.16}$$

where V is the average velocity, ℓ is the pipe length, and ε is a measure of the roughness of the pipe wall. It is clear that Δp should be a function of V, D, and ℓ. The dependence of Δp on the fluid properties μ and ρ is expected because of the dependence of τ on these parameters.

Although the pressure drop for laminar pipe flow is found to be independent of the roughness of the pipe, it is necessary to include this parameter when considering turbulent flow. This can be shown to be due to the random velocity components that account for a momentum transfer (which is a function of the density) and, hence, a shear force.

Since there are seven variables $(k = 7)$ which can be written in terms of the three reference dimensions MLT $(r = 3)$, Eq. 8.16 can be written in dimensionless form in terms of $k - r = 4$ dimensionless groups. One such representation is

$$\frac{\Delta p}{\frac{1}{2}\rho V^2} = \tilde{\phi}\left(\frac{\rho V D}{\mu}, \frac{\ell}{D}, \frac{\varepsilon}{D}\right)$$

This result differs from that used for laminar flow in two ways. First, we have chosen to make the pressure dimensionless by dividing by the dynamic pressure, $\rho V^2/2$, rather than a characteristic viscous shear stress, $\mu V/D$. Second, we have introduced two additional dimensionless parameters, the Reynolds number, $\mathrm{Re} = \rho V D/\mu$, and the *relative roughness*, ε/D, which are not present in the laminar formulation because the two parameters ρ and ε are not important in fully developed laminar pipe flow.

As was done for laminar flow, the functional representation can be simplified by imposing the reasonable assumption that the pressure drop should be proportional to the pipe length. (Such a step is not within the realm of dimensional analysis. It is merely a logical assumption supported by experiments.) The only way that this can be true is if the ℓ/D dependence is factored out as

$$\frac{\Delta p}{\frac{1}{2}\rho V^2} = \frac{\ell}{D} \, \phi \left(\text{Re}, \frac{\varepsilon}{D} \right)$$

The quantity $\Delta p D / (\ell \rho V^2 / 2)$ is termed the friction factor, f. Thus, for a horizontal pipe

$$\Delta p = f \frac{\ell}{D} \frac{\rho V^2}{2} \qquad (8.17)$$

where

$$f = \phi \left(\text{Re}, \frac{\varepsilon}{D} \right)$$

From Eq. 5.57 the energy equation for steady incompressible flow is

$$\frac{p_1}{\gamma} + \frac{V_1^2}{2g} + z_1 = \frac{p_2}{\gamma} + \frac{V_2^2}{2g} + z_2 + h_L$$

where h_L is the head loss between sections (1) and (2). With the assumption of a constant diameter $(D_1 = D_2$ so that $V_1 = V_2)$, horizontal $(z_1 = z_2)$ pipe, this becomes $\Delta p = p_1 - p_2 = \gamma h_L$, which can be combined with Eq. 8.17 to give

$$\boxed{h_L = f \frac{\ell}{D} \frac{V^2}{2g}} \qquad (8.18)$$

Equation 8.18, called the *Darcy–Weisbach equation,* is valid for any fully developed, steady, incompressible pipe flow—whether the pipe is horizontal or on a hill. On the other hand, Eq. 8.17 is valid only for horizontal pipes. In general, with $V_1 = V_2$ the energy equation gives

$$p_1 - p_2 = \gamma(z_2 - z_1) + \gamma h_L = \gamma(z_2 - z_1) + f \frac{\ell}{D} \frac{\rho V^2}{2}$$

Part of the pressure change is due to the elevation change and part is due to the head loss associated with frictional effects, which are given in terms of the friction factor, f.

It is not easy to determine the functional dependence of the friction factor on the Reynolds number and relative roughness. Much of this information is a result of experiments. Figure 8.10 shows the functional dependence of f on Re and ε/D and is called the *Moody chart.* Typical roughness values for various new, clean pipe surfaces are given in Table 8.1.

The following characteristics are observed from the data of Fig. 8.10. For laminar flow, $f = 64/\text{Re}$, which is independent of relative roughness. For very large Reynolds numbers, $f = \phi(\varepsilon/D)$, which is independent of the Reynolds number. Such flows are commonly termed *completely turbulent flow* (or *wholly turbulent flow*). For flows with moderate values of Re, the friction factor is indeed dependent on both the Reynolds number and relative roughness— $f = \phi(\text{Re}, \varepsilon/D)$. Note that even for *hydraulically smooth* pipes $(\varepsilon = 0)$ the friction factor is not zero. That is, there is a head loss in any pipe, no matter how smooth the surface is made.

The following equation is valid for the entire nonlaminar range of the Moody chart

$$\frac{1}{\sqrt{f}} = -2.0 \log \left(\frac{\varepsilon/D}{3.7} + \frac{2.51}{\text{Re}\sqrt{f}} \right) \qquad (8.19)$$

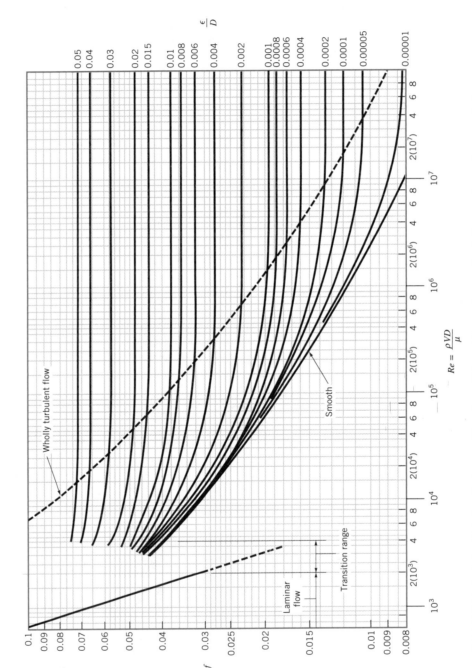

■ **FIGURE 8.10** Friction factor as a function of Reynolds number and relative roughness for round pipes—the Moody chart (Data from Ref. 2 with permission).

■ **TABLE 8.1**
Equivalent Roughness for New Pipes [from Moody
(Ref. 2) and Colebrook (Ref. 3)].

Pipe	Equivalent Roughness, ε	
	Feet	Millimeters
Riveted steel	0.003–0.03	0.9–9.0
Concrete	0.001–0.01	0.3–3.0
Wood stave	0.0006–0.003	0.18–0.9
Cast iron	0.00085	0.26
Galvanized iron	0.0005	0.15
Commercial steel or wrought iron	0.00015	0.045
Drawn tubing	0.000005	0.0015
Plastic, glass	0.0 (smooth)	0.0 (smooth)

In fact, the Moody chart is a graphical representation of this equation, which is an empirical fit of the pipe flow pressure drop data. Equation 8.19 is called the *Colebrook formula.* A difficulty with its use is that it is implicit in the dependence of *f.* That is, for given conditions (Re and ε/D), it is not possible to solve for *f* without some sort of iterative scheme. With the use of modern computers and calculators, such calculations are not difficult.

EXAMPLE 8.3

Air under standard conditions flows through a 4.0-mm-diameter drawn tubing with an average velocity of $V = 50$ m/s. For such conditions the flow would normally be turbulent. However, if precautions are taken to eliminate disturbances to the flow (the entrance to the tube is very smooth, the air is dust-free, the tube does not vibrate, etc.), it may be possible to maintain laminar flow. **(a)** Determine the pressure drop in a 0.1-m section of the tube if the flow is laminar. **(b)** Repeat the calculations if the flow is turbulent.

SOLUTION

Under standard temperature and pressure conditions the density and viscosity are $\rho = 1.23$ kg/m³ and $\mu = 1.79 \times 10^{-5}$ N·s/m². Thus, the Reynolds number is

$$\text{Re} = \frac{\rho V D}{\mu} = \frac{(1.23 \text{ kg/m}^3)(50 \text{ m/s})(0.004 \text{ m})}{1.79 \times 10^{-5} \text{ N·s/m}^2} = 13,700$$

which would normally indicate turbulent flow.
(a) If the flow were laminar, then $f = 64/\text{Re} = 64/13,700 = 0.00467$ and the pressure drop in a 0.1-m-long horizontal section of the pipe would be

$$\Delta p = f \frac{\ell}{D} \frac{1}{2} \rho V^2 = (0.00467) \frac{(0.1 \text{ m})}{(0.004 \text{ m})} \frac{1}{2} (1.23 \text{ kg/m}^3)(50 \text{ m/s})^2$$

or

$$\Delta p = 0.179 \text{ kPa} \qquad \text{(Ans)}$$

Note that the same result is obtained from Eq. 8.8.

$$\Delta p = \frac{32\mu\ell}{D^2}V = \frac{32(1.79 \times 10^{-5} \text{ N·s/m}^2)(0.1 \text{ m})(50 \text{ m/s})}{(0.004 \text{ m})^2} = 179 \text{ N/m}^2$$

(b) If the flow were turbulent, then $f = \phi(\text{Re}, \varepsilon/D)$, where from Table 8.1, $\varepsilon = 0.0015$ mm so that $\varepsilon/D = 0.0015$ mm/4.0 mm $= 0.000375$. From the Moody chart with Re $= 1.37 \times 10^4$ and $\varepsilon/D = 0.000375$ we obtain $f = 0.028$. Thus, the pressure drop in this case would be approximately

$$\Delta p = f\frac{\ell}{D}\frac{1}{2}\rho V^2 = (0.028)\frac{(0.1 \text{ m})}{(0.004 \text{ m})}\frac{1}{2}(1.23 \text{ kg/m}^3)(50 \text{ m/s})^2$$

or

$$\Delta p = 1.076 \text{ kPa} \qquad \text{(Ans)}$$

A considerable savings in effort to force the fluid through the pipe could be realized (0.179 kPa rather than 1.076 kPa) if the flow could be maintained as laminar flow at this Reynolds number. In general this is very difficult to do, although laminar flow in pipes has been maintained up to Re $\approx$ 100,000 in rare instances.

An alternate method to determine the friction factor for the turbulent flow would be to use the Colebrook formula, Eq. 8.19. Thus,

$$\frac{1}{\sqrt{f}} = -2.0 \log\left(\frac{\varepsilon/D}{3.7} + \frac{2.51}{\text{Re}\sqrt{f}}\right) = -2.0 \log\left(\frac{0.000375}{3.7} + \frac{2.51}{1.37 \times 10^4\sqrt{f}}\right)$$

or

$$\frac{1}{\sqrt{f}} = -2.0 \log\left(1.01 \times 10^{-4} + \frac{1.83 \times 10^{-4}}{\sqrt{f}}\right) \qquad \textbf{(1)}$$

An iterative procedure to obtain f can be done as follows. We assume a value of f ($f = 0.02$, for example), substitute it into the right-hand side of Eq. 1, and calculate a new f ($f = 0.0307$ in this case). Since the two values do not agree, the assumed value is not the solution. Hence, we try again. This time we assume $f = 0.0307$ (the last value calculated) and calculate the new value as $f = 0.0289$. Again this is still not the solution. Two more iterations show that the assumed and calculated values converge to the solution $f = 0.0291$, in agreement (within the accuracy of reading the graph) with the Moody chart method of $f = 0.028$.

Numerous other empirical formulas can be found in the literature (Ref. 4) for portions of the Moody chart. For example, an often-used equation, commonly referred to as the Blasius formula, for turbulent flow in smooth pipes ($\varepsilon/D = 0$) with Re $< 10^5$ is

$$f = \frac{0.316}{\text{Re}^{1/4}}$$

For our case this gives

$$f = 0.316(13,700)^{-0.25} = 0.0292$$

which is in agreement with the previous results. Note that the value of f is relatively insensitive to ε/D for this particular situation. Whether the tube was smooth glass ($\varepsilon/D = 0$) or the drawn tubing ($\varepsilon/D = 0.000375$) would not make much difference in the pressure drop. For this flow, an increase in relative roughness by a factor of 30 to $\varepsilon/D = 0.0113$ (equivalent to a commercial steel surface; see Table 8.1) would give $f = 0.043$. This would represent an increase in pressure drop and head loss by a factor of $0.043/0.0291 = 1.48$ compared with that for the original drawn tubing.

The pressure drop of 1.076 kPa in a length of 0.1 m of pipe corresponds to a change in absolute pressure [assuming $p = 101$ kPa (abs) at $x = 0$] of approximately $1.076/101 = 0.0107$, or about 1%. Thus, the incompressible flow assumption on which the above calculations (and all of the formulas in this chapter) are based is reasonable. However, if the pipe were 2-m long the pressure drop would be 21.5 kPa, approximately 20% of the original pressure. In this case the density would not be approximately constant along the pipe, and a compressible flow analysis would be needed.

8.4.2 Minor Losses

Most pipe systems consist of more than straight pipes. These additional components (valves, bends, tees, and the like) add to the overall head loss of the system. Such losses are generally termed *minor losses*. Straight pipe friction losses are termed *major losses*. In this section we indicate how to determine losses that commonly occur in pipe systems.

Head loss information for essentially all components is given in dimensionless form and based on experimental data. The most common method used to determine these head losses or pressure drops is to specify the *loss coefficient, K_L*, which is defined as

$$K_L = \frac{h_L}{(V^2/2g)} = \frac{\Delta p}{\frac{1}{2}\rho V^2}$$

so that

$$\Delta p = K_L \frac{1}{2}\rho V^2$$

or

$$h_L = K_L \frac{V^2}{2g} \tag{8.20}$$

The pressure drop across a component that has a loss coefficient of $K_L = 1$ is equal to the dynamic pressure, $\rho V^2/2$.

Many pipe systems contain various transition sections in which the pipe diameter changes from one size to another. Any change in flow area contributes losses that are not accounted for in the fully developed head loss calculation (the friction factor). The extreme cases involve flow into a pipe from a reservoir (an entrance) or out of a pipe into a reservoir (an exit).

A fluid may flow from a reservoir into a pipe through any number of different shaped entrance regions as are sketched in Fig. 8.11. Each geometry has an associated loss coefficient. An obvious way to reduce the entrance loss is to round the entrance region as is shown in Fig. 8.11c. Typical values for the loss coefficient for entrances with various amounts of

V8.4 Entrance/ exit flows

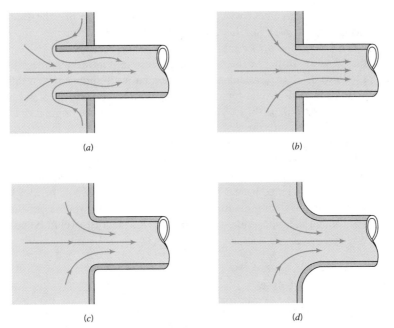

(a) (b)

(c) (d)

■ FIGURE 8.11 **Entrance flow conditions and loss coefficient (Refs. 12, 13). (a) Reentrant, $K_L = 0.8$, (b) sharp-edged, $K_L = 0.5$, (c) slightly rounded, $K_L = 0.2$ (see Fig. 8.12), (d) well-rounded, $K_L = 0.04$ (see Fig. 8.12).**

rounding of the lip are shown in Fig. 8.12. A significant reduction in K_L can be obtained with only slight rounding.

A head loss (the exit loss) is also produced when a fluid flows from a pipe into a tank as is shown in Fig. 8.13. In these cases the entire kinetic energy of the exiting fluid (velocity V_1) is dissipated through viscous effects as the stream of fluid mixes with the fluid in the tank and eventually comes to rest $(V_2 = 0)$. The exit loss from points (1) and (2) is therefore equivalent to one velocity head, or $K_L = 1$.

Losses also occur because of a change in pipe diameter. The loss coefficient for a sudden contraction, $K_L = h_L/(V_2^2/2g)$, is a function of the area ratio, A_2/A_1, as is shown in Fig. 8.14. The value of K_L changes gradually from one extreme of a sharp-edged entrance

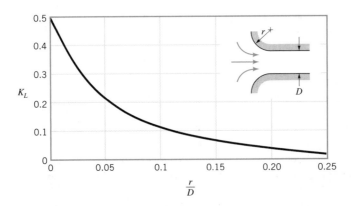

■ FIGURE 8.12
Entrance loss coefficient as a function of rounding of the inlet edge (Ref. 5).

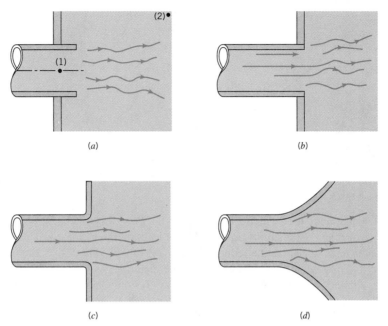

■ **FIGURE 8.13**   **Exit flow conditions and loss coefficient.**
(*a*) **Reentrant,** $K_L = 1.0$, (*b*) **sharp-edged,** $K_L = 1.0$, (*c*) **slightly
rounded,** $K_L = 1.0$, (*d*) **well rounded,** $K_L = 1.0$.

$(A_2/A_1 = 0$ with $K_L = 0.50)$ to the other extreme of no area change $(A_2/A_1 = 1$ with $K_L = 0)$.
The loss coefficient for a sudden expansion is shown in Fig. 8.15.

Bends in pipes produce a greater head loss than if the pipe were straight. The losses
are due to the separated region of flow near the inside of the bend (especially if the bend is
sharp) and the swirling secondary flow that occurs because of the imbalance of centripetal
forces as a result of the curvature of the pipe centerline. These effects and the associated
values of K_L for large Reynolds number flows through a 90° bend are shown in Fig. 8.16.
The friction loss due to the axial length of the pipe bend must be calculated and added to
that given by the loss coefficient of Fig. 8.16.

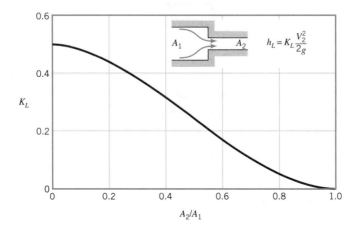

■ **FIGURE 8.14**
**Loss coefficient for a sud-
den contraction (Ref. 6).**

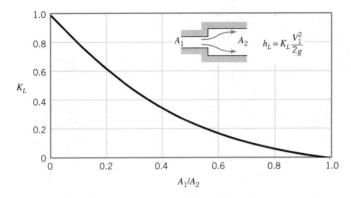

■ **FIGURE 8.15**
Loss coefficient for a sudden expansion (Ref. 6).

V8.5 Car exhaust system

For situations in which space is limited, a flow direction change is often accomplished by use of miter bends, as is shown in Fig. 8.17, rather than smooth bends. The considerable losses in such bends can be reduced by the use of carefully designed guide vanes that help direct the flow with less unwanted swirl and disturbances.

Another important category of pipe system components is that of commercially available pipe fittings such as elbows, tees, reducers, valves, and filters. The values of K_L for such components depend strongly on the shape of the component and only very weakly on the Reynolds number for typical large Re flows. Thus, the loss coefficient for a 90° elbow depends on whether the pipe joints are threaded or flanged, but is, within the accuracy of the data, fairly independent of the pipe diameter, flow rate, or fluid properties (the Reynolds number effect). Typical values of K_L for such components are given in Table 8.2.

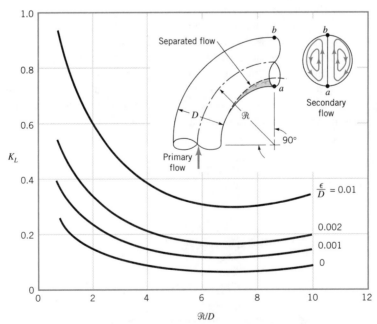

■ **FIGURE 8.16**   **Character of the flow in a 90° bend and the associated loss coefficient (Ref. 4).**

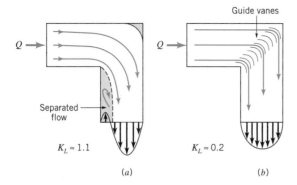

$K_L \approx 1.1$

(a)

$K_L \approx 0.2$

(b)

■ **FIGURE 8.17** **Character of the flow in a 90° miter bend and the associated loss coefficient:** (a) **without guide vanes.** (b) **with guide vanes.**

■ **TABLE 8.2**

Loss Coefficients for Pipe Components $\left(h_L = K_L \dfrac{V^2}{2g} \right)$ **(Data from Refs. 4, 6, 11)**

Component	K_L
a. Elbows	
Regular 90°, flanged	0.3
Regular 90°, threaded	1.5
Long radius 90°, flanged	0.2
Long radius 90°, threaded	0.7
Long radius 45°, flanged	0.2
Regular 45°, threaded	0.4
b. 180° return bends	
180° return bend, flanged	0.2
180° return bend, threaded	1.5
c. Tees	
Line flow, flanged	0.2
Line flow, threaded	0.9
Branch flow, flanged	1.0
Branch flow, threaded	2.0
d. Union, threaded	0.08
*e. Valves	
Globe, fully open	10
Angle, fully open	2
Gate, fully open	0.15
Gate, $\frac{1}{4}$ closed	0.26
Gate, $\frac{1}{2}$ closed	2.1
Gate, $\frac{3}{4}$ closed	17
Swing check, forward flow	2
Swing check, backward flow	∞
Ball valve, fully open	0.05
Ball valve, $\frac{1}{3}$ closed	5.5
Ball valve, $\frac{2}{3}$ closed	210

*See Fig. 8.18 for typical valve geometry

325

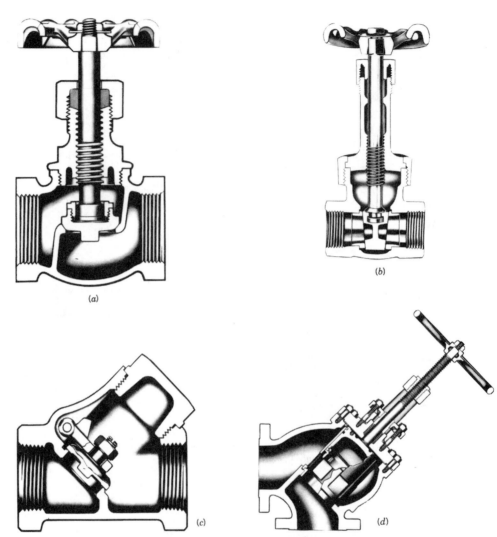

■ **FIGURE 8.18**   **Internal structure of various valves: (a) globe valve, (b) gate valve, (c) swing check valve, (d) stop check valve (courtesy of Crane Co., Valve Division).**

Valves control the flowrate by providing a means to adjust the overall system loss coefficient to the desired value. When the valve is closed, the value of K_L is infinite and no fluid flows. Opening of the valve reduces K_L, producing the desired flowrate. Typical cross-sections of various types of valves are shown in Fig. 8.18. Loss coefficients for typical valves are given in Table 8.2.

*E*XAMPLE 8.4

Air at standard conditions is to flow through the test section [between sections (5) and (6)] of the closed-circuit wind tunnel shown in Fig. E8.4 with a velocity of 200 ft/s. The flow is driven by a fan that essentially increases the static pressure by the amount $p_1 - p_9$ that is

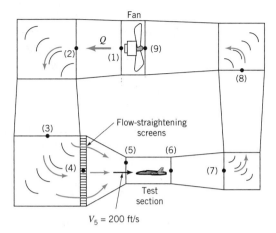

Fan

Q

(2) (1) (9)

(8)

(3)

Flow-straightening screens

(5) (6)

(4) (7)

Test section

$V_5 = 200$ ft/s

■ FIGURE E8.4

needed to overcome the head losses experienced by the fluid as it flows around the circuit. Estimate the value of $p_1 - p_9$ and the horsepower supplied to the fluid by the fan.

SOLUTION

The maximum velocity within the wind tunnel occurs in the test section (smallest area). Thus, the maximum Mach number of the flow is $\text{Ma}_5 = V_5/c_5$, where $V_5 = 200$ ft/s and from Eq. 1.15 the speed of sound is $c_5 = (kRT_5)^{1/2} = \{1.4(1716 \text{ ft·lb/slug·°R})[(460 + 59)°R]\}^{1/2} = 1117$ ft/s. Thus, $\text{Ma}_5 = 200/1117 = 0.179$. As was indicated in Chapter 3, most flows can be considered as incompressible if the Mach number is less than about 0.3. Hence, we can use the incompressible formulas for this problem.

The purpose of the fan in the wind tunnel is to provide the necessary energy to overcome the net head loss experienced by the air as it flows around the circuit. This can be found from the energy equation between points (1) and (9) as

$$\frac{p_1}{\gamma} + \frac{V_1^2}{2g} + z_1 = \frac{p_9}{\gamma} + \frac{V_9^2}{2g} + z_9 + h_{L_{1-9}}$$

where $h_{L_{1-9}}$ is the total head loss from (1) to (9). With $z_1 = z_9$ and $V_1 = V_9$ this gives

$$\frac{p_1}{\gamma} - \frac{p_9}{\gamma} = h_{L_{1-9}} \tag{1}$$

Similarly, by writing the energy equation (Eq. 5.57) across the fan, from (9) to (1), we obtain

$$\frac{p_9}{\gamma} + \frac{V_9^2}{2g} + z_9 + h_p = \frac{p_1}{\gamma} + \frac{V_1^2}{2g} + z_9$$

where h_p is the actual head rise supplied by the pump (fan) to the air. Again since $z_9 = z_1$ and $V_9 = V_1$ this, when combined with Eq. 1, becomes

$$h_p = \frac{(p_1 - p_9)}{\gamma} = h_{L_{1-9}}$$

The actual power supplied to the air (horsepower, $\mathcal{P}_a$) is obtained from the fan head by

$$\mathcal{P}_a = \gamma Q h_p = \gamma A_5 V_5 h_p = \gamma A_5 V_5 h_{L_{1-9}} \tag{2}$$

Thus, the power that the fan must supply to the air depends on the head loss associated with the flow through the wind tunnel. To obtain a reasonable, approximate answer we make the following assumptions. We treat each of the four turning corners as a mitered bend with guide vanes so that from Fig. 8.17 $K_{L_{corner}} = 0.2$. Thus, for each corner

$$h_{L_{corner}} = K_L \frac{V^2}{2g} = 0.2 \frac{V^2}{2g}$$

where, because the flow is assumed incompressible, $V = V_5 A_5/A$. The values of A and the corresponding velocities throughout the tunnel are given in Table E8.4.

■ **TABLE E8.4**

Location	Area (ft²)	Velocity (ft/s)
1	22.0	36.4
2	28.0	28.6
3	35.0	22.9
4	35.0	22.9
5	4.0	200.0
6	4.0	200.0
7	10.0	80.0
8	18.0	44.4
9	22.0	36.4

We also treat the enlarging sections from the end of the test section (6) to the beginning of the nozzle (4) as a conical diffuser with a loss coefficient of $K_{L_{dif}} = 0.6$. This value is larger than that of a well-designed diffuser (see Ref. 4, for example). Since the wind tunnel diffuser is interrupted by the four turning corners and the fan, it may not be possible to obtain a smaller value of $K_{L_{dif}}$ for this situation. Thus,

$$h_{L_{dif}} = K_{L_{dif}} \frac{V_6^2}{2g} = 0.6 \frac{V_6^2}{2g}$$

The loss coefficients for the conical nozzle between section (4) and (5) and the flow-straightening screens are assumed to be $K_{L_{noz}} = 0.2$ and $K_{L_{scr}} = 0.4$ (Ref. 14), respectively. We neglect the head loss in the relatively short test section.

Thus, the total head loss is

$$h_{L_{1-9}} = h_{L_{corner7}} + h_{L_{corner8}} + h_{L_{corner2}} + h_{L_{corner3}} + h_{L_{dif}} + h_{L_{noz}} + h_{L_{scr}}$$

or

$$\begin{aligned}
h_{L_{1-9}} &= [0.2(V_7^2 + V_8^2 + V_2^2 + V_3^2) + 0.6V_6^2 + 0.2V_5^2 + 4.0V_4^2]/2g \\
&= [0.2(80.0^2 + 44.4^2 + 28.6^2 + 22.9^2) + 0.6(200)^2 \\
&\quad + 0.2(200)^2 + 4.0(22.9)^2] \text{ ft}^2/\text{s}^2/[2(32.2 \text{ ft/s}^2)]
\end{aligned}$$

or

$$h_{L_{1-9}} = 560 \text{ ft}$$

Hence, from Eq. 1 we obtain the pressure rise across the fan as

$$\begin{aligned}
p_1 - p_9 &= \gamma h_{L_{1-9}} = (0.0765 \text{ lb/ft}^3)(560 \text{ ft}) \\
&= 42.8 \text{ lb/ft}^2 = 0.298 \text{ psi}
\end{aligned}$$

(Ans)

From Eq. 2 we obtain the power added to the fluid as

$$\mathcal{P}_a = (0.0765 \text{ lb/ft}^3)(4.0 \text{ ft}^2)(200 \text{ ft/s})(560 \text{ ft}) = 34,300 \text{ ft·lb/s}$$

or

$$\mathcal{P}_a = \frac{34,300 \text{ ft·lb/s}}{550 \text{ (ft·lb/s)/hp}} = 62.3 \text{ hp} \qquad \text{(Ans)}$$

With a closed-return wind tunnel of this type, all of the power required to maintain the flow is dissipated through viscous effects, with the energy remaining within the closed tunnel. If heat transfer across the tunnel walls is negligible, the air temperature within the tunnel will increase in time. For steady-state operations of such tunnels, it is often necessary to provide some means of cooling to maintain the temperature at acceptable levels.

It should be noted that the actual size of the motor that powers the fan must be greater than the calculated 62.3 hp because the fan is not 100% efficient. The power calculated above is that needed by the fluid to overcome losses in the tunnel, excluding those in the fan. If the fan were 60% efficient, it would require a shaft power of $\mathcal{P} = 62.3 \text{ hp}/(0.60) = 104 \text{ hp}$ to run the fan. Determination of fan (or pump) efficiencies can be a complex problem that depends on the specific geometry of the fan. Introductory material about fan performance can be found in various references (Refs. 7, 8, 9, for example).

It should also be noted that the above results are only approximate. Clever, careful design of the various components (corners, diffuser, etc.) may lead to improved (i.e., lower) values of the various loss coefficients, and hence lower power requirements. Since h_L is proportional to V^2, the components with the larger V tend to have the larger head loss. Thus, even though $K_L = 0.2$ for each of the four corners, the head loss for corner (7) is $(V_7/V_3)^2 = (80/22.9)^2 = 12.2$ times greater than it is for corner (3).

8.4.3 Noncircular Conduits

Many of the conduits that are used for conveying fluids are not circular in cross section. Although the details of the flows in such conduits depend on the exact cross-sectional shape, many round pipe results can be carried over, with slight modification, to flow in conduits of other shapes.

Practical, easy-to-use results can be obtained by introducing the *hydraulic diameter.* $D_h = 4A/P$, defined as four times the ratio of the cross-sectional flow area divided by the wetted perimeter, P, of the pipe as is illustrated in Fig. 8.19. The hydraulic diameter is used

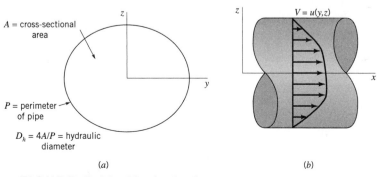

A = cross-sectional area

P = perimeter of pipe

$D_h = 4A/P$ = hydraulic diameter

$V = u(y,z)$

(a)   (b)

■ FIGURE 8.19 **Noncircular duct.**

in the definition of the friction factor, $h_L = f(\ell/D_h)V^2/2g$, the Reynolds number, $\mathrm{Re}_h = \rho V D_h/\mu$, and the relative roughness, ε/D_h.

Calculations for fully developed turbulent flow in ducts of noncircular cross section are usually carried out by using the Moody chart data for round pipes with the diameter replaced by the hydraulic diameter as indicated above. For turbulent flow such calculations are usually accurate to within about 15%. If greater accuracy is needed, a more detailed analysis based on the specific geometry of interest is needed.

EXAMPLE 8.5

Air at a temperature of 120 °F and standard pressure flows from a furnace through an 8-in.-diameter pipe with an average velocity of 10 ft/s. It then passes through a transition section and into a square duct whose side is of length a. The pipe and duct surfaces are smooth ($\varepsilon = 0$). Determine the duct size, a, if the head loss per foot is to be the same for the pipe and the duct.

SOLUTION

We first determine the head loss per foot for the pipe, $h_L/\ell = (f/D)V^2/2g$, and then size the square duct to give the same value. For the given pressure and temperature we obtain (from Table B.3) $\nu = 1.89 \times 10^{-4}$ ft^2/s so that

$$\mathrm{Re} = \frac{VD}{\nu} = \frac{(10 \text{ ft/s})(\frac{8}{12} \text{ ft})}{1.89 \times 10^{-4} \text{ ft}^2/\text{s}} = 35{,}300$$

With this Reynolds number and with $\varepsilon/D = 0$ we obtain the friction factor from Fig. 8.10 as $f = 0.022$ so that

$$\frac{h_L}{\ell} = \frac{0.022}{(\frac{8}{12} \text{ ft})} \frac{(10 \text{ ft/s})^2}{2(32.2 \text{ ft/s}^2)} = 0.0512$$

Thus, for the square duct we must have

$$\frac{h_L}{\ell} = \frac{f}{D_h} \frac{V_s^2}{2g} = 0.0512 \tag{1}$$

where

$$D_h = 4A/P = 4a^2/4a = a \quad \text{and}$$

$$V_s = \frac{Q}{A} = \frac{\frac{\pi}{4}\left(\frac{8}{12} \text{ ft}\right)^2 (10 \text{ ft/s})}{a^2} = \frac{3.49}{a^2} \tag{2}$$

is the velocity in the duct.

By combining Eqs. 1 and 2 we obtain

$$0.0512 = \frac{f}{a} \frac{(3.49/a^2)^2}{2(32.2)}$$

or

$$a = 1.30 f^{1/5} \qquad (3)$$

where a is in feet. Similarly, the Reynolds number based on the hydraulic diameter is

$$\mathrm{Re}_h = \frac{V_s D_h}{\nu} = \frac{(3.49/a^2)a}{1.89 \times 10^{-4}} = \frac{1.85 \times 10^4}{a} \qquad (4)$$

We have three unknowns (a, f, and Re_h) and three equations (Eqs. 3, 4, and the third equation in graphical form, Fig. 8.10, the Moody chart). Thus, a trial-and-error solution is required.

As an initial attempt, assume the friction factor for the duct is the same as for the pipe. That is, assume $f = 0.022$. From Eq. 3 we obtain $a = 0.606$ ft, while from Eq. 4 we have $\mathrm{Re}_h = 3.05 \times 10^4$. From Fig. 8.10, with this Reynolds number and the given smooth duct we obtain $f = 0.023$, which does not quite agree with the assumed value of f. Hence, we do not have the solution. We try again, using the latest calculated value of $f = 0.023$ as our guess. The calculations are repeated until the guessed value of f agrees with the value obtained from Fig. 8.10. The final result (after only two iterations) is $f = 0.023$, $\mathrm{Re}_h = 3.03 \times 10^4$, and

$$a = 0.611 \text{ ft} = 7.34 \text{ in.} \qquad \textbf{(Ans)}$$

Note that the length of the side of the equivalent square duct is $a/D = 7.34/8 = 0.918$, or approximately 92% of the diameter of the equivalent duct. It can be shown that this value, 92%, is a very good approximation for any pipe flow—laminar or turbulent. The cross-sectional area of the duct ($A = a^2 = 53.9$ in.^{2}) is greater than that of the round pipe ($A = \pi D^2/4 = 50.3$ in.^{2}). Also, it takes less material to form the round pipe (perimeter $= \pi D = 25.1$ in.) than the square duct (perimeter $= 4a = 29.4$ in.). Circles are very efficient shapes.

8.5   Pipe Flow Examples

In the previous sections of this chapter we discussed concepts concerning flow in pipes and ducts. The purpose of this section is to apply these ideas to the solutions of various practical problems.

8.5.1   Single Pipes

The nature of the solution process for pipe flow problems can depend strongly on which of the various parameters are independent parameters (the "given") and which is the dependent parameter (the "determine"). The three most common types of problems are discussed below.

In a Type I problem we specify the desired flowrate or average velocity and determine the necessary pressure difference or head loss. For example, if a flowrate of 2.0 gal/min is required for a dishwasher that is connected to the water heater by a given pipe system, what pressure is needed in the water heater?

In a Type II problem we specify the applied driving pressure (or, alternatively, the head loss) and determine the flowrate. For example, how many gal/min of hot water are supplied to the dishwasher if the pressure within the water heater is 60 psi and the pipe system details (length, diameter, roughness of the pipe; number of elbows; etc.) are specified?

In a Type III problem we specify the pressure drop and the flowrate and determine the diameter of the pipe needed. For example, what diameter of pipe is needed between the water heater and dishwasher if the pressure in the water heater is 60 psi (determined by the city water system) and the flowrate is to be not less than 2.0 gal/min (determined by the manufacturer)?

EXAMPLE 8.6 (TYPE I, DETERMINE PRESSURE DROP)

Water at 60 °F flows from the basement to the second floor through the 0.75-in. (0.0625-ft-)-diameter copper pipe (a drawn tubing) at a rate of $Q = 12.0$ gal/min $= 0.0267$ ft^3/s and exits through a faucet of diameter 0.50 in. as shown in Fig. E8.6a. Determine the pressure at point (1) if: **(a)** all losses are neglected, **(b)** the only losses included are major losses, or **(c)** all losses are included.

SOLUTION

Since the fluid velocity in the pipe is given by $V_1 = Q/A_1 = Q/(\pi D^2/4) = (0.0267$ ft^3/s)/$[\pi(0.0625$ ft)$^2/4] = 8.70$ ft/s, and the fluid properties are $\rho = 1.94$ slugs/ft^3 and $\mu = 2.34 \times 10^{-5}$ lb·s/ft^2 (see Table B.1), it follows that Re $= \rho VD/\mu = (1.94$ slugs/ft$^3)(8.70$ ft/s)$(0.0625$ ft)/$(2.34 \times 10^{-5}$ lb·s/ft$^2) = 45,000$. Thus, the flow is turbulent. The governing equation for either case **(a)**, **(b)**, or **(c)** is the following form of the energy equation,

$$\frac{p_1}{\gamma} + \alpha_1 \frac{V_1^2}{2g} + z_1 = \frac{p_2}{\gamma} + \alpha_2 \frac{V_2^2}{2g} + z_2 + h_L$$

where $z_1 = 0$, $z_2 = 20$ ft, $p_2 = 0$ (free jet), $\gamma = \rho g = 62.4$ lb/ft^3, and the outlet velocity is $V_2 = Q/A_2 = (0.0267$ ft^3/s)/$[\pi(0.50/12)^2$ft$^2/4] = 19.6$ ft/s. We assume that the kinetic energy coefficients α_1 and α_2 are unity. This is reasonable because turbulent velocity profiles are nearly uniform across the pipe (see Section 5.3.4). Thus,

$$p_1 = \gamma z_2 + \tfrac{1}{2}\rho(V_2^2 - V_1^2) + \gamma h_L \tag{1}$$

where the head loss is different for each of the three cases.

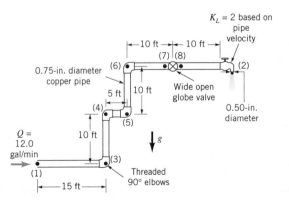

$K_L = 2$ based on pipe velocity

■ FIGURE E8.6a

(a) If all losses are neglected ($h_L = 0$), Eq. 1 gives

$$p_1 = (62.4 \text{ lb/ft}^3)(20 \text{ ft})$$
$$+ \frac{1.94 \text{ slugs/ft}^3}{2}\left[\left(19.6 \frac{\text{ft}}{\text{s}}\right)^2 - \left(8.70 \frac{\text{ft}}{\text{s}}\right)^2\right]$$
$$= (1248 + 299) \text{ lb/ft}^2 = 1547 \text{ lb/ft}^2$$

or

$$p_1 = 10.7 \text{ psi} \qquad \text{(Ans)}$$

Note that for this pressure drop, the amount due to elevation change (the hydrostatic effect) is $\gamma(z_2 - z_1) = 8.67$ psi and the amount due to the increase in kinetic energy is $\rho(V_2^2 - V_1^2)/2 = 2.07$ psi.

(b) If the only losses included are the major losses, the head loss is

$$h_L = f\frac{\ell}{D}\frac{V_1^2}{2g}$$

From Table 8.1 the roughness for a 0.75-in.-diameter copper pipe (drawn tubing) is $\varepsilon = 0.000005$ ft so that $\varepsilon/D = 8 \times 10^{-5}$. With this ε/D and the calculated Reynolds number (Re = 45,000), the value of f is obtained from the Moody chart as $f = 0.0215$. Note that the Colebrook equation (Eq. 8.19) would give the same value of f. Hence, the total length of the pipe as $\ell = (15 + 5 + 10 + 10 + 20)$ ft = 60 ft and the elevation and kinetic energy portions the same as for part **(a)**, Eq. 1 gives

$$p_1 = \gamma z_2 + \frac{1}{2}\rho(V_2^2 - V_1^2) + \rho f\frac{\ell}{D}\frac{V_1^2}{2}$$
$$= (1248 + 299) \text{ lb/ft}^2$$
$$+ (1.94 \text{ slugs/ft}^3)(0.0215)\left(\frac{60 \text{ ft}}{0.0625 \text{ ft}}\right)\frac{(8.70 \text{ ft/s})^2}{2}$$
$$= (1248 + 299 + 1515) \text{ lb/ft}^2 = 3062 \text{ lb/ft}^2$$

or

$$p_1 = 21.3 \text{ psi} \qquad \text{(Ans)}$$

Of this pressure drop, the amount due to pipe friction is approximately $(21.3 - 10.7)$ psi = 10.6 psi.

(c) If major and minor losses are included, Eq. 1 becomes

$$p_1 = \gamma z_2 + \frac{1}{2}\rho(V_2^2 - V_1^2) + f\gamma\frac{\ell}{D}\frac{V_1^2}{2g} + \sum \rho K_L \frac{V^2}{2}$$

or

$$p_1 = 21.3 \text{ psi} + \sum \rho K_L \frac{V^2}{2} \qquad (2)$$

where the 21.3-psi contribution is due to elevation change, kinetic energy change, and major losses [part **(b)**], and the last term represents the sum of all of the minor losses. The loss coefficients of the components ($K_L = 1.5$ for each elbow and $K_L = 10$ for the wide-open globe valve) are given in Table 8.2 (except for the loss coefficient of the faucet, which is given in Fig. E8.6a as $K_L = 2$). Thus,

$$\sum \rho K_L \frac{V^2}{2} = (1.94 \text{ slugs/ft}^3) \frac{(8.70 \text{ ft/s})^2}{2} [10 + 4(1.5) + 2]$$
$$= 1321 \text{ lb/ft}^2$$

or

$$\sum \rho K_L \frac{V^2}{2} = 9.17 \text{ psi} \tag{3}$$

Note that we did not include an entrance or exit loss because points (1) and (2) are located within the fluid streams, not within an attaching reservoir where the kinetic energy is zero. Thus, by combining Eqs. 2 and 3 we obtain the entire pressure drop as

$$p_1 = (21.3 + 9.17) \text{ psi} = 30.5 \text{ psi} \tag{Ans}$$

This pressure drop calculated by including all losses should be the most realistic answer of the three cases considered.

More detailed calculations will show that the pressure distribution along the pipe is as illustrated in Fig. E8.6b for cases **(a)** and **(c)**—neglecting all losses or including all losses. Note that not all of the pressure drop, $p_1 - p_2$, is a "pressure loss." The pressure change due to the elevation and velocity changes are completely reversible. The portion due to the major and minor losses are irreversible.

This flow can be illustrated in terms of the energy line and hydraulic grade line concepts introduced in Section 3.7. As is shown in Fig. E8.6c, for case **(a)** there are no losses and the energy line (EL) is horizontal, one velocity head ($V^2/2g$) above the hydraulic grade line (HGL), which is one pressure head (γz) above the pipe itself. For case **(c)** the energy line is not horizontal. Each bit of friction in the pipe or loss in a

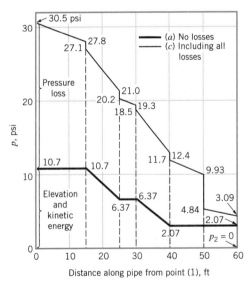

Location: (1)   (3)   (4) (5)   (6)   (7)(8)   (2)   ■ **FIGURE E8.6b**

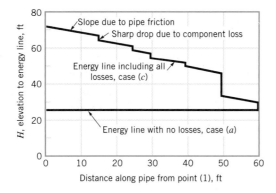

■ FIGURE E8.6c

component reduces the available energy, thereby lowering the energy line. Thus, for case **(a)** the total head remains constant throughout the flow with a value of

$$H = \frac{p_1}{\gamma} + \frac{V_1^2}{2g} + z_1 = \frac{(1547 \text{ lb/ft}^2)}{(62.4 \text{ lb/ft}^3)} + \frac{(8.70 \text{ ft/s})^2}{2(32.2 \text{ ft/s}^2)} + 0$$

$$= 26.0 \text{ ft}$$

$$= \frac{p_2}{\gamma} + \frac{V_2^2}{2g} + z_2 = \frac{p_3}{\gamma} + \frac{V_3^3}{2g} + z_3 = \cdots$$

For case **(c)** the energy line starts at

$$H_1 = \frac{p_1}{\gamma} + \frac{V_1^2}{2g} + z_1 = \frac{(30.5 \times 144)\text{lb/ft}^2}{(62.4 \text{ lb/ft}^3)} + \frac{(8.70 \text{ ft/s})^2}{2(32.2 \text{ ft/s}^2)} + 0 = 71.6 \text{ ft}$$

and falls to a final value of

$$H_2 = \frac{p_2}{\gamma} + \frac{V_2^2}{2g} + z_2 = 0 + \frac{(19.6 \text{ ft/s})^2}{2(32.2 \text{ ft/s}^2)} + 20 \text{ ft} = 26.0 \text{ ft}$$

The elevation of the energy line can be calculated at any point along the pipe. For example, at point (7), 50 ft from point (1),

$$H_7 = \frac{p_7}{\gamma} + \frac{V_7^2}{2g} + z_7 = \frac{(9.93 \times 144) \text{ lb/ft}^2}{(62.4 \text{ lb/ft}^3)} + \frac{(8.70 \text{ ft/s})^2}{2(32.2 \text{ ft/s}^2)} + 20 \text{ ft} = 44.1 \text{ ft}$$

The head loss per foot of pipe is the same all along the pipe. That is,

$$\frac{h_L}{\ell} = f \frac{V^2}{2gD} = \frac{0.0215(8.70 \text{ ft/s})^2}{2(32.2 \text{ ft/s}^2)(0.0625 \text{ ft})} = 0.404 \text{ ft/ft}$$

Thus, the energy line is a set of straight-line segments of the same slope separated by steps whose height equals the head loss of the minor component at that location. As is seen from Fig. E8.6c, the globe valve produces the largest of all the minor losses.

Although the governing pipe flow equations are quite simple, they can provide very reasonable results for a variety of applications as shown in the next example.

EXAMPLE 8.7 (TYPE I, DETERMINE HEAD LOSS)

Crude oil at 140 °F with $\gamma = 53.7$ lb/ft³ and $\mu = 8 \times 10^{-5}$ lb·s/ft² (about four times the viscosity of water) is pumped across Alaska through the Alaskan pipeline, a 799-mile-long, 4-ft-diameter steel pipe, at a maximum rate of $Q = 2.4$ million barrels/day $= 117$ ft³/s, or $V = Q/A = 9.31$ ft/s. Determine the horsepower needed for the pumps that drive this large system.

SOLUTION

From the energy equation (Eq. 5.57) we obtain

$$\frac{p_1}{\gamma} + \frac{V_1^2}{2g} + z_1 + h_p = \frac{p_2}{\gamma} + \frac{V_2^2}{2g} + z_2 + h_L$$

where points (1) and (2) represent locations within the large holding tanks at either end of the line and h_p is the head provided to the oil by the pumps. We assume that $z_1 = z_2$ (pumped from sea level to sea level), $p_1 = p_2 = V_1 = V_2 = 0$ (large, open tanks) and $h_L = (f\ell/D)$ $(V^2/2g)$. Minor losses are negligible because of the large length-to-diameter ratio of the relatively straight, uninterrupted pipe; $\ell/D = (799$ mi)(5280 ft/mi)/(4 ft) $= 1.05 \times 10^6$. Thus,

$$h_p = h_L = f\frac{\ell}{D}\frac{V^2}{2g}$$

where from Fig. 8.10, $f = 0.0125$ since $\varepsilon/D = (0.00015$ ft)/(4 ft) $= 0.0000375$ (see Table 8.1) and Re $= \rho VD/\mu = [(53.7/32.2)$ slugs/ft³](9.31 ft/s)(4.0 ft)/(8 $\times$ 10⁻⁵ lb·s/ft²) $=$ 7.76×10^5. Thus,

$$h_p = 0.0125(1.05 \times 10^6) \frac{(9.31 \text{ ft/s})^2}{2(32.2 \text{ ft/s}^2)} = 17,700 \text{ ft}$$

and the actual power supplied to the fluid, $\mathcal{P}_a$, is

$$\mathcal{P}_a = \gamma Q h_p = (53.7 \text{ lb/ft}^3)(117 \text{ ft}^3/\text{s})(17,700 \text{ ft})$$

$$= 1.11 \times 10^8 \text{ ft·lb/s} \left(\frac{1 \text{ hp}}{550 \text{ ft·lb/s}}\right)$$

$$= 202,000 \text{ hp} \tag{Ans}$$

There are many reasons why it is not practical to drive this flow with a single pump of this size. First, there are no pumps this large! Second, the pressure at the pump outlet would need to be $p = \gamma h_L = (53.7 \text{ lb/ft}^3)(17,700 \text{ ft})(1 \text{ ft}^2/144 \text{ in.}^2) = 6600$ psi. No practical 4-ft-diameter pipe would withstand this pressure. An equally unfeasible alternative would be to place the holding tank at the beginning of the pipe on top of a hill at height $h_L = 17,700$ ft and let gravity force the oil through the 799-mi pipe!

To produce the desired flow, the actual system contains 12 pumping stations positioned at strategic locations along the pipeline. Each station contains four pumps, three of which operate at any one time (the fourth is in reserve in case of emergency). Each pump is driven by a 13,500-hp motor, thereby producing a total horsepower of $\mathcal{P} = 12$ stations (3 pumps/

station)(13,500 hp/pump) = 486,000 hp. If we assume that the pump/motor combination is approximately 60% efficient, there is a total of 0.60 (486,000) hp = 292,000 hp available to drive the fluid. This number compares favorably with the 202,000-hp answer calculated above.

The assumption of a 140 °F oil temperature may not seem reasonable for flow across Alaska. Note, however, that the oil is warm when it is pumped from the ground and that the 202,000 hp needed to pump the oil is dissipated as a head loss (and therefore a temperature rise) along the pipe. However, if the oil temperature were 70 °F rather than 140 °F, the viscosity would be approximately 16×10^{-5} lb·s/ft^2 (twice as large), but the friction factor would only increase from $f = 0.0125$ at 140 °F (Re = 7.76×10^5) to $f = 0.0140$ at 70 °F (Re = 3.88×10^5). This doubling of viscosity would result in only an 11% increase in power (from 202,000 to 226,000 hp). Because of the large Reynolds numbers involved, the shear stress is due mostly to the turbulent nature of the flow. That is, the value of Re for this flow is large enough (on the relatively flat part of the Moody chart) so that f is nearly independent of Re (or viscosity).

Pipe flow problems in which it is desired to determine the flowrate for a given set of conditions (Type II problems) often require trial-and-error solution techniques. This is because it is necessary to know the value of the friction factor to carry out the calculations, but the friction factor is a function of the unknown velocity (flowrate) in terms of the Reynolds number. The solution procedure is indicated in Example 8.8.

EXAMPLE 8.8 (TYPE II, DETERMINE FLOWRATE)

According to an appliance manufacturer, the 4-in.-diameter galvanized iron vent on a clothes dryer is not to contain more than 20 ft of pipe and four 90° elbows. Under these conditions determine the air flowrate if the pressure within the dryer is 0.20 inches of water. Assume a temperature of 100 °F and standard pressure.

SOLUTION

Application of the energy equation (Eq. 5.57) between the inside of the dryer, point (1), and the exit of the vent pipe, point (2), gives

$$\frac{p_1}{\gamma} + \frac{V_1^2}{2g} + z_1 = \frac{p_2}{\gamma} + \frac{V_2^2}{2g} + z_2 + f \frac{\ell}{D} \frac{V^2}{2g} + \sum K_L \frac{V^2}{2g} \tag{1}$$

where K_L for the entrance is assumed to be 0.5 and that for each elbow is assumed to be 1.5. In addition we assume that $V_1 = 0$ and $z_1 = z_2$. (The change in elevation is often negligible for gas flows.) Also, $p_2 = 0$, and $p_1/\gamma_{H_2O} = 0.2$ in., or

$$p_1 = (0.2 \text{ in.}) \left(\frac{1 \text{ ft}}{12 \text{ in.}}\right) (62.4 \text{ lb/ft}^3) = 1.04 \text{ lb/ft}^2$$

Thus, with $\gamma = 0.0709$ lb/ft^3 (see Table B.3) and $V_2 = V$ (the air velocity in the pipe), Eq. 1 becomes

$$\frac{(1.04\ \text{lb/ft}^2)}{(0.0709\ \text{lb/ft}^3)} = \left[1 + f\frac{(20\ \text{ft})}{(\frac{4}{12}\ \text{ft})} + 0.5 + 4(1.5) \right] \frac{V^2}{2(32.2\ \text{ft/s}^2)}$$

or

$$945 = (7.5 + 60f)V^2 \tag{2}$$

where V is in ft/s.

The value of f is dependent on Re, which is dependent on V, an unknown. However, from Table B.3, $\nu = 1.79 \times 10^{-4}\ \text{ft}^2/\text{s}$ and we obtain

$$\text{Re} = \frac{VD}{\nu} = \frac{(\frac{4}{12}\ \text{ft})V}{1.79 \times 10^{-4}\ \text{ft}^2/\text{s}}$$

or

$$\text{Re} = 1860\ V \tag{3}$$

where again V is in ft/s.

Also, since $\varepsilon/D = (0.0005\ \text{ft})/(4/12\ \text{ft}) = 0.0015$ (see Table 8.1 for the value of ε), we know which particular curve of the Moody chart is pertinent to this flow. Thus, we have three relationships (Eqs. 2, 3, and the $\varepsilon/D = 0.0015$ curve of Fig. 8.10) from which we can solve for the three unknowns f, Re, and V. This is done easily by an iterative scheme as follows.

It is usually simplest to assume a value of f, calculate V from Eq. 2, calculate Re from Eq. 3, and look up the appropriate value of f in the Moody chart for this value of Re. If the assumed f and the new f do not agree, the assumed answer is not correct—we do not have the solution to the three equations. Although values of either f, V, or Re could be assumed as starting values, it is usually simplest to assume a value of f because the correct value often lies on the relatively flat portion of the Moody chart for which f is quite insensitive to Re.

Thus, we assume $f = 0.022$, approximately the large Re limit for the given relative roughness. From Eq. 2 we obtain

$$V = \left[\frac{945}{7.5 + 60(0.022)} \right]^{1/2} = 10.4\ \text{ft/s}$$

and from Eq. 3

$$\text{Re} = 1860(10.4) = 19{,}300$$

With this Re and ε/D, Fig. 8.10 gives $f = 0.029$, which is not equal to the assumed solution $f = 0.022$ (although it is close!). We try again, this time with the newly obtained value of $f = 0.029$, which gives $V = 10.1$ ft/s and Re $= 18{,}800$. With these values, Fig. 8.10 gives $f = 0.029$, which agrees with the assumed value. Thus, the solution is $V = 10.1$ ft/s, or

$$Q = AV = \frac{\pi}{4}(\tfrac{4}{12}\ \text{ft})^2(10.1\ \text{ft/s}) = 0.881\ \text{ft}^3/\text{s} \tag{Ans}$$

Note that the need for the iteration scheme is because one of the equations, $f = \phi(\text{Re}, \varepsilon/D)$, is in graphical form (the Moody chart). If the dependence of f on Re and ε/D is known in equation form, this graphical dependency is eliminated, and the solution technique may be easier. Such is the case if the flow is laminar so that the friction factor is simply $f = 64/\text{Re}$. For turbulent flow, we can use the Colebrook equation rather than the Moody chart, although this will normally require an iterative scheme also because of the complexity of the equation. As is shown below, such a formulation is ideally suited for an iterative computer solution.

We keep Eqs. 2 and 3 and use the Colebrook equation (Eq. 8.19, rather than the Moody chart) with $\varepsilon/D = 0.0015$ to give

$$\frac{1}{\sqrt{f}} = -2.0 \log\left(\frac{\varepsilon/D}{3.7} + \frac{2.51}{\text{Re}\sqrt{f}}\right) = -2.0 \log\left(4.05 \times 10^{-4} + \frac{2.51}{\text{Re}\sqrt{f}}\right) \quad (4)$$

From Eq. 2 we have $V = [945/(7.5 + 60f)]^{1/2}$, which can be combined with Eq. 3 to give

$$\text{Re} = \frac{57{,}200}{\sqrt{7.5 + 60f}} \quad (5)$$

The combination of Eqs. 4 and 5 provides a single equation for the determination of f

$$\frac{1}{\sqrt{f}} = -2.0 \log\left(4.05 \times 10^{-4} + 4.39 \times 10^{-5}\sqrt{60 + \frac{7.5}{f}}\right) \quad (6)$$

A simple iterative solution of this equation gives $f = 0.029$, in agreement with the above solution which used the Moody chart. [This iterative solution using the Colebrook equation can be done as follows: (a) assume a value of f, (b) calculate a new value by using the assumed value in the right-hand side of Eq. 6, (c) use this new f to recalculate another value of f, and (d) repeat until the successive values agree.]

Note that unlike the Alaskan pipeline example (Example 8.7) in which we assumed minor losses are negligible, minor losses are of importance in this example because of the relatively small length-to-diameter ratio: $\ell/D = 20/(4/12) = 60$. The ratio of minor to major losses in this case is $K_L/(f\ell/D) = 6.5/[0.029(60)] = 3.74$. The elbows and entrance produce considerably more loss than the pipe itself.

In pipe flow problems for which the diameter is the unknown (Type III), an iterative technique is required since neither the Reynolds number, $\text{Re} = \rho VD/\mu = 4\rho Q/\pi\mu D$, nor the relative roughness, ε/D, are known unless D is known. Example 8.9 illustrates this.

EXAMPLE 8.9 (TYPE III WITHOUT MINOR LOSSES, DETERMINE DIAMETER)

Air at standard temperature and pressure flows through a horizontal, galvanized iron pipe ($\varepsilon = 0.0005$ ft) at a rate of 2.0 ft^3/s. Determine the minimum pipe diameter if the pressure drop is to be no more than 0.50 psi per 100 ft of pipe.

SOLUTION

We assume the flow to be incompressible with $\rho = 0.00238$ slugs/ft^3 and $\mu = 3.74 \times 10^{-7}$ lb·s/ft^2. Note that if the pipe were too long, the pressure drop from one end to the other, $p_1 - p_2$, would not be small relative to the pressure at the beginning, and compressible flow considerations would be required. For example, a pipe length of 200 ft gives $(p_1 - p_2)/p_1 = [(0.50 \text{ psi})/(100 \text{ ft})](200 \text{ ft})/14.7 \text{ psi} = 0.068 = 6.8\%$, which is probably small enough to justify the incompressible assumption.

With $z_1 = z_2$ and $V_1 = V_2$ the energy equation (Eq. 5.57) becomes

$$p_1 = p_2 + f\frac{\ell}{D}\frac{\rho V^2}{2} \tag{1}$$

where $V = Q/A = 4Q/(\pi D^2) = 4(2.0 \text{ ft}^3/\text{s})/\pi D^2$, or

$$V = \frac{2.55}{D^2}$$

where D is in feet. Thus, with $p_1 - p_2 = (0.5 \text{ lb/in.}^2)(144 \text{ in.}^2/\text{ft}^2)$ and $\ell = 100$ ft, Eq. 1 becomes

$$p_1 - p_2 = (0.5)(144) \text{ lb/ft}^2$$
$$= f\frac{(100 \text{ ft})}{D}(0.00238 \text{ slugs/ft}^3)\frac{1}{2}\left(\frac{2.55 \text{ ft}}{D^2 \text{ s}}\right)^2$$

or

$$D = 0.404\,f^{1/5} \tag{2}$$

where D is in feet. Also $\text{Re} = \rho VD/\mu = (0.00238 \text{ slugs/ft}^3)[(2.55/D^2) \text{ ft/s}]D/(3.74 \times 10^{-7} \text{ lb·s/ft}^2)$, or

$$\text{Re} = \frac{1.62 \times 10^4}{D} \tag{3}$$

and

$$\frac{\varepsilon}{D} = \frac{0.0005}{D} \tag{4}$$

Thus, we have four equations (Eqs. 2, 3, 4, and either the Moody chart (Fig. 8.10) or the Colebrook equation (Eq. 8.19)) and four unknowns (f, D, ε/D, and Re) from which the solution can be obtained by trial-and-error methods.

If we use the Moody chart, it is probably easiest to assume a value of f, use Eqs. 2, 3, and 4 to calculate D, Re, and ε/D, and then compare the assumed f with that from the Moody chart. If they do not agree, try again. Thus, we assume $f = 0.02$, a typical value, and obtain $D = 0.404(0.02)^{1/5} = 0.185$ ft, which gives $\varepsilon/D = 0.0005/0.185 = 0.0027$ and $\text{Re} = 1.62 \times 10^4/0.185 = 8.76 \times 10^4$. From the Moody chart we obtain $f = 0.027$ for these values of ε/D and Re. Since this is not the same as our assumed value of f, we try again. With $f = 0.027$, we obtain $D = 0.196$ ft, $\varepsilon/D = 0.0026$, and $\text{Re} = 8.27 \times 10^4$, which in turn give $f = 0.027$, in agreement with the assumed value. Thus, the diameter of the pipe should be

$$D = 0.196 \text{ ft} \tag{Ans}$$

If we use the Colebrook equation (Eq. 8.19) with $\varepsilon/D = 0.0005/0.404\,f^{1/5} = 0.00124/f^{1/5}$ and $\text{Re} = 1.62 \times 10^4/0.404\,f^{1/5} = 4.01 \times 10^4/f^{1/5}$, we obtain

$$\frac{1}{\sqrt{f}} = -2.0 \log\left(\frac{\varepsilon/D}{3.7} + \frac{2.51}{\text{Re}\sqrt{f}}\right)$$

or

$$\frac{1}{\sqrt{f}} = -2.0 \log \left(\frac{3.35 \times 10^{-4}}{f^{1/5}} + \frac{6.26 \times 10^{-5}}{f^{3/10}} \right)$$

An iterative scheme (see solution of Eq. 6 in Example 8.8) to solve this equation for f gives $f = 0.027$, and hence $D = 0.196$ ft, in agreement with the Moody chart method.

8.5.2 Multiple Pipe Systems

In many pipe systems there is more than one pipe involved. The governing mechanisms for the flow in multiple pipe systems are the same as for the single pipes.

One of the simplest multiple pipe systems is that containing pipes in *series,* as is shown in Fig. 8.20a. Every fluid particle that passes through the system passes through each of the pipes. Thus, the flowrate (but not the velocity) is the same in each pipe, and the head loss from point A to point B is the sum of the head losses in each of the pipes. The governing equations can be written as follows

$$Q_1 = Q_2 = Q_3$$

and

$$h_{L_{A-B}} = h_{L_1} + h_{L_2} + h_{L_3}$$

where the subscripts refer to each of the pipes.

Another common multiple pipe system contains pipes in *parallel,* as is shown in Fig. 8.20b. In this system a fluid particle traveling from A to B may take any of the paths available, with the total flowrate equal to the sum of the flowrates in each pipe. However, by writing the energy equation between points A and B it is found that the head loss experienced

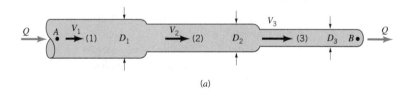

(a)

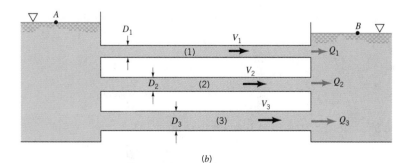

(b)

■ **FIGURE 8.20** Series (*a*) and parallel (*b*) pipe systems.

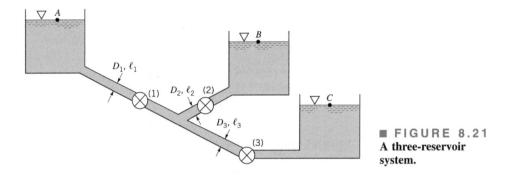

■ **FIGURE 8.21**
A three-reservoir system.

by any fluid particle traveling between these locations is the same, independent of the path taken. Thus, the governing equations for parallel pipes are

$$Q = Q_1 + Q_2 + Q_3$$

and

$$h_{L_1} = h_{L_2} = h_{L_3}$$

The flow in a relatively simple looking multiple pipe system may be more complex than it appears initially. The branching system termed the *three reservoir problem* shown in Fig. 8.21 is such a system. Three reservoirs at known elevations are connected together with three pipes of known properties (lengths, diameters, and roughnesses). The problem is to determine the flowrates into or out of the reservoirs. In general, the flow direction (whether the fluid flows into or out of reservoir B) is not obvious, and the solution process must include the determination of this direction.

8.6 Pipe Flowrate Measurement

Three of the most common devices used to measure the instantaneous flowrate in pipes are the orifice meter, the nozzle meter, and the Venturi meter as shown in Figs. 8.22, 8.24, and 8.26. As was discussed in Section 3.6.3, each of these meters operates on the principle that a decrease in flow area in a pipe causes an increase in velocity that is accompanied by a decrease in pressure. Correlation of the pressure difference with the velocity provides a means of measuring the flowrate.

Based on the results of the previous sections of this chapter, we anticipate that there is a head loss between sections (1) and (2) (see Fig. 8.22) so that the governing equations become

$$Q = A_1 V_1 = A_2 V_2$$

and

$$\frac{p_1}{\gamma} + \frac{V_1^2}{2g} = \frac{p_2}{\gamma} + \frac{V_2^2}{2g} + h_L$$

The ideal situation has $h_L = 0$ and results in

$$Q_{\text{ideal}} = A_2 V_2 = A_2 \sqrt{\frac{2(p_1 - p_2)}{\rho(1 - \beta^4)}} \qquad (8.21)$$

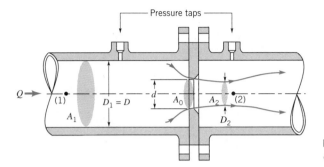

■ **FIGURE 8.22** **Typical orifice meter construction.**

where $\beta = D_2/D_1$ (see section 3.6.3). The difficulty in including the head loss is that there is no accurate expression for it. The net result is that empirical coefficients are used in the flowrate equations to account for the complex "real-world" effect brought on by the nonzero viscosity. The coefficients are discussed below.

A typical *orifice meter* is constructed by inserting between two flanges of a pipe a flat plate with a hole, as shown in Fig. 8.22. An *orifice discharge coefficient, C_o,* is used to take nonideal effects into account. That is,

$$Q = C_o Q_{ideal} = C_o A_o \sqrt{\frac{2(p_1 - p_2)}{\rho(1 - \beta^4)}} \tag{8.22}$$

where $A_0 = \pi d^2/4$ is the area of the hole in the orifice plate. The value of C_o is a function of $\beta = d/D$ and the Reynolds number $Re = \rho VD/\mu$, where $V = Q/A_1$. Typical values of C_o are given in Fig. 8.23.

Another type of pipe flowmeter that is based on the same principles used in the orifice meter is the *nozzle meter,* three variations of which are shown in Fig. 8.24. The flow

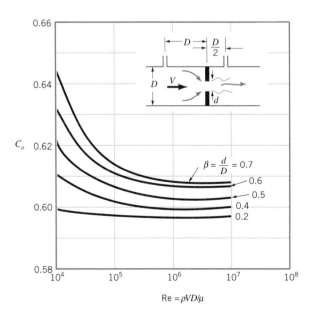

■ **FIGURE 8.23** **Orifice meter discharge coefficient (Ref. 10).**

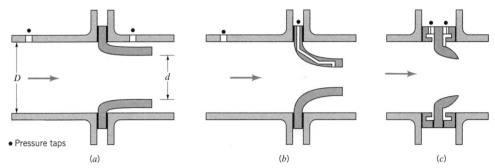

• Pressure taps

(a)   (b)   (c)

■ **FIGURE 8.24**   **Typical nozzle meter construction.**

pattern for the nozzle meter is closer to ideal than the orifice meter flow, but there still are viscous effects. These are accounted for by use of the *nozzle discharge coefficient, C_n*, where

$$Q = C_n Q_{\text{ideal}} = C_n A_n \sqrt{\frac{2(p_1 - p_2)}{\rho(1 - \beta^4)}} \tag{8.23}$$

with $A_n = \pi d^2/4$. As with the orifice meter, the value of C_n is a function of the diameter ratio, $\beta = d/D$, and the Reynolds number, $\text{Re} = \rho VD/\mu$. Typical values obtained from experiments are shown in Fig. 8.25. Note that $C_n > C_o$; the nozzle meter is more efficient (less energy dissipated) than the orifice meter.

The most precise and most expensive of the three obstruction-type flowmeters is the *Venturi meter* shown in Fig. 8.26. It is designed to reduce head losses to a minimum. Most of the head loss that occurs in a well-designed Venturi meter is due to friction losses along the walls rather than losses associated with separated flows and the inefficient mixing motion that accompanies such flow.

The flowrate through a Venturi meter is given by

$$Q = C_v Q_{\text{ideal}} = C_v A_T \sqrt{\frac{2(p_1 - p_2)}{\rho(1 - \beta^4)}} \tag{8.24}$$

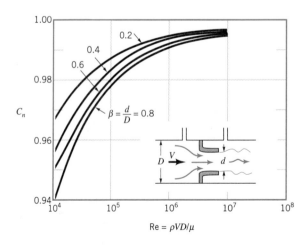

■ **FIGURE 8.25**   **Nozzle meter discharge coefficient (Ref. 10).**

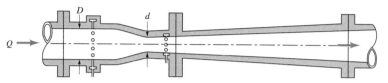

■ **FIGURE 8.26**   **Typical Venturi meter construction.**

where $A_T = \pi d^2/4$ is the throat area. The range of values of C_v, the *Venturi discharge coefficient,* is given in Fig. 8.27. The throat-to-pipe diameter ratio ($\beta = d/D$), the Reynolds number, and the shape of the converging and diverging sections of the meter are among the parameters that affect the value of C_v.

Again, the precise values of C_n, C_o, and C_v depend on the specific geometry of the devices used. Considerable information concerning the design, use, and installation of standard flowmeters can be found in various books (Refs. 10, 15, 16, 17).

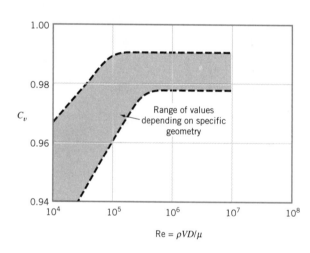

■ **FIGURE 8.27**   **Venturi meter discharge coefficient (Ref. 15).**

EXAMPLE 8.10

Ethyl alcohol flows through a pipe of diameter $D = 60$ mm in a refinery. The pressure drop across the nozzle meter used to measure the flowrate is to be $\Delta p = 4.0$ kPa when the flowrate is $Q = 0.003$ m^3/s. Determine the diameter, d, of the nozzle.

SOLUTION

From Table 1.5 the properties of ethyl alcohol are $\rho = 789$ kg/m^3 and $\mu = 1.19 \times 10^{-3}$ N·s/m^2. Thus,

$$\mathrm{Re} = \frac{\rho V D}{\mu} = \frac{4\rho Q}{\pi D \mu} = \frac{4(789 \text{ kg/m}^3)(0.003 \text{ m}^3/\text{s})}{\pi(0.06 \text{ m})(1.19 \times 10^{-3} \text{ N·s/m}^2)} = 42,200$$

From Eq. 8.23 the flowrate through the nozzle is

$$Q = 0.003 \text{ m}^3/\text{s} = C_n \frac{\pi}{4} d^2 \sqrt{\frac{2(4 \times 10^3 \text{ N/m}^2)}{789 \text{ kg/m}^3 (1 - \beta^4)}}$$

or

$$1.20 \times 10^{-3} = \frac{C_n d^2}{\sqrt{1 - \beta^4}} \qquad (1)$$

where d is in meters. Note that $\beta = d/D = d/0.06$. Equation 1 and Fig. 8.25 represent two equations for the two unknowns d and C_n that must be solved by trial and error.

As a first approximation we assume that the flow is ideal, or $C_n = 1.0$, so that Eq. 1 becomes

$$d = (1.20 \times 10^{-3} \sqrt{1 - \beta^4})^{1/2} \qquad (2)$$

In addition, for many cases $1 - \beta^4 \approx 1$, so that an approximate value of d can be obtained from Eq. 2 as

$$d = (1.20 \times 10^{-3})^{1/2} = 0.0346 \text{ m}$$

Hence, with an initial guess of $d = 0.0346$ m or $\beta = d/D = 0.0346/0.06 = 0.577$, we obtain from Fig. 8.25 (using Re = 42,200) a value of $C_n = 0.972$. Clearly this does not agree with our initial assumption of $C_n = 1.0$. Thus, we do not have the solution to Eq. 1 and Fig. 8.25. Next we assume $\beta = 0.577$ and $C_n = 0.972$ and solve for d from Eq. 1 to obtain

$$d = \left(\frac{1.20 \times 10^{-3}}{0.972} \sqrt{1 - 0.577^4} \right)^{1/2}$$

or $d = 0.0341$ m. With the new value of $\beta = 0.0341/0.060 = 0.568$ and Re = 42,200, we obtain (from Fig. 8.25) $C_n \approx 0.972$ in agreement with the assumed value. Thus,

$$d = 34.1 \text{ mm} \qquad \text{(Ans)}$$

If numerous cases are to be investigated, it may be much easier to replace the discharge coefficient data of Fig. 8.25 by the equivalent equation, $C_n = \phi(\beta, \text{Re})$, and use a computer to iterate for the answer. Such equations are available in the literature (Ref. 10). This would be similar to using the Colebrook equation rather than the Moody chart for pipe friction problems.

V8.6 Rotameter

V8.7 Water meter

Numerous other devices are used to measure the flowrate in pipes. Many of these devices use principles other than the high-speed/low-pressure concept of the orifice, nozzle, and Venturi meters (see Ref. 16). In some instances, it is necessary to know the amount (volume or mass) of fluid that has passed through a pipe during a given time period, rather than the instantaneous flowrate. There are several quantity-measuring devices that provide such information. These including the nutating disk meter used to determine the amount of water used in your house or the amount of gasoline pumped into your car's fuel tank and the bellows meter used to determine the amount of natural gas delivered to the furnace in your house.

References

1. Schlichting, H., *Boundary Layer Theory,* Seventh Edition, McGraw-Hill, New York, 1979.
2. Moody, L. F., "Friction Factors for Pipe Flow," *Transactions of the ASME,* Vol. 66, 1944.
3. Colebrook, C. F., "Turbulent Flow in Pipes with Particular Reference to the Transition Between the Smooth and Rough Pipe Laws," *Journal of the Institute of Civil Engineers London,* Vol. 11, 1939.
4. White, F. M., *Viscous Fluid Flow,* McGraw-Hill, New York, 1979.
5. *ASHRAE Handbook of Fundamentals,* ASHRAE, Atlanta, 1981.
6. Streeter, V. L., ed., *Handbook of Fluid Dynamics,* McGraw-Hill, New York, 1961.
7. Balje, O. E., *Turbomachines: A Guide to Design, Selection and Theory,* Wiley, New York, 1981.
8. Wallis, R. A., *Axial Flow Fans and Ducts,* Wiley, New York, 1983.
9. Karassick, I. J. et al, *Pump Handbook,* Second Edition, McGraw-Hill, New York, 1985.
10. "Measurement of Fluid Flow by Means of Orifice Plates, Nozzles, and Venturi Tubes Inserted in Circular Cross Section Conduits Running Full," Int. Organ. Stand. Rep. DIS-5167, Geneva, 1976.
11. Hydraulic Institute, *Engineering Data Book,* First Edition, Cleveland Hydraulic Institute, 1979.
12. Harris, C. W., *University of Washington Engineering Experimental Station Bulletin,* 48, 1928.
13. Hamilton, J. B., *University of Washington Engineering Experimental Station Bulletin,* 51, 1929.
14. Laws, E. M., and Livesey, J. L., "Flow Through Screens," *Annual Review of Fluid Mechanics,* Vol. 10, Annual Reviews, Inc., Palo Alto, CA, 1978.
15. Bean, H. S., ed., *Fluid Meters: Their Theory and Application,* Sixth Edition, American Society of Mechanical Engineers, New York, 1971.
16. Goldstein, R. J., ed., *Flow Mechanics Measurements,* Hemisphere Publishing, New York, 1983.
17. Spitzer, D. W., ed., *Flow Measurement: Practical Guides for Measurement and Control,* Instrument Society of America, Research Triangle Park, North Carolina, 1991.

Problems

Note: Unless otherwise indicated use the values of fluid properties found in the tables on the inside of the front cover. Problems designated with an (*) are intended to be solved with the aid of a programmable calculator or a computer. Problems designated with a (†) are "open ended" problems and require critical thinking in that to work them one must make various assumptions and provide the necessary data. There is not a unique answer to these problems.

8.1 Rainwater runoff from a parking lot flows through a 3-ft-diameter pipe, completely filling it. Whether flow in a pipe is laminar or turbulent depends on the value of the Reynolds number. (See **Video V8.1.**) Would you expect the flow to be laminar or turbulent? Support your answer with appropriate calculations.

†8.2 Under normal circumstances is the air flow through your trachea (your windpipe) laminar or turbulent? List all assumptions and show all calculations.

8.3 Carbon dioxide at 20 °C and a pressure of 550 kPa (abs) flows in a pipe at a rate of 0.04 N/s. Determine the maximum diameter allowed if the flow is to be turbulent.

8.4   It takes 20 seconds for 0.5 cubic inch of water to flow through the 0.046-in. diameter tube of the capillary tube viscometer shown in **Video V1.3** and Fig. P8.4. Is the flow in the tube laminar or turbulent? Explain.

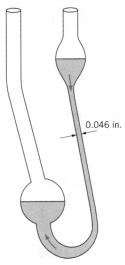

0.046 in.

■ **FIGURE P8.4**

8.5   A soft drink with the properties of 10 °C water is sucked through a 4-mm-diameter, 0.25-m-long straw at a rate of 4 cm³/s. Is the flow at the outlet of the straw laminar? Is it fully developed? Explain.

8.6   To cool a given room it is necessary to supply 4 ft³/s of air through an 8-in.-diameter pipe. Approximately how long is the entrance length in this pipe?

8.7   The pressure drop needed to force water through a horizontal 1-in.-diameter pipe is 0.60 psi for every 12-ft length of pipe. Determine the shear stress on the pipe wall. Determine the shear stress at distances 0.3 and 0.5 in. away from the pipe wall.

8.8   The pressure distribution measured along a straight, horizontal portion of a 50-mm-diameter pipe attached to a tank is shown in the next column. Approximately how long is the entrance length? In the fully developed portion of the flow, what is the value of the wall shear stress?

8.9   Water flows in a constant diameter pipe with the following conditions measured: At section (a) $p_a = 32.4$ psi and $z_a = 56.8$ ft; at section (b) $p_b = 29.7$ psi and $z_b = 68.2$ ft. Is the flow from (a) to (b) or from (b) to (a)? Explain.

8.10   A fluid of specific gravity 0.96 flows steadily in a long, vertical 1-in.-diameter pipe with an average velocity of 0.50 ft/s. If the pressure is constant throughout the fluid, what is the viscosity of the fluid? Determine the shear stress on the pipe wall.

x (m) (± 0.01 m)	p (mm H₂O) (± 5 mm)
0 (tank exit)	520
0.5	427
1.0	351
1.5	288
2.0	236
2.5	188
3.0	145
3.5	109
4.0	73
4.5	36
5.0 (pipe exit)	0

8.11   A fluid flows through a horizontal 0.1-in.-diameter pipe. When the Reynolds number is 1500, the head loss over a 20-ft length of the pipe is 6.4 ft. Determine the fluid velocity.

8.12   Glycerin at 20 °C flows upward in a vertical 75-mm-diameter pipe with a centerline velocity of 1.0 m/s. Determine the head loss and pressure drop in a 10-m length of the pipe.

8.13   Oil (specific weight = 8900 N/m³, viscosity = 0.10 N·s/m²) flows through a horizontal 23-mm-diameter tube as shown in Fig. P8.13. A differential U-tube manometer is used to measure the pressure drop along the tube. Determine the range of values for h for laminar flow.

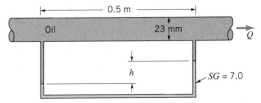

■ **FIGURE P8.13**

8.14   Oil of $SG = 0.87$ and a kinematic viscosity $\nu = 2.2 \times 10^{-4}$ m²/s flows through the vertical pipe shown in Fig. P8.14 at a rate of 4×10^{-4} m³/s. Determine the manometer reading, h.

8.15   Determine the manometer reading, h, for Problem 8.14 if the flow is up rather than down the pipe.

8.16   As shown in **Video V8.3** and Fig. P8.16, the velocity profile for laminar flow in a pipe is quite different from that for turbulent flow. With laminar flow the velocity profile is parabolic; with turbulent flow at Re = 10,000 the velocity profile can be approximated by the power-law profile shown in the figure. **(a)** For laminar flow, determine at what radial location you would place a Pitot tube if it is to measure the average velocity in the pipe. **(b)** Repeat part **(a)** for turbulent flow with Re = 10,000.

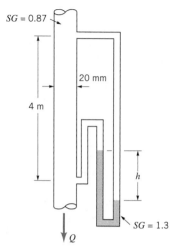

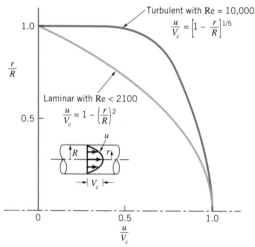

■ FIGURE P8.14

■ FIGURE P8.16

if the flowrate is $Q = 0.00191$ cfs when $h = 1.70$ in. Compare your results with the expression $f = 64/Re$. Is the flow laminar or turbulent?

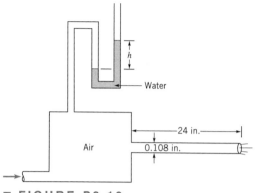

■ FIGURE P8.19

8.17 During a heavy rainstorm, water from a parking lot completely fills an 18-in.-diameter, smooth, concrete storm sewer. If the flowrate is 10 ft³/s, determine the pressure drop in a 100-ft horizontal section of the pipe. Repeat the problem if there is a 2-ft change in elevation of the pipe per 100 ft of its length.

8.18 Carbon dioxide at a temperature of 0 °C and a pressure of 600 kPa (abs) flows through a horizontal 40-mm-diameter pipe with an average velocity of 2 m/s. Determine the friction factor if the pressure drop is 235 N/m² per 10-m length of pipe.

8.19 Air flows through the 0.108-in.-diameter, 24-in.-long tube shown in Fig. P8.19. Determine the friction factor

8.20 Water flows through a 6-in.-diameter horizontal pipe at a rate of 2.0 cfs and a pressure drop of 4.2 psi per 100 ft of pipe. Determine the friction factor.

8.21 A 70-ft-long, 0.5-in.-diameter hose with a roughness of $\varepsilon = 0.0009$ ft is fastened to a water faucet where the pressure is p_1. Determine p_1 if there is no nozzle attached and the average velocity in the hose is 6 ft/s. Neglect minor losses and elevation changes.

8.22 Repeat Problem 8.21 if there is a nozzle of diameter 0.25 in. attached to the end of the hose.

8.23 Determine the pressure drop per 100-m length of horizontal new 0.20-m-diameter cast iron water pipe when the average velocity is 1.7 m/s.

†8.24 A garden hose is attached to a faucet that is fully opened. Without a nozzle on the end of the hose, the water does not shoot very far. However, if you place your thumb over a portion of the end of the hose, it is possible to shoot the water a considerable distance. Explain this phenomenon. (*Note:* The flowrate decreases as the area covered by your thumb increases.)

8.25 Air at standard temperature and pressure flows through a 1-in.-diameter galvanized iron pipe with an average velocity of 10 ft/s. What length of pipe produces a head loss equivalent to (a) a flanged 90° elbow, (b) a wide-open angle valve, or (c) a sharp-edged entrance?

***8.26** Water at 40 °C flows through drawn tubings with diameters of 0.025, 0.050, or 0.075 m. Plot the head loss in each meter length of pipe for flowrates between 5×10^{-4} m³/s and 50×10^{-4} m³/s. In your solution obtain the friction factor from the Colebrook formula.

†8.27 Consider the process of donating blood. Blood flows from a vein in which the pressure is greater than atmospheric, through a long small-diameter tube, and into a plastic bag that is essentially at atmospheric pressure. Based on fluid mechanics principles, estimate the amount of time it takes to donate a pint of blood. List all assumptions and show calculations.

8.28   To conserve water and energy, a "flow reducer" is installed in the shower head as shown in Fig. P8.28. If the pressure at point (1) remains constant and all losses except for that in the "flow reducer" are neglected, determine the value of the loss coefficient (based on the velocity in the pipe) of the "flow reducer" if its presence is to reduce the flowrate by a factor of 2. Neglect gravity.

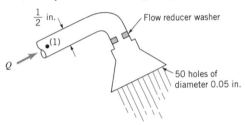

■ **FIGURE P8.28**

8.29   An incompressible fluid flows steadily through a sudden expansion, from diameter D_1 to diameter D_2. Although there is a pressure rise across the expansion as a result of the decrease of kinetic energy, there is also a pressure drop due to the head loss. For what value of D_1/D_2 will $p_1 = p_2$?

8.30   As shown in Fig. P8.30, water flows from one tank to another through a short pipe whose length is n times the pipe diameter. Head losses occur in the pipe and at the entrance and exit. (See **Video V8.4**.) Determine the maximum value of n if the major loss is to be no more than 10% of the minor loss and the friction factor is 0.02.

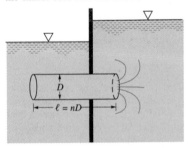

■ **FIGURE P8.30**

†8.31   A 6-in.-diameter water main in your town has become very rough due to rust and corrosion. It has been suggested that the flowrate through this pipe can be increased by inserting a smooth plastic liner into the pipe. Although the new diameter will be smaller, the pipe will be smoother.

Will such a procedure produce a greater flowrate? List all assumptions and show all calculations.

8.32   Natural gas ($\rho = 0.0044$ slugs/ft^3 and $\nu = 5.2 \times 10^{-5}$ ft^2/s) is pumped through a horizontal 6-in.-diameter cast-iron pipe at a rate of 800 lb/hr. If the pressure at section (1) is 50 psi (abs), determine the pressure at section (2) 8 mi downstream if the flow is assumed incompressible. Is the incompressible assumption reasonable? Explain.

8.33   Gasoline flows in a smooth pipe of 40-mm diameter at a rate of 0.001 m^3/s. If it were possible to prevent turbulence from occurring, what would be the ratio of the head loss for the actual turbulent flow compared to that if it were laminar flow?

8.34   A 3-ft-diameter duct is used to carry ventilating air into a vehicular tunnel at a rate of 9000 ft^3/min. Tests show that the pressure drop is 1.5 in. of water per 1500 ft of duct. What is the value of the friction factor for this duct and the approximate size of the equivalent roughness of the surface of the duct?

8.35   Air flows through a rectangular galvanized iron duct of size 0.30 m by 0.15 m at a rate of 0.068 m^3/s. Determine the head loss in 12 m of this duct.

8.36   Air at standard temperature and pressure flows through a horizontal 2 ft by 1.3 ft rectangular galvanized iron duct with a flowrate of 8.2 cfs. Determine the pressure drop in inches of water per 200-ft length of duct.

8.37   When the valve is closed, the pressure throughout the horizontal pipe shown in Fig. P8.37 is 400 kPa, and the water level in the closed surge chamber is $h = 0.4$ m. If the valve is fully opened and the pressure at point (1) remains 400 kPa, determine the new level of the water in the surge chamber. Assume the friction factor is $f = 0.02$ and the fittings are threaded fittings.

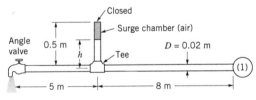

■ **FIGURE P8.37**

8.38   Water flows from a lake as is shown in Fig. P8.38 at a rate of 4.0 cfs. Is the device inside the building a pump or a turbine? Explain and determine the horsepower of the device. Neglect all minor losses and assume the friction factor is 0.025.

8.39   Repeat Problem 8.38 if the flowrate is 1.0 cfs.

8.40   At a ski resort water at 40 °F is pumped through a 3-in.-diameter, 2000-ft-long steel pipe from a pond at an elevation of 4286 ft to a snow-making machine at an eleva-

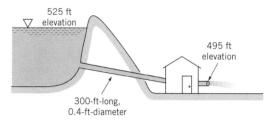

FIGURE P8.38

tion of 4623 ft at a rate of 0.26 ft³/s. If it is necessary to maintain a pressure of 180 psi at the snow-making machine, determine the horsepower added to the water by the pump. Neglect minor losses.

8.41 Water flows through the screen in the pipe shown in Fig. P8.41 as indicated. Determine the loss coefficient for the screen.

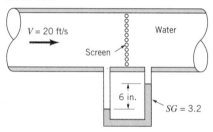

FIGURE P8.41

8.42 Water flows steadily through the 0.75-in. diameter galvanized iron pipe system shown in **Video V8.6** and Fig. P8.42 at a rate of 0.020 cfs. Your boss suggests that friction losses in the straight pipe sections are negligible compared to losses in the threaded elbows and fittings of the system. Do you agree or disagree with your boss? Support your answer with appropriate calculations.

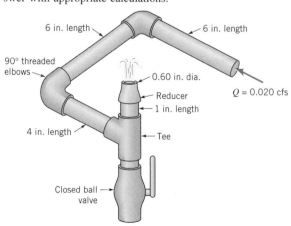

FIGURE P8.42

8.43 Assume a car's exhaust system can be approximated as 14 ft of 0.125-ft-diameter cast-iron pipe with the equivalent of six 90° flanged elbows and a muffler. (See **Video V8.5**.) The muffler acts as a resistor with a loss coefficient of $K_L = 8.5$. Determine the pressure at the beginning of the exhaust system if the flowrate is 0.10 cfs and the temperature is 250 °F.

8.44 Water at 40 °F flows through the coils of the heat exchanger as shown in Fig. P8.44 at a rate of 0.9 gal/min. Determine the pressure drop between the inlet and outlet of the horizontal device.

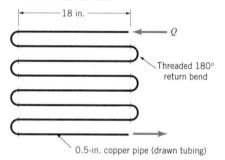

FIGURE P8.44

8.45 Water at 40 °F is pumped from a lake as shown in Fig. P8.45. What is the maximum flowrate possible without cavitation occurring?

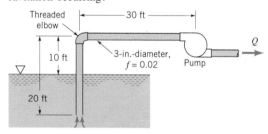

FIGURE P8.45

8.46 The $\frac{1}{2}$-in.-diameter hose shown in Fig. P8.46 can withstand a maximum pressure of 200 psi without rupturing. Determine the maximum length, ℓ, allowed if the friction factor is 0.022 and the flowrate is 0.010 cfs. Neglect minor losses. The fluid is water.

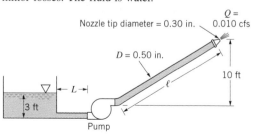

FIGURE P8.46

8.47 The hose shown in Fig. P8.46 will collapse if the pressure within it is lower than 10 psi below atmospheric pressure. Determine the maximum length, L, allowed if the friction factor is 0.015 and the flowrate is 0.010 cfs. Neglect minor losses.

8.48 As shown in **Video V8.6** and Fig. P8.48, water "bubbles up" 3 in. above the exit of the vertical pipe attached to three horizontal pipe segments. The total length of the 0.75-in.-diameter galvanized iron pipe between point (1) and the exit is 21 inches. Determine the pressure needed at point (1) to produce this flow.

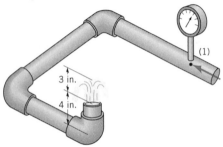

■ **FIGURE P8.48**

8.49 A sign like the one shown in Fig. P8.49 is often attached to the side of a jet engine as a warning to airport workers. Based on **Video V8.4** or Figs. 8.11 and 8.13, explain why the danger areas (indicated in color) are the shape they are.

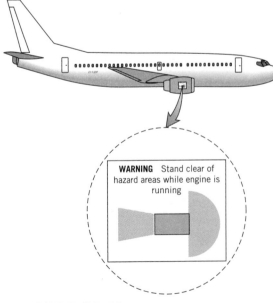

■ **FIGURE P8.49**

8.50 Water flows at a rate of 0.50 cfs from tank A to tank B through a horizontal 3-in.-diameter cast-iron pipe of length 200 ft. If minor losses are neglected, determine the difference in elevation of the free surfaces of the tanks.

8.51 According to fire regulations in a town, the pressure drop in a commercial steel, horizontal pipe must not exceed 1.0 psi per 150 ft pipe for flowrates up to 500 gal/min. If the water temperature is never below 50 °F, what diameter pipe is needed?

8.52 As shown in Fig. P8.52, a standard household water meter is incorporated into a lawn irrigation system to measure the volume of water applied to the lawn. Note that these meters measure volume, not volume flowrate. (See **Video V8.7**.) With an upstream pressure of $p_1 = 50$ psi the meter registered that 120 ft^3 of water was delivered to the lawn during an "on" cycle. Estimate the upstream pressure, p_1, needed if it is desired to have 150 ft^3 delivered during an "on" cycle. List any assumptions needed to arrive at your answer.

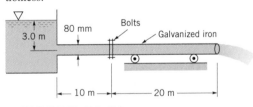

■ **FIGURE P8.52**

8.53 Water flows through the pipe shown in Fig. P8.53. Determine the net tension in the bolts if minor losses are neglected and the wheels on which the pipe rests are frictionless.

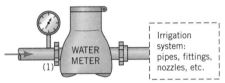

■ **FIGURE P8.53**

8.54 Repeat Problem 3.28 if head losses are included.

8.55 The pump shown in Fig. P8.55 adds 25 kW to the water and causes a flowrate of 0.04 m^3/s. Determine the flowrate expected if the pump is removed from the system. Assume $f = 0.016$ for either case and neglect minor losses.

8.56 Water is circulated from a large tank through a filter, and back to the tank as shown in Fig. P8.56. The power added to the water by the pump is 200 ft·lb/s. Determine the flowrate through the filter.

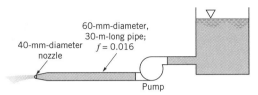

■ **FIGURE P8.55**

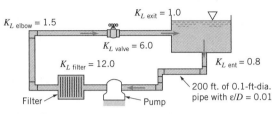

■ **FIGURE P8.56**

8.57   Determine the diameter of a steel pipe that is to carry 2,000 gal/min of gasoline with a pressure drop of 5 psi per 100 ft of horizontal pipe.

8.58   Water is to be moved from a large, closed tank in which the air pressure is 20 psi into a large, open tank through 2000 ft of smooth pipe at the rate of 3 ft³/s. The fluid level in the open tank is 150 ft below that in the closed tank. Determine the required diameter of the pipe. Neglect minor losses.

8.59   Repeat Problem 8.58 if there are numerous components (valves, elbows, etc.) along the pipe so that the minor loss is equal to 40 velocity heads.

8.60   Air, assumed incompressible, flows through the two pipes shown in Fig. P8.60. Determine the flowrate if minor losses are neglected and the friction factor in each pipe is 0.020. Determine the flowrate if the 0.5-in.-diameter pipe were replaced by a 1-in.-diameter pipe. Comment on the assumption of incompressibility.

■ **FIGURE P8.60**

***8.61**   Repeat Problem 8.60 if the pipes are galvanized iron and the friction factors are not known a priori.

8.62   With the valve closed, water flows from tank A to tank B as shown in Fig. P8.62. What is the flowrate into

tank B, when the valve is opened to allow water to flow into tank C also? Neglect all minor losses and assume that the friction factor is 0.02 for all pipes.

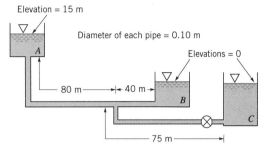

■ **FIGURE P8.62**

8.63   The three water-filled tanks shown in Fig. P8.63 are connected by pipes as indicated. If minor losses are neglected, determine the flowrate in each pipe.

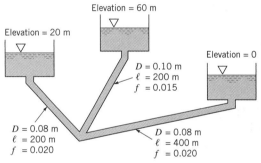

■ **FIGURE P8.63**

***8.64**   Repeat Problem 8.63 if the friction factors are not known, but the pipes are steel pipes.

8.65   Gasoline flows through a 35-mm-diameter pipe at a rate of 0.0032 m³/s. Determine the pressure drop across a flow nozzle placed in the line if the nozzle diameter is 20 mm.

8.66   Air to ventilate an underground mine flows through a large 2-m-diameter pipe. A crude flowrate meter is constructed by placing a sheet metal "washer" between two sections of the pipe. Estimate the flowrate if the hole in the sheet metal has a diameter of 1.6 m and the pressure difference across the sheet metal is 8.0 mm of water.

8.67   A 2.5-in.-diameter nozzle meter is installed in a 3.8-in.-diameter pipe that carries water at 160 °F. If the inverted air-water U-tube manometer used to measure the pressure difference across the meter indicates a reading of 3.1 ft, determine the flowrate.

8.68 Water flows through the Venturi meter shown in Fig. P8.68. The specific gravity of the manometer fluid is 1.52. Determine the flowrate.

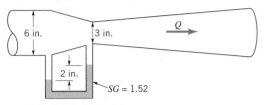

■ FIGURE P8.68

8.69 If the fluid flowing in Problem 8.68 were air, what would the flowrate be? Would compressibility effects be important? Explain.

8.70 Water flows through the orifice meter shown in Fig. P8.70 at a rate of 0.10 cfs. If $d = 0.1$ ft, determine the value of h.

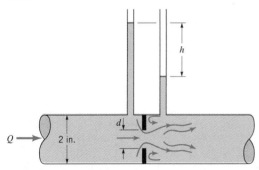

■ FIGURE P8.70

8.71 Water flows through the orifice meter shown in Fig. P8.70 at a rate of 0.10 cfs. If $h = 3.8$ ft, determine the value of d.

8.72 Water flows through the orifice meter shown in Fig. P8.70 such that $h = 1.6$ ft with $d = 1.5$ in. Determine the flowrate.

8.73 The device shown in Fig. P8.73 is used to investigate laminar flow through a pipe and to determine the Reynolds number for transition from laminar to turbulent flow. Air at a temperature of 73 °F and an absolute pressure of 29.93 in. of mercury flows with an average velocity of V through a small diameter, $D = 0.108$ in., tube of length $\ell = 24.0$ in. as indicated. The flowrate, Q, is determined by a rotameter and the pressure within the tank to which the tube is attached is given by the water manometer reading, h.

Experimentally determined values of Q and h are shown in the following table. Use these results to plot a graph on log–log paper of the friction factor, f, for this tube as a function of the Reynolds number based on the tube diameter, $\text{Re} = \rho V D/\mu$. On the same graph, plot the theoretical curve for laminar pipe flow. From the graphed results, determine the value of the Reynolds number for which the flow becomes turbulent in this pipe.

Compare the experimental and theoretical results and discuss some possible reasons for any differences between them.

Q (cm^3/min)	h (in.)
1,100	0.60
1,800	1.08
2,400	1.49
2,900	1.89
3,700	2.70
4,500	3.75
4,600	4.06
4,860	4.57
5,000	5.01
5,150	5.43
5,650	6.47
6,000	7.31
6,200	7.89

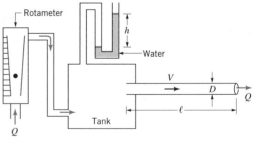

■ FIGURE P8.73

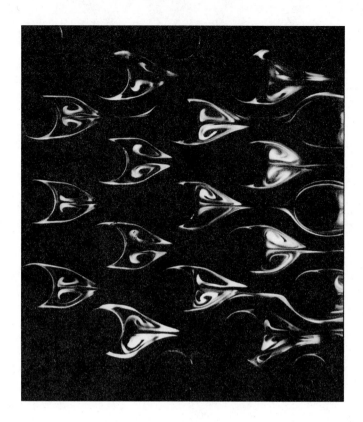

Flow Over Immersed Bodies

*I*n this chapter we consider various aspects of the flow over bodies that are immersed in a fluid. Examples include the flow of air around airplanes, automobiles, and falling snowflakes, or the flow of water around submarines and fish. In these situations the object is completely surrounded by the fluid and the flows are termed *external flows.* Theoretical (i.e., analytical and numerical) techniques can provide much of the needed information about such flows. However, because of the complexities of the governing equations and the complexities of the geometry of the objects involved, the amount of information obtained from purely theoretical methods is limited. Thus, much of the information about external flows comes from experiments carried out, for the most part, on scale models of the actual objects.

9.1 General External Flow Characteristics

A body immersed in a moving fluid experiences a resultant force due to the interaction between the body and the fluid surrounding it. We can fix the coordinate system in the body and treat the situation as fluid flowing past a stationary body with velocity *U,* the *upstream velocity.*

Impulsive start of flow past an array of cylinders: The complex structure of laminar flow past a relatively simple geometric structure illustrates why it is often difficult to obtain exact analytical results for external flows. (Dye in water.) (Photograph courtesy of ONERA, France.)

Three general categories of bodies are shown in Fig. 9.1. They include (a) two-dimensional objects (infinitely long and of constant cross-sectional size and shape), (b) axisymmetric bodies (formed by rotating their cross-sectional shape about the axis of symmetry), and (c) three-dimensional bodies that may or may not possess a line or plane of symmetry.

Another classification of body shape can be made depending on whether the body is streamlined or blunt. The flow characteristics depend strongly on the amount of streamlining present. In general, *streamlined bodies* (i.e., airfoils, racing cars, etc.) have little effect on the surrounding fluid, compared with the effect that *blunt bodies* (i.e., parachutes, buildings, etc.) have on the fluid.

V9.1 Space shuttle landing

9.1.1 Lift and Drag Concepts

When any body moves through a fluid, an interaction between the body and the fluid occurs; this effect can be described in terms of the forces at the fluid–body interface. This can be described in terms of the stresses—wall shear stresses, τ_w, due to viscous effects and normal stresses due to the pressure, p. Typical shear stress and pressure distributions are shown in Figs. 9.2a and 9.2b. Both τ_w and p vary in magnitude and direction along the surface.

The resultant force in the direction of the upstream velocity is termed the *drag,* $\mathcal{D}$, and the resultant force normal to the upstream velocity is termed the *lift,* $\mathcal{L}$, as is indicated in Fig. 9.2c. The resultant of the shear stress and pressure distributions can be obtained by in-

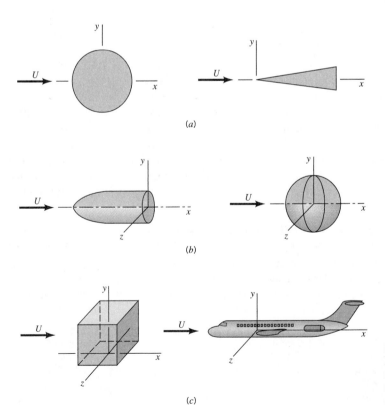

■ **FIGURE 9.1**
Flow classification:
(*a*) two-dimensional,
(*b*) axisymmetric,
(*c*) three-dimensional.

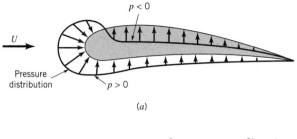

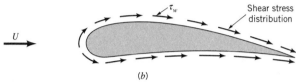

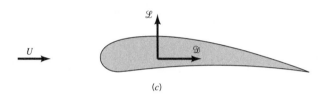

■ **FIGURE 9.2** **Forces from the surrounding fluid on a two-dimensional object: (*a*) pressure force, (*b*) viscous force, (*c*) resultant force (lift and drag).**

tegrating the effect of these two quantities on the body surface as is indicated in Fig. 9.3. The net *x* and *y* components of the force on the object are

$$\mathcal{D} = \int dF_x = \int p \cos \theta \, dA + \int \tau_w \sin \theta \, dA \tag{9.1}$$

and

$$\mathcal{L} = \int dF_y = -\int p \sin \theta \, dA + \int \tau_w \cos \theta \, dA \tag{9.2}$$

Of course, to carry out the integrations and determine the lift and drag, we must know the body shape (i.e., θ as a function of location along the body) and the distribution of τ_w and p along the surface. These distributions are often extremely difficult to obtain, either experimentally or theoretically.

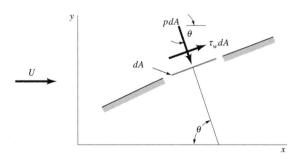

■ **FIGURE 9.3** **Pressure and shear forces on a small element of the surface of a body.**

EXAMPLE 9.1

Air at standard conditions flows past a flat plate as is indicated in Fig. E9.1. In case **(a)** the plate is parallel to the upstream flow, and in case **(b)** it is perpendicular to the upstream flow. If the pressure and shear stress distributions on the surface are as indicated (obtained either by experiment or theory), determine the lift and drag on the plate.

SOLUTION

For either orientation of the plate, the lift and drag are obtained from Eqs. 9.1 and 9.2. With the plate parallel to the upstream flow we have $\theta = 90°$ on the top surface and $\theta = 270°$ on the bottom surface so that the lift and drag are given by

$$\mathscr{L} = -\int_{\text{top}} p \, dA + \int_{\text{bottom}} p \, dA = 0$$

and

$$\mathscr{D} = \int_{\text{top}} \tau_w \, dA + \int_{\text{bottom}} \tau_w \, dA = 2 \int_{\text{top}} \tau_w \, dA \qquad \text{(1)}$$

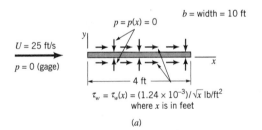

(a)

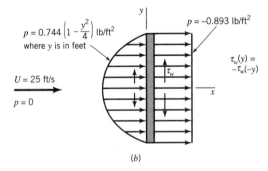

(b)

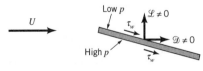

(c)

■ FIGURE E9.1

where we have used the fact that because of symmetry the shear stress distribution is the same on the top and the bottom surfaces, as is the pressure also [whether we use gage ($p = 0$) or absolute ($p = p_{atm}$) pressure]. There is no lift generated—the plate does not know up from down. With the given shear stress distribution, Eq. 1 gives

$$\mathcal{D} = 2 \int_{x=0}^{4\,\text{ft}} \left(\frac{1.24 \times 10^{-3}}{x^{1/2}} \text{ lb/ft}^2 \right) (10 \text{ ft}) \, dx$$

or

$$\mathcal{D} = 0.0992 \text{ lb} \tag{Ans}$$

With the plate perpendicular to the upstream flow, we have $\theta = 0°$ on the front and $\theta = 180°$ on the back. Thus, from Eqs. 9.1 and 9.2

$$\mathcal{L} = \int_{\text{front}} \tau_w \, dA - \int_{\text{back}} \tau_w \, dA = 0$$

and

$$\mathcal{D} = \int_{\text{front}} p \, dA - \int_{\text{back}} p \, dA$$

Again there is no lift because the pressure forces act parallel to the upstream flow (in the direction of $\mathcal{D}$ not $\mathcal{L}$) and the shear stress is symmetrical about the center of the plate. With the given relatively large pressure on the front of the plate (the center of the plate is a stagnation point) and the negative pressure (less than the upstream pressure) on the back of the plate, we obtain the following drag

$$\mathcal{D} = \int_{y=-2}^{2\,\text{ft}} \left[0.744 \left(1 - \frac{y^2}{4} \right) \text{ lb/ft}^2 - (-0.893) \text{lb/ft}^2 \right] (10 \text{ ft}) \, dy$$

or

$$\mathcal{D} = 55.6 \text{ lb} \tag{Ans}$$

Clearly there are two mechanisms responsible for the drag. On the ultimately streamlined body (a zero thickness flat plate parallel to the flow) the drag is entirely due to the shear stress at the surface and, in this example, is relatively small. For the ultimately blunted body (a flat plate normal to the upstream flow) the drag is entirely due to the pressure difference between the front and back portions of the object and, in this example, is relatively large.

If the flat plate were oriented at an arbitrary angle relative to the upstream flow as indicated in Fig. E9.1c, there would be both a lift and a drag, each of which would be dependent on both the shear stress and the pressure. Both the pressure and shear stress distributions would be different for the top and bottom surfaces.

Without detailed information concerning the shear stress and pressure distributions on a body, Eqs. 9.1 and 9.2 cannot be used. The widely used alternative is to define dimensionless lift and drag coefficients and determine their approximate values by means of either a simplified analysis, some numerical technique, or an appropriate experiment. The *lift coefficient*, C_L, and *drag coefficient*, C_D, are defined as

$$C_L = \frac{\mathcal{L}}{\frac{1}{2}\rho U^2 A}$$

and

$$C_D = \frac{\mathscr{D}}{\frac{1}{2}\rho U^2 A}$$

where A is a characteristic area of the object (see Chapter 7). Typically, A is taken to be *frontal area*—the projected area seen by a person looking toward the object from a direction parallel to the upstream velocity, U. In other situations A is taken to be the *planform area*—the projected area seen by an observer looking toward the object from a direction normal to the upstream velocity (i.e., from "above" it).

9.1.2 Characteristics of Flow Past an Object

External flows past objects encompass an extremely wide variety of fluid mechanics phenomena. For a given-shaped object, the characteristics of the flow depend very strongly on various parameters such as size, orientation, speed, and fluid properties. As is discussed in Chapter 7, according to dimensional analysis arguments, the character of the flow should depend on the various dimensionless parameters involved. For typical external flows the most important of these parameters are the Reynolds number, the Mach number, and the Froude number.

For the present, we consider how the external flow and its associated lift and drag vary as a function of Reynolds number. Recall that the Reynolds number represents the ratio of inertial effects to viscous effects. The nature of the flow past a body depends strongly on whether $\text{Re} \gg 1$ or $\text{Re} \ll 1$.

Flows past three flat plates of length ℓ with $\text{Re} = \rho U \ell / \mu = 0.1$, 10, and 10^7 are shown in Fig. 9.4. If the Reynolds number is small, the viscous effects are relatively strong and the plate affects the uniform upstream flow far ahead, above, below, and behind the plate. To reach that portion of the flow field where the velocity has been altered by less than 1% of its undisturbed value (i.e., $U - u < 0.01U$) we must travel relatively far from the plate. In low Reynolds number flows the viscous effects are felt far from the object in all directions.

As the Reynolds number is increased (by increasing U, for example), the region in which viscous effects are important becomes smaller in all directions except downstream, as is shown in Fig. 9.4b. One does not need to travel very far ahead, above, or below the plate to reach areas in which the viscous effects of the plate are not felt. The streamlines are displaced from their original uniform upstream conditions, but the displacement is not as great as for the $\text{Re} = 0.1$ situation shown in Fig. 9.4a.

As suggested by Ludwig Prandtl in 1904, if the Reynolds number is large (but not infinite), the flow is dominated by inertial effects and the viscous effects are negligible everywhere except in a region very close to the plate and in the relatively thin *wake region* behind the plate, as shown in Fig. 9.4c. Since the fluid viscosity is not zero ($\text{Re} < \infty$), it follows that the fluid must stick to the solid surface (the no-slip boundary condition). There is a thin *boundary layer* region of thickness $\delta = \delta(x) \ll \ell$ (i.e., thin relative to the length of the plate) next to the plate in which the fluid velocity changes from the upstream value of $u = U$ to zero velocity on the plate. The existence of the plate has very little effect on the streamlines outside of the boundary layer—either ahead, above, or below the plate. On the other hand, the wake region is due entirely to the viscous interaction between the fluid and the plate.

As with the flow past the flat plate described above, the flow past a blunt object (such as a circular cylinder) also varies with Reynolds number. In general, the larger the Reynolds

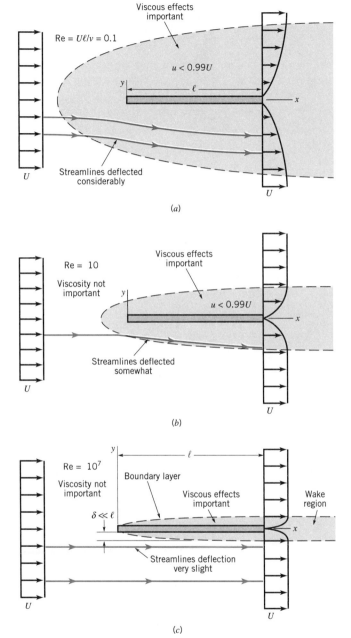

■ **FIGURE 9.4** **Character of the steady, viscous flow past a flat plate parallel to the upstream velocity: (*a*) low Reynolds number flow, (*b*) moderate Reynolds number flow, (*c*) large Reynolds number flow.**

number, the smaller the region of the flow field in which viscous effects are important. For objects that are not sufficiently streamlined, however, an additional characteristic of the flow is observed. This is termed *flow separation* and is illustrated in Fig. 9.5.

Low Reynolds number flow (Re = $UD/\nu < 1$) past a circular cylinder is characterized by the fact that the presence of the cylinder and the accompanying viscous effects are

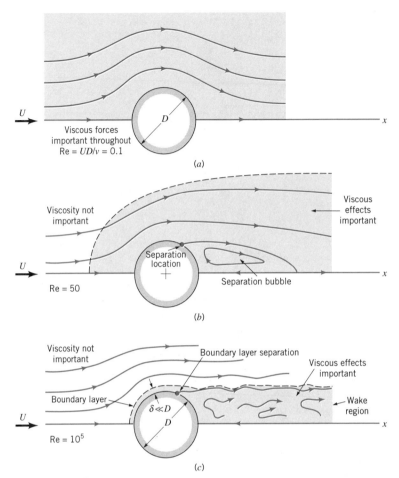

■ **FIGURE 9.5** **Character of the steady, viscous flow past a circular cylinder: (a) low Reynolds number flow, (b) moderate Reynolds number flow, (c) large Reynolds number flow.**

V9.2 Stream-
lined and
blunt bodies

felt throughout a relatively large portion of the flow field. As is indicated in Fig. 9.5a, for Re $= UD/\nu = 0.1$, the viscous effects are important several diameters in any direction from the cylinder.

As the Reynolds number is increased, the region ahead of the cylinder in which viscous effects are important becomes smaller, with the viscous region extending only a short distance ahead of the cylinder. The viscous effects are convected downstream and the flow loses its symmetry. Another characteristic of external flows becomes important—the flow separates from the body at the *separation location* as indicated in Fig. 9.5b.

At still larger Reynolds numbers, the area affected by the viscous forces is forced farther downstream until it involves only a thin ($\delta \ll D$) boundary layer on the front portion of the cylinder and an irregular, unsteady (perhaps turbulent) wake region that extends far downstream of the cylinder. The fluid in the region outside of the boundary layer and wake region flows as if it were inviscid.

9.2   Boundary Layer Characteristics

As was discussed in the previous section, it is often possible to treat flow past an object as a combination of viscous flow in the boundary layer and inviscid flow elsewhere. If the Reynolds number is large enough, viscous effects are important only in the boundary layer regions near the object (and in the wake region behind the object). The boundary layer is needed to allow for the no-slip boundary condition that requires the fluid to cling to any solid surface that it flows past. Outside of the boundary layer the velocity gradients normal to the flow are relatively small, and the fluid acts as if it were inviscid, even though the viscosity is not zero. A necessary condition for this structure of the flow is that the Reynolds number be large.

9.2.1   Boundary Layer Structure and Thickness on a Flat Plate

In this section we consider the situation in which the boundary layer is formed on a long flat plate along which flows a viscous, incompressible fluid as is shown in Fig. 9.6. For a finite length plate, it is clear that the plate length, ℓ, can be used as the characteristic length, with the Reynolds number as $Re = U\ell/\nu$. For the infinitely long flat plate extending from $x = 0$ to $x = \infty$, it is not obvious how to define the Reynolds number because there is no characteristic length. The plate has no thickness and is not of finite length!

For an infinitely long plate we use x, the coordinate distance along the plate from the leading edge, as the characteristic length and define the Reynolds number as $Re_x = Ux/\nu$. Thus, for any fluid or upstream velocity the Reynolds number will be sufficiently large for boundary layer type flow (i.e., Fig. 9.4c) if the plate is long enough. Physically, this means that the flow situations illustrated in Fig. 9.4 could be thought of as occurring on the same plate, but should be viewed by looking at longer portions of the plate as we step away from the plate to see the flows in Fig. 9.4a, 9.4b, and 9.4c, respectively. If the plate is sufficiently long, the Reynolds number $Re = U\ell/\nu$ is sufficiently large so that the flow takes on its boundary layer character (except very near the leading edge).

An appreciation of the structure of the boundary layer flow can be obtained by considering what happens to a fluid particle that flows into the boundary layer. As is indicated

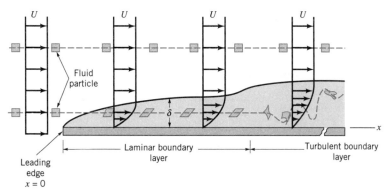

■ **FIGURE 9.6**   **Distortion of a fluid particle as it flows within the boundary layer.**

in Fig. 9.6, a small rectangular particle retains its original shape as it flows in the uniform flow outside of the boundary layer. Once it enters the boundary layer, the particle begins to distort because of the velocity gradient within the boundary layer—the top of the particle has a larger speed than its bottom.

V9.3 Laminar/turbulent transition

At some distance downstream from the leading edge, the boundary layer flow becomes turbulent and the fluid particles become greatly distorted because of the random, irregular nature of the turbulence. The transition from laminar to turbulent flow occurs at a critical value of the Reynolds number, Re_{xcr}, on the order of 2×10^5 to 3×10^6, depending on the roughness of the surface and the amount of turbulence in the upstream flow, as is discussed in Section 9.2.4.

The purpose of the boundary layer on the plate is to allow the fluid to change its velocity from the upstream value of U to zero on the plate. Thus, $\mathbf{V} = 0$ at $y = 0$ and $\mathbf{V} \approx U\hat{\mathbf{i}}$ at $y = \delta$, with the velocity profile, $u = u(x, y)$ bridging the boundary layer thickness. We define the *boundary layer thickness, δ*, as that distance from the plate at which the fluid velocity is within some arbitrary value of the upstream velocity. Typically, as indicated in Fig. 9.7a,

$$\delta = y \quad \text{where} \quad u = 0.99U$$

To remove this arbitrariness (i.e., what is so special about 99%; why not 98%?), the following definitions are introduced. Shown in Fig. 9.7b are two velocity profiles for flow past a flat plate—one if there were no viscosity (a uniform profile) and the other if there is viscosity and zero slip at the wall (the boundary layer profile). Because of the velocity deficit, $U - u$, within the boundary layer, the flowrate across section b–b is less than that across section a–a. However, if we displace the plate at section a–a by an appropriate amount δ^*, the *boundary layer displacement thickness,* the flowrate across each section will be identical. This is true if

$$\delta^* bU = \int_0^\infty (U - u)b \, dy$$

where b is the plate width. Thus,

$$\delta^* = \int_0^\infty \left(1 - \frac{u}{U}\right) dy \tag{9.3}$$

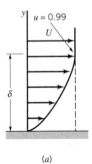

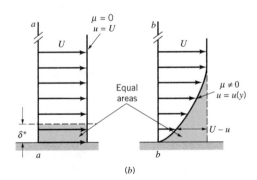

■ **FIGURE 9.7** **Boundary layer thickness: (a) standard boundary layer thickness, (b) boundary layer displacement thickness.**

The displacement thickness represents the amount that the thickness of the body must be increased so that the fictitious uniform inviscid flow has the same mass flowrate properties as the actual viscous flow. It represents the outward displacement of the streamlines caused by the viscous effects on the plate.

Another boundary layer thickness definition, the *boundary layer momentum thickness,* Θ, is often used when determining the drag on an object. Again because of the velocity deficit, $U - u$, in the boundary layer, the momentum flux across section b–b in Fig. 9.7 is less than that across section a–a. This deficit in momentum flux for the actual boundary layer flow is given by

$$\int \rho u(U - u) \, dA = \rho b \int_0^\infty u(U - u) \, dy$$

which by definition is the momentum flux in a layer of uniform speed U and thickness Θ. That is,

$$\rho b U^2 \Theta = \rho b \int_0^\infty u(U - u) \, dy$$

or

$$\Theta = \int_0^\infty \frac{u}{U} \left(1 - \frac{u}{U} \right) dy \tag{9.4}$$

All three boundary layer thickness definitions, δ, δ^*, and Θ, are of use in boundary layer analyses.

9.2.2 Prandtl/Blasius Boundary Layer Solution

In theory, the details of viscous incompressible flow past any object can be obtained by solving the governing Navier–Stokes equations discussed in Section 6.8.2. For steady, two-dimensional laminar flows with negligible gravitational effects, these equations (Eqs. 6.120a, b, and c) reduce to the following

$$u \frac{\partial u}{\partial x} + v \frac{\partial u}{\partial y} = -\frac{1}{\rho} \frac{\partial p}{\partial x} + \nu \left(\frac{\partial^2 u}{\partial x^2} + \frac{\partial^2 u}{\partial y^2} \right) \tag{9.5}$$

$$u \frac{\partial v}{\partial x} + v \frac{\partial v}{\partial y} = -\frac{1}{\rho} \frac{\partial p}{\partial y} + \nu \left(\frac{\partial^2 v}{\partial x^2} + \frac{\partial^2 v}{\partial y^2} \right) \tag{9.6}$$

which express Newton's second law. In addition, the conservation of mass equation, Eq. 6.31, for incompressible flow is

$$\frac{\partial u}{\partial x} + \frac{\partial v}{\partial y} = 0 \tag{9.7}$$

The appropriate boundary conditions are that the fluid velocity far from the body is the upstream velocity and that the fluid sticks to the solid body surfaces. Although the mathematical problem is well-posed, no one has obtained an analytical solution to these equations for flow past any shaped body!

By using boundary layer concepts introduced in the previous sections, Prandtl was able to impose certain approximations (valid for large Reynolds number flows), and thereby to simplify the governing equations. In 1908, H. Blasius, one of Prandtl's students, was able to solve these simplified equations for the boundary layer flow past a flat plate parallel to the flow. Details may be found in the literature (Refs. 1, 2, 3).

From the Blasius solution it is found that the boundary layer thickness is

$$\delta = 5\sqrt{\frac{\nu x}{U}} \tag{9.8}$$

or

$$\frac{\delta}{x} = \frac{5}{\sqrt{Re_x}}$$

where $Re_x = Ux/\nu$. It can also be shown that the displacement and momentum thicknesses are given by

$$\frac{\delta^*}{x} = \frac{1.721}{\sqrt{Re_x}} \tag{9.9}$$

and

$$\frac{\Theta}{x} = \frac{0.664}{\sqrt{Re_x}} \tag{9.10}$$

As postulated, the boundary layer is thin provided that Re_x is large (i.e., $\delta/x \rightarrow 0$ as $Re_x \rightarrow \infty$).

With the velocity profile known it is an easy matter to determine the wall shear stress, $\tau_w = \mu(\partial u/\partial y)_{y=0}$, where the velocity gradient is evaluated at the plate. The value of $\partial u/\partial y$ at $y = 0$ can be obtained from the Blasius solution to give

$$\tau_w = 0.332 U^{3/2} \sqrt{\frac{\rho\mu}{x}} \tag{9.11}$$

Note that the shear stress decreases with increasing x because of the increasing thickness of the boundary layer—the velocity gradient at the wall decreases with increasing x. Also, τ_w varies as $U^{3/2}$, not as U as it does for fully developed laminar pipe flow.

For a flat plate of length ℓ and width b, the net friction drag, $\mathcal{D}_f$, can be expressed in terms of the *friction drag coefficient*, C_{Df}, as

$$C_{Df} = \frac{\mathcal{D}_f}{\frac{1}{2}\rho U^2 b\ell} = \frac{b\int_0^\ell \tau_w \, dx}{\frac{1}{2}\rho U^2 b\ell} \tag{9.12}$$

For the Blasius solution Eq. 9.12 gives

$$C_{Df} = \frac{1.328}{\sqrt{Re_\ell}}$$

where $Re_\ell = U\ell/\nu$ is the Reynolds number based on the plate length.

9.2.3   Momentum Integral Boundary Layer Equation for a Flat Plate

One of the important aspects of boundary layer theory is the determination of the drag caused by shear forces on a body. As was discussed in the previous section, such results can be obtained from the governing differential equations for laminar boundary layer flow. Since these solutions are extremely difficult to obtain, it is of interest to have an alternative approximate method. The momentum integral method described in this section provides such an alternative.

We consider the uniform flow past a flat plate and the fixed control volume as shown in Fig. 9.8. In agreement with advanced theory and experiment, we assume that the pressure is constant throughout the flow field. The flow entering the control volume at the leading edge of the plate [section (1)] is uniform, while the velocity of the flow exiting the control volume [section (2)] varies from the upstream velocity at the edge of the boundary layer to zero velocity on the plate.

The fluid adjacent to the plate makes up the lower portion of the control surface. The upper surface coincides with the streamline just outside the edge of the boundary layer at section (2). It need not (in fact, does not) coincide with the edge of the boundary layer except at section (2). If we apply the x component of the momentum equation (Eq. 5.17) to the steady flow of fluid within this control volume we obtain

$$\sum F_x = \rho \int_{(1)} u\mathbf{V} \cdot \hat{\mathbf{n}} \, dA + \rho \int_{(2)} u\mathbf{V} \cdot \hat{\mathbf{n}} \, dA \tag{9.13}$$

In addition, for a plate of width b the net force that the plate exerts on the fluid is the drag, $\mathcal{D}$, where

$$\sum F_x = -\mathcal{D} = -\int_{\text{plate}} \tau_w \, dA = -b \int_{\text{plate}} \tau_w \, dx \tag{9.14}$$

Thus, by combining Eqs. 9.13 and 9.14,

$$-\mathcal{D} = \rho \int_{(1)} U(-U) \, dA + \rho \int_{(2)} u^2 \, dA$$

or

$$\mathcal{D} = \rho U^2 bh - \rho b \int_0^\delta u^2 \, dy \tag{9.15}$$

Although the height h is not known, it is known that for conservation of mass the flowrate through section (1) must equal that through section (2), or

$$Uh = \int_0^\delta u \, dy$$

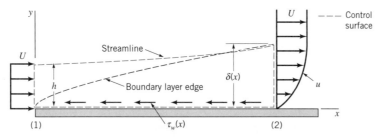

■ **FIGURE 9.8** **Control volume used in the derivation of the momentum integral equation for boundary layer flow.**

which can be written as

$$\rho U^2 bh = \rho b \int_0^\delta Uu \, dy \tag{9.16}$$

Thus, by combining Eqs. 9.15 and 9.16 we obtain the drag in terms of the deficit of momentum flux across the outlet of the control volume as

$$\mathcal{D} = \rho b \int_0^\delta u(U - u) \, dy \tag{9.17}$$

If the flow were inviscid, the drag would be zero, since we would have $u \equiv U$ and the right-hand side of Eq. 9.17 would be zero. (This is consistent with the fact that $\tau_w = 0$ if $\mu = 0$.) Equation 9.17 points out the important fact that boundary layer flow on a flat plate is governed by a balance between shear drag (the left-hand side of Eq. 9.17) and a decrease in the momentum of the fluid (the right-hand side of Eq. 9.17). By comparing Eqs. 9.17 and 9.4 we see that the drag can be written in terms of the momentum thickness, Θ, as

$$\mathcal{D} = \rho b U^2 \Theta \tag{9.18}$$

Note that this equation is valid for laminar or turbulent flows.

The shear stress distribution can be obtained from Eq. 9.18 by differentiating both sides with respect to x to obtain

$$\frac{d\mathcal{D}}{dx} = \rho b U^2 \frac{d\Theta}{dx} \tag{9.19}$$

Since $d\mathcal{D} = \tau_w b \, dx$ (see Eq. 9.14) it follows that

$$\frac{d\mathcal{D}}{dx} = b\tau_w \tag{9.20}$$

Hence, by combining Eqs. 9.19 and 9.20 we obtain the *momentum integral equation* for the boundary layer flow on a flat plate

$$\tau_w = \rho U^2 \frac{d\Theta}{dx} \tag{9.21}$$

The usefulness of this relationship lies in the ability to obtain approximate boundary layer results easily by using rather crude assumptions. This method is illustrated in Example 9.2.

EXAMPLE 9.2

Consider the laminar flow of an incompressible fluid past a flat plate at $y = 0$. The boundary layer velocity profile is approximated as $u = Uy/\delta$ for $0 \le y \le \delta$ and $u = U$ for $y > \delta$, as is shown in Fig. E9.2. Determine the shear stress by using the momentum integral equation. Compare these results with the Blasius results given by Eq. 9.11.

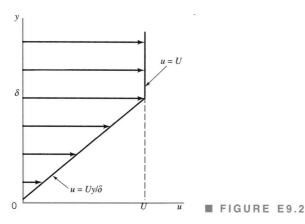

■ FIGURE E9.2

SOLUTION

From Eq. 9.21 the shear stress is given by

$$\tau_w = \rho U^2 \frac{d\Theta}{dx} \tag{1}$$

while for laminar flow we know that $\tau_w = \mu(\partial u/\partial y)_{y=0}$. For the assumed profile we have

$$\tau_w = \mu \frac{U}{\delta} \tag{2}$$

and from Eq. 9.4

$$\Theta = \int_0^\infty \frac{u}{U}\left(1 - \frac{u}{U}\right) dy = \int_0^\delta \frac{u}{U}\left(1 - \frac{u}{U}\right) dy = \int_0^\delta \left(\frac{y}{\delta}\right)\left(1 - \frac{y}{\delta}\right) dy$$

or

$$\Theta = \frac{\delta}{6} \tag{3}$$

Note that as yet we do not know the value of δ (but suspect that it should be a function of x).
By combining Eqs. 1, 2, and 3 we obtain the following differential equation for δ:

$$\frac{\mu U}{\delta} = \frac{\rho U^2}{6} \frac{d\delta}{dx}$$

or

$$\delta \, d\delta = \frac{6\mu}{\rho U} \, dx$$

This can be integrated from the leading edge of the plate, $x = 0$, where $\delta = 0$ to an arbitrary location x where the boundary layer thickness is δ. The result is

$$\frac{\delta^2}{2} = \frac{6\mu}{\rho U} x$$

or

$$\delta = 3.46 \sqrt{\frac{\nu x}{U}} \qquad (4)$$

Note that this approximate result (i.e., the velocity profile is not actually the simple straight line we assumed) compares favorably with the (much more laborious to obtain) Blasius result given by Eq. 9.8.

The wall shear stress can also be obtained by combining Eqs. 1, 3, and 4 to give

$$\tau_w = 0.289 U^{3/2} \sqrt{\frac{\rho \mu}{x}} \qquad \text{(Ans)}$$

Again this approximate result is close (within 13%) to the Blasius value of τ_w given by Eq. 9.11.

9.2.4 Transition from Laminar to Turbulent Flow

The analytical results given in Section 9.2.2 are restricted to laminar boundary layer flows along a flat plate with zero pressure gradient. They agree quite well with experimental results up to the point where the boundary layer flow becomes turbulent, which will occur for any free stream velocity and any fluid provided the plate is long enough. This is true because

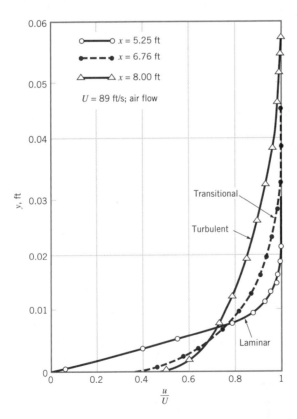

■ **FIGURE 9.9** Typical boundary layer profiles on a flat plate for laminar, transitional, and turbulent flow (Ref. 1).

the parameter that governs the transition to turbulent flow is the Reynolds number—in this case the Reynolds number based on the distance from the leading edge of the plate, $Re_x = Ux/\nu$.

The value of the Reynolds number at the transition location is a rather complex function of various parameters involved, including the roughness of the surface, the curvature of the surface (e.g., a flat plate or a sphere), and some measure of the disturbances in the flow outside the boundary layer. On a flat plate with a sharp leading edge in a typical air stream, the transition takes place at a distance x from the leading edge given by $Re_{xcr} = 2 \times 10^5$ to 3×10^6. Unless otherwise stated, we will use $Re_{xcr} = 5 \times 10^5$ in our calculations.

Transition from laminar to turbulent flow also involves a noticeable change in the shape of the boundary layer velocity profile. Typical profiles obtained in the neighborhood of the transition location are indicated in Fig. 9.9. The turbulent profiles are flatter, have a larger velocity gradient at the wall, and produce a larger boundary layer thickness than do the laminar profiles.

EXAMPLE 9.3

A fluid flows steadily past a flat plate with a velocity of $U = 10$ ft/s. At approximately what location will the boundary layer become turbulent, and how thick is the boundary layer at that point if the fluid is (a) water at 60 °F, (b) standard air, or (c) glycerin at 68 °F?

SOLUTION

For any fluid, the laminar boundary layer thickness is found from Eq. 9.8 as

$$\delta = 5\sqrt{\frac{\nu x}{U}}$$

The boundary layer remains laminar up to

$$x_{cr} = \frac{\nu Re_{xcr}}{U}$$

Thus, if we assume $Re_{xcr} = 5 \times 10^5$ we obtain

$$x_{cr} = \frac{5 \times 10^5}{10 \text{ ft/s}} \nu = 5 \times 10^4 \nu$$

and

$$\delta_{cr} \equiv \delta|_{x=x_{cr}} = 5\left[\frac{\nu}{10}(5 \times 10^4 \nu)\right]^{1/2} = 354 \nu$$

where ν is in ft²/s and x_{cr} and δ_{cr} are in feet. The values of the kinematic viscosity obtained from Tables 1.4 to 1.6 are listed in Table E9.3 along with the corresponding x_{cr} and δ_{cr}.

■ **TABLE E9.3**

Fluid	ν (ft^2/s)	x_{cr} (ft)	δ_{cr} (ft)
a. Water	1.21×10^{-5}	0.605	0.00428
b. Air	1.57×10^{-4}	7.85	0.0556
c. Glycerin	1.28×10^{-2}	640.0	4.53

(Ans)

Laminar flow can be maintained on a longer portion of the plate if the viscosity is increased. However, the boundary layer flow eventually becomes turbulent, provided the plate is long enough. Similarly, the boundary layer thickness is greater if the viscosity is increased.

9.2.5 Turbulent Boundary Layer Flow

The structure of turbulent boundary layer flow is very complex, random, and irregular. It shares many of the characteristics described for turbulent pipe flow in Section 8.3. In particular, the velocity at any given location in the flow is unsteady in a random fashion. The flow can be thought of as a jumbled mix of intertwined eddies (or swirls) of different sizes (diameters and angular velocities). The various fluid quantities involved (i.e., mass, momentum, energy) are convected downstream in the free-stream direction as in a laminar boundary layer. For turbulent flow they are also convected across the boundary layer (in the direction perpendicular to the plate) by the random transport of finite-sized fluid particles associated with the turbulent eddies. There is considerable mixing involved with these finite-sized eddies—considerably more than is associated with the mixing found in laminar flow where it is confined to the molecular scale. Consequently, the shear force for turbulent boundary layer flow is considerably greater than it is for laminar boundary layer flow (see Section 8.3.2).

There are no "exact" solutions for turbulent boundary layer flow. As is discussed in Section 9.2.2, it is possible to solve the Prandtl boundary layer equations for laminar flow past a flat plate to obtain the Blasius solution. Since there is no precise expression for the shear stress in turbulent flow (see Section 8.3), solutions are not available for turbulent flow. Thus, it is necessary to use some empirical relationship for the wall shear stress and corresponding drag coefficient.

In general, the drag coefficient for a flat plate of length ℓ, $C_{Df} = \mathscr{D}_f / \frac{1}{2} \rho U^2 A$, is a function of the Reynolds number, Re_ℓ, and the relative roughness, ε/ℓ. The results of numerous experiments covering a wide range of the parameters of interest are shown in Fig. 9.10. For laminar boundary layer flow the drag coefficient is a function of only the Reynolds number—surface roughness is not important. This is similar to laminar flow in a pipe. However, for turbulent flow, the surface roughness does affect the shear stress and, hence, the drag coefficient. This is similar to turbulent pipe flow. Values of the roughness, ε, for different materials can be obtained from Table 8.1.

The drag coefficient diagram of Fig. 9.10 (boundary layer flow) shares many characteristics in common with the familiar Moody diagram (pipe flow) of Fig. 8.10, even though the mechanisms governing the flow are quite different. Fully developed horizontal pipe flow is governed by a balance between pressure forces and viscous forces. The fluid inertia remains constant throughout the flow. Boundary layer flow on a horizontal flat plate is gov-

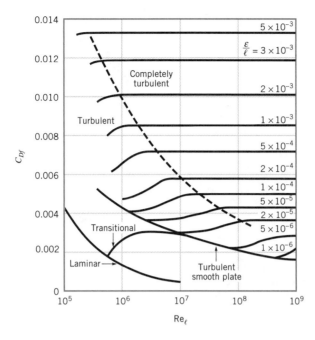

■ FIGURE 9.10 **Friction drag coefficient for a flat plate parallel to the upstream flow (Ref. 12, with permission).**

erned by a balance between inertia effects and viscous forces. The pressure remains constant throughout the flow.

It is often convenient to have an equation for the drag coefficient as a function of the Reynolds number and relative roughness rather than the graphical representation given in Fig. 9.10. Although there is not one equation valid for the entire $\text{Re}_\ell - \varepsilon/\ell$ range, the equations presented in Table 9.1 do work well for the conditions indicated.

■ **TABLE 9.1**

Empirical Equations for the Flat Plate Drag Coefficient (Ref. 1)

Equation	Flow Conditions
$C_{Df} = 1.328/(\text{Re}_\ell)^{0.5}$	Laminar flow
$C_{Df} = 0.455/(\log \text{Re}_\ell)^{2.58} - 1700/\text{Re}_\ell$	Transitional with $\text{Re}_{xcr} = 5 \times 10^5$
$C_{Df} = 0.455/(\log \text{Re}_\ell)^{2.58}$	Turbulent, smooth plate
$C_{Df} = [1.89 - 1.62 \log(\varepsilon/\ell)]^{-2.5}$	Completely turbulent

EXAMPLE 9.4

The water ski shown in Fig. E9.4a moves through 70 °F water with a velocity U. Estimate the drag caused by the shear stress on the bottom of the ski for $0 < U < 30$ ft/s.

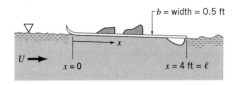

(a)

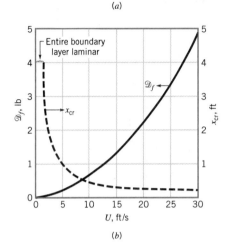

(b)

■ **FIGURE E9.4**

Solution

Clearly the ski is not a flat plate, and it is not aligned exactly parallel to the upstream flow. However, we can obtain a reasonable approximation to the shear force by using the flat plate results. That is, the friction drag, $\mathcal{D}_f$, caused by the shear stress on the bottom of the ski (the wall shear stress) can be determined as

$$\mathcal{D}_f = \tfrac{1}{2}\rho U^2 \ell b C_{Df}$$

With $A = \ell b = 4 \text{ ft} \times 0.5 \text{ ft} = 2 \text{ ft}^2$, $\rho = 1.94 \text{ slugs/ft}^3$, and $\mu = 2.04 \times 10^{-5} \text{ lb·s/ft}^2$ (see Table B.1) we obtain

$$\mathcal{D}_f = \tfrac{1}{2}(1.94 \text{ slugs/ft}^3)(2.0 \text{ ft}^2)U^2 C_{Df}$$
$$= 1.94 \, U^2 C_{Df} \tag{1}$$

where $\mathcal{D}_f$ and U are in pounds and ft/s, respectively.

The friction coefficient, C_{Df}, can be obtained from Fig. 9.10 or from the appropriate equations given in Table 9.1. As we will see, for this problem, much of the flow lies within the transition regime where both the laminar and turbulent portions of the boundary layer flow occupy comparable lengths of the plate. We choose to use the values of C_{Df} from the table.

For the given conditions we obtain

$$\text{Re}_\ell = \frac{\rho U \ell}{\mu} = \frac{(1.94 \text{ slugs/ft}^3)(4 \text{ ft})U}{2.04 \times 10^{-5} \text{ lb·s/ft}^2} = 3.80 \times 10^5 \, U$$

where U is in ft/s. With $U = 10$ ft/s, or $\text{Re}_\ell = 3.80 \times 10^6$, we obtain from Table 9.1 $C_{Df} = 0.455/(\log \text{Re}_\ell)^{2.58} - 1700/\text{Re}_\ell = 0.00308$. From Eq. 1 the corresponding drag is

$$\mathcal{D}_f = 1.94(10)^2(0.00308) = 0.598 \text{ lb}$$

By covering the range of upstream velocities of interest we obtain the results shown in Fig. E9.4b.

If $\text{Re} \lesssim 1000$, the results of boundary layer theory are not valid—inertia effects are not dominant enough and the boundary layer is not thin compared with the length of the plate. For our problem this corresponds to $U = 2.63 \times 10^{-3}$ ft/s. For all practical purposes U is greater than this value, and the flow past the ski is of the boundary layer type.

The approximate location of the transition from laminar to turbulent boundary layer flow as defined by $\text{Re}_{cr} = \rho U x_{cr}/\mu = 5 \times 10^5$ is indicated in Fig. E9.4b. Up to $U = 1.31$ ft/s the entire boundary layer is laminar. The fraction of the boundary layer that is laminar decreases as U increases until only the front 0.18 ft is laminar when $U = 30$ ft/s.

For anyone who has water skied, it is clear that it can require considerably more force to be pulled along at 30 ft/s than the 2×4.88 lb $= 9.76$ lb (two skis) indicated in Fig. E9.4b. As is discussed in Section 9.3, the total drag on an object such as a water ski consists of more than just the friction drag. Other components, including pressure drag and wave-making drag, can add considerably to the total resistance.

9.2.6   Effects of Pressure Gradient

The boundary layer discussions in the previous parts of Section 9.2 have dealt with flow along a flat plate in which the pressure is constant throughout the fluid. In general, when a fluid flows past an object other than a flat plate, the pressure field is not uniform. As shown in Fig. 9.5, if the Reynolds number is large, relatively thin boundary layers will develop along the surfaces. Within these layers the component of the pressure gradient in the streamwise direction (i.e., along the body surface) is not zero, although the pressure gradient normal to the surface is negligibly small. That is, if we were to measure the pressure while moving across the boundary layer from the body to the boundary layer edge, we would find that the pressure is essentially constant. However, the pressure does vary in the direction along the body surface if the body is curved. The variation in the *free-stream velocity*, U_{fs}, the fluid velocity at the edge of the boundary layer, is the cause of the pressure gradient in the boundary layer. The characteristics of the entire flow (both within and outside of the boundary layer) are often highly dependent on the pressure gradient effects on the fluid within the boundary layer.

For a flat plate parallel to the upstream flow, the upstream velocity (that far ahead of the plate) and the free-stream velocity (that at the edge of the boundary layer) are equal—$U = U_{fs}$. This is a consequence of the negligible thickness of the plate. For bodies of nonzero thickness, these two velocities are different. This can be seen in the flow past a circular cylinder of diameter D. The upstream velocity and pressure are U and p_0, respectively. If the fluid were completely inviscid ($\mu = 0$), the Reynolds number would be infinite ($\text{Re} = \rho U D/\mu = \infty$) and the streamlines would be symmetrical, as are shown in Fig. 9.11a. The fluid velocity along the surface would vary from $U_{fs} = 0$ at the very front and rear of the

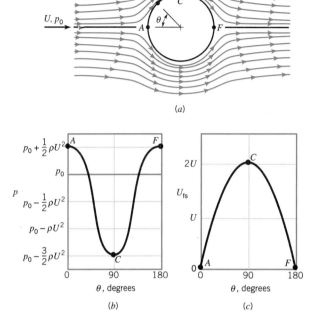

(a)

(b)

(c)

■ **FIGURE 9.11**   **Inviscid flow past a circular cylinder: (a) streamlines for the flow if there were no viscous effects, (b) pressure distribution on the cylinder's surface, (c) free stream velocity on the cylinder's surface.**

cylinder (points A and F are stagnation points) to a maximum of $U_{fs} = 2U$ at the top and bottom of the cylinder (point C). The pressure on the surface of the cylinder would be symmetrical about the vertical midplane of the cylinder, reaching a maximum value of $p_0 + \rho U^2/2$ (the stagnation pressure) at both the front and back of the cylinder, and a minimum of $p_0 - 3\rho U^2/2$ at the top and bottom of the cylinder. The pressure and free-stream velocity distributions are shown in Figs. 9.11b and 9.11c. Because of the absence of viscosity (therefore, $\tau_w = 0$) and the symmetry of the pressure distribution for inviscid flow past a circular cylinder, it is clear that the drag on the cylinder is zero.

Consider large Reynolds number flow of a real (viscous) fluid past a circular cylinder. As was discussed in Section 9.1.2, we expect the viscous effects to be confined to thin boundary layers near the surface. This allows the fluid to stick ($\mathbf{V} = 0$) to the surface—a necessary condition for any fluid, provided $\mu \neq 0$. The basic idea of boundary layer theory is that the boundary layer is thin enough so that it does not greatly disturb the flow outside the boundary layer. Based on this reasoning, for large Reynolds numbers the flow throughout most of the flow field would be expected to be as is indicated in Fig. 9.11a, the inviscid flow field.

The pressure distribution indicated in Fig. 9.11b is imposed on the boundary layer flow along the surface of the cylinder. In fact, there is negligible pressure variation across the thin boundary layer so that the pressure within the boundary layer is that given by the inviscid flow field. This pressure distribution along the cylinder is such that the stationary fluid at the nose of the cylinder ($U_{fs} = 0$ at $\theta = 0$) is accelerated to its maximum velocity ($U_{fs} = 2U$ at $\theta = 90°$) and then is decelerated back to zero velocity at the rear of the cylinder ($U_{fs} = 0$ at $\theta = 180°$). This is accomplished by a balance between pressure and inertia effects; viscous effects are absent for the inviscid flow outside the boundary layer.

Physically, in the absence of viscous effects, a fluid particle traveling from the front to the back of the cylinder coasts down the "pressure hill" from $\theta = 0$ to $\theta = 90°$ (from point A to C in Fig. 9.11b) and then back up the hill to $\theta = 180°$ (from point C to F) without any loss of energy. There is an exchange between kinetic and pressure energy, but there are no energy losses. The same pressure distribution is imposed on the viscous fluid within the boundary layer. The decrease in pressure in the direction of flow along the front half of the cylinder is termed a *favorable pressure gradient*. The increase in pressure in the direction of flow along the rear half of the cylinder is termed an *adverse pressure gradient*.

Consider a fluid particle within the boundary layer indicated in Fig. 9.12. In its attempt to flow from A to F it experiences the same pressure distribution as the particles in the free stream immediately outside the boundary layer—the inviscid flow field pressure. However,

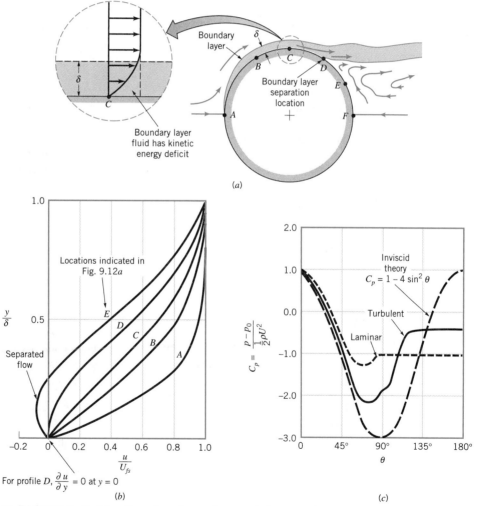

■ **FIGURE 9.12** **Boundary layer characteristics on a circular cylinder: (*a*) boundary layer separation location, (*b*) typical boundary layer velocity profiles at various locations on the cylinder, (*c*) surface pressure distributions for inviscid flow and boundary layer flow.**

because of the viscous effects involved, the particle in the boundary layer experiences a loss of energy as it flows along. This loss means that the particle does not have enough energy to coast all of the way up the pressure hill (from C to F) and to reach point F at the rear of the cylinder. This kinetic energy deficit is seen in the velocity profile detail at point C, shown in Fig. 9.12a. Because of friction, the boundary layer fluid cannot travel from the front to the rear of the cylinder. (This conclusion can also be obtained from the concept that due to viscous effects the particle at C does not have enough momentum to allow it to coast up the pressure hill to F.)

V9.4 Snow drifts

Thus, the fluid flows against the increasing pressure as far as it can, at which point the boundary layer separates from (lifts off) the surface. This *boundary layer separation* is indicated in Fig. 9.12a. Typical velocity profiles at representative locations along the surface are shown in Fig. 9.12b. At the separation location (profile D), the velocity gradient at the wall and the wall shear stress are zero. Beyond that location (from D to E) there is reverse flow in the boundary layer.

As is indicated in Fig. 9.12c, because of the boundary layer separation, the average pressure on the rear half of the cylinder is considerably less than that on the front half. Thus, a large pressure drag is developed, even though (because of small viscosity) the viscous shear drag may be quite small.

The location of separation, the width of the wake region behind the object, and the pressure distribution on the surface depend on the nature of the boundary layer flow. Compared with a laminar boundary layer, a turbulent boundary layer flow has more kinetic energy and momentum associated with it because (1) the velocity profile is fuller, more nearly like the ideal uniform profile, and (2) there can be considerable energy associated with the swirling, random components of the velocity that do not appear in the time-averaged x component of velocity. Thus, as is indicated in Fig. 9.12c, the turbulent boundary layer can flow farther around the cylinder (farther up the pressure hill) before it separates than can the laminar boundary layer.

9.3 Drag

As was discussed in Section 9.1, any object moving through a fluid will experience a drag, $\mathcal{D}$—a net force in the direction of flow due to the pressure and shear forces on the surface of the object. This net force, a combination of flow direction components of the normal and tangential forces on the body, can be determined by use of Eqs. 9.1 and 9.2, provided the distributions of pressure, p, and wall shear stress, τ_w, are known. Only in very rare instances can these distributions be determined analytically.

Most of the information pertaining to drag on objects is a result of numerous experiments with wind tunnels, water tunnels, towing tanks, and other ingenious devices that are used to measure the drag on scale models. Typically, the result for a given shaped object is a drag coefficient, C_D, where

$$C_D = \frac{\mathcal{D}}{\frac{1}{2}\rho U^2 A} \tag{9.22}$$

and C_D is a function of other dimensionless parameters such as Reynolds number, Re, Mach number, Ma, Froude number, Fr, and relative roughness of the surface, ε/ℓ. That is,

$$C_D = \phi(\text{shape, Re, Ma, Fr, } \varepsilon/\ell)$$

9.3.1   Friction Drag

Friction drag, $\mathcal{D}_f$, is that part of the drag that is due directly to the shear stress, τ_w, on the object. It is a function of not only the magnitude of the wall shear stress, but also of the orientation of the surface on which it acts. This is indicated by the factor $\tau_w \sin \theta$ in Eq. 9.1. For highly streamlined bodies or for low Reynolds number flow most of the drag may be due to friction.

The friction drag on a flat plate of width b and length ℓ oriented parallel to the upstream flow can be calculated from

$$\mathcal{D}_f = \tfrac{1}{2}\rho U^2 b\ell C_{Df}$$

where C_{Df} is the friction drag coefficient. The value of C_{Df} is given as a function of Reynolds number, $\text{Re}_\ell = \rho U\ell/\mu$, and relative surface roughness, ε/ℓ, in Fig. 9.10 and Table 9.1.

Most objects are not flat plates parallel to the flow; instead, they are curved surfaces along which the pressure varies. The precise determination of the shear stress along the surface of a curved body is quite difficult to obtain. Although approximate results can be obtained by a variety of techniques (Refs. 1, 2), these are outside the scope of this text.

9.3.2   Pressure Drag

Pressure drag, $\mathcal{D}_p$, is that part of the drag that is due directly to the pressure, p, on an object. It is often referred to as *form drag* because of its strong dependency on the shape or form of the object. Pressure drag is a function of the magnitude of the pressure and the orientation of the surface element on which the pressure force acts. For example, the pressure force on either side of a flat plate parallel to the flow may be very large, but it does not contribute to the drag because it acts in the direction normal to the upstream velocity. On the other hand, the pressure force on a flat plate normal to the flow provides the entire drag.

As previously noted, for most bodies, there are portions of the surface that are parallel to the upstream velocity, others normal to the upstream velocity, and the majority of which are at some angle in between. The pressure drag can be obtained from Eq. 9.1 provided a detailed description of the pressure distribution and the body shape is given. That is,

$$\mathcal{D}_p = \int p \cos \theta \, dA$$

which can be rewritten in terms of the *pressure drag coefficient, C_{Dp}*, as

$$C_{Dp} = \frac{\mathcal{D}_p}{\tfrac{1}{2}\rho U^2 A} = \frac{\displaystyle\int p \cos \theta \, dA}{\tfrac{1}{2}\rho U^2 A} = \frac{\displaystyle\int C_p \cos \theta \, dA}{A} \qquad (9.23)$$

Here $C_p = (p - p_0)/(\rho U^2/2)$ is the *pressure coefficient,* where p_0 is a reference pressure. The level of the reference pressure, p_0, does not influence the drag directly because the net pressure force on a body is zero if the pressure is constant (i.e., p_0) on the entire surface.

9.3.3   Drag Coefficient Data and Examples

As was discussed in previous sections, the net drag is produced by both pressure and shear stress effects. In most instances these two effects are considered together and an overall drag coefficient, C_D, as defined in Eq. 9.22 is used. There is an abundance of such drag coefficient data available in the literature. In this section we consider a small portion of this information for representative situations. Additional data can be obtained from various sources (Refs. 4, 5).

V9.5 Skydiving practice

Shape Dependence.   Clearly the drag coefficient for an object depends on the shape of the object, with shapes ranging from those that are streamlined to those that are blunt. The drag on an ellipse with aspect ratio ℓ/D, where D and ℓ are the thickness and length parallel to the flow, illustrates this dependence. The drag coefficient $C_D = \mathcal{D}/(\rho U^2 bD/2)$, based on the frontal area, $A = bD$, where b is the length normal to the flow, is as shown in Fig. 9.13. The more blunt the body, the larger the drag coefficient. With $\ell/D = 0$ (i.e., a flat plate normal to the flow) we obtain the flat plate value of $C_D = 1.9$. With $\ell/D = 1$ the corresponding value for a circular cylinder is obtained. As ℓ/D becomes larger the value of C_D decreases.

For very large aspect ratios ($\ell/D \rightarrow \infty$) the ellipse behaves as a flat plate parallel to the flow. For such cases, the friction drag is greater than the pressure drag. For extremely thin bodies (i.e., an ellipse with $\ell/D \rightarrow \infty$, a flat plate, or very thin airfoils) it is customary to use the planform area, $A = b\ell$, in defining the drag coefficient. The ellipse drag coefficient based on the planform area, $C_D = \mathcal{D}/(\rho U^2 b\ell/2)$, is also shown in Fig. 9.13. Clearly the drag obtained by using either of these drag coefficients would be the same. They merely represent two different ways to package the same information.

The amount of streamlining can have a considerable effect on the drag. Incredibly, the drag on the two two-dimensional objects drawn to scale in Fig. 9.14 is the same. The width of the wake for the streamlined strut is very thin, on the order of that for the much smaller diameter circular cylinder.

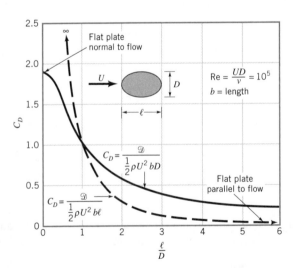

■ **FIGURE 9.13**   Drag coefficient for an ellipse with the characteristic area either the frontal area, $A = bD$, or the planform area, $A = b\ell$ (Ref. 4).

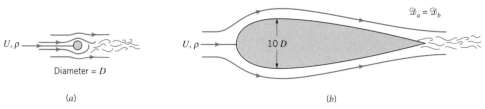

■ **FIGURE 9.14** **Two objects of considerably different size that have the same drag force: (a) circular cylinder $C_D = 1.2$, (b) streamlined strut $C_D = 0.12$.**

Reynolds Number Dependence. Another parameter on which the drag coefficient can be very dependent is the Reynolds number. Low Reynolds number flows (Re < 1) are governed by a balance between viscous and pressure forces. Inertia effects are negligibly small. In such instances the drag is expected to be a function of the upstream velocity, U, the body size, ℓ, and the viscosity, μ. That is,

$$\mathcal{D} = f(U, \ell, \mu)$$

From dimensional considerations (see Section 7.7.1)

$$\mathcal{D} = C\mu\ell U \tag{9.24}$$

where the value of the constant C depends on the shape of the body. If we put Eq. 9.24 into dimensionless form using the standard definition of the drag coefficient, $C_D = \mathcal{D}/\frac{1}{2}\rho U^2 A$, we obtain

$$C_D = \frac{\text{constant}}{\text{Re}}$$

where $\text{Re} = \rho U \ell / \mu$. For a sphere it can be shown that $C_D = 24/\text{Re}$, where $\ell = D$, the sphere diameter. For most objects, the low Reynolds number flow results are valid up to a Reynolds number of about 1.

EXAMPLE 9.5

A small grain of sand diameter $D = 0.10$ mm and specific gravity $SG = 2.3$ settles to the bottom of a lake after having been stirred up by a passing boat. Determine how fast it falls through the still water.

SOLUTION

A free-body diagram of the particle (relative to the moving particle) is shown in Fig. E9.5. The particle moves downward with a constant velocity U that is governed by a balance between the weight of the particle, $\mathcal{W}$, the buoyancy force of the surrounding water, F_B, and the drag of the water on the particle, $\mathcal{D}$.

From the free-body diagram we obtain

$$\mathcal{W} = \mathcal{D} + F_B$$

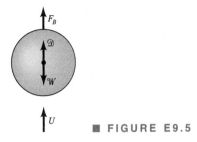

■ FIGURE E9.5

where

$$W = \gamma_{\text{sand}} V = SG\, \gamma_{\text{H}_2\text{O}} \frac{\pi}{6} D^3 \qquad (1)$$

and

$$F_B = \gamma_{\text{H}_2\text{O}} V = \gamma_{\text{H}_2\text{O}} \frac{\pi}{6} D^3 \qquad (2)$$

We assume (because of the smallness of the object) that the flow will be creeping flow (Re < 1) with $C_D = 24/\text{Re}$ so that

$$\mathcal{D} = \frac{1}{2} \rho_{\text{H}_2\text{O}} U^2 \frac{\pi}{4} D^2 C_D = \frac{1}{2} \rho_{\text{H}_2\text{O}} U^2 \frac{\pi}{4} D^2 \left(\frac{24}{\rho_{\text{H}_2\text{O}} UD / \mu_{\text{H}_2\text{O}}} \right)$$

or

$$\mathcal{D} = 3\pi \mu_{\text{H}_2\text{O}} UD \qquad (3)$$

We must eventually check to determine if this assumption is valid or not. Equation 3 is called Stokes law in honor of G. G. Stokes, a British mathematician and a physicist. By combining Eqs. 1, 2, and 3, we obtain

$$SG\, \gamma_{\text{H}_2\text{O}} \frac{\pi}{6} D^3 = 3\pi \mu_{\text{H}_2\text{O}} UD + \gamma_{\text{H}_2\text{O}} \frac{\pi}{6} D^3$$

or, since $\gamma = \rho g$,

$$U = \frac{(SG\rho_{\text{H}_2\text{O}} - \rho_{\text{H}_2\text{O}}) g D^2}{18\mu} \qquad (4)$$

From Table 1.5 for water at 15.6 °C we obtain $\rho_{\text{H}_2\text{O}} = 999$ kg/m^3 and $\mu_{\text{H}_2\text{O}} = 1.12 \times 10^{-3}$ N·s/m^2. Thus, from Eq. 4 we obtain

$$U = \frac{(2.3 - 1)(999 \text{ kg/m}^3)(9.81 \text{ m/s}^2)(0.10 \times 10^{-3} \text{ m})^2}{18(1.12 \times 10^{-3} \text{ N·s/m}^2)}$$

or

$$U = 6.32 \times 10^{-3} \text{ m/s} \qquad \text{(Ans)}$$

Since

$$\text{Re} = \frac{\rho D U}{\mu} = \frac{(999 \text{ kg/m}^3)(0.10 \times 10^{-3} \text{ m})(0.00632 \text{ m/s})}{1.12 \times 10^{-3} \text{ N·s/m}^2} = 0.564$$

we see that Re $<$ 1, and the form of the drag coefficient used is valid.

Note that if the density of the particle were the same as the surrounding fluid, from Eq. 4 we would obtain $U = 0$. This is reasonable since the particle would be neutrally buoyant and there would be no force to overcome the motion-induced drag. Note also that we have assumed that the particle falls at its steady terminal velocity. That is, we have neglected the acceleration of the particle from rest to its terminal velocity. Since the terminal velocity is small, this acceleration time is quite small. For faster objects (such as a free-falling skydiver) it may be important to consider the acceleration portion of the fall.

V9.6 Oscillating sign

Moderate Reynolds number flows tend to take on a boundary layer flow structure. For such flows past streamlined bodies, the drag coefficient tends to decrease slightly with Reynolds number. The $C_D \sim \text{Re}^{-1/2}$ dependence for a laminar boundary layer on a flat plate (see Table 9.1) is such an example. Moderate Reynolds number flows past blunt bodies generally produce drag coefficients that are relatively constant. The C_D values for the spheres and circular cylinders shown in Fig. 9.15a indicate this character in the range $10^3 < \text{Re} < 10^5$.

The structure of the flow field at selected Reynolds numbers indicated in Fig. 9.15a is shown in Fig. 9.15b. For a given object there is a wide variety of flow situations, depending on the Reynolds number involved. The curious reader is strongly encouraged to study the many beautiful photographs of these (and other) flow situations found in Ref. 6.

For many shapes there is a sudden change in the character of the drag coefficient when the boundary layer becomes turbulent. This is illustrated in Fig. 9.10 for the flat plate and in Fig. 9.15 for the sphere and the circular cylinder. The Reynolds number at which this transition takes place is a function of the shape of the body.

For the streamlined bodies, the drag coefficient increases when the boundary layer becomes turbulent because most of the drag is due to the shear force, which is greater for turbulent flow than for laminar flow. On the other hand, the drag coefficient for a relatively blunt object, such as a cylinder or sphere, actually decreases when the boundary layer becomes turbulent. As is discussed in Section 9.2.6, a turbulent boundary layer can travel further along the surface into the adverse pressure gradient on the rear portion of the cylinder before separation occurs. The result is a thinner wake and smaller pressure drag for turbulent boundary layer flow. This is indicated in Fig. 9.15 by the sudden decrease in C_D for $10^5 < \text{Re} < 10^6$.

For extremely blunt bodies, like a flat plate perpendicular to the flow, the flow separates at the edge of the plate regardless of the nature of the boundary layer flow. Thus, the drag coefficient shows very little dependence on the Reynolds number.

The drag coefficients for a series of two-dimensional bodies of varying bluntness are given as a function of Reynolds number in Fig. 9.16. The characteristics described above are evident.

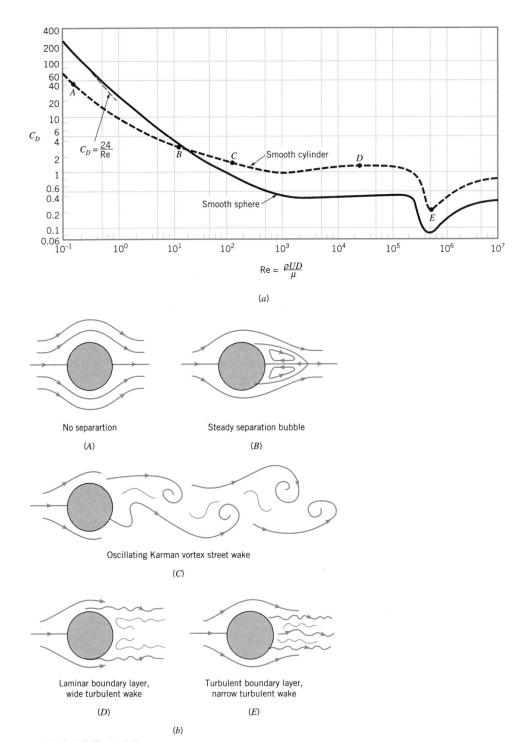

■ **FIGURE 9.15** (*a*) **Drag coefficient as a function of Reynolds number for a smooth circular cylinder and a smooth sphere.** (*b*) **Typical flow patterns for flow past a circular cylinder at various Reynolds numbers as indicated in (*a*).**

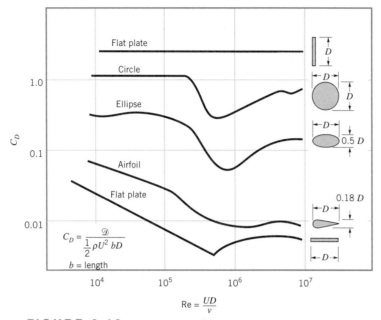

■ FIGURE 9.16 **Character of the drag coefficient as a function of Reynolds number for objects with various degrees of streamlining, from a flat plate normal to the upstream flow to a flat plate parallel to the flow (two-dimensional flow) (Ref. 4).**

EXAMPLE 9.6

Hail is produced by the repeated rising and falling of ice particles in the updraft of a thunderstorm, as is indicated in Fig. E9.6. When the hail becomes large enough, the aerodynamic drag from the updraft can no longer support the weight of the hail, and it falls from the storm cloud. Estimate the velocity, U, of the updraft needed to make D = 1.5-in.-diameter (i.e., "golf ball-sized") hail.

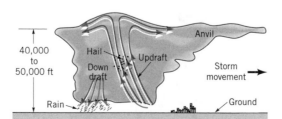

■ FIGURE E9.6

SOLUTION

As is discussed in Example 9.5, for steady state conditions a force balance on an object falling through a fluid gives

$$\mathcal{W} = \mathcal{D} + F_B$$

where $F_B = \gamma_{air}V$ is the buoyant force of the air on the particle, $\mathcal{W} = \gamma_{ice}V$ is the particle weight, and $\mathcal{D}$ is the aerodynamic drag. This equation can be rewritten as

$$\tfrac{1}{2}\rho_{air}U^2\,\frac{\pi}{4}\,D^2 C_D = \mathcal{W} - F_B \tag{1}$$

With $V = \pi D^3/6$ and since $\gamma_{ice} \gg \gamma_{air}$ (i.e., $\mathcal{W} \gg F_B$), Eq. 1 can be simplified to

$$U = \left(\frac{4}{3}\frac{\rho_{ice}}{\rho_{air}}\frac{gD}{C_D}\right)^{1/2} \tag{2}$$

By using $\rho_{ice} = 1.84$ slugs/ft^3, $\rho_{air} = 2.38 \times 10^{-3}$ slugs/ft^3, and $D = 1.5$ in. $= 0.125$ ft, Eq. 2 becomes

$$U = \left[\frac{4(1.84\ \text{slugs/ft}^3)(32.2\ \text{ft/s}^2)(0.125\ \text{ft})}{3(2.38 \times 10^{-3}\ \text{slugs/ft}^3)C_D}\right]^{1/2}$$

or

$$U = \frac{64.5}{\sqrt{C_D}} \tag{3}$$

where U is in ft/s. To determine U, we must know C_D. Unfortunately, C_D is a function of the Reynolds number (see Fig. 9.15), which is not known unless U is known. Thus, we must use an iterative technique similar to that done with the Moody chart for certain types of pipe flow problems (see Section 8.5).

   From Fig. 9.15 we expect that C_D is on the order of 0.5. Thus, we assume $C_D = 0.5$ and from Eq. 3 obtain

$$U = \frac{64.5}{\sqrt{0.5}} = 91.2\ \text{ft/s}$$

The corresponding Reynolds number (assuming $\nu = 1.57 \times 10^{-4}$ ft^2/s) is

$$\text{Re} = \frac{UD}{\nu} = \frac{91.2\ \text{ft/s}\,(0.125\ \text{ft})}{1.57 \times 10^{-4}\ \text{ft}^2/\text{s}} = 7.26 \times 10^4$$

For this value of Re we obtain from Fig. 9.15, $C_D = 0.5$. Thus, our assumed value of $C_D = 0.5$ was correct. The corresponding value of U is

$$U = 91.2\ \text{ft/s} = 62.2\ \text{mph} \tag{Ans}$$

This result was obtained by using standard sea-level properties for the air. If conditions at 20,000 ft altitude are used (i.e., from Table C.1, $\rho_{air} = 1.267 \times 10^{-3}$ slugs/ft^3 and $\mu = 3.324 \times 10^{-7}$ lb·s/ft^2), the corresponding result is $U = 125$ ft/s $= 85.2$ mph.

Clearly, an airplane flying through such an updraft would feel its effects (even if it were able to dodge the hail). As seen from Eq. 2, the larger the hail, the stronger the necessary updraft. Hailstones greater than 6 in. in diameter have been reported. In reality, a hailstone is seldom spherical and often not smooth. However, the calculated updraft velocities are in agreement with measured values.

Compressibility Effects. If the velocity of the object is sufficiently large, compressibility effects become important and the drag coefficient becomes a function of the Mach number, $Ma = U/c$, where c is the speed of sound in the fluid. For low Mach numbers, $Ma < 0.5$ or so, compressibility effects are unimportant and the drag coefficient is essentially independent of Ma. On the other hand, for larger Mach number flows, the drag coefficient can be strongly dependent on Ma.

For most objects, values of C_D increase dramatically in the vicinity of $Ma = 1$ (i.e., sonic flow). This change in character, indicated by Fig. 9.17, is due to the existence of shock waves (extremely narrow regions in the flow field across which the flow parameters change in a nearly discontinuous manner). Shock waves, which cannot exist in subsonic flows, provide a mechanism for the generation of drag that is not present in the relatively low-speed

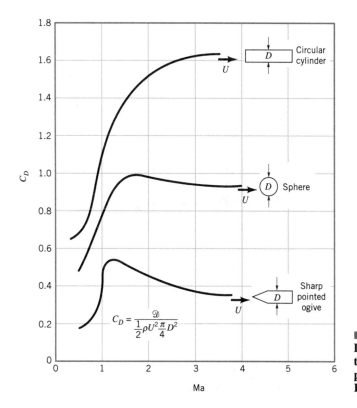

$$C_D = \frac{\mathcal{D}}{\frac{1}{2}\rho U^2 \frac{\pi}{4} D^2}$$

■ **FIGURE 9.17**
Drag coefficient as a function of Mach number for supersonic flow (adapted from Ref. 13).

subsonic flows. More information on these important topics can be found in standard texts about compressible flow and aerodynamics (Refs. 7, 8, 18).

Surface Roughness. In general, for streamlined bodies, the drag increases with increasing surface roughness. Great care is taken to design the surfaces of airplane wings to be as smooth as possible, since protruding rivets or screw heads can cause a considerable increase in the drag. On the other hand, for an extremely blunt body, such as a flat plate normal to the flow, the drag is independent of the surface roughness, since the shear stress is not in the upstream flow direction and contributes nothing to the drag.

For blunt bodies like a circular cylinder or sphere, an increase in surface roughness can actually cause a decrease in the drag. This is illustrated for a sphere in Fig. 9.18. As is discussed in Section 9.2.6, when the Reynolds number reaches the critical value (Re = 3×10^5 for a smooth sphere), the boundary layer becomes turbulent and the wake region behind the sphere becomes considerably narrower than if it were laminar (see Figs. 9.12 and 9.15). The result is a considerable drop in pressure drag with a slight increase in friction drag, combining to give a smaller overall drag (and C_D).

The boundary layer can be tripped into turbulence at a smaller Reynolds number by using a rough-surfaced sphere. For example, the critical Reynolds number for a golf ball is approximately Re = 4×10^4. In the range $4 \times 10^4 <$ Re $< 4 \times 10^5$, the drag on the standard rough (i.e., dimpled) golf ball is considerably less ($C_{D\text{rough}}/C_{D\text{smooth}} \approx 0.25/0.5 = 0.5$) than for the smooth ball. As is shown in Example 9.7, this is precisely the Reynolds number range for well-hit golf balls—hence, the reason for dimples on golf balls. The Reynolds number range for well-hit table tennis balls is less than Re = 4×10^4. Thus, table tennis balls are smooth.

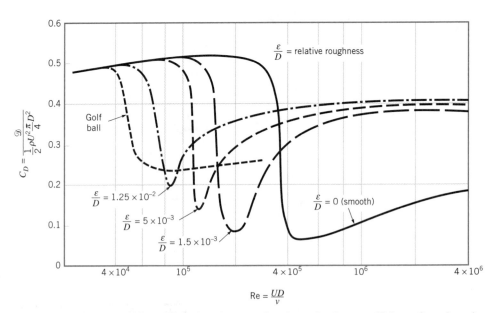

■ **FIGURE 9.18** **The effect of surface roughness on the drag coefficient of a sphere in the Reynolds number range for which the laminar boundary layer becomes turbulent (Ref. 4).**

EXAMPLE 9.7

A well-hit golf ball (diameter $D = 1.69$ in., weight $W = 0.0992$ lb) can travel at $U = 200$ ft/s as it leaves the tee. A well-hit table tennis ball (diameter $D = 1.50$ in., weight $W = 0.00551$ lb) can travel at $U = 60$ ft/s as it leaves the paddle. Determine the drag on a standard golf ball, a smooth golf ball, and a table tennis ball for the conditions given. Also determine the deceleration of each ball for these conditions.

SOLUTION

For either ball, the drag can be obtained from

$$\mathcal{D} = \frac{1}{2}\rho U^2 \frac{\pi}{4} D^2 C_D \tag{1}$$

where the drag coefficient, C_D, is given in Fig. 9.18 as a function of the Reynolds number and surface roughness. For the golf ball in standard air

$$\mathrm{Re} = \frac{UD}{\nu} = \frac{(200 \text{ ft/s})(1.69/12 \text{ ft})}{1.57 \times 10^{-4} \text{ ft}^2/\text{s}} = 1.79 \times 10^5$$

while for the table tennis ball

$$\mathrm{Re} = \frac{UD}{\nu} = \frac{(60 \text{ ft/s})(1.50/12 \text{ ft})}{1.57 \times 10^{-4} \text{ ft}^2/\text{s}} = 4.78 \times 10^4$$

The corresponding drag coefficients are $C_D = 0.25$ for the standard golf ball, $C_D = 0.51$ for the smooth golf ball, and $C_D = 0.50$ for the table tennis ball. Hence, from Eq. 1 for the standard golf ball

$$\mathcal{D} = \frac{1}{2}(2.38 \times 10^{-3} \text{ slugs/ft}^3)(200 \text{ ft/s})^2 \frac{\pi}{4}\left(\frac{1.69}{12}\text{ ft}\right)^2(0.25) = 0.185 \text{ lb} \quad \text{(Ans)}$$

for the smooth golf ball

$$\mathcal{D} = \frac{1}{2}(2.38 \times 10^{-3} \text{ slugs/ft}^3)(200 \text{ ft/s})^2 \frac{\pi}{4}\left(\frac{1.69}{12}\text{ ft}\right)^2(0.51) = 0.378 \text{ lb} \quad \text{(Ans)}$$

and for the table tennis ball

$$\mathcal{D} = \frac{1}{2}(2.38 \times 10^{-3} \text{ slugs/ft}^3)(60 \text{ ft/s})^2 \frac{\pi}{4}\left(\frac{1.50}{12}\text{ ft}\right)^2(0.50) = 0.0263 \text{ lb} \quad \text{(Ans)}$$

The corresponding decelerations are $a = \mathcal{D}/m = g\mathcal{D}/W$, where m is the mass of the ball. Thus, the deceleration relative to the acceleration of gravity, a/g (i.e., the number of g's deceleration) is $a/g = \mathcal{D}/W$ or

$$\frac{a}{g} = \frac{0.185 \text{ lb}}{0.0992 \text{ lb}} = 1.86 \text{ for the standard golf ball} \quad \text{(Ans)}$$

$$\frac{a}{g} = \frac{0.378 \text{ lb}}{0.0992 \text{ lb}} = 3.81 \text{ for the smooth golf ball} \quad \text{(Ans)}$$

and

$$\frac{a}{g} = \frac{0.0263 \text{ lb}}{0.00551 \text{ lb}} = 4.77 \text{ for the table tennis ball} \qquad \text{(Ans)}$$

Note that there is a considerably smaller deceleration for the rough golf ball than for the smooth one. Because of its much larger drag-to-mass ratio, the table tennis ball slows down relatively quickly and does not travel as far as the golf ball. (Note that with $U = 60$ ft/s the standard golf ball has a drag of $\mathcal{D} = 0.0200$ lb and a deceleration of $a/g = 0.202$, considerably less than the $a/g = 4.77$ of the table tennis ball. Conversely, a table tennis ball hit from a tee at 200 ft/s would decelerate at a rate of $a = 1740$ ft/s^2, or $a/g = 54.1$. It would not travel nearly as far as the golf ball.)

The Reynolds number range for which a rough golf ball has smaller drag than a smooth one (i.e., 4×10^4 to 4×10^5) corresponds to a flight velocity range of $45 < U < 450$ ft/s. This is comfortably within the range of most golfers. As is discussed in Section 9.4.2, the dimples (roughness) on a golf ball also help produce a lift (due to the spin of the ball) that allows the ball to travel farther than a smooth ball.

V9.7 Jet ski

Froude Number Effects. Another parameter on which the drag coefficient may be strongly dependent is the Froude number, Fr $= U/\sqrt{g\ell}$. As is discussed in Chapter 10, the Froude number is a ratio of the free-stream speed to a typical wave speed on the interface of two fluids, such as the surface of the ocean. An object moving on the surface, such as a ship, often produces waves that require a source of energy to generate. This energy comes from the ship and is manifest as a drag. [Recall that the rate of energy production (power) equals speed times force.] The nature of the waves produced often depends on the Froude number of the flow and the shape of the object—the waves generated by a water skier "plowing" through the water at a low speed (low Fr) are different than those generated by the skier "planing" along the surface at a high speed (larger Fr).

Composite Body Drag. Approximate drag calculations for a complex body can often be obtained by treating the body as a composite collection of its various parts.

EXAMPLE 9.8

A 60-mph (i.e., 88-fps) wind blows past the water tower shown in Fig. E9.8a. Estimate the moment (torque), M, needed at the base to keep the tower from tipping over.

SOLUTION

We treat the water tower as a sphere resting on a circular cylinder and assume that the total drag is the sum of the drag from these parts. The free-body diagram of the tower is shown in Fig. E9.8b. By summing moments about the base of the tower, we obtain

$$M = \mathcal{D}_s\left(b + \frac{D_s}{2}\right) + \mathcal{D}_c\left(\frac{b}{2}\right) \qquad (1)$$

where

$$\mathcal{D}_s = \frac{1}{2}\rho U^2 \frac{\pi}{4} D_s^2 C_{Ds} \qquad (2)$$

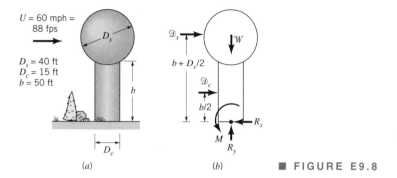

$U = 60$ mph = 88 fps

$D_s = 40$ ft
$D_c = 15$ ft
$b = 50$ ft

(a)   (b)   ■ **FIGURE E9.8**

and

$$\mathcal{D}_c = \frac{1}{2}\rho U^2 b D_c C_{Dc} \tag{3}$$

are the drag on the sphere and cylinder, respectively. For standard atmospheric conditions, the Reynolds numbers are

$$\text{Re}_s = \frac{UD_s}{\nu} = \frac{(88 \text{ ft/s})(40 \text{ ft})}{1.57 \times 10^{-4} \text{ ft}^2/\text{s}} = 2.24 \times 10^7$$

and

$$\text{Re}_c = \frac{UD_c}{\nu} = \frac{(88 \text{ ft/s})(15 \text{ ft})}{1.57 \times 10^{-4} \text{ ft}^2/\text{s}} = 8.41 \times 10^6$$

The corresponding drag coefficients, C_{Ds} and C_{Dc}, can be approximated from Fig. 9.15 as

$$C_{Ds} \approx 0.3 \quad \text{and} \quad C_{Dc} \approx 0.7$$

Note that the value of C_{Ds} was obtained by an extrapolation of the given data to Reynolds numbers beyond those given (a potentially dangerous practice!). From Eqs. 2 and 3 we obtain

$$\mathcal{D}_s = 0.5(2.38 \times 10^{-3} \text{ slugs/ft}^3)(88 \text{ ft/s})^2 \frac{\pi}{4} (40 \text{ ft})^2(0.3) = 3470 \text{ lb}$$

and

$$\mathcal{D}_c = 0.5(2.38 \times 10^{-3} \text{ slugs/ft}^3)(88 \text{ ft/s})^2(50 \text{ ft} \times 15 \text{ ft})(0.7) = 4840 \text{ lb}$$

From Eq. 1 the corresponding moment needed to prevent the tower from tipping is

$$M = 3470 \text{ lb}\left(50 \text{ ft} + \frac{40}{2} \text{ ft}\right) + 4840 \text{ lb}\left(\frac{50}{2} \text{ ft}\right) = 3.64 \times 10^5 \text{ ft·lb} \quad \textbf{(Ans)}$$

The above result is only an estimate because (a) the wind is probably not uniform from the top of the tower to the ground, (b) the tower is not exactly a combination of a smooth sphere and a circular cylinder, (c) the cylinder is not of infinite length, (d) there will be some interaction between the flow past the cylinder and that past the sphere so that the net drag is not exactly the sum of the two, and (e) a drag coefficient value was obtained by extrapolation of the given data. However, such approximate results are often quite accurate.

V9.8 Drag on a truck

Drag coefficient information for a very wide range of objects is available in the literature. Some of this information is given in Figs. 9.19, 9.20, and 9.21 for a variety of two- and three-dimensional, natural and man-made objects. Recall that a drag coefficient of unity is equivalent to the drag produced by the dynamic pressure acting on an area of size A. That is, $\mathcal{D} = \frac{1}{2}\rho U^2 A C_D = \frac{1}{2}\rho U^2 A$ if $C_D = 1$. Typical nonstreamlined objects have drag coefficients on this order.

Shape	Reference area A (b = length)	Drag coefficient $C_D = \dfrac{\mathcal{D}}{\frac{1}{2}\rho U^2 A}$		Reynold number $Re = \rho U D/\mu$
Square rod with rounded corners	$A = bD$	R/D 0 0.02 0.17 0.33	C_D 2.2 2.0 1.2 1.0	$Re = 10^5$
Rounded equilateral triangle	$A = bD$	R/D $\rightarrow$ 0 1.4 0.02 1.2 0.08 1.3 0.25 1.1	$\leftarrow$ 2.1 2.0 1.9 1.3	$Re = 10^5$
Semicircular shell	$A = bD$	$\rightarrow$ 2.3 $\leftarrow$ 1.1		$Re = 2 \times 10^4$
Semicircular cylinder	$A = bD$	$\rightarrow$ 2.15 $\leftarrow$ 1.15		$Re > 10^4$
T-beam	$A = bD$	$\rightarrow$ 1.80 $\leftarrow$ 1.65		$Re > 10^4$
I-beam	$A = bD$	2.05		$Re > 10^4$
Angle	$A = bD$	$\rightarrow$ 1.98 $\leftarrow$ 1.82		$Re > 10^4$
Hexagon	$A = bD$	1.0		$Re > 10^4$
Rectangle	$A = bD$	ℓ/D $\leq$0.1 0.5 0.65 1.0 2.0 3.0	C_D 1.9 2.5 2.9 2.2 1.6 1.3	$Re = 10^5$

■ **FIGURE 9.19** **Typical drag coefficients for regular two-dimensional objects (Refs. 4 and 5).**

Shape	Reference area A	Drag coefficient C_D	Reynolds number $Re = \rho U D/\mu$
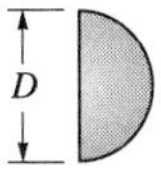 Solid hemisphere	$A = \frac{\pi}{4}D^2$	→ 1.17 ← 0.42	$Re > 10^4$
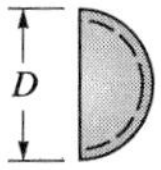 Hollow hemisphere	$A = \frac{\pi}{4}D^2$	→ 1.42 ← 0.38	$Re > 10^4$
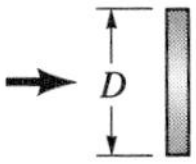 Thin disk	$A = \frac{\pi}{4}D^2$	1.1	$Re > 10^3$
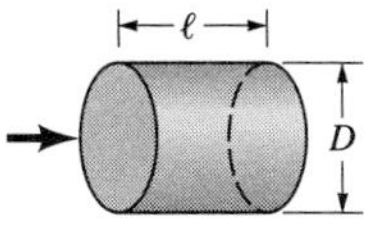 Circular rod parallel to flow	$A = \frac{\pi}{4}D^2$	ℓ/D — C_D 0.5 — 1.1 1.0 — 0.93 2.0 — 0.83 4.0 — 0.85	$Re > 10^5$
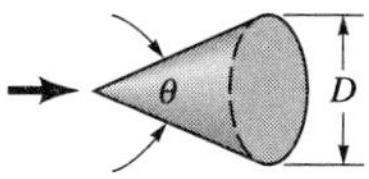 Cone	$A = \frac{\pi}{4}D^2$	θ, degrees — C_D 10 — 0.30 30 — 0.55 60 — 0.80 90 — 1.15	$Re > 10^4$
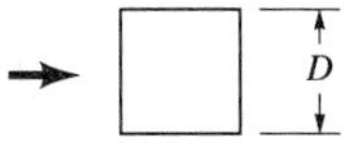 Cube	$A = D^2$	1.05	$Re > 10^4$
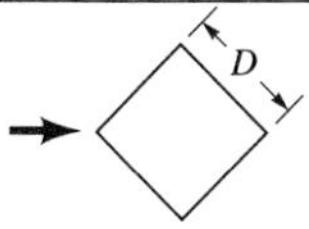 Cube	$A = D^2$	0.80	$Re > 10^4$
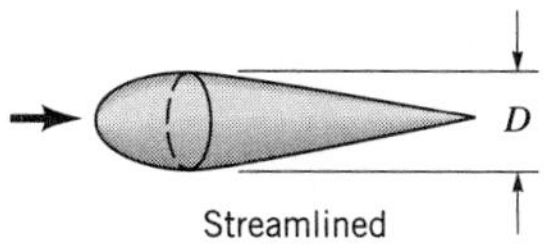 Streamlined body	$A = \frac{\pi}{4}D^2$	0.04	$Re > 10^5$

■ FIGURE 9.20 **Typical drag coefficients for regular three-dimensional objects (Ref. 4).**

Shape	Reference area	Drag coefficient C_D
 Parachute	Frontal area $A = \frac{\pi}{4}D^2$	1.4
Porous parabolic dish	Frontal area $A = \frac{\pi}{4}D^2$	(see table below)

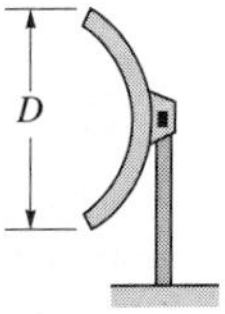

Porosity	0	0.2	0.5
→	1.42	1.20	0.82
←	0.95	0.90	0.80

Porosity = open area/total area

Shape	Reference area	Drag coefficient C_D
 Average person	Standing Sitting Crouching	$C_D A = 9\ \text{ft}^2$ $C_D A = 6\ \text{ft}^2$ $C_D A = 2.5\ \text{ft}^2$
Fluttering flag	$A = \ell D$	(see table below)

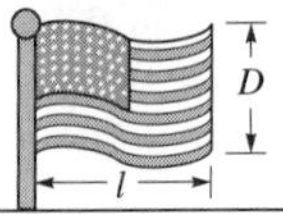

ℓ/D	C_D
1	0.07
2	0.12
3	0.15

Shape	Reference area	Drag coefficient C_D
 Empire State Building	Frontal area	1.4
 Six-car passenger train	Frontal area	1.8
Bikes — Upright commuter	$A = 5.5\ \text{ft}^2$	1.1
 Racing	$A = 3.9\ \text{ft}^2$	0.88
 Drafting	$A = 3.9\ \text{ft}^2$	0.50
 Streamlined	$A = 5.0\ \text{ft}^2$	0.12
Tractor-trailor tucks — Standard	Frontal area	0.96
With fairing	Frontal area	0.76
With fairing and gap seal	Frontal area	0.70
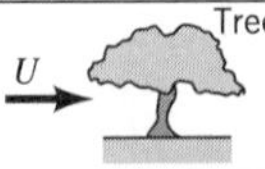 Tree $U = 10$ m/s $U = 20$ m/s $U = 30$ m/s	Frontal area	0.43 0.26 0.20
 Dolphin	Wetted area	0.0036 at Re = 6×10^6 (flat plate has $C_{Df} = 0.0031$)
 Large birds	Frontal area	0.40

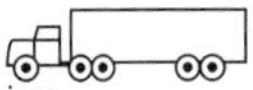

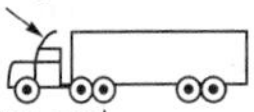

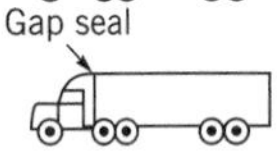

■ FIGURE 9.21 Typical drag coefficients for objects of interest (Refs. 4, 5, 11, and 14).

9.4   Lift

As is indicated in Section 9.1, any object moving through a fluid will experience a net force of the fluid on the object. For symmetrical objects, this force will be in the direction of the free stream—a drag, $\mathcal{D}$. If the object is not symmetrical (or if it does not produce a symmetrical flow field, such as the flow around a rotating sphere), there may also be a force normal to the free stream—a lift, $\mathcal{L}$.

9.4.1   Surface Pressure Distribution

The lift can be determined from Eq. 9.2 if the distributions of pressure and wall shear stress around the entire body are known. As is indicated in Section 9.1, such data are usually not known. Typically, the lift is given in terms of the lift coefficient

$$C_L = \frac{\mathcal{L}}{\frac{1}{2}\rho U^2 A} \tag{9.25}$$

which is obtained from experiments, advanced analysis, or numerical considerations.

The most important parameter that affects the lift coefficient is the shape of the object. Considerable effort has gone into designing optimally shaped lift-producing devices. We will emphasize the effect of the shape on lift—the effects of the other dimensionless parameters can be found in the literature (Refs. 9, 10, 18).

Most common lift-generating devices (i.e., airfoils, fans, spoilers on cars, etc.) operate in the large Reynolds number range in which the flow has a boundary layer character, with viscous effects confined to the boundary layers and wake regions. For such cases the wall shear stress, τ_w, contributes little to the lift. Most of the lift comes from the surface pressure distribution.

A typical device designed to produce lift does so by generating a pressure distribution that is different on the top and bottom surfaces. For large Reynolds number flows these pressure distributions are usually directly proportional to the dynamic pressure, $\rho U^2/2$, with viscous effects being of secondary importance. Two airfoils used to produce lift are indicated in Fig. 9.22. Clearly the symmetrical one cannot produce lift unless the angle of attack, α, is nonzero. Because of the asymmetry of the nonsymmetrical airfoil, the pressure distributions on the upper and lower surfaces are different, and a lift is produced even with $\alpha = 0$.

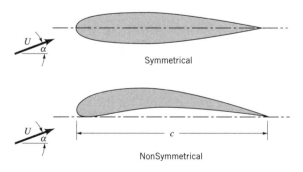

■ FIGURE 9.22   **Symmetrical and nonsymmetrical airfoils.**

Since most airfoils are thin, it is customary to use the planform area, $A = bc$, in the definition of the lift coefficient. Here b is the length of the airfoil and c is the *chord length—* the length from the leading edge to the trailing edge as indicated in Fig. 9.22. Typical lift coefficients so defined are on the order of unity (see Fig. 9.23). That is, the lift force is on the order of the dynamic pressure times the planform area of the wing, $\mathcal{L} \approx (\rho U^2/2)A$. The *wing loading,* defined as the average lift per unit area of the wing, $\mathcal{L}/A$, therefore, increases with speed. For example, the wing loading of the 1903 Wright Flyer aircraft was 1.5 lb/ft^2, while for the present-day Boeing 747 aircraft it is 150 lb/ft^2. The wing loading for a bumble bee is approximately 1 lb/ft^2 (Ref. 11).

In many lift-generating devices the important quantity is the ratio of the lift to drag developed, $\mathcal{L}/\mathcal{D} = C_L/C_D$. Such information is often presented in terms of C_L/C_D versus α, as is shown in Fig. 9.23a, or in a *lift-drag polar* of C_L versus C_D with α as a parameter, as shown in Fig. 9.23b. The most efficient angle of attack (i.e., largest C_L/C_D) can be found by drawing a line tangent to the $C_L - C_D$ curve from the origin, as shown in Fig. 9.23b.

Although viscous effects and the wall shear stress contribute little to the direct generation of lift, they play an extremely important role in the design and use of lifting devices. This is because of the viscosity-induced boundary layer separation that can occur on non-streamlined bodies such as airfoils that have too large an angle of attack. Up to a certain point, the lift coefficient increases rather steadily with the angle of attack. If α is too large,

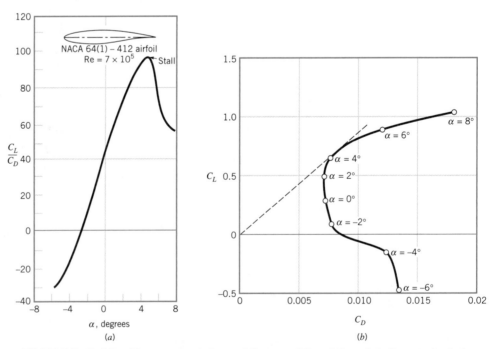

■ **FIGURE 9.23** **Two representations of the same lift and drag data for a typical airfoil: (*a*) lift-to-drag ratio as a function of angle of attack, with the onset of boundary layer separation on the upper surface indicated by the occurrence of stall, (*b*) the lift and drag polar diagram with the angle of attack indicated (Ref. 17).**

the boundary layer on the upper surface separates, the flow over the wing develops a wide, turbulent wake region, the lift decreases, and the drag increases. The airfoil *stalls*. Such conditions are extremely dangerous if they occur while the airplane is flying at a low altitude where there is not sufficient time and altitude to recover from the stall.

As indicated above, the lift and drag on an airfoil can be altered by changing the angle of attack. This actually represents a change in the shape of the object. Other shape changes can be used to alter the lift and drag when desirable. In modern airplanes it is common to utilize leading edge and trailing edge flaps as shown in Fig. 9.24. To generate the necessary lift during the relatively low-speed landing and takeoff procedures, the airfoil shape is altered by extending special flaps on the front and/or rear portions of the wing. Use of the flaps considerably enhances the lift, although it is at the expense of an increase in the drag (the airfoil is in a "dirty" configuration). This increase in drag is not of much concern during landing and takeoff operations—the decrease in landing or takeoff speed is more important than is a temporary increase in drag. During normal flight with the flaps retracted (the "clean" configuration), the drag is relatively small, and the needed lift force is achieved with the smaller lift coefficient and the larger dynamic pressure (higher speed).

A wide variety of lift and drag information for airfoils can be found in standard aerodynamics books (Ref. 9, 10, 18).

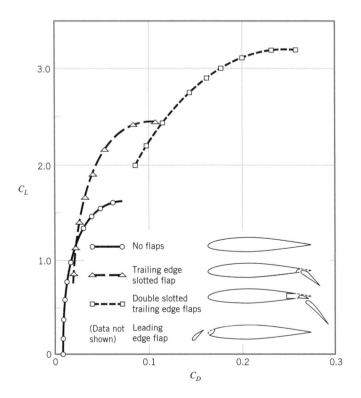

■ FIGURE 9.24
Typical lift and drag alterations possible with the use of various types of flap designs (Ref. 15).

EXAMPLE 9.9

In 1977 the *Gossamer Condor* won the Kremer prize by being the first human-powered aircraft to complete a prescribed figure-of-eight course around two turning points 0.5 mi apart (Ref. 16). The following data pertain to this aircraft:

$$\text{flight speed} = U = 15 \text{ ft/s}$$
$$\text{wing size} = b = 96 \text{ ft}, \, c = 7.5 \text{ ft (average)}$$
$$\text{weight (including pilot)} = \mathcal{W} = 210 \text{ lb}$$
$$\text{drag coefficient} = C_D = 0.046 \text{ (based on planform area)}$$
$$\text{power train efficiency} = \eta = \text{power to overcome drag/pilot power} = 0.8$$

Determine the lift coefficient, C_L, and the power, $\mathcal{P}$, required by the pilot.

SOLUTION

For steady flight conditions the lift must be exactly balanced by the weight, or

$$\mathcal{W} = \mathcal{L} = \tfrac{1}{2}\rho U^2 A C_L$$

Thus,

$$C_L = \frac{2\mathcal{W}}{\rho U^2 A}$$

where $A = bc = 96 \text{ ft} \times 7.5 \text{ ft} = 720 \text{ ft}^2$, $\mathcal{W} = 210 \text{ lb}$, and $\rho = 2.38 \times 10^{-3} \text{ slugs/ft}^3$ for standard air. This gives

$$C_L = \frac{2(210 \text{ lb})}{(2.38 \times 10^{-3} \text{ slugs/ft}^3)(15 \text{ ft/s})^2(720 \text{ ft}^2)}$$

or

$$C_L = 1.09 \tag{Ans}$$

a reasonable number. The overall-lift-to drag ratio for the aircraft is $C_L/C_D = 1.09/0.046 = 23.7$.

    The product of the power that the pilot supplies and the power train efficiency equals the useful power needed to overcome the drag, $\mathcal{D}$. That is,

$$\eta\mathcal{P} = \mathcal{D}U$$

where

$$\mathcal{D} = \tfrac{1}{2}\rho U^2 A C_D$$

Thus,

$$\mathcal{P} = \frac{\mathcal{D}U}{\eta} = \frac{\tfrac{1}{2}\rho U^2 A C_D U}{\eta} = \frac{\rho A C_D U^3}{2\eta} \tag{1}$$

or

$$\mathcal{P} = \frac{(2.38 \times 10^{-3} \text{ slugs/ft}^3)(720 \text{ ft}^2)(0.046)(15 \text{ ft/s})^3}{2(0.8)}$$

$$\mathcal{P} = 166 \text{ ft·lb/s} \left(\frac{1 \text{ hp}}{550 \text{ ft·lb/s}}\right) = 0.302 \text{ hp} \tag{Ans}$$

This power level is obtainable by a well-conditioned athlete (as is indicated by the fact that the flight was successfully completed). Note that only 80% of the pilot's power (i.e., $0.8 \times 0.302 = 0.242$ hp, which corresponds to a drag of $\mathcal{D} = 8.86$ lb) is needed to force the aircraft through the air. The other 20% is lost because of the power train inefficiency. Note from Eq. 1 that for a constant drag coefficient, the power required increases as U^3—a doubling of the speed to 30 ft/s would require an eightfold increase in power (i.e., 2.42 hp, well beyond the range of any human).

9.4.2 Circulation

Consider the flow past a finite length airfoil, as indicated in Fig. 9.25. For lift-generating conditions the average pressure on the lower surface is greater than that on the upper surface. Near the tips of the wing this pressure difference will cause some of the fluid to attempt to migrate from the lower to the upper surface, as indicated in Fig. 9.25*b*. At the same time, this fluid is swept downstream, forming a *trailing vortex* (swirl) from each wing tip (see Fig. 4.3).

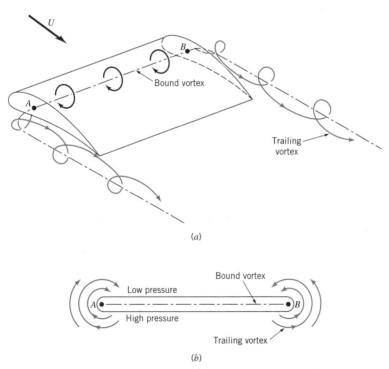

■ **FIGURE 9.25** **Flow past a finite length wing: (*a*) the horseshoe vortex system produced by the bound vortex and the trailing vortices; (*b*) the leakage of air around the wing tips produces the trailing vortices.**

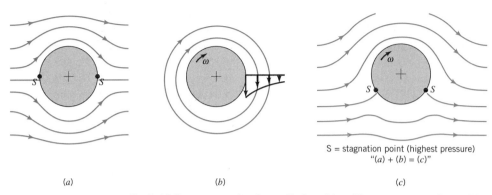

S = stagnation point (highest pressure)
"(a) + (b) = (c)"

(a)   (b)   (c)

■ **FIGURE 9.26** **Inviscid flow past a circular cylinder:** (*a*) **uniform upstream flow without circulation,** (*b*) **free vortex at the center of the cylinder,** (*c*) **combination of free vortex and uniform flow past a circular cylinder giving nonsymmetric flow and a lift.**

V9.9 Wing tip vortices

The trailing vortices from the right and left wing tips are connected by the *bound vortex* along the length of the wing. It is this vortex that generates the *circulation* that produces the lift. The combined vortex system (the bound vortex and the trailing vortices) is termed a horseshoe vortex. The strength of the trailing vortices (which is equal to the strength of the bound vortex) is proportional to the lift generated. Large aircraft (for example, a Boeing 747) can generate very strong trailing vortices that persist for a long time before viscous effects finally cause them to die out. Such vortices are strong enough to flip smaller aircraft out of control if they follow too closely behind the large aircraft.

As indicated above, the generation of lift is directly related to the production of circulation or vortex flow around the object. A nonsymmetric airfoil, by design, generates its own prescribed amount of swirl and lift. A symmetrical object like a circular cylinder or sphere, which normally provides no lift, can generate swirl and lift if it rotates.

As discussed in Section 6.6.2, the inviscid flow past a circular cylinder has the symmetrical flow pattern indicated in Fig. 9.26*a*. By symmetry the lift and drag are zero. However, if the cylinder is rotated about its axis in a stationary real ($\mu \neq 0$) fluid, the rotation will drag some of the fluid around, producing circulation about the cylinder as in Fig. 9.26*b*. When this circulation is combined with an ideal, uniform upstream flow, the flow pattern indicated in Fig. 9.26*c* is obtained. The flow is no longer symmetrical about the horizontal plane through the center of the cylinder; the average pressure is greater on the lower half of the cylinder than on the upper half, and a lift is generated. This effect is called the *Magnus effect*. A similar lift is generated on a rotating sphere. It accounts for the various types of pitches in baseball (i.e., curve ball, floater, sinker, etc.), the ability of a soccer player to hook the ball, and the hook, slice, or lift of a golf ball.

References

1. Schlichting, H., *Boundary Layer Theory*, Seventh Edition, McGraw-Hill, New York, 1979.

2. Rosenhead, L., *Laminar Boundary Layers*, Oxford University Press, London, 1963.

3. White, F. M., *Viscous Fluid Flow,* McGraw-Hill, New York, 1974.

4. Blevins, R. D., *Applied Fluid Dynamics Handbook,* Van Nostrand Reinhold, New York, 1984.

5. Hoerner, S. F., *Fluid-Dynamic Drag,* published by the author, Library of Congress No. 64,19666, 1965.

6. Van Dyke, M., *An Album of Fluid Motion,* Parabolic Press, Stanford, Calif., 1982.

7. Thompson, P. A., *Compressible-Fluid Dynamics,* McGraw-Hill, New York, 1972.

8. Zucrow, M. J., and Hoffman, J. D., *Gas Dynamics, Vol. I,* Wiley, New York, 1976.

9. Shevell, R. S., *Fundamentals of Flight,* Second Edition, Prentice Hall, Englewood Cliffs, NJ, 1989.

10. Kuethe, A. M. and Chow, C. Y., *Foundations of Aerodynamics, Bases of Aerodynamics Design,* Fourth Edition, Wiley, 1986.

11. Vogel, J., *Life in Moving Fluids,* Willard Grant Press, Boston, 1981.

12. White, F. M., *Fluid Mechanics,* McGraw-Hill, New York, 1986.

13. Vennard, J. K., and Street, R. L., *Elementary Fluid Mechanics,* Sixth Edition, Wiley, New York, 1982.

14. Gross, A. C., Kyle, C. R., and Malewicki, D. J., The Aerodynamics of Human Powered Land Vehicles, *Scientific American,* Vol. 249, No. 6, 1983.

15. Abbott, I. H., and Von Doenhoff, A. E., *Theory of Wing Sections,* Dover Publications, New York, 1959.

16. MacReady, P. B., "Flight on 0.33 Horsepower: The Gossamer Condor," *Proc. AIAA 14th Annual Meeting* (Paper No. 78-308), Washington, DC, 1978.

17. Abbott, I. H., von Doenhoff, A. E. and Stivers, L. S., Summary of Airfoil Data, NACA Report No. 824, Langley Field, Va., 1945.

18. Anderson, J. D., *Fundamentals of Aerodynamics,* Second Edition, McGraw-Hill, New York, 1991.

Problems

Note: Unless otherwise indicated use the values of fluid properties found in the tables on the inside of the front cover. Problems designated with an (*) are intended to be solved with the aid of a programmable calculator or a computer. Problems designated with a (†) are "open ended" problems and require critical thinking in that to work them one must make various assumptions and provide the necessary data. There is not a unique answer to these problems.

9.1 Assume that water flowing past the equilateral triangular bar shown in Fig. P9.1 produces the pressure distributions indicated. Determine the lift and drag on the bar and the corresponding lift and drag coefficients (based on frontal area). Neglect shear forces.

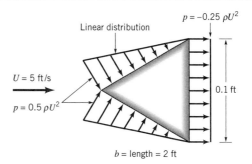

■ **FIGURE P9.1**

9.2 The average pressure and shear stress acting on the surface of the 1-m-square flat plate are as indicated in Fig. P9.2. Determine the lift and drag generated. Determine the lift and drag if the shear stress is neglected. Compare these two sets of results.

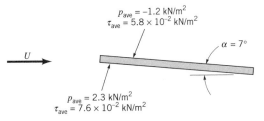

■ **FIGURE P9.2**

9.3 The pressure distribution on a cylinder is approximated by the two straight line segments shown in Fig. P9.3. Determine the drag coefficient for the cylinder. Neglect shear forces.

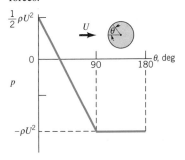

■ **FIGURE P9.3**

9.4 Repeat Problem 9.1 if the object is a cone (made by rotating the equilateral triangle about the horizontal axis through its tip) rather than a triangular bar.

9.5 Typical values of the Reynolds number for various animals moving through air or water are listed below. For which cases is inertia of the fluid important? For which cases do viscous effects dominate? For which cases would the flow be laminar; turbulent? Explain.

Animal	Speed	Re
(a) large whale	10 m/s	300,000,000
(b) flying duck	20 m/s	300,000
(c) large dragonfly	7 m/s	30,000
(d) invertebrate larva	1 mm/s	0.3
(e) bacterium	0.01 mm/s	0.00003

†**9.6** When you walk through still air, would you expect the character of the air flow around you to be most like that depicted in Fig. 9.5a, b, or c? Explain.

9.7 A viscous fluid flows past a flat plate such that the boundary layer thickness at a distance 1.3 m from the leading edge is 12 mm. Determine the boundary layer thickness at distances of 0.20, 2.0, and 20 m from the leading edge. Assume laminar flow.

9.8 Water flows past a flat plate with an upstream velocity of $U = 0.02$ m/s. Determine the water velocity a distance of 10 mm from the plate at distances of $x = 1.5$ m and $x = 15$ m from the leading edge.

9.9 Air enters a square duct through a 1-ft opening as shown in Fig. P9.9. Because the boundary layer displacement thickness increases in the direction of flow, it is necessary to increase the cross-sectional size of the duct if a constant $U = 2$ ft/s velocity is to be maintained outside the boundary layer. Plot a graph of the duct size, d, as a function of x for $0 \leq x \leq 10$ ft if U is to remain constant. Assume laminar flow.

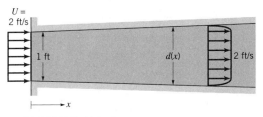

■ **FIGURE P9.9**

9.10 A smooth flat plate of length $\ell = 6$ m and width $b = 4$ m is placed in water with an upstream velocity of $U = 0.5$ m/s. Determine the boundary layer thickness and the wall shear stress at the center and the trailing edge of the plate. Assume a laminar boundary layer.

9.11 An atmospheric boundary layer is formed when the wind blows over the earth's surface. Typically, such velocity profiles can be written as a power law: $u = ay^n$, where the constants a and n depend on the roughness of the terrain. As indicated in Fig. P9.11, typical values are $n = 0.40$

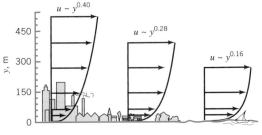

■ **FIGURE P9.11**

for urban areas, $n = 0.28$ for woodland or suburban areas, and $n = 0.16$ for flat open country. **(a)** If the velocity is 20 ft/s at the bottom of the sail on your boat ($y = 4$ ft), what is the velocity at the top of the mast ($y = 30$ ft)? **(b)** If the average velocity is 10 mph on the tenth floor of an urban building, what is the average velocity on the sixtieth floor?

9.12 A 30-story office building (each story is 12 ft tall) is built in a suburban industrial park. Plot the dynamic pressure, $\rho u^2/2$, as a function of elevation if the wind blows at hurricane strength (75 mph) at the top of the building. Use the atmospheric boundary layer information of Problem 9.11.

†**9.13** If the boundary layer on the hood of your car behaves as one on a flat plate, estimate how far from the front edge of the hood the boundary layer becomes turbulent. How thick is the boundary layer at this location?

9.14 A laminar boundary layer velocity profile is approximated by $u/U = 2(y/\delta) - 2(y/\delta)^3 + (y/\delta)^4$ for $y \le \delta$, and $u = U$ for $y > \delta$. **(a)** Show that this profile satisfies the appropriate boundary conditions. **(b)** Use the momentum integral equation to determine the boundary layer thickness, $\delta = \delta(x)$.

9.15 A laminar boundary layer velocity profile is approximated by the two straight-line segments indicated in Fig. P9.15. Use the momentum integral equation to determine the boundary layer thickness, $\delta = \delta(x)$, and wall shear stress, $\tau_w = \tau_w(x)$. Compare these results with those in Eqs. 9.8 and 9.11.

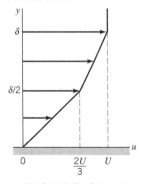

■ **FIGURE P9.15**

*9.16 For a fluid of specific gravity $SG = 0.86$ flowing past a flat plate with an upstream velocity of $U = 5$ m/s, the wall shear stress on a flat plate was determined to be as indicated in the table below. Use the momentum integral equation to determine the boundary layer momentum thickness, $\Theta = \Theta(x)$. Assume $\Theta = 0$ at the leading edge, $x = 0$.

x (m)	τ_w (N/m^2)
0	—
0.2	13.4
0.4	9.25
0.6	7.68
0.8	6.51
1.0	5.89
1.2	6.57
1.4	6.75
1.6	6.23
1.8	5.92
2.0	5.26

9.17 The net drag on one side of the two plates (each of size ℓ by $\ell/2$) parallel to the free stream shown in Fig. P9.17a is $\mathcal{D}$. Determine the drag (in terms of $\mathcal{D}$) on the same two plates when they are connected together as indicated in Fig. P9.17b. Assume laminar boundary flow. Explain your answer physically.

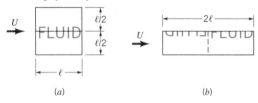

(a)   (b)

■ **FIGURE P9.17**

9.18 If the drag on one side of a flat plate parallel to the upstream flow is $\mathcal{D}$ when the upstream velocity is U, what will the drag be when the upstream velocity is $2U$; or $U/2$? Assume laminar flow.

9.19 It is often assumed that "sharp objects can cut through the air better than blunt ones." Based on this assumption, the drag on the object shown in Fig. P9.19 should be less when the wind blows from right to left than when it blows from left to right. Experiments show that the opposite is true. Explain.

■ **FIGURE P9.19**

9.20 A ceiling fan consists of five blades of 0.80-m length and 0.10-m width which rotate at 100 rpm. Estimate the torque needed to overcome the friction on the blades if they act as flat plates.

9.21   As shown in Video V9.2 and Fig. P9.21*a*, a kayak is a relatively streamlined object. As a first approximation in calculating the drag on a kayak, assume that the kayak acts as if it were a smooth flat plate 17 ft long and 2 ft wide. Determine the drag as a function of speed and compare your results with the measured values given in Fig. P9.21*b*. Comment on reasons why the two sets of values may differ.

9.22   A sphere of diameter D and density ρ_s falls at a steady rate through a liquid of density ρ and viscosity μ. If the Reynolds number, $\text{Re} = \rho D U / \mu$, is less than 1, show that the viscosity can be determined from $\mu = g D^2 (\rho_s - \rho)/18\, U$.

9.23   A hot air balloon roughly spherical in shape has a volume of 70,000 ft³ and a weight of 500 lb (including pas-

sengers, basket, balloon fabric, etc.). If the outside air temperature is 80 °F and the temperature within the balloon is 165 °F, estimate the rate at which it will rise under steady-state conditions if the atmospheric pressure is 14.7 psi.

9.24   A 38.1-mm-diameter, 0.0245-N table tennis ball is released from the bottom of a swimming pool. With what velocity does it rise to the surface? Assume it has reached its terminal velocity.

†9.25   How fast will a toy balloon filled with helium rise through still air? List all of your assumptions.

9.26   A 60-mph wind flows against an outdoor movie screen that is 70 ft wide and 20 ft tall. Estimate the wind force on the screen.

(a)

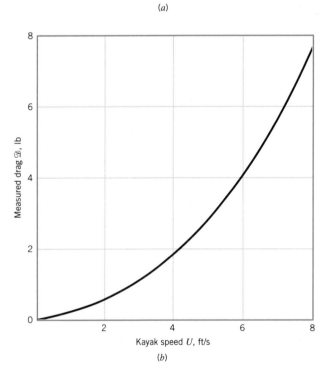

(b)

■ **FIGURE P9.21**

9.27 Determine the moment needed at the base of 30-m-tall, 0.12-m-diameter flag pole to keep it in place in a 20 m/s wind.

9.28 Repeat Problem 9.27 if a 2-m by 2.5-m flag is attached to the top of the pole. See Fig. 9.21 for drag coefficient data for flags.

9.29 If for a given vehicle it takes 20 hp to overcome aerodynamic drag while being driven at 55 mph, estimate the horsepower required at 65 mph.

9.30 Two bicycle racers ride 30 km/hr through still air. By what percentage is the power required to overcome aerodynamic drag for the second cyclist reduced if she drafts closely behind the first cyclist rather than riding alongside her? Neglect any forces other than aerodynamic drag. (See Fig. 9.21).

9.31 It is suggested that the power, $\mathcal{P}$, needed to overcome the aerodynamic drag on a vehicle traveling at a speed U varies as $\mathcal{P} \sim U^n$. What is an appropriate value for the constant n? Explain.

†9.32 Estimate the wind velocity necessary to knock over a garbage can. List your assumptions.

9.33 A 25-ton (50,000-lb) truck coasts down a steep 7% mountain grade without brakes, as shown in Fig. P9.33. The truck's ultimate steady-state speed, V, is determined by a balance between weight, rolling resistance, and aerodynamic drag. Determine V if the rolling resistance for a truck on concrete is 1.2% of the weight and the drag coefficient based on frontal area is 0.76.

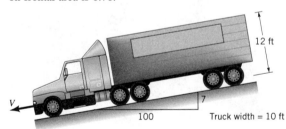

12 ft

V

100   7   Truck width = 10 ft

■ **FIGURE P9.33**

9.34 Estimate the velocity with which you would contact the ground if you jumped from an airplane at an altitude of 5,000 ft and **(a)** air resistance is negligible, **(b)** air resistance is important, but you forgot your parachute, or **(c)** you use a 25-ft-diameter parachute.

9.35 A 2-in.-diameter cork sphere (specific weight = 13 lb/ft³) is attached to the bottom of a river with a thin cable, as illustrated in Fig. P9.35. If the sphere has a drag coefficient of 0.5, determine the river velocity. Both the drag on the cable and its weight are negligible.

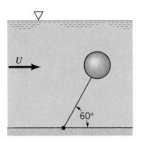

U

60°

■ **FIGURE P9.35**

9.36 A 12-mm-diameter cable is strung between a series of poles that are 60 m apart. Determine the horizontal force this cable puts on each pole if the wind velocity is 30 m/s.

9.37 A 22 in. by 34 in. speed limit sign is supported on a 3-in. wide, 5-ft-long pole. Estimate the bending moment in the pole at ground level when a 30-mph wind blows against the sign. (See Video V9.6.) List any assumptions used in your calculations.

9.38 Estimate the wind force on your hand when you hold it out your car window while driving 55 mph. Repeat your calculations if you were to hold your hand out of the window of an airplane flying 550 mph.

9.39 Estimate the deceleration (in terms of the number of g's) of a 6-ft-diameter, 12,500-lb blunt reentry vehicle traveling 15,000 mph through the atmosphere at an altitude of 30 mi.

9.40 A 30-ft-tall tower is constructed of equal 1-ft segments as is indicated in Fig. P9.40. Each of the four sides is similar. Estimate the drag on the tower when a 75-mph wind blows against it.

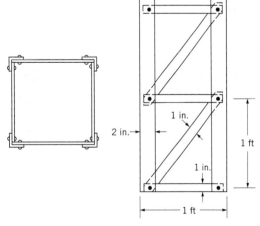

2 in.→   1 in.

1 in.

1 ft

1 ft

■ **FIGURE P9.40**

9.41 The United Nations Building in New York is approximately 87.5 m wide and 154 m tall. **(a)** Determine the drag on this building if the drag coefficient is 1.3 and the wind speed is a uniform 20 m/s. **(b)** Repeat your calculations if the velocity profile against the building is a typical profile for an urban area (see Problem 9.11) and the wind speed half way up the building is 20 m/s.

†9.42 An "air-popper" popcorn machine is shown in Fig. P9.42. The hot $(T = 250 \text{ °F})$ air blows past the kernels with speed U so that the unpopped ones remain in the holder $(U < U_{max})$, but the popped kernels are blown out of the holder $(U > U_{min})$. Estimate the range of air velocity allowed for proper operation of the machine $(U_{min} < U < U_{max})$. List all assumptions and show all calculations.

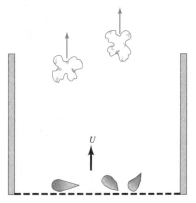

■ **FIGURE P9.42**

9.43 A regulation football is 6.78 in. in diameter and weighs 0.91 lb. If its drag coefficient is $C_D = 0.2$, determine its deceleration if it has a speed of 20 ft/s at the top of its trajectory.

9.44 A strong wind can blow a golf ball off the tee by pivoting it about point 1 as shown in Fig. P9.44. Determine the wind speed necessary to do this.

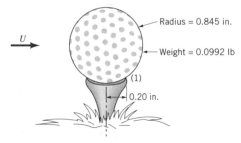

Radius = 0.845 in.

Weight = 0.0992 lb

(1)

0.20 in.

■ **FIGURE P9.44**

9.45 An airplane tows a banner that is $b = 0.8$ m tall and $\ell = 25$ m long at a speed of 150 km/hr. If the drag coefficient based on the area $b\ell$ is $C_D = 0.06$, estimate the power required to tow the banner. Compare the drag force on the banner with that on a rigid flat plate of the same size. Which has the larger drag force and why?

9.46 As shown in **Video V9.8** and Fig. P9.46, the aerodynamic drag on a truck can be reduced by the use of appropriate air deflectors. A reduction in drag coefficient from $C_D = 0.96$ to $C_D = 0.70$ corresponds to a reduction of how many horsepower needed at a highway speed of 65 mph?

b = width = 10 ft

12 ft

(a) $C_D = 0.70$

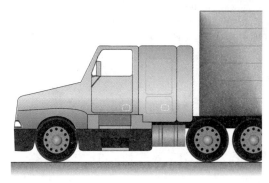

(b) $C_D = 0.96$

■ **FIGURE P9.46**

9.47 Estimate the power needed to overcome the aerodynamic drag of a person who runs at a rate of 100 yds in 10 s in still air. Repeat the calculations if the race is run into a 20-mph headwind.

9.48 As shown in **Video V9.5** and Fig. P9.48, a vertical wind tunnel can be used for skydiving practice. Estimate the vertical wind speed needed if a 150-lb person is to be able to "float" motionless when the person **(a)** curls up as in a crouching position or **(b)** lies flat. See Fig. 9.21 for appropriate drag coefficient data.

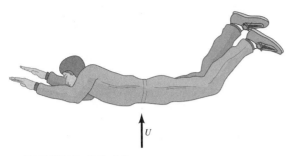

■ FIGURE P9.48

■ FIGURE P9.52

9.49   A 1.2-lb kite with an area of 6 ft² flies in a 20 ft/s wind such that the weightless string makes an angle of 55° relative to the horizontal. If the pull on the string is 1.5 lb, determine the lift and drag coefficients based on the kite area.

9.50   An iceberg floats with approximately $\frac{1}{7}$ of its volume in the air as is shown in Fig. P9.50. If the wind velocity is U and the water is stationary, estimate the speed at which the wind forces the iceberg through the water.

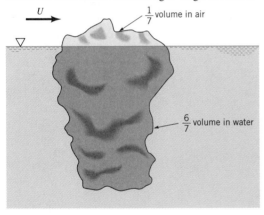

■ FIGURE P9.50

9.51   A Piper Cub airplane has a gross weight of 1750 lb, a cruising speed of 115 mph, and a wing area of 179 ft². Determine the lift coefficient of this airplane for these conditions.

9.52   As shown in **Video V9.9** and Fig. P9.52, a spoiler is used on race cars to produce a negative lift, thereby giving a better tractive force. The lift coefficient for the airfoil shown is $C_L = 1.1$ and the coefficient of friction between the wheels and the pavement is 0.6. At a speed of 200 mph, by how much would use of the spoiler increase the maximum tractive force that could be generated between the wheels and ground? Assume the air speed past the spoiler equals the car speed and that the airfoil acts directly over the drive wheels.

9.53   A wing generates a lift $\mathcal{L}$ when moving through sea-level air with a velocity U. How fast must the wing move through the air at an altitude of 35,000 ft with the same lift coefficient if it is to generate the same lift?

9.54   A Boeing 747 aircraft weighing 580,000 lb when loaded with fuel and 100 passengers takes off with an air speed of 140 mph. With the same configuration (i.e., angle of attack, flap settings, etc.), what is the takeoff speed if it is loaded with 372 passengers? Assume each passenger with luggage weighs 200 lb.

9.55   **(a)** Show that for unpowered flight (for which the lift, drag, and weight forces are in equilibrium) the glide slope angle, θ, is given by $\tan \theta = C_D/C_L$. **(b)** If the lift coefficient for a Boeing 727 aircraft is 16 times greater than its drag coefficient, can it glide from an altitude of 30,000 ft to an airport 60 miles away if it loses power from its engines? Explain.

9.56   For a given airplane, compare the power to maintain level flight at a 5000-ft altitude with that at 30,000 ft at the same velocity. Assume C_D remains constant.

9.57   The landing speed of an airplane such as the Space Shuttle is dependent on the air density. (See **Video V9.1**.) By what percent must the landing speed be increased on a day when the temperature is 110 deg F compared to a day when it is 50 deg F? Assume the atmospheric pressure remains constant.

9.58   The velocity profile within the boundary layer on a flat plate can be determined by means of the device shown in Fig. P9.58. Air at a temperature of 80 °F and an absolute pressure of 29.09 in. of mercury blows steadily along a flat plate. A small diameter, open-ended tube located at various distances, y, above the plate is used to measure the stagnation pressure of the flow at these locations. The static pressure is measured by means of a static pressure tap on the plate as indicated. The difference between the stagnation and static pressures is determined from the inclined manometer reading, ℓ. The manometer is filled with a liquid of specific gravity 0.812.

Values of ℓ and y obtained experimentally at a distance of 15.0 in. from the leading edge of the plate are shown in the table below. Use these results to plot a graph of the air speed, u, as a function of the distance above the plate, y.

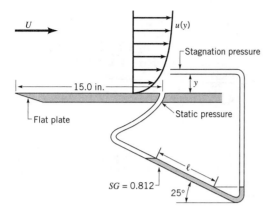

■ **FIGURE P9.58**

Determine the boundary layer thickness at this location. Also calculate the theoretical boundary layer thickness for the conditions corresponding to the above experimental data.

Compare the experimental and theoretical results and discuss some possible reasons for any differences between them.

y (in.)	ℓ (in.)
0.020	0.15
0.035	0.35
0.044	0.40
0.060	0.70
0.096	0.90
0.110	1.30
0.138	1.45
0.178	1.65
0.230	1.95
0.270	2.00
0.322	2.00

CHAPTER

10

*O*pen-Channel Flow

*O*pen-channel flow involves the flow of a liquid in a channel or conduit that is not completely filled. There exists a free surface between the flowing fluid (usually water) and fluid above it (usually the atmosphere). The main driving force for such flows is the fluid weight — gravity forces the fluid to flow downhill. Most open-channel flow results are based on correlations obtained from model and full-scale experiments. Additional information can be gained from various analytical and numerical efforts.

10.1 General Characteristics of Open-Channel Flow

An open-channel flow is classified as *uniform flow* (UF) if the depth of flow does not vary along the channel ($dy/dx = 0$, where y is the fluid depth and x is the distance along the channel). Conversely, it is *nonuniform flow* or *varied flow* if the depth varies with distance ($dy/dx \neq 0$). Nonuniform flows are further classified as *rapidly varying flow* (RVF) if the flow depth changes considerably over a relatively short distance; $dy/dx \sim 1$. *Gradually*

Motion of water induced by surface waves: As a wave passes along the surface of the water, the water particles follow elliptical paths. There is no net motion of the water, just a periodic, cyclic trajectory (neutrally buoyant particles in water). (Photograph by A. Wallet and F. Ruellan, Ref. 10, courtesy of M. C. Vasseur, Sogreah.)

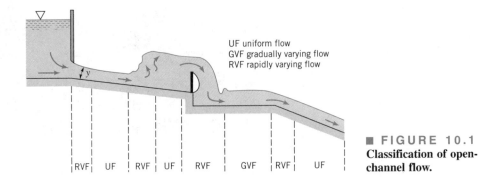

UF uniform flow
GVF gradually varying flow
RVF rapidly varying flow

■ **FIGURE 10.1**
Classification of open-channel flow.

RVF | UF | RVF | UF | RVF | GVF | RVF | UF

varying flows (GVF) are those in which the flow depth changes slowly with distance along the channel; $dy/dx \ll 1$. Examples of these types of flow are illustrated in Fig. 10.1.

As for any flow geometry, open-channel flow may be *larminar, transitional,* or *turbulent,* depending on various conditions involved. Which type of flow occurs depends on the Reynolds number, $\text{Re} = \rho V R_h / \mu$, where V is the average velocity of the fluid and R_h is the hydraulic radius of the channel (see Section 10.4). Since most open-channel flows involve water (which has a fairly small viscosity) and have relatively large characteristic lengths, it is uncommon to have laminar open-channel flows.

Open-channel flows involve a free surface that can deform from its undistorted relatively flat configuration to form waves. The character of an open-channel flow may depend strongly on how fast the fluid is flowing relative to how fast a typical wave moves relative to the fluid. The dimensionless parameter that describes this behavior is termed the Froude number, $\text{Fr} = V/(gy)^{1/2}$, where y is the fluid depth. The special case of a flow with a Froude number of unity, $\text{Fr} = 1$, is termed a *critical flow.* If the Froude number is less than 1, the flow is *subcritical* (or *tranquil*). A flow with the Froude number greater than 1 is termed *supercritical* (or *rapid*).

10.2 Surface Waves

The distinguishing feature of flows involving a free surface (as in open-channel flows) is the opportunity for the free surface to distort into various shapes. The surface of a lake or the ocean is seldom "smooth as a mirror." It is usually distorted into ever-changing patterns associated with surface speeds.

10.2.1 Wave Speed

Consider the situation illustrated in Fig. 10.2a in which a single elementary wave of small height, δy, is produced on the surface of a channel by suddenly moving the initially stationary end wall with speed δV. The water in the channel was stationary at the initial time, $t = 0$. A stationary observer will observe a single wave move down the channel with a *wave speed* c, with no fluid motion ahead of the wave and a fluid velocity of δV behind the wave. The motion is unsteady for such an observer. For an observer moving along the channel with speed c, the flow will appear steady as shown in Fig. 10.2b. To this observer, the fluid velocity will be $\mathbf{V} = -c\hat{\mathbf{i}}$ on the observer's right and $\mathbf{V} = (-c + \delta V)\hat{\mathbf{i}}$ to the left of the observer.

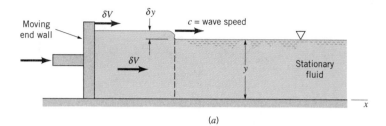

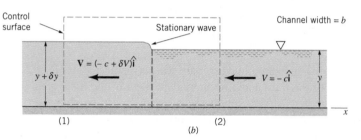

(b)

■ **FIGURE 10.2**
(*a*) **Production of a single elementary wave in a channel as seen by a stationary observer.** (*b*) **Wave as seen by an observer moving with a speed equal to the wave speed.**

The relationship between the various parameters involved for this flow can be obtained by application of the continuity and momentum equations to the control volume shown in Fig. 10.2*b* as follows. With the assumption of uniform one-dimensional flow, the continuity equation (Eq. 5.10) becomes

$$-cyb = (-c + \delta V)(y + \delta y)b$$

where b is the channel width. This simplifies to

$$c = \frac{(y + \delta y)\,\delta V}{\delta y}$$

or in the limit of small amplitude waves with $\delta y \ll y$

$$c = y\,\frac{\delta V}{\delta y} \tag{10.1}$$

Similarly, the momentum equation (Eq. 5.17) is

$$\tfrac{1}{2}\gamma y^2 b - \tfrac{1}{2}\gamma(y + \delta y)^2 b = \rho bcy[(c - \delta V) - c]$$

where we have written the mass flowrate as $m = \rho bcy$ and have assumed that the pressure variation is hydrostatic within the fluid. That is, the pressure forces on the channel across sections (1) and (2) are $F_1 = \gamma y_{c1}A_1 = \gamma(y + \delta y)^2 b/2$ and $F_2 = \gamma y_{c2}A_2 = \gamma y^2 b/2$, respectively. If we again impose the assumption of small amplitude waves [that is, $(\delta y)^2 \ll y\,\delta y$], the momentum equation reduces to

$$\frac{\delta V}{\delta y} = \frac{g}{c} \tag{10.2}$$

Combination of Eqs. 10.1 and 10.2 gives the wave speed as

$$c = \sqrt{gy} \tag{10.3}$$

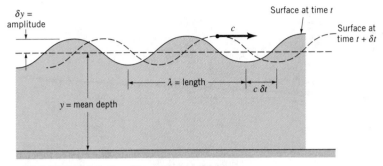

■ FIGURE 10.3 **Sinusoidal surface wave.**

The speed of a small amplitude solitary wave as indicated in Fig. 10.2 is proportional to the square root of the fluid depth, y, and independent of the wave amplitude, δy.

A more general description of wave motion can be obtained by considering continuous (not solitary) waves of sinusoidal shape as is shown in Fig. 10.3. An advanced analysis of such sinusoidal surface waves of small amplitude shows that the wave speed varies with both the wavelength, λ, and fluid depth, y, as (Ref. 1)

$$c = \left[\frac{g\lambda}{2\pi} \tanh\left(\frac{2\pi y}{\lambda}\right) \right]^{1/2} \tag{10.4}$$

where $\tanh(2\pi y/\lambda)$ is the hyperbolic tangent of the argument $2\pi y/\lambda$. This result is plotted in Fig. 10.4. For conditions for which the water depth is much greater than the wavelength ($y \gg \lambda$, as in the ocean), the wave speed is independent of y and given by

$$c = \sqrt{\frac{g\lambda}{2\pi}}$$

On the other hand, if the fluid layer is shallow ($y \ll \lambda$, as often happens in open channels), the wave speed is given by $c = (gy)^{1/2}$, as derived for the solitary wave in Fig. 10.2. These two limiting cases are shown in Fig. 10.4.

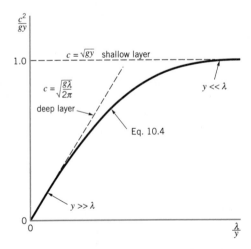

■ FIGURE 10.4 **Wave speed as a function of wavelength.**

10.2.2   Froude Number Effects

V10.1 Bicycle through a puddle

Consider an elementary wave traveling on the surface of a fluid, as is shown in Fig. 10.2*a*. If the fluid layer is stationary, the wave moves to the right with speed c relative to the fluid and the stationary observer. If the fluid is flowing to the left with velocity $V < c$, the wave (which travels with speed c relative to the fluid) will travel to the right with a speed of $c - V$ relative to a fixed observer. If the fluid flows to the left with $V = c$, the wave will remain stationary, but if $V > c$ the wave will be washed to the left with speed $V - c$.

The above ideas can be expressed in dimensionless form by use of the Froude number, $\text{Fr} = V/(gy)^{1/2}$, where we take the characteristic length to be the fluid depth, y. Thus, the Froude number, $\text{Fr} = V/(gy)^{1/2} = V/c$, is the ratio of the fluid velocity to the wave speed.

The following characteristics are observed when a wave is produced on the surface of a moving stream, as happens when a rock is thrown into a river. If the stream is not flowing, the wave spreads equally in all directions. If the stream is nearly stationary or moving in a tranquil manner (i.e., $V < c$), the wave can move upstream. Upstream locations are said to be in hydraulic communication with the downstream locations. That is, an observer upstream of a disturbance can tell that there has been a disturbance on the surface because that disturbance can propagate upstream to the observer. Such conditions, $V < c$ or $\text{Fr} < 1$, are termed subcritical.

On the other hand, if the stream is moving rapidly so that the flow velocity is greater than the wave speed (i.e., $V > c$), no upstream communication with downstream locations is possible. Any disturbance on the surface downstream from the observer will be washed further downstream. Such conditions, $V > c$ or $\text{Fr} > 1$, are termed supercritical. For the special case of $V = c$ or $\text{Fr} = 1$, the upstream propagating wave remains stationary and the flow is termed critical.

10.3   Energy Considerations

A typical segment of an open-channel flow is shown in Fig. 10.5. The slope of the channel bottom (or *bottom slope*), $S_0 = (z_1 - z_2)/\ell$, is assumed constant over the segment shown. The fluid depths and velocities are y_1, y_2, V_1, and V_2 as indicated.

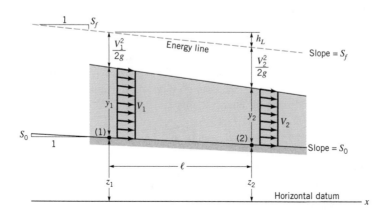

■ **FIGURE 10.5**
Typical open-channel geometry.

With the assumption of a uniform velocity profile across any section of the channel, the one-dimensional energy equation for this flow (Eq. 5.57) becomes

$$\frac{p_1}{\gamma} + \frac{V_1^2}{2g} + z_1 = \frac{p_2}{\gamma} + \frac{V_2^2}{2g} + z_2 + h_L \tag{10.5}$$

where h_L is the head loss due to viscous effects between sections (1) and (2) and $z_1 - z_2 = S_0\ell$. Since the pressure is essentially hydrostatic at any cross section, we find that $p_1/\gamma = y_1$ and $p_2/\gamma = y_2$ so that Eq. 10.5 becomes

$$y_1 + \frac{V_1^2}{2g} + S_0\ell = y_2 + \frac{V_2^2}{2g} + h_L \tag{10.6}$$

We write the head loss in terms of the slope of the energy line, $S_f = h_L/\ell$ (often termed the *friction slope*), as indicated in Fig. 10.5. Recall from Chapter 3 that the energy line is located a distance z (the elevation from some datum to the channel bottom) plus the pressure head (p/γ) plus the velocity head $(V^2/2g)$ above the datum.

10.3.1 Specific Energy

The concept of the *specific energy, E,* defined as

$$E = y + \frac{V^2}{2g} \tag{10.7}$$

is often useful in open-channel flow considerations. The energy equation, Eq. 10.6, can be written in terms of E as

$$E_1 = E_2 + (S_f - S_0)\ell \tag{10.8}$$

If we consider a simple channel whose cross-sectional shape is a rectangle of width b, the specific energy can be written in terms of the flowrate per unit width, $q = Q/b = Vyb/b = Vy$, as

$$E = y + \frac{q^2}{2gy^2} \tag{10.9}$$

For a given channel of constant width, the value of q remains constant along the channel, although the depth, y, may vary. To gain insight into the flow processes involved, we consider the *specific energy diagram*, a graph of $E = E(y)$ with q fixed, as shown in Fig. 10.6.

For given q and E, Eq. 10.9 is a cubic equation with three solutions, y_{sup}, y_{sub}, and y_{neg}. If the specific energy is large enough (i.e., $E > E_{min}$, where E_{min} is a function of q), two of the solutions are positive and the other, y_{neg}, is negative. The negative root, represented by the curved dashed line in Fig. 10.6, has no physical meaning and can be ignored. Thus, for a given flowrate and specific energy there are two possible depths. These two depths are termed *alternate depths*.

It can be shown that critical conditions (Fr $= 1$) occur at the location of E_{min}. Since the layer is deeper and the velocity smaller for the upper part of the specific energy diagram (compared with the conditions at E_{min}), such flows are subcritical (Fr < 1). Conversely, flows for the lower part of the diagram are supercritical. Thus, for a given flowrate, q, if $E > E_{min}$ there are two possible depths of flow, one subcritical and the other supercritical.

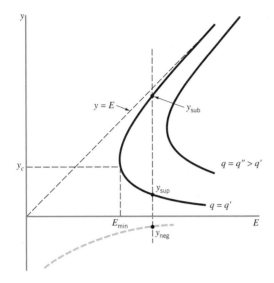

■ FIGURE 10.6   Specific energy diagram.

EXAMPLE 10.1

Water flows under the sluice gate in a constant width rectangular channel as shown in Fig. E10.1a. Describe this flow in terms of the specific energy diagram. Assume inviscid flow.

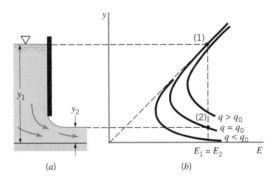

■ FIGURE E10.1a & b

SOLUTION

For this inviscid ($S_f = 0$) flow the channel bottom is horizontal, $z_1 = z_2$ (or $S_0 = 0$), so that the energy equation (Eq. 10.8) reduces to $E_1 = E_2$. Although the flowrate is not given, we do know that $q_1 = q_2$ and that the specific energy diagram for this flow is as shown in Fig. E10.1b. The flow upstream of the gate is subcritical while the flow downstream is super-critical. The particular value of q obtained, $q = q_0$, and hence the specific curve of Fig. E10.1b which is valid for this flow, are illustrated by those that give $E_1 = E_2$ for the given y_1 and y_2.

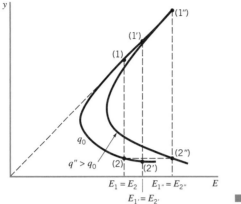

■ FIGURE E10.1c

The flowrate can remain the same for this channel even if the upstream depth is increased. This is indicated by depths $y_{1'}$ and $y_{2'}$ in Fig. E10.1c. Of course, to do this the distance between the bottom of the gate and the channel bottom must be decreased to give a smaller flow area ($y_{2'} < y_2$), and the upstream depth must be increased to give a bigger head ($y_{1'} > y_1$). On the other hand, if the gate remains fixed so that the downstream depth remains fixed ($y_{2''} = y_2$), the flowrate will increase as the upstream depth increases to $y_{1''} > y_1$. This is indicated in Fig. E10.1c by the curve with flowrate $q'' > q_0$.

10.4 Uniform Depth Channel Flow

V10.2 Merging channels

Many channels are designed to carry fluid at a uniform depth all along their length. Uniform depth flow ($dy/dx = 0$, or $y_1 = y_2$ and $V_1 = V_2$) can be accomplished by adjusting the bottom slope, S_0, so that it precisely equals the slope of the energy line, S_f. That is, $S_0 = S_f$ (see Eq. 10.8). From an energy point of view, uniform depth flow is achieved by a balance between the potential energy lost by the fluid as it coasts downhill and the energy that is dissipated by viscous effects (head loss) associated with shear stresses throughout the fluid.

10.4.1 Uniform Flow Approximations

We consider fluid flowing in an open channel of constant cross-sectional size and shape such that the depth of flow remains constant as indicated in Fig. 10.7. The area of the section is A and the *wetted perimeter* (i.e., the length of the perimeter of the cross section in contact

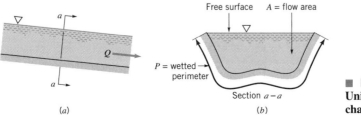

■ FIGURE 10.7
Uniform flow in an open channel.

with the fluid) is P. Reasonable analytical results can be obtained by assuming a uniform velocity profile, V, and a constant wall shear stress, τ_w, along the wetted perimeter.

10.4.2   The Chezy and Manning Equations

Under the assumptions of steady, uniform flow, the x component of the momentum equation (Eq. 5.17) applied to the control volume indicated in Fig. 10.8 simply reduces to

$$\Sigma F_x = \rho Q(V_2 - V_1) = 0$$

since $V_1 = V_2$. There is no acceleration of the fluid, and the momentum flux across section (1) is the same as that across section (2). The flow is governed by a simple balance between the forces in the direction of the flow. Thus, $\Sigma F_x = 0$, or

$$F_1 - F_2 - \tau_w P\ell + \mathcal{W}\sin\theta = 0 \tag{10.10}$$

where F_1 and F_2 are the hydrostatic pressure forces across either end of the control volume. Because the flow is at a uniform depth ($y_1 = y_2$), it follows that $F_1 = F_2$ so that these two forces do not contribute to the force balance. The term $\mathcal{W}\sin\theta$ is the component of the fluid weight that acts down the slope, and $\tau_w P\ell$ is the shear force on the fluid, acting up the slope as a result of the interaction of the water and the channel's wetted perimeter. Thus, Eq. 10.10 becomes

$$\tau_w = \frac{\mathcal{W}\sin\theta}{P\ell} = \frac{\mathcal{W}S_0}{P\ell}$$

where we have used the approximation that $\sin\theta \approx \tan\theta = S_0$, since the bottom slope is typically very small (i.e., $S_0 \ll 1$). Since $\mathcal{W} = \gamma A\ell$ and the *hydraulic radius* is defined as $R_h = A/P$, the force balance equation becomes

$$\tau_w = \frac{\gamma A\ell S_0}{P\ell} = \gamma R_h S_0 \tag{10.11}$$

Most open-channel flows are turbulent (rather than laminar), and the wall shear stress is nearly proportional to the dynamic pressure, $\rho V^2/2$, and independent of the viscosity. That is,

$$\tau_w = K\rho\frac{V^2}{2}$$

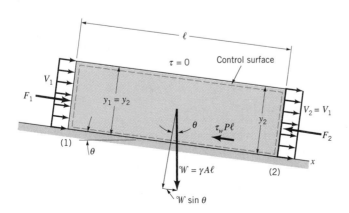

■ **FIGURE 10.8**
Control volume for uniform flow in an open channel.

where K is a constant dependent upon the roughness of the channel. In such situations, Eq. 10.11 becomes

$$K\rho\,\frac{V^2}{2} = \gamma R_h S_0$$

or

$$V = C\sqrt{R_h S_0} \qquad\qquad (10.12)$$

where the constant C is termed the Chezy coefficient and Eq. 10.12 is termed the *Chezy equation.*

From a series of experiments it was found that the slope dependence of Eq. 10.12 ($V \sim S_0^{1/2}$) is reasonable, but that the dependence on the hydraulic radius is actually not as given. The following somewhat modified equation for open-channel flow is used to more accurately describe the R_h dependence:

$$V = \frac{R_h^{2/3} S_0^{1/2}}{n} \qquad\qquad (10.13)$$

Equation 10.13 is termed the *Manning equation,* and the parameter n is the *Manning resistance coefficient.* Its value is dependent on the surface material of the channel's wetted perimeter and is obtained from experiments. It is not dimensionless, having the units of $s/m^{1/3}$ or $s/ft^{1/3}$.

Typical values of the Manning coefficient are indicated in Table 10.1. As expected, the rougher the wetted perimeter, the larger the value of n. The values of n were developed for SI units. Standard practice is to use the same value of n when using the BG system of units, and to insert a conversion factor into the equation.

Thus, uniform flow in an open channel is obtained from the Manning equation written as

V10.3 Uniform channel flow

$$\boxed{V = \frac{\kappa}{n}\,R_h^{2/3} S_0^{1/2}} \qquad\qquad (10.14)$$

and

$$\boxed{Q = \frac{\kappa}{n}\,A R_h^{2/3} S_0^{1/2}} \qquad\qquad (10.15)$$

where $\kappa = 1$ if SI units are used, and $\kappa = 1.49$ if BG units are used. Thus, by using R_h in meters, A in m^2, and $\kappa = 1$, the average velocity is m/s and the flowrate m^3/s. By using R_h in feet, A in ft^2, and $\kappa = 1.49$, the average velocity is ft/s and the flowrate ft^3/s.

10.4.3   Uniform Depth Examples

A variety of interesting and useful results can be obtained from the Manning equation. The following examples illustrate some of the typical considerations.

Determination of the flowrate for a given channel with flow at a given depth (often termed the *normal flowrate* or *normal depth*) is obtained from a straightforward calculation as shown in Example 10.2.

■ **TABLE 10.1**
Values of the Manning Coefficient, *n* (Ref 5)

Wetted Perimeter	*n*
A. *Natural channels*	
Clean and straight	0.030
Sluggish with deep pools	0.040
Major rivers	0.035
B. *Floodplains*	
Pasture, farmland	0.035
Light brush	0.050
Heavy brush	0.075
Trees	0.15
C. *Excavated earth channels*	
Clean	0.022
Gravelly	0.025
Weedy	0.030
Stony, cobbles	0.035
D. *Artifically lined channels*	
Glass	0.010
Brass	0.011
Steel, smooth	0.012
Steel, painted	0.014
Steel, riveted	0.015
Cast iron	0.013
Concrete, finished	0.012
Concrete, unfinished	0.014
Planed wood	0.012
Clay tile	0.014
Brickwork	0.015
Asphalt	0.016
Corrugated metal	0.022
Rubble masonry	0.025

*E*XAMPLE 10.2

Water flows in the canal of trapezoidal cross section shown in Fig. E10.2. The bottom drops 1.4 ft per 1000 ft of length. Determine the flowrate if the canal is lined with new smooth concrete, or if weeds cover the wetted perimeter. Determine the Froude number for each of these flows.

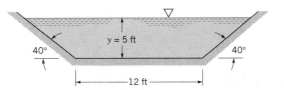

40° $y = 5$ ft   40°

|← 12 ft →|

■ FIGURE E10.2

$\mathcal{S}$OLUTION_____

From Eq. 10.15

$$Q = \frac{1.49}{n} AR_h^{2/3} S_0^{1/2} \tag{1}$$

where we have used $\kappa = 1.49$, since the dimensions are given in BG units. For a depth of $y = 5$ ft, the flow area is

$$A = 12 \text{ ft } (5 \text{ ft}) + 5 \text{ ft} \left(\frac{5}{\tan 40°} \text{ ft} \right) = 89.8 \text{ ft}^2$$

so that with a wetter perimeter of $P = 12 \text{ ft} + 2(5/\sin 40° \text{ ft}) = 27.6$ ft, the hydraulic radius is determined to be $R_h = A/P = 3.25$ ft. Note that even though the channel is quite wide (the free-surface width is 23.9 ft), the hydraulic radius is only 3.25 ft, which is less than the depth.

Thus, with $S_0 = 1.4 \text{ ft}/1000 \text{ ft} = 0.0014$, Eq. 1 becomes

$$Q = \frac{1.49}{n} (89.8 \text{ ft}^2)(3.25 \text{ ft})^{2/3}(0.0014)^{1/2} = \frac{10.98}{n}$$

where Q is in ft^3/s.

From Table 10.1, the values of n are estimated to be $n = 0.012$ for the smooth concrete and $n = 0.030$ for the weedy conditions. Thus,

$$Q = \frac{10.98}{0.012} = 915 \text{ cfs} \tag{Ans}$$

for the new concrete lining and

$$Q = \frac{10.98}{0.030} = 366 \text{ cfs} \tag{Ans}$$

for the weedy lining. The corresponding average velocities, $V = Q/A$, are 10.2 ft/s and 4.08 ft/s, respectively. It does not take a very steep slope ($S_0 = 0.0014$ or $\theta = \tan^{-1}(0.0014) = 0.080°$) for this velocity.

Note that the increased roughness causes a decrease in the flowrate. This is an indication that for the turbulent flows involved, the wall shear stress increases with surface roughness. [For water at 50 °F, the Reynolds number based on the 3.25-ft hydraulic radius of the channel is Re $= R_h V/\nu = 3.25 \text{ ft } (4.08 \text{ ft/s})/(1.41 \times 10^{-5} \text{ ft}^2/\text{s}) = 9.40 \times 10^5$, well into the turbulent regime.]

The Froude numbers based on the maximum depths for the two flows can be determined from Fr $= V/(gy)^{1/2}$. For the new concrete case,

$$\text{Fr} = \frac{10.2 \text{ ft/s}}{(3.22 \text{ ft/s}^2 \times 5 \text{ ft})^{1/2}} = 0.804 \tag{Ans}$$

while for the weedy case

$$\text{Fr} = \frac{4.08 \text{ ft/s}}{(32.2 \text{ ft/s}^2 \times 5 \text{ ft})^{1/2}} = 0.322 \tag{Ans}$$

In either case the flow is subcritical.

The same results would be obtained for the channel if its size were given in meters. We would use the same value of n but set $\kappa = 1$ for this SI units situation.

In some instances a trial-and-error or iteration method must be used to solve for the dependent variable. This is often encountered when the flowrate, channel slope, and channel material are given, and the flow depth is to be determined as illustrated in the following examples.

EXAMPLE 10.3

Water flows in the channel shown in Fig. E10.2 at a rate of $Q = 10.0$ m³/s. If the canal lining is weedy, determine the depth of the flow.

SOLUTION

In this instance neither the flow area nor the hydraulic radius are known, although they can be written in terms of the depth, y, as

$$A = 1.19y^2 + 3.66y$$

where the bottom width is $(12 \text{ ft})(1 \text{ m}/3.281 \text{ ft}) = 3.66$ m and A and y are in square meters and meters, respectively. Also, the wetted perimeter is

$$P = 3.66 + 2\left(\frac{y}{\sin 40°}\right) = 3.11y + 3.66$$

so that

$$R_h = \frac{A}{P} = \frac{1.19y^2 + 3.66y}{3.11y + 3.66}$$

where R_h and y are in meters. Thus, with $n = 0.030$ (from Table 10.1), Eq. 10.15 can be written as

$$Q = 10 = \frac{\kappa}{n} AR_h^{2/3} S_0^{1/2}$$

$$= \frac{1.0}{0.030}(1.19y^2 + 3.66y)\left(\frac{1.19y^2 + 3.66y}{3.11y + 3.66}\right)^{2/3}(0.0014)^{1/2}$$

which can be rearranged into the form

$$(1.19y^2 + 3.66y)^5 - 515(3.11y + 3.66)^2 = 0 \tag{1}$$

where y is in meters. The solution of Eq. 1 can be easily obtained by use of a simple root-finding numerical technique or by trial-and-error methods. The only physically meaningful root of Eq. 1 (i.e., a positive, real number) gives the solution for the normal flow depth at this flowrate as

$$y = 1.50 \text{ m} \tag{Ans}$$

In many man-made channels the surface roughness (and hence the Manning coefficient) varies along the wetted perimeter of the channel. In such cases the channel cross section can be divided into N subsections, each with its own wetted perimeter, P_i, and A_i, and Manning coefficient, n_i. The P_i values do not include the imaginary boundaries between the different subsections. The total flowrate is assumed to be the sum of the flowrates through each section. This technique is illustrated by Example 10.4.

EXAMPLE 10.4

Water flows along the drainage canal having the properties shown in Fig. E10.4. If the bottom slope is $S_0 = 1 \text{ ft}/500 \text{ ft} = 0.002$, estimate the flowrate.

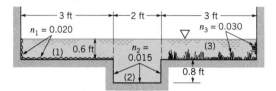

■ FIGURE E10.4

SOLUTION

We divide the cross section into three subsections as is indicated in Fig. E10.4 and write the flowrate as $Q = Q_1 + Q_2 + Q_3$, where for each section

$$Q_i = \frac{1.49}{n_i} A_i R_{hi}^{2/3} S_0^{1/2}$$

The appropriate values of A_i, P_i, R_{hi}, and n_i are listed in Table E10.4. Note that the imaginary portions of the perimeters between sections (denoted by the dashed lines in Fig. E10.4) are not included in the P_i. That is, for section (2)

$$A_2 = 2 \text{ ft} (0.8 + 0.6) \text{ ft} = 2.8 \text{ ft}^2$$

and

$$P_2 = 2 \text{ ft} + 2(0.8 \text{ ft}) = 3.6 \text{ ft}$$

so that

$$R_{h_2} = \frac{A_2}{P_2} = \frac{2.8 \text{ ft}^2}{3.6 \text{ ft}} = 0.778 \text{ ft}$$

■ TABLE E10.4

i	A_i (ft^2)	P_i (ft)	R_{hi} (ft)	n_i
1	1.8	3.6	0.500	0.020
2	2.8	3.6	0.778	0.015
3	1.8	3.6	0.500	0.030

Thus, the total flowrate is

$$Q = Q_1 + Q_2 + Q_3 = 1.49(0.002)^{1/2}$$
$$\times \left[\frac{(1.8 \text{ ft}^2)(0.500 \text{ ft})^{2/3}}{0.020} + \frac{(2.8 \text{ ft}^2)(0.778 \text{ ft})^{2/3}}{0.015} + \frac{(1.8 \text{ ft}^2)(0.500 \text{ ft})^{2/3}}{0.030} \right]$$

or

$$Q = 16.8 \text{ ft}^3/\text{s} \tag{Ans}$$

If the entire channel cross section were considered as one flow area, then $A = A_1 + A_2 + A_3 = 6.4 \text{ ft}^2$ and $P = P_1 + P_2 + P_3 = 10.8 \text{ ft}$, or $R_h = A/P = 6.4 \text{ ft}^2/10.8 \text{ ft} = 0.593 \text{ ft}$. The flowrate is given by Eq. 10.15, which can be written as

$$Q = \frac{1.49}{n_{\text{eff}}} AR_h^{2/3} S_0^{1/2}$$

where n_{eff} is the effective value of n for this channel. With $Q = 16.8 \text{ ft}^3/\text{s}$ as determined above, the value of n_{eff} is found to be

$$n_{\text{eff}} = \frac{1.49 AR_h^{2/3} S_0^{1/2}}{Q}$$

$$= \frac{1.49(6.4)(0.593)^{2/3}(0.002)^{1/2}}{16.8} = 0.0179$$

As expected, the effective roughness (Manning n) is between the minimum ($n_2 = 0.015$) and maximum ($n_3 = 0.030$) values for the individual subsections.

One type of problem often encountered in open-channel flows is that of determining the *best hydraulic cross section* defined as the section of the minimum area for a given flowrate, Q, slope, S_0, and roughness coefficient, n. Example 10.5 illustrates the concept of the best hydraulic cross section for rectangular channels.

EXAMPLE 10.5

Water flows uniformly in a rectangular channel of width b and depth y. Determine the aspect ratio, b/y, for the best hydraulic cross section.

SOLUTION

The uniform flow is given by Eq. 10.15 as

$$Q = \frac{\kappa}{n} AR_h^{2/3} S_0^{1/2} \tag{1}$$

where $A = by$ and $P = b + 2y$, so that $R_h = A/P = by/(b + 2y)$. We rewrite the hydraulic radius in terms of A as

$$R_h = \frac{A}{(2y + b)} = \frac{A}{(2y + A/y)} = \frac{Ay}{(2y^2 + A)}$$

so that Eq. 1 becomes

$$Q = \frac{\kappa}{n} A \left(\frac{Ay}{2y^2 + A} \right)^{2/3} S_0^{1/2}$$

This can be rearranged to give

$$A^{5/2} y = K(2y^2 + A) \tag{2}$$

where $K = (nQ/\kappa S_0^{1/2})^{3/2}$ is a constant. The best hydraulic section is the one that gives the minimum A for all y. That is, $dA/dy = 0$. By differentiating Eq. 2 with respect to y, we obtain

$$\frac{5}{2} A^{3/2} \frac{dA}{dy} y + A^{5/2} = K \left(4y + \frac{dA}{dy} \right)$$

which, with $dA/dy = 0$, reduces to

$$A^{5/2} = 4Ky \tag{3}$$

With $K = A^{5/2} y/(2y^2 + A)$ from Eq. 2, Eq. 3 can be written in the form

$$A^{5/2} = \frac{4A^{5/2}y^2}{(2y^2 + A)}$$

which simplifies to $y = (A/2)^{1/2}$. Thus, since $A = by$, the best hydraulic cross section for a rectangular shape has a width b and a depth

$$y = \left(\frac{A}{2} \right)^{1/2} = \left(\frac{by}{2} \right)^{1/2}$$

or

$$2y^2 = by$$

That is, the rectangle with the best hydraulic cross section is twice as wide as it is deep, or

$$b/y = 2 \tag{Ans}$$

A rectangular channel with $b/y = 2$ will give the smallest area (and smallest wetted perimeter) for a given flowrate. Conversely, for a given area, the largest flowrate in a rectangular channel will occur when $b/y = 2$. For $A = by = $ constant, if $y \rightarrow 0$ then $b \rightarrow \infty$, and the flowrate is small because of the large wetted perimeter $P = b + 2y \rightarrow \infty$. The maximum Q occurs when $y = b/2$. However, as seen in Fig. E10.5a, the maximum represented by this optimal configuration is a rather weak one. For example, for aspect ratios between 1 and 4, the flowrate is within 96% of the maximum flowrate obtained with the same area and $b/y = 2$.

An alternate but equivalent method to obtain the above answer is to use the fact that $dR_h/dy = 0$, which follows from Eq. 1 using $dQ/dy = 0$ (constant flowrate) and $dA/dy = 0$ (best hydraulic cross section has minimum area). Differentiation of $R_h = Ay/(2y^2 + A)$ with constant A gives $b/y = 2$ when $dR_h/dy = 0$.

The best hydraulic cross section can be calculated for other shapes in a similar fashion. The results (given here without proof) for circular, rectangular, trapezoidal (with 60° sides), and triangular shapes are shown in Fig. E10.5b.

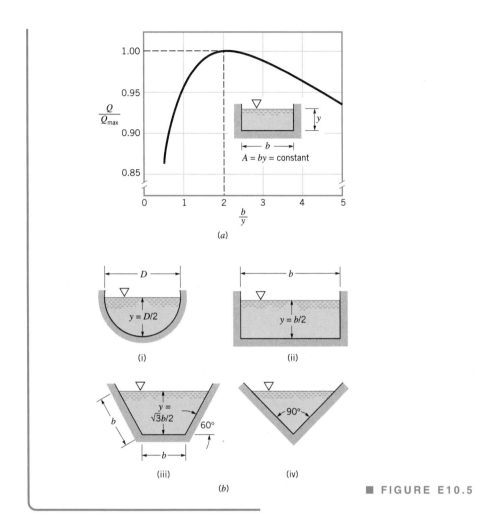

■ FIGURE E10.5

10.5 Gradually Varied Flow

In many situations the flow in an open channel is not of uniform depth ($y = $ constant) along the channel. This can occur because of several reasons: The bottom slope is not constant, the cross-sectional shape and area vary in the flow direction, or there is some obstruction across a portion of the channel. Such flows are classified as gradually varying flows if $dy/dx \ll 1$.

If the bottom slope and the energy line slope are not equal, the flow depth will vary along the channel, either increasing or decreasing in the flow direction. In such cases $dy/dx \neq 0$, $dV/dx \neq 0$ and the right-hand side of Eq. 10.8 is not zero. Physically, the difference between the component of weight and the shear forces in the direction of flow produces a change in the fluid momentum that requires a change in velocity and, from continuity considerations, a change in depth. Whether the depth increases or decreases depends on various parameters of the flow, with a variety of surface profile configurations [flow depth as a function of distance, $y = y(x)$] possible (Refs. 4, 7).

10.6   Rapidly Varied Flow

In many open channels, flow depth changes occur over a relatively short distance so that $dy/dx \sim 1$. Such rapidly varied flow conditions are often quite complex and difficult to analyze in a precise fashion. Fortunately, many useful approximate results can be obtained by using a simple one-dimensional model along with appropriate experimentally determined coefficients when necessary. In this section we discuss several of these flows.

The hydraulic jump is one such case. As indicated in Fig. 10.9, the flow may change from a relatively shallow, high-speed condition into a relatively deep, low-speed condition within a horizontal distance of just a few channel depths. Also, many open-channel flow-measuring devices are based on principles associated with rapidly varied flows. Among these devices are broad-crested weirs, sharp-crested weirs, critical flow flumes, and sluice gates. The operation of such devices is discussed in the following sections.

10.6.1   The Hydraulic Jump

Observations of flows in open channels show that under certain conditions it is possible that the fluid depth will change very rapidly over a short length of the channel without any change in the channel configuration. Such changes in depth can be approximated as a discontinuity in the free-surface elevation ($dy/dx = \infty$). Physically, this near discontinuity, called a *hydraulic jump,* may result when there is a conflict between the upstream and downstream influences that control a particular section (or reach) of a channel.

The simplest type of hydraulic jump occurs in a horizontal, rectangular channel as indicated in Fig. 10.10. Although the flow within the jump itself is extremely complex and agitated, it is reasonable to assume that the flow at sections (1) and (2) is nearly uniform, steady, and one-dimensional. In addition, we neglect any wall shear stresses, τ_w, within the relatively short segment between these two sections. Under these conditions the x component of the momentum equation (Eq. 5.17) for the control volume indicated can be written as

$$F_1 - F_2 = \rho Q(V_2 - V_1) = \rho V_1 y_1 b(V_2 - V_1)$$

where the pressure force at either section is hydrostatic. That is, $F_1 = p_{c1}A_1 = \gamma y_1^2 b/2$ and $F_2 = p_{c2}A_2 = \gamma y_2^2 b/2$, where $p_{c1} = \gamma y_1/2$ and $p_{c2} = \gamma y_2/2$ are the pressures at the centroids

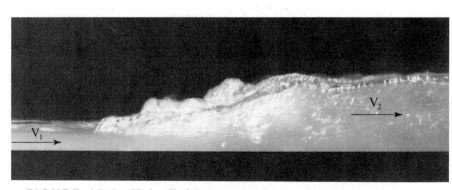

■ **FIGURE 10.9   Hydraulic jump.**

■ FIGURE 10.10 Hydraulic jump geometry.

of the channel cross sections and b is the channel width. Thus, the momentum equation becomes

$$\frac{y_1^2}{2} - \frac{y_2^2}{2} = \frac{V_1 y_1}{g}(V_2 - V_1) \tag{10.16}$$

In addition to the momentum equation, we have the conservation of mass equation (Eq. 5.11)

$$y_1 b V_1 = y_2 b V_2 = Q \tag{10.17}$$

and the energy equation (Eq. 5.57)

$$y_1 + \frac{V_1^2}{2g} = y_2 + \frac{V_2^2}{2g} + h_L \tag{10.18}$$

The head loss, h_L, in Eq. 10.18 is due to the violent turbulent mixing and dissipation that occur within the jump itself. We have neglected any head loss due to wall shear stresses.

Clearly Eqs. 10.16, 10.17, and 10.18 have a solution $y_1 = y_2$, $V_1 = V_2$, and $h_L = 0$. This represents the trivial case of no jump. Since these are nonlinear equations, it may be possible that more than one solution exists. The other solutions can be obtained as follows. By combining Eqs. 10.16 and 10.17 to eliminate V_2 we obtain

$$\frac{y_1^2}{2} - \frac{y_2^2}{2} = \frac{V_1 y_1}{g}\left(\frac{V_1 y_1}{y_2} - V_1\right) = \frac{V_1^2 y_1}{g y_2}(y_1 - y_2)$$

which can be simplified by factoring out a common nonzero factor $y_1 - y_2$ from each side to give

$$\left(\frac{y_2}{y_1}\right)^2 + \left(\frac{y_2}{y_1}\right) - 2\,\mathrm{Fr}_1^2 = 0$$

where $\mathrm{Fr}_1 = V_1/\sqrt{gy_1}$ is the upstream Froude number. By using the quadratic formula we obtain

$$\frac{y_2}{y_1} = \frac{1}{2}\left(-1 \pm \sqrt{1 + 8\mathrm{Fr}_1^2}\right)$$

Clearly the solution with the minus sign is not possible (it would give a negative y_2/y_1). Thus,

$$\frac{y_2}{y_1} = \frac{1}{2}\left(-1 + \sqrt{1 + 8\mathrm{Fr}_1^2}\right) \tag{10.19}$$

V10.6 Hydraulic jump in a sink

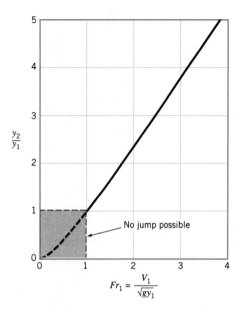

■ FIGURE 10.11 **Depth ratio across a hydraulic jump as a function of upstream Froude number.**

This depth ratio, y_2/y_1, across the hydraulic jump is shown as a function of the upstream Froude number in Fig. 10.11. The portion of the curve for $Fr_1 < 1$ is dashed in recognition of the fact that to have a hydraulic jump the flow must be supercritical. That is, the solution as given in Eq. 10.19 must be restricted to $Fr_1 \geq 1$, for which $y_2/y_1 \geq 1$. This can be shown by consideration of the energy equation, Eq. 10.18, as follows. The dimensionless head loss, h_L/y_1, can be obtained from Eq. 10.18 as

$$\frac{h_L}{y_1} = 1 - \frac{y_2}{y_1} + \frac{Fr_1^2}{2}\left[1 - \left(\frac{y_1}{y_2}\right)^2\right] \tag{10.20}$$

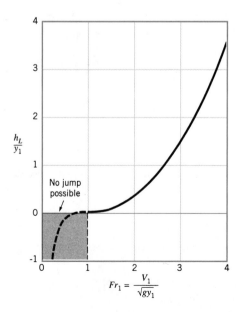

■ FIGURE 10.12 **Dimensionless head loss across a hydraulic jump as a function of upstream Froude number.**

where, for given values of Fr_1, the values of y_2/y_1 are obtained from Eq. 10.19. As indicated in Fig. 10.12, the head loss is negative if $Fr_1 < 1$. Since negative head losses are not possible (viscous effects dissipate energy, they cannot create energy; see Section 5.3), it is not possible to produce a hydraulic jump with $Fr_1 < 1$. The head loss across the jump is indicated by the lowering of the energy line shown in Fig. 10.10.

EXAMPLE 10.6

Water on the horizontal apron of the 100-ft-wide spillway shown in Fig. E10.6a has a depth of 0.60 ft and a velocity of 18 ft/s. Determine the depth, y_2, after the jump, the Froude numbers before and after the jump, Fr_1 and Fr_2, and the power dissipated, $\mathcal{P}_d$, within the jump.

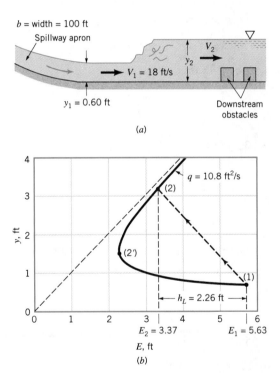

■ FIGURE E10.6

SOLUTION

Conditions across the jump are determined by the upstream Froude number

$$Fr_1 = \frac{V_1}{\sqrt{gy_1}} = \frac{18 \text{ ft/s}}{[(32.2 \text{ ft/s}^2)(0.60 \text{ ft})]^{1/2}} = 4.10 \qquad \text{(Ans)}$$

Thus, the upstream flow is supercritical, and it is possible to generate a hydraulic jump as sketched.

From Eq. 10.19 we obtain the depth ratio across the jump as

$$\frac{y_2}{y_1} = \frac{1}{2}\left(-1 + \sqrt{1 + 8\mathrm{Fr}_1^2}\right) = \frac{1}{2}\left[-1 + \sqrt{1 + 8(4.10)^2}\right] = 5.32$$

or

$$y_2 = 5.32\,(0.60\ \text{ft}) = 3.19\ \text{ft} \tag{Ans}$$

Since $Q_1 = Q_2$, or $V_2 = (y_1V_1)/y_2 = 0.60$ ft $(18$ ft/s$)/3.19$ ft $= 3.39$ ft/s, it follows that

$$\mathrm{Fr}_2 = \frac{V_2}{\sqrt{gy_2}} = \frac{3.39\ \text{ft/s}}{[(32.2\ \text{ft/s}^2)(3.19\ \text{ft})]^{1/2}} = 0.334 \tag{Ans}$$

As is true for any hydraulic jump, the flow changes from supercritical to subcritical flow across the jump.

The power (energy per unit time) dissipated, $\mathcal{P}_d$, by viscous effects within the jump can be determined from the head loss as (see Eq. 5.58)

$$\mathcal{P}_d = \gamma Q h_L = \gamma b y_1 V_1 h_L \tag{1}$$

where h_L is obtained from Eqs. 10.18 or 10.20 as

$$h_L = \left(y_1 + \frac{V_1^2}{2g}\right) - \left(y_2 + \frac{V_2^2}{2g}\right) = \left[0.60\ \text{ft} + \frac{(18.0\ \text{ft/s})^2}{2(32.2\ \text{ft/s}^2)}\right]$$
$$- \left[3.19\ \text{ft} + \frac{(3.39\ \text{ft/s})^2}{2(32.2\ \text{ft/s}^2)}\right]$$

or

$$h_L = 2.26\ \text{ft}$$

Thus, from Eq. 1,

$$\mathcal{P}_d = (62.4\ \text{lb/ft}^3)(100\ \text{ft})(0.60\ \text{ft})(18.0\ \text{ft/s})(2.26\ \text{ft})$$
$$= 1.52 \times 10^5\ \text{ft·lb/s}$$

or

$$\mathcal{P}_d = \frac{1.52 \times 10^5\ \text{ft·lb/s}}{550[(\text{ft·lb/s})/\text{hp}]} = 277\ \text{hp} \tag{Ans}$$

This power, which is dissipated within the highly turbulent motion of the jump, is converted into an increase in water temperature, T. That is, $T_2 > T_1$. Although the power dissipated is considerable, the difference in temperature is not great because the flowrate is quite large.

The hydraulic jump flow process can be illustrated by use of the specific energy concept introduced in Section 10.3 as follows. Equation 10.18 can be written in terms of the specific energy, $E = y + V^2/2g$, as $E_1 = E_2 + h_L$, where $E_1 = y_1 + V_1^2/2g = 5.63$ ft and $E_2 = y_2 + V_2^2/2g = 3.37$ ft. As discussed in Section 10.3, the specific energy diagram for this flow can be obtained by using $V = q/y$, where

$$q = q_1 = q_2 = \frac{Q}{b} = y_1V_1 = 0.60\ \text{ft}\,(18.0\ \text{ft/s}) = 10.8\ \text{ft}^2/\text{s}$$

Thus,

$$E = y + \frac{q^2}{2gy^2} = y + \frac{(10.8 \text{ ft}^2/\text{s})^2}{2(32.2 \text{ ft/s}^2)y^2}$$

or

$$E = y + \frac{1.81}{y^2}$$

where y and E are in feet. The resulting specific energy diagram is shown in Fig. 10.6b. Because of the head loss across the jump, the upstream and downstream values of E are different. In going from state (1) to state (2) the fluid does not proceed along the specific energy curve and pass through the critical condition at state $2'$. Rather, it jumps from (1) to (2) as is represented by the dashed line in the figure. From a one-dimensional consideration, the jump is a discontinuity. In actuality, the jump is a complex three-dimensional flow incapable of being represented on the one-dimensional specific energy diagram.

10.6.2 Sharp-crested Weirs

A weir is an obstruction on a channel bottom over which the fluid must flow. It provides a convenient method of determining the flowrate in an open channel in terms of a single depth measurement. A *sharp-crested weir* is essentially a vertical sharp-edged flat plate placed across the channel in a way such that the fluid must flow across the sharp edge and drop into the pool downstream of the weir plate, as shown in Fig. 10.13. The specific shape of the flow area in the plane of the weir plate is used to designate the type of weir (see Fig. 10.14). The complex nature of the flow over a weir makes it impossible to obtain precise analytical expressions for the flow as a function of other parameters, such as the weir height, P_w, the head of the weir, H, the fluid depth upstream, and the geometry of the weir plate (angle θ for triangular weirs or aspect ratio, b/H, for rectangular weirs).

As a first approximation, we assume that the velocity profile upstream of the weir plate is uniform and that the pressure within the nappe (see Fig. 10.13) is atmospheric. In addition, we assume that the fluid flows horizontally over the weir plate with a nonuniform velocity profile, as indicated in Fig. 10.15. With $p_B = 0$ the Bernoulli equation for flow along the arbitrary streamline A–B indicated can be written as

$$\frac{p_A}{\gamma} + \frac{V_1^2}{2g} + z_A = (H + P_w - h) + \frac{u_2^2}{2g} \tag{10.21}$$

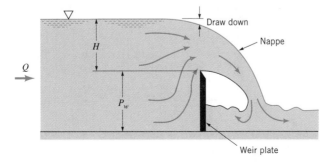

■ **FIGURE 10.13**
Sharp-crested weir geometry.

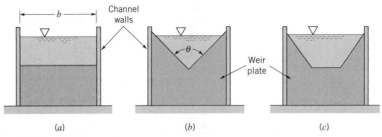

■ **FIGURE 10.14** **Sharp-crested weir plate geometry: (a) rectangular, (b) triangular, (c) trapezoidal.**

where h is the distance that point B is below the free surface. The total head for any particle along the vertical section (1) is the same, $z_A + p_A/\gamma + V_1^2/2g = H + P_w + V_1^2/2g$. Thus, the velocity of the fluid over the weir plate is obtained from Eq. 10.21 as

$$u_2 = \sqrt{2g\left(h + \frac{V_1^2}{2g}\right)}$$

The flowrate can be calculated from

$$Q = \int_{(2)} u_2 \, dA = \int_{h=0}^{h=H} u_2 \ell \, dh \tag{10.22}$$

where $\ell = \ell(h)$ is the cross-channel width of a strip of the weir area, as indicated in Fig. 10.15b. For a rectangular weir ℓ is constant. For other weirs, such as triangular or circular weirs, the value of ℓ is known as a function of h.

For a rectangular weir (see Fig. 10.15a), $\ell = b$, and the flowrate becomes

$$Q = \sqrt{2g}\, b \int_0^H \left(h + \frac{V_1^2}{2g}\right)^{1/2} dh$$

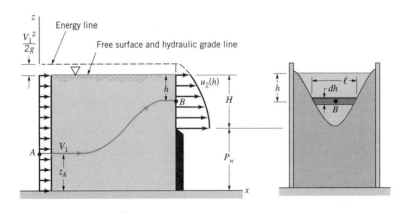

■ **FIGURE 10.15** **Assumed flow structure over a weir.**

or

$$Q = \frac{2}{3}\sqrt{2g}\, b \left[\left(H + \frac{V_1^2}{2g} \right)^{3/2} - \left(\frac{V_1^2}{2g} \right)^{3/2} \right]$$
(10.23)

Equation 10.23 is a rather cumbersome expression that can be simplified by using the fact that with $P_w \gg H$ (as often happens in practical situations) the upstream velocity is negligibly small. That is, $V_1^2/2g \ll H$ and Eq. 10.23 simplifies to the basic rectangular weir equation

$$Q = \tfrac{2}{3}\sqrt{2g}\, b\, H^{3/2}$$
(10.24)

Because of the numerous approximations made to obtain Eq. 10.24, it is not unexpected that an experimentally determined correction factor must be used to obtain the actual flowrate as a function of weir head. Thus, the final form is

$$Q = C_{wr}\tfrac{2}{3}\sqrt{2g}\, b\, H^{3/2}$$
(10.25)

where C_{wr} is the rectangular weir coefficient. In most practical situations the following correlation can be used (Refs. 3 and 6):

$$C_{wr} = 0.611 + 0.075\left(\frac{H}{P_w} \right)$$
(10.26)

More precise values of C_{wr} can be found in the literature, if needed (Refs. 2, 9).

The triangular sharp-crested weir (see Fig. 10.14b) is often used for flow measurements, particularly for measuring flowrates over a wide range of values. For small flowrates, the head, $H,$ for a rectangular weir would be very small and the flowrate could not be measured accurately. However, with the triangular weir, the flow area decreases as H decreases so that even for small flowrates, reasonable heads are developed. Accurate results can be obtained over a wide range of $Q.$

The triangular weir equation can be obtained from Eq. 10.22 by using

$$\ell = 2(H - h)\tan\left(\frac{\theta}{2} \right)$$

where θ is the angle of the vee-notch (see Figs. 10.14 and 10.15). After carrying out the integration and again neglecting the upstream velocity ($V_1^2/2g \ll H$), we obtain

V10.7 Triangular weir

$$Q = C_{wt}\frac{8}{15}\tan\left(\frac{\theta}{2} \right)\sqrt{2g}\, H^{5/2}$$
(10.27)

where the experimentally determined triangular weir coefficient, C_{wt}, is used to account for the real-world effects neglected in the analysis. Typical values of C_{wt} for triangular weirs are in the range of 0.58 to 0.62, as shown in Fig. 10.16.

10.6.3　Broad-crested Weirs

A *broad-crested weir* is a structure in an open channel that has a horizontal crest above which the fluid pressure may be considered hydrostatic. A typical configuration is shown in Fig. 10.17.

The operation of a broad-crested weir is based on the fact that nearly uniform critical flow is achieved in the short reach above the weir block. (If $H/L_w < 0.08$, viscous effects are important, and the flow is subcritical over the weir. On the other hand, if $H/L_w > 0.5$ the streamlines are not horizontal.) If the kinetic energy of the upstream flow is negligible,

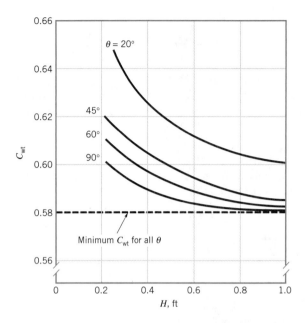

■ **FIGURE 10.16** Weir coefficient for triangular sharp-crested weirs (Ref. 8).

then $V_1^2/2g \ll y_1$ and the upstream specific energy is $E_1 = V_1^2/2g + y_1 \approx y_1$. Observations show that as the flow passes over the weir block, it accelerates and reaches critical conditions, $y_2 = y_c$ and $\mathrm{Fr}_2 = 1$ (i.e., $V_2 = c_2$), corresponding to the nose of the specific energy curve (see Fig. 10.6). The flow does not accelerate to supercritical conditions ($\mathrm{Fr}_2 > 1$).

The Bernoulli equation can be applied between point (1) upstream of the weir and point (2) over the weir where the flow is critical to obtain

$$H + P_w + \frac{V_1^2}{2g} = y_c + P_w + \frac{V_c^2}{2g}$$

or, if the upstream velocity head is negligible

$$H - y_c = \frac{(V_c^2 - V_1^2)}{2g} = \frac{V_c^2}{2g}$$

However, since $V_2 = V_c = (gy_c)^{1/2}$, we find that $V_c^2 = gy_c$ so that we obtain

$$H - y_c = \frac{y_c}{2}$$

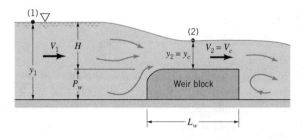

■ **FIGURE 10.17** Broad-crested weir geometry.

or

$$y_c = \frac{2H}{3}$$

V10.8 Low-head dam

Thus, the flowrate is

$$Q = by_2 V_2 = by_c V_c = by_c(gy_c)^{1/2} = b\sqrt{g}\, y_c^{3/2}$$

or

$$Q = b\sqrt{g}\left(\frac{2}{3}\right)^{3/2} H^{3/2}$$

Again an empirical weir coefficient is used to account for the various real-world effects not included in the above simplified analysis. That is

$$Q = C_{wb}\, b\sqrt{g}\left(\frac{2}{3}\right)^{3/2} H^{3/2} \tag{10.28}$$

where typical values of C_{wb}, the broad-crested weir coefficient, can be obtained from the equation (Ref. 5)

$$C_{wb} = \frac{0.65}{(1 + H/P_w)^{1/2}} \tag{10.29}$$

EXAMPLE 10.7

Water flows in a rectangular channel of width $b = 2$ m with flowrates between $Q_{min} = 0.02$ m³/s and $Q_{max} = 0.60$ m³/s. This flowrate is to be measured by using either **(a)** a rectangular sharp-crested weir, **(b)** a triangular sharp-crested weir with $\theta = 90°$, or **(c)** a broad-crested weir. In all cases the bottom of the flow area over the weir is a distance $P_w = 1$ m above the channel bottom. Plot a graph of $Q = Q(H)$ for each weir and comment on which weir would be best for this application.

SOLUTION

For the rectangular weir with $P_w = 1$ m, Eqs. 10.25 and 10.26 give

$$Q = C_{wr}\frac{2}{3}\sqrt{2g}\, bH^{3/2} = \left(0.611 + 0.075\frac{H}{P_w}\right)\frac{2}{3}\sqrt{2g}\, bH^{3/2}$$

Thus,

$$Q = (0.611 + 0.075H)\frac{2}{3}\sqrt{2(9.81\ \text{m/s}^2)}\,(2\ \text{m})\, H^{3/2}$$

or

$$Q = 5.91(0.611 + 0.075H)H^{3/2} \tag{1}$$

where H and Q are in meters and m³/s, respectively. The results from Eq. 1 are plotted in Fig. E10.7.

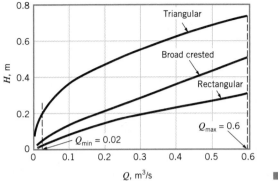

■ **FIGURE E10.7**

Similarly, for the triangular weir, Eq. 10.27 gives

$$Q = C_{wt} \frac{8}{15} \tan\left(\frac{\theta}{2}\right) \sqrt{2g} \, H^{5/2}$$

$$= C_{wt} \frac{8}{15} \tan(45°) \sqrt{2(9.81 \text{ m/s}^2)} \, H^{5/2}$$

or

$$Q = 2.36 C_{wt} H^{5/2} \tag{2}$$

where H and Q are in meters and m³/s and C_{wt} is obtained from Fig. 10.16. For example, with $H = 0.20$ m, we find $C_{wt} = 0.60$, or $Q = 2.36 \,(0.60)(0.20)^{5/2} = 0.0253$ m³/s. The triangular weir results are also plotted in Fig. E10.7.

For the broad-crested weir, Eqs. 10.28 and 10.29 give

$$Q = C_{wb} b \sqrt{g} \left(\frac{2}{3}\right)^{3/2} H^{3/2} = \frac{0.65}{(1 + H/P_w)^{1/2}} \, b \sqrt{g} \left(\frac{2}{3}\right)^{3/2} H^{3/2}$$

Thus, with $P_w = 1$ m

$$Q = \frac{0.65}{(1 + H)^{1/2}} \, (2 \text{ m}) \sqrt{9.81 \text{ m/s}^2} \left(\frac{2}{3}\right)^{3/2} H^{3/2}$$

or

$$Q = \frac{2.22}{(1 + H)^{1/2}} H^{3/2} \tag{3}$$

where, again, H and Q are in meters and m³/s. This result is also plotted in Fig. E10.7.

Although it appears as though any of the three weirs would work well for the upper portion of the flowrate range, neither the rectangular nor the broad-crested weir would be very accurate for small flowrates near $Q = Q_{min}$ because of the small head, H, at these conditions. The triangular weir, however, would allow reasonably large values of H at the lowest flowrates. The corresponding heads with $Q = Q_{min} = 0.02$ m³/s for rectangular, triangular, and broad-crested weirs are 0.0312 m, 0.182 m, and 0.0440 m, respectively.

In addition, as discussed in this section, for proper operation the broad-crested weir geometry is restricted to $0.08 < H/L_w < 0.50$, where L_w is the weir block length. From Eq. 3 with $Q_{max} = 0.60$ m³/s, we obtain $H_{max} = 0.476$. Thus, we must have $L_w > H_{max}/0.5 =$

0.952 m to maintain proper critical flow conditions at the largest flowrate in the channel. On the other hand, with $Q = Q_{min} = 0.02$ m³/s, we obtain $H_{min} = 0.0440$ m. Thus, we must have $L_w < H_{min}/0.08 = 0.549$ m to ensure that frictional effects are not important. Clearly, these two constraints on the geometry of the weir block, L_w, are incompatible.

A broad-crested weir will not function properly under the wide range of flowrates considered in this example. The sharp-crested triangular weir would be the best of the three types considered, provided the channel can handle the $H_{max} = 0.719$-m head.

10.6.4   Underflow Gates

A variety of gate-type structures is available for flowrate control. Three typical types are illustrated in Fig. 10.18.

The flow under a gate is said to be free outflow when the fluid issues as a jet of supercritical flow with a free surface open to the atmosphere as shown in Fig. 10.18. In such

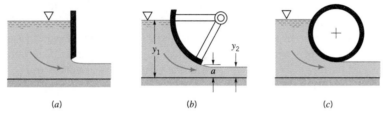

(a)   (b)   (c)

■ **FIGURE 10.18   Three variations of underflow gates:** (*a*) **vertical gate,** (*b*) **radial gate,** (*c*) **drum gate.**

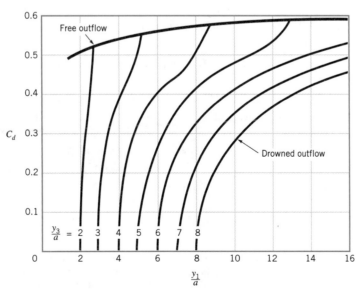

■ **FIGURE 10.19   Typical discharge coefficients for under-flow gates (Ref. 3).**

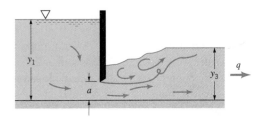

■ **FIGURE 10.20** **Drowned outflow from a sluice gate.**

cases it is customary to write this flowrate as the product of the distance, a, between the channel bottom and the bottom of the gate times the convenient reference velocity $(2gy_1)^{1/2}$. That is

$$q = C_d a \sqrt{2gy_1} \qquad (10.30)$$

where q is the flowrate per unit width. The discharge coefficient, C_d, is a function of the contraction coefficient, $C_c = y_2/a$, and the depth ratio y_1/a. Typical values of the discharge coefficient for free outflow (or free discharge) from a vertical sluice gate are on the order of 0.55 to 0.60 as indicated by the top line in Fig. 10.19 (Ref. 2).

As indicated in Fig. 10.20, in certain situations the jet of water issuing from under the gate is overlaid by a mass of water that is quite turbulent. Typical values of C_d for these drowned outflow cases are indicated as the series of lower curves in Fig. 10.19.

References

1. Currie, I. G., *Fundamental Mechanics of Fluids,* McGraw-Hill, New York, 1974.
2. Henderson, F. M., *Open Channel Flow,* Macmillan, New York, 1966.
3. Rouse, H., *Elementary Fluid Mechanics,* Wiley, New York, 1946.
4. French, R. H., *Open Channel Hydraulics,* McGraw-Hill, New York, 1985.
5. Chow, V. T., *Open Channel Hydraulics,* McGraw-Hill, New York, 1959.
6. Blevins, R. D., *Applied Fluid Dynamics Handbook,* Van Nostrand Reinhold, New York, 1984.
7. Vennard, J. K., and Street, R. L., *Elementary Fluid Mechanics,* Wiley, New York, 1976.
8. Lenz, A. T., "Viscosity and Surface Tension Effects on V-Notch Weir Coefficients," *Transactions of the American Society of Chemical Engineers,* Vol. 108, 759–820, 1943.
9. Spitzer, D. W., editor, *Flow Measurement: Practical Guides for Measurement and Control,* Instrument Society of America, Research Triangle Park, 1991.
10. Wallet, A., and Ruellan, F., *Houille Blanche,* Vol. 5, 1950.

Problems

Note: Unless otherwise indicated, use the values of fluid properties found in the tables on the inside of the front cover. Problems designated with an (*) are intended to be solved with the aid of a programmable calculator or a computer.

10.1 The flowrate per unit width in a wide channel is $q = 2.3$ m²/s. Is the flow subcritical or supercritical if the depth is **(a)** 0.2 m, **(b)** 0.8 m, or **(c)** 2.5 m?

10.2 A bicyclist rides through a 3-in. deep puddle of water as shown in **Video V10.1** and Fig. P10.2. If the angle

■ FIGURE P10.2

made by the V-shaped wave pattern produced by the front wheel is observed to be 40 deg, estimate the speed of the bike through the puddle. *Hint:* Make a sketch of the current location of the bike wheel relative to where it was Δt seconds ago. Also indicate on this sketch the current location of the wave that the wheel made Δt seconds ago. Recall that the wave moves radially outward in all directions with speed c relative to the stationary water.

10.3   Waves on the surface of a tank are observed to travel at a speed of 2 m/s. How fast would these waves travel if **(a)** the tank were in an elevator accelerating upward at a rate of 4 m/s², **(b)** the tank accelerates horizontally at a rate of 9.81 m/s², **(c)** the tank were aboard the orbiting Space Shuttle. Explain.

10.4   Observations at a shallow sandy beach show that even though the waves several hundred yards out from the shore are not parallel to the beach, the waves often "break" on the beach nearly parallel to the shore as is indicated in Fig. P10.4. Explain this behavior based on the wave speed $c = (gy)^{1/2}$.

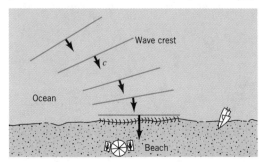

■ FIGURE P10.4

10.5   Often when an earthquake shifts a segment of the ocean floor, a relatively small amplitude wave of very long wavelength is produced. Such waves go unnoticed as they move across the open ocean; only when they approach the shore do they become dangerous (a tsunami or "tidal wave"). Determine the wave speed if the wavelength, λ, is 6000 ft and the ocean depth is 15,000 ft.

10.6   Plot the specific energy diagram for a wide channel carrying $q = 50$ ft²/s. Determine **(a)** the critical depth, **(b)** the minimum specific energy, **(c)** the alternate depth corresponding to a depth of 2.5 ft, and **(d)** the possible flow velocities if $E = 10$ ft.

10.7   Water flows radially outward on a horizontal round disk as shown in **Video V10.6** and Fig. P10.7. **(a)** Show that the specific energy can be written in terms of the flowrate, Q, the radial distance from the axis of symmetry, r, and the fluid depth, y, as

$$E = y + \left(\frac{Q}{2\pi r}\right)^2 \frac{1}{2gy^2}$$

(b) For a constant flowrate, sketch the specific energy diagram. Recall Fig. 10.6, but note that for the present case r is a variable. Explain the important characteristics of your sketch. **(c)** Based on the results of part **(b)**, show that the water depth increases in the flow direction if the flow is subcritical, but that it decreases in the flow direction if the flow is supercritical.

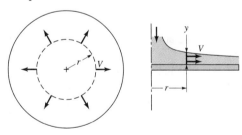

■ FIGURE P10.7

10.8   Water flows in a rectangular channel at a rate of $q = 20$ cfs/ft. When a Pitot tube is placed in the stream, water in the tube rises to a level of 4.5 ft above the channel bottom. Determine the two possible flow depths in the channel. Illustrate this flow on a specific energy diagram.

10.9   Water flows in a 10-ft-wide rectangular channel with a flowrate of $Q = 60$ ft³/s and an upstream depth of $y_1 = 2$ ft as shown in Fig. P10.9. Determine the flow depth and the surface elevation at section (2).

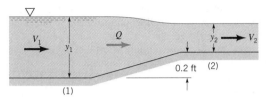

■ **FIGURE P10.9**

10.10 Repeat Problem 10.9 if the upstream depth is $y_1 = 0.5$ ft.

10.11 Water in a rectangular channel flows into a gradual contraction section as indicated in Fig. P10.11. If the flowrate is $Q = 25$ ft³/s and the upstream depth is $y_1 = 2$ ft, determine the downstream depth, y_2.

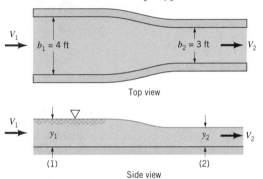

■ **FIGURE P10.11**

10.12 Repeat Problem 10.11 if the upstream depth is $y_1 = 0.5$ ft. Assume that there are no losses between sections (1) and (2).

10.13 Water flows in a horizontal, rectangular channel with an initial depth of 2 ft and initial velocity of 12 ft/s. Determine the depth downstream if losses are negligible. Note that there may be more than one solution. Repeat the problem if the initial depth remains the same, but the initial velocity is 6 ft/s.

*10.14 Water flows over the bump in the bottom of the rectangular channel shown in Fig. P10.14 with a flowrate per unit width of $q = 4$ m²/s. The channel bottom contour is given by $z_B = 0.2e^{-x^2}$, where z_B and x are in meters. The water depth far upstream of the bump is $y_1 = 2$ m. Plot a graph of the wa-

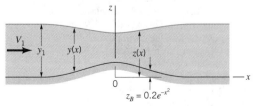

■ **FIGURE P10.14**

ter depth, $y = y(x)$, and the surface elevation, $z = z(x)$, for $-4 \text{ m} \le x \le 4 \text{ m}$. Assume one-dimensional flow.

10.15 Determine the maximum depth in a 3-m-wide rectangular channel if the flow is to be supercritical with a flowrate of $Q = 60$ m³/s.

10.16 The following data are taken from measurements on Indian Fork Creek: $A = 26$ m², $P = 16$ m, and $S_0 = 0.02$ m/62 m. Determine the average shear stress on the wetted perimeter of this channel.

10.17 The following data are obtained for a particular reach of the Provo River in Utah: $A = 183$ ft², free-surface width = 55 ft, average depth = 3.3 ft, $R_h = 3.22$ ft, $V = 6.56$ ft/s, length of reach = 116 ft, and elevation drop of reach = 1.04 ft. Determine **(a)** the average shear stress on the wetted perimeter, **(b)** the Manning coefficient, n, and **(c)** the Froude number of the flow.

10.18 Water flows in an unfinished concrete channel at a rate of 30 m³/s. What flowrate can be expected if the concrete were finished and the depth remains constant?

10.19 By what percent is the flowrate reduced in the rectangular channel shown in Fig. P10.19 because of the addition of the thin center board? All surfaces are of the same material.

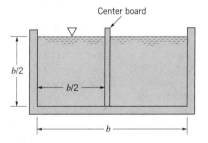

■ **FIGURE P10.19**

10.20 The Blue Ridge Flume, constructed in Shasta County, California, in 1872 to supply water for gold-mining operations, was built of planed wood and had a cross section as shown in Fig. P10.20. Determine the water velocity in a section of this flume if it was full and the elevation change was 27 ft per mile.

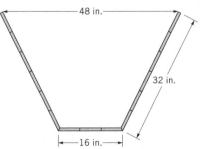

■ **FIGURE P10.20**

10.21   At a particular location the cross section of the Columbia River is as indicated in Fig. P10.21. If on a day without wind it takes 5 min to float 0.5 mi along the river, which drops 0.46 ft in that distance, determine the value of the Manning coefficient, n.

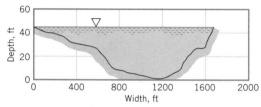

■ **FIGURE P10.21**

10.22   Rainwater runoff from a 200-ft by 500-ft parking lot is to drain through a circular concrete pipe that is laid on a slope of 5 ft/mi. Determine the pipe diameter if it is to be full with a steady rainfall of 1.5 in./hr.

10.23   To prevent weeds from growing in a clean earthen-lined canal, it is recommended that the velocity be no less than 2.5 ft/s. For the symmetrical canal shown in Fig. P10.23, determine the minimum slope needed.

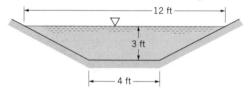

■ **FIGURE P10.23**

10.24   The smooth concrete-lined symmetrical channel shown in **Video V10.3** and Fig. P10.23 carries silt-laden water. If the velocity must be 4.0 ft/s to prevent the silt from settling out (and eventually clogging the channel), determine the minimum slope needed.

10.25   The symmetrical channel shown in Fig. P10.23 is dug in sandy loam soil with $n = 0.020$. For such surface material it is recommended that to prevent scouring of the surface the average velocity be no more than 1.75 ft/s. Determine the maximum slope allowed.

10.26   Water flows in a 2-m-diameter finished concrete pipe so that it is completely full and the pressure is constant all along the pipe. If the slope is $S_0 = 0.005$, determine the flowrate by using open-channel flow methods. Compare this result with that obtained by using pipe flow methods of Chapter 8.

10.27   The flowrate in the clay-lined channel ($n = 0.025$) shown in Fig. P10.27 is to be 300 ft³/s. To prevent erosion of the sides, the velocity must not exceed 5 ft/s. For this maximum velocity, determine the width of the bottom, b, and the slope, S_0.

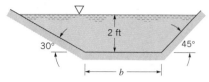

■ **FIGURE P10.27**

10.28   The flowrate through the trapezoidal canal shown in Fig. P10.28 is Q. If it is desired to double the flowrate to $2Q$ without changing the depth, determine the additional width, L, needed. The bottom slope, surface material, and the slope of the walls are to remain the same.

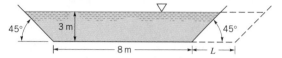

■ **FIGURE P10.28**

10.29   A rectangular, unfinished concrete channel of 28-ft-width is laid on a slope of 8 ft/mi. Determine the flow depth and Froude number of the flow if the flowrate is 400 ft³/s.

10.30   An engineer is to design a channel lined with planed wood to carry water at a flowrate of 2 m³/s on a slope of 10 m/800 m. The channel cross section can be either a 90° triangle or a rectangle with a cross section twice as wide as its depth. Which would require less wood and by what percent?

10.31   Water flows in a channel with an equilateral triangle cross section as shown in Fig. P10.31. For a given Manning coefficient, n, and channel slope, determine the depth that gives the maximum flowrate.

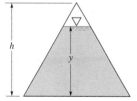

■ **FIGURE P10.31**

10.32   Two canals join to form a larger canal as shown in **Video V10.2** and Fig. P10.32. Each of the three rectangular canals is lined with the same material and has the same bottom slope. The water depth in each is to be 2 m. Determine the width of the merged canal, b. Explain physically (i.e., without using any equations) why it is expected that the width of the merged canal is less than the combined widths of the two original canals (i.e., $b < 4$ m $+ 8$ m $= 12$ m).

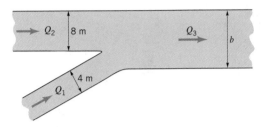

■ **FIGURE P10.32**

10.33 An 8-ft-diameter concrete drainage pipe that flows half-full is to be replaced by a concrete-lined V-shaped open channel having an interior angle of 90°. Determine the depth of fluid that will exist in the V-shaped channel if it is laid on the same slope and carries the same discharge as the drainage pipe.

*10.34 The cross section of a long tunnel carrying water through a mountain is as indicated in Fig. P10.34. Plot a graph of flowrate as a function of water depth, y, for $0 \leq y \leq 18$ ft. The slope is 2 ft/mi and the surface of the tunnel is rough rock (equivalent to rubble masonry). At what depth is the flowrate maximum? Explain.

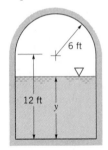

■ **FIGURE P10.34**

10.35 The smooth concrete-lined channel shown in Fig. P10.35 is built on a slope of 2 m/km. Determine the flowrate if the depth is $y = 1.5$ m.

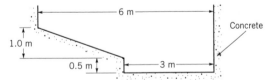

■ **FIGURE P10.35**

10.36 Determine the flow depth for the channel shown in Fig. P10.35 if the flowrate is 15 m³/s.

10.37 The cross section of an ancient Roman aqueduct is drawn to scale in Fig. P10.37. When it was new the channel was essentially rectangular and for a flowrate of 100,000 m³/day, the water depth was as indicated. Archeological evidence indicates that after many years of use, calcium carbonate deposits on the sides and bottom modified the shape

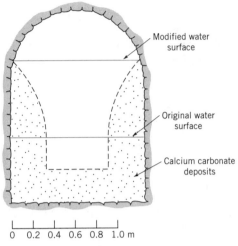

Modified water surface

Original water surface

Calcium carbonate deposits

0 0.2 0.4 0.6 0.8 1.0 m

■ **FIGURE P10.37**

to that shown in the figure. Estimate the flowrate for the modified shape if the slope and surface roughness did not change.

10.38 Determine the maximum flowrate possible for the creek shown in Fig. P10.38 if it is not to overflow onto the flood plain. The creek bed drops an average of 3 ft/half mile of length. Determine the flowrate during a flood if the depth is 8 ft.

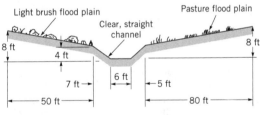

Light brush flood plain

Clear, straight channel

Pasture flood plain

■ **FIGURE P10.38**

10.39 Determine the flowrate for the symmetrical channel shown in Fig. P10.23 if the bottom is smooth concrete and the sides are weedy. The bottom slope is $S_0 = 0.001$.

10.40 A 2.0-ft standing wave is produced at the bottom of the rectangular channel in an amusement park water ride. If the water depth upstream of the wave is estimated to be 1.5 ft, determine how fast the boat is traveling when it passes through this standing wave (hydraulic jump) for its final "splash."

10.41 The water depths upstream and downstream of a hydraulic jump are 0.3 and 1.2 m, respectively. Determine the upstream velocity and the power dissipated if the channel is 50 m wide.

10.42 Water flowing radially outward along a circular plate forms a circular hydraulic jump as shown in **Video**

V10.6 and Fig. P10.42a. **(a)** Sketch a typical specific energy diagram for this flow (see Problem 10.7) and locate points 1, 2, 3, and 4 on the diagram. **(b)** Which of the water depth profiles shown in Fig. P10.42b represents the actual situation? Explain.

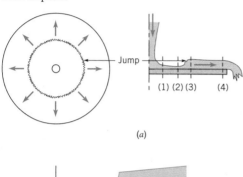

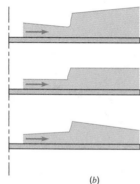

(a)

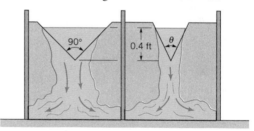

Note: the figure (b) caption below

(b)

■ **FIGURE P10.42**

10.43 Water flows in a 2-ft-wide rectangular channel at a rate of 10 ft^3/s. If the water depth downstream of a hydraulic jump is 2.5 ft, determine **(a)** the water depth upstream of the jump, **(b)** the upstream and downstream Froude numbers, and **(c)** the head loss across the jump.

10.44 A hydraulic jump at the base of a spillway of a dam is such that the depths upstream and downstream of the jump are 0.90 and 3.6 m, respectively (see **Video V10.5.**) If the spillway is 10 m wide, what is the flowrate over the spillway?

10.45 Show that for a hydraulic jump in a rectangular channel, the Froude number upstream, Fr$_1$, and the Froude number downstream, Fr$_2$, are related by

$$\text{Fr}_2^2 = \frac{8\text{Fr}_1^2}{[(1 + 8\text{Fr}_1^2)^{1/2} - 1]^3}$$

Plot Fr$_2$ as a function of Fr$_1$ and show that the flow downstream of a jump is subcritical.

10.46 Water flows in a rectangular channel at a depth of $y = 1$ ft and a velocity of $V = 20$ ft/s. When a gate is suddenly placed across the end of the channel, a wave (a

moving hydraulic jump) travels upstream with velocity V_w as is indicated in Fig. P10.46. Determine V_w. Note that this is an unsteady problem for a stationary observer. However, for an observer moving to the left with velocity V_w, the flow appears as a steady hydraulic jump.

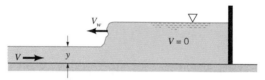

■ **FIGURE P10.46**

10.47 Water flows over a 5-ft-wide, rectangular sharp-crested weir that is $P_w = 4.5$-ft tall. If the depth upstream is 5 ft, determine the flowrate.

10.48 A rectangular sharp-crested weir is used to measure the flowrate in a channel of width 10 ft. It is desired to have the channel flow depth be 6 ft when the flowrate is 50 cfs. Determine the height, P_w, of the weir plate.

10.49 Water flows from a storage tank, over two triangular weirs, and into two irrigation channels as shown in **Video V10.7** and Fig. P10.49. The head for each weir is 0.4 ft and the flowrate in the channel fed by the 90-degree V-notch weir is to be twice the flowrate in the other channel. Determine the angle θ for the second weir.

■ **FIGURE P10.49**

10.50 Water flows over a broad-crested weir that has a width of 4 m and a height of $P_w = 1.5$ m. The free-surface well upstream of the weir is at a height of 0.5 m above the surface of the weir. Determine the flowrate in the channel and the minimum depth of the water above the weir block.

10.51 Determine the flowrate per unit width, q, over a broad-crested weir that is 2.0 m tall if the head, H, is 0.50 m.

10.52 Water flows over the rectangular sharp-crested weir in a wide channel as shown in Fig. P10.52. If the channel is lined with unfinished concrete with a bottom slope of 2 m/300 m, will it be possible to produce a hydraulic jump in the channel downstream of the weir? Explain.

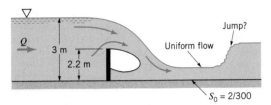

■ FIGURE P10.52

10.53 Water flows in a rectangular channel of width $b = 20$ ft at a rate of 100 ft³/s. The flowrate is to be measured by using either a rectangular weir of height $P_w = 4$ ft or a triangular ($\theta = 90°$) sharp-crested weir. Determine the head, H, necessary. If measurement of the head is accurate to only ± 0.04 ft, determine the accuracy of the measured flowrate expected for each of the weirs. Which weir would be the most accurate? Explain.

10.54 A water-level regulator (not shown) maintains a depth of 2.0 m downstream from a 50-ft-wide drum gate as shown in Fig. P10.54. Plot a graph of flowrate, Q, as a function of water depth upstream of the gate, y_1, for $2.0 \leq y_1 \leq 5.0$ m.

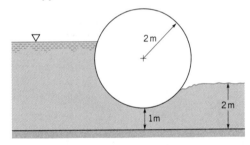

■ FIGURE P10.54

10.55 The device shown in Fig. P10.55 is used to investigate the flowrate of water under a sluice gate. For a given flowrate, the water upstream of the sluice gate is at a

uniform depth of y_1, while that downstream of the gate is y_2. The bottom of the gate is distance $a = 1.0$ in. from the channel bottom. The average velocity in the channel, V_1, is determined by measuring the time, t, it takes a float to travel a known distance, $\ell = 2$ ft. That is, $V_1 = \ell/t$. The flowrate is $Q = V_1A_1$, where A_1 is the cross-sectional area of the channel.

Experimentally determined values of y_1, y_2, and t for various flowrates are shown in the table below. Use these results to plot a graph on log–log graph paper of the flowrate as a function of the upstream depth. On the same graph, plot the theoretical curve assuming that the discharge coefficient, C_d, is equal to one. From the experimental results, determine the value of the discharge coefficient and the contraction coefficient, $C_c = y_2/a$, for this sluice gate.

Discuss some possible sources of error in the results.

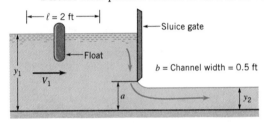

■ FIGURE P10.55

y_1 (ft)	y_2 (ft)	t (s)
0.877	0.057	5.1
0.725	0.057	4.5
0.569	0.059	4.3
0.453	0.059	3.5
0.343	0.060	3.3
0.267	0.060	3.0
0.183	0.060	2.9

*T*urbomachines

*P*umps and turbines (sometimes called *fluid machines*) occur in a wide variety of configurations. In general, pumps add energy to the fluid—they do work on the fluid; turbines extract energy from the fluid—the fluid does work on them. The term "pump" will be used to generically refer to all pumping machines, including *pumps, fans, blowers,* and *compressors.* Fluid machines can be divided into two main categories: *positive displacement machines* (denoted as the static type) and *turbomachines* (denoted as the dynamic type). The majority of this chapter deals with turbomachines.

Positive displacement machines force a fluid into or out of a chamber by changing the volume of the chamber. The pressures developed and the work done are a result of essentially static forces rather than dynamic effects. Typical examples include the common tire pump used to fill bicycle tires, the human heart, and the gear pump.

Turbomachines, on the other hand, involve a collection of blades, buckets, flow channels, or passages arranged around an axis of rotation to form a rotor. Rotation of the rotor produces dynamic effects that either add energy to the fluid or remove energy from the fluid. Examples of turbomachine-type pumps include simple window fans, propellers on ships or

Laser velocimeter measurements of the flow field in the rotor row of a low-speed research turbine. (Photograph courtesy of Dr. D. C. Wisler, Director, Aerodynamics Research Laboratory of GE Aircraft Engines.)

airplanes, squirrel-cage fans on home furnaces, and compressors in automobile turbochargers. Examples of turbines include the turbine portion of gas turbine engines on aircraft, steam turbines used to drive generators at electrical generation stations, and the small, high-speed air turbines that power dentist drills.

11.1   Introduction

Turbomachines are mechanical devices that either extract energy from a fluid (turbine) or add energy to a fluid (pump) as a result of dynamic interactions between the device and the fluid.

Turbomachines contain blades, airfoils, "buckets," flow channels, or passages attached to a rotating shaft. Energy is either supplied to the rotating shaft (by a motor, for example) and transferred to the fluid by the blades (a pump), or the energy is transferred from the fluid to the blades and made available at the rotating shaft as shaft power (a turbine). The fluid used can be either a gas (as with a window fan or a gas turbine engine) or a liquid (as with the water pump on a car or a turbine at a hydroelectric power plant).

Many turbomachines contain some type of housing or casing that surrounds the rotating blades or rotor, thus forming an internal flow passageway through which the fluid flows (see Fig. 11.1). Others, such as a windmill or a window fan, are unducted. Some turbomachines include stationary blades or vanes in addition to rotor blades.

Turbomachines are classified as *axial-flow, mixed-flow,* or *radial-flow* machines depending on the predominant direction of the fluid motion relative to the rotor's axis (see Fig.

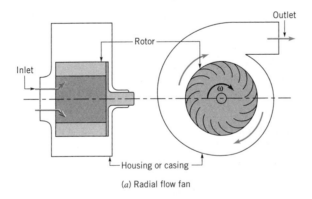

(a) Radial flow fan

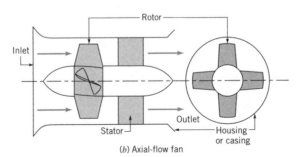

(b) Axial-flow fan

■ **FIGURE 11.1**   (*a*) **A radial-flow turbomachine.** (*b*) **An axial-flow turbomachine.**

11.1). For an axial-flow machine the fluid maintains a significant axial-flow direction component from the inlet to outlet of the rotor. A radial-flow machine involves a substantial radial-flow component at the rotor inlet, exit, or both. In mixed-flow machines there are significant radial- and axial-flow velocity components for the flow through the rotor row.

11.2   Basic Energy Considerations

An understanding of the work transfer in turbomachines can be obtained by considering the basic operation of a household fan (pump) and a windmill (turbine). Although the actual flows in such devices are very complex (i.e., three-dimensional and unsteady), the essential phenomena can be illustrated by use of simplified considerations and velocity triangles.

Consider a fan blade driven at constant angular velocity, ω, by a motor as is shown in Fig. 11.2a. We denote the blade speed as $U = \omega r$, where r is the radial distance from the axis of the fan. The absolute fluid velocity (that seen by a person sitting stationary at the table on which the fan rests) is denoted $\mathbf{V}$, and the relative velocity (that seen by a person riding on the moving fan blade) is denoted $\mathbf{W}$. The actual (absolute) fluid velocity is the vector sum of the relative velocity and the blade velocity

$$\mathbf{V} = \mathbf{W} + \mathbf{U} \qquad\qquad (11.1)$$

A simplified sketch of the fluid velocity as it "enters" and "exits" the fan at radius r is shown in Fig. 11.2b. The shaded surface labeled a-b-c-d is a portion of the cylindrical surface (including a "slice" through the blade) shown in Fig. 11.2a. We assume for simplicity that the flow moves smoothly along the blade so that relative to the moving blade the velocity is parallel to the leading and trailing edges (points 1 and 2) of the blade. For now we assume that the fluid enters and leaves the fan at the same distance from the axis of rotation; thus, $U_1 = U_2 = \omega r$.

With this information we can construct the *velocity triangles* shown in Fig. 11.2b. Note that this view is looking radially toward the axis of rotation. The motion of the blade is down; the motion of the incoming air is assumed to be directed along the axis of rotation. The important concept to grasp from this sketch is that the fan blade (because of its shape and motion) "pushes" the fluid, causing it to change direction. The absolute velocity vector, $\mathbf{V}$, is turned during its flow across the blade from section (1) to section (2). Initially the fluid had no component of absolute velocity in the direction of the motion of the blade, the θ (or tangential) direction. When the fluid leaves the blade, this tangential component of absolute velocity is nonzero. For this to occur, the blade must push on the fluid in the tangential direction. That is, the blade exerts a tangential force component on the fluid in the direction of the motion of the blade. This tangential force component and the blade motion are in the same direction—the blade does work on the fluid. This device is a pump.

On the other hand, consider the windmill shown in Fig. 11.3a. Rather than the rotor being driven by a motor, it is rotated in the opposite direction (compared to the fan in Fig. 11.2) by the wind blowing through the rotor. We again note that because of the blade shape and motion, the absolute velocity vectors at sections (1) and (2), $\mathbf{V}_1$ and $\mathbf{V}_2$, have different directions. For this to happen, the blades must have pushed up on the fluid—opposite to the direction of their motion. Alternatively, because of equal and opposite forces (action/reaction) the fluid must have pushed on the blades in the direction of their motion—the fluid does work on the blades. This extraction of energy from the fluid is the purpose of a turbine.

V11.1 Windmills

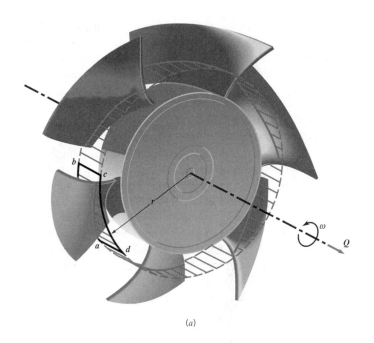

(a)

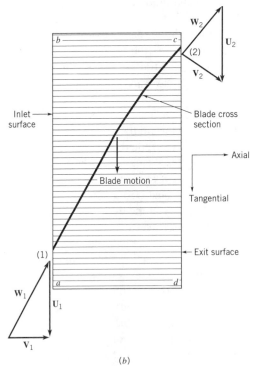

(b)

■ FIGURE 11.2
Idealized flow through a fan:
(a) fan blade geometry; (b)
absolute velocity, V; relative
velocity, W; and blade velocity, U; at the inlet and exit of
the fan blade section.

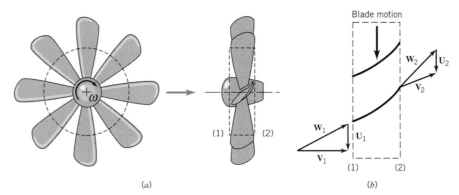

■ **FIGURE 11.3** **Idealized flow through a windmill: (*a*) Windmill blade geometry; (*b*) Absolute velocity, V; relative velocity, W; and blade velocity, U; at the inlet and exit of the windmill blade section.**

*E*XAMPLE 11.1

The rotor shown in Fig. E11.1*a* rotates at a constant angular velocity of $\omega = 100$ rad/s. Although the fluid initially approaches the rotor in an axial direction, the flow across the blades is primarily radial (see Fig. 11.1*a*). Measurements indicate that the absolute velocity at the inlet and outlet are $V_1 = 12$ m/s and $V_2 = 25$ m/s, respectively. Is this device a pump or a turbine?

*S*OLUTION

To answer this question, we need to know if the tangential component of the force of the blade on the fluid is in the direction of the blade motion (a pump) or opposite to it (a turbine). We assume that the blades are tangent to the incoming relative velocity and that the

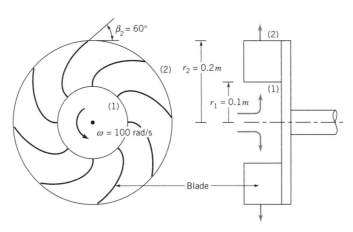

(*a*)

■ FIGURE E11.1

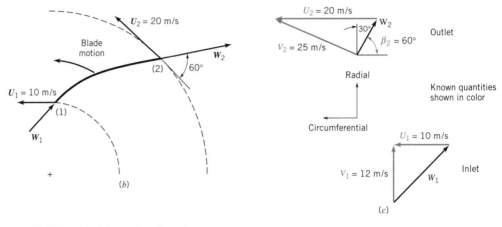

■ **FIGURE E11.1** (*Continued*)

relative flow leaving the rotor is tangent to the blades as shown in Fig. E11.1b. We can also calculate the inlet and outlet blade speeds as

$$U_1 = \omega r_1 = (100 \text{ rad/s})(0.1 \text{ m}) = 10 \text{ m/s}$$

and

$$U_2 = \omega r_2 = (100 \text{ rad/s})(0.2 \text{ m}) = 20 \text{ m/s}$$

With the known absolute fluid velocity and blade velocity at the inlet, we can draw the velocity triangle (the graphical representation of Eq. 11.1) at that location as shown in Fig. E11.1c. Note that we have assumed that the absolute flow at the blade row inlet is radial (i.e., the direction of $\mathbf{V}_1$ is radial). At the outlet we know the blade velocity, $\mathbf{U}_2$, the outlet speed, V_2, and the relative velocity direction, β_2, (because of the blade geometry). Therefore, we can graphically (or trigonometrically) construct the outlet velocity triangle as shown in the figure. By comparing the velocity triangles at the inlet and outlet, it can be seen that as the fluid flows across the blade row, the absolute velocity vector turns in the direction of the blade motion. At the inlet there is no component of absolute velocity in the direction of rotation; at the outlet this component is not zero. That is, the blade pushes the fluid in the direction of the blade motion, thereby doing work on the fluid, adding energy to it.

This device is a pump.   (**Ans**)

11.3   Basic Angular Momentum Considerations

Since turbomachines involve the rotation of an impeller or a rotor about a central axis, it is appropriate to discuss their performance in terms of torque and angular momentum.

Recall that work can be written as force times distance or as torque times angular displacement. Hence, if the shaft torque (the torque that the shaft applies to the rotor) and the rotation of the rotor are in the same direction, energy is transferred from the shaft to the rotor and from the rotor to the fluid—the machine is a pump. Conversely, if the torque exerted by the shaft on the rotor is opposite to the direction of rotation, the energy transfer is from the fluid to the rotor—a turbine. The amount of shaft torque (and hence shaft work) can be obtained from the moment-of-momentum equation derived formally in Section 5.2.3 and discussed as follows.

Consider a fluid particle traveling through the rotor in the radial-flow machine shown in Fig. E11.1a, b, and c. For now, assume that the particle enters the rotor with a radial velocity only (i.e., no "swirl"). After being acted upon by the rotor blades during its passage from the inlet [section (1)] to the outlet [section (2)], the particle exits with radial (r) and circumferential (θ) components of velocity. Thus, the particle enters with no angular momentum about the rotor axis of rotation but leaves with nonzero angular momentum about that axis. (Recall that the axial component of angular momentum for a particle is its mass times the distance from the axis times the θ component of absolute velocity.)

V11.2 Self-propelled lawn sprinkler

In a turbomachine a series of particles (a continuum) passes through the rotor. Thus, the moment-of-momentum equation applied to a control volume as derived in Section 5.2.3 is valid. For steady flow Eq. 5.21 gives

$$\sum (\mathbf{r} \times \mathbf{F}) = \int_{cs} (\mathbf{r} \times \mathbf{V})\rho \mathbf{V} \cdot \hat{\mathbf{n}}\, dA$$

Recall that the left-hand side of this equation represents the sum of the external torques (moments) acting on the contents of the control volume, and the right-hand side is the net rate of flow of moment-of-momentum (angular momentum) through the control surface.

The axial component of this equation applied to the one-dimensional simplification of flow through a turbomachine rotor with section (1) as the inlet and section (2) as the outlet results in

$$T_{shaft} = -\dot{m}_1(r_1 V_{\theta 1}) + \dot{m}_2(r_2 V_{\theta 2}) \tag{11.2}$$

where T_{shaft} is the shaft torque applied to the contents of the control volume. The "−" is associated with mass flowrate into the control volume and the "+" is used with the outflow. The sign of the V_θ component depends on the direction of V_θ and the blade motion, U. If V_θ and U are in the same direction, then V_θ is positive. The sign of the torque exerted by the shaft on the rotor, T_{shaft}, is positive if T_{shaft} is in the same direction as rotation, and negative otherwise.

As seen from Eq. 11.2, the shaft torque is directly proportional to the mass flowrate, $\dot{m} = \rho Q$. (It takes considerably more torque and power to pump water than to pump air with the same volume flowrate.) The torque also depends on the tangential component of the absolute velocity, V_θ. Equation 11.2 is often called the *Euler turbomachine equation*.

Also recall that the shaft power, $\dot{W}_{shaft}$, is related to the shaft torque and angular velocity by

$$\dot{W}_{shaft} = T_{shaft}\, \omega \tag{11.3}$$

By combining Eqs. 11.2 and 11.3 and using the fact that $U = \omega r$, we obtain

$$\dot{W}_{shaft} = -\dot{m}_1(U_1 V_{\theta 1}) + \dot{m}_2(U_2 V_{\theta 2}) \tag{11.4}$$

Again, the value of V_θ is positive when V_θ and U are in the same direction and negative otherwise. Also, $\dot{W}_{shaft}$ is positive when the shaft torque and ω are in the same direction and negative otherwise. Thus, $\dot{W}_{shaft}$ is positive when power is supplied to the contents of the control volume (pumps) and negative otherwise (turbines). This outcome is consistent with the sign convention involving the work term in the energy equation considered in Chapter 5 (see Eq. 5.44).

Finally, in terms of work per unit mass, $w_{shaft} = \dot{W}_{shaft}/\dot{m}$, we obtain

$$w_{shaft} = -U_1 V_{\theta 1} + U_2 V_{\theta 2} \tag{11.5}$$

where we have used the fact that by conservation of mass, $\dot{m}_1 = \dot{m}_2$. Equations 11.3, 11.4, and 11.5 are the basic governing equations for pumps or turbines whether the machines are radial-, mixed-, or axial-flow devices and for compressible and incompressible flows. Note that neither the axial nor the radial component of velocity enter into the specific work (work per unit mass) equation.

11.4   The Centrifugal Pump

V11.3 Wind-shield washer pump

One of the most common radial-flow turbomachines is the *centrifugal pump*. This type of pump has two main components: an *impeller* attached to a rotating shaft, and a stationary *casing, housing,* or *volute* enclosing the impeller. The impeller consists of a number of blades (usually curved) arranged in a regular pattern around the shaft. A sketch showing the essential features of a centrifugal pump is shown in Fig. 11.4. As the impeller rotates, fluid is sucked in through the *eye* of the casing and flows radially outward. Energy is added to the fluid by the rotating blades, and both pressure and absolute velocity are increased as the fluid flows from the eye to the periphery of the blades. For the simplest type of centrifugal pump, the fluid discharges directly into a volute-shaped casing. The casing shape is designed to reduce the velocity as the fluid leaves the impeller, and this decrease in kinetic energy is converted into an increase in pressure. The volute-shaped casing, with its increasing area in the direction of flow, is used to produce an essentially uniform velocity distribution as the fluid moves around the casing into the discharge opening. For large centrifugal pumps, a different design is often used in which diffuser guide vanes surround the impeller.

11.4.1   Theoretical Considerations

Although flow through a pump is very complex (unsteady and three-dimensional), the basic theory of operation of a centrifugal pump can be developed by considering the time aver-

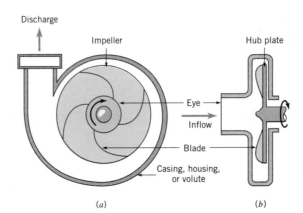

■ **FIGURE 11.4** Schematic diagram of basic elements of a centrifugal pump.

aged, steady, one-dimensional flow of the fluid as it passes between the inlet and the outlet sections of the impeller as the blades rotate. As shown in Fig. 11.5, for a typical blade passage, the absolute velocity, $\mathbf{V}_1$, of the fluid entering the passage is the vector sum of the velocity of the blade, $\mathbf{U}_1$, rotating in a circular path with angular velocity ω, and the relative velocity, $\mathbf{W}_1$, within the blade passage so that $\mathbf{V}_1 = \mathbf{W}_1 + \mathbf{U}_1$. Similarly, at the exit $\mathbf{V}_2 = \mathbf{W}_2 + \mathbf{U}_2$. Note that $U_1 = r_1\omega$ and $U_2 = r_2\omega$. Fluid velocities are taken to be average velocities over the inlet and exit sections of the blade passage. The relationship between the various velocities is shown graphically in Fig. 11.5.

As discussed in Section 11.3, the moment-of-momentum equation indicates that the shaft torque, T_{shaft}, required to rotate the pump impeller is given by equation Eq. 11.2 applied to a pump with $\dot{m}_1 = \dot{m}_2 = \dot{m}$. That is,

$$T_{\text{shaft}} = \dot{m}(r_2 V_{\theta 2} - r_1 V_{\theta 1}) = \rho Q (r_2 V_{\theta 2} - r_1 V_{\theta 1}) \tag{11.6}$$

where $V_{\theta 1}$ and $V_{\theta 2}$ are the tangential components of the absolute velocities, $\mathbf{V}_1$ and $\mathbf{V}_2$ (see Fig. 11.5).

For a rotating shaft, the power transferred is given by $\dot{W}_{\text{shaft}} = T_{\text{shaft}}\omega$ and therefore from Eq. 11.6

$$\dot{W}_{\text{shaft}} = \rho Q \omega (r_2 V_{\theta 2} - r_1 V_{\theta 1})$$

Since $U_1 = r_1\omega$ and $U_2 = r_2\omega$ we obtain

$$\dot{W}_{\text{shaft}} = \rho Q (U_2 V_{\theta 2} - U_1 V_{\theta 1}) \tag{11.7}$$

Equation 11.7 shows how the power supplied to the shaft of the pump is transferred to the flowing fluid. It also follows that the shaft power per unit mass of flowing fluid is

$$w_{\text{shaft}} = \frac{\dot{W}_{\text{shaft}}}{\rho Q} = U_2 V_{\theta 2} - U_1 V_{\theta 1} \tag{11.8}$$

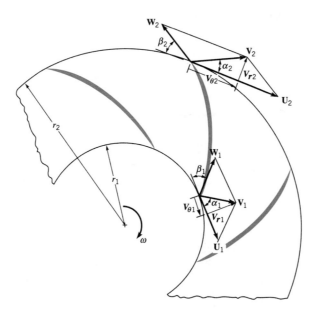

■ FIGURE 11.5 **Velocity diagrams at the inlet and exit of a centrifugal pump impeller.**

Recall from Section 5.3.3 that the energy equation is often written in terms of heads—velocity head, pressure head, elevation head. The head that a pump adds to the fluid is an important parameter. The ideal or maximum head rise possible, h_i, is found from

$$\dot{W}_{shaft} = \rho g Q h_i$$

which is obtained from Eq. 5.57 by setting head loss (h_L) equal to zero and multiplying by the weight flowrate, $\rho g Q$. Combining this result with Eq. 11.8 we get

$$h_i = \frac{1}{g}(U_2 V_{\theta 2} - U_1 V_{\theta 1}) \tag{11.9}$$

This ideal head rise, h_i, is the amount of energy per unit weight of fluid added to the fluid by the pump. The actual head rise realized by the fluid is less than the ideal amount by the head loss suffered.

An appropriate relationship between the flowrate and the pump ideal head rise can be obtained as follows. Often the fluid has no tangential component of velocity $V_{\theta 1}$, or *swirl*, as it enters the impeller; i.e., the angle between the absolute velocity and the tangential direction is 90° ($\alpha_1 = 90°$ in Fig. 11.5). In this case, Eq. 11.19 reduces to

$$h_i = \frac{U_2 V_{\theta 2}}{g} \tag{11.10}$$

From Fig. 11.5

$$\cot \beta_2 = \frac{U_2 - V_{\theta 2}}{V_{r2}}$$

so that Eq. 11.10 can be expressed as

$$h_i = \frac{U_2^2}{g} - \frac{U_2 V_{r2} \cot \beta_2}{g} \tag{11.11}$$

The flowrate, Q, is related to the radial component of the absolute velocity through the equation

$$Q = 2\pi r_2 b_2 V_{r2} \tag{11.12}$$

where b_2 is the impeller blade height at the radius r_2. Thus, combining Eqs. 11.11 and 11.12 yields

$$h_i = \frac{U_2^2}{g} - \frac{U_2 \cot \beta_2}{2\pi r_2 b_2 g} Q \tag{11.13}$$

This equation shows that the ideal or maximum head rise for a centrifugal pump varies linearly with Q for a given blade geometry and angular velocity. For actual pumps, the blade angle β_2 falls in the range of 15°–35°, with a normal range of 20° $< \beta_2 <$ 25°, and with 15° $< \beta_1 <$ 50° (Ref. 1). Blades with $\beta_2 <$ 90° are called *backward curved*, whereas blades with $\beta_2 >$ 90° are called *forward curved*. Pumps are not usually designed with forward curved vanes since such pumps tend to suffer unstable flow conditions.

Figure 11.6 shows the ideal head versus flowrate curve (Eq. 11.13) for a centrifugal pump with backward curved vanes ($\beta_2 <$ 90°). Since there are simplifying assumptions (i.e., zero losses) associated with the equation for h_i, we would expect that the actual rise in head of the fluid, h_a, would be less than the ideal head rise, and this is indeed the case. As shown

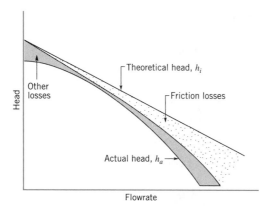

■ **FIGURE 11.6** **Effect of losses on the pump head-flowrate curve.**

in Fig. 11.6, the h_a versus Q curve lies below the ideal head-rise curve and shows a nonlinear variation with Q. The differences between the two curves (as represented by the shaded areas between the curves) arise from several sources. These differences include hydraulic losses due to fluid skin friction in the blade passages, which vary as Q^2, and other losses due to such factors as flow separation, impeller blade-casing clearance flows, and other three-dimensional flow effects. Near the design flowrate, some of these other losses are minimized.

EXAMPLE 11.2

Water is pumped at the rate of 1400 gpm through a centrifugal pump operating at a speed of 1750 rpm. The impeller has a uniform blade height, b, of 2 in. with $r_1 = 1.9$ in. and $r_2 = 7.0$ in., and the exit blade angle β_2 is 23° (see Fig. 11.5). Assume ideal flow conditions and that the tangential velocity component, $V_{\theta 1}$, of the water entering the blade is zero ($\alpha_1 = 90°$). Determine **(a)** the tangential velocity component, $V_{\theta 2}$, at the exit, **(b)** the ideal head rise, h_i, and **(c)** the power, $\dot{W}_{shaft}$, transferred to the fluid.

SOLUTION

(a) At the exit the velocity diagram is as shown in Fig. 11.5, where $\mathbf{V}_2$ is the absolute velocity of the fluid, $\mathbf{W}_2$ is the relative velocity, and $\mathbf{U}_2$ is the tip velocity of the impeller with

$$U_2 = r_2\omega = (7/12 \text{ ft})(2\pi \text{ rad/rev})\frac{(1750 \text{ rpm})}{(60 \text{ s/min})} = 107 \text{ ft/s}$$

Since the flowrate is given, it follows that $Q = 2\pi r_2 b_2 V_{r2}$ or

$$V_{r2} = \frac{Q}{2\pi r_2 b_2} = \frac{1400 \text{ gpm}}{(7.48 \text{ gal/ft}^3)(60 \text{ s/min})(2\pi)(7/12 \text{ ft})(2/12 \text{ ft})} = 5.11 \text{ ft/s}$$

From Fig. 11.5, we see that

$$\cot \beta_2 = \frac{U_2 - V_{\theta 2}}{V_{r2}}$$

so that

$$
\begin{aligned}
V_{\theta 2} &= U_2 - V_{r2} \cot \beta_2 \\
&= (107 - 5.11 \cot 23°) \text{ ft/s} \\
&= 95.0 \text{ ft/s} \quad \text{(Ans)}
\end{aligned}
$$

(b) From Eq. 11.10 the ideal head rise is given by

$$h_i = \frac{U_2 V_{\theta 2}}{g} = \frac{(107 \text{ ft/s})(95.0 \text{ ft/s})}{32.2 \text{ ft/s}^2}$$
$$= 316 \text{ ft} \quad \text{(Ans)}$$

Alternatively, from Eq. 11.11, the ideal head rise is

$$h_i = \frac{U_2^2}{g} - \frac{U_2 V_{r2} \cot \beta_2}{g} = \frac{(107 \text{ ft/s})^2}{32.2 \text{ ft/s}^2} - \frac{(107 \text{ ft/s})(5.11 \text{ ft/s}) \cot 23°}{32.2 \text{ ft/s}^2}$$
$$= 316 \text{ ft} \quad \text{(Ans)}$$

(c) From Eq. 11.7, with $V_{\theta 1} = 0$, the power transferred to the fluid is given by the equation

$$\dot{W}_{\text{shaft}} = \rho Q U_2 V_{\theta 2} = \frac{(1.94 \text{ slugs/ft}^3)(1400 \text{ gpm})(107 \text{ ft/s})(95.0 \text{ ft/s})}{[1(\text{slug·ft/s}^2)/\text{lb}](7.48 \text{ gal/ft}^3)(60 \text{ s/min})}$$
$$= 61,500 \text{ ft·lb/s} = 112 \text{ hp} \quad \text{(Ans)}$$

Note that the ideal head rise and the power transferred are related through the relationship

$$\dot{W}_{\text{shaft}} = \rho g Q h_i$$

It should be emphasized that results given involve the ideal head rise. The actual head-rise performance characteristics of a pump are usually determined by experimental measurements obtained in a testing laboratory.

11.4.2 Pump Performance Characteristics

Centrifugal pump design is a highly developed field, with much known about pump theory and design procedures (see, e.g., Refs. 1, 2, 3, 4, 17). However, due to the general complexity of flow through a centrifugal pump, the actual performance of the pump cannot be accurately predicted on a completely theoretical basis as indicated by the data of Fig. 11.6. Actual pump performance is determined experimentally through tests on the pump. From these tests, pump characteristics are determined and presented as *pump performance curves*. It is this information that is most helpful to the engineer responsible for incorporating pumps into a given flow system.

The actual head rise, h_a, gained by fluid flowing through a pump can be determined with an experimental arrangement of the type shown in Fig. 11.7, using the energy equation

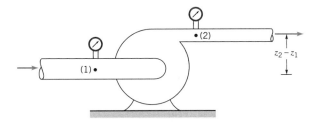

■ **FIGURE 11.7** **Typical experimental arrangement for determining the head rise gained by a fluid flowing through a pump.**

(Eq. 5.57 with $h_a = h_s - h_L$ where h_s is the shaft work head and is identical to h_i, and h_L is the pump head loss)

$$h_a = \frac{p_2 - p_1}{\gamma} + z_2 - z_1 + \frac{V_2^2 - V_1^2}{2g} \tag{11.14}$$

with sections (1) and (2) at the pump inlet and exit, respectively. The head, h_a, is the same as h_p used with the energy equation, Eq. 5.57, where h_p is interpreted to be the net head rise actually gained by the fluid flowing through the pump, i.e., $h_a = h_p = h_s - h_L$. Typically, the differences in elevations and velocities are small so that

$$h_a \approx \frac{p_2 - p_1}{\gamma} \tag{11.15}$$

The power, $\mathscr{P}_f$, gained by the fluid is given by the equation

$$\mathscr{P}_f = \gamma Q h_a \tag{11.16}$$

In addition to the head or power added to the fluid, the *overall efficiency, η,* is of interest, where

$$\eta = \frac{\text{power gained by the fluid}}{\text{shaft power driving the pump}} = \frac{\mathscr{P}_f}{\dot{W}_{\text{shaft}}}$$

The denominator of this relationship represents the total power applied to the shaft of the pump and is often referred to as *brake horsepower* (bhp). Thus,

$$\eta = \frac{\gamma Q h_a / 550}{\text{bhp}} \tag{11.17}$$

The overall pump efficiency is affected by the *hydraulic losses* in the pump and by the *mechanical losses* in the bearings and seals.

Performance characteristics for a given pump geometry and operating speed are usually given in the form of plots of h_a, η, and bhp versus Q (commonly referred to as *capacity*) as illustrated in Fig. 11.8. Actually, only two curves are needed since h_a, η, and bhp are related through Eq. 11.17. For convenience, all three curves are usually provided. The head developed by the pump at zero discharge is called the shutoff head, and it represents the rise in pressure head across the pump with the discharge valve closed. Since there is no flow with the valve closed, the related efficiency is zero, and the power supplied by the pump (bhp at $Q = 0$) is simply dissipated as heat. Although centrifugal pumps can be operated for short periods of time with the discharge valve closed, damage will occur due to overheating and large mechanical stress with any extended operation with the valve closed.

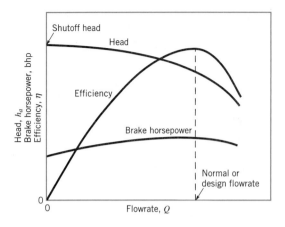

■ **FIGURE 11.8** **Typical performance characteristics for a centrifugal pump of a given size operating at a constant impeller speed.**

As can be seen from Fig. 11.8, as the discharge is increased from zero the brake horsepower increases, with a subsequent fall as the maximum discharge is approached. As previously noted, with h_a and bhp known, the efficiency can be calculated. As shown in Fig. 11.8, the efficiency is a function of the flowrate and reaches a maximum value at some particular value of the flowrate, commonly referred to as the *normal* or *design* flowrate or capacity for the pump. The points on the various curves corresponding to the maximum efficiency are denoted as the *best efficiency points* (BEP). It is apparent that when selecting a pump for a particular application, it is usually desirable to have the pump operate near its maximum efficiency. Thus, performance curves of the type shown in Fig. 11.8 are very important to the engineer responsible for the selection of pumps for a particular flow system. Matching the pump to a particular flow system is discussed in Section 11.4.3.

Pump performance characteristics are also presented in charts of the type shown in Fig. 11.9. Since impellers with different diameters may be used in a given casing, performance characteristics for several impeller diameters can be provided with corresponding lines of constant efficiency and brake horsepower as illustrated in Fig. 11.9. Thus, the same information can be obtained from this type of graph as from the curves shown in Fig. 11.8.

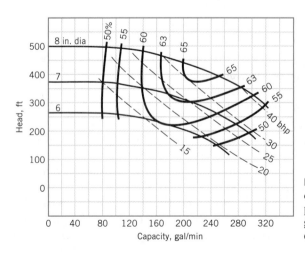

■ **FIGURE 11.9** **Performance curves for a two-stage centrifugal pump operating at 3500 rpm. Data given for three different impeller diameters.**

11.4.3 System Characteristics and Pump Selection

A typical flow system in which a pump is used is shown in Fig. 11.10. The energy equation applied between points (1) and (2) indicates that

$$h_p = z_2 - z_1 + \Sigma h_L \tag{11.18}$$

where h_p is the actual head gained by the fluid from the pump, and Σh_L represents all friction losses in the pipe and minor losses for pipe fittings and valves. From our study of pipe flow, we know that typically h_L varies approximately as the flowrate squared; that is, $h_L \propto Q^2$ (see Section 8.4). Thus, Eq. 11.18 can be written in the form

$$h_p = z_2 - z_1 + KQ^2 \tag{11.19}$$

where K depends on the pipe sizes and lengths, friction factors, and minor loss coefficients. Equation 11.19 is the *system equation* and shows how the actual head gained by the fluid from the pump is related to the system parameters. In this case the parameters include the change in elevation head, $z_2 - z_1$, and the losses due to friction as expressed by KQ^2. Each flow system has its own specific system equation. If the flow is laminar, the frictional losses will be proportional to Q rather than Q^2 (see Section 8.2).

There is also a unique relationship between the actual pump head gained by the fluid and the flowrate, which is governed by the pump design (as indicated by the pump performance curve). To select a pump for a particular application, it is necessary to utilize both the *system curve,* as determined by the system equation, and the pump performance curve. If both curves are plotted on the same graph, as illustrated in Fig. 11.11, their intersection (point A) represents the operating point for the system. That is, this point gives the head and flowrate that satisfies both the system equation and the pump equation. On the same graph the pump efficiency is shown. Ideally, we want the operating point to be near the best efficiency point (BEP) for the pump. For a given pump, it is clear that as the system equation changes, the operating point will shift. For example, if the pipe friction increases due to pipe wall fouling, the system changes, resulting in the operating point A shifting to point B in Fig. 11.11 with a reduction in flowrate and efficiency. The following example shows how the system and pump characteristics can be used to decide if a particular pump is suitable for a given application.

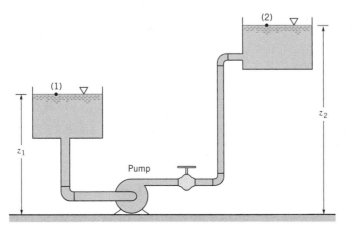

■ FIGURE 11.10
Typical flow system.

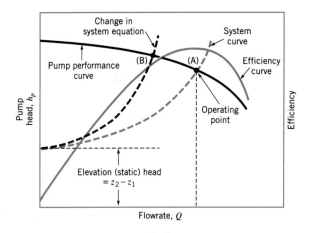

■ **FIGURE 11.11**
Utilization of the system curve and the pump performance curve to obtain the operating point for the system.

EXAMPLE 11.3

Water is to be pumped from one large, open tank to a second large, open tank as shown in Fig. E11.3a. The pipe diameter throughout is 6 in. and the total length of the pipe between the pipe entrance and exit is 200 ft. Minor loss coefficients for the entrance, exit, and the elbow are shown on the figure, and the friction factor for the pipe can be assumed constant and equal to 0.02. A certain centrifugal pump having the performance characteristics shown in Fig. E11.3b is suggested as a good pump for this flow system. With this pump, what would be the flowrate between the tanks? Do you think this pump would be a good choice?

SOLUTION

Application of the energy equation between the two free surfaces, points (1) and (2) as indicated, gives

$$\frac{p_1}{\gamma} + \frac{V_1^2}{2g} + z_1 + h_p = \frac{p_2}{\gamma} + \frac{V_2^2}{2g} + z_2 + f\frac{\ell}{D}\frac{V^2}{2g} + \sum K_L \frac{V^2}{2g} \qquad (1)$$

Thus, with $p_1 = p_2 = 0$, $V_1 = V_2 = 0$, $z_2 - z_1 = 10$ ft, $f = 0.02$, $D = 6/12$ ft, and $\ell = 200$ ft, Eq. (1) becomes

$$h_p = 10 + \left[0.02 \frac{(200 \text{ ft})}{(6/12 \text{ ft})} + (0.5 + 1.5 + 1.0) \right] \frac{V^2}{2(32.2 \text{ ft/s}^2)} \qquad (2)$$

where the given minor loss coefficients have been used. Since

$$V = \frac{Q}{A} = \frac{Q(\text{ft}^3/\text{s})}{(\pi/4)(6/12 \text{ ft})^2}$$

Eq. 2 can be expressed as

$$h_p = 10 + 4.43 \, Q^2 \qquad (3)$$

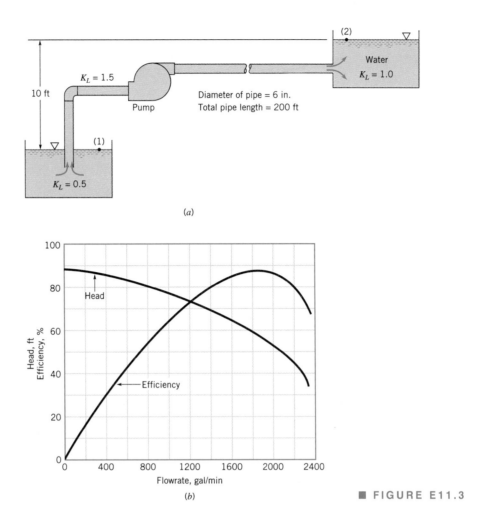

(a)

(b)

■ FIGURE E11.3

where Q is in ft^3/s, or with Q in gal/min.

$$h_p = 10 + 2.20 \times 10^{-5}Q^2 \tag{4}$$

Equation 3 or 4 represents the system equation for this particular flow system and reveals how much actual head the fluid will need to gain from the pump to maintain a certain flowrate. The performance data shown in Fig. E11.3b indicate the actual head the fluid will gain from this particular pump when it operates at a certain flowrate. Thus, when Eq. 4 is plotted on the same graph with the performance data, the intersection of the two curves represents the operating point for the pump and the system. This combination is shown in Fig. E11.3c with the intersection (as obtained graphically) occurring at

$$Q = 1600 \text{ gal/min} \tag{Ans}$$

with the corresponding actual head gained equal to 66.5 ft.

Another concern is whether or not the pump is operating efficiently at the operating point. As can be seen from Fig. E11.3c, although this is not peak efficiency, which is about

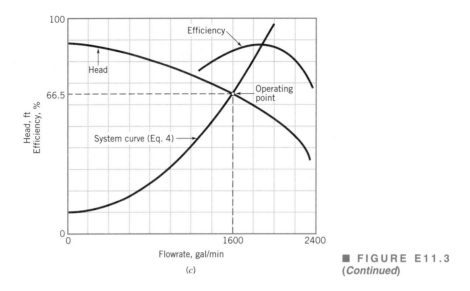

■ **FIGURE E11.3**
(*Continued*)

86%, it is close (about 84%). Thus, this pump would be a satisfactory choice, assuming the 1600 gal/min flowrate is at or near the desired flowrate.

The amount of pump head needed at the pump shaft is 66.5 ft/0.84 = 79.2 ft. The power needed to drive the pump is

$$
\begin{aligned}
\dot{W}_{\text{shaft}} &= \frac{\gamma Q h_a}{\eta} \\
&= \frac{(62.4 \text{ lb/ft}^3)[(1600 \text{ gal/min})/(7.48 \text{ gal/ft}^3)(60 \text{ s/min})](66.5 \text{ ft})}{0.84} \\
&= 17{,}600 \text{ ft} \cdot \text{lb/s} = 32.0 \text{ hp}
\end{aligned}
$$

11.5 Dimensionless Parameters and Similarity Laws

As discussed in Chapter 7, dimensional analysis is particularly useful in the planning and execution of experiments. Since the characteristics of pumps are usually determined experimentally, it is expected that dimensional analysis and similitude considerations will prove to be useful in the study and documentation of these characteristics.

From the previous section we know that the principal, dependent pump variables are the actual head rise, h_a, shaft power, $\dot{W}_{\text{shaft}}$, and efficiency, η. We expect that these variables will depend on the geometrical configuration, which can be represented by some characteristic diameter, D, other pertinent lengths, ℓ_i, and surface roughness, ε. In addition, the other important variables are flowrate, Q, the pump shaft rotational speed, ω, fluid viscosity, μ, and fluid density, ρ. We will only consider incompressible fluids presently, so compressibility effects need not concern us yet. Thus, any one of the dependent variables h_a, $\dot{W}_{\text{shaft}}$, and η can be expressed as

$$\text{dependent variable} = f(D, \ell_i, \varepsilon, Q, \omega, \mu, \rho)$$

and a straightforward application of dimensional analysis leads to

$$\text{dependent pi term} = \phi\left(\frac{\ell_i}{D}, \frac{\varepsilon}{D}, \frac{Q}{\omega D^3}, \frac{\rho\omega D^2}{\mu}\right) \tag{11.20}$$

The dependent pi term involving the head is usually expressed as $C_H = gh_a/\omega^2 D^2$, where gh_a is the actual head rise in terms of energy per unit mass, rather than simply h_a, which is energy per unit weight. This dimensionless parameter is called the *head rise coefficient*. The dependent pi term involving the shaft power is expressed as $C_\mathscr{P} = \dot{W}_{\text{shaft}}/\rho\omega^3 D^5$, and this standard dimensionless parameter is termed the *power coefficient*. The power appearing in this dimensionless parameter is commonly based on the shaft (brake) horsepower, bhp, so that in BG units, $\dot{W}_{\text{shaft}} = 550 \times (\text{bhp})$. The rotational speed, ω, which appears in these dimensionless groups is expressed in rad/s. The final dependent pi term is the efficiency, η, which is already dimensionless. Thus, in terms of dimensionless parameters the performance characteristics are expressed as

$$C_H = \frac{gh_a}{\omega^2 D^2} = \phi_1\left(\frac{\ell_i}{D}, \frac{\varepsilon}{D}, \frac{Q}{\omega D^3}, \frac{\rho\omega D^2}{\mu}\right)$$

$$C_\mathscr{P} = \frac{\dot{W}_{\text{shaft}}}{\rho\omega^3 D^5} = \phi_2\left(\frac{\ell_i}{D}, \frac{\varepsilon}{D}, \frac{Q}{\omega D^3}, \frac{\rho\omega D^2}{\mu}\right)$$

$$\eta = \frac{\rho g Q h_a}{\dot{W}_{\text{shaft}}} = \phi_3\left(\frac{\ell_i}{D}, \frac{\varepsilon}{D}, \frac{Q}{\omega D^3}, \frac{\rho\omega D^2}{\mu}\right)$$

The last pi term in each of the above equations is a form of Reynolds number that represents the relative influence of viscous effects. When the pump flow involves high Reynolds numbers, as is usually the case, experience has shown that the effect of the Reynolds number can be neglected. For simplicity, the relative roughness, ε/D, can also be neglected in pumps since the highly irregular shape of the pump chamber is usually the dominant geometric factor rather than the surface roughness. Thus, with these simplifications and for *geometrically similar* pumps (all pertinent dimensions, ℓ_i, scaled by a common length scale), the dependent pi terms are functions of only $Q/\omega D^3$, so that

$$\frac{gh_a}{\omega^2 D^2} = \phi_1\left(\frac{Q}{\omega D^3}\right) \tag{11.21}$$

$$\frac{\dot{W}_{\text{shaft}}}{\rho\omega^3 D^5} = \phi_2\left(\frac{Q}{\omega D^3}\right) \tag{11.22}$$

$$\eta = \phi_3\left(\frac{Q}{\omega D^3}\right) \tag{11.23}$$

The dimensionless parameter $C_Q = Q/\omega D^3$ is called the *flow coefficient*. These three equations provide the desired similarity relationships among a family of geometrically similar pumps. If two pumps from the family are operated at the same value of flow coefficient

$$\left(\frac{Q}{\omega D^3}\right)_1 = \left(\frac{Q}{\omega D^3}\right)_2 \tag{11.24}$$

it then follows that

$$\left(\frac{gh_a}{\omega^2 D^2}\right)_1 = \left(\frac{gh_a}{\omega^2 D^2}\right)_2 \tag{11.25}$$

$$\left(\frac{\dot{W}_{shaft}}{\rho\omega^3 D^5}\right)_1 = \left(\frac{\dot{W}_{shaft}}{\rho\omega^3 D^5}\right)_2 \tag{11.26}$$

$$\eta_1 = \eta_2 \tag{11.27}$$

where the subscripts 1 and 2 refer to any two pumps from the family of geometrically similar pumps.

With these so-called *pump scaling laws* it is possible to experimentally determine the performance characteristics of one pump in the laboratory and then use these data to predict the corresponding characteristics for other pumps within the family under different operating conditions. Figure 11.12a shows some typical curves obtained for a centrifugal pump. Figure 11.12b shows the results plotted in terms of the dimensionless coefficients, C_Q, C_H, $C_{\mathscr{P}}$, and η. From these curves the performance of different-sized, geometrically similar pumps can be predicted, as can the effect of changing speeds on the performance of the pump from which the curves were obtained. It is to be noted that the efficiency, η, is related to the other coefficients through the relationship $\eta = C_Q C_H C_{\mathscr{P}}^{-1}$. This follows directly from the definition of η.

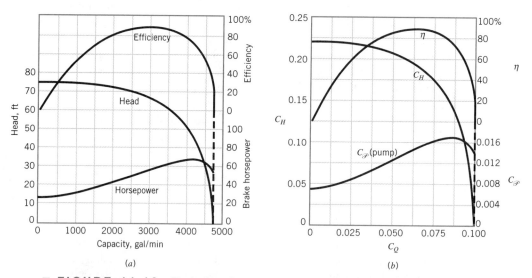

■ **FIGURE 11.12** **Typical performance data for a centrifugal pump: (*a*) characteristic curves for a 12-in. centrifugal pump operating at 1000 rpm, (*b*) dimensionless characteristic curves. (Data from Ref. 5, used by permission.)**

EXAMPLE 11.4

An 8-in.-diameter centrifugal pump operating at 1200 rpm is geometrically similar to the 12-in.-diameter pump having the performance characteristics of Figs. 11.12*a* and 11.12*b* while operating at 1000 rpm. For peak efficiency, predict the discharge, actual head rise, and shaft horsepower for this smaller pump. The working fluid is water at 60 °F.

SOLUTION

As is indicated by Eq. 11.23, for a given efficiency the flow coefficient has the same value for a given family of pumps. From Fig. 11.12*b* we see that at peak efficiency $C_Q = 0.0625$. Thus, for the 8-in. pump

$$Q = C_Q \omega D^3 = (0.0625)(1200/60 \text{ rev/s})(2\pi \text{ rad/rev})(8/12 \text{ ft})^3$$
$$Q = 2.33 \text{ ft}^3/\text{s} \tag{Ans}$$

or in terms of gpm

$$Q = (2.33 \text{ ft}^3/\text{s})(7.48 \text{ gal/ft}^3)(60 \text{ s/min}) = 1046 \text{ gpm} \tag{Ans}$$

The actual head rise and the shaft horsepower can be determined in a similar manner since at peak efficiency $C_H = 0.19$ and $C_{\mathscr{P}} = 0.014$, so that

$$h_a = \frac{C_H \omega^2 D^2}{g} = \frac{(0.19)(1200/60 \text{ rev/s})^2(2\pi \text{ rad/rev})^2(8/12 \text{ ft})^2}{32.2 \text{ ft/s}^2} = 41.4 \text{ ft} \tag{Ans}$$

and

$$\dot{W}_{\text{shaft}} = C_{\mathscr{P}} \rho \omega^3 D^5$$
$$= (0.014)(1.94 \text{ slugs/ft}^3)(1200/60 \text{ rev/s})^2(2\pi \text{ rad/rev})^3(8/12 \text{ ft})^5$$
$$= 7100 \text{ ft·lb/s}$$

$$\dot{W}_{\text{shaft}} = \frac{7100 \text{ ft·lb/s}}{550 \text{ ft·lb/s/hp}} = 12.9 \text{ hp} \tag{Ans}$$

The last result gives the shaft horsepower, which is the power supplied to the pump shaft. The power actually gained by the fluid is equal to $\gamma Q h_a$, which in this example is

$$\mathscr{P}_f = \gamma Q h_a = (62.4 \text{ lb/ft}^3)(2.33 \text{ ft}^3/\text{s})(41.4 \text{ ft}) = 6020 \text{ ft·lb/s}$$

Thus, the efficiency, η, is

$$\eta = \frac{\mathscr{P}_f}{\dot{W}_{\text{shaft}}} = \frac{6020}{7100} = 85\%$$

which checks with the efficiency curve of Fig. 11.12*b*.

11.5.1   Specific Speed

A useful pi term can be obtained by eliminating diameter D between the flow coefficient and the head rise coefficient. This is accomplished by raising the flow coefficient to an appropriate exponent (1/2) and dividing this result by the head coefficient raised to another appropriate exponent (3/4) so that

$$\frac{(Q/\omega D^3)^{1/2}}{(gh_a/\omega^2 D^2)^{3/4}} = \frac{\omega\sqrt{Q}}{(gh_a)^{3/4}} = N_s \tag{11.28}$$

The dimensionless parameter N_s is called the *specific speed*. Specific speed varies with flow coefficient just as the other coefficients and efficiency discussed earlier do. However, for any pump it is customary to specify a value of specific speed at the flow coefficient corresponding to peak efficiency only. For pumps with low Q and high h_a, the specific speed is low compared to a pump with high Q and low h_a. Centrifugal pumps typically are low-capacity, high-head pumps, and therefore have low specific speeds.

Specific speed as defined by Eq. 11.28 is dimensionless, and therefore independent of the system of units used in its evaluation as long as a consistent unit system is used. However, in the United States a modified, dimensional form of specific speed, N_{sd}, is commonly used, where

$$N_{sd} = \frac{\omega(\text{rpm})\sqrt{Q(\text{gpm})}}{[h_a(\text{ft})]^{3/4}} \tag{11.29}$$

In this case N_{sd} is said to be expressed in *U.S. customary units*. Typical values of N_{sd} are in the range $500 < N_{sd} < 4000$ for centrifugal pumps. Both N_s and N_{sd} have the same physical meaning, but their magnitudes will differ by a constant conversion factor ($N_{sd} = 2733\,N_s$) when ω in Eq. 11.28 is expressed in rad/s.

Each family or class of pumps has a particular range of values of specific speed associated with it. Thus, pumps that have low-capacity, high-head characteristics will have specific speeds that are smaller than pumps that have high-capacity, low-head characteristics. The concept of specific speed is very useful to engineers and designers, since if the required

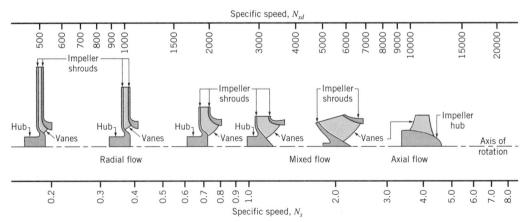

■ **FIGURE 11.13** **Variation in specific speed with type of pump (for pumps operating at peak efficiency). (Adapted from Ref. 6, used with permission.)**

head, flowrate, and speed are specified, it is possible to select an appropriate (most efficient) type of pump for a particular application. As the specific speed, N_{sd}, increases beyond about 2000 the peak efficiency of the purely radial-flow centrifugal pump starts to fall off, and other types of more efficient pump design are preferred. In addition to the centrifugal pump, the *axial-flow* pump is widely used. As discussed in Section 11.6, in an axial-flow pump the direction of the flow is primarily parallel to the rotating shaft rather than radial as in the centrifugal pump. Axial-flow pumps are essentially high-capacity, low-head pumps, and therefore have large specific speeds ($N_{sd} > 9000$) compared to centrifugal pumps. *Mixed-flow* pumps combine features of both radial-flow and axial-flow pumps and have intermediate values of specific speed. Figure 11.13 illustrates how the specific speed changes as the configuration of the pump changes from centrifugal or radial to axial.

11.6   Axial-Flow and Mixed-Flow Pumps

As noted previously, centrifugal pumps are radial-flow machines that operate most efficiently for applications requiring high heads at relatively low flowrates. This head–flowrate combination typically yields specific speeds (N_{sd}) that are less than approximately 4000. For many applications, such as those associated with drainage and irrigation, high flowrates at low heads are required and centrifugal pumps are not suitable. In this case, axial-flow pumps are commonly used. This type of pump consists essentially of a propeller confined within a cylindrical casing. Axial-flow pumps are often called *propeller pumps*. For this type of pump the flow is primarily in the axial direction (parallel to the axis of rotation of the shaft), as opposed to the radial flow found in the centrifugal pump. Whereas the head developed by a centrifugal pump includes a contribution due to centrifugal action, the head developed by an axial-flow pump is due primarily to the tangential force exerted by the rotor blades on the fluid. A schematic of an axial-flow pump arranged for vertical operation is shown in Fig. 11.14. The rotor is connected to a motor through a shaft, and as it rotates (usually at a rela-

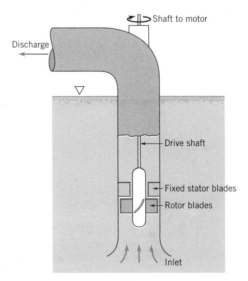

■ FIGURE 11.14   Schematic diagram of an axial-flow pump arranged for vertical operation.

tively high speed) the fluid is sucked in through the inlet. Typically the fluid discharges through a row of fixed stator (guide) vanes used to straighten the flow leaving the rotor. Some axial-flow pumps also have inlet guide vanes upstream of the rotor row, and some are multi-stage in which pairs (*stages*) of rotating blades (*rotor blades*) and fixed vanes (*stator blades*) are arranged in series. Axial-flow pumps usually have specific speeds (N_{sd}) in excess of 9000.

The definitions and broad concepts that were developed for centrifugal pumps are also applicable to axial-flow pumps. The actual flow characteristics, however, are quite different. In Fig. 11.15 typical head, power, and efficiency characteristics are compared for a centrifugal pump and an axial-flow pump. It is noted that at design capacity (maximum efficiency) the head and brake horsepower are the same for the two pumps. But as the flowrate decreases, the power input to the centrifugal pump falls to 180 hp at shutoff, whereas for the axial-flow pump the power input increases to 520 hp at shutoff. This characteristic of the axial-flow pump can cause overloading of the drive motor if the flowrate is reduced significantly from the design capacity. It is also noted that the head curve for the axial-flow pump is much steeper than that for the centrifugal pump. Thus, with axial-flow pumps there will be a large change in head with a small change in the flowrate, whereas for the centrifugal pump, with its relatively flat head curve, there will be only a small change in head with large changes in the flowrate. It is further observed from Fig. 11.15 that, except at design capacity, the efficiency of the axial-flow pump is lower than that of the centrifugal pump. To improve operating characteristics, some axial-flow pumps are constructed with adjustable blades.

For applications requiring specific speeds intermediate to those for centrifugal and axial-flow pumps, mixed-flow pumps have been developed that operate efficiently in the specific speed range $4000 < N_{sd} < 9000$. As the name implies, the flow in a mixed-flow pump has both a radial and an axial component. Figure 11.16 shows some typical data for centrifugal, mixed-flow, and axial-flow pumps, each operating at the same flowrate for peak efficiency. These data indicate that as we proceed from the centrifugal pump to the mixed-flow pump to the axial-flow pump, the specific speed increases, the head decreases, the speed increases, the impeller diameter decreases, and the eye diameter increases. These general trends are commonly found when these three types of pumps are compared.

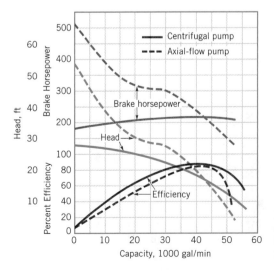

■ **FIGURE 11.15** **Comparison of performance characteristics for a centrifugal pump and an axial-flow pump, each rated 42,000 gal/min at a 17-ft head. (Data from Ref. 7, used with permission.)**

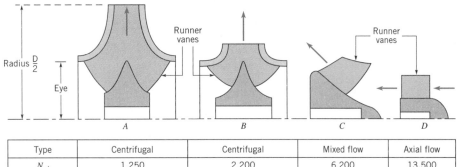

Type	Centrifugal	Centrifugal	Mixed flow	Axial flow
N_{sd}	1,250	2,200	6,200	13,500
Gal/min	2,400	2,400	2,400	2,400
Head, ft	70	48	33	20
Rpm	870	1,160	1,750	2,600
D, in.	19	12	10	7
D_{eye}/D	0.5	0.7	0.9	1.0

■ **FIGURE 11.16** **Comparison of different types of impellers. Specific speed for centrifugal pumps based on single suction. (Adapted from Ref. 7, used with permission.)**

The dimensionless parameters and scaling relationships developed in the previous sections apply to all three types of pumps—centrifugal, mixed-flow, and axial-flow—since the dimensional analysis used is not restricted to a particular type of pump. Additional information about pumps can be found in Refs. 1, 7, 8, 9, and 10.

11.7   Turbines

As discussed in Section 11.2, turbines are devices that extract energy from a flowing fluid. The geometry of turbines is such that the fluid exerts a torque on the rotor in the direction of its rotation. The shaft power generated is available to drive generators or other devices. In the following sections we discuss mainly the operation of hydraulic turbines (those for which the working fluid is water). Although there are numerous ingenious hydraulic turbine designs, most of these turbines can be classified into two basic types—*impulse turbines* and *reaction turbines*. In general, impulse turbines are high-head, low-flowrate devices, while reaction turbines are low-head, high-flowrate devices.

For hydraulic impulse turbines, the pressure drop across the rotor is zero; all of the pressure drop across the turbine stage occurs in the nozzle row. The *Pelton wheel* shown in Fig. 11.17 is a classical example of an impulse turbine. In these machines the total head of the incoming fluid (the sum of the pressure head, velocity head, and elevation head) is converted into a large velocity head at the exit of the supply nozzle (or nozzles if a multiple nozzle configuration is used). Both the pressure drop across the bucket (blade) and the change in relative speed (i.e., fluid speed relative to the moving bucket) of the fluid across the bucket are negligible. The space surrounding the rotor is not completely filled with fluid. It is the impulse of the individual jets of fluid striking the buckets that generates the torque.

For reaction turbines, on the other hand, the rotor is surrounded by a casing (or volute), which is completely filled with the working fluid. There is both a pressure drop and a change in fluid relative speed across the rotor. As shown for the radial-inflow turbine in

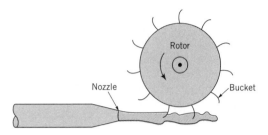

■ **FIGURE 11.17** Schematic diagram of a Pelton wheel turbine.

Fig. 11.18, guide vanes act as nozzles to accelerate the flow and turn it in the appropriate direction as the fluid enters the rotor. Thus, part of the pressure drop occurs across the guide vanes and part occurs across the rotor.

11.7.1 Impulse Turbines

Although there are various types of impulse turbine designs, perhaps the easiest to understand is the Pelton wheel. Lester Pelton, an American mining engineer during the California gold-mining days, is responsible for many of the still-used features of this type of turbine. It is most efficient when operated with a large head (e.g., a water source from a lake located significantly above the turbine nozzle), which is converted into a relatively large velocity at the exit of the nozzle (see Fig. 11.17).

As shown in Fig. 11.19, for a Pelton wheel a high-speed jet of water strikes the buckets and is deflected. The water enters and leaves the control volume surrounding the wheel as free jets (atmospheric pressure). In addition, a person riding on the bucket would note that the speed of the water does not change as it slides across the buckets (assuming viscous effects are negligible). That is, the magnitude of the relative velocity does not change, but its direction does. The change in direction of the velocity of the fluid jet causes a torque on the rotor, resulting in a power output from the turbine.

Design of the optimum, complex shape of the buckets to obtain maximum power output is a very difficult matter. Ideally, the radial component of velocity is zero. (In practice there often is a small but negligible radial component.) In addition, the buckets would ide-

V11.4 Pelton wheel lawn sprinkler

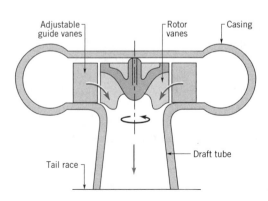

■ **FIGURE 11.18** Schematic diagram of a reaction turbine.

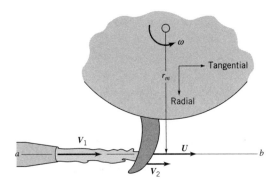

■ **FIGURE 11.19**   **Ideal fluid velocities for a Pelton wheel turbine.**

ally turn the relative velocity vector through a 180° turn, but physical constraints dictate that β, the angle of the exit edge of the blade, is less than 180°. Thus, the fluid leaves with an axial component of velocity as shown in Fig. 11.20.

The inlet and exit velocity triangles at the arithmetic mean radius, r_m, are assumed to be as shown in Fig. 11.21. To calculate the torque and power, we must know the tangential components of the absolute velocities at the inlet and exit. (Recall from the discussion in Section 11.3 that neither the radial nor the axial components of velocity enter into the torque or power equations.) From Fig. 11.21 we see that

$$V_{\theta 1} = V_1 = W_1 + U \tag{11.30}$$

and

$$V_{\theta 2} = W_2 \cos \beta + U \tag{11.31}$$

Thus, with the assumption that $W_1 = W_2$ (i.e., the relative speed of the fluid does not change as it is deflected by the buckets), we can combine Eqs. 11.30 and 11.31 to obtain

$$V_{\theta 2} - V_{\theta 1} = (U - V_1)(1 - \cos \beta) \tag{11.32}$$

This change in tangential component of velocity combined with the torque and power equations developed in Section 11.3 (i.e., Eqs. 11.2 and 11.4) gives

$$T_{\text{shaft}} = \dot{m} r_m (U - V_1)(1 - \cos \beta)$$

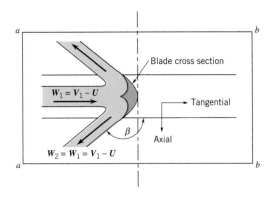

■ **FIGURE 11.20**   **Flow as viewed by an observer riding on the Pelton wheel—relative velocities.**

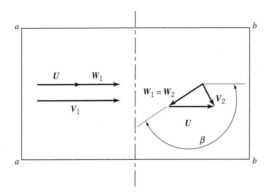

■ **FIGURE 11.21** **Inlet and exit velocity triangles for a Pelton wheel turbine.**

and since $U = \omega r_m$

$$\dot{W}_{shaft} = T_{shaft}\omega = \dot{m}U(U - V_1)(1 - \cos\beta) \tag{11.33}$$

These results are plotted in Fig. 11.22 along with typical experimental results. Note that $V_1 > U$ (i.e., the jet impacts the bucket), and $\dot{W}_{shaft} < 0$ (i.e., the turbine extracts power from the fluid).

Several interesting points can be noted from the above results. First, the power is a function of β. However, a typical value of $\beta = 165°$ (rather than the optimum $180°$) results in a relatively small (less than 2%) reduction in power since $1 - \cos 165 = 1.966$, compared to $1 - \cos 180 = 2$. Second, although the torque is maximum when the wheel is stopped ($U = 0$), there is no power under this condition—to extract power one needs force and motion. On the other hand, the power output is a maximum when

$$U_{\text{max power}} = \frac{V_1}{2} \tag{11.34}$$

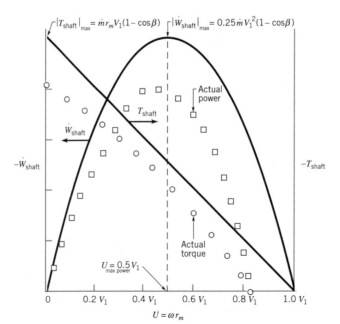

■ **FIGURE 11.22** **Typical theoretical and experimental power and torque for a Pelton wheel turbine as a function of bucket speed.**

This can be shown by using Eq. 11.33 and solving for U that gives $d\dot{W}_{shaft}/dU = 0$. A bucket speed of one-half the speed of the fluid coming from the nozzle gives the maximum power. Third, the maximum speed occurs when $T_{shaft} = 0$ (i.e., the load is completely removed from the turbine, as would happen if the shaft connecting the turbine to the generator were to break and frictional torques were negligible). For this case $U = \omega R = V_1$, the turbine is "free wheeling," and the water simply passes across the rotor without putting any force on the buckets.

EXAMPLE 11.5

Water to drive a Pelton wheel is supplied through a pipe from a lake as indicated in Fig. E11.5a. Determine the nozzle diameter, D_1, that will give the maximum power output. Also determine this maximum power and the angular velocity of the rotor at this condition.

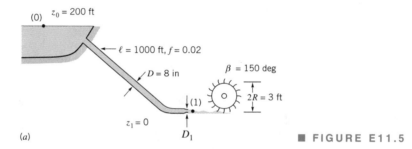

(a)   ■ FIGURE E11.5

SOLUTION

As indicated by Eq. 11.33, the power output depends on the flowrate, $Q = \dot{m}/\rho$, and the jet speed at the nozzle exit, V_1, both of which depend on the diameter of the nozzle, D_1, and the head loss associated with the supply pipe. That is

$$\dot{W}_{shaft} = \rho Q U (U - V_1)(1 - \cos\beta) \tag{1}$$

The nozzle exit speed, V_1, can be obtained by applying the energy equation (Eq. 5.57) between a point on the lake surface (where $V_0 = p_0 = 0$) and the nozzle outlet (where $z_1 = p_1 = 0$) to give

$$z_0 = \frac{V_1^2}{2g} + h_L \tag{2}$$

where the head loss is given in terms of the friction factor, f, as (see Eq. 8.18)

$$h_L = f\frac{\ell}{D}\frac{V^2}{2g}$$

The speed, V, of the fluid in the pipe of diameter D is obtained from the continuity equation

$$V = \frac{A_1 V_1}{A} = \left(\frac{D_1}{D}\right)^2 V_1$$

We have neglected minor losses associated with the pipe entrance and the nozzle. With the given data, Eq. 2 becomes

$$z_0 = \left[1 + f\frac{\ell}{D}\left(\frac{D_1}{D}\right)^4\right]\frac{V_1^2}{2g} \tag{3}$$

or

$$V_1 = \left[\frac{2gz_0}{1 + f\dfrac{\ell}{D}\left(\dfrac{D_1}{D}\right)^4}\right]^{1/2}$$

$$= \left[\frac{2(32.2 \text{ ft/s}^2)(200 \text{ ft})}{1 + 0.02\left(\dfrac{1000 \text{ ft}}{8/12 \text{ ft}}\right)\left(\dfrac{D_1}{8/12}\right)^4}\right]^{1/2} = \frac{113.5}{\sqrt{1 + 152\, D_1^4}} \tag{4}$$

where D_1 is in feet.

By combining Eqs. 1 and 4 and using $Q = \pi D_1^2 V_1/4$ we obtain the power as a function of D_1 and U as

$$\dot{W}_{\text{shaft}} = \frac{323\, U D_1^2}{\sqrt{1 + 152\, D_1^4}}\left[U - \frac{113.5}{\sqrt{1 + 152\, D_1^4}}\right] \tag{5}$$

where U is in ft/s and $\dot{W}_{\text{shaft}}$ is in ft·lb/s. These results are plotted as a function of U for various values of D_1 in Fig. 11.5b.

As shown by Eq. 11.34, the maximum power (in terms of its variation with U) occurs when $U = V_1/2$, which, when used with Eqs. 4 and 5, gives

$$\dot{W}_{\text{shaft}} = -\frac{1.04 \times 10^6\, D_1^2}{(1 + 152\, D_1^4)^{3/2}} \tag{6}$$

The maximum power possible occurs when $d\dot{W}_{\text{shaft}}/dD_1 = 0$, which according to Eq. 6 can be found as follows:

$$\frac{d\dot{W}_{\text{shaft}}}{dD_1} = -1.04 \times 10^6\left[\frac{2\, D_1}{(1 + 152\, D_1^4)^{3/2}} - \left(\frac{3}{2}\right)\frac{4(152)\, D_1^5}{(1 + 152\, D_1^4)^{5/2}}\right] = 0$$

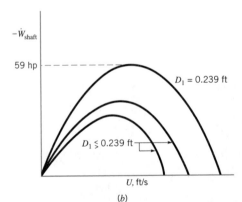

(b)

■ **FIGURE E11.5** (*Continued*)

or

$$304 D_1^4 = 1$$

Thus, the nozzle diameter for maximum power output is

$$D_1 = 0.239 \text{ ft} \qquad \text{(Ans)}$$

The corresponding maximum power can be determined from Eq. 6 as

$$\dot{W}_{\text{shaft}} = -\frac{1.04 \times 10^6 \, (0.239)^2}{[1 + 152(0.239)^4]^{3/2}} = -3.25 \times 10^4 \text{ ft} \cdot \text{lb/s}$$

or

$$\dot{W}_{\text{shaft}} = -3.25 \times 10^4 \text{ ft} \cdot \text{lb/s} \times \frac{1 \text{ hp}}{550 \text{ ft} \cdot \text{lb/s}} = -59.0 \text{ hp} \qquad \text{(Ans)}$$

The rotor speed at the maximum power condition can be obtained from

$$U = \omega R = \frac{V_1}{2}$$

where V_1 is given by Eq. 4. Thus,

$$\omega = \frac{V_1}{2R} = \frac{\dfrac{113.5}{\sqrt{1 + 152(0.239)^4}} \text{ ft/s}}{2\left(\dfrac{3}{2} \text{ ft}\right)}$$

$$= 30.9 \text{ rad/s} \times 1 \text{ rev}/2\pi \text{ rad} \times 60 \text{ s/min} = 295 \text{ rpm} \qquad \text{(Ans)}$$

The reason that an optimum diameter nozzle exists can be explained as follows. A larger diameter nozzle will allow a larger flowrate, but it will produce a smaller jet velocity because of the head loss within the supply side. A smaller diameter nozzle will reduce the flowrate but will produce a larger jet velocity. Since the power depends on a product combination of flowrate and jet velocity (see Eq. 1), there is an optimum-diameter nozzle that gives the maximum power.

The above results can be generalized (i.e., without regard to the specific parameter values of this problem) by considering Eqs. 1 and 3 and the condition that $U = V_1/2$ to obtain

$$\dot{W}_{\text{shaft}|U=V_1/2} = -\frac{\pi}{16} \rho(1 - \cos\beta)(2gz_0)^{3/2} D_1^2 \bigg/ \left(1 + f\frac{\ell}{D^5} D_1^4\right)^{3/2}$$

By setting $d\dot{W}_{\text{shaft}}/dD_1 = 0$, it can be shown (see Problem 11.33) that the maximum power occurs when

$$D_1 = D \bigg/ \left(2f\frac{\ell}{D}\right)^{1/4}$$

which gives the same results obtained above for the specific parameters of the example problem. Note that the optimum condition depends only on the friction factor and the length to diameter ratio of the supply pipe. What happens if the supply pipe is frictionless or of essentially zero length?

A second type of impulse turbine that is widely used (most often with gas as the working fluid) is indicated in Fig. E11.6a. A circumferential series of fluid jets strikes the rotating blades which, as with the Pelton wheel, alter both the direction and magnitude of the absolute velocity. As with the Pelton wheel, the inlet and exit pressures (i.e., on either side of the rotor) are equal, and the magnitude of the relative velocity is unchanged as the fluid slides across the blades (if frictional effects are negligible).

EXAMPLE 11.6

An air turbine used to drive the high-speed drill used by your dentist is shown in Fig. E11.6a. Air exiting from the upstream nozzle holes forces the turbine blades to move in the direction shown. Estimate the shaft energy per unit mass of air flowing through the turbine under the following conditions. The turbine rotor speed is 300,000 rpm, the tangential component of velocity out of the nozzle is twice the blade speed, and the tangential component of the absolute velocity out of the rotor is zero.

SOLUTION

We use the fixed, nondeforming control volume that includes the turbine rotor and the fluid in the rotor blade passages at an instant of time (see Fig. E11.6b). The only torque acting on this control volume is the shaft torque. For simplicity we analyze this problem using an arithmetic mean radius, r_m, where

$$r_m = \frac{1}{2}(r_0 + r_i)$$

A sketch of the velocity triangles at the rotor entrance and exit is shown in Fig. E11.6c.
Application of Eq. 11.5 (a form of the moment-of-momentum equation) gives

$$w_{shaft} = -U_1 V_{\theta 1} + U_2 V_{\theta 2} \tag{1}$$

where w_{shaft} is shaft energy per unit of mass flowing through the turbine. From the problem statement, $V_{\theta 1} = 2U$ and $V_{\theta 2} = 0$, where

$$\begin{aligned} U = \omega r_m &= (300,000 \text{ rev/min})(1 \text{ min/60 s})(2\pi \text{ rad/rev}) \\ &\quad \times (0.168 \text{ in.} + 0.133 \text{ in.})/2(12 \text{ in./ft}) \\ &= 394 \text{ ft/s} \end{aligned} \tag{2}$$

is the mean-radius blade velocity. Thus, Eq. (1) becomes

$$\begin{aligned} w_{shaft} = -U_1 V_{\theta 1} &= -2U^2 = -2(394 \text{ ft/s})^2 = -310,000 \text{ ft}^2/\text{s}^2 \\ &= (-310,000 \text{ ft}^2/\text{s}^2)(1 \text{ lb/slug} \cdot \text{ft/s}^2) = -310,000 \text{ ft} \cdot \text{lb/slug} \end{aligned} \tag{Ans}$$

For each slug of air passing through the turbine there is 310,000 ft·lb of energy available at the shaft to drive the drill. However, because of fluid friction, the actual amount of energy given up by each slug of air will be greater than the amount available at the shaft.

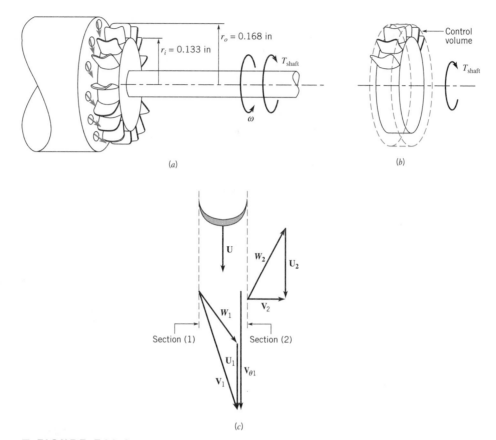

■ FIGURE E11.6

How much greater depends on the efficiency of the fluid-mechanical energy transfer between the fluid and the turbine blades.

Recall that the shaft power is given by $\dot{W}_{shaft} = \dot{m}w_{shaft}$. Hence, to determine the power we need to know the mass flowrate, $\dot{m}$, which depends on the size and number of the nozzles. Although the energy per unit mass is large (i.e., 310,000 ft · lb/slug), the flowrate is small, so the power is not "large."

11.7.2 Reaction Turbines

As indicated in the previous section, impulse turbines are best suited (i.e., most efficient) for lower flowrate and higher head operations. Reaction turbines, on the other hand, are best suited for higher flowrate and lower head situations such as are often encountered in hydro-electric power plants associated with a dammed river, for example.

In a reaction turbine the working fluid completely fills the passageways through which it flows (unlike an impulse turbine, which contains one or more individual unconfined jets of fluid). The angular momentum, pressure, and velocity of the fluid decrease as it flows through the turbine rotor—the turbine rotor extracts energy from the fluid.

As with pumps, turbines are manufactured in a variety of configurations—radial-flow, mixed-flow, and axial-flow. Typical radial- and mixed-flow hydraulic turbines are called *Francis turbines,* named after James Francis, an American engineer. At very low heads the most efficient type of turbine is the axial-flow or propeller turbine. The *Kaplan turbine,* named after Victor Kaplan, a German professor, is an efficient axial-flow hydraulic turbine with adjustable blades. Cross sections of these different turbine types are shown in Fig. 11.23.

As shown in Fig. 11.23*a*, flow across the rotor blades of a radial-inflow turbine has a major component in the radial direction. Inlet guide vanes (which may be adjusted to allow optimum performance) direct the water into the rotor with a tangential component of velocity. The absolute velocity of the water leaving the rotor is essentially without tangential velocity. Hence, the rotor decreases the angular momentum of the fluid, the fluid exerts a torque on the rotor in the direction of rotation, and the rotor extracts energy from the fluid. The Euler turbomachine equation (Eq. 11.2) and the corresponding power equation (Eq. 11.4) are equally valid for this turbine as they are for the centrifugal pump discussed in Section 11.4.

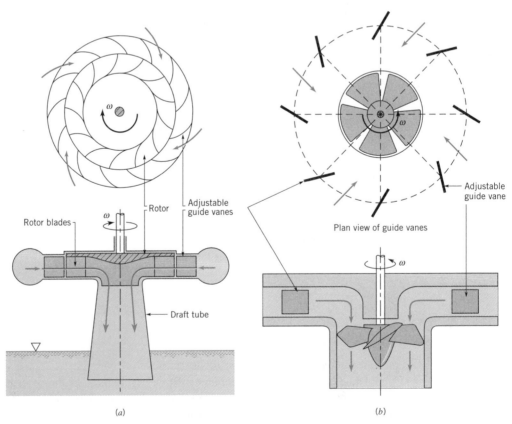

(a) (b)

■ **FIGURE 11.23** (*a*) **Typical radial-flow Francis turbine,** (*b*) **typical axial-flow Kaplan turbine.**

As shown in Fig. 11.23*b*, for an axial-flow Kaplan turbine, the fluid flows through the inlet guide vanes and achieves a tangential velocity in a vortex (swirl) motion before it reaches the rotor. Flow across the rotor contains a major axial component. Both the inlet guide vanes and the turbine blades can be adjusted by changing their setting angles to produce the best match (optimum output) for the specific operating conditions. For example, the operating head available may change from season to season and/or the flowrate through the rotor may vary.

As with pumps, incompressible flow turbine performance is often specified in terms of appropriate dimensionless parameters. The flow coefficient, $C_Q = Q/\omega D^3$, the head coefficient, $C_H = gh_T/\omega^2 D^2$, and the power coefficient, $C_\mathcal{P} = \dot{W}_{shaft}/\rho\omega^3 D^5$, are defined in the same way for pumps and turbines. On the other hand, turbine efficiency, η, is the inverse of pump efficiency. That is, the efficiency is the ratio of the shaft power output to the power available in the flowing fluid, or

$$\eta = \frac{\dot{W}_{shaft}}{\rho g Q h_T}$$

For geometrically similar turbines and for negligible Reynolds number and surface roughness difference effects, the relationships between the dimensionless parameters are given functionally by that shown in Eqs. 11.21, 22, and 23. That is,

$$C_H = \phi_1(C_Q), \qquad C_\mathcal{P} = \phi_2(C_Q), \qquad \text{and} \qquad \eta = \phi_3(C_Q)$$

where the functions ϕ_1, ϕ_2, and ϕ_3 are dependent on the type of turbine involved. Also, for turbines the efficiency, η, is related to the other coefficients according to $\eta = C_\mathcal{P}/C_H C_Q$.

As indicated above, the design engineer has a variety of turbine types available for any given application. It is necessary to determine which type of turbine would best fit the job (i.e., be most efficient) before detailed design work is attempted. As with pumps, the use of a specific speed parameter can help provide this information. For hydraulic turbines, the rotor diameter D is eliminated between the flow coefficient and the power coefficient to obtain the *power specific speed, N'_s*, where

$$N'_s = \frac{\omega\sqrt{\dot{W}_{shaft}/\rho}}{(gh_T)^{5/4}}$$

We use the more common, but not dimensionless, definition of specific speed

$$N'_{sd} = \frac{\omega(\text{rpm})\sqrt{\dot{W}_{shaft}\,(\text{bhp})}}{[h_T(\text{ft})]^{5/4}} \tag{11.35}$$

That is, N'_{sd} is calculated with angular velocity, ω, in rpm; shaft power, $\dot{W}_{shaft}$, in brake horsepower; and head, h_T, in feet. Optimum turbine efficiency (for large turbines) as a function of specific speed is indicated in Fig. 11.24. Also shown are representative rotor and casing cross sections. Note that impulse turbines are best at low specific speeds; that is, when operating with larger heads and small flowrate. The other extreme is axial-flow turbines, which are the most efficient type if the head is low and if the flowrate is large. For intermediate values of specific speeds, radial- and mixed-flow turbines offer the best peformance.

The data shown in Fig. 11.24 are meant only to provide a guide for turbine-type selection. The actual turbine efficiency for a given turbine depends very strongly on the detailed design of the turbine. Considerable analysis, testing, and experience are needed to produce an efficient turbine. However, the data of Fig. 11.24 are representative. Much additional information can be found in the literature (Ref. 11, 17).

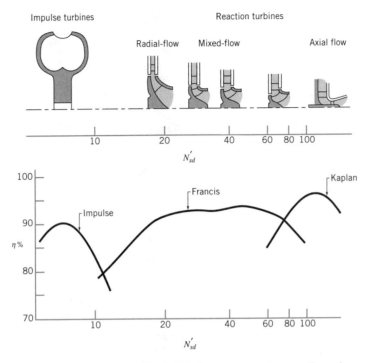

■ **FIGURE 11.24**   **Typical turbine cross sections and maxi-mum efficiencies as a function of specific speed.**

EXAMPLE 11.7

A hydraulic turbine is to operate at an angular velocity of 6 rev/s, a flowrate of 10 ft^3/s, and a head of 20 ft. What type of turbine should be selected? Explain.

SOLUTION

The most efficient type of turbine to use can be obtained by calculating the specific speed, N'_{sd}, and using the information of Fig. 11.24. To use the dimensional form of the specific speed indicated in Fig. 11.24 we must convert the given data into the appropriate units. For the rotor speed we get

$$\omega = 6 \text{ rev/s} \times 60 \text{ s/min} = 360 \text{ rpm}$$

To estimate the shaft power, we assume all of the available head is converted into power and multiply this amount by an assumed efficiency (94%).

$$\dot{W}_{\text{shaft}} = \gamma Q z \eta = (62.4 \text{ lb/ft}^3)(10 \text{ ft}^3/\text{s}) \left[\frac{20 \text{ ft}(0.94)}{550 \text{ ft} \cdot \text{lb/s} \cdot \text{hp}} \right]$$

$$\dot{W}_{\text{shaft}} = 21.3 \text{ hp}$$

Thus for this turbine,

$$N'_{sd} = \frac{\omega \sqrt{\dot{W}_{shaft}}}{(h_T)^{5/4}} = \frac{(360 \text{ rpm})\sqrt{21.3 \text{ hp}}}{(20 \text{ ft})^{5/4}} = 39.3$$

According to the information of Fig. 11.24,

A mixed-flow Francis turbine would
probably give the highest efficiency and
an assumed efficiency of 0.94 is appropriate.   **(Ans)**

What would happen if we wished to use a Pelton wheel for this application? Note that with only a 20-ft head, the maximum jet velocity, V_1, obtainable (neglecting viscous effects) would be

$$V_1 = \sqrt{2 gz} = \sqrt{2 \times 32.2 \text{ ft/s}^2 \times 20 \text{ ft}} = 35.9 \text{ ft/s}$$

As shown by Eq. 11.34, for maximum efficiency of a Pelton wheel the jet velocity is ideally two times the blade velocity. Thus, $V_1 = 2\omega R$, or the wheel diameter, $D = 2R$, is

$$D = \frac{V_1}{\omega} = \frac{35.9 \text{ ft/s}}{(6 \text{ rev/s} \times 2\pi \text{ rad/rev})} = 0.952 \text{ ft}$$

To obtain a flowrate of $Q = 10 \text{ ft}^3/\text{s}$ at a velocity of $V_1 = 39.5 \text{ ft/s}$, the jet diameter, d_1, must be given by

$$Q = \frac{\pi}{4} d_1^2 V_1$$

or

$$d_1 = \left[\frac{4Q}{\pi V_1} \right]^{1/2} = \left[\frac{4(10 \text{ ft}^3/\text{s})}{\pi(35.9 \text{ ft/s})} \right]^{1/2} = 0.596 \text{ ft}$$

A Pelton wheel with a diameter of $D = 0.952$ ft supplied with water through a nozzle of diameter $d_1 = 0.596$ ft is not a practical design. Typically $d_1 \ll D$ (see Fig. 11.17). By using multiple jets it would be possible to reduce the jet diameter. However, even with 8 jets, the jet diameter would be 0.211 ft, which is still too large (relative to the wheel diameter) to be practical. Hence, the above calculations reinforce the results presented in Fig. 11.24—a Pelton wheel would not be practical for this application. If the flowrate were considerably smaller, the specific speed could be reduced to the range where a Pelton wheel would be the type to use (rather than a mixed-flow reaction turbine).

11.8 Compressible Flow Turbomachines

Compressible flow turbomachines are in many ways similar to the incompressible flow pumps and turbines described in previous portions of this chapter. The main difference is that the density of the fluid (a gas or vapor) changes significantly from the inlet to the outlet of the compressible flow machines. This added feature has interesting consequences (e.g., shock waves), benefits (e.g., large pressure changes), and complications (e.g., blade cooling).

An in-depth understanding of compressible flow turbomachines requires mastery of various thermodynamic concepts as well as information provided earlier about basic energy considerations (Section 11.2) and basic angular momentum considerations (Section 11.3). The interested reader is encouraged to read some of the references available for further information (Refs. 12, 13, 14, 15, 16, and 17).

References

1. Stepanoff, H. J., *Centrifugal and Axial Flow Pumps,* 2nd Ed., Wiley, New York, 1957.
2. Shepherd, D. G., *Principles of Turbomachinery,* Macmillan, New York, 1956.
3. Wislicenus, G. F., *Preliminary Design of Turbopumps and Related Machinery,* NASA Reference Publication 1170, 1986.
4. Neumann, B., *The Interaction Between Geometry and Performance of a Centrifugal Pump,* Mechanical Engineering Publications Limited, London, 1991.
5. Rouse, H., *Elementary Mechanics of Fluids,* Wiley, New York, 1946.
6. Hydraulic Institute, *Hydraulic Institute Standards,* 14th Ed., Hydraulic Institute, Cleveland, Ohio, 1983.
7. Kristal, F. A., and Annett, F. A., *Pumps: Types, Selection, Installation, Operation, and Maintenance,* McGraw-Hill, New York, 1953.
8. Garay, P. N., *Pump Application Desk Book,* Fairmont Press, Lilburn, Georgia, 1990.
9. Karassick, I. J., et al., *Pump Handbook,* McGraw-Hill, New York, 1985.
10. Moody, L. F., and Zowski, T., "Hydraulic Machinery," in *Handbook of Applied Hydraulics,* 3rd Ed., by C. V. Davis and K. E. Sorensen, McGraw-Hill, New York, 1969.
11. Balje, O. E., *Turbomachines: A Guide to Design, Selection, and Theory,* Wiley, New York, 1981.
12. Bathie, W. W., *Fundamentals of Gas Turbines,* Wiley, New York, 1984.
13. Boyce, M. P., *Gas Turbine Engineering Handbook,* Gulf Publishing, Houston, 1982.
14. Cohen, H., Rogers, G. F. C., and Saravanamuttoo, H. I. H., *Gas Turbine Theory,* 3rd Ed., Longman Scientific & Technical, Essex, UK, and Wiley, New York, 1987.
15. Johnson, I. A., and Bullock, R. D., Eds., *Aerodynamic Design of Axial-Flow Compressors,* NASA SP-36, National Aeronautics and Space Administration, Washington, 1965.
16. Glassman, A. J., Ed., *Turbine Design and Application,* Vol. 3, NASA SP-290, National Aeronautics and Space Administration, Washington, 1975.
17. Johnson, R. W., Ed. *The Handbook of Fluid Dynamics,* CRC Press, New York, 1998.

Problems

Note: Unless otherwise indicated, use the values of fluid properties found in the tables on the inside of the front cover. Problems designated with a (†) are "open ended" problems and require critical thinking in that to work them one must make various assumptions and provide the necessary data. There is not a unique answer to these problems.

11.1 Water flows through a rotating sprinkler arm as shown in **Video V11.2** and Fig. P11.1. Determine the flowrate if the angular velocity is 120 rpm. Friction is negligible. Is this a turbine or a pump?

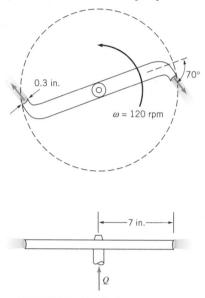

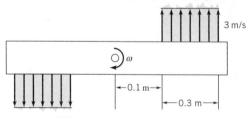

■ **FIGURE P11.1**

11.2 Uniform horizontal sheets of water of 3-mm thickness issue from the slits on the rotating manifold shown in Fig. P11.2. The velocity relative to the arm is a constant 3 m/s along each slit. Determine the torque needed to hold the manifold stationary. What would the angular velocity of the manifold be if the resisting torque is negligible?

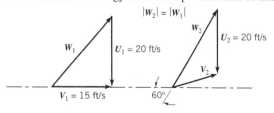

■ **FIGURE P11.2**

11.3 The rotor shown in Fig. P11.3 rotates with an angular velocity of 2000 rpm. Assume that the fluid enters in the radial direction and the relative velocity is tangent to the blades across the entire rotor. Is the device a pump or a turbine? Explain.

11.4 The measured shaft torque on the turbomachine shown in Fig. P11.4 is −60 N·m when the absolute velocities are as indicated. Determine the mass flowrate. What is the angular velocity if the magnitude of the shaft power is 1800 N·m/s? Is this machine a pump or a turbine? Explain.

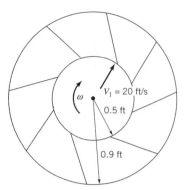

■ **FIGURE P11.3**

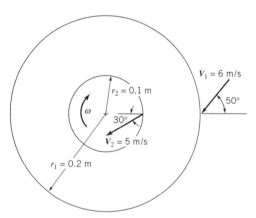

■ **FIGURE P11.4**

11.5 At a given radial location, a 15 ft/s wind against a windmill (see **Video V11.1**) results in the upstream (1) and downstream (2) velocity triangles shown in Fig. P11.5. Sketch an appropriate blade section at that radial location and determine the energy transferred per unit mass of fluid.

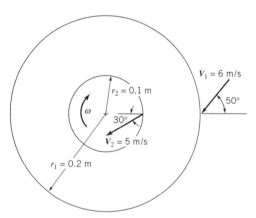

$|W_2| = |W_1|$

$U_2 = 20$ ft/s

W_2

V_2

W_1 $U_1 = 20$ ft/s

$V_1 = 15$ ft/s   60°

■ **FIGURE P11.5**

11.6 A centrifugal pump impeller is rotating at 1200 rpm in the direction shown in Fig. P11.6. The flow enters parallel to the axis of rotation and leaves at an angle of 30° to the radial direction. The absolute exit velocity, V_2, is 90 ft/s. **(a)** Draw the velocity triangle for the impeller exit flow. **(b)** Estimate the torque necessary to turn the impeller if the fluid density is 2.0 slugs/ft³. What will the impeller rotation speed become if the shaft breaks?

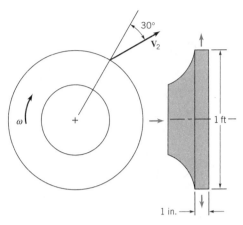

■ **FIGURE P11.6**

11.7 A centrifugal radial water pump has the dimensions shown in Fig. P11.7. The volume rate of flow is 0.25 ft^3/s, and the absolute inlet velocity is directed radially outward. The angular velocity of the impeller is 960 rpm. The exit velocity as seen from a coordinate system attached to the impeller can be assumed to be tangent to the vane at its trailing edge. Calculate the power required to drive the pump.

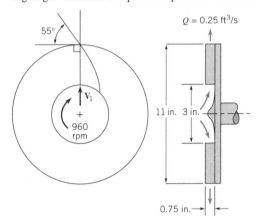

■ **FIGURE P11.7**

11.8 Water is pumped with a centrifugal pump, and measurements made on the pump indicate that for a flowrate of 240 gpm the required input power is 6 hp. For a pump efficiency of 62%, what is the actual head rise of the water being pumped?

11.9 The performance characteristics of a certain centrifugal pump having a 9-in.-diameter impeller and operating at 1750 rpm are determined using an experimental setup similar to that shown in Fig. 11.7. The following data were obtained during a series of tests in which $z_2 - z_1 = 0$, $V_2 = V_1$, and the fluid was water.

Q (gpm)	20	40	60	80	100	120	140
$p_2 - p_1$ (psi)	40.2	40.1	38.1	36.2	33.5	30.1	25.8
Power input (hp)	1.58	2.27	2.67	2.95	3.19	3.49	4.00

Based on these data, show or plot how the actual head rise, h_a, and the pump efficiency, η, vary with the flowrate. What is the design flowrate for this pump?

11.10 The centrifugal pump shown in Fig. P11.10 is not self-priming. That is, if the water is drained from the pump and pipe as shown in Fig. P11.10a, the pump will not draw the water into the pump and start pumping when the pump is turned on. However, if the pump is primed [i.e., filled with water as in Fig. P11.10b], the pump does start pumping water when turned on. Explain this behavior.

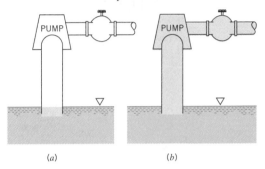

(a)   (b)

■ **FIGURE P11.10**

11.11 Owing to fouling of the pipe wall, the friction factor for the pipe of Example 11.3 increases from 0.02 to 0.03. Determine the new flowrate, assuming all other conditions remain the same. What is the pump efficiency at this new flowrate? Explain how a line valve could be used to vary the flowrate through the pipe of Example 11.3. Would it be better to place the valve upstream or downstream of the pump? Why?

11.12 A centrifugal pump having a head-capacity relationship given by the equation $h_a = 180 - 6.10 \times 10^{-4}Q^2$, with h_a in feet when Q is in gpm, is to be used with a system similar to that shown in Fig. 11.10. For $z_2 - z_1 = 50$ ft, what is the expected flowrate if the total length of constant-diameter pipe is 600 ft and the fluid is water? Assume the pipe diameter to be 4 in. and the friction factor to be equal to 0.02. Neglect all minor losses.

11.13 A centrifugal pump having a 6-in.-diameter impeller and the characteristics shown in Fig. 11.9 is to be used to pump gasoline through 4000 ft of commercial steel 3-in.-diameter pipe. The pipe connects two reservoirs having open surfaces at the same elevation. Determine the flowrate. Do you think this pump is a good choice? Explain.

11.14 A centrifugal pump having the characteristics shown in Example 11.3 is used to pump water between two large open tanks through 100 ft of 8-in.-diameter pipe. The pipeline contains 4 regular flanged 90° elbows, a check valve, and a fully open globe valve. Assume the friction factor $f = 0.02$ for the 100-ft section of pipe. Other minor losses are negligible. If the static head (difference in height of fluid surfaces in the two tanks) is 30 ft, what is the expected flowrate? Do you think this pump is a good choice? Explain.

11.15   In a chemical processing plant a liquid is pumped from an open tank, through a 0.1-m-diameter vertical pipe, and into another open tank as shown in Fig. P11.15a. A valve is located in the pipe, and the minor loss coefficient for the valve as a function of the valve setting is shown in Fig. P11.15b. The pump head-capacity relationship is given by the equation $h_a = 52.0 - 1.01 \times 10^3 Q^2$ with h_a in meters when Q is in m^3/s. Assume the friction factor $f = 0.02$ for the pipe, and all minor losses, except for the valve, are negligible. The fluid levels in the two tanks can be assumed to remain constant. **(a)** Determine the flowrate with the valve wide open. **(b)** Determine the required valve setting (percent open) to reduce the flowrate by 50%.

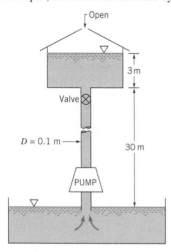

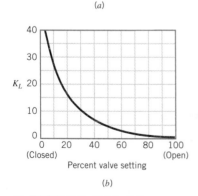

(a)

(b)

■ **FIGURE P11.15**

11.16   A centrifugal pump having an impeller diameter of 1 m is to be constructed so that it will supply a head rise of 200 m at a flowrate of 4.1 m^3/s of water when operating at a speed of 1200 rpm. To study the characteristics of this pump, a 1/5 scale, geometrically similar model operated at

the same speed is to be tested in the laboratory. Determine the required model discharge and head rise. Assume both model and prototype operate with the same efficiency (and therefore the same flow coefficient).

11.17   A small model of a pump is tested in the laboratory and found to have a specific speed, N_{sd}, equal to 1000 when operating at peak efficiency. Predict the discharge of a larger, geometrically similar pump operating at peak efficiency at a speed of 1800 rpm across an actual head rise of 200 ft.

11.18   A centrifugal pump provides a flowrate of 500 gpm when operating at 1760 rpm against a 200-ft head. Determine the pump's flowrate and developed head if the pump speed is increased to 3500 rpm.

11.19   A centrifugal pump with a 12-in.-diameter impeller requires a power input of 60 hp when the flowrate is 3200 gpm against a 60-ft head. The impeller is changed to one with a 10-in. diameter. Determine the expected flowrate, head, and input power if the pump speed remains the same.

11.20   A centrifugal pump has the performance characteristics of the pump with the 6-in.-diameter impeller described in Fig. 11.9. Note that in Fig. 11.9 the pump is operating at 3500 rpm. What is the expected flowrate and head gain if the speed of this pump is reduced to 2800 rpm while operating at peak efficiency?

11.21   A certain axial-flow pump has a specific speed of $N_S = 5.0$. If the pump is expected to deliver 3000 gpm when operating against a 15-ft head, at what speed (rpm) should the pump be run?

11.22   A certain pump is known to have a capacity of 3 m^3/s when operating at a speed of 60 rad/s against a head of 20 m. Based on the information in Fig. 11.13, would you recommend a radial-flow, mixed-flow, or axial-flow pump?

11.23   Fuel oil (sp. wt = 48.0 lb/ft^3, viscosity = 2.0 × 10^{-5} lb·s/ft^2) is pumped through the piping system of Fig. P11.23 with a velocity of 4.6 ft/s. The pressure 200 ft upstream from the pump is 5 psi. Pipe losses downstream from the pump are negligible, but minor losses are not (minor loss coefficients are given on the figure). **(a)** For a pipe diameter of 2 in. with a relative roughness $\varepsilon/D = 0.001$, determine the head that must be added by the pump. **(b)** For a

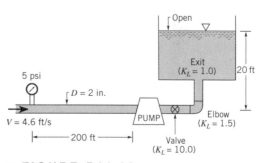

■ **FIGURE P11.23**

pump operating speed of 1750 rpm, what type of pump (radial-flow, mixed-flow, or axial-flow) would you recommend for this application?

†**11.24** Water is pumped between the two tanks described in Example 11.3 once a day, 365 days a year, with each pumping period lasting two hours. The water levels in the two tanks remain essentially constant. Estimate the annual cost of the electrical power needed to operate the pump if it were located in your city. You will have to make a reasonable estimate for the efficiency of the motor used to drive the pump. Due to aging, it can be expected that the overall resistance of the system will increase with time. If the operating point shown in Fig. E11.3c changes to a point where the flowrate has been reduced to 1000 gpm, what will be the new annual cost of operating the pump? Assume the cost of electrical power remains the same.

11.25 A Pelton wheel turbine is illustrated in Fig. P11.25. The radius to the line of action of the tangential reaction force on each vane is 1 ft. Each vane deflects fluid by an angle of 135° as indicated. Assume all of the flow occurs in a horizontal plane. Each of the four jets shown strikes a vane with a velocity of 100 ft/s and a stream diameter of 1 in. The magnitude of velocity of the jet remains constant along the vane surface. **(a)** How much torque is required to hold the wheel stationary? **(b)** How fast will the wheel rotate if shaft torque is negligible and what practical situation is simulated by this condition?

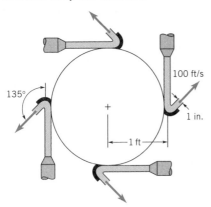

■ **FIGURE P11.25**

11.26 A simplified sketch of a hydraulic turbine runner is shown in Fig. P11.26. Relative to the rotating runner, water enters at section (1) (cylindrical cross section area A_1 at $r_1 = 1.5$ m) at an angle of 100° from the tangential direction and leaves at section (2) (cylindrical cross section area A_2 at $r_2 = 0.85$ m) at an angle of 50° from the tangential direction. The blade height at sections (1) and (2) is 0.45 m and the volume flowrate through the turbine is 30 m³/s. The runner speed is 130 rpm in the direction shown. Determine the shaft power developed. Is the shaft power greater or less than the power lost by the fluid? Explain.

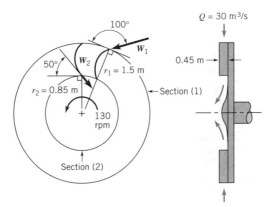

■ **FIGURE P11.26**

11.27 A water turbine wheel rotates at the rate of 100 rpm in the direction shown in Fig. P11.27. The inner radius, r_2, of the blade row is 1 ft, and the outer radius, r_1, is 2 ft. The absolute velocity vector at the turbine rotor entrance makes an angle of 20° with the tangential direction. The inlet blade angle is 60° relative to the tangential direction. The blade outlet angle is 120°. The flowrate is 10 ft³/s. For the flow tangent to the rotor blade surface at inlet and outlet, determine an appropriate constant blade height, b, and the corresponding power available at the rotor shaft. Is the shaft power greater or less than the power lost by the fluid? Explain.

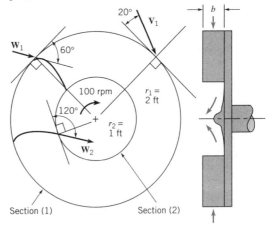

■ **FIGURE P11.27**

11.28 A sketch of the arithmetic mean radius blade sections of an axial-flow water turbine stage is shown in Fig. P11.28. The rotor speed is 1500 rpm. **(a)** Sketch and label velocity triangles for the flow entering and leaving the rotor row. Use **V** for absolute velocity, **W** for relative velocity, and **U** for blade velocity. Assume flow enters and leaves each blade row at the blade angles shown. **(b)** Calculate the work per unit mass delivered at the shaft.

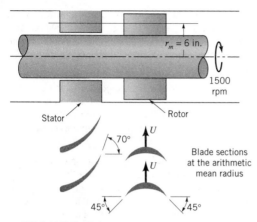

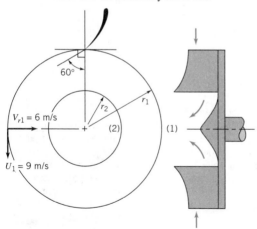

■ FIGURE P11.28

11.29 An inward flow radial turbine (see Fig. P11.29) involves a nozzle angle, α_1, of 60° and an inlet rotor tip speed, U_1, of 9 m/s. The ratio of rotor inlet to outlet diameters is 2.0. The radial component of velocity remains constant at 6 m/s through the rotor and the flow leaving the rotor at section (2) is without angular momentum. If the flowing fluid is water and the stagnation pressure drop across the rotor is 110 kPa, determine the loss of available energy across the rotor and the efficiency involved.

■ FIGURE P11.29

11.30 A 10.9-ft-diameter Pelton wheel operates at 500 rpm with a total head just upstream of the nozzle of 5,330 ft. Estimate the diameter of the nozzle of the single-nozzle wheel if it develops 25,000 horsepower.

11.31 A small Pelton wheel is used to power an oscillating lawn sprinkler as shown in **Video V11.4** and Fig. P11.31. The arithmetic mean radius of the turbine is 1 in. and the exit angle of the blade is 135 degrees relative to the blade motion. Water is supplied through a single 0.20-in. diameter nozzle at a speed of 50 ft/s. Determine the flowrate, the maximum torque developed, and the maximum power developed by this turbine.

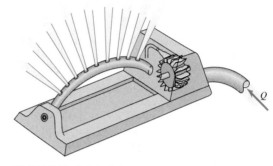

■ FIGURE P11.31

11.32 A Pelton wheel has a diameter of 2 m and develops 500 kW when rotating 180 rpm. What is the average force of the water against the blades? If the turbine is operating at maximum efficiency, determine the speed of the water jet from the nozzle and the mass flowrate.

11.33 Water to run a Pelton wheel is supplied by a penstock of length ℓ and diameter D with a friction factor f. If the only losses associated with the flow in the penstock are due to pipe friction, show that the maximum power output of the turbine occurs when the nozzle diameter, D_1, is given by $D_1 = D/(2f\,\ell/D)^{1/4}$.

11.34 A hydraulic turbine operating at 180 rpm with a head of 170 feet develops 20,000 horsepower. Estimate the power and speed if the turbine were to operate under a head of 190 ft.

11.35 Draft tubes as shown in Fig. P11.35 are often installed at the exit of Kaplan and Francis turbines. Explain why such draft tubes are advantageous.

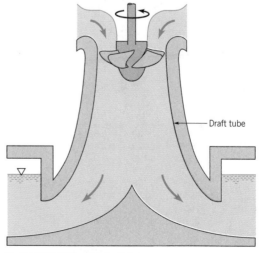

■ FIGURE P11.35

11.36   Turbines are to be designed to develop 30,000 horsepower while operating under a head of 70 ft and an angular velocity of 60 rpm. What type of turbine is best suited for this purpose? Estimate the flowrate needed.

11.37   A 1-m-diameter Pelton wheel rotates at 300 rpm. Which of the following heads (in meters) would be best suited for this turbine: **(a)** 2, **(b)** 5, **(c)** 40, **(d)** 70, or **(e)** 140? Explain.

11.38   Water at 400 psi is available to operate a turbine at 1750 rpm. What type of turbine would you suggest to use if the turbine should have an output of approximately 200 hp?

11.39   A high-speed turbine used to power a dentist's drill is shown in **Video V11.5** and Fig. E11.6. With the conditions stated in Example 11.6, for every slug of air that passes through the turbine there is 310,000 ft·lb of energy available at the shaft to drive the drill. One of the assumptions made to obtain this numerical result is that the tangential component of the absolute velocity out of the rotor is zero. Suppose this assumption were not true (but all other parameter values remain the same). Discuss how and why the value of 310,000 ft·lb/slug would change for these new conditions.

11.40   Test data for the small Francis turbine shown in Fig. P11.40 is given in the table below. The test was run at a constant 32.8 ft head just upstream of the turbine. The Prony brake on the turbine output shaft was adjusted to give various angular velocities, and the force on the brake arm, F, was recorded. Use the given data to plot curves of torque as a function of angular velocity and turbine efficiency as a function of angular velocity.

†11.41   It is possible to generate power by using the water from your garden hose to drive a small Pelton wheel turbine. (See **Video V11.4**.) Provide a preliminary design of such a turbine and estimate the power output expected. List all assumptions and show calculations.

11.42   The device shown in Fig. P11.42 is used to investigate the power produced by a Pelton wheel turbine. Water supplied at a constant flowrate issues from a nozzle and strikes the turbine buckets as indicated. The angular velocity, ω, of the turbine wheel is varied by adjusting the tension on the Prony brake spring, thereby varying the torque, T_{shaft}, applied to the output shaft. This torque can be determined from the measured force, R, needed to keep the brake arm stationary as $T_{shaft} = F\ell$, where ℓ is the moment arm of the brake force.

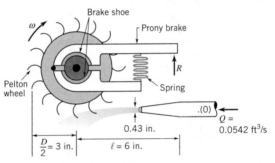

■ **FIGURE P11.42**

Experimentally determined values of ω and R are shown in the following table. Use these results to plot a graph of torque as a function of the angular velocity. On another graph plot the power output, $W_{shaft} = T_{shaft}\,\omega$, as a function of the angular velocity. On each of these graphs plot the theoretical curves for this turbine, assuming 100 percent efficiency.

Compare the experimental and theoretical results and discuss some possible reasons for any differences between them.

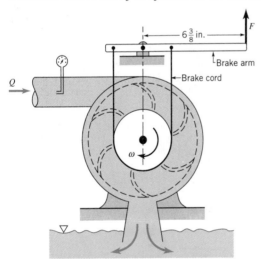

■ **FIGURE P11.40**

ω (rpm)	Q (ft³/s)	F (lb)
0	0.129	2.63
1000	0.129	2.40
1500	0.129	2.22
1870	0.124	1.91
2170	0.118	1.49
2350	0.0942	0.876
2580	0.0766	0.337
2710	0.068	0.089

ω (rpm)	R (lb)
0	2.47
360	1.91
450	1.84
600	1.69
700	1.55
940	1.17
1120	0.89
1480	0.16

*A*ppendices

489

APPENDIX A

Unit Conversion Tables[1]

The following tables express the definitions of miscellaneous units of measure as exact numerical multiples of coherent SI units, and provide multiplying factors for converting numbers and miscellaneous units to corresponding new numbers and SI units.

Conversion factors are expressed using computer exponential notation, and an asterisk follows each number which expresses an exact definition. For example, the entry "2.54 E − 2*" expresses the fact that 1 inch = 2.54 × 10^{-2} meter, exactly by definition. Numbers not followed by an asterisk are only approximate representations of definitions, or are the results of physical measurements. In these tables pound-force is designated as lbf, whereas in the text pound-force is designated as lb.

■ TABLE A.1

Listing by Physical Quantity

To convert from	to	Multiply by
Acceleration		
foot/second²	meter/second²	3.048 E − 1*
free fall, standard	meter/second²	9.806 65 E + 0*
gal (galileo)	meter/second²	1.00 E − 2*
inch/second²	meter/second²	2.54 E − 2*
Area		
acre	meter²	4.046 856 422 4 E + 3*
are	meter²	1.00 E + 2*

---

[1]These tables abridged from Mechtly, E. A., *The International System of Units, 2nd Revision*, NASA SP-7012, 1973.

■ **TABLE A.1** (continued)

To convert from	to	Multiply by
barn	meter^2	1.00 E − 28*
foot^2	meter^2	9.290 304 E − 2*
hectare	meter^2	1.00 E + 4*
inch^2	meter^2	6.4516 E − 4*
mile^2 (U.S. statute)	meter^2	2.589 988 110 336 E + 6*
section	meter^2	2.589 988 110 336 E + 6*
township	meter^2	9.323 957 2 E + 7
yard^2	meter^2	8.361 273 6 E − 1*

Density

gram/centimeter^3	kilogram/meter^3	1.00 E + 3*
lbm/inch^3	kilogram/meter^3	2.767 990 5 E + 4
lbm/foot^3	kilogram/meter^3	1.601 846 3 E + 1
slug/foot^3	kilogram/meter^3	5.153 79 E + 2

Energy

British thermal unit:		
(IST after 1956)	joule	1.055 056 E + 3
British thermal unit (thermochemical)	joule	1.054 350 E + 3
calorie (International Steam Table)	joule	4.1868 E + 0
calorie (thermochemical)	joule	4.184 E + 0*
calorie (kilogram, International Steam Table)	joule	4.1868 E + 3
calorie (kilogram, thermochemical)	joule	4.184 E + 3*
electron volt	joule	1.602 191 7 E − 19
erg	joule	1.00 E − 7*
foot lbf	joule	1.355 817 9 E + 0
foot poundal	joule	4.214 011 0 E − 2
joule (international of 1948)	joule	1.000 165 E + 0
kilocalorie (International Steam Table)	joule	4.1868 E + 3
kilocalorie (thermochemical)	joule	4.184 E + 3*
kilowatt hour	joule	3.60 E + 6*
watt hour	joule	3.60 E + 3*

Force

dyne	newton	1.00 E − 5*
kilogram force (kgf)	newton	9.806 65 E + 0*
kilopond force	newton	9.806 65 E + 0*
kip	newton	4.448 221 615 260 5 E + 3*
lbf (pound force, avoirdupois)	newton	4.448 221 615 260 5 E + 0*
ounce force (avoirdupois)	newton	2.780 138 5 E − 1
pound force, lbf (avoirdupois)	newton	4.448 221 615 260 5 E + 0*
poundal	newton	1.382 549 543 76 E − 1*

Length

angstrom	meter	1.00 E − 10*
astronomical unit (IAU)	meter	1.496 00 E + 11
cubit	meter	4.572 E − 1*
fathom	meter	1.8288 E + 0*
foot	meter	3.048 E − 1*

■ **TABLE A. 1** (continued)

To convert from	to	Multiply by
furlong	meter	2.011 68 E + 2*
hand	meter	1.016 E − 1*
inch	meter	2.54 E − 2*
league (international nautical)	meter	5.556 E + 3*
light year	meter	9.460 55 E + 15
meter	wavelengths Kr 86	1.650 763 73 E + 6*
micron	meter	1.00 E − 6*
mil	meter	2.54 E − 5*
mile (U.S. statute)	meter	1.609 344 E + 3*
nautical mile (U.S.)	meter	1.852 E + 3*
rod	meter	5.0292 E + 0*
yard	meter	9.144 E − 1*

Mass

carat (metric)	kilogram	2.00 E − 4*
grain	kilogram	6.479 891 E − 5*
gram	kilogram	1.00 E − 3*
ounce mass (avoirdupois)	kilogram	2.834 952 312 5 E − 2*
pound mass, lbm (avoirdupois)	kilogram	4.535 923 7 E − 1*
slug	kilogram	1.459 390 29 E + 1
ton (long)	kilogram	1.016 046 908 8 E + 3*
ton (metric)	kilogram	1.00 E + 3*
ton (short, 2000 pound)	kilogram	9.071 847 4 E + 2*
tonne	kilogram	1.00 E + 3*

Power

Btu (thermochemical)/second	watt	1.054 350 264 488 E + 3
calorie (thermochemical)/second	watt	4.184 E + 0*
foot lbf/second	watt	1.355 817 9 E + 0
horsepower (550 foot lbf/second)	watt	7.456 998 7 E + 2
kilocalorie (thermochemical)/second	watt	4.184 E + 3*
watt (international of 1948)	watt	1.000 165 E + 0

Pressure

atmosphere	newton/meter^2	1.013 25 E + 5*
bar	newton/meter^2	1.00 E + 5*
barye	newton/meter^2	1.00 E − 1*
centimeter of mercury (0°C)	newton/meter^2	1.333 22 E + 3
centimeter of water (4° C)	newton/meter^2	9.806 38 E + 1
dyne/centimeter^2	newton/meter^2	1.00 E − 1*
foot of water (39.2° F)	newton/meter^2	2.988 98 E + 3
inch of mercury (32° F)	newton/meter^2	3.386 389 E + 3
inch of mercury (60° F)	newton/meter^2	3.376 85 E + 3
inch of water (39.2° F)	newton/meter^2	2.490 82 E + 2
inch of water (60° F)	newton/meter^2	2.4884 E + 2
kgf/centimeter^2	newton/meter^2	9.806 65 E + 4*
kgf/meter^2	newton/meter^2	9.806 65 E + 0*
lbf/foot^2	newton/meter^2	4.788 025 8 E + 1
lbf/inch^2 (psi)	newton/meter^2	6.894 757 2 E + 3
millibar	newton/meter^2	1.00 E + 2*
millimeter of mercury (0° C)	newton/meter^2	1.333 224 E + 2
pascal	newton/meter^2	1.00 E + 0*
psi (lbf/inch^2)	newton/meter^2	6.894 757 2 E + 3
torr (0° C)	newton/meter^2	1.333 22 E + 2

■ **TABLE A.1** (continued)

To convert from	to	Multiply by
Speed		
foot/second	meter/second	3.048 E − 1*
inch/second	meter/second	2.54 E − 2*
kilometer/hour	meter/second	2.777 777 8 E − 1
knot (international)	meter/second	5.144 444 444 E − 1
mile/hour (U.S. statute)	meter/second	4.4704 E − 1*
Temperature		
Celsius	kelvin	$t_K = t_C + 273.15$
Fahrenheit	kelvin	$t_K = (5/9)(t_F + 459.67)$
Fahrenheit	Celsius	$t_C = (5/9)(t_F - 32)$
Rankine	kelvin	$t_K = (5/9)t_R$
Time		
day (mean solar)	second (mean solar)	8.64 E + 4*
hour (mean solar)	second (mean solar)	3.60 E + 3*
minute (mean solar)	second (mean solar)	6.00 E + 1*
year (calendar)	second (mean solar)	3.1536 E + 7*
Viscosity		
centistoke	meter^2/second	1.00 E − 6*
stoke	meter^2/second	1.00 E − 4*
foot^2/second	meter^2/second	9.290 304 E − 2*
centipoise	newton second/meter^2	1.00 E − 3*
lbm/foot second	newton second/meter^2	1.488 163 9 E + 0
lbf second/foot^2	newton second/meter^2	4.788 025 8 E + 1
poise	newton second/meter^2	1.00 E − 1*
poundal second/foot^2	newton second/meter^2	1.488 163 9 E + 0
slug/foot second	newton second/meter^2	4.788 025 8 E + 1
rhe	meter^2/newton second	1.00 E + 1*
Volume		
acre foot	meter^3	1.233 481 837 547 52 E + 3*
barrel (petroleum, 42 gallons)	meter^3	1.589 873 E − 1
board foot	meter^3	2.359 737 216 E − 3*
bushel (U.S.)	meter^3	3.523 907 016 688 E − 2*
cord	meter^3	3.624 556 3 E + 0
cup	meter^3	2.365 882 365 E − 4*
dram (U.S. fluid)	meter^3	3.696 691 195 312 5 E − 6*
fluid ounce (U.S.)	meter^3	2.957 352 956 25 E − 5*
foot^3	meter^3	2.831 684 659 2 E − 2*
gallon (U.K. liquid)	meter^3	4.546 087 E − 3
gallon (U.S. liquid)	meter^3	3.785 411 784 E − 3*
inch^3	meter^3	1.638 706 4 E − 5*
liter	meter^3	1.00 E − 3*
ounce (U.S. fluid)	meter^3	2.957 352 956 25 E − 5*
peck (U.S.)	meter^3	8.809 767 541 72 E − 3*
pint (U.S. liquid)	meter^3	4.731 764 73 E − 4*
quart (U.S. liquid)	meter^3	9.463 529 5 E − 4
stere	meter^3	1.00 E + 0*
tablespoon	meter^3	1.478 676 478 125 E − 5*
teaspoon	meter^3	4.928 921 593 75 E − 6*
yard^3	meter^3	7.645 548 579 84 E − 1*

APPENDIX B

Physical Properties of Fluids

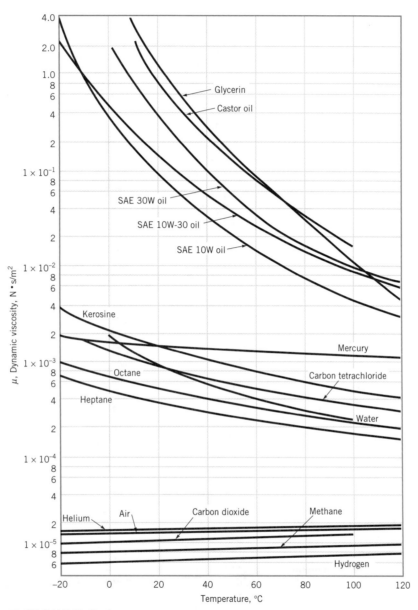

■ **FIGURE B.1**   **Dynamic (absolute) viscosity of common fluids as a function of temperature. To convert to BG units of lb·s/ft² multiply N·s/m² by 2.089 × 10⁻². Curves from R. W. Fox, and A. T. McDonald, *Introduction to Fluid Mechanics*, Third Edition, Wiley, New York, 1985. Used by permission.**

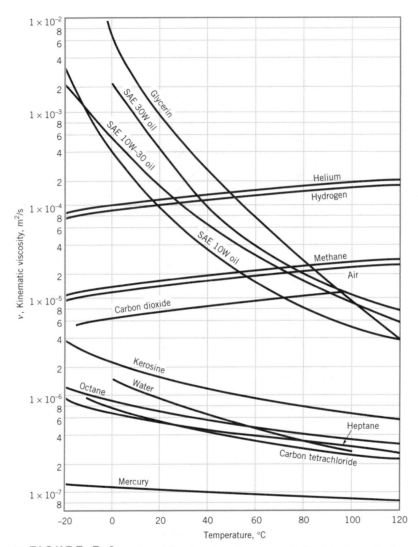

■ **FIGURE B.2** **Kinematic viscosity of common fluids (at atmospheric pressure) as a function of temperature. To convert to BG units of ft^2/s multiply m^2/s by 10.76. Curves from R. W. Fox, and A. T. McDonald, *Introduction to Fluid Mechanics*, Third Edition, Wiley, New York, 1985. Used by permission.**

■ **TABLE B.1**

Physical Properties of Water (BG Units)[a]

Temperature (°F)	Density, ρ (slugs/ft^3)	Specific Weight,[b] γ (lb/ft^3)	Dynamic Viscosity, μ (lb·s/ft^2)	Kinematic Viscosity, ν (ft^2/s)	Surface Tension,[c] σ (lb/ft)	Vapor Pressure, p_v [lb/in.^{2}(abs)]	Speed of Sound,[d] c (ft/s)
32	1.940	62.42	3.732 E − 5	1.924 E − 5	5.18 E − 3	8.854 E − 2	4603
40	1.940	62.43	3.228 E − 5	1.664 E − 5	5.13 E − 3	1.217 E − 1	4672
50	1.940	62.41	2.730 E − 5	1.407 E − 5	5.09 E − 3	1.781 E − 1	4748
60	1.938	62.37	2.344 E − 5	1.210 E − 5	5.03 E − 3	2.563 E − 1	4814
70	1.936	62.30	2.037 E − 5	1.052 E − 5	4.97 E − 3	3.631 E − 1	4871
80	1.934	62.22	1.791 E − 5	9.262 E − 6	4.91 E − 3	5.069 E − 1	4819
90	1.931	62.11	1.500 E − 5	8.233 E − 6	4.86 E − 3	6.979 E − 1	4960
100	1.927	62.00	1.423 E − 5	7.383 E − 6	4.79 E − 3	9.493 E − 1	4995
120	1.918	61.71	1.164 E − 5	6.067 E − 6	4.67 E − 3	1.692 E + 0	5049
140	1.908	61.38	9.743 E − 6	5.106 E − 6	4.53 E − 3	2.888 E + 0	5091
160	1.896	61.00	8.315 E − 6	4.385 E − 6	4.40 E − 3	4.736 E + 0	5101
180	1.883	60.58	7.207 E − 6	3.827 E − 6	4.26 E − 3	7.507 E + 0	5195
200	1.869	60.12	6.342 E − 6	3.393 E − 6	4.12 E − 3	1.152 E + 1	5089
212	1.860	59.83	5.886 E − 6	3.165 E − 6	4.04 E − 3	1.469 E + 1	5062

[a]Based on data from *Handbook of Chemistry and Physics,* 69th Ed., CRC Press, 1988. Where necessary, values obtained by interpolation.
[b]Density and specific weight are related through the equation $\gamma = \rho g$. For this table, $g = 32.174$ ft/s^2.
[c]In contact with air.
[d]From R. D. Blevins, *Applied Fluid Dynamics Handbook,* Van Nostrand Reinhold Co., Inc., New York, 1984.

■ **TABLE B.2**

Physical Properties of Water (SI Units)[a]

Temperature (°C)	Density, ρ (kg/m^3)	Specific Weight,[b] γ (kN/m^3)	Dynamic Viscosity, μ (N·s/m^2)	Kinematic Viscosity, ν (m^2/s)	Surface Tension,[c] σ (N/m)	Vapor Pressure, p_v [N/m^2(abs)]	Speed of Sound,[d] c (m/s)
0	999.9	9.806	1.787 E − 3	1.787 E − 6	7.56 E − 2	6.105 E + 2	1403
5	1000.0	9.807	1.519 E − 3	1.519 E − 6	7.49 E − 2	8.722 E + 2	1427
10	999.7	9.804	1.307 E − 3	1.307 E − 6	7.42 E − 2	1.228 E + 3	1447
20	998.2	9.789	1.002 E − 3	1.004 E − 6	7.28 E − 2	2.338 E + 3	1481
30	995.7	9.765	7.975 E − 4	8.009 E − 7	7.12 E − 2	4.243 E + 3	1507
40	992.2	9.731	6.529 E − 4	6.580 E − 7	6.96 E − 2	7.376 E + 3	1526
50	988.1	9.690	5.468 E − 4	5.534 E − 7	6.79 E − 2	1.233 E + 4	1541
60	983.2	9.642	4.665 E − 4	4.745 E − 7	6.62 E − 2	1.992 E + 4	1552
70	977.8	9.589	4.042 E − 4	4.134 E − 7	6.44 E − 2	3.116 E + 4	1555
80	971.8	9.530	3.547 E − 4	3.650 E − 7	6.26 E − 2	4.734 E + 4	1555
90	965.3	9.467	3.147 E − 4	3.260 E − 7	6.08 E − 2	7.010 E + 4	1550
100	958.4	9.399	2.818 E − 4	2.940 E − 7	5.89 E − 2	1.013 E + 5	1543

[a]Based on data from *Handbook of Chemistry and Physics,* 69th Ed., CRC Press, 1988.
[b]Density and specific weight are related through the equation $\gamma = \rho g$. For this table, $g = 9.807$ m/s^2.
[c]In contact with air.
[d]From R. D. Blevins, *Applied Fluid Dynamics Handbook,* Van Nostrand Reinhold Co., Inc., New York, 1984.

■ **TABLE B.3**

Physical Properties of Air at Standard Atmospheric Pressure (BG Units)[a]

Temperature (°F)	Density, ρ (slugs/ft³)		Specific Weight,[b] γ (lb/ft³)		Dynamic Viscosity, μ (lb·s/ft²)		Kinematic Viscosity, ν (ft²/s)		Specific Heat Ratio, k (—)	Speed of Sound, c (ft/s)
−40	2.939	E − 3	9.456	E − 2	3.29	E − 7	1.12	E − 4	1.401	1004
−20	2.805	E − 3	9.026	E − 2	3.34	E − 7	1.19	E − 4	1.401	1028
0	2.683	E − 3	8.633	E − 2	3.38	E − 7	1.26	E − 4	1.401	1051
10	2.626	E − 3	8.449	E − 2	3.44	E − 7	1.31	E − 4	1.401	1062
20	2.571	E − 3	8.273	E − 2	3.50	E − 7	1.36	E − 4	1.401	1074
30	2.519	E − 3	8.104	E − 2	3.58	E − 7	1.42	E − 4	1.401	1085
40	2.469	E − 3	7.942	E − 2	3.60	E − 7	1.46	E − 4	1.401	1096
50	2.420	E − 3	7.786	E − 2	3.68	E − 7	1.52	E − 4	1.401	1106
60	2.373	E − 3	7.636	E − 2	3.75	E − 7	1.58	E − 4	1.401	1117
70	2.329	E − 3	7.492	E − 2	3.82	E − 7	1.64	E − 4	1.401	1128
80	2.286	E − 3	7.353	E − 2	3.86	E − 7	1.69	E − 4	1.400	1138
90	2.244	E − 3	7.219	E − 2	3.90	E − 7	1.74	E − 4	1.400	1149
100	2.204	E − 3	7.090	E − 2	3.94	E − 7	1.79	E − 4	1.400	1159
120	2.128	E − 3	6.846	E − 2	4.02	E − 7	1.89	E − 4	1.400	1180
140	2.057	E − 3	6.617	E − 2	4.13	E − 7	2.01	E − 4	1.399	1200
160	1.990	E − 3	6.404	E − 2	4.22	E − 7	2.12	E − 4	1.399	1220
180	1.928	E − 3	6.204	E − 2	4.34	E − 7	2.25	E − 4	1.399	1239
200	1.870	E − 3	6.016	E − 2	4.49	E − 7	2.40	E − 4	1.398	1258
300	1.624	E − 3	5.224	E − 2	4.97	E − 7	3.06	E − 4	1.394	1348
400	1.435	E − 3	4.616	E − 2	5.24	E − 7	3.65	E − 4	1.389	1431
500	1.285	E − 3	4.135	E − 2	5.80	E − 7	4.51	E − 4	1.383	1509
750	1.020	E − 3	3.280	E − 2	6.81	E − 7	6.68	E − 4	1.367	1685
1000	8.445	E − 4	2.717	E − 2	7.85	E − 7	9.30	E − 4	1.351	1839
1500	6.291	E − 4	2.024	E − 2	9.50	E − 7	1.51	E − 3	1.329	2114

[a]Based on data from R. D. Blevins, *Applied Fluid Dynamics Handbook,* Van Nostrand Reinhold Co., Inc., New York, 1984.

[b]Density and specific weight are related through the equation $\gamma = \rho g$. For this table $g = 32.174$ ft/s².

■ **TABLE B.4**

Physical Properties of Air at Standard Atmospheric Pressure (SI Units)[a]

Temperature (°C)	Density, ρ (kg/m³)	Specific Weight,[b] γ (N/m³)	Dynamic Viscosity, μ (N·s/m²)	Kinematic Viscosity, ν (m²/s)	Specific Heat Ratio, k (–)	Speed of Sound, c (m/s)
−40	1.514	14.85	1.57 E − 5	1.04 E − 5	1.401	306.2
−20	1.395	13.68	1.63 E − 5	1.17 E − 5	1.401	319.1
0	1.292	12.67	1.71 E − 5	1.32 E − 5	1.401	331.4
5	1.269	12.45	1.73 E − 5	1.36 E − 5	1.401	334.4
10	1.247	12.23	1.76 E − 5	1.41 E − 5	1.401	337.4
15	1.225	12.01	1.80 E − 5	1.47 E − 5	1.401	340.4
20	1.204	11.81	1.82 E − 5	1.51 E − 5	1.401	343.3
25	1.184	11.61	1.85 E − 5	1.56 E − 5	1.401	346.3
30	1.165	11.43	1.86 E − 5	1.60 E − 5	1.400	349.1
40	1.127	11.05	1.87 E − 5	1.66 E − 5	1.400	354.7
50	1.109	10.88	1.95 E − 5	1.76 E − 5	1.400	360.3
60	1.060	10.40	1.97 E − 5	1.86 E − 5	1.399	365.7
70	1.029	10.09	2.03 E − 5	1.97 E − 5	1.399	371.2
80	0.9996	9.803	2.07 E − 5	2.07 E − 5	1.399	376.6
90	0.9721	9.533	2.14 E − 5	2.20 E − 5	1.398	381.7
100	0.9461	9.278	2.17 E − 5	2.29 E − 5	1.397	386.9
200	0.7461	7.317	2.53 E − 5	3.39 E − 5	1.390	434.5
300	0.6159	6.040	2.98 E − 5	4.84 E − 5	1.379	476.3
400	0.5243	5.142	3.32 E − 5	6.34 E − 5	1.368	514.1
500	0.4565	4.477	3.64 E − 5	7.97 E − 5	1.357	548.8
1000	0.2772	2.719	5.04 E − 5	1.82 E − 4	1.321	694.8

[a]Based on data from R. D. Blevins, *Applied Fluid Dynamics Handbook,* Van Nostrand Reinhold Co., Inc., New York, 1984.

[b]Density and specific weight are related through the equation $\gamma = \rho g$. For this table $g = 9.807$ m/s².

APPENDIX C

*P*roperties of the U.S. Standard Atmosphere

■ TABLE C.1
Properties of the U.S. Standard Atmosphere (BG Units)[a]

Altitude (ft)	Temperature (°F)	Acceleration of Gravity, g (ft/s^2)	Pressure, p [lb/in.^{2}(abs)]	Density, ρ (slugs/ft^3)		Dynamic Viscosity, μ (lb·s/ft^2)	
−5000	76.84	32.189	17.554	2.745	E − 3	3.836	E − 7
0	59.00	32.174	14.696	2.377	E − 3	3.737	E − 7
5,000	47.17	32.159	12.228	2.048	E − 3	3.637	E − 7
10,000	23.36	32.143	10.108	1.756	E − 3	3.534	E − 7
15,000	5.55	32.128	8.297	1.496	E − 3	3.430	E − 7
20,000	−12.26	32.112	6.759	1.267	E − 3	3.324	E − 7
25,000	−30.05	32.097	5.461	1.066	E − 3	3.217	E − 7
30,000	−47.83	32.082	4.373	8.907	E − 4	3.107	E − 7
35,000	−65.61	32.066	3.468	7.382	E − 4	2.995	E − 7
40,000	−69.70	32.051	2.730	5.873	E − 4	2.969	E − 7
45,000	−69.70	32.036	2.149	4.623	E − 4	2.969	E − 7
50,000	−69.70	32.020	1.692	3.639	E − 4	2.969	E − 7
60,000	−69.70	31.990	1.049	2.256	E − 4	2.969	E − 7
70,000	−67.42	31.959	0.651	1.392	E − 4	2.984	E − 7
80,000	−61.98	31.929	0.406	8.571	E − 5	3.018	E − 7
90,000	−56.54	31.897	0.255	5.610	E − 5	3.052	E − 7
100,000	−51.10	31.868	0.162	3.318	E − 5	3.087	E − 7
150,000	19.40	31.717	0.020	3.658	E − 6	3.511	E − 7
200,000	−19.78	31.566	0.003	5.328	E − 7	3.279	E − 7
250,000	−88.77	31.415	0.000	6.458	E − 8	2.846	E − 7

[a]Data abridged from *U.S. Standard Atmosphere,* 1976, U.S. Government Printing Office, Washington, D.C.

■ **TABLE C.2**

Properties of the U.S. Standard Atmosphere (SI Units)[a]

Altitude (m)	Temperature (°C)	Acceleration of Gravity, g (m/s^2)	Pressure, p [N/m^2(abs)]		Density, ρ (kg/m^3)		Dynamic Viscosity, μ (N·s/m^2)	
−1,000	21.50	9.810	1.139	E + 5	1.347	E + 0	1.821	E − 5
0	15.00	9.807	1.013	E + 5	1.225	E + 0	1.789	E − 5
1,000	8.50	9.804	8.988	E + 4	1.112	E + 0	1.758	E − 5
2,000	2.00	9.801	7.950	E + 4	1.007	E + 0	1.726	E − 5
3,000	−4.49	9.797	7.012	E + 4	9.093	E − 1	1.694	E − 5
4,000	−10.98	9.794	6.166	E + 4	8.194	E − 1	1.661	E − 5
5,000	−17.47	9.791	5.405	E + 4	7.364	E − 1	1.628	E − 5
6,000	−23.96	9.788	4.722	E + 4	6.601	E − 1	1.595	E − 5
7,000	−30.45	9.785	4.111	E + 4	5.900	E − 1	1.561	E − 5
8,000	−36.94	9.782	3.565	E + 4	5.258	E − 1	1.527	E − 5
9,000	−43.42	9.779	3.080	E + 4	4.671	E − 1	1.493	E − 5
10,000	−49.90	9.776	2.650	E + 4	4.135	E − 1	1.458	E − 5
15,000	−56.50	9.761	1.211	E + 4	1.948	E − 1	1.422	E − 5
20,000	−56.50	9.745	5.529	E + 3	8.891	E − 2	1.422	E − 5
25,000	−51.60	9.730	2.549	E + 3	4.008	E − 2	1.448	E − 5
30,000	−46.64	9.715	1.197	E + 3	1.841	E − 2	1.475	E − 5
40,000	−22.80	9.684	2.871	E + 2	3.996	E − 3	1.601	E − 5
50,000	−2.50	9.654	7.978	E + 1	1.027	E − 3	1.704	E − 5
60,000	−26.13	9.624	2.196	E + 1	3.097	E − 4	1.584	E − 5
70,000	−53.57	9.594	5.221	E + 0	8.283	E − 5	1.438	E − 5
80,000	−74.51	9.564	1.052	E + 0	1.846	E − 5	1.321	E − 5

[a]Data abridged from *U.S. Standard Atmosphere,* 1975, U.S. Government Printing Office, Washington, D.C.

Answers to Selected Even Numbered Homework Problems

Chapter 1

1.6 Yes

1.10 (a) 4.66×10^4 ft; (b) 5.18×10^{-2} lb/ft^3;
(c) 3.12×10^{-3} slugs/ft^3;
(d) 2.36×10^{-2} ft $\cdot$ lb/s;
(e) 5.17×10^{-6} ft/s

1.12 1.25, 1.25

1.14 0.805, 7.90 kN/m^3

1.16 12.0 kN/m^3; 1.22×10^3 kg/m^3; 1.22

1.20 oxygen

1.22 2.02 m^3

1.24 0.277 N $\cdot$ s/m^2

1.26 184

1.28 0.552 U/δ N/m^2 <u>acting to left on plate</u>

1.30 $\mathcal{D} = 0.571 \, b\rho \sqrt{\nu \ell U^3}$

1.32 1.03×10^{-4} ft

1.34 (a) 153 s^{-1}, 4350 ft^{-2} s^{-1};
(b) 5.72×10^{-5} lb/ft^2, 6.94×10^{-5} lb/ft^2

1.36 0.727 N $\cdot$ s/m^2

1.38 286 N

1.40 (a) 1.38 km/s; (b) 1.45 km/s;
(c) 1.51 km/s

1.42 3.77×10^{-3} slugs/ft^3; 280°F

1.44 5.9 kPa (abs)

1.46 97.9 Pa

1.48 3.00 mm

1.50 $\sigma \cos \theta = 4.37 \times 10^{-3}$ lb/ft; $\theta = 29.7°$;
$\sigma = 4.37 \times 10^{-3}$ lb/ft

Chapter 2

2.2 10.4 m

2.4 60.6 MPa, 8790 psi

2.8 464 mm

2.10 19.3 psia

*2.12 10.2 psia

2.14 22.4 psi

2.16 1.55 slugs/ft^3

2.18 0.424 psi

2.20 6.28 ft

2.22 34.2°

2.24 0.100 m

2.26 11.7

2.28 $F_R = 1.48$ MN; $y_R = 13.4$ m

2.30 1350 lb

2.32 33,900 lb; 2.49 ft above base

2.34 $\mathcal{W} = 314$ kN; $R = 497$ kN

2.36 436 kN

2.38 118 kN; 2.03 m below free surface

2.40	1680 lb
2.42	0.146
2.44	294 kN; 328 kN; yes
2.46	22,500 lb
2.48	7.77×10^9 lb acting 406 ft up from base of dam
2.50	(a) 31.4 lb; (b) 581 lb; (c) 0.289 psi
2.52	6.27 kN/m^3; 824 N
2.56	127 lb
2.58	17.2 mm
2.60	158 lb/ft^2

Chapter 3

3.2	(a) $-194(1 + x) - 62.4$ lb/ft^3; (b) 38.6 psi
3.4	-9.99 kPa/m
3.6	(a) 4.97 lb/ft^3; (b) 0.681 lb/ft^3
3.12	61.9 psi
3.14	10.8 lb/ft^2, 124 lb/ft^2
3.16	(a) 138 ft; (b) 0.909 ft; (c) 159 ft
3.18	$Q = 1.56 D^2$ where $Q \sim$ m^3/s, $D \sim$ m
3.20	302 knots
3.22	1.40 mph
3.24	2.54×10^{-4} m^3/s
3.26	$V_2 = \{2g((\rho_m/\rho) - 1) \, h/[1 - (D_2/D_1)^4]\}^{\frac{1}{2}}$
3.28	5.12×10^{-4} m^3/s
3.30	0.0111 m^3/s
3.32	20.8 lb/s
3.34	(a) 0.0555 m^3/s; (b) 0.0253 m; (c) 0
3.36	13.0 psi
3.38	1.79 ft
3.40	20.9 ft/s
3.42	0.0758 ft^3/s, 499 lb/ft^2, 488 lb/ft^2, -11.7 lb/ft^2
3.44	7.53 ft
3.46	6.10×10^{-3} m^3/s
3.50	2.00×10^{-4} m^3/s; 0.129 m
3.54	0.630 ft, 4.48 ft
3.56	6.51 m, 25.4 m; 6.51 m, -9.59 m

Chapter 4

4.4	$y = e^{(x^2/2 - x)} - 1$
4.8	$2\,c^2x^3$; $2\,c^2y^3$; $x = y = 0$
4.10	(a) 4 ft/s^2, 2 ft/s^2; (b) negative
4.12	2880 m/s^2, 5760 m/s^2, 8640 m/s^2
4.14	$-x/t^2$; x/t^2

4.16	0; $(225x + 150)\hat{\mathbf{i}}$ m/s^2; $150\hat{\mathbf{i}}$ m/s^2; $375\hat{\mathbf{i}}$ m/s^2
4.18	200 C/s; 100 C/s
4.20	(a) 10 ft/s^2, 20 ft/s^2; (b) 20 ft/s^2; (c) 22.4 ft/s^2 at 63.4° from streamline
4.22	-225 ft/s^2; -28.1 ft/s^2; -8.33 ft/s^2
4.24	$\rho_0 V_0 b e^{-bt}$
4.28	$7.14\hat{\mathbf{i}}$ slug · ft/s^2

Chapter 5

5.2	13.8 ft
5.4	2.92 ft/s
5.6	1.70 ft/s
5.8	(a) 0.00456 slugs/s; (b) 2.28×10^{-4} (slugs/ft^3)/s
5.10	7/8
5.12	(a) 15.6 gal/min; (b) 62.4 gal/min
5.14	3.63 ft/s
5.16	352 lb to left
5.18	$F_{A,x} = 1890$ lb to left; $F_{A,y} = 0$
5.20	$F_{A,x} = 97$ lb, $F_{A,y} = 0$
5.22	$F_{A,x} = 0$, $F_{A,y} = 66.6$ N
5.24	(a) 6.26 m/s; (b) 392 N; (c) 675 N
5.26	axial-direction momentum flowrate with nonuniform velocity profile is 4/3 times the axial-direction momentum flowrate with uniform velocity profile
5.28	214 lb to left
5.30	2.66×10^{-4} m^3/s
5.32	7.07 ft/s at 45°
5.34	(a) 2.96 ft·lb, (b) 1.35 ft·lb, (c) 920 rpm
5.36	(a) 62.4 N·m/kg, (b) 62.4 N·m/kg
5.38	5460 (ft · lb)/slug
5.40	11.4 (N · m)/kg
5.42	11.6 (N · m)/kg, 0.796
5.44	0.842
5.46	0.469 K
5.48	0.0455 m^3/s
5.50	566 (ft · lb)/slug
5.52	(a) 294 kPa; (b) 324 kPa
5.54	4.54 MW
5.56	930 kW
5.58	(a) 4.08 hp; (b) 9.94 ft
5.60	0.763 ft^3/s
5.62	(a) 54.1 ft; (b) 2.75 lb/ft^2; (c) 46.3 ft^3/s
5.64	14,500 ft · lb/s
5.66	right side; 4.09 lb

5.68 $R_x = -12,850$ lb, $R_y = 1,540$ lb
5.70   3.97 m
5.72   (a) 4.29 m/s, 17.2°; (b) 558 N·m/s

Chapter 6
6.2 $x^2z^2 + xy, 2xyz^2 + x^3, yz$
6.4   (a) 0; (b) $\boldsymbol{\omega} = -(U/2b)\mathbf{k}$;
           (c) $\zeta = -(U/b)\hat{\mathbf{k}}$; (d) $\dot{\gamma} = U/b$
6.6 $\omega = 4yz^2 - 6y^2z$
6.8   (a) $v_r = V\sin\theta, v_\theta = V\cos\theta$;
           (b) $\psi = -Vx + C, \psi = -Vr\cos\theta + C$
6.10 $v = -2y$; (b) 1.41 ft/s
6.12   (b) 1 m^3/s (flow right to left)
6.14 $\psi = 5x^2y - (5/3)y^3 + C$
6.16 $\psi = U_cy[1 - \frac{1}{3}(y/h)^2] + C$; No ϕ
6.18   (a) $\psi = 2xy$; (b) $q = 2x_iy_i$
6.20   (a) $\psi = -Kr^2/2 + c$; (b) No
6.22   (a) $\partial p/\partial r = (1.60 \times 10^3)r^{-3}$ kPa/m;
           (b) 184 kPa
6.24 $C = 0.500$ m
6.26   0.00637 ft to right of slit;
           $y = m\theta/2\pi U$; $H = 0.0200$ ft
6.28 $h^2 = m/2\pi A$
6.30 $p_{stag} - p_A = 0.703\,\rho U^2$
6.34   (a) $p_{max} = p_0 + \rho U^2/2$ (at $\theta = 0$ and π);
           $p_{min} = p_0 - 3\rho U^2/2$ (at $\theta = \pi/2$);
           (b) $(2r/3a)(1 - a^2/r^2)\sin\theta = 1$
6.36 $y/a \geq 10$
6.38 -5.98 kPa; -6.02 kPa, 45.0 Pa
6.40 $\partial p_s/\partial\theta = 4\rho U^2\sin\theta\cos\theta$; θ falls in range
           of $\pm 90°$
6.42   311 lb/ft^3, 1.35 ft/s
6.44 $v\mu/\gamma h^2 = (x/h)^2/2 - (x/h) + (1/3)$
6.46 $U = (b^2/2\mu)\,\partial p/\partial x$
6.48   0.355 N · m
6.52   (a) yes; (b) 57.1 N/m^2 per m
6.54 $v_\theta = R^2\omega/r$
6.56   (b) 1.20 Pa

Chapter 7
7.2   (b)
7.4 $\Delta pD_1/V\mu = \phi(D_2/D_1, \rho D_1V/\mu)$
7.6 $H/a = \phi(\rho_a/\rho, \ell/d, gd/V^2)$
7.8 $\mathcal{D}/d_1^2V^2\rho = \phi(d_2/d_1, \rho Vd_1/\mu)$
7.10 $c\sqrt{\rho/E} = \phi(h/D)$
7.12   If the velocity, V, is doubled the pressure,
           p, will be doubled

7.14 $\mu = C_1t\Delta\gamma$ where C_1 is a constant
7.16   Omit ρ and σ
7.18 $\Delta p_\ell = 40.5\,\mu Q/D^4$
7.20 8.71×10^{-2} ft/s
7.22   11.0 m/s
7.24   1180 km/hr
7.26   249 mph
7.28   (a) $V_m/U_m = V/U$, $V_mD_m/\nu_{sm} = VD/\nu_s$,
           $V_m^2/g_mD_m = V^2/gD$,
           $(\rho - \rho_s)_m/\rho_m = (\rho - \rho_s)/\rho$; (b) no
7.30   (a) $V\ell^2/Q = \phi(\ell_i/\ell, Q^2/\ell^5g, \rho Q/\ell\mu)$, no;
           (b) 0.410 gpm, 2.46 in.
7.32   0.274 lb
7.34   (a) $p/\rho V^2 = \phi(\ell/\ell_i)$; (b) 0.333 ft;
           (c) $p = (V/V_m)^2p_m$, no
7.36   0.440 ft; 2.80 ft^3/s
7.38 -0.0809 lb/ft^2
7.40   (a) 3.58 ft/s; (b) 1.06 ft/s
7.42   (a) $t\sqrt{g/w}, \mu/\rho\sqrt{w^3g}$; (b) $t_m/t = 0.316$,
           no

Chapter 8
8.4   laminar
8.6   17.7 ft
8.8   3m; 8.83 N/m^2
8.10   0.0260 lb · s/ft^2; 1.25 lb/ft^2
8.12   3.43 m; 166 kPa
8.14   18.5 m
8.16   (a) 0.707 R; (b) 0.750 R
8.18   0.0404
8.20   0.0300
8.22   25.1 psi
8.28   9.00
8.30   9
8.32   48.0 psi
8.34   0.0292; 0.0132 ft
8.36   0.00720 in.
8.38   Pump; 127 hp
8.40   24.4 hp
8.44   0.325 psi
8.46   1012 ft
8.48   0.750 psi
8.50   35.5 ft
8.52   78.1 psi
8.54 2.30×10^{-4} m^3/s
8.56   0.0494 ft^3/s
8.58   0.491 ft

8.60	0.108 ft^3/s; 0.440 ft^3/s	**10.10**	0.528 ft; 0.728 ft
8.62	0.0180 m^3/s	**10.12**	0.694 ft
*****8.64**	0.0275 m^3/s; 0.0135 m^3/s; 0.0140 m^3/s	**10.16**	5.14 N/m^2
8.66	18.0 m^3/s	**10.18**	35.0 m^3/s
8.68	0.115 ft^3/s	**10.20**	8.42 ft/s
8.70	5.77 ft	**10.22**	1.49 ft
8.72	0.0936 ft^3/s	**10.24**	0.000505
		10.26	11.7 m^3/s; 12.2 m^3/s
Chapter 9		**10.28**	8.77 m
9.2	3.45 kN; 0.560 kN; 3.47 kN; 0.427 kN	**10.30**	same for each
9.4	0.159 lb; 0.833	**10.32**	10.66 m
9.6	Fig. 9.5c	*****10.34**	17.1 ft
9.8	0.00718 m/s; 0.00229 m/s	**10.36**	1.36 m
9.10	0.0130 m; 0.0716 N/m^2; 0.0183 m; 0.0506 N/m^2	**10.38**	142 ft^3/s; 1180 ft^3/s
		10.40	13.7 ft/s
9.14	$\delta = 5.83\sqrt{\nu x/U}$	**10.44**	84.5 m^3/s
9.18	2.83 $\mathcal{D}$; 0.354 $\mathcal{D}$	**10.46**	4.36 ft/s
9.20	0.0438 N · m	**10.48**	4.70 ft
9.24	1.06 m/s	**10.50**	1.36 m^3/s; 0.333 m
9.26	24,500 lb	**10.52**	yes
9.28	18,800 N · m		
9.30	43.2%	**Chapter 11**	
9.34	(a) 567 ft/s; (b) 118 ft/s; (c) 13.5 ft/s	**11.2**	4.05 N · m; 1.705 rev/s
9.36	558 N	**11.4**	89.7 kg/s, 286 rpm
9.38	1.29 lb; 129 lb	**11.6**	(b) 918 ft · lb; 0 rpm
9.40	859 lb	**11.8**	61.3 ft
9.44	77.0 ft/s	**11.12**	365 gpm
9.46	58.4 hp	**11.14**	1740 gal/min
9.48	(a) 153 mph; (b) 80.7 mph	**11.16**	0.0328 m^3/s, 8.00 m
9.50	0.0187 U	**11.18**	1000 gpm; 800 ft
9.52	405 lb	**11.20**	136 gpm, 147 ft
9.54	146 mph	**11.22**	mixed-flow pump
9.56	power ratio = 2.30	**11.26**	−12.8 MW
9.58	$\delta_{exp} = 0.23$ in.; $\delta_{th} = 0.117$ in.	**11.28**	(b) −7020 ft^2/s^2
		11.30	0.300 ft
Chapter 10		**11.32**	26,600 N; 37.6 m/s; 707 kg/s
10.2	8.30 ft/s	**11.34**	23,500 hp, 190 rpm
10.6	(a) 4.27 ft; (b) 6.41 ft; (c) 8.12 ft; (d) 5.22 ft/s; 22.3 ft/s	**11.36**	Francis, 378 ft^3/s
10.8	1.42 ft; 4.14 ft	**11.38**	impulse

Index